HEALTH LAW: SELECTED STATUTES AND REGULATIONS

2003 STANDARD EDITION

By

Thomas L. Greaney
Professor of Law and Co-Director, Center for Health Law Studies
Saint Louis University

Robert L. Schwartz
Professor of Law and Professor of Pediatrics
University of New Mexico

THOMSON

WEST

Mat #18471647

COPYRIGHT © 2003

By

WEST GROUP

All rights reserved
Printed in the United States of America

ISBN 0–314–26016–1

Preface

This supplement aims to provide students and practitioners with selected statutory provisions and regulations essential to the study and practice of health law. These materials may help deepen and expand what is commonly taught in the health law curriculum in law schools, medical schools and schools of health administration. In addition, the supplement may serve as a handy desk reference book for researchers and practitioners who need quick access to essential statutory and regulatory materials.

The materials contained in this supplement are current as of the preparation of the manuscript. We have attempted to group the statutes and regulatory materials by areas of topical coverage appropriate for courses or for research purposes in health law. Consequently, the book intermingles both state and federal materials and statutory and regulatory materials. Our process of choosing which statutes and materials to include was necessarily a subjective one. As a general matter, we attempted to select statutes that provide useful guides or are representative of the kinds of laws developed in certain areas. In some instances the choice was a matter of selecting statutes that seemed key to the practice of law or understanding fundamental concepts that shape the regulatory environment governing health care. If we omitted your favorite health law statute (or a statute that you think would be helpful as a reference for students or practitioners), please let us know. We will do out best to correct that error before the next edition is published.

With a few exceptions, the text of the statutes and regulatory materials have not been edited except to delete notes, comments and administrative materials. Where we did edit the materials, the following conventions have been observed. Omissions of an entire statutory section have not been indicated. Omissions within a statutory section are indicated by ellipses (...). It should be emphasized that the Medicare and Medicaid statutes are not complete and that practitioners and others needing access to the full statutes are advised to consult the statutes themselves. We have included a large portion of the Medicare and Medicaid statutes with the objective of giving students and researchers an understanding of the detail and comprehensiveness of the statutory regimes and the necessary interrelation of the various parts of these statutes.

We express our appreciation to remarkable research assistants, Kallie Dixon, Jeremy Johnson, Jean Montney, Stephanie Kane, Ed McDonald and Willow Misty Parks, and to Mary Ann Jauer and Joseph Blecha.

THOMAS GREANEY
ROBERT SCHWARTZ

Papeete, 2002

*

iii

Acknowledgements

National Conference of Commissioners on Uniform State Laws, Uniform Determination of Death Act, Copyright 1980, National Conference of Commissioners on Uniform State Laws. Reprinted with permission of the National Conference of Commissioners on Uniform State Laws.

National Conference of Commissioners on Uniform State Laws, Uniform Health Care Decisions Act, Copyright 1993, National Conference of Commissioners on Uniform State Laws. Reprinted with permission of the National Conference of Commissioners on Uniform State Laws.

National Conference of Commissioners on Uniform State Laws, Uniform Parentage Act, Copyright 2000, National Conference of Commissioners on Uniform State Laws. Reprinted with permission of the National Conference of Commissioners on Uniform State Laws.

*

Table of Contents

*

PART ONE: REGULATION OF THE HEALTH CARE INDUSTRY

I. FRAUD AND ABUSE

A. GENERAL FRAUD AND FALSE CLAIMS LAWS

Federal Criminal False Claims Act: 18 U.S.C.A. § 287

§ 287. False, fictitious or fraudulent claims

Whoever makes or presents to any person or officer in the civil, military, or naval service of the United States, or to any department or agency thereof, any claim upon or against the United States, or any department or agency thereof, knowing such claim to be false, fictitious, or fraudulent, shall be imprisoned not more than five years and shall be subject to a fine in the amount provided in this title.

False Statements: 18 U.S.C.A. § 1001

§ 1001. Statements or entries generally

(a) Except as otherwise provided in this section, whoever, in any matter within the jurisdiction of the executive, legislative, or judicial branch of the Government of the United States, knowingly and willfully—

> **(1)** falsifies, conceals, or covers up by any trick, scheme, or device a material fact;

> **(2)** makes any materially false, fictitious, or fraudulent statement or representation; or

> **(3)** makes or uses any false writing or document knowing the same to contain any materially false, fictitious, or fraudulent statement or entry;

shall be fined under this title or imprisoned not more than 5 years, or both.

(b) Subsection (a) does not apply to a party to a judicial proceeding, or that party's counsel, for statements, representations, writings or documents submitted by such party or counsel to a judge or magistrate in that proceeding.

(c) With respect to any matter within the jurisdiction of the legislative branch, subsection (a) shall apply only to—

(1) administrative matters, including a claim for payment, a matter related to the procurement of property or services, personnel or employment practices, or support services, or a document required by law, rule, or regulation to be submitted to the Congress or any office or officer within the legislative branch; or

(2) any investigation or review, conducted pursuant to the authority of any committee, subcommittee, commission or office of the Congress, consistent with applicable rules of the House or Senate.

Mail Fraud: 18 U.S.C.A. § 1341

§ 1341. Frauds and swindles

Whoever, having devised or intending to devise any scheme or artifice to defraud, or for obtaining money or property by means of false or fraudulent pretenses, representations, or promises, or to sell, dispose of, loan, exchange, alter, give away, distribute, supply, or furnish or procure for unlawful use any counterfeit or spurious coin, obligation, security, or other article, or anything represented to be or intimated or held out to be such counterfeit or spurious article, for the purpose of executing such scheme or artifice or attempting so to do, places in any post office or authorized depository for mail matter, any matter or thing whatever to be sent or delivered by the Postal Service, or deposits or causes to be deposited any matter or thing whatever to be sent or delivered by any private or commercial interstate carrier, or takes or receives therefrom, any such matter or thing, or knowingly causes to be delivered by mail or such carrier according to the direction thereon, or at the place at which it is directed to be delivered by the person to whom it is addressed, any such matter or thing, shall be fined under this title or imprisoned not more than five years, or both. If the violation affects a financial institution, such person shall be fined not more than $1,000,000 or imprisoned not more than 30 years, or both.

Federal Qui Tam Statute: 31 U.S.C.A. § 3730

§ 3730. Civil actions for false claims

(a) Responsibilities of the Attorney General.—The Attorney General diligently shall investigate a violation under section 3729. If the Attorney General finds that a person has violated or is violating section 3729, the Attorney General may bring a civil action under this section against the person.

(b) Actions by private persons.—

(1) A person may bring a civil action for a violation of section 3729 for the person and for the United States Government. The action shall be brought in the name of the Government. The action may be dismissed only if the court and the Attorney General give written consent to the dismissal and their reasons for consenting.

(2) A copy of the complaint and written disclosure of substantially all material evidence and information the person possesses shall be served on the Government pursuant to [Rule 4(i) of the Federal Rules of Civil Procedure]. The complaint shall be filed in camera, shall remain under seal for at least 60 days, and shall not be served on the defendant until the court so orders. The Government may elect to intervene and proceed with the action within 60 days after it receives both the complaint and the material evidence and information.

(3) The Government may, for good cause shown, move the court for extensions of the time during which the complaint remains under seal under paragraph (2). Any such motions may be supported by affidavits or other submissions in camera. The defendant shall not be required to respond to any complaint filed under this section until 20 days after the complaint is unsealed and served upon the defendant pursuant to Rule 4 of the Federal Rules of Civil Procedure.

(4) Before the expiration of the 60–day period or any extensions obtained under paragraph (3), the Government shall—

(A) proceed with the action, in which case the action shall be conducted by the Government; or

(B) notify the court that it declines to take over the action, in which case the person bringing the action shall have the right to conduct the action.

(5) When a person brings an action under this subsection, no person other than the Government may intervene or bring a related action based on the facts underlying the pending action.

(c) Rights of the parties to qui tam actions.—**(1)** If the Government proceeds with the action, it shall have the primary responsibility for prosecuting the action, and shall not be bound by an act of the person bringing the action. Such person shall have the right to continue as a party to the action, subject to the limitations set forth in paragraph (2).

(2)(A) The Government may dismiss the action notwithstanding the objections of the person initiating the action if the person has been notified by the Government of the filing of the motion and the court has provided the person with an opportunity for a hearing on the motion.

(B) The Government may settle the action with the defendant notwithstanding the objections of the person initiating the action if the court determines, after a hearing, that the proposed settlement is fair, adequate, and reasonable under all the circumstances. Upon a showing of good cause, such hearing may be held in camera.

(C) Upon a showing by the Government that unrestricted participation during the course of the litigation by the person initiating the action would interfere with or unduly delay the Government's prosecution of the case, or would be repetitious, irrelevant, or for

3

purposes of harassment, the court may, in its discretion, impose limitations on the person's participation, such as—

    (i) limiting the number of witnesses the person may call;

    (ii) limiting the length of the testimony of such witnesses;

    (iii) limiting the person's cross-examination of witnesses; or

    (iv) otherwise limiting the participation by the person in the litigation.

(D) Upon a showing by the defendant that unrestricted participation during the course of the litigation by the person initiating the action would be for purposes of harassment or would cause the defendant undue burden or unnecessary expense, the court may limit the participation by the person in the litigation.

(3) If the Government elects not to proceed with the action, the person who initiated the action shall have the right to conduct the action. If the Government so requests, it shall be served with copies of all pleadings filed in the action and shall be supplied with copies of all deposition transcripts (at the Government's expense). When a person proceeds with the action, the court, without limiting the status and rights of the person initiating the action, may nevertheless permit the Government to intervene at a later date upon a showing of good cause.

(4) Whether or not the Government proceeds with the action, upon a showing by the Government that certain actions of discovery by the person initiating the action would interfere with the Government's investigation or prosecution of a criminal or civil matter arising out of the same facts, the court may stay such discovery for a period of not more than 60 days. Such a showing shall be conducted in camera. The court may extend the 60–day period upon a further showing in camera that the Government has pursued the criminal or civil investigation or proceedings with reasonable diligence and any proposed discovery in the civil action will interfere with the ongoing criminal or civil investigation or proceedings.

(5) Notwithstanding subsection (b), the Government may elect to pursue its claim through any alternate remedy available to the Government, including any administrative proceeding to determine a civil money penalty. If any such alternate remedy is pursued in another proceeding, the person initiating the action shall have the same rights in such proceeding as such person would have had if the action had continued under this section. Any finding of fact or conclusion of law made in such other proceeding that has become final shall be conclusive on all parties to an action under this section. For purposes of the preceding sentence, a finding or conclusion is final if it has been finally determined on appeal to the appropriate court of the United States, if all time for filing such an appeal with respect to the finding or conclusion has expired, or if the finding or conclusion is not subject to judicial review.

(d) Award to qui tam plaintiff.—

(1) If the Government proceeds with an action brought by a person under subsection (b), such person shall, subject to the second sentence of this paragraph, receive at least 15 percent but not more than 25 percent of the proceeds of the action or settlement of the claim, depending upon the extent to which the person substantially contributed to the prosecution of the action. Where the action is one which the court finds to be based primarily on disclosures of specific information (other than information provided by the person bringing the action) relating to allegations or transactions in a criminal, civil, or administrative hearing, in a congressional, administrative, or Government Accounting Office report, hearing, audit, or investigation, or from the news media, the court may award such sums as it considers appropriate, but in no case more than 10 percent of the proceeds, taking into account the significance of the information and the role of the person bringing the action in advancing the case to litigation. Any payment to a person under the first or second sentence of this paragraph shall be made from the proceeds. Any such person shall also receive an amount for reasonable expenses which the court finds to have been necessarily incurred, plus reasonable attorneys' fees and costs. All such expenses, fees, and costs shall be awarded against the defendant.

(2) If the Government does not proceed with an action under this section, the person bringing the action or settling the claim shall receive an amount which the court decides is reasonable for collecting the civil penalty and damages. The amount shall be not less than 25 percent and not more than 30 percent of the proceeds of the action or settlement and shall be paid out of such proceeds. Such person shall also receive an amount for reasonable expenses which the court finds to have been necessarily incurred, plus reasonable attorneys' fees and costs. All such expenses, fees, and costs shall be awarded against the defendant.

(3) Whether or not the Government proceeds with the action, if the court finds that the action was brought by a person who planned and initiated the violation of section 3729 upon which the action was brought, then the court may, to the extent the court considers appropriate, reduce the share of the proceeds of the action which the person would otherwise receive under paragraph (1) or (2) of this subsection, taking into account the role of that person in advancing the case to litigation and any relevant circumstances pertaining to the violation. If the person bringing the action is convicted of criminal conduct arising from his or her role in the violation of section 3729, that person shall be dismissed from the civil action and shall not receive any share of the proceeds of the action. Such dismissal shall not prejudice the right of the United States to continue the action, represented by the Department of Justice.

(4) If the Government does not proceed with the action and the person bringing the action conducts the action, the court may award to the defendant its reasonable attorneys' fees and expenses if the defendant prevails in the action and the court finds that the claim of the person bringing the action was clearly frivolous, clearly vexatious, or brought primarily for purposes of harassment.

(e) Certain actions barred.

(1) No court shall have jurisdiction over an action brought by a former or present member of the armed forces under subsection (b) of this section against a member of the armed forces arising out of such person's service in the armed forces.

(2)(A) No court shall have jurisdiction over an action brought under subsection (b) against a Member of Congress, a member of the judiciary, or a senior executive branch official if the action is based on evidence or information known to the Government when the action was brought.

    (B) For purposes of this paragraph, "senior executive branch official" means any officer or employee listed in paragraphs (1) through (8) of section 101(f) of the Ethics in Government Act of 1978 (5 U.S.C. App.).

(3) In no event may a person bring an action under subsection (b) which is based upon allegations or transactions which are the subject of a civil suit or an administrative civil money penalty proceeding in which the Government is already a party.

(4)(A) No court shall have jurisdiction over an action under this section based upon the public disclosure of allegations or transactions in a criminal, civil, or administrative hearing, in a congressional, administrative, or Government Accounting Office report, hearing, audit, or investigation, or from the news media, unless the action is brought by the Attorney General or the person bringing the action is an original source of the information.

    (B) For purposes of this paragraph, "original source" means an individual who has direct and independent knowledge of the information on which the allegations are based and has voluntarily provided the information to the Government before filing an action under this section which is based on the information.

(f) Government not liable for certain expenses.—The Government is not liable for expenses which a person incurs in bringing an action under this section.

(g) Fees and expenses to prevailing defendant.—In civil actions brought under this section by the United States, the provisions of section 24 12(d) of title 28 shall apply.

(h) Any employee who is discharged, demoted, suspended, threatened, harassed, or in any other manner discriminated against in the terms and conditions of employment by his or her employer because of lawful acts done by the employee on behalf of the employee or others in furtherance of an action under this section, including investigation for, initiation of, testimony for, or assistance in an action filed or to be filed under this section, shall be entitled to all relief necessary to make the employee whole. Such relief shall include reinstatement with the same seniority status such employee would have had but for the discrimination, 2 times the amount of back pay, interest on the back pay, and compensation for any special damages sustained as a result of the discrimination, including litigation costs and reasonable attorneys' fees. An employee may bring an action in the appropriate district court of the United States for the relief provided in this subsection.

Civil False Claims Act: 31 U.S.C.A. § 3729

§ 3729. False claims

(a) Liability for certain acts.—Any person who—

(1) knowingly presents, or causes to be presented, to an officer or employee of the United States Government or a member of the Armed Forces of the United States a false or fraudulent claim for payment or approval;

(2) knowingly makes, uses, or causes to be made or used, a false record or statement to get a false or fraudulent claim paid or approved by the Government;

(3) conspires to defraud the Government by getting a false or fraudulent claim allowed or paid;

(4) has possession, custody, or control of property or money used, or to be used, by the Government and, intending to defraud the Government or willfully to conceal the property, delivers, or causes to be delivered, less property than the amount for which the person receives a certificate or receipt;

(5) authorized to make or deliver a document certifying receipt of property used, or to be used, by the Government and, intending to defraud the Government, makes or delivers the receipt without completely knowing that the information on the receipt is true;

(6) knowingly buys, or receives as a pledge of an obligation or debt, public property from an officer or employee of the Government, or a member of the Armed Forces, who lawfully may not sell or pledge the property; or

(7) knowingly makes, uses, or causes to be made or used, a false record or statement to conceal, avoid, or decrease an obligation to pay or transmit money or property to the Government,

is liable to the United States Government for a civil penalty of not less than $5,000 and not more than $10,000, plus 3 times the amount of damages which the Government sustains because of the act of that person, except that if the court finds that—

(A) the person committing the violation of this subsection furnished officials of the United States responsible for investigating false claims violations with all information known to such person about the violation within 30 days after the date on which the defendant first obtained the information;

    (B) such person fully cooperated with any Government investigation of such violation; and

    (C) at the time such person furnished the United States with the information about the violation, no criminal prosecution, civil action, or administrative action had commenced under this title with respect to such violation, and the person did not have actual knowledge of the existence of an investigation into such violation; the court may assess not less than 2 times the amount of damages which the Government sustains because of the act of the person. A person violating this subsection shall also be liable to the United States Government for the costs of a civil action brought to recover any such penalty or damages.

  (b) Knowing and knowingly defined.—For purposes of this section, the terms "knowing" and "knowingly" mean that a person, with respect to information—

    (1) has actual knowledge of the information;

    (2) acts in deliberate ignorance of the truth or falsity of the information; or

    (3) acts in reckless disregard of the truth or falsity of the information,and no proof of specific intent to defraud is required.

  (c) Claim defined.—For purposes of this section, "claim" includes any request or demand, whether under a contract or otherwise, for money or property which is made to a contractor, grantee, or other recipient if the United States Government provides any portion of the money or property which is requested or demanded, or if the Government will reimburse such contractor, grantee, or other recipient for any portion of the money or property which is requested or demanded.

  (d) Exemption from disclosure.—Any information furnished pursuant to subparagraphs (A) through (C) of subsection (a) shall be exempt from disclosure under section 552 of title 5.

  (e) Exclusion.—This section does not apply to claims, records, or statements made under the Internal Revenue Code of 1986.

B. FEDERAL HEALTH CARE FRAUD & ABUSE LAWS

1. Federal Health Care Offenses and Exclusions: 18 U.S.C.A. §§ 24, 669, 1035, 1347

§ 24. Definitions relating to Federal health care offense

  (a) As used in this title, the term "Federal health care offense" means a violation of, or a criminal conspiracy to violate—

    (1) section 669, 1035, 1347, or 1518 of this title;

(2) section 287, 371, 664, 666, 1001, 1027, 1341, 1343, or 1954 of this title, if the violation or conspiracy relates to a health care benefit program.

(b) As used in this title, the term "health care benefit program" means any public or private plan or contract, affecting commerce, under which any medical benefit, item, or service is provided to any individual, and includes any individual or entity who is providing a medical benefit, item, or service for which payment may be made under the plan or contract.

§ 669.   Theft or embezzlement in connection with health care

(a) Whoever knowingly and willfully embezzles, steals, or otherwise without authority converts to the use of any person other than the rightful owner, or intentionally misapplies any of the moneys, funds, securities, premiums, credits, property, or other assets of a health care benefit program, shall be fined under this title or imprisoned not more than 10 years, or both; but if the value of such property does not exceed the sum of $100 the defendant shall be fined under this title or imprisoned not more than one year, or both.

(b) As used in this section, the term "health care benefit program" has the meaning given such term in section 24(b) of this title.

§ 1035.   False statements relating to health care matters

(a) Whoever, in any matter involving a health care benefit program, knowingly and willfully—

(1) falsifies, conceals, or covers up by any trick, scheme, or device a material fact; or

(2) makes any materially false, fictitious, or fraudulent statements or representations, or makes or uses any materially false writing or document knowing the same to contain any materially false, fictitious, or fraudulent statement or entry, in connection with the delivery of or payment for health care benefits, items, or services, shall be fined under this title or imprisoned not more than 5 years, or both.

(b) As used in this section, the term "health care benefit program" has the meaning given such term in section 24(b) of this title.

§ 1347.   Health care fraud

Whoever knowingly and willfully executes, or attempts to execute, a scheme or artifice—

(1) to defraud any health care benefit program; or

(2) to obtain, by means of false or fraudulent pretenses, representations, or promises, any of the money or property owned by, or under the custody or control of, any health care benefit program,

in connection with the delivery of or payment for health care benefits, items, or services, shall be fined under this title or imprisoned not more than 10 years, or both. If the violation results in serious bodily injury (as defined in section 1365 of this title), such person shall be fined under this title or imprisoned not more than 20 years, or both; and if the violation results in death, such person shall be fined under this title, or imprisoned for any term of years or for life, or both.

False Representations Concerning Requirements of the Social Security Act: 42 U.S.C.A. § 1307

§ 1307. Penalty for fraud

(a) Whoever, with the intent to defraud any person, shall make or cause to be made any false representation concerning the requirements of this chapter, of chapter 2, 21, or 23 of Title 26, or of any provision of subtitle F of such Title which corresponds (within the meaning of section 7852(b) of such Title) to a provision contained in subchapter E of chapter 9 of the Internal Revenue Code of 1939, or of any rules or regulations issued thereunder, knowing such representations to be false, shall be deemed guilty of a misdemeanor, and, upon conviction thereof, shall be punished by a fine not exceeding $1,000, or by imprisonment not exceeding one year, or both.

(b) Whoever, with the intent to elicit information as to the social security account number, date of birth, employment, wages, or benefits of any individual (1) falsely represents to the Commissioner of Social Security or the Secretary that he is such individual, or the wife, husband, widow, widower, divorced wife, divorced husband, surviving divorced wife, surviving divorced husband, surviving divorced mother, surviving divorced father, child, or parent of such individual, or the duly authorized agent of such individual, or of the wife, husband, widow, widower, divorced wife, divorced husband, surviving divorced wife, surviving divorced husband, surviving divorced mother, surviving divorced father, child, or parent of such individual, or (2) falsely represents to any person that he is an employee or agent of the United States, shall be deemed guilty of a felony, and, upon conviction thereof, shall be punished by a fine not exceeding $10,000 for each occurrence of a violation, or by imprisonment not exceeding 5 years, or both.

Exclusions From Participation in Medicare and State Health Care Programs: 42 U.S.C.A. § 1320a–7

§ 1320a–7. Exclusion of certain individuals and entities from participation in Medicare and State health care programs

(a) Mandatory exclusion

The Secretary shall exclude the following individuals and entities from participation in any Federal health care program (as defined in section 1320a–7b(f) of this title):

(1) Conviction of program-related crimes

Any individual or entity that has been convicted of a criminal offense related to the delivery of an item or service under subchapter XVIII of this chapter or under any State health care program.

(2) Conviction relating to patient abuse

Any individual or entity that has been convicted, under Federal or State law, of a criminal offense relating to neglect or abuse of patients in connection with the delivery of a health care item or service.

(3) Felony conviction relating to health care fraud

Any individual or entity that has been convicted for an offense which occurred after August 21, 1996, under Federal or State law, in connection with the delivery of a health care item or service or with respect to any act or omission in a health care program (other than those specifically described in paragraph (1)) operated by or financed in whole or in part by any Federal, State, or local government agency, of a criminal offense consisting of a felony relating to fraud, theft, embezzlement, breach of fiduciary responsibility, or other financial misconduct.

(4) Felony conviction relating to controlled substance

Any individual or entity that has been convicted for an offense which occurred after August 21, 1996, under Federal or State law, of a criminal offense consisting of a felony relating to the unlawful manufacture, distribution, prescription, or dispensing of a controlled substance.

(b) Permissive exclusion

The Secretary may exclude the following individuals and entities from participation in any Federal health care program (as defined in section 1320a–7b(f) of this title):

(1) Conviction relating to fraud

Any individual or entity that has been convicted for an offense which occurred after August 21, 1996, under Federal or State law—

(A) of a criminal offense consisting of a misdemeanor relating to fraud, theft, embezzlement, breach of fiduciary responsibility, or other financial misconduct—

(i) in connection with the delivery of a health care item or service, or

(ii) with respect to any act or omission in a health care program (other than those specifically described in subsection (a)(1) of this section) operated by or financed in whole or in part by any Federal, State, or local government agency; or

(B) of a criminal offense relating to fraud, theft, embezzlement, breach of fiduciary responsibility, or other financial misconduct with respect to any act or omission in a program (other than a health care program) operated by or financed in whole or in part by any Federal, State, or local government agency.

(2) Conviction relating to obstruction of an investigation

Any individual or entity that has been convicted, under Federal or State law, in connection with the interference with or obstruction of any investigation into any criminal offense described in paragraph (1) or in subsection (a) of this section.

(3) Misdemeanor conviction relating to controlled substance

Any individual or entity that has been convicted, under Federal or State law, of a criminal offense consisting of a misdemeanor relating to the unlawful manufacture, distribution, prescription, or dispensing of a controlled substance.

(4) License revocation or suspension

Any individual or entity—

(A) whose license to provide health care has been revoked or suspended by any State licensing authority, or who otherwise lost such a license or the right to apply for or renew such a license, for reasons bearing on the individual's or entity's professional competence, professional performance, or financial integrity, or

(B) who surrendered such a license while a formal disciplinary proceeding was pending before such an authority and the proceeding concerned the individual's or entity's professional competence, professional performance, or financial integrity.

(5) Exclusion or suspension under Federal or State health care program

Any individual or entity which has been suspended or excluded from participation, or otherwise sanctioned, under—

(A) any Federal Program, including programs of the Department of Defense or the Department of Veterans Affairs, involving the provision of health care, or

(B) a State health care program,

for reasons bearing on the individual's or entity's professional competence, professional performance, or financial integrity.

(6) Claims for excessive charges or unnecessary services and failure of certain organizations to furnish medically necessary services

Any individual or entity that the Secretary determines—

(A) has submitted or caused to be submitted bills or requests for payment (where such bills or requests are based on charges or cost) under subchapter XVIII of this chapter or a State health care program containing charges (or, in applicable cases, requests for payment of costs) for items or services furnished substantially in excess of such individual's or entity's usual charges (or, in applicable cases, substantially in excess of such individual's or entity's costs) for such items or services, unless the Secretary finds there is good cause for such bills or requests containing such charges or costs;

(B) has furnished or caused to be furnished items or services to patients (whether or not eligible for benefits under subchapter XVIII of this chapter or under a State health care program) substantially in excess of the needs of such patients or of a quality which fails to meet professionally recognized standards of health care;

(C) is—

(i) a health maintenance organization (as defined in section 1396b(m) of this title) providing items and services under a State plan approved under subchapter XIX of this chapter, or

(ii) an entity furnishing services under a waiver approved under section 1396n(b)(1) of this title, and has failed substantially to provide medically necessary items and services that are required (under law or the contract with the State under subchapter XIX of this chapter) to be provided to individuals covered under that plan or waiver, if the failure has adversely affected (or has a substantial likelihood of adversely affecting) these individuals; or

(D) is an entity providing items and services as an eligible organization under a risk-sharing contract under section 1395mm of this title and has failed substantially to provide medically necessary items and services that are required (under law or such contract) to be provided to individuals covered under the risk-sharing contract, if the failure has adversely affected (or has a substantial likelihood of adversely affecting) these individuals.

(7) Fraud, kickbacks, and other prohibited activities

Any individual or entity that the Secretary determines has committed an act which is described in section 1320a–7a, 1320a–7b, or 1320a–8 of this title.

13

(8) Entities controlled by a sanctioned individual

Any entity with respect to which the Secretary determines that a person—

(A)(i) who has a direct or indirect ownership or control interest of 5 percent or more in the entity or with an ownership or control interest (as defined in section 1320a–3(a)(3) of this title) in that entity,

(ii) who is an officer, director, agent, or managing employee (as defined in section 1320a–5(b) of this title) of that entity; or

(iii) who was described in clause (i) but is no longer so described because of a transfer of ownership or control interest, in anticipation of (or following) a conviction, assessment, or exclusion described in subparagraph (B) against the person, to an immediate family member (as defined in subsection (j)(1) of this section) or a member of the household of the person (as defined in subsection (j)(2) of this section) who continues to maintain an interest described in such clause—

is a person—

(B)(i) who has been convicted of any offense described in subsection (a) of this section or in paragraph (1), (2), or (3) of this subsection;

(ii) against whom a civil monetary penalty has been assessed under section 1320a–7a of this title or 1320a–8 of this title; or

(iii) who has been excluded from participation under a program under subchapter XVIII of this chapter or under a State health care program.

(9) Failure to disclose required information

Any entity that did not fully and accurately make any disclosure required by section 1320a–3 of this title, section 1320a–3a of this title, or section 1320a–5 of this title.

(10) Failure to supply requested information on subcontractors and suppliers

Any disclosing entity (as defined in section 1320a–3(a)(2) of this title) that fails to supply (within such period as may be specified by the Secretary in regulations) upon request specifically addressed to the entity by the Secretary or by the State agency administering or supervising the administration of a State health care program—

(A) full and complete information as to the ownership of a subcontractor (as defined by the Secretary in regulations) with whom the entity has had, during the previous 12 months, business transactions in an aggregate amount in excess of $25,000, or

(B) full and complete information as to any significant business transactions (as defined by the Secretary in regulations), occurring during the five-year period ending on the date of such request, between the entity and any wholly owned supplier or between the entity and any subcontractor.

(11) Failure to supply payment information

Any individual or entity furnishing items or services for which payment may be made under subchapter XVIII of this chapter or a State health care program that fails to provide such information as the Secretary or the appropriate State agency finds necessary to determine whether such payments are or were due and the amounts thereof, or has refused to permit such examination of its records by or on behalf of the Secretary or that agency as may be necessary to verify such information.

(12) Failure to grant immediate access

Any individual or entity that fails to grant immediate access, upon reasonable request (as defined by the Secretary in regulations) to any of the following:

(A) To the Secretary, or to the agency used by the Secretary, for the purpose specified in the first sentence of section 1395aa(a) of this title (relating to compliance with conditions of participation or payment).

(B) To the Secretary or the State agency, to perform the reviews and surveys required under State plans under paragraphs (26), (31), and (33) of section 1396a(a) of this title and under section 1396b(g) of this title.

(C) To the Inspector General of the Department of Health and Human Services, for the purpose of reviewing records, documents, and other data necessary to the performance of the statutory functions of the Inspector General.

(D) To a State medicaid fraud control unit (as defined in section 1396b(q) of this title), for the purpose of conducting activities described in that section.

(13) Failure to take corrective action

Any hospital that fails to comply substantially with a corrective action required under section 1395ww(f)(2)(B) of this title.

(14) Default on health education loan or scholarship obligations

Any individual who the Secretary determines is in default on repayments of scholarship obligations or loans in connection with health professions education made or secured, in whole or in part, by the Secretary and with respect to whom the Secretary has taken all reasonable steps available to the Secretary to secure repayment of such obligations or loans, except that (A) the Secretary shall not exclude pursuant to this paragraph a physician who is the sole community physician or sole

15

source of essential specialized services in a community if a State requests that the physician not be excluded, and (B) the Secretary shall take into account, in determining whether to exclude any other physician pursuant to this paragraph, access of beneficiaries to physician services for which payment may be made under subchapter XVIII or XIX of this chapter.

(15) Individuals controlling a sanctioned entity

(A) Any individual—

(i) who has a direct or indirect ownership or control interest in a sanctioned entity and who knows or should know (as defined in section 1320a–7a(i)(7)) of the action constituting the basis for the conviction or exclusion described in subparagraph (B); or

(ii) who is an officer or managing employee (as defined in section 1320a–5(b) of this title) of such an entity.

(B) For purposes of subparagraph (A), the term "sanctioned entity" means an entity—

(i) that has been convicted of any offense described in subsection (a) of this section or in paragraph (1), (2), or (3) of this subsection; or

(ii) that has been excluded from participation under a program under subchapter XVIII of this chapter or under a State health care program.

(c) Notice, effective date, and period of exclusion

(1) An exclusion under this section or under section 1320a–7a of this title shall be effective at such time and upon such reasonable notice to the public and to the individual or entity excluded as may be specified in regulations consistent with paragraph (2).

(2)(A) Except as provided in subparagraph (B), such an exclusion shall be effective with respect to services furnished to an individual on or after the effective date of the exclusion.

(B) Unless the Secretary determines that the health and safety of individuals receiving services warrants the exclusion taking effect earlier, an exclusion shall not apply to payments made under subchapter XVIII of this chapter or under a State health care program for—

(i) inpatient institutional services furnished to an individual who was admitted to such institution before the date of the exclusion, or

(ii) home health services and hospice care furnished to an individual under a plan of care established before the date of the exclusion, until the passage of 30 days after the effective date of the exclusion.

(3)(A) The Secretary shall specify, in the notice of exclusion under paragraph (1) and the written notice under section 1320a–7a of this title, the minimum period (or, in the case of an exclusion of an individual under subsection (b)(12) of this section or in the case described in subparagraph (G), the period) of the exclusion.

(B) Subject to subparagraph (G), in the case of an exclusion under subsection (a) of this section, the minimum period of exclusion shall be not less than five years, except that, upon the request of a State, the Secretary may waive the exclusion under subsection (a)(1) of this section in the case of an individual or entity that is the sole community physician or sole source of essential specialized services in a community. The Secretary's decision whether to waive the exclusion shall not be reviewable.

(C) In the case of an exclusion of an individual under subsection (b)(12) of this section, the period of the exclusion shall be equal to the sum of—

(i) the length of the period in which the individual failed to grant the immediate access described in that subsection, and

(ii) an additional period, not to exceed 90 days, set by the Secretary.

(D) Subject to subparagraph (G), in the case of an exclusion of an individual or entity under paragraph (1), (2), or (3) of subsection (b) of this section, the period of the exclusion shall be 3 years, unless the Secretary determines in accordance with published regulations that a shorter period is appropriate because of mitigating circumstances or that a longer period is appropriate because of aggravating circumstances.

(E) In the case of an exclusion of an individual or entity under subsection (b)(4) or (b)(5) of this section, the period of the exclusion shall not be less than the period during which the individual's or entity's license to provide health care is revoked, suspended, or surrendered, or the individual or the entity is excluded or suspended from a Federal or State health care program.

(F) In the case of an exclusion of an individual or entity under subsection (b)(6)(B) of this section, the period of the exclusion shall be not less than 1 year.

(G) In the case of an exclusion of an individual under subsection (a) of this section based on a conviction occurring on or after August 5, 1997, if the individual has (before, on, or after August 5, 1997) been convicted—

(i) on one previous occasion of one or more offenses for which an exclusion may be effected under such subsection, the period of the exclusion shall be not less than 10 years, or

(ii) on 2 or more previous occasions of one or more offenses for which an exclusion may be effected under such subsection, the period of the exclusion shall be permanent.

(d) Notice to State agencies and exclusion under State health care programs

(1) Subject to paragraph (3), the Secretary shall exercise the authority under this section and section 1320a–7a of this title in a manner that results in an individual's or entity's exclusion from all the programs under subchapter XVIII of this chapter and all the State health care programs in which the individual or entity may otherwise participate.

(2) The Secretary shall promptly notify each appropriate State agency administering or supervising the administration of each State health care program (and, in the case of an exclusion effected pursuant to subsection (a) of this section and to which section 824(a)(5) of Title 21 may apply, the Attorney General)—

(A) of the fact and circumstances of each exclusion effected against an individual or entity under this section or section 1320a–7a of this title, and

(B) of the period (described in paragraph (3)) for which the State agency is directed to exclude the individual or entity from participation in the State health care program.

(3)(A) Except as provided in subparagraph (B), the period of the exclusion under a State health care program under paragraph (2) shall be the same as any period of exclusion under subchapter XVIII of this chapter.

(B)(i) The Secretary may waive an individual's or entity's exclusion under a State health care program under paragraph (2) if the Secretary receives and approves a request for the waiver with respect to the individual or entity from the State agency administering or supervising the administration of the program.

(ii) A State health care program may provide for a period of exclusion which is longer than the period of exclusion under subchapter XVIII of this chapter.

(e) Notice to State licensing agencies

The Secretary shall—

(1) promptly notify the appropriate State or local agency or authority having responsibility for the licensing or certification of an individual or entity excluded (or directed to be excluded) from participation under this section or section 1320a–7a of this title, of the fact and circumstances of the exclusion,

(2) request that appropriate investigations be made and sanctions invoked in accordance with applicable State law and policy, and

(3) request that the State or local agency or authority keep the Secretary and the Inspector General of the Department of Health and Human Services fully and currently informed with respect to any actions taken in response to the request.

(f) Notice, hearing, and judicial review

(1) Subject to paragraph (2), any individual or entity that is excluded (or directed to be excluded) from participation under this section is entitled to reasonable notice and opportunity for a hearing thereon by the Secretary to the same extent as is provided in section 405(b) of this title, and to judicial review of the Secretary's final decision after such hearing as is provided in section 405(g) of this title, except that, in so applying such sections and section 405(*l*) of this title, any reference therein to the Commissioner of Social Security or the Social Security Administration shall be considered a reference to the Secretary or the Department of Health and Human Services, respectively.

(2) Unless the Secretary determines that the health or safety of individuals receiving services warrants the exclusion taking effect earlier, any individual or entity that is the subject of an adverse determination under subsection (b)(7) of this section shall be entitled to a hearing by an administrative law judge (as provided under section 405(b) of this title) on the determination under subsection (b)(7) of this section before any exclusion based upon the determination takes effect.

(3) The provisions of section 405(h) of this title shall apply with respect to this section and sections 1320a–7a, 1320a–8, and 1320c–5 of this title to the same extent as it is applicable with respect to subchapter II of this chapter, except that, in so applying such section and section 405(*l*) of this title, any reference therein to the Commissioner of Social Security shall be considered a reference to the Secretary.

(g) Application for termination of exclusion

(1) An individual or entity excluded (or directed to be excluded) from participation under this section or section 1320a–7a of this title may apply to the Secretary, in the manner specified by the Secretary in regulations and at the end of the minimum period of exclusion provided under subsection (c)(3) of this section and at such other times as the Secretary may provide, for termination of the exclusion effected under this section or section 1320a–7a of this title.

(2) The Secretary may terminate the exclusion if the Secretary determines, on the basis of the conduct of the applicant which occurred after the date of the notice of exclusion or which was unknown to the Secretary at the time of the exclusion, that—

(A) there is no basis under subsection (a) or (b) of this section or section 1320a–7a(a) of this title for a continuation of the exclusion, and

(B) there are reasonable assurances that the types of actions which formed the basis for the original exclusion have not recurred and will not recur.

(3) The Secretary shall promptly notify each appropriate State agency administering or supervising the administration of each State health care program (and, in the case of an exclusion effected pursuant to subsection (a) of this section and to which section 824(a)(5) of Title 21 may apply, the Attorney General) of the fact and circumstances of each termination of exclusion made under this subsection.

(h) "State health care program" defined

For purposes of this section and sections 1320a–7a and 1320a–7b of this title, the term "State health care program" means—

(1) a State plan approved under subchapter XIX of this chapter,

(2) any program receiving funds under subchapter V of this chapter or from an allotment to a State under such subchapter,

(3) any program receiving funds under subchapter XX of this chapter or from an allotment to a State under such subchapter, or

(4) a State child health plan approved under subchapter XXI of this chapter.

(i) "Convicted" defined

For purposes of subsections (a) and (b) of this section, an individual or entity is considered to have been "convicted" of a criminal offense—

(1) when a judgment of conviction has been entered against the individual or entity by a Federal, State, or local court, regardless of whether there is an appeal pending or whether the judgment of conviction or other record relating to criminal conduct has been expunged;

(2) when there has been a finding of guilt against the individual or entity by a Federal, State, or local court;

(3) when a plea of guilty or nolo contendere by the individual or entity has been accepted by a Federal, State, or local court; or

(4) when the individual or entity has entered into participation in a first offender, deferred adjudication, or other arrangement or program where judgment of conviction has been withheld.

(j) Definition of immediate family member and member of household

For purposes of subsection (b)(8)(A)(iii) of this section:

(1) The term "immediate family member" means, with respect to a person—

(A) the husband or wife of the person;

(B) the natural or adoptive parent, child, or sibling of the person;

(**C**) the stepparent, stepchild, stepbrother, or stepsister of the person;

(**D**) the father-, mother-, daughter-, son-, brother-, or sister-in-law of the person;

(**E**) the grandparent or grandchild of the person; and

(**F**) the spouse of a grandparent or grandchild of the person.

(**2**) The term "member of the household" means, with respect to any person, any individual sharing a common abode as part of a single family unit with the person, including domestic employees and others who live together as a family unit, but not including a roomer or boarder.

Administrative Penalties Under the Federal Health Care False Claims Statute: 42 U.S.C.A. § 1320a–7a

§ 1320a–7a. Civil monetary penalties

(**a**) Improperly filed claims

Any person (including an organization, agency, or other entity, but excluding a beneficiary, as defined in subsection (i)(5) of this section) that—

(**1**) knowingly presents or causes to be presented to an officer, employee, or agent of the United States, or of any department or agency thereof, or of any State agency (as defined in subsection (i)(1) of this section), a claim (as defined in subsection (i)(2) of this section) that the Secretary determines—

(**A**) is for a medical or other item or service that the person knows or should know was not provided as claimed, including any person who engages in a pattern or practice of presenting or causing to be presented a claim for an item or service that is based on a code that the person knows or should know will result in a greater payment to the person than the code the person knows or should know is applicable to the item or service actually provided,

(**B**) is for a medical or other item or service and the person knows or should know the claim is false or fraudulent,

(**C**) is presented for a physician's service (or an item or service incident to a physician's service) by a person who knows or should know that the individual who furnished (or supervised the furnishing of) the service—

(**i**) was not licensed as a physician,

(**ii**) was licensed as a physician, but such license had been obtained through a misrepresentation of material fact (including cheating on an examination required for licensing), or

(**iii**) represented to the patient at the time the service was furnished that the physician was certified in a medical specialty

21

by a medical specialty board when the individual was not so certified,

(D) is for a medical or other item or service furnished during a period in which the person was excluded from the program under which the claim was made pursuant to a determination by the Secretary under this section or under section 1320a–7, 1320c–5, 1320c–9(b) (as in effect on September 2, 1982), 1395y(d) (as in effect on August 18, 1987), or 1395cc(b) of this title or as a result of the application of the provisions of section 1395u(j)(2) of this title, or

(E) is for a pattern of medical or other items or services that a person knows or should know are not medically necessary;

(2) knowingly presents or causes to be presented to any person a request for payment which is in violation of the terms of (A) an assignment under section 1395u(b)(3)(B)(ii) of this title, or (B) an agreement with a State agency (or other requirement of a State plan under subchapter XIX of this chapter) not to charge a person for an item or service in excess of the amount permitted to be charged, or (C) an agreement to be a participating physician or supplier under section 1395u(h)(1) of this title, or (D) an agreement pursuant to section 1395cc(a)(1)(G) of this title;

(3) knowingly gives or causes to be given to any person, with respect to coverage under subchapter XVIII of this chapter of inpatient hospital services subject to the provisions of section 1395ww of this title, information that he knows or should know is false or misleading, and that could reasonably be expected to influence the decision when to discharge such person or another individual from the hospital;

(4) in the case of a person who is not an organization, agency, or other entity, is excluded from participating in a program under subchapter XVIII of this chapter or a State health care program in accordance with this subsection or under section 1320a–7 of this title and who, at the time of a violation of this subsection—

(A) retains a direct or indirect ownership or control interest in an entity that is participating in a program under subchapter XVIII of this chapter or a State health care program, and who knows or should know of the action constituting the basis for the exclusion; or

(B) is an officer or managing employee (as defined in section 1320a–5(b) of this title) of such an entity;

(5) offers to or transfers remuneration to any individual eligible for benefits under subchapter XVIII of this chapter, or under a State health care program (as defined in section 1320a–7(h) of this title) that such person knows or should know is likely to influence such individual to order or receive from a particular provider, practitioner, or supplier any item or service for which payment may be made, in whole or in part, under subchapter XVIII of this chapter, or a State health care program (as so defined);

(6) arranges or contracts (by employment or otherwise) with an individual or entity that the person knows or should know is excluded from participation in a Federal health care program (as defined in section 1320a–7b(f) of this title), for the provision of items or services for which payment may be made under such a program; or

(7) commits an act described in paragraph (1) or (2) of section 1320a–7b(b) of this title; shall be subject, in addition to any other penalties that may be prescribed by law, to a civil money penalty of not more than $10,000 for each item or service (or, in cases under paragraph (3), $15,000 for each individual with respect to whom false or misleading information was given; in cases under paragraph (4), $10,000 for each day the prohibited relationship occurs; or in cases under paragraph (7), $50,000 for each such act). In addition, such a person shall be subject to an assessment of not more than 3 times the amount claimed for each such item or service in lieu of damages sustained by the United States or a State agency because of such claim (or, in cases under paragraph (7), damages of not more than 3 times the total amount of remuneration offered, paid, solicited, or received, without regard to whether a portion of such remuneration was offered, paid, solicited, or received for a lawful purpose). In addition the Secretary may make a determination in the same proceeding to exclude the person from participation in the Federal health care programs (as defined in section 1320a–7b(f)(1) of this title) and to direct the appropriate State agency to exclude the person from participation in any State health care program.

(b) Payments to induce reduction or limitation of services

(1) If a hospital or a critical access hospital knowingly makes a payment, directly or indirectly, to a physician as an inducement to reduce or limit services provided with respect to individuals who—

(A) are entitled to benefits under part A or part B of subchapter XVIII of this chapter or to medical assistance under a State plan approved under subchapter XIX of this chapter, and

(B) are under the direct care of the physician, the hospital or a critical access hospital shall be subject, in addition to any other penalties that may be prescribed by law, to a civil money penalty of not more than $2,000 for each such individual with respect to whom the payment is made.

(2) Any physician who knowingly accepts receipt of a payment described in paragraph (1) shall be subject, in addition to any other penalties that may be prescribed by law, to a civil money penalty of not more than $2,000 for each individual described in such paragraph with respect to whom the payment is made.

(3)(A) Any physician who executes a document described in subparagraph (B) with respect to an individual knowing that all of the requirements referred to in such subparagraph are not met with respect to the individual shall be subject to a civil monetary penalty of not more than the greater of—

(i) $5,000, or

(ii) three times the amount of the payments under subchapter XVIII of this chapter for home health services which are made pursuant to such certification.

(B) A document described in this subparagraph is any document that certifies, for purposes of subchapter XVIII of this chapter, that an individual meets the requirements of section 1395f(a)(2)(C) or 1395n(a)(2)(A) of this title in the case of home health services furnished to the individual.

(c) Initiation of proceeding; authorization by Attorney General, notice, etc.; estoppel, failure to comply with order or procedure

(1) The Secretary may initiate a proceeding to determine whether to impose a civil money penalty, assessment, or exclusion under subsection (a) or (b) of this section only as authorized by the Attorney General pursuant to procedures agreed upon by them. The Secretary may not initiate an action under this section with respect to any claim, request for payment, or other occurrence described in this section later than six years after the date the claim was presented, the request for payment was made, or the occurrence took place. The Secretary may initiate an action under this section by serving notice of the action in any manner authorized by Rule 4 of the Federal Rules of Civil Procedure.

(2) The Secretary shall not make a determination adverse to any person under subsection (a) or (b) of this section until the person has been given written notice and an opportunity for the determination to be made on the record after a hearing at which the person is entitled to be represented by counsel, to present witnesses, and to cross-examine witnesses against the person.

(3) In a proceeding under subsection (a) or (b) of this section which—

(A) is against a person who has been convicted (whether upon a verdict after trial or upon a plea of guilty or nolo contendere) of a Federal crime charging fraud or false statements, and

(B) involves the same transaction as in the criminal action, the person is estopped from denying the essential elements of the criminal offense.

(4) The official conducting a hearing under this section may sanction a person, including any party or attorney, for failing to comply with an order or procedure, failing to defend an action, or other misconduct as would interfere with the speedy, orderly, or fair conduct of the hearing.

Such sanction shall reasonably relate to the severity and nature of the failure or misconduct. Such sanction may include—

(A) in the case of refusal to provide or permit discovery, drawing negative factual inferences or treating such refusal as an admission by deeming the matter, or certain facts, to be established,

(B) prohibiting a party from introducing certain evidence or otherwise supporting a particular claim or defense,

(C) striking pleadings, in whole or in part,

(D) staying the proceedings,

(E) dismissal of the action,

(F) entering a default judgment,

(G) ordering the party or attorney to pay attorneys' fees and other costs caused by the failure or misconduct, and

(H) refusing to consider any motion or other action which is not filed in a timely manner.

(d) Amount or scope of penalty, assessment, or exclusion

In determining the amount or scope of any penalty, assessment, or exclusion imposed pursuant to subsection (a) or (b) of this section, the Secretary shall take into account—

(1) the nature of claims and the circumstances under which they were presented,

(2) the degree of culpability, history of prior offenses, and financial condition of the person presenting the claims, and

(3) such other matters as justice may require.

(e) Review by courts of appeals

Any person adversely affected by a determination of the Secretary under this section may obtain a review of such determination in the United States Court of Appeals for the circuit in which the person resides, or in which the claim was presented, by filing in such court (within sixty days following the date the person is notified of the Secretary's determination) a written petition requesting that the determination be modified or set aside. A copy of the petition shall be forthwith transmitted by the clerk of the court to the Secretary, and thereupon the Secretary shall file in the Court the record in the proceeding as provided in section 2112 of Title 28. Upon such filing, the court shall have jurisdiction of the proceeding and of the question determined therein, and shall have the power to make and enter upon the pleadings, testimony, and proceedings set forth in such record a decree affirming, modifying, remanding for further consideration, or setting aside, in whole or in part, the determination of the Secretary and enforcing the same to the extent that such order is affirmed or modified. No objection that has not been urged before the Secretary shall be considered by the court, unless the failure or neglect to urge such objection shall be excused because of extraordinary circumstances. The findings of the Secretary with respect to questions of fact, if supported by substantial evidence on the record considered as a whole, shall be conclusive. If any party shall apply to the court for leave to adduce additional evidence and shall show to the satisfaction of the court that such additional evidence is material and that there were reasonable grounds for the failure to adduce such evidence in the hearing before the Secretary, the court may order such additional evidence to be taken before the Secretary and to be made a part of the record. The Secretary may modify his findings as to the facts, or make new findings, by reason of additional evidence so taken and filed, and he shall file with the court such modified or new findings, which findings with respect to questions of fact, if supported by substantial evidence on the record considered as a whole, shall be conclusive, and his recommendations, if any, for the modification or setting aside of his original order. Upon the filing of the record with it, the jurisdiction of the court shall be exclusive and its judgment and decree shall be final, except that the same shall be subject to review by the Supreme Court of the United States, as provided in section 1254 of Title 28.

(f) Compromise of penalties and assessments; recovery; use of funds recovered

Civil money penalties and assessments imposed under this section may be compromised by the Secretary and may be recovered in a civil action in the name of the United States brought in United States district court for the district where the claim was presented, or where the claimant resides, as determined by the Secretary. Amounts recovered under this section shall be paid to the Secretary and disposed of as follows:

(1)(A) In the case of amounts recovered arising out of a claim under subchapter XIX of this chapter, there shall be paid to the State agency an amount bearing the same proportion to the total amount recovered as the State's share of the amount paid by the State agency for such claim bears to the total amount paid for such claim.

(B) In the case of amounts recovered arising out of a claim under an allotment to a State under subchapter V of this chapter, there shall be paid to the State agency an amount equal to three-sevenths of the amount recovered.

(2) Such portion of the amounts recovered as is determined to have been paid out of the trust funds under sections 1395i and 1395t of this title shall be repaid to such trust funds.

(3) With respect to amounts recovered arising out of a claim under a Federal health care program (as defined in section 1320a-7b(f) of this title), the portion of such amounts as is determined to have been paid by the program shall be repaid to the program, and the portion of such amounts attributable to the amounts recovered under this section by reason of the amendments made by the Health Insurance Portability and Accountability Act of 1996 (as estimated by the Secretary) shall be deposited into the Federal Hospital Insurance Trust Fund pursuant to section 1395i(k)(2)(C) of this title.

(4) The remainder of the amounts recovered shall be deposited as miscellaneous receipts of the Treasury of the United States.

The amount of such penalty or assessment, when finally determined, or the amount agreed upon in compromise, may be deducted from any sum then or later owing by the United States or a State agency to the person against whom the penalty or assessment has been assessed.

(g) Finality of determination respecting penalty, assessment, or exclusion

A determination by the Secretary to impose a penalty, assessment, or exclusion under subsection (a) or (b) of this section shall be final upon the expiration of the sixty-day period referred to in subsection (e) of this section. Matters that were raised or that could have been raised in a hearing before the Secretary or in an appeal pursuant to subsection (e) of this section may not be raised as a defense to a civil action by the United States to collect a penalty, assessment, or exclusion assessed under this section.

(h) Notification of appropriate entities of finality of determination

Whenever the Secretary's determination to impose a penalty, assessment, or exclusion under subsection (a) or (b) of this section becomes final, he shall notify the appropriate State or local medical or professional organization, the appropriate State agency or agencies administering or supervising the administration of State health care programs (as defined in section 1320a–7(h) of this title), and the appropriate utilization and quality control peer review organization, and the appropriate State or local licensing agency or organization (including the agency specified in section 1395aa(a) and 1396a(a)(33) of this title) that such a penalty, assessment, or exclusion has become final and the reasons therefor.

(i) Definitions

For the purposes of this section:

(1) The term "State agency" means the agency established or designated to administer or supervise the administration of the State plan under subchapter XIX of this chapter or designated to administer the State's program under subchapter V of this chapter or subchapter XX of this chapter.

(2) The term "claim" means an application for payments for items and services under a Federal health care program (as defined in section 1320a–7b(f) of this title).

(3) The term "item or service" includes (A) any particular item, device, medical supply, or service claimed to have been provided to a patient and listed in an itemized claim for payment, and (B) in the case of a claim based on costs, any entry in the cost report, books of account or other documents supporting such claim.

(4) The term "agency of the United States" includes any contractor acting as a fiscal intermediary, carrier, or fiscal agent or any other claims processing agent for a Federal health care program (as so defined).

(5) The term "beneficiary" means an individual who is eligible to receive items or services for which payment may be made under a Federal health care program (as so defined) but does not include a provider, supplier, or practitioner.

(6) The term "remuneration" includes the waiver of coinsurance and deductible amounts (or any part thereof), and transfers of items or services for free or for other than fair market value. The term "remuneration" does not include—

    (A) the waiver of coinsurance and deductible amounts by a person, if—

        (i) the waiver is not offered as part of any advertisement or solicitation;

        (ii) the person does not routinely waive coinsurance or deductible amounts; and

        (iii) the person—

            (I) waives the coinsurance and deductible amounts after determining in good faith that the individual is in financial need; or

            (II) fails to collect coinsurance or deductible amounts after making reasonable collection efforts;

            (III) Repealed. Pub.L. 105–33, Title IV, § 4331(e)(1)(C), Aug. 5, 1997, 111 Stat. 396

    (B) subject to subsection (n), any permissible practice described in any subparagraph of section 1320a–7b(b)(3) of this title or in regulations issued by the Secretary;

    (C) differentials in coinsurance and deductible amounts as part of a benefit plan design as long as the differentials have been disclosed in writing to all beneficiaries, third party payers, and providers, to whom claims are presented and as long as the differentials meet the standards as defined in regulations promulgated by the Secretary not later than 180 days after August 21, 1996; or

    (D) incentives given to individuals to promote the delivery of preventive care as determined by the Secretary in regulations so promulgated.

    (D) [sic] a reduction in the copayment amount for covered OPD services under section 1395l(t)(5)(B) of this title.

(7) The term "should know" means that a person, with respect to information—

    (A) acts in deliberate ignorance of the truth or falsity of the information; or

    (B) acts in reckless disregard of the truth or falsity of the information, and no proof of specific intent to defraud is required.

(j) Subpoenas

(1) The provisions of subsections (d) and (e) of section 405 of this title shall apply with respect to this section to the same extent as they are applicable with respect to subchapter II of this chapter. The Secretary may delegate the authority granted by section 405(d) of this title (as made applicable to this section) to the Inspector General of the Department of Health and Human Services for purposes of any investigation under this section.

(2) The Secretary may delegate authority granted under this section and under section 1320a–7 of this title to the Inspector General of the Department of Health and Human Services.

(k) Injunctions

Whenever the Secretary has reason to believe that any person has engaged, is engaging, or is about to engage in any activity which makes the person subject to a civil monetary penalty under this section, the Secretary may bring an action in an appropriate district court of the United States (or, if applicable, a United States court of any territory) to enjoin such activity, or to enjoin the person from concealing, removing, encumbering, or disposing of assets which may be required in order to pay a civil monetary penalty if any such penalty were to be imposed or to seek other appropriate relief.

(l) Liability of principal for acts of agent

A principal is liable for penalties, assessments, and an exclusion under this section for the actions of the principal's agent acting within the scope of the agency.

(m) Claims within jurisdiction of other departments or agencies

(1) For purposes of this section, with respect to a Federal health care program not contained in this chapter, references to the Secretary in this section shall be deemed to be references to the Secretary or Administrator of the department or agency with jurisdiction over such program and references to the Inspector General of the Department of Health and Human Services in this section shall be deemed to be references to the Inspector General of the applicable department or agency.

(2)(A) The Secretary and Administrator of the departments and agencies referred to in paragraph (1) may include in any action pursuant to this section, claims within the jurisdiction of other Federal departments or agencies as long as the following conditions are satisfied:

(i) The case involves primarily claims submitted to the Federal health care programs of the department or agency initiating the action.

(ii) The Secretary or Administrator of the department or agency initiating the action gives notice and an opportunity to participate in the investigation to the Inspector General of the department or agency with primary jurisdiction over the Federal health care programs to which the claims were submitted.

(B) If the conditions specified in subparagraph (A) are fulfilled, the Inspector General of the department or agency initiating the action is authorized to exercise all powers granted under the Inspector General Act of 1978 (5 U.S.C. App.) with respect to the claims submitted to the other departments or agencies to the same manner and extent as provided in that Act with respect to claims submitted to such departments or agencies.

(n) Safe harbor for payment of Medigap premiums

(1) Subparagraph (B) of subsection (i)(6) shall not apply to a practice described in paragraph unless—

(A) the Secretary, through the Inspector General of the Department of Health and Human Services, promulgates a rule authorizing such a practice as an exception to remuneration; and

(B) the remuneration is offered or transferred by a person under such rule during the 2–year period beginning on the date the rule is first promulgated.

(2) A practice described in this paragraph is a practice under which a health care provider or facility pays, in whole or in part, premiums for medicare supplemental policies for individuals entitled to benefits under part A of title XVIII [42 U.S.C.A. § 1395c et seq.] pursuant to section 426–1 of this title.

2. Antikickback Law

Criminal Penalties for Acts Involving Federal Health Care Programs: 42 U.S.C.A. § 1320a–7b

§ 1320a–7b. Criminal penalties for acts involving Federal health care programs

(a) Making or causing to be made false statements or representations

Whoever—

(1) knowingly and willfully makes or causes to be made any false statement or representation of a material fact in any application for any benefit or payment under a Federal health care program (as defined in subsection (f) of this section),

(2) at any time knowingly and willfully makes or causes to be made any false statement or representation of a material fact for use in determining rights to such benefit or payment,

(3) having knowledge of the occurrence of any event affecting (A) his initial or continued right to any such benefit or payment, or (B) the initial or continued right to any such benefit or payment of any other individual in whose behalf he has applied for or is receiving such benefit or payment, conceals or fails to disclose such event with an intent fraudulently to secure such benefit or payment either in a greater amount or quantity than is due or when no such benefit or payment is authorized,

(4) having made application to receive any such benefit or payment for the use and benefit of another and having received it, knowingly and willfully converts such benefit or payment or any part thereof to a use other than for the use and benefit of such other person,

(5) presents or causes to be presented a claim for a physician's service for which payment may be made under a Federal health care program and knows that the individual who furnished the service was not licensed as a physician, or

(6) for a fee knowingly and willfully counsels or assists an individual to dispose of assets (including by any transfer in trust) in order for the individual to become eligible for medical assistance under a State plan under subchapter XIX of this chapter, if disposing of the assets results in the imposition of a period of ineligibility for such assistance under section 1396p(c) of this title,

shall (i) in the case of such a statement, representation, concealment, failure, or conversion by any person in connection with the furnishing (by that person) of items or services for which payment is or may be made under the program, be guilty of a felony and upon conviction thereof fined not more than $25,000 or imprisoned for not more than five years or both, or (ii) in the case of such a statement, representation, concealment, failure, conversion, or provision of counsel or assistance by any other person, be guilty of a misdemeanor and upon conviction thereof fined not more than $10,000 or imprisoned for not more than one year, or both. In addition, in any case where an individual who is otherwise eligible for assistance under a Federal health care program is convicted of an offense under the preceding provisions of this subsection, the administrator of such program may at its option (notwithstanding any other provision of such program) limit, restrict, or suspend the eligibility of that individual for such period (not exceeding one year) as it deems appropriate; but the imposition of a limitation, restriction, or suspension with respect to the eligibility of any individual under this sentence shall not affect the eligibility of any other person for assistance under the plan, regardless of the relationship between that individual and such other person.

(b) Illegal remunerations

(1) whoever knowingly and willfully solicits or receives any remuneration (including any kickback, bribe, or rebate) directly or indirectly, overtly or covertly, in cash or in kind—

(A) in return for referring an individual to a person for the furnishing or arranging for the furnishing of any item or service for which payment may be made in whole or in part under a Federal health care program, or

(B) in return for purchasing, leasing, ordering, or arranging for or recommending purchasing, leasing, or ordering any good, facility, service, or item for which payment may be made in whole or in part under a Federal health care program,

shall be guilty of a felony and upon conviction thereof, shall be fined not more than $25,000 or imprisoned for not more than five years, or both.

(2) whoever knowingly and willfully offers or pays any remuneration (including any kickback, bribe, or rebate) directly or indirectly, overtly or covertly, in cash or in kind to any person to induce such person—

(A) to refer an individual to a person for the furnishing or arranging for the furnishing of any item or service for which payment may be made in whole or in part under a Federal health care program, or

(B) to purchase, lease, order, or arrange for or recommend purchasing, leasing, or ordering any good, facility, service, or item for which payment may be made in whole or in part under a Federal health care program, shall be guilty of a felony and upon conviction thereof, shall be fined not more than $25,000 or imprisoned for not more than five years, or both.

(3) Paragraphs (1) and (2) shall not apply to—

(A) a discount or other reduction in price obtained by a provider of services or other entity under a Federal health care program if the reduction in price is properly disclosed and appropriately reflected in the costs claimed or charges made by the provider or entity under a Federal health care program;

(B) any amount paid by an employer to an employee (who has a bona fide employment relationship with such employer) for employment in the provision of covered items or services;

(C) any amount paid by a vendor of goods or services to a person authorized to act as a purchasing agent for a group of individuals or entities who are furnishing services reimbursed under a Federal health care program if—

(i) the person has a written contract, with each such individual or entity, which specifies the amount to be paid the person, which amount may be a fixed amount or a fixed percentage of the value of the purchases made by each such individual or entity under the contract, and

(ii) in the case of an entity that is a provider of services (as defined in section 1395x(u) of this title), the person discloses (in such form and manner as the Secretary requires) to the entity and, upon request, to the Secretary the amount received from each such vendor with respect to purchases made by or on behalf of the entity;

(D) a waiver of any coinsurance under part B of subchapter XVIII of this chapter by a Federally qualified health care center with respect to an individual who qualifies for subsidized services under a provision of the Public Health Service Act [42 U.S.C.A. § 201 et seq.];

(E) any payment practice specified by the Secretary in regulations promulgated pursuant to section 14(a) of the Medicare and Medicaid Patient and Program Protection Act of 1987; and

(F) any remuneration between an organization and an individual or entity providing items or services, or a combination thereof, pursuant to a written agreement between the organization and the individual or entity if the organization is an eligible organization under section 1395mm of this title or if the written agreement, through a risk-sharing arrangement, places the individual or entity at substantial financial risk for the cost or utilization of the items or services, or a combination thereof, which the individual or entity is obligated to provide.

(c) False statements or representations with respect to condition or operation of institutions

Whoever knowingly and willfully makes or causes to be made, or induces or seeks to induce the making of, any false statement or representation of a material fact with respect to the conditions or operation of any institution, facility, or entity in order that such institution, facility, or entity may qualify (either upon initial certification or upon recertification) as a hospital, critical access hospital, skilled nursing facility, nursing facility, intermediate care facility for the mentally retarded, home health agency, or other entity (including an eligible organization under section 1395mm(b) of this title) for which certification is required under subchapter XVIII of this chapter or a State health care program (as defined in section 1320a–7(h) of this title), or with respect to information required to be provided under section 1320a–3a of this title, shall be guilty of a felony and upon conviction thereof shall be fined not more than $25,000 or imprisoned for not more than five years, or both.

(d) Illegal patient admittance and retention practices

Whoever knowingly and willfully—

(1) charges, for any service provided to a patient under a State plan approved under subchapter XIX of this chapter, money or other consideration at a rate in excess of the rates established by the State (or, in the case of services provided to an individual enrolled with a medicaid managed care organization under subchapter XIX of this chapter under a contract under section 1396b(m) of this title or under a contractual, referral, or other arrangement under such contract, at a rate in excess of the rate permitted under such contract), or

(2) charges, solicits, accepts, or receives, in addition to any amount otherwise required to be paid under a State plan approved under subchapter XIX of this chapter, any gift, money, donation, or other consideration (other than a charitable, religious, or philanthropic contribution from an organization or from a person unrelated to the patient)—

(A) as a precondition of admitting a patient to a hospital, nursing facility, or intermediate care facility for the mentally retarded, or

(B) as a requirement for the patient's continued stay in such a facility,

when the cost of the services provided therein to the patient is paid for (in whole or in part) under the State plan, shall be guilty of a felony and upon conviction thereof shall be fined not more than $25,000 or imprisoned for not more than five years, or both.

(e) Violation of assignment terms

Whoever accepts assignments described in section 1395u(b)(3)(B)(ii) of this title or agrees to be a participating physician or supplier under section 1395u(h)(1) of this title and knowingly, willfully, and repeatedly violates the term of such assignments or agreement, shall be guilty of a misdemeanor and upon conviction thereof shall be fined not more than $2,000 or imprisoned for not more than six months, or both.

(f) "Federal health care program" defined

For purposes of this section, the term "Federal health care program" means—

(1) any plan or program that provides health benefits, whether directly, through insurance, or otherwise, which is funded directly, in whole or in part, by the United States Government (other than the health insurance program under chapter 89 of Title 5); or

(2) any State health care program, as defined in section 1320a–7(h) of this title.

Fraud and Abuse Safe Harbor Regulations, Department of Health and Human Services: 42 CFR § 1001.952

Current through June 5, 2001; 66 FR 30092

§ 1001.952   Exceptions

The following payment practices shall not be treated as a criminal offense under section 1128B of the Act and shall not serve as the basis for an exclusion:

(a) *Investment interests.* As used in section 1128B of the Act, "remuneration" does not include any payment that is a return on an investment interest, such as a dividend or interest income, made to an investor as long as all of the applicable standards are met within one of the following three categories of entities:

(1) If, within the previous fiscal year or previous 12 month period, the entity possesses more than $50,000,000 in undepreciated net tangible assets (based on the net acquisition cost of purchasing such assets from an unrelated entity) related to the furnishing of health care items and services, all of the following five standards must be met—

(i) With respect to an investment interest that is an equity security, the equity security must be registered with the Securities and Exchange Commission under 15 U.S.C. 78l (b) or (g).

(ii) The investment interest of an investor in a position to make or influence referrals to, furnish items or services to, or otherwise generate business for the entity must be obtained on terms (including any direct or indirect transferability restrictions) and at a price equally available to the public when trading on a registered securities exchange, such as the New York Stock Exchange or the American Stock Exchange, or in accordance with the National Association of Securities Dealers Automated Quotation System.

(iii) The entity or any investor must not market or furnish the entity's items or services (or those of another entity as part of a cross referral agreement) to passive investors differently than to non-investors.

(iv) The entity or any investor (or other individual or entity acting on behalf of the entity or any investor in the entity) must not loan funds to or guarantee a loan for an investor who is in a position to make or influence referrals to, furnish items or services to, or otherwise generate business for the entity if the investor uses any part of such loan to obtain the investment interest.

(v) The amount of payment to an investor in return for the investment interest must be directly proportional to the amount of the capital investment of that investor.

(2) If the entity possesses investment interests that are held by either active or passive investors, all of the following eight applicable standards must be met—

(i) No more than 40 percent of the value of the investment interests of each class of investment interests may be held in the previous fiscal year or previous 12 month period by investors who are in a position to make or influence referrals to, furnish items or services to, or otherwise generate business for the entity. (For purposes of paragraph (a)(2)(i) of this section, equivalent classes of equity investments may be combined, and equivalent classes of debt instruments may be combined.)

35

(ii) The terms on which an investment interest is offered to a passive investor, if any, who is in a position to make or influence referrals to, furnish items or services to, or otherwise generate business for the entity must be no different from the terms offered to other passive investors.

(iii) The terms on which an investment interest is offered to an investor who is in a position to make or influence referrals to, furnish items or services to, or otherwise generate business for the entity must not be related to the previous or expected volume of referrals, items or services furnished, or the amount of business otherwise generated from that investor to the entity.

(iv) There is no requirement that a passive investor, if any, make referrals to, be in a position to make or influence referrals to, furnish items or services to, or otherwise generate business for the entity as a condition for remaining as an investor.

(v) The entity or any investor must not market or furnish the entity's items or services (or those of another entity as part of a cross referral agreement) to passive investors differently than to non-investors.

(vi) No more than 40 percent of the entity's gross revenue related to the furnishing of health care items and services in the previous fiscal year or previous 12–month period may come from referrals or business otherwise generated from investors.

(vii) The entity or any investor (or other individual or entity acting on behalf of the entity or any investor in the entity) must not loan funds to or guarantee a loan for an investor who is in a position to make or influence referrals to, furnish items or services to, or otherwise generate business for the entity if the investor uses any part of such loan to obtain the investment interest.

(viii) The amount of payment to an investor in return for the investment interest must be directly proportional to the amount of the capital investment (including the fair market value of any pre-operational services rendered) of that investor.

(3)(i) If the entity possesses investment interests that are held by either active or passive investors and is located in an underserved area, all of the following eight standards must be met—

(A) No more than 50 percent of the value of the investment interests of each class of investments may be held in the previous fiscal year or previous 12–month period by investors who are in a position to make or influence referrals to, furnish items or services to, or otherwise generate business for, the entity. (For purposes of paragraph (a)(3)(i)(A) of this section, equivalent classes of equity investments may be combined, and equivalent classes of debt instruments may be combined.)

(B) The terms on which an investment interest is offered to a passive investor, if any, who is in a position to make or influence referrals to, furnish items or services to, or otherwise generate business for the entity must be no different from the terms offered to other passive investors.

(C) The terms on which an investment interest is offered to an investor who is in a position to make or influence referrals to, furnish items or services to, or otherwise generate business for the entity must not be related to the previous or expected volume of referrals, items or services furnished, or the amount of business otherwise generated from that investor to the entity.

(D) There is no requirement that a passive investor, if any, make referrals to, be in a position to make or influence referrals to, furnish items or services to, or otherwise generate business for the entity as a condition for remaining as an investor.

(E) The entity or any investor must not market or furnish the entity's items or services (or those of another entity as part of a cross-referral agreement) to passive investors differently than to non-investors.

(F) At least 75 percent of the dollar volume of the entity's business in the previous fiscal year or previous 12–month period must be derived from the service of persons who reside in an underserved area or are members of medically underserved populations.

(G) The entity or any investor (or other individual or entity acting on behalf of the entity or any investor in the entity) must not loan funds to or guarantee a loan for an investor who is in a position to make or influence referrals to, furnish items or services to, or otherwise generate business for the entity if the investor uses any part of such loan to obtain the investment interest.

(H) The amount of payment to an investor in return for the investment interest must be directly proportional to the amount of the capital investment (including the fair market value of any pre-operational services rendered) of that investor.

(ii) If an entity that otherwise meets all of the above standards is located in an area that was an underserved area at the time of the initial investment, but subsequently ceases to be an underserved area, the entity will be deemed to comply with paragraph (a)(3)(i) of this section for a period equal to the lesser of:

(A) The current term of the investment remaining after the date upon which the area ceased to be an underserved area or

(B) Three years from the date the area ceased to be an underserved area.

37

(4) For purposes of paragraph (a) of this section, the following terms apply. Active investor means an investor either who is responsible for the day-to-day management of the entity and is a bona fide general partner in a partnership under the Uniform Partnership Act or who agrees in writing to undertake liability for the actions of the entity's agents acting within the scope of their agency. Investment interest means a security issued by an entity, and may include the following classes of investments: shares in a corporation, interests or units in a partnership or limited liability company, bonds, debentures, notes, or other debt instruments. Investor means an individual or entity either who directly holds an investment interest in an entity, or who holds such investment interest indirectly by, including but not limited to, such means as having a family member hold such investment interest or holding a legal or beneficial interest in another entity (such as a trust or holding company) that holds such investment interest. Passive investor means an investor who is not an active investor, such as a limited partner in a partnership under the Uniform Partnership Act, a shareholder in a corporation, or a holder of a debt security. Underserved area means any defined geographic area that is designated as a Medically Underserved Area (MUA) in accordance with regulations issued by the Department. Medically underserved population means a Medically Underserved Population (MUP) in accordance with regulations issued by the Department.

(b) *Space rental.* As used in section 1128B of the Act, "remuneration" does not include any payment made by a lessee to a lessor for the use of premises, as long as all of the following six standards are met—

(1) The lease agreement is set out in writing and signed by the parties.

(2) The lease covers all of the premises leased between the parties for the term of the lease and specifies the premises covered by the lease.

(3) If the lease is intended to provide the lessee with access to the premises for periodic intervals of time, rather than on a full-time basis for the term of the lease, the lease specifies exactly the schedule of such intervals, their precise length, and the exact rent for such intervals.

(4) The term of the lease is for not less than one year.

(5) The aggregate rental charge is set in advance, is consistent with fair market value in arms-length transactions and is not determined in a manner that takes into account the volume or value of any referrals or business otherwise generated between the parties for which payment may be made in whole or in part under Medicare or a State health care program.

(6) The aggregate space rented does not exceed that which is reasonably necessary to accomplish the commercially reasonable business purpose of the rental.

For purposes of paragraph (b) of this section, the term fair market value means the value of the rental property for general commercial purposes, but shall not be adjusted to reflect the additional value that one party (either the prospective lessee or lessor) would attribute to the property as a result of its proximity or convenience to sources of referrals or business otherwise generated for which payment may be made in whole or in part under Medicare or a State health care program.

(c) Equipment rental. As used in section 1128B of the Act, "remuneration" does not include any payment made by a lessee of equipment to the lessor of the equipment for the use of the equipment, as long as all of the following six standards are met—

(1) The lease agreement is set out in writing and signed by the parties.

(2) The lease covers all of the equipment leased between the parties for the term of the lease and specifies the equipment covered by the lease.

(3) If the lease is intended to provide the lessee with use of the equipment for periodic intervals of time, rather than on a full-time basis for the term of the lease, the lease specifies exactly the schedule of such intervals, their precise length, and the exact rent for such interval.

(4) The term of the lease is for not less than one year.

(5) The aggregate rental charge is set in advance, is consistent with fair market value in arms-length transactions and is not determined in a manner that takes into account the volume or value of any referrals or business otherwise generated between the parties for which payment may be made in whole or in part under Medicare or a State health care program.

(6) The aggregate equipment rental does not exceed that which is reasonably necessary to accomplish the commercially reasonable business purpose of the rental.

For purposes of paragraph (c) of this section, the term fair market value means the value of the equipment when obtained from a manufacturer or professional distributor, but shall not be adjusted to reflect the additional value one party (either the prospective lessee or lessor) would attribute to the equipment as a result of its proximity or convenience to sources of referrals or business otherwise generated for which payment may be made in whole or in part under Medicare or a State health care program.

(d) Personal services and management contracts. As used in section 1128B of the Act, "remuneration" does not include any payment made by a principal to an agent as compensation for the services of the agent, as long as all of the following seven standards are met—

(1) The agency agreement is set out in writing and signed by the parties.

(2) The agency agreement covers all of the services the agent provides to the principal for the term of the agreement and specifies the services to be provided by the agent.

(3) If the agency agreement is intended to provide for the services of the agent on a periodic, sporadic or part-time basis, rather than on a full-time basis for the term of the agreement, the agreement specifies exactly the schedule of such intervals, their precise length, and the exact charge for such intervals.

(4) The term of the agreement is for not less than one year.

(5) The aggregate compensation paid to the agent over the term of the agreement is set in advance, is consistent with fair market value in arms-length transactions and is not determined in a manner that takes into account the volume or value of any referrals or business otherwise generated between the parties for which payment may be made in whole or in part under Medicare or a State health care program.

(6) The services performed under the agreement do not involve the counselling or promotion of a business arrangement or other activity that violates any State or Federal law.

(7) The aggregate services contracted for do not exceed those which are reasonably necessary to accomplish the commercially reasonable business purpose of the services.

For purposes of paragraph (d) of this section, an agent of a principal is any person, other than a bona fide employee of the principal, who has an agreement to perform services for, or on behalf of, the principal.

(e) Sale of practice.

(1) As used in section 1128B of the Act, "remuneration" does not include any payment made to a practitioner by another practitioner where the former practitioner is selling his or her practice to the latter practitioner, as long as both of the following two standards are met—

(i) The period from the date of the first agreement pertaining to the sale to the completion of the sale is not more than one year.

(ii) The practitioner who is selling his or her practice will not be in a professional position to make referrals to, or otherwise generate business for, the purchasing practitioner for which payment may be made in whole or in part under Medicare or a State health care program after one year from the date of the first agreement pertaining to the sale.

(2) As used in section 1128B of the Act, "remuneration" does not include any payment made to a practitioner by a hospital or other entity where the practitioner is selling his or her practice to the hospital or other entity, so long as the following four standards are met:

(i) The period from the date of the first agreement pertaining to the sale to the completion date of the sale is not more than three years.

40

(ii) The practitioner who is selling his or her practice will not be in a professional position after completion of the sale to make or influence referrals to, or otherwise generate business for, the purchasing hospital or entity for which payment may be made in whole or in part under Medicare or a State health care program.

(iii) The practice being acquired must be located in a Health Professional Shortage Area (HPSA), as defined in Departmental regulations, for the practitioner's specialty area.

(iv) Commencing at the time of the first agreement pertaining to the sale, the purchasing hospital or entity must diligently and in good faith engage in commercially reasonable recruitment activities that:

(A) May reasonably be expected to result in the recruitment of a new practitioner to take over the acquired practice within a one year period and

(B) Will satisfy the conditions of the practitioner recruitment safe harbor in accordance with paragraph (n) of this section.

(f) Referral services. As used in section 1128B of the Act, "remuneration" does not include any payment or exchange of anything of value between an individual or entity ("participant") and another entity serving as a referral service ("referral service"), as long as all of the following four standards are met—

(1) The referral service does not exclude as a participant in the referral service any individual or entity who meets the qualifications for participation.

(2) Any payment the participant makes to the referral service is assessed equally against and collected equally from all participants, and is only based on the cost of operating the referral service, and not on the volume or value of any referrals to or business otherwise generated by either party for the other party for which payment may be made in whole or in part under Medicare or a State health care program.

(3) The referral service imposes no requirements on the manner in which the participant provides services to a referred person, except that the referral service may require that the participant charge the person referred at the same rate as it charges other persons not referred by the referral service, or that these services be furnished free of charge or at reduced charge.

(4) The referral service makes the following five disclosures to each person seeking a referral, with each such disclosure maintained by the referral service in a written record certifying such disclosure and signed

41

by either such person seeking a referral or by the individual making the disclosure on behalf of the referral service—

(i) The manner in which it selects the group of participants in the referral service to which it could make a referral;

(ii) Whether the participant has paid a fee to the referral service;

(iii) The manner in which it selects a particular participant from this group for that person;

(iv) The nature of the relationship between the referral service and the group of participants to whom it could make the referral; and

(v) The nature of any restrictions that would exclude such an individual or entity from continuing as a participant.

(g) Warranties. As used in section 1128B of the Act, "remuneration" does not include any payment or exchange of anything of value under a warranty provided by a manufacturer or supplier of an item to the buyer (such as a health care provider or beneficiary) of the item, as long as the buyer complies with all of the following standards in paragraphs (g)(1) and (g)(2) of this section and the manufacturer or supplier complies with all of the following standards in paragraphs (g)(3) and (g)(4) of this section—

(1) The buyer must fully and accurately report any price reduction of the item (including a free item), which was obtained as part of the warranty, in the applicable cost reporting mechanism or claim for payment filed with the Department or a State agency.

(2) The buyer must provide, upon request by the Secretary or a State agency, information provided by the manufacturer or supplier as specified in paragraph (g)(3) of this section.

(3) The manufacturer or supplier must comply with either of the following two standards—

(i) The manufacturer or supplier must fully and accurately report the price reduction of the item (including a free item), which was obtained as part of the warranty, on the invoice or statement submitted to the buyer, and inform the buyer of its obligations under paragraphs (a)(1) and (a)(2) of this section.

(ii) Where the amount of the price reduction is not known at the time of sale, the manufacturer or supplier must fully and accurately report the existence of a warranty on the invoice or statement, inform the buyer of its obligations under paragraphs (g)(1) and (g)(2) of this section, and, when the price reduction becomes known, provide the buyer with documentation of the calculation of the price reduction resulting from the warranty.

(4) The manufacturer or supplier must not pay any remuneration to any individual (other than a beneficiary) or entity for any medical,

surgical, or hospital expense incurred by a beneficiary other than for the cost of the item itself.

For purposes of paragraph (g) of this section, the term warranty means either an agreement made in accordance with the provisions of 15 U.S.C. 2301(6), or a manufacturer's or supplier's agreement to replace another manufacturer's or supplier's defective item (which is covered by an agreement made in accordance with this statutory provision), on terms equal to the agreement that it replaces.

(h) Discounts. As used in section 1128B of the Act, "remuneration" does not include a discount, as defined in paragraph (h)(5) of this section, on an item or service for which payment may be made, in whole or in part, under Medicare or a State health care program for a buyer as long as the buyer complies with the applicable standards of paragraph (h)(1) of this section; a seller as long as the seller complies with the applicable standards of paragraph (h)(2) of this section; and an offeror of a discount who is not a seller under paragraph (h)(2) of this section so long as such offeror complies with the applicable standards of paragraph (h)(3) of this section:

(1) With respect to the following three categories of buyers, the buyer must comply with all of the applicable standards within one of the three following categories—

(i) If the buyer is an entity which is a health maintenance organization (HMO) or a competitive medical plan (CMP) acting in accordance with a risk contract under section 1876(g) or 1903(m) of the Act, or under another State health care program, it need not report the discount except as otherwise may be required under the risk contract.

(ii) If the buyer is an entity which reports its costs on a cost report required by the Department or a State health care program, it must comply with all of the following four standards—

(A) The discount must be earned based on purchases of that same good or service bought within a single fiscal year of the buyer;

(B) The buyer must claim the benefit of the discount in the fiscal year in which the discount is earned or the following year;

(C) The buyer must fully and accurately report the discount in the applicable cost report; and

(D) The buyer must provide, upon request by the Secretary or a State agency, information provided by the seller as specified in paragraph (h)(2)(ii) of this section, or information provided by the offeror as specified in paragraph (h)(3)(ii) of this section.

(iii) If the buyer is an individual or entity in whose name a claim or request for payment is submitted for the discounted item or service and payment may be made, in whole or in part, under Medicare or a State health care program (not including individuals or entities defined as buyers in paragraph (h)(1)(i) or (h)(1)(ii) of this section), the buyer must comply with both of the following standards—

(A) The discount must be made at the time of the sale of the good or service or the terms of the rebate must be fixed and disclosed in writing to the buyer at the time of the initial sale of the good or service; and

(B) The buyer (if submitting the claim) must provide, upon request by the Secretary or a State agency, information provided by the seller as specified in paragraph (h)(2)(iii)(B) of this section, or information provided by the offeror as specified in paragraph (h)(3)(iii)(A) of this section.

(2) The seller is an individual or entity that supplies an item or service for which payment may be made, in whole or in part, under Medicare or a State health care program to the buyer and who permits a discount to be taken off the buyer's purchase price. The seller must comply with all of the applicable standards within the following three categories—

(i) If the buyer is an entity which is an HMO a CMP acting in accordance with a risk contract under section 1876(g) or 1903(m) of the Act, or under another State health care program, the seller need not report the discount to the buyer for purposes of this provision.

(ii) If the buyer is an entity that reports its costs on a cost report required by the Department or a State agency, the seller must comply with either of the following two standards—

(A) Where a discount is required to be reported to Medicare or a State health care program under paragraph (h)(1) of this section, the seller must fully and accurately report such discount on the invoice, coupon or statement submitted to the buyer; inform the buyer in a manner that is reasonably calculated to give notice to the buyer of its obligations to report such discount and to provide information upon request under paragraph (h)(1) of this section; and refrain from doing anything that would impede the buyer from meeting its obligations under this paragraph; or

(B) Where the value of the discount is not known at the time of sale, the seller must fully and accurately report the existence of a discount program on the invoice, coupon or statement submitted to the buyer; inform the buyer in a manner reasonably calculated to give notice to the buyer of its obligations to report such discount and to provide information upon request under paragraph (h)(1) of this section; when the value of the discount becomes known, provide the buyer with documentation of the calculation of the discount identifying the specific goods or services purchased to which the discount will be applied; and refrain from doing anything which would impede the buyer from meeting its obligations under this paragraph.

(iii) If the buyer is an individual or entity not included in paragraph (h)(2)(i) or (h)(2)(ii) of this section, the seller must comply with either of the following two standards—

(A) Where the seller submits a claim or request for payment on behalf of the buyer and the item or service is separately claimed, the seller must provide, upon request by the Secretary or a State agency, information provided by the offeror as specified in paragraph (h)(3)(iii)(A) of this section; or

(B) Where the buyer submits a claim, the seller must fully and accurately report such discount on the invoice, coupon or statement submitted to the buyer; inform the buyer in a manner reasonably calculated to give notice to the buyer of its obligations to report such discount and to provide information upon request under paragraph (h)(1) of this section; and refrain from doing anything that would impede the buyer from meeting its obligations under this paragraph.

(3) The offeror of a discount is an individual or entity who is not a seller under paragraph (h)(2) of this section, but promotes the purchase of an item or service by a buyer under paragraph (h)(1) of this section at a reduced price for which payment may be made, in whole or in part, under Medicare or a State health care program. The offeror must comply with all of the applicable standards within the following three categories—

(i) If the buyer is an entity which is an HMO or a CMP acting in accordance with a risk contract under section 1876(g) or 1903(m) of the Act, or under another State health care program, the offeror need not report the discount to the buyer for purposes of this provision.

(ii) If the buyer is an entity that reports its costs on a cost report required by the Department or a State agency, the offeror must comply with the following two standards—

(A) The offeror must inform the buyer in a manner reasonably calculated to give notice to the buyer of its obligations to report such a discount and to provide information upon request under paragraph (h)(1) of this section; and

(B) The offeror of the discount must refrain from doing anything that would impede the buyer's ability to meet its obligations under this paragraph.

(iii) If the buyer is an individual or entity in whose name a request for payment is submitted for the discounted item or service and payment may be made, in whole or in part, under Medicare or a State health care program (not including individuals or entities defined as buyers in paragraph (h)(1)(i) or (h)(1)(ii) of this section), the offeror must comply with the following two standards—

(A) The offeror must inform the individual or entity submitting the claim or request for payment in a manner reasonably calculated to give notice to the individual or entity of its obligations to report such a discount and to provide information upon request under paragraphs (h)(1) and (h)(2) of this section; and

(B) The offeror of the discount must refrain from doing anything that would impede the buyer's or seller's ability to meet its obligations under this paragraph.

(4) For purposes of this paragraph, a rebate is any discount the terms of which are fixed and disclosed in writing to the buyer at the time of the initial purchase to which the discount applies, but which is not given at the time of sale.

(5) For purposes of this paragraph, the term discount means a reduction in the amount a buyer (who buys either directly or through a wholesaler or a group purchasing organization) is charged for an item or service based on an arms-length transaction. The term discount does not include—

(i) Cash payment or cash equivalents (except that rebates as defined in paragraph (h)(4) of this section may be in the form of a check);

(ii) Supplying one good or service without charge or at a reduced charge to induce the purchase of a different good or service, unless the goods and services are reimbursed by the same Federal health care program using the same methodology and the reduced charge is fully disclosed to the Federal health care program and accurately reflected where appropriate, and as appropriate, to the reimbursement methodology;

(iii) A reduction in price applicable to one payer but not to Medicare or a State health care program;

(iv) A routine reduction or waiver of any coinsurance or deductible amount owed by a program beneficiary;

(v) Warranties;

(vi) Services provided in accordance with a personal or management services contract; or

(vii) Other remuneration, in cash or in kind, not explicitly described in paragraph (h)(5) of this section.

(i) Employees. As used in section 1128B of the Act, "remuneration" does not include any amount paid by an employer to an employee, who has a bona fide employment relationship with the employer, for employment in the furnishing of any item or service for which payment may be made in whole or

in part under Medicare or a State health care program. For purposes of paragraph (i) of this section, the term employee has the same meaning as it does for purposes of 26 U.S.C. 3121(d)(2).

(j) Group purchasing organizations. As used in section 1128B of the Act, "remuneration" does not include any payment by a vendor of goods or services to a group purchasing organization (GPO), as part of an agreement to furnish such goods or services to an individual or entity as long as both of the following two standards are met—

(1) The GPO must have a written agreement with each individual or entity, for which items or services are furnished, that provides for either of the following—

(i) The agreement states that participating vendors from which the individual or entity will purchase goods or services will pay a fee to the GPO of 3 percent or less of the purchase price of the goods or services provided by that vendor.

(ii) In the event the fee paid to the GPO is not fixed at 3 percent or less of the purchase price of the goods or services, the agreement specifies the amount (or if not known, the maximum amount) the GPO will be paid by each vendor (where such amount may be a fixed sum or a fixed percentage of the value of purchases made from the vendor by the members of the group under the contract between the vendor and the GPO).

(2) Where the entity which receives the goods or service from the vendor is a health care provider of services, the GPO must disclose in writing to the entity at least annually, and to the Secretary upon request, the amount received from each vendor with respect to purchases made by or on behalf of the entity.

For purposes of paragraph (j) of this section, the term group purchasing organization (GPO) means an entity authorized to act as a purchasing agent for a group of individuals or entities who are furnishing services for which payment may be made in whole or in part under Medicare or a State health care program, and who are neither wholly-owned by the GPO nor subsidiaries of a parent corporation that wholly owns the GPO (either directly or through another wholly-owned entity).

(k) Waiver of beneficiary coinsurance and deductible amounts. As used in section 1128B of the Act, "remuneration" does not include any reduction or waiver of a Medicare or a State health care program beneficiary's obligation to pay coinsurance or deductible amounts as long as all of the standards are met within either of the following two categories of health care providers:

(1) If the coinsurance or deductible amounts are owed to a hospital for inpatient hospital services for which Medicare pays under the prospective payment system, the hospital must comply with all of the following three standards—

(i) The hospital must not later claim the amount reduced or waived as a bad debt for payment purposes under Medicare or otherwise shift the burden of the reduction or waiver onto Medicare, a State health care program, other payers, or individuals.

(ii) The hospital must offer to reduce or waive the coinsurance or deductible amounts without regard to the reason for admission, the length of stay of the beneficiary, or the diagnostic related group for which the claim for Medicare reimbursement is filed.

(iii) The hospital's offer to reduce or waive the coinsurance or deductible amounts must not be made as part of a price reduction agreement between a hospital and a third-party payer (including a health plan as defined in paragraph (*l*)(2) of this section), unless the agreement is part of a contract for the furnishing of items or services to a beneficiary of a Medicare supplemental policy issued under the terms of section 1882(t)(1) of the Act.

(2) If the coinsurance or deductible amounts are owed by an individual who qualifies for subsidized services under a provision of the Public Health Services Act or under titles V or XIX of the Act to a federally qualified health care center or other health care facility under any Public Health Services Act grant program or under title V of the Act, the health care center or facility may reduce or waive the coinsurance or deductible amounts for items or services for which payment may be made in whole or in part under part B of Medicare or a State health care program.

(l) Increased coverage, reduced cost-sharing amounts, or reduced premium amounts offered by health plans.

(1) As used in section 1128B of the Act, "remuneration" does not include the additional coverage of any item or service offered by a health plan to an enrollee or the reduction of some or all of the enrollee's obligation to pay the health plan or a contract health care provider for cost-sharing amounts (such as coinsurance, deductible, or copayment amounts) or for premium amounts attributable to items or services covered by the health plan, the Medicare program, or a State health care program, as long as the health plan complies with all of the standards within one of the following two categories of health plans:

(i) If the health plan is a risk-based health maintenance organization, competitive medical plan, prepaid health plan, or other health plan under contract with HCFA or a State health care program and operating in accordance with section 1876(g) or 1903(m) of the Act, under a Federal statutory demonstration authority, or under other Federal statutory or regulatory authority, it must offer the same increased coverage or reduced cost-sharing or premium amounts to all Medicare or State health care program enrollees covered by the contract unless otherwise approved by HCFA or by a State health care program.

(ii) If the health plan is a health maintenance organization, competitive medical plan, health care prepayment plan, prepaid health plan or other health plan that has executed a contract or agreement with HCFA or with a State health care program to receive payment for enrollees on a reasonable cost or similar basis, it must comply with both of the following two standards—

(A) The health plan must offer the same increased coverage or reduced cost-sharing or premium amounts to all Medicare or State health care program enrollees covered by the contract or agreement unless otherwise approved by HCFA or by a State health care program; and

(B) The health plan must not claim the costs of the increased coverage or the reduced cost-sharing or premium amounts as a bad debt for payment purposes under Medicare or a State health care program or otherwise shift the burden of the increased coverage or reduced cost-sharing or premium amounts to the extent that increased payments are claimed from Medicare or a State health care program.

(2) For purposes of paragraph (*l*) of this section, the terms—

Contract health care provider means an individual or entity under contract with a health plan to furnish items or services to enrollees who are covered by the health plan, Medicare, or a State health care program.

Enrollee means an individual who has entered into a contractual relationship with a health plan (or on whose behalf an employer, or other private or governmental entity has entered into such a relationship) under which the individual is entitled to receive specified health care items and services, or insurance coverage for such items and services, in return for payment of a premium or a fee.

Health plan means an entity that furnishes or arranges under agreement with contract health care providers for the furnishing of items or services to enrollees, or furnishes insurance coverage for the provision of such items and services, in exchange for a premium or a fee, where such entity:

(i) Operates in accordance with a contract, agreement or statutory demonstration authority approved by HCFA or a State health care program;

(ii) Charges a premium and its premium structure is regulated under a State insurance statute or a State enabling statute governing health maintenance organizations or preferred provider organizations;

(iii) Is an employer, if the enrollees of the plan are current or retired employees, or is a union welfare fund, if the enrollees of the plan are union members; or

(iv) Is licensed in the State, is under contract with an employer, union welfare fund, or a company furnishing health insurance coverage as described in conditions (ii) and (iii) of this definition, and is paid a fee for the administration of the plan which reflects the fair market value of those services.

(m) Price reductions offered to health plans.

(1) As used in section 1128B of the Act, "remuneration" does not include a reduction in price a contract health care provider offers to a health plan in accordance with the terms of a written agreement between the contract health care provider and the health plan for the sole purpose of furnishing to enrollees items or services that are covered by the health plan, Medicare, or a State health care program, as long as both the health plan and contract health care provider comply with all of the applicable standards within one of the following four categories of health plans:

(i) If the health plan is a risk-based health maintenance organization, competitive medical plan, or prepaid health plan under contract with HCFA or a State agency and operating in accordance with section 1876(g) or 1903(m) of the Act, under a Federal statutory demonstration authority, or under other Federal statutory or regulatory authority, the contract health care provider must not claim payment in any form from the Department or the State agency for items or services furnished in accordance with the agreement except as approved by HCFA or the State health care program, or otherwise shift the burden of such an agreement to the extent that increased payments are claimed from Medicare or a State health care program.

(ii) If the health plan is a health maintenance organization, competitive medical plan, health care prepayment plan, prepaid health plan, or other health plan that has executed a contract or agreement with HCFA or a State health care program to receive payment for enrollees on a reasonable cost or similar basis, the health plan and contract health care provider must comply with all of the following four standards—

(A) The term of the agreement between the health plan and the contract health care provider must be for not less than one year;

(B) The agreement between the health plan and the contract health care provider must specify in advance the covered items and services to be furnished to enrollees, and the methodology for computing the payment to the contract health care provider;

(C) The health plan must fully and accurately report, on the applicable cost report or other claim form filed with the Department or the State health care program, the amount it has paid the contract health care provider under the agreement for the covered items and services furnished to enrollees; and

50

(D) The contract health care provider must not claim payment in any form from the Department or the State health care program for items or services furnished in accordance with the agreement except as approved by HCFA or the State health care program, or otherwise shift the burden of such an agreement to the extent that increased payments are claimed from Medicare or a State health care program.

(iii) If the health plan is not described in paragraphs (m)(1)(i) or (m)(1)(ii) of this section and the contract health care provider is not paid on an at-risk, capitated basis, both the health plan and contract health care provider must comply with all of the following six standards—

(A) The term of the agreement between the health plan and the contract health care provider must be for not less than one year;

(B) The agreement between the health plan and the contract health care provider must specify in advance the covered items and services to be furnished to enrollees, which party is to file claims or requests for payment with Medicare or the State health care program for such items and services, and the schedule of fees the contract health care provider will charge for furnishing such items and services to enrollees;

(C) The fee schedule contained in the agreement between the health plan and the contract health care provider must remain in effect throughout the term of the agreement, unless a fee increase results directly from a payment update authorized by Medicare or the State health care program;

(D) The party submitting claims or requests for payment from Medicare or the State health care program for items and services furnished in accordance with the agreement must not claim or request payment for amounts in excess of the fee schedule;

(E) The contract health care provider and the health plan must fully and accurately report on any cost report filed with Medicare or a State health care program the fee schedule amounts charged in accordance with the agreement and, upon request, will report to the Medicare or a State health care program the terms of the agreement and the amounts paid in accordance with the agreement; and

(F) The party to the agreement, which does not have the responsibility under the agreement for filing claims or requests for payment, must not claim or request payment in any form from the Department or the State health care program for items or services furnished in accordance with the agreement, or otherwise shift the burden of such an agreement to the extent that increased payments are claimed from Medicare or a State health care program.

(iv) If the health plan is not described in paragraphs (m)(1)(i) or (m)(1)(ii) of this section, and the contract health care provider is paid on an at-risk, capitated basis, both the health plan and contract health care provider must comply with all of the following five standards—

(A) The term of the agreement between the health plan and the contract health provider must be for not less than one year;

(B) The agreement between the health plan and the contract health provider must specify in advance the covered items and services to be furnished to enrollees and the total amount per enrollee (which may be expressed in a per month or other time period basis) the contract health care provider will be paid by the health plan for furnishing such items and services to enrollees and must set forth any copayments, if any, to be paid by enrollees to the contract health care provider for covered services;

(C) The payment amount contained in the agreement between the health care plan and the contract health care provider must remain in effect throughout the term of the agreement;

(D) The contract health care provider and the health plan must fully and accurately report to the Medicare and State health care program upon request, the terms of the agreement and the amounts paid in accordance with the agreement; and

(E) The contract health care provider must not claim or request payment in any form from the Department, a State health care program or an enrollee (other than copayment amounts described in paragraph (m)(2)(iv)(B) of this section) and the health plan must not pay the contract care provider in excess of the amounts described in paragraph (m)(2)(iv)(B) of this section for items and services covered by the agreement.

(2) For purposes of this paragraph, the terms contract health care provider, enrollee, and health plan have the same meaning as in paragraph (*l*)(2) of this section.

(n) Practitioner recruitment. As used in section 1128B of the Act, "remuneration" does not include any payment or exchange of anything of value by an entity in order to induce a practitioner who has been practicing within his or her current specialty for less than one year to locate, or to induce any other practitioner to relocate, his or her primary place of practice into a HPSA for his or her specialty area, as defined in Departmental regulations, that is served by the entity, as long as all of the following nine standards are met—

(1) The arrangement is set forth in a written agreement signed by the parties that specifies the benefits provided by the entity, the terms under which the benefits are to be provided, and the obligations of each party.

(2) If a practitioner is leaving an established practice, at least 75 percent of the revenues of the new practice must be generated from new patients not previously seen by the practitioner at his or her former practice.

(3) The benefits are provided by the entity for a period not in excess of 3 years, and the terms of the agreement are not renegotiated during this 3–year period in any substantial aspect; provided, however, that if the HPSA to which the practitioner was recruited ceases to be a HPSA during the term of the written agreement, the payments made under the written agreement will continue to satisfy this paragraph for the duration of the written agreement (not to exceed 3 years).

(4) There is no requirement that the practitioner make referrals to, be in a position to make or influence referrals to, or otherwise generate business for the entity as a condition for receiving the benefits; provided, however, that for purposes of this paragraph, the entity may require as a condition for receiving benefits that the practitioner maintain staff privileges at the entity.

(5) The practitioner is not restricted from establishing staff privileges at, referring any service to, or otherwise generating any business for any other entity of his or her choosing.

(6) The amount or value of the benefits provided by the entity may not vary (or be adjusted or renegotiated) in any manner based on the volume or value of any expected referrals to or business otherwise generated for the entity by the practitioner for which payment may be made in whole or in part under Medicare or a State health care program.

(7) The practitioner agrees to treat patients receiving medical benefits or assistance under any Federal health care program in a nondiscriminatory manner.

(8) At least 75 percent of the revenues of the new practice must be generated from patients residing in a HPSA or a Medically Underserved Area (MUA) or who are part of a Medically Underserved Population (MUP), all as defined in paragraph (a) of this section.

(9) The payment or exchange of anything of value may not directly or indirectly benefit any person (other than the practitioner being recruited) or entity in a position to make or influence referrals to the entity providing the recruitment payments or benefits of items or services payable by a Federal health care program.

(o) *Obstetrical malpractice insurance subsidies.* As used in section 1128B of the Act, "remuneration" does not include any payment made by a hospital or other entity to another entity that is providing malpractice insurance (including a self-funded entity), where such payment is used to pay for some or all of the costs of malpractice insurance premiums for a practitioner (including a certified nurse-midwife as defined in section 1861(gg) of the Act) who engages in obstetrical practice as a routine part of his or her medical practice in a primary care HPSA, as long as all of the following seven standards are met—

(1) The payment is made in accordance with a written agreement between the entity paying the premiums and the practitioner, which sets out the payments to be made by the entity, and the terms under which the payments are to be provided.

(2)(i) The practitioner must certify that for the initial coverage period (not to exceed one year) the practitioner has a reasonable basis for believing that at least 75 percent of the practitioner's obstetrical patients treated under the coverage of the malpractice insurance will either—

(A) Reside in a HPSA or MUA, as defined in paragraph (a) of this section; or

(B) Be part of a MUP, as defined in paragraph (a) of this section.

(ii) Thereafter, for each additional coverage period (not to exceed one year), at least 75 percent of the practitioner's obstetrical patients treated under the prior coverage period (not to exceed one year) must have—

(A) Resided in a HPSA or MUA, as defined in paragraph (a) of this section; or

(B) Been part of a MUP, as defined in paragraph (a) of this section.

(3) There is no requirement that the practitioner make referrals to, or otherwise generate business for, the entity as a condition for receiving the benefits.

(4) The practitioner is not restricted from establishing staff privileges at, referring any service to, or otherwise generating any business for any other entity of his or her choosing.

(5) The amount of payment may not vary based on the volume or value of any previous or expected referrals to or business otherwise generated for the entity by the practitioner for which payment may be made in whole or in part under Medicare or a State health care program.

(6) The practitioner must treat obstetrical patients who receive medical benefits or assistance under any Federal health care program in a nondiscriminatory manner.

(7) The insurance is a bona fide malpractice insurance policy or program, and the premium, if any, is calculated based on a bona fide assessment of the liability risk covered under the insurance. For purposes of paragraph (o) of this section, costs of malpractice insurance premiums means:

(i) For practitioners who engage in obstetrical practice full-time, any costs attributable to malpractice insurance; or

(ii) For practitioners who engage in obstetrical practice on a part-time or sporadic basis, the costs:

(A) Attributable exclusively to the obstetrical portion of the practitioner's malpractice insurance and

(B) Related exclusively to obstetrical services provided in a primary care HPSA.

(p) Investments in group practices. As used in section 1128B of the Act, "remuneration" does not include any payment that is a return on an investment interest, such as a dividend or interest income, made to a solo or group practitioner investing in his or her own practice or group practice if the following four standards are met—

(1) The equity interests in the practice or group must be held by licensed health care professionals who practice in the practice or group.

(2) The equity interests must be in the practice or group itself, and not some subdivision of the practice or group.

(3) In the case of group practices, the practice must:

(i) Meet the definition of "group practice" in section 1877(h)(4) of the Social Security Act and implementing regulations; and

(ii) Be a unified business with centralized decision-making, pooling of expenses and revenues, and a compensation/profit distribution system that is not based on satellite offices operating substantially as if they were separate enterprises or profit centers.

(4) Revenues from ancillary services, if any, must be derived from "in-office ancillary services" that meet the definition of such term in section 1877(b)(2) of the Act and implementing regulations.

(q) Cooperative hospital service organizations. As used in section 1128B of the Act, "remuneration" does not include any payment made between a cooperative hospital service organization (CHSO) and its patron-hospital, both of which are described in section 501(e) of the Internal Revenue Code of 1986 and are tax-exempt under section 501(c)(3) of the Internal Revenue Code, where the CHSO is wholly owned by two or more patron-hospitals, as long as the following standards are met—

(1) If the patron-hospital makes a payment to the CHSO, the payment must be for the purpose of paying for the bona fide operating expenses of the CHSO, or

(2) If the CHSO makes a payment to the patron-hospital, the payment must be for the purpose of paying a distribution of net earnings required to be made under section 501(e)(2) of the Internal Revenue Code of 1986.

(r) Ambulatory surgical centers. As used in section 1128B of the Act, "remuneration" does not include any payment that is a return on an investment interest, such as a dividend or interest income, made to an investor, as long as the investment entity is a certified ambulatory surgical center (ASC) under part 416 of this title, whose operating and recovery room space is dedicated exclusively to the ASC, patients referred to the investment entity by an investor are fully informed of the investor's investment interest, and all of the applicable standards are met within one of the following four categories—

(1) Surgeon-owned ASCs—If all of the investors are general surgeons or surgeons engaged in the same surgical specialty, who are in a position to refer patients directly to the entity and perform surgery on such referred patients; surgical group practices (as defined in this paragraph) composed exclusively of such surgeons; or investors who are not employed by the entity or by any investor, are not in a position to provide items or services to the entity or any of its investors, and are not in a position to make or influence referrals directly or indirectly to the entity or any of its investors, all of the following six standards must be met—

(i) The terms on which an investment interest is offered to an investor must not be related to the previous or expected volume of referrals, services furnished, or the amount of business otherwise generated from that investor to the entity.

(ii) At least one-third of each surgeon investor's medical practice income from all sources for the previous fiscal year or previous 12-month period must be derived from the surgeon's performance of procedures (as defined in this paragraph).

(iii) The entity or any investor (or other individual or entity acting on behalf of the entity or any investor) must not loan funds to or guarantee a loan for an investor if the investor uses any part of such loan to obtain the investment interest.

(iv) The amount of payment to an investor in return for the investment must be directly proportional to the amount of the capital investment (including the fair market value of any pre-operational services rendered) of that investor.

(v) All ancillary services for Federal health care program beneficiaries performed at the entity must be directly and integrally related to primary procedures performed at the entity, and none may be separately billed to Medicare or other Federal health care programs.

(vi) The entity and any surgeon investors must treat patients receiving medical benefits or assistance under any Federal health care program in a nondiscriminatory manner.

(2) Single-Specialty ASCs—If all of the investors are physicians engaged in the same medical practice specialty who are in a position to refer patients directly to the entity and perform procedures on such

referred patients; group practices (as defined in this paragraph) composed exclusively of such physicians; or investors who are not employed by the entity or by any investor, are not in a position to provide items or services to the entity or any of its investors, and are not in a position to make or influence referrals directly or indirectly to the entity or any of its investors, all of the following six standards must be met—

(i) The terms on which an investment interest is offered to an investor must not be related to the previous or expected volume of referrals, services furnished, or the amount of business otherwise generated from that investor to the entity.

(ii) At least one-third of each physician investor's medical practice income from all sources for the previous fiscal year or previous 12–month period must be derived from the surgeon's performance of procedures (as defined in this paragraph).

(iii) The entity or any investor (or other individual or entity acting on behalf of the entity or any investor) must not loan funds to or guarantee a loan for an investor if the investor uses any part of such loan to obtain the investment interest.

(iv) The amount of payment to an investor in return for the investment must be directly proportional to the amount of the capital investment (including the fair market value of any pre-operational services rendered) of that investor.

(v) All ancillary services for Federal health care program beneficiaries performed at the entity must be directly and integrally related to primary procedures performed at the entity, and none may be separately billed to Medicare or other Federal health care programs.

(vi) The entity and any physician investors must treat patients receiving medical benefits or assistance under any Federal health care program in a nondiscriminatory manner.

(3) Multi–Specialty ASCs—If all of the investors are physicians who are in a position to refer patients directly to the entity and perform procedures on such referred patients; group practices, as defined in this paragraph, composed exclusively of such physicians; or investors who are not employed by the entity or by any investor, are not in a position to provide items or services to the entity or any of its investors, and are not in a position to make or influence referrals directly or indirectly to the entity or any of its investors, all of the following seven standards must be met—

(i) The terms on which an investment interest is offered to an investor must not be related to the previous or expected volume of referrals, services furnished, or the amount of business otherwise generated from that investor to the entity.

(ii) At least one-third of each physician investor's medical practice income from all sources for the previous fiscal year or previous

12–month period must be derived from the physician's performance of procedures (as defined in this paragraph).

(iii) At least one-third of the procedures (as defined in this paragraph) performed by each physician investor for the previous fiscal year or previous 12–month period must be performed at the investment entity.

(iv) The entity or any investor (or other individual or entity acting on behalf of the entity or any investor) must not loan funds to or guarantee a loan for an investor if the investor uses any part of such loan to obtain the investment interest.

(v) The amount of payment to an investor in return for the investment must be directly proportional to the amount of the capital investment (including the fair market value of any pre-operational services rendered) of that investor.

(vi) All ancillary services for Federal health care program beneficiaries performed at the entity must be directly and integrally related to primary procedures performed at the entity, and none may be separately billed to Medicare or other Federal health care programs.

(vii) The entity and any physician investors must treat patients receiving medical benefits or assistance under any Federal health care program in a nondiscriminatory manner.

(4) Hospital/Physician ASCs—If at least one investor is a hospital, and all of the remaining investors are physicians who meet the requirements of paragraphs (r)(1), (r)(2) or (r)(3) of this section; group practices (as defined in this paragraph) composed of such physicians; surgical group practices (as defined in this paragraph); or investors who are not employed by the entity or by any investor, are not in a position to provide items or services to the entity or any of its investors, and are not in a position to refer patients directly or indirectly to the entity or any of its investors, all of the following eight standards must be met—

(i) The terms on which an investment interest is offered to an investor must not be related to the previous or expected volume of referrals, services furnished, or the amount of business otherwise generated from that investor to the entity.

(ii) The entity or any investor (or other individual or entity acting on behalf of the entity or any investor) must not loan funds to or guarantee a loan for an investor if the investor uses any part of such loan to obtain the investment interest.

(iii) The amount of payment to an investor in return for the investment must be directly proportional to the amount of the capital investment (including the fair market value of any pre-operational services rendered) of that investor.

(iv) The entity and any hospital or physician investor must treat patients receiving medical benefits or assistance under any Federal health care program in a nondiscriminatory manner.

(v) The entity may not use space, including, but not limited to, operating and recovery room space, located in or owned by any hospital investor, unless such space is leased from the hospital in accordance with a lease that complies with all the standards of the space rental safe harbor set forth in paragraph (b) of this section; nor may it use equipment owned by or services provided by the hospital unless such equipment is leased in accordance with a lease that complies with the equipment rental safe harbor set forth in paragraph (c) of this section, and such services are provided in accordance with a contract that complies with the personal services and management contracts safe harbor set forth in paragraph (d) of this section.

(vi) All ancillary services for Federal health care program beneficiaries performed at the entity must be directly and integrally related to primary procedures performed at the entity, and none may be separately billed to Medicare or other Federal health care programs.

(vii) The hospital may not include on its cost report or any claim for payment from a Federal health care program any costs associated with the ASC (unless such costs are required to be included by a Federal health care program).

(viii) The hospital may not be in a position to make or influence referrals directly or indirectly to any investor or the entity.

(5) For purposes of paragraph (r) of this section, procedures means any procedure or procedures on the list of Medicare-covered procedures for ambulatory surgical centers in accordance with regulations issued by the Department and group practice means a group practice that meets all of the standards of paragraph (p) of this section. Surgical group practice means a group practice that meets all of the standards of paragraph (p) of this section and is composed exclusively of surgeons who meet the requirements of paragraph (r)(1) of this section.

(s) *Referral agreements for specialty services.* As used in section 1128B of the Act, remuneration does not include any exchange of value among individuals and entities where one party agrees to refer a patient to the other party for the provision of a specialty service payable in whole or in part under Medicare or a State health care program in return for an agreement on the part of the other party to refer that patient back at a mutually agreed upon time or circumstance as long as the following four standards are met—

(1) The mutually agreed upon time or circumstance for referring the patient back to the originating individual or entity is clinically appropriate.

(2) The service for which the referral is made is not within the medical expertise of the referring individual or entity, but is within the special expertise of the other party receiving the referral.

(3) The parties receive no payment from each other for the referral and do not share or split a global fee from any Federal health care program in connection with the referred patient.

(4) Unless both parties belong to the same group practice as defined in paragraph (p) of this section, the only exchange of value between the parties is the remuneration the parties receive directly from third-party payors or the patient compensating the parties for the services they each have furnished to the patient.

(t) Price reductions offered to eligible managed care organizations.

(1) As used in section 1128(B) of the Act, "remuneration" does not include any payment between:

(i) An eligible managed care organization and any first tier contractor for providing or arranging for items or services, as long as the following three standards are met—

(A) The eligible managed care organization and the first tier contractor have an agreement that:

(1) Is set out in writing and signed by both parties;

(2) Specifies the items and services covered by the agreement;

(3) Is for a period of at least one year; and

(4) Specifies that the first tier contractor cannot claim payment in any form directly or indirectly from a Federal health care program for items or services covered under the agreement, except for:

(i) HMOs and competitive medical plans with cost-based contracts under section 1876 of the Act where the agreement with the eligible managed care organization sets out the arrangements in accordance with which the first tier contractor is billing the Federal health care program;

(ii) Federally qualified HMOs without a contract under sections 1854 or 1876 of the Act, where the agreement with the eligible managed care organization sets out the arrangements in accordance with which the first tier contractor is billing the Federal health care program; or

(iii) First tier contractors that are Federally qualified health centers that claim supplemental payments from a Federal health care program.

(B) In establishing the terms of the agreement, neither party gives or receives remuneration in return for or to induce the provision or acceptance of business (other than business covered by the agreement) for which payment may be made in whole or in part by a Federal health care program on a fee-for-service or cost basis.

(C) Neither party to the agreement shifts the financial burden of the agreement to the extent that increased payments are claimed from a Federal health care program.

(ii) A first tier contractor and a downstream contractor or between two downstream contractors to provide or arrange for items or services, as long as the following four standards are met—

(A) The parties have an agreement that:

(1) Is set out in writing and signed by both parties;

(2) Specifies the items and services covered by the agreement;

(3) Is for a period of at least one year; and

(4) Specifies that the party providing the items or services cannot claim payment in any form from a Federal health care program for items or services covered under the agreement.

(B) In establishing the terms of the agreement, neither party gives or receives remuneration in return for or to induce the provision or acceptance of business (other than business covered by the agreement) for which payment may be made in whole or in part by a Federal health care program on a fee-for-service or cost basis.

(C) Neither party shifts the financial burden of the agreement to the extent that increased payments are claimed from a Federal health care program.

(D) The agreement between the eligible managed care organization and first tier contractor covering the items or services that are covered by the agreement between the parties does not involve:

(1) A Federally qualified health center receiving supplemental payments;

(2) A HMO or CMP with a cost-based contract under section 1876 of the Act; or

(3) A Federally qualified HMO, unless the items or services are covered by a risk based contract under sections 1854 or 1876 of the Act.

(2) For purposes of this paragraph, the following terms are defined as follows:

(i) Downstream contractor means an individual or entity that has a subcontract directly or indirectly with a first tier contractor for the provision or arrangement of items or services that are covered by an agreement between an eligible managed care organization and the first tier contractor.

(ii) Eligible managed care organization[1] means—

(A) A HMO or CMP with a risk or cost based contract in accordance with section 1876 of the Act;

(B) Any Medicare Part C health plan that receives a capitated payment from Medicare and which must have its total Medicare beneficiary cost sharing approved by HCFA under section 1854 of the Act;

(C) Medicaid managed care organizations as defined in section 1903(m)(1)(A) that provide or arrange for items or services for Medicaid enrollees under a contract in accordance with section 1903(m) of the Act (except for fee-for-service plans or medical savings accounts);

(D) Any other health plans that provide or arrange for items and services for Medicaid enrollees in accordance with a risk-based contract with a State agency subject to the upper payment limits in § 447.361 of this title or an equivalent payment cap approved by the Secretary;

(E) Programs For All Inclusive Care For The Elderly (PACE) under sections 1894 and 1934 of the Act, except for for-profit demonstrations under sections 4801(h) and 4802(h) of Pub.L. 105–33; or

(F) A Federally qualified HMO.

(iii) First tier contractor means an individual or entity that has a contract directly with an eligible managed care organization to provide or arrange for items or services.

(iv) Items and services means health care items, devices, supplies or services or those services reasonably related to the provision of health care items, devices, supplies or services including, but not limited to, non-emergency transportation, patient education, attendant services, social services (e.g., case management), utilization review and quality assurance. Marketing and other pre-enrollment activities are not "items or services" for purposes of this section.

1. The eligible managed care organizations in paragraphs (u)(2)(ii)(A)-(F) of this section are only eligible with respect to items or services covered by the contracts specified in those paragraphs.

(u) Price reductions offered by contractors with substantial financial risk to managed care organizations.

(1) As used in section 1128(B) of the Act, "remuneration" does not include any payment between:

(i) A qualified managed care plan and a first tier contractor for providing or arranging for items or services, where the following five standards are met—

(A) The agreement between the qualified managed care plan and first tier contractor must:

(1) Be in writing and signed by the parties;

(2) Specify the items and services covered by the agreement;

(3) Be for a period of a least one year;

(4) Require participation in a quality assurance program that promotes the coordination of care, protects against underutilization and specifies patient goals, including measurable outcomes where appropriate; and

(5) Specify a methodology for determining payment that is commercially reasonable and consistent with fair market value established in an arms-length transaction and includes the intervals at which payments will be made and the formula for calculating incentives and penalties, if any.

(B) If a first tier contractor has an investment interest in a qualified managed care plan, the investment interest must meet the criteria of paragraph (a)(1) of this section.

(C) The first tier contractor must have substantial financial risk for the cost or utilization of services it is obligated to provide through one of the following four payment methodologies:

(1) A periodic fixed payment per patient that does not take into account the dates services are provided, the frequency of services, or the extent or kind of services provided;

(2) Percentage of premium;

(3) Inpatient Federal health care program diagnosis-related groups (DRGs) (other than those for psychiatric services);

(4) Bonus and withhold arrangements, provided—

(i) The target payment for first tier contractors that are individuals or non-institutional providers is at least 20 percent greater than the minimum payment, and for first tier contractors that are institutional providers, i.e., hospitals and nursing homes, is at least 10 percent greater than the minimum payment;

(ii) The amount at risk, i.e., the bonus or withhold, is earned by a first tier contractor in direct proportion to the ratio of the contractor's actual utilization to its target utilization;

(iii) In calculating the percentage in accordance with paragraph (u)(1)(i)(C)(4)(i) of this section, both the target payment amount and the minimum payment amount include any performance bonus, e.g., payments for timely submission of paperwork, continuing medical education, meeting attendance, etc., at a level achieved by 75 percent of the first tier contractors who are eligible for such payments;

(iv) Payment amounts, including any bonus or withhold amounts, are reasonable given the historical utilization patterns and costs for the same or comparable populations in similar managed care arrangements; and

(v) Alternatively, for a first tier contractor that is a physician, the qualified managed care plan has placed the physician at risk for referral services in an amount that exceeds the substantial financial risk threshold set forth in 42 CFR 417.479(f) and the arrangement is in compliance with the stop-loss and beneficiary survey requirements of 42 CFR 417.479(g).

(D) Payments for items and services reimbursable by Federal health care program must comply with the following two standards—

(1) The qualified managed care plan (or in the case of a self-funded employer plan that contracts with a qualified managed care plan to provide administrative services, the self-funded employer plan) must submit the claims directly to the Federal health care program, in accordance with a valid reassignment agreement, for items or services reimbursed by the Federal health care program. (Notwithstanding the foregoing, inpatient hospital services, other than psychiatric services, will be deemed to comply if the hospital is reimbursed by a Federal health care program under a DRG methodology.)

(2) Payments to first tier contractors and any downstream contractors for providing or arranging for items or services reimbursed by a Federal health care program must be identical to payment arrangements to or between such parties for the same items or services provided to other beneficiaries with similar health status, provided that such payments may be adjusted where the adjustments are relat-

ed to utilization patterns or costs of providing items or services to the relevant population.

(E) In establishing the terms of an arrangement—

(1) Neither party gives or receives remuneration in return for or to induce the provision or acceptance of business (other than business covered by the arrangement) for which payment may be made in whole or in part by a Federal health care program on a fee-for-service or cost basis; and

(2) Neither party to the arrangement shifts the financial burden of such arrangement to the extent that increased payments are claimed from a Federal health care program.

(ii) A first tier contractor and a downstream contractor, or between downstream contractors, to provide or arrange for items or services, as long as the following three standards are met—

(A) Both parties are being paid for the provision or arrangement of items or services in accordance with one of the payment methodologies set out in paragraph (u)(1)(i)(C) of this section;

(B) Payment arrangements for items and services reimbursable by a Federal health care program comply with paragraph (u)(1)(i)(D) of this section; and

(C) In establishing the terms of an arrangement—

(1) Neither party gives or receives remuneration in return for or to induce the provision or acceptance of business (other than business covered by the arrangement) for which payment may be made in whole or in part by a Federal health care program on a fee-for-service or cost basis; and

(2) Neither party to the arrangement shifts the financial burden of the arrangement to the extent that increased payments are claimed from a Federal health care program.

(2) For purposes of this paragraph, the following terms are defined as follows:

(i) Downstream contractor means an individual or entity that has a subcontract directly or indirectly with a first tier contractor for the provision or arrangement of items or services that are covered by an agreement between a qualified managed care plan and the first tier contractor.

(ii) First tier contractor means an individual or entity that has a contract directly with a qualified managed care plan to provide or arrange for items or services.

(iii) Is obligated to provide for a contractor refers to items or services:

(A) Provided directly by an individual or entity and its employees;

(B) For which an individual or entity is financially responsible, but which are provided by downstream contractors;

(C) For which an individual or entity makes referrals or arrangements; or

(D) For which an individual or entity receives financial incentives based on its own, its provider group's, or its qualified managed care plan's performance (or combination thereof).

(iv) Items and services means health care items, devices, supplies or services or those services reasonably related to the provision of health care items, devices, supplies or services including, but not limited to, non-emergency transportation, patient education, attendant services, social services (e.g., case management), utilization review and quality assurance. Marketing or other pre-enrollment activities are not "items or services" for purposes of this definition in this paragraph.

(v) Minimum payment is the guaranteed amount that a provider is entitled to receive under an agreement with a first tier or downstream contractor or a qualified managed care plan.

(vi) Qualified managed care plan means a health plan as defined in paragraph $(l)(2)$ of this section that:

(A) Provides a comprehensive range of health services;

(B) Provides or arranges for—

(1) Reasonable utilization goals to avoid inappropriate utilization;

(2) An operational utilization review program;

(3) A quality assurance program that promotes the coordination of care, protects against underutilization, and specifies patient goals, including measurable outcomes where appropriate;

(4) Grievance and hearing procedures;

(5) Protection of enrollees from incurring financial liability other than copayments and deductibles; and

(6) Treatment for Federal health care program beneficiaries that is not different than treatment for other enrollees because of their status as Federal health care program beneficiaries; and

(C) Covers a beneficiary population of which either—

(1) No more than 10 percent are Medicare beneficiaries, not including persons for whom a Federal health care program is the secondary payer; or

(2) No more than 50 percent are Medicare beneficiaries (not including persons for whom a Federal health care program is the secondary payer), provided that payment of premiums is on a periodic basis that does not take into account the dates services are rendered, the frequency of services, or the extent or kind of services rendered, and provided further that such periodic payments for the non-Federal health care program beneficiaries do not take into account the number of Federal health care program fee-for-service beneficiaries covered by the agreement or the amount of services generated by such beneficiaries.

(vii) Target payment means the fair market value payment established through arms length negotiations that will be earned by an individual or entity that:

(A) Is dependent on the individual or entity's meeting a utilization target or range of utilization targets that are set consistent with historical utilization rates for the same or comparable populations in similar managed care arrangements, whether based on its own, its provider group's or the qualified managed care plan's utilization (or a combination thereof); and

(B) Does not include any bonus or fees that the individual or entity may earn from exceeding the utilization target.

3.   Other Penalties

Civil Monetary Penalties and Assessments:
42 U.S.C.A. § 1320a–8

§ 1320a–8.   Civil Monetary Penalties and Assessments for Subchapters II, VIII and XVI

(a) False statements or representations of material fact; proceedings to exclude

(1) Any person (including an organization, agency, or other entity) who makes, or causes to be made, a statement or representation of a material fact for use in determining any initial or continuing right to or the amount of—

(A) monthly insurance benefits under subchapter II of this chapter,

(B) benefits or payments under subchapter VIII of this chapter [42 U.S.C.A. § 1001 et seq.], or

(C) benefits or payments under title subchapter XVI of this chapter[42 U.S.C.A. § 1381 et seq.], that the person knows or should know is false or misleading or knows or should know omits a material fact or makes such a statement with knowing disregard for the truth shall be subject to, in addition to any other penalties that may be prescribed by law, a civil money penalty of not more than $5,000 for each such statement or representation. Such person also shall be subject to an assessment, in lieu of damages sustained by the United States because of such statement or representation, of not more than twice the amount of benefits or payments paid as a result of such a statement or representation. In addition, the Commissioner of Social Security may make a determination in the same proceeding to recommend that the Secretary exclude, as provided in section 1320a–7 of this title, such a person who is a medical provider or physician from participation in the programs under subchapter XVIII of this chapter.

(2) For purposes of this section, a material fact is one which the Commissioner of Social Security may consider in evaluating whether an applicant is entitled to benefits under subchapter II [42 U.S.C.A. § 401 et seq.] or subchapter VIII [42 U.S.C.A. § 1001 et seq.], of this chapter or eligible for benefits or payments under subchapter XVI of this chapter [42 U.S.C.A. § 1381 et seq.].

(b) Initiation of proceedings; hearing; sanctions

(1) The Commissioner of Social Security may initiate a proceeding to determine whether to impose a civil money penalty or assessment, or whether to recommend exclusion under subsection (a) of this section only as authorized by the Attorney General pursuant to procedures agreed upon by the Commissioner of Social Security and the Attorney General. The Commissioner of Social Security may not initiate an action under this section with respect to any violation described in subsection (a) of this section later than 6 years after the date the violation was committed. The Commissioner of Social Security may initiate an action under this section by serving notice of the action in any manner authorized by Rule 4 of the Federal Rules of Civil Procedure.

(2) The Commissioner of Social Security shall not make a determination adverse to any person under this section until the person has been given written notice and an opportunity for the determination to be made on the record after a hearing at which the person is entitled to be represented by counsel, to present witnesses, and to cross-examine witnesses against the person.

(3) In a proceeding under this section which—

(A) is against a person who has been convicted (whether upon a verdict after trial or upon a plea of guilty or nolo contendere) of a Federal or State crime charging fraud or false statements; and

(B) involves the same transaction as in the criminal action; the person is estopped from denying the essential elements of the criminal offense.

(4) The official conducting a hearing under this section may sanction a person, including any party or attorney, for failing to comply with an order or procedure, for failing to defend an action, or for such other misconduct as would interfere with the speedy, orderly, or fair conduct of the hearing. Such sanction shall reasonably relate to the severity and nature of the failure or misconduct. Such sanction may include—

 (A) in the case of refusal to provide or permit discovery, drawing negative factual inference or treating such refusal as an admission by deeming the matter, or certain facts, to be established;

 (B) prohibiting a party from introducing certain evidence or otherwise supporting a particular claim or defense;

 (C) striking pleadings, in whole or in part;

 (D) staying the proceedings;

 (E) dismissal of the action;

 (F) entering a default judgment;

 (G) ordering the party or attorney to pay attorneys' fees and other costs caused by the failure or misconduct; and

 (H) refusing to consider any motion or other action which is not filed in a timely manner.

(c) Amount or scope of penalties, assessments, or exclusions

In determining pursuant to subsection (a) of this section the amount or scope of any penalty or assessment, or whether to recommend an exclusion, the Commissioner of Social Security shall take into account—

 (1) the nature of the statements and representations referred to in subsection (a) of this section and the circumstances under which they occurred;

 (2) the degree of culpability, history of prior offenses, and financial condition of the person committing the offense; and

 (3) such other matters as justice may require.

(d) Judicial review

 (1) Any person adversely affected by a determination of the Commissioner of Social Security under this section may obtain a review of such determination in the United States Court of Appeals for the circuit in which the person resides, or in which the statement or representation referred to in subsection (a) of this section was made, by filing in such court (within 60 days following the date the person is notified of the Commissioner's determination) a written petition requesting that the determination be modified or set aside. A copy of the petition shall be forthwith transmitted by the clerk of the court to the Commissioner of Social Security, and thereupon the Commissioner of Social Security shall file in the court the record in the proceeding as provided in section 2112 of Title 28. Upon such filing, the court shall have jurisdiction of the proceeding and of the question determined therein, and shall have the power to make and enter upon the pleadings, testimony, and proceedings set forth in such record a decree affirming, modifying, remanding for further consideration, or setting aside, in whole or in part, the determination of the Commissioner of Social Security and enforcing the same to the extent that such order is affirmed or modified. No objection that has not been urged before the Commissioner of Social Security shall be considered by the court, unless the failure or neglect to urge such objection shall be excused because of extraordinary circumstances.

(2) The findings of the Commissioner of Social Security with respect to questions of fact, if supported by substantial evidence on the record considered as a whole, shall be conclusive in the review described in paragraph (1). If any party shall apply to the court for leave to adduce additional evidence and shall show to the satisfaction of the court that such additional evidence is material and that there were reasonable grounds for the failure to adduce such evidence in the hearing before the Commissioner of Social Security, the court may order such additional evidence to be taken before the Commissioner of Social Security and to be made a part of the record. The Commissioner of Social Security may modify such findings as to the facts, or make new findings, by reason of additional evidence so taken and filed, and the Commissioner of Social Security shall file with the court such modified or new findings, which findings with respect to questions of fact, if supported by substantial evidence on the record considered as a whole shall be conclusive, and the Commissioner's recommendations, if any, for the modification or setting aside of the Commissioner's original order.

(3) Upon the filing of the record and the Commissioner's original or modified order with the court, the jurisdiction of the court shall be exclusive and its judgment and decree shall be final, except that the same shall be subject to review by the Supreme Court of the United States, as provided in section 1254 of Title 28.

(e) Compromise of money penalties and assessments; recovery; use of funds recovered

(1) Civil money penalties and assessments imposed under this section may be compromised by the Commissioner of Social Security and may be recovered—

(A) in a civil action in the name of the United States brought in United States district court for the district where the statement or representation referred to in subsection (a) of this section was made, or where the person resides, as determined by the Commissioner of Social Security;

(B) by means of reduction in tax refunds to which the person is entitled, based on notice to the Commissioner of Social Security of the Treasury as permitted under section 3720A of Title 31;

(C)(i) by decrease of any payment of monthly insurance benefits under subchapter II of this chapter [42 U.S.C.A. § 401 et seq.], notwithstanding section 407 of this title,

(ii) by decrease of any payment under subchapter VIII of this chapter [42 U.S.C.A. § 1001 et seq.] to which the person is entitled, or

(iii) by decrease of any payment under subchapter XVI of this chapter [42 U.S.C.A. § 1381 et seq.] for which the person is eligible, notwithstanding section 407 of this title, as made applicable to subchapter XVI of this chapter by reason of section 1383(d)(1) of this title;

(D) by authorities provided under the Debt Collection Act of 1982, as amended [31 U.S.C.A. § 3711 et seq.], to the extent applicable to debts arising under this chapter;

(E) by deduction of the amount of such penalty or assessment, when finally determined, or the amount agreed upon in compromise, from any sum then or later owing by the United States to the person against whom the penalty or assessment has been assessed; or

(F) by any combination of the foregoing.

(2) Amounts recovered under this section shall be recovered by the Commissioner of Social Security and shall be disposed of as follows:

(A) In the case of amounts recovered arising out of a determination relating to subchapter II of this chapter, the amounts shall be transferred to the Managing Trustee of the Federal Old–Age and Survivors Insurance Trust Fund or the Federal Disability Insurance Trust Fund, as determined appropriate by the Commissioner of Social Security, and such amounts shall be deposited by the Managing Trustee into such Trust Fund.

(B) In the case of amounts recovered arising out of a determination relating to subchapter VIII or subchapter or XVI of this chapter [42 U.S.C.A. § 1001 et seq. or 1381 et seq.], the amounts shall be deposited by the Commissioner of Social Security into the general fund of the Treasury as miscellaneous receipts.

(f) Finality of determination respecting penalty, assessment, or exclusion

A determination pursuant to subsection (a) of this section by the Commissioner of Social Security to impose a penalty or assessment, or to recommend an exclusion shall be final upon the expiration of the 60–day period referred to in subsection (d) of this section. Matters that were raised or that could have been raised in a hearing before the Commissioner of Social Security or in an appeal pursuant to subsection (d) of this section may not be raised as a defense to a civil action by the United States to collect a penalty or assessment imposed under this section.

71

(g) Notification of appropriate entities of finality of determination

Whenever the Commissioner's determination to impose a penalty or assessment under this section with respect to a medical provider or physician becomes final, the Commissioner shall notify the Secretary of the final determination and the reasons therefor, and the Secretary shall then notify the entities described in section 1320a–7a(h) of this title of such final determination.

(h) Injunction

Whenever the Commissioner of Social Security has reason to believe that any person has engaged, is engaging, or is about to engage in any activity which makes the person subject to a civil monetary penalty under this section, the Commissioner of Social Security may bring an action in an appropriate district court of the United States (or, if applicable, a United States court of any territory) to enjoin such activity, or to enjoin the person from concealing, removing, encumbering, or disposing of assets which may be required in order to pay a civil monetary penalty and assessment if any such penalty were to be imposed or to seek other appropriate relief.

(i) Delegation of authority

(1) The provisions of subsections (d) and (e) of section 405 of this title shall apply with respect to this section to the same extent as they are applicable with respect to subchapter II of this chapter. The Commissioner of Social Security may delegate the authority granted by section 405(d) of this title (as made applicable to this section) to the Inspector General for purposes of any investigation under this section.

(2) The Commissioner of Social Security may delegate authority granted under this section to the Inspector General.

(j) "State agency" defined

For purposes of this section, the term "State agency" shall have the same meaning as in section 1320a–7a(i)(1) of this title.

(k) Liability of principal for acts of agents

A principal is liable for penalties and assessments under subsection (a) of this section, and for an exclusion under section 1320a–7 of this title based on a recommendation under subsection (a) of this section, for the actions of the principal's agent acting within the scope of the agency.

(*l*) Protection of ongoing criminal investigations

As soon as the Inspector General, Social Security Administration, has reason to believe that fraud was involved in the application of an individual for monthly insurance benefits under subchapter II of this chapter or for benefits under subchapter VIII or subchapter XVI of this chapter [42 U.S.C.A. § 1001 et seq. or 1381 et seq.], the Inspector General shall make available to the Commissioner of Social Security information identifying the individual, unless a United States attorney, or equivalent State prosecutor, with jurisdiction over potential or actual related criminal cases, certifies, in writing, that there is a substantial risk that making the information so available in a particular investigation or redetermining the eligibility of the individual for such benefits would jeopardize the criminal prosecution of any person who is a subject of the investigation from which the information is derived.

Penalties Involving HMOs Failing to Provide Medically Necessary Services or Imposing Premiums in Excess of Permitted Amounts: 42 U.S.C.A. § 1395mm

§ 1395mm.   Payments to health maintenance organizations and competitive medical plans

* * *

(i) Duration, Terminations, effective date, and terms of contract; powers of Secretary

(6)(A) If the Secretary determines that an eligible organization with a contract under this section—

(i) fails substantially to provide medically necessary items and services that are required (under law or under the contract) to be provided to an individual covered under the contract, if the failure has adversely affected (or has substantial likelihood of adversely affecting) the individual;

(ii) imposes premiums on individuals enrolled under this section in excess of the premiums permitted;

(iii) acts to expel or to refuse to re-enroll an individual in violation of the provisions of this section;

(iv) engages in any practice that would reasonably be expected to have the effect of denying or discouraging enrollment (except as permitted by this section) by eligible individuals with the organization whose medical condition or history indicates a need for substantial future medical services;

(v) misrepresents or falsifies information that is furnished—

(I) to the Secretary under this section, or

(II) to an individual or to any other entity under this section;

(vi) fails to comply with the requirements of subsection (g)(6)(A) or paragraph (8) of this section; or

(vii) in the case of a risk-sharing contract, employs or contracts with any individual or entity that is excluded from participation under this subchapter under section 1320a–7 or 1320a–7a of this title for the provision of health care, utilization review, medical social work, or administrative services or employs or contracts with any entity for the provision (directly or indirectly) through such an excluded individual or entity of such services; the Secretary may

73

provide, in addition to any other remedies authorized by law, for any of the remedies described in subparagraph (B).

(B) The remedies described in this subparagraph are—

(i) civil money penalties of not more than $25,000 for each determination under subparagraph (A) or, with respect to a determination under clause (iv) or (v)(I) of such subparagraph, of not more than $100,000 for each such determination, plus, with respect to a determination under subparagraph (A)(ii), double the excess amount charged in violation of such subparagraph (and the excess amount charged shall be deducted from the penalty and returned to the individual concerned), and plus, with respect to a determination under subparagraph (A)(iv), $15,000 for each individual not enrolled as a result of the practice involved,

(ii) suspension of enrollment of individuals under this section after the date the Secretary notifies the organization of a determination under subparagraph (A) and until the Secretary is satisfied that the basis for such determination has been corrected and is not likely to recur, or

(iii) suspension of payment to the organization under this section for individuals enrolled after the date the Secretary notifies the organization of a determination under subparagraph (A) and until the Secretary is satisfied that the basis for such determination has been corrected and is not likely to recur.

(C) In the case of an eligible organization for which the Secretary makes a determination under paragraph (1), the basis of which is not described in subparagraph (A), the Secretary may apply the following intermediate sanctions:

(i) Civil money penalties of not more than $25,000 for each determination under paragraph (1) if the deficiency that is the basis of the determination has directly adversely affected (or has the substantial likelihood of adversely affecting) an individual covered under the organization's contract.

(ii) Civil money penalties of not more than $10,000 for each week beginning after the initiation of procedures by the Secretary under paragraph (9) during which the deficiency that is the basis of a determination under paragraph (1) exists.

(iii) Suspension of enrollment of individuals under this section after the date the Secretary notifies the organization of a determination under paragraph (1) and until the Secretary is satisfied that the deficiency that is the basis for the determination has been corrected and is not likely to recur.

(D) The provisions of section 1320a–7a of this title (other than subsections (a) and (b)) shall apply to a civil money penalty under subparagraph (B)(i) or (C)(i) in the same manner as such provisions apply to a civil money penalty or proceeding under section 1320a–7(a) of this title.

4.   Law: 42 U.S.C.A. § 1395nn

Limitation on Certain Physician Referrals

(a) Prohibition of certain referrals

(1) In general

Except as provided in subsection (b) of this section, if a physician (or an immediate family member of such physician) has a financial relationship with an entity specified in paragraph (2), then—

   (A) the physician may not make a referral to the entity for the furnishing of designated health services for which payment otherwise may be made under this subchapter, and

   (B) the entity may not present or cause to be presented a claim under this subchapter or bill to any individual, third party payor, or other entity for designated health services furnished pursuant to a referral prohibited under subparagraph (A).

(2) Financial relationship specified

For purposes of this section, a financial relationship of a physician (or an immediate family member of such physician) with an entity specified in this paragraph is—

   (A) except as provided in subsections (c) and (d) of this section, an ownership or investment interest in the entity, or

   (B) except as provided in subsection (e) of this section, a compensation arrangement (as defined in subsection (h)(1) of this section) between the physician (or an immediate family member of such physician) and the entity.

An ownership or investment interest described in subparagraph (A) may be through equity, debt, or other means and includes an interest in an entity that holds an ownership or investment interest in any entity providing the designated health service.

(b) General exceptions to both ownership and compensation arrangement prohibitions

Subsection (a)(1) of this section shall not apply in the following cases:

(1) Physicians' services

In the case of physicians' services (as defined in section 1395x(q) of this title) provided personally by (or under the personal supervision of) another physician in the same group practice (as defined in subsection (h)(4) of this section) as the referring physician.

(2) In-office ancillary services

In the case of services (other than durable medical equipment (excluding infusion pumps) and parenteral and enteral nutrients, equipment, and supplies)—

(A) that are furnished—

(i) personally by the referring physician, personally by a physician who is a member of the same group practice as the referring physician, or personally by individuals who are directly supervised by the physician or by another physician in the group practice, and

(ii)(I) in a building in which the referring physician (or another physician who is a member of the same group practice) furnishes physicians' services unrelated to the furnishing of designated health services, or

(II) in the case of a referring physician who is a member of a group practice, in another building which is used by the group practice—

(aa) for the provision of some or all of the group's clinical laboratory services, or

(bb) for the centralized provision of the group's designated health services (other than clinical laboratory services),

unless the Secretary determines other terms and conditions under which the provision of such services does not present a risk of program or patient abuse, and

(B) that are billed by the physician performing or supervising the services, by a group practice of which such physician is a member under a billing number assigned to the group practice, or by an entity that is wholly owned by such physician or such group practice, if the ownership or investment interest in such services meets such other requirements as the Secretary may impose by regulation as needed to protect against program or patient abuse.

(3) Prepaid plans

In the case of services furnished by an organization—

(A) with a contract under section 1395mm of this title to an individual enrolled with the organization,

(B) described in section 1395l(a)(1)(A) of this title to an individual enrolled with the organization,

(C) receiving payments on a prepaid basis, under a demonstration project under section 1395b–1(a) of this title or under section 222(a) of the Social Security Amendments of 1972, to an individual enrolled with the organization,

(D) that is a qualified health maintenance organization (within the meaning of section 300e–9(d) of this title) to an individual enrolled with the organization, or

(E) that is a Medicare + Choice organization under part C [42 U.S.C.A. § 1395w–21 et seq.] that is offering a coordinated care plan described in section 1395w–21(a)(2)(A) of this title to an individual enrolled with the organization.

(4) Other permissible exceptions

In the case of any other financial relationship which the Secretary determines, and specifies in regulations, does not pose a risk of program or patient abuse.

(c) General exception related only to ownership or investment prohibition for ownership in publicly traded securities and mutual funds

Ownership of the following shall not be considered to be an ownership or investment interest described in subsection (a)(2)(A) of this section:

(1) Ownership of investment securities (including shares or bonds, debentures, notes, or other debt instruments) which may be purchased on terms generally available to the public and which are—

(A)(i) securities listed on the New York Stock Exchange, the American Stock Exchange, or any regional exchange in which quotations are published on a daily basis, or foreign securities listed on a recognized foreign, national, or regional exchange in which quotations are published on a daily basis, or

(ii) traded under an automated interdealer quotation system operated by the National Association of Securities Dealers, and

(B) in a corporation that had, at the end of the corporation's most recent fiscal year, or on average during the previous 3 fiscal years, stockholder equity exceeding $75,000,000.

(2) Ownership of shares in a regulated investment company as defined in section 851(a) of Title 26, if such company had, at the end of the company's most recent fiscal year, or on average during the previous 3 fiscal years, total assets exceeding $75,000,000.

(d) Additional exceptions related only to ownership or investment prohibition

The following, if not otherwise excepted under subsection (b) of this section, shall not be considered to be an ownership or investment interest described in subsection (a)(2)(A) of this section:

(1) Hospitals in Puerto Rico

In the case of designated health services provided by a hospital located in Puerto Rico.

(2) Rural provider

In the case of designated health services furnished in a rural area (as defined in section 1395ww(d)(2)(D) of this title) by an entity, if substantially all of the designated health services furnished by such entity are furnished to individuals residing in such a rural area.

(3) Hospital ownership

In the case of designated health services provided by a hospital (other than a hospital described in paragraph (1)) if—

(A) the referring physician is authorized to perform services at the hospital, and

(B) the ownership or investment interest is in the hospital itself (and not merely in a subdivision of the hospital).

(e) Exceptions relating to other compensation arrangements

The following shall not be considered to be a compensation arrangement described in subsection (a)(2)(B) of this section:

(1) Rental of office space; rental of equipment

(A) Office space

Payments made by a lessee to a lessor for the use of premises if—

(i) the lease is set out in writing, signed by the parties, and specifies the premises covered by the lease,

(ii) the space rented or leased does not exceed that which is reasonable and necessary for the legitimate business purposes of the lease or rental and is used exclusively by the lessee when being used by the lessee, except that the lessee may make payments for the use of space consisting of common areas if such payments do not exceed the lessee's pro rata share of expenses for such space based upon the ratio of the space used exclusively by the lessee to the total amount of space (other than common areas) occupied by all persons using such common areas,

(iii) the lease provides for a term of rental or lease for at least 1 year,

(iv) the rental charges over the term of the lease are set in advance, are consistent with fair market value, and are not determined in a manner that takes into account the volume or value of any referrals or other business generated between the parties,

(v) the lease would be commercially reasonable even if no referrals were made between the parties, and

(vi) the lease meets such other requirements as the Secretary may impose by regulation as needed to protect against program or patient abuse.

(B) Equipment

Payments made by a lessee of equipment to the lessor of the equipment for the use of the equipment if—

(i) the lease is set out in writing, signed by the parties, and specifies the equipment covered by the lease,

(ii) the equipment rented or leased does not exceed that which is reasonable and necessary for the legitimate business purposes of the lease or rental and is used exclusively by the lessee when being used by the lessee,

(iii) the lease provides for a term of rental or lease of at least 1 year,

(iv) the rental charges over the term of the lease are set in advance, are consistent with fair market value, and are not determined in a manner that takes into account the volume or value of any referrals or other business generated between the parties,

(v) the lease would be commercially reasonable even if no referrals were made between the parties, and

(vi) the lease meets such other requirements as the Secretary may impose by regulation as needed to protect against program or patient abuse.

(2) Bona fide employment relationships

Any amount paid by an employer to a physician (or an immediate family member of such physician) who has a bona fide employment relationship with the employer for the provision of services if—

(A) the employment is for identifiable services,

(B) the amount of the remuneration under the employment—

(i) is consistent with the fair market value of the services, and

(ii) is not determined in a manner that takes into account (directly or indirectly) the volume or value of any referrals by the referring physician,

(C) the remuneration is provided pursuant to an agreement which would be commercially reasonable even if no referrals were made to the employer, and

(D) the employment meets such other requirements as the Secretary may impose by regulation as needed to protect against program or patient abuse.

Subparagraph (B)(ii) shall not prohibit the payment of remuneration in the form of a productivity bonus based on services performed personally by the physician (or an immediate family member of such physician).

(3) Personal service arrangements

(A) In general

Remuneration from an entity under an arrangement (including remuneration for specific physicians' services furnished to a nonprofit blood center) if—

(i) the arrangement is set out in writing, signed by the parties, and specifies the services covered by the arrangement,

(ii) the arrangement covers all of the services to be provided by the physician (or an immediate family member of such physician) to the entity,

(iii) the aggregate services contracted for do not exceed those that are reasonable and necessary for the legitimate business purposes of the arrangement,

(iv) the term of the arrangement is for at least 1 year,

(v) the compensation to be paid over the term of the arrangement is set in advance, does not exceed fair market value, and except in the case of a physician incentive plan described in subparagraph (B), is not determined in a manner that takes into account the volume or value of any referrals or other business generated between the parties,

(vi) the services to be performed under the arrangement do not involve the counseling or promotion or a business arrangement or other activity that violates any State or Federal law, and

(vii) the arrangement meets such other requirements as the Secretary may impose by regulation as needed to protect against program or patient abuse.

(B) Physician incentive plan exception

(i) In general

In the case of a physician incentive plan (as defined in clause (ii)) between a physician and an entity, the compensation may be determined in a manner (through a withhold, capitation, bonus, or otherwise) that takes into account directly or indirectly the volume or value of any referrals or other business generated between the parties, if the plan meets the following requirements:

(I) No specific payment is made directly or indirectly under the plan to a physician or a physician group as an inducement to reduce or limit medically necessary services provided with respect to a specific individual enrolled with the entity.

(II) In the case of a plan that places a physician or a physician group at substantial financial risk as determined by the Secretary pursuant to section 1395mm(i)(8)(A)(ii) of

80

this title, the plan complies with any requirements the Secretary may impose pursuant to such section.

(III) Upon request by the Secretary, the entity provides the Secretary with access to descriptive information regarding the plan, in order to permit the Secretary to determine whether the plan is in compliance with the requirements of this clause.

(ii) Physician incentive plan defined

For purposes of this subparagraph, the term "physician incentive plan" means any compensation arrangement between an entity and a physician or physician group that may directly or indirectly have the effect of reducing or limiting services provided with respect to individuals enrolled with the entity.

(4) Remuneration unrelated to the provision of designated health services

In the case of remuneration which is provided by a hospital to a physician if such remuneration does not relate to the provision of designated health services.

(5) Physician recruitment

In the case of remuneration which is provided by a hospital to a physician to induce the physician to relocate to the geographic area served by the hospital in order to be a member of the medical staff of the hospital, if—

(A) the physician is not required to refer patients to the hospital,

(B) the amount of the remuneration under the arrangement is not determined in a manner that takes into account (directly or indirectly) the volume or value of any referrals by the referring physician, and

(C) the arrangement meets such other requirements as the Secretary may impose by regulation as needed to protect against program or patient abuse.

(6) Isolated transactions

In the case of an isolated financial transaction, such as a one-time sale of property or practice, if—

(A) the requirements described in subparagraphs (B) and (C) of paragraph (2) are met with respect to the entity in the same manner as they apply to an employer, and

(B) the transaction meets such other requirements as the Secretary may impose by regulation as needed to protect against program or patient abuse.

(7) Certain group practice arrangements with a hospital

(A) In general

An arrangement between a hospital and a group under which designated health services are provided by the group but are billed by the hospital if—

(i) with respect to services provided to an inpatient of the hospital, the arrangement is pursuant to the provision of inpatient hospital services under section 1395x(b)(3) of this title,

(ii) the arrangement began before December 19, 1989, and has continued in effect without interruption since such date,

(iii) with respect to the designated health services covered under the arrangement, substantially all of such services furnished to patients of the hospital are furnished by the group under the arrangement,

(iv) the arrangement is pursuant to an agreement that is set out in writing and that specifies the services to be provided by the parties and the compensation for services provided under the agreement,

(v) the compensation paid over the term of the agreement is consistent with fair market value and the compensation per unit of services is fixed in advance and is not determined in a manner that takes into account the volume or value of any referrals or other business generated between the parties,

(vi) the compensation is provided pursuant to an agreement which would be commercially reasonable even if no referrals were made to the entity, and

(vii) the arrangement between the parties meets such other requirements as the Secretary may impose by regulation as needed to protect against program or patient abuse.

(8) Payments by a physician for items and services

Payments made by a physician—

(A) to a laboratory in exchange for the provision of clinical laboratory services, or

(B) to an entity as compensation for other items or services if the items or services are furnished at a price that is consistent with fair market value.

(f) Reporting requirements

Each entity providing covered items or services for which payment may be made under this subchapter shall provide the Secretary with the information concerning the entity's ownership, investment, and compensation arrangements, including—

(1) the covered items and services provided by the entity, and

(2) the names and unique physician identification numbers of all physicians with an ownership or investment interest (as described in subsection (a)(2)(A) of this section), or with a compensation arrangement (as described in subsection (a)(2)(B) of this section), in the entity, or whose immediate relatives have such an ownership or investment interest or who have such a compensation relationship with the entity.

Such information shall be provided in such form, manner, and at such times as the Secretary shall specify. The requirement of this subsection shall not apply to designated health services provided outside the United States or to entities which the Secretary determines provides services for which payment may be made under this subchapter very infrequently.

(g) Sanctions

(1) Denial of payment

No payment may be made under this subchapter for a designated health service which is provided in violation of subsection (a)(1) of this section.

(2) Requiring refunds for certain claims

If a person collects any amounts that were billed in violation of subsection (a)(1) of this section, the person shall be liable to the individual for, and shall refund on a timely basis to the individual, any amounts so collected.

(3) Civil money penalty and exclusion for improper claims

Any person that presents or causes to be presented a bill or a claim for a service that such person knows or should know is for a service for which payment may not be made under paragraph (1) or for which a refund has not been made under paragraph (2) shall be subject to a civil money penalty of not more than $15,000 for each such service. The provisions of section 1320a–7a of this title (other than the first sentence of subsection (a) and other than subsection (b)) shall apply to a civil money penalty under the previous sentence in the same manner as such provisions apply to a penalty or proceeding under section 1320a–7a(a) of this title.

(4) Civil money penalty and exclusion for circumvention schemes

Any physician or other entity that enters into an arrangement or scheme (such as a cross-referral arrangement) which the physician or entity knows or should know has a principal purpose of assuring referrals by the physician to a particular entity which, if the physician directly made referrals to such entity, would be in violation of this section, shall be subject to a civil money penalty of not more than $100,000 for each such arrangement or scheme. The provisions of section 1320a–7a of this title (other than the first sentence of subsection (a) and other than subsection (b)) shall apply to a civil money penalty under the previous sentence in the same manner as such provisions apply to a penalty or proceeding under section 1320a–7a(a) of this title.

(5) Failure to report information

Any person who is required, but fails, to meet a reporting requirement of subsection (f) of this section is subject to a civil money penalty of not more than $10,000 for each day for which reporting is required to have been made. The provisions of section 1320a–7a of this title (other than the first sentence of subsection (a) and other than subsection (b)) shall apply to a civil money penalty under the previous sentence in the same manner as such provisions apply to a penalty or proceeding under section 1320a–7a(a) of this title.

(6) Advisory opinions

(A) In general

The Secretary shall issue written advisory opinions concerning whether a referral relating to designated health services (other than clinical laboratory services) is prohibited under this section. Each advisory opinion issued by the Secretary shall be binding as to the Secretary and the party or parties requesting the opinion.

(B) Application of certain rules

The Secretary shall, to the extent practicable, apply the rules under subsections (b)(3) and (b)(4) of this section and take into account the regulations promulgated under subsection (b)(5) of section 1320a–7d of this title in the issuance of advisory opinions under this paragraph.

(C) Regulations

In order to implement this paragraph in a timely manner, the Secretary may promulgate regulations that take effect on an interim basis, after notice and pending opportunity for public comment.

(D) Applicability

This paragraph shall apply to requests for advisory opinions made after the date which is 90 days after August 5, 1997 and before the close of the period described in section 1320a–7d(b)(6) of this title.

(h) Definitions and special rules

For purposes of this section:

(1) Compensation arrangement; remuneration

(A) The term "compensation arrangement" means any arrangement involving any remuneration between a physician (or an immediate family member of such physician) and an entity other than an arrangement involving only remuneration described in subparagraph (C).

(B) The term "remuneration" includes any remuneration, directly or indirectly, overtly or covertly, in cash or in kind.

(C) Remuneration described in this subparagraph is any remuneration consisting of any of the following:

(i) The forgiveness of amounts owed for inaccurate tests or procedures, mistakenly performed tests or procedures, or the correction of minor billing errors.

(ii) The provision of items, devices, or supplies that are used solely to—

(I) collect, transport, process, or store specimens for the entity providing the item, device, or supply, or

(II) order or communicate the results of tests or procedures for such entity.

(iii) A payment made by an insurer or a self-insured plan to a physician to satisfy a claim, submitted on a fee for service basis, for the furnishing of health services by that physician to an individual who is covered by a policy with the insurer or by the self-insured plan, if—

(I) the health services are not furnished, and the payment is not made, pursuant to a contract or other arrangement between the insurer or the plan and the physician,

(II) the payment is made to the physician on behalf of the covered individual and would otherwise be made directly to such individual,

(III) the amount of the payment is set in advance, does not exceed fair market value, and is not determined in a manner that takes into account directly or indirectly the volume or value of any referrals, and

(IV) the payment meets such other requirements as the Secretary may impose by regulation as needed to protect against program or patient abuse.

(2) Employee

An individual is considered to be "employed by" or an "employee" of an entity if the individual would be considered to be an employee of the entity under the usual common law rules applicable in determining the employer-employee relationship (as applied for purposes of section 3121(d)(2) of Title 26).

(3) Fair market value

The term "fair market value" means the value in arms length transactions, consistent with the general market value, and, with respect to rentals or leases, the value of rental property for general commercial purposes (not taking into account its intended use) and, in the case of a lease of space, not adjusted to reflect the additional value the prospective lessee or lessor would attribute to the proximity or convenience to the lessor where the lessor is a potential source of patient referrals to the lessee.

(4) Group practice

(A) Definition of group practice

The term "group practice" means a group of 2 or more physicians legally organized as a partnership, professional corporation, foundation, not-for-profit corporation, faculty practice plan, or similar association—

(i) in which each physician who is a member of the group provides substantially the full range of services which the physician routinely provides, including medical care, consultation, diagnosis, or treatment, through the joint use of shared office space, facilities, equipment and personnel,

(ii) for which substantially all of the services of the physicians who are members of the group are provided through the group and are billed under a billing number assigned to the group and amounts so received are treated as receipts of the group,

(iii) in which the overhead expenses of and the income from the practice are distributed in accordance with methods previously determined,

(iv) except as provided in subparagraph (B)(i), in which no physician who is a member of the group directly or indirectly receives compensation based on the volume or value of referrals by the physician,

(v) in which members of the group personally conduct no less than 75 percent of the physician-patient encounters of the group practice, and

(vi) which meets such other standards as the Secretary may impose by regulation.

(B) Special rules

(i) Profits and productivity bonuses

A physician in a group practice may be paid a share of overall profits of the group, or a productivity bonus based on services personally performed or services incident to such personally performed services, so long as the share or bonus is not determined in any manner which is directly related to the volume or value of referrals by such physician.

(ii) Faculty practice plans

In the case of a faculty practice plan associated with a hospital, institution of higher education, or medical school with an approved medical residency training program in which physician members may provide a variety of different specialty services and provide professional services both within and outside the group, as well as perform other tasks such as research, subparagraph

(A) shall be applied only with respect to the services provided within the faculty practice plan.

(5) Referral; referring physician

(A) Physicians' services

Except as provided in subparagraph (C), in the case of an item or service for which payment may be made under part B, the request by a physician for the item or service, including the request by a physician for a consultation with another physician (and any test or procedure ordered by, or to be performed by (or under the supervision of) that other physician), constitutes a "referral" by a "referring physician".

(B) Other items

Except as provided in subparagraph (C), the request or establishment of a plan of care by a physician which includes the provision of the designated health service constitutes a "referral" by a "referring physician".

(C) Clarification respecting certain services integral to a consultation by certain specialists

A request by a pathologist for clinical diagnostic laboratory tests and pathological examination services, a request by a radiologist for diagnostic radiology services, and a request by a radiation oncologist for radiation therapy, if such services are furnished by (or under the supervision of) such pathologist, radiologist, or radiation oncologist pursuant to a consultation requested by another physician does not constitute a "referral" by a "referring physician".

(6) Designated health services

The term "designated health services" means any of the following items or services:

(A) Clinical laboratory services.

(B) Physical therapy services.

(C) Occupational therapy services.

(D) Radiology services, including magnetic resonance imaging, computerized axial tomography scans, and ultrasound services.

(E) Radiation therapy services and supplies.

(F) Durable medical equipment and supplies.

(G) Parenteral and enteral nutrients, equipment, and supplies.

(H) Prosthetics, orthotics, and prosthetic devices and supplies.

(I) Home health services.

(J) Outpatient prescription drugs.

(K) Inpatient and outpatient hospital services.

C. STATE FRAUD AND ABUSE LAWS AND SELF REFERRAL LAWS

California Fraud and Abuse Law: Ca. Bus. & Prof. § 650

§ 650. Consideration for referral of patients, clients, or customers; violations; penalty

Except as provided in Chapter 2.3 (commencing with Section 1400) of Division 2 of the Health and Safety Code, the offer, delivery, receipt, or acceptance by any person licensed under this division of any rebate, refund, commission, preference, patronage dividend, discount, or other consideration, whether in the form of money or otherwise, as compensation or inducement for referring patients, clients, or customers to any person, irrespective of any membership, proprietary interest or coownership in or with any person to whom these patients, clients or customers are referred is unlawful.

The payment or receipt of consideration for services other than the referral of patients which is based on a percentage of gross revenue or similar type of contractual arrangement shall not be unlawful if the consideration is commensurate with the value of the services furnished or with the fair rental value of any premises or equipment leased or provided by the recipient to the payer.

Except as provided in Chapter 2.3 (commencing with Section 1400) of Division 2 of the Health and Safety Code and in Sections 654.1 and 654.2, it shall not be unlawful for any person licensed under this division to refer a person to any laboratory, pharmacy, clinic (including entities exempt from licensure pursuant to Section 1206 of the Health and Safety Code), or health care facility solely because the licensee has a proprietary interest or coowner-ship in the laboratory, pharmacy, clinic, or health care facility; provided, however, that the licensee's return on investment for that proprietary interest or coownership shall be based upon the amount of the capital investment or proportional ownership of the licensee which ownership interest is not based on the number or value of any patients referred. Any referral excepted under this section shall be unlawful if the prosecutor proves that there was no valid medical need for the referral.

"Health care facility" means a general acute care hospital, acute psychiatric hospital, skilled nursing facility, intermediate care facility, and any other health facility licensed by the State Department of Health Services under Chapter 2 (commencing with Section 1250) of Division 2 of the Health and Safety Code.

A violation of this section is a public offense and is punishable upon a first conviction by imprisonment in the county jail for not more than one year, or by imprisonment in the state prison, or by a fine not exceeding fifty thousand dollars ($50,000), or by both that imprisonment and fine. A second or subsequent conviction is punishable by imprisonment in the state prison or by imprisonment in the state prison and a fine of fifty thousand dollars ($50,000).

California Self Referral Law: Ca. Bus. & Prof. Code § 650.01

§ 650.01 Referral to health care provider in which practitioner or immediate family member has financial interest; prohibition; cross-referral arrangements; disclosure to patients

(a) Notwithstanding Section 650, or any other provision of law, it is unlawful for a licensee to refer a person for laboratory, diagnostic nuclear medicine, radiation oncology, physical therapy, physical rehabilitation, psychometric testing, home infusion therapy, or diagnostic imaging goods or services if the licensee or his or her immediate family has a financial interest with the person or in the entity that receives the referral.

(b) For purposes of this section and Section 650.02, the following shall apply:

(1) "Diagnostic imaging" includes, but is not limited to, all X-ray, computed axial tomography, magnetic resonance imaging nuclear medicine, positron emission tomography, mammography, and ultrasound goods and services.

(2) A "financial interest" includes, but is not limited to, any type of ownership interest, debt, loan, lease, compensation, remuneration, discount, rebate, refund, dividend, distribution, subsidy, or other form of direct or indirect payment, whether in money or otherwise, between a licensee and a person or entity to whom the licensee refers a person for a good or service specified in subdivision (a). A financial interest also exists if there is an indirect financial relationship between a licensee and the referral recipient including, but not limited to, an arrangement whereby a licensee has an ownership interest in an entity that leases property to the referral recipient. Any financial interest transferred by a licensee to any person or entity or otherwise established in any person or entity for the purpose of avoiding the prohibition of this section shall be deemed a financial interest of the licensee. For purposes of this paragraph, "direct or indirect payment" shall not include a royalty or consulting fee received by a physician and surgeon who has completed a recognized residency training program in orthopedics from a manufacturer or distributor as a result of his or her research and development of medical devices and techniques for that manufacturer or distributor. For purposes of this paragraph, "consulting fees" means those fees paid by the manufacturer or distributor to a physician and surgeon who has completed a recognized residency training program in orthopedics only for his or her ongoing services in making refinements to his or her medical devices or techniques marketed or distributed by the manufacturer or distributor, if the manufacturer or distributor does not own or control the facility to which the physician is referring the patient. A "financial interest" shall not include the receipt of capitation payments or other fixed amounts that are prepaid in exchange for a promise of a licensee to provide specified health care services to specified beneficiaries. A "financial interest" shall not include the receipt of remuneration by a medical director of a hospice, as defined in Section 1746 of the Health and Safety Code, for specified services if the arrangement is set out in writing, and specifies all services to be provided by the medical director, the term of the arrangement is for at least one year, and the compensation to be paid over the term of the arrangement is set in advance, does not exceed fair market value, and is not determined in a manner that takes into account the volume or value of any referrals or other business generated between parties.

(3) For the purposes of this section, "immediate family" includes the spouse and children of the licensee, the parents of the licensee, and the spouses of the children of the licensee.

(4) "Licensee" means a physician as defined in Section 3209.3 of the Labor Code.

(5) "Licensee's office" means either of the following:

(A) An office of a licensee in solo practice.

(B) An office in which services or goods are personally provided by the licensee or by employees in that office, or personally by independent contractors in that office, in accordance with other provisions of law. Employees and independent contractors shall be licensed or certified when licensure or certification is required by law.

(6) "Office of a group practice" means an office or offices in which two or more licensees are legally organized as a partnership, professional corporation, or not-for-profit corporation, licensed pursuant to subdivision (a) of Section 1204 of the Health and Safety Code, for which all of the following apply:

(A) Each licensee who is a member of the group provides substantially the full range of services that the licensee routinely provides, including medical care, consultation, diagnosis, or treatment through the joint use of shared office space, facilities, equipment, and personnel.

(B) Substantially all of the services of the licensees who are members of the group are provided through the group and are billed in the name of the group and amounts so received are treated as receipts of the group, except in the case of a multispecialty clinic, as defined in subdivision (*l*) of Section 1206 of the Health and Safety Code, physician services are billed in the name of the multispecialty clinic and amounts so received are treated as receipts of the multispecialty clinic.

(C) The overhead expenses of, and the income from, the practice are distributed in accordance with methods previously determined by members of the group.

(c) It is unlawful for a licensee to enter into an arrangement or scheme, such as a cross-referral arrangement, that the licensee knows, or should know, has a principal purpose of ensuring referrals by the licensee to a particular entity that, if the licensee directly made referrals to that entity, would be in violation of this section.

(d) No claim for payment shall be presented by an entity to any individual, third party payer, or other entity for a good or service furnished pursuant to a referral prohibited under this section.

(e) No insurer, self-insurer, or other payer shall pay a charge or lien for any good or service resulting from a referral in violation of this section.

(f) A licensee who refers a person to, or seeks consultation from, an organization in which the licensee has a financial interest, other than as prohibited by subdivision (a), shall disclose the financial interest to the patient, or the parent or legal guardian of the patient, in writing, at the time of the referral or request for consultation.

(1) If a referral, billing, or other solicitation is between one or more licensees who contract with a multispecialty clinic pursuant to subdivision (*l*) of Section 1206 of the Health and Safety Code or who conduct their practice as members of the same professional corporation or partnership, and the services are rendered on the same physical premises, or under the same professional corporation or partnership name, the requirements of this subdivision may be met by posting a conspicuous disclosure statement at the registration area or by providing a patient with a written disclosure statement.

(2) If a licensee is under contract with the Department of Corrections or the California Youth Authority, and the patient is an inmate or parolee of either respective department, the requirements of this subdivision shall be satisfied by disclosing financial interests to either the Department of Corrections or the California Youth Authority.

(g) A violation of subdivision (a) shall be a misdemeanor. The Medical Board of California shall review the facts and circumstances of any conviction pursuant to subdivision (a) and take appropriate disciplinary action if the licensee has committed unprofessional conduct. Violations of this section may also be subject to civil penalties of up to five thousand dollars ($5,000) for each offense, which may be enforced by the Insurance Commissioner, Attorney General, or a district attorney. A violation of subdivision (c), (d), or (e) is a public offense and is punishable upon conviction by a fine not exceeding fifteen thousand dollars ($15,000) for each violation and appropriate disciplinary action, including revocation of professional licensure, by the Medical Board of California or other appropriate governmental agency.

(h) This section shall not apply to referrals for services that are described in and covered by Sections 139.3 and 139.31 of the Labor Code.

(i) This section shall become operative on January 1, 1995.

§ 650.02 Exemptions; referrals by financially interested licensees

The prohibition of Section 650.01 shall not apply to or restrict any of the following:

(a) A licensee may refer a patient for a good or service otherwise prohibited by subdivision (a) of Section 650.01 if the licensee's regular practice is located where there is no alternative provider of the service within either 25 miles or 40 minutes traveling time, via the shortest route on a paved road. If an alternative provider commences furnishing the good or service for which a patient was referred pursuant to this subdivision, the licensee shall cease referrals under this subdivision within six months of the time at which the licensee knew or should have known that the alternative provider is furnishing the good or service. A licensee who refers to or seeks consultation from an organization in which the licensee has a financial interest under this subdivision shall disclose this interest to the patient or the patient's parents or legal guardian in writing at the time of referral.

(b) A licensee, when the licensee or his or her immediate family has one or more of the following arrangements with another licensee, a person, or an entity, is not prohibited from referring a patient to the licensee, person, or entity because of the arrangement:

(1) A loan between a licensee and the recipient of the referral, if the loan has commercially reasonable terms, bears interest at the prime rate or a higher rate that does not constitute usury, is adequately secured, and the loan terms are not affected by either party's referral of any person or the volume of services provided by either party.

(2) A lease of space or equipment between a licensee and the recipient of the referral, if the lease is written, has commercially reasonable terms, has a fixed periodic rent payment, has a term of one year or more, and the lease payments are not affected by either party's referral of any person or the volume of services provided by either party.

(3) Ownership of corporate investment securities, including shares, bonds, or other debt instruments that may be purchased on terms generally available to the public and that are traded on a licensed securities exchange or NASDAQ, do not base profit distributions or other transfers of value on the licensee's referral of persons to the corporation, do not have a separate class or accounting for any persons or for any licensees who may refer persons to the corporation, and are in a corporation that had, at the end of the corporation's most recent fiscal year, or on average during the previous three fiscal years, stockholder equity exceeding seventy-five million dollars ($75,000,000).

(4) Ownership of shares in a regulated investment company as defined in Section 851(a) of the federal Internal Revenue Code, if the company had, at the end of the company's most recent fiscal year, or on average during the previous three fiscal years, total assets exceeding seventy-five million dollars ($75,000,000).

(5) A one-time sale or transfer of a practice or property or other financial interest between a licensee and the recipient of the referral if the sale or transfer is for commercially reasonable terms and the consideration is not affected by either party's referral of any person or the volume of services provided by either party.

(c)(1) A licensee may refer a person to a health facility, as defined in Section 1250 of the Health and Safety Code, or to any facility owned or leased by a health facility, if the recipient of the referral does not compensate the licensee for the patient referral, and any equipment lease arrangement between the licensee and the referral recipient complies with the requirements of paragraph (2) of subdivision (b).

(2) Nothing shall preclude this subdivision from applying to a licensee solely because the licensee has an ownership or leasehold interest in an entire health facility or an entity that owns or leases an entire health facility.

(3) A licensee may refer a person to a health facility for any service classified as an emergency under subdivision (a) or (b) of Section 1317.1 of the Health and Safety Code.

(4) A licensee may refer a person to any organization that owns or leases a health facility licensed pursuant to subdivision (a), (b), or (f) of Section 1250 of the Health and Safety Code if the licensee is not compensated for the patient referral, the licensee does not receive any payment from the recipient of the referral that is based or determined on the number or value of any patient referrals, and any equipment lease arrangement between the licensee and the referral recipient complies with the requirements of paragraph (2) of subdivision (b). For purposes of this paragraph, the ownership may be through stock or membership, and may be represented by a parent holding company that solely owns or controls both the health facility organization and the affiliated organization.

(d) A licensee may refer a person to a nonprofit corporation that provides physician services pursuant to subdivision (*l*) of Section 1206 of the Health and Safety Code if the nonprofit corporation is controlled through membership by one or more health facilities or health facility systems and the amount of compensation or other transfer of funds from the health facility or nonprofit corporation to the licensee is fixed annually, except for adjustments caused by physicians joining or leaving the groups during the year, and is not based on the number of persons utilizing goods or services specified in Section 650.01.

(e) A licensee compensated or employed by a university may refer a person for a physician service, to any facility owned or operated by the university, or to another licensee employed by the university, provided that the facility or university does not compensate the referring licensee for the patient referral. In the case of a facility that is totally or partially owned by an entity other than the university, but that is staffed by university physicians, those physicians may not refer patients to the facility if the facility compensates the referring physicians for those referrals.

(f) The prohibition of Section 650.01 shall not apply to any service for a specific patient that is performed within, or goods that are supplied by, a licensee's office, or the office of a group practice. Further, the provisions of Section 650.01 shall not alter, limit, or expand a licensee's ability to deliver, or to direct or supervise the delivery of, in-office goods or services according to the laws, rules, and regulations governing his or her scope of practice.

(g) The prohibition of Section 650.01 shall not apply to cardiac rehabilitation services provided by a licensee or by a suitably trained individual under the direct or general supervision of a licensee, if the services are provided to patients meeting the criteria for Medicare reimbursement for the services.

(h) The prohibition of Section 650.01 shall not apply if a licensee is in the office of a group practice and refers a person for services or goods specified in Section 650.01 to a multispecialty clinic, as defined in subdivision (*l*) of Section 1206 of the Health and Safety Code.

(i) The prohibition of Section 650.01 shall not apply to health care services provided to an enrollee of a health care service plan licensed pursuant to the Knox–Keene Health Care Service Plan Act of 1975 (Chapter 2.2 (commencing with Section 1340) of Division 2 of the Health and Safety Code).

(j) The prohibition of Section 650.01 shall not apply to a request by a pathologist for clinical diagnostic laboratory tests and pathological examination services, a request by a radiologist for diagnostic radiology services, or a request by a radiation oncologist for radiation therapy if those services are furnished by, or under the supervision of, the pathologist, radiologist, or radiation oncologist pursuant to a consultation requested by another physician.

(k) This section shall not apply to referrals for services that are described in and covered by Sections 139.3 and 139.31 of the Labor Code.

(*l*) This section shall become operative on January 1, 1995.

II. ANTITRUST

A. FEDERAL ANTITRUST LAW

Sherman Act

Restraints of Trade: 15 U.S.C.A. § 1

§ 1. Trusts, etc., in restraint of trade illegal; penalty

Every contract, combination in the form of trust or otherwise, or conspiracy, in restraint of trade or commerce among the several States, or with foreign nations, is hereby declared to be illegal. Every person who shall make any contract or engage in any combination or conspiracy hereby declared to be illegal shall be deemed guilty of a felony, and, on conviction thereof, shall be punished by fine not exceeding $10,000,000 if a corporation, or, if any other person, $350,000, or by imprisonment not exceeding three years, or by both said punishments, in the discretion of the court.

Monopolization: 15 U.S.C.A. § 2

§ 2. Monopolizing trade a felony; penalty

Every person who shall monopolize, or attempt to monopolize, or combine or conspire with any other person or persons, to monopolize any part of the trade or commerce among the several States, or with foreign nations, shall be deemed guilty of a felony, and, on conviction thereof, shall be punished by fine not exceeding $10,000,000 if a corporation, or, if any other person, $350,000, or by imprisonment not exceeding three years, or by both said punishments, in the discretion of the court.

Robinson-Patman Act
Price Discrimination: 15 U.S.C.A. §§ 13 et seq.

§ 13. Discrimination in price, services, or facilities

(a) Price; selection of customers

It shall be unlawful for any person engaged in commerce, in the course of such commerce, either directly or indirectly, to discriminate in price between different purchasers of commodities of like grade and quality, where either or any of the purchases involved in such discrimination are in commerce, where such commodities are sold for use, consumption, or resale within the United States or any Territory thereof or the District of Columbia or any insular possession or other place under the jurisdiction of the United States, and where the effect of such discrimination may be substantially to lessen competition or tend to create a monopoly in any line of commerce, or to injure, destroy, or prevent competition with any person who either grants or knowingly receives the benefit of such discrimination, or with customers of either of them: Provided, That nothing herein contained shall prevent differentials which make only due allowance for differences in the cost of manufacture, sale, or delivery resulting from the differing methods or quantities in which such commodities are to such purchasers sold or delivered: Provided, however, That the Federal Trade Commission may, after due investigation and hearing to all interested parties, fix and establish quantity limits, and revise the same as it finds necessary, as to particular commodities or classes of commodities, where it finds that available purchasers in greater quantities are so few as to render differentials on account thereof unjustly discriminatory or promotive of monopoly in any line of commerce; and the foregoing shall then not be construed to permit differentials based on differences in quantities greater than those so fixed and established: And provided further, That nothing herein contained shall prevent persons engaged in selling goods, wares, or merchandise in commerce from selecting their own customers in bona fide transactions and not in restraint of trade: And provided further, That nothing herein contained shall prevent price changes from time to time where in response to changing conditions affecting the market for or the marketability of the goods concerned, such as but not limited to actual or imminent deterioration of perishable goods, obsolescence of seasonal goods, distress sales under court process, or sales in good faith in discontinuance of business in the goods concerned.

(b) Burden of rebutting prima-facie case of discrimination

Upon proof being made, at any hearing on a complaint under this section, that there has been discrimination in price or services or facilities furnished, the burden of rebutting the prima-facie case thus made by showing justification shall be upon the person charged with a violation of this section, and unless justification shall be affirmatively shown, the Commission is authorized to issue an order terminating the discrimination: Provided, however, That nothing herein contained shall prevent a seller rebutting the prima-facie case thus made by showing that his lower price or the furnishing of services or facilities to any purchaser or purchasers was made in good faith to meet an equally low price of a competitor, or the services or facilities furnished by a competitor.

(c) Payment or acceptance of commission, brokerage, or other compensation

It shall be unlawful for any person engaged in commerce, in the course of such commerce, to pay or grant, or to receive or accept, anything of value as a commission, brokerage, or other compensation, or any allowance or discount in lieu thereof, except for services rendered in connection with the sale or purchase of goods, wares, or merchandise, either to the other party to such transaction or to an agent, representative, or other intermediary therein where such intermediary is acting in fact for or in behalf, or is subject to the direct or indirect control, of any party to such transaction other than the person by whom such compensation is so granted or paid.

(d) Payment for services or facilities for processing or sale

It shall be unlawful for any person engaged in commerce to pay or contract for the payment of anything of value to or for the benefit of a customer of such person in the course of such commerce as compensation or in consideration for any services or facilities furnished by or through such customer in connection with the processing, handling, sale, or offering for sale of any products or commodities manufactured, sold, or offered for sale by such person, unless such payment or consideration is available on proportionally equal terms to all other customers competing in the distribution of such products or commodities.

(e) Furnishing services or facilities for processing, handling, etc.

It shall be unlawful for any person to discriminate in favor of one purchaser against another purchaser or purchasers of a commodity bought for resale, with or without processing, by contracting to furnish or furnishing, or by contributing to the furnishing of, any services or facilities connected with the processing, handling, sale, or offering for sale of such commodity so purchased upon terms not accorded to all purchasers on proportionally equal terms.

(f) Knowingly inducing or receiving discriminatory price

It shall be unlawful for any person engaged in commerce, in the course of such commerce, knowingly to induce or receive a discrimination in price which is prohibited by this section.

Suits By Persons Injured Clayton Act § 4: 15 U.S.C.A. § 15

§ 15. Suits by persons injured

(a) Amount of recovery; prejudgment interest

Except as provided in subsection (b) of this section, any person who shall be injured in his business or property by reason of anything forbidden in the antitrust laws may sue therefor in any district court of the United States in the district in which the defendant resides or is found or has an agent, without respect to the amount in controversy, and shall recover threefold the damages by him sustained, and the cost of suit, including a reasonable attorney's fee. The court may award under this section, pursuant to a motion by such person promptly made, simple interest on actual damages for the period beginning on the date of service of such person's pleading setting forth a claim under the antitrust laws and ending on the date of judgment, or for any shorter period therein, if the court finds that the award of such interest for such period is just in the circumstances. In determining whether an award of interest under this section for any period is just in the circumstances, the court shall consider only—

    (1) whether such person or the opposing party, or either party's representative, made motions or asserted claims or defenses so lacking in merit as to show that such party or representative acted intentionally for delay, or otherwise acted in bad faith;

(2) whether, in the course of the action involved, such person or the opposing party, or either party's representative, violated any applicable rule, statute, or court order providing for sanctions for dilatory behavior or otherwise providing for expeditious proceedings; and

(3) whether such person or the opposing party, or either party's representative, engaged in conduct primarily for the purpose of delaying the litigation or increasing the cost thereof.

(b) Amount of damages payable to foreign states and instrumentalities of foreign states

(1) Except as provided in paragraph (2), any person who is a foreign state may not recover under subsection (a) of this section an amount in excess of the actual damages sustained by it and the cost of suit, including a reasonable attorney's fee.

(2) Paragraph (1) shall not apply to a foreign state if—

(A) such foreign state would be denied, under section 1605(a)(2) of Title 28, immunity in a case in which the action is based upon a commercial activity, or an act, that is the subject matter of its claim under this section;

(B) such foreign state waives all defenses based upon or arising out of its status as a foreign state, to any claims brought against it in the same action;

(C) such foreign state engages primarily in commercial activities; and

(D) such foreign state does not function, with respect to the commercial activity, or the act, that is the subject matter of its claim under this section as a procurement entity for itself or for another foreign state.

(c) Definitions

For purposes of this section—

(1) the term "commercial activity" shall have the meaning given it in section 1603(d) of Title 28, and

(2) the term "foreign state" shall have the meaning given it in section 1603(a) of Title 28.

Actions by State attorneys general:

§ 15c(a) Parens patriae; monetary relief; damages; prejudgment interest

(1) Any attorney general of a State may bring a civil action in the name of such State, as parens patriae on behalf of natural persons residing in such State, in any district court of the United States having jurisdiction of the defendant, to secure monetary relief as provided in this section for injury sustained by such natural persons to their property by reason of any violation of sections 1 to 7 of this title. The court shall exclude from the amount of monetary relief awarded in such action any amount of monetary relief (A) which duplicates amounts which have been awarded for the same injury, or (B) which is properly allocable to (i) natural persons who have excluded their claims pursuant to subsection (b)(2) of this section, and (ii) any business entity.

(2) The court shall award the State as monetary relief threefold the total damage sustained as described in paragraph (1) of this subsection, and the cost of suit, including a reasonable attorney's fee. The court may award under this paragraph, pursuant to a motion by such State promptly made, simple interest on the total damage for the period beginning on the date of service of such State's pleading setting forth a claim under the antitrust laws and ending on the date of judgment, or for any shorter period therein, if the court finds that the award of such interest for such period is just in the circumstances. In determining whether an award of interest under this paragraph for any period is just in the circumstances, the court shall consider only—

(A) whether such State or the opposing party, or either party's representative, made motions or asserted claims or defenses so lacking in merit as to show that such party or representative acted intentionally for delay or otherwise acted in bad faith;

(B) whether, in the course of the action involved, such State or the opposing party, or either party's representative, violated any applicable rule, statute, or court order providing for sanctions for dilatory behavior or otherwise providing for expeditious proceedings; and

(C) whether such State or the opposing party, or either party's representative, engaged in conduct primarily for the purpose of delaying the litigation or increasing the cost thereof.

(b) Notice; exclusion election; final judgment

(1) In any action brought under subsection (a)(1) of this section, the State attorney general shall, at such times, in such manner, and with such content as the court may direct, cause notice thereof to be given by publication. If the court finds that notice given solely by publication would deny due process of law to any person or persons, the court may direct further notice to such person or persons according to the circumstances of the case.

(2) Any person on whose behalf an action is brought under subsection (a)(1) of this section may elect to exclude from adjudication the portion of the State claim for monetary relief attributable to him by filing notice of such election with the court within such time as specified in the notice given pursuant to paragraph (1) of this subsection.

(3) The final judgment in an action under subsection (a)(1) of this section shall be res judicata as to any claim under section 15 of this title by any person on behalf of whom such action was brought and who fails to give such notice within the period specified in the notice given pursuant to paragraph (1) of this subsection.

(c) Dismissal or compromise of action

An action under subsection (a)(1) of this section shall not be dismissed or compromised without the approval of the court, and notice of any proposed dismissal or compromise shall be given in such manner as the court directs.

(d) Attorneys' fees

In any action under subsection (a) of this section—

(1) the amount of the plaintiffs' attorney's fee, if any, shall be determined by the court; and

(2) the court may, in its discretion, award a reasonable attorney's fee to a prevailing defendant upon a finding that the State attorney general has acted in bad faith, vexatiously, wantonly, or for oppressive reasons.

Mergers and Acquisitions, Clayton Act, § 7: 15 U.S.C.A. § 18

§ 18. Acquisition by one corporation of stock of another

No person engaged in commerce or in any activity affecting commerce shall acquire, directly or indirectly, the whole or any part of the stock or other share capital and no person subject to the jurisdiction of the Federal Trade Commission shall acquire the whole or any part of the assets of another person engaged also in commerce or in any activity affecting commerce, where in any line of commerce or in any activity affecting commerce in any section of the country, the effect of such acquisition may be substantially to lessen competition, or to tend to create a monopoly.

No person shall acquire, directly or indirectly, the whole or any part of the stock or other share capital and no person subject to the jurisdiction of the Federal Trade Commission shall acquire the whole or any part of the assets of one or more persons engaged in commerce or in any activity affecting commerce, where in any line of commerce or in any activity affecting commerce in any section of the country, the effect of such acquisition, of such stocks or assets, or of the use of such stock by the voting or granting of proxies or otherwise, may be substantially to lessen competition, or to tend to create a monopoly.

This section shall not apply to persons purchasing such stock solely for investment and not using the same by voting or otherwise to bring about, or in attempting to bring about, the substantial lessening of competition. Nor shall anything contained in this section prevent a corporation engaged in commerce or in any activity affecting commerce from causing the formation of subsidiary corporations for the actual carrying on of their immediate lawful business, or the natural and legitimate branches or extensions thereof, or from owning and holding all or a part of the stock of such subsidiary corporations, when the effect of such formation is not to substantially lessen competition.

Nor shall anything herein contained be construed to prohibit any common carrier subject to the laws to regulate commerce from aiding in the construction of branches or short lines so located as to become feeders to the main line of the company so aiding in such construction or from acquiring or owning all or any part of the stock of such branch lines, nor to prevent any such common carrier from acquiring and owning all or any part of the stock of a branch or short line constructed by an independent company where there is no substantial competition between the company owning the branch line so constructed and the company owning the main line acquiring the property or an interest therein, nor to prevent such common carrier from extending any of its lines through the medium of the acquisition of stock or otherwise of any other common carrier where there is no substantial competition between the company extending its lines and the company whose stock, property, or an interest therein is so acquired.

Nothing contained in this section shall be held to affect or impair any right heretofore legally acquired: Provided, That nothing in this section shall be held or construed to authorize or make lawful anything heretofore prohibited or made illegal by the antitrust laws, nor to exempt any person from the penal provisions thereof or the civil remedies therein provided.

Nothing contained in this section shall apply to transactions duly consummated pursuant to authority given by the Secretary of Transportation, Federal Power Commission, Surface Transportation Board, the Securities and Exchange Commission in the exercise of its jurisdiction under section 79j of this title, the United States Maritime Commission, or the Secretary of Agriculture under any statutory provision vesting such power in such Commission, Board, or Secretary.

Interlocking Directorates and Officers, Clayton Act, § 8: 15 U.S.C.A. § 19

§ 19.   Interlocking directorates and officers

(a)(1) No person shall, at the same time, serve as a director or officer in any two corporations (other than banks, banking associations, and trust companies) that are—

(A) engaged in whole or in part in commerce; and

(B) by virtue of their business and location of operation, competitors, so that the elimination of competition by agreement between them would constitute a violation of any of the antitrust laws; if each of the corporations has capital, surplus, and undivided profits aggregating more than $10,000,000 as adjusted pursuant to paragraph (5) of this subsection.

(2) Notwithstanding the provisions of paragraph (1), simultaneous service as a director or officer in any two corporations shall not be prohibited by this section if—

(A) the competitive sales of either corporation are less than $1,000,000, as adjusted pursuant to paragraph (5) of this subsection;

(B) the competitive sales of either corporation are less than 2 per centum of that corporation's total sales; or

(C) the competitive sales of each corporation are less than 4 per centum of that corporation's total sales.

For purposes of this paragraph, "competitive sales" means the gross revenues for all products and services sold by one corporation in competition with the other, determined on the basis of annual gross revenues for such products and services in that corporation's last completed fiscal year. For the purposes of this paragraph, "total sales" means the gross revenues for all products and services sold by one corporation over that corporation's last completed fiscal year.

(3) The eligibility of a director or officer under the provisions of paragraph (1) shall be determined by the capital, surplus and undivided profits, exclusive of dividends declared but not paid to stockholders, of each corporation at the end of that corporation's last completed fiscal year.

(4) For purposes of this section, the term "officer" means an officer elected or chosen by the Board of Directors.

(5) For each fiscal year commencing after September 30, 1990, the $10,000,000 and $1,000,000 thresholds in this subsection shall be increased (or decreased) as of October 1 each year by an amount equal to the percentage increase (or decrease) in the gross national product, as determined by the Department of Commerce or its successor, for the year then ended over the level so established for the year ending September 30, 1989. As soon as practicable, but not later than January 31 of each year, the Federal Trade Commission shall publish the adjusted amounts required by this paragraph.

(b) When any person elected or chosen as a director or officer of any corporation subject to the provisions hereof is eligible at the time of his election or selection to act for such corporation in such capacity, his eligibility to act in such capacity shall not be affected by any of the provisions hereof by reason of any change in the capital, surplus and undivided profits, or affairs of such corporation from whatever cause, until the expiration of one year from the date on which the event causing ineligibility occurred.

Federal Trade Commission Act: 15 U.S.C.A. § 41 et seq.

§ 41.   Federal Trade Commission established; membership; vacancies; seal

A commission is created and established, to be known as the Federal Trade Commission (hereinafter referred to as the Commission), which shall be composed of five Commissioners, who shall be appointed by the President, by and with the advice and consent of the Senate. Not more than three of the Commissioners shall be members of the same political party. The first Commissioners appointed shall continue in office for terms of three, four, five, six, and seven years, respectively, from September 26, 1914, the term of each to be designated by the President, but their successors shall be appointed for terms of seven years, except that any person chosen to fill a vacancy shall be appointed only for the unexpired term of the Commissioner whom he shall succeed: Provided, however, That upon the expiration of his term of office a Commissioner shall continue to serve until his successor shall have been appointed and shall have qualified. The President shall choose a chairman from the Commission's membership. No Commissioner shall engage in any other business, vocation, or employment. Any Commissioner may be removed by the President for inefficiency, neglect of duty, or malfeasance in office. A vacancy in the Commission shall not impair the right of the remaining Commissioners to exercise all the powers of the Commission.

The Commission shall have an official seal, which shall be judicially noticed.

§ 45.   Unfair methods of competition unlawful; prevention by Commission

(a) Declaration of unlawfulness; power to prohibit unfair practices; inapplicability to foreign trade

(1) Unfair methods of competition in or affecting commerce, and unfair or deceptive acts or practices in or affecting commerce, are hereby declared unlawful.

(2) The Commission is hereby empowered and directed to prevent persons, partnerships, or corporations, except banks, savings and loan institutions described in section 57a(f)(3) of this title, Federal credit unions described in section 57a(f)(4) of this title, common carriers subject to the Acts to regulate commerce, air carriers and foreign air carriers subject to part A of subtitle VII of Title 49, and persons, partnerships, or corporations insofar as they are subject to the Packers and Stockyards Act, 1921, as amended [7 U.S.C.A. § 181 et seq.], except as provided in section 406(b) of said Act [7 U.S.C.A. § 227(b)], from using unfair methods of competition in or affecting commerce and unfair or deceptive acts or practices in or affecting commerce.

(3) This subsection shall not apply to unfair methods of competition involving commerce with foreign nations (other than import commerce) unless—

(A) such methods of competition have a direct, substantial, and reasonably foreseeable effect—

(i) on commerce which is not commerce with foreign nations, or on import commerce with foreign nations; or

(ii) on export commerce with foreign nations, of a person engaged in such commerce in the United States; and

(B) such effect gives rise to a claim under the provisions of this subsection, other than this paragraph.

If this subsection applies to such methods of competition only because of the operation of subparagraph (A)(ii), this subsection shall apply to such conduct only for injury to export business in the United States.

(b) Proceeding by Commission; modifying and setting aside orders

Whenever the Commission shall have reason to believe that any such person, partnership, or corporation has been or is using any unfair method of competition or unfair or deceptive act or practice in or affecting commerce, and if it shall appear to the Commission that a proceeding by it in respect thereof would be to the interest of the public, it shall issue and serve upon such person, partnership, or corporation a complaint stating its charges in that respect and containing a notice of a hearing upon a day and at a place therein fixed at least thirty days after the service of said complaint. The person, partnership, or corporation so complained of shall have the right to appear at the place and time so fixed and show cause why an order should not be entered by the Commission requiring such person, partnership, or corporation to cease and desist from the violation of the law so charged in said complaint. Any person, partnership, or corporation may make application, and upon good cause shown may be allowed by the Commission to intervene and appear in said proceeding by counsel or in person. The testimony in any such proceeding shall be reduced to writing and filed in the office of the Commission. If upon such hearing the Commission shall be of the opinion that the method of competition or the act or practice in question is prohibited by this subchapter, it shall make a report in writing in which it shall state its findings as to the facts and shall issue and cause to be served on such person, partnership, or corporation an order requiring such person, partnership, or corporation to cease and desist from using such method of competition or such act or practice. Until the expiration of the time allowed for filing a petition for review, if no such petition has been duly filed within such time, or, if a petition for review has been filed within such time then until the record in the proceeding has been filed in a court of appeals of the United States, as hereinafter provided, the Commission may at any time, upon such notice and in such manner as it shall deem proper, modify or set aside, in whole or in part, any report or any order made or issued by it under this section. After the expiration of the time allowed for filing a petition for review, if no such petition has been duly filed within such time, the Commission may at any time, after notice and opportunity for hearing, reopen and alter, modify, or set aside, in whole or in part, any report or order made or issued by it under this section, whenever in the opinion of the Commission conditions of fact or of law have so changed as to require such action or if the public interest shall so require, except that (1) the said person, partnership, or corporation may, within sixty days after service upon him or it of said report or order entered after such a reopening, obtain a review thereof in the appropriate court of appeals of the United States, in the manner provided in subsection (c) of this section; and (2) in the case of an order, the Commission shall reopen any such order to consider whether such order (including any affirmative relief provision contained in such order) should be altered, modified, or set aside, in whole or in part, if the person, partnership, or corporation involved files a request with the Commission which makes a satisfactory showing that changed conditions of law or fact require such order to be altered, modified, or set aside, in whole or in part. The Commission shall determine whether to alter, modify, or set aside any order of the Commission in response to a request made by a person, partnership, or corporation under paragraph (2) not later than 120 days after the date of the filing of such request.

(c) Review of order; rehearing

Any person, partnership, or corporation required by an order of the Commission to cease and desist from using any method of competition or act or practice may obtain a review of such order in the court of appeals of the United States, within any circuit where the method of competition or the act or practice in question was used or where such person, partnership, or corporation resides or carries on business, by filing in the court, within sixty days from the date of the service of such order, a written petition praying that the order of the Commission be set aside. A copy of such petition shall be forthwith transmitted by the clerk of the court to the Commission, and thereupon the Commission shall file in the court the record in the proceeding, as provided in section 2112 of Title 28. Upon such filing of the petition the court shall have jurisdiction of the proceeding and of the question determined therein concurrently with the Commission until the filing of the record and shall have power to make and enter a decree affirming, modifying, or setting aside the order of the Commission, and enforcing the same to the extent that such order is affirmed and to issue such writs as are ancillary to its jurisdiction or are necessary in its judgment to prevent injury to the public or to competitors pendente lite. The findings of the Commission as to the facts, if supported by evidence, shall be conclusive. To the extent that the order of the Commission is affirmed, the court shall thereupon issue its own order commanding obedience to the terms of such order of the Commission. If either party shall apply to the court for leave to adduce additional evidence, and shall show to the satisfaction of the court that such additional evidence is material and that there were reasonable grounds for the failure to adduce such evidence in the proceeding before the Commission, the court may order such additional evidence to be taken before the Commission and to be adduced upon the hearing in such manner and upon such terms and conditions as to the court may seem proper. The Commission may modify its findings as to the facts, or make new findings, by reason of the additional evidence so taken, and it shall file such modified or new findings, which, if supported by evidence, shall be conclusive, and its recommendation, if any, for the modification or setting aside of its original order, with the return of such additional evidence. The judgment and decree of the court shall be final, except that the same shall be subject to review by the Supreme Court upon certiorari, as provided in section 1254 of Title 28.

(d) Jurisdiction of court

Upon the filing of the record with it the jurisdiction of the court of appeals of the United States to affirm, enforce, modify, or set aside orders of the Commission shall be exclusive.

(e) Exemption from liability

No order of the Commission or judgment of court to enforce the same shall in anywise relieve or absolve any person, partnership, or corporation from any liability under the Antitrust Acts.

(f) Service of complaints, orders and other processes; return

Complaints, orders, and other processes of the Commission under this section may be served by anyone duly authorized by the Commission, either (a) by delivering a copy thereof to the person to be served, or to a member of the partnership to be served, or the president, secretary, or other executive officer or a director of the corporation to be served; or (b) by leaving a copy thereof at the residence or the principal office or place of business of such person, partnership, or corporation; or (c) by mailing a copy thereof by registered mail or by certified mail addressed to such person, partnership, or corporation at his or its residence or principal office or place of business. The verified return by the person so serving said complaint, order, or other process setting forth the manner of said service shall be proof of the same, and the return post office receipt for said complaint, order, or other process mailed by registered mail or by certified mail as aforesaid shall be proof of the service of the same.

(g) Finality of order

An order of the Commission to cease and desist shall become final—

(1) Upon the expiration of the time allowed for filing a petition for review, if no such petition has been duly filed within such time; but the Commission may thereafter modify or set aside its order to the extent provided in the last sentence of subsection (b) of this section.

(2) Except as to any order provision subject to paragraph (4), upon the sixtieth day after such order is served, if a petition for review has been duly filed; except that any such order may be stayed, in whole or in part and subject to such conditions as may be appropriate, by—

(A) the Commission;

(B) an appropriate court of appeals of the United States, if (i) a petition for review of such order is pending in such court, and (ii) an application for such a stay was previously submitted to the Commission and the Commission, within the 30–day period beginning on the date the application was received by the Commission, either denied the application or did not grant or deny the application; or

(C) the Supreme Court, if an applicable petition for certiorari is pending.

(3) For purposes of subsection (m)(1)(B) of this section and of section 57b(a)(2) of this title, if a petition for review of the order of the Commission has been filed—

(A) upon the expiration of the time allowed for filing a petition for certiorari, if the order of the Commission has been affirmed or the petition for review has been dismissed by the court of appeals and no petition for certiorari has been duly filed;

(B) upon the denial of a petition for certiorari, if the order of the Commission has been affirmed or the petition for review has been dismissed by the court of appeals; or

(C) upon the expiration of 30 days from the date of issuance of a mandate of the Supreme Court directing that the order of the Commission be affirmed or the petition for review be dismissed.

(4) In the case of an order provision requiring a person, partnership, or corporation to divest itself of stock, other share capital, or assets, if a petition for review of such order of the Commission has been filed—

(A) upon the expiration of the time allowed for filing a petition for certiorari, if the order of the Commission has been affirmed or the petition for review has been dismissed by the court of appeals and no petition for certiorari has been duly filed;

(B) upon the denial of a petition for certiorari, if the order of the Commission has been affirmed or the petition for review has been dismissed by the court of appeals; or

(C) upon the expiration of 30 days from the date of issuance of a mandate of the Supreme Court directing that the order of the Commission be affirmed or the petition for review be dismissed.

(h) Modification or setting aside of order by Supreme Court

If the Supreme Court directs that the order of the Commission be modified or set aside, the order of the Commission rendered in accordance with the mandate of the Supreme Court shall become final upon the expiration of thirty days from the time it was rendered, unless within such thirty days either party has instituted proceedings to have such order corrected to accord with the mandate, in which event the order of the Commission shall become final when so corrected.

(i) Modification or setting aside of order by Court of Appeals

If the order of the Commission is modified or set aside by the court of appeals, and if (1) the time allowed for filing a petition for certiorari has expired and no such petition has been duly filed, or (2) the petition for certiorari has been denied, or (3) the decision of the court has been affirmed by the Supreme Court, then the order of the Commission rendered in accordance with the mandate of the court of appeals shall become final on the expiration of thirty days from the time such order of the Commission was rendered, unless within such thirty days either party has instituted proceedings to have such order corrected so that it will accord with the mandate, in which event the order of the Commission shall become final when so corrected.

(j) Rehearing upon order or remand

If the Supreme Court orders a rehearing; or if the case is remanded by the court of appeals to the Commission for a rehearing, and if (1) the time allowed for filing a petition for certiorari has expired, and no such petition has been duly filed, or (2) the petition for certiorari has been denied, or (3) the decision of the court has been affirmed by the Supreme Court, then the order of the Commission rendered upon such rehearing shall become final in the same manner as though no prior order of the Commission had been rendered.

(k) "Mandate" defined

As used in this section the term "mandate", in case a mandate has been recalled prior to the expiration of thirty days from the date of issuance thereof, means the final mandate.

(*l*) Penalty for violation of order; injunctions and other appropriate equitable relief

Any person, partnership, or corporation who violates an order of the Commission after it has become final, and while such order is in effect, shall forfeit and pay to the United States a civil penalty of not more than $10,000 for each violation, which shall accrue to the United States and may be recovered in a civil action brought by the Attorney General of the United States. Each separate violation of such an order shall be a separate offense, except that in the case of a violation through continuing failure to obey or neglect to obey a final order of the Commission, each day of continuance of such failure or neglect shall be deemed a separate offense. In such actions, the United States district courts are empowered to grant mandatory injunctions and such other and further equitable relief as they deem appropriate in the enforcement of such final orders of the Commission.

(m) Civil actions for recovery of penalties for knowing violations of rules and cease and desist orders respecting unfair or deceptive acts or practices; jurisdiction; maximum amount of penalties; continuing violations; de novo determinations; compromise or settlement procedure

(1)(A) The Commission may commence a civil action to recover a civil penalty in a district court of the United States against any person, partnership, or corporation which violates any rule under this chapter respecting unfair or deceptive acts or practices (other than an interpretive rule or a rule violation of which the Commission has provided is not an unfair or deceptive act or practice in violation of subsection (a)(1) of this section) with actual knowledge or knowledge fairly implied on the basis of objective circumstances that such act is unfair or deceptive and is prohibited by such rule. In such action, such person, partnership, or corporation shall be liable for a civil penalty of not more than $10,000 for each violation.

(B) If the Commission determines in a proceeding under subsection (b) of this section that any act or practice is unfair or deceptive, and issues a final cease and desist order, other than a consent order, with respect to such act or practice, then the Commission may commence a civil action to obtain a civil penalty in a district court of the United States against any person, partnership, or corporation which engages in such act or practice—

(1) after such cease and desist order becomes final (whether or not such person, partnership, or corporation was subject to such cease and desist order), and

(2) with actual knowledge that such act or practice is unfair or deceptive and is unlawful under subsection (a)(1) of this section.

In such action, such person, partnership, or corporation shall be liable for a civil penalty of not more than $10,000 for each violation.

(C) In the case of a violation through continuing failure to comply with a rule or with subsection (a)(1) of this section, each day of continuance of such failure shall be treated as a separate violation, for purposes of subparagraphs (A) and (B). In determining the amount of such a civil penalty, the court shall take into account the degree of culpability, any history of prior such conduct, ability to pay, effect on ability to continue to do business, and such other matters as justice may require.

(2) If the cease and desist order establishing that the act or practice is unfair or deceptive was not issued against the defendant in a civil penalty action under paragraph (1)(B) the issues of fact in such action against such defendant shall be tried de novo. Upon request of any party to such an action against such defendant, the court shall also review the determination of law made by the Commission in the proceeding under subsection (b) of this section that the act or practice which was the subject of such proceeding constituted an unfair or deceptive act or practice in violation of subsection (a) of this section.

(3) The Commission may compromise or settle any action for a civil penalty if such compromise or settlement is accompanied by a public statement of its reasons and is approved by the court.

(n) Standard of proof; public policy considerations

The Commission shall have no authority under this section or section 57a of this title to declare unlawful an act or practice on the grounds that such act or practice is unfair unless the act or practice causes or is likely to cause substantial injury to consumers which is not reasonably avoidable by consumers themselves and not outweighed by countervailing benefits to consumers or to competition. In determining whether an act or practice is unfair, the Commission may consider established public policies as evidence to be considered with all other evidence. Such public policy considerations may not serve as a primary basis for such determination.

B. EXEMPTIONS AND IMMUNITIES

McCarran–Ferguson Act: 15 U.S.C.A. § 1011 et seq.

§ 1011. Declaration of policy

Congress hereby declares that the continued regulation and taxation by the several States of the business of insurance is in the public interest, and that silence on the part of the Congress shall not be construed to impose any barrier to the regulation or taxation of such business by the several States.

§ 1012. Regulation by State law; Federal law relating specifically to insurance; applicability of certain Federal laws after June 30, 1948

(a) State regulation

The business of insurance, and every person engaged therein, shall be subject to the laws of the several States which relate to the regulation or taxation of such business.

(b) Federal regulation

No Act of Congress shall be construed to invalidate, impair, or supersede any law enacted by any State for the purpose of regulating the business of insurance, or which imposes a fee or tax upon such business, unless such Act specifically relates to the business of insurance: Provided, That after June 30, 1948, the Act of July 2, 1890, as amended, known as the Sherman Act, and the Act of October 15, 1914, as amended, known as the Clayton Act, and the Act of September 26, 1914, known as the Federal Trade Commission Act, as amended [15 U.S.C.A. 41 et seq.], shall be applicable to the business of insurance to the extent that such business is not regulated by State law.

§ 1013.   Suspension until June 30, 1948, of application of certain Federal laws; Sherman Act applicable to agreements to, or acts of, boycott, coercion, or intimidation

(a) Until June 30, 1948, the Act of July 2, 1890, as amended, known as the Sherman Act, and the Act of October 15, 1914, as amended, known as the Clayton Act, and the Act of September 26, 1914, known as the Federal Trade Commission Act [15 U.S.C.A. 41 et seq.], and the Act of June 19, 1936, known as the Robinson–Patman Anti–Discrimination Act, shall not apply to the business of insurance or to acts in the conduct thereof.

(b) Nothing contained in this chapter shall render the said Sherman Act inapplicable to any agreement to boycott, coerce, or intimidate, or act of boycott, coercion, or intimidation.

§ 1015.   "State" defined

As used in this chapter, the term "State" includes the several States, Alaska, Hawaii, Puerto Rico, Guam, and the District of Columbia.

Health Care Quality Improvement Act: 42 U.S.C.A. § 11101, et seq.

§ 11101.   Findings

The Congress finds the following:

(1) The increasing occurrence of medical malpractice and the need to improve the quality of medical care have become nationwide problems that warrant greater efforts than those that can be undertaken by any individual State.

(2) There is a national need to restrict the ability of incompetent physicians to move from State to State without disclosure or discovery of the physician's previous damaging or incompetent performance.

(3) This nationwide problem can be remedied through effective professional peer review.

(4) The threat of private money damage liability under Federal laws, including treble damage liability under Federal antitrust law, unreasonably discourages physicians from participating in effective professional peer review.

(5) There is an overriding national need to provide incentive and protection for physicians engaging in effective professional peer review.

§ 11111.   Professional review

(a) In general

(1) Limitation on damages for professional review actions

If a professional review action (as defined in section 11151(9) of this title) of a professional review body meets all the standards specified in

111

section 11112(a) of this title, except as provided in subsection (b) of this section—

> **(A)** the professional review body,
>
> **(B)** any person acting as a member or staff to the body,
>
> **(C)** any person under a contract or other formal agreement with the body, and
>
> **(D)** any person who participates with or assists the body with respect to the action,
>
> shall not be liable in damages under any law of the United States or of any State (or political subdivision thereof) with respect to the action. The preceding sentence shall not apply to damages under any law of the United States or any State relating to the civil rights of any person or persons, including the Civil Rights Act of 1964, 42 U.S.C. 2000e, et seq. and the Civil Rights Acts, 42 U.S.C. 1981, et seq. Nothing in this paragraph shall prevent the United States or any Attorney General of a State from bringing an action, including an action under section 15c of title 15, where such an action is otherwise authorized.

(2) Protection for those providing information to professional review bodies

Notwithstanding any other provision of law, no person (whether as a witness or otherwise) providing information to a professional review body regarding the competence or professional conduct of a physician shall be held, by reason of having provided such information, to be liable in damages under any law of the United States or of any State (or political subdivision thereof) unless such information is false and the person providing it knew that such information was false.

(b) Exception

If the Secretary has reason to believe that a health care entity has failed to report information in accordance with section 1133(a) of this title, the Secretary shall conduct an investigation. If, after providing notice of noncompliance, an opportunity to correct the noncompliance, and an opportunity for a hearing, the Secretary determines that a health care entity has failed substantially to report information in accordance with section 11133(a) of this title, the Secretary shall publish the name of the entity in the Federal Register. The protections of subsection (a)(1) of this section shall not apply to an entity the name of which is published in the Federal Register under the previous sentence with respect to professional review actions of the entity commenced during the 3–year period beginning 30 days after the date of publication of the name.

(c) Treatment under State laws

(1) Professional review actions taken on or after October 14, 1989

Except as provided in paragraph (2), subsection (a) of this section shall apply to State laws in a State only for professional review actions commenced on or after October 14,1989.

(2) Exceptions

(A) State early opt-in

Subsection (a) of this section shall apply to State laws in a State for actions commenced before October 14, 1989, if the State by legislation elects such treatment.

(B) Effective date of election

An election under State law is not effective, for purposes of,[1] for actions commenced before the effective date of the State law, which may not be earlier than the date of the enactment of that law.

---

1. So in original. Probably should be "for purposes of subparagraph (A),".

§ 11112.   Standards for professional review actions

(a) In general

For purposes of the protection set forth in section 11111(a) of this title, a professional review action must be taken—

(1) in the reasonable belief that the action was in the furtherance of quality health care,

(2) after a reasonable effort to obtain the facts of the matter,

(3) after adequate notice and hearing procedures are afforded to the physician involved or after such other procedures as are fair to the physician under the circumstances, and

(4) in the reasonable belief that the action was warranted by the facts known after such reasonable effort to obtain facts and after meeting the requirement of paragraph (3).

A professional review action shall be presumed to have met the preceding standards necessary for the protection set out in section 11111(a) of this title unless the presumption is rebutted by a preponderance of the evidence.

(b) Adequate notice and hearing

A health care entity is deemed to have met the adequate notice and hearing requirement of subsection (a)(3) of this section with respect to a physician if the following conditions are met (or are waived voluntarily by the physician):

(1) Notice of proposed action

The physician has been given notice stating—

(A)(i) that a professional review action has been proposed to be taken against the physician,

113

(ii) reasons for the proposed action,

(B)(i) that the physician has the right to request a hearing on the proposed action,

(ii) any time limit (of not less than 30 days) within which to request such a hearing, and

(C) a summary of the rights in the hearing under paragraph (3).

(2) Notice of hearing

If a hearing is requested on a timely basis under paragraph (1)(B), the physician involved must be given notice stating—

(A) the place, time, and date, of the hearing, which date shall not be less than 30 days after the date of the notice, and

(B) a list of the witnesses (if any) expected to testify at the hearing on behalf of the professional review body.

(3) Conduct of hearing and notice

If a hearing is requested on a timely basis under paragraph (1)(B)—

(A) subject to subparagraph (B), the hearing shall be held (as determined by the health care entity)—

(i) before an arbitrator mutually acceptable to the physician and the health care entity,

(ii) before a hearing officer who is appointed by the entity and who is not in direct economic competition with the physician involved, or

(iii) before a panel of individuals who are appointed by the entity and are not in direct economic competition with the physician involved;

(B) the right to the hearing may be forfeited if the physician fails, without good cause, to appear;

(C) in the hearing the physician involved has the right—

(i) to representation by an attorney or other person of the physician's choice,

(ii) to have a record made of the proceedings, copies of which may be obtained by the physician upon payment of any reasonable charges associated with the preparation thereof,

(iii) to call, examine, and cross-examine witnesses,

(iv) to present evidence determined to be relevant by the hearing officer, regardless of its admissibility in a court of law, and

(v) to submit a written statement at the close of the hearing; and

(D) upon completion of the hearing, the physician involved has the right—

(i) to receive the written recommendation of the arbitrator, officer, or panel, including a statement of the basis for the recommendations, and

(ii) to receive a written decision of the health care entity, including a statement of the basis for the decision.

A professional review body's failure to meet the conditions described in this subsection shall not, in itself, constitute failure to meet the standards of subsection (a)(3) of this section.

(c) Adequate procedures in investigations or health emergencies

For purposes of section 11111(a) of this title, nothing in this section shall be construed as—

(1) requiring the procedures referred to in subsection (a)(3) of this section—

(A) where there is no adverse professional review action taken, or

(B) in the case of a suspension or restriction of clinical privileges, for a period of not longer than 14 days, during which an investigation is being conducted to determine the need for a professional review action; or

(2) precluding an immediate suspension or restriction of clinical privileges, subject to subsequent notice and hearing or other adequate procedures, where the failure to take such an action may result in an imminent danger to the health of any individual.

§ 11113. Payment of reasonable attorneys' fees and costs in defense of suit

In any suit brought against a defendant, to the extent that a defendant has met the standards set forth under section 11112(a) of this title and the defendant substantially prevails, the court shall, at the conclusion of the action, award to a substantially prevailing party defending against any such claim the cost of the suit attributable to such claim, including a reasonable attorney's fee, if the claim, or the claimant's conduct during the litigation of the claim, was frivolous, unreasonable, without foundation, or in bad faith. For the purposes of this section, a defendant shall not be considered to have substantially prevailed when the plaintiff obtains an award for damages or permanent injunctive or declaratory relief.

§ 11114. Guidelines of Secretary

The Secretary may establish, after notice and opportunity for comment, such voluntary guidelines as may assist the professional review bodies in meeting the standards described in section11112(a) of this title.

§ 11115. Construction

(a) In general

Except as specifically provided in this subchapter, nothing in this subchapter shall be construed as changing the liabilities or immunities under law or as preempting or overriding any State law which provides incentives, immunities, or protection for those engaged in a professional review action that is in addition to or greater than that provided by this subchapter.

(b) Scope of clinical privileges

Nothing in this subchapter shall be construed as requiring health care entities to provide clinical privileges to any or all classes or types of physicians or other licensed health care practitioners.

(c) Treatment of nurses and other practitioners

Nothing in this subchapter shall be construed as affecting, or modifying any provision of Federal or State law, with respect to activities of professional review bodies regarding nurses, other licensed health care practitioners, or other health professionals who are not physicians.

(d) Treatment of patient malpractice claims

Nothing in this chapter shall be construed as affecting in any manner the rights and remedies afforded patients under any provision of Federal or State law to seek redress for any harm or injury suffered as a result of negligent treatment or care by any physician, health care practitioner, or health care entity, or as limiting any defenses or immunities available to any physician, health care practitioner, or health care entity.

Reporting of Information: 42 U.S.C.A. § 11131–§ 11152

§ 11131. Requiring reports on medical malpractice payments

(a) In general

Each entity (including an insurance company) which makes payment under a policy of insurance, self-insurance, or otherwise in settlement (or partial settlement) of, or in satisfaction of a judgment in, a medical malpractice action or claim shall report, in accordance with section 11134 of this title, information respecting the payment and circumstances thereof.

(b) Information to be reported

The information to be reported under subsection (a) of this section includes—

    (1) the name of any physician or licensed health care practitioner for whose benefit the payment is made,

    (2) the amount of the payment,

    (3) the name (if known) of any hospital with which the physician or practitioner is affiliated or associated,

(4) a description of the acts or omissions and injuries or illnesses upon which the action or claim was based, and

(5) such other information as the Secretary determines is required for appropriate interpretation of information reported under this section.

(c) Sanctions for failure to report

Any entity that fails to report information on a payment required to be reported under this section shall be subject to a civil money penalty of not more than $10,000 for each such payment involved. Such penalty shall be imposed and collected in the same manner as civil money penalties under subsection (a) of section 1320a–7a of this title are imposed and collected under that section.

(d) Report on treatment of small payments

The Secretary shall study and report to Congress, not later than two years after November 14, 1986, on whether information respecting small payments should continue to be required to be reported under subsection (a) of this section and whether information respecting all claims made concerning a medical malpractice action should be required to be reported under such subsection.

§ 11132. Reporting of sanctions taken by Boards of Medical Examiners

(a) In general

(1) Actions subject to reporting

Each Board of Medical Examiners—

(A) which revokes or suspends (or otherwise restricts) a physician's license or censures, reprimands, or places on probation a physician, for reasons relating to the physician's professional competence or professional conduct, or

(B) to which a physician's license is surrendered, shall report, in accordance with section 11134 of this title, the information described in paragraph (2).

(2) Information to be reported

The information to be reported under paragraph (1) is—

(A) the name of the physician involved,

(B) a description of the acts or omissions or other reasons (if known) for the revocation, suspension, or surrender of license, and

(C) such other information respecting the circumstances of the action or surrender as the Secretary deems appropriate.

(b) Failure to report

If, after notice of noncompliance and providing opportunity to correct noncompliance, the Secretary determines that a Board of Medical Examiners has failed to report information in accordance with subsection (a) of this section, the Secretary shall designate another qualified entity for the reporting of information under section 11133 of this title.

§ 11133. Reporting of certain professional review actions taken by health care entities

(a) Reporting by health care entities

(1) On physicians

Each health care entity which—

(A) takes a professional review action that adversely affects the clinical privileges of a physician for a period longer than 30 days;

(B) accepts the surrender of clinical privileges of a physician—

(i) while the physician is under an investigation by the entity relating to possible incompetence or improper professional conduct, or

(ii) in return for not conducting such an investigation or proceeding; or

(C) in the case of such an entity which is a professional society, takes a professional review action which adversely affects the membership of a physician in the society,

shall report to the Board of Medical Examiners, in accordance with section 11134(a) of this title, the information described in paragraph (3).

(2) Permissive reporting on other licensed health care practitioners

A health care entity may report to the Board of Medical Examiners, in accordance with section 11134(a) of this title, the information described in paragraph (3) in the case of a licensed health care practitioner who is not a physician, if the entity would be required to report such information under paragraph (1) with respect to the practitioner if the practitioner were a physician.

(3) Information to be reported

The information to be reported under this subsection is—

(A) the name of the physician or practitioner involved,

(B) a description of the acts or omissions or other reasons for the action or, if known, for the surrender, and

(C) such other information respecting the circumstances of the action or surrender as the Secretary deems appropriate.

(b) Reporting by Board of Medical Examiners

Each Board of Medical Examiners shall report, in accordance with section 11134 of this title, the information reported to it under subsection (a) of this section and known instances of a health care entity's failure to report information under subsection (a)(1) of this section.

(c) Sanctions

(1) Health care entities

A health care entity that fails substantially to meet the requirement of subsection (a)(1) of this section shall lose the protections of section 11111(a)(1) of this title if the Secretary publishes the name of the entity under section 11111(b) of this title.

(2) Board of Medical Examiners

If, after notice of noncompliance and providing an opportunity to correct noncompliance, the Secretary determines that a Board of Medical Examiners has failed to report information in accordance with subsection (b) of this section, the Secretary shall designate another qualified entity for the reporting of information under subsection (b) of this section.

(d) References to Board of Medical Examiners

Any reference in this subchapter to a Board of Medical Examiners includes, in the case of a Board in a State that fails to meet the reporting requirements of section 11132(a) of this title or subsection (b) of this section, a reference to such other qualified entity as the Secretary designates.

§ 11134.　Form of reporting

(a) Timing and form

The information required to be reported under sections 11131, 11132(a), and 11133 of this title shall be reported regularly (but not less often than monthly) and in such form and manner as the Secretary prescribes. Such information shall first be required to be reported on a date (not later than one year after November 14, 1986) specified by the Secretary.

(b) To whom reported

The information required to be reported under sections 11131, 11132(a), and 11133(b) of this title shall be reported to the Secretary, or, in the Secretary's discretion, to an appropriate private or public agency which has made suitable arrangements with the Secretary with respect to receipt, storage, protection of confidentiality, and dissemination of the information under this subchapter.

(c) Reporting to State licensing boards

(1) Malpractice payments

Information required to be reported under section 11131 of this title shall also be reported to the appropriate State licensing board (or boards) in the State in which the medical malpractice claim arose.

(2) Reporting to other licensing boards

Information required to be reported under section 11133(b) of this title shall also be reported to the appropriate State licensing board in the State in which the health care entity is located if it is not otherwise reported to such board under subsection (b) of this section.

§ 11135. Duty of hospitals to obtain information

(a) In general

It is the duty of each hospital to request from the Secretary (or the agency designated under section 11134(b) of this title), on and after the date information is first required to be reported under section 11134(a) of this title)—

(1) at the time a physician or licensed health care practitioner applies to be on the medical staff (courtesy or otherwise) of, or for clinical privileges at, the hospital, information reported under this subchapter concerning the physician or practitioner, and

(2) once every 2 years information reported under this subchapter concerning any physician or such practitioner who is on the medical staff (courtesy or otherwise) of, or has been granted clinical privileges at, the hospital.

A hospital may request such information at other times.

(b) Failure to obtain information

With respect to a medical malpractice action, a hospital which does not request information respecting a physician or practitioner as required under subsection (a) of this section is presumed to have knowledge of any information reported under this subchapter to the Secretary with respect to the physician or practitioner.

(c) Reliance on information provided

Each hospital may rely upon information provided to the hospital under this chapter and shall not be held liable for such reliance in the absence of the hospital's knowledge that the information provided was false.

§ 11136. Disclosure and correction of information

With respect to the information reported to the Secretary (or the agency designated under section 11134(b) of this title) under this subchapter respecting a physician or other licensed health care practitioner, the Secretary shall, by regulation, provide for—

(1) disclosure of the information, upon request, to the physician or practitioner, and

(2) procedures in the case of disputed accuracy of the information.

§ 11137. Miscellaneous provisions

(a) Providing licensing boards and other health care entities with access to information

The Secretary (or the agency designated under section 11134(b) of this title) shall, upon request, provide information reported under this subchapter with respect to a physician or other licensed health care practitioner to State licensing boards, to hospitals, and to other health care entities (including health maintenance organizations) that have entered (or may be entering) into an employment or affiliation relationship with the physician or practitioner or to which the physician or practitioner has applied for clinical privileges or appointment to the medical staff.

(b) Confidentiality of information

(1) In general

Information reported under this subchapter is considered confidential and shall not be disclosed (other than to the physician or practitioner involved) except with respect to professional review activity, as necessary to carry out subsections (b) and (c) of section 11135 of this title (as specified in regulations by the Secretary), or in accordance with regulations of the Secretary promulgated pursuant to subsection(a) of this section. Nothing in this subsection shall prevent the disclosure of such information by a party which is otherwise authorized, under applicable State law, to make such disclosure. Information reported under this subchapter that is in a form that does not permit the identification of any particular health care entity, physician, other health care practitioner, or patient shall not be considered confidential. The Secretary (or the agency designated under section 11134(b) of this title), on application by any person, shall prepare such information in such form and shall disclose such information in such form.

(2) Penalty for violations

Any person who violates paragraph (1) shall be subject to a civil money penalty of not more than $10,000 for each such violation involved. Such penalty shall be imposed and collected in the same manner as civil money penalties under subsection (a) of section 1320a–7a of this title are imposed and collected under that section.

(3) Use of information

Subject to paragraph (1), information provided under section11135 of this title and subsection (a) of this section is intended to be used solely with respect to activities in the furtherance of the quality of health care.

(4) Fees

The Secretary may establish or approve reasonable fees for the disclosure of information under this section or section 11136 of this title. The amount of such a fee may not exceed the costs of processing the requests for disclosure and of providing such information. Such fees shall be available to the Secretary (or, in the Secretary's discretion, to the agency designated under section 11134(b) of this title) to cover such costs.

(c) Relief from liability for reporting

No person or entity (including the agency designated under section 11134(b) of this title) shall be held liable in any civil action with respect to any report made under this subchapter (including information provided under subsection (a) of this section without knowledge of the falsity of the information contained in the report.

(d) Interpretation of information

In interpreting information reported under this subchapter, a payment in settlement of a medical malpractice action or claim shall not be construed as creating a presumption that medical malpractice has occurred.

§ 11151. Definitions

In this chapter:

(1) The term "adversely affecting" includes reducing, restricting, suspending, revoking, denying, or failing to renew clinical privileges or membership in a health care entity.

(2) The term "Board of Medical Examiners" includes a body comparable to such a Board (as determined by the State) with responsibility for the licensing of physicians and also includes a subdivision of such a Board or body.

(3) The term "clinical privileges" includes privileges, membership on the medical staff, and the other circumstances pertaining to the furnishing of medical care under which a physician or other licensed health care practitioner is permitted to furnish such care by a health care entity.

(4)(A) The term "health care entity" means—

 (i) a hospital that is licensed to provide health care services by the State in which it is located,

 (ii) an entity (including a health maintenance organization or group medical practice) that provides health care services and that follows a formal peer review process for the purpose of furthering quality health care (as determined under regulations of the Secretary), and

 (iii) subject to subparagraph (B), a professional society (or committee thereof) of physicians or other licensed health care practitioners that follows a formal peer review process for the purpose of furthering quality health care (as determined under regulations of the Secretary).

(B) The term "health care entity" does not include a professional society (or committee thereof) if, within the previous 5 years, the society has been found by the Federal Trade Commission or any court to have engaged in any anti-competitive practice which had the effect of restricting the practice of licensed health care practitioners.

(5) The term "hospital" means an entity described in paragraphs (1) and (7) of section 1395x(e) of this title.

(6) The terms "licensed health care practitioner" and "practitioner" mean, with respect to a State, an individual (other than a physician) who is licensed or otherwise authorized by the State to provide health care services.

(7) The term "medical malpractice action or claim" means a written claim or demand for payment based on a health care provider's furnishing (or failure to furnish) health care services, and includes the filing of a cause of action, based on the law of tort, brought in any court of any State or the United States seeking monetary damages.

(8) The term "physician" means a doctor of medicine or osteopathy or a doctor of dental surgery or medical dentistry legally authorized to practice medicine and surgery or dentistry by a State (or any individual who, without authority holds himself or herself out to be so authorized).

(9) The term "professional review action" means an action or recommendation of a professional review body which is taken or made in the conduct of professional review activity, which is based on the competence or professional conduct of an individual physician (which conduct affects or could affect adversely the health or welfare of a patient or patients), and which affects (or may affect) adversely the clinical privileges, or membership in a professional society, of the physician. Such term includes a formal decision of a professional review body not to take an action or make a recommendation described in the previous sentence and also includes professional review activities relating to a professional review action. In this chapter, an action is not considered to be based on the competence or professional conduct of a physician if the action is primarily based on—

(A) the physician's association, or lack of association, with a professional society or association,

(B) the physician's fees or the physician's advertising or engaging in other competitive acts intended to solicit or retain business,

(C) the physician's participation in prepaid group health plans, salaried employment, or any other manner of delivering health services whether on a fee-for-service or other basis,

(D) a physician's association with, supervision of, delegation of authority to, support for, training of, or participation in a private group practice with, a member or members of a particular class of health care practitioner or professional, or

(E) any other matter that does not relate to the competence or professional conduct of a physician.

123

(10) The term "professional review activity" means an activity of a health care entity with respect to an individual physician—

(A) to determine whether the physician may have clinical privileges with respect to, or membership in, the entity,

(B) to determine the scope or conditions of such privileges or membership, or

(C) to change or modify such privileges or membership.

(11) The term "professional review body" means a health care entity and the governing body or any committee of a health care entity which conducts professional review activity, and includes any committee of the medical staff of such an entity when assisting the governing body in a professional review activity.

(12) The term "Secretary" means the Secretary of Health and Human Services.

(13) The term "State" means the 50 States, the District of Columbia, Puerto Rico, the Virgin Islands, Guam, American Samoa, and the Northern Mariana Islands.

(14) The term "State licensing board" means, with respect to a physician or health care provider in a State, the agency of the State which is primarily responsible for the licensing of the physician or provider to furnish health care services.

§ 11152. Reports and memoranda of understanding

(a) Annual reports to Congress

The Secretary shall report to Congress, annually during the three years after November 14, 1986, on the implementation of this chapter.

(b) Memoranda of understanding

The Secretary of Health and Human Services shall seek to enter into memoranda of understanding with the Secretary of Defense and the Administrator of Veterans' Affairs to apply the provisions of subchapter II of this chapter to hospitals and other facilities and health care providers under the jurisdiction of the Secretary or Administrator, respectively. The Secretary shall report to Congress, not later than two years after November 14, 1986, on any such memoranda and on the cooperation among such officials in establishing such memoranda.

(c) Memorandum of understanding with Drug Enforcement Administration

The Secretary of Health and Human Services shall seek to enter into a memorandum of understanding with the Administrator of Drug Enforcement relating to providing for the reporting 824 of title 21. The Secretary shall report to Congress, not later than two years after November 14, 1986, on any such memorandum and on the cooperation between the Secretary and the Administrator in establishing such a memorandum.

C. FEDERAL ANTITRUST POLICY STATEMENTS AND GUIDELINES

Horizontal Merger Guidelines: U.S. Department of Justice and Federal Trade Commission 1992

The U.S. Department of Justice ("Department") and Federal Trade Commission ("Commission") today jointly issued Horizontal Merger Guidelines revising the Department's 1984 Merger Guidelines and the Commission's 1982 Statement Concerning Horizontal Merger Guidelines. The release marks the first time that the two federal agencies that share antitrust enforcement jurisdiction have issued joint guidelines.

Central to the 1992 Department of Justice and Federal Trade Commission Horizontal Merger Guidelines is a recognition that sound merger enforcement is an essential component of our free enterprise system benefiting the competitiveness of American firms and the welfare of American consumers. Sound merger enforcement must prevent anticompetitive mergers yet avoid deterring the larger universe of procompetitive or competitively neutral mergers.

The 1992 Horizontal Merger Guidelines implement this objective by describing the analytical foundations of merger enforcement and providing guidance enabling the business community to avoid antitrust problems when planning mergers. The Department first released Merger Guidelines in 1968 in order to inform the business community of the analysis applied by the Department to mergers under the federal antitrust laws. The 1968 Merger Guidelines eventually fell into disuse, both internally and externally, as they were eclipsed by developments in legal and economic thinking about mergers.

In 1982, the Department released revised Merger Guidelines which, reflecting those developments, departed dramatically from the 1968 version. Relative to the Department's actual practice, however, the 1982 Merger Guidelines represented an evolutionary not revolutionary change. On the same date, the Commission released its Statement Concerning Horizontal Mergers highlighting the principal considerations guiding the Commission's horizontal merger enforcement and noting the "considerable weight" given by the Commission to the Department's 1982 Merger Guidelines.

The Department's current Merger Guidelines, released in 1984, refined and clarified the analytical framework of the 1982 Merger Guidelines. Although the agencies' experience with the 1982 Merger Guidelines reaffirmed the soundness of its underlying principles, the Department concluded that there remained room for improvement.

The revisions embodied in the 1992 Horizontal Merger Guidelines reflect the next logical step in the development of the agencies' analysis of mergers. They reflect the Department's experience in applying the 1982 and 1984 Merger Guidelines as well as the Commission's experience in applying those guidelines and the Commission's 1982 Statement. Both the Department and the Commission believed that their respective Guidelines and Statement presented sound frameworks for antitrust analysis of mergers, but that improvements could be made to reflect advances in legal and economic thinking. The 1992 Horizontal Merger Guidelines accomplish this objective and also clarify certain aspects of the Merger Guidelines that proved to be ambiguous or were interpreted by observers in ways that were inconsistent with the actual policy of the agencies.

The 1992 Horizontal Merger Guidelines do not include a discussion of horizontal effects from non-horizontal mergers (e.g., elimination of specific potential entrants and competitive problems from vertical mergers). Neither agency has changed its policy with respect to non-horizontal mergers. Specific guidance on non-horizontal mergers is provided in Section 4 of the Department's 1984 Merger Guidelines, read in the context of today's revisions to the treatment of horizontal mergers.

A number of today's revisions are largely technical or stylistic. One major objective of the revisions is to strengthen the document as an analytical road map for the evaluation of mergers. The language, therefore, is intended to be burden-neutral, without altering the burdens of proof or burdens of coming forward as those standards have been established by the courts. In addition, the revisions principally address two areas.

The most significant revision to the Merger Guidelines is to explain more clearly how mergers may lead to adverse competitive effects and how particular market factors relate to the analysis of those effects. These revisions are found in Section 2 of the Horizontal Merger Guidelines. The second principal revision is to sharpen the distinction between the treatment of various types of supply responses and to articulate the framework for analyzing the timeliness, likelihood and sufficiency of entry. These revisions are found in Sections 1.3 and 3.

The new Horizontal Merger Guidelines observe, as did the 1984 Guidelines, that because the specific standards they set out must be applied in widely varied factual circumstances, mechanical application of those standards could produce misleading results. Thus, the Guidelines state that the agencies will apply those standards reasonably and flexibly to the particular facts and circumstances of each proposed merger.

0. PURPOSE, UNDERLYING POLICY ASSUMPTIONS AND OVERVIEW

These Guidelines outline the present enforcement policy of the Department of Justice and the Federal Trade Commission (the "Agency") concerning horizontal acquisitions and mergers ("mergers") subject to section 7 of the Clayton Act, (1) to section 1 of the Sherman Act, (2) or to section 5 of the FTC Act. (3) They describe the analytical framework and specific standards normally used by the Agency in analyzing mergers. (4) By stating its policy as simply and clearly as possible, the Agency hopes to reduce the uncertainty associated with enforcement of the antitrust laws in this area.

Although the Guidelines should improve the predictability of the Agency's merger enforcement policy, it is not possible to remove the exercise of judgment from the evaluation of mergers under the antitrust laws. Because the specific standards set forth in the Guidelines must be applied to a broad range of possible factual circumstances, mechanical application of those standards may provide misleading answers to the economic questions raised under the antitrust laws. Moreover, information is often incomplete and the picture of competitive conditions that develops from historical evidence may provide an incomplete answer to the forward-looking inquiry of the Guidelines. Therefore, the Agency will apply the standards of the Guidelines reasonably and flexibly to the particular facts and circumstances of each proposed merger.

0.1 Purpose and Underlying Policy Assumptions of the Guidelines

The Guidelines are designed primarily to articulate the analytical framework the Agency applies in determining whether a merger is likely substantially to lessen competition, not to describe how the Agency will conduct the litigation of cases that it decides to bring. Although relevant in the latter context, the factors contemplated in the Guidelines neither dictate nor exhaust the range of evidence that the Agency must or may introduce in litigation. Consistent with their objective, the Guidelines do not attempt to assign the burden of proof, or the burden of coming forward with evidence, on any particular issue. Nor do the Guidelines attempt to adjust or reapportion burdens of proof or burdens of coming forward as those standards have been established by the courts. (5) Instead, the Guidelines set forth a methodology for analyzing issues once the necessary facts are available. The necessary facts may be derived from the documents and statements of both the merging firms and other sources.

Throughout the Guidelines, the analysis is focused on whether consumers or producers "likely would" take certain actions, that is, whether the action is in the actor's economic interest. References to the profitability of certain actions focus on economic profits rather than accounting profits. Economic profits may be defined as the excess of revenues over costs where costs include the opportunity cost of invested capital.

Mergers are motivated by the prospect of financial gains. The possible sources of the financial gains from mergers are many, and the Guidelines do not attempt to identify all possible sources of gain in every merger. Instead, the Guidelines focus on the one potential source of gain that is of concern under the antitrust laws: market power.

The unifying theme of the Guidelines is that mergers should not be permitted to create or enhance market power or to facilitate its exercise. Market power to a seller is the ability profitably to maintain prices above competitive levels for a significant period of time. (6) In some circumstances, a sole seller (a "monopolist") of a product with no good substitutes can maintain a selling price that is above the level that would prevail if the market were competitive. Similarly, in some circumstances, where only a few firms account for most of the sales of a product, those firms can exercise market power, perhaps even approximating the performance of a monopolist, by either explicitly or implicitly coordinating their actions. Circumstances also may permit a single firm, not a monopolist, to exercise market power through unilateral or non-coordinated conduct—conduct the success of which does not rely on the concurrence of other firms in the market or on coordinated responses by those firms. In any case, the result of the exercise of market power is a transfer of wealth from buyers to sellers or a misallocation of resources.

Market power also encompasses the ability of a single buyer (a "monopsonist"), a coordinating group of buyers, or a single buyer, not a monopsonist, to depress the price paid for a product to a level that is below the competitive price and thereby depress output. The exercise of market power by buyers ("monopsony power") has adverse effects comparable to those associated with the exercise of market power by sellers. In order to assess potential monopsony concerns, the Agency will apply an analytical framework analogous to the framework of these Guidelines.

While challenging competitively harmful mergers, the Agency seeks to avoid unnecessary interference with the larger universe of mergers that are either competitively beneficial or neutral. In implementing this objective, however, the Guidelines reflect the congressional intent that merger enforcement should interdict competitive problems in their incipiency.

0.2 Overview

The Guidelines describe the analytical process that the Agency will employ in determining whether to challenge a horizontal merger. First, the Agency assesses whether the merger would significantly increase concentration and result in a concentrated market, properly defined and measured. Second, the Agency assesses whether the merger, in light of market concentration and other factors that characterize the market, raises concern about potential adverse competitive effects. Third, the Agency assesses whether entry would be timely, likely and sufficient either to deter or to counteract the competitive effects of concern. Fourth, the Agency assesses any efficiency gains that reasonably cannot be achieved by the parties through other means. Finally the Agency assesses whether, but for the merger, either party to the transaction would be likely to fail, causing its assets to exit the market. The process of assessing market concentration, potential adverse competitive effects, entry, efficiency and failure is a tool that allows the Agency to answer the ultimate inquiry in merger analysis: whether the merger is likely to create or enhance market power or to facilitate its exercise.

1. MARKET DEFINITION, MEASUREMENT AND CONCENTRATION

1.0 Overview

A merger is unlikely to create or enhance market power or to facilitate its exercise unless it significantly increases concentration and results in a concentrated market, properly defined and measured. Mergers that either do not significantly increase concentration or do not result in a concentrated market ordinarily require no further analysis.

The analytic process described in this section ensures that the Agency evaluates the likely competitive impact of a merger within the context of economically meaningful markets—i.e., markets that could be subject to the exercise of market power. Accordingly, for each product or service (hereafter "product") of each merging firm, the Agency seeks to define a market in which firms could effectively exercise market power if they were able to coordinate their actions.

Market definition focuses solely on demand substitution factors—i.e., possible consumer responses. Supply substitution factors—i.e., possible production responses—are considered elsewhere in the Guidelines in the identification of firms that participate in the relevant market and the analysis of entry. See Sections 1.3 and 3. A market is defined as a product or group of products and a geographic area in which it is produced or sold such that a hypothetical profit-maximizing firm, not subject to price regulation, that was the only present and future producer or seller of those products in that area likely would impose at least a "small but significant and nontransitory" increase in price, assuming the terms of sale of all other products are held constant. A relevant market is a group of products and a geographic area that is no bigger than necessary to satisfy this test. The "small but significant and non-transitory" increase in price is employed solely as a methodological tool for the analysis of mergers: it is not a tolerance level for price increases.

Absent price discrimination, a relevant market is described by a product or group of products and a geographic area. In determining whether a hypothetical monopolist would be in a position to exercise market power, it is necessary to evaluate the likely demand responses of consumers to a price increase. A price increase could be made unprofitable by consumers either switching to other products or switching to the same product produced by firms at other locations. The nature and magnitude of these two types of demand responses respectively determine the scope of the product market and the geographic market.

In contrast, where a hypothetical monopolist likely would discriminate in prices charged to different groups of buyers, distinguished, for example, by their uses or locations, the Agency may delineate different relevant markets corresponding to each such buyer group. Competition for sales to each such group may be affected differently by a particular merger and markets are delineated by evaluating the demand response of each such buyer group. A relevant market of this kind is described by a collection of products for sale to a given group of buyers.

Once defined, a relevant market must be measured in terms of its participants and concentration. Participants include firms currently producing or selling the market's products in the market's geographic area. In addition, participants may include other firms depending on their likely supply responses to a "small but significant and nontransitory" price increase. A firm is viewed as a participant if, in response to a "small but significant and nontransitory" price increase, it likely would enter rapidly into production or sale of a market product in the market's area, without incurring significant sunk costs of entry and exit. Firms likely to make any of these supply responses are considered to be "uncommitted" entrants because their supply response would create new production or sale in the relevant market and because that production or sale could be quickly terminated without significant loss. (7)

Uncommitted entrants are capable of making such quick and uncommitted supply responses that they likely influenced the market premerger, would influence it post-merger, and accordingly are considered as market participants at both times. This analysis of market definition and market measurement applies equally to foreign and domestic firms.

If the process of market definition and market measurement identifies one or more relevant markets in which the merging firms are both participants, then the merger is considered to be horizontal. Sections 1.1 through 1.5 describe in greater detail how product and geographic markets will be defined, how market shares will be calculated and how market concentration will be assessed.

1.1 Product Market Definition

The Agency will first define the relevant product market with respect to each of the products of each of the merging firms. (8)

1.11 General Standards

Absent price discrimination, the Agency will delineate the product market to be a product or group of products such that a hypothetical profit-maximizing firm that was the only present and future seller of those products ("monopolist") likely would impose at least a "small but significant and nontransitory" increase in price. That is, assuming that buyers likely would respond to an increase in price for a tentatively identified product group only by shifting to other products, what would happen? If the alternatives were, in the aggregate, sufficiently attractive at their existing terms of sale, an attempt to raise prices would result in a reduction of sales large enough that the price increase would not prove profitable, and the tentatively identified product group would prove to be too narrow.

Specifically, the Agency will begin with each product (narrowly defined) produced or sold by each merging firm and ask what would happen if a hypothetical monopolist of that product imposed at least a "small but significant and nontransitory" increase in price, but the terms of sale of all other products remained constant. If, in response to the price increase, the reduction in sales of the product would be large enough that a hypothetical monopolist would not find it profitable to impose such an increase in price, then the Agency will add to the product group the product that is the next-best substitute for the merging firm's product. (9)

In considering the likely reaction of buyers to a price increase, the Agency will take into account all relevant evidence, including, but not limited to, the following:

(1) evidence that buyers have shifted or have considered shifting purchases between products in response to relative changes in price or other competitive variables;

(2) evidence that sellers base business decisions on the prospect of buyer substitution between products in response to relative changes in price or other competitive variables;

(3) the influence of downstream competition faced by buyers in their output markets; and

(4) the timing and costs of switching products.

The price increase question is then asked for a hypothetical monopolist controlling the expanded product group. In performing successive iterations of the price increase test, the hypothetical monopolist will be assumed to pursue maximum profits in deciding whether to raise the prices of any or all of the additional products under its control. This process will continue until a group of products is identified such that a hypothetical monopolist over that group of products would profitably impose at least a "small but significant and nontransitory" increase, including the price of a product of one of the merging firms. The Agency generally will consider the relevant product market to be the smallest group of products that satisfies this test.

In the above analysis, the Agency will use prevailing prices of the products of the merging firms and possible substitutes for such products, unless premerger circumstances are strongly suggestive of coordinated interaction, in which case the Agency will use a price more reflective of the competitive price. (10)

However, the Agency may use likely future prices, absent the merger, when changes in the prevailing prices can be predicted with reasonable reliability. Changes in price may be predicted on the basis of, for example, changes in regulation which affect price either directly or indirectly by affecting costs or demand.

In general, the price for which an increase will be postulated will be whatever is considered to be the price of the product at the stage of the industry being examined. (11) In attempting to determine objectively the effect of a "small but significant and nontransitory" increase in price, the Agency, in most contexts, will use a price increase of five percent lasting for the foreseeable future. However, what constitutes a "small but significant and nontransitory" increase in price will depend on the nature of the industry, and the Agency at times may use a price increase that is larger or smaller than five percent.

1.12 Product Market Definition in the Presence of Price Discrimination

The analysis of product market definition to this point has assumed that price discrimination—charging different buyers different prices for the same product, for example—would not be profitable for a hypothetical monopolist. A different analysis applies where price discrimination would be profitable for a hypothetical monopolist.

Existing buyers sometimes will differ significantly in their likelihood of switching to other products in response to a "small but significant and nontransitory" price increase. If a hypothetical monopolist can identify and price differently to those buyers ("targeted buyers") who would not defeat the targeted price increase by substituting to other products in response to a "small but significant and nontransitory" price increase for the relevant product, and if other buyers likely would not purchase the relevant product and resell to targeted buyers, then a hypothetical monopolist would profitably impose a discriminatory price increase on sales to targeted buyers. This is true regardless of whether a general increase in price would cause such significant substitution that the price increase would not be profitable. The Agency will consider additional relevant product markets consisting of a particular use or uses by groups of buyers of the product for which a hypothetical monopolist would profitably and separately impose at least a "small but significant and nontransitory" increase in price.

1.2 Geographic Market Definition

For each product market in which both merging firms participate, the Agency will determine the geographic market or markets in which the firms produce or sell. A single firm may operate in a number of different geographic markets.

1.21 General Standards

Absent price discrimination, the Agency will delineate the geographic market to be a region such that a hypothetical monopolist that was the only present or future producer of the relevant product at locations in that region would profitably impose at least a "small but significant and nontransitory" increase in price, holding constant the terms of sale for all products produced elsewhere. That is, assuming that buyers likely would respond to a price increase on products produced within the tentatively identified region only by shifting to products produced at locations of production outside the region, what would happen? If those locations of production outside the region were, in the aggregate, sufficiently attractive at their existing terms of sale, an attempt to raise price would result in a reduction in sales large enough that the price increase would not prove profitable, and the tentatively identified geographic area would prove to be too narrow.

In defining the geographic market or markets affected by a merger, the Agency will begin with the location of each merging firm (or each plant of a multiplant firm) and ask what would happen if a hypothetical monopolist of the relevant product at that point imposed at least a "small but significant and nontransitory" increase in price, but the terms of sale at all other locations remained constant. If, in response to the price increase, the reduction in sales of the product at that location would be large enough that a hypothetical monopolist producing or selling the relevant product at the merging firm's location would not find it profitable to impose such an increase in price, then the Agency will add the location from which production is the next-best substitute for production at the merging firm's location. In considering the likely reaction of buyers to a price increase, the Agency will take into account all relevant evidence, including, but not limited to, the following:

(1) evidence that buyers have shifted or have considered shifting purchases between different geographic locations in response to relative changes in price or other competitive variables;

(2) evidence that sellers base business decisions on the prospect of buyer substitution between geographic locations in response to relative changes in price or other competitive variables;

(3) the influence of downstream competition faced by buyers in their output markets; and

(4) the timing and costs of switching suppliers.

The price increase question is then asked for a hypothetical monopolist controlling the expanded group of locations. In performing successive iterations of the price increase test, the hypothetical monopolist will be assumed to pursue maximum profits in deciding whether to raise the price at any or all of the additional locations under its control. This process will continue until a group of locations is identified such that a hypothetical monopolist over that group of locations would profitably impose at least a "small but significant and nontransitory" increase, including the price charged at a location of one of the merging firms.

The "smallest market" principle will be applied as it is in product market definition. The price for which an increase will be postulated, what constitutes a "small but significant and nontransitory" increase in price, and the substitution decisions of consumers all will be determined in the same way in which they are determined in product market definition.

1.22 Geographic Market Definition in the Presence of Price Discrimination

The analysis of geographic market definition to this point has assumed that geographic price discrimination—charging different prices net of transportation costs for the same product to buyers in different areas, for example—would not be profitable for a hypothetical monopolist. However, if a hypothetical monopolist can identify and price differently to buyers in certain areas ("targeted buyers") who would not defeat the targeted price increase by substituting to more distant sellers in response to a "small but significant and nontransitory" price increase for the relevant product, and if other buyers likely would not purchase the relevant product and resell to targeted buyers,

(12) then a hypothetical monopolist would profitably impose a discriminatory price increase. This is true even where a general price increase would cause such significant substitution that the price increase would not be profitable. The Agency will consider additional geographic markets consisting of particular locations of buyers for which a hypothetical monopolist would profitably and separately impose at least a "small but significant and nontransitory" increase in price.

1.3 Identification of Firms that Participate in the Relevant Market

1.31 Current Producers or Sellers

The Agency's identification of firms that participate in the relevant market begins with all firms that currently produce or sell in the relevant market. This includes vertically integrated firms to the extent that such inclusion accurately reflects their competitive significance in the relevant market prior to the merger. To the extent that the analysis under Section 1.1 indicates that used, reconditioned or recycled goods are included in the relevant market, market participants will include firms that produce or sell such goods and that likely would offer those goods in competition with other relevant products.

1.32 Firms That Participate Through Supply Response

In addition, the Agency will identify other firms not currently producing or selling the relevant product in the relevant area as participating in the relevant market if their inclusion would more accurately reflect probable supply responses. These firms are termed "uncommitted entrants." These supply responses must be likely to occur within one year and without the expenditure of significant sunk costs of entry and exit, in response to a "small but significant and nontransitory" price increase. If a firm has the technological capability to achieve such an uncommitted supply response, but likely would not (e.g., because difficulties in achieving product acceptance, distribution, or production would render such a response unprofitable), that firm will not be considered to be a market participant. The competitive significance of supply responses that require more time or that require firms to incur significant sunk costs of entry and exit will be considered in entry analysis. See Section 3. (13)

Sunk costs are the acquisition costs of tangible and intangible assets that cannot be recovered through the redeployment of these assets outside the relevant market, i.e., costs uniquely incurred to supply the relevant product and geographic market. Examples of sunk costs may include market-specific investments in production facilities, technologies, marketing (including product acceptance), research and development, regulatory approvals, and testing. A significant sunk cost is one which would not be recouped within one year of the commencement of the supply response, assuming a "small but significant and nontransitory" price increase in the relevant market. In this context, a "small but significant and nontransitory" price increase will be determined in the same way in which it is determined in product market definition, except the price increase will be assumed to last one year. In some instances, it may be difficult to calculate sunk costs with precision. Accordingly, when necessary, the Agency will make an overall assessment of the extent of sunk costs for firms likely to participate through supply responses.

These supply responses may give rise to new production of products in the relevant product market or new sources of supply in the relevant geographic market. Alternatively, where price discrimination is likely so that the relevant market is defined in terms of a targeted group of buyers, these supply responses serve to identify new sellers to the targeted buyers. Uncommitted supply responses may occur in several different ways: by the switching or extension of existing assets to production or sale in the relevant market; or by the construction or acquisition of assets that enable production or sale in the relevant market.

1.321 Production Substitution and Extension: The Switching or Extension of Existing Assets to Production or Sale in the Relevant Market

The productive and distributive assets of a firm sometimes can be used to produce and sell either the relevant products or products that buyers do not regard as good substitutes. Production substitution refers to the shift by a firm in the use of assets from producing and selling one product to producing and selling another. Production extension refers to the use of those assets, for example, existing brand names and reputation, both for their current production and for production of the relevant product. Depending upon the speed of that shift and the extent of sunk costs incurred in the shift or extension, the potential for production substitution or extension may necessitate treating as market participants firms that do not currently produce the relevant product. (14)

If a firm has existing assets that likely would be shifted or extended into production and sale of the relevant product within one year, and without incurring significant sunk costs of entry and exit, in response to a "small but significant and nontransitory" increase in price for only the relevant product, the Agency will treat that firm as a market participant. In assessing whether a firm is such a market participant, the Agency will take into account the costs of substitution or extension relative to the profitability of sales at the elevated price, and whether the firm's capacity is elsewhere committed or elsewhere so profitably employed that such capacity likely would not be available to respond to an increase in price in the market.

1.322 Obtaining New Assets for Production or Sale of the Relevant Product

A firm may also be able to enter into production or sale in the relevant market within one year and without the expenditure of significant sunk costs of entry and exit, in response to a "small but significant and nontransitory" increase in price for only the relevant product, even if the firm is newly organized or is an existing firm without products or productive assets closely related to the relevant market. If new firms, or existing firms without closely related products or productive assets, likely would enter into production or sale in the relevant market within one year without the expenditure of significant sunk costs of entry and exit, the Agency will treat those firms as market participants.

1.4 Calculating Market Shares

1.41 General Approach

The Agency normally will calculate market shares for all firms (or plants) identified as market participants in Section 1.3 based on the total sales or capacity currently devoted to the relevant market together with that which likely would be devoted to the relevant market in response to a "small but significant and nontransitory" price increase. Market shares can be expressed either in dollar terms through measurement of sales, shipments, or production, or in physical terms through measurement of sales, shipments, production, capacity, or reserves.

Market shares will be calculated using the best indicator of firms' future competitive significance. Dollar sales or shipments generally will be used if firms are distinguished primarily by differentiation of their products. Unit sales generally will be used if firms are distinguished primarily on the basis of their relative advantages in serving different buyers or groups of buyers. Physical capacity or reserves generally will be used if it is these measures that most effectively distinguish firms. (15) Typically, annual data are used, but where individual sales are large and infrequent so that annual data may be unrepresentative, the Agency may measure market shares over a longer period of time.

In measuring a firm's market share, the Agency will not include its sales or capacity to the extent that the firm's capacity is committed or so profitably employed outside the relevant market that it would not be available to respond to an increase in price in the market.

1.42 Price Discrimination Markets

When markets are defined on the basis of price discrimination (Sections 1.12 and 1.22), the Agency will include only sales likely to be made into, or capacity likely to be used to supply, the relevant market in response to a "small but significant and nontransitory" price increase.

1.43 Special Factors Affecting Foreign Firms

Market shares will be assigned to foreign competitors in the same way in which they are assigned to domestic competitors. However, if exchange rates fluctuate significantly, so that comparable dollar calculations on an annual basis may be unrepresentative, the Agency may measure market shares over a period longer than one year.

If shipments from a particular country to the United States are subject to a quota, the market shares assigned to firms in that country will not exceed the amount of shipments by such firms allowed under the quota. (16)

In the case of restraints that limit imports to some percentage of the total amount of the product sold in the United States (i.e., percentage quotas), a domestic price increase that reduced domestic consumption also would reduce the volume of imports into the United States. Accordingly, actual import sales and capacity data will be reduced for purposes of calculating market shares. Finally, a single market share may be assigned to a country or group of countries if firms in that country or group of countries act in coordination.

1.5 Concentration and Market Shares

Market concentration is a function of the number of firms in a market and their respective market shares. As an aid to the interpretation of market data, the Agency will use the Herfindahl–Hirschman Index ("HHI") of market concentration. The HHI is calculated by summing the squares of the individual market shares of all the participants. (17) Unlike the four-firm concentration ratio, the HHI reflects both the distribution of the market shares of the top four firms and the composition of the market outside the top four firms. It also gives proportionately greater weight to the market shares of the larger firms, in accord with their relative importance in competitive interactions.

The Agency divides the spectrum of market concentration as measured by the HHI into three regions that can be broadly characterized as unconcentrated (HHI below 1000), moderately concentrated (HHI between 1000 and 1800), and highly concentrated (HHI above 1800). Although the resulting regions provide a useful framework for merger analysis, the numerical divisions suggest greater precision than is possible with the available economic tools and information. Other things being equal, cases falling just above and just below a threshold present comparable competitive issues.

1.51 General Standards

In evaluating horizontal mergers, the Agency will consider both the post-merger market concentration and the increase in concentration resulting from the merger. (18)

Market concentration is a useful indicator of the likely potential competitive effect of a merger. The general standards for horizontal mergers are as follows:

(a) Post–Merger HHI Below 1000. The Agency regards markets in this region to be unconcentrated. Mergers resulting in unconcentrated markets are unlikely to have adverse competitive effects and ordinarily require no further analysis.

(b) Post–Merger HHI Between 1000 and 1800. The Agency regards markets in this region to be moderately concentrated. Mergers producing an increase in the HHI of less than 100 points in moderately concentrated markets post-merger are unlikely to have adverse competitive consequences and ordinarily require no further analysis. Mergers producing an increase in the HHI of more than 100 points in moderately concentrated markets post-merger potentially raise significant competitive concerns depending on the factors set forth in Sections 2–5 of the Guidelines.

(c) Post–Merger HHI Above 1800. The Agency regards markets in this region to be highly concentrated. Mergers producing an increase in the HHI of less than 50 points, even in highly concentrated markets post-merger, are unlikely to have adverse competitive consequences and ordinarily require no further analysis. Mergers producing an increase in the HHI of more than 50 points in highly concentrated markets post-merger potentially raise significant competitive concerns, depending on the factors set forth in Sections 2–5 of the Guidelines. Where the post-merger HHI exceeds 1800, it will be presumed that mergers producing an increase in the HHI of more than 100 points are likely to create or enhance market power or facilitate its exercise. The presumption may be overcome by a showing that factors set forth in Sections 2–5 of the Guidelines make it unlikely that the merger will create or enhance market power or facilitate its exercise, in light of market concentration and market shares.

1.52 Factors Affecting the Significance of Market Shares and Concentration

The post-merger level of market concentration and the change in concentration resulting from a merger affect the degree to which a merger raises competitive concerns. However, in some situations, market share and market concentration data may either understate or overstate the likely future competitive significance of a firm or firms in the market or the impact of a merger. The following are examples of such situations.

1.521 Changing Market Conditions

Market concentration and market share data of necessity are based on historical evidence. However, recent or ongoing changes in the market may indicate that the current market share of a particular firm either understates or overstates the firm's future competitive significance. For example, if a new technology that is important to long-term competitive viability is available to other firms in the market, but is not available to a particular firm, the Agency may conclude that the historical market share of that firm overstates its future competitive significance. The Agency will consider reasonably predictable effects of recent or ongoing changes in market conditions in interpreting market concentration and market share data.

1.522 Degree of Difference Between the Products and Locations in the Market and Substitutes Outside the Market

All else equal, the magnitude of potential competitive harm from a merger is greater if a hypothetical monopolist would raise price within the relevant market by substantially more than a "small but significant and nontransitory" amount. This may occur when the demand substitutes outside the relevant market, as a group, are not close substitutes for the products and locations within the relevant market. There thus may be a wide gap in the chain of demand substitutes at the edge of the product and geographic market. Under such circumstances, more market power is at stake in the relevant market than in a market in which a hypothetical monopolist would raise price by exactly five percent.

2. THE POTENTIAL ADVERSE COMPETITIVE EFFECTS OF MERGERS

2.0 Overview

Other things being equal, market concentration affects the likelihood that one firm, or a small group of firms, could successfully exercise market power. The smaller the percentage of total supply that a firm controls, the more severely it must restrict its own output in order to produce a given price increase, and the less likely it is that an output restriction will be profitable. If collective action is necessary for the exercise of market power, as the number of firms necessary to control a given percentage of total supply decreases, the difficulties and costs of reaching and enforcing an understanding with respect to the control of that supply might be reduced. However, market share and concentration data provide only the starting point for analyzing the competitive impact of a merger. Before determining whether to challenge a merger, the Agency also will assess the other market factors that pertain to competitive effects, as well as entry, efficiencies and failure. This section considers some of the potential adverse competitive effects of mergers and the factors in addition to market concentration relevant to each. Because an individual merger may threaten to harm competition through more than one of these effects, mergers will be analyzed in terms of as many potential adverse competitive effects as are appropriate. Entry, efficiencies, and failure are treated in Sections 3–5.

2.1 Lessening of Competition Through Coordinated Interaction

A merger may diminish competition by enabling the firms selling in the relevant market more likely, more successfully, or more completely to engage in coordinated interaction that harms consumers. Coordinated interaction is comprised of actions by a group of firms that are profitable for each of them only as a result of the accommodating reactions of the others. This behavior includes tacit or express collusion, and may or may not be lawful in and of itself.

Successful coordinated interaction entails reaching terms of coordination that are profitable to the firms involved and an ability to detect and punish deviations that would undermine the coordinated interaction. Detection and punishment of deviations ensure that coordinating firms will find it more profitable to adhere to the terms of coordination than to pursue short-term profits from deviating, given the costs of reprisal. In this phase of the analysis, the Agency will examine the extent to which post-merger market conditions are conducive to reaching terms of coordination, detecting deviations from those terms, and punishing such deviations. Depending upon the circumstances, the following market factors, among others, may be relevant: the availability of key information concerning market conditions, transactions and individual competitors; the extent of firm and product heterogeneity; pricing or marketing practices typically employed by firms in the market; the characteristics of buyers and sellers; and the characteristics of typical transactions.

Certain market conditions that are conducive to reaching terms of coordination also may be conducive to detecting or punishing deviations from those terms. For example, the extent of information available to firms in the market, or the extent of homogeneity, may be relevant to both the ability to reach terms of coordination and to detect or punish deviations from those terms. The extent to which any specific market condition will be relevant to one or more of the conditions necessary to coordinated interaction will depend on the circumstances of the particular case.

It is likely that market conditions are conducive to coordinated interaction when the firms in the market previously have engaged in express collusion and when the salient characteristics of the market have not changed appreciably since the most recent such incident. Previous express collusion in another geographic market will have the same weight when the salient characteristics of that other market at the time of the collusion are comparable to those in the relevant market.

In analyzing the effect of a particular merger on coordinated interaction, the Agency is mindful of the difficulties of predicting likely future behavior based on the types of incomplete and sometimes contradictory information typically generated in merger investigations. Whether a merger is likely to diminish competition by enabling firms more likely, more successfully or more completely to engage in coordinated interaction depends on whether market conditions, on the whole, are conducive to reaching terms of coordination and detecting and punishing deviations from those terms.

2.11 Conditions Conducive to Reaching Terms of Coordination

Firms coordinating their interactions need not reach complex terms concerning the allocation of the market output across firms or the level of the market prices but may, instead, follow simple terms such as a common price, fixed price differentials, stable market shares, or customer or territorial restrictions. Terms of coordination need not perfectly achieve the monopoly outcome in order to be harmful to consumers. Instead, the terms of coordination may be imperfect and incomplete—inasmuch as they omit some market participants, omit some dimensions of competition, omit some customers, yield elevated prices short of monopoly levels, or lapse into episodic price wars—and still result in significant competitive harm. At some point, however, imperfections cause the profitability of abiding by the terms of coordination to decrease and, depending on their extent, may make coordinated interaction unlikely in the first instance.

Market conditions may be conducive to or hinder reaching terms of coordination. For example, reaching terms of coordination may be facilitated by product or firm homogeneity and by existing practices among firms, practices not necessarily themselves antitrust violations, such as standardization of pricing or product variables on which firms could compete. Key information about rival firms and the market may also facilitate reaching terms of coordination. Conversely, reaching terms of coordination may be limited or impeded by product heterogeneity or by firms having substantially incomplete information about the conditions and prospects of their rival's businesses, perhaps because of important differences among their current business operations. In addition, reaching terms of coordination may be limited or impeded by firm heterogeneity, for example, differences in vertical integration or the production of another product that tends to be used together with the relevant product.

2.12   Conditions Conducive to Detecting and Punishing Deviations

Where market conditions are conducive to timely detection and punishment of significant deviations, a firm will find it more profitable to abide by the terms of coordination than to deviate from them. Deviation from the terms of coordination will be deterred where the threat of punishment is credible. Credible punishment, however, may not need to be any more complex than temporary abandonment of the terms of coordination by other firms in the market.

Where detection and punishment likely would be rapid, incentives to deviate are diminished and coordination is likely to be successful. The detection and punishment of deviations may be facilitated by existing practices among firms, themselves not necessarily antitrust violations, and by the characteristics of typical transactions. For example, if key information about specific transactions or individual price or output levels is available routinely to competitors, it may be difficult for a firm to deviate secretly. If orders for the relevant product are frequent, regular and small relative to the total output of a firm in a market, it may be difficult for the firm to deviate in a substantial way without the knowledge of rivals and without the opportunity for rivals to react. If demand or cost fluctuations are relatively infrequent and small, deviations may be relatively easy to deter.

By contrast, where detection or punishment is likely to be slow, incentives to deviate are enhanced and coordinated interaction is unlikely to be successful. If demand or cost fluctuations are relatively frequent and large, deviations may be relatively difficult to distinguish from these other sources of market price fluctuations, and, in consequence, deviations may be relatively difficult to deter.

In certain circumstances, buyer characteristics and the nature of the procurement process may affect the incentives to deviate from terms of coordination. Buyer size alone is not the determining characteristic. Where large buyers likely would engage in long-term contracting, so that the sales covered by such contracts can be large relative to the total output of a firm in the market, firms may have the incentive to deviate. However, this only can be accomplished where the duration, volume and profitability of the business covered by such contracts are sufficiently large as to make deviation more profitable in the long term than honoring the terms of coordination, and buyers likely would switch suppliers.

In some circumstances, coordinated interaction can be effectively prevented or limited by maverick firms—firms that have a greater economic incentive to deviate from the terms of coordination than do most of their rivals (e.g., firms that are unusually disruptive and competitive influences in the market). Consequently, acquisition of a maverick firm is one way in which a merger may make coordinated interaction more likely, more successful, or more complete. For example, in a market where capacity constraints are significant for many competitors, a firm is more likely to be a maverick the greater is its excess or divertable capacity in relation to its sales or its total capacity, and the lower are its direct and opportunity costs of expanding sales in the relevant market. (19)

This is so because a firm's incentive to deviate from price-elevating and output-limiting terms of coordination is greater the more the firm is able profitably to expand its output as a proportion of the sales it would obtain if it adhered to the terms of coordination and the smaller is the base of sales on which it enjoys elevated profits prior to the price cutting deviation.(20) A firm also may be a maverick if it has an unusual ability secretly to expand its sales in relation to the sales it would obtain if it adhered to the terms of coordination. This ability might arise from opportunities to expand captive production for a downstream affiliate.

2.2 Lessening of Competition Through Unilateral Effects

A merger may diminish competition even if it does not lead to increased likelihood of successful coordinated interaction, because merging firms may find it profitable to alter their behavior unilaterally following the acquisition by elevating price and suppressing output. Unilateral competitive effects can arise in a variety of different settings. In each setting, particular other factors describing the relevant market affect the likelihood of unilateral competitive effects. The settings differ by the primary characteristics that distinguish firms and shape the nature of their competition.

2.21 Firms Distinguished Primarily by Differentiated Products

In some markets the products are differentiated, so that products sold by different participants in the market are not perfect substitutes for one another. Moreover, different products in the market may vary in the degree of their substitutability for one another. In this setting, competition may be non-uniform (i.e., localized), so that individual sellers compete more directly with those rivals selling closer substitutes.(21)

A merger between firms in a market for differentiated products may diminish competition by enabling the merged firm to profit by unilaterally raising the price of one or both products above the premerger level. Some of the sales loss due to the price rise merely will be diverted to the product of the merger partner and, depending on relative margins, capturing such sales loss through merger may make the price increase profitable even though it would not have been profitable premerger. Substantial unilateral price elevation in a market for differentiated products requires that there be a significant share of sales in the market accounted for by consumers who regard the products of the merging firms as their first and second choices, and that repositioning of the non-parties' product lines to replace the localized competition lost through the merger be unlikely. The price rise will be greater the closer substitutes are the products of the merging firms, i.e., the more the buyers of one product consider the other product to be their next choice.

2.211 Closeness of the Products of the Merging Firms

The market concentration measures articulated in Section 1 may help assess the extent of the likely competitive effect from a unilateral price elevation by the merged firm notwithstanding the fact that the affected products are differentiated. The market concentration measures provide a measure of this effect if each product's market share is reflective of not only its relative appeal as a first choice to consumers of the merging firms' products but also its relative appeal as a second choice, and hence as a competitive constraint to the first choice(22) where this circumstance holds, market concentration data fall outside the safeharbor regions of Section 1.5, and the merging firms have a combined market share of at least thirty-five percent, the Agency will presume that a significant share of sales in the market are accounted for by consumers who regard the products of the merging firms as their first and second choices.

Purchasers of one of the merging firms, products may be more or less likely to make the other their second choice than market shares alone would indicate. The market shares of the merging firms, products may understate the competitive effect of concern, when, for example, the products of the merging firms are relatively more similar in their various attributes to one another than to other products in the relevant market. On the other hand, the market shares alone may overstate the competitive effects of concern when, for example, the relevant products are less similar in their attributes to one another than to other products in the relevant market.

Where market concentration data fall outside the safeharbor regions of Section 1.5, the merging firms have a combined market share of at least thirty-five percent, and where data on product attributes and relative product appeal show that a significant share of purchasers of one merging firm's product regard the other as their second choice, then market share data may be relied upon to demonstrate that there is a significant share of sales in the market accounted for by consumers who would be adversely affected by the merger.

2.212 Ability of Rival Sellers to Replace Lost Competition

A merger is not likely to lead to unilateral elevation of prices of differentiated products if, in response to such an effect, rival sellers likely would replace any localized competition lost through the merger by repositioning their product lines.(23)

In markets where it is costly for buyers to evaluate product quality, buyers who consider purchasing from both merging parties may limit the total number of sellers they consider. If either of the merging firms would be replaced in such buyers, consideration by an equally competitive seller not formerly considered, then the merger is not likely to lead to a unilateral elevation of prices.

2.22 Firms Distinguished Primarily by Their Capacities

Where products are relatively undifferentiated and capacity primarily distinguishes firms and shapes the nature of their competition, the merged firm may find it profitable unilaterally to raise price and suppress output. The merger provides the merged firm a larger base of sales on which to enjoy the resulting price rise and also eliminates a competitor to which customers otherwise would have diverted their sales. Where the merging firms have a combined market share of at least thirty-five percent, merged firms may find it profitable to raise price and reduce joint output below the sum of their premerger outputs because the lost markups on the foregone sales may be outweighed by the resulting price increase on the merged base of sales.

This unilateral effect is unlikely unless a sufficiently large number of the merged firm's customers would not be able to find economical alternative sources of supply, i.e., competitors of the merged firm likely would not respond to the price increase and output reduction by the merged firm with increases in their own outputs sufficient in the aggregate to make the unilateral action of the merged firm unprofitable. Such non-party expansion is unlikely if those firms face binding capacity constraints that could not be economically relaxed within two years or if existing excess capacity is significantly more costly to operate than capacity currently in use.(24)

3. ENTRY ANALYSIS

3.0 Overview

A merger is not likely to create or enhance market power or to facilitate its exercise, if entry into the market is so easy that market participants, after the merger, either collectively or unilaterally could not profitably maintain a price increase above premerger levels. Such entry likely will deter an anticompetitive merger in its incipiency, or deter or counteract the competitive effects of concern.

Entry is that easy if entry would be timely, likely, and sufficient in its magnitude, character and scope to deter or counteract the competitive effects of concern. In markets where entry is that easy (i.e., where entry passes these tests of timeliness, likelihood, and sufficiency), the merger raises no antitrust concern and ordinarily requires no further analysis.

The committed entry treated in this Section is defined as new competition that requires expenditure of significant sunk costs of entry and exit.(25) The

Agency employs a three step methodology to assess whether committed entry would deter or counteract a competitive effect of concern.

The first step assesses whether entry can achieve significant market impact within a timely period. If significant market impact would require a longer period, entry will not deter or counteract the competitive effect of concern.

The second step assesses whether committed entry would be a profitable and, hence, a likely response to a merger having competitive effects of concern. Firms considering entry that requires significant sunk costs must evaluate the profitability of the entry on the basis of long term participation in the market, because the underlying assets will be committed to the market until they are economically depreciated. Entry that is sufficient to counteract the competitive effects of concern will cause prices to fall to their premerger levels or lower. Thus, the profitability of such committed entry-must be determined on the basis of premerger market prices over the long-term.

A merger having anticompetitive effects can attract committed entry, profitable at premerger prices, that would not have occurred premerger at these same prices. But following the merger, the reduction in industry output and increase in prices associated with the competitive effect of concern may allow the same entry to occur without driving market prices below premerger levels. After a merger that results in decreased output and increased prices, the likely sales opportunities available to entrants at premerger prices will be larger than they were premerger, larger by the output reduction caused by the merger. If entry could be profitable at premerger prices without exceeding the likely sales opportunities—opportunities that include pre-existing pertinent factors as well as the merger-induced output reduction—then such entry is likely in response to the merger.

The third step assesses whether timely and likely entry would be sufficient to return market prices to their premerger levels. This end may be accomplished either through multiple entry or individual entry at a sufficient scale. Entry may not be sufficient, even though timely and likely, where the constraints on availability of essential assets, due to incumbent control, make it impossible for entry profitably to achieve the necessary level of sales. Also, the character and scope of entrants' products might not be fully responsive to the localized sales opportunities created by the removal of direct competition among sellers of differentiated products. In assessing whether entry will be timely, likely, and sufficient, the Agency recognizes that precise and detailed information may be difficult or impossible to obtain. In such instances, the Agency will rely on all available evidence bearing on whether entry will satisfy the conditions of timeliness, likelihood, and sufficiency.

3.1 Entry Alternatives

The Agency will examine the timeliness, likelihood, and sufficiency of the means of entry (entry alternatives) a potential entrant might practically employ, without attempting to identify who might be potential entrants. An entry alternative is defined by the actions the firm must take in order to produce and sell in the market. All phases of the entry effort will be considered, including, where relevant, planning, design, and management; permitting, licensing, and other approvals; construction, debugging, and operation of production facilities; and promotion (including necessary introductory discounts), marketing, distribution, and satisfaction of customer testing and qualification requirements.(26)

Recent examples of entry, whether successful or unsuccessful, may provide a useful starting point for identifying the necessary actions, time requirements, and characteristics of possible entry alternatives.

3.2 Timeliness of Entry

In order to deter or counteract the competitive effects of concern, entrants quickly must achieve a significant impact on price in the relevant market. The Agency generally will consider timely only those committed entry alternatives that can be achieved within two years from initial planning to significant market impact.(27) Where the relevant product is a durable good, consumers, in response to a significant commitment to entry, may defer purchases by making additional investments to extend the useful life of previously purchased goods and in this way deter or counteract for a time the competitive effects of concern. In these circumstances, if entry only can occur outside of the two year period, the Agency will consider entry to be timely so long as it would deter or counteract the competitive effects of concern within the two year period and subsequently.

3.3 Likelihood of Entry

An entry alternative is likely if it would be profitable at premerger prices, and if such prices could be secured by the entrant.(28) The committed entrant will be unable to secure prices at premerger levels if its output is too large for the market to absorb without depressing prices further. Thus, entry is unlikely if the minimum viable scale is larger than the likely sales opportunity available to entrants. Minimum viable scale is the smallest average annual level of sales that the committed entrant must persistently achieve for profitability at premerger prices.(29) Minimum viable scale is a function of expected revenues, based upon premerger prices,(30) and all categories of costs associated with the entry alternative, including an appropriate rate of return on invested capital given that entry could fail and sunk costs, if any, will be lost.(31)

Sources of sales opportunities available to entrants include:

(a) the output reduction associated with the competitive effect of concern, (32)

(b) entrants' ability to capture a share of reasonably expected growth in market demand, (33)

(c) entrants' ability securely to divert sales from incumbents, for example, through vertical integration or through forward contracting, and

(d) any additional anticipated contraction in incumbents' output in response to entry. (34)

Factors that reduce the sales opportunities available to entrants include:

(a) the prospect that an entrant will share in a reasonably expected decline in market demand,

(b) the exclusion of an entrant from a portion of the market over the long term because of vertical integration or forward contracting by incumbents, and

(c) any anticipated sales expansion by incumbents in reaction to entry, either generalized or targeted at customers approached by the entrant, that utilizes prior irreversible investments in excess production capacity.

Demand growth or decline will be viewed as relevant only if total market demand is projected to experience long-lasting change during at least the two year period following the competitive effect of concern.

3.4 Sufficiency of Entry

Inasmuch as multiple entry generally is possible and individual entrants may flexibly choose their scale, committed entry generally will be sufficient to deter or counteract the competitive effects of concern whenever entry is likely under the analysis of Section 3.3. However, entry, although likely, will not be sufficient if, as a result of incumbent control, the tangible and intangible assets required for entry are not adequately available for entrants to respond fully to their sales opportunities. In addition, where the competitive effect of concern is not uniform across the relevant market, in order for entry to be sufficient, the character and scope of entrants' products must be responsive to the localized sales opportunities that include the output reduction associated with the competitive effect of concern. For example, where the concern is unilateral price elevation as a result of a merger between producers of differentiated products, entry, in order to be sufficient, must involve a product so close to the products of the merging firms that the merged firm will be unable to internalize enough of the sales loss due to the price rise, rendering the price increase unprofitable.

4. Efficiencies

Competition usually spurs firms to achieve efficiencies internally. Nevertheless, mergers have the potential to generate significant efficiencies by permitting a better utilization of existing assets, enabling the combined firm to achieve lower costs in producing a given quantity and quality than either firm could have achieved without the proposed transaction. Indeed, the primary benefit of mergers to the economy is their potential to generate such efficiencies.

Efficiencies generated through merger can enhance the merged firm's ability and incentive to compete, which may result in lower prices, improved quality, enhanced service, or new products. For example, merger-generated efficiencies may enhance competition by permitting two ineffective (e.g., high cost) competitors to become one effective (e.g., lower cost) competitor. In a coordinated interaction context (see Section 2.1), marginal cost reductions may make coordination less likely or effective by enhancing the incentive of a maverick to lower price or by creating a new maverick firm. In a unilateral effects context (see Section 2.2), marginal cost reductions may reduce the merged firm's incentive to elevate price. Efficiencies also may result in benefits in the form of new or improved products, and efficiencies may result in benefits even when price is not immediately and directly affected. Even when efficiencies generated through merger enhance a firm's ability to compete, however, a merger may have other effects that may lessen competition and ultimately may make the merger anticompetitive.

The Agency will consider only those efficiencies likely to be accomplished with the proposed merger and unlikely to be accomplished in the absence of either the proposed merger or another means having comparable anticompetitive effects. These are termed merger-specific efficiencies.(35) Only alternatives that are practical in the business situation faced by the merging firms will be considered in making this determination; the Agency will not insist upon a less restrictive alternative that is merely theoretical.

Efficiencies are difficult to verify and quantify, in part because much of the information relating to efficiencies is uniquely in the possession of the merging firms. Moreover, efficiencies projected reasonably and in good faith by the merging firms may not be realized. Therefore, the merging firms must substantiate efficiency claims so that the Agency can verify by reasonable means the likelihood and magnitude of each asserted efficiency, how and when each would be achieved (and any costs of doing so), how each would enhance the merged firm's ability and incentive to compete, and why each would be merger-specific. Efficiency claims will not be considered if they are vague or speculative or otherwise cannot be verified by reasonable means.

Cognizable efficiencies are merger-specific efficiencies that have been verified and do not arise from anticompetitive reductions in output or service. Cognizable efficiencies are assessed net of costs produced by the merger or incurred in achieving those efficiencies.

The Agency will not challenge a merger if cognizable efficiencies are of a character and magnitude such that the merger is not likely to be anticompetitive in any relevant market.(36) To make the requisite determination, the Agency considers whether cognizable efficiencies likely would be sufficient to reverse the merger's potential to harm consumers in the relevant market, e.g., by preventing price increases in that market. In conducting this analysis,(37) the Agency will not simply compare the magnitude of the cognizable efficiencies with the magnitude of the likely harm to competition absent the efficiencies. The greater the potential adverse competitive effect of a merger—as indicated by the increase in the HHI and post-merger HHI from Section 1, the analysis of potential adverse competitive effects from Section 2, and the timeliness, likelihood, and sufficiency of entry from Section 3—the greater must be cognizable efficiencies in order for the Agency to conclude that the merger will not have an anticompetitive effect in the relevant market. When the potential adverse competitive effect of a merger is likely to be particularly large, extraordinarily great cognizable efficiencies would be necessary to prevent the merger from being anticompetitive.

In the Agency's experience, efficiencies are most likely to make a difference in merger analysis when the likely adverse competitive effects, absent the efficiencies, are not great. Efficiencies almost never justify a merger to monopoly or near-monopoly.

The Agency has found that certain types of efficiencies are more likely to be cognizable and substantial than others. For example, efficiencies resulting from shifting production among facilities formerly owned separately, which enable the merging firms to reduce the marginal cost of production, are more likely to be susceptible to verification, merger-specific, and substantial, and are less likely to result from anticompetitive reductions in output. Other efficiencies, such as those relating to research and development, are potentially substantial but are generally less susceptible to verification and may be the result of anticompetitive output reductions. Yet others, such as those relating to procurement, management, or capital cost are less likely to be merger-specific or substantial, or may not be cognizable for other reasons.

5. FAILURE AND EXITING ASSETS

5.0 Overview

Notwithstanding the analysis of Sections 1–4 of the Guidelines, a merger is not likely to create or enhance market power or to facilitate its exercise, if imminent failure, as defined below, of one of the merging firms would cause the assets of that firm to exit the relevant market. In such circumstances, post-merger performance in the relevant market may be no worse than market performance had the merger been blocked and the assets left the market.

5.1 Failing Firm

A merger is not likely to create or enhance market power or facilitate its exercise if the following circumstances are met: 1) the allegedly failing firm would be unable to meet its financial obligations in the near future; 2) it would not be able to reorganize successfully under Chapter 11 of the Bankruptcy Act;(38) 3) it has made unsuccessful good-faith efforts to elicit reasonable alternative offers of acquisition of the assets of the failing firm(39) that would both keep its tangible and intangible assets in the relevant market and pose a less severe danger to competition than does the proposed merger; and 4) absent the acquisition, the assets of the failing firm would exit the relevant market.

5.2 Failing Division

A similar argument can be made for ''failing'' divisions as for failing firms. First, upon applying appropriate cost allocation rules, the division must

149

have a negative cash flow on an operating basis. Second, absent the acquisition, it must be that the assets of the division would exit the relevant market in the near future if not sold. Due to the ability of the parent firm to allocate costs, revenues, and intracompany transactions among itself and its subsidiaries and divisions, the Agency will require evidence, not based solely on management plans that could be prepared solely for the purpose of demonstrating negative cash flow or the prospect of exit from the relevant market. Third, the owner of the failing division also must have complied with the competitively-preferable purchaser requirement of Section 5.1.

Footnotes

1.   15 U.S.C. Section 18 (1988). Mergers subject to section 7 are prohibited if their effect "may be substantially to lessen competition, or to tend to create a monopoly."

2.   15 U.S.C. Section 1 (1988). Mergers subject to section 1 are prohibited if they constitute a "contract, combination or conspiracy in restraint of trade."

3.   15 U.S.C. Section 45 (1988). Mergers subject to section 5 are prohibited if they constitute an "unfair method of competition."

4.   These Guidelines update the Merger Guidelines issued by the U.S. Department of Justice in 1984 and the Statement of Federal Trade Commission Concerning Horizontal Mergers issued in 1982. The Merger Guidelines may be revised from time to time as necessary to reflect any significant changes in enforcement policy or to clarify aspects of existing policy.

5.   For example, the burden with respect to efficiency and failure continues to reside with the proponents of the merger.

6.   Sellers with market power also may lessen competition on dimensions other than price, such as product quality, service, or innovation.

7.   Probable supply responses that require the entrant to incur significant sunk costs of entry and exit are not part of market measurement, but are included in the analysis of the significance of entry. See Section 3. Entrants that must commit substantial sunk costs are regarded as "committed" entrants because those sunk costs make entry irreversible in the short term without foregoing that investment; thus the likelihood of their entry must be evaluated with regard to their long-term profitability.

8.   Although discussed separately, product market definition and geographic market definition are interrelated. In particular, the extent to which buyers of a particular product would shift to other products in the event of a "small but significant and nontransitory" increase in price must be evaluated in the context of the relevant geographic market.

9.   Throughout the Guidelines, the term "next best substitute" refers to the alternative which, if available in unlimited quantities at constant prices, would account for the greatest value of diversion of demand in response to a "small but significant and nontransitory" price increase.

10.   The terms of sale of all other products are held constant in order to focus market definition on the behavior of consumers. Movements in the terms of sale for other products, as may result from the behavior of producers of those products, are accounted for in the analysis of competitive effects and entry. See Sections 2 and 3.

11.   For example, in a merger between retailers, the relevant price would be the retail price of a product to consumers. In the case of a merger among oil pipelines, the relevant price would be the tariff—the price of the transportation service.

12.   This arbitrage is inherently impossible for many services and is particularly difficult where the product is sold on a delivered basis and where transportation costs are a significant percentage of the final cost.

13.   If uncommitted entrants likely would also remain in the market and would meet the entry tests of timeliness, likelihood and sufficiency, and thus would likely deter anticompetitive mergers or deter or counteract the competitive effects of concern (see Section 3, infra), the Agency will consider the impact of those firms in the entry analysis.

14.   Under other analytical approaches, production substitution sometimes has been reflected in the description of the product market. For example, the product market for stamped metal products such as automobile hub caps might be described as "light metal stamping," a production process rather than a product. The Agency believes that the approach described in the text provides a more clearly focused method of incorporating this factor in merger analysis. If production substitution among a group of products is nearly universal among the firms selling one or more of those products, however, the Agency may use an aggregate description of those markets as a matter of convenience.

15.   Where all firms have, on a forward-looking basis, an equal likelihood of securing sales, the Agency will assign firms equal shares.

16.   The constraining effect of the quota on the importer's ability to expand sales is relevant to the evaluation of potential adverse competitive effects. See Section 2.

17.   For example, a market consisting of four firms with market shares of 30 percent, 30 percent, 20 percent and 20 percent has an HHI of 2600 (30^2 + 30^2 + 20^2 + 20^2 = 2600). The HHI ranges from 10,000 (in the case of a pure monopoly) to a number approaching zero (in the case of an atomistic market). Although it is desirable to include all firms in the calculation, lack of information about small firms is not critical because such firms do not affect the HHI significantly.

18.   The increase in concentration as measured by the HHI can be calculated independently of the overall market concentration by doubling the product of the market shares of the merging firms. For example, the merger of firms with shares of 5 percent and 10 percent of the market would increase the HHI by 100 (5 x 10 x 2 = 100). The explanation for this technique is as

follows: In calculating the HHI before the merger, the market shares of the merging firms are squared individually: $(a)2 + (b)2$. After the merger, the sum of those shares would be squared: $(a + b)2$, which equals $a2 + 2ab + b2$. The increase in the HHI therefore is represented by $2ab$.

19.   But excess capacity in the hands of non-maverick firms may be a potent weapon with which to punish deviations from the terms of coordination.

20.   Similarly, in a market where product design or quality is significant, a firm is more likely to be an effective maverick the greater is the sales potential of its products among customers of its rivals, in relation to the sales it would obtain if it adhered to the terms of coordination. The likelihood of expansion responses by a maverick will be analyzed in the same fashion as uncommitted entry or committed entry (see Sections 1.3 and 3) depending on the significance of the sunk costs entailed in expansion.

21.   Similarly, in some markets sellers are primarily distinguished by their relative advantages in serving different buyers or groups of buyers, and buyers negotiate individually with sellers. Here, for example, sellers may formally bid against one another for the business of a buyer, or each buyer may elicit individual price quotes from multiple sellers. A seller may find it relatively inexpensive to meet the demands of particular buyers or types of buyers, and relatively expensive to meet others' demands. Competition, again, may be localized: sellers compete more directly with those rivals having similar relative advantages in serving particular buyers or groups of buyers. For example, in open outcry auctions, price is determined by the cost of the second lowest-cost seller. A merger involving the first and second lowest-cost sellers could cause prices to rise to the constraining level of the next lowest-cost seller.

22.   Information about consumers' actual first and second product choices may be provided by marketing surveys, information from bidding structures, or normal course of business documents from industry participants.

23.   The timeliness and likelihood of repositioning responses will be analyzed using the same methodology as used in analyzing uncommitted entry or committed entry (see Sections 1.3 and 3), depending on the significance of the sunk costs entailed in repositioning.

24.   The timeliness and likelihood of non-party expansion will be analyzed using the same methodology as used in analyzing uncommitted or committed entry (see Sections 1.3 and 3) depending on the significance of the sunk costs entailed in expansion.

25.   Supply responses that require less than one year and insignificant sunk costs to effectuate are analyzed as uncommitted entry in Section 1.3.

26.   Many of these phases may be undertaken simultaneously.

27.   Firms which have committed to entering the market prior to the merger generally will be included in the measurement of the market. Only

committed entry or adjustments to pre-existing entry plans that are induced by the merger will be considered as possibly deterring or counteracting the competitive effects of concern.

28. Where conditions indicate that entry may be profitable at prices below premerger levels, the Agency will assess the likelihood of entry at the lowest price at which such entry would be profitable.

29. The concept of minimum viable scale ("MVS") differs from the concept of minimum efficient scale ("MES"). While MES is the smallest scale at which average costs are minimized, MVS is the smallest scale at which average costs equal the premerger price.

30. The expected path of future prices, absent the merger, may be used if future price changes can be predicted with reasonable reliability.

31. The minimum viable scale of an entry alternative will be relatively large when the fixed costs of entry are large, when the fixed costs of entry are largely sunk, when the marginal costs of production are high at low levels of output, and when a plant is underutilized for a long time because of delays in achieving market acceptance.

32. Five percent of total market sales typically is used because where a monopolist profitably would raise price by five percent or more across the entire relevant market, it is likely that the accompanying reduction in sales would be no less than five percent.

33. Entrants' anticipated share of growth in demand depends on incumbents' capacity constraints and irreversible investments in capacity expansion, as well as on the relative appeal, acceptability and reputation of incumbents' and entrants' products to the new demand.

34. For example, in a bidding market where all bidders are on equal footing, the market share of incumbents will contract as a result of entry.

35. The Agency will not deem efficiencies to be merger-specific if they could be preserved by practical alternatives that mitigate competitive concerns, such as divestiture or licensing. If a merger affects not whether but only when an efficiency would be achieved, only the timing advantage is a merger-specific efficiency.

36. Section 7 of the Clayton Act prohibits mergers that may substantially lessen competition "in any line of commerce ... in any section of the country." Accordingly, the Agency normally assesses competition in each relevant market affected by a merger independently and normally will challenge the merger if it is likely to be anticompetitive in any relevant market. In some cases, however, the Agency in its prosecutorial discretion will consider efficiencies not strictly in the relevant market, but so inextricably linked with it that a partial divestiture or other remedy could not feasibly eliminate the anticompetitive effect in the relevant market without sacrificing the efficiencies in the other market(s). Inextricably linked efficiencies rarely are a significant factor in the Agency's determination not to challenge a merger.

They are most likely to make a difference when they are great and the likely anticompetitive effect in the relevant market(s) is small.

37.   The result of this analysis over the short term will determine the Agency's enforcement decision in most cases. The Agency also will consider the effects of cognizable efficiencies with no short-term, direct effect on prices in the relevant market. Delayed benefits from efficiencies (due to delay in the achievement of, or the realization of consumer benefits from, the efficiencies) will be given less weight because they are less proximate and more difficult to predict.

38.   11 U.S.C. Sections 1101–1174 (1988).

39.   Any offer to purchase the assets of the failing firm for a price above the liquidation value of those assets—the highest valued use outside the relevant market or equivalent offer to purchase the stock of the failing firm— will be regarded as a reasonable alternative offer.

Statements of Antitrust Enforcement Policy in Health Care Issued by the U.S. Department of Justice and the Federal Trade Commission
August 1996

TABLE OF CONTENTS

DEPARTMENT OF JUSTICE AND FEDERAL TRADE COMMISSION STATEMENTS OF ANTITRUST ENFORCEMENT POLICY IN HEALTH CARE

Introduction

In September 1993, the Department of Justice and the Federal Trade Commission (the "Agencies") issued six statements of their antitrust enforcement policies regarding mergers and various joint activities in the health care area. The six policy statements addressed: (1) hospital mergers; (2) hospital joint ventures involving high-technology or other expensive medical equipment; (3) physicians' provision of information to purchasers of health care services; (4) hospital participation in exchanges of price and cost information; (5) health care providers' joint purchasing arrangements; and (6) physician network joint ventures. The Agencies also committed to issuing expedited Department of Justice business reviews and Federal Trade Commission advisory opinions in response to requests for antitrust guidance on specific proposed conduct involving the health care industry.

The 1993 policy statements and expedited specific Agency guidance were designed to advise the health care community in a time of tremendous change, and to address, as completely as possible, the problem of uncertainty concerning the Agencies' enforcement policy that some had said might deter mergers, joint ventures, or other activities that could lower health care costs. Sound antitrust enforcement, of course, continued to protect consumers against anticompetitive activities.

When the Agencies issued the 1993 health care antitrust enforcement policy statements, they recognized that additional guidance might be desirable in the areas covered by those statements as well as in other health care areas, and committed to issuing revised and additional policy statements as warranted. In light of the comments the Agencies received on the 1993 statements and the Agencies' own experience, the Agencies revised and expanded the health care antitrust enforcement policy statements in September 1994. The 1994 statements, which superseded the 1993 statements, added new statements addressing hospital joint ventures involving specialized clinical or other expensive health care services, providers' collective provision of fee-related information to purchasers of health care services, and analytical principles relating to a broad range of health care provider networks (termed "multiprovider networks"), and expanded the antitrust "safety zones" for several other statements.

Since issuance of the 1994 statements, health care markets have continued to evolve in response to consumer demand and competition in the marketplace. New arrangements and variations on existing arrangements involving joint activity by health care providers continue to emerge to meet consumers', purchasers', and payers' desire for more efficient delivery of high quality health care services. During this period, the Agencies have gained additional experience with arrangements involving joint provider activity. As a result of these developments, the Agencies have decided to amplify the enforcement policy statement on physician network joint ventures and the more general statement on multiprovider networks.

In these revised statements, the Agencies continue to analyze all types of health care provider networks under general antitrust principles. These principles are sufficiently flexible to take into account the particular characteristics of health care markets and the rapid changes that are occurring in those markets. The Agencies emphasize that it is not their intent to treat such networks either more strictly or more leniently than joint ventures in other industries, or to favor any particular procompetitive organization or structure of health care delivery over other forms that consumers may desire. Rather, their goal is to ensure a competitive marketplace in which consumers will have the benefit of high quality, cost-effective health care and a wide range of choices, including new provider-controlled networks that expand consumer choice and increase competition.

The revisions to the statements on physician network joint ventures and multiprovider networks are summarized below. In addition to these revisions, various changes have been made to the language of both statements to improve their clarity. No revisions have been made to any of the other statements.

Physician Network Joint Ventures

The revised statement on physician network joint ventures provides an expanded discussion of the antitrust principles that apply to such ventures. The revisions focus on the analysis of networks that fall outside the safety zones contained in the existing statement, particularly those networks that do not involve the sharing of substantial financial risk by their physician participants. The revised statement explains that where physicians' integration through the network is likely to produce significant efficiencies, any agreements on price reasonably necessary to accomplish the venture's procompetitive benefits will be analyzed under the rule of reason.

The revised statement adds three hypothetical examples to further illustrate the application of these principles: (1) a physician network joint venture that does not involve the sharing of substantial financial risk, but receives rule of reason treatment due to the extensive integration among its physician participants; (2) a network that involves both risk-sharing and non-risk-sharing activities, and receives rule of reason treatment; and (3) a network that involves little or no integration among its physician participants, and is per se illegal.

The safety zones for physician network joint ventures remain unchanged, but the revised statement identifies additional types of financial risk-sharing arrangements that can qualify a network for the safety zones. It also further emphasizes two points previously made in the 1994 statements. First, the enumeration in the statements of particular examples of substantial financial risk sharing does not foreclose consideration of other arrangements through which physicians may share substantial financial risk. Second, a physician network that falls outside the safety zones is not necessarily anticompetitive.

Multiprovider Networks

In 1994, the Agencies issued a new statement on multiprovider health care networks that described the general antitrust analysis of such networks. The revised statement on multiprovider networks emphasizes that it is intended to articulate general principles relating to a wide range of health care provider networks. Many of the revisions to this statement reflect changes made to the revised statement on physician network joint ventures. In addition, four hypothetical examples involving PHOs ("physician-hospital organizations"), including one involving "messenger model" arrangements, have been added.

Safety Zones and Hypothetical Examples

Most of the nine statements give health care providers guidance in the form of antitrust safety zones, which describe conduct that the Agencies will not challenge under the antitrust laws, absent extraordinary circumstances. The Agencies are aware that some parties have interpreted the safety zones as defining the limits of joint conduct that is permissible under the antitrust laws. This view is incorrect. The inclusion of certain conduct within the antitrust safety zones does not imply that conduct falling outside the safety zones is likely to be challenged by the Agencies. Antitrust analysis is inherently fact-intensive. The safety zones are designed to require consideration of only a few factors that are relatively easy to apply, and to provide the Agencies with a high degree of confidence that arrangements falling within them are unlikely to raise substantial competitive concerns. Thus, the safety zones encompass only a subset of provider arrangements that the Agencies are unlikely to challenge under the antitrust laws. The statements outline the analysis the Agencies will use to review conduct that falls outside the safety zones.

Likewise, the statements' hypothetical examples concluding that the Agencies would not challenge the particular arrangement do not mean that conduct varying from the examples is likely to be challenged by the Agencies. The hypothetical examples are designed to illustrate how the statements' general principles apply to specific situations. Interested parties should examine the business review letters issued by the Department of Justice and the advisory opinions issued by the Federal Trade Commission and its staff for additional guidance on the application and interpretation of these statements. Copies of those letters and opinions and summaries of the letters and opinions are available from the Agencies at the mailing and Internet addresses listed at the end of the statements.

The statements also set forth the Department of Justice's business review procedure and the Federal Trade Commission's advisory opinion procedure under which the health care community can obtain the Agencies' antitrust enforcement intentions regarding specific proposed conduct on an expedited basis. The statements continue the commitment of the Agencies to respond to requests for business reviews or advisory opinions from the health care community no later than 90 days after all necessary information is received regarding any matter addressed in the statements, except requests relating to hospital mergers outside the antitrust safety zone and multiprovider networks. The Agencies also will respond to business review or advisory opinion requests regarding multiprovider networks or other non-merger health care matters within 120 days after all necessary information is received. The Agencies intend to work closely with persons making requests to clarify what information is necessary and to provide guidance throughout the process. The Agencies continue this commitment to expedited review in an effort to reduce antitrust uncertainty for the health care industry in what the Agencies recognize is a time of fundamental change.

The Agencies recognize the importance of antitrust guidance in evolving health care contexts. Consequently, the Agencies continue their commitment to issue additional guidance as warranted.

1. STATEMENT OF DEPARTMENT OF JUSTICE AND FEDERAL TRADE COMMISSION ENFORCEMENT POLICY ON MERGERS AMONG HOSPITALS

Introduction

Most hospital mergers and acquisitions ("mergers") do not present competitive concerns. While careful analysis may be necessary to determine the likely competitive effect of a particular hospital merger, the competitive effect of many hospital mergers is relatively easy to assess. This statement sets forth an antitrust safety zone for certain mergers in light of the Agencies' extensive experience analyzing hospital mergers. Mergers that fall within the antitrust safety zone will not be challenged by the Agencies under the antitrust laws, absent extraordinary circumstances.[1] This policy statement also briefly describes the Agencies' antitrust analysis of hospital mergers that fall outside the antitrust safety zone.

A. Antitrust Safety Zone: Mergers Of Hospitals That Will Not Be Challenged, Absent Extraordinary Circumstances, By The Agencies

The Agencies will not challenge any merger between two general acute-care hospitals where one of the hospitals (1) has an average of fewer than 100 licensed beds over the three most recent years, and (2) has an average daily inpatient census of fewer than 40 patients over the three most recent years, absent extraordinary circumstances. This antitrust safety zone will not apply if that hospital is less than 5 years old.

The Agencies recognize that in some cases a general acute care hospital with fewer than 100 licensed beds and an average daily inpatient census of fewer than 40 patients will be the only hospital in a relevant market. As such, the hospital does not compete in any significant way with other hospitals. Accordingly, mergers involving such hospitals are unlikely to reduce competition substantially.

The Agencies also recognize that many general acute care hospitals, especially rural hospitals, with fewer than 100 licensed beds and an average daily inpatient census of fewer than 40 patients are unlikely to achieve the efficiencies that larger hospitals enjoy. Some of those cost-saving efficiencies may be realized, however, through a merger with another hospital.

B. The Agencies' Analysis Of Hospital Mergers That Fall Outside The Antitrust Safety Zone

Hospital mergers that fall outside the antitrust safety zone are not necessarily anticompetitive, and may be procompetitive. The Agencies' analysis of hospital mergers follows the five steps set forth in the Department of Justice/ Federal Trade Commission 1992 Horizontal Merger Guidelines.

Applying the analytical framework of the Merger Guidelines to particular facts of specific hospital mergers, the Agencies often have concluded that an investigated hospital merger will not result in a substantial lessening of competition in situations where market concentration might otherwise raise an inference of anticompetitive effects. Such situations include transactions where the Agencies found that:

1. The Agencies are confident that conduct falling within the antitrust safety zones contained in these policy statements is very unlikely to raise competitive concerns. Accordingly, the Agencies anticipate that extraordinary circumstances warranting a challenge to such conduct will be rare.

(1) the merger would not increase the likelihood of the exercise of market power either because of the existence post-merger of strong competitors or because the merging hospitals were sufficiently differentiated;

(2) the merger would allow the hospitals to realize significant cost savings that could not otherwise be realized; or

(3) the merger would eliminate a hospital that likely would fail with its assets exiting the market.

Antitrust challenges to hospital mergers are relatively rare. Of the hundreds of hospital mergers in the United States since 1987, the Agencies have challenged only a handful, and in several cases sought relief only as to part of the transaction. Most reviews of hospital mergers conducted by the Agencies are concluded within one month.

* * *

If hospitals are considering mergers that appear to fall within the antitrust safety zone and believe they need additional certainty regarding the legality of their conduct under the antitrust laws, they can take advantage of the Department's business review procedure (28 C.F.R. § 50.6 (1992)) or the Federal Trade Commission's advisory opinion procedure (16 C.F.R. §§ 1.1–1.4 (1993)). The Agencies will respond to business review or advisory opinion requests on behalf of hospitals considering mergers that appear to fall within the antitrust safety zone within 90 days after all necessary information is submitted.

2. STATEMENT OF DEPARTMENT OF JUSTICE AND FEDERAL TRADE COMMISSION ENFORCEMENT POLICY ON HOSPITAL JOINT VENTURES INVOLVING HIGH–TECHNOLOGY OR OTHER EXPENSIVE HEALTH CARE EQUIPMENT

Introduction

Most hospital joint ventures to purchase or otherwise share the ownership cost of, operate, and market high-technology or other expensive health care equipment and related services do not create antitrust problems. In most cases, these collaborative activities create procompetitive efficiencies that benefit consumers. These efficiencies include the provision of services at a lower cost or the provision of services that would not have been provided absent the joint venture. Sound antitrust enforcement policy distinguishes those joint ventures that on balance benefit the public from those that may increase prices without providing a countervailing benefit, and seeks to prevent only those that are harmful to consumers. The Agencies have never challenged a joint venture among hospitals to purchase or otherwise share the ownership cost of, operate and market high-technology or other expensive health care equipment and related services.

This statement of enforcement policy sets forth an antitrust safety zone that describes hospital high-technology or other expensive health care equipment joint ventures that will not be challenged, absent extraordinary circumstances, by the Agencies under the antitrust laws. It then describes the Agencies' antitrust analysis of hospital high-technology or other expensive health care equipment joint ventures that fall outside the antitrust safety zone. Finally, this statement includes examples of its application to hospital high-technology or other expensive health care equipment joint ventures.

A. Antitrust Safety Zone: Hospital High–Technology Joint Ventures That Will Not Be Challenged, Absent Extraordinary Circumstances, By The Agencies

The Agencies will not challenge under the antitrust laws any joint venture among hospitals to purchase or otherwise share the ownership cost of, operate, and market the related services of, high-technology or other expensive health care equipment if the joint venture includes only the number of hospitals whose participation is needed to support the equipment, absent extraordinary circumstances.[2] This applies to joint ventures involving purchases of new equipment as well as to joint ventures involving existing equipment.[3] A joint venture that includes additional hospitals also will not be challenged if the additional hospitals could not support the equipment on their own or through the formation of a competing joint venture, absent extraordinary circumstances.

For example, if two hospitals are each unlikely to recover the cost of individually purchasing, operating, and marketing the services of a magnetic resonance imager (MRI) over its useful life, their joint venture with respect to the MRI would not be challenged by the Agencies. On the other hand, if the same two hospitals entered into a joint venture with a third hospital that independently could have purchased, operated, and marketed an MRI in a financially viable manner, the joint venture would not be in this antitrust safety zone. If, however, none of the three hospitals could have supported an MRI by itself, the Agencies would not challenge the joint venture.[4]

Information necessary to determine whether the costs of a piece of high-technology health care equipment could be recovered over its useful life is normally available to any hospital or group of hospitals considering such a purchase. This information may include the cost of the equipment, its expected useful life, the minimum number of procedures that must be done to

2. A hospital or group of hospitals will be considered able to support high-technology or other expensive health care equipment for purposes of this antitrust safety zone if it could recover the costs of owning, operating, and marketing the equipment over its useful life. If the joint venture is limited to ownership, only the ownership costs are relevant. If the joint venture is limited to owning and operating, only the owning and operating costs are relevant.

3. Consequently, the safety zone would apply in a situation in which one hospital had already purchased the health care equipment, but was not recovering the costs of the equip-

ment and sought a joint venture with one or more hospitals in order to recover the costs of the equipment.

4. The antitrust safety zone described in this statement applies only to the joint venture and agreements reasonably necessary to the venture. The safety zone does not apply to or protect agreements made by participants in a joint venture that are related to a service not provided by the venture. For example, the antitrust safety zone that would apply to the MRI joint venture would not apply to protect an agreement among the hospitals with respect to charges for an overnight stay.

meet a machine's financial breakeven point, the expected number of procedures the equipment will be used for given the population served by the joint venture and the expected price to be charged for the use of the equipment. Expected prices and costs should be confirmed by objective evidence, such as experiences in similar markets for similar technologies.

B. The Agencies' Analysis Of Hospital High–Technology Or Other Expensive Health Care Equipment Joint Ventures That Fall Outside The Antitrust Safety Zone

The Agencies recognize that joint ventures that fall outside the antitrust safety zone do not necessarily raise significant antitrust concerns. The Agencies will apply a rule of reason analysis in their antitrust review of such joint ventures.[5] The objective of this analysis is to determine whether the joint venture may reduce competition substantially, and, if it might, whether it is likely to produce procompetitive efficiencies that outweigh its anticompetitive potential. This analysis is flexible and takes into account the nature and effect of the joint venture, the characteristics of the venture and of the hospital industry generally, and the reasons for, and purposes of, the venture. It also allows for consideration of efficiencies that will result from the venture. The steps involved in a rule of reason analysis are set forth below.[6]

Step one: Define the relevant market. The rule of reason analysis first identifies what is produced through the joint venture. The relevant product and geographic markets are then properly defined. This process seeks to identify any other provider that could offer what patients or physicians generally would consider a good substitute for that provided by the joint venture. Thus, if a joint venture were to purchase and jointly operate and market the related services of an MRI, the relevant market would include all other MRIs in the area that are reasonable alternatives for the same patients, but would *not* include providers with only traditional X-ray equipment.

Step two: Evaluate the competitive effects of the venture. This step begins with an analysis of the structure of the relevant market. If many providers would compete with the joint venture, competitive harm is unlikely and the analysis would continue with step four described below.

If the structural analysis of the relevant market showed that the joint venture would eliminate an existing or potentially viable competing provider

---

5. This statement assumes that the joint venture arrangement is not one that uses the joint venture label but is likely merely to restrict competition and decrease output. For example, two hospitals that independently operate profitable MRI services could not avoid charges of price fixing by labeling as a joint venture their plan to obtain higher prices through joint marketing of their existing MRI services.

6. Many joint ventures that could provide substantial efficiencies also may present little likelihood of competitive harm. Where it is clear initially that any joint venture presents

little likelihood of competitive harm, the step-by-step analysis described in the text below will not be necessary. For example, when two hospitals propose to merge existing expensive health care equipment into a joint venture in a properly defined market in which many other hospitals or other health care facilities operate the same equipment, such that the market will be unconcentrated, then the combination is unlikely to be anticompetitive and further analysis ordinarily would not be required. *See* Department of Justice/Federal Trade Commission 1992 Horizontal Merger Guidelines.

and that there were few competing providers of that service, or that cooperation in the joint venture market may spill over into a market in which the
parties to the joint venture are competitors, it then would be necessary to
assess the extent of the potential anticompetitive effects of the joint venture.
In addition to the number and size of competing providers, factors that could
restrain the ability of the joint venture to raise prices either unilaterally or
through collusive agreements with other providers would include: (1) characteristics of the market that make anticompetitive coordination unlikely; (2)
the likelihood that other providers would enter the market; and (3) the effects
of government regulation.

The extent to which the joint venture restricts competition among the
hospitals participating in the venture is evaluated during this step. In some
cases, a joint venture to purchase or otherwise share the cost of high-
technology equipment may not substantially eliminate competition among the
hospitals in providing the related service made possible by the equipment. For
example, two hospitals might purchase a mobile MRI jointly, but operate and
market MRI services separately. In such instances, the potential impact on
competition of the joint venture would be substantially reduced.[7]

Step three: Evaluate the impact of procompetitive efficiencies. This step
requires an examination of the joint venture's potential to create procompetitive efficiencies, and the balancing of these efficiencies against any potential
anticompetitive effects. The greater the venture's likely anticompetitive effects, the greater must be the venture's likely efficiencies. In certain circumstances, efficiencies can be substantial because of the need to spread the cost
of expensive equipment over a large number of patients and the potential for
improvements in quality to occur as providers gain experience and skill from
performing a larger number of procedures.

Step four: Evaluate collateral agreements. This step examines whether
the joint venture includes collateral agreements or conditions that unreasonably restrict competition and are unlikely to contribute significantly to the
legitimate purposes of the joint venture. The Agencies will examine whether
the collateral agreements are reasonably necessary to achieve the efficiencies
sought by the joint venture. For example, if the participants in a joint venture
formed to purchase a mobile lithotripter also agreed on the daily room rate to
be charged lithotripsy patients who required overnight hospitalization, this
collateral agreement as to room rates would not be necessary to achieve the
benefits of the lithotripter joint venture. Although the joint venture itself
would be legal, the collateral agreement on hospital room rates would not be
legal and would be subject to challenge.

C. Examples Of Hospital High–Technology Joint Ventures

The following are examples of hospital joint ventures that are unlikely to
raise significant antitrust concerns. Each is intended to demonstrate an
aspect of the analysis that would be used to evaluate the venture.

---

7. If steps one and two reveal no competitive concerns with the joint venture, step three
is unnecessary, and the analysis continues with
step four described below.

1. New Equipment That Can Be Offered Only By A Joint Venture

All the hospitals in a relevant market agree that they jointly will purchase, operate and market a helicopter to provide emergency transportation for patients. The community's need for the helicopter is not great enough to justify having more than one helicopter operating in the area and studies of similarly sized communities indicate that a second helicopter service could not be supported. This joint venture falls within the antitrust safety zone. It would make available a service that would not otherwise be available, and for which duplication would be inefficient.

2. Joint Venture To Purchase Expensive Equipment

All five hospitals in a relevant market agree to jointly purchase a mobile health care device that provides a service for which consumers have no reasonable alternatives. The hospitals will share equally in the cost of maintaining the equipment, and the equipment will travel from one hospital to another and be available one day each week at each hospital. The hospitals' agreement contains no provisions for joint marketing of, and protects against exchanges of competitively sensitive information regarding, the equipment.[8] There are also no limitations on the prices that each hospital will charge for use of the equipment, on the number of procedures that each hospital can perform, or on each hospital's ability to purchase the equipment on its own. Although any combination of two of the hospitals could afford to purchase the equipment and recover their costs within the equipment's useful life, patient volume from all five hospitals is required to maximize the efficient use of the equipment and lead to significant cost savings. In addition, patient demand would be satisfied by provision of the equipment one day each week at each hospital. The joint venture would result in higher use of the equipment, thus lowering the cost per patient and potentially improving quality.

This joint venture does not fall within the antitrust safety zone because smaller groups of hospitals could afford to purchase and operate the equipment and recover their costs. Therefore, the joint venture would be analyzed under the rule of reason. The first step is to define the relevant market. In this example, the relevant market consists of the services provided by the equipment, and the five hospitals all potentially compete against each other for patients requiring this service.

The second step in the analysis is to determine the competitive effects of the joint venture. Because the joint venture is likely to reduce the number of these health care devices in the market, there is a potential restraint on competition. The restraint would not be substantial, however, for several reasons. First, the joint venture is limited to the purchase of the equipment and would not eliminate competition among the hospitals in the provision of the services. The hospitals will market the services independently, and will not exchange competitively sensitive information. In addition, the venture

8. Examples of such information include prices and marketing plans.

does not preclude a hospital from purchasing another unit should the demand for these services increase.

Because the joint venture raises some competitive concerns, however, it is necessary to examine the potential efficiencies associated with the venture. As noted above, by sharing the equipment among the five hospitals significant cost savings can be achieved. The joint venture would produce substantial efficiencies while providing access to high quality care. Thus, this joint venture would on balance benefit consumers since it would not lessen competition substantially, and it would allow the hospitals to serve the community's need in a more efficient manner. Finally, in this example the joint venture does not involve any collateral agreements that raise competitive concerns. On these facts, the joint venture would not be challenged by the Agencies.

3. Joint Venture Of Existing Expensive Equipment Where One Of The Hospitals In The Venture Already Owns The Equipment

Metropolis has three hospitals and a population of 300,000. Mercy and University Hospitals each own and operate their own magnetic resonance imaging device ("MRI"). General Hospital does not. Three independent physician clinics also own and operate MRIs. All of the existing MRIs have similar capabilities. The acquisition of an MRI is not subject to review under a certificate of need law in the state in which Metropolis is located.

Managed care plans have told General Hospital that, unless it can provide MRI services, it will be a less attractive contracting partner than the other two hospitals in town. The five existing MRIs are slightly underutilized—that is, the average cost per scan could be reduced if utilization of the machines increased. There is insufficient demand in Metropolis for six fully-utilized MRIs.

General has considered purchasing its own MRI so that it can compete on equal terms with Mercy and University Hospitals. However, it has decided based on its analysis of demand for MRI services and the cost of acquiring and operating the equipment that it would be better to share the equipment with another hospital. General proposes forming a joint venture in which it will purchase a 50 percent share in Mercy's MRI, and the two hospitals will work out an arrangement by which each hospital has equal access to the MRI. Each hospital in the joint venture will independently market and set prices for those MRI services, and the joint venture agreement protects against exchanges of competitively sensitive information among the hospitals. There is no restriction on the ability of each hospital to purchase its own equipment.

The proposed joint venture does not fall within the antitrust safety zone because General apparently could independently support the purchase and operation of its own MRI. Accordingly, the Agencies would analyze the joint venture under a rule of reason.

The first step of the rule of reason analysis is defining the relevant product and geographic markets. Assuming there are no good substitutes for MRI services, the relevant product market in this case is MRI services. Most patients currently receiving MRI services are unwilling to travel outside of Metropolis for those services, so the relevant geographic market is Metropolis. Mercy, University, and the three physician clinics are already offering MRI services in this market. Because General intends to offer MRI services within the next year, even if there is no joint venture, it is viewed as a market participant.

The second step is determining the competitive impact of the joint venture. Absent the joint venture, there would have been six independent MRIs in the market. This raises some competitive concerns with the joint venture. The fact that the joint venture will not entail joint price setting or marketing of MRI services to purchasers reduces the venture's potential anticompetitive effect. The competitive analysis would also consider the likelihood of additional entry in the market. If, for example, another physician clinic is likely to purchase an MRI in the event that the price of MRI services were to increase, any anticompetitive effect from the joint venture becomes less likely. Entry may be more likely in Metropolis than other areas because new entrants are not required to obtain certificates of need.

The third step of the analysis is assessing the likely efficiencies associated with the joint venture. The magnitude of any likely anticompetitive effects associated with the joint venture is important; the greater the venture's likely anticompetitive effects, the greater must be the venture's likely efficiencies. In this instance, the joint venture will avoid the costly duplication associated with General purchasing an MRI, and will allow Mercy to reduce the average cost of operating its MRI by increasing the number of procedures done. The competition between the Mercy/General venture and the other MRI providers in the market will provide some incentive for the joint venture to operate the MRI in as low-cost a manner as possible. Thus, there are efficiencies associated with the joint venture that could not be achieved in a less restrictive manner.

The final step of the analysis is determining whether the joint venture has any collateral agreements or conditions that reduce competition and are not reasonably necessary to achieve the efficiencies sought by the venture. For example, if the joint venture required managed care plans desiring MRI services to contract with both joint venture participants for those services, that condition would be viewed as anticompetitive and unnecessary to achieve the legitimate procompetitive goals of the joint venture. This example does not include any unnecessary collateral restraints.

On balance, when weighing the likelihood that the joint venture will significantly reduce competition for these services against its potential to result in efficiencies, the Agencies would view this joint venture favorably under a rule of reason analysis.

4. Joint Venture Of Existing Equipment Where Both Hospitals In The Venture Already Own The Equipment

Valley Town has a population of 30,000 and is located in a valley surrounded by mountains. The closest urbanized area is over 75 miles away.

166

There are two hospitals in Valley Town: Valley Medical Center and St. Mary's. Valley Medical Center offers a full range of primary and secondary services. St. Mary's offers primary and some secondary services. Although both hospitals have a CT scanner, Valley Medical Center's scanner is more sophisticated. Because of its greater sophistication, Valley Medical Center's scanner is more expensive to operate, and can conduct fewer scans in a day. A physician clinic in Valley Town operates a third CT scanner that is comparable to St. Mary's scanner and is not fully utilized.

Valley Medical Center has found that many of the scans that it conducts do not require the sophisticated features of its scanner. Because scans on its machine take so long, and so many patients require scans, Valley Medical Center also is experiencing significant scheduling problems. St. Mary's scanner, on the other hand, is underutilized, partially because many individuals go to Valley Medical Center because they need the more sophisticated scans that only Valley Medical Center's scanner can provide. Despite the underutilization of St. Mary's scanner, and the higher costs of Valley Medical Center's scanner, neither hospital has any intention of discontinuing its CT services. Valley Medical Center and St. Mary's are proposing a joint venture that would own and operate both hospitals' CT scanners. The two hospitals will then independently market and set the prices they charge for those services, and the joint venture agreement protects against exchanges of competitively sensitive information between the hospitals. There is no restriction on the ability of each hospital to purchase its own equipment.

The proposed joint venture does not qualify under the Agencies' safety zone because the participating hospitals can independently support their own equipment. Accordingly, the Agencies would analyze the joint venture under a rule of reason. The first step of the analysis is to determine the relevant product and geographic markets. As long as other diagnostic services such as conventional X-rays or MRI scans are not viewed as a good substitute for CT scans, the relevant product market is CT scans. If patients currently receiving CT scans in Valley Town would be unlikely to switch to providers offering CT scans outside of Valley Town in the event that the price of CT scans in Valley Town increased by a small but significant amount, the relevant geographic market is Valley Town. There are three participants in this relevant market: Valley Medical Center, St. Mary's, and the physician clinic.

The second step of the analysis is determining the competitive effect of the joint venture. Because the joint venture does not entail joint pricing or marketing of CT services, the joint venture does not effectively reduce the number of market participants. This reduces the venture's potential anticompetitive effect. In fact, by increasing the scope of the CT services that each hospital can provide, the joint venture may increase competition between Valley Medical Center and St. Mary's since now both hospitals can provide sophisticated scans. Competitive concerns with this joint venture would be further ameliorated if other health care providers were likely to acquire CT scanners in response to a price increase following the formation of the joint venture.

The third step is assessing whether the efficiencies associated with the joint venture outweigh any anticompetitive effect associated with the joint venture. This joint venture will allow both hospitals to make either the sophisticated CT scanner or the less sophisticated, but less costly, CT scanner available to patients at those hospitals.

Thus, the joint venture should increase quality of care by allowing for better utilization and scheduling of the equipment, while also reducing the cost of providing that care, thereby benefitting the community. The joint venture may also increase quality of care by making more capacity available to Valley Medical Center; while Valley Medical Center faced capacity constraints prior to the joint venture, it can now take advantage of St. Mary's underutilized CT scanner. The joint venture will also improve access by allowing patients requiring routine scans to be moved from the sophisticated scanner at Valley Medical Center to St. Mary's scanner where the scans can be performed more quickly.

The last step of the analysis is to determine whether there are any collateral agreements or conditions associated with the joint venture that reduce competition and are not reasonably necessary to achieve the efficiencies sought by the joint venture. Assuming there are no such agreements or conditions, the Agencies would view this joint venture favorably under a rule of reason analysis.

As noted in the previous example, excluding price setting and marketing from the scope of the joint venture reduces the probability and magnitude of any anticompetitive effect of the joint venture, and thus reduces the likelihood that the Agencies will find the joint venture to be anticompetitive. If joint price setting and marketing were, however, a part of that joint venture, the Agencies would have to determine whether the cost savings and quality improvements associated with the joint venture offset the loss of competition between the two hospitals.

Also, if neither of the hospitals in Valley Town had a CT scanner, and they proposed a similar joint venture for the purchase of two CT scanners, one sophisticated and one less sophisticated, the Agencies would be unlikely to view that joint venture as anticompetitive, even though each hospital could independently support the purchase of its own CT scanner. This conclusion would be based upon a rule of reason analysis that was virtually identical to the one described above.

* * *

Hospitals that are considering high-technology or other expensive equipment joint ventures and are unsure of the legality of their conduct under the antitrust laws can take advantage of the Department's expedited business review procedure for joint ventures and information exchanges announced on December 1, 1992 (58 Fed. Reg. 6132 (1993)) or the Federal Trade Commission's advisory opinion procedure contained at 16 C.F.R. §§ 1.1–1.4 (1993). The Agencies will respond to a business review or advisory opinion request on behalf of hospitals that are considering a high-technology joint venture within

90 days after all necessary information is submitted. The Department's December 1, 1992 announcement contains specific guidance as to the information that should be submitted.

3. STATEMENT OF DEPARTMENT OF JUSTICE AND FEDERAL TRADE COMMISSION ENFORCEMENT POLICY ON HOSPITAL JOINT VENTURES INVOLVING SPECIALIZED CLINICAL OR OTHER EXPENSIVE HEALTH CARE SERVICES

Introduction

Most hospital joint ventures to provide specialized clinical or other expensive health care services do not create antitrust problems. The Agencies have never challenged an integrated joint venture among hospitals to provide a specialized clinical or other expensive health care service.

Many hospitals wish to enter into joint ventures to offer these services because the development of these services involves investments—such as the recruitment and training of specialized personnel—that a single hospital may not be able to support. In many cases, these collaborative activities could create procompetitive efficiencies that benefit consumers, including the provision of services at a lower cost or the provision of a service that would not have been provided absent the joint venture. Sound antitrust enforcement policy distinguishes those joint ventures that on balance benefit the public from those that may increase prices without providing a countervailing benefit, and seeks to prevent only those that are harmful to consumers.

This statement of enforcement policy sets forth the Agencies' antitrust analysis of joint ventures between hospitals to provide specialized clinical or other expensive health care services and includes an example of its application to such ventures. It does not include a safety zone for such ventures since the Agencies believe that they must acquire more expertise in evaluating the cost of, demand for, and potential benefits from such joint ventures before they can articulate a meaningful safety zone. The absence of a safety zone for such collaborative activities does not imply that they create any greater antitrust risk than other types of collaborative activities.

A. The Agencies' Analysis Of Hospital Joint Ventures Involving Specialized Clinical Or Other Expensive Health Care Services

The Agencies apply a rule of reason analysis in their antitrust review of hospital joint ventures involving specialized clinical or other expensive health care services.[9] The objective of this analysis is to determine whether the joint venture may reduce competition substantially, and if it might, whether it is likely to produce procompetitive efficiencies that outweigh its anticompetitive

---

9. This statement assumes that the joint venture is not likely merely to restrict competition and decrease output. For example, if two hospitals that both profitably provide open heart surgery and a burn unit simply agree without entering into an integrated joint venture that in the future each of the services will be offered exclusively at only one of the hospitals, the agreement would be viewed as an illegal market allocation.

potential. This analysis is flexible and takes into account the nature and effect of the joint venture, the characteristics of the services involved and of the hospital industry generally, and the reasons for, and purposes of, the venture. It also allows for consideration of efficiencies that will result from the venture. The steps involved in a rule of reason analysis are set forth below.[10]

Step one: Define the relevant market. The rule of reason analysis first identifies the service that is produced through the joint venture. The relevant product and geographic markets that include the service are then properly defined. This process seeks to identify any other provider that could offer a service that patients or physicians generally would consider a good substitute for that provided by the joint venture. Thus, if a joint venture were to produce intensive care neonatology services, the relevant market would include only other neonatal intensive care nurseries that patients or physicians would view as reasonable alternatives.

Step two: Evaluate the competitive effects of the venture. This step begins with an analysis of the structure of the relevant market. If many providers compete with the joint venture, competitive harm is unlikely and the analysis would continue with step four described below.

If the structural analysis of the relevant market showed that the joint venture would eliminate an existing or potentially viable competing provider of a service and that there were few competing providers of that service, or that cooperation in the joint venture market might spill over into a market in which the parties to the joint venture are competitors, it then would be necessary to assess the extent of the potential anticompetitive effects of the joint venture. In addition to the number and size of competing providers, factors that could restrain the ability of the joint venture to act anticompetitively either unilaterally or through collusive agreements with other providers would include:

(1) characteristics of the market that make anticompetitive coordination unlikely;

(2) the likelihood that others would enter the market; and

(3) the effects of government regulation.

The extent to which the joint venture restricts competition among the hospitals participating in the venture is evaluated during this step. In some cases, a joint venture to provide a specialized clinical or other expensive health care service may not substantially limit competition. For example, if the only two hospitals providing primary and secondary acute care inpatient services in a relevant geographic market for such services were to form a joint venture to provide a tertiary service, they would continue to compete on primary and secondary services. Because the geographic market for a tertiary service may in certain cases be larger than the geographic market for primary or secondary services, the hospitals may also face substantial competition for the joint-ventured tertiary service.[11]

---

10. Many joint venturers that could provide substantial efficiencies also may present little likelihood of competitive harm. Where it is clear initially that any joint venture presents little likelihood of competitive harm, it will not be necessary to complete all steps in the analysis to conclude that the joint venture should not be challenged. See note 7, above.

11. If steps one and two reveal no competitive concerns with the joint venture, step three is unnecessary, and the analysis continues with step four described below.

Step three: Evaluate the impact of procompetitive efficiencies. This step requires an examination of the joint venture's potential to create procompetitive efficiencies, and the balancing of these efficiencies against any potential anticompetitive effects. The greater the venture's likely anticompetitive effects, the greater must be the venture's likely efficiencies. In certain circumstances, efficiencies can be substantial because of the need to spread the cost of the investment associated with the recruitment and training of personnel over a large number of patients and the potential for improvement in quality to occur as providers gain experience and skill from performing a larger number of procedures. In the case of certain specialized clinical services, such as open heart surgery, the joint venture may permit the program to generate sufficient patient volume to meet well-accepted minimum standards for assuring quality and patient safety.

Step four: Evaluate collateral agreements. This step examines whether the joint venture includes collateral agreements or conditions that unreasonably restrict competition and are unlikely to contribute significantly to the legitimate purposes of the joint venture. The Agencies will examine whether the collateral agreements are reasonably necessary to achieve the efficiencies sought by the venture. For example, if the participants in a joint venture to provide highly sophisticated oncology services were to agree on the prices to be charged for all radiology services regardless of whether the services are provided to patients undergoing oncology radiation therapy, this collateral agreement as to radiology services for non-oncology patients would be unnecessary to achieve the benefits of the sophisticated oncology joint venture. Although the joint venture itself would be legal, the collateral agreement would not be legal and would be subject to challenge.

B. Example—Hospital Joint Venture For New Specialized Clinical Service Not Involving Purchase Of High–Technology Or Other Expensive Health Care Equipment

Midvale has a population of about 75,000, and is geographically isolated in a rural part of its state. Midvale has two general acute care hospitals, Community Hospital and Religious Hospital, each of which performs a mix of basic primary, secondary, and some tertiary care services. The two hospitals have largely non-overlapping medical staffs. Neither hospital currently offers open-heart surgery services, nor has plans to do so on its own. Local residents, physicians, employers, and hospital managers all believe that Midvale has sufficient demand to support one local open-heart surgery unit.

The two hospitals in Midvale propose a joint venture whereby they will share the costs of recruiting a cardiac surgery team and establishing an open-heart surgery program, to be located at one of the hospitals. Patients will be referred to the program from both hospitals, who will share expenses and revenues of the program. The hospitals' agreement protects against exchanges of competitively sensitive information.

171

As stated above, the Agencies would analyze such a joint venture under a rule of reason. The first step of the rule of reason analysis is defining the relevant product and geographic markets. The relevant product market in this case is open-heart surgery services, because there are no reasonable alternatives for patients needing such surgery. The relevant geographic market may be limited to Midvale. Although patients now travel to distant hospitals for open-heart surgery, it is significantly more costly for patients to obtain surgery from them than from a provider located in Midvale. Physicians, patients, and purchasers believe that after the open heart surgery program is operational, most Midvale residents will choose to receive these services locally.

The second step is determining the competitive impact of the joint venture. Here, the joint venture does not eliminate any existing competition, because neither of the two hospitals previously was providing open-heart surgery. Nor does the joint venture eliminate any potential competition, because there is insufficient patient volume for more than one viable open-heart surgery program. Thus, only one such program could exist in Midvale, regardless of whether it was established unilaterally or through a joint venture.

Normally, the third step in the rule of reason analysis would be to assess the procompetitive effects of, and likely efficiencies associated with, the joint venture. In this instance, this step is unnecessary, since the analysis has concluded under step two that the joint venture will not result in any significant anticompetitive effects.

The final step of the analysis is to determine whether the joint venture has any collateral agreements or conditions that reduce competition and are not reasonably necessary to achieve the efficiencies sought by the venture. The joint venture does not appear to involve any such agreements or conditions; it does not eliminate or reduce competition between the two hospitals for any other services, or impose any conditions on use of the open-heart surgery program that would affect other competition.

Because the joint venture described above is unlikely significantly to reduce competition among hospitals for open-heart surgery services, and will in fact increase the services available to consumers, the Agencies would view this joint venture favorably under a rule of reason analysis.

* * *

Hospitals that are considering specialized clinical or other expensive health care services joint ventures and are unsure of the legality of their conduct under the antitrust laws can take advantage of the Department of Justice's expedited business review procedure announced on December 1, 1992 (58 Fed. Reg. 6132 (1993)) or the Federal Trade Commission's advisory opinion procedure contained at 16 C.F.R. §§ 1.1–1.4 (1993). The Agencies will respond to a business review or advisory opinion request on behalf of hospitals that are considering jointly providing such services within 90 days after all necessary information is submitted. The Department's December 1,

1992 announcement contains specific guidance as to the information that should be submitted.

4. STATEMENT OF DEPARTMENT OF JUSTICE AND FEDERAL TRADE COMMISSION ENFORCEMENT POLICY ON PROVIDERS' COLLECTIVE PROVISION OF NON-FEE–RELATED INFORMATION TO PURCHASERS OF HEALTH CARE SERVICES

Introduction

The collective provision of non-fee-related information by competing health care providers to a purchaser in an effort to influence the terms upon which the purchaser deals with the providers does not necessarily raise antitrust concerns. Generally, providers' collective provision of certain types of information to a purchaser is likely either to raise little risk of anticompetitive effects or to provide procompetitive benefits.

This statement sets forth an antitrust safety zone that describes providers' collective provision of non-fee-related information that will not be challenged by the Agencies under the antitrust laws, absent extraordinary circumstances.[12] It also describes conduct that is expressly excluded from the antitrust safety zone.

A. Antitrust Safety Zone: Providers' Collective Provision Of Non–Fee–Related Information That Will Not Be Challenged, Absent Extraordinary Circumstances, By The Agencies

Providers' collective provision of underlying medical data that may improve purchasers' resolution of issues relating to the mode, quality, or efficiency of treatment is unlikely to raise any significant antitrust concern and will not be challenged by the Agencies, absent extraordinary circumstances. Thus, the Agencies will not challenge, absent extraordinary circumstances, a medical society's collection of outcome data from its members about a particular procedure that they believe should be covered by a purchaser and the provision of such information to the purchaser. The Agencies also will not challenge, absent extraordinary circumstances, providers' development of suggested practice parameters—standards for patient management developed to assist providers in clinical decisionmaking—that also may provide useful information to patients, providers, and purchasers. Because providers' collective provision of such information poses little risk of restraining competition and may help in the development of protocols that increase quality and efficiency, the Agencies will not challenge such activity, absent extraordinary circumstances.

---

12. This statement addresses only providers' collective activities. As a general proposition, providers acting individually may provide any information to any purchaser without incurring liability under federal antitrust law. This statement also does not address the collective provision of information through an integrated joint venture or the exchange of information that necessarily occurs among providers involved in legitimate joint venture activities. Those activities generally do not raise antitrust concerns.

In the course of providing underlying medical data, providers may collectively engage in discussions with purchasers about the scientific merit of that data. However, the antitrust safety zone excludes any attempt by providers to coerce a purchaser's decisionmaking by implying or threatening a boycott of any plan that does not follow the providers' joint recommendation. Providers who collectively threaten to or actually refuse to deal with a purchaser because they object to the purchaser's administrative, clinical, or other terms governing the provision of services run a substantial antitrust risk. For example, providers' collective refusal to provide X-rays to a purchaser that seeks them before covering a particular treatment regimen would constitute an antitrust violation. Similarly, providers' collective attempt to force purchasers to adopt recommended practice parameters by threatening to or actually boycotting purchasers that refuse to accept their joint recommendation also would risk antitrust challenge.

* * *

Competing providers who are considering jointly providing non-fee-related information to a purchaser and are unsure of the legality of their conduct under the antitrust laws can take advantage of the Department of Justice's expedited business review procedure announced on December 1, 1992 (58 Fed. Reg. 6132 (1993)) or the Federal Trade Commission's advisory opinion procedure contained at 16 C.F.R. §§ 1.1–1.4 (1993). The Agencies will respond to a business review or advisory opinion request on behalf of providers who are considering jointly providing such information within 90 days after all necessary information is submitted. The Department's December 1, 1992 announcement contains specific guidance as to the information that should be submitted.

5. STATEMENT OF DEPARTMENT OF JUSTICE AND FEDERAL
TRADE COMMISSION ENFORCEMENT POLICY
ON PROVIDERS' COLLECTIVE PROVISION
OF FEE–RELATED INFORMATION TO
PURCHASERS OF HEALTH CARE SERVICES

Introduction

The collective provision by competing health care providers to purchasers of health care services of factual information concerning the fees charged currently or in the past for the providers' services, and other factual information concerning the amounts, levels, or methods of fees or reimbursement, does not necessarily raise antitrust concerns. With reasonable safeguards, providers' collective provision of this type of factual information to a purchaser of health care services may provide procompetitive benefits and raise little risk of anticompetitive effects.

This statement sets forth an antitrust safety zone that describes collective provision of fee-related information that will not be challenged by the Agencies under the antitrust laws, absent extraordinary circumstances.[13] It also describes types of conduct that are expressly excluded from the antitrust safety zone, some clearly unlawful, and others that may be lawful depending on the circumstances.

A. Antitrust Safety Zone: Providers' Collective Provision Of Fee–Related Information That Will Not Be Challenged, Absent Extraordinary Circumstances, By The Agencies

Providers' collective provision to purchasers of health care services of factual information concerning the providers' current or historical fees or other aspects of reimbursement, such as discounts or alternative reimbursement methods accepted (including capitation arrangements, risk-withhold fee arrangements, or use of all-inclusive fees), is unlikely to raise significant antitrust concern and will not be challenged by the Agencies, absent extraordinary circumstances. Such factual information can help purchasers efficiently develop reimbursement terms to be offered to providers and may be useful to a purchaser when provided in response to a request from the purchaser or at the initiative of providers.

In assembling information to be collectively provided to purchasers, providers need to be aware of the potential antitrust consequences of information exchanges among competitors. The principles expressed in the Agencies' statement on provider participation in exchanges of price and cost information are applicable in this context. Accordingly, in order to qualify for this safety zone, the collection of information to be provided to purchasers must satisfy the following conditions:

(1) the collection is managed by a third party (*e.g.*, a purchaser, government agency, health care consultant, academic institution, or trade association);

(2) although current fee-related information may be provided to purchasers, any information that is shared among or is available to the competing providers furnishing the data must be more than three months old; and

(3) for any information that is available to the providers furnishing data, there are at least five providers reporting data upon which each disseminated statistic is based, no individual provider's data may represent more than 25 percent on a weighted basis of that statistic, and any information disseminated must be sufficiently aggregated such that it would not allow recipients to identify the prices charged by any individual provider.

---

13. This statement addresses only providers' collective activities. As a general proposition, providers acting individually may provide any information to any purchaser without incurring liability under federal antitrust law. This statement also does not address the collective provision of information through an integrated joint venture or the exchange of information that necessarily occurs among providers involved in legitimate joint venture activities. Those activities generally do not raise antitrust concerns.

The conditions that must be met for an information exchange among providers to fall within the antitrust safety zone are intended to ensure that an exchange of price or cost data is not used by competing providers for discussion or coordination of provider prices or costs. They represent a careful balancing of a provider's individual interest in obtaining information useful in adjusting the prices it charges or the wages it pays in response to changing market conditions against the risk that the exchange of such information may permit competing providers to communicate with each other regarding a mutually acceptable level of prices for health care services or compensation for employees.

B. The Agencies' Analysis Of Providers' Collective Provision Of Fee–Related Information That Falls Outside The Antitrust Safety Zone

The safety zone set forth in this policy statement does not apply to collective negotiations between unintegrated providers and purchasers in contemplation or in furtherance of any agreement among the providers on fees or other terms or aspects of reimbursement,[14] or to any agreement among unintegrated providers to deal with purchasers only on agreed terms. Providers also may not collectively threaten, implicitly or explicitly, to engage in a boycott or similar conduct, or actually undertake such a boycott or conduct, to coerce any purchaser to accept collectively-determined fees or other terms or aspects of reimbursement. These types of conduct likely would violate the antitrust laws and, in many instances, might be per se illegal.

Also excluded from the safety zone is providers' collective provision of information or views concerning prospective fee-related matters. In some circumstances, the collective provision of this type of fee-related information also may be helpful to a purchaser and, as long as independent decisions on whether to accept a purchaser's offer are truly preserved, may not raise antitrust concerns. However, in other circumstances, the collective provision of prospective fee-related information or views may evidence or facilitate an agreement on prices or other competitively significant terms by the competing providers. It also may exert a coercive effect on the purchaser by implying or threatening a collective refusal to deal on terms other than those proposed, or amount to an implied threat to boycott any plan that does not follow the providers' collective proposal.

The Agencies recognize the need carefully to distinguish possibly procompetitive collective provision of prospective fee-related information or views from anticompetitive situations that involve unlawful price agreements, boycott threats, refusals to deal except on collectively determined terms, collective negotiations, or conduct that signals or facilitates collective price terms. Therefore, the collective provision of such prospective fee-related information or views will be assessed on a case-by-case basis. In their case-by-case

14. Whether communications between providers and purchasers will amount to negotiations depends on the nature and context of the communications, not solely the number of such communications.

analysis, the Agencies will look at all the facts and circumstances surrounding the provision of the information, including, but not limited to, the nature of the information provided, the nature and extent of the communications among the providers and between the providers and the purchaser, the rationale for providing the information, and the nature of the market in which the information is provided.

In addition, because the collective provision of prospective fee-related information and views can easily lead to or accompany unlawful collective negotiations, price agreements, or the other types of collective conduct noted above, providers need to be aware of the potential antitrust consequences of information exchanges among competitors in assembling information or views concerning prospective fee-related matters. Consequently, such protections as the use of a third party to manage the collection of information and views, and the adoption of mechanisms to assure that the information is not disseminated or used in a manner that facilitates unlawful agreements or coordinated conduct by the providers, likely would reduce antitrust concerns.

* * *

Competing providers who are considering collectively providing fee-related information to purchasers, and are unsure of the legality of their conduct under the antitrust laws, can take advantage of the Department of Justice's expedited business review procedure announced on December 1, 1992 (58 Fed. Reg. 6132 (1993)) or the Federal Trade Commission's advisory opinion procedure contained at 16 C.F.R. §§ 1.1–1.4 (1993). The Agencies will respond to a business review or advisory opinion request on behalf of providers who are considering collectively providing fee-related information within 90 days after all necessary information is submitted. The Department's December 1, 1992 announcement contains specific guidance as to the information that should be submitted.

6. STATEMENT OF DEPARTMENT OF JUSTICE AND FEDERAL TRADE COMMISSION ENFORCEMENT POLICY ON PROVIDER PARTICIPATION IN EXCHANGES OF PRICE AND COST INFORMATION

Introduction

Participation by competing providers in surveys of prices for health care services, or surveys of salaries, wages or benefits of personnel, does not necessarily raise antitrust concerns. In fact, such surveys can have significant benefits for health care consumers. Providers can use information derived from price and compensation surveys to price their services more competitively and to offer compensation that attracts highly qualified personnel. Purchasers can use price survey information to make more informed decisions when buying health care services. Without appropriate safeguards, however, information exchanges among competing providers may facilitate collusion or otherwise reduce competition on prices or compensation, resulting in increased prices, or reduced quality and availability of health care services. A collusive restriction on the compensation paid to health care employees, for example, could adversely affect the availability of health care personnel.

This statement sets forth an antitrust safety zone that describes exchanges of price and cost information among providers that will not be challenged by the Agencies under the antitrust laws, absent extraordinary circumstances. It also briefly describes the Agencies' antitrust analysis of information exchanges that fall outside the antitrust safety zone.

A. Antitrust Safety Zone: Exchanges Of Price And Cost Information Among Providers That Will Not Be Challenged, Absent Extraordinary Circumstances, By The Agencies

The Agencies will not challenge, absent extraordinary circumstances, provider participation in written surveys of (a) prices for health care services,[15] or (b) wages, salaries, or benefits of health care personnel, if the following conditions are satisfied:

(1) the survey is managed by a third-party (*e.g.*, a purchaser, government agency, health care consultant, academic institution, or trade association);

(2) the information provided by survey participants is based on data more than 3 months old; and

(3) there are at least five providers reporting data upon which each disseminated statistic is based, no individual provider's data represents more than 25 percent on a weighted basis of that statistic, and any information disseminated is sufficiently aggregated such that it would not allow recipients to identify the prices charged or compensation paid by any particular provider.

The conditions that must be met for an information exchange among providers to fall within the antitrust safety zone are intended to ensure that an exchange of price or cost data is not used by competing providers for discussion or coordination of provider prices or costs. They represent a careful balancing of a provider's individual interest in obtaining information useful in adjusting the prices it charges or the wages it pays in response to changing market conditions against the risk that the exchange of such information may permit competing providers to communicate with each other regarding a mutually acceptable level of prices for health care services or compensation for employees.

B. The Agencies' Analysis of Provider Exchanges Of Information That Fall Outside The Antitrust Safety Zone

Exchanges of price and cost information that fall outside the antitrust safety zone generally will be evaluated to determine whether the information exchange may have an anticompetitive effect that outweighs any procompeti-

---

15. The "prices" at which providers offer their services to purchasers can take many forms, including billed charges for individual services, discounts off billed charges, or per diem, capitated, or diagnosis related group rates.

tive justification for the exchange. Depending on the circumstances, public, non-provider initiated surveys may not raise competitive concerns. Such surveys could allow purchasers to have useful information that they can use for procompetitive purposes.

Exchanges of future prices for provider services or future compensation of employees are very likely to be considered anticompetitive. If an exchange among competing providers of price or cost information results in an agreement among competitors as to the prices for health care services or the wages to be paid to health care employees, that agreement will be considered unlawful per se.

* * *

Competing providers that are considering participating in a survey of price or cost information and are unsure of the legality of their conduct under the antitrust laws can take advantage of the Department's expedited business review procedure announced on December 1, 1992 (58 Fed. Reg. 6132 (1993)) or the Federal Trade Commission's advisory opinion procedure contained at 16 C.F.R. §§ 1.1–1.4 (1993). The Agencies will respond to a business review or advisory opinion request on behalf of providers who are considering participating in a survey of price or cost information within 90 days after all necessary information is submitted. The Department's December 1, 1992 announcement contains specific guidance as to the information that should be submitted.

7. STATEMENT OF DEPARTMENT OF JUSTICE AND FEDERAL TRADE COMMISSION ENFORCEMENT POLICY ON JOINT PURCHASING ARRANGEMENTS AMONG HEALTH CARE PROVIDERS

Introduction

Most joint purchasing arrangements among hospitals or other health care providers do not raise antitrust concerns. Such collaborative activities typically allow the participants to achieve efficiencies that will benefit consumers. Joint purchasing arrangements usually involve the purchase of a product or service used in providing the ultimate package of health care services or products sold by the participants. Examples include the purchase of laundry or food services by hospitals, the purchase of computer or data processing services by hospitals or other groups of providers, and the purchase of prescription drugs and other pharmaceutical products. Through such joint purchasing arrangements, the participants frequently can obtain volume discounts, reduce transaction costs, and have access to consulting advice that may not be available to each participant on its own.

Joint purchasing arrangements are unlikely to raise antitrust concerns unless (1) the arrangement accounts for so large a portion of the purchases of a product or service that it can effectively exercise market power[16] in the

16. In the case of a purchaser, this is the power to drive the price of goods or services purchased below competitive levels.

purchase of the product or service, or (2) the products or services being purchased jointly account for so large a proportion of the total cost of the services being sold by the participants that the joint purchasing arrangement may facilitate price fixing or otherwise reduce competition. If neither factor is present, the joint purchasing arrangement will not present competitive concerns.[17]

This statement sets forth an antitrust safety zone that describes joint purchasing arrangements among health care providers that will not be challenged, absent extraordinary circumstances, by the Agencies under the antitrust laws. It also describes factors that mitigate any competitive concerns with joint purchasing arrangements that fall outside the antitrust safety zone.[18]

A. Antitrust Safety Zone: Joint Purchasing Arrangements Among Health Care Providers That Will Not Be Challenged, Absent Extraordinary Circumstances, By The Agencies

The Agencies will not challenge, absent extraordinary circumstances, any joint purchasing arrangement among health care providers where two conditions are present: (1) the purchases account for less than 35 percent of the total sales of the purchased product or service in the relevant market; and (2) the cost of the products and services purchased jointly accounts for less than 20 percent of the total revenues from all products or services sold by each competing participant in the joint purchasing arrangement.

The first condition compares the purchases accounted for by a joint purchasing arrangement to the total purchases of the purchased product or service in the relevant market. Its purpose is to determine whether the joint purchasing arrangement might be able to drive down the price of the product or service being purchased below competitive levels. For example, a joint purchasing arrangement may account for all or most of the purchases of laundry services by hospitals in a particular market, but represent less than 35 percent of the purchases of all commercial laundry services in that market. Unless there are special costs that cannot be easily recovered associated with providing laundry services to hospitals, such a purchasing arrangement is not likely to force prices below competitive levels. The same principle applies to joint purchasing arrangements for food services, data processing, and many other products and services.

The second condition addresses any possibility that a joint purchasing arrangement might result in standardized costs, thus facilitating price fixing

---

17. An agreement among purchasers that simply fixes the price that each purchaser will pay or offer to pay for a product or service is not a legitimate joint purchasing arrangement and is a per se antitrust violation. Legitimate joint purchasing arrangements provide some integration of purchasing functions to achieve efficiencies.

18. This statement applies to purchasing arrangements through which the participants acquire products or services for their own use, not arrangements in which the participants are jointly investing in equipment or providing a service. Joint ventures involving investment in equipment and the provision of services are discussed in separate policy statements.

or otherwise having anticompetitive effects. This condition applies only where some or all of the participants are direct competitors. For example, if a nationwide purchasing cooperative limits its membership to one hospital in each geographic area, there is not likely to be any concern about reduction of competition among its members. Even where a purchasing arrangement's membership includes hospitals or other health care providers that compete with one another, the arrangement is not likely to facilitate collusion if the goods and services being purchased jointly account for a small fraction of the final price of the services provided by the participants. In the health care field, it may be difficult to determine the specific final service in which the jointly purchased products are used, as well as the price at which that final service is sold.[19] Therefore, the Agencies will examine whether the cost of the products or services being purchased jointly accounts, in the aggregate, for less than 20 percent of the total revenues from all health care services of each competing participant.

B. Factors Mitigating Competitive Concerns With Joint Purchasing Arrangements That Fall Outside The Antitrust Safety Zone

Joint purchasing arrangements among hospitals or other health care providers that fall outside the antitrust safety zone do not necessarily raise antitrust concerns. There are several safeguards that joint purchasing arrangements can adopt to mitigate concerns that might otherwise arise. First, antitrust concern is lessened if members are not required to use the arrangement for all their purchases of a particular product or service. Members can, however, be asked to commit to purchase a voluntarily specified amount through the arrangement so that a volume discount or other favorable contract can be negotiated. Second, where negotiations are conducted on behalf of the joint purchasing arrangement by an independent employee or agent who is not also an employee of a participant, antitrust risk is lowered. Third, the likelihood of anticompetitive communications is lessened where communications between the purchasing group and each individual participant are kept confidential, and not discussed with, or disseminated to, other participants.

These safeguards will reduce substantially, if not completely eliminate, use of the purchasing arrangement as a vehicle for discussing and coordinating the prices of health care services offered by the participants.[20] The adoption of these safeguards also will help demonstrate that the joint purchasing arrangement is intended to achieve economic efficiencies rather than to serve an anticompetitive purpose. Where there appear to be significant efficiencies from a joint purchasing arrangement, the Agencies will not challenge the arrangement absent substantial risk of anticompetitive effects.

---

19. This especially is true because some large purchasers negotiate prices with hospitals and other providers that encompass a group of services, while others pay separately for each service.

20. Obviously, if the members of a legitimate purchasing group engage in price fixing or other collusive anticompetitive conduct as to services sold by the participants, whether through the arrangement or independently, they remain subject to antitrust challenge.

The existence of a large number and variety of purchasing groups in the health care field suggests that entry barriers to forming new groups currently are not great. Thus, in most circumstances at present, it is not necessary to open a joint purchasing arrangement to all competitors in the market. However, if some competitors excluded from the arrangement are unable to compete effectively without access to the arrangement, and competition is thereby harmed, antitrust concerns will exist.

C. Example—Joint Purchasing Arrangement Involving Both Hospitals In Rural Community That The Agencies Would Not Challenge

Smalltown is the county seat of Rural County. There are two general acute care hospitals, County Hospital ("County") and Smalltown Medical Center ("SMC"), both located in Smalltown. The nearest other hospitals are located in Big City, about 100 miles from Smalltown.

County and SMC propose to join a joint venture being formed by several of the hospitals in Big City through which they will purchase various hospital supplies—such as bandages, antiseptics, surgical gowns, and masks. The joint venture will likely be the vehicle for the purchase of most such products by the Smalltown hospitals, but under the joint venture agreement, both retain the option to purchase supplies independently.

The joint venture will be an independent corporation, jointly owned by the participating hospitals. It will purchase the supplies needed by the hospitals and then resell them to the hospitals at average variable cost plus a reasonable return on capital. The joint venture will periodically solicit from each participating hospital its expected needs for various hospital supplies, and negotiate the best terms possible for the combined purchases. It will also purchase supplies for its member hospitals on an ad hoc basis.

Competitive Analysis

The first issue is whether the proposed joint purchasing arrangement would fall within the safety zone set forth in this policy statement. In order to make this determination, the Agencies would first inquire whether the joint purchases would account for less than 35 percent of the total sales of the purchased products in the relevant markets for the sales of those products. Here, the relevant hospital supply markets are likely to be national or at least regional in scope. Thus, while County and SMC might well account for more than 35 percent of the total sales of many hospital supplies in Smalltown or Rural County, they and the other hospitals in Big City that will participate in the arrangement together would likely not account for significant percentages of sales in the actual relevant markets. Thus, the first criterion for inclusion in the safety zone is likely to be satisfied.

The Agencies would then inquire whether the supplies to be purchased jointly account for less than 20 percent of the total revenues from all products and services sold by each of the competing hospitals that participate in the arrangement. In this case, County and SMC are competing hospitals, but this second criterion for inclusion in the safety zone is also likely to be satisfied, and the Agencies would not challenge the joint purchasing arrangement.

* * *

Hospitals or other health care providers that are considering joint purchasing arrangements and are unsure of the legality of their conduct under the antitrust laws can take advantage of the Department of Justice's expedited business review procedure for joint ventures and information exchanges announced on December 1, 1992 (58 Fed. Reg. 6132 (1993)) or the Federal Trade Commission's advisory opinion procedure contained at 16 C.F.R. §§ 1.1–1.4 (1993). The Agencies will respond to a business review or advisory opinion request on behalf of health care providers considering a joint purchasing arrangement within 90 days after all necessary information is submitted. The Department's December 1, 1992 announcement contains specific guidance as to the information that should be submitted.

8. STATEMENT OF DEPARTMENT OF JUSTICE AND FEDERAL TRADE COMMISSION ENFORCEMENT POLICY ON PHYSICIAN NETWORK JOINT VENTURES

Introduction

In recent years, health plans and other purchasers of health care services have developed a variety of managed care programs that seek to reduce the costs and assure the quality of health care services. Many physicians and physician groups have organized physician network joint ventures, such as individual practice associations ("IPAs"), preferred provider organizations ("PPOs"), and other arrangements to market their services to these plans.[21] Typically, such networks contract with the plans to provide physician services to plan subscribers at predetermined prices, and the physician participants in the networks agree to controls aimed at containing costs and assuring the appropriate and efficient provision of high quality physician services. By developing and implementing mechanisms that encourage physicians to collaborate in practicing efficiently as part of the network, many physician network joint ventures promise significant procompetitive benefits for consumers of health care services.

As used in this statement, a physician network joint venture is a physician-controlled venture in which the network's physician participants collectively agree on prices or price-related terms and jointly market their services.[22] Other types of health care network joint ventures are not directly

---

21. An IPA or PPO typically provides medical services to the subscribers of health plans but does not act as their insurer. In addition, an IPA or PPO does not require complete integration of the medical practices of its physician participants. Such physicians typically continue to compete fully for patients who are enrolled in health plans not served by the IPA or PPO, or who have indemnity insurance or

pay for the physician's services directly "out of pocket."

22. Although this statement refers to IPAs and PPOs as examples of physician network joint ventures, the Agencies' competitive analysis focuses on the substance of such arrangements, not on their formal titles. This policy statement applies, therefore, to all entities that addressed by this statement.[23]

This statement of enforcement policy describes the Agencies' antitrust analysis of physician network joint ventures, and presents several examples of its application to specific hypothetical physician network joint ventures. Before describing the general antitrust analysis, the statement sets forth antitrust safety zones that describe physician network joint ventures that are highly unlikely to raise substantial competitive concerns, and therefore will not be challenged by the Agencies under the antitrust laws, absent extraordinary circumstances.

The Agencies emphasize that merely because a physician network joint venture does not come within a safety zone in no way indicates that it is unlawful under the antitrust laws. On the contrary, such arrangements may be procompetitive and lawful, and many such arrangements have received favorable business review letters or advisory opinions from the Agencies.[24] The safety zones use a few factors that are relatively easy to apply, to define a category of ventures for which the Agencies presume no anticompetitive harm, without examining competitive conditions in the particular case. A determination about the lawfulness of physician network joint ventures that fall outside the safety zones must be made on a case-by-case basis according to general antitrust principles and the more specific analysis described in this statement.

A. Antitrust Safety Zones

This section describes those physician network joint ventures that will fall within the antitrust safety zones designated by the Agencies. The antitrust safety zones differ for "exclusive" and "non-exclusive" physician net-

are substantively equivalent to the physician network joint ventures described in this statement.

23. The physician network joint ventures discussed in this statement are one type of the multiprovider network joint ventures discussed below in the Agencies' Statement Of Enforcement Policy On Multiprovider Networks. That statement also covers other types of networks, such as networks that include both hospitals and physicians, and networks involving non-physician health professionals. In addition, that statement, and Example 7 of this statement, address networks that do not include agreements among competitors on prices or price-related terms, through use of various "messenger model" arrangements. Many of the issues relating to physician network joint ventures are the same as those that arise and are addressed in connection with multiprovider networks generally, and the analysis often will be very similar for all such arrangements.

24. For example, the Agencies have approved a number of non-exclusive physician or provider networks in which the percentage of participating physicians or providers in the market exceeded the 30% criterion of the safety zone. See, e.g., Letter from Anne K. Bingaman, Assistant Attorney General, Department of Justice, to John F. Fischer (Oklahoma Physicians Network, Inc.) (Jan. 17, 1996) ("substantially more" than 30% of several specialties in a number of local markets, including more than 50% in one specialty); Letter from Anne K. Bingaman to Melissa J. Fields (Dermnet, Inc.) (Dec. 5, 1995) (44% of board-certified dermatologists); Letter from Anne K. Bingaman to Dee Hartzog (International Chiropractor's Association of California) (Oct. 27, 1994) (up to 50% of chiropractors); Letter from Mark Horoschak, Assistant Director, Federal Trade Commission, to Stephen P. Nash (Eastern Ohio Physicians Organization) (Sept. 28, 1995) (safety zone's 30% criterion exceeded for primary care physicians by a small amount, and for certain subspecialty fields "to a greater extent"); Letter from Mark Horoschak to John A. Cook (Oakland Physician Network) (Mar. 28, 1995) (multispecialty network with 44% of physicians in one specialty).

work joint ventures. In an "exclusive" venture, the network's physician participants are restricted in their ability to, or do not in practice, individually contract or affiliate with other network joint ventures or health plans. In a "non-exclusive" venture, on the other hand, the physician participants in fact do, or are available to, affiliate with other networks or contract individually with health plans. This section explains how the Agencies will determine whether a physician network joint venture is exclusive or non-exclusive. It also illustrates types of arrangements that can involve the sharing of substantial financial risk among a network's physician participants, which is necessary for a network to come within the safety zones.

1. Exclusive Physician Network Joint Ventures That The Agencies Will Not Challenge, Absent Extraordinary Circumstances

The Agencies will not challenge, absent extraordinary circumstances, an exclusive physician network joint venture whose physician participants share substantial financial risk and constitute 20 percent or less of the physicians[25] in each physician specialty with active hospital staff privileges who practice in the relevant geographic market.[26] In relevant markets with fewer than five physicians in a particular specialty, an exclusive physician network joint venture otherwise qualifying for the antitrust safety zone may include one physician from that specialty, on a non-exclusive basis, even though the inclusion of that physician results in the venture consisting of more than 20 percent of the physicians in that specialty.

2. Non–Exclusive Physician Network Joint Ventures That The Agencies Will Not Challenge, Absent Extraordinary Circumstances

The Agencies will not challenge, absent extraordinary circumstances, a non-exclusive physician network joint venture whose physician participants share substantial financial risk and constitute 30 percent or less of the physicians in each physician specialty with active hospital staff privileges who practice in the relevant geographic market. In relevant markets with fewer than four physicians in a particular specialty, a non-exclusive physician network joint venture otherwise qualifying for the antitrust safety zone may include one physician from that specialty, even though the inclusion of that physician results in the venture consisting of more than 30 percent of the physicians in that specialty.

3. Indicia Of Non–Exclusivity

Because of the different market share thresholds for the safety zones for exclusive and non-exclusive physician network joint ventures, the Agencies

25. For purposes of the antitrust safety zones, in calculating the number of physicians in a relevant market and the number of physician participants in a physician network joint venture, each physician ordinarily will be counted individually, whether the physician practices in a group or solo practice.

26. Generally, relevant geographic markets for the delivery of physician services are local.

caution physician participants in a non-exclusive physician network joint venture to be sure that the network is non-exclusive in fact and not just in name. The Agencies will determine whether a physician network joint venture is exclusive or non-exclusive by its physician participants' activities, and not simply by the terms of the contractual relationship. In making that determination, the Agencies will examine the following indicia of non-exclusivity, among others:

(1) that viable competing networks or managed care plans with adequate physician participation currently exist in the market;

(2) that physicians in the network actually individually participate in, or contract with, other networks or managed care plans, or there is other evidence of their willingness and incentive to do so;

(3) that physicians in the network earn substantial revenue from other networks or through individual contracts with managed care plans;

(4) the absence of any indications of significant de-participation from other networks or managed care plans in the market; and

(5) the absence of any indications of coordination among the physicians in the network regarding price or other competitively significant terms of participation in other networks or managed care plans.

Networks also may limit or condition physician participants' freedom to contract outside the network in ways that fall short of a commitment of full exclusivity. If those provisions significantly restrict the ability or willingness of a network's physicians to join other networks or contract individually with managed care plans, the network will be considered exclusive for purposes of the safety zones.

4. Sharing Of Substantial Financial Risk By Physicians In A Physician Network Joint Venture

To qualify for either antitrust safety zone, the participants in a physician network joint venture must share substantial financial risk in providing all the services that are jointly priced through the network.[27] The safety zones are limited to networks involving substantial financial risk sharing not because such risk sharing is a desired end in itself, but because it normally is a clear and reliable indicator that a physician network involves sufficient integration by its physician participants to achieve significant efficiencies.[28]

---

27. Physician network joint ventures that involve both risk-sharing and non-risk-sharing arrangements do not fall within the safety zones. For example, a network may have both risk-sharing and non-risk-sharing contracts. It also may have contracts that involve risk sharing, but not all the physicians in the network participate in risk sharing or not all of the services are paid for on a risk-sharing basis. The Agencies will consider each of the network's arrangements separately, as well as the activities of the venture as a whole, to determine whether the joint pricing with respect to the non-risk-sharing aspects of the venture is appropriately analyzed under the rule of reason. *See infra* Example 2. The mere presence of some risk-sharing arrangements, however, will not necessarily result in rule of reason analysis of the non-risk-sharing aspects of the venture.

28. The existence of financial risk sharing does not depend on whether, under applicable state law, the network is considered an insurer.

Risk sharing provides incentives for the physicians to cooperate in controlling costs and improving quality by managing the provision of services by network physicians.

The following are examples of some types of arrangements through which participants in a physician network joint venture can share substantial financial risk:[29]

(1) agreement by the venture to provide services to a health plan at a "capitated" rate;[30]

(2) agreement by the venture to provide designated services or classes of services to a health plan for a predetermined percentage of premium or revenue from the plan;[31]

(3) use by the venture of significant financial incentives for its physician participants, as a group, to achieve specified cost-containment goals. Two methods by which the venture can accomplish this are:

(a) withholding from all physician participants in the network a substantial amount of the compensation due to them, with distribution of that amount to the physician participants based on group performance in meeting the cost-containment goals of the network as a whole; or

(b) establishing overall cost or utilization targets for the network as a whole, with the network's physician participants subject to subsequent substantial financial rewards or penalties based on group performance in meeting the targets; and

(4) agreement by the venture to provide a complex or extended course of treatment that requires the substantial coordination of care by physicians in different specialities offering a complementary mix of services, for a fixed, predetermined payment, where the costs of that course of treatment for any individual patient can vary greatly due to the individual patient's condition, the choice, complexity, or length of treatment, or other factors.[32]

---

29. Physician participants in a single network need not all be involved in the same risk-sharing arrangement within the network to fall within the safety zones. For example, primary care physicians may be capitated and specialists subject to a withhold, or groups of physicians may be in separate risk pools.

30. A "capitated" rate is a fixed, predetermined payment per covered life (the "capitation") from a health plan to the joint venture in exchange for the joint venture's (not merely an individual physician's) providing and guaranteeing provision of a defined set of covered services to covered individuals for a specified period, regardless of the amount of services actually provided.

31. This is similar to a capitation arrangement, except that the amount of payment to the network can vary in response to changes in the health plan's premiums or revenues.

32. Such arrangements are sometimes referred to as "global fees" or "all-inclusive case rates." Global fee or all-inclusive case rate arrangements that involve financial risk sharing as contemplated by this example will require that the joint venture (not merely an individual physician participant) assume the risk or benefit that the treatment provided through the network may either exceed, or cost less than, the predetermined payment.

The Agencies recognize that new types of risk-sharing arrangements may develop. The preceding examples do not foreclose consideration of other arrangements through which the participants in a physician network joint venture may share substantial financial risk in the provision of medical services through the network.[33] Organizers of physician networks who are uncertain whether their proposed arrangements constitute substantial financial risk sharing for purposes of this policy statement are encouraged to take advantage of the Agencies' expedited business review and advisory opinion procedures.

B.   The Agencies' Analysis Of Physician Network Joint Ventures That Fall Outside The Antitrust Safety Zones

Physician network joint ventures that fall outside the antitrust safety zones also may have the potential to create significant efficiencies, and do not necessarily raise substantial antitrust concerns. For example, physician network joint ventures in which the physician participants share substantial financial risk, but which involve a higher percentage of physicians in a relevant market than specified in the safety zones, may be lawful if they are not anticompetitive on balance.Likewise, physician network joint ventures that do not involve the sharing of substantial financial risk also may be lawful if the physicians' integration through the joint venture creates significant efficiencies and the venture, on balance, is not anticompetitive.[34]

The Agencies emphasize that it is not their intent to treat such networks either more strictly or more leniently than joint ventures in other industries, or to favor any particular procompetitive organization or structure of health care delivery over other forms that consumers may desire. Rather, their goal is to ensure a competitive marketplace in which consumers will have the benefit of high quality, cost-effective health care and a wide range of choices, including new provider-controlled networks that expand consumer choice and increase competition.

1.   Determining When Agreements Among Physicians In A Physician Network Joint Venture Are Analyzed Under The Rule Of Reason

Antitrust law treats naked agreements among competitors that fix prices or allocate markets as per se illegal. Where competitors economically integrate in a joint venture, however, such agreements, if reasonably necessary to accomplish the procompetitive benefits of the integration, are analyzed under

33. The manner of dividing revenues among the network's physician participants generally does not raise antitrust issues so long as the competing physicians in a network share substantial financial risk. For example, capitated networks may distribute income among their physician participants using fee-for-service payment with a partial withhold fund to cover the risk of having to provide more services than were originally anticipated.

34. See infra Examples 5 and 6. Many such physician networks have received favorable business review or advisory opinion letters from the Agencies. The percentages used in the safety zones define areas in which the lack of anticompetitive effects ordinarily will be presumed.

the rule of reason.[35] In accord with general antitrust principles, physician network joint ventures will be analyzed under the rule of reason, and will not be viewed as per se illegal, if the physicians' integration through the network is likely to produce significant efficiencies that benefit consumers, and any price agreements (or other agreements that would otherwise be per se illegal) by the network physicians are reasonably necessary to realize those efficiencies.[36]

Where the participants in a physician network joint venture have agreed to share substantial financial risk as defined in Section A.4. of this policy statement, their risk-sharing arrangement generally establishes both an overall efficiency goal for the venture and the incentives for the physicians to meet that goal. The setting of price is integral to the venture's use of such an arrangement and therefore warrants evaluation under the rule of reason.

Physician network joint ventures that do not involve the sharing of substantial financial risk may also involve sufficient integration to demonstrate that the venture is likely to produce significant efficiencies. Such integration can be evidenced by the network implementing an active and ongoing program to evaluate and modify practice patterns by the network's physician participants and create a high degree of interdependence and cooperation among the physicians to control costs and ensure quality. This program may include: (1) establishing mechanisms to monitor and control utilization of health care services that are designed to control costs and assure quality of care; (2) selectively choosing network physicians who are likely to further these efficiency objectives; and (3) the significant investment of capital, both monetary and human, in the necessary infrastructure and capability to realize the claimed efficiencies.

The foregoing are not, however, the only types of arrangements that can evidence sufficient integration to warrant rule of reason analysis, and the Agencies will consider other arrangements that also may evidence such integration. However, in all cases, the Agencies' analysis will focus on substance, rather than form, in assessing a network's likelihood of producing significant efficiencies. To the extent that agreements on prices to be charged for the integrated provision of services are reasonably necessary to the venture's achievement of efficiencies, they will be evaluated under the rule of reason.

---

35. In a network limited to providers who are not actual or potential competitors, the providers generally can agree on the prices to be charged for their services without the kinds of economic integration discussed below.

36. In some cases, the combination of the competing physicians in the network may enable them to offer what could be considered to be a new product producing substantial efficiencies, and therefore the venture will be analyzed under the rule of reason. *See Broadcast Music, Inc. v. Columbia Broadcasting System, Inc.*, 441 U.S. 1, 21–22 (1979) (competitors' integration and creation of a blanket license for use of copyrighted compositions results in efficiencies so great as to make the blanket license a "different product" from the mere combination of individual competitors and, therefore, joint pricing of the blanket license is subject to rule of reason analysis, rather than the per se rule against price fixing). The Agencies' analysis will focus on the efficiencies likely to be produced by the venture, and the relationship of any price agreements to the achievement of those efficiencies, rather than on whether the venture creates a product that can be labeled "new" or "different."

In contrast to integrated physician network joint ventures, such as these discussed above, there have been arrangements among physicians that have taken the form of networks, but which in purpose or effect were little more than efforts by their participants to prevent or impede competitive forces from operating in the market. These arrangements are not likely to produce significant procompetitive efficiencies. Such arrangements have been, and will continue to be, treated as unlawful conspiracies or cartels, whose price agreements are per se illegal.

Determining that an arrangement is merely a vehicle to fix prices or engage in naked anticompetitive conduct is a factual inquiry that must be done on a case-by-case basis to determine the arrangement's true nature and likely competitive effects. However, a variety of factors may tend to corroborate a network's anticompetitive nature, including: statements evidencing anticompetitive purpose; a recent history of anticompetitive behavior or collusion in the market, including efforts to obstruct or undermine the development of managed care; obvious anticompetitive structure of the network (*e.g.*, a network comprising a very high percentage of local area physicians, whose participation in the network is exclusive, without any plausible business or efficiency justification); the absence of any mechanisms with the potential for generating significant efficiencies or otherwise increasing competition through the network; the presence of anticompetitive collateral agreements; and the absence of mechanisms to prevent the network's operation from having anticompetitive spillover effects outside the network.

2. Applying The Rule Of Reason

A rule of reason analysis determines whether the formation and operation of the joint venture may have a substantial anticompetitive effect and, if so, whether that potential effect is outweighed by any procompetitive efficiencies resulting from the joint venture. The rule of reason analysis takes into account characteristics of the particular physician network joint venture, and the competitive environment in which it operates, that bear on the venture's likely effect on competition.

A determination about the lawfulness of a network's activity under the rule of reason sometimes can be reached without an extensive inquiry under each step of the analysis. For example, a physician network joint venture that involves substantial clinical integration may include a relatively small percentage of the physicians in the relevant markets on a non-exclusive basis. In that case, the Agencies may be able to conclude expeditiously that the network is unlikely to be anticompetitive, based on the competitive environment in which it operates. In assessing the competitive environment, the Agencies would consider such market factors as the number, types, and size of managed care plans operating in the area, the extent of physician participation in those plans, and the economic importance of the managed care plans to area physicians. *See infra* Example 1. Alternatively, for example, if a restraint that facially appears to be of a kind that would always or almost always tend to reduce output or increase prices, but has not been considered per se unlawful, is not reasonably necessary to the creation of efficiencies, the Agencies will likely challenge the restraint without an elaborate analysis of market definition and market power.[37]

The steps ordinarily involved in a rule of reason analysis of physician network joint ventures are set forth below.

Step one: Define the relevant market. The Agencies evaluate the competitive effects of a physician network joint venture in each relevant market in which it operates or has substantial impact. In defining the relevant product and geographic markets, the Agencies look to what substitutes, as a practical matter, are reasonably available to consumers for the services in question.[38] The Agencies will first identify the relevant services that the physician network joint venture provides. Although all services provided by each physician specialty might be a separate relevant service market, there may be instances in which significant overlap of services provided by different physician specialties, or in some circumstances, certain nonphysician health care providers, justifies including services from more than one physician specialty or category of providers in the same market. For each relevant service market, the relevant geographic market will include all physicians (or other providers) who are good substitutes for the physician participants in the joint venture.

Step two: Evaluate the competitive effects of the physician joint venture. The Agencies examine the structure and activities of the physician network joint venture and the nature of competition in the relevant market to determine whether the formation or operation of the venture is likely to have an anticompetitive effect. Two key areas of competitive concern are whether a physician network joint venture could raise the prices for physician services charged to health plans above competitive levels, or could prevent or impede the formation or operation of other networks or plans.

In assessing whether a particular network arrangement could raise prices or exclude competition, the Agencies will examine whether the network physicians collectively have the ability and incentive to engage in such conduct. The Agencies will consider not only the proportion of the physicians in any relevant market who are in the network, but also the incentives faced by physicians in the network, and whether different groups of physicians in a network may have significantly different incentives that would reduce the likelihood of anticompetitive conduct. The Department of Justice has entered into final judgments that permit a network to include a relatively large proportion of physicians in a relevant market where the percentage of physicians with an ownership interest in the network is strictly limited, and the network subcontracts with additional physicians under terms that create a sufficient divergence of economic interest between the subcontracting physicians and the owner physicians so that the owner physicians have an incen-

---

37. See FTC v. Indiana Federation of Dentists, 476 U.S. 447, 459–60 (1986).

38. A more extensive discussion of how the Agencies define relevant markets is contained in the Agencies' *1992 Horizontal Merger Guidelines*.

tive to control the costs to the network of the subcontracting physicians.[39] Evaluating the incentives faced by network physicians requires an examination of the facts and circumstances of each particular case. The Agencies will assess whether different groups of physicians in the network actually have significantly divergent incentives that would override any shared interest, such as the incentive to profit from higher fees for their medical services. The Agencies will also consider whether the behavior of network physicians or other market evidence indicates that the differing incentives among groups of physicians will not prevent anticompetitive conduct.

If, in the relevant market, there are many other networks or many physicians who would be available to form competing networks or to contract directly with health plans, it is unlikely that the joint venture would raise significant competitive concerns. The Agencies will analyze the availability of suitable physicians to form competing networks, including the exclusive or non-exclusive nature of the physician network joint venture.

The Agencies recognize that the competitive impact of exclusive arrangements or other limitations on the ability of a network's physician participants to contract outside the network can vary greatly. For example, in some circumstances exclusivity may help a network serve its subscribers and increase its physician participants' incentives to further the interests of the network. In other situations, however, the anticompetitive risks posed by such exclusivity may outweigh its procompetitive benefits. Accordingly, the Agencies will evaluate the actual or likely effects of particular limitations on contracting in the market situation in which they occur.

An additional area of possible anticompetitive concern involves the risk of "spillover" effects from the venture. For example, a joint venture may involve the exchange of competitively sensitive information among competing physicians and thereby become a vehicle for the network's physician participants to coordinate their activities outside the venture. Ventures that are structured to reduce the likelihood of such spillover are less likely to result in anticompetitive effects. For example, a network that uses an outside agent to collect and analyze fee data from physicians for use in developing the network's fee schedule, and avoids the sharing of such sensitive information among the network's physician participants, may reduce concerns that the information could be used by the network's physician participants to set prices for services they provide outside the network.

Step three: Evaluate the impact of procompetitive efficiencies.[40] This step requires an examination of the joint venture's likely procompetitive efficiencies, and the balancing of these efficiencies against any likely anticompetitive

---

39. *See, e.g.,* Competitive Impact Statements in *United States v. Health Choice of Northwest Missouri, Inc.,* Case No. 95–6171–CV–SJ–6 (W.D. Mo.; filed Sept. 13, 1995), 60 Fed. Reg. 51808, 51815 (Oct. 3, 1995); *United States and State of Connecticut v. HealthCare Partners, Inc.,* Case No. 395–CV–01946–RNC

(D. Conn.; filed Sept. 13, 1995), 60 Fed. Reg. 52018, 52020 (Oct. 4, 1995).

40. If steps one and two reveal no competitive concerns with the physician network joint venture, step three is unnecessary, and the analysis continues with step four, below.

effects. The greater the venture's likely anticompetitive effects, the greater must be the venture's likely efficiencies. In assessing efficiency claims, the Agencies focus on net efficiencies that will be derived from the operation of the network and that result in lower prices or higher quality to consumers. The Agencies will not accept claims of efficiencies if the parties reasonably can achieve equivalent or comparable savings through significantly less anticompetitive means. In making this assessment, however, the Agencies will not search for a theoretically least restrictive alternative that is not practical given business realities.

Experience indicates that, in general, more significant efficiencies are likely to result from a physician network joint venture's substantial financial risk sharing or substantial clinical integration. However, the Agencies will consider a broad range of possible cost savings, including improved cost controls, case management and quality assurance, economies of scale, and reduced administrative or transaction costs.

In assessing the likelihood that efficiencies will be realized, the Agencies recognize that competition is one of the strongest motivations for firms to lower prices, reduce costs, and provide higher quality. Thus, the greater the competition facing the network, the more likely it is that the network will actually realize potential efficiencies that would benefit consumers.

Step four: Evaluation of collateral agreements. This step examines whether the physician network joint venture includes collateral agreements or conditions that unreasonably restrict competition and are unlikely to contribute significantly to the legitimate purposes of the physician network joint venture. The Agencies will examine whether the collateral agreements are reasonably necessary to achieve the efficiencies sought by the joint venture. For example, if the physician participants in a physician network joint venture agree on the prices they will charge patients who are not covered by the health plans with which their network contracts, such an agreement plainly is not reasonably necessary to the success of the joint venture and is an antitrust violation.[41] Similarly, attempts by a physician network joint venture to exclude competitors or classes of competitors of the network's physician participants from the market could have anticompetitive effects, without advancing any legitimate, procompetitive goal of the network. This could happen, for example, if the network facilitated agreements among the physicians to refuse to deal with such competitors outside the network, or to pressure other market participants to refuse to deal with such competitors or deny them necessary access to key facilities.

C. Examples Of Physician Network Joint Ventures

The following are examples of how the Agencies would apply the principles set forth in this statement to specific physician network joint ventures. The first three are new examples: 1) a network involving substantial clinical

41. This analysis of collateral agreements also applies to physician network joint ventures that fall within the safety zones.

integration, that is unlikely to raise significant competitive concerns under the rule of reason; 2) a network involving both substantial financial risk-sharing and non-risk-sharing arrangements, which would be analyzed under the rule of reason; and 3) a network involving neither substantial financial risk-sharing nor substantial clinical integration, and whose price agreements likely would be challenged as per se unlawful. The last four examples involve networks that operate in a variety of market settings and with different levels of physician participants; three are networks that involve substantial financial risk-sharing and one is a network in which the physician participants do not jointly agree on, or negotiate, price.

1. Physician Network Joint Venture Involving Clinical Integration

Charlestown is a relatively isolated, medium-sized city. For the purposes of this example, the services provided by primary care physicians and those provided by the different physician specialties each constitute a relevant product market; and the relevant geographic market for each of them is Charlestown.

Several HMOs and other significant managed care plans operate in Charlestown. A substantial proportion of insured individuals are enrolled in these plans, and enrollment in managed care is expected to increase. Many physicians in each of the specialties participate in more than one of these plans. There is no significant overlap among the participants on the physician panels of many of these plans.

A group of Charlestown physicians establishes an IPA to assume greater responsibility for managing the cost and quality of care rendered to Charlestown residents who are members of health plans. They hope to reduce costs while maintaining or improving the quality of care, and thus to attract more managed care patients to their practices.

The IPA will implement systems to establish goals relating to quality and appropriate utilization of services by IPA participants, regularly evaluate both individual participants' and the network's aggregate performance with respect to those goals, and modify individual participants' actual practices, where necessary, based on those evaluations. The IPA will engage in case management, preauthorization of some services, and concurrent and retrospective review of inpatient stays. In addition, the IPA is developing practice standards and protocols to govern treatment and utilization of services, and it will actively review the care rendered by each doctor in light of these standards and protocols.

There is a significant investment of capital to purchase the information systems necessary to gather aggregate and individual data on the cost, quantity, and nature of services provided or ordered by the IPA physicians; to measure performance of the group and the individual doctors against cost and quality benchmarks; and to monitor patient satisfaction. The IPA will provide payers with detailed reports on the cost and quantity of services provided, and on the network's success in meeting its goals.

The IPA will hire a medical director and a support staff to perform the above functions and to coordinate patient care in specific cases. The doctors also have invested appreciable time in developing the practice standards and protocols, and will continue actively to monitor care provided through the IPA. Network participants who fail to adhere to the network's standards and protocols will be subject to remedial action, including the possibility of expulsion from the network.

The IPA physicians will be paid by health plans on a fee-for-service basis; the physicians will not share substantial financial risk for the cost of services rendered to covered individuals through the network. The IPA will retain an agent to develop a fee schedule, negotiate fees, and contract with payers on behalf of the venture. Information about what participating doctors charge non-network patients will not be disseminated to participants in the IPA, and the doctors will not agree on the prices they will charge patients not covered by IPA contracts.

The IPA is built around three geographically dispersed primary care group practices that together account for 25 percent of the primary care doctors in Charlestown. A number of specialists to whom the primary care doctors most often refer their patients also are invited to participate in the IPA. These specialists are selected based on their established referral relationships with the primary care doctors, the quality of care provided by the doctors, their willingness to cooperate with the goals of the IPA, and the need to provide convenient referral services to patients of the primary care doctors. Specialist services that are needed less frequently will be provided by doctors who are not IPA participants. Participating specialists constitute from 20 to 35 percent of the specialists in each relevant market, depending on the specialty. Physician participation in the IPA is non-exclusive. Many IPA participants already do and are expected to continue to participate in other managed care plans and earn substantial income from those plans.

Competitive Analysis

Although the IPA does not fall within the antitrust safety zone because the physicians do not share substantial financial risk, the Agencies would analyze the IPA under the rule of reason because it offers the potential for creating significant efficiencies and the price agreement is reasonably necessary to realize those efficiencies. Prior to contracting on behalf of competing doctors, the IPA will develop and invest in mechanisms to provide cost-effective quality care, including standards and protocols to govern treatment and utilization of services, information systems to measure and monitor individual physician and aggregate network performance, and procedures to modify physician behavior and assure adherence to network standards and protocols. The network is structured to achieve its efficiencies through a high degree of interdependence and cooperation among its physician participants. The price agreement, under these circumstances, is subordinate to and reasonably necessary to achieve these objectives.[42]

42. Although the physicians in this example have not directly agreed with one another on the prices to be charged for services rendered through the network, the venture's use

Furthermore, the Agencies would not challenge under the rule of reason the doctors' agreement to establish and operate the IPA. In conducting the rule of reason analysis, the Agencies would evaluate the likely competitive effects of the venture in each relevant market. In this case, the IPA does not appear likely to limit competition in any relevant market either by hampering the ability of health plans to contract individually with area physicians or with other physician network joint ventures, or by enabling the physicians to raise prices above competitive levels. The IPA does not appear to be overinclusive: many primary care physicians and specialists are available to other plans, and the doctors in the IPA have been selected to achieve the network's procompetitive potential. Many IPA participants also participate in other managed care plans and are expected to continue to do so in the future. Moreover, several significant managed care plans are not dependent on the IPA participants to offer their products to consumers. Finally, the venture is structured so that physician participants do not share competitively sensitive information, thus reducing the likelihood of anticompetitive spillover effects outside the network where the physicians still compete, and the venture avoids any anticompetitive collateral agreements.

Since the venture is not likely to be anticompetitive, there is no need for further detailed evaluation of the venture's potential for generating procompetitive efficiencies. For these reasons, the Agencies would not challenge the joint venture. However, they would reexamine this conclusion and do a more complete analysis of the procompetitive efficiencies if evidence of actual anticompetitive effects were to develop.

2. Physician Network Joint Venture Involving Risk–Sharing And Non–Risk–Sharing Contracts

An IPA has capitation contracts with three insurer-developed HMOs. Under its contracts with the HMOs, the IPA receives a set fee per member per month for all covered services required by enrollees in a particular health plan. Physician participants in the IPA are paid on a fee-for-service basis, pursuant to a fee schedule developed by the IPA. Physicians participate in the IPA on a non-exclusive basis. Many of the IPA's physicians participate in managed care plans outside the IPA, and earn substantial income from those plans.

The IPA uses a variety of mechanisms to assure appropriate use of services under its capitation contracts so that it can provide contract services within its capitation budgets. In part because the IPA has managed the provision of care effectively, enrollment in the HMOs has grown to the point where HMO patients are a significant share of the IPA doctors' patients.

of an agent, subject to its control, to establish fees and to negotiate and execute contracts on behalf of the venture amounts to a price agreement among competitors. However, the use of such an agent should reduce the risk of the network's activities having anticompetitive spillover effects on competition among the physicians for non-network patients.

The three insurers that offer the HMOs also offer PPO options in response to the request of employers who want to give their employees greater choice of plans. Although the capitation contracts are a substantial majority of the IPA's business, it also contracts with the insurers to provide services to the PPO programs on a fee-for-service basis. The physicians are paid /according to the same fee schedule used to pay them under the IPA's capitated contracts. The IPA uses the same panel of providers and the same utilization management mechanisms that are involved in the HMO contracts. The IPA has tracked utilization for HMO and PPO patients, which shows similar utilization patterns for both types of patients.

Competitive Analysis

Because the IPA negotiates and enters into both capitated and fee-for-service contracts on behalf of its physicians, the venture is not within a safety zone. However, the IPA's HMO contracts are analyzed under the rule of reason because they involve substantial financial risk-sharing. The PPO contracts also are analyzed under the rule of reason because there are significant efficiencies from the capitated arrangements that carry over to the fee-for-service business. The IPA's procedures for managing the provision of care under its capitation contracts and its related fee schedules produce significant efficiencies; and since those same procedures and fees are used for the PPO contracts and result in similar utilization patterns, they will likely result in significant efficiencies for the PPO arrangements as well.

3. Physician Network That Is Per Se Unlawful

A group of physicians in Clarksville forms an IPA to contract with managed care plans. There is some limited managed care presence in the area, and new plans have announced their interest in entering. The physicians agree that the only way they can effectively combat the power of the plans and protect themselves from low fees and intrusive utilization review is to organize and negotiate with the plans collectively through the IPA, rather than individually.

Membership in the IPA is open to any licensed physician in Clarksville. Members contribute $2,000 each to fund the legal fees associated with incorporating the IPA and its operating expenses, including the salary of an executive director who will negotiate contracts on behalf of the IPA. The IPA will enter only into fee-for-service contracts. The doctors will not share substantial financial risk under the contracts. The Contracting Committee, in consultation with the executive director, develops a fee schedule.

The IPA establishes a Quality Assurance and Utilization Review Committee. Upon recommendation of this committee, the members vote to have the IPA adopt two basic utilization review parameters: strict limits on documentation to be provided by physicians to the payers, and arbitration of disputes regarding plan utilization review decisions by a committee of the local medical society. The IPA refuses to contract with plans that do not accept these utilization review parameters. The IPA claims to have its own utilization review/quality assurance programs in development, but has taken very few steps to create such a program. It decides to rely instead on the hospital's established peer review mechanisms.

Although there is no formal exclusivity agreement, IPA physicians who are approached by managed care plans seeking contracts refer the plans to the IPA. Except for some contracts predating the formation of the IPA, the physicians do not contract individually with managed care plans on terms other than those set by the IPA.

Competitive Analysis

This IPA is merely a vehicle for collective decisions by its physicians on price and other significant terms of dealing. The physicians' purpose in forming the IPA is to increase their bargaining power with payers. The IPA makes no effort to selectively choose physicians who are likely to further the network's achievement of efficiencies, and the IPA involves no significant integration, financial or otherwise. IPA physicians' participation in the hospital's general peer review procedures does not evidence integration by those physicians that is likely to result in significant efficiencies in the provision of services through the IPA. The IPA does not manage the provision of care or offer any substantial potential for significant procompetitive efficiencies. The physicians are merely collectively agreeing on prices they will receive for services rendered under IPA contracts and not to accept certain aspects of utilization review that they do not like.

The physicians' contribution of capital to form the IPA does not make it a legitimate joint venture. In some circumstances, capital contributions by an IPA's participants can indicate that the participants have made a significant commitment to the creation of an efficiency-producing competitive entity in the market.[43] Capital contributions, however, can also be used to fund a cartel. The key inquiry is whether the contributed capital is being used to further the network's capability to achieve substantial efficiencies. In this case, the funds are being used primarily to support the joint negotiation, and not to achieve substantial procompetitive efficiencies. Thus, the physicians' agreement to bargain through the joint venture will be treated as per se illegal price fixing.

4. Exclusive Physician Network Joint Venture With Financial Risk–Sharing And Comprising More Than Twenty Percent Of Physicians With Active Admitting Privileges At A Hospital

County Seat is a relatively isolated, medium-sized community of about 350,000 residents. The closest town is 50 miles away. County Seat has five general acute care hospitals that offer a mix of basic primary, secondary, and tertiary care services.

---

43. *See supra* Example 1.

Five hundred physicians have medical practices based in County Seat, and all maintain active admitting privileges at one or more of County Seat's hospitals. No physician from outside County Seat has any type of admitting privileges at a County Seat hospital. The physicians represent 10 different specialties and are distributed evenly among the specialties, with 50 doctors practicing each specialty.

One hundred physicians (also distributed evenly among specialties) maintain active admitting privileges at County Seat Medical Center. County Seat's other 400 physicians maintain active admitting privileges at other County Seat hospitals.

Half of County Seat Medical Center's 100 active admitting physicians propose to form an IPA to market their services to purchasers of health care services. The physicians are divided evenly among the specialties. Under the proposed arrangement, the physicians in the network joint venture would agree to meaningful cost containment and quality goals, including utilization review, quality assurance, and other measures designed to reduce the provision of unnecessary care to the plan's subscribers, and a substantial amount (in this example 20 percent) of the compensation due to the network's physician participants would be withheld and distributed only if these measures are successfully met. This physician network joint venture would be exclusive: Its physician participants would not be free to contract individually with health plans or to join other physician joint ventures.

A number of health plans that contract selectively with hospitals and physicians already operate in County Seat. These plans and local employers agree that other County Seat physicians, and the hospitals to which they admit, are good substitutes for the active admitting physicians and the inpatient services provided at County Seat Medical Center. Physicians with medical practices based outside County Seat, however, are not good substitutes for area physicians, because such physicians would find it inconvenient to practice at County Seat hospitals due to the distance between their practice locations and County Seat.

Competitive Analysis

A key issue is whether a physician network joint venture, such as this IPA, comprising 50 percent of the physicians in each specialty with active privileges at one of five comparable hospitals in County Seat would fall within the antitrust safety zone. The physicians within the joint venture represent less than 20 percent of all the physicians in each specialty in County Seat.

County Seat is the relevant geographic market for purposes of analyzing the competitive effects of this proposed physician joint venture. Within each specialty, physicians with admitting privileges at area hospitals are good substitutes for one another. However, physicians with practices based elsewhere are not considered good substitutes.

For purposes of analyzing the effects of the venture, all of the physicians in County Seat should be considered market participants. Purchasers of health care services consider all physicians within each specialty, and the hospitals at which they have admitting privileges, to be relatively interchangeable. Thus, in this example, any attempt by the joint venture's physician participants collectively to increase the price of physician services above competitive levels would likely lead third-party purchasers to recruit non-network physicians at County Seat Medical Center or other area hospitals.

Because physician network joint venture participants constitute less than 20 percent of each group of specialists in County Seat and agree to share substantial financial risk, this proposed joint venture would fall within the antitrust safety zone.

5. Physician Network Joint Venture With Financial Risk–Sharing And A Large Percentage Of Physicians In A Relatively Small Community

Smalltown has a population of 25,000, a single hospital, and 50 physicians, most of whom are family practitioners. All of the physicians practice exclusively in Smalltown and have active admitting privileges at the Smalltown hospital. The closest urban area, Big City, is located some 35 miles away and has a population of 500,000. A little more than half of Smalltown's working adults commute to work in Big City. Some of the health plans used by employers in Big City are interested in extending their network of providers to Smalltown to provide coverage for subscribers who live in Smalltown, but commute to work in Big City (coverage is to include the families of commuting subscribers). However, the number of commuting Smalltown subscribers is a small fraction of the Big City employers' total workforce.

Responding to these employers' needs, a few health plans have asked physicians in Smalltown to organize a non-exclusive IPA large enough to provide a reasonable choice to subscribers who reside in Smalltown, but commute to work in Big City. Because of the relatively small number of potential enrollees in Smalltown, the plans prefer to contract with such a physician network joint venture, rather than engage in what may prove to be a time-consuming series of negotiations with individual Smalltown physicians to establish a panel of physician providers there.

A number of Smalltown physicians have agreed to form a physician network joint venture. The joint venture will contract with health plans to provide physician services to subscribers of the plans in exchange for a monthly capitation fee paid for each of the plans' subscribers. The physicians forming this joint venture would constitute about half of the total number of physicians in Smalltown. They would represent about 35 percent of the town's family practitioners, but higher percentages of the town's general surgeons (50 percent), pediatricians (50 percent), and obstetricians (67 percent). The health plans that serve Big City employers say that the IPA must have a large percentage of Smalltown physicians to provide adequate coverage for employees and their families in Smalltown and in a few scattered rural communities in the immediate area and to allow the doctors to provide coverage for each other.

In this example, other health plans already have entered Smalltown, and contracted with individual physicians. They have made substantial inroads with Smalltown employers, signing up a large number of enrollees. None of these plans has had any difficulty contracting with individual physicians, including many who would participate in the proposed joint venture.

Finally, the evidence indicates that Smalltown is the relevant geographic market for all physician services. Physicians in Big City are not good substitutes for a significant number of Smalltown residents.

Competitive Analysis

This proposed physician network joint venture would not fall within the antitrust safety zone because it would comprise over 30 percent of the physicians in a number of relevant specialties in the geographic market. However, the Agencies would not challenge the joint venture because a rule of reason analysis indicates that its formation would not likely hamper the ability of health plans to contract individually with area physicians or with other physician network joint ventures, or enable the physicians to raise prices above competitive levels. In addition, the joint venture's agreement to accept capitated fees creates incentives for its physicians to achieve cost savings.

That health plans have requested formation of this venture also is significant, for it suggests that the joint venture would offer additional efficiencies. In this instance, it appears to be a low-cost method for plans to enter an area without investing in costly negotiations to identify and contract with individual physicians.

Moreover, in small markets such as Smalltown, it may be necessary for purchasers of health care services to contract with a relatively large number of physicians to provide adequate coverage and choice for enrollees. For instance, if there were only three obstetricians in Smalltown, it would not be possible for a physician network joint venture offering obstetrical services to have less than 33 percent of the obstetricians in the relevant area. Furthermore, it may be impractical to have less than 67 percent in the plan, because two obstetricians may be needed in the venture to provide coverage for each other.

Although the joint venture has a relatively large percentage of some specialties, it appears unlikely to present competitive concerns under the rule of reason because of three factors:

> (1) the demonstrated ability of health plans to contract with physicians individually;

> (2) the possibility that other physician network joint ventures could be formed; and

> (3) the potential benefits from the coverage to be provided by this physician network joint venture. Therefore, the Agencies would not challenge the joint venture.

6. Physician Network Joint Venture With Financial Risk Sharing And A Large Percentage Of Physicians In A Small, Rural County

Rural County has a population of 15,000, a small primary care hospital, and ten physicians, including seven general and family practitioners, an obstetrician, a pediatrician, and a general surgeon. All of the physicians are solo practitioners. The nearest urban area is about 60 miles away in Big City, which has a population of 300,000, and three major hospitals to which patients from Rural County are referred or transferred for higher levels of hospital care. However, Big City is too far away for most residents of Rural County routinely to use its physicians for services available in Rural County.

Insurance Company, which operates throughout the state, is attempting to offer managed care programs in all areas of the state, and has asked the local physicians in Rural County to form an IPA to provide services under the program to covered persons living in the County. No other managed care plan has attempted to enter the County previously.

Initially, two of the general practitioners and two of the specialists express interest in forming a network, but Insurance Company says that it intends to market its plan to the larger local employers, who need broader geographic and specialty coverage for their employees. Consequently, Insurance Company needs more of the local general practitioners and the one remaining specialist in the IPA to provide adequate geographic, specialty, and backup coverage to subscribers in Rural County. Eventually, four of the seven general practitioners and the one remaining specialist join the IPA and agree to provide services to Insurance Company's subscribers, under contracts providing for capitation. While the physicians' participation in the IPA is structured to be non-exclusive, no other managed care plan has yet entered the local market or approached any of the physicians about joining a different provider panel. In discussing the formation of the IPA with Insurance Company, a number of the physicians have made clear their intention to continue to practice outside the IPA and have indicated they would be interested in contracting individually with other managed care plans when those plans expand into Rural County.

Competitive Analysis

This proposed physician network joint venture would not fall within the antitrust safety zone because it would comprise over 30 percent of the general practitioners in the geographic market. Under the circumstances, a rule of reason analysis indicates that the Agencies would not challenge the formation of the joint venture, for the reasons discussed below.

For purposes of this analysis, Rural County is considered the relevant geographic market. Generally, the Agencies will closely examine joint ventures that comprise a large percentage of physicians in the relevant market. However, in this case, the establishment of the IPA and its inclusion of more than half of the general practitioners and all of the specialists in the network is the result of the payer's expressed need to have more of the local physicians in its network to sell its product in the market. Thus, the level of physician participation in the network does not appear to be overinclusive, but rather appears to be the minimum necessary to meet the employers' needs.

Although the IPA has more than half of the general practitioners and all of the specialists in it, under the particular circumstances this does not, by itself, raise sufficient concerns of possible foreclosure of entry by other managed care plans, or of the collective ability to raise prices above competitive levels, to warrant antitrust challenge to the joint venture by the Agencies. Because it is the first such joint venture in the county, there is no way absolutely to verify at the outset that the joint venture in fact will be nonexclusive. However, the physicians' participation in the IPA is formally nonexclusive, and they have expressed a willingness to consider joining other managed care programs if they begin operating in the area. Moreover, the three general practitioners who are not members of the IPA are available to contract with other managed care plans. The IPA also was established with participation by the local area physicians at the request of Insurance Company, indicating that this structure was not undertaken as a means for the physicians to increase prices or prevent entry of managed care plans.

Finally, the joint venture can benefit consumers in Rural County through the creation of efficiencies. The physicians have jointly put themselves at financial risk to control the use and cost of health care services through capitation. To make the capitation arrangement financially viable, the physicians will have to control the use and cost of health care services they provide under Insurance Company's program. Through the physicians' network joint venture, Rural County residents will be offered a beneficial product, while competition among the physicians outside the network will continue.

Given these facts, the Agencies would not challenge the joint venture. If, however, it later became apparent that the physicians' participation in the joint venture in fact was exclusive, and consequently other managed care plans that wanted to enter the market and contract with some or all of the physicians at competitive terms were unable to do so, the Agencies would reexamine the joint venture's legality. The joint venture also would raise antitrust concerns if it appeared that participation by most of the local physicians in the joint venture resulted in anticompetitive effects in markets outside the joint venture, such as uniformity of fees charged by the physicians in their solo medical practices.

7. Physician Network Joint Venture With No Price Agreement And Involving All Of The Physicians In A Small, Rural County

Rural County has a population of 10,000, a small primary care hospital, and six physicians, consisting of a group practice of three family practitioners, a general practitioner, an obstetrician, and a general surgeon. The nearest urban area is about 75 miles away in Big City, which has a population of 200,000, and two major hospitals to which patients from Rural County are referred or transferred for higher levels of hospital care. Big City is too far away, however, for most residents of Rural County to use for services available in Rural County.

HealthCare, a managed care plan headquartered in another state, is thinking of marketing a plan to the larger employers in Rural County. However, it finds that the cost of contracting individually with providers, administering the system, and overseeing the quality of care in Rural County is too high on a per capita basis to allow it to convince employers to switch from indemnity plans to its plan. HealthCare believes its plan would be more successful if it offered higher quality and better access to care by opening a clinic in the northern part of the county where no physicians currently practice.

All of the local physicians approach HealthCare about contracting with their recently-formed, non-exclusive, IPA. The physicians are willing to agree through their IPA to provide services at the new clinic that HealthCare will establish in the northern part of the county and to implement the utilization review procedures that HealthCare has adopted in other parts of the state.

HealthCare wants to negotiate with the new IPA. It believes that the local physicians collectively can operate the new clinic more efficiently than it can from its distant headquarters, but HealthCare also believes that collectively negotiating with all of the physicians will result in it having to pay higher fees or capitation rates. Thus, it encourages the IPA to appoint an agent to negotiate the non-fee related aspects of the contracts and to facilitate fee negotiations with the group practice and the individual doctors. The group practice and the individual physicians each will sign and negotiate their own individual contracts regarding fees and will unilaterally determine whether to contract with HealthCare, but will agree through the IPA to provide physician, administrative, and utilization review services. The agent will facilitate these individual fee negotiations by discussing separately and confidentially with each physician the physician's fee demands and presenting the information to HealthCare. No fee information will be shared among the physicians.

Competitive Analysis

For purposes of this analysis, Rural County is considered the relevant geographic market. Generally, the Agencies are concerned with joint ventures that comprise all or a large percentage of the physicians in the relevant market. In this case, however, the joint venture appears on balance to be procompetitive. The potential for competitive harm from the venture is not great and is outweighed by the efficiencies likely to be generated by the arrangement.

The physicians are not jointly negotiating fees or engaging in other activities that would be viewed as per se antitrust violations. Therefore, the IPA would be evaluated under the rule of reason. Any possible competitive harm would be balanced against any likely efficiencies to be realized by the venture to see whether, on balance, the IPA is anticompetitive or procompetitive.

Because the IPA is non-exclusive, the potential for competitive harm from foreclosure of competition is reduced. Its physicians are free to contract with other managed care plans or individually with HealthCare if they desire. In addition, potential concerns over anticompetitive pricing are minimized because physicians will continue to negotiate prices individually. Although the physicians are jointly negotiating non-price terms of the contract, agreement on these terms appears to be necessary to the successful operation of the joint venture.

The small risk of anticompetitive harm from this venture is outweighed by the substantial procompetitive benefits of improved quality of care and access to physician services that the venture will engender. The new clinic in the northern part of the county will make it easier for residents of that area to receive the care they need. Given these facts, the Agencies would not challenge the joint venture.

* * *

Physicians who are considering forming physician network joint ventures and are unsure of the legality of their conduct under the antitrust laws can take advantage of the Department of Justice's expedited business review procedure announced on December 1, 1992 (58 Fed. Reg. 6132 (1993)) or the Federal Trade Commission's advisory opinion procedure contained at 16 C.F.R. §§ 1.1–1.4 (1993). The Agencies will respond to a business review or advisory opinion request on behalf of physicians who are considering forming a network joint venture within 90 days after all necessary information is submitted. The Department's December 1, 1992 announcement contains specific guidance about the information that should be submitted.

9. STATEMENT OF DEPARTMENT OF JUSTICE AND FEDERAL TRADE COMMISSION ENFORCEMENT POLICY ON MULTIPROVIDER NETWORKS

Introduction

The health care industry is changing rapidly as it looks for innovative ways to control costs and efficiently provide quality services. Health care providers are forming a wide range of new relationships and affiliations, including networks among otherwise competing providers, as well as networks of providers offering complementary or unrelated services.[44] These affiliations, referred to herein as multiprovider networks, can offer significant procompeti-

---

44. The multiprovider networks covered by this statement include all types and combinations of health care providers, such as networks involving just a single type of provider (e.g., dentists or hospitals) or a single provider specialty (e.g., orthodontists), as well as networks involving more than one type of provider (e.g., physician-hospital organizations or networks involving both physician and non-physician professionals). Networks containing only physicians, which are addressed in detail in the preceding enforcement policy statement, are a particular category of multiprovider network. Many of the issues relating to multiprovider networks in general are the same as those that arise, and are addressed, in connection with physician network joint ventures, and the analysis often will be very similar for all such arrangements.

tive benefits to consumers. They also can present antitrust questions, particularly if the network includes otherwise competing providers.

As used in this statement, multiprovider networks are ventures among providers that jointly market their health care services to health plans and other purchasers. Such ventures may contract to provide services to subscribers at jointly determined prices and agree to controls aimed at containing costs and assuring quality. Multiprovider networks vary greatly regarding the providers they include, the contractual relationships among those providers, and the efficiencies likely to be realized by the networks. Competitive conditions in the markets in which such networks operate also may vary greatly.

In this statement, the Agencies describe the antitrust principles that they apply in evaluating multiprovider networks, address some issues commonly raised in connection with the formation and operation of such networks, and present examples of the application of antitrust principles to hypothetical multiprovider networks. Because multiprovider networks involve a large variety of structures and relationships among many different types of health care providers, and new arrangements are continually developing, the Agencies are unable to establish a meaningful safety zone for these entities.

A. Determining When Agreements Among Providers In A Multiprovider Network Are Analyzed Under The Rule Of Reason

Antitrust law condemns as per se illegal naked agreements among competitors that fix prices or allocate markets. Where competitors economically integrate in a joint venture, however, such agreements, if reasonably necessary to accomplish the procompetitive benefits of the integration, are analyzed under the rule of reason.[45] In accord with general antitrust principles, multiprovider networks will be evaluated under the rule of reason, and will not be viewed as per se illegal, if the providers' integration through the network is likely to produce significant efficiencies that benefit consumers, and any price agreements (or other agreements that would otherwise be per se illegal) by the network providers are reasonably necessary to realize those efficiencies.[46]

In some multiprovider networks, significant efficiencies may be achieved through agreement by the competing providers to share substantial financial

---

45. In a network limited to providers who are not actual or potential competitors, the providers generally can agree on the prices to be charged for their services without the kinds of economic integration discussed below.

46. In some cases, the combination of the competing providers in the network may enable them to offer what could be considered to be a new product producing substantial efficiencies, and therefore the venture will be analyzed under the rule of reason. *See Broadcast Music, Inc. v. Columbia Broadcasting System, Inc.*, 441 U.S. 1 (1979) (competitors' integration and creation of a blanket license for use of copyrighted compositions result in efficiencies so great as to make the blanket license a "different product" from the mere combination of individual competitors and, therefore, joint pricing of the blanket license is subject to rule of reason analysis, rather than the per se rule against price fixing). The Agencies' analysis will focus on the efficiencies likely to be produced by the venture, and the relationship of any price agreements to the achievement of those efficiencies, rather than on whether the venture creates a product that can be labeled "new" or "different."

risk for the services provided through the network.[47] In such cases, the setting of price would be integral to the network's use of such an arrangement and, therefore, would warrant evaluation under the rule of reason.

The following are examples of some types of arrangements through which substantial financial risk can be shared among competitors in a multiprovider network:

(1) agreement by the venture to provide services to a health plan at a "capitated" rate;[48]

(2) agreement by the venture to provide designated services or classes of services to a health plan for a predetermined percentage of premium or revenue from the plan;[49]

(3) use by the venture of significant financial incentives for its provider participants, as a group, to achieve specified cost-containment goals. Two methods by which the venture can accomplish this are:

(a) withholding from all provider participants a substantial amount of the compensation due to them, with distribution of that amount to the participants based on group performance in meeting the cost-containment goals of the network as a whole; or

(b) establishing overall cost or utilization targets for the network as a whole, with the provider participants subject to subsequent substantial financial rewards or penalties based on group performance in meeting the targets; and

(4) agreement by the venture to provide a complex or extended course of treatment that requires the substantial coordination of care by different types of providers offering a complementary mix of services, for a fixed, predetermined payment, where the costs of that course of treatment for any individual patient can vary greatly due to the individual patient's condition, the choice, complexity, or length of treatment, or other factors.[50]

The Agencies recognize that new types of risk-sharing arrangements may develop. The preceding examples do not foreclose consideration of other arrangements through which the participants in a multiprovider network joint venture may share substantial financial risk in the provision of health

---

47. The existence of financial risk sharing does not depend on whether, under applicable state law, the network is considered an insurer.

48. A "capitated" rate is a fixed, predetermined payment per covered life (the "capitation") from a health plan to the joint venture in exchange for the joint venture's (not merely an individual provider's) furnishing and guaranteeing provision of a defined set of covered services to covered individuals for a specified period, regardless of the amount of services actually provided.

49. This is similar to a capitation arrangement, except that the amount of payment to the network can vary in response to changes in the health plan's premiums or revenues.

50. Such arrangements are sometimes referred to either as "global fees" or "all-inclusive case rates." Global fee or all-inclusive case rate arrangements that involve financial risk sharing as contemplated by this example will require that the joint venture (not merely an individual provider participant) assume the risk or benefit that the treatment provided through the network may either exceed, or cost less than, the predetermined payment.

care services or products through the network.[51] Organizers of multiprovider networks who are uncertain whether their proposed arrangements constitute substantial financial risk sharing for purposes of this policy statement are encouraged to take advantage of the Agencies' expedited business review and advisory opinion procedures.

Multiprovider networks that do not involve the sharing of substantial financial risk may also involve sufficient integration to demonstrate that the venture is likely to produce significant efficiencies. For example, as discussed in the Statement Of Enforcement Policy On Physician Network Joint Ventures, substantial clinical integration among competing physicians in a network who do not share substantial financial risk may produce efficiency benefits that justify joint pricing.[52] However, given the wide range of providers who may participate in multiprovider networks, the types of clinical integration and efficiencies available to physician network joint ventures may not be relevant to all multiprovider networks. Accordingly, the Agencies will consider the particular nature of the services provided by the network in assessing whether the network has the potential for producing efficiencies that warrant rule of reason treatment. In all cases, the Agencies' analysis will focus on substance, not form, in assessing a network's likelihood of producing significant efficiencies. To the extent that agreements on prices to be charged for the integrated provision of services promote the venture's achievement of efficiencies, they will be evaluated under the rule of reason.

A multiprovider network also might include an agreement among competitors on service allocation or specialization. The Agencies would examine the relationship between the agreement and efficiency-enhancing joint activity. If such an agreement is reasonably necessary for the network to realize significant procompetitive benefits, it similarly would be subject to rule of reason analysis.[53] For example, competing hospitals in an integrated multiprovider network might need to agree that only certain hospitals would provide certain services to network patients in order to achieve the benefits of the integration.[54] The hospitals, however, would not necessarily be permitted to agree

---

51. The manner of dividing revenues among the network's provider participants generally does not raise antitrust issues so long as the competing providers in a network share substantial financial risk. For example, capitated networks frequently distribute income among their participants using fee-for-service payment with a partial withhold fund to cover the risk of having to provide more services than were originally anticipated.

52. *See* Section B(1) of the Agencies' Statement Of Enforcement Policy On Physician Network Joint Ventures (pp. 71–74).

53. A unilateral decision to eliminate a service or specialization, however, does not generally present antitrust issues. For example, a hospital or other provider unilaterally may decide to concentrate on its more profitable services and not offer other less profitable

services, and seek to enter a network joint venture with competitors that still provides the latter services. If such a decision is made unilaterally, rather than pursuant to an express or implied agreement, the arrangement would not be considered a per se illegal market allocation.

54. Hospitals, even if they do not belong to a multiprovider network, also could agree jointly to develop and operate new services that the participants could not profitably support individually or through a less inclusive joint venture, and to decide where the jointly operated services are to be located. Such joint ventures would be analyzed by the Agencies under the rule of reason. The Statement of Enforcement Policy On Hospital Joint Ventures Involving Specialized Clinical Or Other Expensive Health Care Services offers addion what services they would provide to non-network patients.[55]

B. Applying The Rule Of Reason

A rule of reason analysis determines whether the formation and operation of the joint venture may have a substantial anticompetitive effect and, if so, whether that potential effect is outweighed by any procompetitive efficiencies resulting from the venture. The rule of reason analysis takes into account characteristics of the particular multiprovider network and the competitive environment in which it operates to determine the network's likely effect on competition.

A determination about the lawfulness of a multiprovider network's activity under the rule of reason sometimes can be reached without an extensive inquiry under each step of the analysis. For example, a multiprovider network that involves substantial integration may include a relatively small percentage of the providers in each relevant product market on a non-exclusive basis. In that case, the Agencies may be able to conclude expeditiously that the network is unlikely to be anticompetitive, based on the competitive environment in which it operates. In assessing the competitive environment, the Agencies would consider such market factors as the number, type, and size of managed care plans operating in the area, the extent of provider participation in those plans, and the economic importance of the managed care plans to area providers. Alternatively, for example, if a restraint that facially appears to be of a kind that would always or almost always tend to reduce output or increase prices, but has not been considered per se unlawful, is not reasonably necessary to the creation of efficiencies, the Agencies will likely challenge the restraint without an elaborate analysis of market definition and market power.[56]

The steps ordinarily involved in a rule of reason analysis of multiprovider networks are set forth below.

1. Market Definition

The Agencies will evaluate the competitive effects of multiprovider networks in each of the relevant markets in which they operate or have substantial impact. In defining the relevant product and geographic markets, the Agencies look to what substitutes, as a practical matter, are reasonably available to consumers for the services in question.[57]

A multiprovider network can affect markets for the provision of hospital, medical, and other health care services, and health insurance/financing mar-

---

tional guidance on joint ventures among hospitals to provide such services.

55. The Agencies' analysis would take into account that agreements among multiprovider network participants relating to the offering of services might be more likely than those relating to price to affect participants' competition outside the network, and to persist even if the network is disbanded.

56. *See FTC v. Indiana Federation of Dentists*, 476 U.S. 447, 459–60 (1986).

57. A more extensive discussion of how the Agencies define relevant markets is contained in the Agencies' *1992 Horizontal Merger Guidelines*.

kets. The possible product markets for analyzing the competitive effects of multiprovider networks likely would include both the market for such networks themselves, if there is a distinct market for such networks, and the markets for service components of the network that are, or could be, sold separately outside the network. For example, if two hospitals formed a multiprovider network with their medical and other health care professional staffs, the Agencies would consider potential competitive effects in each market affected by the network, including but not necessarily limited to the markets for inpatient hospital services, outpatient services, each physician and non-physician health care service provided by network members, and health insurance/financing markets whose participants may deal with the network and its various types of health care providers.

The relevant geographic market for each relevant product market affected by the multiprovider network will be determined through a fact-specific analysis that focuses on the location of reasonable alternatives. The relevant geographic markets may be broader for some product markets than for others.

2. Competitive Effects

In applying the rule of reason, the Agencies will examine both the potential "horizontal" and "vertical" effects of the arrangement. Agreements between or among competitors (e.g., competing hospitals or competing physicians) are considered "horizontal" under the antitrust laws. Agreements between or among parties that are not competitors (such as a hospital and a physician in a physician-hospital organization ("PHO")), may be considered "vertical" in nature.

a. Horizontal Analysis

In evaluating the possible horizontal competitive effects of multiprovider networks, the Agencies will define the relevant markets (as discussed earlier) and evaluate the network's likely overall competitive effects considering all market conditions. Determining market share and concentration in the relevant markets is often an important first step in analyzing a network's competitive effects. For example, in analyzing a PHO, the Agencies will consider the network's market share (and the market concentration) in such service components as inpatient hospital services (as measured by such indicia as number of institutions, number of hospital beds, patient census, and revenues), physician services (in individual physician specialty or other appropriate service markets),[58] and any other services provided by competing health care providers, institutional or noninstitutional, participating in the network.

If a particular multiprovider network had a substantial share of any of the relevant service markets, it could, depending on other factors, increase the price of such services above competitive levels. For example, a network that

---

58. Although all services provided by each physician specialty or category of non-physician provider might be a separate relevant service market, there may be instances in which significant overlap of services provided by different physician specialties or categories of providers justifies including services from more than one physician specialty or provider category in the same market.

included most or all of the surgeons in a relevant geographic market could create market power in the market for surgical services and thereby permit the surgeons to increase prices.

If there is only one hospital in the market, a multiprovider network, by definition, cannot reduce any existing competition among hospitals. Such a network could, however, reduce competition among other providers, for example, among physicians in the network and, thereby, reduce the ability of payers to control the costs of both physician and hospital services.[59] It also could reduce competition between the hospital and non-hospital providers of certain services, such as outpatient surgery.

Although market share and concentration are useful starting points in analyzing the competitive effects of multiprovider networks, the Agencies' ultimate conclusion is based upon a more comprehensive analysis. This will include an analysis of collateral agreements and spillover effects.[60] In addition, in assessing the likely competitive effects of a multiprovider network, the Agencies are particularly interested in the ability and willingness of health plans and other purchasers of health care services to switch between different health care providers or networks in response to a price increase, and the factors that determine the ability and willingness of plans to make such changes. The Agencies will consider not only the proportion of the providers in any relevant market who are in the network, but also the incentives faced by providers in the network, and whether different groups of providers in a network may have significantly different incentives that would reduce the likelihood of anticompetitive conduct.[61] If plans can contract at competitive terms with other networks or with individual providers, and can obtain a similar quality and range of services for their enrollees, the network is less likely to raise competitive concerns.

In examining a multiprovider network's overall competitive effect, the Agencies will examine whether the competing providers in the network have agreed among themselves to offer their services exclusively through the network or are otherwise operating, or are likely to operate, exclusively. Such exclusive arrangements are not necessarily anticompetitive.[62] Exclusive networks, however, mean that the providers in the network are not available to join other networks or contract individually with health plans, and thus, in some circumstances, exclusive networks can impede or preclude competition among networks and among individual providers. In determining whether an exclusive arrangement of this type raises antitrust concerns, the Agencies will examine the market share of the providers subject to the exclusivity arrangement; the terms of the exclusive arrangement, such as its duration and

59. By aligning itself with a large share of physicians in the market, a monopoly hospital may effectively be able to insulate itself from payer efforts to control utilization of its services and thus protect its monopoly profits.

60. *See* Statement of Enforcement Policy on Physician Network Joint Ventures.

61. *See* discussion in Statement of Enforcement Policy on Physician Network Joint Ventures, pp. 61–105.

62. For example, an exclusive arrangement may help ensure the multiprovider network's ability to serve its subscribers and increase its providers' incentives to further the interests of the network.

providers' ability and financial incentives or disincentives to withdraw from the arrangement; the number of providers that need to be included for the network and potentially competing networks to compete effectively; and the justification for the exclusivity arrangement.

Networks also may limit or condition provider participants' freedom to contract outside the network in ways that fall short of a commitment of full exclusivity. The Agencies recognize that the competitive impact of exclusive arrangements or other limitations on the ability of a network's provider participants to contract outside the network can vary greatly.

b. Vertical Analysis

In addition to the horizontal issues discussed above, multiprovider networks also can raise vertical issues. Generally, vertical concerns can arise if a network's power in one market in which it operates enables it to limit competition in another market.

Some multiprovider networks involve "vertical" exclusive arrangements that restrict the providers in one market from dealing with non-network providers that compete in a different market, or that restrict network provider participants' dealings with health plans or other purchasers. For example, a multiprovider network owned by a hospital and individually contracting with its participating physicians might limit the incentives or ability of those physicians to participate in other networks. Similarly, a hospital might use a multiprovider network to block or impede other hospitals from entering a market or from offering competing services.

In evaluating whether such exclusive arrangements raise antitrust concerns, the Agencies will examine the degree to which the arrangement may limit the ability of other networks or health plans to compete in the market. The factors the Agencies will consider include those set forth in the discussion of exclusive arrangements on pages 118–119, above.

For example, if the multiprovider network has exclusive arrangements with only a small percentage of the physicians in a relevant market, and there are enough suitable alternative physicians in the market to allow other competing networks to form, the exclusive arrangement is unlikely to raise antitrust concerns. On the other hand, a network might contract exclusively with a large percentage of physicians in a relevant market, for example general surgeons. In that case, if purchasers or payers could not form a satisfactory competing network using the remaining general surgeons in the market, and could not induce new general surgeons to enter the market, those purchasers and payers would be forced to use this network, rather than put together a panel consisting of those providers of each needed service who offer the most attractive combination of price and quality. Thus, the exclusive arrangement would be likely to restrict competition unreasonably, both among general surgeons (the horizontal effect) and among health care providers in other service markets and payers (the vertical effects).

The Agencies recognize that exclusive arrangements, whether they are horizontal or vertical, may not be explicit, so that labeling a multiprovider network as "non-exclusive" will not be determinative. In some cases, providers will refuse to contract with other networks or purchasers, even though they have not entered into an agreement specifically forbidding them from doing so. For example, if a network includes a large percentage of physicians in a certain market, those physicians may perceive that they are likely to obtain more favorable terms from plans by dealing collectively through one network, rather than as individuals.

In determining whether a network is truly non-exclusive, the Agencies will consider a number of factors, including the following:

(1) that viable competing networks or managed care plans with adequate provider participation currently exist in the market;

(2) that providers in the network actually individually participate in, or contract with, other networks or managed care plans, or there is other evidence of their willingness and incentive to do so;

(3) that providers in the network earn substantial revenue from other networks or through individual contracts with managed care plans;

(4) the absence of any indications of substantial departicipation from other networks or managed care plans in the market; and

(5) the absence of any indications of coordination among the providers in the network regarding price or other competitively significant terms of participation in other networks or managed care plans.

c. Exclusion Of Particular Providers

Most multiprovider networks will contract with some, but not all, providers in an area. Such selective contracting may be a method through which networks limit their provider panels in an effort to achieve quality and cost-containment goals, and thus enhance their ability to compete against other networks. One reason often advanced for selective contracting is to ensure that the network can direct a sufficient patient volume to its providers to justify price concessions or adherence to strict quality controls by the providers. It may also help the network create a favorable market reputation based on careful selection of high quality, cost-effective providers. In addition, selective contracting may be procompetitive by giving non-participant providers an incentive to form competing networks. A rule of reason analysis usually is applied in judging the legality of a multiprovider network's exclusion of providers or classes of providers from the network, or its policies on referring enrollees to network providers. The focus of the analysis is not on whether a particular provider has been harmed by the exclusion or referral policies, but rather whether the conduct reduces competition among providers in the market and thereby harms consumers. Where other networks offering the same types of services exist or could be formed, there are not likely to be significant competitive concerns associated with the exclusion of particular providers by particular networks. Exclusion or referral policies may present competitive concerns, however, if providers or classes of providers are unable to compete effectively without access to the network, and competition is thereby harmed. In assessing such situations, the Agencies will consider whether there are procompetitive reasons for the exclusion or referral policies.

3. Efficiencies

Finally, the Agencies will balance any potential anticompetitive effects of the multiprovider network against the potential efficiencies associated with its formation and operation. The greater the network's likely anticompetitive effects, the greater must be the network's likely efficiencies. In assessing efficiency claims, the Agencies focus on net efficiencies that will be derived from the operation of the network and that result in lower prices or higher quality to consumers. The Agencies will not accept claims of efficiencies if the parties reasonably can achieve equivalent or comparable savings through significantly less anticompetitive means. In making this assessment, however, the Agencies will not search for a theoretically least restrictive alternative that is not practical given business realities.

Experience indicates that, in general, more significant efficiencies are likely to result from a multiprovider network joint venture's substantial financial risk-sharing or substantial clinical integration. However, the Agencies will consider a broad range of possible cost savings, including improved cost controls, case management and quality assurance, economies of scale, and reduced administrative or transaction costs.

In assessing the likelihood that efficiencies will be realized, the Agencies recognize that competition is one of the strongest motivations for firms to lower prices, reduce costs, and provide higher quality. Thus, the greater the competition facing the network, the more likely the network will actually realize potential efficiencies that would benefit consumers.

4. Information Used In The Analysis

In conducting a rule of reason analysis, the Agencies rely upon a wide variety of data and information, including the information supplied by the participants in the multiprovider network, purchasers, providers, consumers, and others familiar with the market in question. The Agencies may interview purchasers of health care services, including self-insured employers and other employers that offer health benefits, and health plans (such as HMOs and PPOs), competitors of the providers in the network, and any other parties who may have relevant information for analyzing the competitive effects of the network.

The Agencies do not simply count the number of parties who support or oppose the formation of the multiprovider network. Instead, the Agencies seek information concerning the competitive dynamics in the particular community where the network is forming. For example, in defining relevant markets, the Agencies are likely to give substantial weight to information provided by purchasers or payers who have attempted to switch between providers in the face of a price increase. Similarly, an employer or payer with locations in several communities may have had experience with a network comparable to the proposed network, and thus be able to provide the Agencies with useful information about the likely effect of the proposed network, including its potential competitive benefits.

In assessing the information provided by various parties, the Agencies take into account the parties' economic incentives and interests. In addition, the Agencies attach less significance to opinions that are based on incomplete, biased, or inaccurate information, or opinions of those who, for whatever reason, may be simply indifferent to the potential for anticompetitive harm.

C. Arrangements That Do Not Involve Horizontal Agreements On Prices Or Price–Related Terms

Some networks that are not substantially integrated use a variety of "messenger model" arrangements to facilitate contracting between providers and payers and avoid price-fixing agreements among competing network providers. Arrangements that are designed simply to minimize the costs associated with the contracting process, and that do not result in a collective determination by the competing network providers on prices or price-related terms, are not per se illegal price fixing.[63]

Messenger models can be organized and operate in a variety of ways. For example, network providers may use an agent or third party to convey to purchasers information obtained individually from the providers about the prices or price-related terms that the providers are willing to accept.[64] In some cases, the agent may convey to the providers all contract offers made by purchasers, and each provider then makes an independent, unilateral decision to accept or reject the contract offers. In others, the agent may have received from individual providers some authority to accept contract offers on their behalf. The agent also may help providers understand the contracts offered, for example by providing objective or empirical information about the terms of an offer (such as a comparison of the offered terms to other contracts agreed to by network participants).

The key issue in any messenger model arrangement is whether the arrangement creates or facilitates an agreement among competitors on prices or price-related terms. Determining whether there is such an agreement is a question of fact in each case. The Agencies will examine whether the agent facilitates collective decision-making by network providers, rather than independent, unilateral, decisions.[65] In particular, the Agencies will examine whether the agent coordinates the providers' responses to a particular proposal, disseminates to network providers the views or intentions of other network

---

63. *See infra* Example 4.

64. Guidance about the antitrust standards applicable to collection and exchange of fee information can be found in the Statement of Enforcement Policy On Providers' Collective Provision Of Fee–Related Information To Purchasers Of Health Care Services, and the Statement of Enforcement Policy On Provider Participation In Exchanges Of Price And Cost Information.

65. Use of an intermediary or "independent" third party to convey collectively determined price offers to purchasers or to negotiate agreements with purchasers, or giving to individual providers an opportunity to "opt" into, or out of, such agreements does not negate the existence of an agreement.

providers as to the proposal, expresses an opinion on the terms offered, collectively negotiates for the providers, or decides whether or not to convey an offer based on the agent's judgment about the attractiveness of the prices or price-related terms. If the agent engages in such activities, the arrangement may amount to a per se illegal price-fixing agreement.

D. Examples Of Multiprovider Network Joint Ventures

The following are four examples of how the Agencies would apply the principles set forth in this statement to specific multiprovider network joint ventures, including: 1) a PHO involving substantial clinical integration, that does not raise significant competitive concerns under the rule of reason; 2) a PHO providing services on a per case basis, that would be analyzed under the rule of reason; 3) a PHO involving substantial financial risk sharing and including all the physicians in a small rural county, that does not raise competitive concerns under the rule of reason; and 4) a PHO that does not involve horizontal agreements on price.

1. PHO Involving Substantial Clinical Integration

Roxbury is a relatively isolated, medium-sized city. For the purposes of this example, the services provided by primary care physicians and those provided by the different physician specialists each constitute a relevant product market; and the relevant geographic market for each of them is Roxbury.

Several HMOs and other significant managed care plans operate in Roxbury. A substantial proportion of insured individuals are enrolled in these plans, and enrollment in managed care is expected to increase. Many physicians in each of the specialties and Roxbury's four hospitals participate in more than one of these plans. There is no significant overlap among the participants on the physician panels of many of these plans, nor among the active medical staffs of the hospitals, except in a few specialties. Most plans include only 2 or 3 of Roxbury's hospitals, and each hospital is a substitute for any other.

One of Roxbury's hospitals and the physicians on its active medical staff establish a PHO to assume greater responsibility for managing the cost and quality of care rendered to Roxbury residents who are members of health plans. They hope to reduce costs while maintaining or improving the quality of care, and thus to attract more managed care patients to the hospital and their practices.

The PHO will implement systems to establish goals relating to quality and appropriate utilization of services by PHO participants, regularly evaluate both the hospital's and each individual doctor's and the network's aggregate performance concerning those goals, and modify the hospital's and individual participants' actual practices, where necessary, based on those evaluations. The PHO will engage in case management, preadmission authorization of some services, and concurrent and retrospective review of inpatient stays. In addition, the PHO is developing practice standards and protocols to govern treatment and utilization of services, and it will actively review the care rendered by each doctor in light of these standards and protocols.

There is a significant investment of capital to purchase the information systems necessary to gather aggregate and individual data on the cost, quantity, and nature of services provided or ordered by the hospital and PHO physicians; to measure performance of the PHO, the hospital, and the individual doctors against cost and quality benchmarks; and to monitor patient satisfaction. The PHO will provide payers with detailed reports on the cost and quantity of services provided, and on the network's success in meeting its goals.

The PHO will hire a medical director and support staff to perform the above functions and to coordinate patient care in specific cases. The doctors and the hospital's administrative staff also have invested appreciable time in developing the practice standards and protocols, and will continue actively to monitor care provided through the PHO. PHO physicians who fail to adhere to the network's standards and protocols will be subject to remedial action, including the possibility of expulsion from the network.

Under PHO contracts, physicians will be paid by health plans on a fee-for-service basis; the hospital will be paid a set amount for each day a covered patient is in the hospital, and will be paid on a fee-for-service basis for other services. The physicians will not share substantial financial risk for the cost of services rendered to covered individuals through the network. The PHO will retain an agent to develop a fee schedule, negotiate fees, and contract with payers. Information about what participating doctors charge non-network patients will not be disseminated to participants of the PHO, and the doctors will not agree on the prices they will charge patients not covered by PHO contracts.

All members of the hospital's medical staff join the PHO, including its three geographically dispersed primary care group practices that together account for about 25 percent of the primary care doctors in Roxbury. These primary care doctors generally refer their patients to specialists on the hospital's active medical staff. The PHO includes all primary care doctors and specialists on the hospital's medical staff because of those established referral relationships with the primary care doctors, the admitting privileges all have at the hospital, the quality of care provided by the medical staff, their commitment to cooperate with the goals of the PHO, and the need to provide convenient referral services to patients of the primary care doctors. Participating specialists include from 20 to 35 percent of specialists in each relevant market, depending on the specialty. Hospital and physician participation in the PHO is non-exclusive. Many PHO participants, including the hospital, already do and are expected to continue to participate in other managed care plans and earn substantial income from those plans.

Competitive Analysis

The Agencies would analyze the PHO under the rule of reason because it offers the potential for creating significant efficiencies and the price agreement among the physicians is reasonably necessary to realize those efficiencies. Prior to contracting on behalf of competing physicians, the PHO will develop mechanisms to provide cost-effective, quality care, including standards and protocols to govern treatment and utilization of services, information systems to measure and monitor both the individual performance of the hospital and physicians and aggregate network performance, and procedures to modify hospital and physician behavior and assure adherence to network standards and protocols. The network is structured to achieve its efficiencies through a high degree of interdependence and cooperation among its participants. The price agreement for physician services, under these circumstances, is subordinate to and reasonably necessary to achieve these objectives.[66]

Furthermore, the Agencies would not challenge establishment and operation of the PHO under the rule of reason. In conducting the rule of reason analysis, the Agencies would evaluate the likely competitive effects of the venture in each relevant market. In this case, the PHO does not appear likely to limit competition in any relevant market either by hampering the ability of health plans to contract individually with area hospitals or physicians or with other network joint ventures, or by enabling the hospital or physicians to raise prices above competitive levels. The PHO does not appear to be overinclusive: many primary care physicians as well as specialists are available to other plans, and the doctors in the PHO have been included to achieve the network's procompetitive potential. Many PHO doctors also participate in other managed care plans and are expected to continue to do so in the future. Moreover, several significant managed care plans are not dependent on the PHO doctors to offer their products to consumers. Finally, the venture is structured so that physician participants do not share competitively sensitive information, thus reducing the likelihood of anticompetitive spillover effects outside the network where the physicians still compete, and the venture avoids any anticompetitive collateral agreements.

Since the venture is not likely to be anticompetitive, there is no need for further detailed evaluation of the venture's potential for generating procompetitive efficiencies. For these reasons, the Agencies would not challenge the joint venture. They would reexamine this conclusion, however, and do a more complete analysis of the procompetitive efficiencies if evidence of actual anticompetitive effects were to develop.

2. PHO That Provides Services On A Per Case Basis

Goodville is a large city with a number of hospitals. One of Goodville's hospitals, together with its oncologists and other relevant health care providers, establishes a joint venture to contract with health plans and other payers of health care services to provide bone marrow transplants and related cancer

---

66. Although the physicians have not directly agreed among themselves on the prices to be charged, their use of an agent subject to the control of the PHO to establish fees and to negotiate and execute contracts on behalf of the venture would amount to a price agreement among competitors. The use of such an agent, however, should reduce the risk of the PHO's activities having anticompetitive spillover effects on competition among provider participants for non-network patients.

care for certain types of cancers based on an all inclusive per case payment. Under these contracts, the venture will receive a single payment for all hospital, physician, and ancillary services rendered to covered patients requiring bone marrow transplants. The venture will be responsible for paying for and coordinating the various forms of care provided. At first, it will pay its providers using a fee schedule with a withhold to cover unanticipated losses on the case rate. Based on its operational experience, the venture intends to explore other payment methodologies that may most effectively provide the venture's providers with financial incentives to allocate resources efficiently in their treatment of patients.

Competitive Analysis

The joint venture is a multiprovider network in which competitors share substantial financial risk, and the price agreement among members of the venture will be analyzed under the rule of reason. The per case payment arrangement involves the sharing of substantial financial risk because the venture will receive a single, predetermined payment for a course of treatment that requires the substantial coordination of care by different types of providers and can vary significantly in cost and complexity from patient to patient. The venture will pay its provider participants in a way that gives them incentives to allocate resources efficiently, and that spreads among the participants the risk of loss and the possibility of gain on any particular case. The venture adds to the market another contracting option for health plans and other payers that is likely to result in cost savings because of its use of a per case payment method. Establishment of the case rate is an integral part of the risk sharing arrangement.

3. PHO With All The Physicians In A Small, Rural County

Frederick County has a population of 15,000, and a 50–bed hospital that offers primary and some secondary services. There are 12 physicians on the active medical staff of the hospital (six general and family practitioners, one internist, two pediatricians, one otolaryngologist, and two general surgeons) as well as a part-time pathologist, anesthesiologist, and radiologist. Outside of Frederick County, the nearest hospitals are in Big City, 25 miles away. Most Frederick County residents receive basic physician and hospital care in Frederick County, and are referred or transferred to the Big City physician specialists and hospitals for higher levels of care.

No managed care plans currently operate in Frederick County. Nor are there any large employers who selectively contract with Frederick County physicians. Increasingly, Frederick County residents who work for employers in Big City are covered under managed care contracts that direct Frederick County residents to hospitals and to numerous primary care and specialty physicians in Big City. Providers in Frederick County who are losing patients to hospitals and doctors in Big City want to contract with payers and employers so that they can retain these patients. However, the Frederick County hospital and doctors have been unsuccessful in their efforts to obtain contracts individually; too few potential enrollees are involved to justify payers' undertaking the expense and effort of individually contracting with Frederick County providers and administering a utilization review and quality assurance program for a provider network in Frederick County.

The hospital and all the physicians in Frederick County want to establish a PHO to contract with managed care plans and employers operating in Big City. Managed care plans have expressed interest in contracting with all Frederick County physicians under a single risk-sharing contract. The PHO also will offer its network to employers operating in Frederick County.

The PHO will market the services of the hospital on a per diem basis, and physician services on the basis of a fee schedule that is significantly discounted from the doctors' current charges. The PHO will be eligible for a bonus of up to 20 percent of the total payments made to it, depending on the PHO's success in meeting utilization targets agreed to with the payers. An employee of the hospital will develop a fee schedule, negotiate fees, and contract with payers on behalf of the PHO. Information about what participating doctors charge non-PHO patients will not be disseminated to the doctors, and they will not agree on the prices they will charge patients not covered by PHO contracts.

Physicians' participation in the PHO is structured to be non-exclusive. Because no other managed care plans operate in the area, PHO physicians do not now participate in other plans and have not been approached by other plans. The PHO physicians have made clear their intention to continue to practice outside the PHO and to be available to contract individually with any other managed care plans that expand into Frederick County.

Competitive Analysis

The agreement of the physicians on the prices they will charge through the PHO would be analyzed under the rule of reason, because they share substantial financial risk through the use of a pricing arrangement that provides significant financial incentives for the physicians, as a group, to achieve specified cost-containment goals. The venture thus has the potential for creating significant efficiencies, and the setting of price promotes the venture's use of the risk-sharing arrangement.

The Agencies would not challenge formation and operation of the PHO under the rule of reason. Under the rule of reason analysis, the Agencies would evaluate the likely competitive effects of the venture. The venture does not appear likely to limit competition in any relevant market. Managed care plans' current practice of directing patients from Frederick County to Big City suggests that the physicians in the PHO face significant competition from providers and managed care plans that operate in Big City. Moreover, the absence of managed care contracting in Frederick County, either now or in the foreseeable future, indicates that the network is not likely to reduce any actual or likely competition for patients who do not travel to Big City for care.

While the venture involves all of the doctors in Frederick County, this was necessary to respond to competition from Big City providers. It is not possible to verify at the outset that the venture will in fact be non-exclusive, but the physicians' participation in the venture is structured to be non-exclusive, and the doctors have expressed a willingness to consider joining other managed care plans if they begin operating in the area.

For these reasons, the Agencies would not challenge the joint venture. However, if it later became apparent that the physicians' participation in the PHO was exclusive in fact, and consequently managed care plans or employers that wanted to contract with some or all of the physicians at competitive terms were unable to do so, or that the PHO doctors entered into collateral agreements that restrained competition for services furnished outside the PHO, the Agencies likely would challenge the joint venture.

4. PHO That Does Not Involve Horizontal Agreements On Price

A hospital and doctors and other health care providers on its medical staff have established a PHO to market their services to payers, including employers with self-funded health benefits plans. The PHO contracts on a fee-for-service basis. The physicians and other health care providers who are participants in the PHO do not share substantial financial risk or otherwise integrate their services so as to provide significant efficiencies. The payers prefer to continue to use their existing third-party administrators for contract administration and utilization management, or to do it in-house.

There is no agreement among the PHO's participants to deal only through the PHO, and many of them participate in other networks and HMOs on a variety of terms. Some payers have chosen to contract with the hospital and some or all of the PHO physicians and other providers without going through the PHO, and a significant proportion of the PHO's participants contract with payers in this manner.

In an effort to avoid horizontal price agreements among competing participants in the PHO while facilitating the contracting process, the PHO considers using the following mechanisms:

A. An agent of the PHO, not otherwise affiliated with any PHO participant, will obtain from each participant a fee schedule or conversion factor that represents the minimum payment that participant will accept from a payer. The agent is authorized to contract on the participants' behalf with payers offering prices at this level or better. The agent does not negotiate pricing terms with the payer and does not share pricing information among competing participants. Price offers that do not meet the authorized fee are conveyed to the individual participant.

B. The same as option A, with the added feature that the agent is authorized, for a specified time, to bind the participant to any contract offers with prices equal, to or better than, those in a contract that the participant has already approved.

C. The same as option A, except that in order to assist payers in developing contract offers, the agent takes the fee authorizations of the various participants and develops a schedule that can be presented to a payer showing the percentages of participants in the network who have authorized contracts at various price levels.

D. The venture hires an agent to negotiate prices with payers on behalf of the PHO's participants. The agent does not disclose to the payer the prices the participants are willing to accept, as in option C, but attempts to obtain the best possible prices for all the participants. The resulting contract offer then is relayed to each participant for acceptance or rejection.

Competitive Analysis

In the circumstances described in options A through D, the Agencies would determine whether there was a horizontal agreement on price or any other competitively significant terms among PHO participants. The Agencies would determine whether such agreements were subject to the per se rule or the rule of reason, and evaluate them accordingly.

The existence of an agreement is a factual question. The PHO's use of options A through C does not establish the existence of a horizontal price agreement. Nor is there sharing of price information or other evidence of explicit or implicit agreements among network participants on price. The agent does not inform PHO participants about others' acceptance or rejection of contract offers; there is no agreement or understanding that PHO participants will only contract through the PHO; and participants deal outside the network on competitive terms.

The PHO's use of option D amounts to a per se unlawful price agreement. The participants' joint negotiation through a common agent confronts the payer with the combined bargaining power of the PHO participants, even though they ultimately have to agree individually to the contract negotiated on their behalf.

* * *

Persons who are considering forming multiprovider networks and are unsure of the legality of their conduct under the antitrust laws can take advantage of the Department of Justice's expedited business review procedure for joint ventures and information exchange programs announced on December 1, 1992 (58 Fed. Reg. 6132 (1993)) or the Federal Trade Commission's advisory opinion procedure contained at 16 C.F.R. §§ 1.1–1.4 (1993). The Agencies will respond to a business review or advisory opinion request on behalf of parties considering the formation of a multiprovider network within 120 days after all necessary information is submitted. The Department's December 1, 1992 announcement contains guidance as to information that should be submitted.

III. TAX EXEMPT ORGANIZATIONS

A. FEDERAL TAX EXEMPTION: 26 U.S.C.A. § 501 et seq.

§ 501. Exemption from tax on corporations, certain trusts, etc.

(a) Exemption from taxation.—An organization described in subsection (c) or (d) or section 401(a) shall be exempt from taxation under this subtitle unless such exemption is denied under section 502 or 503.

(b) Tax on unrelated business income and certain other activities.—An organization exempt from taxation under subsection (a) shall be subject to tax to the extent provided in parts II, III, and VI of this subchapter, but (notwithstanding parts II, III, and VI of this subchapter) shall be considered an organization exempt from income taxes for the purpose of any law which refers to organizations exempt from income taxes.

(c) List of exempt organizations.—The following organizations are referred to in subsection (a):

(1) Any corporation organized under Act of Congress which is an instrumentality of the United States but only if such corporation—

(A) is exempt from Federal income taxes—

(i) under such Act as amended and supplemented before July 18, 1984, or

(ii) under this title without regard to any provision of law which is not contained in this title and which is not contained in a revenue Act, or

(B) is described in subsection (l).

(2) Corporations organized for the exclusive purpose of holding title to property, collecting income therefrom, and turning over the entire amount thereof, less expenses, to an organization which itself is exempt under this section. Rules similar to the rules of subparagraph (G) of paragraph (25) shall apply for purposes of this paragraph.

(3) Corporations, and any community chest, fund, or foundation, organized and operated exclusively for religious, charitable, scientific, testing for public safety, literary, or educational purposes, or to foster national or international amateur sports competition (but only if no part of its activities involve the provision of athletic facilities or equipment), or for the prevention of cruelty to children or animals, no part of the net earnings of which inures to the benefit of any private shareholder or individual, no substantial part of the activities of which is carrying on propaganda, or otherwise attempting, to influence legislation (except as

223

otherwise provided in subsection (h)), and which does not participate in, or intervene in (including the publishing or distributing of statements), any political campaign on behalf of (or in opposition to) any candidate for public office.

(4)(A) Civic leagues or organizations not organized for profit but operated exclusively for the promotion of social welfare, or local associations of employees, the membership of which is limited to the employees of a designated person or persons in a particular municipality, and the net earnings of which are devoted exclusively to charitable, educational, or recreational purposes.

(B) Subparagraph (A) shall not apply to an entity unless no part of the net earnings of such entity inures to the benefit of any private shareholder or individual.

(e) Cooperative hospital service organizations.—For purposes of this title, an organization shall be treated as an organization organized and operated exclusively for charitable purposes, if—

(1) such organization is organized and operated solely—

(A) to perform, on a centralized basis, one or more of the following services which, if performed on its own behalf by a hospital which is an organization described in subsection (c)(3) and exempt from taxation under subsection (a), would constitute activities in exercising or performing the purpose or function constituting the basis for its exemption: data processing, purchasing (including the purchasing of insurance on a group basis), warehousing, billing and collection (including the purchase of patron accounts receivable on a recourse basis), food, clinical, industrial engineering, laboratory, printing, communications, record center, and personnel (including selection, testing, training, and education of personnel) services; and

(B) to perform such services solely for two or more hospitals each of which is—

(i) an organization described in subsection (c)(3) which is exempt from taxation under subsection (a),

(ii) a constituent part of an organization described in subsection (c)(3) which is exempt from taxation under subsection (a) and which, if organized and operated as a separate entity, would constitute an organization described in subsection (c)(3), or

(iii) owned and operated by the United States, a State, the District of Columbia, or a possession of the United States, or a political subdivision or an agency or instrumentality of any of the foregoing;

(2) such organization is organized and operated on a cooperative basis and allocates or pays, within 8 1/2 months after the close of its taxable year, all net earnings to patrons on the basis of services performed for them; and

(3) if such organization has capital stock, all of such stock outstanding is owned by its patrons.

For purposes of this title, any organization which, by reason of the preceding sentence, is an organization described in subsection (c)(3) and exempt from taxation under subsection (a), shall be treated as a hospital and as an organization referred to in section 170(b)(1)(A)(iii).

(h) Expenditures by public charities to influence legislation.—

(1) General rule.—In the case of an organization to which this subsection applies, exemption from taxation under subsection (a) shall be denied because a substantial part of the activities of such organization consists of carrying on propaganda, or otherwise attempting, to influence legislation, but only if such organization normally—

(A) makes lobbying expenditures in excess of the lobbying ceiling amount for such organization for each taxable year, or

(B) makes grass roots expenditures in excess of the grass roots ceiling amount for such organization for each taxable year.

(2) Definitions.—For purposes of this subsection—

(A) Lobbying expenditures.—The term "lobbying expenditures" means expenditures for the purpose of influencing legislation (as defined in section 4911(d)).

(B) Lobbying ceiling amount.—The lobbying ceiling amount for any organization for any taxable year is 150 percent of the lobbying nontaxable amount for such organization for such taxable year, determined under section 4911.

(C) Grass roots expenditures.—The term "grass roots expenditures" means expenditures for the purpose of influencing legislation (as defined in section 4911(d) without regard to paragraph (1)(B) thereof).

(D) Grass roots ceiling amount.—The grass roots ceiling amount for any organization for any taxable year is 150 percent of the grass roots nontaxable amount for such organization for such taxable year, determined under section 4911.

(3) Organizations to which this subsection applies.—This subsection shall apply to any organization which has elected (in such manner and at such time as the Secretary may prescribe) to have the provisions of this subsection apply to such organization and which, for the taxable year which includes the date the election is made, is described in subsection (c)(3) and—

(A) is described in paragraph (4), and

(B) is not a disqualified organization under paragraph (5).

(4) Organizations permitted to elect to have this subsection apply.—An organization is described in this paragraph if it is described in—

    (A) section 170(b)(1)(A)(ii) (relating to educational institutions),

    (B) section 170(b)(1)(A)(iii) (relating to hospitals and medical research organizations),

    (C) section 170(b)(1)(A)(iv) (relating to organizations supporting government schools),

    (D) section 170(b)(1)(A)(vi) (relating to organizations publicly supported by charitable contributions),

    (E) section 509(a)(2) (relating to organizations publicly supported by admissions, sales, etc.), or

    (F) section 509(a)(3) (relating to organizations supporting certain types of public charities) except that for purposes of this subparagraph, section 509(a)(3) shall be applied without regard to the last sentence of section 509(a).

(5) Disqualified organizations.—For purposes of paragraph (3) an organization is a disqualified organization if it is—

    (A) described in section 170(b)(1)(A)(i) (relating to churches),

    (B) an integrated auxiliary of a church or of a convention or association of churches, or

    (C) a member of an affiliated group of organizations (within the meaning of section 4911(f) (2)) if one or more members of such group is described in subparagraph (A) or (B).

(6) Years for which election is effective.—An election by an organization under this subsection shall be effective for all taxable years of such organization which—

    (A) end after the date the election is made, and

    (B) begin before the date the election is revoked by such organization (under regulations prescribed by the Secretary).

(7) No effect on certain organizations.—With respect to any organization for a taxable year for which—

    (A) such organization is a disqualified organization (within the meaning of paragraph (5)), or

    (B) an election under this subsection is not in effect for such organization,

nothing in this subsection or in section 4911 shall be construed to affect the interpretation of the phrase, "no substantial part of the activities of which is carrying on propaganda, or otherwise attempting, to influence legislation," under subsection (c)(3).

(8) Affiliated organizations.—

For rules regarding affiliated organizations, see section 4911(f).

(m) Certain organizations providing commercial-type insurance not exempt from tax.—

(1) Denial of tax exemption where providing commercial-type insurance is substantial part of activities.—An organization described in paragraph (3) or (4) of subsection (c) shall be exempt from tax under subsection (a) only if no substantial part of its activities consists of providing commercial-type insurance.

(2) Other organizations taxed as insurance companies on insurance business.—In the case of an organization described in paragraph (3) or (4) of subsection (c) which is exempt from tax under subsection (a) after the application of paragraph (1) of this subsection—

(A) the activity of providing commercial-type insurance shall be treated as an unrelated trade or business (as defined in section 513), and

(B) in lieu of the tax imposed by section 511 with respect to such activity, such organization shall be treated as an insurance company for purposes of applying subchapter L with respect to such activity.

(3) Commercial-type insurance.—For purposes of this subsection, the term "commercial-type insurance" shall not include—

(A) insurance provided at substantially below cost to a class of charitable recipients,

(B) incidental health insurance provided by a health maintenance organization of a kind customarily provided by such organizations,

(C) property or casualty insurance provided (directly or through an organization described in section 414(e)(3)(B)(ii)) by a church or convention or association of churches for such church or convention or association of churches,

(D) providing retirement or welfare benefits (or both) by a church or a convention or association of churches (directly or through an organization described in section 414(e)(3)(A) or 414(e)(3)(B)(ii)) for the employees (including employees described in section 414(e)(3)(B)) of such church or convention or association of churches or the beneficiaries of such employees, and

(E) charitable gift annuities.

(4) Insurance includes annuities.—For purposes of this subsection, the issuance of annuity contracts shall be treated as providing insurance.

(5) Charitable gift annuity.—For purposes of paragraph (3)(E), the term "charitable gift annuity" means an annuity if—

(A) a portion of the amount paid in connection with the issuance of the annuity is allowable as a deduction under section 170 or 2055, and

(B) the annuity is described in section 514(c)(5) (determined as if any amount paid in cash in connection with such issuance were property).

(o) Treatment of hospitals participating in provider-sponsored organizations.—An organization shall not fail to be treated as organized and operated exclusively for a charitable purpose for purposes of subsection (c)(3) solely because a hospital which is owned and operated by such organization participates in a provider-sponsored organization (as defined in section 1855(d) of the Social Security Act), whether or not the provider-sponsored organization is exempt from tax. For purposes of subsection (c)(3), any person with a material financial interest in such a provider-sponsored organization shall be treated as a private shareholder or individual with respect to the hospital.

Tax on Unrelated Business Income of Charitable, Etc., Organizations: 26 U.S.C.A. § 511

§ 511. Imposition of tax on unrelated business income of charitable, etc., organizations

(a) Charitable, etc., organizations taxable at corporation rates.—

(1) Imposition of tax.—There is hereby imposed for each taxable year on the unrelated business taxable income (as defined in section 512) of every organization described in paragraph (2) a tax computed as provided in section 11. In making such computation for purposes of this section, the term "taxable income" as used in section 11 shall be read as "unrelated business taxable income".

(2) Organizations subject to tax.—

(A) Organizations described in sections 401(a) and 501(c).—The tax imposed by paragraph (1) shall apply in the case of any organization (other than a trust described in subsection (b) or an organization described in section 501(c)(1)) which is exempt, except as provided in this part or part II (relating to private foundations), from taxation under this subtitle by reason of section 501(a).

(B) State colleges and universities.—The tax imposed by paragraph (1) shall apply in the case of any college or university which is an agency or instrumentality of any government or any political subdivision thereof, or which is owned or operated by a government or any political subdivision thereof, or by any agency or instrumentality of one or more governments or political subdivisions. Such tax shall also apply in the case of any corporation wholly owned by one or more such colleges or universities.

(b) Tax on charitable, etc., trusts.—

(1) Imposition of tax.—There is hereby imposed for each taxable year on the unrelated business taxable income of every trust described in paragraph (2) a tax computed as provided in section 1(e). In making such computation for purposes of this section, the term "taxable income" as used in section 1 shall be read as "unrelated business taxable income" as defined in section 512.

(2) Charitable, etc., trusts subject to tax.—The tax imposed by paragraph (1) shall apply in the case of any trust which is exempt, except as provided in this part or part II (relating to private foundations), from taxation under this subtitle by reason of section 501(a) and which, if it were not for such exemption, would be subject to subchapter J (sec. 641 and following, relating to estates, trusts, beneficiaries, and decedents).

(c) Special rule for section 501(c)(2) corporations.—If a corporation described in section 501(c)(2)—

(1) pays any amount of its net income for a taxable year to an organization exempt from taxation under section 501(a) (or which would pay such an amount but for the fact that the expenses of collecting its income exceed its income), and

(2) such corporation and such organization file a consolidated return for the taxable year,

such corporation shall be treated, for purposes of the tax imposed by subsection (a), as being organized and operated for the same purposes as such organization, in addition to the purposes described in section 501(c)(2).

[(d) Repealed. Pub.L. 100–647, Title I, § 1007(g)(6), Nov. 10, 1988, 102 Stat. 3435]

§ 512. Unrelated business taxable income

(a) Definition.—For purposes of this title–

(1) General rule.—Except as otherwise provided in this subsection, the term "unrelated business taxable income" means the gross income derived by any organization from any unrelated trade or business (as defined in section 513) regularly carried on by it, less the deductions allowed by this chapter which are directly connected with the carrying on of such trade or business, both computed with the modifications provided in subsection (b).

(2) Special rule for foreign organizations.—In the case of an organization described in section 511 which is a foreign organization, the unrelated business taxable income shall be—

(A) its unrelated business taxable income which is derived from sources within the United States and which is not effectively connected with the conduct of a trade or business within the United States, plus

(B) its unrelated business taxable income which is effectively connected with the conduct of a trade or business within the United States.

(3) Special rules applicable to organizations described in paragraph (7), (9), (17), or (20) of section 501(c).—

(A) General rule.—In the case of an organization described in paragraph (7), (9), (17), or (20) of section 501(c), the term "unrelated business taxable income" means the gross income (excluding any exempt function income), less the deductions allowed by this chapter which are directly connected with the production of the gross income (excluding exempt function income), both computed with the modifications provided in paragraphs (6), (10), (11), and (12) of subsection (b). For purposes of the preceding sentence, the deductions provided by sections 243, 244, and 245 (relating to dividends received by corporations) shall be treated as not directly connected with the production of gross income.

(B) Exempt function income.—For purposes of subparagraph (A), the term "exempt function income" means the gross income from dues, fees, charges, or similar amounts paid by members of the organization as consideration for providing such members or their dependents or guests goods, facilities, or services in furtherance of the purposes constituting the basis for the exemption of the organization to which such income is paid. Such term also means all income (other than an amount equal to the gross income derived from any unrelated trade or business regularly carried on by such organization computed as if the organization were subject to paragraph (1)), which is set aside—

(i) for a purpose specified in section 170(c)(4), or

(ii) in the case of an organization described in paragraph (9), (17), or (20) of section 501(c), to provide for the payment of life, sick, accident, or other benefits,

including reasonable costs of administration directly connected with a purpose described in clause (i) or (ii). If during the taxable year, an amount which is attributable to income so set aside is used for a purpose other than that described in clause (i) or (ii), such amount shall be included, under subparagraph (A), in unrelated business taxable income for the taxable year.

(C) Applicability to certain corporations described in section 501(c)(2).—In the case of a corporation described in section 501(c)(2), the income of which is payable to an organization described in paragraph (7), (9), (17), or (20) of section 501(c), subparagraph (A) shall apply as if such corporation were the organization to which the income is payable. For purposes of the preceding sentence, such corporation shall be treated as having exempt function income for a taxable year only if it files a consolidated return with such organization for such year.

(D) Nonrecognition of gain.—If property used directly in the performance of the exempt function of an organization described in paragraph (7), (9), (17), or (20) of section 501(c) is sold by such organization, and within a period beginning 1 year before the date of such sale, and ending 3 years after such date, other property is purchased and used by such organization directly in the performance of its exempt function, gain (if any) from such sale shall be recognized only to the extent that such organization's sales price of the old property exceeds the organization's cost of purchasing the other property. For purposes of this subparagraph, the destruction in whole or in part, theft, seizure, requisition, or condemnation of property, shall be treated as the sale of such property, and rules similar to the rules provided by subsections (b), (c), (e), and (j) of section 1034 (as in effect on the day before the date of the enactment of the Taxpayer Relief Act of 1997) shall apply.

(E) Limitation on amount of set aside in the case of organizations described in paragraph (9), (17), or (20) of section 501(c).—

(i) In general.—In the case of any organization described in paragraph (9), (17), or (20) of section 501(c), a set-aside for any purpose specified in clause (ii) of subparagraph (B) may be taken into account under subparagraph (B) only to the extent that such set-aside does not result in an amount of assets set aside for such purpose in excess of the account limit determined under section 419A (without regard to subsection (f)(6) thereof) for the taxable year (not taking into account any reserve described in section 419A(c)(2)(A) for post-retirement medical benefits).

(ii) Treatment of existing reserves for post-retirement medical or life insurance benefits.—

(I) Clause (i) shall not apply to any income attributable to an existing reserve for post-retirement medical or life insurance benefits.

(II) For purposes of subclause (I), the term "reserve for post-retirement medical or life insurance benefits" means the greater of the amount of assets set aside for purposes of post-retirement medical or life insurance benefits to be provided to covered employees as of the close of the last plan year ending before the date of the enactment of the Tax Reform Act of 1984 or on July 18, 1984.

(III) All payments during plan years ending on or after the date of the enactment of the Tax Reform Act of 1984 of post-retirement medical benefits or life insurance benefits shall be charged against the reserve referred to in subclause (II). Except to the extent provided in regulations prescribed by the Secretary, all plans of an employer shall be treated as 1 plan for purposes of the preceding sentence.

(iii) Treatment of tax exempt organizations.—This subparagraph shall not apply to any organization if substantially all of

231

the contributions to such organization are made by employers who were exempt from tax under this chapter throughout the 5–taxable year period ending with the taxable year in which the contributions are made.

(4) Special rule applicable to organizations described in section 501(c)(19).—In the case of an organization described in section 501(c)(19), the term "unrelated business taxable income" does not include any amount attributable to payments for life, sick, accident, or health insurance with respect to members of such organizations or their dependents which is set aside for the purpose of providing for the payment of insurance benefits or for a purpose specified in section 170(c)(4). If an amount set aside under the preceding sentence is used during the taxable year for a purpose other than a purpose described in the preceding sentence, such amount shall be included, under paragraph (1), in unrelated business taxable income for the taxable year.

(5) Definition of payments with respect to securities loans.—

(A) The term "payments with respect to securities loans" includes all amounts received in respect of a security (as defined in section 1236(c)) transferred by the owner to another person in a transaction to which section 1058 applies (whether or not title to the security remains in the name of the lender) including—

(i) amounts in respect of dividends, interest, or other distributions,

(ii) fees computed by reference to the period beginning with the transfer of securities by the owner and ending with the transfer of identical securities back to the transferor by the transferee and the fair market value of the security during such period,

(iii) income from collateral security for such loan, and

(iv) income from the investment of collateral security.

(B) Subparagraph (A) shall apply only with respect to securities transferred pursuant to an agreement between the transferor and the transferee which provides for—

(i) reasonable procedures to implement the obligation of the transferee to furnish to the transferor, for each business day during such period, collateral with a fair market value not less than the fair market value of the security at the close of business on the preceding business day,

(ii) termination of the loan by the transferor upon notice of not more than 5 business days, and

(iii) return to the transferor of securities identical to the transferred securities upon termination of the loan.

(b) Modifications.—The modifications referred to in subsection (a) are the following:

(1) There shall be excluded all dividends, interest, payments with respect to securities loans (as defined in section 512(a)(5)), amounts received or accrued as consideration for entering into agreements to make loans, and annuities, and all deductions directly connected with such income.

(2) There shall be excluded all royalties (including overriding royalties) whether measured by production or by gross or taxable income from the property, and all deductions directly connected with such income.

(3) In the case of rents—

(A) Except as provided in subparagraph (B), there shall be excluded—

(i) all rents from real property (including property described in section 1245(a)(3)(C)), and

(ii) all rents from personal property (including for purposes of this paragraph as personal property any property described in section 1245(a)(3) (B)) leased with such real property, if the rents attributable to such personal property are an incidental amount of the total rents received or accrued under the lease, determined at the time the personal property is placed in service.

(B) Subparagraph (A) shall not apply—

(i) if more than 50 percent of the total rent received or accrued under the lease is attributable to personal property described in subparagraph (A)(ii), or

(ii) if the determination of the amount of such rent depends in whole or in part on the income or profits derived by any person from the property leased (other than an amount based on a fixed percentage or percentages of receipts or sales).

(C) There shall be excluded all deductions directly connected with rents excluded under subparagraph (A).

(4) Notwithstanding paragraph (1), (2), (3), or (5), in the case of debt-financed property (as defined in section 514) there shall be included, as an item of gross income derived from an unrelated trade or business, the amount ascertained under section 514(a)(1), and there shall be allowed, as a deduction, the amount ascertained under section 514(a)(2).

(5) There shall be excluded all gains or losses from the sale, exchange, or other disposition of property other than—

(A) stock in trade or other property of a kind which would properly be includible in inventory if on hand at the close of the taxable year, or

233

(B) property held primarily for sale to customers in the ordinary course of the trade or business.

There shall also be excluded all gains or losses recognized, in connection with the organization's investment activities, from the lapse or termination of options to buy or sell securities (as defined in section 1236(c)) or real property and all gains or losses from the forfeiture of good-faith deposits (that are consistent with established business practice) for the purchase, sale, or lease of real property in connection with the organization's investment activities. This paragraph shall not apply with respect to the cutting of timber which is considered, on the application of section 631, as a sale or exchange of such timber.

(6) The net operating loss deduction provided in section 172 shall be allowed, except that—

(A) the net operating loss for any taxable year, the amount of the net operating loss carryback or carryover to any taxable year, and the net operating loss deduction for any taxable year shall be determined under section 172 without taking into account any amount of income or deduction which is excluded under this part in computing the unrelated business taxable income; and

(B) the terms "preceding taxable year" and "preceding taxable years" as used in section 172 shall not include any taxable year for which the organization was not subject to the provisions of this part.

(7) There shall be excluded all income derived from research for (A) the United States, or any of its agencies or instrumentalities, or (B) any State or political subdivision thereof; and there shall be excluded all deductions directly connected with such income.

(8) In the case of a college, university, or hospital, there shall be excluded all income derived from research performed for any person, and all deductions directly connected with such income.

(9) In the case of an organization operated primarily for purposes of carrying on fundamental research the results of which are freely available to the general public, there shall be excluded all income derived from research performed for any person, and all deductions directly connected with such income.

(10) In the case of any organization described in section 511(a), the deduction allowed by section 170 (relating to charitable etc. contributions and gifts) shall be allowed (whether or not directly connected with the carrying on of the trade or business), but shall not exceed 10 percent of the unrelated business taxable income computed without the benefit of this paragraph.

(11) In the case of any trust described in section 511(b), the deduction allowed by section 170 (relating to charitable etc. contributions and gifts) shall be allowed (whether or not directly connected with the carrying on of the trade or business), and for such purpose a distribution made by the trust to a beneficiary described in section 170 shall be considered as a gift or contribution. The deduction allowed by this paragraph shall be allowed with the limitations prescribed in section 170(b)(1)(A) and (B) determined with reference to the unrelated business taxable income computed without the benefit of this paragraph (in lieu of with reference to adjusted gross income).

(12) Except for purposes of computing the net operating loss under section 172 and paragraph (6), there shall be allowed a specific deduction of $1,000. In the case of a diocese, province of a religious order, or a convention or association of churches, there shall also be allowed, with respect to each parish, individual church, district, or other local unit, a specific deduction equal to the lower of—

(A) $1,000, or

(B) the gross income derived from any unrelated trade or business regularly carried on by such local unit.

(13) Special rules for certain amounts received from controlled entities.—

(A) In general.—If an organization (in this paragraph referred to as the "controlling organization") receives or accrues (directly or indirectly) a specified payment from another entity which it controls (in this paragraph referred to as the "controlled entity"), notwithstanding paragraphs (1), (2), and (3), the controlling organization shall include such payment as an item of gross income derived from an unrelated trade or business to the extent such payment reduces the net unrelated income of the controlled entity (or increases any net unrelated loss of the controlled entity). There shall be allowed all deductions of the controlling organization directly connected with amounts treated as derived from an unrelated trade or business under the preceding sentence.

(B) Net unrelated income or loss.—For purposes of this paragraph–

(i) Net unrelated income.—The term "net unrelated income" means—

(I) in the case of a controlled entity which is not exempt from tax under section 501(a), the portion of such entity's taxable income which would be unrelated business taxable income if such entity were exempt from tax under section 501(a) and had the same exempt purposes as the controlling organization, or

(II) in the case of a controlled entity which is exempt from tax under section 501(a), the amount of the unrelated business taxable income of the controlled entity.

(ii) Net unrelated loss.—The term "net unrelated loss" means the net operating loss adjusted under rules similar to the rules of clause (i).

(C) Specified payment.—For purposes of this paragraph, the term "specified payment" means any interest, annuity, royalty, or rent.

(D) Definition of control.—For purposes of this paragraph—

(i) Control.—The term "control" means—

(I) in the case of a corporation, ownership (by vote or value) of more than 50 percent of the stock in such corporation,

(II) in the case of a partnership, ownership of more than 50 percent of the profits interests or capital interests in such partnership, or

(III) in any other case, ownership of more than 50 percent of the beneficial interests in the entity.

(ii) Constructive ownership.—Section 318 (relating to constructive ownership of stock) shall apply for purposes of determining ownership of stock in a corporation. Similar principles shall apply for purposes of determining ownership of interests in any other entity.

(E) Related persons.—The Secretary shall prescribe such rules as may be necessary or appropriate to prevent avoidance of the purposes of this paragraph through the use of related persons.

[**(14)** Repealed. Pub.L. 101–508, Title XI, § 11801(a)(23), Nov. 5, 1990, 104 Stat. 1388–521]

(15) Except as provided in paragraph (4), in the case of a trade or business—

(A) which consists of providing services under license issued by a Federal regulatory agency,

(B) which is carried on by a religious order or by an educational organization described in section 170(b)(1)(A)(ii) maintained by such religious order, and which was so carried on before May 27, 1959, and

(C) less than 10 percent of the net income of which for each taxable year is used for activities which are not related to the purpose constituting the basis for the religious order's exemption,

there shall be excluded all gross income derived from such trade or business and all deductions directly connected with the carrying on of such trade or business, so long as it is established to the satisfaction of the Secretary that the rates or other charges for such services are competitive with rates or other charges charged for similar services by persons not exempt from taxation.

(16)(A) Notwithstanding paragraph (5)(B), there shall be excluded all gains or losses from the sale, exchange, or other disposition of any real property described in subparagraph (B) if—

> **(i)** such property was acquired by the organization from—

>> **(I)** a financial institution described in section 581 or 591(a) which is in conservatorship or receivership, or

>> **(II)** the conservator or receiver of such an institution (or any government agency or corporation succeeding to the rights or interests of the conservator or receiver),

> **(ii)** such property is designated by the organization within the 9–month period beginning on the date of its acquisition as property held for sale, except that not more than one-half (by value determined as of such date) of property acquired in a single transaction may be so designated,

> **(iii)** such sale, exchange, or disposition occurs before the later of—

>> **(I)** the date which is 30 months after the date of the acquisition of such property, or

>> **(II)** the date specified by the Secretary in order to assure an orderly disposition of property held by persons described in subparagraph (A), and

> **(iv)** while such property was held by the organization, the aggregate expenditures on improvements and development activities included in the basis of the property are (or were) not in excess of 20 percent of the net selling price of such property.

(B) Property is described in this subparagraph if it is real property which—

> **(i)** was held by the financial institution at the time it entered into conservatorship or receivership, or

> **(ii)** was foreclosure property (as defined in section 514(c)(9)(H)(v)) which secured indebtedness held by the financial institution at such time.

For purposes of this subparagraph, real property includes an interest in a mortgage.

(17) Treatment of certain amounts derived from foreign corporations.—

(A) In general.—Notwithstanding paragraph (1), any amount included in gross income under section 951(a)(1)(A) shall be included as an item of gross income derived from an unrelated trade or business to the extent the amount so included is attributable to insurance income (as defined in section 953) which, if derived directly by the organization, would be treated as gross income from an unrelated trade or business. There shall be allowed all deductions directly connected with amounts included in gross income under the preceding sentence.

(B) Exception.—

(i) In general.—Subparagraph (A) shall not apply to income attributable to a policy of insurance or reinsurance with respect to which the person (directly or indirectly) insured is—

(I) such organization,

(II) an affiliate of such organization which is exempt from tax under section 501(a), or

(III) a director or officer of, or an individual who (directly or indirectly) performs services for, such organization or affiliate but only if the insurance covers primarily risks associated with the performance of services in connection with such organization or affiliate.

(ii) Affiliate.—For purposes of this subparagraph—

(I) In general.—The determination as to whether an entity is an affiliate of an organization shall be made under rules similar to the rules of section 168(h)(4)(B).

(II) Special rule.—Two or more organizations (and any affiliates of such organizations) shall be treated as affiliates if such organizations are colleges or universities described in section 170(b)(1)(A)(ii) or organizations described in section 170(b)(1)(A)(iii) and participate in an insurance arrangement that provides for any profits from such arrangement to be returned to the policyholders in their capacity as such.

(C) Regulations.—The Secretary shall prescribe such regulations as may be necessary or appropriate to carry out the purposes of this paragraph, including regulations for the application of this paragraph in the case of income paid through 1 or more entities or between 2 or more chains of entities.

(c) Special rules for partnerships.—

(1) In general.—If a trade or business regularly carried on by a partnership of which an organization is a member is an unrelated trade or business with respect to such organization, such organization in computing its unrelated business taxable income shall, subject to the exceptions, additions, and limitations contained in subsection (b), include its share (whether or not distributed) of the gross income of the partnership from such unrelated trade or business and its share of the partnership deductions directly connected with such gross income.

(2) Special rule where partnership year is different from organization's year.—If the taxable year of the organization is different from that of the partnership, the amounts to be included or deducted in computing the unrelated business taxable income under paragraph (1) shall be based upon the income and deductions of the partnership for any taxable year of the partnership ending within or with the taxable year of the organization.

[(3) Redesignated (2)]

(d) Treatment of dues of agricultural or horticultural organizations.—

(1) In general.—If—

(A) an agricultural or horticultural organization described in section 501(c)(5) requires annual dues to be paid in order to be a member of such organization, and

(B) the amount of such required annual dues does not exceed $100,

in no event shall any portion of such dues be treated as derived by such organization from an unrelated trade or business by reason of any benefits or privileges to which members of such organization are entitled.

(2) Indexation of $100 amount.—In the case of any taxable year beginning in a calendar year after 1995, the $100 amount in paragraph (1) shall be increased by an amount equal to–

(A) $100, multiplied by

(B) the cost-of-living adjustment determined under section 1(f)(3) for the calendar year in which the taxable year begins, by substituting "calendar year 1994" for "calendar year 1992" in subparagraph (B) thereof.

(3) Dues.—For purposes of this subsection, the term "dues" means any payment (whether or not designated as dues) which is required to be made in order to be recognized by the organization as a member of the organization.

(e) Special rules applicable to S corporations.—

(1) In general.—If an organization described in section 1361(c)(6) holds stock in an S corporation—

(A) such interest shall be treated as an interest in an unrelated trade or business, and

(B) notwithstanding any other provision of this part—

(i) all items of income, loss, or deduction taken into account under section 1366(a), and

(ii) any gain or loss on the disposition of the stock in the S corporation,

shall be taken into account in computing the unrelated business taxable income of such organization.

(2) Basis reduction.—Except as provided in regulations, for purposes of paragraph (1), the basis of any stock acquired by purchase (as defined in section 1361(e)(1)(C)) shall be reduced by the amount of any dividends received by the organization with respect to the stock.

(3) Exception for ESOPS.—This subsection shall not apply to employer securities (within the meaning of section 409(l)) held by an employee stock ownership plan described in section 4975(e)(7).

B. TAXES ON EXCESS BENEFIT TRANSACTION

Excess Benefit Statute: 26 U.S.C.A. § 4958

§ 4958. Taxes on excess benefit transactions

(a) Initial taxes.—

(1) On the disqualified person.—There is hereby imposed on each excess benefit transaction a tax equal to 25 percent of the excess benefit. The tax imposed by this paragraph shall be paid by any disqualified person referred to in subsection (f)(1) with respect to such transaction.

(2) On the management.—In any case in which a tax is imposed by paragraph (1), there is hereby imposed on the participation of any organization manager in the excess benefit transaction, knowing that it is such a transaction, a tax equal to 10 percent of the excess benefit, unless such participation is not willful and is due to reasonable cause. The tax imposed by this paragraph shall be paid by any organization manager who participated in the excess benefit transaction.

(b) Additional tax on the disqualified person.—In any case in which an initial tax is imposed by subsection (a)(1) on an excess benefit transaction and the excess benefit involved in such transaction is not corrected within the taxable period, there is hereby imposed a tax equal to 200 percent of the excess benefit involved. The tax imposed by this subsection shall be paid by any disqualified person referred to in subsection (f)(1) with respect to such transaction.

(c) Excess benefit transaction; excess benefit.—For purposes of this section—

(1) Excess benefit transaction.—

(A) In general.—The term "excess benefit transaction" means any transaction in which an economic benefit is provided by an applicable tax-exempt organization directly or indirectly to or for the use of any disqualified person if the value of the economic benefit provided exceeds the value of the consideration (including the performance of services) received for providing such benefit. For purposes of the preceding sentence, an economic benefit shall not be treated as consideration for the performance of services unless such organization clearly indicated its intent to so treat such benefit.

(B) Excess benefit.—The term "excess benefit" means the excess referred to in subparagraph (A).

(2) Authority to include certain other private inurement.—To the extent provided in regulations prescribed by the Secretary, the term "excess benefit transaction" includes any transaction in which the amount of any economic benefit provided to or for the use of a disqualified person is determined in whole or in part by the revenues of 1 or more activities of the organization but only if such transaction results in inurement not permitted under paragraph (3) or (4) of section 501(c), as the case may be. In the case of any such transaction, the excess benefit shall be the amount of the inurement not so permitted.

(d) Special rules.—For purposes of this section—

(1) Joint and several liability.—If more than 1 person is liable for any tax imposed by subsection (a) or subsection (b), all such persons shall be jointly and severally liable for such tax.

(2) Limit for management.—With respect to any 1 excess benefit transaction, the maximum amount of the tax imposed by subsection (a)(2) shall not exceed $10,000.

(e) Applicable tax-exempt organization.—For purposes of this subchapter, the term "applicable tax-exempt organization" means—

(1) any organization which (without regard to any excess benefit) would be described in paragraph (3) or (4) of section 501(c) and exempt from tax under section 501(a), and

(2) any organization which was described in paragraph (1) at any time during the 5–year period ending on the date of the transaction.

Such term shall not include a private foundation (as defined in section 509(a)).

(f) Other definitions.—For purposes of this section—

(1) Disqualified person.—The term "disqualified person" means, with respect to any transaction—

(A) any person who was, at any time during the 5–year period ending on the date of such transaction, in a position to exercise substantial influence over the affairs of the organization.

(B) a member of the family of an individual described in subparagraph (A), and

(C) a 35–percent controlled entity.

(2) Organization manager.—The term "organization manager" means, with respect to any applicable tax-exempt organization, any officer, director, or trustee of such organization (or any individual having

241

powers or responsibilities similar to those of officers, directors, or trustees of the organization).

(3) 35–Percent controlled entity.—

(A) In general.—The term "35–percent controlled entity" means—

(i) a corporation in which persons described in subparagraph (A) or (B) of paragraph (1) own more than 35 percent of the total combined voting power,

(ii) a partnership in which such persons own more than 35 percent of the profits interest, and

(iii) a trust or estate in which such persons own more than 35 percent of the beneficial interest.

(B) Constructive ownership rules.—Rules similar to the rules of paragraphs (3) and (4) of section 4946(a) shall apply for purposes of this paragraph.

(4) Family members.—The members of an individual's family shall be determined under section 4946(d); except that such members also shall include the brothers and sisters (whether by the whole or half blood) of the individual and their spouses.

(5) Taxable period.—The term "taxable period" means, with respect to any excess benefit transaction, the period beginning with the date on which the transaction occurs and ending on the earliest of—

(A) the date of mailing a notice of deficiency under section 6212 with respect to the tax imposed by subsection (a)(1), or

(B) the date on which the tax imposed by subsection (a)(1) is assessed.

(6) Correction.—The terms "correction" and "correct" mean, with respect to any excess benefit transaction, undoing the excess benefit to the extent possible, and taking any additional measures necessary to place the organization in a financial position not worse than that in which it would be if the disqualified person were dealing under the highest fiduciary standards.

Excess Benefit Tax Regulations

DEPARTMENT OF THE TREASURY, Internal Revenue Service

26 CFR Parts 53, 301, and 602

Excise Taxes on Excess Benefit Transactions Final Regulations

SUMMARY: This document contains final regulations relating to the excise taxes on excess benefit transactions under section 4958 of the Internal Revenue Code, as well as certain amendments and additions to existing Income Tax Regulations affected by section 4958. Section 4958 was enacted by the Taxpayer Bill of Rights 2. Section 4958 imposes excise taxes on any transaction that provides excess economic benefits to a person in a position to exercise substantial influence over the affairs of a public charity or a social welfare organization.

DATES: Effective Date: These regulations are effective January 23, 2002.

Applicability Date: These regulations apply as of January 23, 2002.

Background

Section 4958 was added to the Internal Revenue Code (Code) by the Taxpayer Bill of Rights 2, Public Law 104–168 (110 Stat. 1452), enacted July 30, 1996. The section 4958 excise taxes generally apply to excess benefit transactions occurring on or after September 14, 1995. Any disqualified person who benefits from an excess benefit transaction with an applicable tax-exempt organization is liable for a tax of 25 percent of the excess benefit. The person is also liable for a tax of 200 percent of the excess benefit if the excess benefit is not corrected by a certain date. A disqualified person is generally defined as a person in a position to exercise substantial influence over the affairs of the applicable tax-exempt organization. An applicable tax-exempt organization is an organization described in Code section 501(c)(3) or (4) and exempt from tax under section 501(a). Additionally, organization managers who participate in an excess benefit transaction knowingly, willfully, and without reasonable cause, are liable for a tax of 10 percent of the excess benefit. The tax for which all participating organization managers are liable cannot exceed $10,000 for any one excess benefit transaction.

On August 4, 1998, a notice of proposed rulemaking (REG–246256–96) clarifying certain definitions and rules contained in section 4958 was published in the Federal Register (63 FR 41486). The IRS received numerous written comments responding to this notice. A public hearing was held on March 16 and 17, 1999. Those proposed regulations were revised in response to written and oral comments, and replaced by temporary regulations (TD 8920, 66 FR 2144) and a cross-referencing notice of proposed rulemaking (REG–246256–96, 66 FR 2173) on January 10, 2001. A few written comments were received in response to the notice of proposed rulemaking of January 10, 2001. A public hearing was held July 31, 2001. After consideration of all comments received, the January 2001 cross-referencing proposed regulations under section 4958 are revised and published in final form, and the temporary regulations removed. The major areas of the comments and revisions are discussed below.

Explanation and Summary of Comments

Tax Paid by Organization Managers

Organization managers who participate in an excess benefit transaction knowingly, willfully, and without reasonable cause, are liable for a tax equal to 10 percent of the excess benefit. The temporary regulations provide that an organization manager's participation in an excess benefit transaction will ordinarily not be considered knowing to the extent that, after full disclosure of the factual situation to an appropriate professional, the organization manager relies on a reasoned written opinion of that professional with respect to elements of the transaction within the professional's expertise. For this purpose, appropriate professionals are legal counsel (including in-house counsel), certified public accountants or accounting firms with expertise regarding the relevant tax law matters, and independent valuation experts who meet specified requirements. Oral comments at the public hearing objected to this safe harbor, suggesting instances of the unreliability of appraisers and accountants. The final regulations retain this safe harbor. The IRS and the Treasury Department believe that an organization manager who has sought and relied upon an appropriate professional opinion has not "fail[ed] to make reasonable attempts to ascertain whether the transaction is an excess benefit transaction", which is a required element of knowing for this purpose.

The temporary regulations provide an additional safe harbor: that an organization manager's participation in a transaction will ordinarily not be considered knowing if the manager relies on the fact that the requirements giving rise to the rebuttable presumption of reasonableness are satisfied with respect to the transaction. Several comments were received requesting that the safe harbor be modified, either to apply if the organization manager "reasonably believes" that the requirements for the presumption are satisfied, or to eliminate the reliance requirement. In response to these comments, the final regulations no longer require that the organization manager rely on the fact that the requirements of the rebuttable presumption of reasonableness are satisfied. The final regulations state that the organization manager's participation in a transaction will ordinarily not be considered knowing if the appropriate authorized body has met the requirements of the rebuttable presumption with respect to the transaction. The IRS and the Treasury Department note that the relief given by this provision is only a safe harbor, so that failure to satisfy its requirements does not necessarily mean that the organization manager acted knowingly.

Definition of Applicable Tax–Exempt Organization

The temporary regulations provide that any governmental entity that is exempt from (or not subject to) taxation without regard to section 501(a) is not an applicable tax-exempt organization for purposes of section 4958. A comment was received requesting that the final regulations clarify whether section 115 entities are excepted from the definition of applicable tax-exempt organization. Because section 115 exempts certain income, and not the entity itself, the reference in the temporary regulations to any governmental entity "exempt from tax" without regard to section 501(a) is unclear. The final regulations provide that for purposes of section 4958, a governmental unit or an affiliate of a governmental unit is not an applicable tax-exempt organization if it is: (1) Exempt from (or not subject to) taxation without regard to section 501(a); or (2) relieved from filing an annual return pursuant to the authority of Treasury Regulations under section 6033.

Regulations under section 6033 grant the Commissioner authority to relieve organizations from filing an annual return required by that section in cases where the returns are not necessary for the efficient administration of the internal revenue laws. Under this authority, Rev. Proc. 95–48 (1995–2 C.B. 418) relieves "governmental units" and certain "affiliates of governmental units" from the annual filing requirement. A governmental unit as defined in this revenue procedure already falls within the exception provided in the section 4958 temporary regulations for "any governmental entity that is exempt from (or not subject to) taxation without regard to section 501(a)". An affiliate of a governmental unit that is relieved from filing an annual return by Rev. Proc. 95–48 (and thus also excepted from the definition of an applicable tax-exempt organization under these section 4958 final regulations) includes any organization described in section 501(c) that has a ruling or determination from the IRS that: (1) Its income, derived from activities constituting the basis for its exemption under section 501(c), is excluded from gross income under section 115; (2) it is entitled to receive deductible charitable contributions under section 170(c)(1) on the basis that the contributions are "for the use of" governmental units; or (3) it is a wholly owned instrumentality of a State for employment tax purposes. An organization described in section 501(c) that does not have such a ruling or determination may also qualify as an affiliate of a governmental unit for purposes of the revenue procedure if: (1) It is either "operated, supervised, or controlled by" governmental units within the meaning of regulations under section 509; (2) it possesses at least two affiliation factors listed in Rev. Proc. 95–48; and (3) its filing of Form 990, "Return of Organization Exempt From Income Tax", is not otherwise necessary to the efficient administration of the internal revenue laws.

A comment was also received requesting that the final regulations exclude from the definition of applicable tax-exempt organization collectively bargained apprenticeship funds subject to the rules of the Labor Management Relations Act of 1947 (61 Stat. 157) and the Employee Retirement Income Security Act of 1974 (88 Stat. 854) (ERISA). The commenter stated that, like governmental entities, these funds seek recognition under Code section 501(c)(3) on a strictly voluntary basis, and are also eligible for tax exemption under Code section 501(c)(5). The commenter also stated that applying section 4958 to these funds would provide an unnecessary layer of regulation, because these plans already are subject to ERISA.

The final regulations do not except collectively bargained apprenticeship funds from the definition of applicable tax-exempt organization. However, in response to this comment, the final regulations provide a special exception under section 4958 for transactions that are covered by a final individual prohibited transaction exemption issued by the Department of Labor. The final regulations provide that section 4958 does not apply to any payment made pursuant to, and in accordance with, a final individual prohibited transaction exemption issued by the Department of Labor under ERISA with respect to a transaction involving a plan that is an applicable tax-exempt organization. Before granting an individual prohibited transaction exemption under ERISA, the Department of Labor must determine that the particular transaction is in the interests of the plan and its participants, and is protective of the rights of participants in the plan. The IRS and the Treasury Department believe that the similarity between the ERISA standard ("in the interests of" and "protective of the rights of" participants) and the fair market value standard of section 4958 warrants this special exception.

Definition of Disqualified Person

The preamble of the temporary regulations noted that the IRS and the Treasury Department considered adopting a special rule with respect to so-called donor-advised funds maintained by applicable tax-exempt organizations, and requested comments regarding potential issues raised by applying the fair market value standard of section 4958 to distributions from a donor-advised fund to (or for the use of) the donor or advisor. Several comments were received on this issue. Most of the comments objected to treating a donor or advisor to this type of fund as a disqualified person based solely on influence over a donor-advised fund. Others stated that the existing factors contained in the temporary regulations were adequate to find disqualified person status in appropriate circumstances. One commenter requested that if section 4958 were to apply to transactions involving donor-advised funds, the fair market standard should apply, and requested additional definitions and exclusions if the final regulations contained specific rules for these types of funds.

In response to these comments, the final regulations do not adopt a special rule regarding any donor or advisor to a donor-advised fund. Thus, the general rules of § 53.4958–3 will apply to determine if a donor or advisor is a disqualified person.

Some additional comments were received on other specific rules of the disqualified person definition contained in the temporary regulations. The final regulations do not change the rules or descriptions contained in the definition. However, several of the comments are discussed below to explain why the IRS and the Treasury Department concluded that changes were not necessary or desirable. Other comments suggested changes to the examples. In response to those comments, several examples in this section of the final regulations were revised from the temporary regulations, as discussed below.

The temporary regulations state that an organization described in section 501(c)(4) is deemed not to have substantial influence with respect to another applicable tax-exempt organization described in section 501(c)(4). A section 501(c)(4) organization can, however, have substantial influence with respect to an organization described in section 501(c)(3). A commenter requested that section 501(c)(4) organizations be excluded from disqualified person status with respect to all applicable tax-exempt organizations.

The IRS and the Treasury Department decline to expand the exclusion for section 501(c)(4) organizations. A section 501(c)(4) organization can engage in certain activities (such as political campaign activities) that a section

501(c)(3) organization cannot. Accordingly, the IRS and the Treasury Department are concerned about transactions in which a section 501(c)(3) organization may provide an excess benefit to a section 501(c)(4) organization to avoid limitations of section 501(c)(3).

Oral comments at the public hearing objected to including, as one of the factors tending to show no substantial influence, the fact that the person's sole relationship to an applicable tax-exempt organization is as a contractor (such as an attorney, accountant, or investment manager or advisor) providing professional advice to the organization. The commenter suggested that these providers of professional advice have a great deal of influence over applicable tax-exempt organizations, but choose not to exercise that influence. The IRS and the Treasury Department believe that the description of this factor in the temporary regulations includes sufficient safeguards to protect the organization. Accordingly, the final regulations retain this factor. Additionally, being in this category of persons is merely a factor tending to show no substantial influence. In appropriate circumstances, the IRS could still conclude that a person ostensibly described in this category was a disqualified person based on all relevant facts and circumstances.

Another comment objected to the standard of one of the factors tending to show substantial influence: that a person's compensation is primarily based on revenues derived from activities of the organization that the person controls. The commenter suggested that this factor be modified to provide that revenues controlled by the person also represent a substantial part of the organization's total revenues. The IRS and the Treasury Department do not believe that a change is necessary. The factor at issue is only one of many factors that may be considered, and will be considered in conjunction with all relevant facts and circumstances.

Another comment requested further revision to two factors tending to show substantial influence. The first factor states that the person has or shares authority to control or determine a substantial portion of the organization's capital expenditures, operating budget, or compensation for employees. The second factor states that the person manages a discrete segment or activity of the organization that represents a substantial portion of the activities, assets, income, or expense of the organization, as compared to the organization as a whole. The commenter suggested that the first factor is sufficient, and requested that the second factor be deleted. Alternatively, the commenter requested that the final regulations define the term substantial, and recommended a safe harbor percentage of 15 percent.

The IRS and the Treasury Department did not revise these two factors tending to show substantial influence. The IRS and the Treasury Department do not believe that these two factors are redundant, as they address budget and management authority, respectively, and these two functions may reside in different persons. In addition, as with any of the listed factors, these two factors are considered along with all other relevant facts and circumstances.

In response to a comment regarding the examples of this section, the final regulations revise an example that concludes that a hospital management company is a disqualified person with respect to the applicable tax-exempt organization. The comment stated that the example could create confusion because its language does not match neatly with the factors tending to show substantial influence listed in the temporary regulations. The commenter also pointed out that, under the facts of the example, the functions of the management company seemed close to those of a president, chief executive officer, or chief operating officer, one of the categories of persons who are deemed to have substantial influence. The example is revised in the final regulations to illustrate that the management company is a disqualified person per se, because it has ultimate responsibility for supervising the management of the hospital, consistent with the regulatory description of the functions of a president, chief executive officer, or chief operating officer. By concluding that the management company is a disqualified person, this example also addresses a comment requesting that final regulations clarify whether only individuals could be persons having substantial influence.

Economic Benefit Provided Indirectly

One comment analyzed examples in the temporary regulations defining an indirect excess benefit transaction. The commenter questioned one example in which the benefits provided to a disqualified person by an applicable tax-exempt organization and an entity controlled by the organization are evaluated in the aggregate, and the excess over reasonable compensation for the services performed by the disqualified person for both entities is treated as an excess benefit. The commenter recommended that the example be deleted or revised so that the reasonableness of compensation provided by each entity is evaluated separately.

The rules governing an indirect excess benefit transaction are intended to prevent an applicable tax-exempt organization from avoiding section 4958 by using a controlled entity to provide excess benefits to a disqualified person. Thus, for purposes of section 4958, economic benefits provided by a controlled entity will be treated as provided by the applicable tax-exempt organization. Likewise, the IRS and the Treasury Department believe that any services performed by the disqualified person for a controlled entity should be taken into account in determining the reasonableness of compensation paid by the applicable tax-exempt organization. Accordingly, this example is not changed in the final regulations. However, the IRS and the Treasury Department agree with the commenter that the payment of compensation by an applicable tax-exempt organization to a disqualified person for services provided to a controlled entity, other than a wholly-owned subsidiary, may raise private benefit issues if the other investors in the entity do not make a proportional contribution. Accordingly, another example in this section is modified to clarify that the controlled entity for which the disqualified person performs services is a wholly-owned subsidiary of the applicable tax-exempt organization.

Initial Contract Exception

The temporary regulations provide that section 4958 does not apply to any fixed payment made to a person pursuant to an initial contract, regardless of whether the payment would otherwise constitute an excess benefit transaction. For this purpose, an initial contract is defined as a binding written contract between an applicable tax-exempt organization and a person who was not a disqualified person immediately prior to entering into the contract. A fixed payment means an amount of cash or other property specified in the contract, or determined by a fixed formula specified in the contract, which is paid or transferred in exchange for the provision of specified services or property. A fixed formula may incorporate an amount that depends upon future specified events or contingencies (e.g., revenues generated by activities of the organization), provided that no person exercises discretion when calculating the amount of a payment or deciding whether to make a payment. The temporary regulations include examples to illustrate the application of the initial contract rule.

Several comments were received on this section of the temporary regulations, including comments on specific examples. Several commentators requested a more liberal definition of initial contract. For instance, requests were received to extend the initial contract exception to cases where there is other contemporaneous written evidence of the terms of employment (but not a binding contract), or for the rule to cover cases where the parties agree to substantial terms of the person's employment, but where a final contract has not been signed before the person begins performing services for the organization. As the term binding written contract is governed by State law, in some cases that term may in fact be satisfied by an exchange of writings indicating the substantial terms of an agreement. However, the IRS and the Treasury Department decline to revise the regulatory definition of this term from that contained in the temporary regulations.

One commenter at the public hearing requested that the final regulations eliminate the initial contract exception. In this commenter's view, the Seventh Circuit in United Cancer Council, Inc. v. Commissioner of Internal Revenue, 165 F.3d 1173 (7th Cir. 1999), rev'ing and remanding 109 T.C. 326 (1997), focused on the wrong moment in time to determine insider status (analogous to disqualified person status under section 4958). The commenter suggested that a person's insider status should be determined at the time payments are made to the person. Therefore, the commenter recommended that the IRS and the Treasury Department decline to follow the reasoning of the Seventh Circuit's decision in the United Cancer Council case in the final regulations. Alternatively, the commenter requested that, if the initial contract exception is retained in the section 4958 final regulations, the IRS and the Treasury Department revise the private benefit standard under the section 501(c)(3) regulations to require that any private benefit conferred by a transaction must be insubstantial relative to the public benefit resulting from the transaction (rather than the public benefit resulting from the organization's overall activities).

Although the United Cancer Council case addressed the issue of private inurement under the standards of section 501(c)(3) in connection with revocation of the organization's tax exemption, the temporary regulations address the concerns expressed in the Seventh Circuit's opinion in United Cancer Council in the context of section 4958. The Seventh Circuit concluded that prohibited inurement under section 501(c)(3) cannot result from a contractual relationship negotiated at arm's length with a party having no prior relationship with the organization, regardless of the relative bargaining strength of the parties or resultant control over the tax-exempt organization created by the terms of the contract. The temporary regulations provide that, to the extent that an applicable tax-exempt organization and a person who is not yet a disqualified person enter into a binding written contract that specifies the amounts to be paid to the person (or specifies an objective formula for calculating those amounts), those fixed payments are not subject to scrutiny under section 4958, even if paid after the person becomes a disqualified person. However, the initial contract exception does not apply if the contract is materially modified or if the person fails to substantially perform his or her obligations under the contract. The IRS and the Treasury Department believe that the fact that the initial contract is scrutinized again when either of these situations occurs provides adequate protection to the applicable tax-exempt organization. In addition, the suggested revisions to the regulations under section 501(c)(3) are beyond the scope of this regulations project.

Several comments on specific examples in the initial contract exception section of the temporary regulations were received. One writer commented that in the example involving a hospital management company, the structure of the management fee gives the management company an incentive to provide charity care regardless of whether the hospital has the financial resources to pay for it. The intent of that example is merely to illustrate a fixed payment determined by a fixed formula specified in the contract, where the formula incorporates an amount that is dependent on future specified events, but where no person exercises discretion when calculating the amount of a payment under the contract. Therefore, the example remains unchanged in the final regulations.

Additional comments were received addressing the example in which the same hospital management company also received reimbursements for certain expenses in addition to the fixed management fee. The temporary regulations provide that any amount paid to a person under a reimbursement (or similar) arrangement where discretion is exercised with respect to the amount of expenses incurred or reimbursed is not a fixed payment for purposes of the section 4958 initial contract exception. A request was made to distinguish such reimbursement arrangements from payments determined by a fixed formula based on revenues from a particular activity, where a person has discretion over the extent of the activity. The IRS and the Treasury Department believe that reimbursement payments should generally be evaluated for reasonableness for purposes of section 4958. Consequently, the example is not modified in the final regulations, except to clarify that the management fee is a fixed payment, even though the reimbursement payments under the contract are not. However, as discussed below, the IRS and the Treasury Department also believe that reimbursement arrangements that meet the requirements of § 1.62–2(c) (expense reimbursements pursuant to an accountable plan) do not raise the same concerns as other reimbursement payments, because of the requirements to qualify as an accountable plan. Accordingly, the final regulations disregard amounts reimbursed to employees pursuant to an accountable plan (see the discussion of this topic in this preamble under the heading "Disregarded Economic Benefits"). Because the hospital management company in the example is a contractor, and not an employee, the expense reimbursements do not fall within this exception for expense reimbursements pursuant to an accountable plan.

Disregarded Economic Benefits

The temporary regulations provide that all fringe benefits excluded from income under section 132 (except for certain liability insurance premiums, payments or reimbursements) are disregarded for section 4958 purposes. To provide consistent treatment of benefits provided in cash and in kind, the final regulations also disregard expense reimbursements paid pursuant to an accountable plan that meets the requirements of § 1.62–2(c). Thus, as is the case with section 132(d) working condition fringe benefits, existing standards under section 162 and section 274 will apply to determine whether employee expense reimbursements are disregarded for section 4958 purposes, or are treated as part of the disqualified person's compensation for purposes of determining reasonableness under section 4958.

Several comments were received requesting that lodging furnished for the convenience of the employer (i.e., meeting the requirements of section 119) be disregarded for section 4958 purposes. These comments suggested that benefits excluded from gross income under section 119 should be disregarded for purposes of section 4958 because the policy rationale underlying section 119 is the same as that underlying section 132. However, there are differences between the two sections. In general, section 132 benefits are subject to nondiscrimination rules or are de minimis in amount, which is not the case with section 119 benefits. The value of housing benefits is potentially much larger than many of the section 132 benefits, and therefore a greater potential for abuse exists in the section 119 area. Accordingly, the IRS and the Treasury Department believe it is appropriate to treat section 119 benefits differently from section 132 benefits by requiring an evaluation for reasonableness.

The temporary regulations disregard economic benefits provided to a donor solely on account of a contribution deductible under section 170 if two requirements are met. First, any non-disqualified person making a contribution above a specified amount to the organization is given the option of receiving substantially the same economic benefit. Second, the disqualified person and a significant number of non-disqualified persons in fact make a contribution of at least the specified amount. Several comments were received requesting additional guidance with respect to these disregarded benefits. One commenter asked that the rule be revised to address contributions that are not deductible by the donor in the current year because of the percentage limitations under section 170(b). That commenter also requested that the final regulations provide for situations where no other donor makes a comparable contribution to the specific applicable tax-exempt organization. In that instance, the commenter requested that the benefits be considered in relation to benefits customarily provided by similar organizations for that level of contribution. Another commenter requested that any benefit provided to a donor be disregarded if the value of the benefit does not exceed the value of the donation and the donor treats the benefit as a quid pro quo that reduces the donor's charitable contribution deduction.

The IRS and the Treasury Department decline to address situations where a disqualified person makes a unique contribution to an applicable tax-exempt organization. As a practical matter, an excess benefit transaction would never arise in connection with a contribution to an applicable tax-exempt organization, where the value of the contribution exceeds the value of any benefit the donor receives in return. However, in response to comments, the final regulations clarify that economic benefits made available on equal terms to a disqualified person and a significant number of other donors who make charitable contributions (within the meaning of section 170) above a specified amount may be disregarded for purposes of section 4958, even if the disqualified person cannot claim a deduction under section 170 with respect to the contribution, because the disqualified person does not itemize deductions, or is subject to the percentage limitations under section 170(b).

Timing of Reasonableness Determination

The temporary regulations provide that reasonableness is determined with respect to any fixed payment (as defined for purposes of the initial contract rule) at the time the parties enter into the contract. For non-fixed payments, reasonableness is determined based on all facts and circumstances, up to and including circumstances as of the date of payment. A comment requested that final regulations clarify that the timing for determining the reasonableness of a benefit is not affected by the existence of a substantial risk of forfeiture. In response to this comment, the final regulations are revised to clarify that the general timing rules apply to property subject to a substantial risk of forfeiture. Therefore, if the property subject to a substantial risk of forfeiture satisfies the definition of fixed payment, reasonableness is determined at the time the parties enter into the contract providing for the transfer of the property. If the property is not a fixed payment, then reasonableness is determined based on all facts and circumstances, up to and including circumstances as of the date of payment. An example is also added to illustrate how the regular timing rules for determining reasonableness for section 4958 purposes apply to property that is subject to a substantial risk of forfeiture.

Contemporaneous Substantiation

The temporary regulations provide that an organization must provide written substantiation that is contemporaneous with the transfer of benefits at issue in order to provide clear and convincing evidence of its intent to treat benefits provided to a disqualified person as compensation for services. This requirement may be satisfied by either: (1) The organization reporting the economic benefit as compensation on an original Federal tax information return, or on an amended Federal tax information return filed prior to the commencement of an IRS examination of the applicable tax-exempt organization or the disqualified person for the taxable year in which the transaction occurred; or (2) the recipient disqualified person reporting the benefit as income on the person's original Federal tax return, or on the person's amended Federal tax return filed prior to the commencement of an IRS examination. The final regulations clarify that for an amended return filed by a disqualified person to be considered contemporaneous substantiation, the person must file an amended return prior to the earlier of the following dates: (1) Commencement of an IRS examination; or (2) the first documentation in writing by the IRS of a potential excess benefit transaction.

The temporary regulations provide that, if a benefit is not reported on a return filed with the IRS, other written contemporaneous evidence (such as an approved written employment contract executed on or before the date of the transfer) may be used to demonstrate that the appropriate decision-making body or an authorized officer approved a transfer as compensation for services in accordance with established procedures. A comment was received requesting that the reference to "established procedures" be deleted.

The final regulations retain the reference to "established procedures" because it appears in the legislative history to section 4958 (See H. REP. NO. 506, 104th Congress, 2d Sess. (1996), 53, 57). The IRS will interpret the term established procedures to refer to the organization's usual practice for approving compensation, not to require an organization to have a formal written procedure for approving compensation. For clarity, the final regulations replace the term authorized officer with "officer authorized to approve compensation".

The final regulations also clarify that written evidence upon which the applicable tax-exempt organization based a reasonable belief that a benefit was nontaxable can serve as written contemporaneous evidence demonstrating that a transfer was approved as compensation, even if the organization's belief later proves to be erroneous. The written evidence must have been in existence on or before the due date of the applicable Federal tax return (including extensions but not amendments). The final regulations include an example illustrating this rule.

Finally, the final regulations provide that in no event will an economic benefit that a disqualified person obtains by theft or fraud be treated as consideration for the performance of services.

Transaction in Which the Amount of the Economic Benefit is Determined in Whole or in Part by the Revenues of One or More Activities of the Organization

Section 4958(c)(2) identifies a second type of excess benefit transaction: any transaction in which the amount of any economic benefit provided to or for the use of a disqualified person is determined in whole or in part by the revenues of one or more activities of the applicable tax-exempt organization, where the transaction results in impermissible inurement under section 501(c)(3) or (4). The statute provides, however, that this type of transaction is only an excess benefit transaction to the extent provided in regulations prescribed by the Secretary.

The August 1998 proposed regulations provided standards for determining when a revenue-sharing transaction constitutes an excess benefit transaction. Numerous comments were received on this section of the proposed regulations. Commenters offered multiple, often conflicting, suggestions and recommendations to address the many issues raised with respect to revenue-sharing transactions.

The temporary regulations reserve the section of the regulations governing revenue-sharing transactions. The temporary regulations provide that, until specific rules are issued to regulate such transactions, all transactions with disqualified persons (regardless of whether the person's compensation is computed by reference to revenues of the organization) will be evaluated under general rules defining an excess benefit transaction in § 53.4958–4T. A written comment was received supporting the decision to reserve that section of the regulations. However, a speaker at the public hearing objected to the lack of specific limits on revenue-sharing transactions in the temporary regulations. The speaker would allow only a small percentage of a disqualified person's salary to be based on an applicable tax-exempt organization's revenues.

Another comment asked whether revenue-sharing transactions that are reasonable in amount may nonetheless violate the inurement prohibition, so that they jeopardize the organization's tax-exempt status. The temporary regulations and these final regulations make clear that the general exemption standards of sections 501(c)(3) and (4) still apply. Under these standards, inurement may exist even though a disqualified person receives a reasonable amount from a revenue-sharing arrangement. However, most situations that constitute inurement will also violate the general rules of § 53.4958–4 (e.g., exceed reasonable compensation).

The final regulations continue to reserve the separate section governing revenue-sharing transactions. The IRS and the Treasury Department will continue to monitor these types of transactions, and if appropriate, will consider issuing specific rules to regulate them. Any later regulations that may become necessary will be issued in proposed form.

The final regulations provide that the general rules of § 53.4958–4 apply to all transactions with disqualified persons, regardless of whether the amount of the benefit provided is determined, in whole or in part, by the revenues of one or more activities of the organization.

Rebuttable Presumption That a Transaction Is Not an Excess Benefit Transaction

An informal question was presented with respect to the definition of authorized body contained in the temporary regulations for purposes of the rebuttable presumption of reasonableness. The IRS was asked whether approval by one authorized official of an applicable tax-exempt organization could satisfy the requirement of approval by an authorized body for purposes of establishing the presumption. Under the regulatory definition of authorized body in both the temporary regulations and these final regulations, a single individual may constitute either a committee of the governing body or a party authorized by the governing body to act on its behalf, if State law allows a single individual to act in either of these capacities.

Correction

Several comments were received with respect to the specific correction rules contained in the temporary regulations. One commenter requested that, in the case of an excess benefit involving a transfer of property by an applicable tax-exempt organization to a disqualified person, the final regulations be modified to require the return of the specific property if the organization wants the property back. The commenter suggested that such a rule would be consistent with the private foundation self-dealing regulations under section 4941, which require rescission of the transaction where possible. Rescission is appropriate under section 4941, where most transactions between a private foundation and a disqualified person are absolutely prohibited. By contrast, section 4958 is intended to ensure that transactions between an applicable tax-exempt organization and a disqualified person, which are permissible, do not result in an excess benefit to the disqualified person. Therefore, no change has been made in the final regulations on this point.

Another commenter requested additional guidance on the rules governing correction in the case of an applicable tax-exempt organization that has ceased to exist, or is no longer tax-exempt. The temporary regulations provide that, in such cases, the correction amount may not be paid to an organization that is related to the disqualified person. The commenter noted that the "related to" standard is imprecise. The commenter suggested replacing this standard with a requirement that the recipient organization in these instances either be a publicly-supported charity with respect to which the disqualified person has no authority to make or recommend grants, or an organization selected with the consent of the appropriate State official.

In response to this comment, the final regulations require that a section 501(c)(3) organization receiving the correction amount be a publicly-supported charity that has been in existence as such for a continuous period of at least 60 calendar months ending on the correction date. The time in existence requirement prevents the disqualified person from creating a new organization to receive the correction amount. The final regulations also require that the organization receiving the correction amount does not allow the disqualified person to make or recommend any grants or distributions by the organization. The final regulations replace the relatedness standard with a requirement that the disqualified person is not also a disqualified person with respect to the organization receiving the correction amount. Similar requirements, except for the publicly-supported charity requirement, apply to a section 501(c)(4) organization receiving the correction amount.

Factors To Determine Whether Revocation Is Appropriate

The preamble of the August 1998 proposed regulations listed four factors that the IRS will consider in determining whether to revoke an applicable tax-exempt organization's exempt status: (1) Whether the organization has been involved in repeated excess benefit transactions; (2) the size and scope of the excess benefit transaction; (3) whether, after concluding that it has been party to an excess benefit transaction, the organization has implemented safeguards to prevent future recurrences; and (4) whether there was compliance with other applicable laws. The preamble of the temporary regulations indicates that the IRS will publish guidance regarding the factors that it will consider in enforcing the requirements of sections 4958, 501(c)(3), and 501(c)(4), as it gains more experience in administering section 4958. One comment was received recommending several factors in addition to the four factors. The IRS continues to consider the suggested additions and revisions. Until it publishes a revised or expanded list of factors, the IRS will consider all relevant facts and circumstances in the administration of section 4958 cases.

Other Substantiation Requirements

The final regulations add a special rule clarifying that compliance with the specific substantiation rules of the regulations does not relieve applicable tax-exempt organizations of other rules and requirements of the Code, regulations, Revenue Rulings, and other guidance issued by the IRS (such as the substantiation rules of sections 162 and 274, or § 1.6001–1(a) and (c)).

Special Analyses

It has been determined that this Treasury decision is not a significant regulatory action as defined in Executive Order 12866. Therefore, a regulatory assessment is not required. A final regulatory flexibility analysis has been prepared for a collection of information in this Treasury decision under 5 U.S.C. 604.

Final Regulatory Flexibility Analysis

These final regulations clarifying section 4958 of the Code (Taxes on excess benefit transactions) may have an impact on small organizations if those organizations avail themselves of the rebuttable presumption of reasonableness described in the regulations (26 CFR 53.4958–6(a)(2), 53.4958–6(a)(3), 53.4958–6(c)(2), and 53.4958–6(c)(3)). The rebuttable presumption is available because the legislative history of section 4958 (H. REP. 104–506 at 56–7, March 28, 1996) stated that parties to a transaction should be entitled to rely on such a rebuttable presumption that a compensation arrangement or a property transaction between certain organizations and disqualified persons of the organizations is reasonable or at fair market value. The legislative history further instructed the Secretary of the Treasury and the IRS to issue guidance in connection with the standard for establishing reasonable compensation or fair market value that incorporates this presumption.

The objective for the rebuttable presumption is to allow organizations that satisfy the three requirements to presume that compensation arrangements and property transactions entered into with disqualified persons pursuant to satisfaction of those requirements are reasonable or at fair market value. In such cases, the section 4958 excise taxes can be imposed only if the IRS develops sufficient contrary evidence to rebut the probative value of the evidence put forth by the parties to the transaction. The legal basis for the proposed rule is Code sections 4958 and 7805.

The final rule affects organizations described in Code sections 501(c)(3) and (4) (applicable tax-exempt organizations). Some applicable tax-exempt organizations may be small organizations, defined in 5 U.S.C. 601(4) as any not-for-profit enterprise which is independently owned and operated and is not dominant in its field.

The proposed recordkeeping burden entails obtaining and relying on appropriate comparability data and documenting the basis of an organization's determination that compensation is reasonable, or a property transfer (or transfer of the right to use property) is at fair market value. These actions are necessary to meet two of the requirements specified in the legislative history for obtaining the rebuttable presumption of reasonableness. The skills necessary for these actions are of the type required for obtaining and considering comparability data, and for documenting the membership and actions of the governing board or relevant committee of the organization. Applicable tax-exempt organizations that are small entities of the class that files Form 990–EZ, "Short Form Return of Organization Exempt From Income Tax" (i.e., those with gross receipts of less than $100,000 and assets of less than $250,000), are unlikely to undertake fulfilling the requirements of the rebuttable presumption of reasonableness, and therefore will not be affected by the recordkeeping burden. All other classes of applicable tax-exempt organizations that file Form 990, "Return of Organization Exempt from Income Tax", up to organizations with assets of $50 million, are likely to be small organizations that avail themselves of the rebuttable presumption of reasonableness. These classes range from organizations with assets of $100,000 to $50 million. The final rule contains a less burdensome safe harbor for one of the requirements (obtaining comparability data on compensation) for organizations with annual gross receipts of less than $1 million. The IRS is not aware of any other relevant Federal rules which may duplicate, overlap, or conflict with the final rule. A less burdensome alternative for small organizations would be to exempt those entities from the requirements for establishing the rebuttable presumption of reasonableness. However, it is not consistent with the statute to allow organizations to rely on this presumption without satisfying some conditions. Satisfaction of the requirements as outlined in the legislative history leads to a benefit, but failure to satisfy them does not necessarily lead to a penalty. A more burdensome alternative would be to require all applicable tax-exempt organizations under Code section 4958 to satisfy the three requirements of the rebuttable presumption of reasonableness under all circumstances.

Pursuant to section 7805(f) of the Code, this final regulation will be submitted to the Chief Counsel for Advocacy of the Small Business Administration for comment on its impact on business.

Drafting Information

The principal author of these regulations is Phyllis D. Haney, Office of Division Counsel/Associate Chief Counsel (Tax Exempt and Government Entities). However, other personnel from the IRS and the Treasury Department participated in their development.

§ 53.4958–1   Taxes on excess benefit transactions

(a) In general. Section 4958 imposes excise taxes on each excess benefit transaction (as defined in section 4958(c) and § 53.4958–4) between an applicable tax-exempt organization (as defined in section 4958(e) and § 53.4958–2) and a disqualified person (as defined in section 4958(f)(1) and § 53.4958–3). A disqualified person who receives an excess benefit from an excess benefit transaction is liable for payment of a section 4958(a)(1) excise tax equal to 25 percent of the excess benefit. If an initial tax is imposed by section 4958(a)(1) on an excess benefit transaction and the transaction is not corrected (as defined in section 4958(f)(6) and § 53.4958–7) within the taxable period (as defined in section 4958(f)(5) and paragraph (c)(2)(ii) of this section), then any disqualified person who received an excess benefit from the excess benefit transaction on which the initial tax was imposed is liable for an additional tax of 200 percent of the excess benefit. An organization manager (as defined in section 4958(f)(2) and paragraph (d) of this section) who participates in an excess benefit transaction, knowing that it was such a transaction, is liable for payment of a section 4958(a)(2) excise tax equal to 10 percent of the excess benefit, unless the participation was not willful and was due to reasonable cause. If an organization manager also receives an excess benefit from an excess benefit transaction, the manager may be liable for both taxes imposed by section 4958(a).

(b) Excess benefit defined. An excess benefit is the amount by which the value of the economic benefit provided by an applicable tax-exempt organization directly or indirectly to or for the use of any disqualified person exceeds the value of the consideration (including the performance of services) received for providing such benefit.

(c) Taxes paid by disqualified person—

(1) Initial tax. Section 4958(a)(1) imposes a tax equal to 25 percent of the excess benefit on each excess benefit transaction. The section 4958(a)(1) tax shall be paid by any disqualified person who received an excess benefit from that excess benefit transaction. With respect to any excess benefit transaction, if more than one disqualified person is liable for the tax imposed by section 4958(a)(1), all such persons are jointly and severally liable for that tax.

(2) Additional tax on disqualified person—

(i) In general. Section 4958(b) imposes a tax equal to 200 percent of the excess benefit in any case in which section 4958(a)(1) imposes a 25–percent tax on an excess benefit transaction and the transaction is not corrected (as defined in section 4958(f)(6) and § 53.4958–7) within the taxable period (as defined in section 4958(f)(5) and paragraph (c)(2)(ii) of this section). If a disqualified person makes a payment of less than the full correction amount under the rules of § 53.4958–7, the 200–percent tax is imposed only on the unpaid portion of the correction amount (as described in § 53.4958–7(c)). The tax imposed by section 4958(b) is payable by any disqualified person who received an excess benefit from the excess benefit transaction on which the initial tax was imposed by section 4958(a)(1). With respect to any excess benefit transaction, if more than one disqualified person is liable for the tax imposed by section 4958(b), all such persons are jointly and severally liable for that tax.

(ii) Taxable period. Taxable period means, with respect to any excess benefit transaction, the period beginning with the date on which the transaction occurs and ending on the earlier of—

(A) The date of mailing a notice of deficiency under section 6212 with respect to the section 4958(a)(1) tax; or

(B) The date on which the tax imposed by section 4958(a)(1) is assessed.

(iii) Abatement if correction during the correction period. For rules relating to abatement of taxes on excess benefit transactions that are corrected within the correction period, as defined in section 4963(e), see sections 4961(a), 4962(a), and the regulations thereunder. The abatement rules of section 4961 specifically provide for a 90–day correction period after the date of mailing a notice of deficiency under section 6212 with respect to the section 4958(b) 200–percent tax. If the excess benefit is corrected during that correction period, the 200–percent tax imposed shall not be assessed, and if assessed the assessment shall be abated, and if collected shall be credited or refunded as an overpayment. For special rules relating to abatement of the 25–percent tax, see section 4962.

(d) Tax paid by organization managers—

(1) In general. In any case in which section 4958(a)(1) imposes a tax, section 4958(a)(2) imposes a tax equal to 10 percent of the excess benefit on the participation of any organization manager who knowingly participated in the excess benefit transaction, unless such participation was not willful and was due to reasonable cause. Any organization manager who so participated in the excess benefit transaction must pay the tax.

(2) Organization manager defined—

(i) In general. An organization manager is, with respect to any applicable tax-exempt organization, any officer, director, or trustee of such organization, or any individual having powers or responsibilities similar to those of officers, directors, or trustees of the organization, regardless of title. A person is an officer of an organization if that person—

(A) Is specifically so designated under the certificate of incorporation, by-laws, or other constitutive documents of the organization; or

(B) Regularly exercises general authority to make administrative or policy decisions on behalf of the organization. A contractor who acts solely in a capacity as an attorney, accountant, or investment manager or advisor, is not an officer. For purposes of this paragraph (d)(2)(i)(B), any person who has authority merely to recommend particular administrative or policy decisions, but not to implement them without approval of a superior, is not an officer.

(ii) Special rule for certain committee members. An individual who is not an officer, director, or trustee, yet serves on a committee of the governing body of an applicable tax-exempt organization (or as a designee of the governing body described in § 53.4958–6(c)(1)) that is attempting to invoke the rebuttable presumption of reasonableness described in § 53.4958–6 based on the committee's (or designee's) actions, is an organization manager for purposes of the tax imposed by section 4958(a)(2).

(3) Participation. For purposes of section 4958(a)(2) and this paragraph (d), participation includes silence or inaction on the part of an organization manager where the manager is under a duty to speak or act, as well as any affirmative action by such manager. An organization manager is not considered to have participated in an excess benefit transaction, however, where the manager has opposed the transaction in a manner consistent with the fulfillment of the manager's responsibilities to the applicable tax-exempt organization.

(4) Knowing—

(i) In general. For purposes of section 4958(a)(2) and this paragraph (d), a manager participates in a transaction knowingly only if the person—

(A) Has actual knowledge of sufficient facts so that, based solely upon those facts, such transaction would be an excess benefit transaction;

(B) Is aware that such a transaction under these circumstances may violate the provisions of Federal tax law governing excess benefit transactions; and

(C) Negligently fails to make reasonable attempts to ascertain whether the transaction is an excess benefit transaction, or the manager is in fact aware that it is such a transaction.

(ii) Amplification of general rule. Knowing does not mean having reason to know. However, evidence tending to show that a manager has reason to know of a particular fact or particular rule is relevant in determining whether the manager had actual knowledge of such a fact or rule. Thus, for example, evidence tending to show that a manager has reason to know of sufficient facts so that, based solely upon such facts, a transaction would be an excess benefit transaction is relevant in determining whether the manager has actual knowledge of such facts.

(iii) Reliance on professional advice. An organization manager's participation in a transaction is ordinarily not considered knowing within the meaning of section 4958(a)(2), even though the transaction is subsequently held to be an excess benefit transaction, to the extent that, after full disclosure of the factual situation to an appropriate professional, the organization manager relies on a reasoned written opinion of that professional with respect to elements of the transaction within the professional's expertise. For purposes of section 4958(a)(2) and this paragraph (d), a written opinion is reasoned even though it reaches a conclusion that is subsequently determined to be incorrect so long as the opinion addresses itself to the facts and the applicable standards. However, a written opinion is not reasoned if it does nothing more than recite the facts and express a conclusion. The absence of a written opinion of an appropriate professional with respect to a transaction shall not, by itself, however, give rise to any inference that an organization manager participated in the transaction knowingly. For purposes of this paragraph, appropriate professionals on whose written opinion an organization manager may rely, are limited to—

(A) Legal counsel, including in-house counsel;

(B) Certified public accountants or accounting firms with expertise regarding the relevant tax law matters; and

(C) Independent valuation experts who—

(1) Hold themselves out to the public as appraisers or compensation consultants;

(2) Perform the relevant valuations on a regular basis;

(3) Are qualified to make valuations of the type of property or services involved; and

(4) Include in the written opinion a certification that the requirements of paragraphs (d)(4)(iii)(C)(1) through (3) of this section are met.

(iv) Satisfaction of rebuttable presumption of reasonableness. An organization manager's participation in a transaction is ordinarily not considered knowing within the meaning of section 4958(a)(2), even though the transaction is subsequently held to be an excess benefit transaction, if the appropriate authorized body has met the requirements of § 53.4958–6(a) with respect to the transaction.

(5) Willful. For purposes of section 4958(a)(2) and this paragraph (d), participation by an organization manager is willful if it is voluntary, conscious, and intentional. No motive to avoid the restrictions of the law or the incurrence of any tax is necessary to make the participation willful. However, participation by an organization manager is not willful if the manager does not know that the transaction in which the manager is participating is an excess benefit transaction.

(6) Due to reasonable cause. An organization manager's participation is due to reasonable cause if the manager has exercised responsibility on behalf of the organization with ordinary business care and prudence.

(7) Limits on liability for management. The maximum aggregate amount of tax collectible under section 4958(a)(2) and this paragraph (d) from organization managers with respect to any one excess benefit transaction is $10,000.

(8) Joint and several liability. In any case where more than one person is liable for a tax imposed by section 4958(a)(2), all such persons shall be jointly and severally liable for the taxes imposed under section 4958(a)(2) with respect to that excess benefit transaction.

(9) Burden of proof. For provisions relating to the burden of proof in cases involving the issue of whether an organization manager has knowingly participated in an excess benefit transaction, see section 7454(b) and § 301.7454–2 of this chapter. In these cases, the Commissioner bears the burden of proof.

(e) Date of occurrence—

(1) In general. Except as otherwise provided, an excess benefit transaction occurs on the date on which the disqualified person receives the economic benefit for Federal income tax purposes. When a single contractual arrangement provides for a series of compensation or other payments to (or for the use of) a disqualified person over the course of the disqualified person's taxable year (or part of a taxable year), any excess benefit transaction with respect to these aggregate payments is deemed to occur on the last day of the taxable year (or if the payments continue for part of the year, the date of the last payment in the series).

(2) Special rules. In the case of benefits provided pursuant to a qualified pension, profit-sharing, or stock bonus plan, the transaction occurs on the date the benefit is vested. In the case of a transfer of property that is subject to a substantial risk of forfeiture or in the case of rights to future compensation or property (including benefits under a nonqualified deferred compensation plan), the transaction occurs on the date the property, or the rights to future compensation or property, is not subject to a substantial risk of forfeiture. However, where the disqualified person elects to include an amount in gross income in the taxable year of transfer pursuant to section 83(b), the general rule of paragraph (e)(1) of this section applies to the property with respect to which the section 83(b) election is made. Any excess benefit transaction with respect to benefits under a deferred compensation plan which vest during any taxable year of the disqualified person is deemed to occur on the last day of such taxable year. For the rules governing the timing of the reasonableness determination for deferred, contingent, and certain other noncash compensation, see § 53.4958–4(b)(2).

(3) Statute of limitations rules. See sections 6501(e)(3) and (*l*) and the regulations thereunder for statute of limitations rules as they apply to section 4958 excise taxes.

(f) Effective date for imposition of taxes—

(1) In general. The section 4958 taxes imposed on excess benefit transactions or on participation in excess benefit transactions apply to transactions occurring on or after September 14, 1995.

(2) Existing binding contracts. The section 4958 taxes do not apply to any transaction occurring pursuant to a written contract that was binding on September 13, 1995, and at all times thereafter before the transaction occurs. A written binding contract that is terminable or subject to cancellation by the applicable tax-exempt organization without the disqualified person's consent (including as the result of a breach of contract by the disqualified person) and without substantial penalty to the organization, is no longer treated as a binding contract as of the earliest date that any such termination or cancellation, if made, would be effective. If a binding written contract is materially changed, it is treated as a new contract entered into as of the date the material change is effective. A material change includes an extension or renewal of the contract (other than an extension or renewal that results from the person contracting with the applicable tax-exempt organization unilaterally exercising an option expressly granted by the contract), or a more than incidental change to any payment under the contract.

§ 53.4958–2   Definition of applicable tax-exempt organization

(a) Organizations described in section 501(c)(3) or (4) and exempt from tax under section 501(a)—

(1) In general. An applicable tax-exempt organization is any organization that, without regard to any excess benefit, would be described in section 501(c)(3) or (4) and exempt from tax under section 501(a). An applicable tax-exempt organization also includes any organization that was described in section 501(c)(3) or (4) and was exempt from tax under section 501(a) at any time during a five-year period ending on the date of an excess benefit transaction (the lookback period).

(2) Exceptions from definition of applicable tax-exempt organization—

(i) Private foundation. A private foundation as defined in section 509(a) is not an applicable tax-exempt organization for section 4958 purposes.

(ii) Governmental unit or affiliate. A governmental unit or an affiliate of a governmental unit is not an applicable tax-exempt organization for section 4958 purposes if it is—

(A) Exempt from (or not subject to) taxation without regard to section 501(a); or

(B) Relieved from filing an annual return pursuant to the authority of § 1.6033–2(g)(6).

(3) Organizations described in section 501(c)(3). An organization is described in section 501(c)(3) for purposes of section 4958 only if the organization—

(i) Provides the notice described in section 508; or

(ii) Is described in section 501(c)(3) and specifically is excluded from the requirements of section 508 by that section.

(4) Organizations described in section 501(c)(4). An organization is described in section 501(c)(4) for purposes of section 4958 only if the organization—

(i) Has applied for and received recognition from the Internal Revenue Service as an organization described in section 501(c)(4); or

(ii) Has filed an application for recognition under section 501(c)(4) with the Internal Revenue Service, has filed an annual information return as a section 501(c)(4) organization under the Internal Revenue Code or regulations promulgated thereunder, or has otherwise held itself out as being described in section 501(c)(4) and exempt from tax under section 501(a).

(5) Effect of non-recognition or revocation of exempt status. An organization is not described in paragraph (a)(3) or (4) of this section during any period covered by a final determination or adjudication that the organization is not exempt from tax under section 501(a) as an organization described in section 501(c)(3) or (4), so long as that determination or adjudication is not based upon participation in inurement or one or more excess benefit transactions. However, the organization may be an applicable tax-exempt organization for that period as a result of the five-year lookback period described in paragraph (a)(1) of this section.

(b) Special rules—

(1) Transition rule for lookback period. In the case of any excess benefit transaction occurring before September 14, 2000, the lookback period described in paragraph (a)(1) of this section begins on September 14, 1995, and ends on the date of the transaction.

(2) Certain foreign organizations. A foreign organization, recognized by the Internal Revenue Service or by treaty, that receives substantially all of its support (other than gross investment income) from sources outside of the United States is not an organization described in section 501(c)(3) or (4) for purposes of section 4958.

§ 53.4958–3   Definition of disqualified person

(a) In general—

(1) Scope of definition. Section 4958(f)(1) defines disqualified person, with respect to any transaction, as any person who was in a position to exercise substantial influence over the affairs of an applicable tax-exempt organization at any time during the five-year period ending on the date of the transaction (the lookback period). Paragraph (b) of this section describes persons who are defined to be disqualified persons under the statute, including certain family members of an individual in a position to exercise substantial influence, and certain 35–percent controlled entities. Paragraph (c) of this section describes persons in a position to exercise substantial influence over the affairs of an applicable tax-exempt organization by virtue of their powers and responsibilities or certain interests they hold. Paragraph (d) of this section describes persons deemed not to be in a position to exercise substantial influence. Whether any person who is not described in paragraph (b), (c) or (d) of this section is a disqualified person with respect to a transaction for purposes of section 4958 is based on all relevant facts and circumstances, as described in paragraph (e) of this section. Paragraph (f) of this section describes special rules for affiliated organizations. Examples in paragraph (g) of this section illustrate these categories of persons.

(2) Transition rule for lookback period. In the case of any excess benefit transaction occurring before September 14, 2000, the lookback period described in paragraph (a)(1) of this section begins on September 14, 1995, and ends on the date of the transaction.

(b) Statutory categories of disqualified persons—

(1) Family members. A person is a disqualified person with respect to any transaction with an applicable tax-exempt organization if the person is a member of the family of a person who is a disqualified person described in paragraph (a) of this section (other than as a result of this paragraph) with respect to any transaction with the same organization.

For purposes of the following sentence, a legally adopted child of an individual is treated as a child of such individual by blood. A person's family is limited to—

(i) Spouse;

(ii) Brothers or sisters (by whole or half blood);

(iii) Spouses of brothers or sisters (by whole or half blood);

(iv) Ancestors;

(v) Children;

(vi) Grandchildren;

(vii) Great grandchildren; and

(viii) Spouses of children, grandchildren, and great grandchildren.

(2) Thirty-five percent controlled entities—

(i) In general. A person is a disqualified person with respect to any transaction with an applicable tax-exempt organization if the person is a 35–percent controlled entity. A 35–percent controlled entity is—

(A) A corporation in which persons described in this section (except in paragraphs (b)(2) and (d) of this section) own more than 35 percent of the combined voting power;

(B) A partnership in which persons described in this section (except in paragraphs (b)(2) and (d) of this section) own more than 35 percent of the profits interest; or

(C) A trust or estate in which persons described in this section (except in paragraphs (b)(2) and (d) of this section) own more than 35 percent of the beneficial interest.

(ii) Combined voting power. For purposes of this paragraph (b)(2), combined voting power includes voting power represented by holdings of voting stock, direct or indirect, but does not include voting rights held only as a director, trustee, or other fiduciary.

(iii) Constructive ownership rules—(A) Stockholdings. For purposes of section 4958(f)(3) and this paragraph (b)(2), indirect stockholdings are taken into account as under section 267(c), except that in applying section 267(c)(4), the family of an individual shall include the members of the family specified in section 4958(f)(4) and paragraph (b)(1) of this section.

(B) Profits or beneficial interest. For purposes of section 4958(f)(3) and this paragraph (b)(2), the ownership of profits or beneficial interests shall be determined in accordance with the rules for constructive ownership of stock provided in section 267(c) (other than section 267(c)(3)), except that in applying section 267(c)(4), the family of an individual shall include the members of the family specified in section 4958(f)(4) and paragraph (b)(1) of this section.

(c) Persons having substantial influence. A person who holds any of the following powers, responsibilities, or interests is in a position to exercise substantial influence over the affairs of an applicable tax-exempt organization:

(1) Voting members of the governing body. This category includes any individual serving on the governing body of the organization who is entitled to vote on any matter over which the governing body has authority.

(2) Presidents, chief executive officers, or chief operating officers. This category includes any person who, regardless of title, has ultimate responsibility for implementing the decisions of the governing body or for supervising the management, administration, or operation of the organization. A person who serves as president, chief executive officer, or chief operating officer has this ultimate responsibility unless the person demonstrates otherwise. If this ultimate responsibility resides with two or more individuals (e.g., co-presidents), who may exercise such responsibility in concert or individually, then each individual is in a position to exercise substantial influence over the affairs of the organization.

(3) Treasurers and chief financial officers. This category includes any person who, regardless of title, has ultimate responsibility for managing the finances of the organization. A person who serves as treasurer or chief financial officer has this ultimate responsibility unless the person demonstrates otherwise. If this ultimate responsibility resides with two or more individuals who may exercise the responsibility in concert or individually, then each individual is in a position to exercise substantial influence over the affairs of the organization.

(4) Persons with a material financial interest in a provider-sponsored organization. For purposes of section 4958, if a hospital that participates in a provider-sponsored organization (as defined in section 1855(e) of the Social Security Act, 42 U.S.C. 1395w–25) is an applicable tax-exempt organization, then any person with a material financial interest (within the meaning of section 501(*o*)) in the provider-sponsored organization has substantial influence with respect to the hospital.

(d) Persons deemed not to have substantial influence. A person is deemed not to be in a position to exercise substantial influence over the affairs of an applicable tax-exempt organization if that person is described in one of the following categories:

(1) Tax-exempt organizations described in section 501(c)(3). This category includes any organization described in section 501(c)(3) and exempt from tax under section 501(a).

(2) Certain section 501(c)(4) organizations. Only with respect to an applicable tax-exempt organization described in section 501(c)(4) and

§ 53.4958–2(a)(4), this category includes any other organization so described.

(3) Employees receiving economic benefits of less than a specified amount in a taxable year. This category includes, for the taxable year in which benefits are provided, any full-or part-time employee of the applicable tax-exempt organization who—

(i) Receives economic benefits, directly or indirectly from the organization, of less than the amount referenced for a highly compensated employee in section 414(q)(1)(B)(i);

(ii) Is not described in paragraph (b) or (c) of this section with respect to the organization; and

(iii) Is not a substantial contributor to the organization within the meaning of section 507(d)(2)(A), taking into account only contributions received by the organization during its current taxable year and the four preceding taxable years.

(e) Facts and circumstances govern in all other cases—

(1) In general. Whether a person who is not described in paragraph (b), (c) or (d) of this section is a disqualified person depends upon all relevant facts and circumstances.

(2) Facts and circumstances tending to show substantial influence. Facts and circumstances tending to show that a person has substantial influence over the affairs of an organization include, but are not limited to, the following—

(i) The person founded the organization;

(ii) The person is a substantial contributor to the organization (within the meaning of section 507(d)(2)(A)), taking into account only contributions received by the organization during its current taxable year and the four preceding taxable years;

(iii) The person's compensation is primarily based on revenues derived from activities of the organization, or of a particular department or function of the organization, that the person controls;

(iv) The person has or shares authority to control or determine a substantial portion of the organization's capital expenditures, operating budget, or compensation for employees;

(v) The person manages a discrete segment or activity of the organization that represents a substantial portion of the activities, assets, income, or expenses of the organization, as compared to the organization as a whole;

(vi) The person owns a controlling interest (measured by either vote or value) in a corporation, partnership, or trust that is a disqualified person; or

(vii) The person is a non-stock organization controlled, directly or indirectly, by one or more disqualified persons.

(3) *Facts and circumstances tending to show no substantial influence.* Facts and circumstances tending to show that a person does not have substantial influence over the affairs of an organization include, but are not limited to, the following—

(i) The person has taken a bona fide vow of poverty as an employee, agent, or on behalf, of a religious organization;

(ii) The person is a contractor (such as an attorney, accountant, or investment manager or advisor) whose sole relationship to the organization is providing professional advice (without having decision-making authority) with respect to transactions from which the contractor will not economically benefit either directly or indirectly (aside from customary fees received for the professional advice rendered);

(iii) The direct supervisor of the individual is not a disqualified person;

(iv) The person does not participate in any management decisions affecting the organization as a whole or a discrete segment or activity of the organization that represents a substantial portion of the activities, assets, income, or expenses of the organization, as compared to the organization as a whole; or

(v) Any preferential treatment a person receives based on the size of that person's contribution is also offered to all other donors making a comparable contribution as part of a solicitation intended to attract a substantial number of contributions.

(f) *Affiliated organizations.* In the case of multiple organizations affiliated by common control or governing documents, the determination of whether a person does or does not have substantial influence shall be made separately for each applicable tax-exempt organization. A person may be a disqualified person with respect to transactions with more than one applicable tax-exempt organization.

(g) *Examples.* The following examples illustrate the principles of this section. A finding that a person is a disqualified person in the following examples does not indicate that an excess benefit transaction has occurred. If a person is a disqualified person, the rules of section 4958(c) and § 53.4958-4 apply to determine whether an excess benefit transaction has occurred. The examples are as follows:

Example 1. N, an artist by profession, works part-time at R, a local museum. In the first taxable year in which R employs N, R pays N a salary and provides no additional benefits to N except for free admission to the museum, a benefit R provides to all of its employees and volunteers. The total economic benefits N receives from R during the taxable year are less than the amount referenced for a highly compensated employee in section 414(q)(1)(B)(i). The part-time job constitutes N's only relationship with R. N is not related to any other disqualified person with respect to R. N is deemed not to be in a position to exercise substantial influence over the affairs of R. Therefore, N is not a disqualified person with respect to R in that year.

Example 2. The facts are the same as in Example 1, except that in addition to the salary that R pays N for N's services during the taxable year, R also purchases one of N's paintings for $x. The total of N's salary plus $x exceeds the amount referenced for highly compensated employees in section 414(q)(1)(B)(i). Consequently, whether N is in a position to exercise substantial influence over the affairs of R for that taxable year depends upon all of the relevant facts and circumstances.

Example 3. Q is a member of K, a section 501(c)(3)organization with a broad-based public membership. Members of K are entitled to vote only with respect to the annual election of directors and the approval of major organizational transactions such as a merger or dissolution. Q is not related to any other disqualified person of K. Q has no other relationship to K besides being a member of K and occasionally making modest donations to K. Whether Q is a disqualified person is determined by all relevant facts and circumstances. Q's voting rights, which are the same as granted to all members of K, do not place Q in a position to exercise substantial influence over K. Under these facts and circumstances, Q is not a disqualified person with respect to K.

Example 4. E is the headmaster of Z, a school that is an applicable tax-exempt organization for purposes of section 4958. E reports to Z's board of trustees and has ultimate responsibility for supervising Z's day-to-day operations. For example, E can hire faculty members and staff, make changes to the school's curriculum and discipline students without specific board approval. Because E has ultimate responsibility for supervising the operation of Z, E is in a position to exercise substantial influence over the affairs of Z. Therefore, E is a disqualified person with respect to Z.

Example 5. Y is an applicable tax-exempt organization for purposes of section 4958 that decides to use bingo games as a method of generating revenue. Y enters into a contract with B, a company that operates bingo games. Under the contract, B manages the promotion and operation of the bingo activity, provides all necessary staff, equipment, and services, and pays Y q percent of the revenue from this activity. B retains the balance of the proceeds. Y provides no goods or services in connection with the bingo operation other than the use of its hall for the bingo games. The annual gross revenue earned from the bingo games represents more than half of Y's total annual revenue. B's compensation is primarily based on revenues from an activity B controls. B also manages a discrete activity of Y that represents a substantial portion of Y's income compared to the organization as a whole. Under these facts and circumstances, B is in a position to exercise substantial influence over the affairs of Y. Therefore, B is a disqualified person with respect to Y.

Example 6. The facts are the same as in Example 5, with the additional fact that P owns a majority of the stock of B and is actively involved in managing B. Because P owns a controlling interest (measured by either vote or value) in and actively manages B, P is also in a position to exercise substantial influence over the affairs of Y. Therefore, under these facts and circumstances, P is a disqualified person with respect to Y.

Example 7. A, an applicable tax-exempt organization for purposes of section 4958, owns and operates one acute care hospital. B, a for-profit corporation, owns and operates a number of hospitals. A and B form C, a limited liability company. In exchange for proportional ownership interests, A contributes its hospital, and B contributes other assets, to C. All of A's assets then consist of its membership interest in C. A continues to be operated for exempt purposes based almost exclusively on the activities it conducts through C. C enters into a management agreement with a management company, M, to provide day to day management services to C. Subject to supervision by C's board, M is given broad discretion to manage C's day to day operation and has ultimate responsibility for supervising the management of the hospital. Because M has ultimate responsibility for supervising the management of the hospital operated by C, A's ownership interest in C is its primary asset, and C's activities form the basis for A's continued exemption as an organization described in section 501(c)(3), M is in a position to exercise substantial influence over the affairs of A. Therefore, M is a disqualified person with respect to A.

Example 8. T is a large university and an applicable tax-exempt organization for purposes of section 4958. L is the dean of the College of Law of T, a substantial source of revenue for T, including contributions from alumni and foundations. L is not related to any other disqualified person of T. L does not serve on T's governing body or have ultimate responsibility for managing the university as whole. However, as dean of the College of Law, L plays a key role in faculty hiring and determines a substantial portion of the capital expenditures and operating budget of the College of Law. L's compensation is greater than the amount referenced for a highly compensated employee in section 414(q)(1)(B)(i) in the year benefits are provided. L's management of a discrete segment of T that represents a substantial portion of the income of T (as compared to T as a whole) places L in a position to exercise substantial influence over the affairs of T. Under these facts and circumstances L is a disqualified person with respect to T.

Example 9. S chairs a small academic department in the College of Arts and Sciences of the same university T described in Example 8. S is not related to any other disqualified person of T. S does not serve on T's governing body or as an officer of T. As department chair, S supervises faculty in the department, approves the course curriculum, and oversees the operating budget for the department. S's compensation is greater than the amount referenced for a highly compensated employee in section 414(q)(1)(B)(i) in the year benefits are provided. Even though S manages the department, that department does not represent a substantial portion of T's activities, assets, income, expenses, or operating budget. Therefore, S does not participate in any management decisions affecting either T as a whole, or a discrete segment or activity of T that represents a substantial portion of its activities, assets, income, or expenses. Under these facts and circumstances, S does not have substantial influence over the affairs of T, and therefore S is not a disqualified person with respect to T.

Example 10.   U is a large acute-care hospital that is an applicable tax-exempt organization for purposes of section 4958. U employs X as a radiologist. X gives instructions to staff with respect to the radiology work X conducts, but X does not supervise other U employees or manage any substantial part of U's operations. X's compensation is primarily in the form of a fixed salary. In addition, X is eligible to receive an incentive award based on revenues of the radiology department. X's compensation is greater than the amount referenced for a highly compensated employee in section 414(q)(1)(B)(i) in the year benefits are provided. X is not related to any other disqualified person of U. X does not serve on U's governing body or as an officer of U. Although U participates in a provider-sponsored organization (as defined in section 1855(e) of the Social Security Act), X does not have a material financial interest in that organization. X does not receive compensation primarily based on revenues derived from activities of U that X controls. X does not participate in any management decisions affecting either U as a whole or a discrete segment of U that represents a substantial portion of its activities, assets, income, or expenses. Under these facts and circumstances, X does not have substantial influence over the affairs of U, and therefore X is not a disqualified person with respect to U.

Example 11.   W is a cardiologist and head of the cardiology department of the same hospital U described in Example 10. The cardiology department is a major source of patients admitted to U and consequently represents a substantial portion of U's income, as compared to U as a whole. W does not serve on U's governing board or as an officer of U. W does not have a material financial interest in the provider-sponsored organization (as defined in section 1855(e) of the Social Security Act) in which U participates. W receives a salary and retirement and welfare benefits fixed by a three-year renewable employment contract with U. W's compensation is greater than the amount referenced for a highly compensated employee in section 414(q)(1)(B)(i) in the year benefits are provided. As department head, W manages the cardiology department and has authority to allocate the budget for that department, which includes authority to distribute incentive bonuses among cardiologists according to criteria that W has authority to set. W's management of a discrete segment of U that represents a substantial portion of its income and activities (as compared to U as a whole) places W in a position to exercise substantial influence over the affairs of U. Under these facts and circumstances, W is a disqualified person with respect to U.

272

Example 12. M is a museum that is an applicable tax-exempt organization for purposes of section 4958. D provides accounting services and tax advice to M as a contractor in return for a fee. D has no other relationship with M and is not related to any disqualified person of M. D does not provide professional advice with respect to any transaction from which D might economically benefit either directly or indirectly (aside from fees received for the professional advice rendered). Because D's sole relationship to M is providing professional advice (without having decision-making authority) with respect to transactions from which D will not economically benefit either directly or indirectly (aside from customary fees received for the professional advice rendered), under these facts and circumstances, D is not a disqualified person with respect to M.

Example 13. F is a repertory theater company that is an applicable tax-exempt organization for purposes of section 4958. F holds a fund-raising campaign to pay for the construction of a new theater. J is a regular subscriber to F's productions who has made modest gifts to F in the past. J has no relationship to F other than as a subscriber and contributor. F solicits contributions as part of a broad public campaign intended to attract a large number of donors, including a substantial number of donors making large gifts. In its solicitations for contributions, F promises to invite all contributors giving $z or more to a special opening production and party held at the new theater. These contributors are also given a special number to call in F's office to reserve tickets for performances, make ticket exchanges, and make other special arrangements for their convenience. J makes a contribution of $z to F, which makes J a substantial contributor within the meaning of section 507(d)(2)(A), taking into account only contributions received by F during its current and the four preceding taxable years. J receives the benefits described in F's solicitation. Because F offers the same benefit to all donors of $z or more, the preferential treatment that J receives does not indicate that J is in a position to exercise substantial influence over the affairs of the organization. Therefore, under these facts and circumstances, J is not a disqualified person with respect to F.

§ 53.4958–4 Excess benefit transaction

(a) Definition of excess benefit transaction—

(1) In general. An excess benefit transaction means any transaction in which an economic benefit is provided by an applicable tax-exempt organization directly or indirectly to or for the use of any disqualified person, and the value of the economic benefit provided exceeds the value of the consideration (including the performance of services) received for providing the benefit. Subject to the limitations of paragraph (c) of this section (relating to the treatment of economic benefits as compensation for the performance of services), to determine whether an excess benefit transaction has occurred, all consideration and benefits (except disregarded benefits described in paragraph (a)(4) of this section) exchanged between a disqualified person and the applicable tax-exempt organization and all entities the organization controls (within the meaning of paragraph (a)(2)(ii)(B) of this section) are taken into account. For example, in determining the reasonableness of compensation that is paid (or vests, or is no longer subject to a substantial risk of forfeiture) in one year, services performed in prior years may be taken into account. The rules of this section apply to all transactions with disqualified persons, regardless of whether the amount of the benefit provided is determined, in whole or in part, by the revenues of one or more activities of the organization. For rules regarding valuation standards, see paragraph (b) of this section. For the requirement that an applicable tax-exempt organization clearly indicate its intent to treat a benefit as compensation for services when paid, see paragraph (c) of this section.

(2) Economic benefit provided indirectly—

(i) In general. A transaction that would be an excess benefit transaction if the applicable tax-exempt organization engaged in it directly with a disqualified person is likewise an excess benefit transaction when it is accomplished indirectly. An applicable tax-exempt organization may provide an excess benefit indirectly to a disqualified person through a controlled entity or through an intermediary, as described in paragraphs (a)(2)(ii) and (iii) of this section, respectively.

(ii) Through a controlled entity—(A) In general. An applicable tax-exempt organization may provide an excess benefit indirectly through the use of one or more entities it controls. For purposes of section 4958, economic benefits provided by a controlled entity will be treated as provided by the applicable tax-exempt organization.

(B) Definition of control—

(1) In general. For purposes of this paragraph, control by an applicable tax-exempt organization means—

(i) In the case of a stock corporation, ownership (by vote or value) of more than 50 percent of the stock in such corporation;

(ii) In the case of a partnership, ownership of more than 50 percent of the profits interests or capital interests in the partnership;

(iii) In the case of a nonstock organization (i.e., an entity in which no person holds a proprietary interest), that at least 50 percent of the directors or trustees of the organization are either representatives (including trustees, directors, agents, or employees) of, or directly or indirectly controlled by, an applicable tax-exempt organization; or

(iv) In the case of any other entity, ownership of more than 50 percent of the beneficial interest in the entity.

(2) Constructive ownership. Section 318 (relating to constructive ownership of stock) shall apply for purposes of determining ownership of stock in a corporation. Similar principles shall apply for purposes of determining ownership of interests in any other entity.

(iii) Through an intermediary. An applicable tax-exempt organization may provide an excess benefit indirectly through an intermediary. An intermediary is any person (including an individual or a taxable or tax-exempt entity) who participates in a transaction with one or more disqualified persons of an applicable tax-exempt organization. For purposes of section 4958, economic benefits provided by an intermediary will be treated as provided by the applicable tax-exempt organization when—

(A) An applicable tax-exempt organization provides an economic benefit to an intermediary; and

(B) In connection with the receipt of the benefit by the intermediary—

(1) There is evidence of an oral or written agreement or understanding that the intermediary will provide economic benefits to or for the use of a disqualified person; or

(2) The intermediary provides economic benefits to or for the use of a disqualified person without a significant business purpose or exempt purpose of its own.

(iv) Examples. The following examples illustrate when economic benefits are provided indirectly under the rules of this paragraph (a)(2):

Example 1.   K is an applicable tax-exempt organization for purposes of section 4958. L is a wholly-owned taxable subsidiary of K. J is employed by K, and is a disqualified person with respect to K. K pays J an annual salary of $12m, and reports that amount as compensation during calendar year 2001. Although J only performed services for K for nine months of 2001, J performed equivalent services for L during the remaining three months of 2001. Taking into account all of the economic benefits K provided to J, and all of the services J performed for K and L, $12m does not exceed the fair market value of the services J performed for K and L during 2001. Therefore, under these facts, K does not provide an excess benefit to J directly or indirectly.

Example 2.   F is an applicable tax-exempt organization for purposes of section 4958. D is an entity controlled by F within the meaning of paragraph (a)(2)(ii)(B) of this section. T is the chief executive officer (CEO) of F. As CEO, T is responsible for overseeing the activities of F. T's duties as CEO make him a disqualified person with respect to F. T's compensation package with F represents the maximum reasonable compensation for T's services as CEO. Thus, any additional economic benefits that F provides to T without T providing additional consideration constitute an excess benefit. D contracts with T to provide enumerated consulting services to D. However, the contract does not require T to perform any additional services for D that T is not already obligated to perform as F's chief executive officer. Therefore, any payment to T pursuant to the consulting contract with D represents an indirect excess benefit that F provides through a controlled entity, even if F, D, or T treats the additional payment to T as compensation.

Example 3. P is an applicable tax-exempt organization for purposes of section 4958. S is a taxable entity controlled by P within the meaning of paragraph (a)(2)(ii)(B) of this section. V is the chief executive officer of S, for which S pays V $w in salary and benefits. V also serves as a voting member of P's governing body. Consequently, V is a disqualified person with respect to P. P provides V with $x representing compensation for the services V provides P as a member of its governing body. Although $x represents reasonable compensation for the services V provides directly to P as a member of its governing body, the total compensation of $w + $x exceeds reasonable compensation for the services V provides to P and S collectively. Therefore, the portion of total compensation that exceeds reasonable compensation is an excess benefit provided to V.

Example 4. G is an applicable tax-exempt organization for section 4958 purposes. F is a disqualified person who was last employed by G in a position of substantial influence three years ago. H is an entity engaged in scientific research and is unrelated to either F or G. G makes a grant to H to fund a research position. H subsequently advertises for qualified candidates for the research position. F is among several highly qualified candidates who apply for the research position. H hires F. There was no evidence of an oral or written agreement or understanding with G that H will use G's grant to provide economic benefits to or for the use of F. Although G provided economic benefits to H, and in connection with the receipt of such benefits, H will provide economic benefits to or for the use of F, H acted with a significant business purpose or exempt purpose of its own. Under these facts, G did not provide an economic benefit to F indirectly through the use of an intermediary.

(3) Exception for fixed payments made pursuant to an initial contract—

(i) In general. Except as provided in paragraph (a)(3)(iv) of this section, section 4958 does not apply to any fixed payment made to a person pursuant to an initial contract.

(ii) Fixed payment—

(A) In general. For purposes of paragraph (a)(3)(i) of this section, fixed payment means an amount of cash or other property specified in the contract, or determined by a fixed formula specified in the contract, which is to be paid or transferred in exchange for the provision of specified services or property. A fixed formula may incorporate an amount that depends upon future specified events or contingencies, provided that no person exercises discretion when calculating the amount of a payment or deciding whether to make a payment (such as a bonus). A specified event or contingency may include the amount of revenues generated by (or other objective measure of) one or more activities of the applicable tax-exempt organization. A fixed payment does not include any amount paid to a person under a reimbursement (or similar) arrangement where discretion is exercised by any person with respect to the amount of expenses incurred or reimbursed.

(B) Special rules. Amounts payable pursuant to a qualified pension, profit-sharing, or stock bonus plan under section 401(a), or pursuant to an employee benefit program that is subject to and satisfies coverage and nondiscrimination rules under the Internal Revenue Code (e.g., sections 127 and 137), other than nondiscrimination rules under section 9802, are treated as fixed payments for purposes of this section, regardless of the applicable tax-exempt organization's discretion with respect to the plan or program. The fact that a person contracting with an applicable tax-exempt organization is expressly granted the choice whether to accept or reject any economic benefit is disregarded in determining whether the benefit constitutes a fixed payment for purposes of this paragraph.

(iii) Initial contract. For purposes of paragraph (a)(3)(i) of this section, initial contract means a binding written contract between an applicable tax-exempt organization and a person who was not a disqualified person within the meaning of section 4958(f)(1) and § 53.4958-3 immediately prior to entering into the contract.

(iv) Substantial performance required. Paragraph (a)(3)(i) of this section does not apply to any fixed payment made pursuant to the initial contract during any taxable year of the person contracting with the applicable tax-exempt organization if the person fails to perform substantially the person's obligations under the initial contract during that year.

(v) Treatment as a new contract. A written binding contract that provides that the contract is terminable or subject to cancellation by the applicable tax-exempt organization (other than as a result of a lack of substantial performance by the disqualified person, as described in paragraph (a)(3)(iv) of this section) without the other party's consent and without substantial penalty to the organization is treated as a new contract as of the earliest date that any such termination or cancellation, if made, would be effective. Additionally, if the parties make a material change to a contract, it is treated as a new contract as of the date the material change is effective. A material change includes an extension or renewal of the contract (other than an extension or renewal that results from the person contracting with the applicable tax-exempt organization unilaterally exercising an option expressly granted by the contract), or a more than incidental change to any amount payable under the contract. The new contract is tested under paragraph (a)(3)(iii) of this section to determine whether it is an initial contract for purposes of this section.

(vi) Evaluation of non-fixed payments. Any payment that is not a fixed payment (within the meaning of paragraph (a)(3)(ii) of this section) is evaluated to determine whether it constitutes an excess benefit transaction under section 4958. In making this determination, all payments and consideration exchanged between the parties are taken into account, including any fixed payments made pursuant to an initial contract with respect to which section 4958 does not apply.

(vii) Examples. The following examples illustrate the rules governing fixed payments made pursuant to an initial contract. Unless otherwise stated, assume that the person contracting with the applicable tax-exempt organization has performed substantially the person's obligations under the contract with respect to the payment. The examples are as follows:

Example 1.   T is an applicable tax-exempt organization for purposes of section 4958. On January 1, 2002, T hires S as its chief financial officer by entering into a five-year written employment contract with S. S was not a disqualified person within the meaning of section 4958(f)(1) and § 53.4958–3 immediately prior to entering into the January 1, 2002, contract (initial contract). S's duties and responsibilities under the contract make S a disqualified person with respect to T (see § 53.4958–3(a)). Under the initial contract, T agrees to pay S an annual salary of $200,000, payable in monthly installments. The contract provides that, beginning in 2003, S's annual salary will be adjusted by the increase in the Consumer Price Index (CPI) for the prior year. Section 4958 does not apply because S's compensation under the contract is a fixed payment pursuant to an initial contract within the meaning of paragraph (a)(3) of this section. Thus, for section 4958 purposes, it is unnecessary to evaluate whether any portion of the compensation paid to S pursuant to the initial contract is an excess benefit transaction.

Example 2.   The facts are the same as in Example 1, except that the initial contract provides that, in addition to a base salary of $200,000, T may pay S an annual performance-based bonus. The contract provides that T's governing body will determine the amount of the annual bonus as of the end of each year during the term of the contract, based on the board's evaluation of S's performance, but the bonus cannot exceed $100,000 per year. Unlike the base salary portion of S's compensation, the bonus portion of S's compensation is not a fixed payment pursuant to an initial contract, because the governing body has discretion over the amount, if any, of the bonus payment. Section 4958 does not apply to payment of the $200,000 base salary (as adjusted for inflation), because it is a fixed payment pursuant to an initial contract within the meaning of paragraph (a)(3) of this section. By contrast, the annual bonuses that may be paid to S under the initial contract are not protected by the initial contract exception. Therefore, each bonus payment will be evaluated under section 4958, taking into account all payments and consideration exchanged between the parties.

Example 3.   The facts are the same as in Example 1, except that in 2003, T changes its payroll system, such that T makes biweekly, rather than monthly, salary payments to its employees. Beginning in 2003, T also grants its employees an additional two days of paid vacation each year. Neither change is a material change to S's initial contract within the meaning of paragraph (a)(3)(v) of this section. Therefore, section 4958 does not apply to the base salary payments to S due to the initial contract exception.

Example 4.   The facts are the same as in Example 1, except that on January 1, 2003, S becomes the chief executive officer of T and a new chief financial officer is hired. At the same time, T's board of directors approves an increase in S's annual base salary from $200,000 to $240,000, effective on that day. These changes in S's employment relationship constitute material changes of the initial contract within the meaning of paragraph (a)(3)(v) of this section. As a result, S is treated as entering into a new contract with T on January 1, 2003, at which time S is a disqualified person within the meaning of section 4958(f)(1) and § 53.4958–3. T's payments to S made pursuant to the new contract will be evaluated under section 4958, taking into account all payments and consideration exchanged between the parties.

Example 5.   J is a performing arts organization and an applicable tax-exempt organization for purposes of section 4958. J hires W to become the chief executive officer of J. W was not a disqualified person within the meaning of section 4958(f)(1) and § 53.4958–3 immediately prior to entering into the employment contract with J. As a result of this employment contract, W's duties and responsibilities make W a disqualified person with respect to J (see § 53.4958–3(c)(2)). Under the contract, J will pay W $x (a specified amount) plus a bonus equal to 2 percent of the total season subscription sales that exceed $100z. The $x base salary is a fixed payment pursuant to an initial contract within the meaning of paragraph (a)(3) of this section. The bonus payment is also a fixed payment pursuant to an initial contract within the meaning of paragraph (a)(3) of this section, because no person exercises discretion when calculating the amount of the bonus payment or deciding whether the bonus will be paid. Therefore, section 4958 does not apply to any of J's payments to W pursuant to the employment contract due to the initial contract exception.

Example 6. Hospital B is an applicable tax-exempt organization for purposes of section 4958. Hospital B hires E as its chief operating officer. E was not a disqualified person within the meaning of section 4958(f)(1) and § 53.4958–3 immediately prior to entering into the employment contract with Hospital B. As a result of this employment contract, E's duties and responsibilities make E a disqualified person with respect to Hospital B (see § 53.4958–3(c)(2)). E's initial employment contract provides that E will have authority to enter into hospital management arrangements on behalf of Hospital B. In E's personal capacity, E owns more than 35 percent of the combined voting power of Company X. Consequently, at the time E becomes a disqualified person with respect to B, Company X also becomes a disqualified person with respect to B (see § 53.4958–3(b)(2)(i)(A)). E, acting on behalf of Hospital B as chief operating officer, enters into a contract with Company X under which Company X will provide billing and collection services to Hospital B. The initial contract exception of paragraph (a)(3)(i) of this section does not apply to the billing and collection services contract, because at the time that this contractual arrangement was entered into, Company X was a disqualified person with respect to Hospital B. Although E's employment contract (which is an initial contract) authorizes E to enter into hospital management arrangements on behalf of Hospital B, the payments made to Company X are not made pursuant to E's employment contract, but rather are made by Hospital B pursuant to a separate contractual arrangement with Company X. Therefore, even if payments made to Company X under the billing and collection services contract are fixed payments (within the meaning of paragraph (a)(3)(ii) of this section), section 4958 nonetheless applies to payments made by Hospital B to Company X because the billing and collection services contract itself does not constitute an initial contract under paragraph (a)(3)(iii) of this section. Accordingly, all payments made to Company X under the billing and collection services contract will be evaluated under section 4958.

Example 7. Hospital C, an applicable tax-exempt organization, enters into a contract with Company Y, under which Company Y will provide a wide range of hospital management services to Hospital C. Upon entering into this contractual arrangement, Company Y becomes a disqualified person with respect to Hospital C. The contract provides that Hospital C will pay Company Y a management fee of x percent of adjusted gross revenue (i.e., gross revenue increased by the cost of charity care provided to indigents) annually for a five-year period. The management services contract specifies the cost accounting system and the standards for indigents to be used in calculating the cost of charity care. The cost accounting system objectively defines the direct and indirect costs of all health care goods and services provided as charity care. Because Company Y was not a disqualified person with respect to Hospital C immediately before entering into the management services contract, that contract is an initial contract within the meaning of paragraph (a)(3)(iii) of this section. The annual management fee paid to Company Y is determined by a fixed formula specified in the contract, and is therefore a fixed payment within the meaning of paragraph (a)(3)(ii) of this section. Accordingly, section 4958 does not apply to the annual management fee due to the initial contract exception.

Example 8.   The facts are the same as in Example 7, except that the management services contract also provides that Hospital C will reimburse Company Y on a monthly basis for certain expenses incurred by Company Y that are attributable to management services provided to Hospital C (e.g., legal fees and travel expenses). Although the management fee itself is a fixed payment not subject to section 4958, the reimbursement payments that Hospital C makes to Company Y for the various expenses covered by the contract are not fixed payments within the meaning of paragraph (a)(3)(ii) of this section, because Company Y exercises discretion with respect to the amount of expenses incurred. Therefore, any reimbursement payments that Hospital C pays pursuant to the contract will be evaluated under section 4958.

Example 9   X, an applicable tax-exempt organization for purposes of section 4958, hires C to conduct scientific research. On January 1, 2003, C enters into a three-year written employment contract with X (initial contract). Under the terms of the contract, C is required to work full-time at X's laboratory for a fixed annual salary of $90,000. Immediately prior to entering into the employment contract, C was not a disqualified person within the meaning of section 4958(f)(1) and § 53.4958–3, nor did C become a disqualified person pursuant to the initial contract. However, two years after joining X, C marries D, who is the child of X's president. As D's spouse, C is a disqualified person within the meaning of section 4958(f)(1) and § 53.4958–3 with respect to X. Nonetheless, section 4958 does not apply to X's salary payments to C due to the initial contract exception.

Example 10.   The facts are the same as in Example 9, except that the initial contract included a below-market loan provision under which C has the unilateral right to borrow up to a specified dollar amount from X at a specified interest rate for a specified term. After

C's marriage to D, C borrows money from X to purchase a home under the terms of the initial contract. Section 4958 does not apply to X's loan to C due to the initial contract exception.

Example 11. The facts are the same as in Example 9, except that after C's marriage to D, C works only sporadically at the laboratory, and performs no other services for X. Notwithstanding that C fails to perform substantially C's obligations under the initial contract, X does not exercise its right to terminate the initial contract for nonperformance and continues to pay full salary to C. Pursuant to paragraph (a)(3)(iv) of this section, the initial contract exception does not apply to any payments made pursuant to the initial contract during any taxable year of C in which C fails to perform substantially C's obligations under the initial contract.

(4) Certain economic benefits disregarded for purposes of section 4958. The following economic benefits are disregarded for purposes of section 4958—

(i) Nontaxable fringe benefits. An economic benefit that is excluded from income under section 132, except any liability insurance premium, payment, or reimbursement that must be taken into account under paragraph (b)(1)(ii)(B)(2) of this section;

(ii) Expense reimbursement payments pursuant to accountable plans. Amounts paid under reimbursement arrangements that meet the requirements of § 1.62–2(c) of this chapter;

(iii) Certain economic benefits provided to a volunteer for the organization. An economic benefit provided to a volunteer for the organization if the benefit is provided to the general public in exchange for a membership fee or contribution of $75 or less per year;

(iv) Certain economic benefits provided to a member of, or donor to, the organization. An economic benefit provided to a member of an organization solely on account of the payment of a membership fee, or to a donor solely on account of a contribution for which a deduction is allowable under section 170 (charitable contribution), regardless of whether the donor is eligible to claim the deduction, if—

(A) Any non-disqualified person paying a membership fee or making a charitable contribution above a specified amount to the organization is given the option of receiving substantially the same economic benefit; and

(B) The disqualified person and a significant number of non-disqualified persons make a payment or charitable contribution of at least the specified amount;

(v) Economic benefits provided to a charitable beneficiary. An economic benefit provided to a person solely because the person is a member of a charitable class that the applicable tax-exempt organization intends to benefit as part of the accomplishment of the organization's exempt purpose; and

(vi) Certain economic benefits provided to a governmental unit. Any transfer of an economic benefit to or for the use of a governmental unit defined in section 170(c)(1), if the transfer is for exclusively public purposes.

(5) Exception for certain payments made pursuant to an exemption granted by the Department of Labor under ERISA. Section 4958 does not apply to any payment made pursuant to, and in accordance with, a final individual prohibited transaction exemption issued by the Department of Labor under section 408(a) of the Employee Retirement Income Security Act of 1974 (88 Stat. 854) (ERISA) with respect to a transaction involving a plan (as defined in section 3(3) of ERISA) that is an applicable tax exempt organization.

(b) Valuation standards—

(1) In general. This section provides rules for determining the value of economic benefits for purposes of section 4958.

(i) Fair market value of property. The value of property, including the right to use property, for purposes of section 4958 is the fair market value (i.e., the price at which property or the right to use property would change hands between a willing buyer and a willing seller, neither being under any compulsion to buy, sell or transfer property or the right to use property, and both having reasonable knowledge of relevant facts).

(ii) Reasonable compensation—

(A) In general. The value of services is the amount that would ordinarily be paid for like services by like enterprises (whether taxable or tax-exempt) under like circumstances (i.e., reasonable compensation). Section 162 standards apply in determining reasonableness of compensation, taking into account the aggregate benefits (other than any benefits specifically disregarded under paragraph (a)(4) of this section) provided to a person and the rate at which any deferred compensation accrues. The fact that a compensation arrangement is subject to a cap is a relevant factor in determining the reasonableness of compensation. The fact that a State or local legislative or agency body or court has authorized or approved a particular compensation package paid to a disqualified person is not determinative of the reasonableness of compensation for purposes of section 4958.

(B) Items included in determining the value of compensation for purposes of determining reasonableness under section 4958. Except for economic benefits that are disregarded for purposes of section 4958 under paragraph (a)(4) of this section, compensation for purposes of determining reasonableness under section 4958 includes all economic benefits provided by an applicable tax-exempt organization in exchange for the performance of services. These benefits include, but are not limited to—

(1) All forms of cash and noncash compensation, including salary, fees, bonuses, severance payments, and deferred and noncash compensation described in § 53.4958–1(e)(2);

(2) Unless excludable from income as a de minimis fringe benefit pursuant to section 132(a)(4), the payment of liability insurance premiums for, or the payment or reimbursement by the organization of—

(i) Any penalty, tax, or expense of correction owed under section 4958;

(ii) Any expense not reasonably incurred by the person in connection with a civil judicial or civil administrative proceeding arising out of the person's performance of services on behalf of the applicable tax-exempt organization; or

(iii) Any expense resulting from an act or failure to act with respect to which the person has acted willfully and without reasonable cause; and

(3) All other compensatory benefits, whether or not included in gross income for income tax purposes, including payments to welfare benefit plans, such as plans providing medical, dental, life insurance, severance pay, and disability benefits, and both taxable and nontaxable fringe benefits (other than fringe benefits described in section 132), including expense allowances or reimbursements (other than expense reimbursements pursuant to an accountable plan that meets the requirements of § 1.62–2(c)), and the economic benefit of a below-market loan (within the meaning of section 7872(e)(1)). (For this purpose, the economic benefit of a below-market loan is the amount deemed transferred to the disqualified person under section 7872(a) or (b), regardless of whether section 7872 otherwise applies to the loan).

(C) Inclusion in compensation for reasonableness determination does not govern income tax treatment. The determination of whether any item listed in paragraph (b)(1)(ii)(B) of this section is included in the disqualified person's gross income for income tax purposes is made on the basis of the provisions of chapter 1 of Subtitle A of the Internal Revenue Code, without regard to whether the item is taken into account for purposes of determining reasonableness of compensation under section 4958.

284

(2) Timing of reasonableness determination—

(i) In general. The facts and circumstances to be taken into consideration in determining reasonableness of a fixed payment (within the meaning of paragraph (a)(3)(ii) of this section) are those existing on the date the parties enter into the contract pursuant to which the payment is made. However, in the event of substantial non-performance, reasonableness is determined based on all facts and circumstances, up to and including circumstances as of the date of payment. In the case of any payment that is not a fixed payment under a contract, reasonableness is determined based on all facts and circumstances, up to and including circumstances as of the date of payment. In no event shall circumstances existing at the date when the payment is questioned be considered in making a determination of the reasonableness of the payment. These general timing rules also apply to property subject to a substantial risk of forfeiture. Therefore, if the property subject to a substantial risk of forfeiture satisfies the definition of fixed payment (within the meaning of paragraph (a)(3)(ii) of this section), reasonableness is determined at the time the parties enter into the contract providing for the transfer of the property. If the property is not a fixed payment, then reasonableness is determined based on all facts and circumstances up to and including circumstances as of the date of payment.

(ii) Treatment as a new contract. For purposes of paragraph (b)(2)(i) of this section, a written binding contract that provides that the contract is terminable or subject to cancellation by the applicable tax-exempt organization without the other party's consent and without substantial penalty to the organization is treated as a new contract as of the earliest date that any such termination or cancellation, if made, would be effective. Additionally, if the parties make a material change to a contract (within the meaning of paragraph (a)(3)(v) of this section), it is treated as a new contract as of the date the material change is effective.

(iii) Examples. The following examples illustrate the timing of the reasonableness determination under the rules of this paragraph (b)(2):

Example 1.   G is an applicable tax-exempt organization for purposes of section 4958. H is an employee of G and a disqualified person with respect to G. H's new multi-year employment contract provides for payment of a salary and provision of specific benefits pursuant to a qualified pension plan under section 401(a) and an accident and health plan that meets the requirements of section 105(h)(2). The contract provides that H's salary will be adjusted by the increase in the Consumer Price Index (CPI) for the prior year. The contributions G makes to the qualified pension plan are equal to the maximum amount G is permitted to contribute under the rules applicable to qualified plans. Under these facts, all items comprising H's total compensation are treated as fixed payments within the meaning of paragraph (a)(3)(ii) of this section. Therefore, the reasonableness of H's compensation is determined based on the circumstances existing at the time G and H enter into the employment contract.

Example 2. The facts are the same as in Example 1, except that the multi-year employment contract provides, in addition, that G will transfer title to a car to H under the condition that if H fails to complete x years of service with G, title to the car will be forfeited back to G. All relevant information about the type of car to be provided (including the make, model, and year) is included in the contract. Although ultimate vesting of title to the car is contingent on H continuing to work for G for x years, the amount of property to be vested (i.e., the type of car) is specified in the contract, and no person exercises discretion regarding the type of property or whether H will retain title to the property at the time of vesting. Under these facts, the car is a fixed payment within the meaning of paragraph (a)(3)(ii) of this section. Therefore, the reasonableness of H's compensation, including the value of the car, is determined based on the circumstances existing at the time G and H enter into the employment contract.

Example 3. N is an applicable tax-exempt organization for purposes of section 4958. On January 2, N's governing body enters into a new one-year employment contract with K, its executive director, who is a disqualified person with respect to N. The contract provides that K will receive a specified amount of salary, contributions to a qualified pension plan under section 401(a), and other benefits pursuant to a section 125 cafeteria plan. In addition, the contract provides that N's governing body may, in its discretion, declare a bonus to be paid to K at any time during the year covered by the contract. K's salary and other specified benefits constitute fixed payments within the meaning of paragraph (a)(3)(ii) of this section. Therefore, the reasonableness of those economic benefits is determined on the date when the contract was made. However, because the bonus payment is not a fixed payment within the meaning of paragraph (a)(3)(ii) of this section, the determination of whether any bonus awarded to N is reasonable must be made based on all facts and circumstances (including all payments and consideration exchanged between the parties), up to and including circumstances as of the date of payment of the bonus.

(c) Establishing intent to treat economic benefit as consideration for the performance of services—

(1) In general. An economic benefit is not treated as consideration for the performance of services unless the organization providing the benefit clearly indicates its intent to treat the benefit as compensation when the benefit is paid. Except as provided in paragraph (c)(2) of this section, an applicable tax-exempt organization (or entity controlled by an applicable tax-exempt organization, within the meaning of paragraph (a)(2)(ii)(B) of this section) is treated as clearly indicating its intent to provide an economic benefit as compensation for services only if the organization provides written substantiation that is contemporaneous with the transfer of the economic benefit at issue. If an organization fails to provide this contemporaneous substantiation, any services provided by the disqualified person will not be treated as provided in consideration for the economic benefit for purposes of determining the reasonableness of the transaction. In no event shall an economic benefit that a disqualified person obtains by theft or fraud be treated as consideration for the performance of services.

(2) Nontaxable benefits. For purposes of section 4958(c)(1)(A) and this section, an applicable tax-exempt organization is not required to indicate its intent to provide an economic benefit as compensation for services if the economic benefit is excluded from the disqualified person's gross income for income tax purposes on the basis of the provisions of chapter 1 of Subtitle A of the Internal Revenue Code. Examples of these benefits include, but are not limited to, employer-provided health benefits and contributions to a qualified pension, profit-sharing, or stock bonus plan under section 401(a), and benefits described in sections 127 and 137. However, except for economic benefits that are disregarded for purposes of section 4958 under paragraph (a)(4) of this section, all compensatory benefits (regardless of the Federal income tax treatment) provided by an organization in exchange for the performance of services are taken into account in determining the reasonableness of a person's compensation for purposes of section 4958.

(3) Contemporaneous substantiation—

(i) Reporting of benefit—

(A) In general. An applicable tax-exempt organization provides contemporaneous written substantiation of its intent to provide an economic benefit as compensation if—

(1) The organization reports the economic benefit as compensation on an original Federal tax information return with respect to the payment (e.g., Form W–2, "Wage and Tax Statement", or Form 1099, "Miscellaneous Income") or with respect to the organization (e.g., Form 990, "Return of Organization Exempt From Income Tax"), or on an amended Federal tax information return filed prior to the commencement of an Internal Revenue Service examination of the applicable tax-exempt organization or the disqualified person for the taxable year in which the transaction occurred (as determined under § 53.4958–1(e)); or

(2) The recipient disqualified person reports the benefit as income on the person's original Federal tax return (e.g., Form 1040, "U.S. Individual Income Tax Return"), or on

287

the person's amended Federal tax return filed prior to the earlier of the following dates—

(i) Commencement of an Internal Revenue Service examination described in paragraph (c)(3)(i)(A)(1) of this section; or

(ii) The first documentation in writing by the Internal Revenue Service of a potential excess benefit transaction involving either the applicable tax-exempt organization or the disqualified person.

(B) Failure to report due to reasonable cause. If an applicable tax-exempt organization's failure to report an economic benefit as required under the Internal Revenue Code is due to reasonable cause (within the meaning of § 301.6724–1 of this chapter), then the organization will be treated as having clearly indicated its intent to provide an economic benefit as compensation for services. To show that its failure to report an economic benefit that should have been reported on an information return was due to reasonable cause, an applicable tax-exempt organization must establish that there were significant mitigating factors with respect to its failure to report (as described in § 301.6724–1(b) of this chapter), or the failure arose from events beyond the organization's control (as described in § 301.6724–1(c) of this chapter), and that the organization acted in a responsible manner both before and after the failure occurred (as described in § 301.6724–1(d) of this chapter).

(ii) Other written contemporaneous evidence. In addition, other written contemporaneous evidence may be used to demonstrate that the appropriate decision-making body or an officer authorized to approve compensation approved a transfer as compensation for services in accordance with established procedures, including but not limited to—

(A) An approved written employment contract executed on or before the date of the transfer;

(B) Documentation satisfying the requirements of § 53.4958–6(a)(3) indicating that an authorized body approved the transfer as compensation for services on or before the date of the transfer; or

(C) Written evidence that was in existence on or before the due date of the applicable Federal tax return described in paragraph (c)(3)(i)(A)(1) or (2) of this section (including extensions but not amendments), of a reasonable belief by the applicable tax-exempt organization that a benefit was a nontaxable benefit as defined in paragraph (c)(2) of this section.

(4) Examples. The following examples illustrate the requirement that an organization contemporaneously substantiate its intent to provide an economic benefit as compensation for services, as defined in paragraph (c) of this section:

Example 1.   G is an applicable tax-exempt organization for purposes of section 4958. G hires an individual contractor, P, who is also the child of a disqualified person of G, to design a computer program for it. G executes a contract with P for that purpose in accordance with G's established procedures, and pays P $1,000 during the year pursuant to the contract. Before January 31 of the next year, G reports the full amount paid to P under the contract on a Form 1099 filed with the Internal Revenue Service. G will be treated as providing contemporaneous written substantiation of its intent to provide the $1,000 paid to P as compensation for the services P performed under the contract by virtue of either the Form 1099 filed with the Internal Revenue Service reporting the amount, or by virtue of the written contract executed between G and P.

Example 2.   G is an applicable tax-exempt organization for purposes of section 4958. D is the chief operating officer of G, and a disqualified person with respect to G. D receives a bonus at the end of the year. G's accounting department determines that the bonus is to be reported on D's Form W–2. Due to events beyond G's control, the bonus is not reflected on D's Form W–2. As a result, D fails to report the bonus on his individual income tax return. G acts to amend Forms W–2 affected as soon as G is made aware of the error during an Internal Revenue Service examination. G's failure to report the bonus on an information return issued to D arose from events beyond G's control, and G acted in a responsible manner both before and after the failure occurred. Thus, because G had reasonable cause (within the meaning § 301.6724–1 of this chapter) for failing to report D's bonus, G will be treated as providing contemporaneous written substantiation of its intent to provide the bonus as compensation for services when paid.

Example 3.   H is an applicable tax-exempt organization and J is a disqualified person with respect to H. J's written employment agreement provides for a fixed salary of $y. J's duties include soliciting funds for various programs of H. H raises a large portion of its funds in a major metropolitan area. Accordingly, H maintains an apartment there in order to provide a place to entertain potential donors. H makes the apartment available exclusively to J to assist in the fundraising. J's written employment contract does not mention the use of the apartment. H obtains the written opinion of a benefits compensation expert that the rental value of the apartment is not includable in J's income by reason of section 119, based on the expectation that the apartment will be used for fundraising activities. Consequently, H does not report the rental value of the apartment on

J's Form W–2, which otherwise correctly reports J's taxable compensation. J does not report the rental value of the apartment on J's individual Form 1040. Later, the Internal Revenue Service correctly determines that the requirements of section 119 were not satisfied. Because of the written expert opinion, H has written evidence of its reasonable belief that use of the apartment was a nontaxable benefit as defined in paragraph (c)(2) of this section. That evidence was in existence on or before the due date of the applicable Federal tax return. Therefore, H has demonstrated its intent to treat the use of the apartment as compensation for services performed by J.

§ 53.4958–5 Transaction in which the amount of the economic benefit is determined in whole or in part by the revenues of one or more activities of the organization. [Reserved]

§ 53.4958–6 Rebuttable presumption that a transaction is not an excess benefit transaction

(a) In general. Payments under a compensation arrangement are presumed to be reasonable, and a transfer of property, or the right to use property, is presumed to be at fair market value, if the following conditions are satisfied—

(1) The compensation arrangement or the terms of the property transfer are approved in advance by an authorized body of the applicable tax-exempt organization (or an entity controlled by the organization within the meaning of § 53.4958–4(a)(2)(ii)(B)) composed entirely of individuals who do not have a conflict of interest (within the meaning of paragraph (c)(1)(iii) of this section) with respect to the compensation arrangement or property transfer, as described in paragraph (c)(1) of this section;

(2) The authorized body obtained and relied upon appropriate data as to comparability prior to making its determination, as described in paragraph (c)(2) of this section; and

(3) The authorized body adequately documented the basis for its determination concurrently with making that determination, as described in paragraph (c)(3) of this section.

(b) Rebutting the presumption. If the three requirements of paragraph (a) of this section are satisfied, then the Internal Revenue Service may rebut the presumption that arises under paragraph (a) of this section only if it develops sufficient contrary evidence to rebut the probative value of the comparability data relied upon by the authorized body. With respect to any fixed payment (within the meaning of § 53.4958–4(a)(3)(ii)), rebuttal evidence is limited to evidence relating to facts and circumstances existing on the date the parties enter into the contract pursuant to which the payment is made (except in the event of substantial nonperformance). With respect to all other payments (including non-fixed payments subject to a cap, as described in paragraph (d)(2) of this section), rebuttal evidence may include facts and circumstances up to and including the date of payment. See § 53.4958–4(b)(2)(i).

(**c**) Requirements for invoking rebuttable presumption—

(**1**) Approval by an authorized body—

(**i**) In general. An authorized body means—

(**A**) The governing body (i.e., the board of directors, board of trustees, or equivalent controlling body) of the organization;

(**B**) A committee of the governing body, which may be composed of any individuals permitted under State law to serve on such a committee, to the extent that the committee is permitted by State law to act on behalf of the governing body; or

(**C**) To the extent permitted under State law, other parties authorized by the governing body of the organization to act on its behalf by following procedures specified by the governing body in approving compensation arrangements or property transfers.

(**ii**) Individuals not included on authorized body. For purposes of determining whether the requirements of paragraph (a) of this section have been met with respect to a specific compensation arrangement or property transfer, an individual is not included on the authorized body when it is reviewing a transaction if that individual meets with other members only to answer questions, and otherwise recuses himself or herself from the meeting and is not present during debate and voting on the compensation arrangement or property transfer.

(**iii**) Absence of conflict of interest. A member of the authorized body does not have a conflict of interest with respect to a compensation arrangement or property transfer only if the member—

(**A**) Is not a disqualified person participating in or economically benefitting from the compensation arrangement or property transfer, and is not a member of the family of any such disqualified person, as described in section 4958(f)(4) or § 53.4958–3(b)(1);

(**B**) Is not in an employment relationship subject to the direction or control of any disqualified person participating in or economically benefitting from the compensation arrangement or property transfer;

(**C**) Does not receive compensation or other payments subject to approval by any disqualified person participating in or economically benefitting from the compensation arrangement or property transfer;

(D) Has no material financial interest affected by the compensation arrangement or property transfer; and

(E) Does not approve a transaction providing economic benefits to any disqualified person participating in the compensation arrangement or property transfer, who in turn has approved or will approve a transaction providing economic benefits to the member.

(2) Appropriate data as to comparability—

(i) In general. An authorized body has appropriate data as to comparability if, given the knowledge and expertise of its members, it has information sufficient to determine whether, under the standards set forth in § 53.4958–4(b), the compensation arrangement in its entirety is reasonable or the property transfer is at fair market value. In the case of compensation, relevant information includes, but is not limited to, compensation levels paid by similarly situated organizations, both taxable and tax-exempt, for functionally comparable positions; the availability of similar services in the geographic area of the applicable tax-exempt organization; current compensation surveys compiled by independent firms; and actual written offers from similar institutions competing for the services of the disqualified person. In the case of property, relevant information includes, but is not limited to, current independent appraisals of the value of all property to be transferred; and offers received as part of an open and competitive bidding process.

(ii) Special rule for compensation paid by small organizations. For organizations with annual gross receipts (including contributions) of less than $1 million reviewing compensation arrangements, the authorized body will be considered to have appropriate data as to comparability if it has data on compensation paid by three comparable organizations in the same or similar communities for similar services. No inference is intended with respect to whether circumstances falling outside this safe harbor will meet the requirement with respect to the collection of appropriate data.

(iii) Application of special rule for small organizations. For purposes of determining whether the special rule for small organizations described in paragraph (c)(2)(ii) of this section applies, an organization may calculate its annual gross receipts based on an average of its gross receipts during the three prior taxable years. If any applicable tax-exempt organization is controlled by or controls another entity (as defined in § 53.4958–4(a)(2)(ii)(B)), the annual gross receipts of such organizations must be aggregated to determine applicability of the special rule stated in paragraph (c)(2)(ii) of this section.

(iv) *Examples.* The following examples illustrate the rules for appropriate data as to comparability for purposes of invoking the rebuttable presumption of reasonableness described in this section. In all examples, compensation refers to the aggregate value of all benefits provided in exchange for services. The examples are as follows:

Example 1. Z is a university that is an applicable tax-exempt organization for purposes of section 4958. Z is negotiating a new contract with Q, its president, because the old contract will expire at the end of the year. In setting Q's compensation for its president at $600x per annum, the executive committee of the Board of Trustees relies solely on a national survey of compensation for university presidents that indicates university presidents receive annual compensation in the range of $100x to $700x; this survey does not divide its data by any criteria, such as the number of students served by the institution, annual revenues, academic ranking, or geographic location. Although many members of the executive committee have significant business experience, none of the members has any particular expertise in higher education compensation matters. Given the failure of the survey to provide information specific to universities comparable to Z, and because no other information was presented, the executive committee's decision with respect to Q's compensation was not based upon appropriate data as to comparability.

Example 2. The facts are the same as Example 1, except that the national compensation survey divides the data regarding compensation for university presidents into categories based on various university-specific factors, including the size of the institution (in terms of the number of students it serves and the amount of its revenues) and geographic area. The survey data shows that university presidents at institutions comparable to and in the same geographic area as Z receive annual compensation in the range of $200x to $300x. The executive committee of the Board of Trustees of Z relies on the survey data and its evaluation of Q's many years of service as a tenured professor and high-ranking university official at Z in setting Q's compensation at $275x annually. The data relied upon by the executive committee constitutes appropriate data as to comparability.

Example 3. X is a tax-exempt hospital that is an applicable tax-exempt organization for purposes of section 4958. Before renewing the contracts of X's chief executive officer and chief financial officer, X's governing board commissioned a customized compensation survey from an independent firm that specializes in consulting on issues related to executive placement and compensation. The survey covered executives with comparable responsibilities at a significant number of taxable and tax-exempt hospitals. The survey data are sorted by a number of different variables, including the size of the hospitals and the nature of the services they provide, the level of experience and specific responsibilities of the executives, and the composition of the annual compensation packages. The board members were provided with the survey results, a detailed written analysis comparing the hospital's executives to those covered by the survey, and an opportunity to ask questions of a member of the firm that prepared the survey. The survey, as prepared and presented to X's board, constitutes appropriate data as to comparability.

Example 4. The facts are the same as Example 3, except that one year later, X is negotiating a new contract with its chief executive officer. The governing board of X obtains information indicating that the relevant market conditions have not changed materially, and possesses no other information indicating that the results of the prior year's survey are no longer valid. Therefore, X may continue to rely on the independent compensation survey prepared for the prior year in setting annual compensation under the new contract.

Example 5. W is a local repertory theater and an applicable tax-exempt organization for purposes of section 4958. W has had annual gross receipts ranging from $400,000 to $800,000 over its past three taxable years. In determining the next year's compensation for W's artistic director, the board of directors of W relies on data compiled from a telephone survey of three other unrelated performing arts organizations of similar size in similar communities. A member of the board drafts a brief written summary of the annual compensation information obtained from this informal survey. The annual compensation information obtained in the telephone survey is appropriate data as to comparability.

(3) Documentation—

(i) For a decision to be documented adequately, the written or electronic records of the authorized body must note—

(A) The terms of the transaction that was approved and the date it was approved;

(B) The members of the authorized body who were present during debate on the transaction that was approved and those who voted on it;

(C) The comparability data obtained and relied upon by the authorized body and how the data was obtained; and

(D) Any actions taken with respect to consideration of the transaction by anyone who is otherwise a member of the authorized body but who had a conflict of interest with respect to the transaction.

(ii) If the authorized body determines that reasonable compensation for a specific arrangement or fair market value in a specific property transfer is higher or lower than the range of comparability data obtained, the authorized body must record the basis for its determination. For a decision to be documented concurrently, records must be prepared before the later of the next meeting of the authorized body or 60 days after the final action or actions of the authorized body are taken. Records must be reviewed and approved by the authorized body as reasonable, accurate and complete within a reasonable time period thereafter.

(d) No presumption with respect to non-fixed payments until amounts are determined—

(1) In general. Except as provided in paragraph (d)(2) of this section, in the case of a payment that is not a fixed payment (within the meaning of § 53.4958–4(a)(3)(ii)), the rebuttable presumption of this section arises only after the exact amount of the payment is determined, or a fixed formula for calculating the payment is specified, and the three requirements for the presumption under paragraph (a) of this section subsequently are satisfied. See § 53.4958–4(b)(2)(i).

(2) Special rule for certain non-fixed payments subject to a cap. If the authorized body approves an employment contract with a disqualified person that includes a non-fixed payment (such as a discretionary bonus) subject to a specified cap, the authorized body may establish a rebuttable presumption with respect to the non-fixed payment at the time the employment contract is entered into if—

(i) Prior to approving the contract, the authorized body obtains appropriate comparability data indicating that a fixed payment of up to a certain amount to the particular disqualified person would represent reasonable compensation;

(ii) The maximum amount payable under the contract (taking into account both fixed and non-fixed payments) does not exceed the amount referred to in paragraph (d)(2)(i) of this section; and

(iii) The other requirements for the rebuttable presumption of reasonableness under paragraph (a) of this section are satisfied.

(e) No inference from absence of presumption. The fact that a transaction between an applicable tax-exempt organization and a disqualified person is not subject to the presumption described in this section neither creates any inference that the transaction is an excess benefit transaction, nor exempts or relieves any person from compliance with any Federal or state law imposing any obligation, duty, responsibility, or other standard of conduct with respect to the operation or administration of any applicable tax-exempt organization.

(f) Period of reliance on rebuttable presumption. Except as provided in paragraph (d) of this section with respect to non-fixed payments, the rebuttable presumption applies to all payments made or transactions completed in accordance with a contract, provided that the provisions of paragraph (a) of this section were met at the time the parties entered into the contract.

§ 53.4958–7 Correction

(a) In general. An excess benefit transaction is corrected by undoing the excess benefit to the extent possible, and taking any additional measures necessary to place the applicable tax-exempt organization involved in the excess benefit transaction in a financial position not worse than that in which it would be if the disqualified person were dealing under the highest fiduciary standards. Paragraph (b) of this section describes the acceptable forms of correction. Paragraph (c) of this section defines the correction amount. Paragraph (d) of this section describes correction where a contract has been partially performed. Paragraph (e) of this section describes correction where the applicable tax-exempt organization involved in the transaction has ceased to exist or is no longer tax-exempt. Paragraph (f) of this section provides examples illustrating correction.

(b) Form of correction—

(1) Cash or cash equivalents. Except as provided in paragraphs (b)(3) and (4) of this section, a disqualified person corrects an excess benefit only by making a payment in cash or cash equivalents, excluding payment by a promissory note, to the applicable tax-exempt organization equal to the correction amount, as defined in paragraph (c) of this section.

(2) Anti-abuse rule. A disqualified person will not satisfy the requirements of paragraph (b)(1) of this section if the Commissioner determines that the disqualified person engaged in one or more transactions with the applicable tax-exempt organization to circumvent the requirements of this correction section, and as a result, the disqualified person effectively transferred property other than cash or cash equivalents.

(3) Special rule relating to nonqualified deferred compensation. If an excess benefit transaction results, in whole or in part, from the vesting (as described in § 53.4958–1(e)(2)) of benefits provided under a nonqualified deferred compensation plan, then, to the extent that such benefits have not yet been distributed to the disqualified person, the disqualified person may correct the portion of the excess benefit resulting from the undistributed deferred compensation by relinquishing any right to receive the excess portion of the undistributed deferred compensation (including any earnings thereon).

(4) Return of specific property—

(i) In general. A disqualified person may, with the agreement of the applicable tax-exempt organization, make a payment by returning specific property previously transferred in the excess benefit transaction. In this case, the disqualified person is treated as making a payment equal to the lesser of—

(A) The fair market value of the property determined on the date the property is returned to the organization; or

(B) The fair market value of the property on the date the excess benefit transaction occurred.

(ii) *Payment not equal to correction amount.* If the payment described in paragraph (b)(4)(i) of this section is less than the correction amount (as described in paragraph (c) of this section), the disqualified person must make an additional cash payment to the organization equal to the difference. Conversely, if the payment described in paragraph (b)(4)(i) of this section exceeds the correction amount (as described in paragraph (c) of this section), the organization may make a cash payment to the disqualified person equal to the difference.

(iii) *Disqualified person may not participate in decision.* Any disqualified person who received an excess benefit from the excess benefit transaction may not participate in the applicable tax-exempt organization's decision whether to accept the return of specific property under paragraph (b)(4)(i) of this section.

(c) *Correction amount.* The correction amount with respect to an excess benefit transaction equals the sum of the excess benefit (as defined in § 53.4958–1(b)) and interest on the excess benefit. The amount of the interest charge for purposes of this section is determined by multiplying the excess benefit by an interest rate, compounded annually, for the period from the date the excess benefit transaction occurred (as defined in § 53.4958–1(e)) to the date of correction. The interest rate used for this purpose must be a rate that equals or exceeds the applicable Federal rate (AFR), compounded annually, for the month in which the transaction occurred. The period from the date the excess benefit transaction occurred to the date of correction is used to determine whether the appropriate AFR is the Federal short-term rate, the Federal mid-term rate, or the Federal long-term rate. See section 1274(d)(1)(A).

(d) *Correction where contract has been partially performed.* If the excess benefit transaction arises under a contract that has been partially performed, termination of the contractual relationship between the organization and the disqualified person is not required in order to correct. However, the parties may need to modify the terms of any ongoing contract to avoid future excess benefit transactions.

(e) *Correction in the case of an applicable tax-exempt organization that has ceased to exist, or is no longer tax-exempt*—

(1) *In general.* A disqualified person must correct an excess benefit transaction in accordance with this paragraph where the applicable tax-exempt organization that engaged in the transaction no longer exists or is no longer described in section 501(c)(3) or (4) and exempt from tax under section 501(a).

(2) *Section 501(c)(3) organizations.* In the case of an excess benefit transaction with a section 501(c)(3) applicable tax-exempt organization, the disqualified person must pay the correction amount, as defined in paragraph (c) of this section, to another organization described in section 501(c)(3) and exempt from tax under section 501(a) in accordance with

297

the dissolution clause contained in the constitutive documents of the applicable tax-exempt organization involved in the excess benefit transaction, provided that—

(i) The organization receiving the correction amount is described in section 170(b)(1)(A) (other than in section 170(b)(1)(A)(vii) and (viii)) and has been in existence and so described for a continuous period of at least 60 calendar months ending on the correction date;

(ii) The disqualified person is not also a disqualified person (as defined in § 53.4958–3) with respect to the organization receiving the correction amount; and

(iii) The organization receiving the correction amount does not allow the disqualified person (or persons described in § 53.4958–3(b) with respect to that person) to make or recommend any grants or distributions by the organization.

(3) Section 501(c)(4) organizations. In the case of an excess benefit transaction with a section 501(c)(4) applicable tax-exempt organization, the disqualified person must pay the correction amount, as defined in paragraph (c) of this section, to a successor section 501(c)(4) organization or, if no tax-exempt successor, to any organization described in section 501(c)(3) or (4) and exempt from tax under section 501(a), provided that the requirements of paragraphs (e)(2)(i) through (iii) of this section are satisfied (except that the requirement that the organization receiving the correction amount is described in section 170(b)(1)(A) (other than in section 170(b)(1)(A)(vii) and (viii)) shall not apply if the organization is described in section 501(c)(4)).

(f) Examples. The following examples illustrate the principles of this section describing the requirements of correction:

Example 1. W is an applicable tax-exempt organization for purposes of section 4958. D is a disqualified person with respect to W. W employed D in 1999 and made payments totaling $12t to D as compensation throughout the taxable year. The fair market value of D's services in 1999 was $7t. Thus, D received excess compensation in the amount of $5t, the excess benefit for purposes of section 4958. In accordance with § 53.4958–1(e)(1), the excess benefit transaction with respect to the series of compensatory payments during 1999 is deemed to occur on December 31, 1999, the last day of D's taxable year. In order to correct the excess benefit transaction on June 30, 2002, D must pay W, in cash or cash equivalents, excluding payment with a promissory note, $5t (the excess benefit) plus interest on $5t for the period from the date the excess benefit transaction occurred to the date of correction (i.e., December 31, 1999, to June 30, 2002). Because this period is not more than three years, the interest rate D must use to determine the interest on the excess benefit must equal or exceed the short-term AFR, compounded annually, for December, 1999 (5.74%, compounded annually).

Example 2.   X is an applicable tax-exempt organization for purposes of section 4958. B is a disqualified person with respect to X. On January 1, 2000, B paid X $6v for Property F. Property F had a fair market value of $10v on January 1, 2000. Thus, the sales transaction on that date provided an excess benefit to B in the amount of $4v. In order to correct the excess benefit on July 5, 2005, B pays X, in cash or cash equivalents, excluding payment with a promissory note, $4v (the excess benefit) plus interest on $4v for the period from the date the excess benefit transaction occurred to the date of correction (i.e., January 1, 2000, to July 5, 2005). Because this period is over three but not over nine years, the interest rate B must use to determine the interest on the excess benefit must equal or exceed the mid-term AFR, compounded annually, for January, 2000 (6.21%, compounded annually).

Example 3.   The facts are the same as in Example 2, except that B offers to return Property F. X agrees to accept the return of Property F, a decision in which B does not participate. Property F has declined in value since the date of the excess benefit transaction. On July 5, 2005, the property has a fair market value of $9v. For purposes of correction, B's return of Property F to X is treated as a payment of $9v, the fair market value of the property determined on the date the property is returned to the organization. If $9v is greater than the correction amount ($4v plus interest on $4v at a rate that equals or exceeds 6.21%, compounded annually, for the period from January 1, 2000, to July 5, 2005), then X may make a cash payment to B equal to the difference.

Example 4.   The facts are the same as in Example 3, except that Property F has increased in value since January 1, 2000, the date the excess benefit transaction occurred, and on July 5, 2005, has a fair market value of $13v. For purposes of correction, B's return of Property F to X is treated as a payment of $10v, the fair market value of the property on the date the excess benefit transaction occurred. If $10v is greater than the correction amount ($4v plus interest on $4v at a rate that equals or exceeds 6.21%, compounded annually, for the period from January 1, 2000, to July 5, 2005), then X may make a cash payment to B equal to the difference.

Example 5.   The facts are the same as in Example 2. Assume that the correction amount B paid X in cash on July 5, 2005, was $5.58v. On July 4, 2005, X loaned $5.58v to B, in exchange for a promissory note signed by B in the amount of $5.58v, payable with interest at a future date. These facts indicate that B engaged in the loan transaction to circumvent the requirement of this section that (except as provided in paragraph (b)(3) or (4) of this section), the correction amount must be paid only in cash or cash equivalents. As a result, the Commissioner may determine that B effectively transferred property other than cash or cash equivalents, and therefore did not satisfy the correction requirements of this section.

§ 53.4958–8   Special rules

(a) Substantive requirements for exemption still apply. Section 4958 does not affect the substantive standards for tax exemption under section 501(c)(3) or (4), including the requirements that the organization be organized and operated exclusively for exempt purposes, and that no part of its net earnings inure to the benefit of any private shareholder or individual. Thus, regardless of whether a particular transaction is subject to excise taxes under section 4958, existing principles and rules may be implicated, such as the limitation on private benefit. For example, transactions that are not subject to section 4958 because of the initial contract exception described in § 53.4958–4(a)(3) may, under certain circumstances, jeopardize the organization's tax-exempt status.

(b) Interaction between section 4958 and section 7611 rules for church tax inquiries and examinations. The procedures of section 7611 will be used in initiating and conducting any inquiry or examination into whether an excess benefit transaction has occurred between a church and a disqualified person. For purposes of this rule, the reasonable belief required to initiate a church tax inquiry is satisfied if there is a reasonable belief that a section 4958 tax is due from a disqualified person with respect to a transaction involving a church. See § 301.7611–1 Q & A 19 of this chapter.

(c) Other substantiation requirements. These regulations, in § 53.4958–4(c)(3), set forth specific substantiation rules. Compliance with the specific substantiation rules of that section does not relieve applicable tax-exempt organizations of other rules and requirements of the Internal Revenue Code, regulations, Revenue Rulings, and other guidance issued by the Internal Revenue Service (including the substantiation rules of sections 162 and 274, or § 1.6001–1(a) and (c) of this chapter).

C. CONVERSION TRANSACTIONS INVOLVING NON PROFIT CORPORATIONS

National Association of Attorneys General, Model Act for Nonprofit Healthcare Conversion Transactions (Adopted July, 1998)

Section 1—Definitions

1.01 "Nonprofit healthcare entity" means:

any nonprofit hospital (including corporations and hospitals created under a trust or a will), nonprofit health maintenance organization, or nonprofit healthcare insurer, including entities affiliated with any of these through ownership, governance or membership, such as a holding company or subsidiary. Nonprofit healthcare entity shall include, but not be limited to nonprofit entities which are licensed as hospitals, HMOs or healthcare insurers (including mutual corporations holding assets in charitable trust) under the laws of this State.

1.02   "Nonprofit healthcare conversion transaction" means:

(**1**) the sale, transfer, lease, exchange, optioning, conveyance, or other disposition of a material amount of the assets or operations of a licensed nonprofit hospital, nonprofit health maintenance organization or nonprofit healthcare insurer, including a mutual corporation holding assets in charitable trust, to an entity or person other than a charity; and

(**2**) the transfer of control or governance of a material amount of the assets or operations of a licensed hospital, nonprofit health maintenance organization or nonprofit healthcare insurer, including a mutual corporation holding assets in charitable trust, to an entity or person other than a charity.

1.03   "Nonprofit healthcare insurer" means;

any nonprofit provider of healthcare insurance, including hospital service associations, health service corporations, and physician service organizations.

1.04   "Person" means:

any individual, partnership, trust, estate, corporation, association, joint venture, joint stock company, insurance company, or other organization.

Section 2—Notice to and Approval of Attorney General

2.01   Any nonprofit healthcare entity shall be required to provide written notice to, and obtain the approval of, the Attorney General [or the appropriate Court on advice of the Attorney General in mandatory *cy pres* proceeding states] prior to entering into any nonprofit healthcare conversion transaction. At the time of providing notice to the Attorney General [Court], the nonprofit healthcare entity shall provide the Attorney General [Court] with written certification that a copy of this statute has been given in its entirety to each member of the board of trustees of the nonprofit healthcare entity.

2.02   The notice to the Attorney General provided for in this Section shall include and contain all the information the Attorney General determines is required. No notice shall be effective until the Attorney General has acknowledged receipt of a complete notice in accordance with regulations to be adopted pursuant to Section 6 of this article or in accordance with protocol established by the Attorney General.

2.03   This article shall not apply to a nonprofit healthcare entity if the nonprofit healthcare conversion transaction is in the usual and regular course of its activities and if the Attorney General has given the nonprofit healthcare corporation a written waiver of this article as to the nonprofit healthcare conversion transaction.

Section 3—Approval or disapproval; Written Notice; Time Period; Extension

3.01 Within 90 days of a complete written notice as required by Section 2 of this article, the Attorney General shall notify the nonprofit healthcare entity in writing of its decision to approve, [or advise the Court in mandatory *cy pres* proceeding states] or disapprove the proposed nonprofit healthcare conversion transaction. The Attorney General may extend this period for an additional 60 day period, provided the extension is necessary to obtain information pursuant to subdivision 6.02 or subdivision 7.01 of this article. [Longer time periods should be established for states which opt for attorney general review of health care impact under Section 5.02.]

Section 4—Public Meetings: Notice of Time and Place

4.01 Prior to issuing any written decision pursuant to Section 3 of this article, the Attorney General shall conduct one or more public meetings, one of which shall be held in the county where the nonprofit healthcare entity's assets to be transferred are located. At the public meeting, the Attorney General shall hear comments from interested persons desiring to make statements regarding the proposed nonprofit healthcare conversion transaction. At least 14 days before the meeting, the Attorney General shall cause written notice to be provided of the time and place of the meeting through publication in one or more newspapers of general circulation in the affected community, to the county board of supervisors, and if applicable, to the city council of the city where the nonprofit healthcare entity's assets to be transferred are located.

Section 5—Discretion of Attorney General; Review Elements

5.01 In making a decision whether to approve or disapprove a proposed nonprofit healthcare conversion transaction [or advise the Court in a mandatory *cy pres* proceeding state], the Attorney General shall consider:

(1) Whether the nonprofit healthcare entity will receive full and fair market value for its charitable or social welfare assets;

(2) Whether the fair market value of the nonprofit healthcare entity's assets to be transferred has been manipulated by the actions of the parties in a manner that causes the fair market value of the assets to decrease;

(3) Whether the proceeds of the proposed nonprofit healthcare conversion transaction will be used consistent with the trust under which the assets are held by the nonprofit healthcare entity and whether the proceeds will be controlled as funds independently of the acquiring or related entities;

(4) Whether the proposed nonprofit healthcare conversion transaction will result in a breach of fiduciary duty, as determined by the Attorney General, including conflicts of interest related to payments or benefits to officers, directors, board members, executives, and experts employed or retained by the parties;

(5) Whether the governing body of the nonprofit healthcare entity exercised due diligence in deciding to dispose of nonprofit healthcare entity's assets, selecting the acquiring entity, and negotiating the terms and conditions of the disposition;

(6) Whether the nonprofit healthcare conversion transaction will result in private inurement to any person;

(7) Whether healthcare providers will be offered the opportunity to invest or own an interest in the acquiring entity or a related party, and whether procedures or safeguards are in place to avoid conflict of interest in patient referrals;

(8) Whether the terms of any management or services contract negotiated in conjunction with the proposed nonprofit healthcare conversion transaction are reasonable;

(9) Whether any foundation established to hold the proceeds of the sale will be broadly based in the community and be representative of the affected community, taking into consideration the structure and governance of such foundation; and,

(10) Whether the Attorney General has been provided with sufficient information and data by the nonprofit healthcare entity to evaluate adequately the proposed nonprofit healthcare conversion transaction or the effects thereof on the public, provided the Attorney General has notified the nonprofit healthcare entity or the acquiring entity of any inadequacy of the information or data and has provided a reasonable opportunity to remedy such inadequacy;

(11) Any other criteria the Attorney General considers necessary to determine whether the nonprofit healthcare entity will receive full and fair market value for its assets to be transferred as required in rules adopted by the Attorney General under Section 6 of this article.

5.02 [THIS SUBDIVISION IS OPTIONAL FOR ATTORNEYS GENERAL WHO DEEM IT APPROPRIATE TO ALSO CONSIDER ISSUES OF HEALTH IMPACT IN THEIR REVIEW]

In making a decision whether to approve or disapprove an application, the attorney general shall also determine whether the proposed nonprofit healthcare conversion transaction may have a significant effect on the availability or accessibility of healthcare services to the affected community. In making this determination, the Attorney General shall consider:

(1) Whether sufficient safeguards are included to assure the affected community continued access to affordable care;

(2) Whether the proposed nonprofit healthcare conversion transaction creates or has the likelihood of creating an adverse effect on the access to or availability or cost of healthcare services to the community;

(3) Whether the acquiring entities have made a commitment, at least comparable to the nonprofit healthcare entity, to provide healthcare to the disadvantaged, the uninsured, and the underinsured and to provide benefits to the affected community to promote improved healthcare. Activities and funding provided by the nonprofit healthcare entity or its successor nonprofit healthcare entity or foundation to provide such healthcare or to provide support or medical education and teaching programs or medical research programs shall be considered in evaluating compliance with this commitment;

(4) Whether the nonprofit healthcare conversion transaction will result in the revocation of hospital privileges;

(5) Whether sufficient safeguards are included to maintain appropriate capacity for health science research and healthcare provider education; and,

(6) Whether the proposed nonprofit healthcare conversion transaction demonstrates that the public interest will be served considering the essential medical services needed to provide safe and adequate treatment, appropriate access and balanced healthcare delivery to the residents.

Section 6—Regulations; Authority to Adopt; Information Requests; Consequences of Refusal to Provide Information

6.01 The Attorney General may adopt such regulations as the Attorney General deems appropriate to implement this article and/or establish such protocols as are necessary to implement this article.

6.02 The Attorney General may demand that the nonprofit healthcare entity giving notice under Section 2 of this article provide such information as the Attorney General reasonably deems necessary to complete his/her review of any proposed nonprofit healthcare conversion transaction described in Section 5 of this article. A failure by the nonprofit healthcare entity giving notice under Section 2 of this article to provide timely information as required by the Attorney General shall be a sufficient ground for the Attorney General to disapprove the proposed nonprofit healthcare conversion transaction.

Section 7—Contracts with Agencies and Consultants; Reimbursement for Costs and Expenses of Review; Failure to Pay

7.01 Within the time periods designated in Section 3 of this article, the Attorney General may do any of the following to assist in the review of the proposed nonprofit healthcare conversion transaction described in Section 2 of this article:

(1) Contract with, consult, and receive advice from any agency of the state or the United States on such terms and conditions the Attorney General deems appropriate; or,

(2) In the Attorney General=s sole discretion, contract with such experts or consultants the Attorney General deems appropriate to assist

the Attorney General in reviewing the proposed nonprofit healthcare conversion transaction.

7.02   Any contract costs incurred by the Attorney General pursuant to this Section shall not exceed an amount that is reasonable and necessary to conduct the review of the proposed nonprofit healthcare conversion transaction. The Attorney General shall be exempt from the provisions of [any applicable state laws regarding public bidding procedures] for purposes of entering into contracts pursuant to this Section. The nonprofit healthcare entity giving notice under Section 2 of this article, upon request, shall pay the Attorney General promptly for all costs of contracts entered into by the Attorney General pursuant to this Section.

7.03   The Attorney General shall be entitled to reimbursement from the nonprofit healthcare entity giving notice under Section 2 of this article for all reasonable and actual costs incurred by the Attorney General in reviewing any proposed nonprofit healthcare conversion transaction under this article, including attorney fees at the billing rate used by the Attorney General to bill state agencies for legal services. The nonprofit healthcare entity giving notice under Section 2 of this article, upon request, shall pay the Attorney General promptly for all such costs.

7.04   The failure by the nonprofit healthcare entity giving notice under Section 2 of this article to promptly reimburse the Attorney General for all costs pursuant to subparagraphs 7.02 or 7.03 shall be sufficient ground for the Attorney General to disapprove the proposed nonprofit healthcare conversion transaction.

Section 8—Public Records

8.01   All documents submitted to the Attorney General by any person, including nonprofit healthcare entities giving notice under Section 2 of this article, in connection with the Attorney General's review of the proposed nonprofit healthcare conversion transaction pursuant to this article shall be public records subject to all provisions of the applicable state public records act, [assuming the state public records act contains an exception for trade secrets or other commercially competitive information.]

Section 9—Penalties; Remedies

9.01   Any nonprofit healthcare conversion transactions entered into in violation of the notice, review or approval requirements of this article shall be null and void and each member of the governing boards and the chief financial officers of the parties to the nonprofit healthcare conversion transaction may be subject to a civil penalty of up to $1,000,000, the amount to be determined by the [court of competent jurisdiction] in the county in which the nonprofit healthcare entity's assets to be transferred are located. The Attorney General shall institute proceedings to impose such a penalty. In addition, no permit to operate a hospital may be issued or renewed under this Chapter or under any other applicable statute or regulation if there is a nonprofit healthcare conversion transaction entered into in violation of the notice, review and approval requirements of this article.

9.02   Nothing in this Section shall be construed to limit the common law authority of the Attorney General and the [director of charitable trusts] to protect charitable trusts and charitable assets in this state. These penalties and remedies are in addition to, and not a replacement for, any other civil or criminal actions which the Attorney General may take under either the common law or statutory law, including rescinding the nonprofit healthcare conversion transaction, granting injunctive relief or any combination of these and other remedies available under common law or statutory law.

Notes to the Proposed Model Act

Section 1.01.   Definitions

The scope of the model act is broad, bringing hospitals, HMOs, and health care insurers, as well as nonprofit organizations affiliated with these entities, within the scope of the Attorney General's review authority. Including the affiliated organizations within which a hospital, HMO or insurer operates into the definition is important not only because of the rapid development of integrated healthcare systems, but also because conversion transactions often involve the transfer of assets from multiple corporate entities within a system, rather than the primary entity alone. It is a policy decision for each state whether the sale of subsidiary assets alone, which could constitute a material amount of a healthcare system's wealth, will trigger the statute.

The definition of the term "hospital" varies from state to state, with many states defining hospital as meaning an acute-care hospital. In other states, "hospital" may be defined more broadly to include psychiatric and rehabilitative hospitals. Each state adopting this model act should check its own existing statutes to determine precisely how broadly the term will be defined.

Section 1.02(2).   Definitions

The model act uses the term "material amount" as a trigger for the statute. This is a flexible and imprecise concept but has advantages for the Attorney General. Two factors weigh in favor of a materiality standard. First, in states where there are limited resources at the Attorney General's Office, the Attorney General retains more discretion in deciding when to investigate a proposed transaction. Second, using a specific percentage in the statute may invite gaming or manipulation of the percentage cut-off, either by pre-transaction mechanisms or by fragmenting or staggering the transaction over a number of years and coming in under the statutory percentage trigger. The model act allows attorneys general to issue interpretative releases, creating "safe harbors" with specific percentages indicating with greater specificity what is material and what is not material. Local corporate attorneys might benefit from the predictability of such interpretative releases.

Section 2.01. Court Approval/Cy Pres

This section of the model act requires approval of the Attorney General for such transactions. However, a number of states have existing cy pres statutes which require court approval for such conversions. If your state has such a cy pres statute, you must consider the options available: substituting the Attorney General for the court procedure and approval; requiring both court and Attorney General approval; or retaining only court approval. In one state, the merger statute preserves court approval where a for-profit entity is acquiring a nonprofit entity (cy pres) but requires the Attorney General's approval where two nonprofit healthcare entities are involved. The cy pres statutes set a very high standard in these matters (the entity must prove illegality, impracticability, etc.). The model act has a more flexible standard; and how to proceed is a policy question for each state to decide. Because of concerns that members of governing boards be fully informed of their fiduciary duties in these complex transactions, Section 2.01 requires that a copy of the statute be given to each member of the governing board, with a certification to the Attorney General that this has been done.

Section 2.02. Notice and Filing

The model act requires the filing of "all the information the Attorney General determines is required." There is a need for regulations or interpretative releases to define this provision in more specific language and to alert attorneys representing the parties in advance as to what documents are required. Creating such a list will avoid having the Attorney General continually go back to the applicant to request additional documents, will save time and will allow for greater efficiency. Required documents would include purchase and sale agreements, joint venture agreements, side agreements, employment contracts, financial data and expert analysis, including valuation studies, financial statements, certified board resolutions, minutes related to the approval and deliberations on the transaction, and a description of the corporate and management structures, to name a few items. (See the attached Commentary for a more specific list). The Attorney General must make clear that the 90 day time period does not begin to run until the filing is deemed "complete" by the Attorney General. The 90 day time period is a very brief period for the type of review which the Attorney General's office must undertake.

Section 2.03. Waivers

This section speaks of waivers for transactions in the usual and regular course of its activities. This allows for routine sales of equipment to avoid exhaustive reviews. Regulations or guidelines must be clear on how broad the scope of this exemption is. Is it limited, for example, to the sale of used MRI equipment? This waiver provides an opening for attorneys representing healthcare entities to craft exemptions which were not originally contemplated; consequently, the use of the word "and" (requiring the Attorney General's written approval of any waiver) is important.

Section 4.01.   Public Meetings

The public has a right to be heard on any proposed healthcare transaction. This is so because public charities are responsible to their public beneficiaries. This section makes such public hearings mandatory in all transactions. (In some states because of limited staff and resources, the public hearing is in the discretion of the Attorney General.) Public hearings should be tape-recorded and written statements should be invited. Because parties to the transaction—or opponents of the transaction—may "pack" the meeting, consideration should be given to an orderly process for selecting speakers and the time periods for speakers to present their materials. Community cable programs may ask to videotape the proceedings. If so, thought should be given to ensuring an orderly process where public comment is fully received in a way which ensures fairness to all. Section 4.01 does not limit the scope of the public comments. For those states reluctant to adopt a mandatory public hearing requirement, some provision must be made for receiving formal, written public comment, especially since the proposed transaction will be scrutinized both by the local communities affected and by national health care advocates.

Section 5.01.   Discretion of Attorney General; Review Elements

Section 5.01(1).   Full and Fair Market Value

If a bidding process has been used to determine fair market value and an investment advisor has been retained, the process is generally fair but the challenge is comparing bids which contain many different provisions (cash, stock, promissory notes, differing pay-out periods, etc.). When no bidding process has been used, determining full and fair value can be fraught with difficulty. In these instances, experts need to be retained to represent the Attorney General in making a determination; and the fact that the parties themselves have already retained their own experts is not always decisive.

Section 5.01(4).   Fiduciary Duties

Among the items to be considered in determining whether to approve or disapprove a transaction is whether there are breaches of fiduciary duties by the governing board or officers of the entity. Because fiduciary duties are not always clearly understood, even by the most sophisticated board members (see the Adelphi University controversy), the Attorney General may wish to provide general commentary on fiduciary duties in the regulations or in releases or the Commentary to the model act. More specifically, the duty of care and the duty of loyalty need to be explained in these complex transactions, if only to prepare board members to ask questions and scrutinize the recommendations of management. There are a number of excellent articles on the duty of directors of healthcare entities in complex, integrated transactions.

Section 5.01(9).   The New Foundation

The establishment of the new charitable foundation is a critical outcome of the transaction. However, because of the pressure of time and the attention paid to issues of valuation, this aspect often does not get the attention it deserves during the review process. Over 50 new healthcare foundations have been established as a result of healthcare conversions in the 1990s with assets of over four billion dollars; and the Attorneys General should consider taking an active role in the drafting of the articles and bylaws, the identification of the disadvantaged groups to be served, the defining of the charitable mission, and the critical selection of the members of the first governing board.

Of considerable importance is the obtaining of public comment on the new foundation and the healthcare needs that foundation should address. The public comment may be obtained during the public hearings required under Section 4.01 of the model act and that hearing may be supplemented with an opportunity for the public to submit additional written comments on this aspect.

In addition, existing resources are available without charge to advise the Attorney General and the parties to the transaction in defining the charitable mission. Existing needs assessments are available from hospitals, healthcare groups and governmental agencies (state health and human services departments in particular), among others. Depending on the quality and currency of available data, it may be advisable to commission a particularized needs study. There is also a growing number of resources available to the parties and to the Attorney General: consumer groups, other state attorneys general, as well as literature and newspaper analysis on the existing 50 foundations. There are also sample articles, bylaws and mission statements now available from other attorneys general, as well as information on how to assure diversity on the governing board. The establishment of a broad-based charitable foundation, independent of the parties involved in the merger, deserves to be high on the checklist of things to be done and not left until the last moment. Once the transaction is completed, the role which the Attorney General has in the development of the new foundation diminishes significantly. However, it is worth considering a system for monitoring the grant-making activity of the resultant foundation. For example, the Attorney General may wish by rule to establish a policy to review the initial round of grant-making to ensure that grants fall within the appropriate range of charitable purposes. Further, the Attorney General may wish to establish a policy to appoint an ex officio board representative to serve for one term and report the board=s activity to the Attorney General.

Section 5.02. Impact upon Health Care

This section of the model act is optional. However, the issues which the section addresses are critical and are of enormous public concern: the adverse impact which the transaction may have upon free care for the indigent or upon the affordability of care after the transaction is consummated. Some Attorneys General may view these issues as falling outside the scope of their abilities and resources; however, these issues will be high on the list of concerns of the communities affected by the transaction. If adoption of this optional section is deemed to be inappropriate, it is strongly recommended that oversight for these issues be placed within an existing public health authority for review by that agency.

Section 6.01. Regulations

Once the model act is adopted, the Attorney General should move quickly either (1) to adopt regulations or (2) to issue Interpretative Guidelines or Interpretative Releases to alert the legal community and educate the health-care industry on the impact and significance of the new statute. Adopting the model act is just a first step in obtaining compliance. Educating the legal and healthcare communities on the scope and significance of the model act and on the Attorney General's interpretation and procedures is also important, since it will help ensure efficiency and compliance. The Attorney General should consider offering or participating in seminars or CLEs and contacting the healthcare section of the state bar association. Direct mailings of the statute and a commentary to the regulated hospitals and other regulated entities might also be considered. (See the attached sample Commentary on the Model Act, which could serve this purpose.) If the new regulatory structure is to work effectively, the Attorney General should alert board members on compliance and enforcement issues. In addition, regulations or a commentary will protect against charges of unfair treatment in what is becoming a highly charged, rapidly changing area of the law.

The Attorney General should seek to reassure directors, not intimidate them or cause good individuals to avoid serving on governing boards.

Section 7.02. Retention of Experts

When experts must be retained in a complex transaction, the Attorney General will find his/her office in a difficult position. The model act contains restricted time limitations on the Attorney General's review, with 90 days from a completed filing and an additional 60 additional days if experts need to be retained. Identifying outside legal counsel and financial experts and bringing them up to speed are always time-consuming. The model act contemplates retention of experts outside the scope of a state's purchase regulations, thereby avoiding lengthy RFP procedures. In states where this is not possible, an alternative is to pre-qualify a pool of experts in advance, thereby enabling all parties to proceed expeditiously with the selection. Contract negotiations and conflict-of-interest analysis will still have to be undertaken for each specific engagement, but the time period for this can be greatly compressed.

Two related problems present themselves in connection with the retention of experts. First, financial experts and outside legal counsel are very costly. To control costs, specific issues and tasks should be identified at the start of the engagement and expanded only as needed. If possible, there should be agreement on specific team members for the experts and regular, monthly billings should be required. Second, ensuring that all information has been filed under section 2.02 of the model act will be difficult, since first document production requests often lead to supplemental document requests.

No decision as to whether the filing is complete should be made without consulting with the retained experts.

Section 8.01.   Public Records

Although the model act emphasizes public access to the filed documents, full investigation by the Attorney General requires disclosure of trade secret or other commercially competitive material. This material may be subject to third-party confidentiality agreements under which the nonprofit entity is subject to liability if disclosed without a promise of confidentiality. In addition, some filed material necessary to the Attorney Generals expert to determine valuation (such as rate levels or on-going medical service agreements) will have value to the buyer only if the information remains confidential. In order to ensure full disclosure of all information, the Attorney General should have the ability to promise confidentiality for this very narrow category of information, either under an existing public access/public records statute or by explicit provisions in the new legislation.

Section 9.01.   Penalties

The penalties contained in this section may, at first glance, appear stringent. However, the assets involved in these transactions are charitable assets involving public charities for which the public has granted tax-exemptions to build the value of the entity over time. Because these transactions involve healthcare entities and raise critical issues of healthcare availability and accessibility, the standards contained in the model act are appropriate and warranted.

IV. FEDERAL REGULATION OF HEALTH COVERAGE

A. HEALTH INSURANCE PORTABILITY AND ACCOUNTABILITY ACT: 29 U.S.C.A. §§ 1181 ET SEQ.

29 U.S.C.A. § 1181. Increased portability through limitation on preexisting condition exclusions

(a) Limitation on preexisting condition exclusion period; crediting for periods of previous coverage

Subject to subsection (d) of this section, a group health plan, and a health insurance issuer offering group health insurance coverage, may, with respect to a participant or beneficiary, impose a preexisting condition exclusion only if—

(1) such exclusion relates to a condition (whether physical or mental), regardless of the cause of the condition, for which medical advice, diagnosis, care, or treatment was recommended or received within the 6–month period ending on the enrollment date;

(2) such exclusion extends for a period of not more than 12 months (or 18 months in the case of a late enrollee) after the enrollment date; and

(3) the period of any such preexisting condition exclusion is reduced by the aggregate of the periods of creditable coverage (if any, as defined in subsection (c)(1) of this section) applicable to the participant or beneficiary as of the enrollment date.

(b) Definitions

For purposes of this part—

(1) Preexisting condition exclusion

* See also 42 USC § 300gg (amending Health Services Act).

(A) In general

The term "preexisting condition exclusion" means, with respect to coverage, a limitation or exclusion of benefits relating to a condition based on the fact that the condition was present before the date of enrollment for such coverage, whether or not any medical advice, diagnosis, care, or treatment was recommended or received before such date.

(B) Treatment of genetic information

Genetic information shall not be treated as a condition described in subsection (a)(1) of this section in the absence of a diagnosis of the condition related to such information.

(2) Enrollment date

The term "enrollment date" means, with respect to an individual covered under a group health plan or health insurance coverage, the date of enrollment of the individual in the plan or coverage or, if earlier, the first day of the waiting period for such enrollment.

(3) Late enrollee

The term "late enrollee" means, with respect to coverage under a group health plan, a participant or beneficiary who enrolls under the plan other than during—

    (A) the first period in which the individual is eligible to enroll under the plan, or

    (B) a special enrollment period under subsection (f) of this section.

(4) Waiting period

The term "waiting period" means, with respect to a group health plan and an individual who is a potential participant or beneficiary in the plan, the period that must pass with respect to the individual before the individual is eligible to be covered for benefits under the terms of the plan.

(c) Rules relating to crediting previous coverage

(1) "Creditable coverage" defined

For purposes of this part, the term "creditable coverage" means, with respect to an individual, coverage of the individual under any of the following:

    (A) A group health plan.

    (B) Health insurance coverage.

    (C) Part A or part B of title XVIII of the Social Security Act [42 U.S.C.A. § 1395c et seq. or § 1395j et seq.].

    (D) Title XIX of the Social Security Act [42 U.S.C.A. § 1396 et seq.], other than coverage consisting solely of benefits under section 1928 [42 U.S.C.A. § 1396s].

    (E) Chapter 55 of Title 10.

    (F) A medical care program of the Indian Health Service or of a tribal organization.

    (G) A State health benefits risk pool.

    (H) A health plan offered under chapter 89 of Title 5.

    (I) A public health plan (as defined in regulations).

(J) A health benefit plan under section 2504(e) of Title 22.

Such term does not include coverage consisting solely of coverage of excepted benefits (as defined in section 1191b(c) of this title).

(2) Not counting periods before significant breaks in coverage

(A) In general

A period of creditable coverage shall not be counted, with respect to enrollment of an individual under a group health plan, if, after such period and before the enrollment date, there was a 63–day period during all of which the individual was not covered under any creditable coverage.

(B) Waiting period not treated as a break in coverage

For purposes of subparagraph (A) and subsection (d)(4) of this section, any period that an individual is in a waiting period for any coverage under a group health plan (or for group health insurance coverage) or is in an affiliation period (as defined in subsection (g)(2) of this section) shall not be taken into account in determining the continuous period under subparagraph (A).

(3) Method of crediting coverage

(A) Standard method

Except as otherwise provided under subparagraph (B), for purposes of applying subsection (a)(3) of this section, a group health plan, and a health insurance issuer offering group health insurance coverage, shall count a period of creditable coverage without regard to the specific benefits covered during the period.

(B) Election of alternative method

A group health plan, or a health insurance issuer offering group health insurance coverage, may elect to apply subsection (a)(3)of this section based on coverage of benefits within each of several classes or categories of benefits specified in regulations rather than as provided under subparagraph (A). Such election shall be made on a uniform basis for all participants and beneficiaries. Under such election a group health plan or issuer shall count a period of creditable coverage with respect to any class or category of benefits if any level of benefits is covered within such class or category.

(C) Plan notice

In the case of an election with respect to a group health plan under subparagraph (B) (whether or not health insurance coverage is provided in connection with such plan), the plan shall—

(i) prominently state in any disclosure statements concerning the plan, and state to each enrollee at the time of enrollment under the plan, that the plan has made such election, and

314

(ii) include in such statements a description of the effect of this election.

(4) Establishment of period

Periods of creditable coverage with respect to an individual shall be established through presentation of certifications described in subsection (e) of this section or in such other manner as may be specified in regulations.

(d) Exceptions

(1) Exclusion not applicable to certain newborns

Subject to paragraph (4), a group health plan, and a health insurance issuer offering group health insurance coverage, may not impose any preexisting condition exclusion in the case of an individual who, as of the last day of the 30–day period beginning with the date of birth, is covered under creditable coverage.

(2) Exclusion not applicable to certain adopted children

Subject to paragraph (4), a group health plan, and a health insurance issuer offering group health insurance coverage, may not impose any preexisting condition exclusion in the case of a child who is adopted or placed for adoption before attaining 18 years of age and who, as of the last day of the 30–day period beginning on the date of the adoption or placement for adoption, is covered under creditable coverage. The previous sentence shall not apply to coverage before the date of such adoption or placement for adoption.

(3) Exclusion not applicable to pregnancy

A group health plan, and health insurance issuer offering group health insurance coverage, may not impose any preexisting condition exclusion relating to pregnancy as a preexisting condition.

(4) Loss if break in coverage

Paragraphs (1) and (2) shall no longer apply to an individual after the end of the first 63–day period during all of which the individual was not covered under any creditable coverage.

(e) Certifications and disclosure of coverage

(1) Requirement for certification of period of creditable coverage

(A) In general

A group health plan, and a health insurance issuer offering group health insurance coverage, shall provide the certification described in subparagraph (B)—

(i) at the time an individual ceases to be covered under the plan or otherwise becomes covered under a COBRA continuation provision,

(ii) in the case of an individual becoming covered under such a provision, at the time the individual ceases to be covered under such provision, and

(iii) on the request on behalf of an individual made not later than 24 months after the date of cessation of the coverage described in clause (i) or (ii), whichever is later.

The certification under clause (i) may be provided, to the extent practicable, at a time consistent with notices required under any applicable COBRA continuation provision.

(B) Certification

The certification described in this subparagraph is a written certification of—

(i) the period of creditable coverage of the individual under such plan and the coverage (if any) under such COBRA continuation provision, and

(ii) the waiting period (if any) (and affiliation period, if applicable) imposed with respect to the individual for any coverage under such plan.

(C) Issuer compliance

To the extent that medical care under a group health plan consists of group health insurance coverage, the plan is deemed to have satisfied the certification requirement under this paragraph if the health insurance issuer offering the coverage provides for such certification in accordance with this paragraph.

(2) Disclosure of information on previous benefits

In the case of an election described in subsection (c)(3)(B) of this section by a group health plan or health insurance issuer, if the plan or issuer enrolls an individual for coverage under the plan and the individual provides a certification of coverage of the individual under paragraph (1)—

(A) upon request of such plan or issuer, the entity which issued the certification provided by the individual shall promptly disclose to such requesting plan or issuer information on coverage of classes and categories of health benefits available under such entity's plan or coverage, and

(B) such entity may charge the requesting plan or issuer for the reasonable cost of disclosing such information.

(3) Regulations

The Secretary shall establish rules to prevent an entity's failure to provide information under paragraph (1) or (2) with respect to previous coverage of an individual from adversely affecting any subsequent coverage of the individual under another group health plan or health insurance coverage.

(f) Special enrollment periods

(1) Individuals losing other coverage

A group health plan, and a health insurance issuer offering group health insurance coverage in connection with a group health plan, shall permit an employee who is eligible, but not enrolled, for coverage under the terms of the plan (or a dependent of such an employee if the dependent is eligible, but not enrolled, for coverage under such terms) to enroll for coverage under the terms of the plan if each of the following conditions is met:

(A) The employee or dependent was covered under a group health plan or had health insurance coverage at the time coverage was previously offered to the employee or dependent.

(B) The employee stated in writing at such time that coverage under a group health plan or health insurance coverage was the reason for declining enrollment, but only if the plan sponsor or issuer (if applicable) required such a statement at such time and provided the employee with notice of such requirement (and the consequences of such requirement) at such time.

(C) The employee's or dependent's coverage described in subparagraph (A)—

(i) was under a COBRA continuation provision and the coverage under such provision was exhausted; or

(ii) was not under such a provision and either the coverage was terminated as a result of loss of eligibility for the coverage (including as a result of legal separation, divorce, death, termination of employment, or reduction in the number of hours of employment) or employer contributions toward such coverage were terminated.

(D) Under the terms of the plan, the employee requests such enrollment not later than 30 days after the date of exhaustion of coverage described in subparagraph (C)(i) or termination of coverage or employer contribution described in subparagraph (C)(ii).

(2) For dependent beneficiaries

(A) In general

If—

(i) a group health plan makes coverage available with respect to a dependent of an individual,

(ii) the individual is a participant under the plan (or has met any waiting period applicable to becoming a participant

317

under the plan and is eligible to be enrolled under the plan but for a failure to enroll during a previous enrollment period), and

(iii) a person becomes such a dependent of the individual through marriage, birth, or adoption or placement for adoption,

the group health plan shall provide for a dependent special enrollment period described in subparagraph (B) during which the person (or, if not otherwise enrolled, the individual) may be enrolled under the plan as a dependent of the individual, and in the case of the birth or adoption of a child, the spouse of the individual may be enrolled as a dependent of the individual if such spouse is otherwise eligible for coverage.

(B) Dependent special enrollment period

A dependent special enrollment period under this subparagraph shall be a period of not less than 30 days and shall begin on the later of—

(i) the date dependent coverage is made available, or

(ii) the date of the marriage, birth, or adoption or placement for adoption (as the case may be) described in subparagraph (A)(iii).

(C) No waiting period

If an individual seeks to enroll a dependent during the first 30 days of such a dependent special enrollment period, the coverage of the dependent shall become effective—

(i) in the case of marriage, not later than the first day of the first month beginning after the date the completed request for enrollment is received;

(ii) in the case of a dependent's birth, as of the date of such birth; or

(iii) in the case of a dependent's adoption or placement for adoption, the date of such adoption or placement for adoption.

(g) Use of affiliation period by HMOs as alternative to preexisting condition exclusion

(1) In general

In the case of a group health plan that offers medical care through health insurance coverage offered by a health maintenance organization, the plan may provide for an affiliation period with respect to coverage through the organization only if—

(A) no preexisting condition exclusion is imposed with respect to coverage through the organization,

(B) the period is applied uniformly without regard to any health status-related factors, and

(C) such period does not exceed 2 months (or 3 months in the case of a late enrollee).

(2) Affiliation period

(A) Defined

For purposes of this part, the term "affiliation period" means a period which, under the terms of the health insurance coverage offered by the health maintenance organization, must expire before the health insurance coverage becomes effective. The organization is not required to provide health care services or benefits during such period and no premium shall be charged to the participant or beneficiary for any coverage during the period.

(B) Beginning

Such period shall begin on the enrollment date.

(C) Runs concurrently with waiting periods

An affiliation period under a plan shall run concurrently with any waiting period under the plan.

(3) Alternative methods

A health maintenance organization described in paragraph (1) may use alternative methods, from those described in such paragraph, to address adverse selection as approved by the State insurance commissioner or official or officials designated by the State to enforce the requirements of part A of title XXVII of the Public Health Service Act [42 U.S.C.A. §§ 300gg et seq.] for the State involved with respect to such issuer.

29 U.S.C.A. § 1182. Prohibiting discrimination against individual participants and beneficiaries based on health status

(a) In eligibility to enroll

(1) In general

Subject to paragraph (2), a group health plan, and a health insurance issuer offering group health insurance coverage in connection with a group health plan, may not establish rules for eligibility (including continued eligibility) of any individual to enroll under the terms of the plan based on any of the following health status-related factors in relation to the individual or a dependent of the individual:

(A) Health status.

(B) Medical condition (including both physical and mental illnesses).

(C) Claims experience.

(D) Receipt of health care.

(E) Medical history.

(F) Genetic information.

(G) Evidence of insurability (including conditions arising out of acts of domestic violence).

(H) Disability.

(2) No application to benefits or exclusions

To the extent consistent with section 1181 of this title, paragraph (1) shall not be construed—

  (A) to require a group health plan, or group health insurance coverage, to provide particular benefits other than those provided under the terms of such plan or coverage, or

  (B) to prevent such a plan or coverage from establishing limitations or restrictions on the amount, level, extent, or nature of the benefits or coverage for similarly situated individuals enrolled in the plan or coverage.

(3) Construction

For purposes of paragraph (1), rules for eligibility to enroll under a plan include rules defining any applicable waiting periods for such enrollment.

(b) In premium contributions

(1) In general

A group health plan, and a health insurance issuer offering health insurance coverage in connection with a group health plan, may not require any individual (as a condition of enrollment or continued enrollment under the plan) to pay a premium or contribution which is greater than such premium or contribution for a similarly situated individual enrolled in the plan on the basis of any health status-related factor in relation to the individual or to an individual enrolled under the plan as a dependent of the individual.

(2) Construction

Nothing in paragraph (1) shall be construed—

  (A) to restrict the amount that an employer may be charged for coverage under a group health plan; or

  (B) to prevent a group health plan, and a health insurance issuer offering group health insurance coverage, from establishing premium discounts or rebates or modifying otherwise applicable copayments or deductibles in return for adherence to programs of health promotion and disease prevention.

42 U.S.C.A. § 300gg–11. Guaranteed availability of coverage for employers in the group market

(a) Issuance of coverage in the small group market

(1) In general

Subject to subsections (c) through (f) of this section, each health insurance issuer that offers health insurance coverage in the small group market in a State—

  (A) must accept every small employer (as defined in section 300gg–91(e)(4) of this title) in the State that applies for such coverage; and

(B) must accept for enrollment under such coverage every eligible individual (as defined in paragraph (2)) who applies for enrollment during the period in which the individual first becomes eligible to enroll under the terms of the group health plan and may not place any restriction which is inconsistent with section 300gg–1 of this title on an eligible individual being a participant or beneficiary.

(2) Eligible individual defined

For purposes of this section, the term "eligible individual" means, with respect to a health insurance issuer that offers health insurance coverage to a small employer in connection with a group health plan in the small group market, such an individual in relation to the employer as shall be determined—

(A) in accordance with the terms of such plan,

(B) as provided by the issuer under rules of the issuer which are uniformly applicable in a State to small employers in the small group market, and

(C) in accordance with all applicable State laws governing such issuer and such market.

(b) Assuring access in the large group market

(1) Reports to HHS

The Secretary shall request that the chief executive officer of each State submit to the Secretary, by not later December 31, 2000, and every 3 years thereafter a report on—

(A) the access of large employers to health insurance coverage in the State, and

(B) the circumstances for lack of access (if any) of large employers (or one or more classes of such employers) in the State to such coverage.

(2) Triennial reports to Congress

The Secretary, based on the reports submitted under paragraph (1) and such other information as the Secretary may use, shall prepare and submit to Congress, every 3 years, a report describing the extent to which large employers (and classes of such employers) that seek health insurance coverage in the different States are able to obtain access to such coverage. Such report shall include such recommendations as the Secretary determines to be appropriate.

321

(3) GAO report on large employer access to health insurance coverage

The Comptroller General shall provide for a study of the extent to which classes of large employers in the different States are able to obtain access to health insurance coverage and the circumstances for lack of access (if any) to such coverage. The Comptroller General shall submit to Congress a report on such study not later than 18 months after August 21, 1996.

(c) Special rules for network plans

(1) In general

In the case of a health insurance issuer that offers health insurance coverage in the small group market through a network plan, the issuer may—

(A) limit the employers that may apply for such coverage to those with eligible individuals who live, work, or reside in the service area for such network plan; and

(B) within the service area of such plan, deny such coverage to such employers if the issuer has demonstrated, if required, to the applicable State authority that—

(i) it will not have the capacity to deliver services adequately to enrollees of any additional groups because of its obligations to existing group contract holders and enrollees, and

(ii) it is applying this paragraph uniformly to all employers without regard to the claims experience of those employers and their employees (and their dependents) or any health status-related factor relating to such employees and dependents.

(2) 180–day suspension upon denial of coverage

An issuer, upon denying health insurance coverage in any service area in accordance with paragraph (1)(B), may not offer coverage in the small group market within such service area for a period of 180 days after the date such coverage is denied.

(d) Application of financial capacity limits

(1) In general

A health insurance issuer may deny health insurance coverage in the small group market if the issuer has demonstrated, if required, to the applicable State authority that—

(A) it does not have the financial reserves necessary to underwrite additional coverage; and

(B) it is applying this paragraph uniformly to all employers in the small group market in the State consistent with applicable State law and without regard to the claims experience of those employers and their employees (and their dependents) or any health status-related factor relating to such employees and dependents.

(2) 180–day suspension upon denial of coverage

A health insurance issuer upon denying health insurance coverage in connection with group health plans in accordance with paragraph (1) in a State may not offer coverage in connection with group health plans in the small group market in the State for a period of 180 days after the date such coverage is denied or until the issuer has demonstrated to the applicable State authority, if required under applicable State law, that the issuer has sufficient financial reserves to underwrite additional coverage, whichever is later. An applicable State authority may provide for the application of this subsection on a service-area-specific basis.

(e) Exception to requirement for failure to meet certain minimum participation or contribution rules

(1) In general

Subsection (a) of this section shall not be construed to preclude a health insurance issuer from establishing employer contribution rules or group participation rules for the offering of health insurance coverage in connection with a group health plan in the small group market, as allowed under applicable State law.

(2) Rules defined

For purposes of paragraph (1)—

(A) the term "employer contribution rule" means a requirement relating to the minimum level or amount of employer contribution toward the premium for enrollment of participants and beneficiaries; and

(B) the term "group participation rule" means a requirement relating to the minimum number of participants or beneficiaries that must be enrolled in relation to a specified percentage or number of eligible individuals or employees of an employer.

(f) Exception for coverage offered only to bona fide association members

Subsection (a) of this section shall not apply to health insurance coverage offered by a health insurance issuer if such coverage is made available in the small group market only through one or more bona fide associations (as defined in section 300gg–91(d)(3) of this title.

42 U.S.C.A. § 300gg–12. Guaranteed renewability of coverage for employers in the group market

(a) In general

Except as provided in this section, if a health insurance issuer offers health insurance coverage in the small or large group market in connection with a group health plan, the issuer must renew or continue in force such coverage at the option of the plan sponsor of the plan.

(b) General exceptions

A health insurance issuer may nonrenew or discontinue health insurance coverage offered in connection with a group health plan in the small or large group market based only on one or more of the following:

(1) Nonpayment of premiums

The plan sponsor has failed to pay premiums or contributions in accordance with the terms of the health insurance coverage or the issuer has not received timely premium payments.

(2) Fraud

The plan sponsor has performed an act or practice that constitutes fraud or made an intentional misrepresentation of material fact under the terms of the coverage.

(3) Violation of participation or contribution rules

The plan sponsor has failed to comply with a material plan provision relating to employer contribution or group participation rules, as permitted under section 300gg–11(e) of this title in the case of the small group market or pursuant to applicable State law in the case of the large group market.

(4) Termination of coverage

The issuer is ceasing to offer coverage in such market in accordance with subsection (c) of this section and applicable State law.

(5) Movement outside service area

In the case of a health insurance issuer that offers health insurance coverage in the market through a network plan, there is no longer any enrollee in connection with such plan who lives, resides, or works in the service area of the issuer (or in the area for which the issuer is authorized to do business) and, in the case of the small group market, the issuer would deny enrollment with respect to such plan under section 300gg–11(c)(1)(A) of this title.

(6) Association membership ceases

In the case of health insurance coverage that is made available in the small or large group market (as the case may be) only through one or more bona fide associations, the membership of an employer in the association (on the basis of which the coverage is provided) ceases but only if such coverage is terminated under this paragraph uniformly without regard to any health status-related factor relating to any covered individual.

(c) Requirements for uniform termination of coverage

(1) Particular type of coverage not offered

In any case in which an issuer decides to discontinue offering a particular type of group health insurance coverage offered in the small or large group market, coverage of such type may be discontinued by the issuer in accordance with applicable State law in such market only if—

(**A**) the issuer provides notice to each plan sponsor provided coverage of this type in such market (and participants and beneficiaries covered under such coverage) of such discontinuation at least 90 days prior to the date of the discontinuation of such coverage;

(**B**) the issuer offers to each plan sponsor provided coverage of this type in such market, the option to purchase all (or, in the case of the large group market, any) other health insurance coverage currently being offered by the issuer to a group health plan in such market; and

(**C**) in exercising the option to discontinue coverage of this type and in offering the option of coverage under subparagraph (B), the issuer acts uniformly without regard to the claims experience of those sponsors or any health status-related factor relating to any participants or beneficiaries covered or new participants or beneficiaries who may become eligible for such coverage.

(**2**) Discontinuance of all coverage

(**A**) In general

In any case in which a health insurance issuer elects to discontinue offering all health insurance coverage in the small group market or the large group market, or both markets, in a State, health insurance coverage may be discontinued by the issuer only in accordance with applicable State law and if—

(**i**) the issuer provides notice to the applicable State authority and to each plan sponsor (and participants and beneficiaries covered under such coverage) of such discontinuation at least 180 days prior to the date of the discontinuation of such coverage; and

(**ii**) all health insurance issued or delivered for issuance in the State in such market (or markets) are discontinued and coverage under such health insurance coverage in such market (or markets) is not renewed.

(**B**) Prohibition on market reentry

In the case of a discontinuation under subparagraph (A) in a market, the issuer may not provide for the issuance of any health insurance coverage in the market and State involved during the 5–year period beginning on the date of the discontinuation of the last health insurance coverage not so renewed.

(d) Exception for uniform modification of coverage

At the time of coverage renewal, a health insurance issuer may modify the health insurance coverage for a product offered to a group health plan—

    (1) in the large group market; or

    (2) in the small group market if, for coverage that is available in such market other than only through one or more bona fide associations, such modification is consistent with State law and effective on a uniform basis among group health plans with that product.

(e) Application to coverage offered only through associations

In applying this section in the case of health insurance coverage that is made available by a health insurance issuer in the small or large group market to employers only through one or more associations, a reference to "plan sponsor" is deemed, with respect to coverage provided to an employer member of the association, to include a reference to such employer.

42 U.S.C.A. § 300gg–41. Guaranteed availability of individual health insurance coverage to certain individuals with prior group coverage

(a) Guaranteed availability

    (1) In general

Subject to the succeeding subsections of this section and section 300gg–44 of this title, each health insurance issuer that offers health insurance coverage (as defined in section 300gg–91(b)(1) of this title) in the individual market in a State may not, with respect to an eligible individual (as defined in subsection (b) of this section) desiring to enroll in individual health insurance coverage—

        (A) decline to offer such coverage to, or deny enrollment of, such individual; or

        (B) impose any preexisting condition exclusion (as defined in section 300gg(b)(1)(A) of this title) with respect to such coverage.

    (2) Substitution by State of acceptable alternative mechanism

The requirement of paragraph (1) shall not apply to health insurance coverage offered in the individual market in a State in which the State is implementing an acceptable alternative mechanism under section 300gg–44 of this title.

(b) Eligible individual defined

In this part, the term "eligible individual" means an individual—

    (1)(A) for whom, as of the date on which the individual seeks coverage under this section, the aggregate of the periods of creditable coverage (as defined in section 300gg(c) of this title) is 18 or more months and

        (B) whose most recent prior creditable coverage was under a group health plan, governmental plan, or church plan (or health insurance coverage offered in connection with any such plan);

(2) who is not eligible for coverage under (A) a group health plan, (B) part A or part B of title XVIII of the Social Security Act [42 U.S.C.A. § 1395c et seq., § 1395j et seq.], or (C) a State plan under title XIX of such Act [42 U.S.C.A. § 1396 et seq.] (or any successor program), and does not have other health insurance coverage;

(3) with respect to whom the most recent coverage within the coverage period described in paragraph (1)(A) was not terminated based on a factor described in paragraph (1) or (2) of section 300gg–12(b) of this title (relating to nonpayment of premiums or fraud);

(4) if the individual had been offered the option of continuation coverage under a COBRA continuation provision or under a similar State program, who elected such coverage; and

(5) who, if the individual elected such continuation coverage, has exhausted such continuation coverage under such provision or program.

(c) Alternative coverage permitted where no State mechanism

(1) In general

In the case of health insurance coverage offered in the individual market in a State in which the State is not implementing an acceptable alternative mechanism under section 300gg–44 of this title, the health insurance issuer may elect to limit the coverage offered under subsection (a) of this section so long as it offers at least two different policy forms of health insurance coverage both of which—

(A) are designed for, made generally available to, and actively marketed to, and enroll both eligible and other individuals by the issuer; and

(B) meet the requirement of paragraph (2) or (3), as elected by the issuer.

For purposes of this subsection, policy forms which have different cost-sharing arrangements or different riders shall be considered to be different policy forms.

(2) Choice of most popular policy forms

The requirement of this paragraph is met, for health insurance coverage policy forms offered by an issuer in the individual market, if the issuer offers the policy forms for individual health insurance coverage with the largest, and next to largest, premium volume of all such policy forms offered by the issuer in the State or applicable marketing or service area (as may be prescribed in regulation) by the issuer in the individual market in the period involved.

(3) Choice of 2 policy forms with representative coverage

(A) In general

The requirement of this paragraph is met, for health insurance coverage policy forms offered by an issuer in the individual market, if

327

the issuer offers a lower-level coverage policy form (as defined in subparagraph (B)) and a higher-level coverage policy form (as defined in subparagraph (C)) each of which includes benefits substantially similar to other individual health insurance coverage offered by the issuer in that State and each of which is covered under a method described in section 300gg–44(c)(3)(A) of this title (relating to risk adjustment, risk spreading, or financial subsidization).

(B) Lower-level of coverage described

A policy form is described in this subparagraph if the actuarial value of the benefits under the coverage is at least 85 percent but not greater than 100 percent of a weighted average (described in subparagraph (D)).

(C) Higher-level of coverage described

A policy form is described in this subparagraph if—

(i) the actuarial value of the benefits under the coverage is at least 15 percent greater than the actuarial value of the coverage described in subparagraph (B) offered by the issuer in the area involved; and

(ii) the actuarial value of the benefits under the coverage is at least 100 percent but not greater than 120 percent of a weighted average (described in subparagraph (D)).

(D) Weighted average

For purposes of this paragraph, the weighted average described in this subparagraph is the average actuarial value of the benefits provided by all the health insurance coverage issued (as elected by the issuer) either by that issuer or by all issuers in the State in the individual market during the previous year (not including coverage issued under this section), weighted by enrollment for the different coverage.

(4) Election

The issuer elections under this subsection shall apply uniformly to all eligible individuals in the State for that issuer. Such an election shall be effective for policies offered during a period of not shorter than 2 years.

(5) Assumptions

For purposes of paragraph (3), the actuarial value of benefits provided under individual health insurance coverage shall be calculated based on a standardized population and a set of standardized utilization and cost factors.

(d) Special rules for network plans

(1) In general

In the case of a health insurance issuer that offers health insurance coverage in the individual market through a network plan, the issuer may—

    (A) limit the individuals who may be enrolled under such coverage to those who live, reside, or work within the service area for such network plan; and

    (B) within the service area of such plan, deny such coverage to such individuals if the issuer has demonstrated, if required, to the applicable State authority that—

        (i) it will not have the capacity to deliver services adequately to additional individual enrollees because of its obligations to existing group contract holders and enrollees and individual enrollees, and

        (ii) it is applying this paragraph uniformly to individuals without regard to any health status-related factor of such individuals and without regard to whether the individuals are eligible individuals.

(2) 180–day suspension upon denial of coverage

An issuer, upon denying health insurance coverage in any service area in accordance with paragraph (1)(B), may not offer coverage in the individual market within such service area for a period of 180 days after such coverage is denied.

(e) [Sic] Application of financial capacity limits

(1) In general

A health insurance issuer may deny health insurance coverage in the individual market to an eligible individual if the issuer has demonstrated, if required, to the applicable State authority that—

    (A) it does not have the financial reserves necessary to underwrite additional coverage; and

    (B) it is applying this paragraph uniformly to all individuals in the individual market in the State consistent with applicable State law and without regard to any health status-related factor of such individuals and without regard to whether the individuals are eligible individuals.

(2) 180–day suspension upon denial of coverage

An issuer upon denying individual health insurance coverage in any service area in accordance with paragraph (1) may not offer such coverage in the individual market within such service area for a period of 180 days after the date such coverage is denied or until the issuer has demonstrated, if required under applicable State law, to the applicable State authority that the issuer has sufficient financial reserves to underwrite additional coverage, whichever is later. A State may provide for the application of this paragraph on a service-area-specific basis.

(e) [Sic] Market requirements

(1) In general

The provisions of subsection (a) of this section shall not be construed to require that a health insurance issuer offering health insurance coverage only in connection with group health plans or through one or more bona fide associations, or both, offer such health insurance coverage in the individual market.

(2) Conversion policies

A health insurance issuer offering health insurance coverage in connection with group health plans under this subchapter shall not be deemed to be a health insurance issuer offering individual health insurance coverage solely because such issuer offers a conversion policy.

(f) Construction

Nothing in this section shall be construed—

(1) to restrict the amount of the premium rates that an issuer may charge an individual for health insurance coverage provided in the individual market under applicable State law; or

(2) to prevent a health insurance issuer offering health insurance coverage in the individual market from establishing premium discounts or rebates or modifying otherwise applicable copayments or deductibles in return for adherence to programs of health promotion and disease prevention.

42 U.S.C.A. § 300gg–44. State flexibility in individual market reforms

(a) Waiver of requirements where implementation of acceptable alternative mechanism

(1) In general

The requirements of section 300gg–41 of this title shall not apply with respect to health insurance coverage offered in the individual market in the State so long as a State is found to be implementing, in accordance with this section and consistent with section 300gg–62(b) of this title, an alternative mechanism (in this section referred to as an "acceptable alternative mechanism")—

(A) under which all eligible individuals are provided a choice of health insurance coverage;

(B) under which such coverage does not impose any preexisting condition exclusion with respect to such coverage;

(C) under which such choice of coverage includes at least one policy form of coverage that is comparable to comprehensive health insurance coverage offered in the individual market in such State or

330

that is comparable to a standard option of coverage available under the group or individual health insurance laws of such State; and

(D) in a State which is implementing—

(i) a model act described in subsection (c)(1) of this title,

(ii) a qualified high risk pool described in subsection (c)(2) of this section, or

(iii) a mechanism described in subsection (c)(3) of this section.

(2) Permissible forms of mechanisms

A private or public individual health insurance mechanism (such as a health insurance coverage pool or programs, mandatory group conversion policies, guaranteed issue of one or more plans of individual health insurance coverage, or open enrollment by one or more health insurance issuers), or combination of such mechanisms, that is designed to provide access to health benefits for individuals in the individual market in the State in accordance with this section may constitute an acceptable alternative mechanism.

(b) Application of acceptable alternative mechanisms

(1) Presumption

(A) In general

Subject to the succeeding provisions of this subsection, a State is presumed to be implementing an acceptable alternative mechanism in accordance with this section as of July 1, 1997, if, by not later than April 1, 1997, the chief executive officer of a State—

(i) notifies the Secretary that the State has enacted or intends to enact (by not later than January 1, 1998, or July 1, 1998, in the case of a State described in subparagraph (B)(ii)) any necessary legislation to provide for the implementation of a mechanism reasonably designed to be an acceptable alternative mechanism as of January 1, 1998, [FN1] (or, in the case of a State described in subparagraph (B)(ii), July 1, 1998); and

(ii) provides the Secretary with such information as the Secretary may require to review the mechanism and its implementation (or proposed implementation) under this subsection.

(B) Delay permitted for certain States

(i) Effect of delay

In the case of a State described in clause (ii) that provides notice under subparagraph (A)(i), for the presumption to continue on and after July 1, 1998, the chief executive officer of the State by April 1, 1998—

(I) must notify the Secretary that the State has enacted any necessary legislation to provide for the implementation of a mechanism reasonably designed to be an acceptable alternative mechanism as of July 1, 1998; and

(II) must provide the Secretary with such information as the Secretary may require to review the mechanism and its implementation (or proposed implementation) under this subsection.

(ii) States described

A State described in this clause is a State that has a legislature that does not meet within the 12–month period beginning on August 21, 1996.

(C) Continued application

In order for a mechanism to continue to be presumed to be an acceptable alternative mechanism, the State shall provide the Secretary every 3 years with information described in subparagraph (A)(ii) or (B)(i)(II) (as the case may be).

(2) Notice

If the Secretary finds, after review of information provided under paragraph (1) and in consultation with the chief executive officer of the State and the insurance commissioner or chief insurance regulatory official of the State, that such a mechanism is not an acceptable alternative mechanism or is not (or no longer) being implemented, the Secretary—

(A) shall notify the State of—

(i) such preliminary determination, and

(ii) the consequences under paragraph (3) of a failure to implement such a mechanism; and

(B) shall permit the State a reasonable opportunity in which to modify the mechanism (or to adopt another mechanism) in a manner so that may be an acceptable alternative mechanism or to provide for implementation of such a mechanism.

(3) Final determination

If, after providing notice and opportunity under paragraph (2), the Secretary finds that the mechanism is not an acceptable alternative mechanism or the State is not implementing such a mechanism, the Secretary shall notify the State that the State is no longer considered to be implementing an acceptable alternative mechanism and that the requirements of section 300gg–41 of this title shall apply to health insurance coverage offered in the individual market in the State, effective as of a date specified in the notice.

(4) Limitation on secretarial authority

The Secretary shall not make a determination under paragraph (2) or (3) on any basis other than the basis that a mechanism is not an acceptable alternative mechanism or is not being implemented.

(5) Future adoption of mechanisms

If a State, after January 1, 1997, submits the notice and information described in paragraph (1), unless the Secretary makes a finding described in paragraph (3) within the 90–day period beginning on the date of submission of the notice and information, the mechanism shall be considered to be an acceptable alternative mechanism for purposes of this section, effective 90 days after the end of such period, subject to the second sentence of paragraph (1).

(c) Provision related to risk

(1) Adoption of NAIC models

The model act referred to in subsection (a)(1)(D)(i) of this section is the Small Employer and Individual Health Insurance Availability Model Act (adopted by the National Association of Insurance Commissioners on June 3, 1996) insofar as it applies to individual health insurance coverage or the Individual Health Insurance Portability Model Act (also adopted by such Association on such date).

(2) Qualified high risk pool

For purposes of subsection (a)(1)(D)(ii) of this section, a "qualified high risk pool" described in this paragraph is a high risk pool that—

(A) provides to all eligible individuals health insurance coverage (or comparable coverage) that does not impose any preexisting condition exclusion with respect to such coverage for all eligible individuals, and

(B) provides for premium rates and covered benefits for such coverage consistent with standards included in the NAIC Model Health Plan for Uninsurable Individuals Act (as in effect as of August 21, 1996).

(3) Other mechanisms

For purposes of subsection (a)(1)(D)(iii) of this section, a mechanism described in this paragraph—

(A) provides for risk adjustment, risk spreading, or a risk spreading mechanism (among issuers or policies of an issuer) or otherwise provides for some financial subsidization for eligible individuals, including through assistance to participating issuers; or

(B) is a mechanism under which each eligible individual is provided a choice of all individual health insurance coverage otherwise available.

B. PROVISIONS OF THE EMPLOYEE RETIREMENT INCOME SECURITY ACT, APPLYING TO EMPLOYEE HEALTH BENEFITS (ERISA): 29 U.S.C.A. § 1003 ET SEQ.

§ 1003. Coverage

(a) Except as provided in subsection (b) and in sections 201, 301, and 401 [*29 USCA §§ 1051,* 1081, and 1101], this title shall apply to any employee benefit plan if it is established or maintained—

(1) by any employer engaged in commerce or in any industry or activity affecting commerce; or

(2) by any employee organization or organizations representing employees engaged in commerce or in any industry or activity affecting commerce; or

(3) by both.

(b) The provisions of this title shall not apply to any employee benefit plan if—

(1) such plan is a governmental plan (as defined in section 3(32) [*29 USCA § 1002*(32)]);

(2) such plan is a church plan (as defined in section 3(33) [*29 USCA § 1002*(33)]) with respect to which no election has been made under section 410(d) of the Internal Revenue Code of 1986 [*26 USCA § 410*(d)];

(3) such plan is maintained solely for the purpose of complying with applicable workmen's compensation laws or unemployment compensation or disability insurance laws;

(4) such plan is maintained outside of the United States primarily for the benefit of persons substantially all of whom are nonresident aliens; or

(5) such plan is an excess benefit plan (as defined in section 3(36) [*29 USCA § 1002*(36)]) and is unfunded.

The provisions of part 7 of subtitle B [*29 USCA §§ 1181* et seq.] shall not apply to a health insurance issuer (as defined in section 733(b)(2) [*29 USCA § 1191b*(b)(2)]) solely by reason of health insurance coverage (as defined in section 733(b)(1) [*29 USCA § 1191b*(b)(1)]) provided by such issuer in connection with a group health plan (as defined in section 733(a)(1) [*29 USCA § 1191b*(a)(1)]) if the provisions of this title do not apply to such group health plan.

§ 1021. Duty of disclosure and reporting

(a) Summary plan description and information to be furnished to participants and beneficiaries.

The administrator of each employee benefit plan shall cause to be furnished in accordance with section 104(b) [*29 USCA § 1024*(b)] to each participant covered under the plan and to each beneficiary who is receiving benefits under the plan—

    (1) a summary plan description described in section 102(a)(1) [*29 USCA § 1022*(a)(1)]; and

    (2) the information described in sections 104(b)(3) and 105(a) and (c) [*29 USCA §§ 1024*(b)(3), 1025(a) and (c)].

(b) Plan description, modifications and changes, and reports to be filed with Secretary of Labor.

The administrator shall, in accordance with section 104(a) [*29 USCA § 1024*(a)], file with the Secretary—

    (1) the annual report containing the information required by section 103 [*29 USCA § 1023*]; and

    (2) terminal and supplementary reports as required by subsection (c) of this section.

(c) Terminal and supplementary reports.

    (1) Each administrator of an employee pension benefit plan which is winding up its affairs (without regard to the number of participants remaining in the plan) shall, in accordance with regulations prescribed by the Secretary, file such terminal reports as the Secretary may consider necessary. A copy of such report shall also be filed with the Pension Benefit Guaranty Corporation.

    (2) The Secretary may require terminal reports to be filed with regard to any employee welfare benefit plan which is winding up its affairs in accordance with regulations promulgated by the Secretary.

    (3) The Secretary may require that a plan described in paragraph (1) or (2) file a supplementary or terminal report with the annual report in the year such plan is terminated and that a copy of such supplementary or terminal report in the case of a plan described in paragraph (1) be also filed with the Pension Benefit Guaranty Corporation.

(d) Notice of failure to meet minimum funding standards.

    (1) In general. If an employer maintaining a plan other than a multiemployer plan fails to make a required installment or other payment required to meet the minimum funding standard under section 302 [*29 USCA § 1082*] to a plan before the 60th day following the due date for such installment or other payment, the employer shall notify each participant and beneficiary (including an alternate payee as defined in section 206(d)(3)(K) [*29 USCA § 1056*(d)(3)(K)]) of such plan of such failure. Such notice shall be made at such time and in such manner as the Secretary may prescribe.

    (2) Subsection not to apply if waiver pending. This subsection shall not apply to any failure if the employer has filed a waiver request under section 303 [*29 USCA § 1083*] with respect to the plan year to which the required installment relates, except that if the waiver request is denied, notice under paragraph (1) shall be provided within 60 days after the date of such denial.

(3) Definitions. For purposes of this subsection, the terms "required installment" and "due date" have the same meanings given such terms by section 302(e) [*29 USCA § 1082*(e)].

(e) Notice of transfer of excess pension assets to health benefits accounts.

(1) Notice to participants.

Not later than 60 days before the date of a qualified transfer by an employee pension benefit plan of excess pension assets to a health benefits account, the administrator of the plan shall notify (in such manner as the Secretary may prescribe) each participant and beneficiary under the plan of such transfer. Such notice shall include information with respect to the amount of excess pension assets, the portion to be transferred, the amount of health benefits liabilities expected to be provided with the assets transferred, and the amount of pension benefits of the participant which will be nonforfeitable immediately after the transfer.

(2) Notice to Secretaries, administrator, and employee organizations.

(A) In general.

Not later than 60 days before the date of any qualified transfer by an employee pension benefit plan of excess pension assets to a health benefits account, the employer maintaining the plan from which the transfer is made shall provide the Secretary, the Secretary of the Treasury, the administrator, and each employee organization representing participants in the plan a written notice of such transfer. A copy of any such notice shall be available for inspection in the principal office of the administrator.

(B) Information relating to transfer.

Such notice shall identify the plan from which the transfer is made, the amount of the transfer, a detailed accounting of assets projected to be held by the plan immediately before and immediately after the transfer, and the current liabilities under the plan at the time of the transfer.

(C) Authority for additional reporting requirements.

The Secretary may prescribe such additional reporting requirements as may be necessary to carry out the purposes of this section.

(3) Definitions.

For purposes of paragraph (1), any term used in such paragraph which is also used in section 420 of the Internal Revenue Code of 1986 [*26 USCA § 420*] (as in effect on the date of the enactment of the Tax Relief Extension Act of 1999 [enacted Dec. 17, 1999]) shall have the same meaning as when used in such section.

(f) [Repealed]

(g) Reporting by certain arrangements.

The Secretary may, by regulation, require multiple employer welfare

arrangements providing benefits consisting of medical care (within the meaning of section 733(a)(2) [*29 USCA § 1191b*(a)(2)]) which are not group health plans to report, not more frequently than annually, in such form and such manner as the Secretary may require for the purpose of determining the extent to which the requirements of part 7 [*29 USCA §§ 1181* et seq.] are being carried out in connection with such benefits.

§ 1022. Summary plan description

(a) A summary plan description of any employee benefit plan shall be furnished to participants and beneficiaries as provided in section 104(b) [*29 USCA § 1024*(b)]. The summary plan description shall include the information described in subsection (b), shall be written in a manner calculated to be understood by the average plan participant, and shall be sufficiently accurate and comprehensive to reasonably apprise such participants and beneficiaries of their rights and obligations under the plan. A summary of any material modification in the terms of the plan and any change in the information required under subsection (b) shall be written in a manner calculated to be understood by the average plan participant and shall be furnished in accordance with section 104(b)(1) [*29 USCA § 1024*(b)(1)].

(b) The summary plan description shall contain the following information: The name and type of administration of the plan; in the case of a group health plan (as defined in section 733(a)(1) [*29 USCA § 1191b*(a)(1)]), whether a health insurance issuer (as defined in section 733(b)(2) [*29 USCA § 1191b*(b)(2)]) is responsible for the financing or administration (including payment of claims) of the plan and (if so) the name and address of such issuer; the name and address of the person designated as agent for the service of legal process, if such person is not the administrator; the name and address of the administrator; names, titles and addresses of any trustee or trustees (if they are persons different from the administrator); a description of the relevant provisions of any applicable collective bargaining agreement; the plan's requirements respecting eligibility for participation and benefits; a description of the provisions providing for nonforfeitable pension benefits; circumstances which may result in disqualification, ineligibility, or denial or loss of benefits; the source of financing of the plan and the identity of any organization through which benefits are provided; the date of the end of the plan year and whether the records of the plan are kept on a calendar, policy, or fiscal year basis; the procedures to be followed in presenting claims for benefits under the plan including the office at the Department of Labor through which participants and beneficiaries may seek assistance or information regarding their rights under this Act and the Health Insurance Portability and Accountability Act of 1996 with respect to health benefits that are offered through a group health plan (as defined in section 733(a)(1) [*29 USCA*

§ 1191b(a)(1)]) and the remedies available under the plan for the redress of claims which are denied in whole or in part (including procedures required under section 503 of this Act [*29 USCA § 1133]*).

§ 1101. Coverage

(a) Scope of of coverage

This part [*29 USCA §§ 1101* et seq.] shall apply to any employee benefit plan described in section 4(a) [*29 USCA § 1003*(a)] (and not exempted under section 4(b) [*29 USCA § 1003*(b)]), other than—

(1) a plan which is unfunded and is maintained by an employer primarily for the purpose of providing deferred compensation for a select group of management or highly compensated employees; or

(2) any agreement described in section 736 of the Internal Revenue Code of 1986 [*26 USCA § 736]*, which provides payments to a retired partner or deceased partner or a deceased partner's successor in interest.

(b) Securities or policies deemed to be included in plan assets

For purposes of this part [*29 USCA §§ 1101* et seq.]:

(1) In the case of a plan which invests in any security issued by an investment company registered under the Investment Company Act of 1940, the assets of such plan shall be deemed to include such security but shall not, solely by reason of such investment, be deemed to include any assets of such investment company.

(2) In the case of a plan to which a guaranteed benefit policy is issued by an insurer, the assets of such plan shall be deemed to include such policy, but shall not, solely by reason of the issuance of such policy, be deemed to include any assets of such insurer. For purposes of this paragraph:

(A) The term "insurer" means an insurance company, insurance service, or insurance organization, qualified to do business in a State.

(B) The term "guaranteed benefit policy" means an insurance policy or contract to the extent that such policy or contract provides for benefits the amount of which is guaranteed by the insurer. Such term includes any surplus in a separate account, but excludes any other portion of a separate account.

(c) Clarification of application of ERISA to insurance company general accounts

(1)(A) Not later than June 30, 1997, the Secretary shall issue proposed regulations to provide guidance for the purpose of determining, in cases where an insurer issues 1 or more policies to or for the benefit of an employee benefit plan (and such policies are supported by assets of such insurer's general account), which assets held by the insurer (other than plan assets held in its separate accounts) constitute assets of the plan for purposes of this part [*29 USCA §§ 1101* et seq.] and section 4975 of the Internal Revenue Code of 1986 [*26 USCA § 4975*] and to provide guidance with respect to the application of this title to the general account assets of insurers.

(B) The proposed regulations under subparagraph (A) shall be subject to public notice and comment until September 30, 1997.

(C) The Secretary shall issue final regulations providing the guidance described in subparagraph (A) not later than December 31, 1997.

(D) Such regulations shall only apply with respect to policies which are issued by an insurer on or before December 31, 1998, to or for the benefit of an employee benefit plan which is supported by assets of such insurer's general account. With respect to policies issued on or before December 31, 1998, such regulations shall take effect at the end of the 18–month period following the date on which such regulations become final.

(2) The Secretary shall ensure that the regulations issued under paragraph (1)—

(A) are administratively feasible, and

(B) protect the interests and rights of the plan and of its participants and beneficiaries (including meeting the requirements of paragraph (3)).

(3) The regulations prescribed by the Secretary pursuant to paragraph (1) shall require, in connection with any policy issued by an insurer to or for the benefit of an employee benefit plan to the extent that the policy is not a guaranteed benefit policy (as defined in subsection (b)(2)(B))—

(A) that a plan fiduciary totally independent of the insurer authorize the purchase of such policy (unless such purchase is a transaction exempt under section 408(b)(5) [*29 USCA § 1108*(b)(5)]),

(B) that the insurer describe (in such form and manner as shall be prescribed in such regulations), in annual reports and in policies issued to the policyholder after the date on which such regulations are issued in final form pursuant to paragraph (1)(C)—

(i) a description of the method by which any income and expenses of the insurer's general account are allocated to the policy during the term of the policy and upon the termination of the policy, and

(ii) for each report, the actual return to the plan under the policy and such other financial information as the Secretary may deem appropriate for the period covered by each such annual report,

(C) that the insurer disclose to the plan fiduciary the extent to which alternative arrangements supported by assets of separate accounts of the insurer (which generally hold plan assets) are available, whether there is a right under the policy to transfer funds to a separate account and the terms governing any such right, and the extent to which support by assets of the insurer's general account and support by assets of separate accounts of the insurer might pose differing risks to the plan, and

(D) that the insurer manage those assets of the insurer which are assets of such insurer's general account (irrespective of whether any such assets are plan assets) with the care, skill, prudence, and diligence under the circumstances then prevailing that a prudent man acting in a like capacity and familiar with such matters would use in the conduct of an enterprise of a like character and with like aims, taking into account all obligations supported by such enterprise.

(4) Compliance by the insurer with all requirements of the regulations issued by the Secretary pursuant to paragraph (1) shall be deemed compliance by such insurer with sections 404, 406, and 407 [*29 USCA §§ 1104,* 1106, 1107] with respect to those assets of the insurer's general account which support a policy described in paragraph (3).

(5)(A) Subject to subparagraph (B), any regulations issued under paragraph (1) shall not take effect before the date on which such regulations become final.

(B) No person shall be subject to liability under this part [*29 USCA §§ 1101* et seq.] or section 4975 of the Internal Revenue Code of 1986 [*26 USCA § 4975*] for conduct which occurred before the date which is 18 months following the date described in subparagraph (A) on the basis of a claim that the assets of an insurer (other than plan assets held in a separate account) constitute assets of the plan, except—

(i) as otherwise provided by the Secretary in regulations intended to prevent avoidance of the regulations issued under paragraph (1), or

(ii) as provided in an action brought by the Secretary pursuant to paragraph (2) or (5) of section 502(a) for a breach of fiduciary responsibilities which would also constitute a violation of Federal or State criminal law.

The Secretary shall bring a cause of action described in clause (ii) if a participant, beneficiary, or fiduciary demonstrates to the satisfaction of the Secretary that a breach described in clause (ii) has occurred.

(6) Nothing in this subsection shall preclude the application of any Federal criminal law.

(7) For purposes of this subsection, the term "policy" includes a contract.

§ 1102. Establishment of plan

(a) Named fiduciaries

(1) Every employee benefit plan shall be established and maintained pursuant to a written instrument. Such instrument shall provide for one or more named fiduciaries who jointly or severally shall have authority to control and manage the operation and administration of the plan.

(2) For purposes of this title, the term "named fiduciary" means a fiduciary who is named in the plan instrument, or who, pursuant to a procedure specified in the plan, is identified as a fiduciary (A) by a person who is an employer or employee organization with respect to the plan or (B) by such an employer and such an employee organization acting jointly.

(b) Requisite features of plan. Every employee benefit plan shall—

(1) provide a procedure for establishing and carrying out a funding policy and method consistent with the objectives of the plan and the requirements of this title,

(2) describe any procedure under the plan for the allocation of responsibilities for the operation and administration of the plan (including any procedure described in section 405(c)(1) [*29 USCA § 1105*(c)(1)]),

(3) provide a procedure for amending such plan, and for identifying the persons who have authority to amend the plan, and

(4) specify the basis on which payments are made to and from the plan.

(c) Optional features of plan. Any employee benefit plan may provide—

(1) that any person or group of persons may serve in more than one fiduciary capacity with respect to the plan (including service both as trustee and administrator);

(2) that a named fiduciary, or a fiduciary designated by a named fiduciary pursuant to a plan procedure described in section 405(c)(1) [*29 USCA § 1105*(c)(1)], may employ one or more persons to render advice with regard to any responsibility such fiduciary has under the plan; or

(3) that a person who is a named fiduciary with respect to control or management of the assets of the plan may appoint an investment manager or managers to manage (including the power to acquire and dispose of) any assets of a plan.

§ 1161. Plans must provide continuation coverage to certain individuals

(a) In general.

The plan sponsor of each group health plan shall provide, in accordance with this part [*29 USCA §§ 1161* et seq.], that each qualified beneficiary who would lose coverage under the plan as a result of a qualifying event is entitled, under the plan, to elect, within the election period, continuation coverage under the plan.

(b) Exception for certain plans.

Subsection (a) shall not apply to any group health plan for any calendar year if all employers maintaining such plan normally employed fewer than 20 employees on a typical business day during the preceding calendar year.

§ 1162. Continuation coverage

For purposes of section 601 [*29 USCA § 1161*], the term "continuation coverage" means coverage under the plan which meets the following requirements:

(1) Type of benefit coverage

The coverage must consist of coverage which, as of the time the coverage is being provided, is identical to the coverage provided under the plan to similarly situated beneficiaries under the plan with respect to whom a qualifying event has not occurred. If coverage is modified under the plan for any group of similarly situated beneficiaries, such coverage shall also be modified in the same manner for all individuals who are qualified beneficiaries under the plan pursuant to this part [*29 USCA §§ 1161* et seq.] in connection with such group.

(2) Period of coverage

The coverage must extend for at least the period beginning on the date of the qualifying event and ending not earlier than the earliest of the following:

(A) Maximum required period

(i) General rule for terminations and reduced hours

In the case of a qualifying event described in section 603(2) [*29 USCA § 1163*(2)], except as provided in clause (ii), the date which is 18 months after the date of the qualifying event.

(ii) Special rule for multiple qualifying events

If a qualifying event (other than a qualifying event described in section 603(6) [*29 USCA § 1163*(6)]) occurs during the 18 months after the date of a qualifying event described in section 603(2) [*29 USCA § 1163*(2)], the date which is 36 months after the date of the qualifying event described in section 603(2) [*29 USCA § 1163*(2)].

342

(iii) Special rule for certain bankruptcy proceedings

In the case of a qualifying event described in section 603(6) [*29 USCA § 1163*(6)] (relating to bankruptcy proceedings), the date of the death of the covered employee or qualified beneficiary (described in section 607(3)(C)(iii) [*29 USCA § 1167*(3)(C)(iii)]), or in the case of the surviving spouse or dependent children of the covered employee, 36 months after the date of the death of the covered employee.

(iv) General rule for other qualifying events

In the case of a qualifying event not described in section 603(2) or 603(6) [*29 USCA § 1163*(2) or (6)], the date which is 36 months after the date of the qualifying event.

(v) Medicare entitlement followed by qualifying event

In the case of a qualifying event described in section 603(2) [*29 USCA § 1163*(2)] that occurs less than 18 months after the date the covered employee became entitled to benefits under title XVIII of the Social Security Act [*42 USCA §§ 1395* et seq.], the period of coverage for qualified beneficiaries other than the covered employee shall not terminate under this subparagraph before the close of the 36–month period beginning on the date the covered employee became so entitled.

In the case of a qualified beneficiary who is determined, under title II or XVI of the Social Security Act [*42 USCA §§ 401* et seq. or 1381 et seq.], to have been disabled at any time during the first 60 days of continuation coverage under this part [*29 USCA §§ 1161* et seq.], any reference in clause (i) or (ii) to 18 months is deemed a reference to 29 months (with respect to all qualified beneficiaries), but only if the qualified beneficiary has provided notice of such determination under section 606(3) [*29 USCA § 1166*(3)] before the end of such 18 months.

(B) End of plan

The date on which the employer ceases to provide any group health plan to any employee.

(C) Failure to pay premium

The date on which coverage ceases under the plan by reason of a failure to make timely payment of any premium required under the plan with respect to the qualified beneficiary. The payment of any premium (other than any payment referred to in the last sentence of paragraph (3)) shall be considered to be timely if made within 30 days after the date due or within such longer period as applies to or under the plan.

(D) Group health plan coverage or Medicare entitlement

The date on which the qualified beneficiary first becomes, after the date of the election—

(i) covered under any other group health plan (as an employee or otherwise) which does not contain any exclusion or limitation with respect to any preexisting condition of such beneficiary (other than such an exclusion or limitation which does not apply to (or is satisfied by) such beneficiary by reason of chapter 100 of the Internal Revenue Code of 1986 [*26 USCA §§ 9801* et seq.], part 7 of this subtitle [*29 USCA §§ 1181* et seq.], or title XXVII of the Public Health Service Act [*42 USCA §§ 300gg* et seq.]), or

(ii) in the case of a qualified beneficiary other than a qualified beneficiary described in section 607(3)(C) [*29 USCA § 1167*(3)(C)], entitled to benefits under title XVIII of the Social Security Act [*42 USCA §§ 1395* et seq.].

(E) Termination of extended coverage for disability

In the case of a qualified beneficiary who is disabled at any time during the first 60 days of continuation coverage under this part [*29 USCA §§ 1161* et seq.], the month that begins more than 30 days after the date of the final determination under title II or XVI of the Social Security Act [*42 USCA §§ 401* et seq. or 1381 et seq.] that the qualified beneficiary is no longer disabled.

(3) Premium requirements

The plan may require payment of a premium for any period of continuation coverage, except that such premium—

(A) shall not exceed 102 percent of the applicable premium for such period, and

(B) may, at the election of the payor, be made in monthly installments.

In no event may the plan require the payment of any premium before the day which is 45 days after the day on which the qualified beneficiary made the initial election for continuation coverage. In the case of an individual described in the last sentence of paragraph (2)(A), any reference in subparagraph (A) of this paragraph to "102 percent" is deemed a reference to "150 percent" for any month after the 18th month of continuation coverage described in clause (i) or (ii) of paragraph (2)(A).

(4) No requirement of insurability

The coverage may not be conditioned upon, or discriminate on the basis of lack of, evidence of insurability.

(5) Conversion option

In the case of a qualified beneficiary whose period of continuation coverage expires under paragraph (2)(A), the plan must, during the 180–day period ending on such expiration date, provide to the qualified beneficiary the option of enrollment under a conversion health plan otherwise generally available under the plan.

§ 1163. Qualifying event

For purposes of this part [*29 USCA §§ 1161* et seq.], the term "qualifying event" means, with respect to any covered employee, any of the following events which, but for the continuation coverage required under this part [*29 USCA §§ 1161* et seq.], would result in the loss of coverage of a qualified beneficiary:

(1) The death of the covered employee.

(2) The termination (other than by reason of such employee's gross misconduct), or reduction of hours, of the covered employee's employment.

(3) The divorce or legal separation of the covered employee from the employee's spouse.

(4) The covered employee becoming entitled to benefits under title XVIII of the Social Security Act [*42 USCA §§ 1395* et seq.].

(5) A dependent child ceasing to be a dependent child under the generally applicable requirements of the plan.

(6) A proceeding in a case under title 11, United States Code, commencing on or after July 1, 1986, with respect to the employer from whose employment the covered employee retired at any time.

In the case of an event described in paragraph (6), a loss of coverage includes a substantial elimination of coverage with respect to a qualified beneficiary described in section 607(3)(C) [*29 USCA § 1167*(3)(C)] within one year before or after the date of commencement of the proceeding.

§ 1164. Applicable premium

For purposes of this part [*29 USCA §§ 1161* et seq.]—

(1) In general

The term "applicable premium" means, with respect to any period of continuation coverage of qualified beneficiaries, the cost to the plan for such period of the coverage for similarly situated beneficiaries with respect to whom a qualifying event has not occurred (without regard to whether such cost is paid by the employer or employee).

(2) Special rule for self-insured plans

To the extent that a plan is a self-insured plan

(A) In general

Except as provided in subparagraph (B), the applicable premium for any period of continuation coverage of qualified beneficiaries shall be equal to a reasonable estimate of the cost of providing coverage for such period for similarly situated beneficiaries which—

(i) is determined on an actuarial basis, and

(ii) takes into account such factors as the Secretary may prescribe I n regulations.

(B) Determination on basis of past cost

If an administrator elects to have this subparagraph apply, the applicable premium for any period of continuation coverage of qualified beneficiaries shall be equal to—

(i) the cost to the plan for similarly situated beneficiaries for the same period occurring during the preceding determination period under paragraph (3), adjusted by

(ii) the percentage increase or decrease in the implicit price deflator of the gross national product (calculated by the Department of Commerce and published in the Survey of Current Business) for the 12–month period ending on the last day of the sixth month of such preceding determination period.

(C) Subparagraph (B) not to apply where significant change

An administrator may not elect to have subparagraph (B) apply in any case in which there is any significant difference, between the determination period and the preceding determination period, in coverage under, or in employees covered by, the plan. The determination under the preceding sentence for any determination period shall be made at the same time as the determination under paragraph (3).

(3) Determination period

The determination of any applicable premium shall be made for a period of 12 months and shall be made before the beginning of such period.

§ 1166. Notice requirements

(a) In general

In accordance with regulations prescribed by the Secretary—

(1) the group health plan shall provide, at the time of commencement of coverage under the plan, written notice to each covered employee and spouse of the employee (if any) of the rights provided under this subsection [part],

(2) the employer of an employee under a plan must notify the administrator of a qualifying event described in paragraph (1), (2), (4), or (6) of section 603 [*29 USCA § 1163*(1), (2), (4), or (6)] within 30 days (or, in the case of a group health plan which is a multiemployer plan, such longer period of time as may be provided in the terms of the plan) of the date of the qualifying event,

(3) each covered employee or qualified beneficiary is responsible for notifying the administrator of the occurrence of any qualifying event described in paragraph (3) or (5) of section 603 [*29 USCA § 1163*(3) or (5)] within 60 days after the date of the qualifying event and each qualified beneficiary who is determined, under title II or XVI of the Social Security Act [*42 USCA §§ 401* et seq. or 1381 et seq.], to have been disabled at any time during the first 60 days of continuation coverage under this part [*29 USCA §§ 1161* et seq.] is responsible for notifying the plan administrator of such determination within 60 days after the date of the determination and for notifying the plan administrator within 30 days after the date of any final determination under such title or titles [*42 USCA §§ 401* et seq. or 1381 et seq.] that the qualified beneficiary is no longer disabled, and

(4) the administrator shall notify—

(A) in the case of a qualifying event described in paragraph (1), (2), (4), or (6) of section 603 [*29 USCA § 1163*(1), (2), (4), or (6)], any qualified beneficiary with respect to such event, and

(B) in the case of a qualifying event described in paragraph (3) or (5) of section 603 [*29 USCA § 1163*(3) or (5)] where the covered employee notifies the administrator under paragraph (3), any qualified beneficiary with respect to such event, of such beneficiary's rights under this subsection [part].

(b) Alternative means of compliance with requirement for notification of multiemployer plans by employers

The requirements of subsection (a)(2) shall be considered satisfied in the case of a multiemployer plan in connection with a qualifying event described in paragraph (2) of section 603 [*29 USCA § 1163*(2)] if the plan provides that the determination of the occurrence of such qualifying event will be made by the plan administrator.

(c) Rules relating to notification of qualified beneficiaries by plan administrator

For purposes of subsection (a)(4), any notification shall be made within 14 days (or, in the case of a group health plan which is a multiemployer plan, such longer period of time as may be provided in the terms of the plan) of the date on which the administrator is notified under paragraph (2) or (3), whichever is applicable, and any such notification to an individual who is a qualified beneficiary as the spouse of the covered employee shall be treated as notification to all other qualified beneficiaries residing with such spouse at the time such notification is made.

§ 1167. Definitions and special rules

For purposes of this part [*29 USCA §§ 1161* et seq.]—

(1) Group health plan

The term "group health plan" means an employee welfare benefit plan providing medical care (as defined in section 213(d) of the Internal Revenue Code of 1986 [*26 USCA § 213*(d)]) to participants or beneficiaries directly or through insurance, reimbursement, or otherwise. Such term shall not include any plan substantially all of the coverage under which is for qualified long-term care services (as defined in section 7702B(c) of such Code [*26 USCA § 7702B*(c)]).

(2) Covered employee

The term "covered employee" means an individual who is (or was) provided coverage under a group health plan by virtue of the performance of services by the individual for 1 or more persons maintaining the plan (including as an employee defined in section 401(c)(1) of the Internal Revenue Code of 1986) [*26 USCA § 401*(c)(1)].

(3) Qualified beneficiary

(A) In general

The term "qualified beneficiary" means, with respect to a covered employee under a group health plan, any other individual who, on the day before the qualifying event for that employee, is a beneficiary under the plan—

(i) as the spouse of the covered employee, or

(ii) as the dependent child of the employee.

Such term shall also include a child who is born to or placed for adoption with the covered employee during the period of continuation coverage under this part [*29 USCA §§ 1161* et seq.].

(B) Special rule for terminations and reduced employment

In the case of a qualifying event described in section 603(2) [*29 USCA § 1163*(2)], the term "qualified beneficiary" includes the covered employee.

(C) Special rule for retirees and widows

In the case of a qualifying event described in section 603(6) [*29 USCA § 1163*(6)], the term "qualified beneficiary" includes a covered employee who had retired on or before the date of substantial elimination of coverage and any other individual who, on the day before such qualifying event, is a beneficiary under the plan—

(i) as the spouse of the covered employee,

(ii) as the dependent child of the employee, or

(iii) as the surviving spouse of the covered employee.

(4) Employer

Subsection (n) (relating to leased employees) and subsection (t) (relating to application of controlled group rules to certain employee benefits) of section 414 of the Internal Revenue Code of 1986 [*26 USCA § 414*] shall apply for purposes of this part [*29 USCA §§ 1161* et seq.] in the same manner and to the same extent as such subsections apply for purposes of section 106 of such Code [*26 USCA § 106*]. Any regulations prescribed by the Secretary pursuant to the preceding sentence shall be consistent and coextensive with any regulations prescribed for similar purposes by the Secretary of the Treasury (or such Secretary's delegate) under such subsections.

(5) Optional extension of required periods

A group health plan shall not be treated as failing to meet the requirements of this part solely because the plan provides both—

(A) that the period of extended coverage referred to in section 602(2) [*29 USCA § 1162*(2)] commences with the date of the loss of coverage, and

(B) that the applicable notice period provided under section 606(a)(2) [*29 USCA § 1166*(a)(2)] commences with the date of the loss of coverage.

§ 1169. Additional standards for group health plans

(a) Group health plan coverage pursuant to medical child support orders.

(1) In general

Each group health plan shall provide benefits in accordance with the applicable requirements of any qualified medical child support order. A qualified medical child support order with respect to any participant or beneficiary shall be deemed to apply to each group health plan which has received such order, from which the participant or beneficiary is eligible to receive benefits, and with respect to which the requirements of paragraph (4) are met.

(2) Definitions. For purposes of this subsection—

(A) Qualified medical child support order. The term "qualified medical child support order" means a medical child support order—

(i) which creates or recognizes the existence of an alternate recipient's right to, or assigns to an alternate recipient the right to, receive benefits for which a participant or beneficiary is eligible under a group health plan, and

(ii) with respect to which the requirements of paragraphs (3) and (4) are met.

(B) Medical child support order. The term "medical child support order" means any judgment, decree, or order (including approval of a settlement agreement) which—

(i) provides for child support with respect to a child of a participant under a group health plan or provides for health benefit coverage to such a child, is made pursuant to a State domestic relations law (including a community property law), and relates to benefits under such plan, or

(ii) is made pursuant to a law relating to medical child support described in section 1908 of the Social Security Act [*42 USCA § 1396g–1*] (as added by section 13822 [13623(b)] of the Omnibus Budget Reconciliation Act of 1993) with respect to a group health plan, if such judgment, decree, or order

(I) is issued by a court of competent jurisdiction or

(II) is issued through an administrative process established under State law and has the force and effect of law under applicable State law. For purposes of this subparagraph, an administrative notice which is issued pursuant to an administrative process referred to in subclause (II) of the preceding sentence and which has the effect of an order described in clause (i) or (ii) of the preceding sentence shall be treated as such an order.

(C) Alternate recipient

The term "alternate recipient" means any child of a participant who is recognized under a medical child support order as having a right to enrollment under a group health plan with respect to such participant.

(D) Child

The term "child" includes any child adopted by, or placed for adoption with, a participant of a group health plan.

(3) Information to be included in qualified order

A medical child support order meets the requirements of this paragraph only if such order clearly specifies—

(A) the name and the last known mailing address (if any) of the participant and the name and mailing address of each alternate recipient covered by the order, except that, to the extent provided in the order, the name and mailing address of an official of a State or a political subdivision thereof may be substituted for the mailing address of any such alternate recipient,

(B) a reasonable description of the type of coverage to be provided to each such alternate recipient, or the manner in which such type of coverage is to be determined, and

(C) the period to which such order applies.

(4) Restriction on new types or forms of benefits

A medical child support order meets the requirements of this paragraph only if such order does not require a plan to provide any type or form of benefit, or any option, not otherwise provided under the plan, except to the extent necessary to meet the requirements of a law relating to medical child support described in section 1908 of the Social Security Act [*42 USCA § 1396g–1*] (as added by section 13822 [13623(b)] of the Omnibus Budget Reconciliation Act of 1993).

(5) Procedural requirements

(A) Timely notifications and determinations

In the case of any medical child support order received by a group health plan—

(i) the plan administrator shall promptly notify the participant and each alternate recipient of the receipt of such order and the plan's procedures for determining whether medical child support orders are qualified medical child support orders, and

(ii) within a reasonable period after receipt of such order, the plan administrator shall determine whether such order is a qualified medical child support order and notify the participant and each alternate recipient of such determination.

(B) Establishment of procedures for determining qualified status of orders

Each group health plan shall establish reasonable procedures to determine whether medical child support orders are qualified medical child support orders and to administer the provision of benefits under such qualified orders. Such procedures—

(i) shall be in writing,

(ii) shall provide for the notification of each person specified in a medical child support order as eligible to receive benefits under the plan (at the address included in the medical child support order) of such procedures promptly upon receipt by the plan of the medical child support order, and

(iii) shall permit an alternate recipient to designate a representative for receipt of copies of notices that are sent to the alternate recipient with respect to a medical child support order.

(C) National Medical Support Notice deemed to be a qualified medical child support order

(i) In general

If the plan administrator of a group health plan which is maintained by the employer of a noncustodial parent of a child or to which such an employer contributes receives an appropriately completed National Medical Support Notice promulgated pursuant to section 401(b) of the Child Support Performance and Incentive Act of 1998 [*42 USCA § 651* note] in the case of such child, and the Notice meets the requirements of paragraphs (3) and (4), the Notice shall be deemed to be a qualified medical child support order in the case of such child.

(ii) Enrollment of child in plan

In any case in which an appropriately completed National Medical Support Notice is issued in the case of a child of a participant under a group health plan who is a noncustodial parent of the child, and the Notice is deemed under clause (i) to be a qualified medical child support order, the plan administrator, within 40 business days after the date of the Notice, shall—

(I) notify the State agency issuing the Notice with respect to such child whether coverage of the child is available under the terms of the plan and, if so, whether such child is covered under the plan and either the effective date of the coverage or, if necessary, any steps to be taken by the custodial parent (or by the official of a State or political subdivision thereof substituted for the name of such child pursuant to paragraph (3)(A)) to effectuate the coverage; and

(II) provide to the custodial parent (or such substituted official) a description of the coverage available and any forms or documents necessary to effectuate such coverage.

(iii) Rule of construction

Nothing in this subparagraph shall be construed as requiring a group health plan, upon receipt of a National Medical Support Notice, to provide benefits under the plan (or eligibility for such benefits) in addition to benefits (or eligibility for benefits) provided under the terms of the plan as of immediately before receipt of such Notice.

(6) Actions taken by fiduciaries

If a plan fiduciary acts in accordance with part 4 of this subtitle [*29 USCA §§ 1101* et seq.] in treating a medical child support order as being (or not being) a qualified medical child support order, then the plan's obligation to the participant and each alternate recipient shall be discharged to the extent of any payment made pursuant to such act of the fiduciary.

(7) Treatment of alternate recipients

(A) Treatment as beneficiary generally

A person who is an alternate recipient under a qualified medical child support order shall be considered a beneficiary under the plan for purposes of any provision of this Act.

(B) Treatment as participant for purposes of reporting and disclosure requirements

A person who is an alternate recipient under any medical child support order shall be considered a participant under the plan for purposes of the reporting and disclosure requirements of part 1 [*29 USCA §§ 1021* et seq.].

(8) Direct provision of benefits provided to alternate recipients

Any payment for benefits made by a group health plan pursuant to a medical child support order in reimbursement for expenses paid by an alternate recipient or an alternate recipient's custodial parent or legal guardian shall be made to the alternate recipient or the alternate recipient's custodial parent or legal guardian.

(9) Payment to State official treated as satisfaction of plan's obligation to make payment to alternate recipient

Payment of benefits by a group health plan to an official of a State or a political subdivision thereof whose name and address have been substituted for the address of an alternate recipient in a qualified medical child support order, pursuant to paragraph (3)(A), shall be treated, for purposes of this title [*29 USCA §§ 1001* et seq.], as payment of benefits to the alternate recipient.

(b) Rights of States with respect to group health plans where participants or beneficiaries thereunder are eligible for Medicaid benefits

(1) Compliance by plans with assignment of rights

A group health plan shall provide that payment for benefits with respect to a participant under the plan will be made in accordance with any assignment of rights made by or on behalf of such participant or a beneficiary of the participant as required by a State plan for medical assistance approved under title XIX of the Social Security Act [*42 USCA §§ 1396* et seq.] pursuant to section 1912(a)(1)(A) of such Act [*42 USCA § 1396k*(a)(1)(A)] (as in effect on the date of the enactment of the Omnibus Budget Reconciliation Act of 1993 [enacted Aug. 10, 1993]).

(2) Enrollment and provision of benefits without regard to Medicaid eligibility

A group health plan shall provide that, in enrolling an individual as a participant or beneficiary or in determining or making any payments for benefits of an individual as a participant or beneficiary, the fact that the individual is eligible for or is provided medical assistance under a State plan for medical assistance approved under title XIX of the Social Security Act [*42 USCA §§ 1396* et seq.] will not be taken into account.

(3) Acquisition by States of rights of third parties

A group health plan shall provide that, to the extent that payment has been made under a State plan for medical assistance approved under title XIX of the Social Security Act [*42 USCA §§ 1396* et seq.] in any case in which a group health plan has a legal liability to make payment for items or services constituting such assistance, payment for benefits under the plan will be made in accordance with any State law which provides that the State has acquired the rights with respect to a participant to such payment for such items or services.

(c) Group health plan coverage of dependent children in cases of adoption

(1) Coverage effective upon placement for adoption

In any case in which a group health plan provides coverage for dependent children of participants or beneficiaries, such plan shall provide benefits to dependent children placed with participants or beneficiaries for adoption under the same terms and conditions as apply in the case of dependent children who are natural children of participants or beneficiaries under the plan, irrespective of whether the adoption has become final.

(2) Restrictions based on preexisting conditions at time of placement for adoption prohibited

A group health plan may not restrict coverage under the plan of any dependent child adopted by a participant or beneficiary, or placed with a participant or beneficiary for adoption, solely on the basis of a preexisting condition of such child at the time that such child would otherwise become eligible for coverage under the plan, if the adoption or placement for adoption occurs while the participant or beneficiary is eligible for coverage under the plan.

(3) Definitions

For purposes of this subsection—

(A) Child

The term "child" means, in connection with any adoption, or placement for adoption, of the child, an individual who has not attained age 18 as of the date of such adoption or placement for adoption.

(B) Placement for adoption

The term "placement", or being "placed", for adoption, in connection with any placement for adoption of a child with any person, means the assumption and retention by such person of a legal obligation for total or partial support of such child in anticipation of adoption of such child. The child's placement with such person terminates upon the termination of such legal obligation.

(d) Continued coverage of costs of a pediatric vaccine under group health plans

A group health plan may not reduce its coverage of the costs of pediatric vaccines (as defined under section 1928(h)(6) of the Social Security Act [*42 USCA § 1396s*(h)(6)] as amended by section 13830 [13631(b)] of the Omnibus Budget Reconciliation Act of 1993) below the coverage it provided as of May 1, 1993.

(e) Regulations

Any regulations prescribed under this section shall be prescribed by the Secretary of Labor, in consultation with the Secretary of Health and Human Services.

§ 1181. Increased portability through limitation on preexisting condition exclusions

(a) Limitation on preexisting condition exclusion period; crediting for periods of previous coverage

Subject to subsection (d), a group health plan, and a health insurance issuer offering group health insurance coverage, may, with respect to a participant or beneficiary, impose a preexisting condition exclusion only if—

(1) such exclusion relates to a condition (whether physical or mental), regardless of the cause of the condition, for which medical advice, diagnosis, care, or treatment was recommended or received within the 6–month period ending on the enrollment date;

(2) such exclusion extends for a period of not more than 12 months (or 18 months in the case of a late enrollee) after the enrollment date; and

(3) the period of any such preexisting condition exclusion is reduced by the aggregate of the periods of creditable coverage (if any, as defined in subsection (c)(1)) applicable to the participant or beneficiary as of the enrollment date.

(b) Definitions

For purposes of this part [*29 USCA §§ 1181* et seq.]—

(1) Preexisting condition exclusion

(A) In general

The term "preexisting condition exclusion" means, with respect to coverage, a limitation or exclusion of benefits relating to a condition based on the fact that the condition was present before the date of enrollment for such coverage, whether or not any medical advice, diagnosis, care, or treatment was recommended or received before such date.

(B) Treatment of genetic information

Genetic information shall not be treated as a condition described in subsection (a)(1) in the absence of a diagnosis of the condition related to such information.

(2) Enrollment date

The term "enrollment date" means, with respect to an individual covered under a group health plan or health insurance coverage, the date of enrollment of the individual in the plan or coverage or, if earlier, the first day of the waiting period for such enrollment.

(3) Late enrollee

The term "late enrollee" means, with respect to coverage under a group health plan, a participant or beneficiary who enrolls under the plan other than during—

(A) the first period in which the individual is eligible to enroll under the plan, or

(B) a special enrollment period under subsection (f).

(4) Waiting period

The term "waiting period" means, with respect to a group health plan and an individual who is a potential participant or beneficiary in the plan, the period that must pass with respect to the individual before the individual is eligible to be covered for benefits under the terms of the plan.

(c) Rules relating to crediting previous coverage

(1) Creditable coverage defined

For purposes of this part [*29 USCA §§ 1181* et seq.], the term "creditable coverage" means, with respect to an individual, coverage of the individual under any of the following:

(A) A group health plan.

(B) Health insurance coverage.

(C) Part A or part B of title XVIII of the Social Security Act [*42 USCA §§ 1395c* et seq. or 1395j et seq.].

(D) Title XIX of the Social Security Act [*42 USCA §§ 1396* et seq.], other than coverage consisting solely of benefits under section 1928 [*42 USCA § 1396s*].

(E) Chapter 55 of title 10, United States Code [*10 USCA §§ 1071* et seq.].

(F) A medical care program of the Indian Health Service or of a tribal organization.

(G) A State health benefits risk pool.

(H) A health plan offered under chapter 89 of title 5, United States Code [*5 USCA §§ 8901* et seq.].

(I) A public health plan (as defined in regulations).

(J) A health benefit plan under section 5(e) of the Peace Corps Act *(22 U.S.C. 2504*(e)).

Such term does not include coverage consisting solely of coverage of excepted benefits (as defined in section 733(c) [*29 USCA § 1191b*(c)]).

(2) Not counting periods before significant breaks in coverage

(A) In general

A period of creditable coverage shall not be counted, with respect to enrollment of an individual under a group health plan, if, after such period and before the enrollment date, there was a 63–day period during all of which the individual was not covered under any creditable coverage.

(B) Waiting period not treated as a break in coverage. For purposes of subparagraph (A) and subsection (d)(4), any period that an individual is in a waiting period for any coverage under a group health plan (or for group health insurance coverage) or is in an affiliation period (as defined in subsection (g)(2)) shall not be taken into account in determining the continuous period under subparagraph (A).

(3) Method of crediting coverage

(A) Standard method. Except as otherwise provided under subparagraph (B), for purposes of applying subsection (a)(3), a group health plan, and a health insurance issuer offering group health insurance coverage, shall count a period of creditable coverage without regard to the specific benefits covered during the period.

(B) Election of alternative method. A group health plan, or a health insurance issuer offering group health insurance coverage, may elect to apply subsection (a)(3) based on coverage of benefits within each of several classes or categories of benefits specified in regulations rather than as provided under subparagraph (A). Such election shall be made on a uniform basis for all participants and beneficiaries. Under such election a group health plan or issuer shall count a period of creditable coverage with respect to any class or category of benefits if any level of benefits is covered within such class or category.

(C) Plan notice. In the case of an election with respect to a group health plan under subparagraph (B) (whether or not health insurance coverage is provided in connection with such plan), the plan shall—

(i) prominently state in any disclosure statements concerning the plan, and state to each enrollee at the time of enrollment under the plan, that the plan has made such election, and

(ii) include in such statements a description of the effect of this election.

(4) Establishment of period. Periods of creditable coverage with respect to an individual shall be established through presentation of certifications described in subsection (e) or in such other manner as may be specified in regulations.

(d) Exceptions

(1) Exclusion not applicable to certain newborns. Subject to paragraph (4), a group health plan, and a health insurance issuer offering group health insurance coverage, may not impose any preexisting condition exclusion in the case of an individual who, as of the last day of the 30–day period beginning with the date of birth, is covered under creditable coverage.

357

(2) Exclusion not applicable to certain adopted children. Subject to paragraph (4), a group health plan, and a health insurance issuer offering group health insurance coverage, may not impose any preexisting condition exclusion in the case of a child who is adopted or placed for adoption before attaining 18 years of age and who, as of the last day of the 30–day period beginning on the date of the adoption or placement for adoption, is covered under creditable coverage. The previous sentence shall not apply to coverage before the date of such adoption or placement for adoption.

(3) Exclusion not applicable to pregnancy. A group health plan, and health insurance issuer offering group health insurance coverage, may not impose any preexisting condition exclusion relating to pregnancy as a preexisting condition.

(4) Loss if break in coverage. Paragraphs (1) and (2) shall no longer apply to an individual after the end of the first 63–day period during all of which the individual was not covered under any creditable coverage.

(e) Certifications and disclosure of coverage

(1) Requirement for certification of period of creditable coverage

(A) In general

A group health plan, and a health insurance issuer offering group health insurance coverage, shall provide the certification described in subparagraph (B)—

(i) at the time an individual ceases to be covered under the plan or otherwise becomes covered under a COBRA continuation provision,

(ii) in the case of an individual becoming covered under such a provision, at the time the individual ceases to be covered under such provision, and

(iii) on the request on behalf of an individual made not later than 24 months after the date of cessation of the coverage described in clause (i) or (ii), whichever is later.

The certification under clause (i) may be provided, to the extent practicable, at a time consistent with notices required under any applicable COBRA continuation provision.

(B) Certification

The certification described in this subparagraph I is a written certification of—

(i) the period of creditable coverage of the individual under such plan and the coverage (if any) under such COBRA continuation provision, and

(ii) the waiting period (if any) (and affiliation period, if applicable) imposed with respect to the individual for any coverage under such plan.

(C) Issuer compliance

To the extent that medical care under a group health plan consists of group health insurance coverage, the plan is deemed to have satisfied the certification requirement under this paragraph if the health insurance issuer offering the coverage provides for such certification in accordance with this paragraph.

(2) Disclosure of information on previous benefits

In the case of an election described in subsection (c)(3)(B) by a group health plan or health insurance issuer, if the plan or issuer enrolls an individual for coverage under the plan and the individual provides a certification of coverage of the individual under paragraph (1)—

(A) upon request of such plan or issuer, the entity which issued the certification provided by the individual shall promptly disclose to such requesting plan or issuer information on coverage of classes and categories of health benefits available under such entity's plan or coverage, and

(B) such entity may charge the requesting plan or issuer for the reasonable cost of disclosing such information.

(3) Regulations

The Secretary shall establish rules to prevent an entity's failure to provide information under paragraph (1) or (2) with respect to previous coverage of an individual from adversely affecting any subsequent coverage of the individual under another group health plan or health insurance coverage.

(f) Special enrollment periods

(1) Individuals losing other coverage. A group health plan, and a health insurance issuer offering group health insurance coverage in connection with a group health plan, shall permit an employee who is eligible, but not enrolled, for coverage under the terms of the plan (or a dependent of such an employee if the dependent is eligible, but not enrolled, for coverage under such terms) to enroll for coverage under the terms of the plan if each of the following conditions is met:

(A) The employee or dependent was covered under a group health plan or had health insurance coverage at the time coverage was previously offered to the employee or dependent.

(B) The employee stated in writing at such time that coverage under a group health plan or health insurance coverage was the reason for declining enrollment, but only if the plan sponsor or issuer (if applicable) required such a statement at such time and provided the employee with notice of such requirement (and the consequences of such requirement) at such time.

(C) The employee's or dependent's coverage described in subparagraph (A)—

(i) was under a COBRA continuation provision and the coverage under such provision was exhausted; or

(ii) was not under such a provision and either the coverage was terminated as a result of loss of eligibility for the coverage (including as a result of legal separation, divorce, death, termination of employment, or reduction in the number of hours of employment) or employer contributions toward such coverage were terminated.

(D) Under the terms of the plan, the employee requests such enrollment not later than 30 days after the date of exhaustion of coverage described in subparagraph (C)(i) or termination of coverage or employer contribution described in subparagraph (C)(ii).

(2) For dependent beneficiaries

(A) In general. If—

(i) a group health plan makes coverage available with respect to a dependent of an individual,

(ii) the individual is a participant under the plan (or has met any waiting period applicable to becoming a participant under the plan and is eligible to be enrolled under the plan but for a failure to enroll during a previous enrollment period), and

(iii) a person becomes such a dependent of the individual through marriage, birth, or adoption or placement for adoption,

the group health plan shall provide for a dependent special enrollment period described in subparagraph (B) during which the person (or, if not otherwise enrolled, the individual) may be enrolled under the plan as a dependent of the individual, and in the case of the birth or adoption of a child, the spouse of the individual may be enrolled as a dependent of the individual if such spouse is otherwise eligible for coverage.

(B) Dependent special enrollment period. A dependent special enrollment period under this subparagraph shall be a period of not less than 30 days and shall begin on the later of—

(i) the date dependent coverage is made available, or

(ii) the date of the marriage, birth, or adoption or placement for adoption (as the case may be) described in subparagraph (A)(iii).

(C) No waiting period. If an individual seeks to enroll a dependent during the first 30 days of such a dependent special enrollment period, the coverage of the dependent shall become effective—

(i) in the case of marriage, not later than the first day of the first month beginning after the date the completed request for enrollment is received;

(ii) in the case of a dependent's birth, as of the date of such birth; or

(iii) in the case of a dependent's adoption or placement for adoption, the date of such adoption or placement for adoption.

(g) Use of affiliation period by HMOs as alternative to preexisting condition exclusion

(1) In general

In the case of a group health plan that offers medical care through health insurance coverage offered by a health maintenance organization, the plan may provide for an affiliation period with respect to coverage through the organization only if—

(A) no preexisting condition exclusion is imposed with respect to coverage through the organization,

(B) the period is applied uniformly without regard to any health status-related factors, and

(C) such period does not exceed 2 months (or 3 months in the case of a late enrollee).

(2) Affiliation period

(A) Defined

For purposes of this part [*29 USCA §§ 1181* et seq.], the term "affiliation period" means a period which, under the terms of the health insurance coverage offered by the health maintenance organization, must expire before the health insurance coverage becomes effective. The organization is not required to provide health care services or benefits during such period and no premium shall be charged to the participant or beneficiary for any coverage during the period.

(B) Beginning

Such period shall begin on the enrollment date.

(C) Runs concurrently with waiting periods

An affiliation period under a plan shall run concurrently with any waiting period under the plan.

(3) Alternative methods

A health maintenance organization described in paragraph (1) may use alternative methods, from those described in such paragraph, to address adverse selection as approved by the State insurance commissioner or official or officials designated by the State to enforce the requirements of part A of title XXVII of the Public Health Service Act [*42 USCA §§ 300gg* et seq.] for the State involved with respect to such issuer.

361

§ 1182. Prohibiting discrimination against individual participants and beneficiaries based on health status

(a) In eligibility to enroll

(1) In general

Subject to paragraph (2), a group health plan, and a health insurance issuer offering group health insurance coverage in connection with a group health plan, may not establish rules for eligibility (including continued eligibility) of any individual to enroll under the terms of the plan based on any of the following health status-related factors in relation to the individual or a dependent of the individual:

(A) Health status.

(B) Medical condition (including both physical and mental illnesses).

(C) Claims experience.

(D) Receipt of health care.

(E) Medical history.

(F) Genetic information.

(G) Evidence of insurability (including conditions arising out of acts of domestic violence).

(H) Disability.

(2) No application to benefits or exclusions. To the extent consistent with section 701 [*29 USCA § 1181*], paragraph (1) shall not be construed—

(A) to require a group health plan, or group health insurance coverage, to provide particular benefits other than those provided under the terms of such plan or coverage, or

(B) to prevent such a plan or coverage from establishing limitations or restrictions on the amount, level, extent, or nature of the benefits or coverage for similarly situated individuals enrolled in the plan or coverage.

(3) Construction

For purposes of paragraph (1), rules for eligibility to enroll under a plan include rules defining any applicable waiting periods for such enrollment.

(b) In premium contributions.

(1) In general

A group health plan, and a health insurance issuer offering health insurance coverage in connection with a group health plan, may not require any individual (as a condition of enrollment or continued enrollment under the plan) to pay a premium or contribution which is greater than such premium or contribution for a similarly situated individual enrolled in the plan on the basis of any health status-related factor in relation to the individual or to an individual enrolled under the plan as a dependent of the individual.

(2) Construction

Nothing in paragraph (1) shall be construed—

(A) to restrict the amount that an employer may be charged for coverage under a group health plan; or

(B) to prevent a group health plan, and a health insurance issuer offering group health insurance coverage, from establishing premium discounts or rebates or modifying otherwise applicable copayments or deductibles in return for adherence to programs of health promotion and disease prevention.

§ 1183. Guaranteed renewability in multiemployer plans and multiple employer welfare arrangements

A group health plan which is a multiemployer plan or which is a multiple employer welfare arrangement may not deny an employer whose employees are covered under such a plan continued access to the same or different coverage under the terms of such a plan, other than—

(1) for nonpayment of contributions;

(2) for fraud or other intentional misrepresentation of material fact by the employer;

(3) for noncompliance with material plan provisions;

(4) because the plan is ceasing to offer any coverage in a geographic area;

(5) in the case of a plan that offers benefits through a network plan, there is no longer any individual enrolled through the employer who lives, resides, or works in the service area of the network plan and the plan applies this paragraph uniformly without regard to the claims experience of employers or any health status-related factor in relation to such individuals or their dependents; and

(6) for failure to meet the terms of an applicable collective bargaining agreement, to renew a collective bargaining or other agreement requiring or authorizing contributions to the plan, or to employ employees covered by such an agreement.

§ 1185. Standards relating to benefits for mothers and newborns

(a) Requirements for minimum hospital stay following birth

(1) In general

A group health plan, and a health insurance issuer offering group health insurance coverage, may not—

(A) except as provided in paragraph (2)—

363

(i) restrict benefits for any hospital length of stay in connection with childbirth for the mother or newborn child, following a normal vaginal delivery, to less than 48 hours, or

(ii) restrict benefits for any hospital length of stay in connection with childbirth for the mother or newborn child, following a cesarean section, to less than 96 hours; or

(B) require that a provider obtain authorization from the plan or the issuer for prescribing any length of stay required under subparagraph (A) (without regard to paragraph (2)).

(2) Exception

Paragraph (1)(A) shall not apply in connection with any group health plan or health insurance issuer in any case in which the decision to discharge the mother or her newborn child prior to the expiration of the minimum length of stay otherwise required under paragraph (1)(A) is made by an attending provider in consultation with the mother.

(b) Prohibitions

A group health plan, and a health insurance issuer offering group health insurance coverage in connection with a group health plan, may not—

(1) deny to the mother or her newborn child eligibility, or continued eligibility, to enroll or to renew coverage under the terms of the plan, solely for the purpose of avoiding the requirements of this section;

(2) provide monetary payments or rebates to mothers to encourage such mothers to accept less than the minimum protections available under this section;

(3) penalize or otherwise reduce or limit the reimbursement of an attending provider because such provider provided care to an individual participant or beneficiary in accordance with this section;

(4) provide incentives (monetary or otherwise) to an attending provider to induce such provider to provide care to an individual participant or beneficiary in a manner inconsistent with this section; or

(5) subject to subsection (c)(3), restrict benefits for any portion of a period within a hospital length of stay required under subsection (a) in a manner which is less favorable than the benefits provided for any preceding portion of such stay.

(c) Rules of construction

(1) Nothing in this section shall be construed to require a mother who is a participant or beneficiary—

(A) to give birth in a hospital; or

364

(B) to stay in the hospital for a fixed period of time following the birth of her child.

(2) This section shall not apply with respect to any group health plan, or any group health insurance coverage offered by a health insurance issuer, which does not provide benefits for hospital lengths of stay in connection with childbirth for a mother or her newborn child.

(3) Nothing in this section shall be construed as preventing a group health plan or issuer from imposing deductibles, coinsurance, or other cost-sharing in relation to benefits for hospital lengths of stay in connection with childbirth for a mother or newborn child under the plan (or under health insurance coverage offered in connection with a group health plan), except that such coinsurance or other cost-sharing for any portion of a period within a hospital length of stay required under subsection (a) may not be greater than such coinsurance or cost-sharing for any preceding portion of such stay.

(d) Notice under group health plan

The imposition of the requirements of this section shall be treated as a material modification in the terms of the plan described in section 102(a)(1) [*29 USCA § 1022*(a)(1)], for purposes of assuring notice of such requirements under the plan; except that the summary description required to be provided under the last sentence of section 104(b)(1) [*29 USCA § 1024*(b)(1)] with respect to such modification shall be provided by not later than 60 days after the first day of the first plan year in which such requirements apply.

(e) Level and type of reimbursements.

Nothing in this section shall be construed to prevent a group health plan or a health insurance issuer offering group health insurance coverage from negotiating the level and type of reimbursement with a provider for care provided in accordance with this section.

(f) Preemption; exception for health insurance coverage in certain States.

(1) In general

The requirements of this section shall not apply with respect to health insurance coverage if there is a State law (as defined in section 731(d)(1) [*29 USCA § 1191*(d)(1)]) for a State that regulates such coverage that is described in any of the following subparagraphs:

(A) Such State law requires such coverage to provide for at least a 48–hour hospital length of stay following a normal vaginal delivery and at least a 96–hour hospital length of stay following a cesarean section.

(B) Such State law requires such coverage to provide for maternity and pediatric care in accordance with guidelines established by the American College of Obstetricians and Gynecologists, the American Academy of Pediatrics, or other established professional medical associations.

(C) Such State law requires, in connection with such coverage for maternity care, that the hospital length of stay for such care is left to the decision of (or required to be made by) the attending provider in consultation with the mother.

(2) Construction

Section 731(a)(1) [*29 USCA § 1191*(a)(1)] shall not be construed as superseding a State law described in paragraph (1).

§ 1185a. Parity in the application of certain limits to mental health benefits

(a) In general

(1) Aggregate lifetime limits

In the case of a group health plan (or health insurance coverage offered in connection with such a plan) that provides both medical and surgical benefits and mental health benefits—

(A) No lifetime limit

If the plan or coverage does not include an aggregate lifetime limit on substantially all medical and surgical benefits, the plan or coverage may not impose any aggregate lifetime limit on mental health benefits.

(B) Lifetime limit

If the plan or coverage includes an aggregate lifetime limit on substantially all medical and surgical benefits (in this paragraph referred to as the "applicable lifetime limit"), the plan or coverage shall either—

(i) apply the applicable lifetime limit both to the medical and surgical benefits to which it otherwise would apply and to mental health benefits and not distinguish in the application of such limit between such medical and surgical benefits and mental health benefits; or

(ii) not include any aggregate lifetime limit on mental health benefits that is less than the applicable lifetime limit.

(C) Rule in case of different limits

In the case of a plan or coverage that is not described in subparagraph (A) or (B) and that includes no or different aggregate lifetime limits on different categories of medical and surgical benefits, the Secretary shall establish rules under which subparagraph (B) is applied to such plan or coverage with respect to mental health benefits by substituting for the applicable lifetime limit an average aggregate lifetime limit that is computed taking into account the weighted average of the aggregate lifetime limits applicable to such categories.

(2) Annual limits

In the case of a group health plan (or health insurance coverage offered in connection with such a plan) that provides both medical and surgical benefits and mental health benefits—

(A) No annual limit

If the plan or coverage does not include an annual limit on substantially all medical and surgical benefits, the plan or coverage may not impose any annual limit on mental health benefits.

(B) Annual limit

If the plan or coverage includes an annual limit on substantially all medical and surgical benefits (in this paragraph referred to as the "applicable annual limit"), the plan or coverage shall either—

(i) apply the applicable annual limit both to medical and surgical benefits to which it otherwise would apply and to mental health benefits and not distinguish in the application of such limit between such medical and surgical benefits and mental health benefits; or

(ii) not include any annual limit on mental health benefits that is less than the applicable annual limit.

(C) Rule in case of different limits.

In the case of a plan or coverage that is not described in subparagraph (A) or (B) and that includes no or different annual limits on different categories of medical and surgical benefits, the Secretary shall establish rules under which subparagraph (B) is applied to such plan or coverage with respect to mental health benefits by substituting for the applicable annual limit an average annual limit that is computed taking into account the weighted average of the annual limits applicable to such categories.

(b) Construction

Nothing in this section shall be construed—

(1) as requiring a group health plan (or health insurance coverage offered in connection with such a plan) to provide any mental health benefits; or

(2) in the case of a group health plan (or health insurance coverage offered in connection with such a plan) that provides mental health benefits, as affecting the terms and conditions (including cost sharing, limits on numbers of visits or days of coverage, and requirements relating to medical necessity) relating to the amount, duration, or scope of mental health benefits under the plan or coverage, except as specifically provided in subsection (a) (in regard to parity in the imposition of aggregate lifetime limits and annual limits for mental health benefits).

(c) Exemptions

(1) Small employer exemption

(A) In general

This section shall not apply to any group health plan (and group health insurance coverage offered in connection with a group health plan) for any plan year of a small employer.

(B) Small employer

For purposes of subparagraph (A), the term "small employer" means, in connection with a group health plan with respect to a calendar year and a plan year, an employer who employed an average of at least 2 but not more than 50 employees on business days during the preceding calendar year and who employs at least 2 employees on the first day of the plan year.

(C) Application of certain rules in determination of employer size

For purposes of this paragraph—

(i) Application of aggregation rule for employers

Rules similar to the rules under subsections (b), (c), (m), and (*o*) of section 414 of the Internal Revenue Code of 1986 [*26 USCA § 414*] shall apply for purposes of treating persons as a single employer.

(ii) Employers not in existence in preceding year

In the case of an employer which was not in existence throughout the preceding calendar year, the determination of whether such employer is a small employer shall be based on the average number of employees that it is reasonably expected such employer will employ on business days in the current calendar year.

(iii) Predecessors

Any reference in this paragraph to an employer shall include a reference to any predecessor of such employer.

(2) Increased cost exemption

This section shall not apply with respect to a group health plan (or health insurance coverage offered in connection with a group health plan) if the application of this section to such plan (or to such coverage) results in an increase in the cost under the plan (or for such coverage) of at least 1 percent.

(d) Separate application to each option offered

In the case of a group health plan that offers a participant or beneficiary two or more benefit package options under the plan, the requirements of this section shall be applied separately with respect to each such option.

(e) Definitions

For purposes of this section—

    (1) Aggregate lifetime limit

The term "aggregate lifetime limit" means, with respect to benefits under a group health plan or health insurance coverage, a dollar limitation on the total amount that may be paid with respect to such benefits under the plan or health insurance coverage with respect to an individual or other coverage unit.

    (2) Annual limit

The term "annual limit" means, with respect to benefits under a group health plan or health insurance coverage, a dollar limitation on the total amount of benefits that may be paid with respect to such benefits in a 12–month period under the plan or health insurance coverage with respect to an individual or other coverage unit.

    (3) Medical or surgical benefits

The term "medical or surgical benefits" means benefits with respect to medical or surgical services, as defined under the terms of the plan or coverage (as the case may be), but does not include mental health benefits.

    (4) Mental health benefits

The term "mental health benefits" means benefits with respect to mental health services, as defined under the terms of the plan or coverage (as the case may be), but does not include benefits with respect to treatment of substance abuse or chemical dependency.

(f) Sunset

This section shall not apply to benefits for services furnished on or after September 30, 2001.

§ 1185b. Required coverage for reconstructive surgery following mastectomies

(a) In general

A group health plan, and a health insurance issuer providing health insurance coverage in connection with a group health plan, that provides medical and surgical benefits with respect to a mastectomy shall provide, in a case of a participant or beneficiary who is receiving benefits in connection with a mastectomy and who elects breast reconstruction in connection with such mastectomy, coverage for—

    (1) reconstruction of the breast on which the mastectomy has been performed;

(2) surgery and reconstruction of the other breast to produce a symmetrical appearance; and

(3) prostheses and physical complications all stages of mastectomy, including lymphedemas;

in a manner determined in consultation with the attending physician and the patient. Such coverage may be subject to annual deductibles and coinsurance provisions as may be deemed appropriate and as are consistent with those established for other benefits under the plan or coverage. Written notice of the availability of such coverage shall be delivered to the participant upon enrollment and annually thereafter.

(b) Notice

A group health plan, and a health insurance issuer providing health insurance coverage in connection with a group health plan shall provide notice to each participant and beneficiary under such plan regarding the coverage required by this section in accordance with regulations promulgated by the Secretary. Such notice shall be in writing and prominently positioned in any literature or correspondence made available or distributed by the plan or issuer and shall be transmitted—

(1) in the next mailing made by the plan or issuer to the participant or beneficiary;

(2) as part of any yearly informational packet sent to the participant or beneficiary; or

(3) not later than January 1, 1999;

whichever is earlier.

(c) Prohibitions

A group health plan, and a health insurance issuer offering group health insurance coverage in connection with a group health plan, may not—

(1) deny to a patient eligibility, or continued eligibility, to enroll or to renew coverage under the terms of the plan, solely for the purpose of avoiding the requirements of this section; and

(2) penalize or otherwise reduce or limit the reimbursement of an attending provider, or provide incentives (monetary or otherwise) to an attending provider, to induce such provider to provide care to an individual participant or beneficiary in a manner inconsistent with this section.

(d) Rule of construction

Nothing in this section shall be construed to prevent a group health plan or a health insurance issuer offering group health insurance coverage from negotiating the level and type of reimbursement with a provider for care provided in accordance with this section.

(e) Preemption, relation to State laws

(1) In general

Nothing in this section shall be construed to preempt any State law in effect on the date of enactment of this section [enacted Oct. 21, 1998] with respect to health insurance coverage that requires coverage of at least the coverage of reconstructive breast surgery otherwise required under this section.

(2) ERISA

Nothing in this section shall be construed to affect or modify the provisions of section 514 with respect to group health plans [*29 USCA § 1144*].

§ 1191. Preemption; State flexibility; construction

(a) Continued applicability of State law with respect to health insurance issuers

(1) In general

Subject to paragraph (2) and except as provided in subsection (b), this part [*29 USCA §§ 1181* et seq.] shall not be construed to supersede any provision of State law which establishes, implements, or continues in effect any standard or requirement solely relating to health insurance issuers in connection with group health insurance coverage except to the extent that such standard or requirement prevents the application of a requirement of this part [*29 USCA §§ 1181* et seq.].

(2) Continued preemption with respect to group health plans.

Nothing in this part [*29 USCA §§ 1181* et seq.] shall be construed to affect or modify the provisions of section 514 [*29 USCA § 1144]* with respect to group health plans.

(b) Special rules in case of portability requirements

(1) In general

Subject to paragraph (2), the provisions of this part [*29 USCA §§ 1181* et seq.] relating to health insurance coverage offered by a health insurance issuer supersede any provision of State law which establishes, implements, or continues in effect a standard or requirement applicable to imposition of a preexisting condition exclusion specifically governed by section 701 [*29 USCA § 1181]* which differs from the standards or requirements specified in such section.

(2) Exceptions

Only in relation to health insurance coverage offered by a health insurance issuer, the provisions of this part [*29 USCA §§ 1181* et seq.] do not supersede any provision of State law to the extent that such provision—

　　(A) substitutes for the reference to "6–month period" in section 701(a)(1) [*29 USCA § 1181*(a)(1)] a reference to any shorter period of time;

(B) substitutes for the reference to "12 months" and "18 months" in section 701(a)(2) [*29 USCA § 1181*(a)(2)] a reference to any shorter period of time;

(C) substitutes for the references to "63 days" in sections 701(c)(2)(A) and (d)(4)(A) [*29 USCA § 1181*(c)(2)(A), (d)(4)(A)] a reference to any greater number of days;

(D) substitutes for the reference to "30–day period" in sections 701(b)(2) and (d)(1) [*29 USCA § 1181*(b)(2), (d)(1)] a reference to any greater period;

(E) prohibits the imposition of any preexisting condition exclusion in cases not described in section 701(d) [*29 USCA § 1181*(d)] or expands the exceptions described in such section;

(F) requires special enrollment periods in addition to those required under section 701(f) [*29 USCA § 1181*(f)]; or

(G) reduces the maximum period permitted in an affiliation period under section 701(g)(1)(B) [*29 USCA § 1181*(g)(1)(B)].

(c) Rules of construction

Except as provided in section 711 [*29 USCA § 1185*], nothing in this part [*29 USCA §§ 1181* et seq.] shall be construed as requiring a group health plan or health insurance coverage to provide specific benefits under the terms of such plan or coverage.

(d) Definitions

For purposes of this section—

(1) State law

The term "State law" includes all laws, decisions, rules, regulations, or other State action having the effect of law, of any State. A law of the United States applicable only to the District of Columbia shall be treated as a State law rather than a law of the United States.

(2) State

The term "State" includes a State, the Northern Mariana Islands, any political subdivisions of a State or such Islands, or any agency or instrumentality of either.

§ 1191a. Special rules relating to group health plans

(a) General exception for certain small group health plans

The requirements of this part [*29 USCA §§ 1181* et seq.] (other than section 711 [*29 USCA § 1185*]) shall not apply to any group health plan (and group health insurance coverage offered in connection with a group health plan) for any plan year if, on the first day of such plan year, such plan has less than 2 participants who are current employees.

(b) Exception for certain benefits

The requirements of this part [*29 USCA §§ 1181* et seq.] shall not apply to any group health plan (and group health insurance coverage) in relation to its provision of excepted benefits described in section 731(c)(1) [*29 USCA § 1191*(c)(1)].

(c) Exception for certain benefits if certain conditions met

    (1) Limited, excepted benefits

The requirements of this part [*29 USCA §§ 1181* et seq.] shall not apply to any group health plan (and group health insurance coverage offered in connection with a group health plan) in relation to its provision of excepted benefits described in section 731(c)(2) [*29 USCA § 1191*(c)(2)] if the benefits—

        (A) are provided under a separate policy, certificate, or contract of insurance; or

        (B) are otherwise not an integral part of the plan.

    (2) Noncoordinated, excepted benefits

The requirements of this part [*29 USCA §§ 1181* et seq.] shall not apply to any group health plan (and group health insurance coverage offered in connection with a group health plan) in relation to its provision of excepted benefits described in section 733(c)(3) [*29 USCA § 1191b*(c)(3)] if all of the following conditions are met:

        (A) The benefits are provided under a separate policy, certificate, or contract of insurance.

        (B) There is no coordination between the provision of such benefits and any exclusion of benefits under any group health plan maintained by the same plan sponsor.

        (C) Such benefits are paid with respect to an event without regard to whether benefits are provided with respect to such an event under any group health plan maintained by the same plan sponsor.

    (3) Supplemental excepted benefits

The requirements of this part [*29 USCA §§ 1181* et seq.] shall not apply to any group health plan (and group health insurance coverage) in relation to its provision of excepted benefits described in section 733(c)(4) [*29 USCA § 1191b*(c)(4)] if the benefits are provided under a separate policy, certificate, or contract of insurance.

(d) Treatment of partnerships

For purposes of this part [*29 USCA §§ 1181* et seq.]—

    (1) Treatment as a group health plan

Any plan, fund, or program which would not be (but for this subsection) an employee welfare benefit plan and which is established or maintained by a partnership, to the extent that such plan, fund, or program provides medical care (including items and services paid for as medical care) to present or former partners in the partnership or to their dependents (as defined under the terms of the plan, fund, or program), directly or through insurance, reimbursement, or otherwise, shall be treated (subject to paragraph (2)) as an employee welfare benefit plan which is a group health plan.

(2) Employer

In the case of a group health plan, the term 'employer' also includes the partnership in relation to any partner.

(3) Participants of group health plans

In the case of a group health plan, the term "participant" also includes—

    (A) in connection with a group health plan maintained by a partnership, an individual who is a partner in relation to the partnership, or

    (B) in connection with a group health plan maintained by a self-employed individual (under which one or more employees are participants), the self-employed individual,

if such individual is, or may become, eligible to receive a benefit under the plan or such individual's beneficiaries may be eligible to receive any such benefit.

§ 1191b. Definitions

(a) Group health plan

For purposes of this part [*29 USCA §§ 1181* et seq.]—

    (1) In general

The term "group health plan" means an employee welfare benefit plan to the extent that the plan provides medical care (as defined in paragraph (2) and including items and services paid for as medical care) to employees or their dependents (as defined under the terms of the plan) directly or through insurance, reimbursement, or otherwise.

    (2) Medical care

The term "medical care" means amounts paid for—

    (A) the diagnosis, cure, mitigation, treatment, or prevention of disease, or amounts paid for the purpose of affecting any structure or function of the body,

    (B) amounts paid for transportation primarily for and essential to medical care referred to in subparagraph (A), and

    (C) amounts paid for insurance covering medical care referred to in subparagraphs (A) and (B).

(b) Definitions relating to health insurance

For purposes of this part [*29 USCA §§ 1181* et seq.]—

    (1) Health insurance coverage

The term "health insurance coverage" means benefits consisting of medical care (provided directly, through insurance or reimbursement, or otherwise and including items and services paid for as medical care) under any hospital or medical service policy or certificate, hospital or medical service plan contract, or health maintenance organization contract offered by a health insurance issuer.

(2) Health insurance issuer

The term "health insurance issuer" means an insurance company, insurance service, or insurance organization (including a health maintenance organization, as defined in paragraph (3)) which is licensed to engage in the business of insurance in a State and which is subject to State law which regulates insurance (within the meaning of section 514(b)(2) [*29 USCA § 1144*(b)(2)]). Such term does not include a group health plan.

(3) Health maintenance organization

The term "health maintenance organization" means—

    (A) a federally qualified health maintenance organization (as defined in section 1301(a) of the Public Health Service Act *(42 U.S.C. 300e*(a))),

    (B) an organization recognized under State law as a health maintenance organization, or

    (C) a similar organization regulated under State law for solvency in the same manner and to the same extent as such a health maintenance organization.

(4) Group health insurance coverage

The term "group health insurance coverage" means, in connection with a group health plan, health insurance coverage offered in connection with such plan.

(c) Excepted benefits

For purposes of this part [*29 USCA §§ 1181* et seq.], the term "excepted benefits" means benefits under one or more (or any combination thereof) of the following:

(1) Benefits not subject to requirements

    (A) Coverage only for accident, or disability income insurance, or any combination thereof.

    (B) Coverage issued as a supplement to liability insurance.

    (C) Liability insurance, including general liability insurance and automobile liability insurance.

    (D) Workers' compensation or similar insurance.

    (E) Automobile medical payment insurance.

    (F) Credit-only insurance.

(G) Coverage for on-site medical clinics.

(H) Other similar insurance coverage, specified in regulations, under which benefits for medical care are secondary or incidental to other insurance benefits.

(2) Benefits not subject to requirements if offered separately

(A) Limited scope dental or vision benefits.

(B) Benefits for long-term care, nursing home care, home health care, community-based care, or any combination thereof.

(C) Such other similar, limited benefits as are specified in regulations.

(3) Benefits not subject to requirements if offered as independent, noncoordinated benefits

(A) Coverage only for a specified disease or illness.

(B) Hospital indemnity or other fixed indemnity insurance.

(4) Benefits not subject to requirements if offered as separate insurance policy

Medicare supplemental health insurance (as defined under section 1882(g)(1) of the Social Security Act [*42 USCA § 1395ss*(g)(1)]), coverage supplemental to the coverage provided under chapter 55 of title 10, United States Code, and similar supplemental coverage provided to coverage under a group health plan.

(d) Other definitions

For purposes of this part [*29 USCA §§ 1181* et seq.]—

(1) COBRA continuation provision

The term "COBRA continuation provision" means any of the following:

(A) Part 6 of this subtitle [*29 USCA §§ 1161* et seq.].

(B) Section 4980B of the Internal Revenue Code of 1986 [*26 USCA § 4980B]*, other than subsection (f)(1) of such section insofar as it relates to pediatric vaccines.

(C) Title XXII of the Public Health Service Act [*42 USCA §§ 350gg* et seq.].

(2) Health status-related factor

The term "health status-related factor" means any of the factors described in section 702(a)(1) [*29 USCA § 1182*(a)(1)].

(3) Network plan

The term "network plan" means health insurance coverage offered by a health insurance issuer under which the financing and delivery of medical care (including items and services paid for as medical care) are provided, in whole or in part, through a defined set of providers under contract with the issuer.

(4) Placed for adoption

The term "placement", or being "placed", for adoption, has the meaning given such term in section 609(c)(3)(B) [*29 USCA § 1169*(c)(3)(B)].

§ 1191c.   Regulations

The Secretary, consistent with section 104 of the Health Care Portability and Accountability Act of 1996 [*42 USCA § 300gg–92* note], may promulgate such regulations as may be necessary or appropriate to carry out the provisions of this part [*29 USCA §§ 1181* et seq.]. The Secretary may promulgate any interim final rules as the Secretary determines are appropriate to carry out this part [*29 USCA §§ 1181* et seq.].

C.   Emergency Medical Treatment and Labor Act (EMTALA): 42 USCA § 1395dd

§ 1395dd.   Examination and treatment for emergency medical conditions and women in labor

(a) Medical screening requirement

In the case of a hospital that has a hospital emergency department, if any individual (whether or not eligible for benefits under this subchapter) comes to the emergency department and a request is made on the individual's behalf for examination or treatment for a medical condition, the hospital must provide for an appropriate medical screening examination within the capability of the hospital's emergency department, including ancillary services routinely available to the emergency department, to determine whether or not an emergency medical condition (within the meaning of subsection (e)(1) of this section) exists.

(b) Necessary stabilizing treatment for emergency medical conditions and labor

(1) In general

If any individual (whether or not eligible for benefits under this subchapter) comes to a hospital and the hospital determines that the individual has an emergency medical condition, the hospital must provide either—

(A) within the staff and facilities available at the hospital, for such further medical examination and such treatment as may be required to stabilize the medical condition, or

(B) for transfer of the individual to another medical facility in accordance with subsection (c) of this section.

(2) Refusal to consent to treatment

A hospital is deemed to meet the requirement of paragraph (1)(A) with respect to an individual if the hospital offers the individual the further medical examination and treatment described in that paragraph and informs the individual (or a person acting on the individual's behalf) of the risks and benefits to the individual of such examination and treatment, but the individual (or a person acting on the individual's behalf) refuses to consent to the examination and treatment. The hospital shall take all reasonable steps to secure the individual's (or person's) written informed consent to refuse such examination and treatment.

(3) Refusal to consent to transfer

A hospital is deemed to meet the requirement of paragraph (1) with respect to an individual if the hospital offers to transfer the individual to another medical facility in accordance with subsection (c) of this section and informs the individual (or a person acting on the individual's behalf) of the risks and benefits to the individual of such transfer, but the individual (or a person acting on the individual's behalf) refuses to consent to the transfer. The hospital shall take all reasonable steps to secure the individual's (or person's) written informed consent to refuse such transfer.

(c) Restricting transfers until individual stabilized

(1) Rule

If an individual at a hospital has an emergency medical condition which has not been stabilized (within the meaning of subsection (e)(3)(B) of this section), the hospital may not transfer the individual unless—

(A)(i) the individual (or a legally responsible person acting on the individual's behalf) after being informed of the hospital's obligations under this section and of the risk of transfer, in writing requests transfer to another medical facility,

(ii) a physician (within the meaning of section 1395x(r)(1) of this title) has signed a certification that based upon the information available at the time of transfer, the medical benefits reasonably expected from the provision of appropriate medical treatment at another medical facility outweigh the increased risks to the individual and, in the case of labor, to the unborn child from effecting the transfer, or

(iii) if a physician is not physically present in the emergency department at the time an individual is transferred, a qualified medical person (as defined by the Secretary in regulations) has signed a certification described in clause (ii) after a physician (as defined in section 1395x(r)(1) of this title), in consultation with the person, has made the determination described in such clause, and subsequently countersigns the certification; and

(B) the transfer is an appropriate transfer (within the meaning of paragraph (2)) to that facility.

A certification described in clause (ii) or (iii) of subparagraph (A) shall include a summary of the risks and benefits upon which the certification is based.

(2) Appropriate transfer

An appropriate transfer to a medical facility is a transfer—

(A) in which the transferring hospital provides the medical treatment within its capacity which minimizes the risks to the individual's health and, in the case of a woman in labor, the health of the unborn child;

(B) in which the receiving facility—

    (i) has available space and qualified personnel for the treatment of the individual, and

    (ii) has agreed to accept transfer of the individual and to provide appropriate medical treatment;

(C) in which the transferring hospital sends to the receiving facility all medical records (or copies thereof), related to the emergency condition for which the individual has presented, available at the time of the transfer, including records related to the individual's emergency medical condition, observations of signs or symptoms, preliminary diagnosis, treatment provided, results of any tests and the informed written consent or certification (or copy thereof) provided under paragraph (1)(A), and the name and address of any on-call physician (described in subsection (d)(1)(C) of this section) who has refused or failed to appear within a reasonable time to provide necessary stabilizing treatment;

(D) in which the transfer is effected through qualified personnel and transportation equipment, as required including the use of necessary and medically appropriate life support measures during the transfer; and

(E) which meets such other requirements as the Secretary may find necessary in the interest of the health and safety of individuals transferred.

(d) Enforcement

(1) Civil money penalties

(A) A participating hospital that negligently violates a requirement of this section is subject to a civil money penalty of not more than $50,000 (or not more than $25,000 in the case of a hospital with less than 100 beds) for each such violation. The provisions of section 1320a–7a of this title (other than subsections (a) and (b)) shall apply to a civil money penalty under this subparagraph in the same manner as such provisions apply with respect to a penalty or proceeding under section 1320a–7a(a) of this title.

(B) Subject to subparagraph (C), any physician who is responsible for the examination, treatment, or transfer of an individual in a participating hospital, including a physician on-call for the care of such an individual, and who negligently violates a requirement of this section, including a physician who—

    (i) signs a certification under subsection (c)(1)(A) of this section that the medical benefits reasonably to be expected from a transfer to another facility outweigh the risks associated with the transfer, if the physician knew or should have known that the benefits did not outweigh the risks, or

    (ii) misrepresents an individual's condition or other information, including a hospital's obligations under this section,

is subject to a civil money penalty of not more than $50,000 for each such violation and, if the violation is gross and flagrant or is repeated, to exclusion from participation in this subchapter and State health care programs. The provisions of section 1320a–7a of this title (other than the first and second sentences of subsection (a) and subsection (b)) shall apply to a civil money penalty and exclusion under this subparagraph in the same manner as such provisions apply with respect to a penalty, exclusion, or proceeding under section 1320a–7a(a) of this title.

(C) If, after an initial examination, a physician determines that the individual requires the services of a physician listed by the hospital on its list of on-call physicians (required to be maintained under section 1395cc(a)(1)(I) of this title) and notifies the on-call physician and the on-call physician fails or refuses to appear within a reasonable period of time, and the physician orders the transfer of the individual because the physician determines that without the services of the on-call physician the benefits of transfer outweigh the risks of transfer, the physician authorizing the transfer shall not be subject to a penalty under subparagraph (B). However, the previous sentence shall not apply to the hospital or to the on-call physician who failed or refused to appear.

(2) Civil enforcement

(A) Personal harm

Any individual who suffers personal harm as a direct result of a participating hospital's violation of a requirement of this section may, in a civil action against the participating hospital, obtain those damages available for personal injury under the law of the State in which the hospital is located, and such equitable relief as is appropriate.

(B) Financial loss to other medical facility

Any medical facility that suffers a financial loss as a direct result of a participating hospital's violation of a requirement of this section may, in a civil action against the participating hospital, obtain those damages available for financial loss, under the law of the State in which the hospital is located, and such equitable relief as is appropriate.

(C) Limitations on actions

No action may be brought under this paragraph more than two years after the date of the violation with respect to which the action is brought.

(3) Consultation with peer review organizations

In considering allegations of violations of the requirements of this section in imposing sanctions under paragraph (1), the Secretary shall request the appropriate utilization and quality control peer review organization (with a contract under part B of subchapter XI of this chapter) to assess whether the individual involved had an emergency medical condition which had not been stabilized, and provide a report on its findings. Except in the case in which a delay would jeopardize the health or safety of individuals, the Secretary shall request such a review before effecting a sanction under paragraph (1) and shall provide a period of at least 60 days for such review.

(e) Definitions

In this section:

(1) The term "emergency medical condition" means—

(A) a medical condition manifesting itself by acute symptoms of sufficient severity (including severe pain) such that the absence of immediate medical attention could reasonably be expected to result in—

(i) placing the health of the individual (or, with respect to a pregnant woman, the health of the woman or her unborn child) in serious jeopardy,

(ii) serious impairment to bodily functions, or

(iii) serious dysfunction of any bodily organ or part; or

(B) with respect to a pregnant women who is having contractions—

(i) that there is inadequate time to effect a safe transfer to another hospital before delivery, or

(ii) that transfer may pose a threat to the health or safety of the woman or the unborn child.

(2) The term "participating hospital" means hospital that has entered into a provider agreement under section 1395cc of this title.

(3)(A) The term "to stabilize" means, with respect to an emergency medical condition described in paragraph (1)(A), to provide such medical treatment of the condition as may be necessary to assure, within reasonable medical probability, that no material deterioration of the condition is likely to result from or occur during the transfer of the individual from a facility, or, with respect to an emergency medical condition described in paragraph (1)(B), to deliver (including the placenta).

(B) The term "stabilized" means, with respect to an emergency medical condition described in paragraph (1)(A), that no material deterioration of the condition is likely, within reasonable medical probability, to result from or occur during the transfer of the individual from a facility, or, with respect to an emergency medical condition described in paragraph (1)(B), that the woman has delivered (including the placenta).

(4) The term "transfer" means the movement (including the discharge) of an individual outside a hospital's facilities at the direction of any person employed by (or affiliated or associated, directly or indirectly, with) the hospital, but does not include such a movement of an individual who (A) has been declared dead, or (B) leaves the facility without the permission of any such person.

(5) The term "hospital" includes a critical access hospital (as defined in section 1395x(mm)(1) of this title).

(f) Preemption

The provisions of this section do not preempt any State or local law requirement, except to the extent that the requirement directly conflicts with a requirement of this section.

(g) Nondiscrimination

A participating hospital that has specialized capabilities or facilities (such as burn units, shock-trauma units, neonatal intensive care units, or (with respect to rural areas) regional referral centers as identified by the Secretary in regulation) shall not refuse to accept an appropriate transfer of an individual who requires such specialized capabilities or facilities if the hospital has the capacity to treat the individual.

(h) No delay in examination or treatment

A participating hospital may not delay provision of an appropriate medical screening examination required under subsection (a) of this section or further medical examination and treatment required under subsection (b) of this section in order to inquire about the individual's method of payment or insurance status.

(i) Whistleblower protections

A participating hospital may not penalize or take adverse action against a qualified medical person described in subsection (c)(1)(A)(iii) or a physician because the person or physician refuses to authorize the transfer of an individual with an emergency medical condition that has not been stabilized or against any hospital employee because the employee reports a violation of a requirement of this section.

PART TWO: FEDERAL FINANCING OF HEALTH CARE

V. MEDICARE, MEDICAID AND S-CHIP

A. MEDICARE: 42 U.S.C.A. § 1395

§ 1395. Prohibition against any Federal interference

Nothing in this subchapter shall be construed to authorize any Federal officer or employee to exercise any supervision or control over the practice of medicine or the manner in which medical services are provided, or over the selection, tenure, or compensation of any officer or employee of any institution, agency, or person providing health services; or to exercise any supervision or control over the administration or operation of any such institution, agency, or person.

§ 1395a. Free Choice by Patient Guaranteed

(a) Basic freedom of choice

Any individual entitled to insurance benefits under this subchapter may obtain health services from any institution, agency, or person qualified to participate under this subchapter if such institution, agency, or person undertakes to provide him such services.

(b) Use of private contracts by medicare beneficiaries

(1) In general

Subject to the provisions of this subsection, nothing in this title shall prohibit a physician or practitioner from entering into a private contract with a medicare beneficiary for any item or service—

(A) for which no claim for payment is to be submitted under this title, and

(B) for which the physician or practitioner receives—

(i) no reimbursement under this title directly or on a capitated basis, and

(ii) receives no amount for such item or service from an organization which receives reimbursement for such item or service under this title directly or on a capitated basis.

(2) Beneficiary protections

(A) In general

Paragraph (1) shall not apply to any contract unless—

(i) the contract is in writing and is signed by the medicare beneficiary before any item or service is provided pursuant to the contract;

(ii) the contract contains the items described in subparagraph (B); and

(iii) the contract is not entered into at a time when the medicare beneficiary is facing an emergency or urgent health care situation.

(B) Items required to be included in contract

Any contract to provide items and services to which paragraph (1) applies shall clearly indicate to the medicare beneficiary that by signing such contract the beneficiary—

(i) agrees not to submit a claim (or to request that the physician or practitioner submit a claim) under this title for such items or services even if such items or services are otherwise covered by this subchapter;

(ii) agrees to be responsible, whether through insurance or otherwise, for payment of such items or services and understands that no reimbursement will be provided under this title for such items or services;

(iii) acknowledges that no limits under this title (including the limits under section 1395w–4(g) of this title) apply to amounts that may be charged for such items or services;

(iv) acknowledges that Medigap plans under section 1395ss of this title do not, and other supplemental insurance plans may elect not to, make payments for such items and services because payment is not made under this title; and

(v) acknowledges that the medicare beneficiary has the right to have such items or services provided by other physicians or practitioners for whom payment would be made under this title.

Such contract shall also clearly indicate whether the physician or practitioner is excluded from participation under the medicare program under section 1320a–7 of this title.

(3) Physician or practitioner requirements

(A) In general

Paragraph (1) shall not apply to any contract entered into by a physician or practitioner unless an affidavit described in subparagraph (B) is in effect during the period any item or service is to be provided pursuant to the contract.

(B) Affidavit

An affidavit is described in this subparagraph if—

(i) the affidavit identifies the physician or practitioner and is in writing and is signed by the physician or practitioner;

(ii) the affidavit provides that the physician or practitioner will not submit any claim under this title for any item or service provided to any medicare beneficiary (and will not receive any reimbursement or amount described in paragraph (1)(B) for any such item or service) during the 2–year period beginning on the date the affidavit is signed; and

(iii) a copy of the affidavit is filed with the Secretary no later than 10 days after the first contract to which such affidavit applies is entered into.

(C) Enforcement

If a physician or practitioner signing an affidavit under subparagraph (B) knowingly and willfully submits a claim under this title for any item or service provided during the 2–year period described in subparagraph (B)(ii) (or receives any reimbursement or amount described in paragraph (1)(B) for any such item or service) with respect to such affidavit—

(i) this subsection shall not apply with respect to any items and services provided by the physician or practitioner pursuant to any contract on and after the date of such submission and before the end of such period; and

(ii) no payment shall be made under this subchapter for any item or service furnished by the physician or practitioner during the period described in clause (i) (and no reimbursement or payment of any amount described in paragraph (1)(B) shall be made for any such item or service).

(4) Limitation on actual charge and claim submission requirement not applicable.

Section 1395w–4(g) of this title shall not apply with respect to any item or service provided to a medicare beneficiary under a contract described in paragraph (1).

(5) Definitions

In this subsection:

(A) Medicare beneficiary

The term "medicare beneficiary" means an individual who is entitled to benefits under part A of this subchapter or enrolled under part B of this subchapter.

(B) Physician

The term "physician" has the meaning given such term by section 1395x(r)(1) of this title.

(C) Practitioner

The term "practitioner" has the meaning given such term by section 1395u(b)(18)(C) of this title.

§ 1395d.   Scope of benefits

(a) Entitlement to payment for inpatient hospital services, post-hospital extended care services, home health services, and hospice care.

The benefits provided to an individual by the insurance program under this part shall consist of entitlement to have payment made on his behalf or, in the case of payments referred to in section 1395f(d)(2) of this title to him (subject to the provisions of this part) for—

(1) inpatient hospital services or inpatient critical access hospital services for up to 150 days during any spell of illness minus 1 day for each day of such services in excess of 90 received during any preceding spell of illness (if such individual was entitled to have payment for such services made under this part unless he specifies in accordance with regulations of the Secretary that he does not desire to have such payment made);

(2) (A) post-hospital extended care services for up to 100 days during any spell of illness, and (B) to the extent provided in subsection (f) of this section, extended care services that are not post-hospital extended care services;

(3) for individuals not enrolled in part B of this subchapter, home health services, and for individuals so enrolled, post-institutional home health services furnished during a home health spell of illness for up to 100 visits during such spell of illness; and

(4) in lieu of certain other benefits, hospice care with respect to the individual during up to two periods of 90 days each and an unlimited number of subsequent periods of 60 days each with respect to which the individual makes an election under subsection (d)(1) of this section.

(b) Services not covered

Payment under this part for services furnished an individual during a spell of illness may not (subject to subsection (c) of this section) be made for—

(1) inpatient hospital services furnished to him during such spell after such services have been furnished to him for 150 days during such spell minus 1 day for each day of inpatient hospital services in excess of 90 received during any preceding spell of illness (if such individual was entitled to have payment for such services made under this part unless he specifies in accordance with regulations of the Secretary that he does not desire to have such payment made);

(2) post-hospital extended care services furnished to him during such spell after such services have been furnished to him for 100 days during such spell; or

(3) inpatient psychiatric hospital services furnished to him after such services have been furnished to him for a total of 190 days during his lifetime.

Payment under this part for post-institutional home health services furnished an individual during a home health spell of illness may not be made for such services beginning after such services have been furnished for a total of 100 visits during such spell.

(c) Inpatients of psychiatric hospitals

If an individual is an inpatient of a psychiatric hospital on the first day of the first month for which he is entitled to benefits under this part, the days on which he was an inpatient of such a hospital in the 150–day period immediately before such first day shall be included in determining the number of days limit under subsection (b)(1) of this section insofar as such limit applies to (1) inpatient psychiatric hospital services, or (2) inpatient hospital services for an individual who is an inpatient primarily for the diagnosis or treatment of mental illness (but shall not be included in determining such number of days limit insofar as it applies to other inpatient hospital services or in determining the 190–day limit under subsection (b)(3) of this section).

(d) Hospice care; election; waiver of rights; revocation; change of election

(1) Payment under this part may be made for hospice care provided with respect to an individual only during two periods of 90 days each and an unlimited number of subsequent periods of 60 days each during the individual's lifetime and only, with respect to each such period, if the individual makes an election under this paragraph to receive hospice care under this part provided by, or under arrangements made by, a particular hospice program instead of certain other benefits under this subchapter.

(2)(A) Except as provided in subparagraphs (B) and (C) and except in such exceptional and unusual circumstances as the Secretary may provide, if an individual makes such an election for a period with respect to a particular hospice program, the individual shall be deemed to have waived all rights to have payment made under this subchapter with respect to—

    (i) hospice care provided by another hospice program (other than under arrangements made by the particular hospice program) during the period, and

    (ii) services furnished during the period that are determined (in accordance with guidelines of the Secretary) to be—

        (I) related to the treatment of the individual's condition with respect to which a diagnosis of terminal illness has been made or

        (II) equivalent to (or duplicative of) hospice care;

except that clause (ii) shall not apply to physicians' services furnished by the individual's attending physician (if not an employee of the hospice program) or to services provided by (or under arrangements made by) the hospice program.

(B) After an individual makes such an election with respect to a 90–day period or a subsequent 60–day period, the individual may revoke the election during the period, in which case—

    (i) the revocation shall act as a waiver of the right to have payment made under this part for any hospice care benefits for the remaining time in such period and (for purposes of subsection (a)(4) of this section and subparagraph (A)) the individual shall be deemed to have been provided such benefits during such entire period, and

    (ii) the individual may at any time after the revocation execute a new election for a subsequent period, if the individual otherwise is entitled to hospice care benefits with respect to such a period.

(C) An individual may, once in each such period, change the hospice program with respect to which the election is made and such change shall not be considered a revocation of an election under subparagraph (B).

(D) For purposes of this subchapter, an individual's election with respect to a hospice program shall no longer be considered to be in effect with respect to that hospice program after the date the individual's revocation or change of election with respect to that election takes effect.

(e) Services taken into account

For purposes of subsections (b) and (c) of this section, inpatient hospital services, inpatient psychiatric hospital services, and post-hospital extended care services shall be taken into account only if payment is or would be, except for this section or the failure to comply with the request and certification requirements of or under section 1395f(a) of this title, made with respect to such services under this part.

(f) Coverage of extended care services without regard to three-day prior hospitalization requirement

(1) The Secretary shall provide for coverage, under clause (B) of subsection (a)(2) of this section, of extended care services which are not post-hospital extended care services at such time and for so long as the Secretary determines, and under such terms and conditions (described in paragraph (2)) as the Secretary finds appropriate, that the inclusion of such services will not result in any increase in the total of payments made under this subchapter and will not alter the acute care nature of the benefit described in subsection (a)(2) of this section.

(2) The Secretary may provide—

(A) for such limitations on the scope and extent of services described in subsection (a)(2)(B) of this section and on the categories of individuals who may be eligible to receive such services, and

(B) notwithstanding sections 1395f, 1395x(v), and 1395ww of this title, for such restrictions and alternatives on the amounts and methods of payment for services described in such subsection,

as may be necessary to carry out paragraph (1).

(g) "Spell of illness" defined

For definition of "spell of illness", and for definitions of other terms used in this part, see section 1395x of this title.

§ 1395e. Deductibles and coinsurance

(a) Inpatient hospital services; outpatient hospital diagnostic services; blood; post-hospital extended care services.

(1) The amount payable for inpatient hospital services or inpatient critical access hospital services furnished an individual during any spell of illness shall be reduced by a deduction equal to the inpatient hospital deductible or, if less, the charges imposed with respect to such individual for such services, except that, if the customary charges for such services are greater than the charges so imposed, such customary charges shall be considered to be the charges so imposed. Such amount shall be further reduced by a coinsurance amount equal to—

(A) one-fourth of the inpatient hospital deductible for each day (before the 91st day) on which such individual is furnished such services during such spell of illness after such services have been furnished to him for 60 days during such spell; and

(B) one-half of the inpatient hospital deductible for each day (before the day following the last day for which such individual is entitled under section 1395d(a)(1) of this title to have payment made on his behalf for inpatient hospital services or inpatient critical access hospital services during such spell of illness) on which such individual is furnished such services during such spell of illness after such services have been furnished to him for 90 days during such spell;

except that the reduction under this sentence for any day shall not exceed the charges imposed for that day with respect to such individual for such services (and for this purpose, if the customary charges for such services are greater than the charges so imposed, such customary charges shall be considered to be the charges so imposed).

(2)(A) The amount payable to any provider of services under this part for services furnished an individual shall be further reduced by a deduction equal to the expenses incurred for the first three pints of whole blood (or equivalent quantities of packed red blood cells, as defined under regulations) furnished to the individual during each calendar year, except that such deductible for such blood shall in accordance with regulations be appropriately reduced to the extent that there has been a replacement of such blood (or equivalent quantities of packed red blood cells, as so defined); and for such purposes blood (or equivalent quantities of packed red blood cells, as so defined) furnished such individual shall be deemed replaced when the institution or other person furnishing such blood (or such equivalent quantities of packed red bloodcells, as so defined) is given one pint of blood for each pint of blood (or equivalent quantities of packed red blood cells, as so defined) furnished such individual with respect to which a deduction is made under this sentence.

(B) The deductible under subparagraph (A) for blood or blood cells furnished an individual in a year shall be reduced to the extent that a deductible has been imposed under section 1395l(b) of this title to blood or blood cells furnished the individual in the year.

(3) The amount payable for post-hospital extended care services furnished an individual during any spell of illness shall be reduced by a coinsurance amount equal to one-eighth of the inpatient hospital deductible for each day (before the 101st day) on which he is furnished such services after such services have been furnished to him for 20 days during such spell.

(4)(A) The amount payable for hospice care shall be reduced—

(i) in the case of drugs and biologicals provided on an outpatient basis by (or under arrangements made by) the hospice program, by a coinsurance amount equal to an amount (not to exceed $5 per prescription) determined in accordance with a drug copayment schedule (established by the hospice program) which is related to, and approximates 5 percent of, the cost of the drug or biological to the program, and

(ii) in the case of respite care provided by (or under arrangements made by) the hospice program, by a coinsurance amount equal to 5 percent of the amount estimated by the hospice program (in accordance with regulations of the Secretary) to be equal to the amount of payment under section 1395f(i) of this title to that program for respite care;

except that the total of the coinsurance required under clause (ii) for an individual may not exceed for a hospice coinsurance period the inpatient hospital deductible applicable for the year in which the period began. For purposes of this subparagraph, the term "hospice coinsurance period" means, for an individual, a period of consecutive days beginning with the first day for which an election under section 1395d(d) of this title is in effect for the individual and ending with the close of the first period of 14 consecutive days on each of which such an election is not in effect for the individual.

(B) During the period of an election by an individual under section 1395d(d)(1) of this title, no copayments or deductibles other than those under subparagraph (A) shall apply with respect to services furnished to such individual which constitute hospice care, regardless of the setting in which such services are furnished.

(b) Inpatient hospital deductible; application

(1) The inpatient hospital deductible for 1987 shall be $520. The inpatient hospital deductible for any succeeding year shall be an amount equal to the inpatient hospital deductible for the preceding calendar year, changed by the Secretary's best estimate of the payment-weighted average of the applicable percentage increases (as defined in section 1395ww(b)(3)(B) of this title) which are applied under section 1395ww(d)(3)(A) of this title for discharges in the fiscal year that begins on October 1 of such preceding calendar year, and adjusted to reflect changes in real case mix (determined on the basis of the most recent case mix data available). Any amount determined under the preceding sentence which is not a multiple of $4 shall be rounded to the nearest multiple of $4 (or, if it is midway between two multiples of $4, to the next higher multiple of $4).

(2) The Secretary shall promulgate the inpatient hospital deductible and all coinsurance amounts under this section between September 1 and September 15 of the year preceding the year to which they will apply.

(3) The inpatient hospital deductible for a year shall apply to—

(A) the deduction under the first sentence of subsection (a)(1) of this section for the year in which the first day of inpatient hospital services, inpatient critical access hospital services occurs in a spell of illness, and

(B) to the coinsurance amounts under subsection (a) of this section for inpatient hospital services, inpatient critical access hospital services and post-hospital extended care services furnished in that year.

§ 1395f. Conditions of and limitations on payment for services

(a) Requirement of requests and certifications

Except as provided in subsections (d) and (g) of this section and in section 1395mm of this title, payment for services furnished an individual may be made only to providers of services which are eligible therefor under section 1395cc of this title and only if—

(1) written request, signed by such individual, except in cases in which the Secretary finds it impracticable for the individual to do so, is filed for such payment in such form, in such manner, and by such person or persons as the Secretary may by regulation prescribe, no later than the close of the period of 3 calendar years following the year in which such services are furnished (deeming any services furnished in the last 3 calendar months of any calendar year to have been furnished in the succeeding calendar year) except that where the Secretary deems that efficient administration so requires, such period may be reduced to not less than 1 calendar year;

(2) a physician, or, in the case of services described in subparagraph (B), a physician, or a nurse practitioner or clinical nurse specialist who does not have a direct or indirect employment relationship with the facility but is working in collaboration with a physician, certifies (and recertifies, where such services are furnished over a period of time, in such cases, with such frequency, and accompanied by such supporting material, appropriate to the case involved, as may be provided by regulations, except that the first of such recertifications shall be required in each case of inpatient hospital services not later than the 20th day of such period) that—

(A) in the case of inpatient psychiatric hospital services, such services are or were required to be given on an inpatient basis, by or under the supervision of a physician, for the psychiatric treatment of an individual; and (i) such treatment can or could reasonably be expected to improve the condition for which such treatment is or was necessary or (ii) inpatient diagnostic study is or was medically required and such services are or were necessary for such purposes;

(B) in the case of post-hospital extended care services, such services are or were required to be given because the individual needs or needed on a daily basis skilled nursing care (provided directly by or requiring the supervision of skilled nursing personnel) or other skilled rehabilitation services, which as a practical matter can only be provided in a skilled nursing facility on an inpatient basis, for any of the conditions with respect to which he was receiving inpatient hospital services (or services which would constitute inpatient hospital services if the institution met the requirements of paragraphs (6) and (9) of section 1395x(e) of this title) prior to transfer to the skilled nursing facility or for a condition requiring such extended care services which arose after such transfer and while he was still in the facility for treatment of the condition or conditions for which he was receiving such inpatient hospital services;

(C) in the case of home health services, such services are or were required because the individual is or was confined to his home (except when receiving items and services referred to in section 1395x(m)(7) of this title) and needs or needed skilled nursing care (other than solely venipuncture for the purpose of obtaining a blood sample) on an intermittent basis or physical or speech therapy or, in the case of an individual who has been furnished home health services based on such a need and who no longer has such a need for such care or therapy, continues or continued to need occupational therapy; a plan for furnishing such services to such individual has been established and is periodically reviewed by a physician; and such services are or were furnished while the individual was under the care of a physician; or

(D) in the case of inpatient hospital services in connection with the care, treatment, filling, removal, or replacement of teeth or structures directly supporting teeth, the individual, because of his underlying medical condition and clinical status or because of the severity of the dental procedure, requires hospitalization in connection with the provision of such services;

(3) with respect to inpatient hospital services (other than inpatient psychiatric hospital services) which are furnished over a period of time, a physician certifies that such services are required to be given on an inpatient basis for such individual's medical treatment, or that inpatient diagnostic study is medically required and such services are necessary for such purpose, except that (A) such certification shall be furnished only in such cases, with such frequency, and accompanied by such supporting material, appropriate to the cases involved, as may be provided by regulations, and (B) the first such certification required in accordance with clause (A) shall be furnished no later than the 20th day of such period;

(4) in the case of inpatient psychiatric hospital services, the services are those which the records of the hospital indicate were furnished to the individual during periods when he was receiving (A) intensive treatment services, (B) admission and related services necessary for a diagnostic study, or (C) equivalent services;

(5) with respect to inpatient hospital services furnished such individual after the 20th day of a continuous period of such services, there was not in effect, at the time of admission of such individual to the hospital, a decision under section 1395cc(d) of this title (based on a finding that utilization review of long-stay cases is not being made in such hospital);

(6) with respect to inpatient hospital services or post-hospital extended care services furnished such individual during a continuous period, a finding has not been made (by the physician members of the committee or group, as described in section 1395x(k)(4) of this title, including any finding made in the course of a sample or other review of admissions to the institution) pursuant to the system of utilization review that further inpatient hospital services or further post-hospital extended care services, as the case may be, are not medically necessary; except that, if such a finding has been made, payment may be made for such services furnished before the 4th day after the day on which the hospital or skilled nursing facility, as the case may be, received notice of such finding;

(7) in the case of hospice care provided an individual—

(A)(i) in the first 90–day period and

    (I) the individual's attending physician (as defined in section 1395x(dd)(3)(B) of this title), and

(II) the medical director (or physician member of the interdisciplinary group described in section 1395x(dd)(2)(B) of this title) of the hospice program providing (or arranging for) the care,

each certify in writing at the beginning of the period, that the individual is terminally ill (as defined in section 1395x(dd)(3)(A) of this title),

(ii) in a subsequent 90–or 60–day period, the medical director or physician described in clause (i)(II) recertifies at the beginning of the period that the individual is terminally ill;

(iii) Repealed. Pub.L. 105–33, Title IV, § 4443(b)(2)(C), Aug. 5, 1997, 111 Stat. 423

(B) a written plan for providing hospice care with respect to such individual has been established (before such care is provided by, or under arrangements made by, that hospice program) and is periodically reviewed by the individual's attending physician and by the medical director (and the interdisciplinary group described in section 1395x(dd)(2)(B) of this title) of the hospice program; and

(C) such care is being or was provided pursuant to such plan of care; and

(8) in the case of inpatient critical access hospital services, a physician certifies that the individual may reasonably be expected to be discharged or transferred to a hospital within 96 hours after admission to the critical access hospital.

To the extent provided by regulations, the certification and recertification requirements of paragraph (2) shall be deemed satisfied where, at a later date, a physician, nurse practitioner, or clinical nurse specialist (as the case may be) makes certification of the kind provided in subparagraph (A), (B), (C), or (D) of paragraph (2) (whichever would have applied), but only where such certification is accompanied by such medical and other evidence as may be required by such regulations. With respect to the physician certification required by paragraph (2) for home health services furnished to any individual by a home health agency (other than an agency which is a governmental entity) and with respect to the establishment and review of a plan for such services, the Secretary shall prescribe regulations which shall become effective no later than July 1, 1981, and which prohibit a physician who has a significant ownership interest in, or a significant financial or contractual relationship with, such home health agency from performing such certification and from establishing or reviewing such plan, except that such prohibition shall not apply with respect to a home health agency which is a sole community home health agency (as determined by the Secretary). For purposes of the preceding sentence, service by a physician as an uncompensated officer or director of a home health agency shall not constitute having a significant ownership interest in, or a significant financial or contractual relationship with, such agency. For purposes of paragraph (2)(C), an individual shall be considered to be "confined to his home" if the individual has a condition, due to an illness or injury, that restricts the ability of the individual to leave his or her home except with the assistance of another individual or the aid of a supportive device (such as crutches, a cane, a wheelchair, or a walker), or if the individual has a condition such that leaving his or her home is medically contraindicated. While an individual does not have to be bedridden to be considered "confined to his home", the condition of the individual should be such that there exists a normal inability to leave home, that leaving home requires a considerable and taxing effort by the individual. The certification regarding terminal illness of an individual under paragraph (7) shall be based on the physician's or medical director's clinical judgment regarding the normal course of the individual's illness. Any absence of an individual from the home attributable to the need to receive health care treatment, including regular absences for the purpose of participating in therapeutic, psychosocial, or medical treatment in an adult day-care program that is licensed or certified by a State, or accredited, to furnish adult day-care services in the State shall not disqualify an individual from being considered to be "confined to his home". Any other absence of an individual from the home shall not so disqualify an individual if the absence is of infrequent or of relatively short duration. For purposes of the preceding sentence, any absence for the purpose of attending a religious service shall be deemed to be an absence of infrequent or short duration.

(b) Amount paid to provider of services

The amount paid to any provider of services (other than a hospice program providing hospice care, other than a critical access hospital providing inpatient critical access hospital services, and other than a home health agency with respect to durable medical equipment) with respect to services for which payment may be made under this part shall, subject to the provisions of sections 1395e 1395ww, and 1395fff of this title, be—

(1) except as provided in paragraph (3), the lesser of (A) the reasonable cost of such services, as determined under section 1395x(v) of this title and as further limited by section 1395rr(b)(2)(B) of this title, or (B) the customary charges with respect to such services;

(2) if such services are furnished by a public provider of services, or by another provider which demonstrates to the satisfaction of the Secretary that a significant portion of its patients are low-income (and requests that payment be made under this paragraph), free of charge or at nominal charges to the public, the amount determined on the basis of those items (specified in regulations prescribed by the Secretary) included in the determination of such reasonable cost which the Secretary finds will provide fair compensation to such provider for such services; or

(3) if some or all of the hospitals in a State have been reimbursed for services (for which payment may be made under this part) pursuant to a reimbursement system approved as a demonstration project under section 402 of the Social Security Amendments of 1967 or section 222 of the Social Security Amendments of 1972, if the rate of increase in such hospitals in their costs per hospital inpatient admission of individuals entitled to benefits under this part over the duration of such project was equal to or less than such rate of increase for admissions of such individuals with respect to all hospitals in the United States during such period, and if either the State has legislative authority to operate such system and the State elects to have reimbursement to such hospitals made in accordance with this paragraph or the system is operated through a voluntary agreement of hospitals and such hospitals elect to have reimbursement to those hospitals made in accordance with this paragraph, then the Secretary may provide for continuation of reimbursement to such hospitals under such system until the Secretary determines that—

    (A) a third-party payor reimburses such a hospital on a basis other than under such system, or

    (B) the aggregate rate of increase from January 1, 1981, to the most recent date for which annual data are available in such hospitals in costs per hospital inpatient admission of individuals entitled to benefits under this part is greater than such rate of increase for admissions of such individuals with respect to all hospitals in the United States for such period.

In the case of any State which has had such a demonstration project reimbursement system in continuous operation since July 1, 1977, the Secretary shall provide under paragraph (3) for continuation of reimbursement to hospitals in the State under such system until the first day of the 37th month beginning after the date the Secretary determines and notifies the Governor of the State that either of the conditions described in subparagraph (A) or (B) of such paragraph has occurred. If, by the end of such 36–month period, the Secretary determines, based on evidence submitted by the Governor of the State, that neither of the conditions described in subparagraph (A) or (B) of paragraph (3) continues to apply, the Secretary shall continue without interruption payment to hospitals in the State under the State's system. If, by the end of such 36–month period, the Secretary determines, based on such evidence, that either of the conditions described in subparagraph (A) or (B) of such paragraph continues to apply, the Secretary shall (i) collect any net excess reimbursement to hospitals in the State during such 36–month period (basing such net excess reimbursement on the net difference, if any, in the rate of increase in costs per hospital inpatient admission under the State system compared to the rate of increase in such costs with respect to all hospitals in the United States over the 36–month period, as measured by including the cumulative savings under the State system based on the difference in the rate of increase in costs per hospital inpatient admission under the State system as compared to the rate of increase in such costs with respect to all hospitals in the United States between January 1, 1981, and the date of the Secretary's initial notice), and (ii) provide a reasonable period, not to exceed 2 years, for transition from the State system to the national payment system.

(c) No payments to Federal providers of services

Subject to section 1395qq of this title, no payment may be made under this part (except under subsection (d) or subsection (h) of this section) to any Federal provider of services, except a provider of services which the Secretary determines is providing services to the public generally as a community institution or agency; and no such payment may be made to any provider of services for any item or service which such provider is obligated by a law of, or a contract with, the United States to render at public expense.

(d) Payments for emergency hospital services

(1) Payments shall also be made to any hospital for inpatient hospital services furnished in a calendar year, by the hospital or under arrangements (as defined in section 1395x(w) of this title) with it, to an individual entitled to hospital insurance benefits under section 426 of this title even though such hospital does not have an agreement in effect under this subchapter if (A) such services were emergency services, (B) the Secretary would be required to make such payment if the hospital had such an agreement in effect and otherwise met the conditions of payment hereunder, and (C) such hospital has elected to claim payments for all such inpatient emergency services and for the emergency outpatient services referred to in section 1395n(b) of this title furnished during such year. Such payments shall be made only in the amounts provided under subsection (b) of this section and then only if such hospital agrees to comply, with respect to the emergency services provided, with the provisions of section 1395cc(a) of this title.

(2) Payment may be made on the basis of an itemized bill to an individual entitled to hospital insurance benefits under section 426 of this title for services described in paragraph (1) which are emergency services if (A) payment cannot be made under paragraph (1) solely because the hospital does not elect to claim such payment, and (B) such individual files application (submitted within such time and in such form and manner and by such person, and containing and supported by such information as the Secretary shall by regulations prescribe) for reimbursement.

(3) The amounts payable under the preceding paragraph with respect to services described therein shall, subject to the provisions of section 1395e of this title, be equal to 60 percent of the hospital's reasonable charges for routine services furnished in the accommodations occupied by the individual or in semiprivate accommodations (as defined in section 1395x(v)(4) of this title), whichever is less, plus 80 percent of the hospital's reasonable charges for ancillary services. If separate charges for routine and ancillary services are not made by the hospital, reimbursement may be based on two-thirds of the hospital's reasonable charges for the services received but not to exceed the charges which would have been made if the patient had occupied semiprivate accommodations. For purposes of the preceding provisions of this paragraph, the term "routine services" shall mean the regular room, dietary, and nursing services, minor medical and surgical supplies and the use of equipment and facilities for which a separate charge is not customarily made; the term "ancillary services" shall mean those special services for which charges are customarily made in addition to routine services.

(e) Payment for inpatient hospital services prior to notification of noneligibility

Notwithstanding that an individual is not entitled to have payment made under this part for inpatient hospital services furnished by any hospital, payment shall be made to such hospital (unless it elects not to receive such payment or, if payment has already been made by or on behalf of such individual, fails to refund such payment within the time specified by the Secretary) for such services which are furnished to the individual prior to notification to such hospital from the Secretary of his lack of entitlement, if such payments are precluded only by reason of section 1395d of this title and if such hospital complies with the requirements of and regulations under this subchapter with respect to such payments, has acted in good faith and without knowledge of such lack of entitlement, and has acted reasonably in assuming entitlement existed. Payment under the preceding sentence may not be made for services furnished an individual pursuant to any admission after the 6th elapsed day (not including as an elapsed day Saturday, Sunday, or a legal holiday) after the day on which such admission occurred.

(f) Payment for certain inpatient hospital services furnished outside United States

(1) Payment shall be made for inpatient hospital services furnished to an individual entitled to hospital insurance benefits under section 426 of this title by a hospital located outside the United States, or under arrangements (as defined in section 1395x(w) of this title) with it, if—

(A) such individual is a resident of the United States, and

(B) such hospital was closer to, or substantially more accessible from, the residence of such individual than the nearest hospital within the United States which was adequately equipped to deal with, and was available for the treatment of, such individual's illness or injury.

(2) Payment may also be made for emergency inpatient hospital services furnished to an individual entitled to hospital insurance benefits under section 426 of this title by a hospital located outside the United States if—

(A) such individual was physically present—

(i) in a place within the United States; or

(ii) at a place within Canada while traveling without unreasonable delay by the most direct route (as determined by the Secretary) between Alaska and another State;

at the time the emergency which necessitated such inpatient hospital services occurred, and

(B) such hospital was closer to, or substantially more accessible from, such place than the nearest hospital within the United States which was adequately equipped to deal with, and was available for the treatment of, such individual's illness or injury.

(3) Payment shall be made in the amount provided under subsection (b) of this section to any hospital for the inpatient hospital services described in paragraph (1) or (2) furnished to an individual by the hospital or under arrangements (as defined in section 1395x(w) of this title) with it if (A) the Secretary would be required to make such payment if the hospital had an agreement in effect under this subchapter and otherwise met the conditions of payment hereunder, (B) such hospital elects to claim such payment, and (C) such hospital agrees to comply, with respect to such services, with the provisions of section 1395cc(a) of this title.

(4) Payment for the inpatient hospital services described in paragraph (1) or (2) furnished to an individual entitled to hospital insurance benefits under section 426 of this title may be made on the basis of an itemized bill to such individual if (A) payment for such services cannot be made under paragraph (3) solely because the hospital does not elect to claim such payment, and (B) such individual files application (submitted within such time and in such form and manner and by such person, and continuing and supported by such information as the Secretary shall by regulations prescribe) for reimbursement. The amount payable with respect to such services shall, subject to the provisions of section 1395e of this title, be equal to the amount which would be payable under subsection (d)(3) of this section.

(g) Payments to physicians for services rendered in teaching hospitals

For purposes of services for which the reasonable cost thereof is determined under section 1395x(v)(1)(D) of this title (or would be if section 1395ww of this title did not apply), payment under this part shall be made to such fund as may be designated by the organized medical staff of the hospital in which such services were furnished or, if such services were furnished in such hospital by the faculty of a medical school, to such fund as may be designated by such faculty, but only if—

(1) such hospital has an agreement with the Secretary under section 1395cc of this title, and

(2) the Secretary has received written assurances that (A) such payment will be used by such fund solely for the improvement of care of hospital patients or for educational or charitable purposes and (B) the individuals who were furnished such services or any other persons will not be charged for such services (or if charged, provision will be made for return of any moneys incorrectly collected).

(h) Payment for specified hospital services provided in Department of Veterans Affairs hospitals; amount of payment

(1) Payments shall also be made to any hospital operated by the Department of Veterans Affairs for inpatient hospital services furnished in a calendar year by the hospital, or under arrangements (as defined in section 1395x(w) of this title) with it, to an individual entitled to hospital benefits under section 426 of this title even though the hospital is a Federal provider of services if (A) the individual was not entitled to have the services furnished to him free of charge by the hospital, (B) the individual was admitted to the hospital in the reasonable belief on the part of the admitting authorities that the individual was a person who was entitled to have the services furnished to him free of charge, (C) the authorities of the hospital, in admitting the individual, and the individual, acted in good faith, and (D) the services were furnished during a period ending with the close of the day on which the authorities operating the hospital first became aware of the fact that the individual was not entitled to have the services furnished to him by the hospital free of charge, or (if later) ending with the first day on which it was medically feasible to remove the individual from the hospital by discharging him therefrom or transferring him to a hospital which has in effect an agreement under this subchapter.

(2) Payment for services described in paragraph (1) shall be in an amount equal to the charge imposed by the Secretary of Veterans Affairs for such services, or (if less) the amount that would be payable for such services under subsection (b) of this section and section 1395ww of this title (as estimated by the Secretary). Any such payment shall be made to the entity to which payment for the services involved would have been payable, if payment for such services had been made by the individual receiving the services involved (or by another private person acting on behalf of such individual).

(i) Payment for hospice care

(1)(A) Subject to the limitation under paragraph (2) and the provisions of section 1395e(a)(4) of this title and except as otherwise provided in this paragraph, the amount paid to a hospice program with respect to hospice care for which payment may be made under this part shall be an amount equal to the costs which are reasonable and related to the cost of providing hospice care or which are based on such other tests of reasonableness as the Secretary may prescribe in regulations (including those authorized under section 1395x(v)(1)(A) of this title), except that no payment may be made for bereavement counseling and no reimbursement may be made for other counseling services (including nutritional and dietary counseling) as separate services.

(B) Notwithstanding subparagraph (A), for hospice care furnished on or after April 1, 1986, the daily rate of payment per day for routine home care shall be $63.17 and the daily rate of payment for other services included in hospice care shall be the daily rate of payment recognized under subparagraph (A) as of July 1, 1985, increased by $10.

(C)(i) With respect to routine home care and other services included in hospice care furnished on or after January 1, 1990, and on or before September 30, 1990, the payment rates for such care and services shall be 120 percent of such rates in effect as of September 30, 1989.

(ii) With respect to routine home care and other services included in hospice care furnished during a subsequent fiscal year, the payment rates for such care and services shall be the payment rates in effect under this subparagraph during the previous fiscal year increased by—

(I) for a fiscal year ending on or before September 30, 1993, the market basket percentage increase (as defined in section 1395ww(b)(3)(B)(iii) of this title) for the fiscal year;

(II) for fiscal year 1994, the market basket percentage increase for the fiscal year minus 2.0 percentage points;

(III) for fiscal year 1995, the market basket percentage increase for the fiscal year minus 1.5 percentage points;

(IV) for fiscal year 1996, the market basket percentage increase for the fiscal year minus 1.5 percentage points;

(V) for fiscal year 1997, the market basket percentage increase for the fiscal year minus 0.5 percentage point;

(VI) for each of fiscal years 1998 through 2002, the market basket percentage increase for the fiscal year involved minus 1.0 percentage points, plus, in the case of fiscal year 2001, 5.0 percentage points; and

(VII) for a subsequent fiscal year, the market basket percentage increase for the fiscal year.

(2)(A) The amount of payment made under this part for hospice care provided by (or under arrangements made by) a hospice program for an accounting year may not exceed the "cap amount" for the year (computed under subparagraph (B)) multiplied by the number of medicare beneficiaries in the hospice program in that year (determined under subparagraph (C)).

(B) For purposes of subparagraph (A), the "cap amount" for a year is $6,500, increased or decreased, for accounting years that end after October 1, 1984, by the same percentage as the percentage increase or decrease, respectively, in the medical care expenditure category of the Consumer Price Index for All Urban Consumers (United States city average), published by the Bureau of Labor Statistics, from March 1984 to the fifth month of the accounting year.

(C) For purposes of subparagraph (A), the "number of medicare beneficiaries" in a hospice program in an accounting year is equal to the number of individuals who have made an election under subsection (d) of this section with respect to the hospice program and have been provided hospice care by (or under arrangements made by) the hospice program under this part in the accounting year, such number reduced to reflect the proportion of hospice care that each such individual was provided in a previous or subsequent accounting year or under a plan of care established by another hospice program.

(D) A hospice program shall submit claims for payment for hospice care furnished in an individual's home under this title only on the basis of the geographic location at which the service is furnished, as determined by the Secretary.

(3) Hospice programs providing hospice care for which payment is made under this subsection shall submit to the Secretary such data with respect to the costs for providing such care for each fiscal year, beginning with fiscal year 1999, as the Secretary determines necessary.

(j) Elimination of lesser-of-cost-or-charges provision

(1) The lesser-of-cost-or-charges provisions (described in paragraph (2)) will not apply in the case of services provided by a class of provider of services if the Secretary determines and certifies to Congress that the failure of such provisions to apply to the services provided by that class of providers will not result in any increase in the amount of payments made for those services under this subchapter. Such change will take effect with respect to services furnished, or cost reporting periods of providers, on or after such date as the Secretary shall provide in the certification. Such change for a class of provider shall be discontinued if the Secretary determines and notifies Congress that such change has resulted in an increase in the amount of payments made under this subchapter for services provided by that class of provider.

(2) The lesser-of-cost-or-charges provisions referred to in paragraph (1) are as follows:

(A) Clause (B) of paragraph (1) and paragraph (2) of subsection (b) of this section.

(B) Section 1395m(a)(1)(B) of this title.

(C) So much of subparagraph (A) of section 1395l(a)(2) of this title as provides for payment other than of the reasonable cost of such services, as determined under section 1395x(v) of this title.

(D) Subclause (II) of clause (i) and clause (ii) of section 1395l(a)(2)(B) of this title.

(k) Payments to home health agencies for durable medical equipment

The amount paid to any home health agency with respect to durable medical equipment for which payment may be made under this part shall be the amount described in section 1395m(a)(1) of this title.

(*l*) Payment for inpatient critical access hospital services

The amount of payment under this part for inpatient critical access hospital services is the reasonable costs of the critical access hospital in providing such services.

§ 1395h. Use of public or private agencies or organizations to facilitate payment to providers of services

(a) Authorization for agreement by Secretary for implementation; scope of agreement

If any group or association of providers of services wishes to have payments under this part to such providers made through a national, State, or other public or private agency or organization and nominates such agency or organization for this purpose, the Secretary is authorized to enter into an agreement with such agency or organization providing for the determination by such agency or organization (subject to the provisions of section 1395oo of this title and to such review by the Secretary as may be provided for by the agreement) of the amount of the payments required pursuant to this part to be made to such providers (and to providers assigned to such agency or organization under subsection (e) of this section), and for the making of such payments by such agency or organization to such providers (and to providers assigned to such agency or organization under subsection (e) of this section). Such agreement may also include provision for the agency or organization to do all or any part of the following: (1) to provide consultative services to institutions or agencies to enable them to establish and maintain fiscal records necessary for purposes of this part and otherwise to qualify as hospitals, extended care facilities, or home health agencies, and (2) with respect to the providers of services which are to receive payments through it (A) to serve as a center for, and communicate to providers, any information or instructions furnished to it by the Secretary, and serve as a channel of communication from providers to the Secretary; (B) to make such audits of the records of providers as may be necessary to insure that proper payments are made under this part; and (C) to perform such other functions as are necessary to carry out this subsection. As used in this subchapter and part B of subchapter XI of this chapter, the term "fiscal intermediary" means an agency or organization with a contract under this section.

(b) Prerequisites for agreement or renewal of agreement by Secretary

The Secretary shall not enter into or renew an agreement with any agency or organization under this section unless—

(1) he finds—

(A) after applying the standards, criteria, and procedures developed under subsection (f) of this section, that to do so is consistent with the effective and efficient administration of this part, and

(B) that such agency or organization is willing and able to assist the providers to which payments are made through it under this part in the application of safeguards against unnecessary utilization of services furnished by them to individuals entitled to hospital insurance benefits under section 426 of this title, and the agreement provides for such assistance; and

(2) such agency or organization agrees—

(A) to furnish to the Secretary such of the information acquired by it in carrying out its agreement under this section, and

(B) to provide the Secretary with access to all such data, information, and claims processing operations,

as the Secretary may find necessary in performing his functions under this part.

(c) Terms and conditions of agreements; prompt payment of claims

(1) An agreement with any agency or organization under this section may contain such terms and conditions as the Secretary finds necessary or appropriate, may provide for advances of funds to the agency or organization for the making of payments by it under subsection (a) of this section, and shall provide for payment of so much of the cost of administration of the agency or organization as is determined by the Secretary to be necessary and proper for carrying out the functions covered by the agreement. The Secretary shall provide that in determining the necessary and proper cost of administration, the Secretary shall, with respect to each agreement, take into account the amount that is reasonable and adequate to meet the costs which must be incurred by an efficiently and economically operated agency or organization in carrying out the terms of its agreement. The Secretary shall cause to have published in the Federal Register, by not later than September 1 before each fiscal year, data, standards, and methodology to be used to establish budgets for fiscal intermediaries under this section for that fiscal year, and shall cause to be published in the Federal Register for public comment, at least 90 days before such data, standards, and methodology are published, the data, standards, and methodology proposed to be used. The Secretary may not require, as a condition of entering into or renewing an agreement under

this section or under section 1395hh of this title, that a fiscal intermediary match data obtained other than in its activities under this part with data used in the administration of this part for purposes of identifying situations in which the provisions of section 1395y(b) of this title may apply.

(2)(A) Each agreement under this section shall provide that payment shall be issued, mailed, or otherwise transmitted with respect to not less than 95 percent of all claims submitted under this subchapter—

(i) which are clean claims, and

(ii) for which payment is not made on a periodic interim payment basis,

within the applicable number of calendar days after the date on which the claim is received.

(B) In this paragraph:

(i) The term "clean claim" means a claim that has no defect or impropriety (including any lack of any required substantiating documentation) or particular circumstance requiring special treatment that prevents timely payment from being made on the claim under this subchapter.

(ii) The term "applicable number of calendar days" means—

(I) with respect to claims received in the 12–month period beginning October 1, 1986, 30 calendar days,

(II) with respect to claims received in the 12–month period beginning October 1, 1987, 26 calendar days,

(III) with respect to claims received in the12–month period beginning October 1, 1988, 25 calendar days, and

(IV) with respect to claims received in the 12–month period beginning October 1, 1989, and claims received in any succeeding 12–month period ending on or before September 30, 1993, 24 calendar days.

(V) with respect to claims received in the 12–month period beginning October 1, 1993, and claims received in any succeeding 12–month period, 30 calendar days.

(C) If payment is not issued, mailed, or otherwise transmitted within the applicable number of calendar days (as defined in clause (ii) of subparagraph (B)) after a clean claim (as defined in clause (i) of such subparagraph) is received from a hospital, critical access hospital, skilled nursing facility, home health agency, hospice program, comprehensive outpatient rehabilitation facility, or rehabilitation agency that is not receiving payments on a periodic interim payment basis with respect to such services, interest shall be paid at the rate used for purposes of section 3902(a) of Title 31 (relating to interest penalties for failure to made prompt payments) for the period beginning on the day after the required payment date and ending on the date on which payment is made.

(3)(A) Each agreement under this section shall provide that no payment shall be issued, mailed, or otherwise transmitted with respect to any claim submitted under this subchapter within the applicable number of calendar days after the date on which the claim is received.

(B) In this paragraph, the term "applicable number of calendar days" means—

(i) with respect to claims submitted electronically as prescribed by the Secretary, 13 days, and

(ii) with respect to claims submitted otherwise, 26 days.

(d) Nomination of agency or organization; withdrawal

If the nomination of an agency or organization as provided in this section is made by a group or association of providers of services, it shall not be binding on members of the group or association which notify the Secretary of their election to that effect. Any provider may, upon such notice as may be specified in the agreement under this section with an agency or organization, withdraw its nomination to receive payments through such agency or organization. Any provider which has withdrawn its nomination, and any provider which has not made a nomination, may elect to receive payments from any agency or organization which has entered into an agreement with the Secretary under this section if the Secretary and such agency or organization agree to it.

(e) Assignment or reassignment of provider of services; designation of agency or organization to perform provider services and home health agency functions

(1) Notwithstanding subsections (a) and (d) of this section, the Secretary, after taking into consideration any preferences of providers of services, may assign or reassign any provider of services to any agency or organization which has entered into an agreement with him under this section, if he determines, after applying the standards, criteria, and procedures developed under subsection (f) of this section, that such assignment or reassignment would result in the more effective and efficient administration of this part.

(2) Notwithstanding subsections (a) and (d) of this section, the Secretary may (subject to the provisions of paragraph (4)) designate a national or regional agency or organization which has entered into an agreement with him under this section to perform functions under the agreement with respect to a class of providers of services in the Nation or region (as the case may be), if he determines, after applying the standards, criteria, and procedures developed under subsection (f) of this section, that such designation would result in more effective and efficient administration of this part.

(3)(A) Before the Secretary makes an assignment or reassignment under paragraph (1) of a provider of services to other than the agency or organization nominated by the provider, he shall furnish (i) the provider and such agency or organization with a full explanation of the reasons for his determination as to the efficiency and effectiveness of the agency or organization to perform the functions required under this part with respect to the provider, and (ii) such agency or organization with opportunity for a hearing, and such determination shall be subject to judicial review in accordance with chapter 7 of Title 5.

(B) Before the Secretary makes a designation under paragraph (2) with respect to a class of providers of services, he shall furnish (i) such providers and the agencies and organizations adversely affected by such designation with a full explanation of the reasons for his determination as to the efficiency and effectiveness of such agencies and organizations to perform the functions required under this part with respect to such providers, and (ii) the agencies and organizations adversely affected by such designation with opportunity for a hearing, and such determination shall be subject to judicial review in accordance with chapter 7 of Title 5.

(4) Notwithstanding subsections (a) and (d) of this section and paragraphs (1), (2), and (3) of this subsection, the Secretary shall designate regional agencies or organizations which have entered into an agreement with him under this section to perform functions under such agreement with respect to home health agencies (as defined in section 1395x(*o*) of this title) in the region, except that in assigning such agencies to such designated regional agencies or organizations the Secretary shall assign a home health agency which is a subdivision of a hospital (and such agency and hospital are affiliated or under common control) only if, after applying such criteria relating to administrative efficiency and effectiveness as he shall promulgate, he determines that such assignment would result in the more effective and efficient administration of this subchapter. By not later than July 1, 1987, the Secretary shall limit the number of such regional agencies or organizations to not more than ten.

(5) Notwithstanding any other provision of this subchapter, the Secretary shall designate the agency or organization which has entered into an agreement under this section to perform functions under such an agreement with respect to each hospice program, except that with respect to a hospice program which is a subdivision of a provider of services (and such hospice program and provider of services are under common control) due regard shall be given to the agency or organization which performs the functions under this section for the provider of services.

(f) Development of standards, criteria, and procedures by Secretary for evaluation of agency or organization performance

(1) In order to determine whether the Secretary should enter into, renew, or terminate an agreement under this section with an agency or organization, whether the Secretary should assign or reassign a provider of services to an agency or organization, and whether the Secretary should designate an agency or organization to perform services with respect to a class of providers of services, the Secretary shall develop standards, criteria, and procedures to evaluate such agency's or organization's (A) overall performance of claims processing (including the agency's or organization's success in recovering payments made under this subchapter for services for which payment has been or could be made under a primary plan (as defined in section 1395y(b)(2)(A) of this title)) and other related functions required to be performed by such an agency or organization under an agreement entered into under this section, and (B) performance of such functions with respect to specific providers of services, and the Secretary shall establish, standards and criteria with respect to the efficient and effective administration of this part. No agency or organization shall be found under such standards and criteria not to be efficient or effective or to be less efficient or effective solely on the ground that the agency or organization serves only providers located in a single State.

(2) The standards and criteria established under paragraph (1) shall include—

(A) with respect to claims for services furnished under this part by any provider of services other than a hospital—

(i) whether such agency or organization is able to process 75 percent of reconsiderations within 60 days (except in the case of fiscal year 1989, 66 percent of reconsiderations) and 90 percent of reconsiderations within 90 days, and

(ii) the extent to which such agency's or organization's determinations are reversed on appeal; and

(B) with respect to applications for an exemption from or exception or adjustment to the target amount applicable under section 1395ww(b) of this title to a hospital that is not a subsection (d) hospital (as defined in section 1395ww(d)(1)(B) of this title)—

(i) if such agency or organization receives a completed application, whether such agency or organization is able to process such application not later than 75 days after the application is filed, and

(ii) if such agency or organization receives an incomplete application, whether such agency or organization is able to return the application with instructions on how to complete the application not later than 60 days after the application is filed

(g) Termination of agreement; procedures applicable

An agreement with the Secretary under this section may be terminated—

(1) by the agency or organization which entered into such agreement at such time and upon such notice to the Secretary, to the public, and to the providers as may be provided in regulations, or

(2) by the Secretary at such time and upon such notice to the agency or organization, to the providers which have nominated it for purposes of this section, and to the public, as may be provided in regulations, but only if he finds, after applying the standards, criteria, and procedures developed under subsection (f) of this section and after reasonable notice and opportunity for hearing to the agency or organization, that (A) the agency or organization has failed substantially to carry out the agreement, or (B) the continuation of some or all of the functions provided for in the agreement with the agency or organization is disadvantageous or is inconsistent with the efficient administration of this part.

(h) Bonding requirement under agreement for officers and employees of agency or organization

An agreement with an agency or organization under this section may require any of its officers or employees certifying payments or disbursing funds pursuant to the agreement, or otherwise participating in carrying out the agreement, to give surety bond to the United States in such amount as the Secretary may deem appropriate.

(i) Liability of certifying and disbursing officers designated under agreement for negligent, etc., payments

(1) No individual designated pursuant to an agreement under this section as a certifying officer shall, in the absence of gross negligence or intent to defraud the United States, be liable with respect to any payments certified by him under this section.

(2) No disbursing officer shall, in the absence of gross negligence or intent to defraud the United States, be liable with respect to any payment by him under this section if it was based upon a voucher signed by a certifying officer designated as provided in paragraph (1) of this subsection.

(3) No such agency or organization shall be liable to the United States for any payments referred to in paragraph (1) or (2).

(j) Denial of claim; notification and reconsideration

An agreement with an agency or organization under this section shall require that, with respect to a claim for home health services, extended care services, or post-hospital extended care services submitted by a provider to such agency or organization that is denied, such agency or organization—

(1) furnish the provider and the individual with respect to whom the claim is made with a written explanation of the denial and of the statutory or regulatory basis for the denial; and

(2) in the case of a request for reconsideration of a denial, promptly notify such individual and the provider of the disposition of such reconsideration.

(k) Annual reporting requirement on erroneous payment recovery

An agreement with an agency or organization under this section shall require that such agency or organization submit an annual report to the Secretary describing the steps taken to recover payments made for items or services for which payment has been or could be made under a primary plan (as defined in section 1395y(b)(2)(A) of this title).

(*l*) Responsibilities of fiscal intermediaries

No agency or organization may carry out (or receive payment for carrying out) any activity pursuant to an agreement under this section to the extent that the activity is carried out pursuant to a contract under the Medicare Integrity Program under section 1395ddd of this title.

§ 1395j. Establishment of supplementary medical insurance program for aged and disabled

There is hereby established a voluntary insurance program to provide medical insurance benefits in accordance with the provisions of this part for aged and disabled individuals who elect to enroll under such program, to be financed from premium payments by enrollees together with contributions from funds appropriated by the Federal Government.

§ 1395k. Scope of benefits; extension of coverage of immunosuppressive drugs; definitions

(a) Scope of benefits

The benefits provided to an individual by the insurance program established by this part shall consist of—

(1) entitlement to have payment made to him or on his behalf (subject to the provisions of this part) for medical and other health services, except those described in subparagraphs (B) and (D) of paragraph (2) and subparagraphs (E) and (F) of section 1395u(b)(6) of this title; and

(2) entitlement to have payment made on his behalf (subject to the provisions of this part) for—

(A) home health services (other than items described in subparagraph (G) or subparagraph (I));

(B) medical and other health services (other than items described in subparagraph (G) or subparagraph (I)) furnished by a provider of services or by others under arrangement with them made by a provider of services, excluding—

(i) physician services except where furnished by—

(I) a resident or intern of a hospital, or

410

(**II**) a physician to a patient in a hospital which has a teaching program approved as specified in paragraph (6) of section 1395x(b) of this title (including services in conjunction with the teaching programs of such hospital whether or not such patient is an inpatient of such hospital) where the conditions specified in paragraph (7) of such section are met,

(**ii**) services for which payment may be made pursuant to section 1395n(b)(2) of this title,

(**iii**) services described by section 1395x(s)(2)(K)(i) of this title, certified nurse-midwife services, qualified psychologist services, and services of a certified registered nurse anesthetist;

(**iv**) services of a nurse practitioner or clinical nurse specialist but only if no facility or other provider charges or is paid any amounts with respect to the furnishing of such services; and

(**C**) outpatient physical therapy services (other than services to which the second sentence of section 1395x(p) of this title applies) and outpatient occupational therapy services (other than services to which such sentence applies through the operation of section 1395x(g) of this title);

(**D**)(i) rural health clinic services and (ii) Federally qualified health center services;

(**E**) comprehensive outpatient rehabilitation facility services;

(**F**) facility services furnished in connection with surgical procedures specified by the Secretary—

(**i**) pursuant to section 1395l(i)(1)(A) of this title and performed in an ambulatory surgical center (which meets health, safety, and other standards specified by the Secretary in regulations) if the center has an agreement in effect with the Secretary by which the center agrees to accept the standard overhead amount determined under section 1395l(i)(2)(A) of this title as full payment for such services (including intraocular lens in cases described in section 1395l(i)(2)(A)(iii) of this title) and to accept an assignment described in section 1395u(b)(3)(B)(ii) of this title with respect to payment for all such services (including intraocular lens in cases described in section 1395l(i)(2)(A)(iii) of this title) furnished by the center to individuals enrolled under this part, or

(**ii**) pursuant to section 1395l(i)(1)(B) of this title and performed by a physician, described in paragraph (1), (2), or (3) of section 1395x(r) of this title, in his office, if the Secretary has determined that—

(**I**) a quality control and peer review organization (having a contract with the Secretary under part B of subchapter

XI of this chapter [42 U.S.C.A. § 1320c et seq.]) is willing, able, and has agreed to carry out a review (on a sample or other reasonable basis) of the physician's performing such procedures in the physician's office,

(II) the particular physician involved has agreed to make available to such organization such records as the Secretary determines to be necessary to carry out the review, and

(III) the physician is authorized to perform the procedure in a hospital located in the area in which the office is located,

and if the physician agrees to accept the standard overhead amount determined under section 1395l(i)(2)(B) of this title as full payment for such services and to accept payment on an assignment-related basis with respect to payment for all services (including all pre-and post-operative services) described in paragraphs (1) and (2)(A) of section 1395x(s) of this title and furnished in connection with such surgical procedure to individuals enrolled under this part;

(G) covered items (described in section 1395m(a)(13) of this title) furnished by a provider of services or by others under arrangements with them made by a provider of services;

(H) outpatient critical access hospital services (as defined in section 1395x(mm)(3) of this title);

(I) prosthetic devices and orthotics and prosthetics (described in section 1395m(h)(4) of this title) furnished by a provider of services or by others under arrangements with them made by a provider of services; and

(J) partial hospitalization services provided by a community mental health center (as described in section 1395x(ff)(2)(B) of this title).

(b) Definitions

For definitions of "spell of illness", "medical and other health services", and other terms used in this part, see section 1395x of this title.

§ 1395l. Payment of benefits

(a) Amounts

Except as provided in section 1395mm of this title, and subject to the succeeding provisions of this section, there shall be paid from the Federal Supplementary Medical Insurance Trust Fund, in the case of each individual who is covered under the insurance program established by this part and incurs expenses for services with respect to which benefits are payable under this part, amounts equal to—

(1) in the case of services described in section 1395k(a)(1) of this title—80 percent of the reasonable charges for the services; except that

(A) an organization which provides medical and other health services (or arranges for their availability) on a prepayment basis (and either is sponsored by a union or employer, or does not provide, or arrange for the provision of, any inpatient hospital services) may elect to be paid 80 percent of the reasonable cost of services for which payment may be made under this part on behalf of individuals enrolled in such organization in lieu of 80 percent of the reasonable charges for such services if the organization undertakes to charge such individuals no more than 20 percent of such reasonable cost plus any amounts payable by them as a result of subsection (b) of this section,

(B) with respect to items and services described in section 1395x(s)(10)(A) of this title, the amounts paid shall be 100 percent of the reasonable charges for such items and services,

(C) with respect to expenses incurred for those physicians' services for which payment may be made under this part that are described in section 1395y(a)(4) of this title, the amounts paid shall be subject to such limitations as may be prescribed by regulations,

(D) with respect to clinical diagnostic laboratory tests for which payment is made under this part (i) on the basis of a fee schedule under subsection (h)(1) of this section or section 1395m(d)(1) of this title, the amount paid shall be equal to 80 percent (or 100 percent, in the case of such tests for which payment is made on an assignment-related basis) of the lesser of the amount determined under such fee schedule, the limitation amount for that test determined under subsection (h)(4)(B) of this section, or the amount of the charges billed for the tests, or (ii) on the basis of a negotiated rate established under subsection (h)(6) of this section, the amount paid shall be equal to 100 percent of such negotiated rate,

(E) with respect to services furnished to individuals who have been determined to have end stage renal disease, the amounts paid shall be determined subject to the provisions of section 1395rr of this title,

(F) with respect to clinical social worker services under section 1395x(s)(2)(N) of this title, the amounts paid shall be 80 percent of the lesser of (i) the actual charge for the services or (ii) 75 percent of the amount determined for payment of a psychologist under clause (L),

(G) Repealed. Pub.L. 103–432, Title I, § 156(a)(2)(B)(ii), Oct. 31, 1994, 108 Stat. 4440

(H) with respect to services of a certified registered nurse anesthetist under section 1395x(s)(11) of this title, the amounts paid shall be 80 percent of the least of the actual charge, the prevailing charge that would be recognized (or, for services furnished on or after January 1, 1992, the fee schedule amount provided under section 1395w–4 of this title) if the services had been performed by an anesthesiologist, or the fee schedule for such services established by the Secretary in accordance with subsection (*l*) of this section,

(I) with respect to covered items (described in section 1395m(a)(13) of this title), the amounts paid shall be the amounts described in section 1395m(a)(1) of this title, and

(J) with respect to expenses incurred for radiologist services (as defined in section 1395m(b)(6) of this title) or physician pathology services, subject to section 1395w–4 of this title, the amounts paid shall be 80 percent of the lesser of the actual charge for the services or the amount provided under the fee schedule established under section 1395m(b) of this title or section 1395m(f) of this title, respectively,

(K) with respect to certified nurse-midwife services under section 1395x(s)(2)(L) of this title, the amounts paid shall be 80 percent of the lesser of the actual charge for the services or the amount determined by a fee schedule established by the Secretary for the purposes of this subparagraph (but in no event shall such fee schedule exceed 65 percent of the prevailing charge that would be allowed for the same service performed by a physician, or, for services furnished on or after January 1, 1992, 65 percent of the fee schedule amount provided under section 1395w–4 of this title for the same service performed by a physician),

(L) with respect to qualified psychologist services under section 1395x(s)(2)(M) of this title, the amounts paid shall be 80 percent of the lesser of the actual charge for the services or the amount determined by a fee schedule established by the Secretary for the purposes of this subparagraph,

(M) with respect to prosthetic devices and orthotics and prosthetics (as defined in section 1395m(h)(4) of this title), the amounts paid shall be the amounts described in section 1395m(h)(1) of this title,

(N) with respect to expenses incurred for physicians' services (as defined in section 1395w–4(j)(3) of this title), the amounts paid shall be 80 percent of the payment basis determined under section 1395w–4(a)(1) of this title,

(O) with respect to services described in section 1395x(s)(2)(K) of this title (relating to services furnished by physician assistants, nurse practitioners, or clinical nurse specialists), the amounts paid shall be equal to 80 percent of (i) the lesser of the actual charge or 85

percent of the fee schedule amount provided under section 1395w–4 of this title, or (ii) in the case of services as an assistant at surgery, the lesser of the actual charge or 85 percent of the amount that would otherwise be recognized if performed by a physician who is serving as an assistant at surgery,

(P) with respect to surgical dressings, the amounts paid shall be the amounts determined under section 1395m(i) of this title,

(Q) with respect to items or services for which fee schedules are established pursuant to section 1395u of this title, the amounts paid shall be 80 percent of the lesser of the actual charge or the fee schedule established in such section,

(R) with respect to ambulance services, (i) the amounts paid shall be 80 percent of the lesser of the actual charge for the services or the amount determined by a fee schedule established by the Secretary under section 1395m(l) of this title and (ii) with respect to ambulance services described in section 1395l(a)(1)(R) of this title, the amounts paid shall be the amounts determined under section 1395m(g) of this title for outpatient critical access hospital services, and

(S) with respect to drugs and biologicals not paid on a cost or prospective payment basis as otherwise provided in this part (other than items and services described in subparagraph (B)), the amounts paid shall be 80 percent of the lesser of the actual charge or the payment amount established in section 1395u(o) of this title;

(2) in the case of services described in section 1395k(a)(2) of this title (except those services described in subparagraphs (C), (D), (E), (F), (G), (H), and (I) of such section and unless otherwise specified in section 1395rr of this title)—

(A) with respect to home health services (other than a covered osteoporosis drug) (as defined in section 1395(kk) of this title), the amount determined under the prospective payment system under section 1395fff of this title;

(B) with respect to other items and services (except those described in subparagraph (C), (D), or (E) of this paragraph and except as may be provided in section 1395ww of this title or section 1395yy(e)(9) of this title)—

(i) furnished before January 1, 1999, the lesser of—

(I) the reasonable cost of such services, as determined under section 1395x(v) of this title, or

(II) the customary charges with respect to such services, less the amount a provider may charge as described in clause (ii) of section 1395cc(a)(2)(A) of this title, but in no case may the payment for such other services exceed 80 percent of such reasonable cost, or

    (ii) if such services are furnished before January 1, 1999, by a public provider of services, or by another provider which demonstrates to the satisfaction of the Secretary that a significant portion of its patients are low-income (and requests that payment be made under this clause), free of charge or at nominal charges to the public, 80 percent of the amount determined in accordance with section 1395f(b)(2) of this title, or

    (iii) if such services are furnished on or after January 1, 1999, the amount determined under subsection (t) of this section, or

    (iv) if (and for so long as) the conditions described in section 1395f(b)(3) of this title are met, the amounts determined under the reimbursement system described in such section;

(C) with respect to services described in the second sentence of section 1395x(p) of this title, 80 percent of the reasonable charges for such services;

(D) with respect to clinical diagnostic laboratory tests for which payment is made under this part (i) on the basis of a fee schedule determined under subsection (h)(1) of this section or section 1395m(d)(1) of this title, the amount paid shall be equal to 80 percent (or 100 percent, in the case of such tests for which payment is made on an assignment-related basis or to a provider having an agreement under section 1395cc of this title) of the lesser of the amount determined under such fee schedule, the limitation amount for that test determined under subsection (h)(4)(B) of this section, or the amount of the charges billed for the tests, or (ii) on the basis of a negotiated rate established under subsection (h)(6) of this section, the amount paid shall be equal to 100 percent of such negotiated rate for such tests;

(E) with respect to—

    (i) outpatient hospital radiology services (including diagnostic and therapeutic radiology, nuclear medicine and CAT scan procedures, magnetic resonance imaging, and ultrasound and other imaging services, but excluding screening mammography), and

    (ii) effective for procedures performed on or after October 1, 1989, diagnostic procedures (as defined by the Secretary) described in section 1395x(s)(3) of this title (other than diagnostic x-ray tests and diagnostic laboratory tests), the amount determined under subsection (n) of this section or, for services or procedures performed on or after January 1, 1999, subsection (t);

(F) with respect to a covered osteoporosis drug (as defined in section 1395x(kk) of this title) furnished by a home health agency, 80 percent of the reasonable cost of such service, as determined under section 1395x(v) of this title; and

(G) with respect to items and services described in section 1395(s)(10)(A) of this title, the lesser of—

(i) the reasonable cost of such services, as determined under section 1395(v)of this title, or

(ii) the customary charges with respect to such services,

or, if such services are furnished by a public provider of services, or by another provider which demonstrates to the satisfaction of the Secretary that a significant portion of its patients are low-income (and requests that payment be made under this provision), free of charge or at nominal charges to the public, the amount determined in accordance with section 1395f(b)(2) of this title;

(3) in the case of services described in section 1395k(a)(2)(D) of this title, the costs which are reasonable and related to the cost of furnishing such services or which are based on such other tests of reasonableness as the Secretary may prescribe in regulations, including those authorized under section 1395x(v)(1)(A) of this title, less the amount a provider may charge as described in clause (ii) of section 1395cc(a)(2)(A) of this title, but in no case may the payment for such services (other than for items and services described in section 1395x(s)(10)(A) of this title) exceed 80 percent of such costs;

(4) in the case of facility services described in section 1395k(a)(2)(F) of this title, and outpatient hospital facility services furnished in connection with surgical procedures specified by the Secretary pursuant to subsection (i)(1)(A) of this section, the applicable amount as determined under paragraph (2) or (3) of subsection (i) of this section or subsection (t);

(5) in the case of covered items (described in section 1395m(a)(13) of this title) the amounts described in section 1395m(a)(1) of this title;

(6) in the case of outpatient critical access hospital services, the amounts described in section 1395m(g) of this title;

(7) in the case of prosthetic devices and orthotics and prosthetics (as described in section 1395m(h)(4) of this title), the amounts described in section 1395m(h) of this title;

(8) in the case of—

(A) outpatient physical therapy services (which includes outpatient speech-language pathology services) and outpatient occupational therapy services furnished—

(i) by a rehabilitation agency, public health agency, clinic, comprehensive outpatient rehabilitation facility, or skilled nursing facility,

(ii) by a home health agency to an individual who is not homebound, or

(iii) by another entity under an arrangement with an entity described in clause (i) or (ii); and

(B) outpatient physical therapy services (which includes outpatient speech-language pathology services) and outpatient occupational therapy services furnished—

(i) by a hospital to an outpatient or to a hospital inpatient who is entitled to benefits under part A of this subchapter but has exhausted benefits for inpatient hospital services during a spell of illness or is not so entitled to benefits under part A of this subchapter, or

(ii) by another entity under an arrangement with a hospital described in clause (i),

the amounts described in section 1395m(k) of this title; and

(9) in the case of services described in section 1395m(a)(2)(E) of this title that are not described in paragraph (8), the amounts described in section 1395m(k) of this title.

(b) Deductible provision

Before applying subsection (a) of this section with respect to expenses incurred by an individual during any calendar year, the total amount of the expenses incurred by such individual during such year (which would, except for this subsection, constitute incurred expenses from which benefits payable under subsection (a) of this section are determinable) shall be reduced by a deductible of $75 for calendar years before 1991 and $100 for 1991 and subsequent years; except that (1) such total amount shall not include expenses incurred for items and services described in section 1395x(s)(10)(A) of this title, (2) such deductible shall not apply with respect to home health services (other than a covered osteoporosis drug (as defined in section 1395x(kk) of this title)), (3) such deductible shall not apply with respect to clinical diagnostic laboratory tests for which payment is made under this part (A) under subsection (a)(1)(D)(i) or (a)(2)(D)(i) of this section on an assignment-related basis, or to a provider having an agreement under section 1395cc of this title, or (B) on the basis of a negotiated rate determined under subsection (h)(6) of this section, (4) such deductible shall not apply to Federally qualified health center services, (5) such deductible shall not apply with respect to screening mammography (as described in section 1395x(jj) of this title), and (6) such deductible shall not apply with respect to screening pap smear and screening pelvic exam (as described in section 1395x(nn) of this title). The total amount of the expenses incurred by an individual as determined under the preceding sentence shall, after the reduction specified in such sentence, be further reduced by an amount equal to the expenses incurred for the first three pints of whole blood (or equivalent quantities of packed red blood cells, as defined under regulations) furnished to the individual during the calendar year, except that such deductible for such blood shall in accordance with regulations be appropriately reduced to the extent that there has been a replacement of such blood (or equivalent quantities of packed red blood cells, as so defined); and for such purposes blood (or equivalent quantities of packed red blood cells, as so defined) furnished such individual shall be deemed replaced when the institution or other person furnishing such blood (or such equivalent quantities of packed red blood cells, as so defined) is given one pint of blood for each pint of blood (or equivalent quantities of packed red blood cells, as so defined) furnished such individual with respect to which a deduction is made under this sentence. The deductible under the previous sentence for blood or blood cells furnished an individual in a year shall be reduced to the extent that a deductible has been imposed under section 1395e(a)(2) of this title to blood or blood cells furnished the individual in the year.

(c) Mental disorders

Notwithstanding any other provision of this part, with respect to expenses incurred in any calendar year in connection with the treatment of mental, psychoneurotic, and personality disorders of an individual who is not an inpatient of a hospital at the time such expenses are incurred, there shall be considered as incurred expenses for purposes of subsections (a) and (b) of this section only 62 1/2 percent of such expenses. For purposes of this subsection, the term "treatment" does not include brief office visits (as defined by the Secretary) for the sole purpose of monitoring or changing drug prescriptions used in the treatment of such disorders or partial hospitalization services that are not directly provided by a physician.

(d) Nonduplication of payments

No payment may be made under this part with respect to any services furnished an individual to the extent that such individual is entitled (or would be entitled except for section 1395e of this title) to have payment made with respect to such services under part A of this subchapter.

(e) Information for determination of amounts due

No payment shall be made to any provider of services or other person under this part unless there has been furnished such information as may be necessary in order to determine the amounts due such provider or other person under this part for the period with respect to which the amounts are being paid or for any prior period.

419

(f) Maximum rate of payment per visit for independent rural health clinics

In establishing limits under subsection (a) of this section on payment for rural health clinic services provided by rural health clinics (other than such clinics in hospitals with less than 50 beds), the Secretary shall establish such limit, for services provided—

(1) in 1988, after March 31, at $46 per visit, and

(2) in a subsequent year, at the limit established under this subsection for the previous year increased by the percentage increase in the MEI (as defined in section 1395u(i)(3) of this title) applicable to primary care services (as defined in section 1395u(i)(4) of this title) furnished as of the first day of that year.

(g) Physical therapy services

(1) Subject to paragraph (4), in the case of physical therapy services of the type described in section 1395x(p) of this title, but not described in subsection (a)(8)(B) of this section, and physical therapy services of such type which are furnished by a physician or as incident to physicians' services, with respect to expenses incurred in any calendar year, no more than the amount specified in paragraph (2) for the year shall be considered as incurred expenses for purposes of subsections (a) and (b) of this section.

(2) The amount specified in this paragraph—

(A) for 1999, 2000, and 2001, is $1,500, and

(B) for a subsequent year is the amount specified in this paragraph for the preceding year increased by the percentage increase in the MEI (as defined in section 1395u(i)(3) of this title) for such subsequent year;

except that if an increase under subparagraph (B) for a year is not a multiple of $10, it shall be rounded to the nearest multiple of $10.

(3) Subject to paragraph (4), in the case of occupational therapy services (of the type that described in section 1395x(p) of this title (but not described in subsection (a)(8)(B) of this section)) through the operation of section 1395x(g) of this title and of such type which are furnished by a physician or as incident to physicians' services, with respect to expenses incurred in any calendar year, no more than the amount specified in paragraph (2) for the year shall be considered as incurred expenses for purposes of subsections (a) and (b) of this section.

(4) This subsection shall not apply to expenses incurred with respect to services furnished during 2000, 2001, and 2002.

(h) Fee schedules for clinical diagnostic laboratory tests; percentage of prevailing charge level; nominal fee for samples; adjustments; recipients of payments; negotiated payment rate

(1)(A) Subject to section 1395m(d)(1) of this title, the Secretary shall establish fee schedules for clinical diagnostic laboratory tests (including prostate cancer screening tests under section 1395x(oo) of this title consisting of prostate-specific antigen blood tests) for which payment is made under this part, other than such tests performed by a provider of services for an inpatient of such provider.

(B) In the case of clinical diagnostic laboratory tests performed by a physician or by a laboratory (other than tests performed by a qualified hospital laboratory (as defined in subparagraph (D)) for outpatients of such hospital), the fee schedules established under subparagraph (A) shall be established on a regional, statewide, or carrier service area basis (as the Secretary may determine to be appropriate) for tests furnished on or after July 1, 1984.

(C) In the case of clinical diagnostic laboratory tests performed by a qualified hospital laboratory (as defined in subparagraph (D)) for outpatients of such hospital, the fee schedules established under subparagraph (A) shall be established on a regional, statewide, or carrier service area basis (as the Secretary may determine to be appropriate) for tests furnished on or after July 1, 1984.

(D) In this subsection, the term "qualified hospital laboratory" means a hospital laboratory, in a sole community hospital (as defined in section 1395ww(d)(5)(D)(iii) of this title), which provides some clinical diagnostic laboratory tests 24 hours a day in order to serve a hospital emergency room which is available to provide services 24 hours a day and 7 days a week.

(2)(A)(i) Except as provided in paragraph (4), the Secretary shall set the fee schedules at 60 percent (or, in the case of a test performed by a qualified hospital laboratory (as defined in paragraph (1)(D)) for outpatients of such hospital, 62 percent) of the prevailing charge level determined pursuant to the third and fourth sentences of section 1395u(b)(3) of this title for similar clinical diagnostic laboratory tests for the applicable region, State, or area for the 12–month period beginning July 1, 1984, adjusted annually (to become effective on January 1 of each year) by a percentage increase or decrease equal to the percentage increase or decrease in the Consumer Price Index for All Urban Consumers (United States city average), and subject to such other adjustments as the Secretary determines are justified by technological changes.

(ii) Notwithstanding clause (i)—

(I) any change in the fee schedules which would have become effective under this subsection for tests furnished on or after January 1, 1988, shall not be effective for tests furnished during the 3–month period beginning on January 1, 1988,

(II) the Secretary shall not adjust the fee schedules under clause (i) to take into account any increase in the consumer price index for 1988,

(III) the annual adjustment in the fee schedules determined under clause (i) for each of the years 1991, 1992, and 1993 shall be 2 percent, and

(IV) the annual adjustment in the fee schedules determined under clause (i) for each of the years 1994 and 1995 and 1998 through 2002 shall be 0 percent.

(iii) In establishing fee schedules under clause (i) with respect to automated tests and tests (other than cytopathology tests) which before July 1, 1984, the Secretary made subject to a limit based on lowest charge levels under the sixth sentence of section 1395u(b)(3) of this title performed after March 31, 1988, the Secretary shall reduce by 8.3 percent the fee schedules otherwise established for 1988, and such reduced fee schedules shall serve as the base for 1989 and subsequent years.

(B) The Secretary may make further adjustments or exceptions to the fee schedules to assure adequate reimbursement of (i) emergency laboratory tests needed for the provision of bona fide emergency services, and (ii) certain low volume high-cost tests where highly sophisticated equipment or extremely skilled personnel are necessary to assure quality.

(3) In addition to the amounts provided under the fee schedules, the Secretary shall provide for and establish (A) a nominal fee to cover the appropriate costs in collecting the sample on which a clinical diagnostic laboratory test was performed and for which payment is made under this part, except that not more than one such fee may be provided under this paragraph with respect to samples collected in the same encounter, and (B) a fee to cover the transportation and personnel expenses for trained personnel to travel to the location of an individual to collect the sample, except that such a fee may be provided only with respect to an individual who is homebound or an inpatient in an inpatient facility (other than a hospital). In establishing a fee to cover the transportation and personnel expenses for trained personnel to travel to the location of an individual to collect a sample, the Secretary shall provide a method for computing the fee based on the number of miles traveled and the personnel costs associated with the collection of each individual sample, but the Secretary shall only be required to apply such method in the case of tests furnished during the period beginning on April 1, 1989, and ending on December 31, 1990, by a laboratory that establishes to the satisfaction of the Secretary (based on data for the 12–month period ending June 30, 1988) that (i) the laboratory is dependent upon payments under this subchapter for at least 80 percent of its collected revenues for clinical diagnostic laboratory tests, (ii) at least 85 percent of its gross revenues for such tests are attributable to tests performed with respect to individuals who are homebound or who are residents in a nursing facility, and (iii) the laboratory provided such tests for residents in nursing facilities representing at least 20 percent of the number of such facilities in the State in which the laboratory is located.

(4)(A) In establishing any fee schedule under this subsection, the Secretary may provide for an adjustment to take into account, with respect to the portion of the expenses of clinical diagnostic laboratory tests attributable to wages, the relative difference between a region's or local area's wage rates and the wage rate presumed in the data on which the schedule is based.

(B) For purposes of subsections (a)(1)(D)(i) and (a)(2)(D)(i) of this section, the limitation amount for a clinical diagnostic laboratory test performed—

(i) on or after July 1, 1986, and before April 1, 1988, is equal to 115 percent of the median of all the fee schedules established for that test for that laboratory setting under paragraph (1),

(ii) after March 31, 1988, and before January 1, 1990, is equal to the median of all the fee schedules established for that test for that laboratory setting under paragraph (1),

(iii) after December 31, 1989, and before January 1, 1991, is equal to 93 percent of the median of all the fee schedules established for that test for that laboratory setting under paragraph (1),

(iv) after December 31, 1990, and before January 1, 1994, is equal to 88 percent of such median,

(v) after December 31, 1993, and before January 1, 1995, is equal to 84 percent of such median,

(vi) after December 31, 1994, and before January 1, 1996, is equal to 80 percent of such median,

(vii) after December 31, 1995, and before January 1, 1998, is equal to 76 percent of such median, and

(viii) after December 31, 1997, is equal to 74 percent of such median (or 100 percent of such median in the case of a clinical diagnostic laboratory test performed on or after January 1, 2001, that the Secretary determines is a new test for which no limitation amount has previously been established under this subparagraph).

(5)(A) In the case of a bill or request for payment for a clinical diagnostic laboratory test for which payment may otherwise be made under this part on an assignment-related basis or under a provider agreement under section 1395cc of this title, payment may be made only to the person or entity which performed or supervised the performance of such test; except that—

(i) if a physician performed or supervised the performance of such test, payment may be made to another physician with whom he shares his practice,

(ii) in the case of a test performed at the request of a laboratory by another laboratory, payment may be made to the referring laboratory but only if—

(I) the referring laboratory is located in, or is part of, a rural hospital,

(II) the referring laboratory is wholly owned by the entity performing such test, the referring laboratory wholly owns the entity performing such test, or both the referring laboratory and the entity performing such test are wholly-owned by a third entity, or

(III) not more than 30 percent of the clinical diagnostic laboratory tests for which such referring laboratory (but not including a laboratory described in subclause (II)), receives requests for testing during the year in which the test is performed are performed by another laboratory, and

(iii) in the case of a clinical diagnostic laboratory test provided under an arrangement (as defined in section 1395x(w)(1) of this title) made by a hospital, critical access hospital, or skilled nursing facility, payment shall be made to the hospital or critical access hospital or skilled nursing facility.

(B) In the case of such a bill or request for payment for a clinical diagnostic laboratory test for which payment may otherwise be made under this part, and which is not described in subparagraph (A), payment may be made to the beneficiary only on the basis of the itemized bill of the person or entity which performed or supervised the performance of the test.

(C) Payment for a clinical diagnostic laboratory test, including a test performed in a physician's office but excluding a test performed by a rural health clinic, may only be made on an assignment-related basis or to a provider of services with an agreement in effect under section 1395cc of this title.

(D) A person may not bill for a clinical diagnostic laboratory test, including a test performed in a physician's office but excluding a test performed by a rural health clinic, other than on an assignment-related basis. If a person knowingly and willfully and on a repeated basis bills for a clinical diagnostic laboratory test in violation of the previous sentence, the Secretary may apply sanctions against the person in the same manner as the Secretary may apply sanctions against a physician in accordance with paragraph (2) of section 1395u(j) of this title in the same manner such paragraphs apply with respect to a physician. Paragraph (4) of such section shall apply in this subparagraph in the same manner as such paragraph applies to such section.

(6) In the case of any diagnostic laboratory test payment for which is not made on the basis of a fee schedule under paragraph (1), the Secretary may establish a payment rate which is acceptable to the person or entity performing the test and which would be considered the full charge for such tests. Such negotiated rate shall be limited to an amount not in excess of the total payment that would have been made for the services in the absence of such rate.

(7) Notwithstanding paragraphs (1) and (4), the Secretary shall establish a national minimum payment amount under this subsection for a diagnostic or screening pap smear laboratory test (including all cervical cancer screening technologies that have been approved by the Food and Drug Administration as a primary screening method for detection of cervical cancer) equal to $14.60 for tests furnished in 2000. For such tests furnished in subsequent years, such national minimum payment amount shall be adjusted annually as provided in paragraph (2).

(i) Outpatient surgery

(1) The Secretary shall, in consultation with appropriate medical organizations—

> **(A)** specify those surgical procedures which are appropriately (when considered in terms of the proper utilization of hospital inpatient facilities) performed on an inpatient basis in a hospital but which also can be performed safely on an ambulatory basis in an ambulatory surgical center (meeting the standards specified under section 1395k(a)(2)(F)(i) of this title), critical access hospital, or hospital outpatient department, and

> **(B)** specify those surgical procedures which are appropriately (when considered in terms of the proper utilization of hospital inpatient facilities) performed on an inpatient basis in a hospital but which also can be performed safely on an ambulatory basis in a physician's office.

The lists of procedures established under subparagraphs (A) and (B) shall be reviewed and updated not less often than every 2 years, in consultation with appropriate trade and professional organizations.

(2)(A) The amount of payment to be made for facility services furnished in connection with a surgical procedure specified pursuant to paragraph (1)(A) and furnished to an individual in an ambulatory surgical center described in such paragraph shall be equal to 80 percent of a standard overhead amount established by the Secretary (with respect to each such procedure) on the basis of the Secretary's estimate of a fair fee which—

> **(i)** takes into account the costs incurred by such centers, or classes of centers, generally in providing services furnished in

425

connection with the performance of such procedure, as determined in accordance with a survey (based upon a representative sample of procedures and facilities) taken not later than January 1, 1995, and every 5 years thereafter, of the actual audited costs incurred by such centers in providing such services,

(ii) takes such costs into account in such a manner as will assure that the performance of the procedure in such a center will result in substantially less amounts paid under this subchapter than would have been paid if the procedure had been performed on an inpatient basis in a hospital, and

(iii) in the case of insertion of an intraocular lens during or subsequent to cataract surgery includes payment which is reasonable and related to the cost of acquiring the class of lens involved.

Each amount so established shall be reviewed and updated not later than July 1, 1987, and annually thereafter to take account of varying conditions in different areas.

(B) The amount of payment to be made under this part for facility services furnished, in connection with a surgical procedure specified pursuant to paragraph (1)(B), in a physician's office shall be equal to 80 percent of a standard overhead amount established by the Secretary (with respect to each such procedure) on the basis of the Secretary's estimate of a fair fee which—

(i) takes into account additional costs, not usually included in the professional fee, incurred by physicians in securing, maintaining, and staffing the facilities and ancillary services appropriate for the performance of such procedure in the physician's office, and

(ii) takes such items into account in such a manner which will assure that the performance of such procedure in the physician's office will result in substantially less amounts paid under this subchapter than would have been paid if the services had been furnished on an inpatient basis in a hospital.

Each amount so established shall be reviewed and updated not later than July 1, 1987, and annually thereafter to take account of varying conditions in different areas.

(C) Notwithstanding the second sentence of subparagraph (A) or the second sentence of subparagraph (B), if the Secretary has not updated amounts established under such subparagraphs with respect to facility services furnished during a fiscal year (beginning with fiscal year 1996), such amounts shall be increased by the percentage increase in the consumer price index for all urban consumers (U.S. city average) as estimated by the Secretary for the 12–month period ending with the midpoint of the year involved. In each of the fiscal years 1998 through 2002, the increase under this subparagraph shall be reduced (but not below zero) by 2.0 percentage points.

(3)(A) The aggregate amount of the payments to be made under this part for outpatient hospital facility services or critical access hospital services furnished before January 1, 1999, in connection with surgical procedures specified under paragraph (1)(A) shall be equal to the lesser of—

    (i) the amount determined with respect to such services under subsection (a)(2)(B) of this section; or

    (ii) the blend amount (described in subparagraph (B)).

(B)(i) The blend amount for a cost reporting period is the sum of—

    (I) the cost proportion (as defined in clause (ii)(I)) of the amount described in subparagraph (A)(i), and

    (II) the ASC proportion (as defined in clause (ii)(II)) of the standard overhead amount payable with respect to the same surgical procedure as if it were provided in an ambulatory surgical center in the same area, as determined under paragraph (2)(A), less the amount a provider may charge as described in clause (ii) of section 1395cc(a)(2)(A) of this title.

    (ii) Subject to paragraph (4), in this paragraph:

    (I) The term "cost proportion" means 75 percent for cost reporting periods beginning in fiscal year 1988, 50 percent for portions of cost reporting periods beginning on or after October 1, 1988, and ending on or before December 31, 1990, and 42 percent for portions of cost reporting periods beginning on or after January 1, 1991.

    (II) The term "ASC proportion" means 25 percent for cost reporting periods beginning in fiscal year 1988, 50 percent for portions of cost reporting periods beginning on or after October 1, 1988, and ending on or before December 31, 1990, and 58 percent for portions of cost reporting periods beginning on or after January 1, 1991.

(4)(A) In the case of a hospital that—

    (i) makes application to the Secretary and demonstrates that it specializes in eye services or eye and ear services (as determined by the Secretary),

    (ii) receives more than 30 percent of its total revenues from outpatient services, and

    (iii) on October 1, 1987—

    (I) was an eye specialty hospital or an eye and ear specialty hospital, or

(II) was operated as an eye or eye and ear unit (as defined in subparagraph (B)) of a general acute care hospital which, on the date of the application described in clause (i), operates less than 20 percent of the beds that the hospital operated on October 1, 1987, and has sold or otherwise disposed of a substantial portion of the hospital's other acute care operations, the cost proportion and ASC proportion in effect under subclauses (I) and (II) of paragraph (3)(B)(ii) for cost reporting periods beginning in fiscal year 1988 shall remain in effect for cost reporting periods beginning on or after October 1, 1988, and before January 1, 1995.

(B) For purposes of this subparagraph (A)(iii)(II), the term "eye or eye and ear unit" means a physically separate or distinct unit containing separate surgical suites devoted solely to eye or eye and ear services.

(5)(A) The Secretary is authorized to provide by regulations that in the case of a surgical procedure, specified by the Secretary pursuant to paragraph (1)(A), performed in an ambulatory surgical center described in such paragraph, there shall be paid (in lieu of any amounts otherwise payable under this part) with respect to the facility services furnished by such center and with respect to all related services (including physicians' services, laboratory, X-ray, and diagnostic services) a single all-inclusive fee established pursuant to subparagraph (B), if all parties furnishing all such services agree to accept such fee (to be divided among the parties involved in such manner as they shall have previously agreed upon) as full payment for the services furnished.

(B) In implementing this paragraph, the Secretary shall establish with respect to each surgical procedure specified pursuant to paragraph (1)(A) the amount of the all-inclusive fee for such procedure, taking into account such factors as may be appropriate. The amount so established with respect to any surgical procedure shall be reviewed periodically and may be adjusted by the Secretary, when appropriate, to take account of varying conditions in different areas.

(6) Any person, including a facility having an agreement under section 1395k(a)(2)(F)(i) of this title, who knowingly and willfully presents, or causes to be presented, a bill or request for payment, for an intraocular lens inserted during or subsequent to cataract surgery for which payment may be made under paragraph (2)(A)(iii), is subject to a civil money penalty of not to exceed $2,000. The provisions of section 1320a–7a of this title (other than subsections (a) and (b)) shall apply to a civil money penalty under the previous sentence in the same manner as such provisions apply to a penalty or proceeding under section 1320a–7a(a) of this title.

(j) Accrual of interest on balance of excess or deficit not paid

Whenever a final determination is made that the amount of payment made under this part either to a provider of services or to another person pursuant to an assignment under section 1395u(b)(3)(B)(ii) of this title was in excess of or less than the amount of payment that is due, and payment of such excess or deficit is not made (or effected by offset) within 30 days of the date of the determination, interest shall accrue on the balance of such excess or deficit not paid or offset (to the extent that the balance is owed by or owing to the provider) at a rate determined in accordance with the regulations of the Secretary of the Treasury applicable to charges for late payments.

(k) Hepatitis B vaccine

With respect to services described in section 1395x(s)(10)(B) of this title, the Secretary may provide, instead of the amount of payment otherwise provided under this part, for payment of such an amount or amounts as reasonably reflects the general cost of efficiently providing such services.

(*l*) Fee schedule for services of certified registered nurse anesthetists

(1)(A) The Secretary shall establish a fee schedule for services of certified registered nurse anesthetists under section 1395x(s)(11) of this title.

(B) In establishing the fee schedule under this paragraph the Secretary may utilize a system of time units, a system of base and time units, or any appropriate methodology.

(C) The provisions of this subsection shall not apply to certain services furnished in certain hospitals in rural areas under the provisions of section 9320(k) of the Omnibus Budget Reconciliation Act of 1986, as amended by section 6132 of the Omnibus Budget Reconciliation Act of 1989.

(2) Except as provided in paragraph (3), the fee schedule established under paragraph (1) shall be initially based on audited data from cost reporting periods ending in fiscal year 1985 and such other data as the Secretary determines necessary.

(3)(A) In establishing the initial fee schedule for those services, the Secretary shall adjust the fee schedule to the extent necessary to ensure that the estimated total amount which will be paid under this subchapter for those services plus applicable coinsurance in 1989 will equal the estimated total amount which would be paid under this subchapter for those services in 1989 if the services were included as inpatient hospital services and payment for such services was made under part A of this subchapter in the same manner as payment was made in fiscal year 1987, adjusted to take into account changes in prices and technology relating to the administration of anesthesia.

(B) The Secretary shall also reduce the prevailing charge of physicians for medical direction of a certified registered nurse anesthetist, or the fee schedule for services of certified registered nurse anesthetists, or both, to the extent necessary to ensure that the estimated total amount which will be paid under this subchapter plus applicable coinsurance for such medical direction and such services in 1989 and 1990 will not exceed the estimated total amount which would have been paid plus applicable coinsurance but for the enactment of the amendments made by section 9320 of the Omnibus Budget Reconciliation Act of 1986. A reduced prevailing charge under this subparagraph shall become the prevailing charge but for subsequent years for purposes of applying the economic index under the fourth sentence of section 1395u(b)(3) of this title.

(4)(A) Except as provided in subparagraphs (C) and (D), in determining the amount paid under the fee schedule under this subsection for services furnished on or after January 1, 1991, by a certified registered nurse anesthetist who is not medically directed—

    (i) the conversion factor shall be—

        (I) for services furnished in 1991, $15.50,

        (II) for services furnished in 1992, $15.75,

        (III) for services furnished in 1993, $16.00,

        (IV) for services furnished in 1994, $16.25,

        (V) for services furnished in 1995, $16.50,

        (VI) for services furnished in 1996, $16.75, and

        (VII) for services furnished in calendar years after 1996, the previous year's conversion factor increased by the update determined under section 1395w–4(d) of this title for physician anesthesia services for that year;

    (ii) the payment areas to be used shall be the fee schedule areas used under section 1395w–4 of this title (or, in the case of services furnished during 1991, the localities used under section 1395u(b) of this title) for purposes of computing payments for physicians' services that are anesthesia services;

    (iii) the geographic adjustment factors to be applied to the conversion factor under clause (i) for services in a fee schedule area or locality is—

        (I) in the case of services furnished in 1991, the geographic work index value and the geographic practice cost index value specified in section 1395u(q)(1)(B) of this title for physicians' services that are anesthesia services furnished in the area or locality, and

        (II) in the case of services furnished after 1991, the geographic work index value, the geographic practice cost index value, and the geographic malpractice index value used for determining payments for physicians' services that are anesthesia services under section 1395w–4 of this title, with 70 percent of the conversion factor treated as attributable to work and 30 percent as attributable to overhead for services furnished in 1991 (and the portions attributable to work, practice expenses, and malpractice expenses in 1992 and thereafter being the same as is applied under section 1395w–4 of this title).

(B)(i) Except as provided in clause (ii) and subparagraph (D), in determining the amount paid under the fee schedule under this subsection for services furnished on or after January 1, 1991, and before January 1, 1994, by a certified registered nurse anesthetist who is medically directed, the Secretary shall apply the same methodology specified in subparagraph (A).

(ii) The conversion factor used under clause (i) shall be—

(I) for services furnished in 1991, $10.50,

(II) for services furnished in 1992, $10.75, and

(III) for services furnished in 1993, $11.00.

(IV) to (VII) Repealed. Pub.L. 103–66, Title XIII, § 13516(b)(2)(C), Aug. 10, 1993, 107 Stat. 584

(iii) In the case of services of a certified registered nurse anesthetist who is medically directed or medically supervised by a physician which are furnished on or after January 1, 1994, the fee schedule amount shall be one-half of the amount described in section 1395w–4(a)(5)(B) [FN2] of this title with respect to the physician.

(C) Notwithstanding subclauses (I) through (V) of subparagraph (A)(i)—

(i) in the case of a 1990 conversion factor that is greater than $16.50, the conversion factor for a calendar year after 1990 and before 1996 shall be the 1990 conversion factor reduced by the product of the last digit of the calendar year and one-fifth of the amount by which the 1990 conversion factor exceeds $16.50; and

(ii) in the case of a 1990 conversion factor that is greater than $15.49 but less than $16.51, the conversion factor for a calendar year after 1990 and before 1996 shall be the greater of—

(I) the 1990 conversion factor, or

(II) the conversion factor specified in subparagraph (A)(i) for the year involved.

(D) Notwithstanding subparagraph (C), in no case may the conversion factor used to determine payment for services in a fee schedule area or locality under this subsection, as adjusted by the adjustment factors specified in subparagraphs (A)(iii), exceed the

431

conversion factor used to determine the amount paid for physicians' services that are anesthesia services in the area or locality.

(5)(A) Payment for the services of a certified registered nurse anesthetist (for which payment may otherwise be made under this part) may be made on the basis of a claim or request for payment presented by the certified registered nurse anesthetist furnishing such services, or by a hospital, critical access hospital, physician, group practice, or ambulatory surgical center with which the certified registered nurse anesthetist furnishing such services has an employment or contractual relationship that provides for payment to be made under this part for such services to such hospital, critical access hospital, physician, group practice, or ambulatory surgical center.

(B) No hospital or critical access hospital that presents a claim or request for payment for services of a certified nurse anesthetist under this part may treat any uncollected coinsurance amount imposed under this part with respect to such services as a bad debt of such hospital or rural primary care hospital for purposes of this subchapter.

(6) If an adjustment under paragraph (3)(B) results in a reduction in the reasonable charge for a physicians' service and a nonparticipating physician furnishes the service to an individual entitled to benefits under this part after the effective date of the reduction, the physician's actual charge is subject to a limit under section 1395u(j)(1)(D) of this title.

(m) Incentive payments for physicians' services furnished in underserved areas

In the case of physicians' services furnished to an individual, who is covered under the insurance program established by this part and who incurs expenses for such services, in an area that is designated (under section 254e(a)(1)(A) of this title) as a health professional shortage area, in addition to the amount otherwise paid under this part, there also shall be paid to the physician (or to an employer or facility in the cases described in clause (A) of section 1395u(b)(6) of this title) (on a monthly or quarterly basis) from the Federal Supplementary Medical Insurance Trust Fund an amount equal to 10 percent of the payment amount for the service under this part.

(n) Payments to hospital outpatient departments for radiology; amount; definitions

(1)(A) The aggregate amount of the payments to be made for all or part of a cost reporting period for services described in subsection (a)(2)(E)(i) of this section furnished under this part on or after October 1, 1988, and before January 1, 1999, and for services described in subsection (a)(2)(E)(ii) of this section furnished under this part on or after October 1, 1989, and before January 1, 1999, shall be equal to the lesser of—

(i) the amount determined with respect to such services under subsection (a)(2)(B) of this section, or

(ii) the blend amount for radiology services and diagnostic procedures determined in accordance with subparagraph (B).

(B)(i) The blend amount for radiology services and diagnostic procedures for a cost reporting period is the sum of—

(I) the cost proportion (as defined in clause (ii)) of the amount described in subparagraph (A)(i); and

(II) the charge proportion (as defined in clause (ii)(II)) of 62 percent (for services described in subsection (a)(2)(E)(i) of this section), or (for procedures described in subsection (a)(2)(E)(ii) of this section), 42 percent or such other percent established by the Secretary (or carriers acting pursuant to guidelines issued by the Secretary) based on prevailing charges established with actual charge data, of the prevailing charge or (for services described in subsection (a)(2)(E)(i) of this section furnished on or after April 1, 1989 and for services described in subsection (a)(2)(E)(ii) of this section furnished on or after January 1, 1992) the fee schedule amount established for participating physicians for the same services as if they were furnished in a physician's office in the same locality as determined under section 1395u(b) of this title (or, in the case of services furnished on or after January 1, 1992, under section 1395w–4 of this title), less the amount the provider may charge as described in clause (ii) of section 1395cc(a)(2)(A) of this title.

(ii) In this subparagraph:

(I) The term "cost proportion" means 50 percent, except that such term means 65 percent in the case of outpatient radiology services for portions of cost reporting periods which occur in fiscal year 1989 and in the case of diagnostic procedures described in subsection (a)(2)(E)(ii) of this section for portions of cost reporting periods which occur in fiscal year 1990, and such term means 42 percent in the case of outpatient radiology services for portions of cost reporting periods beginning on or after January 1, 1991.

(II) The term "charge proportion" means 100 percent minus the cost proportion.

(o) Limitation on benefit for payment for therapeutic shoes for individuals with severe diabetic foot disease

(1) In the case of shoes described in section 1395x(s)(12) of this title—

(A) no payment may be made under this part, with respect to any individual for any year, for the furnishing of—

(i) more than one pair of custom molded shoes (including inserts provided with such shoes) and 2 additional pairs of inserts for such shoes, or

433

(ii) more than one pair of extra-depth shoes (not including inserts provided with such shoes) and 3 pairs of inserts for such shoes, and

(B) with respect to expenses incurred in any calendar year, no more than the limits established under paragraph (2) shall be considered as incurred expenses for purposes of subsections (a) and (b) of this section.

Payment for shoes (or inserts) under this part shall be considered to include payment for any expenses for the fitting of such shoes (or inserts).

(2)(A) Except as provided by the Secretary under subparagraphs (B) and (C), the limits established under this paragraph—

(i) for the furnishing of—

(I) one pair of custom molded shoes (including any inserts that are provided initially with the shoes) is $300, and

(II) any additional pair of inserts with respect to such shoes is $50; and

(ii) for the furnishing of extra-depth shoes and inserts is—

(I) $100 for the pair of shoes itself, and

(II) $50 for any pairs of inserts for a pair of shoes.

(B) The Secretary or a carrier may establish limits for shoes that are lower than the limits established under subparagraph (A) if the Secretary finds that shoes and inserts of an appropriate quality are readily available at or below such lower limits.

(C) For each year after 1988, each dollar amount under subparagraph (A) or (B) (as previously adjusted under this subparagraph) shall be increased by the same percentage increase as the Secretary provides with respect to durable medical equipment for that year, except that if such increase is not a multiple of $1, it shall be rounded to the nearest multiple of $1.

(D) In accordance with procedures established by the Secretary, an individual entitled to benefits with respect to shoes described in section 1395x(s)(12) of this title may substitute modification of such shoes instead of obtaining one (or more, as specified by the Secretary) pairs of inserts (other than the original pair of inserts with respect to such shoes). In such case, the Secretary shall substitute, for the limits established under subparagraph (A), such limits as the Secretary estimates will assure that there is no net increase in expenditures under this subsection as a result of this subparagraph.

(3) In this subchapter, the term "shoes" includes, except for purposes of subparagraphs (A)(ii) and (B) of paragraph (2), inserts for extra-depth shoes.

(p) Repealed. Pub.L. 103–432, Title I, § 123(b)(2)(A)(ii), Oct. 31, 1994, 108 Stat. 4411

(q) Requests for payment to include information on referring physician

(1) Each request for payment, or bill submitted, for an item or service furnished by an entity for which payment may be made under this part and for which the entity knows or has reason to believe there has been a referral by a referring physician (within the meaning of section 1395nn of this title) shall include the name and unique physician identification number for the referring physician.

(2)(A) In the case of a request for payment for an item or service furnished by an entity under this part on an assignment-related basis and for which information is required to be provided under paragraph (1) but not included, payment may be denied under this part.

(B) In the case of a request for payment for an item or service furnished by an entity under this part not submitted on an assignment-related basis and for which information is required to be provided under paragraph (1) but not included—

(i) if the entity knowingly and willfully fails to provide such information promptly upon request of the Secretary or a carrier, the entity may be subject to a civil money penalty in an amount not to exceed $2,000, and

(ii) if the entity knowingly, willfully, and in repeated cases fails, after being notified by the Secretary of the obligations and requirements of this subsection to provide the information required under paragraph (1), the entity may be subject to exclusion from participation in the programs under this chapter for a period not to exceed 5 years, in accordance with the procedures of subsections (c), (f), and (g) of section 1320a–7 of this title.

The provisions of section 1320a–7a of this title (other than subsections (a) and (b)) shall apply to civil money penalties under clause (i) in the same manner as they apply to a penalty or proceeding under section 1320a–7a(a) of this title.

(r) Cap on prevailing charge; billing only on assignment-related basis

(1) With respect to services described in section 1395x(s)(2)(K)(ii) of this title (relating to nurse practitioner or clinical nurse specialist services), payment may be made on the basis of a claim or request for payment presented by the nurse practitioner or clinical nurse specialist furnishing such services, or by a hospital, critical access hospital, skilled nursing facility or nursing facility (as defined in section 1396r(a) of this title), physician, group practice, or ambulatory surgical center with which the nurse practitioner or clinical nurse specialist has an employment or contractual relationship that provides for payment to be made under this part for such services to such hospital, physician, group practice, or ambulatory surgical center.

(2) No hospital or critical access hospital that presents a claim or request for payment under this part for services described in section 1395x(s)(2)(K)(ii) of this title may treat any uncollected coinsurance amount imposed under this part with respect to such services as a bad debt of such hospital for purposes of this subchapter.

(3) Redesignated (2)

(4) Redesignated (3)

(s) Other prepaid organizations

The Secretary may not provide for payment under subsection (a)(1)(A) of this section with respect to an organization unless the organization provides assurances satisfactory to the Secretary that the organization meets the requirement of section 1395cc(f) of this title (relating to maintaining written policies and procedures respecting advance directives).

(t) Prospective payment system for hospital outpatient department services

(1) Amount of payment.

(A) In general

With respect to covered OPD services (as defined in subparagraph (B)) furnished during a year beginning with 1999, the amount of payment under this part shall be determined under a prospective payment system established by the Secretary in accordance with this subsection.

(B) Definition of covered OPD services

For purposes of this subsection, the term "covered OPD services"—

(i) means hospital outpatient services designated by the Secretary;

(ii) subject to clause (iv), includes inpatient hospital services designated by the Secretary that are covered under this part and furnished to a hospital inpatient who (I) is entitled to benefits under part A of this subchapter but has exhausted benefits for inpatient hospital services during a spell of illness, or (II) is not so entitled;

(iii) includes implantable items described in paragraph (3), (6), or (8) of section 1395x(s) of this title; but

(iv) does not include any therapy services described in subsection (a)(8) of this section or ambulance services, for which payment is made under a fee schedule described in section 1395m(k) of this section or section 1395m(l) of this section.

(2) System requirements

Under the payment system—

(A) the Secretary shall develop a classification system for covered OPD services;

(B) the Secretary may establish groups of covered OPD services, within the classification system described in subparagraph (A), so that services classified within each group are comparable clinically and with respect to the use of resources and so that an implantable item is classified to the group that includes the service to which the item relates;

(C) the Secretary shall, using data on claims from 1996 and using data from the most recent available cost reports, establish relative payment weights for covered OPD services (and any groups of such services described in subparagraph (B)) based on median (or, at the election of the Secretary, mean) hospital costs and shall determine projections of the frequency of utilization of each such service (or group of services) in 1999;

(D) the Secretary shall determine a wage adjustment factor to adjust the portion of payment and coinsurance attributable to labor-related costs for relative differences in labor and labor-related costs across geographic regions in a budget neutral manner;

(E) the Secretary shall establish , in a budget neutral manner, outlier adjustments under paragraph (5) and transitional pass-through payments under paragraph (6) and other adjustments as determined to be necessary to ensure equitable payments, such as adjustments for certain classes of hospitals; and

(F) the Secretary shall develop a method for controlling unnecessary increases in the volume of covered OPD services.

For purposes of subparagraph (B), items and services within a group shall not be treated as "comparable with respect to the use of resources" if the highest median cost (or mean cost, if elected by the Secretary under subparagraph (C)) for an item or service within the group is more than 2 times greater than the lowest median cost (or mean cost, if so elected) for an item or service within the group; except that the Secretary may make exceptions in unusual cases, such as low volume items and services, but may not make such an exception in the case of a drug or biological that has been designated as an orphan drug under section 360bb of Title 21.

(3) Calculation of base amounts

(A) Aggregate amounts that would be payable if deductibles were disregarded

The Secretary shall estimate the sum of—

(i) the total amounts that would be payable from the Trust Fund under this part for covered OPD services in 1999, determined without regard to this subsection, as though the deductible under subsection (b) of this section did not apply, and

(ii) the total amounts of copayments estimated to be paid under this subsection by beneficiaries to hospitals for covered OPD services in 1999, as though the deductible under subsection (b) of this section did not apply.

(B) Unadjusted copayment amount

(i) In general

For purposes of this subsection, subject to clause (ii), the "unadjusted copayment amount" applicable to a covered OPD service (or group of such services) is 20 percent of the national median of the charges for the service (or services within the group) furnished during 1996, updated to 1999 using the Secretary's estimate of charge growth during the period.

(ii) Adjusted to be 20 percent when fully phased in

If the pre-deductible payment percentage for a covered OPD service (or group of such services) furnished in a year would be equal to or exceed 80 percent, then the unadjusted copayment amount shall be 20 percent of amount determined under subparagraph (D).

(iii) Rules for new services

The Secretary shall establish rules for establishment of an unadjusted copayment amount for a covered OPD service not furnished during 1996, based upon its classification within a group of such services.

(C) Calculation of conversion factors

(i) For 1999

(I) In general

The Secretary shall establish a 1999 conversion factor for determining the medicare OPD fee schedule amounts for each covered OPD service (or group of such services) furnished in 1999. Such conversion factor shall be established on the basis of the weights and frequencies described in paragraph (2)(C) and in such a manner that the sum for all services and groups of the products (described in subclause (II) for each such service or group) equals the total projected amount described in subparagraph (A).

(II) Product described

The Secretary shall determine for each service or group the product of the medicare OPD fee schedule amounts (taking into account appropriate adjustments described in paragraphs (2)(D) and (2)(E)) and the estimated frequencies for such service or group.

(ii) Subsequent years

Subject to paragraph (8)(B), the Secretary shall establish a conversion factor for covered OPD services furnished in subsequent years in an amount equal to the conversion factor established under this subparagraph and applicable to such services furnished in the previous year increased by the OPD fee schedule increase factor specified under clause (iii) for the year involved.

(iii) Adjustment for service mix changes

Insofar as the Secretary determines that the adjustments for service mix under paragraph (2) for a previous year (or estimates that such adjustments for a future year) did (or are likely to) result in a change in aggregate payments under this subsection during the year that are a result of changes in the coding or classification of covered OPD services that do not reflect real changes in service mix, the Secretary may adjust the conversion factor computed under this subparagraph for subsequent years so as to eliminate the effect of such coding or classification changes.

(iv) OPD fee schedule increase factor

For purposes of this subparagraph, the "OPD fee schedule increase factor" for services furnished in a year is equal to the market basket percentage increase applicable under section 1395ww(b)(3)(B)(iii) of this title to hospital discharges occurring during the fiscal year ending in such year, reduced by 1 percentage point for such factor for services furnished in each of 2000 and 2002. In applying the previous sentence for years beginning with 2000, the Secretary may substitute for the market basket percentage increase an annual percentage increase that is computed and applied with respect to covered OPD services furnished in a year in the same manner as the market basket percentage increase is determined and applied to inpatient hospital services for discharges occurring in a fiscal year.

(D) Calculation of medicare OPD fee schedule amounts

The Secretary shall compute a medicare OPD fee schedule amount for each covered OPD service (or group of such services) furnished in a year, in an amount equal to the product of—

(i) the conversion factor computed under subparagraph (C) for the year, and

(ii) the relative payment weight (determined under paragraph (2)(C)) for the service or group.

439

(E) Pre-deductible payment percentage

The pre-deductible payment percentage for a covered OPD service (or group of such services) furnished in a year is equal to the ratio of—

(i) the medicare OPD fee schedule amount established under subparagraph (D) for the year, minus the unadjusted copayment amount determined under subparagraph (B) for the service or group, to

(ii) the medicare OPD fee schedule amount determined under subparagraph (D) for the year for such service or group.

(4) Medicare payment amount

The amount of payment made from the Trust Fund under this part for a covered OPD service (and such services classified within a group) furnished in a year is determined, subject to paragraph (7), as follows:

(A) Fee schedule adjustments.

The medicare OPD fee schedule amount (computed under paragraph (3)(D)) for the service or group and year is adjusted for relative differences in the cost of labor and other factors determined by the Secretary, as computed under paragraphs (2)(D) and (2)(E).

(B) Subtract applicable deductible

Reduce the adjusted amount determined under subparagraph (A) by the amount of the deductible under section 1833(b), to the extent applicable.

(C) Apply payment proportion to remainder

The amount of payment is the amount so determined under subparagraph (B) multiplied by the pre-deductible payment percentage (as determined under paragraph (3)(E)) for the service or group and year involved, plus the amount of any reduction in the copayment amount attributable to paragraph (8)(C).

(5) Outlier adjustment

(A) In general.

Subject to subparagraph (D), the Secretary shall provide for an additional payment for each covered OPD service (or group of services) for which a hospital's charges, adjusted to cost, exceed—

(i) a fixed multiple of the sum of—

(I) the applicable medicare OPD fee schedule amount determined under paragraph (3)(D), as adjusted under paragraph (4)(A) (other than for adjustments under this paragraph or paragraph (6)); and

(II) any transitional pass-through payment under paragraph (6); and

440

(ii) at the option of the Secretary, such fixed dollar amount as the Secretary may establish.

(B) Amount of adjustment

The amount of the additional payment under subparagraph (A) shall be determined by the Secretary and shall approximate the marginal cost of care beyond the applicable cutoff point under such subparagraph.

(C) Limit on aggregate outlier adjustments

(i) In general.

The total of the additional payments made under this paragraph for covered OPD services furnished in a year (as estimated by the Secretary before the beginning of the year) may not exceed the applicable percentage (specified in clause (ii)) of the total program payments estimated to be made under this subsection for all covered OPD services furnished in that year. If this paragraph is first applied to less than a full year, the previous sentence shall apply only to the portion of such year.

(ii) Applicable percentage

For purposes of clause (i), the term "applicable percentage" means a percentage specified by the Secretary up to (but not to exceed)—

(I) for a year (or portion of a year) before 2004, 2.5 percent; and

(II) for 2004 and thereafter, 3.0 percent.

(D) Transitional authority

In applying subparagraph (A) for covered OPD services furnished before January 1, 2002, the Secretary may—

(i) apply such subparagraph to a bill for such services related to an outpatient encounter (rather than for a specific service or group of services) using OPD fee schedule amounts and transitional pass-through payments covered under the bill; and

(ii) use an appropriate cost-to-charge ratio for the hospital involved (as determined by the Secretary), rather than for specific departments within the hospital.

(6) Transitional pass-through for additional costs of innovative medical devices, drugs, and biologicals.

(A) In general

The Secretary shall provide for an additional payment under this paragraph for any of the following that are provided as part of a covered OPD service (or group of services):

(i) Current orphan drugs

A drug or biological that is used for a rare disease or condition with respect to which the drug or biological has been

441

designated as an orphan drug under section 360bb of Title 21 if payment for the drug or biological as an outpatient hospital service under this part was being made on the first date that the system under this subsection is implemented.

(ii) Current cancer therapy drugs and biologicals and brachytherapy

A drug or biological that is used in cancer therapy, including (but not limited to) a chemotherapeutic agent, an antiemetic, a hematopoietic growth factor, a colony stimulating factor, a biological response modifier, a bisphosphonate, and a device of brachytherapy or temperature monitored cryoablation, if payment for such drug, biological, or device as an outpatient hospital service under this part was being made on such first date.

(iii) Current radiopharmaceutical drugs and biological products

A radiopharmaceutical drug or biological product used in diagnostic, monitoring, and therapeutic nuclear medicine procedures if payment for the drug or biological as an outpatient hospital service under this part was being made on such first date.

(iv) New medical devices, drugs, and biologicals

A medical device, drug, or biological not described in clause (i), (ii), or (iii) if—

(I) payment for the device, drug, or biological as an outpatient hospital service under this part was not being made as of December 31, 1996; and

(II) the cost of the drug or biological or the average cost of the category of devices is not insignificant in relation to the OPD fee schedule amount (as calculated under paragraph (3)(D)) payable for the service (or group of services) involved.

(B) Use of categories in determining eligibility of a device for pass-through payments

The following provisions apply for purposes of determining whether a medical device qualifies for additional payments under clause (ii) or (iv) of subparagraph (A):

(i) Establishment of initial categories

(I) In general

The Secretary shall initially establish under this clause categories of medical devices based on type of device by April

442

1, 2001. Such categories shall be established in a manner such that each medical device that meets the requirements of clause (ii) or (iv) of subparagraph (A) as of January 1, 2001, is included in such a category and no such device is included in more than one category. For purposes of the preceding sentence, whether a medical device meets such requirements as of such date shall be determined on the basis of the program memoranda issued before such date.

(II) Authorization of implementation other than through regulations

The categories may be established under this clause by program memorandum or otherwise, after consultation with groups representing hospitals, manufacturers of medical devices, and other affected parties.

(ii) Establishing criteria for additional categories

(I) In general

The Secretary shall establish criteria that will be used for creation of additional categories (other than those established under clause (i)) through rulemaking (which may include use of an interim final rule with comment period).

(II) Standard

Such categories shall be established under this clause in a manner such that no medical device is described by more than one category. Such criteria shall include a test of whether the average cost of devices that would be included in a category and are in use at the time the category is established is not insignificant, as described in subparagraph (A)(iv)(II).

(III) Deadline

Criteria shall first be established under this clause by July 1, 2001. The Secretary may establish in compelling circumstances categories under this clause before the date such criteria are established.

(IV) Adding categories

The Secretary shall promptly establish a new category of medical devices under this clause for any medical device that meets the requirements of subparagraph (A)(iv) and for which none of the categories in effect (or that were previously in effect) is appropriate.

443

(iii) Period for which category is in effect

A category of medical devices established under clause (i) or (ii) shall be in effect for a period of at least 2 years, but not more than 3 years, that begins—

    (I) in the case of a category established under clause (i), on the first date on which payment was made under this paragraph for any device described by such category (including payments made during the period before April 1, 2001); and

    (II) in the case of any other category, on the first date on which payment is made under this paragraph for any medical device that is described by such category.

(iv) Requirements treated as met

A medical device shall be treated as meeting the requirements of subparagraph (A)(iv), regardless of whether the device meets the requirement of subclause (I) of such subparagraph, if—

    (I) the device is described by a category established and in effect under clause (i); or

    (II) the device is described by a category established and in effect under clause (ii) and an application under section 360e of Title 21 has been approved with respect to the device, or the device has been cleared for market under section 360(k) of Title 21, or the device is exempt from the requirements of section 360(k) of Title 21 pursuant to subsection (*l*) or (m) of section 360 of Title 21 or section 360j(g) of Title 21.

    Nothing in this clause shall be construed as requiring an application or prior approval (other than that described in subclause (II)) in order for a covered device described by a category to qualify for payment under this paragraph.

(C) Limited period of payment

(i) Drugs and biologicals

The payment under this paragraph with respect to a drug or biological shall only apply during a period of at least 2 years, but not more than 3 years, that begins—

    (I) on the first date this subsection is implemented in the case of a drug or biological described in clause (i), (ii), or (iii) of subparagraph (A) and in the case of a drug or biological described in subparagraph (A)(iv) and for which payment under this part is made as an outpatient hospital service before such first date; or

    (II) in the case of a drug or biological described in subparagraph (A)(iv) not described in subclause (I), on the first date on which payment is made under this part for the drug or biological as an outpatient hospital service.

(ii) Medical devices

Payment shall be made under this paragraph with respect to a medical device only if such device—

(I) is described by a category of medical devices established and in effect under subparagraph (B); and

(II) is provided as part of a service (or group of services) paid for under this subsection and provided during the period for which such category is in effect under such subparagraph.

(D) Amount of additional payment

Subject to subparagraph (E)(iii), the amount of the payment under this paragraph with respect to a device, drug, or biological provided as part of a covered OPD service is—

(i) in the case of a drug or biological, the amount by which the amount determined under section 1395u(o) of this title for the drug or biological exceeds the portion of the otherwise applicable medicare OPD fee schedule that the Secretary determines is associated with the drug or biological; or

(ii) in the case of a medical device, the amount by which the hospital's charges for the device, adjusted to cost, exceeds the portion of the otherwise applicable medicare OPD fee schedule that the Secretary determines is associated with the device.

(E) Limit on aggregate annual adjustment

(i) In general

The total of the additional payments made under this paragraph for covered OPD services furnished in a year (as estimated by the Secretary before the beginning of the year) may not exceed the applicable percentage (specified in clause (ii)) of the total program payments estimated to be made under this subsection for all covered OPD services furnished in that year. If this paragraph is first applied to less than a full year, the previous sentence shall apply only to the portion of such year.

(ii) Applicable percentage

For purposes of clause (i), the term "applicable percentage" means—

(I) for a year (or portion of a year) before 2004, 2.5 percent; and

(II) for 2004 and thereafter, a percentage specified by the Secretary up to (but not to exceed) 2.0 percent.

(iii) Uniform prospective reduction if aggregate limit projected to be exceeded

If the Secretary estimates before the beginning of a year that the amount of the additional payments under this paragraph for the year (or portion thereof) as determined under clause (i) without regard to this clause will exceed the limit established under such clause, the Secretary shall reduce pro rata the amount of each of the additional payments under this paragraph for that year (or portion thereof) in order to ensure that the aggregate additional payments under this paragraph (as so estimated) do not exceed such limit.

(7) Transitional adjustment to limit decline in payment

(A) Before 2002

Subject to subparagraph (D), for covered OPD services furnished before January 1, 2002, for which the PPS amount (as defined in subparagraph (E)) is—

(i) at least 90 percent, but less than 100 percent, of the pre-BBA amount (as defined in subparagraph (F)), the amount of payment under this subsection shall be increased by 80 percent of the amount of such difference;

(ii) at least 80 percent, but less than 90 percent, of the pre-BBA amount, the amount of payment under this subsection shall be increased by the amount by which (I) the product of 0.71 and the pre-BBA amount, exceeds (II) the product of 0.70 and the PPS amount;

(iii) at least 70 percent, but less than 80 percent, of the pre-BBA amount, the amount of payment under this subsection shall be increased by the amount by which (I) the product of 0.63 and the pre-BBA amount, exceeds (II) the product of 0.60 and the PPS amount; or

(iv) less than 70 percent of the pre-BBA amount, the amount of payment under this subsection shall be increased by 21 percent of the pre-BBA amount.

(B) 2002

Subject to subparagraph (D), for covered OPD services furnished during 2002, for which the PPS amount is—

(i) at least 90 percent, but less than 100 percent, of the pre-BBA amount, the amount of payment under this subsection shall be increased by 70 percent of the amount of such difference;

(ii) at least 80 percent, but less than 90 percent, of the pre-BBA amount, the amount of payment under this subsection shall be increased by the amount by which (I) the product of 0.61 and the pre-BBA amount, exceeds (II) the product of 0.60 and the PPS amount; or

(iii) less than 80 percent of the pre-BBA amount, the amount of payment under this subsection shall be increased by 13 percent of the pre-BBA amount.

(C) 2003

Subject to subparagraph (D), for covered OPD services furnished during 2003, for which the PPS amount is—

(i) at least 90 percent, but less than 100 percent, of the pre-BBA amount, the amount of payment under this subsection shall be increased by 60 percent of the amount of such difference; or

(ii) less than 90 percent of the pre-BBA amount, the amount of payment under this subsection shall be increased by 6 percent of the pre-BBA amount.

(D) Hold harmless provisions

(i) Temporary treatment for small rural hospitals

In the case of a hospital located in a rural area and that has not more than 100 beds, for covered OPD services furnished before January 1, 2004, for which the PPS amount is less than the pre-BBA amount, the amount of payment under this subsection shall be increased by the amount of such difference.

(ii) Permanent treatment for cancer hospitals and children's hospitals

In the case of a hospital described in clause (iii) or (v) of section 1395ww(d)(1)(B) of this title, for covered OPD services for which the PPS amount is less than the pre-BBA amount, the amount of payment under this subsection shall be increased by the amount of such difference.

(E) PPS amount defined

In this paragraph, the term "PPS amount" means, with respect to covered OPD services, the amount payable under this subchapter for such services (determined without regard to this paragraph), including amounts payable as copayment under paragraph (8), coinsurance under section 1395ww(a)(2)(A)(ii) of this title, and the deductible under section 1395l(b) of this title.

(F) Pre–BBA amount defined

(i) In general

In this paragraph, the "pre-BBA amount" means, with respect to covered OPD services furnished by a hospital in a year, an amount equal to the product of the reasonable cost of the hospital for such services for the portions of the hospital's cost reporting period (or periods) occurring in the year and the base OPD payment-to-cost ratio for the hospital (as defined in clause (ii)).

(ii) Base payment-to-cost-ratio defined

For purposes of this subparagraph, the "base payment-to-cost ratio" for a hospital means the ratio of—

(I) the hospital's reimbursement under this part for covered OPD services furnished during the cost reporting period ending in 1996 (or in the case of a hospital that did not submit a cost report for such period, during the first subsequent cost reporting period ending before 2001 for which the hospital submitted a cost report), including any reimbursement for such services through cost-sharing described in subparagraph (E), to

(II) the reasonable cost of such services for such period.

The Secretary shall determine such ratios as if the amendments made by section 4521 of the Balanced Budget Act of 1997 were in effect in 1996.

(G) Interim payments

The Secretary shall make payments under this paragraph to hospitals on an interim basis, subject to retrospective adjustments based on settled cost reports.

(H) No effect on copayments

Nothing in this paragraph shall be construed to affect the unadjusted copayment amount described in paragraph (3)(B) or the copayment amount under paragraph (8).

(I) Application without regard to budget neutrality

The additional payments made under this paragraph—

(i) shall not be considered an adjustment under paragraph (2)(E); and

(ii) shall not be implemented in a budget neutral manner.

(8) Copayment amount

(A) In general

Except as provided in subparagraphs (B) and (C), the copayment amount under this subsection is the amount by which the amount described in paragraph (4)(B) exceeds the amount of payment determined under paragraph (4)(C).

(B) Election to offer reduced copayment amount

The Secretary shall establish a procedure under which a hospital, before the beginning of a year (beginning with 1999), may elect to reduce the copayment amount otherwise established under subparagraph (A) for some or all covered OPD services to an amount that is

448

not less than 20 percent of the medicare OPD fee schedule amount (computed under paragraph (3)(D)) for the service involved. Under such procedures, such reduced copayment amount may not be further reduced or increased during the year involved and the hospital may disseminate information on the reduction of copayment amount effected under this subparagraph.

(C) Limitation on copayment amount

(i) To inpatient hospital deductible amount

In no case shall the copayment amount for a procedure performed in a year exceed the amount of the inpatient hospital deductible established under section 1395e(b) of this title for that year.

(ii) To specified percentage

The Secretary shall reduce the national unadjusted copayment amount for a covered OPD service (or group of such services) furnished in a year in a manner so that the effective copayment rate (determined on a national unadjusted basis) for that service in the year does not exceed the following percentage:

(I) For procedures performed in 2001, on or after April 1, 2001, 57 percent.

(II) For procedures performed in 2002 or 2003, 55 percent.

(III) For procedures performed in 2004, 50 percent.

(IV) For procedures performed in 2005, 45 percent.

(V) For procedures performed in 2006 and thereafter, 40 percent.

(D) No impact on deductibles

Nothing in this paragraph shall be construed as affecting a hospital's authority to waive the charging of a deductible under section 1395l(b) of this title.

(E) Computation ignoring outlier and pass-through adjustments

The copayment amount shall be computed under subparagraph (A) as if the adjustments under paragraphs (5) and (6) (and any adjustment made under paragraph (2)(E) in relation to such adjustments) had not occurred.

(9) Periodic review and adjustments components of prospective payment system

(A) Periodic review

The Secretary shall review not less often than annually and revise the groups, the relative payment weights, and the wage and other adjustments described in paragraph (2) to take into account changes in medical practice, changes in technology, the addition of new services, new cost data, and other relevant information and factors. The Secretary shall consult with an expert outside advisory panel composed of an appropriate selection of representatives of providers to review (and advise the Secretary concerning) the clinical integrity of the groups and weights. Such panel may use data collected or developed by entities and organizations (other than the Department of Health and Human Services) in conducting such review.

(B) Budget neutrality adjustment

If the Secretary makes adjustments under subparagraph (A), then the adjustments for a year may not cause the estimated amount of expenditures under this part for the year to increase or decrease from the estimated amount of expenditures under this part that would have been made if the adjustments had not been made.

(C) Update factor

If the Secretary determines under methodologies described in paragraph (2)(F) that the volume of services paid for under this subsection increased beyond amounts established through those methodologies, the Secretary may appropriately adjust the update to the conversion factor otherwise applicable in a subsequent year.

(10) Special rule for ambulance services

The Secretary shall pay for hospital outpatient services that are ambulance services on the basis described section 1395x(v)(1)(U) of this title, or, if applicable, the fee schedule established under section 1395m(*l*) of this title.

(11) Special rules for certain hospitals

In the case of hospitals described in clause (iii) or (v) of section 1395ww(d)(1)(B) of this title—

(A) the system under this subsection shall not apply to covered OPD services furnished before January 1, 2000; and

(B) the Secretary may establish a separate conversion factor for such services in a manner that specifically takes into account the unique costs incurred by such hospitals by virtue of their patient population and service intensity.

(12) Limitation on review

There shall be no administrative or judicial review under section 1395ff, 1395oo, of this title, or otherwise of—

(A) the development of the classification system under paragraph (2), including the establishment of groups and relative payment weights for covered OPD services, of wage adjustment factors, other adjustments, and methods described in paragraph (2)(F);

(B) the calculation of base amounts under paragraph (3);

(C) periodic adjustments made under paragraph (6);

(D) the establishment of a separate conversion factor under paragraph (8)(B); and

(E) the determination of the fixed multiple, or a fixed dollar cutoff amount, the marginal cost of care, or applicable percentage under paragraph (5) or the determination of insignificance of cost, the duration of the additional payments, the determination and deletion of initial and new categories (consistent with subparagraphs (B) and (C) of paragraph (6)), the portion of the medicare OPD fee schedule amount associated with particular devices, drugs, or biologicals, and the application of any pro rata reduction under paragraph (6).

(13) Miscellaneous provisions

(A) Application of reclassification of certain hospitals

If a hospital is being treated as being located in a rural area under section 1886(d)(8)(E), that hospital shall be treated under this subsection as being located in that rural area.

§ 1395m.   Special payment rules for particular items and services

(a) Payment for durable medical equipment

(1) General rule for payment

(A) In general

With respect to a covered item (as defined in paragraph (13)) for which payment is determined under this subsection, payment shall be made in the frequency specified in paragraphs (2) through (7) and in an amount equal to 80 percent of the payment basis described in subparagraph (B).

(B) Payment basis

The payment basis described in this subparagraph is the lesser of—

(i) the actual charge for the item, or

(ii) the payment amount recognized under paragraphs (2) through (7) of this subsection for the item; except that clause (i) shall not apply if the covered item is furnished by a public home health agency (or by another home health agency which demonstrates to the satisfaction of the Secretary that a significant portion of its patients are low income) free of charge or at nominal charges to the public.

451

(C) Exclusive payment rule

This subsection shall constitute the exclusive provision of this subchapter for payment for covered items under this part or under part A of this subchapter to a home health agency.

(D) Reduction in fee schedules for certain items

With respect to a seat-lift chair or transcutaneous electrical nerve stimulator furnished on or after April 1, 1990, the Secretary shall reduce the payment amount applied under subparagraph (B)(ii) for such an item by 15 percent, and, in the case of a transcutaneous electrical nerve stimulator furnished on or after January 1, 1991, the Secretary shall further reduce such payment amount (as previously reduced) by 45 percent.

(2) Payment for inexpensive and other routinely purchased durable medical equipment

(A) In general

Payment for an item of durable medical equipment (as defined in paragraph (13))—

(i) the purchase price of which does not exceed $150,

(ii) which the Secretary determines is acquired at least 75 percent of the time by purchase, or

(iii) which is an accessory used in conjunction with a nebulizer, aspirator, or a ventilator excluded under paragraph (3)(A), shall be made on a rental basis or in a lump-sum amount for the purchase of the item. The payment amount recognized for purchase or rental of such equipment is the amount specified in subparagraph (B) for purchase or rental, except that the total amount of payments with respect to an item may not exceed the payment amount specified in subparagraph (B) with respect to the purchase of the item.

(B) Payment amount

For purposes of subparagraph (A), the amount specified in this subparagraph, with respect to the purchase or rental of an item furnished in a carrier service area—

(i) in 1989 and in 1990 is the average reasonable charge in the area for the purchase or rental, respectively, of the item for the 12-month period ending on June 30, 1987, increased by the percentage increase in the consumer price index for all urban consumers (U.S. city average) for the 6-month period ending with December 1987;

(ii) in 1991 is the sum of (I) 67 percent of the local payment amount for the item or device computed under subparagraph (C)(i)(I) for 1991, and (II) 33 percent of the national limited payment amount for the item or device computed under subparagraph (C)(ii) for 1991;

452

(iii) in 1992 is the sum of (I) 33 percent of the local payment amount for the item or device computed under subparagraph (C)(i)(II) for 1992, and (II) 67 percent of the national limited payment amount for the item or device computed under subparagraph (C)(ii) for 1992; and

(iv) in 1993 and each subsequent year is the national limited payment amount for the item or device computed under subparagraph (C)(ii) for that year (reduced by 10 percent, in the case of a blood glucose testing strip furnished after 1997 for an individual with diabetes).

(C) Computation of local payment amount and national limited payment amount.

For purposes of subparagraph (B)—

(i) the local payment amount for an item or device for a year is equal to—

(I) for 1991, the amount specified in subparagraph (B)(i) for 1990 increased by the covered item update for 1991, and

(II) for 1992, 1993, and 1994, the amount determined under this clause for the preceding year increased by the covered item update for the year; and

(ii) the national limited payment amount for an item or device for a year is equal to—

(I) for 1991, the local payment amount determined under clause (i) for such item or device for that year, except that the national limited payment amount may not exceed 100 percent of the weighted average of all local payment amounts determined under such clause for such item for that year and may not be less than 85 percent of the weighted average of all local payment amounts determined under such clause for such item,

(II) for 1992 and 1993, the amount determined under this clause for the preceding year increased by the covered item update for such subsequent year,

(III) for 1994, the local payment amount determined under clause (i) for such item or device for that year, except that the national limited payment amount may not exceed 100 percent of the median of all local payment amounts determined under such clause for such item for that year and may not be less than 85 percent of the median of all local payment amounts determined under such clause for such item or device for that year, and

(IV) for each subsequent year, the amount determined under this clause for the preceding year increased by the covered item update for such subsequent year.

(3) Payment for items requiring frequent and substantial servicing.

(A) In general

Payment for a covered item (such as IPPB machines and ventilators, excluding ventilators that are either continuous airway pressure devices or intermittent assist devices with continuous airway pressure devices) for which there must be frequent and substantial servicing in order to avoid risk to the patient's health shall be made on a monthly basis for the rental of the item and the amount recognized is the amount specified in subparagraph (B).

(B) Payment amount

For purposes of subparagraph (A), the amount specified in this subparagraph, with respect to an item or device furnished in a carrier service area—

(i) in 1989 and in 1990 is the average reasonable charge in the area for the rental of the item or device for the 12-month period ending with June 1987, increased by the percentage increase in the consumer price index for all urban consumers (U.S. city average) for the 6-month period ending with December 1987;

(ii) in 1991 is the sum of (I) 67 percent of the local payment amount for the item or device computed under subparagraph (C)(i)(I) for 1991, and (II) 33 percent of the national limited payment amount for the item or device computed under subparagraph (C)(ii) for 1991;

(iii) in 1992 is the sum of (I) 33 percent of the local payment amount for the item or device computed under subparagraph (C)(i)(II) for 1992, and (II) 67 percent of the national limited payment amount for the item or device computed under subparagraph (C)(ii) for 1992; and

(iv) in 1993 and each subsequent year is the national limited payment amount for the item or device computed under subparagraph (C)(ii) for that year.

(C) Computation of local payment amount and national limited payment amount.

For purposes of subparagraph (B)—

(i) the local payment amount for an item or device for a year is equal to—

(I) for 1991, the amount specified in subparagraph (B)(i) for 1990 increased by the covered item update for 1991, and

(II) for 1992, 1993, and 1994, the amount determined under this clause for the preceding year increased by the covered item update for the year; and

(ii) the national limited payment amount for an item or device for a year is equal to—

(I) for 1991, the local payment amount determined under clause (i) for such item or device for that year, except that the national limited payment amount may not exceed 100 percent of the weighted average of all local payment amounts determined under such clause for such item for that year and may not be less than 85 percent of the weighted average of all local payment amounts determined under such clause for such item,

(II) for 1992 and 1993, the amount determined under this clause for the preceding year increased by the covered item update for such subsequent year,

(III) for 1994, the local payment amount determined under clause (i) for such item or device for that year, except that the national limited payment amount may not exceed 100 percent of the median of all local payment amounts determined under such clause for such item for that year and may not be less than 85 percent of the median of all local payment amounts determined under such clause for such item or device for that year, and

(IV) for each subsequent year, the amount determined under this clause for the preceding year increased by the covered item update for such subsequent year.

(D) Repealed. Pub.L. 103–432, Title I, § 135(e)(5), Oct. 31, 1994, 108 Stat. 4424.

(4) Payment for certain customized items

Payment with respect to a covered item that is uniquely constructed or substantially modified to meet the specific needs of an individual patient, and for that reason cannot be grouped with similar items for purposes of payment under this subchapter, shall be made in a lump-sum amount (A) for the purchase of the item in a payment amount based upon the carrier's individual consideration for that item, and (B) for the reasonable and necessary maintenance and servicing for parts and labor not covered by the supplier's or manufacturer's warranty, when necessary during the period of medical need, and the amount recognized for such maintenance and servicing shall be paid on a lump-sum, as needed basis based upon the carrier's individual consideration for that item.

(5) Payment for oxygen and oxygen equipment

(A) In general

Payment for oxygen and oxygen equipment shall be made on a monthly basis in the monthly payment amount recognized under paragraph (9) for oxygen and oxygen equipment (other than portable oxygen equipment), subject to subparagraphs (B), (C), and (E).

(B) Add-on for portable oxygen equipment

When portable oxygen equipment is used, but subject to subparagraph (D), the payment amount recognized under subparagraph (A) shall be increased by the monthly payment amount recognized under paragraph (9) for portable oxygen equipment.

(C) Volume adjustment

When the attending physician prescribes an oxygen flow rate—

(i) exceeding 4 liters per minute, the payment amount recognized under subparagraph (A), subject to subparagraph (D), shall be increased by 50 percent, or

(ii) of less than 1 liter per minute, the payment amount recognized under subparagraph (A) shall be decreased by 50 percent.

(D) Limit on adjustment

When portable oxygen equipment is used and the attending physician prescribes an oxygen flow rate exceeding 4 liters per minute, there shall only be an increase under either subparagraph (B) or (C), whichever increase is larger, and not under both such subparagraphs.

(E) Recertification for patients receiving home oxygen therapy

In the case of a patient receiving home oxygen therapy services who, at the time such services are initiated, has an initial arterial blood gas value at or above a partial pressure of 56 or an arterial oxygen saturation at or above 89 percent (or such other values, pressures, or criteria as the Secretary may specify) no payment may be made under this part for such services after the expiration of the 90–day period that begins on the date the patient first receives such services unless the patient's attending physician certifies that, on the basis of a follow-up test of the patient's arterial blood gas value or arterial oxygen saturation conducted during the final 30 days of such 90–day period, there is a medical need for the patient to continue to receive such services.

(6) Payment for other covered items (other than durable medical equipment)

Payment for other covered items (other than durable medical equipment and other covered items described in paragraph (3), (4), or (5)) shall be made in a lump-sum amount for the purchase of the item in the amount of the purchase price recognized under paragraph (8).

(7) Payment for other items of durable medical equipment

(A) In general

In the case of an item of durable medical equipment not described in paragraphs (2) through (6)—

(i) payment shall be made on a monthly basis for the rental of such item during the period of medical need (but payments under this clause may not extend over a period of continuous use of longer than 15 months, or, in the case of an item for which a purchase agreement has been entered into under clause (iii), a period of continuous use of longer than 13 months), and, subject to subparagraph (B), the amount recognized for each of the first 3 months of such period is 10 percent of the purchase price recognized under paragraph (8) with respect to the item, and for each of the remaining months of such period is 7.5 percent of such purchase price;

(ii) in the case of a power-driven wheelchair, at the time the supplier furnishes the item, the supplier shall offer the individual patient the option to purchase the item, and payment for such item shall be made on a lump-sum basis if the patient exercises such option;

(iii) during the 10th continuous month during which payment is made for the rental of an item under clause (i), the supplier of such item shall offer the individual patient the option to enter into a purchase agreement under which, if the patient notifies the supplier not later than 1 month after the supplier makes such offer that the patient agrees to accept such offer and exercise such option—

(I) the supplier shall transfer title to the item to the individual patient on the first day that begins after the 13th continuous month during which payment is made for the rental of the item under clause (i),

(II) after the supplier transfers title to the item under subclause (I), maintenance and servicing payments shall be made in accordance with clause (vi);

(iv) in the case of an item for which a purchase agreement has not been entered into under clause (ii) or clause (iii), during the first 6–month period of medical need that follows the period of medical need during which payment is made under clause (i), no payment shall be made for rental or maintenance and servicing of the item;

(v) in the case of an item for which a purchase agreement has not been entered into under clause (ii) or clause (iii), during the first month of each succeeding 6–month period of medical need, a maintenance and servicing payment may be made (for parts and labor not covered by the supplier's or manufacturer's

457

warranty, as determined by the Secretary to be appropriate for the particular type of durable medical equipment) and the amount recognized for each such 6–month period is the lower of (I) a reasonable and necessary maintenance and servicing fee or fees established by the Secretary, or (II) 10 percent of the total of the purchase price recognized under paragraph (8) with respect to the item; and

(vi) in the case of an item for which a purchase agreement has been entered into under clause (ii) or clause (iii), maintenance and servicing payments may be made (for parts and labor not covered by the supplier's or manufacturer's warranty, as determined by the Secretary to be appropriate for the particular type of durable medical equipment), and such payments shall be in an amount established by the Secretary on the basis of reasonable charges in the locality for maintenance and servicing.

The Secretary shall determine the meaning of the term "continuous" in subparagraph (A).

(B) Range for rental amounts

(i) For 1989

For items furnished during 1989, the payment amount recognized under subparagraph (A)(i) shall not be more than 115 percent, and shall not be less than 85 percent, of the prevailing charge established for rental of the item in January 1987, increased by the percentage increase in the consumer price index for all urban consumers (U.S. city average) for the 6–month period ending with December 1987.

(ii) For 1990

For items furnished during 1990, clause (i) shall apply in the same manner as it applies to items furnished during 1989.

(C) Replacement of items

(i) Establishment of reasonable useful lifetime

In accordance with clause (iii), the Secretary shall determine and establish a reasonable useful lifetime for items of durable medical equipment for which payment may be made under this paragraph.

(ii) Payment for replacement items

If the reasonable lifetime of such an item, as so established, has been reached during a continuous period of medical need, or the carrier determines that the item is lost or irreparably damaged, the patient may elect to have payment for an item serving as a replacement for such item made—

(I) on a monthly basis for the rental of the replacement item in accordance with subparagraph (A); or

(II) in the case of an item for which a purchase agreement has been entered into under subparagraph (A)(ii) or (A)(iii), in a lump-sum amount for the purchase of the item.

(iii) Length of reasonable useful lifetime

The reasonable useful lifetime of an item of durable medical equipment under this subparagraph shall be equal to 5 years, except that, if the Secretary determines that, on the basis of prior experience in making payments for such an item under this subchapter, a reasonable useful lifetime of 5 years is not appropriate with respect to a particular item, the Secretary shall establish an alternative reasonable lifetime for such item.

(8) Purchase price recognized for miscellaneous devices and items

For purposes of paragraphs (6) and (7), the amount that is recognized under this paragraph as the purchase price for a covered item is the amount described in subparagraph (C) of this paragraph, determined as follows:

(A) Computation of local purchase price.

Each carrier under section 1395u of this title shall compute a base local purchase price for the item as follows:

(i) The carrier shall compute a base local purchase price, for each item described—

(I) in paragraph (6) equal to the average reasonable charge in the locality for the purchase of the item for the 12–month period ending with June 1987, or

(II) in paragraph (7) equal to the average of the purchase prices on the claims submitted on an assignment-related basis for the unused item supplied during the 6–month period ending with December 1986.

(ii) The carrier shall compute a local purchase price, with respect to the furnishing of each particular item—

(I) in 1989 and 1990, equal to the base local purchase price computed under clause (i) increased by the percentage increase in the consumer price index for all urban consumers (U.S. city average) for the 6–month period ending with December 1987,

(II) in 1991, equal to the local purchase price computed under this clause for the previous year, increased by the covered item update for 1991, and decreased by the percentage by which the average of the reasonable charges for claims paid for all items described in paragraph (7) is lower than the average of the purchase prices submitted for such items during the final 9 months of 1988; or

(III) in 1992, 1993, and 1994, equal to the local purchase price computed under this clause for the previous year increased by the covered item update for the year.

(B) Computation of national limited purchase price

With respect to the furnishing of a particular item in a year, the Secretary shall compute a national limited purchase price—

(i) for 1991, equal to the local purchase price computed under subparagraph (A)(ii) for the item for the year, except that such national limited purchase price may not exceed 100 percent of the weighted average of all local purchase prices for the item computed under such subparagraph for the year, and may not be less than 85 percent of the weighted average of all local purchase prices for the item computed under such subparagraph for the year;

(ii) for 1992 and 1993, the amount determined under this subparagraph for the preceding year increased by the covered item update for such subsequent year;

(iii) for 1994, the local purchase price computed under subparagraph (A)(ii) for the item for the year, except that such national limited purchase price may not exceed 100 percent of the median of all local purchase prices computed for the item under such subparagraph for the year and may not be less than 85 percent of the median of all local purchase prices computed under such subparagraph for the item for the year; and

(iv) for each subsequent year, equal to the amount determined under this subparagraph for the preceding year increased by the covered item update for such subsequent year.

(C) Purchase price recognized

For purposes of paragraphs (6) and (7), the amount that is recognized under this paragraph as the purchase price for each item furnished—

(i) in 1989 or 1990, is 100 percent of the local purchase price computed under subparagraph (A)(ii)(I);

(ii) in 1991, is the sum of (I) 67 percent of the local purchase price computed under subparagraph (A)(ii)(II) for 1991, and (II) 33 percent of the national limited purchase price computed under subparagraph (B) for 1991;

(iii) in 1992, is the sum of (I) 33 percent of the local purchase price computed under subparagraph (A)(ii)(III) for 1992, and (II) 67 percent of the national limited purchase price computed under subparagraph (B) for 1992; and

(iv) in 1993 or a subsequent year, is the national limited purchase price computed under subparagraph (B) for that year.

(9) Monthly payment amount recognized with respect to oxygen and oxygen equipment.

For purposes of paragraph (5), the amount that is recognized under this paragraph for payment for oxygen and oxygen equipment is the monthly payment amount described in subparagraph (C) of this paragraph. Such amount shall be computed separately (i) for all items of oxygen and oxygen equipment (other than portable oxygen equipment) and (ii) for portable oxygen equipment (each such group referred to in this paragraph as an "item").

(A) Computation of local monthly payment rate

Each carrier under this section shall compute a base local payment rate for each item as follows:

(i) The carrier shall compute a base local average monthly payment rate per beneficiary as an amount equal to (I) the total reasonable charges for the item during the 12–month period ending with December 1986, divided by (II) the total number of months for all beneficiaries receiving the item in the area during the 12–month period for which the carrier made payment for the item under this subchapter.

(ii) The carrier shall compute a local average monthly payment rate for the item applicable—

(I) to 1989 and 1990, equal to 95 percent of the base local average monthly payment rate computed under clause (i) for the item increased by the percentage increase in the consumer price index for all urban consumers (U.S. city average) for the 6–month period ending with December 1987, or

(II) to 1991, 1992, 1993, and 1994, equal to the local average monthly payment rate computed under this clause for the item for the previous year increased by the covered item increase for the year.

(B) Computation of national limited monthly payment rate

With respect to the furnishing of an item in a year, the Secretary shall compute a national limited monthly payment rate equal to—

(i) for 1991, the local monthly payment rate computed under subparagraph (A)(ii)(II) for the item for the year, except that such national limited monthly payment rate may not exceed 100 percent of the weighted average of all local monthly payment rates computed for the item under such subparagraph for the year, and may not be less than 85 percent of the weighted average of all local monthly payment rates computed for the item under such subparagraph for the year;

461

(ii) for 1992 and 1993, the amount determined under this subparagraph for the preceding year increased by the covered item update for such subsequent year;

(iii) for 1994, the local monthly payment rate computed under subparagraph (A)(ii) for the item for the year, except that such national limited monthly payment rate may not exceed 100 percent of the median of all local monthly payment rates computed for the item under such subparagraph for the year and may not be less than 85 percent of the median of all local monthly payment rates computed for the item under such subparagraph for the year;

(iv) for 1995, 1996, and 1997, equal to the amount determined under this subparagraph for the preceding year increased by the covered item update for such subsequent year;

(v) for 1998, 75 percent of the amount determined under this subparagraph for 1997; and

(vi) for 1999 and each subsequent year, 70 percent of the amount determined under this subparagraph for 1997.

(C) Monthly payment amount recognized

For purposes of paragraph (5), the amount that is recognized under this paragraph as the base monthly payment amount for each item furnished—

(i) in 1989 and in 1990, is 100 percent of the local average monthly payment rate computed under subparagraph (A)(ii) for the item;

(ii) in 1991, is the sum of (I) 67 percent of the local average monthly payment rate computed under subparagraph (A)(ii)(II) for the item for 1991, and (II) 33 percent of the national limited monthly payment rate computed under subparagraph (B)(i) for the item for 1991;

(iii) in 1992, is the sum of (I) 33 percent of the local average monthly payment rate computed under subparagraph (A)(ii)(II) for the item for 1992, and (II) 67 percent of the national limited monthly payment rate computed under subparagraph (B)(ii) for the item for 1992; and

(iv) in a subsequent year, is the national limited monthly payment rate computed under subparagraph (B) for the item for that year.

(D) Authority to create classes

(i) In general

Subject to clause (ii), the secretary may establish separate classes for any item of oxygen and oxygen equipment and sepa-

462

rate national limited monthly payment rates for each of such classes.

(ii) Budget neutrality

the secretary may take actions under clause (i) only to the extent such actions do not result in expenditures for any year to be more or less than the expenditures which would have been made if such actions had not been taken.

(10) Exceptions and adjustments

(A) Areas outside continental United States

Exceptions to the amounts recognized under the previous provisions of this subsection shall be made to take into account the unique circumstances of covered items furnished in Alaska, Hawaii, or Puerto Rico.

(B) Adjustment for inherent reasonableness

The Secretary is authorized to apply the provisions of paragraphs (8) and (9) of section 1395u(b) of this title to covered items and suppliers of such items and payments under this subsection.

(C) Transcutaneous electrical nerve stimulator (TENS)

In order to permit an attending physician time to determine whether the purchase of a transcutaneous electrical nerve stimulator is medically appropriate for a particular patient, the Secretary may determine an appropriate payment amount for the initial rental of such item for a period of not more than 2 months. If such item is subsequently purchased, the payment amount with respect to such purchase is the payment amount determined under paragraph (2).

(11) Improper billing and requirement of physician order

(A) Improper billing for certain rental items

Notwithstanding any other provision of this subchapter, a supplier of a covered item for which payment is made under this subsection and which is furnished on a rental basis shall continue to supply the item without charge (other than a charge provided under this subsection for the maintenance and servicing of the item) after rental payments may no longer be made under this subsection. If a supplier knowingly and willfully violates the previous sentence, the Secretary may apply sanctions against the supplier under section 1395u(j)(2) of this title in the same manner such sanctions may apply with respect to a physician.

(B) Requirement of physician order

The Secretary is authorized to require, for specified covered items, that payment may be made under this subsection with respect to the item only if a physician has communicated to the supplier, before delivery of the item, a written order for the item.

(12) Regional carriers

The Secretary may designate, by regulation under section 1395u of this title, one carrier for one or more entire regions to process all claims within the region for covered items under this section.

(13) "Covered item" defined

In this subsection, the term "covered item" means durable medical equipment (as defined in section 1395x(n) of this title, but not including implantable items for which payment may be made under section 1395l(t) of this title), including such equipment described in section 1395x(m)(5) of this title.

(14) Covered item update

In this subsection, the term "covered item update" means, with respect to a year—

(A) for 1991 and 1992, the percentage increase in the consumer price index for all urban consumers (U.S. city average) for the 12–month period ending with June of the previous year reduced by 1 percentage point;

(B) for 1993, 1994, 1995, 1996, and 1997, the percentage increase in the consumer price index for all urban consumers (U.S. city average) for the 12–month period ending with June of the previous year;

(C) for each of the years 1998 through 2000, 0 percentage points;

(D) for 2001, the percentage increase in the consumer price index for all urban consumers (U.S. city average) for the 12–month period ending with June 2000;

(E) for 2002, 0 percentage points; and

(F) for a subsequent year, the percentage increase in the consumer price index for all urban consumers (U.S. urban average) for the 12–month period ending with June of the previous year.

(15) Advance determinations of coverage for certain items

(A) Development of lists of items by Secretary

The Secretary may develop and periodically update a list of items for which payment may be made under this subsection that the Secretary determines, on the basis of prior payment experience, are frequently subject to unnecessary utilization throughout a carrier's entire service area or a portion of such area.

(B) Development of lists of suppliers by Secretary

The Secretary may develop and periodically update a list of suppliers of items for which payment may be made under this subsection with respect to whom—

(i) the Secretary has found that a substantial number of claims for payment under this part for items furnished by the supplier have been denied on the basis of the application of section 1395y(a)(1) of this title; or

(ii) the Secretary has identified a pattern of overutilization resulting from the business practice of the supplier.

(C) Determinations of coverage in advance

A carrier shall determine in advance of delivery of an item whether payment for the item may not be made because the item is not covered or because of the application of section 1395y(a)(1) of this title if—

(i) the item is included on the list developed by the Secretary under subparagraph (A);

(ii) the item is furnished by a supplier included on the list developed by the Secretary under subparagraph (B); or

(iii) the item is a customized item (other than inexpensive items specified by the Secretary) and the patient to whom the item is to be furnished or the supplier requests that such advance determination be made.

(16) Disclosure of information and surety bond

The Secretary shall not provide for the issuance (or renewal) of a provider number for a supplier of durable medical equipment, for purposes of payment under this part for durable medical equipment furnished by the supplier, unless the supplier provides the Secretary on a continuing basis. The Secretary, at the Secretary's discretion, may impose the requirements of the first sentence with respect to some or all providers of items or services under part A of this subchapter or some or all suppliers or other persons (other than physicians or other practitioners, as defined in section 1395u(b)(18)(C) of this title) who furnish items or services under this part.

(A) with—

(i) full and complete information as to the identity of each person with an ownership or control interest (as defined in section 1320a–3(a)(3) of this title) in the supplier or in any subcontractor (as defined by the Secretary in regulations) in which the supplier directly or indirectly has a 5 percent or more ownership interest; and

(ii) to the extent determined to be feasible under regulations of the Secretary, the name of any disclosing entity (as defined in section 1320(a)(2) of this title) with respect to which a person with such an ownership or control interest in the supplier is a person with such an ownership or control interest in the disclosing entity; and

465

(B) with a surety bond in a form specified by the Secretary and in an amount that is not less than $50,000.

The Secretary may waive the requirement of a bond under subparagraph (B) in the case of a supplier that provides a comparable surety bond under State law.

(17) Prohibition against unsolicited telephone contacts by suppliers

(A) In general

A supplier of a covered item under this subsection may not contact an individual enrolled under this part by telephone regarding the furnishing of a covered item to the individual unless 1 of the following applies:

(i) The individual has given written permission to the supplier to make contact by telephone regarding the furnishing of a covered item.

(ii) The supplier has furnished a covered item to the individual and the supplier is contacting the individual only regarding the furnishing of such covered item.

(iii) If the contact is regarding the furnishing of a covered item other than a covered item already furnished to the individual, the supplier has furnished at least 1 covered item to the individual during the 15–month period preceding the date on which the supplier makes such contact.

(B) Prohibiting payment for items furnished subsequent to unsolicited contacts

If a supplier knowingly contacts an individual in violation of subparagraph (A), no payment may be made under this part for any item subsequently furnished to the individual by the supplier.

(C) Exclusion from program for suppliers engaging in pattern of unsolicited contacts

If a supplier knowingly contacts individuals in violation of subparagraph (A) to such an extent that the supplier's conduct establishes a pattern of contacts in violation of such subparagraph, the Secretary shall exclude the supplier from participation in the programs under this chapter, in accordance with the procedures set forth in subsections (c), (f), and (g) of section 1320a–7 of this title.

(18) Certain upgraded items

(A) Individual's right to choose upgraded item

Notwithstanding any other provision of this title, the Secretary may issue regulations under which an individual may purchase or rent from a supplier an item of upgraded durable medical equipment for which payment would be made under this subsection if the item were a standard item.

(B) Payments to supplier

In the case of the purchase or rental of an upgraded item under subparagraph (A)—

(i) the supplier shall receive payment under this subsection with respect to such item as if such item were a standard item; and

(ii) the individual purchasing or renting the item shall pay the supplier an amount equal to the difference between the supplier's charge and the amount under clause (i).

In no event may the supplier's charge for an upgraded item exceed the applicable fee schedule amount (if any) for such item.

(C) Consumer protection safeguards

Any regulations under subparagraph (A) shall provide for consumer protection standards with respect to the furnishing of upgraded equipment under subparagraph (A). Such regulations shall provide for—

(i) determination of fair market prices with respect to an upgraded item;

(ii) full disclosure of the availability and price of standard items and proof of receipt of such disclosure information by the beneficiary before the furnishing of the upgraded item;

(iii) conditions of participation for suppliers in the billing arrangement;

(iv) sanctions of suppliers who are determined to engage in coercive or abusive practices, including exclusion; and

(v) such other safeguards as the Secretary determines are necessary.

(19) Refund of amounts collected for certain disallowed items

(A) In general

If a nonparticipating supplier furnishes to an individual enrolled under this part a covered item for which no payment may be made under this part by reason of paragraph (17)(B), the supplier shall refund on a timely basis to the patient (and shall be liable to the patient for) any amounts collected from the patient for the item, unless—

(i) the supplier establishes that the supplier did not know and could not reasonably have been expected to know that payment may not be made for the item by reason of paragraph (17)(B), or

(ii) before the item was furnished, the patient was informed that payment under this part may not be made for that item and the patient has agreed to pay for that item.

(B) Sanctions

If a supplier knowingly and willfully fails to make refunds in violation of subparagraph (A), the Secretary may apply sanctions against the supplier in accordance with section 1395u(j)(2) of this title.

(C) Notice

Each carrier with a contract in effect under this part with respect to suppliers of covered items shall send any notice of denial of payment for covered items by reason of paragraph (17)(B) and for which payment is not requested on an assignment-related basis to the supplier and the patient involved.

(D) Timely basis defined

A refund under subparagraph (A) is considered to be on a timely basis only if—

(i) in the case of a supplier who does not request reconsideration or seek appeal on a timely basis, the refund is made within 30 days after the date the supplier receives a denial notice under subparagraph (C), or

(ii) in the case in which such a reconsideration or appeal is taken, the refund is made within 15 days after the date the supplier receives notice of an adverse determination on reconsideration or appeal.

(b) Fee schedules for radiologist services

(1) Development

The Secretary shall develop—

(A) a relative value scale to serve as the basis for the payment for radiologist services under this part, and

(B) using such scale and appropriate conversion factors and subject to subsection (c)(1)(A) of this section, fee schedules (on a regional, statewide, locality, or carrier service area basis) for payment for radiologist services under this part, to be implemented for such services furnished during 1989.

(2) Consultation

In carrying out paragraph (1), the Secretary shall regularly consult closely with the Physician Payment Review Commission, the American College of Radiology, and other organizations representing physicians or suppliers who furnish radiologist services and shall share with them the data and data analysis being used to make the determinations under paragraph (1), including data on variations in current medicare payments by geographic area, and by service and physician specialty.

(3) Considerations

In developing the relative value scale and fee schedules under paragraph (1), the Secretary—

(A) shall take into consideration variations in the cost of furnishing such services among geographic areas and among different sites where services are furnished, and

(B) may also take into consideration such other factors respecting the manner in which physicians in different specialties furnish such services as may be appropriate to assure that payment amounts are equitable and designed to promote effective and efficient provision of radiologist services by physicians in the different specialties.

(4) Savings

(A) Budget neutral fee schedules

The Secretary shall develop preliminary fee schedules for 1989, which are designed to result in the same amount of aggregate payments (net of any coinsurance and deductibles under sections 1395l(a)(1)(J) and 1395l(b) of this title) for radiologist services furnished in 1989 as would have been made if this subsection had not been enacted.

(B) Initial savings

The fee schedules established for payment purposes under this subsection for services furnished in 1989 shall be 97 percent of the amounts permitted under the preliminary fee schedules developed under subparagraph (A).

(C) 1990 fee schedules

For radiologist services (other than portable X-ray services) furnished under this part during 1990, after March 31 of such year, the conversion factors used under this subsection shall be 96 percent of the conversion factors that applied under this subsection as of December 31, 1989.

(D) 1991 fee schedules

For radiologist services (other than portable X-ray services) furnished under this part during 1991, the conversion factors used in a locality under this subsection shall, subject to clause (vii), be reduced to the adjusted conversion factor for the locality determined as follows:

(i) National weighted average conversion factor

The Secretary shall estimate the national weighted average of the conversion factors used under this subsection for services furnished during 1990 beginning on April 1, using the best available data.

(ii) Reduced national weighted average

The national weighted average estimated under clause (i) shall be reduced by 13 percent.

(iii) Computation of 1990 locality index relative to national average

The Secretary shall establish an index which reflects, for each locality, the ratio of the conversion factor used in the locality under this subsection to the national weighted average estimated under clause (i).

(iv) Adjusted conversion factor

The adjusted conversion factor for the professional or technical component of a service in a locality is the sum of 1/2 of the locally-adjusted amount determined under clause (v) and 1/2 of the GPCI-adjusted amount determined under clauses (vi).

(v) Locally-adjusted amount

For purposes of clause (iv), the locally adjusted amount determined under this clause is the product of (I) the national weighted average conversion factor computed under clause (ii), and (II) the index value established under clause (iii) for the locality.

(vi) GPCI-adjusted amount

For purposes of clause (iv), the GPCI-adjusted amount determined under this clause is the sum of—

(I) the product of (a) the portion of the reduced national weighted average conversion factor computed under clause (ii) which is attributable to physician work and (b) the geographic work index value for the locality (specified in Addendum C to the Model Fee Schedule for Physician Services (published on September 4, 1990, 55 Federal Register pp. 36238–36243)); and

(II) the product of (a) the remaining portion of the reduced national weighted average conversion factor computed under clause (ii), and (b) the geographic practice cost index value specified in section 1395u(b)(14)(C)(iv) of this title for the locality.

In applying this clause with respect to the professional component of a service, 80 percent of the conversion factor shall be considered to be attributable to physician work and with respect to the technical component of the service, 0 percent shall be considered to be attributable to physician work.

(vii) Limits on conversion factor

The conversion factor to be applied to a locality to the professional or technical component of a service shall not be reduced under this subparagraph by more than 9.5 percent below the conversion factor applied in the locality under subparagraph (C) to such component, but in no case shall the conversion factor be less than 60 percent of the national weighted average of the conversion factors (computed under clause (i)).

(E) Rule for certain scanning services

In the case of the technical components of magnetic resonance imaging (MRI) services and computer assisted tomography (CAT) services furnished after December 31, 1990, the amount otherwise payable shall be reduced by 10 percent.

(F) Subsequent updating

For radiologist services furnished in subsequent years, the fee schedules shall be the schedules for the previous year updated by the percentage increase in the MEI (as defined in section 1395u(i)(3) of this title) for the year.

(G) Nonparticipating physicians and suppliers

Each fee schedule so established shall provide that the payment rate recognized for nonparticipating physicians and suppliers is equal to the appropriate percent (as defined in section 1395u(b)(4)(A)(iv) of this title) of the payment rate recognized for participating physicians and suppliers.

(5) Limiting charges of nonparticipating physicians and suppliers

(A) In general

In the case of radiologist services furnished after January 1, 1989, for which payment is made under a fee schedule under this subsection, if a nonparticipating physician or supplier furnishes the service to an individual entitled to benefits under this part, the physician or supplier may not charge the individual more than the limiting charge (as defined in subparagraph (B)).

(B) "Limiting charge" defined

In subparagraph (A), the term "limiting charge" means, with respect to a service furnished—

(i) in 1989, 125 percent of the amount specified for the service in the appropriate fee schedule established under paragraph (1),

(ii) in 1990, 120 percent of the amount specified for the service in the appropriate fee schedule established under paragraph (1), and

(iii) after 1990, 115 percent of the amount specified for the service in the appropriate fee schedule established under paragraph (1).

(C) Enforcement

If a physician or supplier knowingly and willfully bills in violation of subparagraph (A), the Secretary may apply sanctions against such physician or supplier in accordance with section 1395u(j)(2) of this title in the same manner as such sanctions may apply to a physician.

(6) "Radiologist services" defined

For the purposes of this subsection and section 1395l(a)(1)(J) of this title, the term "radiologist services" only includes radiology services performed by, or under the direction or supervision of, a physician—

(A) who is certified, or eligible to be certified, by the American Board of Radiology, or

(B) for whom radiology services account for at least 50 percent of the total amount of charges made under this part.

(c) Payments and standards for screening mammography

(1) In general

Notwithstanding any other provision of this part, with respect to expenses incurred for screening mammography (as defined in section 1395x(jj) of this title)—

(A) payment may be made only for screening mammography conducted consistent with the frequency permitted under paragraph (2);

(B) payment may be made only if the screening mammography is conducted by a facility that has a certificate (or provisional certificate) issued under section 263b of this title; and

(C) the amount of the payment under this part shall be equal to 80 percent of the least of—

(i) the actual charge for the screening,

(ii) the fee schedule established under subsection (b) of this section or the fee schedule established under section 1395w–4 of this title, whichever is applicable, with respect to both the professional and technical components of the screening mammography, or

(iii) the limit established under paragraph (3) for the screening mammography.

(2) Frequency covered

(A) In general

Subject to revision by the Secretary under subparagraph (B)—

(i) No payment may be made under this part for screening mammography performed on a woman under 35 years of age.

472

(ii) Payment may be made under this part for only 1 screening mammography performed on a woman over 34 years of age, but under 40 years of age.

(iii) In the case of a woman over 39 years of age, payment may not be made under this part for screening mammography performed within 11 months following the month in which a previous screening mammography was performed.

(iv), (v) Repealed. Pub.L. 105–33, Title IV, § 4101(a), Aug. 5, 1997, 111 Stat. 360

(B) Revision of frequency

(i) Review

The Secretary, in consultation with the Director of the National Cancer Institute, shall review periodically the appropriate frequency for performing screening mammography, based on age and such other factors as the Secretary believes to be pertinent.

(ii) Revision of frequency

The Secretary, taking into consideration the review made under clause (i), may revise from time to time the frequency with which screening mammography may be paid for under this subsection, but no such revision shall apply to screening mammography performed before January 1, 1992.

(3) Limit

(A) $55, indexed

Except as provided by the Secretary under subparagraph (B), the limit established under this paragraph—

(i) for screening mammography performed in 1991, is $55, and

(ii) for screening mammography performed in a subsequent year is the limit established under this paragraph for the preceding year increased by the percentage increase in the MEI for that subsequent year.

(B) Reduction of limit

The Secretary shall review from time to time the appropriateness of the amount of the limit established under this paragraph. The Secretary may, with respect to screening mammography performed in a year after 1992, reduce the amount of such limit as it applies nationally or in any area to the amount that the Secretary estimates is required to assure that screening mammography of an appropriate quality is readily and conveniently available during the year.

(C) Application of limit in hospital outpatient setting

The Secretary shall provide for an appropriate allocation of the limit established under this paragraph between professional and technical components in the case of hospital outpatient screening mammography (and comparable situations) where there is a claim for professional services separate from the claim for the radiologic procedure.

(4) Limiting charges of nonparticipating physicians

(A) In general

In the case of mammography screening performed on or after January 1, 1991, for which payment is made under this subsection, if a nonparticipating physician or supplier provides the screening to an individual entitled to benefits under this part, the physician or supplier may not charge the individual more than the limiting charge (as defined in subparagraph (B), or if less, as defined in subsection (b)(5)(B) of this section or as defined in section 1395w–4(g)(2) of this title).

(B) Limiting charge defined

In subparagraph (A), the term "limiting charge" means, with respect to screening mammography performed—

(i) in 1991, 125 percent of the limit established under paragraph (4),

(ii) in 1992, 120 percent of the limit established under paragraph (4), or

(iii) after 1992, 115 percent of the limit established under paragraph (4).

(C) Enforcement

If a physician or supplier knowing and willfully imposes a charge in violation of subparagraph (A), the Secretary may apply sanctions against such physician or supplier in accordance with section 1395u(j)(2) of this title.

(5) Redesignated (4)

(d) Frequency limits and payment for colorectal cancer screening tests

(1) Screening fecal-occult blood tests

(A) Payment amount

The payment amount for colorectal cancer screening tests consisting of screening fecal-occult blood tests is equal to the payment amount established for diagnostic fecal-occult blood tests under section 1395l(h) of this title.

(B) Frequency limit

No payment may be made under this part for a colorectal cancer screening test consisting of a screening fecal-occult blood test—

(i) if the individual is under 50 years of age; or

(ii) if the test is performed within the 11 months after a previous screening fecal-occult blood test.

(2) Screening flexible sigmoidoscopies

(A) Fee schedule

With respect to colorectal cancer screening tests consisting of screening flexible sigmoidoscopies, payment under section 1395w–4 of this title shall be consistent with payment under such section for similar or related services.

(B) Payment limit

In the case of screening flexible sigmoidoscopy services, payment under this part shall not exceed such amount as the Secretary specifies, based upon the rates recognized for diagnostic flexible sigmoidoscopy services.

(C) Facility payment limit

(i) In general

Notwithstanding subsections (i)(2)(A) and (t) of section 1395l of this title, in the case of screening flexible sigmoidoscopy services furnished on or after January 1, 1999, that—

(I) in accordance with regulations, may be performed in an ambulatory surgical center and for which the Secretary permits ambulatory surgical center payments under this part, and

(II) are performed in an ambulatory surgical center or hospital outpatient department,

payment under this part shall be based on the lesser of the amount under the fee schedule that would apply to such services if they were performed in a hospital outpatient department in an area or the amount under the fee schedule that would apply to such services if they were performed in an ambulatory surgical center in the same area.

(ii) Limitation on deductible and coinsurance

Notwithstanding any other provision of this title, in the case of a beneficiary who receives the services described in clause (i)—

(I) in computing the amount of any applicable deductible or copayment, the computation of such deductible or coinsurance shall be based upon the fee schedule under which payment is made for the services, and

(II) the amount of such coinsurance is equal to 25 percent of the payment amount under the fee schedule described in subclause (I).

(D) Special rule for detected lesions

If during the course of such screening flexible sigmoidoscopy, a lesion or growth is detected which results in a biopsy or removal of the lesion or growth, payment under this part shall not be made for the screening flexible sigmoidoscopy but shall be made for the procedure classified as a flexible sigmoidoscopy with such biopsy or removal.

(E) Frequency limit

No payment may be made under this part for a colorectal cancer screening test consisting of a screening flexible sigmoidoscopy—

   (i) if the individual is under 50 years of age; or

   (ii) if the procedure is performed within the 47 months after a previous screening flexible sigmoidoscopy.

(3) Screening colonoscopy for individuals at high risk for colorectal cancer

(A) Fee schedule

With respect to colorectal cancer screening test consisting of a screening colonoscopy for individuals at high risk for colorectal cancer (as defined in section 1395x(pp)(2) of this title), payment under section 1395w–4 of this title shall be consistent with payment amounts under such section for similar or related services.

(B) Payment limit

In the case of screening colonoscopy services, payment under this part shall not exceed such amount as the Secretary specifies, based upon the rates recognized for diagnostic colonoscopy services.

(C) Facility payment limit

   (i) In general

   Notwithstanding subsections (i)(2)(A) and (t) of section 1395l, in the case of screening colonoscopy services furnished on or after January 1, 1999, that are performed in an ambulatory surgical center or a hospital outpatient department, payment under this part shall be based on the lesser of the amount under the fee schedule that would apply to such services if they were performed in a hospital outpatient department in an area or the amount under the fee schedule that would apply to such services if they were performed in an ambulatory surgical center in the same area.

   (ii) Limitation on deductible and coinsurance

   Notwithstanding any other provision of this title, in the case of a beneficiary who receives the services described in clause (i)—

      (I) in computing the amount of any applicable deductible or coinsurance, the computation of such deductible or

476

coinsurance shall be based upon the fee schedule under which payment is made for the services, and

(II) the amount of such coinsurance is equal to 25 percent of the payment amount under the fee schedule described in subclause (I).

(D) Special rule for detected lesions

If during the course of such screening colonoscopy, a lesion or growth is detected which results in a biopsy or removal of the lesion or growth, payment under this part shall not be made for the screening colonoscopy but shall be made for the procedure classified as a colonoscopy with such biopsy or removal.

(E) Frequency limit

No payment may be made under this part for a colorectal cancer screening test consisting of a screening colonoscopy for individuals at high risk for colorectal cancer if the procedure is performed within the 23 months after a previous screening colonoscopy.

(e) Repealed. Pub.L. 101–234, Title II, § 201(a)(1), Dec. 13, 1989, 103 Stat. 1981

(f) Reduction in payments for physician pathology services during 1991

(1) In general

For physician pathology services furnished under this part during 1991, the prevailing charges used in a locality under this part shall be 7 percent below the prevailing charges used in the locality under this part in 1990 after March 31.

(2) Limitation

The prevailing charge for the technical and professional components of an physician pathology service furnished by a physician through an independent laboratory shall not be reduced pursuant to paragraph (1) to the extent that such reduction would reduce such prevailing charge below 115 percent of the prevailing charge for the professional component of such service when furnished by a hospital-based physician in the same locality. For purposes of the preceding sentence, an independent laboratory is a laboratory that is independent of a hospital and separate from the attending or consulting physicians' office.

(g) Payment for outpatient critical access hospital services

(1) In general

The amount of payment for outpatient critical access hospital services of a critical access hospital is the reasonable costs of the hospital in providing such services, unless the hospital makes the election under paragraph (2).

(2) Election of cost-based hospital outpatient service payment plus fee schedule for professional services.

A critical access hospital may elect to be paid for outpatient critical access hospital services amounts equal to the sum of the following, less the amount that such hospital may charge as described in section 1395cc(a)(2)(A) of this title:

(A) Facility fee

With respect to facility services, not including any services for which payment may be made under subparagraph (B), the reasonable costs of the critical access hospital in providing such services.

(B) Fee schedule for professional services

With respect to professional services otherwise included within outpatient critical access hospital services, such amounts as would otherwise be paid under this part if such services were not included in outpatient critical access hospital services.

(3) Disregarding charges

The payment amounts under this subsection shall be determined without regard to the amount of the customary or other charge.

(4) No beneficiary cost-sharing for clinical diagnostic laboratory services

No coinsurance, deductible, copayment, or other cost-sharing otherwise applicable under this part shall apply with respect to clinical diagnostic laboratory services furnished as an outpatient critical access hospital service. Nothing in this subchapter shall be construed as providing for payment for clinical diagnostic laboratory services furnished as part of outpatient critical access hospital services, other than on the basis described in this subsection.

(h) Payment for prosthetic devices and orthotics and prosthetics

(1) General rule for payment

(A) In general

Payment under this subsection for prosthetic devices and orthotics and prosthetics shall be made in a lump-sum amount for the purchase of the item in an amount equal to 80 percent of the payment basis described in subparagraph (B).

(B) Payment basis

Except as provided in subparagraphs (C) and (E), the payment basis described in this subparagraph is the lesser of—

(i) the actual charge for the item; or

(ii) the amount recognized under paragraph (2) as the purchase price for the item.

(C) Exception for certain public home health agencies

Subparagraph (B)(i) shall not apply to an item furnished by a public home health agency (or by another home health agency which demonstrates to the satisfaction of the Secretary that a significant portion of its patients are low income) free of charge or at nominal charges to the public.

(D) Exclusive payment rule

This subsection shall constitute the exclusive provision of this subchapter for payment for prosthetic devices, orthotics, and prosthetics under this part or under part A of this subchapter to a home health agency.

(E) Exception for certain items

Payment for ostomy supplies, tracheostomy supplies, and urologicals shall be made in accordance with subparagraphs (B) and (C) of subsection (a)(2) of this section.

(F) Special payment rules for certain prosthetics and custom-fabricated orthotics

(i) In general

No payment shall be made under this subsection for an item of custom-fabricated orthotics described in clause (ii) or for an item of prosthetics unless such item is—

(I) furnished by a qualified practitioner; and

(II) fabricated by a qualified practitioner or a qualified supplier at a facility that meets such criteria as the Secretary determines appropriate.

(ii) Description of custom-fabricated item

(I) In general

An item described in this clause is an item of custom-fabricated orthotics that requires education, training, and experience to custom-fabricate and that is included in a list established by the Secretary in subclause (II). Such an item does not include shoes and shoe inserts.

(II) List of items

The Secretary, in consultation with appropriate experts in orthotics (including national organizations representing manufacturers of orthotics), shall establish and update as appropriate a list of items to which this subparagraph applies. No item may be included in such list unless the item is individually fabricated for the patient over a positive model of the patient.

(iii) Qualified practitioner defined

In this subparagraph, the term "qualified practitioner" means a physician or other individual who—

(I) is a qualified physical therapist or a qualified occupational therapist;

479

(II) in the case of a State that provides for the licensing of orthotics and prosthetics, is licensed in orthotics or prosthetics by the State in which the item is supplied; or

(III) in the case of a State that does not provide for the licensing of orthotics and prosthetics, is specifically trained and educated to provide or manage the provision of prosthetics and custom-designed or-fabricated orthotics, and is certified by the American Board for Certification in Orthotics and Prosthetics, Inc. or by the Board for Orthotist/Prosthetist Certification, or is credentialed and approved by a program that the Secretary determines, in consultation with appropriate experts in orthotics and prosthetics, has training and education standards that are necessary to provide such prosthetics and orthotics.

(iv) Qualified supplier defined

In this subparagraph, the term "qualified supplier" means any entity that is accredited by the American Board for Certification in Orthotics and Prosthetics, Inc. or by the Board for Orthotist/Prosthetist Certification, or accredited and approved by a program that the Secretary determines has accreditation and approval standards that are essentially equivalent to those of such Board.

(G) Replacement of prosthetic devices and parts

(i) In general

Payment shall be made for the replacement of prosthetic devices which are artificial limbs, or for the replacement of any part of such devices, without regard to continuous use or useful lifetime restrictions if an ordering physician determines that the provision of a replacement device, or a replacement part of such a device, is necessary because of any of the following:

(I) A change in the physiological condition of the patient.

(II) An irreparable change in the condition of the device, or in a part of the device.

(III) The condition of the device, or the part of the device, requires repairs and the cost of such repairs would be more than 60 percent of the cost of a replacement device, or, as the case may be, of the part being replaced.

(ii) Confirmation may be required if device or part being replaced is less than 3 years old.

If a physician determines that a replacement device, or a replacement part, is necessary pursuant to clause (i)—

(I) such determination shall be controlling; and

(II) such replacement device or part shall be deemed to be reasonable and necessary for purposes of section 1395y(a)(1)(A) of this title; except that if the device, or part, being replaced is less than 3 years old (calculated from the date on which the beneficiary began to use the device or part), the Secretary may also require confirmation of necessity of the replacement device or replacement part, as the case may be.

(2) Purchase price recognized

For purposes of paragraph (1), the amount that is recognized under this paragraph as the purchase price for prosthetic devices, orthotics, and prosthetics is the amount described in subparagraph (C) of this paragraph, determined as follows:

(A) Computation of local purchase price

Each carrier under section 1395u of this title shall compute a base local purchase price for the item as follows:

(i) The carrier shall compute a base local purchase price for each item equal to the average reasonable charge in the locality for the purchase of the item for the 12–month period ending with June 1987.

(ii) The carrier shall compute a local purchase price, with respect to the furnishing of each particular item—

(I) in 1989 and 1990, equal to the base local purchase price computed under clause (i) increased by the percentage increase in the consumer price index for all urban consumers (United States city average) for the 6–month period ending with December 1987, or

(II) in 1991, 1992 or 1993, equal to the local purchase price computed under this clause for the previous year increased by the applicable percentage increase for the year.

(B) Computation of regional purchase price

With respect to the furnishing of a particular item in each region (as defined by the Secretary), the Secretary shall compute a regional purchase price—

(i) for 1992, equal to the average (weighted by relative volume of all claims among carriers) of the local purchase prices for the carriers in the region computed under subparagraph (A)(ii)(II) for the year, and

481

(ii) for each subsequent year, equal to the regional purchase price computed under this subparagraph for the previous year increased by the applicable percentage increase for the year.

(C) Purchase price recognized

For purposes of paragraph (1) and subject to subparagraph (D), the amount that is recognized under this paragraph as the purchase price for each item furnished—

(i) in 1989, 1990, or 1991, is 100 percent of the local purchase price computed under subparagraph (A)(ii);

(ii) in 1992, is the sum of (I) 75 percent of the local purchase price computed under subparagraph (A)(ii)(II) for 1992, and (II) 25 percent of the regional purchase price computed under subparagraph (B) for 1992;

(iii) in 1993, is the sum of (I) 50 percent of the local purchase price computed under subparagraph (A)(ii)(II) for 1993, and (II) 50 percent of the regional purchase price computed under subparagraph (B) for 1993; and

(iv) in 1994 or a subsequent year, is the regional purchase price computed under subparagraph (B) for that year.

(D) Range on amount recognized

The amount that is recognized under subparagraph (C) as the purchase price for an item furnished—

(i) in 1992, may not exceed 125 percent, and may not be lower than 85 percent, of the average of the purchase prices recognized under such subparagraph for all the carrier service areas in the United States in that year; and

(ii) in a subsequent year, may not exceed 120 percent, and may not be lower than 90 percent, of the average of the purchase prices recognized under such subparagraph for all the carrier service areas in the United States in that year.

(3) Applicability of certain provisions relating to durable medical equipment

Paragraphs (12), (15), and (17) and subparagraphs (A) and (B) of paragraph (10) and paragraph (11) of subsection (a) of this section shall apply to prosthetic devices, orthotics, and prosthetics in the same manner as such provisions apply to covered items under such subsection.

(4) Definitions

In this subsection—

(A) the term "applicable percentage increase" means—

(i) for 1991, 0 percent;

(ii) for 1992 and 1993, the percentage increase in the consumer price index for all urban consumers (United States city average) for the 12–month period ending with June of the previous year;

(iii) for 1994 and 1995, 0 percent;

(iv) for 1996 and 1997, the percentage increase in the consumer price index for all urban consumers (United States city average) for the 12–month period ending with June of the previous year;

(v) for each of the years 1998 through 2000, 1 percent;

(vi) for 2001, the percentage increase in the consumer price index for all urban consumers (U.S. city average) for the 12–month period ending with June 2000;

(vii) for 2002, 1 percent; and

(viii) for a subsequent year, the percentage increase in the consumer price index for all urban consumers (United States city average) for the 12–month period ending with June of the previous year;

(B) the term "prosthetic devices" has the meaning given such term in section 1395x(s)(8) of this title, except that such term does not include parenteral and enteral nutrition nutrients, supplies, and equipment and does not include an implantable item for which payment may be made under section 1395(t)of this title; and

(C) the term "orthotics and prosthetics" has the meaning given such term in section 1395x(s)(9) of this title, but does not include intraocular lenses or medical supplies (including catheters, catheter supplies, ostomy bags, and supplies related to ostomy care) furnished by a home health agency under section 1395x(m)(5) of this title.

(i) Payment for surgical dressings

(1) In general

. Payment under this subsection for surgical dressings (described in section 1395x(s)(5) of this title) shall be made in a lump sum amount for the purchase of the item in an amount equal to 80 percent of the lesser of—

(A) the actual charge for the item; or

(B) a payment amount determined in accordance with the methodology described in subparagraphs (B) and (C) of subsection (a)(2) of this section (except that in applying such methodology, the national limited payment amount referred to in such subparagraphs shall be initially computed based on local payment amounts using average reasonable charges for the 12–month period ending December 31, 1992, increased by the covered item updates described in such subsection for 1993 and 1994).

(2) Exceptions

Paragraph (1) shall not apply to surgical dressings that are—

(A) furnished as an incident to a physician's professional service; or

(B) furnished by a home health agency

(j) Requirements for suppliers of medical equipment and supplies

(1) Issuance and renewal of supplier number

(A) Payment

Except as provided in subparagraph (C), no payment may be made under this part after October 31, 1994, for items furnished by a supplier of medical equipment and supplies unless such supplier obtains (and renews at such intervals as the Secretary may require) a supplier number.

(B) Standards for possessing a supplier number

A supplier may not obtain a supplier number unless—

(i) for medical equipment and supplies furnished on or after October 31, 1994, and before January 1, 1996, the supplier meets standards prescribed by the Secretary in regulations issued on June 18, 1992; and

(ii) for medical equipment and supplies furnished on or after January 1, 1996, the supplier meets revised standards prescribed by the Secretary (in consultation with representatives of suppliers of medical equipment and supplies, carriers, and consumers) that shall include requirements that the supplier—

(I) comply with all applicable State and Federal licensure and regulatory requirements;

(II) maintain a physical facility on an appropriate site;

(III) have proof of appropriate liability insurance; and

(IV) meet such other requirements as the Secretary may specify.

(C) Exception for items furnished as incident to a physician's service

Subparagraph (A) shall not apply with respect to medical equipment and supplies furnished incident to a physician's service.

(D) Prohibition against multiple supplier numbers

The Secretary may not issue more than one supplier number to any supplier of medical equipment and supplies unless the issuance of more than one number is appropriate to identify subsidiary or regional entities under the supplier's ownership or control.

(E) Prohibition against delegation of supplier determinations

The Secretary may not delegate (other than by contract under section 1395u of this title) the responsibility to determine whether suppliers meet the standards necessary to obtain a supplier number.

(2) Certificates of medical necessity

(A) Limitation on information provided by suppliers on certificates of medical necessity

(i) In general

Effective 60 days after October 31, 1994, a supplier of medical equipment and supplies may distribute to physicians, or to individuals entitled to benefits under this part, a certificate of medical necessity for commercial purposes which contains no more than the following information completed by the supplier:

(I) An identification of the supplier and the beneficiary to whom such medical equipment and supplies are furnished.

(II) A description of such medical equipment and supplies.

(III) Any product code identifying such medical equipment and supplies.

(IV) Any other administrative information (other than information relating to the beneficiary's medical condition) identified by the Secretary.

(ii) Information on payment amount and charges

If a supplier distributes a certificate of medical necessity containing any of the information permitted to be supplied under clause (i), the supplier shall also list on the certificate of medical necessity the fee schedule amount and the supplier's charge for the medical equipment or supplies being furnished prior to distribution of such certificate to the physician.

(iii) Penalty

Any supplier of medical equipment and supplies who knowingly and willfully distributes a certificate of medical necessity in violation of clause (i) or fails to provide the information required under clause (ii) is subject to a civil money penalty in an amount not to exceed $1,000 for each such certificate of medical necessity so distributed. The provisions of section 1320a–7a of this title (other than subsections (a) and (b) of such section) shall apply to civil money penalties under this subparagraph in the same manner as they apply to a penalty or proceeding under section 1320a–7a(a) of this title.

(B) Definition

For purposes of this paragraph, the term "certificate of medical necessity" means a form or other document containing information required by the carrier to be submitted to show that an item is reasonable and necessary for the diagnosis or treatment of illness or injury or to improve the functioning of a malformed body member.

(3) Coverage and review criteria

The Secretary shall annually review the coverage and utilization of items of medical equipment and supplies to determine whether such items should be made subject to coverage and utilization review criteria, and if appropriate, shall develop and apply such criteria to such items.

(4) Limitation on patient liability

If a supplier of medical equipment and supplies (as defined in paragraph (5))—

(A) furnishes an item or service to a beneficiary for which no payment may be made by reason of paragraph (1);

(B) furnishes an item or service to a beneficiary for which payment is denied in advance under subsection (a)(15) of this section; or

(C) furnishes an item or service to a beneficiary for which payment is denied under section 1395y(a)(1) of this title; any expenses incurred for items and services furnished to an individual by such a supplier not on an assigned basis shall be the responsibility of such supplier. The individual shall have no financial responsibility for such expenses and the supplier shall refund on a timely basis to the individual (and shall be liable to the individual for) any amounts collected from the individual for such items or services. The provisions of subsection (a)(18) of this section shall apply to refunds required under the previous sentence in the same manner as such provisions apply to refunds under such subsection.

(5) Definition

The term "medical equipment and supplies" means—

(A) durable medical equipment (as defined in section 1395x(n) of this title);

(B) prosthetic devices (as described in section 1395x(s)(8) of this title);

(C) orthotics and prosthetics (as described in section 1395x(s)(9) of this title);

(D) surgical dressings (as described in section 1395x(s)(5) of this title);

(E) such other items as the Secretary may determine; and

(F) for purposes of paragraphs (1) and (3)—

(i) home dialysis supplies and equipment (as described in section 1395x(s)(2)(F) of this title),

(ii) immunosuppressive drugs (as described in section 1395x(s)(2)(J) of this title),

(iii) therapeutic shoes for diabetics (as described in section 1395x(s)(12) of this title),

(iv) oral drugs prescribed for use as an anticancer therapeutic agent (as described in section 1395x(s)(2)(Q) of this title), and

(v) self-administered erythropoetin (as described in section 1395x(s)(2)(P) of this title).

(k) Payment for outpatient therapy services and comprehensive outpatient rehabilitation services.

(1) In general

With respect to services described in section 1395l(a)(8) of this title or 1395l(a)(9) of this title for which payment is determined under this subsection, the payment basis shall be—

(A) for services furnished during 1998, the amount determined under paragraph (2); or

(B) for services furnished during a subsequent year, 80 percent of the lesser of—

(i) the actual charge for the services, or

(ii) the applicable fee schedule amount (as defined in paragraph (3)) for the services.

(2) Payment in 1998 based upon adjusted reasonable costs

The amount under this paragraph for services is the lesser of—

(A) the charges imposed for the services, or

(B) the adjusted reasonable costs (as defined in paragraph (4)) for the services, less 20 percent of the amount of the charges imposed for such services.

(3) Applicable fee schedule amount

In this subsection, the term "applicable fee schedule amount" means, with respect to services furnished in a year, the amount determined under the fee schedule established under section 1395w–4 of this title for such services furnished during the year or, if there is no such fee schedule established for such services, the amount determined under the fee schedule established for such comparable services as the Secretary specifies.

(4) Adjusted reasonable costs

In paragraph (2), the term "adjusted reasonable costs" means, with respect to any services, reasonable costs determined for such services, reduced by 10 percent. The 10–percent reduction shall not apply to services described in section 1395l(a)(8)(B) of this title (relating to services provided by hospitals).

487

(5) Uniform coding

For claims for services submitted on or after April 1, 1988, for which the amount of payment is determined under this subsection, the claim shall include a code (or codes) under a uniform coding system specified by the Secretary that identifies the services furnished.

(6) Restraint on billing

The provisions of subparagraphs (A) and (B) of section 1395u(b)(18) of this title shall apply to therapy services for which payment is made under this subsection in the same manner as they apply to services provided by a practitioner described in section 1395u(b)(18)(C) of this title.

(l) Establishment of fee schedule for ambulance services

(1) In general

The Secretary shall establish a fee schedule for payment for ambulance services whether provided directly by a supplier or provider or under arrangement with a provider under this part through a negotiated rulemaking process described in Title 5, and in accordance with the requirements of this subsection.

(2) Considerations

In establishing such fee schedule, the Secretary shall—

(A) establish mechanisms to control increases in expenditures for ambulance services under this part;

(B) establish definitions for ambulance services which link payments to the type of services provided;

(C) consider appropriate regional and operational differences;

(D) consider adjustments to payment rates to account for inflation and other relevant factors; and

(E) phase in the application of the payment rates under the fee schedule in an efficient and fair manner.

(3) Savings

In establishing such fee schedule, the Secretary shall—

(A) ensure that the aggregate amount of payments made for ambulance services under this part during 2000 does not exceed the aggregate amount of payments which would have been made for such services under this part during such year if the amendments made by section 4531(a) of the Balanced Budget Act of 1997 continued in effect, except that in making such determination the Secretary shall assume an update in such payments for 2002 equal to percentage increase in the consumer price index for all urban consumers (U.S. city average) for the 12–month period ending with June of the previous year reduced in the case of 2002 by 1.0 percentage points; and

(B) set the payment amounts provided under the fee schedule for services furnished in 2001 and each subsequent year at amounts equal to the payment amounts under the fee schedule for services furnished during the previous year, increased by the percentage increase in the consumer price index for all urban consumers (U.S. city average) for the 12–month period ending with June of the previous year reduced in the case of 2002 by 1.0 percentage points.

(4) Consultation

In establishing the fee schedule for ambulance services under this subsection, the Secretary shall consult with various national organizations representing individuals and entities who furnish and regulate ambulance services and share with such organizations relevant data in establishing such schedule.

(5) Limitation on review

There shall be no administrative or judicial review under section 1869 or otherwise of the amounts established under the fee schedule for ambulance services under this subsection, including matters described in paragraph (2).

(6) Restraint on billing

The provisions of subparagraphs (A) and (B) of section 1395u(b)(18) of this title shall apply to ambulance services for which payment is made under this subsection in the same manner as they apply to services provided by a practitioner described in section 1395u(b)(18)(C) of this title.

(7) Coding system

The Secretary may require the claim for any services for which the amount of payment is determined under this subsection to include a code (or codes) under a uniform coding system specified by the Secretary that identifies the services furnished.

(8) Services furnished by critical access hospitals

Notwithstanding any other provision of this subsection, the Secretary shall pay the reasonable costs incurred in furnishing ambulance services if such services are furnished—

> **(A)** by a critical access hospital (as defined in section 1395x(mm)(1) of this title), or

> **(B)** by an entity that is owned and operated by a critical access hospital, but only if the critical access hospital or entity is the only provider or supplier of ambulance services that is located within a 35–mile drive of such critical access hospital.

§ 1395n. Procedure for payment of claims of providers of services

(a) Conditions for payment for services described in section 1395k(a)(2) of this title

Except as provided in subsections (b), (c), and (e) of this section, payment for services described in section 1395k(a)(2) of this title furnished an individual may be made only to providers of services which are eligible therefor under section 1395cc(a) of this title, and only if—

(1) written request, signed by such individual, except in cases in which the Secretary finds it impracticable for the individual to do so, is filed for such payment in such form, in such manner and by such person or persons as the Secretary may by regulation prescribe, no later than the close of the period of 3 calendar years following the year in which such services are furnished (deeming any services furnished in the last 3 calendar months of any calendar year to have been furnished in the succeeding calendar year) except that, where the Secretary deems that efficient administration so requires, such period may be reduced to not less than 1 calendar year; and

(2) a physician certifies (and recertifies, where such services are furnished over a period of time, in such cases, with such frequency, and accompanied by such supporting material, appropriate to the case involved, as may be provided by regulations) that—

(A) in the case of home health services

(i) such services are or were required because the individual is or was confined to his home (except when receiving items and services referred to in section 1395x(m)(7) of this title) and needs or needed skilled nursing care (other than solely venipuncture for the purpose of obtaining a blood sample) on an intermittent basis or physical or speech therapy or, in the case of an individual who has been furnished home health services based on such a need and who no longer has such a need for such care or therapy, continues or continued to need occupational therapy,

(ii) a plan for furnishing such services to such individual has been established and is periodically reviewed by a physician, and

(iii) such services are or were furnished while the individual is or was under the care of a physician;

(B) in the case of medical and other health services, except services described in subparagraphs (B), (C), and (D) of section 1395x(s)(2) of this title, such services are or were medically required;

(C) in the case of outpatient physical therapy services or occupational therapy services,

(i) such services are or were required because the individual needed physical therapy services or outpatient occupational therapy services, respectively,

(ii) a plan for furnishing such services has been established by a physician or by the qualified physical therapist or qualified occupational therapist, respectively, providing such services and is periodically reviewed by a physician, and

  (iii) such services are or were furnished while the individual is or was under the care of a physician;

  (D) in the case of outpatient speech pathology services,

   (i) such services are or were required because the individual needed speech pathology services,

   (ii) a plan for furnishing such services has been established by a physician or by the speech pathologist providing such services and is periodically reviewed by a physician, and

   (iii) such services are or were furnished while the individual is or was under the care of a physician;

  (E) in the case of comprehensive outpatient rehabilitation facility services,

   (i) such services are or were required because the individual needed skilled rehabilitation services,

   (ii) a plan for furnishing such services has been established and is periodically reviewed by a physician, and

   (iii) such services are or were furnished while the individual is or was under the care of a physician; and

  (F) in the case of partial hospitalization services,

   (i) the individual would require inpatient psychiatric care in the absence of such services,

   (ii) an individualized, written plan for furnishing such services has been established by a physician and is reviewed periodically by a physician, and

   (iii) such services are or were furnished while the individual is or was under the care of a physician.

For purposes of this section, the term "provider of services" shall include a clinic, rehabilitation agency, or public health agency if, in the case of a clinic or rehabilitation agency, such clinic or agency meets the requirements of section 1395x(p)(4)(A) of this title (or meets the requirements of such section through the operation of section 1395x(g) of this title), or if, in the case of a public health agency, such agency meets the requirements of section 1395x(p)(4)(B) of this title (or meets the requirements of such section through the operation of section 1395x(g) of this title), but only with respect to the furnishing of outpatient physical therapy services (as therein defined) or (through the operation of section 1395x(g) of this title) with respect to the furnishing of outpatient occupational therapy services.

  To the extent provided by regulations, the certification and recertification requirements of paragraph (2) shall be deemed satisfied where, at a later date, a physician makes a certification of the kind provided in subparagraph (A) or (B) of paragraph (2) (whichever would have applied), but only where such certification is accompanied by such medical and other evidence as may be required by such regulations. With respect to the physician certification required by paragraph (2) for home health services furnished to any individual by a home health agency (other than an agency which is a governmental entity) and with respect to the establishment and review of a plan for such services, the Secretary shall prescribe regulations which shall become effective no later than July 1, 1981, and which prohibit a physician who has a significant ownership interest in, or a significant financial or contractual relationship with, such home health agency from performing such certification and from establishing or reviewing such plan, except that such prohibition shall not apply with respect to a home health agency which is a sole community home health agency (as determined by the Secretary). For purposes of the preceding sentence, service by a physician as an uncompensated officer or director of a home health agency shall not constitute having a significant ownership interest in, or a significant financial or contractual relationship with, such agency. For purposes of paragraph (2)(A), an individual shall be considered to be "confined to his home" if the individual has a condition, due to an illness or injury, that restricts the ability of the individual to leave his or her home except with the assistance of another individual or the aid of a supportive device (such as crutches, a cane, a wheelchair, or a walker), or if the individual has a condition such that leaving his or her home is medically contraindicated. While an individual does not have to be bedridden to be considered "confined to his home", the condition of the individual should be such that there exists a normal inability to leave home, that leaving home requires a considerable and taxing effort by the individual. Any absence of an individual from the home attributable to the need to receive health care treatment, including regular absences for the purpose of participating in therapeutic, psychosocial, or medical treatment in an adult day-care program that is licensed or certified by a State, or accredited, to furnish adult day-care services in the State shall not disqualify an individual from being considered to be "confined to his home". Any other absence of an individual from the home shall not so disqualify an individual if the absence is of infrequent or of relatively short duration. For purposes of the preceding sentence, any absence for the purpose of attending a religious service shall be deemed to be an absence of infrequent or short duration.

(b) Conditions for payment for services described in section 1395x(s) of this title

(1) Payment may also be made to any hospital for services described in section 1395x(s) of this title furnished as an outpatient service by a hospital or by others under arrangements made by it to an individual entitled to benefits under this part even though such hospital does not have an agreement in effect under this subchapter if

(A) such services were emergency services,

(B) the Secretary would be required to make such payment if the hospital had such an agreement in effect and otherwise met the conditions of payment hereunder, and

492

(C) such hospital has made an election pursuant to section 1395f(d)(1)(C) of this title with respect to the calendar year in which such emergency services are provided. Such payments shall be made only in the amounts provided under section 1395l(a)(2) of this title and then only if such hospital agrees to comply, with respect to the emergency services provided, with the provisions of section 1395cc(a) of this title.

(2) Payment may also be made on the basis of an itemized bill to an individual for services described in paragraph (1) of this subsection if

(A) payment cannot be made under such paragraph (1) solely because the hospital does not elect, in accordance with section 1395f(d)(1)(C) of this title, to claim such payments and

(B) such individual files application (submitted within such time and in such form and manner, and containing and supported by such information as the Secretary shall by regulations prescribe) for reimbursement. The amounts payable under this paragraph shall, subject to the provisions of section 1395l of this title, be equal to 80 percent of the hospital's reasonable charges for such services.

(c) Collection of charges from individuals for services specified in section 1395x(s) of this title

Notwithstanding the provisions of this section and sections 1395k, 1395l, and 1395cc(a)(1)(A) of this title, a hospital or a critical access hospital may, subject to such limitations as may be prescribed by regulations, collect from an individual the customary charges for services specified in section 1395x(s) of this title and furnished to him by such hospital as an outpatient, but only if such charges for such services do not exceed the applicable supplementary medical insurance deductible, and such customary charges shall be regarded as expenses incurred by such individual with respect to which benefits are payable in accordance with section 1395l(a)(1) of this title. Payments under this subchapter to hospitals which have elected to make collections from individuals in accordance with the preceding sentence shall be adjusted periodically to place the hospital in the same position it would have been had it instead been reimbursed in accordance with section 1395l(a)(2) of this title (or, in the case of a critical access hospital, in accordance with section 1395l(a)(6) of this title).

(d) Payment to Federal provider of services or other Federal agencies prohibited

Subject to section 1395qq of this title, no payment may be made under this part to any Federal provider of services or other Federal agency, except a provider of services which the Secretary determines is providing services to the public generally as a community institution or agency; and no such payment may be made to any provider of services or other person for any item or service which such provider or person is obligated by a law of, or a contract with, the United States to render at public expense.

(e) Payment to fund designated by medical staff or faculty of medical school

For purposes of services

(1) which are inpatient hospital services by reason of paragraph (7) of section 1395x(b) of this title or for which entitlement exists by reason of clause (II) of section 1395k(a)(2)(B)(i) of this title, and

(2) for which the reasonable cost thereof is determined under section 1395x(v)(1)(D) of this title (or would be if section 1395ww of this title did not apply), payment under this part shall be made to such fund as may be designated by the organized medical staff of the hospital in which such services were furnished or, if such services were furnished in such hospital by the faculty of a medical school, to such fund as may be designated by such faculty, but only if—

(A) such hospital has an agreement with the Secretary under section 1395cc of this title, and

(B) the Secretary has received written assurances that

(i) such payment will be used by such fund solely for the improvement of care to patients in such hospital or for educational or charitable purposes and

(ii) the individuals who were furnished such services or any other persons will not be charged for such services (or if charged, provision will be made for return of any moneys incorrectly collected).

§ 1395o.   Eligible individuals

Every individual who—

(1) is entitled to hospital insurance benefits under part A of this subchapter, or

(2) has attained age 65 and is a resident of the United States, and is either (A) a citizen or (B) an alien lawfully admitted for permanent residence who has resided in the United States continuously during the 5 years immediately preceding the month in which he applies for enrollment under this part, is eligible to enroll in the insurance program established by this part.

§ 1395u.   Use of carriers for administration of benefits

(a) Authority of Secretary to enter into contracts with carriers

In order to provide for the administration of the benefits under this part with maximum efficiency and convenience for individuals entitled to benefits under this part and for providers of services and other persons furnishing services to such individuals, and with a view to furthering coordination of the administration of the benefits under part A of this subchapter and under this part, the Secretary is authorized to enter into contracts with carriers, including carriers with which agreements under section 1395h of this title are in effect, which will perform some or all of the following functions (or, to the extent provided in such contracts, will secure performance thereof by other organizations); and, with respect to any of the following functions which involve payments for physicians' services on a reasonable charge basis, the Secretary shall to the extent possible enter into such contracts:

(1)(A) make determinations of the rates and amounts of payments required pursuant to this part to be made to providers of services and other persons on a reasonable cost or reasonable charge basis (as may be applicable);

(B) receive, disburse, and account for funds in making such payments; and

(C) make such audits of the records of providers of services as may be necessary to assure that proper payments are made under this part;

(2)(A) determine compliance with the requirements of section 1395x(k) of this title as to utilization review; and

(B) assist providers of services and other persons who furnish services for which payment may be made under this part in the development of procedures relating to utilization practices, make studies of the effectiveness of such procedures and methods for their improvement, assist in the application of safeguards against unnecessary utilization of services furnished by providers of services and other persons to individuals entitled to benefits under this part, and provide procedures for and assist in arranging, where necessary, the establishment of groups outside hospitals (meeting the requirements of section 1395x(k)(2) of this title) to make reviews of utilization;

(3) serve as a channel of communication of information relating to the administration of this part; and

(4) otherwise assist, in such manner as the contract may provide, in discharging administrative duties necessary to carry out the purposes of this part.

(b) Applicability of competitive bidding provisions; findings as to financial responsibility, etc., of carrier; contractual duties imposed by contract

(1) Contracts with carriers under subsection (a) of this section may be entered into without regard to section 5 of Title 41 or any other provision of law requiring competitive bidding.

(2)(A) No such contract shall be entered into with any carrier unless the Secretary finds that such carrier will perform its obligations under the contract efficiently and effectively and will meet such requirements as to financial responsibility, legal authority, and other matters as he finds pertinent. The Secretary shall publish in the Federal Register standards and criteria for the efficient and effective performance of contract obligations under this section, and opportunity shall be provided for public comment prior to implementation. In establishing such standards and criteria, the Secretary shall provide a system to measure a carrier's performance of responsibilities described in paragraph (3)(H), subsection (h) of this section, and section 1395w–1(e)(2) of this title. The Secretary may not require, as a condition of entering into or renewing a contract under this section or under section 1395hh of this title, that a carrier match data obtained other than in its activities under this part with data used in the administration of this part for purposes of identifying situations in which section 1395y(b) of this title may apply.

(B) The Secretary shall establish standards for evaluating carriers' performance of reviews of initial carrier determinations and of fair hearings under paragraph (3)(C), under which a carrier is expected—

(i) to complete such reviews, within 45 days after the date of a request by an individual enrolled under this part for such a review, in 95 percent of such requests, and

(ii) to make a final determination, within 120 days after the date of receipt of a request by an individual enrolled under this part for a fair hearing under paragraph (3)(C), in 90 percent of such cases.

(C) In the case of residents of nursing facilities who receive services described in clause (i) or (ii) of section 1395x(s)(2)(K) of this title performed by a member of a team, the Secretary shall instruct carriers to develop mechanisms which permit routine payment under this part for up to 1.5 visits per month per resident. In the previous sentence, the term "team" refers to a physician and includes a physician assistant acting under the supervision of the physician or a nurse practitioner working in collaboration with that physician, or both.

(D) In addition to any other standards and criteria established by the Secretary for evaluating carrier performance under this paragraph relating to avoiding erroneous payments, the carrier shall be subject to standards and criteria relating to the carrier's success in recovering payments made under this part for items or services for which payment has been or could be made under a primary plan (as defined in section 1395y(b)(2)(A) of this title).

(E) With respect to the payment of claims for home health services under this part that, but for the amendments made by section 4611 of the Balanced Budget Act of 1997, would be payable under part A of this subchapter instead of under this part, the Secretary shall continue administration of such claims through fiscal intermediaries under section 1395h of this title.

(3) Each such contract shall provide that the carrier—

(A) will take such action as may be necessary to assure that, where payment under this part for a service is on a cost basis, the cost is reasonable cost (as determined under section 1395x(v) of this title);

(B) will take such action as may be necessary to assure that, where payment under this part for a service is on a charge basis, such charge will be reasonable and not higher than the charge applicable, for a comparable service and under comparable circumstances, to the policyholders and subscribers of the carrier, and such payment will (except as otherwise provided in section 1395gg(f) of this title) be made—

    (i) on the basis of an itemized bill; or

    (ii) on the basis of an assignment under the terms of which (I) the reasonable charge is the full charge for the service, (II) the physician or other person furnishing such service agrees not to charge (and to refund amounts already collected) for services for which payment under this subchapter is denied under section 1320c–3(a)(2) of this title by reason of a determination under section 1320c–3(a)(1)(B) of this title, and (III) the physician or other person furnishing such service agrees not to charge (and to refund amounts already collected) for such service if payment may not be made therefor by reason of the provisions of paragraph (1) of section 1395y(a) of this title, and if the individual to whom such service was furnished was without fault in incurring the expenses of such service, and if the Secretary's determination that payment (pursuant to such assignment) was incorrect and was made subsequent to the third year following the year in which notice of such payment was sent to such individual; except that the Secretary may reduce such three-year period to not less than one year if he finds such reduction is consistent with the objectives of this subchapter (except in the case of physicians' services and ambulance service furnished as described in section 1395y(a)(4) of this title, other than for purposes of section 1395gg(f) of this title); but (in the case of bills submitted, or requests for payment made, after March 1968) only if the bill is submitted, or a written request for payment is made in such other form as may be permitted under regulations, no later than the close of the calendar year following the year in which such service is furnished (deeming any service furnished in the last 3 months of any calendar year to have been furnished in the succeeding calendar year);

(C) will establish and maintain procedures pursuant to which an individual enrolled under this part will be granted an opportunity for a fair hearing by the carrier, in any case where the amount in controversy is at least $100, but less than $500, when requests for payment under this part with respect to services furnished him are denied or are not acted upon with reasonable promptness or when the amount of such payment is in controversy;

(D) will furnish to the Secretary such timely information and reports as he may find necessary in performing his functions under this part;

(E) will maintain such records and afford such access thereto as the Secretary finds necessary to assure the correctness and verification of the information and reports under subparagraph (D) and otherwise to carry out the purposes of this part;

(F) will take such action as may be necessary to assure that where payment under this part for a service rendered is on a charge basis, such payment shall be determined on the basis of the charge that is determined in accordance with this section on the basis of customary and prevailing charge levels in effect at the time the service was rendered or, in the case of services rendered more than 12 months before the year in which the bill is submitted or request for payment is made, on the basis of such levels in effect for the 12–month period preceding such year;

(G) will, for a service that is furnished with respect to an individual enrolled under this part, that is not paid on an assignment-related basis, and that is subject to a limiting charge under section 1395w–4(g) of this title—

(i) determine, prior to making payment, whether the amount billed for such service exceeds the limiting charge applicable under section 1395w–4(g)(2) of this title;

(ii) notify the physician, supplier, or other person periodically (but not less often than once every 30 days) of determinations that amounts billed exceeded such applicable limiting charges; and

(iii) provide for prompt response to inquiries of physicians, suppliers, and other persons concerning the accuracy of such limiting charges for their services;

(H) if it makes determinations or payments with respect to physicians' services, will implement—

(i) programs to recruit and retain physicians as participating physicians in the area served by the carrier, including educational and outreach activities and the use of professional relations personnel to handle billing and other problems relating to payment of claims of participating physicians; and

(ii) programs to familiarize beneficiaries with the participating physician program and to assist such beneficiaries in locating participating physicians;

(I) will submit annual reports to the Secretary describing the steps taken to recover payments made under this part for items or services for which payment has been or could be made under a primary plan (as defined in section 1395y(b)(2)(A) of this title); and

(J), (K) Repealed. Pub.L. 101–234, Title II, § 201(a), Dec. 13, 1989, 103 Stat. 1981

(L) will monitor and profile physicians' billing patterns within each area or locality and provide comparative data to physicians whose utilization patterns vary significantly from other physicians in the same payment area or locality;

and shall contain such other terms and conditions not inconsistent with this section as the Secretary may find necessary or appropriate. In determining the reasonable charge for services for purposes of this paragraph, there shall be taken into consideration the customary charges for similar services generally made by the physician or other person furnishing such services, as well as the prevailing charges in the locality for similar services. No charge may be determined to be reasonable in the case of bills submitted or requests for payment made under this part after December 31, 1970, if it exceeds the higher of (i) the prevailing charge recognized by the carrier and found acceptable by the Secretary for similar services in the same locality in administering this part on December 31, 1970, or (ii) the prevailing charge level that, on the basis of statistical data and methodology acceptable to the Secretary, would cover 75 percent of the customary charges made for similar services in the same locality during the 12–month period ending on the June 30 last preceding the start of the calendar year in which the service is rendered. In the case of physicians' services the prevailing charge level determined for purposes of clause (ii) of the preceding sentence for any twelve-month period (beginning after June 30, 1973) specified in clause (ii) of such sentence may not exceed (in the aggregate) the level determined under such clause for the fiscal year ending June 30, 1973, or (with respect to physicians' services furnished in a year after 1987) the level determined under this sentence (or under any other provision of law affecting the prevailing charge level) for the previous year except to the extent that the Secretary finds, on the basis of appropriate economic index data, that such higher level is justified by year-to-year economic changes. With respect to power-operated wheelchairs for which payment may be made in accordance with section 1395x(s)(6) of this title, charges determined to be reasonable may not exceed the lowest charge at which power-operated wheelchairs are available in the locality. In the case of medical services, supplies, and equipment (including equipment servicing) that, in the judgment of the Secretary, do not generally vary significantly in quality from one supplier to another, the charges incurred after December 31, 1972, determined to be reasonable may not exceed the lowest charge levels at which such services, supplies, and equipment are widely and consistently available in a locality except to the extent and under the circumstances specified by the Secretary. The requirement in subparagraph (B) that a bill be submitted or request for payment be made by the close of the following calendar year shall not apply if (I) failure to submit the bill or request the payment by the close of such year is due to the error or misrepresentation of an officer, employee, fiscal intermediary, carrier, or agent of the Department of Health and Human Services performing functions under this subchapter and acting within the scope of his or its authority, and (II) the bill is submitted or the payment is requested promptly after such error or misrepresentation is eliminated or corrected. Notwithstanding the provisions of the third and fourth sentences preceding this sentence, the prevailing charge level in the case of a physician service in a particular locality determined pursuant to such third and fourth sentences for any calendar year after 1974 shall, if lower than the prevailing charge level for the fiscal year ending June 30, 1975, in the case of a similar physician service in the same locality by reason of the application of economic index data, be raised to such prevailing charge level for the fiscal year ending June 30, 1975, and shall remain at such prevailing charge level until the prevailing charge for a year (as adjusted by economic index data) equals or exceeds such prevailing charge level. The amount of any charges for outpatient services which shall be considered reasonable shall be subject to the limitations established by regulations issued by the Secretary pursuant to section 1395x(v)(1)(K) of this title, and in determining the reasonable charge for such services, the Secretary may limit such reasonable charge to a percentage of the amount of the prevailing charge for similar services furnished in a physician's office, taking into account the extent to which overhead costs associated with such outpatient services have been included in the reasonable cost or charge of the facility.

(4)(A)(i) In determining the prevailing charge levels under the third and fourth sentences of paragraph (3) for physicians' services furnished during the 15–month period beginning July 1, 1984, the Secretary shall not set any level higher than the same level as was set for the 12–month period beginning July 1, 1983.

(ii)(I) In determining the prevailing charge levels under the third and fourth sentences of paragraph (3) for physicians' services furnished during the 8–month period beginning May 1, 1986, by a physician who is not a participating physician (as defined in subsection (h)(1) of this section) at the time of furnishing the services, the Secretary shall not set any level higher than the same level as was set for the 12–month period beginning July 1, 1983.

(II) In determining the prevailing charge levels under the fourth sentence of paragraph (3) for physicians' services furnished during the 8–month period beginning May 1, 1986, by a physician who is a participating physician (as defined in subsection (h)(1) of this section) at the time of furnishing the services, the Secretary shall permit an additional one percentage point increase in the increase otherwise permitted under that sentence.

(iii) In determining the maximum allowable prevailing charges which may be recognized consistent with the index described in the fourth sentence of paragraph (3) for physicians' services furnished on or after January 1, 1987, by participating physicians, the Secretary shall treat the maximum allowable prevailing charges recognized as of December 31, 1986, under such sentence with respect to participating physicians as having been justified by economic changes.

(iv) The reasonable charge for physicians' services furnished on or after January 1, 1987, and before January 1, 1992, by a nonparticipating physician shall be no greater than the applicable percent of the prevailing charge levels established under the third and fourth sentences of paragraph (3) (or under any other applicable provision of law affecting the prevailing charge level). In the previous sentence, the term "applicable percent" means for services furnished (I) on or after January 1, 1987, and before April 1, 1988, 96 percent, (II) on or after April 1, 1988, and before January 1, 1989, 95.5 percent, and (III) on or after January 1, 1989, 95 percent.

(v) In determining the prevailing charge levels under the third and fourth sentences of paragraph (3) for physicians' services furnished during the 3–month period beginning January 1, 1988, the Secretary shall not set any level higher than the same level as was set for the 12–month period beginning January 1, 1987.

(vi) Before each year (beginning with 1989), the Secretary shall establish a prevailing charge floor for primary care services (as defined in subsection (i)(4) of this section) equal to 60 percent of the estimated average prevailing charge levels based on the best available data (determined, under the third and fourth sentences of paragraph (3) and under paragraph (4), without regard to this clause and without regard to physician specialty) for such service for all localities in the United States (weighted by the relative frequency of the service in each locality) for the year.

(vii) Beginning with 1987, the percentage increase in the MEI (as defined in subsection (i)(3) of this section) for each year shall be the same for nonparticipating physicians as for participating physicians.

(B)(i) In determining the reasonable charge under paragraph (3) for physicians' services furnished during the 15–month period beginning July 1, 1984, the customary charges shall be the same customary charges as were recognized under this section for the 12–month period beginning July 1, 1983.

(ii) In determining the reasonable charge under paragraph (3) for physicians' services furnished during the 8–month period beginning May 1, 1986, by a physician who is not a participating physician (as defined in subsection (h)(1) of this section) at the time of furnishing the services—

(I) if the physician was not a participating physician at any time during the 12–month period beginning on October 1, 1984, the customary charges shall be the same customary charges as were recognized under this section for the 12–month period beginning July 1, 1983, and

(II) if the physician was a participating physician at any time during the 12–month period beginning on October 1, 1984, the physician's customary charges shall be determined based upon the physician's actual charges billed during the 12–month period ending on March 31, 1985.

(iii) In determining the reasonable charge under paragraph (3) for physicians' services furnished during the 3–month period beginning January 1, 1988, the customary charges shall be the same customary charges as were recognized under this section for the 12–month period beginning January 1, 1987.

(iv) In determining the reasonable charge under paragraph (3) for physicians' services (other than primary care services, as defined in subsection (i)(4) of this section) furnished during 1991, the customary charges shall be the same customary charges as were recognized under this section for the 9–month period beginning April 1, 1990. In a case in which subparagraph (F) applies (relating to new physicians) so as to limit the customary charges of a physician during 1990 to a percent of prevailing charges, the previous sentence shall not prevent such limit on customary charges under such subparagraph from increasing in 1991 to a higher percent of such prevailing charges.

(C) In determining the prevailing charge levels under the third and fourth sentences of paragraph (3) for physicians' services furnished during periods beginning after September 30, 1985, the Secretary shall treat the level as set under subparagraph (A)(i) as having fully provided for the economic changes which would have been taken into account but for the limitations contained in subparagraph (A)(i).

(D)(i) In determining the customary charges for physicians' services furnished during the 8–month period beginning May 1, 1986, or the 12–month period beginning January 1, 1987, by a physician who was not a participating physician (as defined in subsection (h)(1) of this section) on September 30, 1985, the Secretary shall not recognize increases in actual charges for services furnished during the 15–month period beginning on July 1, 1984, above the level of the physician's actual charges billed in the 3–month period ending on June 30, 1984.

(ii) In determining the customary charges for physicians' services furnished during the 12–month period beginning January 1, 1987, by a physician who is not a participating physician (as defined in subsection (h)(1) of this section) on April 30, 1986, the Secretary shall not recognize increases in actual charges for services furnished during the 7–month period beginning on October 1, 1985, above the level of the physician's actual charges billed during the 3–month period ending on June 30, 1984.

(iii) In determining the customary charges for physicians' services furnished during the 12–month period beginning January 1, 1987, or January 1, 1988, by a physician who is not a participating physician (as defined in subsection (h)(1) of this section) on December 31, 1986, the Secretary shall not recognize increases in actual charges for services furnished during the 8–month period beginning on May 1, 1986, above the level of the physician's actual charges billed during the 3–month period ending on June 30, 1984.

(iv) In determining the customary charges for a physicians' service furnished on or after January 1, 1988, if a physician was a nonparticipating physician in a previous year (beginning with 1987), the Secretary shall not recognize any amount of such actual charges (for that service furnished during such previous year) that exceeds the maximum allowable actual charge for such service established under subsection (j)(1)(C) of this section.

(E)(i) For purposes of this part for physicians' services furnished in 1987, the percentage increase in the MEI is 3.2 percent.

(ii) For purposes of this part for physicians' services furnished in 1988, on or after April 1, the percentage increase in the MEI is—

(I) 3.6 percent for primary care services (as defined in subsection (i)(4) of this section), and

(II) 1 percent for other physicians' services.

(iii) For purposes of this part for physicians' services furnished in 1989, the percentage increase in the MEI is—

(I) 3.0 percent for primary care services, and

(II) 1 percent for other physicians' services.

(iv) For purposes of this part for items and services furnished in 1990, after March 31, 1990, the percentage increase in the MEI is—

(I) 0 percent for radiology services, for anesthesia services, and for other services specified in the list referred to in paragraph (14)(C)(i),

503

(II) 2 percent for other services (other than primary care services), and

(III) such percentage increase in the MEI (as defined in subsection (i)(3)) as would be otherwise determined for primary care services (as defined in subsection (i)(4)) of this section.

(v) For purposes of this part for items and services furnished in 1991, the percentage increase in the MEI is—

(I) 0 percent for services (other than primary care services), and

(II) 2 percent for primary care services (as defined in subsection (i)(4) of this section).

(F) Repealed. Pub.L. 103–66, Title XIII, § 13515(a)(2), Aug. 10, 1993, 107 Stat. 583.

(5) Each contract under this section shall be for a term of at least one year, and may be made automatically renewable from term to term in the absence of notice by either party of intention to terminate at the end of the current term; except that the Secretary may terminate any such contract at any time (after such reasonable notice and opportunity for hearing to the carrier involved as he may provide in regulations) if he finds that the carrier has failed substantially to carry out the contract or is carrying out the contract in a manner inconsistent with the efficient and effective administration of the insurance program established by this part.

(6) No payment under this part for a service provided to any individual shall (except as provided in section 1395gg of this title) be made to anyone other than such individual or (pursuant to an assignment described in subparagraph (B)(ii) of paragraph (3)) the physician or other person who provided the service, except that

(A) payment may be made

(i) to the employer of such physician or other person if such physician or other person is required as a condition of his employment to turn over his fee for such service to his employer, or

(ii) (where the service was provided in a hospital, critical access hospital, clinic, or other facility) to the facility in which the service was provided if there is a contractual arrangement between such physician or other person and such facility under which such facility submits the bill for such service,

(B) payment may be made to an entity

(i) which provides coverage of the services under a health benefits plan, but only to the extent that payment is not made under this part,

(ii) which has paid the person who provided the service an amount (including the amount payable under this part) which that person has accepted as payment in full for the service, and

(iii) to which the individual has agreed in writing that payment may be made under this part,

(C) in the case of services described in clause (i) of section 1395x(s)(2)(K) of this title, payment shall be made to either

(i) the employer of the physician assistant involved, or

(ii) with respect to a physician assistant who was the owner of a rural health clinic (as described in section 1395x(aa)(2) of this title) for a continuous period beginning prior to August 5, 1997 and ending on the date that the Secretary determines such rural health clinic no longer meets the requirements of section 1395x(aa)(2) of this title, payment may be made directly to the physician assistant,

(D) payment may be made to a physician for physicians' services (and services furnished incident to such services) furnished by a second physician to patients of the first physician if

(i) the first physician is unavailable to provide the services;

(ii) the services are furnished pursuant to an arrangement between the two physicians that

(I) is informal and reciprocal, or

(II) involves per diem or other fee-for-time compensation for such services;

(iii) the services are not provided by the second physician over a continuous period of more than 60 days; and

(iv) the claim form submitted to the carrier for such services includes the second physician's unique identifier (provided under the system established under subsection (r) of this section) and indicates that the claim meets the requirements of this subparagraph for payment to the first physician. No payment which under the preceding sentence may be made directly to the physician or other person providing the service involved (pursuant to an assignment described in subparagraph (B)(ii) of paragraph (3)) shall be made to anyone else under a reassignment or power of attorney (except to an employer or facility as described in clause (A) of such sentence); but nothing in this subsection shall be construed

(I) to prevent the making of such a payment in accordance with an assignment from the individual to whom the service was provided or a reassignment from the physician or other person providing such service if such assignment or reassignment is made to a governmental agency or entity or is established by or pursuant to the order of a court of competent jurisdiction, or

(II) to preclude an agent of the physician or other person providing the service from receiving any such payment if (but only if) such agent does so pursuant to an agency agreement under which the compensation to be paid to the agent for his services for or in connection with the

505

billing or collection of payments due such physician or other person under this subchapter is unrelated (directly or indirectly) to the amount of such payments or the billings therefor, and is not dependent upon the actual collection of any such payment. For purposes of subparagraph (C) of the first sentence of this paragraph, an employment relationship may include any independent contractor arrangement, and employer status shall be determined in accordance with the law of the State in which the services described in such clause are performed,

(E) in the case of an item or service (other than services described in section 1395yy(e)(2)(A)(ii) of this title) furnished by, or under arrangements made by, a skilled nursing facility to an individual who (at the time the item or service is furnished) is a resident of a skilled nursing facility, payment shall be made to the facility, and

(F) in the case of home health services (including medical supplies described in section 1395x(m)(5)of this title, but excluding durable medical equipment to the extent provided for in such section) furnished to an individual who (at the time the item or service is furnished) is under a plan of care of a home health agency, payment shall be made to the agency (without regard to whether or not the item or service was furnished by the agency, by others under arrangement with them made by the agency, or when any other contracting or consulting arrangement, or otherwise).

(7)(A) In the case of physicians' services furnished to a patient in a hospital with a teaching program approved as specified in section 1395x(b)(6) of this title but which does not meet the conditions described in section 1395x(b)(7) of this title, the carrier shall not provide (except on the basis described in subparagraph (C)) for payment for such services under this part—

(i) unless—

(I) the physician renders sufficient personal and identifiable physicians' services to the patient to exercise full, personal control over the management of the portion of the case for which the payment is sought,

(II) the services are of the same character as the services the physician furnishes to patients not entitled to benefits under this subchapter, and

(III) at least 25 percent of the hospital's patients (during a representative past period, as determined by the Secretary) who were not entitled to benefits under this subchapter and who were furnished services described in subclauses (I) and (II) paid all or a substantial part of charges (other than nominal charges) imposed for such services; and

(ii) to the extent that the payment is based upon a reasonable charge for the services in excess of the customary charge as determined in accordance with subparagraph (B).

(B) The customary charge for such services in a hospital shall be determined in accordance with regulations issued by the Secretary and taking into account the following factors:

(i) In the case of a physician who is not a teaching physician (as defined by the Secretary), the carrier shall take into account the amounts the physician charges for similar services in the physician's practice outside the teaching setting.

(ii) In the case of a teaching physician, if the hospital, its physicians, or other appropriate billing entity has established one or more schedules of charges which are collected for medical and surgical services, the carrier shall base payment under this subchapter on the greatest of—

(I) the charges (other than nominal charges) which are most frequently collected in full or substantial part with respect to patients who were not entitled to benefits under this subchapter and who were furnished services described in subclauses (I) and (II) of subparagraph (A)(i),

(II) the meaning of the charges (other than nominal charges) which were collected in full or substantial part with respect to such patients, or

(III) 85 percent of the prevailing charges paid for similar services in the same locality.

(iii) If all the teaching physicians in a hospital agree to have payment made for all of their physicians' services under this part furnished to patients in such hospital on an assignment-related basis, the customary charge for such services shall be equal to 90 percent of the prevailing charges paid for similar services in the same locality.

(C) In the case of physicians' services furnished to a patient in a hospital with a teaching program approved as specified in section 1395x(b)(6) of this title but which does not meet the conditions described in section 1395x(b)(7) of this title, if the conditions described in subclauses (I) and (II) of subparagraph (A)(i) are met and if the physician elects payment to be determined under this subparagraph, the carrier shall provide for payment for such services under this part on the basis of regulations of the Secretary governing reimbursement for the services of hospital-based physicians (and not on any other basis).

(D)(i) In the case of physicians' services furnished to a patient in a hospital with a teaching program approved as specified in section 1395x(b)(6) of this title but which does not meet the conditions described in section 1395x(b)(7) of this title, no payment shall be made under this part for services of assistants at surgery with respect to a surgical procedure if such hospital has a training program relating to the medical specialty required for such surgical procedure and a qualified individual on the staff of the hospital is available to provide such services; except that payment may be made under this part for such services, to the extent that such payment is otherwise allowed under this paragraph, if such services, as determined under regulations of the Secretary—

(I) are required due to exceptional medical circumstances,

(II) are performed by team physicians needed to perform complex medical procedures, or

(III) constitute concurrent medical care relating to a medical condition which requires the presence of, and active care by, a physician of another specialty during surgery, and under such other circumstances as the Secretary determines by regulation to be appropriate.

(ii) For purposes of this subparagraph, the term "assistant at surgery" means a physician who actively assists the physician in charge of a case in performing a surgical procedure.

(iii) The Secretary shall determine appropriate methods of reimbursement of assistants at surgery where such services are reimbursable under this part.

(8)(A)(i) The Secretary shall by regulation—

(I) describe the factors to be used in determining the cases (of particular items or services) in which the application of this subchapter to payment under this part (other than to physicians' services paid under section 1395w–4 of this title) results in the determination of an amount that, because of its being grossly excessive or grossly deficient, is not inherently reasonable, and

(II) provide in those cases for the factors to be considered in determining an amount that is realistic and equitable.

(ii) Notwithstanding the determination made in clause (i), the Secretary may not apply factors that would increase or decrease the payment under this part during any year for any particular item or service by more than 15 percent from such payment during the preceding year except as provided in subparagraph (B).

(B) The Secretary may make a determination under this subparagraph that would result in an increase or decrease under subparagraph (A) of more than 15 percent of the payment amount for a year, but only if—

(i) the Secretary's determination takes into account the factors described in subparagraph (C) and any additional factors the Secretary determines appropriate,

(ii) the Secretary's determination takes into account the potential impacts described in subparagraph (D), and

(iii) the Secretary complies with the procedural requirements of paragraph (9).

(C) The factors described in this subparagraph are as follows:

(i) The programs established under this subchapter and subchapter XIX are the sole or primary sources of payment for an item or service.

(ii) The payment amount does not reflect changing technology, increased facility with that technology, or reductions in acquisition or production costs.

(iii) The payment amount for an item or service under this part is substantially higher or lower than the payment made for the item or service by other purchasers.

(D) The potential impacts of a determination under subparagraph (B) on quality, access, and beneficiary liability, including the likely effects on assignment rates and participation rates.

(9)(A) The Secretary shall consult with representatives of suppliers or other individuals who furnish an item or service before making a determination under paragraph (8)(B) with regard to that item or service.

(B) The Secretary shall publish notice of a proposed determination under paragraph (8)(B) in the Federal Register—

(i) specifying the payment amount proposed to be established with respect to an item or service,

(ii) explaining the factors and data that the Secretary took into account in determining the payment amount so specified, and

(iii) explaining the potential impacts described in paragraph (8)(D).

(C) After publication of the notice required by subparagraph (B), the Secretary shall allow not less than 60 days for public comment on the proposed determination.

(D)(i) Taking into consideration the comments made by the public, the Secretary shall publish in the Federal Register a final determination under paragraph (8)(B) with respect to the payment amount to be established with respect to the item or service.

(ii) A final determination published pursuant to clause (i) shall explain the factors and data that the Secretary took into consideration in making the final determination.

(10)(A)(i) In determining the reasonable charge for procedures described in subparagraph (B) and performed during the 9–month period beginning on April 1, 1988, the prevailing charge for such procedure shall be the prevailing charge otherwise recognized for such procedure for 1987—

(I) subject to clause (iii), reduced by 2.0 percent, and

(II) further reduced by the applicable percentage specified in clause (ii).

(ii) For purposes of clause (i), the applicable percentage specified in this clause is—

(I) 15 percent, in the case of a prevailing charge otherwise recognized (without regard to this paragraph and determined without regard to physician specialty) that is at least 150 percent of the weighted national average (as determined by the Secretary) of such prevailing charges for such procedure for all localities in the United States for 1987;

(II) 0 percent, in the case of a prevailing charge that does not exceed 85 percent of such weighted national average; and

(III) in the case of any other prevailing charge, a percent determined on the basis of a straight-line sliding scale, equal to 3/13 of a percentage point for each percent by which the prevailing charge exceeds 85 percent of such weighted national average.

(iii) In no case shall the reduction under clause (i) for a procedure result in a prevailing charge in a locality for 1988 which is less than 85 percent of the Secretary's estimate of the weighted national average of such prevailing charges for such procedure for all localities in the United States for 1987 (based upon the best available data and determined without regard to physician specialty) after making the reduction described in clause (i)(I).

(B) The procedures described in this subparagraph are as follows: bronchoscopy, carpal tunnel repair, cataract surgery (including subsequent insertion of an intraocular lens), coronary artery bypass surgery, diagnostic and/or therapeutic dilation and curettage, knee arthroscopy, knee arthroplasty, pacemaker implantation surgery, total hip replacement, subrapubic prostatectomy, transurethral resection of the prostate, and upper gastrointestinal endoscopy.

(C) In the case of a reduction in the reasonable charge for a physicians' service under subparagraph (A), if a nonparticipating physician furnishes the service to an individual entitled to benefits under this part, after the effective date of such reduction, the physician's actual charge is subject to a limit under subsection (j)(1)(D) of this section.

(D) There shall be no administrative or judicial review under section 1395ff of this title or otherwise of any determination under subparagraph (A) or under paragraph (11)(B)(ii).

(11)(A) In providing payment for cataract eyeglasses and cataract contact lenses, and professional services relating to them, under this part, each carrier shall—

(i) provide for separate determinations of the payment amount for the eyeglasses and lenses and of the payment amount for the professional services of a physician (as defined in section 1395x(r) of this title), and

(ii) not recognize as reasonable for such eyeglasses and lenses more than such amount as the Secretary establishes in guidelines relating to the inherent reasonableness of charges for such eyeglasses and lenses.

(B)(i) In determining the reasonable charge under paragraph (3) for a cataract surgical procedure, subject to clause (ii), the prevailing charge for such procedure otherwise recognized for participating and nonparticipating physicians shall be reduced by 10 percent with respect to procedures performed in 1987.

(ii) In no case shall the reduction under clause (i) for a surgical procedure result in a prevailing charge in a locality for a year which is less than 75 percent of the weighted national average of such prevailing charges for such procedure for all the localities in the United States for 1986.

(C)(i) The prevailing charge level determined with respect to A-mode ophthalmic ultrasound procedures may not exceed 5 percent of the prevailing charge level established with respect to extracapsular cataract removal with lens insertion.

(ii) The reasonable charge for an intraocular lens inserted during or subsequent to cataract surgery in a physician's office may not exceed the actual acquisition cost for the lens (taking into account any discount) plus a handling fee (not to exceed 5 percent of such actual acquisition cost).

(D) In the case of a reduction in the reasonable charge for a physicians' service or item under subparagraph (B) or (C), if a nonparticipating physician furnishes the service or item to an individual entitled to benefits under this part after the effective date of such reduction, the physician's actual charge is subject to a limit under subsection (j)(1)(D) of this section.

(12) Repealed. Pub.L. 105–33, Title IV, § 4512(b)(2), Aug. 5, 1997, 111 Stat. 444.

(13)(A) In determining payments under section 1395l(*l*) of this title and section 1395w–4 of this title for anesthesia services furnished on or after January 1, 1994, the methodology for determining the base and time units used shall be the same for services furnished by physicians, for medical direction by physicians of two, three, or four certified registered nurse anesthetists, or for services furnished by a certified registered nurse anesthetist (whether or not medically directed) and shall be based on the methodology in effect, for anesthesia services furnished by physicians, as of August 10, 1993.

(B) The Secretary shall require claims for physicians' services for medical direction of nurse anesthetists during the periods in which the provisions of subparagraph (A) apply to indicate the number of such anesthetists being medically directed concurrently at any time during the procedure, the name of each nurse anesthetist being directed, and the type of procedure for which the services are provided.

(C) Redesignated (B)

(14)(A)(i) In determining the reasonable charge for a physicians' service specified in subparagraph (C)(i) and furnished during the 9–month period beginning on April 1, 1990, the prevailing charge for such service shall be the prevailing charge otherwise recognized for such service for 1989 reduced by 15 percent or, if less, 1/3 of the percent (if any) by which the prevailing charge otherwise applied in the locality in 1989 exceeds the locally-adjusted reduced prevailing amount (as determined under subparagraph (B)(i)) for the service.

(ii) In determining the reasonable charge for a physicians' service specified in subparagraph (C)(i) and furnished during 1991, the prevailing charge for such service shall be the prevailing charge otherwise recognized for such service for the period during 1990 beginning on April 1, reduced by the same amount as the amount of the reduction effected under this paragraph (as amended by the Omnibus Budget Reconciliation Act of 1990) for such service during such period.

(B) For purposes of this paragraph:

(i) The "locally-adjusted reduced prevailing amount" for a locality for a physicians' service is equal to the product of—

(I) the reduced national weighted average prevailing charge for the service (specified under clause (ii)), and

(II) the adjustment factor (specified under clause (iii)) for the locality.

(ii) The "reduced national weighted average prevailing charge" for a physicians' service is equal to the national weighted average prevailing charge for the service (specified in subparagraph (C)(ii)) reduced by the percentage change (specified in subparagraph (C)(iii)) for the service.

(iii) The "adjustment factor", for a physicians' service for a locality, is the sum of—

(I) The practice expense component (percent), divided by 100, specified in appendix A (pages 187 through 194) of the Report of the Medicare and Medicaid Health Budget Reconciliation Amendments of 1989, prepared by the Subcommittee on Health and the Environment of the Committee on Energy and Commerce, House of Representatives, (Committee Print 101–M, 101st Congress, 1st Session) for the service, multiplied by the geographic practice cost index value (specified in subparagraph (C)(iv) for the locality, and

(II) 1 minus the practice expense component (percent), divided by 100.

(C) For purposes of this paragraph:

(i) The procedures specified (by code and description) in the Overvalued Procedures List for Finance Committee, Revised September 20, 1989, prepared by the Physician Payment Review Commission which specification is of physicians' services that have been identified as overvalued by at least 10 percent based on a comparison of payments for such services under a resource-based relative value scale and of the national average prevailing charges under this part.

(ii) The "national weighted average prevailing charge" specified in this clause, for a physicians' service specified in clause (i), is the national weighted average prevailing charge for the service in 1989 as determined by the Secretary using the best data available.

(iii) The "percentage change" specified in this clause, for a physicians' service specified in clause (i), is the percent difference (but expressed as a positive number) specified for the service in the list referred to in clause (i).

(iv) The geographic practice cost index value specified in this clause for a locality is the Geographic Overhead Costs Index specified for the locality in table 1 of the September 1989 Supplement to the Geographic Medicare Economic Index: Alternative Approaches (prepared by the Urban Institute and the Center for Health Economics Research).

(D) In the case of a reduction in the prevailing charge for a physicians' service under subparagraph (A), if a nonparticipating physician furnishes the service to an individual entitled to benefits under this part, after the effective date of such reduction, the physician's actual charge is subject to a limit under subsection (j)(1)(D) of this section.

(15)(A) In determining the reasonable charge for surgery, radiology, and diagnostic physicians' services which the Secretary shall designate (based on their high volume of expenditures under this part) and for which the prevailing charge (but for this paragraph) differs by physician specialty, the prevailing charge for such a service may not exceed the prevailing charge or fee schedule amount for that specialty of physicians that furnish the service most frequently nationally.

(B) In the case of a reduction in the prevailing charge for a physician's service under subparagraph (A), if a nonparticipating physician furnishes the service to an individual entitled to benefits under this part, after the effective date of the reduction, the physician's actual charge is subject to a limit under subsection (j)(1)(D) of this section.

(16)(A) In determining the reasonable charge for all physicians' services other than physicians' services specified in subparagraph (B) furnished during 1991, the prevailing charge for a locality shall be 6.5 percent below the prevailing charges used in the locality under this part in 1990 after March 31.

(B) For purposes of subparagraph (A), the physicians' services specified in this subparagraph are as follows:

(i) Radiology, anesthesia and physician pathology services, the technical components of diagnostic tests specified in paragraph (17) and physicians' services specified in paragraph (14)(C)(i).

(ii) Primary care services specified in subsection (i)(4) of this section, hospital inpatient medical services, consultations, other visits, preventive medicine visits, psychiatric services, emergency care facility services, and critical care services.

(iii) Partial mastectomy; tendon sheath injections and small joint arthrocentesis; femoral fracture treatments; trochanteric fracture and endotracheal intubation; thoracentesis; thoracostomy; aneurysm repair; cystourethroscopy; transurethral fulguration and resection; tympanoplasty with mastoidectomy; and ophthalmoscopy.

(17) With respect to payment under this part for the technical (as distinct from professional) component of diagnostic tests (other than clinical diagnostic laboratory tests, tests specified in paragraph (14)(C)(i), and radiology services, including portable x-ray services) which the Secretary shall designate (based on their high volume of expenditures under this part), the reasonable charge for such technical component (including the applicable portion of a global service) may not exceed the national median of such charges for all localities, as estimated by the Secretary using the best available data.

(18)(A) Payment for any service furnished by a practitioner described in subparagraph (C) and for which payment may be made under this part on a reasonable charge or fee schedule basis may only be made under this part on an assignment-related basis.

(B) A practitioner described in subparagraph (C) or other person may not bill (or collect any amount from) the individual or another person for any service described in subparagraph (A), except for deductible and coinsurance amounts applicable under this part. No person is liable for payment of any amounts billed for such a service in violation of the previous sentence. If a practitioner or other person knowingly and willfully bills (or collects an amount) for such a

514

service in violation of such sentence, the Secretary may apply sanctions against the practitioner or other person in the same manner as the Secretary may apply sanctions against a physician in accordance with subsection (j)(2) of this section in the same manner as such section applies with respect to a physician. Paragraph (4) of subsection (j) of this section shall apply in this subparagraph in the same manner as such paragraph applies to such section.

(C) A practitioner described in this subparagraph is any of the following:

(i) A physician assistant, nurse practitioner, or clinical nurse specialist (as defined in section 1395x(aa)(5) of this title).

(ii) A certified registered nurse anesthetist (as defined in section 1395x(bb)(2) of this title).

(iii) A certified nurse-midwife (as defined in section 1395x(gg)(2) of this title).

(iv) A clinical social worker (as defined in section 1395x(hh)(1) of this title).

(v) A clinical psychologist (as defined by the Secretary for purposes of section 1395x(ii) of this title).

(D) For purposes of this paragraph, a service furnished by a practitioner described in subparagraph (C) includes any services and supplies furnished as incident to the service as would otherwise be covered under this part if furnished by a physician or as incident to a physician's service.

(19) For purposes of section 1395l(a)(1) of this title, the reasonable charge for ambulance services (as described in section 1861(s)(7)) provided during calendar year 1998 and calendar year 1999 may not exceed the reasonable charge for such services provided during the previous calendar year (after application of this paragraph), increased by the percentage increase in the consumer price index for all urban consumers (U.S. city average) as estimated by the Secretary for the 12–month period ending with the midpoint of the year involved reduced by 1.0 percentage point.

(c) Advances of funds to carrier; prompt payment of claims.

(1) Any contract entered into with a carrier under this section shall provide for advances of funds to the carrier for the making of payments by it under this part, and shall provide for payment of the cost of administration of the carrier, as determined by the Secretary to be necessary and proper for carrying out the functions covered by the contract. The Secretary shall provide that in determining a carrier's necessary and proper cost of administration, the Secretary shall, with respect to each contract, take into account the amount that is reasonable and adequate to meet the costs which must be incurred by an efficiently and economically operated carrier in carrying out the terms of its contract. The Secretary shall cause to have published in the Federal Register, by not later than September 1 before each fiscal year, data, standards, and methodology to be used to establish budgets for carriers under this section for that fiscal year, and shall cause to be published in the Federal Register for public comment, at least 90 days before such data, standards, and methodology are published, the data, standards, and methodology proposed to be used.

(2)(A) Each contract under this section which provides for the disbursement of funds, as described in subsection (a)(1)(B) of this section, shall provide that payment shall be issued, mailed, or otherwise transmitted with respect to not less than 95 percent of all claims submitted under this part—

(i) which are clean claims, and

(ii) for which payment is not made on a periodic interim payment basis,

within the applicable number of calendar days after the date on which the claim is received.

(B) In this paragraph:

(i) The term "clean claim" means a claim that has no defect or impropriety (including any lack of any required substantiating documentation) or particular circumstance requiring special treatment that prevents timely payment from being made on the claim under this part.

(ii) The term "applicable number of calendar days" means—

(I) with respect to claims received in the 12–month period beginning October 1, 1986, 30 calendar days,

(II) with respect to claims received in the 12–month period beginning October 1, 1987, 26 calendar days (or 19 calendar days with respect to claims submitted by participating physicians),

(III) with respect to claims received in the 12–month period beginning October 1, 1988, 25 calendar days (or 18 calendar days with respect to claims submitted by participating physicians), and

(IV) with respect to claims received in the 12–month period beginning October 1, 1989, and claims received in any succeeding 12–month period ending on or before September 30, 1993, 24 calendar days (or 17 calendar days with respect to claims submitted by participating physicians).

(V) with respect to claims received in the 12–month period beginning October 1, 1993, and claims received in any succeeding 12–month period, 30 calendar days.

(C) If payment is not issued, mailed, or otherwise transmitted within the applicable number of calendar days (as defined in clause (ii) of subparagraph (B)) after a clean claim (as defined in clause (i) of such subparagraph) is received, interest shall be paid at the rate used for purposes of section 3902(a) of Title 31 (relating to interest penalties for failure to make prompt payments) for the period beginning on the day after the required payment date and ending on the date on which payment is made.

(3)(A) Each contract under this section which provides for the disbursement of funds, as described in subsection (a)(1)(B) of this section, shall provide that no payment shall be issued, mailed, or otherwise transmitted with respect to any claim submitted under this subchapter within the applicable number of calendar days after the date on which the claim is received.

(B) In this paragraph, the term "applicable number of calendar days" means—

(i) with respect to claims submitted electronically as prescribed by the Secretary, 13 days, and

(ii) with respect to claims submitted otherwise, 26 days.

(4) Neither a carrier nor the Secretary may impose a fee under this subchapter—

(A) for the filing of claims related to physicians' services,

(B) for an error in filing a claim relating to physicians' services or for such a claim which is denied,

(C) for any appeal under this subchapter with respect to physicians' services,

(D) for applying for (or obtaining) a unique identifier under subsection (r) of this section, or

(E) for responding to inquiries respecting physicians' services or for providing information with respect to medical review of such services.

(5) Each contract under this section which provides for the disbursement of funds, as described in subsection (a)(1)(B) of this section, shall require the carrier to meet criteria developed by the Secretary to measure the timeliness of carrier responses to requests for payment of items described in section 1395m(a)(15)(C) of this title.

(6) No carrier may carry out (or receive payment for carrying out) any activity pursuant to a contract under this subsection to the extent that the activity is carried out pursuant to a contract under the Medicare Integrity Program under section 1395ddd of this title. The previous sentence shall not apply with respect to the activity described in section 1395ddd(b)(5) of this title (relating to prior authorization of certain items of durable medical equipment under section 1395m(a)(15) of this title).

517

(d) Surety bonds

Any contract with a carrier under this section may require such carrier or any of its officers or employees certifying payments or disbursing funds pursuant to the contract, or otherwise participating in carrying out the contract, to give surety bond to the United States in such amount as the Secretary may deem appropriate.

(e) Liability of certifying or disbursing officers or carriers

(1) No individual designated pursuant to a contract under this section as a certifying officer shall, in the absence of gross negligence or intent to defraud the United States, be liable with respect to any payments certified by him under this section.

(2) No disbursing officer shall, in the absence of gross negligence or intent to defraud the United States, be liable with respect to any payment by him under this section if it was based upon a voucher signed by a certifying officer designated as provided in paragraph (1) of this subsection.

(3) No such carrier shall be liable to the United States for any payments referred to in paragraph (1) or (2).

(f) "Carrier" defined

For purposes of this part, the term "carrier" means—

(1) with respect to providers of services and other persons, a voluntary association, corporation, partnership, or other nongovernmental organization which is lawfully engaged in providing, paying for, or reimbursing the cost of, health services under group insurance policies or contracts, medical or hospital service agreements, membership or subscription contracts, or similar group arrangements, in consideration of premiums or other periodic charges payable to the carrier, including a health benefits plan duly sponsored or underwritten by an employee organization; and

(2) with respect to providers of services only, any agency or organization (not described in paragraph (1)) with which an agreement is in effect under section 1395h of this title.

(g) Authority of Railroad Retirement Board to enter into contracts with carriers

The Railroad Retirement Board shall, in accordance with such regulations as the Secretary may prescribe, contract with a carrier or carriers to perform the functions set out in this section with respect to individuals entitled to benefits as qualified railroad retirement beneficiaries pursuant to section 426(a) of this title and section 231f(d) of Title 45.

(h) Participating physician or supplier; agreement with Secretary; publication of directories; availability; inclusion of program in explanation of benefits; payment of claims on assignment-related basis

(1) Any physician or supplier may voluntarily enter into an agreement with the Secretary to become a participating physician or supplier.

For purposes of this section, the term "participating physician or supplier" means a physician or supplier (excluding any provider of services) who, before the beginning of any year beginning with 1984, enters into an agreement with the Secretary which provides that such physician or supplier will accept payment under this part on an assignment-related basis for all items and services furnished to individuals enrolled under this part during such year. In the case of a newly licensed physician or a physician who begins a practice in a new area, or in the case of a new supplier who begins a new business, or in such similar cases as the Secretary may specify, such physician or supplier may enter into such an agreement after the beginning of a year, for items and services furnished during the remainder of the year.

(2) Each carrier having an agreement with the Secretary under subsection (a) of this section shall maintain a toll-free telephone number or numbers at which individuals enrolled under this part may obtain the names, addresses, specialty, and telephone numbers of participating physicians and suppliers and may request a copy of an appropriate directory published under paragraph (4). Each such carrier shall, without charge, mail a copy of such directory upon such a request.

(3)(A) In any case in which a carrier having an agreement with the Secretary under subsection (a) of this section is able to develop a system for the electronic transmission to such carrier of bills for services, such carrier shall establish direct lines for the electronic receipt of claims from participating physicians and suppliers.

(B) The Secretary shall establish a procedure whereby an individual enrolled under this part may assign, in an appropriate manner on the form claiming a benefit under this part for an item or service furnished by a participating physician or supplier, the individual's rights of payment under a medicare supplemental policy (described in section 1395ss(g)(1) of this title) in which the individual is enrolled. In the case such an assignment is properly executed and a payment determination is made by a carrier with a contract under this section, the carrier shall transmit to the private entity issuing the medicare supplemental policy notice of such fact and shall include an explanation of benefits and any additional information that the Secretary may determine to be appropriate in order to enable the entity to decide whether (and the amount of) any payment is due under the policy. The Secretary may enter into agreements for the transmittal of such information to entities electronically. The Secretary shall impose user fees for the transmittal of information under this subparagraph by a carrier, whether electronically or otherwise, and such user fees shall be collected and retained by the carrier.

(4) At the beginning of each year the Secretary shall publish directories (for appropriate local geographic areas) containing the name, address, and specialty of all participating physicians and suppliers (as defined in paragraph (1)) for that area for that year. Each directory shall be organized to make the most useful presentation of the information (as determined by the Secretary) for individuals enrolled under this part. Each participating physician directory for an area shall provide an alphabetical listing of all participating physicians practicing in the area and an alphabetical listing by locality and specialty of such physicians.

(5)(A) The Secretary shall promptly notify individuals enrolled under this part through an annual mailing of the participation program under this subsection and the publication and availability of the directories and shall make the appropriate area directory or directories available in each district and branch office of the Social Security Administration, in the offices of carriers, and to senior citizen organizations.

(B) The annual notice provided under subparagraph (A) shall include—

(i) a description of the participation program,

(ii) an explanation of the advantages to beneficiaries of obtaining covered services through a participating physician or supplier,

(iii) an explanation of the assistance offered by carriers in obtaining the names of participating physicians and suppliers, and

(iv) the toll-free telephone number under paragraph (2)(A) for inquiries concerning the program and for requests for free copies of appropriate directories.

(6) The Secretary shall provide that the directories shall be available for purchase by the public. The Secretary shall provide that each appropriate area directory is sent to each participating physician located in that area and that an appropriate number of copies of each such directory is sent to hospitals located in the area. Such copies shall be sent free of charge.

(7) The Secretary shall provide that each explanation of benefits provided under this part for services furnished in the United States, in conjunction with the payment of claims under section 1395l(a)(1) of this title (made other than on an assignment-related basis), shall include—

(A) a prominent reminder of the participating physician and supplier program established under this subsection (including the limitation on charges that may be imposed by such physicians and suppliers and a clear statement of any amounts charged for the particular items or services on the claim involved above the amount recognized under this part),

(B) the toll-free telephone number or numbers, maintained under paragraph (2), at which an individual enrolled under this part may obtain information on participating physicians and suppliers,

(C)(i) an offer of assistance to such an individual in obtaining the names of participating physicians of appropriate specialty and (ii) an offer to provide a free copy of the appropriate participating physician directory, and

(D) in the case of services for which the billed amount exceeds the limiting charge imposed under section 1395w–4(g) of this title, information regarding such applicable limiting charge (including information concerning the right to a refund under section 1395w–4(g)(1)(A)(iv) of this title).

(8) The Secretary may refuse to enter into an agreement with a physician or supplier under this subsection, or may terminate or refuse to renew such agreement, in the event that such physician or supplier has been convicted of a felony under Federal or State law for an offense which the Secretary determines is detrimental to the best interests of the program or program beneficiaries.

(i) Definitions

For purposes of this subchapter:

(1) A claim is considered to be paid on an "assignment-related basis" if the claim is paid on the basis of an assignment described in subsection (b)(3)(B)(ii) of this section, in accordance with subsection (b)(6)(B) of this section, or under the procedure described in section 1395gg(f)(1) of this title.

(2) The term "participating physician" refers, with respect to the furnishing of services, to a physician who at the time of furnishing the services is a participating physician (under subsection (h)(1) of this section); the term "nonparticipating physician" refers, with respect to the furnishing of services, a physician who at the time of furnishing the services is not a participating physician; and the term "nonparticipating supplier or other person" means a supplier or other person (excluding a provider of services) that is not a participating physician or supplier (as defined in subsection (h)(1) of this section).

(3) The term "percentage increase in the MEI" means, with respect to physicians' services furnished in a year, the percentage increase in the medicare economic index (referred to in the fourth sentence of subsection (b)(3) of this section) applicable to such services furnished as of the first day of that year.

(4) The term "primary care services" means physicians' services which constitute office medical services, emergency department services, home medical services, skilled nursing, intermediate care, and long-term care medical services, or nursing home, boarding home, domiciliary, or custodial care medical services.

(j) Monitoring of charges of nonparticipating physicians; sanctions; restitution

(1)(A) In the case of a physician who is not a participating physician for items and services furnished during a portion of the 30–month period beginning July 1, 1984, the Secretary shall monitor the physician's actual charges to individuals enrolled under this part for physicians' services during that portion of that period. If such physician knowingly and willfully bills individuals enrolled under this part for actual charges in excess of such physician's actual charges for the calendar quarter beginning on April 1, 1984, the Secretary may apply sanctions against such physician in accordance with paragraph (2).

(B)(i) During any period (on or after January 1, 1987, and before the date specified in clause (ii)), during which a physician is a nonparticipating physician, the Secretary shall monitor the actual charges of each such physician for physicians' services furnished to individuals enrolled under this part. If such physician knowingly and willfully bills on a repeated basis for such a service an actual charge in excess of the maximum allowable actual charge determined under subparagraph (C) for that service, the Secretary may apply sanctions against such physician in accordance with paragraph (2).

(ii) Clause (i) shall not apply to services furnished after December 31, 1990.

(C)(i) For a particular physicians' service furnished by a nonparticipating physician to individuals enrolled under this part during a year, for purposes of subparagraph (B), the maximum allowable actual charge is determined as follows: If the physician's maximum allowable actual charge for that service in the previous year was—

(I) less than 115 percent of the applicable percent (as defined in subsection (b)(4)(A)(iv) of this section) of the prevailing charge for the year and service involved, the maximum allowable actual charge for the year involved is the greater of the maximum allowable actual charge described in subclause (II) or the charge described in clause (ii), or

(II) equal to, or greater than, 115 percent of the applicable percent (as defined in subsection (b)(4)(A)(iv) of this section) of the prevailing charge for the year and service involved, the maximum allowable actual charge is 101 percent of the physician's maximum allowable actual charge for the service for the previous year.

(ii) For purposes of clause (i)(I), the charge described in this clause for a particular physicians' service furnished in a year is the maximum allowable actual charge for the service of the physician for the previous year plus the product of (I) the applicable fraction (as defined in clause (iii)) and (II) the amount by which 115 percent of the prevailing charge for the year involved for such service furnished by nonparticipating physicians, exceeds the physician's maximum allowable actual charge for the service for the previous year.

(iii) In clause (ii), the "applicable fraction" is—

(I) for 1987, 1/4,

(II) for 1988, 1/3,

(III) for 1989, 1/2, and

(IV) for any subsequent year, 1.

(iv) For purposes of determining the maximum allowable actual charge under clauses (i) and (ii) for 1987, in the case of a physicians' service for which the physician has actual charges for the calendar quarter beginning on April 1, 1984, the "maximum allowable actual charge" for 1986 is the physician's actual charge for such service furnished during such quarter.

(v) For purposes of determining the maximum allowable actual charge under clauses (i) and (ii) for a year after 1986, in the case of a physicians' service for which the physician has no actual charges for the calendar quarter beginning on April 1, 1984, and for which a maximum allowable actual charge has not been previously established under this clause, the "maximum allowable actual charge" for the previous year shall be the 50th percentile of the customary charges for the service (weighted by frequency of the service) performed by nonparticipating physicians in the locality during the 12–month period ending June 30 of that previous year.

(vi) For purposes of this subparagraph, a "physician's actual charge" for a physicians' service furnished in a year or other period is the weighted average (or, at the option of the Secretary for a service furnished in the calendar quarter beginning April 1, 1984, the median) of the physician's charges for such service furnished in the year or other period.

(vii) In the case of a nonparticipating physician who was a participating physician during a previous period, for the purpose of computing the physician's maximum allowable actual charge during the physician's period of nonparticipation, the physician shall be deemed to have had a maximum allowable actual charge during the period of participation, and such deemed maximum allowable actual charge shall be determined according to clauses (i) through (vi).

(viii) Notwithstanding any other provision of this subparagraph, the maximum allowable actual charge for a particular physician's service furnished by a nonparticipating physician to individuals enrolled under this part during the 3–month period beginning on January 1, 1988, shall be the amount determined under this subparagraph for 1987. The maximum allowable actual charge for any such service otherwise determined under this subparagraph for 1988 shall take effect on April 1, 1988.

(ix) If there is a reduction under subsection (b)(13) of this section in the reasonable charge for medical direction furnished by a nonparticipating physician, the maximum allowable actual charge otherwise permitted under this subsection for such services shall be reduced in the same manner and in the same percentage as the reduction in such reasonable charge.

(D)(i) If an action described in clause (ii) results in a reduction in a reasonable charge for a physicians' service or item and a nonparticipating physician furnishes the service or item to an individual entitled to benefits under this part after the effective date of such action, the physician may not charge the individual more than 125 percent of the reduced payment allowance (as defined in clause (iii)) plus (for services or items furnished during the 12–month period (or 9–month period in the case of an action described in clause (ii)(II)) beginning on the effective date of the action) 1/2 of the amount by which the physician's maximum allowable actual charge for the service or item for the previous 12–month period exceeds such 125 percent level.

(ii) The first sentence of clause (i) shall apply to—

(I) an adjustment under subsection (b)(8)(B) of this section (relating to inherent reasonableness),

(II) a reduction under subsection (b)(10)(A) or (b)(14)(A) of this section (relating to certain overpriced procedures),

(III) a reduction under subsection (b)(11)(B) of this section (relating to certain cataract procedures),

(IV) a prevailing charge limit established under subsection (b)(11)(C)(i) or (b)(15)(A) of this section,

(V) a reasonable charge limit established under subsection (b)(11)(C)(ii) of this section, and

(VI) an adjustment under section 1395l(*l*)(3)(B) of this title (relating to physician supervision of certified registered nurse anesthetists).

(iii) In clause (i), the term "reduced payment allowance" means, with respect to an action—

(I) under subsection (b)(8)(B) of this section, the inherently reasonable charge established under subsection (b)(8) of this section;

(II) under subsection (b)(10)(A), (b)(11)(B), (b)(11)(C)(i), (b)(14)(A), or (b)(15)(A) of this section or under section 1395l(*l*)(3)(B) of this title, the prevailing charge for the service after the action; or

(III) under subsection (b)(11)(C)(ii) of this section, the payment allowance established under such subsection.

(iv) If a physician knowingly and willfully bills in violation of clause (i) (whether or not such charge violates subparagraph (B)), the Secretary may apply sanctions against such physician in accordance with paragraph (2).

(v) Clause (i) shall not apply to items and services furnished after December 31, 1990.

(2) Subject to paragraph (3), the sanctions which the Secretary may apply under this paragraph are—

(A) excluding a physician from participation in the programs under this chapter for a period not to exceed 5 years, in accordance with the procedures of subsections (c), (f), and (g) of section 1320a–7 of this title, or

(B) civil monetary penalties and assessments, in the same manner as such penalties and assessments are authorized under section 1320a–7a(a) of this title,

or both. The provisions of section 1320a–7a of this title (other than the first 2 sentences of subsection (a) and other than subsection (b)) shall apply to a civil money penalty and assessment under subparagraph (B) in the same manner as such provisions apply to a penalty, assessment, or proceeding under section 1320a–7a(a) of this title, except to the extent such provisions are inconsistent with subparagraph (A) or paragraph (3).

(3)(A) The Secretary may not exclude a physician pursuant to paragraph (2)(A) if such physician is a sole community physician or sole source of essential specialized services in a community.

(B) The Secretary shall take into account access of beneficiaries to physicians' services for which payment may be made under this part in determining whether to bar a physician from participation under paragraph (2)(A).

(4) The Secretary may, out of any civil monetary penalty or assessment collected from a physician pursuant to this subsection, make a payment to a beneficiary enrolled under this part in the nature of restitution for amounts paid by such beneficiary to such physician which was determined to be an excess charge under paragraph (1).

(k) Sanctions for billing for services of assistant at cataract operations

(1) If a physician knowingly and willfully presents or causes to be presented a claim or bills an individual enrolled under this part for charges for services as an assistant at surgery for which payment may not be made by reason of section 1395y(a)(15) of this title, the Secretary may apply sanctions against such physician in accordance with subsection (j)(2) of this section in the case of surgery performed on or after March 1, 1987.

(2) If a physician knowingly and willfully presents or causes to be presented a claim or bills an individual enrolled under this part for charges that includes a charge for an assistant at surgery for which payment may not be made by reason of section 1395y(a)(15) of this title, the Secretary may apply sanctions against such physician in accordance with subsection (j)(2) of this section in the case of surgery performed on or after March 1, 1987.

(*l*) Prohibition of unassigned billing of services determined to be medically unnecessary by carrier

(1)(A) Subject to subparagraph (C), if—

> **(i)** a nonparticipating physician furnishes services to an individual enrolled for benefits under this part,

> **(ii)** payment for such services is not accepted on an assignment-related basis,

> **(iii)(I)** a carrier determines under this part or a peer review organization determines under part B of subchapter XI of this chapter that payment may not be made by reason of section 1395y(a)(1) of this title because a service otherwise covered under this subchapter is not reasonable and necessary under the standards described in that section or

>> **(II)** payment under this subchapter for such services is denied under section 1320c–3(a)(2) of this title by reason of a determination under section 1320c–3(a)(1)(B) of this title, and

> **(iv)** the physician has collected any amounts for such services,

the physician shall refund on a timely basis to the individual (and shall be liable to the individual for) any amounts so collected.

(B) A refund under subparagraph (A) is considered to be on a timely basis only if—

> **(i)** in the case of a physician who does not request reconsideration or seek appeal on a timely basis, the refund is made within 30 days after the date the physician receives a denial notice under paragraph (2), or

> **(ii)** in the case in which such a reconsideration or appeal is taken, the refund is made within 15 days after the date the physician receives notice of an adverse determination on reconsideration or appeal.

(C) Subparagraph (A) shall not apply to the furnishing of a service by a physician to an individual in the case described in subparagraph (A)(iii)(I) if—

> **(i)** the physician establishes that the physician did not know and could not reasonably have been expected to know that payment may not be made for the service by reason of section 1395y(a)(1) of this title, or

> **(ii)** before the service was provided, the individual was informed that payment under this part may not be made for the specific service and the individual has agreed to pay for that service.

(2) Each carrier with a contract in effect under this section with respect to physicians and each peer review organization with a contract under part B of subchapter XI of this chapter shall send any notice of denial of payment for physicians' services based on section 1395y(a)(1) of this title and for which payment is not requested on an assignment-related basis to the physician and the individual involved.

(3) If a physician knowingly and willfully fails to make refunds in violation of paragraph (1)(A), the Secretary may apply sanctions against such physician in accordance with subsection (j)(2) of this section.

(m) Disclosure of information of unassigned claims for certain physicians' services

(1) In the case of a nonparticipating physician who—

> **(A)** performs an elective surgical procedure for an individual enrolled for benefits under this part and for which the physician's actual charge is at least $500, and

> **(B)** does not accept payment for such procedure on an assignment-related basis,

the physician must disclose to the individual, in writing and in a form approved by the Secretary, the physician's estimated actual charge for the procedure, the estimated approved charge under this part for the procedure, the excess of the physician's actual charge over the approved charge, and the coinsurance amount applicable to the procedure. The written estimate may not be used as the basis for, or evidence in, a civil suit.

(2) A physician who fails to make a disclosure required under paragraph (1) with respect to a procedure shall refund on a timely basis to the individual (and shall be liable to the individual for) any amounts collected for the procedure in excess of the charges recognized and approved under this part.

(3) If a physician knowingly and willfully fails to comply with paragraph (2), the Secretary may apply sanctions against such physician in accordance with subsection (j)(2) of this section.

(4) The Secretary shall provide for such monitoring of requests for payment for physicians' services to which paragraph (1) applies as is necessary to assure compliance with paragraph (2).

527

(n) Elimination of markup for certain purchased services

(1) If a physician's bill or a request for payment for services billed by a physician includes a charge for a diagnostic test described in section 1395x(s)(3) of this title (other than a clinical diagnostic laboratory test) for which the bill or request for payment does not indicate that the billing physician personally performed or supervised the performance of the test or that another physician with whom the physician who shares a practice personally performed or supervised the performance of the test, the amount payable with respect to the test shall be determined as follows:

(A) If the bill or request for payment indicates that the test was performed by a supplier, identifies the supplier, and indicates the amount the supplier charged the billing physician, payment for the test (less the applicable deductible and coinsurance amounts) shall be the actual acquisition costs (net of any discounts) or, if lower, the supplier's reasonable charge (or other applicable limit) for the test.

(B) If the bill or request for payment (i) does not indicate who performed the test, or (ii) indicates that the test was performed by a supplier but does not identify the supplier or include the amount charged by the supplier, no payment shall be made under this part.

(2) A physician may not bill an individual enrolled under this part—

(A) any amount other than the payment amount specified in paragraph (1)(A) and any applicable deductible and coinsurance for a diagnostic test for which payment is made pursuant to paragraph (1)(A), or

(B) any amount for a diagnostic test for which payment may not be made pursuant to paragraph (1)(B).

(3) If a physician knowingly and willfully in repeated cases bills one or more individuals in violation of paragraph (2), the Secretary may apply sanctions against such physician in accordance with subsection (j)(2) of this section.

(o) Reimbursement for drugs and biologicals

(1) If a physician's supplier's, or any other person's bill or request for payment for services includes a charge for a drug or biological for which payment may be made under this part and the drug or biological is not paid on a cost or prospective payment basis as otherwise provided in this part, the amount payable for the drug or biological is equal to 95 percent of the average wholesale price.

(2) If payment for a drug or biological is made to a licensed pharmacy approved to dispense drugs or biologicals under this part, the Secretary may pay a dispensing fee (less the applicable deductible and coinsurance amounts) to the pharmacy.

528

(3)(A) Payment for a charge for any drug or biological for which payment may be made under this part may be made only on an assignment-related basis.

(B) The provisions of subsection (b)(18)(B) shall apply to charges for such drugs or biologicals in the same manner as they apply to services furnished by a practitioner described in subsection (b)(18)(C).

(p) Requiring submission of diagnostic information

(1) Each request for payment, or bill submitted, for an item or service furnished by a physician or practitioner specified in subsection (b)(18)(C) of this section for which payment may be made under this part shall include the appropriate diagnosis code (or codes) as established by the Secretary for such item or service.

(2) In the case of a request for payment for an item or service furnished by a physician or practitioner specified in subsection (b)(18)(C) of this section on an assignment-related basis which does not include the code (or codes) required under paragraph (1), payment may be denied under this part.

(3) In the case of a request for payment for an item or service furnished by a physician not submitted on an assignment-related basis and which does not include the code (or codes) required under paragraph (1)—

(A) if the physician knowingly and willfully fails to provide the code (or codes) promptly upon request of the Secretary or a carrier, the physician may be subject to a civil money penalty in an amount not to exceed $2,000, and

(B) if the physician knowingly, willfully, and in repeated cases fails, after being notified by the Secretary of the obligations and requirements of this subsection, to include the code (or codes) required under paragraph (1), the physician may be subject to the sanction described in subsection (j)(2)(A) of this section.

The provisions of section 1320a–7a of this title (other than subsections (a) and (b)) shall apply to civil money penalties under subparagraph (A) in the same manner as they apply to a penalty or proceeding under section 1320a–7a(a) of this title.

(4) In the case of an item or service defined in paragraph (3), (6), (8), or (9) of subsection 1395x(s) of this title ordered by a physician or a practitioner specified in subsection (b)(18)(C) of this section, but furnished by another entity, if the Secretary (or fiscal agent of the Secretary) requires the entity furnishing the item or service to provide diagnostic or other medical information in order for payment to be made to the entity, the physician or practitioner shall provide that information to the entity at the time that the item or service is ordered by the physician or practitioner.

(q) Anesthesia services; counting actual time units

(1)(A) The Secretary, in consultation with groups representing physicians who furnish anesthesia services, shall establish by regulation a relative value guide for use in all carrier localities in making payment for physician anesthesia services furnished under this part. Such guide shall be designed so as to result in expenditures under this subchapter for such services in an amount that would not exceed the amount of such expenditures which would otherwise occur.

(B) For physician anesthesia services furnished under this part during 1991, the prevailing charge conversion factor used in a locality under this subsection shall, subject to clause (iv), be reduced to the adjusted prevailing charge conversion factor for the locality determined as follows:

(i) The Secretary shall estimate the national weighted average of the prevailing charge conversion factors used under this subsection for services furnished during 1990 after March 31, using the best available data.

(ii) The national weighted average estimated under clause (i) shall be reduced by 7 percent.

(iii) The adjusted prevailing charge conversion factor for a locality is the sum of—

(I) the product of (a) the portion of the reduced national weighted average prevailing charge conversion factor computed under clause (ii) which is attributable to physician work and (b) the geographic work index value for the locality (specified in Addendum C to the Model Fee Schedule for Physician Services (published on September 4, 1990, 55 Federal Register pp. 36238–36243)); and

(II) the product of (a) the remaining portion of the reduced national weighted average prevailing charge conversion factor computed under clause (ii) and (b) the geographic practice cost index value specified in subsec. (b)(14)(C)(iv) of this section for the locality.

In applying this clause, 70 percent of the prevailing charge conversion factor shall be considered to be attributable to physician work.

(iv) The prevailing charge conversion factor to be applied to a locality under this subparagraph shall not be reduced by more than 15 percent below the prevailing charge conversion factor applied in the locality for the period during 1990 after March 31, but in no case shall the prevailing charge conversion factor be less than 60 percent of the national weighted average of the prevailing charge conversion factors (computed under clause (i)).

(2) For purposes of payment for anesthesia services (whether furnished by physicians or by certified registered nurse anesthetists) under this part, the time units shall be counted based on actual time rather than rounded to full time units.

(r) Establishment of physician identification system

The Secretary shall establish a system which provides for a unique identifier for each physician who furnishes services for which payment may be made under this subchapter. Under such system, the Secretary may impose appropriate fees on such physicians to cover the costs of investigation and recertification activities with respect to the issuance of the identifiers.

(s) Application of fee schedule

(1) The Secretary may implement a statewide or other areawide fee schedule to be used for payment of any item or service described in paragraph (2) which is paid on a reasonable charge basis. Any fee schedule established under this paragraph for such item or service shall be updated each year by the percentage increase in the consumer price index for all urban consumers (United States city average) for the 12–month period ending with June of the preceding year, except that in no event shall a fee schedule for an item described in paragraph (2)(D) be updated before 2003.

(2) The items and services described in this paragraph are as follows:

(A) Medical supplies.

(B) Home dialysis supplies and equipment (as defined in section 1395rr(b)(8) of this title).

(C) Therapeutic shoes.

(D) Parenteral and enteral nutrients, equipment, and supplies.

(E) Electromyogram devices.

(F) Salivation devices.

(G) Blood products.

(H) Transfusion medicine

(t) Requests for payment or bill submitted to include medicare provider number.

Each request for payment, or bill submitted, for an item or service furnished to an individual who is a resident of a skilled nursing facility for which payment may be made under this part shall include the facility's medicare provider number.

§ 1395w–4. Payment for physicians' services

(a) Payment based on fee schedule

(1) In general

Effective for all physicians' services (as defined in subsection (j)(3) of this section) furnished under this part during a year (beginning with

1992) for which payment is otherwise made on the basis of a reasonable charge or on the basis of a fee schedule under section 1395m(b) of this title, payment under this part shall instead be based on the lesser of—

(A) the actual charge for the service, or

(B) subject to the succeeding provisions of this subsection, the amount determined under the fee schedule established under subsection (b) of this section for services furnished during that year (in this subsection referred to as the "fee schedule amount").

(2) Transition to full fee schedule

(A) Limiting reductions and increases to 15 percent in 1992

(i) Limit on increase

In the case of a service in a fee schedule area (as defined in subsection (j)(2) of this section) for which the adjusted historical payment basis (as defined in subparagraph (D)) is less than 85 percent of the fee schedule amount for services furnished in 1992, there shall be substituted for the fee schedule amount an amount equal to the adjusted historical payment basis plus 15 percent of the fee schedule amount otherwise established (without regard to this paragraph).

(ii) Limit in reduction

In the case of a service in a fee schedule area for which the adjusted historical payment basis exceeds 115 percent of the fee schedule amount for services furnished in 1992, there shall be substituted for the fee schedule amount an amount equal to the adjusted historical payment basis minus 15 percent of the fee schedule amount otherwise established (without regard to this paragraph).

(B) Special rule for 1993, 1994, and 1995

If a physicians' service in a fee schedule area is subject to the provisions of subparagraph (A) in 1992, for physicians' services furnished in the area—

(i) during 1993, there shall be substituted for the fee schedule amount an amount equal to the sum of—

(I) 75 percent of the fee schedule amount determined under subparagraph (A), adjusted by the update established under subsection (d)(3) of this section for 1993, and

(II) 25 percent of the fee schedule amount determined under paragraph (1) for 1993 without regard to this paragraph;

(ii) during 1994, there shall be substituted for the fee schedule amount an amount equal to the sum of—

(I) 67 percent of the fee schedule amount determined under clause (i), adjusted by the update established under subsection (d)(3) of this section for 1994 and as adjusted under subsection (c)(2)(F)(ii) of this section and under section 13515(b) of the Omnibus Budget Reconciliation Act of 1993, and

(II) 33 percent of the fee schedule amount determined under paragraph (1) for 1994 without regard to this paragraph; and

(iii) during 1995, there shall be substituted for the fee schedule amount an amount equal to the sum of—

(I) 50 percent of the fee schedule amount determined under clause (ii) adjusted by the update established under subsection (d)(3) of this section for 1995, and

(II) 50 percent of the fee schedule amount determined under paragraph (1) for 1995 without regard to this paragraph.

(C) Special rule for anesthesia and radiology services

With respect to physicians' services which are anesthesia services, the Secretary shall provide for a transition in the same manner as a transition is provided for other services under subparagraph (B). With respect to radiology services, "109 percent" and "9 percent" shall be substituted for "115 percent" and "15 percent", respectively, in subparagraph (A)(ii).

(D) "Adjusted historical payment basis" defined

(i) In general

In this paragraph, the term "adjusted historical payment basis" means, with respect to a physicians' service furnished in a fee schedule area, the weighted average prevailing charge applied in the area for the service in 1991 (as determined by the Secretary without regard to physician specialty and as adjusted to reflect payments for services with customary charges below the prevailing charge or other payment limitations imposed by law or regulation) adjusted by the update established under subsection (d)(3) of this section for 1992.

(ii) Application to radiology services

In applying clause (i) in the case of physicians' services which are radiology services (including radiologist services, as defined in section 1395m(b)(6) of this title), but excluding nuclear medicine services that are subject to section 6105(b) of the Omnibus Budget Reconciliation Act of 1989, there shall be substituted for the weighted average prevailing charge the amount provided under the fee schedule established for the service for the fee schedule area under section 1395m(b) of this title.

(iii) Nuclear medicine services

In applying clause (i) in the case of physicians' services which are nuclear medicine services, there shall be substituted for the weighted average prevailing charge the amount provided under section 6105(b) of the Omnibus Budget Reconciliation Act of 1989.

(3) Incentives for participating physicians and suppliers

In applying paragraph (1)(B) in the case of a nonparticipating physician or a nonparticipating supplier or other person, the fee schedule amount shall be 95 percent of such amount otherwise applied under this subsection (without regard to this paragraph). In the case of physicians' services (including services which the Secretary excludes pursuant to subsection (j)(3) of this section) of a nonparticipating physician, supplier, or other person for which payment is made under this part on a basis other than the fee schedule amount, the payment shall be based on 95 percent of the payment basis for such services furnished by a participating physician, supplier, or other person.

(4) Special rule for medical direction

(A) In general

With respect to physicians' services furnished on or after January 1, 1994, and consisting of medical direction of two, three, or four concurrent anesthesia cases, the fee schedule amount to be applied shall be equal to one-half of the amount described in subparagraph (B).

(B) Amount

The amount described in this subparagraph, for a physician's medical direction of the performance of anesthesia services, is the following percentage of the fee schedule amount otherwise applicable under this section if the anesthesia services were personally performed by the physician alone:

(i) For services furnished during 1994, 120 percent.

(ii) For services furnished during 1995, 115 percent.

(iii) For services furnished during 1996, 110 percent.

(iv) For services furnished during 1997, 105 percent.

(v) For services furnished after 1997, 100 percent.

(b) Establishment of fee schedules.

(1) In general

Before November 1 of the preceding year, for each year beginning with 1998, the Secretary shall establish, by regulation, fee schedules that establish payment amounts for all physicians' services furnished in all fee schedule areas (as defined in subsection (j)(2) of this section) for the year. Except as provided in paragraph (2), each such payment amount for a service shall be equal to the product of—

(A) the relative value for the service (as determined in subsection (c)(2) of this section),

(B) the conversion factor (established under subsection (d) of this section) for the year, and

(C) the geographic adjustment factor (established under subsection (e)(2) of this section) for the service for the fee schedule area.

(2) Treatment of radiology services and anesthesia services

(A) Radiology services

With respect to radiology services (including radiologist services, as defined in section 1395m(b)(6) of this title), the Secretary shall base the relative values on the relative value scale developed under section 1395m(b)(1)(A) of this title, with appropriate modifications of the relative values to assure that the relative values established for radiology services which are similar or related to other physicians' services are consistent with the relative values established for those similar or related services.

(B) Anesthesia services

In establishing the fee schedule for anesthesia services for which a relative value guide has been established under section 4048(b) of the Omnibus Budget Reconciliation Act of 1987, the Secretary shall use, to the extent practicable, such relative value guide, with appropriate adjustment of the conversion factor, in a manner to assure that the fee schedule amounts for anesthesia services are consistent with the fee schedule amounts for other services determined by the Secretary to be of comparable value. In applying the previous sentence, the Secretary shall adjust the conversion factor by geographic adjustment factors in the same manner as such adjustment is made under paragraph (1)(C).

(C) Consultation

The Secretary shall consult with the Physician Payment Review Commission and organizations representing physicians or suppliers who furnish radiology services and anesthesia services in applying subparagraphs (A) and (B).

(3) Treatment of interpretation of electrocardiograms.

The Secretary—

(A) shall make separate payment under this section for the interpretation of electrocardiograms performed or ordered to be

535

performed as part of or in conjunction with a visit to or a consultation with a physician, and

(B) shall adjust the relative values established for visits and consultations under subsection (c) of this section so as not to include relative value units for interpretations of electrocardiograms in the relative value for visits and consultations.

(c) Determination of relative values for physicians' services

(1) Division of physicians' services into components.

In this section, with respect to a physicians' service:

(A) "Work component" defined

The term "work component" means the portion of the resources used in furnishing the service that reflects physician time and intensity in furnishing the service. Such portion shall—

(i) include activities before and after direct patient contact, and

(ii) be defined, with respect to surgical procedures, to reflect a global definition including pre-operative and post-operative physicians' services.

(B) "Practice expense component" defined

The term "practice expense component" means the portion of the resources used in furnishing the service that reflects the general categories of expenses (such as office rent and wages of personnel, but excluding malpractice expenses) comprising practice expenses.

(C) "Malpractice component" defined

The term "malpractice component" means the portion of the resources used in furnishing the service that reflects malpractice expenses in furnishing the service.

(2) Determination of relative values

(A) In general

(i) Combination of units for components

The Secretary shall develop a methodology for combining the work, practice expense, and malpractice relative value units, determined under subparagraph (C), for each service in a manner to produce a single relative value for that service. Such relative values are subject to adjustment under subparagraph (F)(i) and section 13515(b) of the Omnibus Budget Reconciliation Act of 1993.

(ii) Extrapolation

The Secretary may use extrapolation and other techniques to determine the number of relative value units for physicians' services for which specific data are not available and shall take into account recommendations of the Physician Payment Review Commission and the results of consultations with organizations representing physicians who provide such services.

(B) Periodic review and adjustments in relative values

(i) Periodic review

The Secretary, not less often than every 5 years, shall review the relative values established under this paragraph for all physicians' services.

(ii) Adjustments

(I) In general

The Secretary shall, to the extent the Secretary determines to be necessary and subject to subclause (II), adjust the number of such units to take into account changes in medical practice, coding changes, new data on relative value components, or the addition of new procedures. The Secretary shall publish an explanation of the basis for such adjustments.

(II) Limitation on annual adjustments

The adjustments under subclause (I) for a year may not cause the amount of expenditures under this part for the year to differ by more than $20,000,000 from the amount of expenditures under this part that would have been made if such adjustments had not been made.

(iii) Consultation

The Secretary, in making adjustments under clause (ii), shall consult with the Medicare Payment Advisory Commission and organizations representing physicians.

(C) Computation of relative value units for components

For purposes of this section for each physicians' service—

(i) Work relative value units

The Secretary shall determine a number of work relative value units for the service based on the relative resources incorporating physician time and intensity required in furnishing the service.

(ii) Practice expense relative value units

The Secretary shall determine a number of practice expense relative value units for the service for years before 1999 equal to the product of—

(I) the base allowed charges (as defined in subparagraph (D)) for the service, and

(II) the practice expense percentage for the service (as determined under paragraph (3)(C)(ii)). For 1999, such number of units shall be determined based 75 percent on such product and based 25 percent on the relative practice expense resources involved in furnishing the service. For 2000, such number of units shall be determined based 50 percent on such product and based 50 percent on such relative practice expense resources. For 2001, such number of units shall be determined based 25 percent on such product and based 75 percent on such relative practice expense resources. For a subsequent year, such number of units shall be determined based entirely on such relative practice expense resources.

and for years beginning with 1999 based on the relative practice expense resources involved in furnishing the service.

(iii) Malpractice relative value units

The Secretary shall determine a number of malpractice relative value units for the service for years before 2000 equal to the product of—

    (I) the base allowed charges (as defined in subparagraph (D)) for the service, and

    (II) the malpractice percentage for the service (as determined under paragraph (3)(C)(iii)),

and for years beginning with 2000 based on the malpractice expense resources involved in furnishing the service.

(D) "Base allowed charges" defined.

In this paragraph, the term "base allowed charges" means, with respect to a physician's service, the national average allowed charges for the service under this part for services furnished during 1991, as estimated by the Secretary using the most recent data available.

(E) Reduction in practice expense relative value units for certain services

    (i) In general

Subject to clause (ii), the Secretary shall reduce the practice expense relative value units applied to services described in clause (iii) furnished in—

    (I) 1994, by 25 percent of the number by which the number of practice expense relative value units (determined for 1994 without regard to this subparagraph) exceeds the number of work relative value units determined for 1994,

    (II) 1995, by an additional 25 percent of such excess, and

(III) 1996, by an additional 25 percent of such excess.

(ii) Floor on reductions

The practice expense relative value units for a physician's service shall not be reduced under this subparagraph to a number less than 128 percent of the number of work relative value units.

(iii) Services covered

For purposes of clause (i), the services described in this clause are physicians' services that are not described in clause (iv) and for which—

(I) there are work relative value units, and

(II) the number of practice expense relative value units (determined for 1994) exceeds 128 percent of the number of work relative value units (determined for such year).

(iv) Excluded services

For purposes of clause (iii), the services described in this clause are services which the Secretary determines at least 75 percent of which are provided under this subchapter in an office setting.

(F) Budget neutrality adjustments

The Secretary—

(i) shall reduce the relative values for all services (other than anesthesia services) established under this paragraph (and, in the case of anesthesia services, the conversion factor established by the Secretary for such services) by such percentage as the Secretary determines to be necessary so that, beginning in 1996, the amendment made by section 13514(a) of the Omnibus Budget Reconciliation Act of 1993 would not result in expenditures under this section that exceed the amount of such expenditures that would have been made if such amendment had not been made, and

(ii) shall reduce the amounts determined under subsection (a)(2)(B)(ii)(I) of this section by such percentage as the Secretary determines to be required to assure that, taking into account the reductions made under clause (i), the amendment made by section 13514(a) of the Omnibus Budget Reconciliation Act of 1993 would not result in expenditures under this section in 1994 that exceed the amount of such expenditures that would have been made if such amendment had not been made.

(G) Adjustments in relative value units for 1998

(i) In general

The Secretary shall—

(I) subject to clauses (iv) and (v), reduce the practice expense relative value units applied to any services described in clause (ii) furnished in 1998 to a number equal to 110 percent of the number of work relative value units, and

(II) increase the practice expense relative value units for office visit procedure codes during 1998 by a uniform percentage which the Secretary estimates will result in an aggregate increase in payments for such services equal to the aggregate decrease in payments by reason of subclause (I).

(ii) Services covered

For purposes of clause (i), the services described in this clause are physicians' services that are not described in clause (iii) and for which—

(I) there are work relative value units, and

(II) the number of practice expense relative value units (determined for 1998) exceeds 110 percent of the number of work relative value units (determined for such year).

(iii) Excluded services

For purposes of clause (ii), the services described in this clause are services which the Secretary determines at least 75 percent of which are provided under this title in an office setting.

(iv) Limitation on aggregate reallocation

If the application of clause (i)(I) would result in an aggregate amount of reductions under such clause in excess of $390,000,000, such clause shall be applied by substituting for 110 percent such greater percentage as the Secretary estimates will result in the aggregate amount of such reductions equaling $390,000,000.

(v) No reduction for certain services

Practice expense relative value units for a procedure performed in an office or in a setting out of an office shall not be reduced under clause (i) if the in-office or out-of-office practice expense relative value, respectively, for the procedure would increase under the proposed rule on resource-based practice expenses issued by the Secretary on June 18, 1997 (62 Federal Register 33158 et seq.).

(3) Component percentages

For purposes of paragraph (2), the Secretary shall determine a work percentage, a practice expense percentage, and a malpractice percentage for each physician's service as follows:

(A) Division of services by specialty

For each physician's service or class of physicians' services, the Secretary shall determine the average percentage of each such service or class of services that is performed, nationwide, under this part by physicians in each of the different physician specialties (as identified by the Secretary).

(B) Division of specialty by component

The Secretary shall determine the average percentage division of resources, among the work component, the practice expense component, and the malpractice component, used by physicians in each of such specialties in furnishing physicians' services. Such percentages shall be based on national data that describe the elements of physician practice costs and revenues, by physician specialty. The Secretary may use extrapolation and other techniques to determine practice costs and revenues for specialties for which adequate data are not available.

(C) Determination of component percentages

(i) Work percentage

The work percentage for a service (or class of services) is equal to the sum (for all physician specialties) of—

(I) the average percentage division for the work component for each physician specialty (determined under subparagraph (B)), multiplied by

(II) the proportion (determined under subparagraph (A)) of such service (or services) performed by physicians in that specialty.

(ii) Practice expense percentage

For years before 2002, the practice expense percentage for a service (or class of services) is equal to the sum (for all physician specialties) of—

(I) the average percentage division for the practice expense component for each physician specialty (determined under subparagraph (B)), multiplied by

(II) the proportion (determined under subparagraph (A)) of such service (or services) performed by physicians in that specialty.

(iii) Malpractice percentage

For years before 1999, the malpractice percentage for a service (or class of services) is equal to the sum (for all physician specialties) of—

(I) the average percentage division for the malpractice component for each physician specialty (determined under subparagraph (B)), multiplied by

(II) the proportion (determined under subparagraph (A)) of such service (or services) performed by physicians in that specialty.

(D) Periodic recomputation

The Secretary may, from time to time, provide for the recomputation of work percentages, practice expense percentages, and malpractice percentages determined under this paragraph.

(4) Ancillary policies

The Secretary may establish ancillary policies (with respect to the use of modifiers, local codes, and other matters) as may be necessary to implement this section.

(5) Coding

The Secretary shall establish a uniform procedure coding system for the coding of all physicians' services. The Secretary shall provide for an appropriate coding structure for visits and consultations. The Secretary may incorporate the use of time in the coding for visits and consultations. The Secretary, in establishing such coding system, shall consult with the Physician Payment Review Commission and other organizations representing physicians.

(6) No variation for specialists

The Secretary may not vary the conversion factor or the number of relative value units for a physicians' service based on whether the physician furnishing the service is a specialist or based on the type of specialty of the physician.

(d) Conversion factors

(1) Establishment

(A) In general

The conversion factor for each year shall be the conversion factor established under this subsection for the previous year (or, in the case of 1992, specified in subparagraph (B)) adjusted by the update (established under paragraph (3)) for the year involved (for years before 2001) and, for years beginning with 2001, multiplied by the update (established under paragraph (4)) for the year involved.

(B) Special provision for 1992

For purposes of subparagraph (A), the conversion factor specified in this subparagraph is a conversion factor (determined by the Secretary) which, if this section were to apply during 1991 using such conversion factor, would result in the same aggregate amount of payments under this part for physicians' services as the estimated aggregate amount of the payments under this part for such services in 1991.

542

(C) Special rules for 1998

Except as provided in subparagraph (D), the single conversion factor for 1998 under this subsection shall be the conversion factor for primary care services for 1997, increased by the Secretary's estimate of the weighted average of the three separate updates that would otherwise occur were it not for the enactment of chapter 1 of subtitle F of title IV of the Balanced Budget Act of 1997.

(D) Special rules for anesthesia services

The separate conversion factor for anesthesia services for a year shall be equal to 46 percent of the single conversion factor established for other physicians' services, except as adjusted for changes in work, practice expense, or malpractice relative value units.

(E) Publication and dissemination of information

The Secretary shall—

    (i) cause to have published in the Federal Register not later than November 1 of each year (beginning with 2000) the conversion factor which will apply to physicians' services for the succeeding year, the update determined under paragraph (4) for such succeeding year, and the allowed expenditures under such paragraph for such succeeding year; and

    (ii) make available to the Medicare Payment Advisory Commission and the public by March 1 of each year (beginning with 2000) an estimate of the sustainable growth rate and of the conversion factor which will apply to physicians' services for the succeeding year and data used in making such estimate.

(2) Repealed. Pub.L. 105–33, Title IV, § 4502(b), Aug. 5, 1997, 111 Stat. 433.

(3) Update for 1999 and 2000

(A) In general

Unless otherwise provided by law, subject to subparagraph (D) and the budget-neutrality factor determined by the Secretary under subsection (c)(2)(B)(ii), the update to the single conversion factor established in paragraph (1)(C) for 1999 and 2000 is equal to the product of—

    (i) 1 plus the Secretary's estimate of the percentage increase in the MEI (as defined in section 1395u(i)(3) of this title) for the year (divided by 100), and

    (ii) 1 plus the Secretary's estimate of the update adjustment factor for the year (divided by 100), minus 1 and multiplied by 100.

(B) Update adjustment factor

For purposes of subparagraph (A)(ii), the "update adjustment factor" for a year is equal (as estimated by the Secretary) to—

    (i) the difference between (I) the sum of the allowed expenditures for physicians' services (as determined under subparagraph (C)) for the period beginning April 1, 1997, and ending on March 31 of the year involved, and (II) the amount of actual expenditures for physicians' services furnished during the period beginning April 1, 1997, and ending on March 31 of the preceding year; divided by

(ii) the actual expenditures for physicians' services for the 12–month period ending on March 31 of the preceding year, increased by the sustainable growth rate under subsection (f) of this section for the fiscal year which begins during such 12–month period.

(C) Determination of allowed expenditures

For purposes of this paragraph and paragraph (4), the allowed expenditures for physicians' services for the 12–month period ending with March 31 of—

(i) 1997 is equal to the actual expenditures for physicians' services furnished during such 12–month period, as estimated by the Secretary; or

(ii) a subsequent year is equal to the allowed expenditures for physicians' services for the previous year, increased by the sustainable growth rate under subsection (f) of this section for the fiscal year which begins during such 12–month period.

(D) Restriction on variation from medicare economic index

Notwithstanding the amount of the update adjustment factor determined under subparagraph (B) for a year, the update in the conversion factor under this paragraph for the year may not be—

(i) greater than 100 times the following amount: (1.03 + (MEI percentage/100))—1; or

(ii) less than 100 times the following amount: (0.93 + (MEI percentage/100))—1,

where "MEI percentage" means the Secretary's estimate of the percentage increase in the MEI (as defined in section 1395(i)(3)) for the year involved.

(4) Update for years beginning with 2001

(A) In general

Unless otherwise provided by law, subject to the budget-neutrality factor determined by the Secretary under subsection (c)(2)(B)(ii) and subject to adjustment under subparagraph (F), the update to the single conversion factor established in paragraph (1)(C) for a year beginning with 2001 is equal to the product of—

(i) 1 plus the Secretary's estimate of the percentage increase in the MEI (as defined in section 1395u(i)(3) of this title) for the year (divided by 100); and

(ii) 1 plus the Secretary's estimate of the update adjustment factor under subparagraph (B) for the year.

(B) Update adjustment factor

For purposes of subparagraph (A)(ii), subject to subparagraph (D), the "update adjustment factor" for a year is equal (as estimated by the Secretary) to the sum of the following:

(i) Prior year adjustment component

An amount determined by—

    (I) computing the difference (which may be positive or negative) between the amount of the allowed expenditures for physicians' services for the prior year (as determined under subparagraph (C)) and the amount of the actual expenditures for such services for that year;

    (II) dividing that difference by the amount of the actual expenditures for such services for that year; and

    (III) multiplying that quotient by 0.75.

(ii) Cumulative adjustment component

An amount determined by—

    (I) computing the difference (which may be positive or negative) between the amount of the allowed expenditures for physicians' services (as determined under subparagraph (C)) from April 1, 1996, through the end of the prior year and the amount of the actual expenditures for such services during that period;

    (II) dividing that difference by actual expenditures for such services for the prior year as increased by the sustainable growth rate under subsection (f) for the year for which the update adjustment factor is to be determined; and

    (III) multiplying that quotient by 0.33.

(C) Determination of allowed expenditures

For purposes of this paragraph:

(i) Period up to april 1, 1999

The allowed expenditures for physicians' services for a period before April 1, 1999, shall be the amount of the allowed expenditures for such period as determined under paragraph (3)(C).

(ii) Transition to calendar year allowed expenditures

Subject to subparagraph (E), the allowed expenditures for—

    (I) the 9–month period beginning April 1, 1999, shall be the Secretary's estimate of the amount of the allowed expenditures that would be permitted under paragraph (3)(C) for such period; and

(II) the year of 1999, shall be the Secretary's estimate of the amount of the allowed expenditures that would be permitted under paragraph (3)(C) for such year.

(iii) Years beginning with 2000

The allowed expenditures for a year (beginning with 2000) is equal to the allowed expenditures for physicians' services for the previous year, increased by the sustainable growth rate under subsection (f) for the year involved.

(D) Restriction on update adjustment factor

The update adjustment factor determined under subparagraph (B) for a year may not be less than–0.07 or greater than 0.03.

(E) Recalculation of allowed expenditures for updates beginning with 2001

For purposes of determining the update adjustment factor for a year beginning with 2001, the Secretary shall recompute the allowed expenditures for previous periods beginning on or after April 1, 1999, consistent with subsection (f)(3).

(F) Transitional adjustment designed to provide for budget neutrality

Under this subparagraph the Secretary shall provide for an adjustment to the update under subparagraph (A)—

(i) for each of 2001, 2002, 2003, and 2004, of–0.2 percent; and

(ii) for 2005 of + 0.8 percent.

(e) Geographic adjustment factors

(1) Establishment of geographic indices

(A) In general

Subject to subparagraphs (B) and (C), the Secretary shall establish—

(i) an index which reflects the relative costs of the mix of goods and services comprising practice expenses (other than malpractice expenses) in the different fee schedule areas compared to the national average of such costs,

(ii) an index which reflects the relative costs of malpractice expenses in the different fee schedule areas compared to the national average of such costs, and

(iii) an index which reflects ¼ of the difference between the relative value of physicians' work effort in each of the different fee schedule areas and the national average of such work effort.

(B) Class-specific geographic cost-of-practice indices

The Secretary may establish more than one index under subparagraph (A)(i) in the case of classes of physicians' services, if, because of differences in the mix of goods and services comprising practice expenses for the different classes of services, the application of a single index under such clause to different classes of such services would be substantially inequitable.

(C) Periodic review and adjustments in geographic adjustment factors

The Secretary, not less often than every 3 years, shall, in consultation with appropriate representatives of physicians, review the indices established under subparagraph (A) and the geographic index values applied under this subsection for all fee schedule areas. Based on such review, the Secretary may revise such index and adjust such index values, except that, if more than 1 year has elasped since the date of the last previous adjustment, the adjustment to be applied in the first year of the next adjustment shall be 1/2 of the adjustment that otherwise would be made.

(D) Use of recent data

In establishing indices and index values under this paragraph, the Secretary shall use the most recent data available relating to practice expenses, malpractice expenses, and physician work effort in different fee schedule areas.

(2) Computation of geographic adjustment factor

For purposes of subsection (b)(1)(C) of this section, for all physicians' services for each fee schedule area the Secretary shall establish a geographic adjustment factor equal to the sum of the geographic cost-of-practice adjustment factor (specified in paragraph (3)), the geographic malpractice adjustment factor (specified in paragraph (4)), and the geographic physician work adjustment factor (specified in paragraph (5)) for the service and the area.

(3) Geographic cost-of-practice adjustment factor

For purposes of paragraph (2), the "geographic cost-of-practice adjustment factor", for a service for a fee schedule area, is the product of—

(A) the proportion of the total relative value for the service that reflects the relative value units for the practice expense component, and

547

(B) the geographic cost-of-practice index value for the area for the service, based on the index established under paragraph (1)(A)(i) or (1)(B) (as the case may be).

(4) Geographic malpractice adjustment factor

For purposes of paragraph (2), the "geographic malpractice adjustment factor", for a service for a fee schedule area, is the product of—

(A) the proportion of the total relative value for the service that reflects the relative value units for the malpractice component, and

(B) the geographic malpractice index value for the area, based on the index established under paragraph (1)(A)(ii).

(5) Geographic physician work adjustment factor

For purposes of paragraph (2), the "geographic physician work adjustment factor", for a service for a fee schedule area, is the product of—

(A) the proportion of the total relative value for the service that reflects the relative value units for the work component, and

(B) the geographic physician work index value for the area, based on the index established under paragraph (1)(A)(iii).

(f) Sustainable growth rate

(1) Publication

The Secretary shall cause to have published in the Federal Register not later than—

(A) November 1, 2000, the sustainable growth rate for 2000 and 2001; and

(B) November 1 of each succeeding year the sustainable growth rate for such succeeding year and each of the preceding 2 years.

(2) Specification of growth rate

The sustainable growth rate for all physicians' services for a fiscal year (beginning with fiscal year 1998 and ending with fiscal year 2000) and a year beginning with 2000 shall be equal to the product of—

(A) 1 plus the Secretary's estimate of the weighted average percentage increase (divided by 100) in the fees for all physicians' services in the applicable period involved,

(B) 1 plus the Secretary's estimate of the percentage change (divided by 100) in the average number of individuals enrolled under this part (other than Medicare + Choice plan enrollees) from the previous applicable period to the applicable period involved,

(C) 1 plus the Secretary's estimate of the projected percentage growth in real gross domestic product per capita (divided by 100) from the previous applicable period to the applicable period involved, and

(D) 1 plus the Secretary's estimate of the percentage change (divided by 100) in expenditures for all physicians' services in the applicable period (compared with the previous applicable period) which will result from changes in law and regulations, determined without taking into account estimated changes in expenditures resulting from the update adjustment factor determined under subsection (d)(3)(B) or (d)(4)(B), as the case may be of this section,

minus 1 and multiplied by 100.

(3) Data to be used

For purposes of determining the update adjustment factor under subsection (d)(4)(B) for a year beginning with 2001, the sustainable growth rates taken into consideration in the determination under paragraph (2) shall be determined as follows:

(A) For 2001

For purposes of such calculations for 2001, the sustainable growth rates for fiscal year 2000 and the years 2000 and 2001 shall be determined on the basis of the best data available to the Secretary as of September 1, 2000.

(B) For 2002

For purposes of such calculations for 2002, the sustainable growth rates for fiscal year 2000 and for years 2000, 2001, and 2002 shall be determined on the basis of the best data available to the Secretary as of September 1, 2001.

(C) For 2003 and succeeding years

For purposes of such calculations for a year after 2002—

(i) the sustainable growth rates for that year and the preceding 2 years shall be determined on the basis of the best data available to the Secretary as of September 1 of the year preceding the year for which the calculation is made; and

(ii) the sustainable growth rate for any year before a year described in clause (i) shall be the rate as most recently determined for that year under this subsection.

Nothing in this paragraph shall be construed as affecting the sustainable growth rates established for fiscal year 1998 or fiscal year 1999.

(4) Definitions

In this subsection:

(A) Services included in physicians' services

The term "physicians' services" includes other items and services (such as clinical diagnostic laboratory tests and radiology services), specified by the Secretary, that are commonly performed or furnished by a physician or in a physician's office, but does not include services furnished to a Medicare + Choice plan enrollee.

(B) Medicare + Choice plan enrollee

The term "Medicare + Choice plan enrollee" means, with respect to a fiscal year, an individual enrolled under this part who has elected to receive benefits under this title for the fiscal year through a Medicare + Choice plan offered under part C of this subchapter, and also includes an individual who is receiving benefits under this part through enrollment with an eligible organization with a risk-sharing contract under section 1395mm of this title.

(C) Applicable period

The term "applicable period" means—

(i) a fiscal year, in the case of fiscal year 1998, fiscal year 1999, and fiscal year 2000; or

(ii) a calendar year with respect to a year beginning with 2000; as the case may be.

(5) Repealed. Pub.L. 105–33, Title IV, § 4503(a), Aug. 5, 1997, 111 Stat. 433

(g) Limitation on beneficiary liability

(1) Limitation on actual charges

(A) In general

In the case of a nonparticipating physician or nonparticipating supplier or other person (as defined in section 1395u(i)(2) of this title) who does not accept payment on an assignment-related basis for a physician's service furnished with respect to an individual enrolled under this part, the following rules apply:

(i) Application of limiting charge

No person may bill or collect an actual charge for the service in excess of the limiting charge described in paragraph (2) for such service.

(ii) No liability for excess charges

No person is liable for payment of any amounts billed for the service in excess of such limiting charge.

(iii) Correction of excess charges

If such a physician, supplier, or other person bills, but does not collect, an actual charge for a service in violation of clause (i), the physician, supplier, or other person shall reduce on a timely basis the actual charge billed for the service to an amount not to exceed the limiting charge for the service.

(iv) Refund of excess collections

If such a physician, supplier, or other person collects an actual charge for a service in violation of clause (i), the physician, supplier, or other person shall provide on a timely basis a refund to the individual charged in the amount by which the amount collected exceeded the limiting charge for the service. The amount of such a refund shall be reduced to the extent the individual has an outstanding balance owed by the individual to the physician.

(B) Sanctions

If a physician, supplier, or other person—

(i) knowingly and willfully bills or collects for services in violation of subparagraph (A)(i) on a repeated basis, or

(ii) fails to comply with clause (iii) or (iv) of subparagraph (A) on a timely basis,

the Secretary may apply sanctions against the physician, supplier, or other person in accordance with paragraph (2) of section 1395u(j) of this title. In applying this subparagraph, paragraph (4) of such section applies in the same manner as such paragraph applies to such section and any reference in such section to a physician is deemed also to include a reference to a supplier or other person under this subparagraph.

(C) Timely basis

For purposes of this paragraph, a correction of a bill for an excess charge or refund of an amount with respect to a violation of subparagraph (A)(i) in the case of a service is considered to be provided 'on a timely basis', if the reduction or refund is made not later than 30 days after the date the physician, supplier, or other person is notified by the carrier under this part of such violation and of the requirements of subparagraph (A).

(2) "Limiting charge" defined

(A) For 1991

For physicians' services of a physician furnished during 1991, other than radiologist services subject to section 1395m(b) of this title, the "limiting charge" shall be the same percentage (or, if less, 25 percent) above the recognized payment amount under this part with respect to the physician (as a nonparticipating physician) as the percentage by which—

(i) the maximum allowable actual charge (as determined under section 1395u(j)(1)(C) of this title as of December 31, 1990, or, if less, the maximum actual charge otherwise permitted for the service under this part as of such date) for the service of the physician, exceeds

551

(ii) the recognized payment amount for the service of the physician (as a nonparticipating physician) as of such date.

In the case of evaluation and management services (as specified in section 1395u(b)(16)(B)(ii) of this title), the preceding sentence shall be applied by substituting "40 percent" for "25 percent".

(B) For 1992

For physicians' services furnished during 1992, other than radiologist services subject to section 1395m(b) of this title, the "limiting charge" shall be the same percentage (or, if less, 20 percent) above the recognized payment amount under this part for nonparticipating physicians as the percentage by which—

(i) the limiting charge (as determined under subparagraph (a) as of December 31, 1991) for the service, exceeds

(ii) the recognized payment amount for the service for nonparticipating physicians as of such date.

(C) After 1992

For physicians' services furnished in a year after 1992, the "limiting charge" shall be 115 percent of the recognized payment amount under this part for nonparticipating physicians or for nonparticipating suppliers or other persons.

(D) Recognized payment amount

In this section, the term "recognized payment amount" means, for services furnished on or after January 1, 1992, the fee schedule amount determined under subsection (a) of this section (or, if payment under this part is made on a basis other than the fee schedule under this section, 95 percent of the other payment basis), and, for services furnished during 1991, the applicable percentage (as defined in section 1395u(b)(4)(A)(IV) of this title) of the prevailing charge (or fee schedule amount) for nonparticipating physicians for that year.

(3) Limitation on charges for medicare beneficiaries eligible for medicaid benefits

(A) In general

Payment for physicians' services furnished on or after April 1, 1990, to an individual who is enrolled under this part and eligible for any medical assistance (including as a qualified medicare beneficiary, as defined in section 1396d(p)(1) of this title) with respect to such services under a State plan approved under subchapter XIX of this chapter may only be made on an assignment-related basis and the provisions of section 1396a(n)(3)(A) of this title apply to further limit permissible charges under this section.

(B) Penalty

A person may not bill for physicians' services subject to subparagraph (A) other than on an assignment-related basis. No person is liable for payment of any amounts billed for such a service in violation of the previous sentence. If a person knowingly and willfully bills for physicians' services in violation of the first sentence, the Secretary may apply sanctions against the person in accordance with section 1395u(j)(2) of this title.

(4) Physician submission of claims

(A) In general

For services furnished on or after September 1, 1990, within 1 year after the date of providing a service for which payment is made under this part on a reasonable charge or fee schedule basis, a physician, supplier, or other person (or an employer or facility in the cases described in section 1395u(b)(6)(A) of this title)—

    (i) shall complete and submit a claim for such service on a standard claim form specified by the Secretary to the carrier on behalf of a beneficiary, and

    (ii) may not impose any charge relating to completing and submitting such a form.

(B) Penalty

    (i) With respect to an assigned claim wherever a physician, provider, supplier or other person (or an employer or facility in the cases described in section 1395u(b)(6)(A) of this title) fails to submit such a claim as required in subparagraph (A), the Secretary shall reduce by 10 percent the amount that would otherwise be paid for such claim under this part.

    (ii) If a physician, supplier, or other person (or an employer or facility in the cases described in section 1395u(b)(6)(A) of this title) fails to submit a claim required to be submitted under subparagraph (A) or imposes a charge in violation of such subparagraph, the Secretary shall apply the sanction with respect to such a violation in the same manner as a sanction may be imposed under section 1395u(p)(3) of this title for a violation of section 1395u(p)(1) of this title.

(5) Electronic billing; direct deposit

The Secretary shall encourage and develop a system providing for expedited payment for claims submitted electronically. The Secretary shall also encourage and provide incentives allowing for direct deposit as payments for services furnished by participating physicians. The Secretary shall provide physicians with such technical information as necessary to enable such physicians to submit claims electronically. The Secretary shall submit a plan to Congress on this paragraph by May 1, 1990.

(6) Monitoring of charges

(A) In general

The Secretary shall monitor—

(i) the actual charges of nonparticipating physicians for physicians' services furnished on or after January 1, 1991, to individuals enrolled under this part, and

(ii) changes (by specialty, type of service, and geographic area) in (I) the proportion of expenditures for physicians' services provided under this part by participating physicians, (II) the proportion of expenditures for such services for which payment is made under this part on an assignment-related basis, and (III) the amounts charged above the recognized payment amounts under this part.

(B) Report

The Secretary shall, by not later than April 15 of each year (beginning in 1992), report to the Congress information on the extent to which actual charges exceed limiting charges, the number and types of services involved, and the average amount of excess charges and information regarding the changes described in subparagraph (A)(ii).

(C) Plan

If the Secretary finds that there has been a significant decrease in the proportions described in subclauses (I) and (II) of subparagraph (A)(ii) or an increase in the amounts described in subclause (III) of that subparagraph, the Secretary shall develop a plan to address such a problem and transmit to Congress recommendations regarding the plan. The Medicare Payment Advisory Commission shall review the Secretary's plan and recommendations and transmit to Congress its comments regarding such plan and recommendations.

(7) Monitoring of utilization and access

(A) In general

The Secretary shall monitor—

(i) changes in the utilization of and access to services furnished under this part within geographic, population, and service related categories,

(ii) possible sources of inappropriate utilization of services furnished under this part which contribute to the overall level of expenditures under this part, and

(iii) factors underlying these changes and their interrelationships.

(B) Report

The Secretary shall by not later than April 15, of each year (beginning with 1991) report to the Congress on the changes described in subparagraph (A)(i) and shall include in the report an examination of the factors (including factors relating to different services and specific categories and groups of services and geographic and demographic variations in utilization) which may contribute to such changes.

(C) Recommendations

The Secretary shall include in each annual report under subparagraph (B) recommendations—

(**i**) addressing any identified patterns of inappropriate utilization,

(**ii**) on utilization review,

(**iii**) on physician education or patient education,

(**iv**) addressing any problems of beneficiary access to care made evident by the monitoring process, and

(**v**) on such other matters as the Secretary deems appropriate.

The Medicare Payment Advisory Commission shall comment on the Secretary's recommendations and in developing its comments, the Commission shall convene and consult a panel of physician experts to evaluate the implications of medical utilization patterns for the quality of and access to patient care.

(h) Sending information to physicians

Before the beginning of each year (beginning with 1992), the Secretary shall send to each physician or nonparticipating supplier or other person furnishing physicians' services (as defined in subsection (j)(3) of this section) furnishing physicians', suppliers, and other persons services under this part, for services commonly performed by the physician, supplier, or other person, information on fee schedule amounts that apply for the year in the fee schedule area for participating and non-participating physicians, and the maximum amount that may be charged consistent with subsection (g)(2) of this section. Such information shall be transmitted in conjunction with notices to physicians, suppliers, and other persons under section 1395u(h) of this title (relating to the participating physician program) for a year.

(i) Miscellaneous provisions

(1) Restriction on administrative and judicial review

There shall be no administrative or judicial review under section 1395ff of this title or otherwise of—

(**A**) the determination of the adjusted historical payment basis (as defined in subsection (a)(2)(D)(i) of this section),

(**B**) the determination of relative values and relative value units under subsection (c) of this section, including adjustments under subsection (c)(2)(F) of this section and section 13515(b) of the Omnibus Budget Reconciliation Act of 1993,

(C) the determination of conversion factors under subsection (d) of this section,

(D) the establishment of geographic adjustment factors under subsection (e) of this section, and

(E) the establishment of the system for the coding of physicians' services under this section.

(2) Assistants-at-surgery

(A) In general

Subject to subparagraph (B), in the case of a surgical service furnished by a physician, if payment is made separately under this part for the services of a physician serving as an assistant-at-surgery, the fee schedule amount shall not exceed 16 percent of the fee schedule amount otherwise determined under this section for the global surgical service involved.

(B) Denial of payment in certain cases

If the Secretary determines, based on the most recent data available, that for a surgical procedure (or class of surgical procedures) the national average percentage of such procedure performed under this part which involve the use of a physician as an assistant at surgery is less than 5 percent, no payment may be made under this part for services of an assistant at surgery involved in the procedure.

(3) No comparability adjustment

For physicians' services for which payment under this part is determined under this section—

(A) a carrier may not make any adjustment in the payment amount under section 1395u(b)(3)(B) of this title on the basis that the payment amount is higher than the charge applicable, for a comparable services and under comparable circumstances, to the policyholders and subscribers of the carrier,

(B) no payment adjustment may be made under section 1395u(b)(8) of this title, and

(C) section 1395u(b)(9) of this title shall not apply.

(j) Definitions

In this section:

(1) Category

For services furnished before January 1, 1998, the term "category" means, with respect to physicians' services, surgical services, and all physicians' services other than surgical services (as defined by the Secretary and including anesthesia services), primary care services (as defined in section 1395u(i)(4) of this title), and all other physicians' services. The Secretary shall define surgical services and publish such definition in the Federal Register no later than May 1, 1990, after consultation with organizations representing physicians.

(2) Fee schedule area

The term "fee schedule area" means a locality used under section 1395u(b) of this title for purposes of computing payment amounts for physicians' services.

(3) Physicians' services

The term "physicians' services" includes items and services described in paragraphs (1), (2)(A), (2)(D), (2)(G), (2)(P) (with respect to services described in subparagraphs (A) and (C) of section 1395x(oo)(2) of this title), (2)(R) (with respect to services described in subparagraphs (B), (C), and (D) of section 1395x(pp)(1) of this title), (2)(S), (3), (4), (14) (with respect to services described in section 1395x(nn)(2) of this title), and (15) of section 1395x(s) of this title (other than clinical diagnostic laboratory tests and, except for purposes of subsections (a)(3), (g), and (h) of this section such other items and services as the Secretary may specify).

(4) Practice expenses

The term "practice expenses" includes all expenses for furnishing physicians' services, excluding malpractice expenses, physician compensation, and other physician fringe benefits.

§ 1395w–21. Eligibility, election, and enrollment

(a) Choice of medicare benefits through Medicare + Choice plans

(1) In general

Subject to the provisions of this section, each Medicare + Choice eligible individual (as defined in paragraph (3)) is entitled to elect to receive benefits under this title—

>**(A)** through the original medicare fee-for-service program under parts A and B of this subchapter, or

>**(B)** through enrollment in a Medicare + Choice plan under this part.

(2) Types of Medicare + Choice plans that may be available

A Medicare + Choice plan may be any of the following types of plans of health insurance:

>**(A)** Coordinated care plans

>Coordinated care plans which provide health care services, including but not limited to health maintenance organization plans (with or without point of service options), plans offered by provider-sponsored organizations (as defined in section 1395w–25(d) of this title), and preferred provider organization plans.

(B) Combination of MSA plan and contributions to Medicare + Choice MSA

An MSA plan, as defined in section 1395w–28(b)(3) of this title, and a contribution into a Medicare + Choice medical savings account (MSA).

(C) Private fee-for-service plans

A Medicare + Choice private fee-for-service plan, as defined in section 1395w-28(b)(2) of this title.

(3) Medicare + Choice eligible individual

(A) In general

In this title, subject to subparagraph (B), the term "Medicare + Choice eligible individual" means an individual who is entitled to benefits under part A of this subchapter and enrolled under part B of this subchapter.

(B) Special rule for end-stage renal disease

Such term shall not include an individual medically determined to have end-stage renal disease, except that—

    (i) an individual who develops end-stage renal disease while enrolled in a Medicare + Choice plan may continue to be enrolled in that plan; and

    (ii) in the case of such an individual who is enrolled in a Medicare + Choice plan under clause (i) (or subsequently under this clause), if the enrollment is discontinued under circumstances described in subsection (e)(4)(A) of this section, then the individual will be treated as a "Medicare + Choice eligible individual" for purposes of electing to continue enrollment in another Medicare + Choice plan.

(b) Special rules

(1) Residence requirement

(A) In general

Except as the Secretary may otherwise provide and except as provided in subparagraph (C), an individual is eligible to elect a Medicare + Choice plan offered by a Medicare + Choice organization only if the plan serves the geographic area in which the individual resides.

(B) Continuation of enrollment permitted

Pursuant to rules specified by the Secretary, the Secretary shall provide that a plan may offer to all individuals residing in a geographic area the option to continue enrollment in the plan, notwithstanding that the individual no longer resides in the service area of the plan, so long as the plan provides that individuals exercising this option have, as part of the basic benefits described in section 1395w–

22(a)(1)(A), reasonable access within that geographic area to the full range of basic benefits, subject to reasonable cost sharing liability in obtaining such benefits.

(C) Continuation of enrollment permitted where service changed

Notwithstanding subparagraph (A) and in addition to subparagraph (B), if a Medicare + Choice organization eliminates from its service area a Medicare + Choice payment area that was previously within its service area, the organization may elect to offer individuals residing in all or portions of the affected area who would otherwise be ineligible to continue enrollment the option to continue enrollment in a Medicare + Choice plan it offers so long as—

(i) the enrollee agrees to receive the full range of basic benefits (excluding emergency and urgently needed care) exclusively at facilities designated by the organization within the plan service area; and

(ii) there is no other Medicare + Choice plan offered in the area in which the enrollee resides at the time of the organization's election.

(2) Special rule for certain individuals covered under FEHBP or eligible for veterans or military health benefits, veterans

(A) FEHBP

An individual who is enrolled in a health benefit plan under chapter 89 of Title 5 [5 U.S.C.A. § 8901 et seq.], is not eligible to enroll in an MSA plan until such time as the Director of the Office of Management and Budget certifies to the Secretary that the Office of Personnel Management has adopted policies which will ensure that the enrollment of such individuals in such plans will not result in increased expenditures for the Federal Government for health benefit plans under such chapter.

(B) VA and DOD

The Secretary may apply rules similar to the rules described in subparagraph (A) in the case of individuals who are eligible for health care benefits under chapter 55 of Title 10 [10 U.S.C.A. § 1071 et seq.], or under chapter 17 of Title 38 [38 U.S.C.A. § 1701 et seq.].

(3) Limitation on eligibility of qualified medicare beneficiaries and other medicaid beneficiaries to enroll in an MSA plan

An individual who is a qualified medicare beneficiary (as defined in section 1396d(p)(1) of this title), a qualified disabled and working individual (described in section 1396d(s) of this title), an individual described in section 1396a(a)(10)(E)(iii) of this title, or otherwise entitled to medicare cost-sharing under a State plan under subchapter XIX of this chapter is not eligible to enroll in an MSA plan.

(4) Coverage under MSA plans on a demonstration basis

(A) In general

An individual is not eligible to enroll in an MSA plan under this part—

(i) on or after January 1, 2003, unless the enrollment is the continuation of such an enrollment in effect as of such date; or

(ii) as of any date if the number of such individuals so enrolled as of such date has reached 390,000.

Under rules established by the Secretary, an individual is not eligible to enroll (or continue enrollment) in an MSA plan for a year unless the individual provides assurances satisfactory to the Secretary that the individual will reside in the United States for at least 183 days during the year.

(B) Evaluation

The Secretary shall regularly evaluate the impact of permitting enrollment in MSA plans under this part on selection (including adverse selection), use of preventive care, access to care, and the financial status of the Trust Funds under this subchapter.

(C) Reports

The Secretary shall submit to Congress periodic reports on the numbers of individuals enrolled in such plans and on the evaluation being conducted under subparagraph (B). The Secretary shall submit such a report, by not later than March 1, 2002, on whether the time limitation under subparagraph (A)(i) should be extended or removed and whether to change the numerical limitation under subparagraph (A)(ii).

(c) Process for exercising choice

(1) In general

The Secretary shall establish a process through which elections described in subsection (a) are made and changed, including the form and manner in which such elections are made and changed. Such elections shall be made or changed only during coverage election periods specified under subsection (e) of this section and shall become effective as provided in subsection (f) of this section.

(2) Coordination through Medicare + Choice organizations

(A) Enrollment

Such process shall permit an individual who wishes to elect a Medicare + Choice plan offered by a Medicare + Choice organization to make such election through the filing of an appropriate election form with the organization.

(B) Disenrollment

Such process shall permit an individual, who has elected a Medicare + Choice plan offered by a Medicare + Choice organization and who wishes to terminate such election, to terminate such election through the filing of an appropriate election form with the organization.

(3) Default

(A) Initial election

(i) In general

Subject to clause (ii), an individual who fails to make an election during an initial election period under subsection (e)(1) of this section is deemed to have chosen the original medicare fee-for-service program option.

(ii) Seamless continuation of coverage

The Secretary may establish procedures under which an individual who is enrolled in a health plan (other than Medicare + Choice plan) offered by a Medicare + Choice organization at the time of the initial election period and who fails to elect to receive coverage other than through the organization is deemed to have elected the Medicare + Choice plan offered by the organization (or, if the organization offers more than one such plan, such plan or plans as the Secretary identifies under such procedures).

(B) Continuing periods

An individual who has made (or is deemed to have made) an election under this section is considered to have continued to make such election until such time as—

(i) the individual changes the election under this section, or

(ii) the Medicare + Choice plan with respect to which such election is in effect is discontinued or, subject to subsection (b)(1)(B) of this section, no longer serves the area in which the individual resides.

(d) Providing information to promote informed choice

(1) In general

The Secretary shall provide for activities under this subsection to broadly disseminate information to medicare beneficiaries (and prospective medicare beneficiaries) on the coverage options provided under this section in order to promote an active, informed selection among such options.

(2) Provision of notice

(A) Open season notification

At least 15 days before the beginning of each annual, coordinated election period (as defined in subsection (e)(3)(B) of this section), the

Secretary shall mail to each Medicare + Choice eligible individual residing in an area the following:

    (i) General information

The general information described in paragraph (3).

    (ii) List of plans and comparison of plan options

A list identifying the Medicare + Choice plans that are (or will be) available to residents of the area and information described in paragraph (4) concerning such plans. Such information shall be presented in a comparative form.

    (iii) Additional information

Any other information that the Secretary determines will assist the individual in making the election under this section.

The mailing of such information shall be coordinated, to the extent practicable, with the mailing of any annual notice under section 1395b–2 of this title.

    (B) Notification to newly eligible Medicare + Choice eligible individuals

To the extent practicable, the Secretary shall, not later than 30 days before the beginning of the initial Medicare + Choice enrollment period for an individual described in subsection (e)(1) of this section, mail to the individual the information described in subparagraph (A).

    (C) Form

The information disseminated under this paragraph shall be written and formatted using language that is easily understandable by medicare beneficiaries.

    (D) Periodic updating

The information described in subparagraph (A) shall be updated on at least an annual basis to reflect changes in the availability of Medicare + Choice plans and the benefits and Medicare + Choice monthly basic and supplemental beneficiary premiums for such plans.

(3) General information

General information under this paragraph, with respect to coverage under this part during a year, shall include the following:

    (A) Benefits under original medicare fee-for-service program option

A general description of the benefits covered under the original medicare fee-for-service program under parts A and B of this subchapter, including—

    (i) covered items and services,

(ii) beneficiary cost sharing, such as deductibles, coinsurance, and copayment amounts, and

(iii) any beneficiary liability for balance billing.

(B) Election procedures

Information and instructions on how to exercise election options under this section.

(C) Rights

A general description of procedural rights (including grievance and appeals procedures) of beneficiaries under the original medicare fee-for-service program and the Medicare + Choice program and the right to be protected against discrimination based on health status-related factors under section 1395w-22(b) of this title.

(D) Information on medigap and medicare select

A general description of the benefits, enrollment rights, and other requirements applicable to medicare supplemental policies under section 1395ss of this title and provisions relating to medicare select policies described in section 1395ss(t) of this title.

(E) Potential for contract termination

The fact that a Medicare + Choice organization may terminate its contract, refuse to renew its contract, or reduce the service area included in its contract, under this part, and the effect of such a termination, nonrenewal, or service area reduction may have on individuals enrolled with the Medicare + Choice plan under this part.

(4) Information comparing plan options

Information under this paragraph, with respect to a Medicare + Choice plan for a year, shall include the following:

(A) Benefits

The benefits covered under the plan, including the following:

(i) Covered items and services beyond those provided under the original medicare fee-for-service program.

(ii) Any beneficiary cost sharing.

(iii) Any maximum limitations on out-of-pocket expenses.

(iv) In the case of an MSA plan, differences in cost sharing, premiums, and balance billing under such a plan compared to under other Medicare + Choice plans.

(v) In the case of a Medicare + Choice private fee-for-service plan, differences in cost sharing, premiums, and balance billing under such a plan compared to under other Medicare + Choice plans.

(vi) The extent to which an enrollee may obtain benefits through out-of-network health care providers.

(vii) The extent to which an enrollee may select among in-network providers and the types of providers participating in the plan's network.

(viii) The organization's coverage of emergency and urgently needed care.

(B) Premiums

The Medicare + Choice monthly basic beneficiary premium and Medicare + Choice monthly supplemental beneficiary premium, if any, for the plan or, in the case of an MSA plan, the Medicare + Choice monthly MSA premium.

(C) Service area

The service area of the plan.

(D) Quality and performance

To the extent available, plan quality and performance indicators for the benefits under the plan (and how they compare to such indicators under the original medicare fee-for-service program under parts A and B of this subchapter in the area involved), including—

(i) disenrollment rates for medicare enrollees electing to receive benefits through the plan for the previous 2 years (excluding disenrollment due to death or moving outside the plan's service area),

(ii) information on medicare enrollee satisfaction,

(iii) information on health outcomes, and

(iv) the recent record regarding compliance of the plan with requirements of this part (as determined by the Secretary).

(E) Supplemental benefits

Whether the organization offering the plan includes mandatory supplemental benefits in its base benefit package or offers optional supplemental benefits and the terms and conditions (including premiums) for such coverage.

(5) Maintaining a toll-free number and Internet site

The Secretary shall maintain a toll-free number for inquiries regarding Medicare + Choice options and the operation of this part in all areas in which Medicare + Choice plans are offered and an Internet site through which individuals may electronically obtain information on such options and Medicare + Choice plans.

(6) Use of non-Federal entities

The Secretary may enter into contracts with non-Federal entities to carry out activities under this subsection.

(7) Provision of information

A Medicare + Choice organization shall provide the Secretary with such information on the organization and each Medicare + Choice plan it offers as may be required for the preparation of the information referred to in paragraph (2)(A).

(e) Coverage election periods

(1) Initial choice upon eligibility to make election if Medicare + Choice plans available to individual

If, at the time an individual first becomes entitled to benefits under part A of this subchapter and enrolled under part B of this subchapter, there is one or more Medicare + Choice plans offered in the area in which the individual resides, the individual shall make the election under this section during a period specified by the Secretary such that if the individual elects a Medicare + Choice plan during the period, coverage under the plan becomes effective as of the first date on which the individual may receive such coverage.

(2) Open enrollment and disenrollment opportunities

Subject to paragraph (5)—

(A) Continuous open enrollment and disenrollment through 2001

At any time during 1998, 1999, 2000, and 2001, a Medicare + Choice eligible individual may change the election under subsection (a)(1).

(B) Continuous open enrollment and disenrollment for first 6 months during 2002

(i) In general

Subject to clause (ii) and subparagraph (D), at any time during the first 6 months of 2002, or, if the individual first becomes a Medicare + Choice eligible individual during 2002, during the first 6 months during 2002 in which the individual is a Medicare + Choice eligible individual, a Medicare + Choice eligible individual may change the election under subsection (a)(1) of this section.

(ii) Limitation of one change

An individual may exercise the right under clause (i) only once. The limitation under this clause shall not apply to changes in elections effected during an annual, coordinated election period under paragraph (3) or during a special enrollment period under the first sentence of paragraph (4).

(C) Continuous open enrollment and disenrollment for first 3 months in subsequent years

(i) In general

Subject to clause (ii) and subparagraph (D), at any time during the first 3 months of a year after 2002, or, if the individual first becomes a Medicare + Choice eligible individual during a year after 2002, during the first 3 months of such year in which the individual is a Medicare + Choice eligible individual,a Medicare + Choice eligible individual may change the election under subsection (a)(1) if this section.

(ii) Limitation of one change during open enrollment period each year

An individual may exercise the right under clause (i) only once during the applicable 3–month period described in such clause in each year. The limitation under this clause shall not apply to changes in elections effected during an annual, coordinated election period under paragraph (3) or during a special enrollment period under paragraph (4).

(D) Continuous open enrollment for institutionalized individuals

At any time after 2001 in the case of a Medicare + Choice eligible individual who is institutionalized (as defined by the Secretary), the individual may elect under subsection (a)(1)—

(i) to enroll in a Medicare + Choice plan; or

(ii) to change the Medicare + Choice plan in which the individual is enrolled.

(3) Annual, coordinated election period

(A) In general

Subject to paragraph (5), each individual who is eligible to make an election under this section may change such election during an annual, coordinated election period.

(B) Annual, coordinated election period

For purposes of this section, the term "annual, coordinated election period" means, with respect to a calendar year (beginning with 2000), the month of November before such year.

(C) Medicare + Choice health information fairs

During the fall season of each year (beginning with 1999), in conjunction with the annual coordinated election period defined in subparagraph (B), the Secretary shall provide for a nationally coordinated educational and publicity campaign to inform Medicare + Choice eligible individuals about Medicare + Choice plans and the election process provided under this section.

(D) Special information campaign in 1998

During November 1998 the Secretary shall provide for an educational and publicity campaign to inform Medicare + Choice eligible individuals about the availability of Medicare + Choice plans, and eligible organizations with risk-sharing contracts under section 1395mm of this title, offered in different areas and the election process provided under this section.

(4) Special election periods

Effective as of January 1, 2002, an individual may discontinue an election of a Medicare + Choice plan offered by a Medicare + Choice organization other than during an annual, coordinated election period and make a new election under this section if—

(A)(i) the certification of the organization or plan under this part has been terminated, or the organization or plan has notified the individual of an impending termination of such certification; or

(ii) the organization has terminated or otherwise discontinued providing the plan in the area in which the individual resides, or has notified the individual of an impending termination or discontinuation of such plan;

(B) the individual is no longer eligible to elect the plan because of a change in the individual's place of residence or other change in circumstances (specified by the Secretary, but not including termination of the individual's enrollment on the basis described in clause (i) or (ii) of subsection (g)(3)(B) of this section);

(C) the individual demonstrates (in accordance with guidelines established by the Secretary) that—

(i) the organization offering the plan substantially violated a material provision of the organization's contract under this part in relation to the individual (including the failure to provide an enrollee on a timely basis medically necessary care for which benefits are available under the plan or the failure to provide such covered care in accordance with applicable quality standards); or

(ii) the organization (or an agent or other entity acting on the organization's behalf) materially misrepresented the plan's provisions in marketing the plan to the individual; or

(D) the individual meets such other exceptional conditions as the Secretary may provide.

Effective as of January 1, 2002, an individual who, upon first becoming eligible for benefits under part A of this subchapter at age 65, enrolls in a Medicare + Choice plan under this part, the individual may discontinue the election of such plan, and elect coverage under the original fee-for-service plan, at any time during the 12–month period beginning on the effective date of such enrollment.

(5) Special rules for MSA plans

Notwithstanding the preceding provisions of this subsection, an individual—

(A) may elect an MSA plan only during—

(i) an initial open enrollment period described in paragraph (1),

(ii) an annual, coordinated election period described in paragraph (3)(B), or

(iii) the month of November 1998;

(B) subject to subparagraph (C), may not discontinue an election of an MSA plan except during the periods described in clause (ii) or (iii) of subparagraph (A) and under the first sentence of paragraph (4); and

(C) who elects an MSA plan during an annual, coordinated election period, and who never previously had elected such a plan, may revoke such election, in a manner determined by the Secretary, by not later than December 15 following the date of the election.

(6) Open enrollment periods

Subject to paragraph (5), a Medicare + Choice organization—

(A) shall accept elections or changes to elections during the initial enrollment periods described in paragraph (1), during the month of November 1998 and each subsequent year (as provided in paragraph (3)), and during special election periods described in the first sentence of paragraph (4); and

(B) may accept other changes to elections at such other times as the organization provides.

(f) Effectiveness of elections and changes of elections

(1) During initial coverage election period

An election of coverage made during the initial coverage election period under subsection (e)(1)(A) shall take effect upon the date the individual becomes entitled to benefits under part A of this subchapter and enrolled under part B of this subchapter, except as the Secretary may provide (consistent with section 1395q of this title) in order to prevent retroactive coverage.

(2) During continuous open enrollment periods

An election or change of coverage made under subsection (e)(2) of this section shall take effect with the first day of the first calendar month following the date on which the election or change is made.

(3) Annual, coordinated election period

An election or change of coverage made during an annual, coordinated election period (as defined in subsection (e)(3)(B) of this section) in a year shall take effect as of the first day of the following year.

(4) Other periods

An election or change of coverage made during any other period under subsection (e)(4) of this section shall take effect in such manner as the Secretary provides in a manner consistent (to the extent practicable) with protecting continuity of health benefit coverage.

(g) Guaranteed issue and renewal

(1) In general

Except as provided in this subsection, a Medicare + Choice organization shall provide that at any time during which elections are accepted under this section with respect to a Medicare + Choice plan offered by the organization, the organization will accept without restrictions individuals who are eligible to make such election.

(2) Priority

If the Secretary determines that a Medicare + Choice organization, in relation to a Medicare + Choice plan it offers, has a capacity limit and the number of Medicare + Choice eligible individuals who elect the plan under this section exceeds the capacity limit, the organization may limit the election of individuals of the plan under this section but only if priority in election is provided—

(A) first to such individuals as have elected the plan at the time of the determination, and

(B) then to other such individuals in such a manner that does not discriminate, on a basis described in section 1395w–22(b) of this title, among the individuals (who seek to elect the plan).

The preceding sentence shall not apply if it would result in the enrollment of enrollees substantially nonrepresentative, as determined in accordance with regulations of the Secretary, of the medicare population in the service area of the plan.

(3) Limitation on termination of election

(A) In general

Subject to subparagraph (B), a Medicare + Choice organization may not for any reason terminate the election of any individual under this section for a Medicare + Choice plan it offers.

(B) Basis for termination of election

A Medicare + Choice organization may terminate an individual's election under this section with respect to a Medicare + Choice plan it offers if—

(i) any Medicare + Choice monthly basic and supplemental beneficiary premiums required with respect to such plan are not paid on a timely basis (consistent with standards under section 1395w–26 of this title that provide for a grace period for late payment of such premiums),

569

(ii) the individual has engaged in disruptive behavior (as specified in such standards), or

(iii) the plan is terminated with respect to all individuals under this part in the area in which the individual resides.

(C) Consequence of termination

(i) Terminations for cause

Any individual whose election is terminated under clause (i) or (ii) of subparagraph (B) is deemed to have elected the original medicare fee-for-service program option described in subsection (a)(1)(A) of this section.

(ii) Termination based on plan termination or service area reduction ·

Any individual whose election is terminated under subparagraph (B)(iii) shall have a special election period under subsection (e)(4)(A) of this section in which to change coverage to coverage under another Medicare + Choice plan. Such an individual who fails to make an election during such period is deemed to have chosen to change coverage to the original medicare fee-for-service program option described in subsection (a)(1)(A) of this section.

(D) Organization obligation with respect to election forms

Pursuant to a contract under section 1395w–27, each Medicare + Choice organization receiving an election form under subsection (c)(2) of this section shall transmit to the Secretary (at such time and in such manner as the Secretary may specify) a copy of such form or such other information respecting the election as the Secretary may specify.

(h) Approval of marketing material and application forms

(1) Submission

No marketing material or application form may be distributed by a Medicare + Choice organization to (or for the use of) Medicare + Choice eligible individuals unless—

(A) at least 45 days (or 10 days in the case described in paragraph (5)) before the date of distribution the organization has submitted the material or form to the Secretary for review, and

(B) the Secretary has not disapproved the distribution of such material or form.

(2) Review

The standards established under section 1395w–26 shall include guidelines for the review of any material or form submitted and under such guidelines the Secretary shall disapprove (or later require the correction of) such material or form if the material or form is materially inaccurate or misleading or otherwise makes a material misrepresentation.

(3) Deemed approval (1–stop shopping)

In the case of material or form that is submitted under paragraph (1)(A) to the Secretary or a regional office of the Department of Health and Human Services and the Secretary or the office has not disapproved the distribution of marketing material or form under paragraph (1)(B) with respect to a Medicare + Choice plan in an area, the Secretary is deemed not to have disapproved such distribution in all other areas covered by the plan and organization except with regard to that portion of such material or form that is specific only to an area involved.

(4) Prohibition of certain marketing practices

Each Medicare + Choice organization shall conform to fair marketing standards, in relation to Medicare + Choice plans offered under this part, included in the standards established under section 1395w–26. Such standards—

> **(A)** shall not permit a Medicare + Choice organization to provide for cash or other monetary rebates as an inducement for enrollment or otherwise, and

> **(B)** may include a prohibition against a Medicare + Choice organization (or agent of such an organization) completing any portion of any election form used to carry out elections under this section on behalf of any individual.

(5) Special treatment of marketing material following model marketing language

In the case of marketing material of an organization that uses, without modification, proposed model language specified by the Secretary, the period specified in paragraph (1)(A) shall be reduced from 45 days to 10 days.

(i) Effect of election of Medicare + Choice plan option

(1) Payments to organizations

Subject to sections 1395w–22(a)(5), 1395w–23(g), 1395w–23(h), 1395ww(d)(11), and 1395ww(h)(3)(D) of this title, payments under a contract with a Medicare + Choice organization under section 1395w–23(a) of this title with respect to an individual electing a Medicare + Choice plan offered by the organization shall be instead of the amounts which (in the absence of the contract) would otherwise be payable under parts A and B of this subchapter for items and services furnished to the individual.

(2) Only organization entitled to payment

Subject to sections 13952w–23(e), 1395w–23(g), 1395w–23(h), 1395w–27(f)(2), 1395ww(d)(11), and 1395ww(h)(3)(D) of this title, only the Medicare + Choice organization shall be entitled to receive payments from the Secretary under this title for services furnished to the individual.

1395x. Definitions

For purposes of this subchapter—

(a) Spell of illness

The term "spell of illness" with respect to any individual means a period of consecutive days—

(1) beginning with the first day (not included in a previous spell of illness)

(A) on which such individual is furnished inpatient hospital services, inpatient critical access hospital services or extended care services, and

(B) which occurs in a month for which he is entitled to benefits under part A of this subchapter, and

(2) ending with the close of the first period of 60 consecutive days thereafter on each of which he is neither an inpatient of a hospital or critical access hospital nor an inpatient of a facility described in section 1395i–3(a)(1) of this title or subsection (y)(1) of this section.

(b) Inpatient hospital services

The term "inpatient hospital services" means the following items and services furnished to an inpatient of a hospital and (except as provided in paragraph (3)) by the hospital—

(1) bed and board;

(2) such nursing services and other related services, such use of hospital facilities, and such medical social services as are ordinarily furnished by the hospital for the care and treatment of inpatients, and such drugs, biologicals, supplies, appliances, and equipment, for use in the hospital, as are ordinarily furnished by such hospital for the care and treatment of inpatients; and

(3) such other diagnostic or therapeutic items or services, furnished by the hospital or by others under arrangements with them made by the hospital, as are ordinarily furnished to inpatients either by such hospital or by others under such arrangements;

excluding, however—

(4) medical or surgical services provided by a physician, resident, or intern, services described by subsection (s)(2)(K) of this section, certified nurse-midwife services, qualified psychologist services, and services of a certified registered nurse anesthetist; and

(5) the services of a private-duty nurse or other private-duty attendant.

Paragraph (4) shall not apply to services provided in a hospital by—

(6) an intern or a resident-in-training under a teaching program approved by the Council on Medical Education of the American Medical Association or, in the case of an osteopathic hospital, approved by the

572

Committee on Hospitals of the Bureau of Professional Education of the American Osteopathic Association, or, in the case of services in a hospital or osteopathic hospital by an intern or resident-in-training in the field of dentistry, approved by the Council on Dental Education of the American Dental Association, or in the case of services in a hospital or osteopathic hospital by an intern or resident-in-training in the field of podiatry, approved by the Council on Podiatric Medical Education of the American Podiatric Medical Association; or

(7) a physician where the hospital has a teaching program approved as specified in paragraph (6), if

(A) the hospital elects to receive any payment due under this subchapter for reasonable costs of such services, and

(B) all physicians in such hospital agree not to bill charges for professional services rendered in such hospital to individuals covered under the insurance program established by this subchapter.

(c) Inpatient psychiatric hospital services

The term "inpatient psychiatric hospital services" means inpatient hospital services furnished to an inpatient of a psychiatric hospital.

(d) Repealed. *Pub.L. 98–369*, Div. B, Title III, § 2335(b)(1), July 18, 1984, 98 Stat. 1090

(e) Hospital

The term "hospital" (except for purposes of sections 1395f(d), 1395f(f), and 1395n(b) of this title, subsection (a)(2) of this section, paragraph (7) of this subsection, and subsection (i) of this section) means an institution which—

(1) is primarily engaged in providing, by or under the supervision of physicians, to inpatients

(A) diagnostic services and therapeutic services for medical diagnosis, treatment, and care of injured, disabled, or sick persons, or

(B) rehabilitation services for the rehabilitation of injured, disabled, or sick persons;

(2) maintains clinical records on all patients;

(3) has bylaws in effect with respect to its staff of physicians;

(4) has a requirement that every patient with respect to whom payment may be made under this subchapter must be under the care of a physician, except that a patient receiving qualified psychologist services (as defined in subsection (ii) of this section) may be under the care of a clinical psychologist with respect to such services to the extent permitted under State law;

(5) provides 24–hour nursing service rendered or supervised by a registered professional nurse, and has a licensed practical nurse or registered professional nurse on duty at all times; except that until January 1, 1979, the Secretary is authorized to waive the requirement of this paragraph for any one-year period with respect to any institution, insofar as such requirement relates to the provision of twenty-four-hour nursing service rendered or supervised by a registered professional nurse

573

(except that in any event a registered professional nurse must be present on the premises to render or supervise the nursing service provided, during at least the regular daytime shift), where immediately preceding such one-year period he finds that—

    (A) such institution is located in a rural area and the supply of hospital services in such area is not sufficient to meet the needs of individuals residing therein,

    (B) the failure of such institution to qualify as a hospital would seriously reduce the availability of such services to such individuals, and

    (C) such institution has made and continues to make a good faith effort to comply with this paragraph, but such compliance is impeded by the lack of qualified nursing personnel in such area;

(6)(A) has in effect a hospital utilization review plan which meets the requirements of subsection (k) of this section and

    (B) has in place a discharge planning process that meets the requirements of subsection (ee) of this section;

(7) in the case of an institution in any State in which State or applicable local law provides for the licensing of hospitals,

    (A) is licensed pursuant to such law or

    (B) is approved, by the agency of such State or locality responsible for licensing hospitals, as meeting the standards established for such licensing;

(8) has in effect an overall plan and budget that meets the requirements of subsection (z) of this section; and

(9) meets such other requirements as the Secretary finds necessary in the interest of the health and safety of individuals who are furnished services in the institution.

For purposes of subsection (a)(2) of this section, such term includes any institution which meets the requirements of paragraph (1) of this subsection. For purposes of sections 1395f(d) and 1395n(b) of this title (including determination of whether an individual received inpatient hospital services or diagnostic services for purposes of such sections), section 1395f(f)(2) of this title, and subsection (i) of this section, such term includes any institution which

    (i) meets the requirements of paragraphs (5) and (7) of this subsection,

    (ii) is not primarily engaged in providing the services described in subsection (j)(1)(A) of this section and

    (iii) is primarily engaged in providing, by or under the supervision of individuals referred to in paragraph (1) of subsection (r) of this section, to inpatients diagnostic services and therapeutic services for medical diagnosis, treatment, and care of injured, disabled, or sick persons, or rehabilitation services for the rehabilitation of injured, disabled, or sick persons.

For purposes of section 1395f(f)(1) of this title, such term includes an institution which

(i) is a hospital for purposes of sections 1395f(d), 1395f(f)(2), and 1395n(b) of this title and

(ii) is accredited by the Joint Commission on Accreditation of Hospitals, or is accredited by or approved by a program of the country in which such institution is located if the Secretary finds the accreditation or comparable approval standards of such program to be essentially equivalent to those of the Joint Commission on Accreditation of Hospitals. Notwithstanding the preceding provisions of this subsection, such term shall not, except for purposes of subsection (a)(2) of this section, include any institution which is primarily for the care and treatment of mental diseases unless it is a psychiatric hospital (as defined in subsection (f) of this section). The term "hospital" also includes a religious nonmedical health care institution (as defined in subsection (ss)(1) of this section), with respect to items and services ordinarily furnished by such institution to inpatients, and payment may be made with respect to services provided by or in such an institution only to such extent and under such conditions, limitations, and requirements (in addition to or in lieu of the conditions, limitations, and requirements otherwise applicable) as may be provided in regulations consistent with section 1395i-5 of this title. For provisions deeming certain requirements of this subsection to be met in the case of accredited institutions, see section 1395bb of this title. The term "hospital" also includes a facility of fifty beds or less which is located in an area determined by the Secretary to meet the definition relating to a rural area described in subparagraph (A) of paragraph (5) of this subsection and which meets the other requirements of this subsection, except that—

(A) with respect to the requirements for nursing services applicable after December 31, 1978, such requirements shall provide for temporary waiver of the requirements, for such period as the Secretary deems appropriate, where

(i) the facility's failure to fully comply with the requirements is attributable to a temporary shortage of qualified nursing personnel in the area in which the facility is located,

(ii) a registered professional nurse is present on the premises to render or supervise the nursing service provided during at least the regular daytime shift, and

(iii) the Secretary determines that the employment of such nursing personnel as are available to the facility during such temporary period will not adversely affect the health and safety of patients;

(B) with respect to the health and safety requirements promulgated under paragraph (9), such requirements shall be applied by the Secretary to a facility herein defined in such manner as to assure that personnel requirements take into account the availability of technical personnel and the educational opportunities for technical personnel in the area in which such facility is located, and the scope of services rendered by such facility; and the Secretary, by regulations, shall provide for the continued participation of such a facility where such personnel requirements are not fully met, for such period as the Secretary determines that

(i) the facility is making good faith efforts to fully comply with the personnel requirements,

(ii) the employment by the facility of such personnel as are available to the facility will not adversely affect the health and safety of patients, and

(iii) if the Secretary has determined that because of the facility's waiver under this subparagraph, the facility should limit its scope of services in order not to adversely affect the health and safety of the facility's patients, the facility is so limiting the scope of services it provides; and

(C) with respect to the fire and safety requirements promulgated under paragraph (9), the Secretary

(i) may waive, for such period as he deems appropriate, specific provisions of such requirements which if rigidly applied would result in unreasonable hardship for such a facility and which, if not applied, would not jeopardize the health and safety of patients, and

(ii) may accept a facility's compliance with all applicable State codes relating to fire and safety in lieu of compliance with the fire and safety requirements promulgated under paragraph (9), if he determines that such State has in effect fire and safety codes, imposed by State law, which adequately protect patients.

The term "hospital" does not include, unless the context otherwise requires, a critical **access hospital (as defined in subsection (mm)(1) of this section).**

(f) Psychiatric hospital

The term "psychiatric hospital" means an institution which—

(1) is primarily engaged in providing, by or under the supervision of a physician, psychiatric services for the diagnosis and treatment of mentally ill persons;

(2) satisfies the requirements of paragraphs (3) through (9) of subsection (e) of this section;

(3) maintains clinical records on all patients and maintains such records as the Secretary finds to be necessary to determine the degree and intensity of the treatment provided to individuals entitled to hospital insurance benefits under part A of this subchapter; and

(4) meets such staffing requirements as the Secretary finds necessary for the institution to carry out an active program of treatment for individuals who are furnished services in the institution.

In the case of an institution which satisfies paragraphs (1) and (2) of the preceding sentence and which contains a distinct part which also satisfies paragraphs (3) and (4) of such sentence, such distinct part shall be considered to be a "psychiatric hospital".

(g) Outpatient occupational therapy services

The term "outpatient occupational therapy services" has the meaning given the term "outpatient physical therapy services" in subsection (p) of this section, except that "occupational" shall be substituted for "physical" each place it appears therein.

(h) Extended care services

The term "extended care services" means the following items and services furnished to an inpatient of a skilled nursing facility and (except as provided in paragraphs (3), (6), and (7) by such skilled nursing facility—

(1) nursing care provided by or under the supervision of a registered professional nurse;

(2) bed and board in connection with the furnishing of such nursing care;

(3) physical or occupational therapy or speech-language pathology services furnished by the skilled nursing facility or by others under arrangements with them made by the facility;

(4) medical social services;

(5) such drugs, biologicals, supplies, appliances, and equipment, furnished for use in the skilled nursing facility, as are ordinarily furnished by such facility for the care and treatment of inpatients;

(6) medical services provided by an intern or resident-in-training of a hospital with which the facility has in effect a transfer agreement (meeting the requirements of subsection (*l*) of this section), under a teaching program of such hospital approved as provided in the last sentence of subsection (b) of this section, and other diagnostic or therapeutic services provided by a hospital with which the facility has such an agreement in effect; and

(7) such other services necessary to the health of the patients as are generally provided by skilled nursing facilities, or by others under arrangements with them made by the facility;

excluding, however, any item or service if it would not be included under subsection (b) of this section if furnished to an inpatient of a hospital.

(i) Post-hospital extended care services

The term "post-hospital extended care services" means extended care services furnished an individual after transfer from a hospital in which he was an inpatient for not less than 3 consecutive days before his discharge from the hospital in connection with such transfer. For purposes of the preceding sentence, items and services shall be deemed to have been furnished to an individual after transfer from a hospital, and he shall be deemed to have been an inpatient in the hospital immediately before transfer therefrom, if he is admitted to the skilled nursing facility

(A) within 30 days after discharge from such hospital, or

(B) within such time as it would be medically appropriate to begin an active course of treatment, in the case of an individual whose condition is such that skilled nursing facility care would not be medically appropriate within 30 days after discharge from a hospital; and an individual shall be deemed not to have been discharged from a skilled nursing facility if, within 30 days after discharge therefrom, he is admitted to such facility or any other skilled nursing facility.

(j) Skilled nursing facility

The term "skilled nursing facility" has the meaning given such term in section 1395i–3(a) of this title.

(k) Utilization review

A utilization review plan of a hospital or skilled nursing facility shall be considered sufficient if it is applicable to services furnished by the institution to individuals entitled to insurance benefits under this subchapter and if it provides—

(1) for the review, on a sample or other basis, of admissions to the institution, the duration of stays therein, and the professional services (including drugs and biologicals) furnished,

(A) with respect to the medical necessity of the services, and

(B) for the purpose of promoting the most efficient use of available health facilities and services;

(2) for such review to be made by either

(A) a staff committee of the institution composed of two or more physicians (of which at least two must be physicians described in subsection (r)(1) of this section), with or without participation of other professional personnel, or

(B) a group outside the institution which is similarly composed and

(i) which is established by the local medical society and some or all of the hospitals and skilled nursing facilities in the locality, or

(ii) if (and for as long as) there has not been established such a group which serves such institution, which is established in such other manner as may be approved by the Secretary;

(3) for such review, in each case of inpatient hospital services or extended care services furnished to such an individual during a continuous period of extended duration, as of such days of such period (which may differ for different classes of cases) as may be specified in regulations, with such review to be made as promptly as possible, after each day so specified, and in no event later than one week following such day; and

(4) for prompt notification to the institution, the individual, and his attending physician of any finding (made after opportunity for consultation to such attending physician) by the physician members of such committee or group that any further stay in the institution is not medically necessary.

The review committee must be composed as provided in clause (B) of paragraph (2) rather than as provided in clause (A) of such paragraph in the case of any hospital or skilled nursing facility where, because of the small size of the institution, or (in the case of a skilled nursing facility) because of lack of an organized medical staff, or for such other reason or reasons as may be included in regulations, it is impracticable for the institution to have a properly functioning staff committee for the purposes of this subsection. If the Secretary determines that the utilization review procedures established pursuant to subchapter XIX of this chapter are superior in their effectiveness to the procedures required under this section, he may, to the extent that he deems it appropriate, require for purposes of this subchapter that the procedures established pursuant to subchapter XIX of this chapter be utilized instead of the procedures required by this section.

(*l*) Agreements for transfer between skilled nursing facilities and hospitals

A hospital and a skilled nursing facility shall be considered to have a transfer agreement in effect if, by reason of a written agreement between them or (in case the two institutions are under common control) by reason of a written undertaking by the person or body which controls them, there is reasonable assurance that—

(1) transfer of patients will be effected between the hospital and the skilled nursing facility whenever such transfer is medically appropriate as determined by the attending physician; and

(2) there will be interchange of medical and other information necessary or useful in the care and treatment of individuals transferred between the institutions, or in determining whether such individuals can be adequately cared for otherwise than in either of such institutions.

Any skilled nursing facility which does not have such an agreement in effect, but which is found by a State agency (of the State in which such facility is situated) with which an agreement under section 1395aa of this title is in effect (or, in the case of a State in which no such agency has an agreement under section 1395aa of this title, by the Secretary) to have attempted in good faith to enter into such an agreement with a hospital sufficiently close to the facility to make feasible the transfer between them of patients and the information referred to in paragraph (2), shall be considered to have such an agreement in effect if and for so long as such agency (or the Secretary, as the case may be) finds that to do so is in the public interest and essential to assuring extended care services for persons in the community who are eligible for payments with respect to such services under this subchapter.

(m) Home health services

The term "home health services" means the following items and services furnished to an individual, who is under the care of a physician, by a home health agency or by others under arrangements with them made by such agency, under a plan (for furnishing such items and services to such individual) established and periodically reviewed by a physician, which items and services are, except as provided in paragraph (7), provided on a visiting basis in a place of residence used as such individual's home—

(1) part-time or intermittent nursing care provided by or under the supervision of a registered professional nurse;

(2) physical or occupational therapy or speech-language pathology services;

(3) medical social services under the direction of a physician;

(4) to the extent permitted in regulations, part-time or intermittent services of a home health aide who has successfully completed a training program approved by the Secretary;

(5) medical supplies (including catheters, catheter supplies, ostomy bags, and supplies related to ostomy care, and a covered osteoporosis drug (as defined in subsection (kk) of this section), but excluding other drugs and biologicals) and durable medical equipment while under such a plan;

(6) in the case of a home health agency which is affiliated or under common control with a hospital, medical services provided by an intern or resident-in-training of such hospital, under a teaching program of such hospital approved as provided in the last sentence of subsection (b) of this section; and

(7) any of the foregoing items and services which are provided on an outpatient basis, under arrangements made by the home health agency, at a hospital or skilled nursing facility, or at a rehabilitation center which meets such standards as may be prescribed in regulations, and—

   (A) the furnishing of which involves the use of equipment of such a nature that the items and services cannot readily be made available to the individual in such place of residence, or

   (B) which are furnished at such facility while he is there to receive any such item or service described in clause (A),

but not including transportation of the individual in connection with any such item or service;

excluding, however, any item or service if it would not be included under subsection (b) of this section if furnished to an inpatient of a hospital. For purposes of paragraphs (1) and (4), the term "part-time or intermittent services" means skilled nursing and home health aide services furnished any number of days per week as long as they are furnished (combined) less than 8 hours each day and 28 or fewer hours each week (or, subject to review on a case-by-case basis as to the need for care, less than 8 hours each day and 35 or fewer hours per week). For purposes of sections 1395f(a)(2)(C) and 1395n(a)(2)(A) of this title, "intermittent" means skilled nursing care that is either provided or needed on fewer than 7 days each week, or less than 8 hours of each day for periods of 21 days or less (with extensions in exceptional circumstances when the need for additional care is finite and predictable).

(n) Durable medical equipment

The term "durable medical equipment" includes iron lungs, oxygen tents, hospital beds, and wheelchairs (which may include a power-operated vehicle that may be appropriately used as a wheelchair, but only where the use of such a vehicle is determined to be necessary on the basis of the individual's medical and physical condition and the vehicle meets such safety requirements as the Secretary may prescribe) used in the patient's home (including an institution used as his home other than an institution that meets the requirements of subsection (e)(1) of this section or section 1395i–3(a)(1) of this title), whether furnished on a rental basis or purchased, and includes blood-testing strips and blood glucose monitors for individuals with diabetes without regard to whether the individual has Type I or Type II diabetes or to the individual's use of insulin (as determined under standards established by the Secretary in consultation with the appropriate organizations); except that such term does not include such equipment furnished by a supplier who has used, for the demonstration and use of specific equipment, an individual who has not met such minimum training standards as the Secretary may establish with respect to the demonstration and use of such specific equipment. With respect to a seat-lift chair, such term includes only the seat-lift mechanism and does not include the chair.

(*o*) Home health agency

The term "home health agency" means a public agency or private organization, or a subdivision of such an agency or organization, which—

(**1**) is primarily engaged in providing skilled nursing services and other therapeutic services;

(**2**) has policies, established by a group of professional personnel (associated with the agency or organization), including one or more physicians and one or more registered professional nurses, to govern the services (referred to in paragraph (1)) which it provides, and provides for supervision of such services by a physician or registered professional nurse;

(**3**) maintains clinical records on all patients;

(**4**) in the case of an agency or organization in any State in which State or applicable local law provides for the licensing of agencies or organizations of this nature,

(**A**) is licensed pursuant to such law, or

(**B**) is approved, by the agency of such State or locality responsible for licensing agencies or organizations of this nature, as meeting the standards established for such licensing;

(**5**) has in effect an overall plan and budget that meets the requirements of subsection (z) of this section;

(**6**) meets the conditions of participation specified in section 1395bbb(a) of this title and such other conditions of participation as the Secretary may find necessary in the interest of the health and safety of individuals who are furnished services by such agency or organization;

(**7**) provides the Secretary with a surety bond—

(**A**) effective for a period of 4 years (as specified by the Secretary) or in the case of a change in the ownership or control of the agency (as determined by the Secretary) during or after such 4–year period, an additional period of time that the Secretary determines appropriate, such additional period not to exceed 4 years from the date of such change in ownership or control;

(B) in a form specified by the Secretary; and

(C) for a year in the period described in subparagraph (A) in an amount that is equal to the lesser of $50,000 or 10 percent of the aggregate amount of payments to the agency under this subchapter and subchapter XIX of this chapter [*42 U.S.C.A. § 1396* et seq.] for that year, as estimated by the Secretary; and

(8) meets such additional requirements (including conditions relating to bonding or establishing of escrow accounts as the Secretary finds necessary for the financial security of the program) as the Secretary finds necessary for the effective and efficient operation of the program;

except that for purposes of part A of this subchapter such term shall not include any agency or organization which is primarily for the care and treatment of mental diseases. The Secretary may waive the requirement of a surety bond under paragraph (7) in the case of an agency or organization that provides a comparable surety bond under State law.

(p) Outpatient physical therapy services

The term "outpatient physical therapy services" means physical therapy services furnished by a provider of services, a clinic, rehabilitation agency, or a public health agency, or by others under an arrangement with, and under the supervision of, such provider, clinic, rehabilitation agency, or public health agency to an individual as an outpatient—

(1) who is under the care of a physician (as defined in paragraph (1), (3), or (4) of subsection (r) of this section), and

(2) with respect to whom a plan prescribing the type, amount, and duration of physical therapy services that are to be furnished such individual has been established by a physician (as so defined) or by a qualified physical therapist and is periodically reviewed by a physician (as so defined);

excluding, however—

(3) any item or service if it would not be included under subsection (b) of this section if furnished to an inpatient of a hospital; and

(4) any such service—

(A) if furnished by a clinic or rehabilitation agency, or by others under arrangements with such clinic or agency, unless such clinic or rehabilitation agency—

(i) provides an adequate program of physical therapy services for outpatients and has the facilities and personnel required for such program or required for the supervision of such a program, in accordance with such requirements as the Secretary may specify,

(ii) has policies, established by a group of professional personnel, including one or more physicians (associated with the clinic or rehabilitation agency) and one or more qualified physical therapists, to govern the services (referred to in clause (i)) it provides,

    (iii) maintains clinical records on all patients,

    (iv) if such clinic or agency is situated in a State in which State or applicable local law provides for the licensing of institutions of this nature,

        (I) is licensed pursuant to such law, or

        (II) is approved by the agency of such State or locality responsible for licensing institutions of this nature, as meeting the standards established for such licensing; and

    (v) meets such other conditions relating to the health and safety of individuals who are furnished services by such clinic or agency on an outpatient basis, as the Secretary may find necessary, and provides the Secretary on a continuing basis with a surety bond in a form specified by the Secretary and in an amount that is not less than $50,000, or

    (B) if furnished by a public health agency, unless such agency meets such other conditions relating to health and safety of individuals who are furnished services by such agency on an outpatient basis, as the Secretary may find necessary.

The term "outpatient physical therapy services" also includes physical therapy services furnished an individual by a physical therapist (in his office or in such individual's home) who meets licensing and other standards prescribed by the Secretary in regulations, otherwise than under an arrangement with and under the supervision of a provider of services, clinic, rehabilitation agency, or public health agency, if the furnishing of such services meets such conditions relating to health and safety as the Secretary may find necessary. In addition, such term includes physical therapy services which meet the requirements of the first sentence of this subsection except that they are furnished to an individual as an inpatient of a hospital or extended care facility. The term "outpatient physical therapy services" also includes speech-language pathology services furnished by a provider of services, a clinic, rehabilitation agency, or by a public health agency, or by others under an arrangement with, and under the supervision of, such provider, clinic, rehabilitation agency, or public health agency to an individual as an outpatient, subject to the conditions prescribed in this subsection. Nothing in this subsection shall be construed as requiring, with respect to outpatients who are not entitled to benefits under this subchapter, a physical therapist to provide outpatient physical therapy services only to outpatients who are under the care of a physician or pursuant to a plan of care established by a physician. The Secretary may waive the requirement of a surety bond under paragraph (4)(A)(v) in the case of a clinic or agency that provides a comparable surety bond under State law.

    (q) Physicians' services

    The term "physicians' services" means professional services performed by physicians, including surgery, consultation, and home, office, and institutional calls (but not including services described in subsection (b)(6) of this section).

(r) Physician

The term "physician", when used in connection with the performance of any function or action, means

(1) a doctor of medicine or osteopathy legally authorized to practice medicine and surgery by the State in which he performs such function or action (including a physician within the meaning of section 1301(a)(7) of this title),

(2) a doctor of dental surgery or of dental medicine who is legally authorized to practice dentistry by the State in which he performs such function and who is acting within the scope of his license when he performs such functions,

(3) a doctor of podiatric medicine for the purposes of subsections (k), (m), (p)(1), and (s) of this section and sections 1395f(a), 1395k(a)(2)(F)(ii), and 1395n of this title but only with respect to functions which he is legally authorized to perform as such by the State in which he performs them,

(4) a doctor of optometry, but only for purposes of subsection (p)(1) and with respect to the provision of items or services described in subsection (s) of this section which he is legally authorized to perform as a doctor of optometry by the State in which he performs them, or

(5) a chiropractor who is licensed as such by the State (or in a State which does not license chiropractors as such, is legally authorized to perform the services of a chiropractor in the jurisdiction in which he performs such services), and who meets uniform minimum standards promulgated by the Secretary, but only for the purpose of subsections (s)(1) and (s)(2)(A) of this section and only with respect to treatment by means of manual manipulation of the spine (to correct a subluxation) which he is legally authorized to perform by the State or jurisdiction in which such treatment is provided. For the purposes of section 1395y(a)(4) of this title and subject to the limitations and conditions provided in the previous sentence, such term includes a doctor of one of the arts, specified in such previous sentence, legally authorized to practice such art in the country in which the inpatient hospital services (referred to in such section 1395y(a)(4) of this title) are furnished.

(s) Medical and other health services

The term "medical and other health services" means any of the following items or services:

(1) physicians' services;

(2)(A) services and supplies (including drugs and biologicals which are not usually self-administered by the patient) furnished as an incident to a physician's professional service, of kinds which are commonly furnished in physicians' offices and are commonly either rendered without charge or included in the physicians' bills;

(B) hospital services (including drugs and biologicals which are not usually self-administered by the patient) incident to physicians' services rendered to outpatients and partial hospitalization services incident to such services;

(C) diagnostic services which are—

(i) furnished to an individual as an outpatient by a hospital or by others under arrangements with them made by a hospital, and

(ii) ordinarily furnished by such hospital (or by others under such arrangements) to its outpatients for the purpose of diagnostic study;

(D) outpatient physical therapy services and outpatient occupational therapy services;

(E) rural health clinic services and Federally qualified health center services;

(F) home dialysis supplies and equipment, self-care home dialysis support services, and institutional dialysis services and supplies;

(G) antigens (subject to quantity limitations prescribed in regulations by the Secretary) prepared by a physician, as defined in subsection (r)(1) of this section, for a particular patient, including antigens so prepared which are forwarded to another qualified person (including a rural health clinic) for administration to such patient, from time to time, by or under the supervision of another such physician;

(H)(i) services furnished pursuant to a contract under section 1395mm of this title to a member of an eligible organization by a physician assistant or by a nurse practitioner (as defined in subsection (aa)(5) of this section) and such services and supplies furnished as an incident to his service to such a member as would otherwise be covered under this part if furnished by a physician or as an incident to a physician's service; and

(ii) services furnished pursuant to a risk-sharing contract under section 1395mm(g) of this title to a member of an eligible organization by a clinical psychologist (as defined by the Secretary) or by a clinical social worker (as defined in subsection (hh)(2) of this section), and such services and supplies furnished as an incident to such clinical psychologist's services or clinical social worker's services to such a member as would otherwise be covered under this part if furnished by a physician or as an incident to a physician's service;

(I) blood clotting factors, for hemophilia patients competent to use such factors to control bleeding without medical or other supervision, and items related to the administration of such factors, subject to utilization controls deemed necessary by the Secretary for the efficient use of such factors;

(J) prescription drugs used in immunosuppressive therapy furnished, to an individual who receives an organ transplant for which payment is made under this subchapter;

(K)(i) services which would be physicians' services if furnished by a physician (as defined in subsection (r)(1) of this section) and which are performed by a physician assistant (as defined in subsec-

585

tion (aa)(5) of this section) under the supervision of a physician (as so defined) and which the physician assistant is legally authorized to perform by the State in which the services are performed, and such services and supplies furnished as incident to such services as would be covered under subparagraph (A) if furnished incident to a physician's professional service; and but only if no facility or other provider charges or is paid any amounts with respect to the furnishing of such services,

(ii) services which would be physicians' services if furnished by a physician (as defined in subsection (r)(1) of this section) and which are performed by a nurse practitioner or clinical nurse specialist (as defined in subsection (aa)(5) of this section) working in collaboration (as defined in subsection (aa)(6) of this section) with a physician (as defined in subsection (r)(1) of this section) which the nurse practitioner or clinical nurse specialist is legally authorized to perform by the State in which the services are performed, and such services and supplies furnished as an incident to such services as would be covered under subparagraph (A) if furnished incident to a physician's professional service, but only if no facility or other provider charges or is paid any amounts with respect to the furnishing of such services;

(iii), (iv) Repealed. *Pub.L. 105–33, Title IV, § 4511(a)(2)(A)(ii)*, Aug. 5, 1997, 111 Stat. 442

(L) certified nurse-midwife services;

(M) qualified psychologist services; and

(N) clinical social worker services (as defined in subsection (hh)(2) of this section);

(O) erythropoietin for dialysis patients competent to use such drug without medical or other supervision with respect to the administration of such drug, subject to methods and standards established by the Secretary by regulation for the safe and effective use of such drug, and items related to the administration of such drug;

(P) prostate cancer screening tests (as defined in subsection (oo) of this title);

(Q) an oral drug (which is approved by the Federal Food and Drug Administration) prescribed for use as an anticancer chemotherapeutic agent for a given indication, and containing an active ingredient (or ingredients), which is the same indication and active ingredient (or ingredients) as a drug which the carrier determines would be covered pursuant to subparagraph (A) or (B) if the drug could not be self-administered;

(R) colorectal cancer screening tests (as defined in subsection (pp) of this section);

(S) diabetes outpatient self-management training services (as defined in subsection (qq) of this section);

(T) an oral drug (which is approved by the Federal Food and Drug Administration) prescribed for use as an acute anti-emetic used as part of an anticancer chemotherapeutic regimen if the drug is administered by a physician (or as prescribed by a physician)—

    (i) for use immediately before, at, or within 48 hours after the time of the administration of the anticancer chemotherapeutic agent; and

    (ii) as a full replacement for the anti-emetic therapy which would otherwise be administered intravenously;

(U) screening for glaucoma (as defined in subsection (uu)) for individuals determined to be at high risk for glaucoma, individuals with a family history of glaucoma and individuals with diabetes; and

(V) medical nutrition therapy services (as defined in subsection (vv)(1)) in the case of a beneficiary with diabetes or a renal disease who—

    (i) has not received diabetes outpatient self-management training services within a time period determined by the Secretary;

    (ii) is not receiving maintenance dialysis for which payment is made under section 1395rr of this title; and

    (iii) meets such other criteria determined by the Secretary after consideration of protocols established by dietitian or nutrition professional organizations;

(3) diagnostic X-ray tests (including tests under the supervision of a physician, furnished in a place of residence used as the patient's home, if the performance of such tests meets such conditions relating to health and safety as the Secretary may find necessary and including diagnostic mammography if conducted by a facility that has a certificate (or provisional certificate) issued under section 263b of this title, diagnostic laboratory tests, and other diagnostic tests;

(4) X-ray, radium, and radioactive isotope therapy, including materials and services of technicians;

(5) surgical dressings, and splints, casts, and other devices used for reduction of fractures and dislocations;

(6) durable medical equipment;

(7) ambulance service where the use of other methods of transportation is contraindicated by the individual's condition, but only to the extent provided in regulations;

(8) prosthetic devices (other than dental) which replace all or part of an internal body organ (including colostomy bags and supplies directly related to colostomy care), including replacement of such devices, and including one pair of conventional eyeglasses or contact lenses furnished subsequent to each cataract surgery with insertion of an intraocular lens;

(9) leg, arm, back, and neck braces, and artificial legs, arms, and eyes, including replacements if required because of a change in the patient's physical condition;

(10)(A) pneumococcal vaccine and its administration and, subject to section 4071(b) of the Omnibus Budget Reconciliation Act of 1987, influenza vaccine and its administration; and

> **(B)** hepatitis B vaccine and its administration, furnished to an individual who is at high or intermediate risk of contracting hepatitis B (as determined by the Secretary under regulations);

(11) services of a certified registered nurse anesthetist (as defined in subsection (bb));

(12) subject to section 4072(e) of the Omnibus Budget Reconciliation Act of 1987, extra-depth shoes with inserts or custom molded shoes with inserts for an individual with diabetes, if—

> **(A)** the physician who is managing the individual's diabetic condition

>> **(i)** documents that the individual has peripheral neuropathy with evidence of callus formation, a history of pre-ulcerative calluses, a history of previous ulceration, foot deformity, or previous amputation, or poor circulation, and

>> **(ii)** certifies that the individual needs such shoes under a comprehensive plan of care related to the individual's diabetic condition;

> **(B)** the particular type of shoes are prescribed by a podiatrist or other qualified physician (as established by the Secretary); and

> **(C)** the shoes are fitted and furnished by a podiatrist or other qualified individual (such as a pedorthist or orthotist, as established by the Secretary) who is not the physician described in subparagraph (A) (unless the Secretary finds that the physician is the only such qualified individual in the area);

(13) screening mammography (as defined in subsection (jj) of this section);

(14) screening pap smear and screening pelvic exam; and

(15) bone mass measurement (as defined in subsection (rr) of this section).

No diagnostic tests performed in any laboratory, including a laboratory that is part of a rural health clinic, or a hospital (which, for purposes of this sentence, means an institution considered a hospital for purposes of section 1395f(d) of this title) shall be included within paragraph (3) unless such laboratory—

(16) if situated in any State in which State or applicable local law provides for licensing of establishments of this nature,

> **(A)** is licensed pursuant to such law, or

(B) is approved, by the agency of such State or locality responsible for licensing establishments of this nature, as meeting the standards established for such licensing; and

(17)(A) meets the certification requirements under section 263a of this title; and

(B) meets such other conditions relating to the health and safety of individuals with respect to whom such tests are performed as the Secretary may find necessary.

There shall be excluded from the diagnostic services specified in paragraph (2)(C) any item or service (except services referred to in paragraph (1)) which would not be included under subsection (b) of this section if it were furnished to an inpatient of a hospital. None of the items and services referred to in the preceding paragraphs (other than paragraphs (1) and (2)(A)) of this subsection which are furnished to a patient of an institution which meets the definition of a hospital for purposes of section 1395f(d) of this title shall be included unless such other conditions are met as the Secretary may find necessary relating to health and safety of individuals with respect to whom such items and services are furnished.

(t) Drugs and biologicals

(1) The term "drugs" and the term "biologicals", except for purposes of subsection (m)(5) of this section and paragraph (2) include only such drugs (including contrast agents) and biologicals, respectively, as are included (or approved for inclusion) in the United States Pharmacopoeia, the National Formulary, or the United States Homeopathic Pharmacopoeia, or in New Drugs or Accepted Dental Remedies (except for any drugs and biologicals unfavorably evaluated therein), or as are approved by the pharmacy and drug therapeutics committee (or equivalent committee) of the medical staff of the hospital furnishing such drugs and biologicals for use in such hospital.

(2)(A) For purposes of paragraph (1), the term "drugs" also includes any drugs or biologicals used in an anticancer chemotherapeutic regimen for a medically accepted indication (as described in subparagraph (B)).

(B) In subparagraph (A), the term "medically accepted indication", with respect to the use of a drug, includes any use which has been approved by the Food and Drug Administration for the drug, and includes another use of the drug if—

(i) the drug has been approved by the Food and Drug Administration; and

(ii)(I) such use is supported by one or more citations which are included (or approved for inclusion) in one or more of the following compendia: the American Hospital Formulary Service–Drug Information, the American Medical Association Drug Evaluations, the United States Pharmacopoeia–Drug Information, and other authoritative compendia as identified by the Secretary, unless the Secretary has determined that the use is not medically appropriate or the use is identified as not indicated in one or more such compendia, or

> **(II)** the carrier involved determines, based upon guidance provided by the Secretary to carriers for determining accepted uses of drugs, that such use is medically accepted based on supportive clinical evidence in peer reviewed medical literature appearing in publications which have been identified for purposes of this subclause by the Secretary.

The Secretary may revise the list of compendia in clause (ii)(I) as is appropriate for identifying medically accepted indications for drugs.

(u) Provider of services

The term "provider of services" means a hospital, critical access hospital, skilled nursing facility, comprehensive outpatient rehabilitation facility, home health agency, hospice program, or, for purposes of section 1395f(g) and section 1395n(e) of this title, a fund.

(v) Reasonable costs

(1)(A) The reasonable cost of any services shall be the cost actually incurred, excluding therefrom any part of incurred cost found to be unnecessary in the efficient delivery of needed health services, and shall be determined in accordance with regulations establishing the method or methods to be used, and the items to be included, in determining such costs for various types or classes of institutions, agencies, and services; except that in any case to which paragraph (2) or (3) applies, the amount of the payment determined under such paragraph with respect to the services involved shall be considered the reasonable cost of such services. In prescribing the regulations referred to in the preceding sentence, the Secretary shall consider, among other things, the principles generally applied by national organizations or established prepayment organizations (which have developed such principles) in computing the amount of payment, to be made by persons other than the recipients of services, to providers of services on account of services furnished to such recipients by such providers. Such regulations may provide for determination of the costs of services on a per diem, per unit, per capita, or other basis, may provide for using different methods in different circumstances, may provide for the use of estimates of costs of particular items or services, may provide for the establishment of limits on the direct or indirect overall incurred costs or incurred costs of specific items or services or groups of items or services to be recognized as reasonable based on estimates of the costs necessary in the efficient delivery of needed health services to individuals covered by the insurance programs established under this subchapter, and may provide for the use of charges or a percentage of charges where this method reasonably reflects the costs. Such regulations shall

> **(i)** take into account both direct and indirect costs of providers of services (excluding therefrom any such costs, including

standby costs, which are determined in accordance with regulations to be unnecessary in the efficient delivery of services covered by the insurance programs established under this subchapter) in order that, under the methods of determining costs, the necessary costs of efficiently delivering covered services to individuals covered by the insurance programs established by this subchapter will not be borne by individuals not so covered, and the costs with respect to individuals not so covered will not be borne by such insurance programs, and

(ii) provide for the making of suitable retroactive corrective adjustments where, for a provider of services for any fiscal period, the aggregate reimbursement produced by the methods of determining costs proves to be either inadequate or excessive.

(B) In the case of extended care services, the regulations under subparagraph (A) shall not include provision for specific recognition of a return on equity capital.

(C) Where a hospital has an arrangement with a medical school under which the faculty of such school provides services at such hospital, an amount not in excess of the reasonable cost of such services to the medical school shall be included in determining the reasonable cost to the hospital of furnishing services—

(i) for which payment may be made under part A of this subchapter, but only if—

(I) payment for such services as furnished under such arrangement would be made under part A of this subchapter to the hospital had such services been furnished by the hospital, and

(II) such hospital pays to the medical school at least the reasonable cost of such services to the medical school, or

(ii) for which payment may be made under part B of this subchapter, but only if such hospital pays to the medical school at least the reasonable cost of such services to the medical school.

(D) Where

(i) physicians furnish services which are either inpatient hospital services (including services in conjunction with the teaching programs of such hospital) by reason of paragraph (7) of subsection (b) of this section or for which entitlement exists by reason of clause (II) of section 1395k(a)(2)(B)(i) of this title, and

(ii) such hospital (or medical school under arrangement with such hospital) incurs no actual cost in the furnishing of such services, the reasonable cost of such services shall (under regulations of the Secretary) be deemed to be the cost such hospital or medical school would have incurred had it paid a salary to such physicians rendering such services approximately equivalent to the average salary paid to all physicians employed by such hospital (or if such employment does not exist, or is

591

minimal in such hospital, by similar hospitals in a geographic area of sufficient size to assure reasonable inclusion of sufficient physicians in development of such average salary).

(E) Such regulations may, in the case of skilled nursing facilities in any State, provide for the use of rates, developed by the State in which such facilities are located, for the payment of the cost of skilled nursing facility services furnished under the State's plan approved under subchapter XIX of this chapter (and such rates may be increased by the Secretary on a class or size of institution or on a geographical basis by a percentage factor not in excess of 10 percent to take into account determinable items or services or other requirements under this subchapter not otherwise included in the computation of such State rates), if the Secretary finds that such rates are reasonably related to (but not necessarily limited to) analyses undertaken by such State of costs of care in comparable facilities in such State. Notwithstanding the previous sentence, such regulations with respect to skilled nursing facilities shall take into account (in a manner consistent with subparagraph (A) and based on patient-days of services furnished) the costs (including the costs of services required to attain or maintain the highest practicable physical, mental, and psychosocial well-being of each resident eligible for benefits under this subchapter) of such facilities complying with the requirements of subsections (b), (c), and (d) of section 1395i–3 of this title (including the costs of conducting nurse aide training and competency evaluation programs and competency evaluation programs).

(F) Such regulations shall require each provider of services (other than a fund) to make reports to the Secretary of information described in section 1320a(a) of this title in accordance with the uniform reporting system (established under such section) for that type of provider.

(G)(i) In any case in which a hospital provides inpatient services to an individual that would constitute post-hospital extended care services if provided by a skilled nursing facility and a quality control and peer review organization (or, in the absence of such a qualified organization, the Secretary or such agent as the Secretary may designate) determines that inpatient hospital services for the individual are not medically necessary but post-hospital extended care services for the individual are medically necessary and such extended care services are not otherwise available to the individual (as determined in accordance with criteria established by the Secretary) at the time of such determination, payment for such services provided to the individual shall continue to be made under this subchapter at the payment rate described in clause (ii) during the period in which—

> **(I)** such post-hospital extended care services for the individual are medically necessary and not otherwise available to the individual (as so determined),

(II) inpatient hospital services for the individual are not medically necessary, and

(III) the individual is entitled to have payment made for post-hospital extended care services under this subchapter,

except that if the Secretary determines that there is not an excess of hospital beds in such hospital and (subject to clause (iv)) there is not an excess of hospital beds in the area of such hospital, such payment shall be made (during such period) on the basis of the amount otherwise payable under part A with respect to inpatient hospital services.

(ii)(I) Except as provided in subclause (II), the payment rate referred to in clause (i) is a rate equal to the estimated adjusted State-wide average rate per patient-day paid for services provided in skilled nursing facilities under the State plan approved under subchapter XIX of this chapter for the State in which such hospital is located, or, if the State in which the hospital is located does not have a State plan approved under subchapter XIX of this chapter, the estimated adjusted State-wide average allowable costs per patient-day for extended care services under this subchapter in that State.

(II) If a hospital has a unit which is a skilled nursing facility, the payment rate referred to in clause (i) for the hospital is a rate equal to the lesser of the rate described in subclause (I) or the allowable costs in effect under this subchapter for extended care services provided to patients of such unit.

(iii) Any day on which an individual receives inpatient services for which payment is made under this subparagraph shall, for purposes of this chapter (other than this subparagraph), be deemed to be a day on which the individual received inpatient hospital services.

(iv) In determining under clause (i), in the case of a public hospital, whether or not there is an excess of hospital beds in the area of such hospital, such determination shall be made on the basis of only the public hospitals (including the hospital) which are in the area of the hospital and which are under common ownership with that hospital.

(H) In determining such reasonable cost with respect to home health agencies, the Secretary may not include—

(i) any costs incurred in connection with bonding or establishing an escrow account by any such agency as a result of the surety bond requirement described in subsection (o)(7) of this section and the financial security requirement described in subsection (*o*)(8) of this section;

(ii) in the case of home health agencies to which the surety bond requirement described in subsection (*o*)(7) of this section and the financial security requirement described in subsection (*o*)(8) of this section apply, any costs attributed to interest charged such an agency in connection with amounts borrowed by the agency to repay overpayments made under this subchapter to the agency, except that such costs may be included in reasonable cost if the Secretary determines that the agency was acting in good faith in borrowing the amounts;

(iii) in the case of contracts entered into by a home health agency after December 5, 1980, for the purpose of having services furnished for or on behalf of such agency, any cost incurred by such agency pursuant to any such contract which is entered into for a period exceeding five years; and

(iv) in the case of contracts entered into by a home health agency before December 5, 1980, for the purpose of having services furnished for or on behalf of such agency, any cost incurred by such agency pursuant to any such contract, which determines the amount payable by the home health agency on the basis of a percentage of the agency's reimbursement or claim for reimbursement for services furnished by the agency, to the extent that such cost exceeds the reasonable value of the services furnished on behalf of such agency.

(I) In determining such reasonable cost, the Secretary may not include any costs incurred by a provider with respect to any services furnished in connection with matters for which payment may be made under this subchapter and furnished pursuant to a contract between the provider and any of its subcontractors which is entered into after December 5, 1980, and the value or cost of which is $10,000 or more over a twelve-month period unless the contract contains a clause to the effect that—

(i) until the expiration of four years after the furnishing of such services pursuant to such contract, the subcontractor shall make available, upon written request by the Secretary, or upon request by the Comptroller General, or any of their duly authorized representatives, the contract, and books, documents and records of such subcontractor that are necessary to certify the nature and extent of such costs, and

(ii) if the subcontractor carries out any of the duties of the contract through a subcontract, with a value or cost of $10,000 or more over a twelve-month period, with a related organization, such subcontract shall contain a clause to the effect that until the expiration of four years after the furnishing of such services pursuant to such subcontract, the related organization shall make available, upon written request by the Secretary, or upon request by the Comptroller General, or any of their duly authorized representatives, the subcontract, and books, documents and records of such organization that are necessary to verify the nature and extent of such costs.

The Secretary shall prescribe in regulation criteria and procedures which the Secretary shall use in obtaining access to books, documents, and records under clauses required in contracts and subcontracts under this subparagraph.

(J) Such regulations may not provide for any inpatient routine salary cost differential as a reimbursable cost for hospitals and skilled nursing facilities.

(K)(i) The Secretary shall issue regulations that provide, to the extent feasible, for the establishment of limitations on the amount of any costs or charges that shall be considered reasonable with respect to services provided on an outpatient basis by hospitals (other than bona fide emergency services as defined in clause (ii)) or clinics (other than rural health clinics), which are reimbursed on a cost basis or on the basis of cost related charges, and by physicians utilizing such outpatient facilities. Such limitations shall be reasonably related to the charges in the same area for similar services provided in physicians' offices. Such regulations shall provide for exceptions to such limitations in cases where similar services are not generally available in physicians' offices in the area to individuals entitled to benefits under this subchapter.

(ii) For purposes of clause (i), the term "bona fide emergency services" means services provided in a hospital emergency room after the sudden onset of a medical condition manifesting itself by acute symptoms of sufficient severity (including severe pain) such that the absence of immediate medical attention could reasonably be expected to result in—

(I) placing the patient's health in serious jeopardy;

(II) serious impairment to bodily functions; or

(III) serious dysfunction of any bodily organ or part.

(L)(i) The Secretary, in determining the amount of the payments that may be made under this subchapter with respect to services furnished by home health agencies, may not recognize as reasonable (in the efficient delivery of such services) costs for the provision of such services by an agency to the extent these costs exceed (on the aggregate for the agency) for cost reporting periods beginning on or after—

(I) July 1, 1985, and before July 1, 1986, 120 percent of the mean of the labor-related and nonlabor per visit costs for freestanding home health agencies,

595

(II) July 1, 1986, and before July 1, 1987, 115 percent of such mean,

(III) July 1, 1987, and before October 1, 1997, 112 percent of such mean,

(IV) October 1, 1997, and before October 1, 1998, 105 percent of the median of the labor-related and nonlabor per visit costs for freestanding home health agencies, or

(V) October 1, 1998, 106 percent of such median.

(ii) Effective for cost reporting periods beginning on or after July 1, 1986, such limitations shall be applied on an aggregate basis for the agency, rather than on a discipline specific basis. The Secretary may provide for such exemptions and exceptions to such limitation as he deems appropriate.

(iii) Not later than July 1, 1991, and annually thereafter (but not for cost reporting periods beginning on or after July 1, 1994, and before July 1, 1996, or on or after July 1, 1997, and before October 1, 1997), the Secretary shall establish limits under this subparagraph for cost reporting periods beginning on or after such date by utilizing the area wage index applicable under section 1395ww(d)(3)(E) of this title and determined using the survey of the most recent available wages and wage-related costs of hospitals located in the geographic area in which the home health service is furnished (determined without regard to whether such hospitals have been reclassified to a new geographic area pursuant to section 1395ww(d)(8)(B) of this title, a decision of the Medicare Geographic Classification Review Board under section 1395ww(d)(10) of this title, or a decision of the Secretary).

(iv) In establishing limits under this subparagraph for cost reporting periods beginning after September 30, 1997, the Secretary shall not take into account any changes in the home health market basket, as determined by the Secretary, with respect to cost reporting periods which began on or after July 1, 1994, and before July 1, 1996.

(v) For services furnished by home health agencies for cost reporting periods beginning on or after October 1, 1997, subject to clause (viii)(I), the Secretary shall provide for an interim system of limits. Payment shall not exceed the costs determined under the preceding provisions of this subparagraph or, if lower, the product of—

(I) an agency-specific per beneficiary annual limitation calculated based 75 percent on 98 percent of the reasonable costs (including nonroutine medical supplies) for the agency's 12–month cost reporting period ending during fiscal year 1994, and based 25 percent on 98 percent of the standardized regional average of such costs for the agency's census division, as applied to such agency, for cost reporting periods ending during fiscal year 1994, such costs updated by the home health market basket index; and

(**II**) the agency's unduplicated census count of patients (entitled to benefits under this subchapter) for the cost reporting period subject to the limitation.

(**vi**) For services furnished by home health agencies for cost reporting periods beginning on or after October 1, 1997, the following rules apply:

(**I**) For new providers and those providers without a 12–month cost reporting period ending in fiscal year 1994, subject to clauses (viii)(II) and (viii)(III) the per beneficiary limitation shall be equal to the median of these limits (or the Secretary's best estimates thereof) applied to other home health agencies as determined by the Secretary. A home health agency that has altered its corporate structure or name shall not be considered a new provider for this purpose.

(**II**) For beneficiaries who use services furnished by more than one home health agency, the per beneficiary limitations shall be prorated among the agencies.

(**vii**)(**I**) Not later than January 1, 1998, the Secretary shall establish per visit limits applicable for fiscal year 1998, and not later than April 1, 1998, the Secretary shall establish per beneficiary limits under clause (v)(I) for fiscal year 1998.

(**II**) Not later than August 1 of each year (beginning in 1998) the Secretary shall establish the limits applicable under this subparagraph for services furnished during the fiscal year beginning October 1 of the year.

(**viii**)(**I**) In the case of a provider with a 12–month cost reporting period ending in fiscal year 1994, if the limit imposed under clause (v) (determined without regard to this subclause) for a cost reporting period beginning during or after fiscal year 1999 is less than the median described in clause (vi)(I) (but determined as if any reference in clause (v) to "98 percent" were a reference to "100 percent"), the limit otherwise imposed under clause (v) for such provider and period shall be increased by ⅓ of such difference.

(II) Subject to subclause (IV), for new providers and those providers without a 12–month cost reporting period ending in fiscal year 1994, but for which the first cost reporting period begins before fiscal year 1999, for cost reporting periods beginning during or after fiscal year 1999, the per beneficiary limitation described in clause (vi)(I) shall be equal to the median described in such clause (determined as if any reference in clause (v) to "98 percent" were a reference to "100 percent").

(III) Subject to subclause (IV), in the case of a new provider for which the first cost reporting period begins during or after fiscal year 1999, the limitation applied under clause (vi)(I) (but only with respect to such provider) shall be equal to 75 percent of the median described in clause (vi)(I).

(IV) In the case of a new provider or a provider without a 12–month cost reporting period ending in fiscal year 1994, subclause (II) shall apply, instead of subclause (III), to a home health agency which filed an application for home health agency provider status under this subchapter before September 15, 1998, or which was approved as a branch of its parent agency before such date and becomes a subunit of the parent agency or a separate agency on or after such date.

(V) Each of the amounts specified in subclauses (I) through (III) are such amounts as adjusted under clause (iii) to reflect variations in wages among different areas.

(ix) Notwithstanding the per beneficiary limit under clause (viii), if the limit imposed under clause (v) (determined without regard to this clause) for a cost reporting period beginning during or after fiscal year 2000 is less than the median described in clause (vi)(I) (but determined as if any reference in clause (v) to "98 percent" were a reference to "100 percent"), the limit otherwise imposed under clause (v) for such provider and period shall be increased by 2 percent.

(x) Notwithstanding any other provision of this subparagraph, in updating any limit under this subparagraph by a home health market basket index for cost reporting periods beginning during each of fiscal years 2000, 2002, and 2003, the update otherwise provided shall be reduced by 1.1 percentage points. With respect to cost reporting periods beginning during fiscal year 2001, the update to any limit under this subparagraph shall be the home health market basket index.

(M) Such regulations shall provide that costs respecting care provided by a provider of services, pursuant to an assurance under subchapter IV or XIV of chapter 6A of this title [*42 U.S.C.A. § 291* et seq. or 300q et seq.] that the provider will make available a reasonable volume of services to persons unable to pay therefor, shall not be allowable as reasonable costs.

(N) In determining such reasonable costs, costs incurred for activities directly related to influencing employees respecting unionization may not be included.

(O)(i) In establishing an appropriate allowance for depreciation and for interest on capital indebtedness with respect to an asset of a provider of services which has undergone a change of ownership, such regulations shall provide, except as provided in clause (iii), that the valuation of the asset after such change of ownership shall be the historical cost of the asset, as recognized under this subchapter, less depreciation allowed, to the owner of record as of August 5, 1997 (or, in the case of an asset not in existence as of August 5, 1997, the first owner of record of the asset after August 5, 1997).

(ii) Such regulations shall not recognize, as reasonable in the provision of health care services, costs (including legal fees, accounting and administrative costs, travel costs, and the costs of feasibility studies) attributable to the negotiation or settlement of the sale or purchase of any capital asset (by acquisition or merger) for which any payment has previously been made under this subchapter.

(iii) In the case of the transfer of a hospital from ownership by a State to ownership by a nonprofit corporation without monetary consideration, the basis for capital allowances to the new owner shall be the book value of the hospital to the State at the time of the transfer.

(iv) Redesignated (iii)

(P) If such regulations provide for the payment for a return on equity capital (other than with respect to costs of inpatient hospital services), the rate of return to be recognized, for determining the reasonable cost of services furnished in a cost reporting period, shall be equal to the average of the rates of interest, for each of the months any part of which is included in the period, on obligations issued for purchase by the Federal Hospital Insurance Trust Fund.

(Q) Except as otherwise explicitly authorized, the Secretary is not authorized to limit the rate of increase on allowable costs of approved medical educational activities.

(R) In determining such reasonable cost, costs incurred by a provider of services representing a beneficiary in an unsuccessful appeal of a determination described in section 1395ff(b) of this title shall not be allowable as reasonable costs.

(S)(i) Such regulations shall not include provision for specific recognition of any return on equity capital with respect to hospital outpatient departments.

(ii)(I) Such regulations shall provide that, in determining the amount of the payments that may be made under this subchapter with respect to all the capital-related costs of outpatient hospital services, the Secretary shall reduce the amounts of such payments otherwise established under this subchapter by 15 percent for payments attributable to portions of cost reporting periods occurring during fiscal year 1990, by 15 percent for payments attributable to portions of cost reporting periods occurring during fiscal year 1991, and by 10 percent for payments attributable to portions of cost reporting periods occurring during fiscal years 1992 through 1999 and until the first date that the prospective payment system under section 1395l(t) of this title is implemented.

(II) The Secretary shall reduce the reasonable cost of outpatient hospital services (other than the capital-related costs of such services) otherwise determined pursuant to section 1395l(a)(2)(B)(i)(I) of this title by 5.8 percent for payments attributable to portions of cost reporting periods occurring during fiscal years 1991 through 1999 and until the first date that the prospective payment system under section 1395l(t) of this title is implemented.

(III) Subclauses (I) and (II) shall not apply to payments with respect to the capital-related costs of any hospital that is a sole community hospital (as defined in section 1395ww(d)(5)(D)(iii) of this title or a critical access hospital (as defined in subsection (mm)(1) of this section).

(IV) In applying subclauses (I) and (II) to services for which payment is made on the basis of a blend amount under section 1395l(i)(3)(A)(ii) or 1395l(n)(1)(A)(ii) of this title, the costs reflected in the amounts described in sections 1395l(i)(3)(B)(i)(I) and 1395l(n)(1)(B)(i)(I) of this title, respectively, shall be reduced in accordance with such subclause.

(T) In determining such reasonable costs for hospitals, no reduction in copayments under section 1395l(t)(5)(B) of this title shall be treated as a bad debt and the amount of bad debts otherwise treated as allowable costs which are attributable to the deductibles and coinsurance amounts under this subchapter shall be reduced—

(i) for cost reporting periods beginning during fiscal year 1998, by 25 percent of such amount otherwise allowable,

(ii) for cost reporting periods beginning during fiscal year 1999, by 40 percent of such amount otherwise allowable,

(iii) for cost reporting periods beginning during fiscal year 2000, by 45 percent of such amount otherwise allowable, and

(iv) for cost reporting periods beginning during a subsequent fiscal year, by 30 percent of such amount otherwise allowable.

(U) In determining the reasonable cost of ambulance services (as described in subsection (s)(7) of this section) provided during fiscal year 1998, during fiscal year 1999, and during so much of fiscal year 2000 as precedes January 1, 2000, the Secretary shall not recognize the costs per trip in excess of costs recognized as reasonable for ambulance services provided on a per trip basis during the previous fiscal year (after application of this subparagraph), increased by the percentage increase in the consumer price index for all urban consumers (U.S. city average) as estimated by the Secretary for the 12–month period ending with the midpoint of the fiscal year involved reduced by 1.0 percentage point. For ambulance services provided after June 30, 1998, the Secretary may provide that claims for such services must include a code (or codes) under a uniform coding system specified by the Secretary that identifies the services furnished.

(2)(A) If the bed and board furnished as part of inpatient hospital services (including inpatient tuberculosis hospital services and inpatient psychiatric hospital services) or post-hospital extended care services is in accommodations more expensive than semi-private accommodations, the amount taken into account for purposes of payment under this subchapter with respect to such services may not exceed the amount that would be taken into account with respect to such services if furnished in such semi-private accommodations unless the more expensive accommodations were required for medical reasons.

(B) Where a provider of services which has an agreement in effect under this subchapter furnishes to an individual, items or services which are in excess of or more expensive than the items or services with respect to which payment may be made under part A or part B of this subchapter, as the case may be, the Secretary shall take into account for purposes of payment to such provider of services only the items or services with respect to which such payment may be made.

(3) If the bed and board furnished as part of inpatient hospital services (including inpatient tuberculosis hospital services and inpatient psychiatric hospital services) or post-hospital extended care services is in accommodations other than, but not more expensive than, semi-private accommodations and the use of such other accommodations rather than semi-private accommodations was neither at the request of the patient nor for a reason which the Secretary determines is consistent with the purposes of this subchapter, the amount of the payment with respect to

601

such bed and board under part A of this subchapter shall be the amount otherwise payable under this subchapter for such bed and board furnished in semi-private accommodations minus the difference between the charge customarily made by the hospital or skilled nursing facility for bed and board in semi-private accommodations and the charge customarily made by it for bed and board in the accommodations furnished.

(4) If a provider of services furnishes items or services to an individual which are in excess of or more expensive than the items or services determined to be necessary in the efficient delivery of needed health services and charges are imposed for such more expensive items or services under the authority granted in section 1395cc(a)(2)(B)(ii) of this title, the amount of payment with respect to such items or services otherwise due such provider in any fiscal period shall be reduced to the extent that such payment plus such charges exceed the cost actually incurred for such items or services in the fiscal period in which such charges are imposed.

(5)(A) Where physical therapy services, occupational therapy services, speech therapy services, or other therapy services or services of other health-related personnel (other than physicians) are furnished under an arrangement with a provider of services or other organization, specified in the first sentence of subsection (p) of this section (including through the operation of subsection (g) of this section) the amount included in any payment to such provider or other organization under this subchapter as the reasonable cost of such services (as furnished under such arrangements) shall not exceed an amount equal to the salary which would reasonably have been paid for such services (together with any additional costs that would have been incurred by the provider or other organization) to the person performing them if they had been performed in an employment relationship with such provider or other organization (rather than under such arrangement) plus the cost of such other expenses (including a reasonable allowance for traveltime and other reasonable types of expense related to any differences in acceptable methods of organization for the provision of such therapy) incurred by such person, as the Secretary may in regulations determine to be appropriate.

(B) Notwithstanding the provisions of subparagraph (A), if a provider of services or other organization specified in the first sentence of subsection (p) of this section requires the services of a therapist on a limited part-time basis, or only to perform intermittent services, the Secretary may make payment on the basis of a reasonable rate per unit of service, even though such rate is greater per unit of time than salary related amounts, where he finds that such greater payment is, in the aggregate, less than the amount that would have been paid if such organization had employed a therapist on a full- or part-time salary basis.

(6) For purposes of this subsection, the term "semi-private accommodations" means two-bed, three-bed, or four-bed accommodations.

(7)(A) For limitation on Federal participation for capital expenditures which are out of conformity with a comprehensive plan of a State or areawide planning agency, see section 1320a–1 of this title.

(B) For further limitations on reasonable cost and determination of payment amounts for operating costs of inpatient hospital services and waivers for certain States, see section 1395ww of this title.

(C) For provisions restricting payment for provider-based physicians' services and for payments under certain percentage arrangements, see section 1395xx of this title.

(D) For further limitations on reasonable cost and determination of payment amounts for routine service costs of skilled nursing facilities, see subsections (a) through (c) of section 1395yy of this title.

(8) Items unrelated to patient care.—Reasonable costs do not include costs for the following—

(i) entertainment, including tickets to sporting and other entertainment events;

(ii) gifts or donations;

(iii) personal use of motor vehicles;

(iv) costs for fines and penalties resulting from violations of Federal, State, or local laws; and

(v) education expenses for spouses or other dependents of providers of services, their employees or contractors.

(w) Arrangements for certain services; payments pursuant to arrangements for utilization review activities

(1) The term "arrangements" is limited to arrangements under which receipt of payment by the hospital, critical access hospital, skilled nursing facility, home health agency, or hospice program (whether in its own right or as agent), with respect to services for which an individual is entitled to have payment made under this subchapter, discharges the liability of such individual or any other person to pay for the services.

(2) Utilization review activities conducted, in accordance with the requirements of the program established under part B of subchapter XI of this chapter with respect to services furnished by a hospital or critical access hospital to patients insured under part A of this subchapter or entitled to have payment made for such services under part B of this subchapter or under a State plan approved under subchapter XIX of this chapter, by a quality control and peer review organization designated for the area in which such hospital or critical access hospital is located shall be deemed to have been conducted pursuant to arrangements between

603

such hospital or critical access hospital and such organization under which such hospital or critical access hospital is obligated to pay to such organization, as a condition of receiving payment for hospital or critical access hospital services so furnished under this part or under such a State plan, such amount as is reasonably incurred and requested (as determined under regulations of the Secretary) by such organization in conducting such review activities with respect to services furnished by such hospital or critical access hospital to such patients.

(x) State and United States

The terms "State" and "United States" have the meaning given to them by subsections (h) and (i), respectively, of section 410 of this title.

(y) Extended care in religious nonmedical health care institutions

(1) The term "skilled nursing facility" also includes a religious nonmedical health care institution (as defined in subsection (ss)(1) of this section), (except for purposes of subsection (a)(2) of this section) with respect to items and services ordinarily furnished by such an institution to inpatients, and payment may be made with respect to services provided by or in such an institution only to such extent and under such conditions, limitations, and requirements (in addition to or in lieu of the conditions, limitations, and requirements otherwise applicable) as may be provided in regulations consistent with section 1395i–5 of this title.

(2) Notwithstanding any other provision of this subchapter, payment under part A of this subchapter may not be made for services furnished an individual in a skilled nursing facility to which paragraph (1) applies unless such individual elects, in accordance with regulations, for a spell of illness to have such services treated as post-hospital extended care services for purposes of such part; and payment under part A of this subchapter may not be made for post-hospital extended care services—

(A) furnished an individual during such spell of illness in a skilled nursing facility to which paragraph (1) applies after—

(i) such services have been furnished to him in such a facility for 30 days during such spell, or

(ii) such services have been furnished to him during such spell in a skilled nursing facility to which such paragraph does not apply; or

(B) furnished an individual during such spell of illness in a skilled nursing facility to which paragraph (1) does not apply after such services have been furnished to him during such spell in a skilled nursing facility to which such paragraph applies.

(3) The amount payable under part A of this subchapter for post-hospital extended care services furnished an individual during any spell of illness in a skilled nursing facility to which paragraph (1) applies shall be reduced by a coinsurance amount equal to one-eighth of the inpatient hospital deductible for each day before the 31st day on which he is furnished such services in such a facility during such spell (and the reduction under this paragraph shall be in lieu of any reduction under section 1395e(a)(3) of this title).

(4) For purposes of subsection (i) of this section, the determination of whether services furnished by or in an institution described in paragraph (1) constitute post-hospital extended care services shall be made in accordance with and subject to such conditions, limitations, and requirements as may be provided in regulations.

(z) Institutional planning

An overall plan and budget of a hospital, skilled nursing facility, comprehensive outpatient rehabilitation facility, or home health agency shall be considered sufficient if it—

(1) provides for an annual operating budget which includes all anticipated income and expenses related to items which would, under generally accepted accounting principles, be considered income and expense items (except that nothing in this paragraph shall require that there be prepared, in connection with any budget, an item-by-item identification of the components of each type of anticipated expenditure or income);

(2)(A) provides for a capital expenditures plan for at least a 3–year period (including the year to which the operating budget described in paragraph (1) is applicable) which includes and identifies in detail the anticipated sources of financing for, and the objectives of, each anticipated expenditure in excess of $600,000 (or such lesser amount as may be established by the State under section 1320a–1(g)(1) of this title in which the hospital is located) related to the acquisition of land, the improvement of land, buildings, and equipment, and the replacement, modernization, and expansion of the buildings and equipment which would, under generally accepted accounting principles, be considered capital items;

(B) provides that such plan is submitted to the agency designated under section 1320a–1(b) of this title, or if no such agency is designated, to the appropriate health planning agency in the State (but this subparagraph shall not apply in the case of a facility exempt from review under section 1320a–1 of this title by reason of section 1320a–1(j) of this title);

(3) provides for review and updating at least annually; and

(4) is prepared, under the direction of the governing body of the institution or agency, by a committee consisting of representatives of the governing body, the administrative staff, and the medical staff (if any) of the institution or agency.

(aa) Rural health clinic services and Federally qualified health center services

(1) The term "rural health clinic services" means—

(A) physicians' services and such services and supplies as are covered under subsection (s)(2)(A) of this section if furnished as an incident to a physician's professional service and items and services described in subsection (s)(10) of this section,

(B) such services furnished by a physician assistant or a nurse practitioner (as defined in paragraph (5)), by a clinical psychologist (as defined by the Secretary) or by a clinical social worker (as defined in subsection (hh)(1) of this section), and such services and supplies furnished as an incident to his service as would otherwise be covered if furnished by a physician or as an incident to a physician's service, and

(C) in the case of a rural health clinic located in an area in which there exists a shortage of home health agencies, part-time or intermittent nursing care and related medical supplies (other than drugs and biologicals) furnished by a registered professional nurse or licensed practical nurse to a homebound individual under a written plan of treatment

    (i) established and periodically reviewed by a physician described in paragraph (2)(B), or

    (ii) established by a nurse practitioner or physician assistant and periodically reviewed and approved by a physician described in paragraph (2)(B),

when furnished to an individual as an outpatient of a rural health clinic.

(2) The term "rural health clinic" means a facility which—

(A) is primarily engaged in furnishing to outpatients services described in subparagraphs (A) and (B) of paragraph (1);

(B) in the case of a facility which is not a physician-directed clinic, has an arrangement (consistent with the provisions of State and local law relative to the practice, performance, and delivery of health services) with one or more physicians (as defined in subsection (r)(1) of this section) under which provision is made for the periodic review by such physicians of covered services furnished by physician assistants and nurse practitioners, the supervision and guidance by such physicians of physician assistants and nurse practitioners, the preparation by such physicians of such medical orders for care and treatment of clinic patients as may be necessary, and the availability of such physicians for such referral of and consultation for patients as is necessary and for advice and assistance in the management of medical emergencies; and, in the case of a physician-directed clinic, has one or more of its staff physicians perform the activities accomplished through such an arrangement;

(C) maintains clinical records on all patients;

(D) has arrangements with one or more hospitals, having agreements in effect under section 1395cc of this title, for the referral and admission of patients requiring inpatient services or such diagnostic or other specialized services as are not available at the clinic;

(E) has written policies, which are developed with the advice of (and with provision for review of such policies from time to time by) a group of professional personnel, including one or more physicians and one or more physician assistants or nurse practitioners, to govern those services described in paragraph (1) which it furnishes;

(F) has a physician, physician assistant, or nurse practitioner responsible for the execution of policies described in subparagraph (E) and relating to the provision of the clinic's services;

(G) directly provides routine diagnostic services, including clinical laboratory services, as prescribed in regulations by the Secretary, and has prompt access to additional diagnostic services from facilities meeting requirements under this subchapter;

(H) in compliance with State and Federal law, has available for administering to patients of the clinic at least such drugs and biologicals as are determined by the Secretary to be necessary for the treatment of emergency cases (as defined in regulations) and has appropriate procedures or arrangements for storing, administering, and dispensing any drugs and biologicals;

(I) has a quality assessment and performance improvement program, and appropriate procedures for review of utilization of clinic services, as the Secretary may specify;

(J) has a nurse practitioner, a physician assistant, or a certified nurse-midwife (as defined in subsection (gg) of this section) available to furnish patient care services not less than 50 percent of the time the clinic operates; and

(K) meets such other requirements as the Secretary may find necessary in the interest of the health and safety of the individuals who are furnished services by the clinic.

For the purposes of this subchapter, such term includes only a facility which

(i) is located in an area that is not an urbanized area (as defined by the Bureau of the Census) and in which there are insufficient numbers of needed health care practitioners (as determined by the Secretary), and that, within the previous 3–year period, has been designated by the chief executive officer of the State and certified by the Secretary as an area with a shortage of personal health services or designated by the Secretary either

(I) as an area with a shortage of personal health services under section 254c(b)(3) or 300e–1(7) of this title, or

(II) as a health professional shortage area described in section 254e(a)(1)(A) of this title because of its shortage of primary medical care manpower,

(III) as a high impact area described in section 254b(a)(5) of this title, or

(IV) as an area which includes a population group which the Secretary determines has a health professional shortage under section 254e(a)(1)(B) of this title,

(ii) has filed an agreement with the Secretary by which it agrees not to charge any individual or other person for items or services for which such individual is entitled to have payment made under this subchapter, except for the amount of any

607

deductible or coinsurance amount imposed with respect to such items or services (not in excess of the amount customarily charged for such items and services by such clinic), pursuant to subsections (a) and (b) of section 1395l of this title,

(iii) employs a physician assistant or nurse practitioner, and

(iv) is not a rehabilitation agency or a facility which is primarily for the care and treatment of mental diseases. A facility that is in operation and qualifies as a rural health clinic under this subchapter or subchapter XIX of this chapter and that subsequently fails to satisfy the requirement of clause (i) shall be considered, for purposes of this subchapter and subchapter XIX of this chapter, as still satisfying the requirement of such clause if it is determined, in accordance with criteria established by the Secretary in regulations, to be essential to the delivery of primary care services that would otherwise be unavailable in the geographic area served by the clinic. If a State agency has determined under section 1395aa(a) of this title that a facility is a rural health clinic and the facility has applied to the Secretary for approval as such a clinic, the Secretary shall notify the facility of the Secretary's approval or disapproval not later than 60 days after the date of the State agency determination or the application (whichever is later).

(3) The term "Federally qualified health center services" means—

(A) services of the type described in subparagraphs (A) through (C) of paragraph (1), and

(B) preventive primary health services that a center is required to provide under sections 254b, 254c, and 256 of this title,

when furnished to an individual as an outpatient of a Federally qualified health center and, for this purpose, any reference to a rural health clinic or a physician described in paragraph (2)(B) is deemed a reference to a Federally qualified health center or a physician at the center, respectively.

(4) The term "Federally qualified health center" means an entity which—

(A)(i) is receiving a grant under section 254b of this title (other than subsection (h)), or

(ii)(I) is receiving funding from such a grant under a contract with the recipient of such a grant, and

(II) meets the requirements to receive a grant under section 254b of this title (other than subsection (h));

(B) based on the recommendation of the Health Resources and Services Administration within the Public Health Service, is determined by the Secretary to meet the requirements for receiving such a grant;

(C) was treated by the Secretary, for purposes of part B of this subchapter, as a comprehensive Federally funded health center as of January 1, 1990; or

(D) is an outpatient health program or facility operated by a tribe or tribal organization under the Indian Self–Determination Act [*25 U.S.C.A. § 450f* et seq.] or by an urban Indian organization receiving funds under title V of the Indian Health Care Improvement Act [*25 U.S.C.A. § 1651* et seq.].

(5)(A) The term "physician assistant" and the term "nurse practitioner" mean, for purposes of this subchapter, a physician assistant or nurse practitioner who performs such services as such individual is legally authorized to perform (in the State in which the individual performs such services) in accordance with State law (or the State regulatory mechanism provided by State law), and who meets such training, education, and experience requirements (or any combination thereof) as the Secretary may prescribe in regulations.

(B) The term "clinical nurse specialist" means, for purposes of this subchapter, an individual who—

    (i) is a registered nurse and is licensed to practice nursing in the State in which the clinical nurse specialist services are performed; and

    (ii) holds a master's degree in a defined clinical area of nursing from an accredited educational institution.

(6) The term "collaboration" means a process in which a nurse practitioner works with a physician to deliver health care services within the scope of the practitioner's professional expertise, with medical direction and appropriate supervision as provided for in jointly developed guidelines or other mechanisms as defined by the law of the State in which the services are performed.

(7)(A) The Secretary shall waive for a 1–year period the requirements of paragraph (2) that a rural health clinic employ a physician assistant, nurse practitioner or certified nurse midwife or that such clinic require such providers to furnish services at least 50 percent of the time that the clinic operates for any facility that requests such waiver if the facility demonstrates that the facility has been unable, despite reasonable efforts, to hire a physician assistant, nurse practitioner, or certified nurse-midwife in the previous 90–day period.

(B) The Secretary may not grant such a waiver under subparagraph (A) to a facility if the request for the waiver is made less than 6 months after the date of the expiration of any previous such waiver for the facility, or if the facility has not yet been determined to meet the requirements (including subparagraph (J) of the first sentence of paragraph (2)) of a rural health clinic.

(C) A waiver which is requested under this paragraph shall be deemed granted unless such request is denied by the Secretary within 60 days after the date such request is received.

(bb) Services of a certified registered nurse anesthetist

(1) The term "services of a certified registered nurse anesthetist" means anesthesia services and related care furnished by a certified registered nurse anesthetist (as defined in paragraph (2)) which the nurse anesthetist is legally authorized to perform as such by the State in which the services are furnished.

(2) The term "certified registered nurse anesthetist" means a certified registered nurse anesthetist licensed by the State who meets such education, training, and other requirements relating to anesthesia services and related care as the Secretary may prescribe. In prescribing such requirements the Secretary may use the same requirements as those established by a national organization for the certification of nurse anesthetists. Such term also includes, as prescribed by the Secretary, an anesthesiologist assistant.

(cc) Comprehensive outpatient rehabilitation facility services

(1) The term "comprehensive outpatient rehabilitation facility services" means the following items and services furnished by a physician or other qualified professional personnel (as defined in regulations by the Secretary) to an individual who is an outpatient of a comprehensive outpatient rehabilitation facility under a plan (for furnishing such items and services to such individual) established and periodically reviewed by a physician—

(A) physicians' services;

(B) physical therapy, occupational therapy, speech-language pathology services, and respiratory therapy;

(C) prosthetic and orthotic devices, including testing, fitting, or training in the use of prosthetic and orthotic devices;

(D) social and psychological services;

(E) nursing care provided by or under the supervision of a registered professional nurse;

(F) drugs and biologicals which cannot, as determined in accordance with regulations, be self-administered;

(G) supplies and durable medical equipment; and

(H) such other items and services as are medically necessary for the rehabilitation of the patient and are ordinarily furnished by comprehensive outpatient rehabilitation facilities,

excluding, however, any item or service if it would not be included under subsection (b) of this section if furnished to an inpatient of a hospital. In the case of physical therapy, occupational therapy, and speech pathology services, there shall be no requirement that the item or service be furnished at any single fixed location if the item or service is furnished pursuant to such plan and payments are not otherwise made for the item or service under this subchapter.

610

(2) The term "comprehensive outpatient rehabilitation facility" means a facility which—

(A) is primarily engaged in providing (by or under the supervision of physicians) diagnostic, therapeutic, and restorative services to outpatients for the rehabilitation of injured, disabled, or sick persons;

(B) provides at least the following comprehensive outpatient rehabilitation services:

(i) physicians' services (rendered by physicians, as defined in subsection (r)(1) of this section, who are available at the facility on a full- or part-time basis);

(ii) physical therapy; and

(iii) social or psychological services;

(C) maintains clinical records on all patients;

(D) has policies established by a group of professional personnel (associated with the facility), including one or more physicians defined in subsection (r)(1) of this section to govern the comprehensive outpatient rehabilitation services it furnishes, and provides for the carrying out of such policies by a full- or part-time physician referred to in subparagraph (B)(i);

(E) has a requirement that every patient must be under the care of a physician;

(F) in the case of a facility in any State in which State or applicable local law provides for the licensing of facilities of this nature

(i) is licensed pursuant to such law, or

(ii) is approved by the agency of such State or locality, responsible for licensing facilities of this nature, as meeting the standards established for such licensing;

(G) has in effect a utilization review plan in accordance with regulations prescribed by the Secretary;

(H) has in effect an overall plan and budget that meets the requirements of subsection (z) of this section;

(I) provides the Secretary on a continuing basis with a surety bond in a form specified by the Secretary and in an amount that is not less than $50,000; and

(J) meets such other conditions of participation as the Secretary may find necessary in the interest of the health and safety of individuals who are furnished services by such facility, including conditions concerning qualifications of personnel in these facilities.

The Secretary may waive the requirement of a surety bond under subparagraph (I) in the case of a facility that provides a comparable surety bond under State law.

(dd) Hospice care; hospice program; definitions; certification; waiver by Secretary

(1) The term "hospice care" means the following items and services provided to a terminally ill individual by, or by others under arrangements made by, a hospice program under a written plan (for providing such care to such individual) established and periodically reviewed by the individual's attending physician and by the medical director (and by the interdisciplinary group described in paragraph (2)(B)) of the program—

(A) nursing care provided by or under the supervision of a registered professional nurse,

(B) physical or occupational therapy, or speech-language pathology services,

(C) medical social services under the direction of a physician,

(D)(i) services of a home health aide who has successfully completed a training program approved by the Secretary and

(ii) homemaker services,

(E) medical supplies (including drugs and biologicals) and the use of medical appliances, while under such a plan,

(F) physicians' services,

(G) short-term inpatient care (including both respite care and procedures necessary for pain control and acute and chronic symptom management) in an inpatient facility meeting such conditions as the Secretary determines to be appropriate to provide such care, but such respite care may be provided only on an intermittent, nonroutine, and occasional basis and may not be provided consecutively over longer than five days,

(H) counseling (including dietary counseling) with respect to care of the terminally ill individual and adjustment to his death, and

(I) any other item or service which is specified in the plan and for which payment may otherwise be made under this subchapter.

The care and services described in subparagraphs (A) and (D) may be provided on a 24–hour, continuous basis only during periods of crisis (meeting criteria established by the Secretary) and only as necessary to maintain the terminally ill individual at home.

(2) The term "hospice program" means a public agency or private organization (or a subdivision thereof) which—

(A)(i) is primarily engaged in providing the care and services described in paragraph (1) and makes such services available (as needed) on a 24–hour basis and which also provides bereavement counseling for the immediate family of terminally ill individuals,

(ii) provides for such care and services in individuals' homes, on an outpatient basis, and on a short-term inpatient basis, directly or under arrangements made by the agency or organization, except that—

(I) the agency or organization must routinely provide directly substantially all of each of the services described in subparagraphs (A), (C), and (H) of paragraph (1), except as otherwise provided in paragraph (5), and

(II) in the case of other services described in paragraph (1) which are not provided directly by the agency or organization, the agency or organization must maintain professional management responsibility for all such services furnished to an individual, regardless of the location or facility in which such services are furnished; and

(iii) provides assurances satisfactory to the Secretary that the aggregate number of days of inpatient care described in paragraph (1)(G) provided in any 12–month period to individuals who have an election in effect under section 1395d(d) of this title with respect to that agency or organization does not exceed 20 percent of the aggregate number of days during that period on which such elections for such individuals are in effect;

(B) has an interdisciplinary group of personnel which—

(i) includes at least—

(I) one physician (as defined in subsection (r)(1) of this section),

(II) one registered professional nurse, and

(III) one social worker,

employed by or, in the case of a physician described in subclause (I), under contract with the agency or organization, and also includes at least one pastoral or other counselor,

(ii) provides (or supervises the provision of) the care and services described in paragraph (1), and

(iii) establishes the policies governing the provision of such care and services;

(C) maintains central clinical records on all patients;

(D) does not discontinue the hospice care it provides with respect to a patient because of the inability of the patient to pay for such care;

(E)(i) utilizes volunteers in its provision of care and services in accordance with standards set by the Secretary, which standards shall ensure a continuing level of effort to utilize such volunteers, and

(ii) maintains records on the use of these volunteers and the cost savings and expansion of care and services achieved through the use of these volunteers;

(F) in the case of an agency or organization in any State in which State or applicable local law provides for the licensing of agencies or organizations of this nature, is licensed pursuant to such law; and

(G) meets such other requirements as the Secretary may find necessary in the interest of the health and safety of the individuals who are provided care and services by such agency or organization.

(3)(A) An individual is considered to be "terminally ill" if the individual has a medical prognosis that the individual's life expectancy is 6 months or less.

(B) The term "attending physician" means, with respect to an individual, the physician (as defined in subsection (r)(1) of this section), who may be employed by a hospice program, whom the individual identifies as having the most significant role in the determination and delivery of medical care to the individual at the time the individual makes an election to receive hospice care.

(4)(A) An entity which is certified as a provider of services other than a hospice program shall be considered, for purposes of certification as a hospice program, to have met any requirements under paragraph (2) which are also the same requirements for certification as such other type of provider. The Secretary shall coordinate surveys for determining certification under this subchapter so as to provide, to the extent feasible, for simultaneous surveys of an entity which seeks to be certified as a hospice program and as a provider of services of another type.

(B) Any entity which is certified as a hospice program and as a provider of another type shall have separate provider agreements under section 1395cc of this title and shall file separate cost reports with respect to costs incurred in providing hospice care and in providing other services and items under this subchapter.

(5)(A) The Secretary may waive the requirements of paragraph (2)(A)(ii)(I) for an agency or organization with respect to all or part of the nursing care described in paragraph (1)(A) if such agency or organization—

(i) is located in an area which is not an urbanized area (as defined by the Bureau of the Census);

(ii) was in operation on or before January 1, 1983; and

(iii) has demonstrated a good faith effort (as determined by the Secretary) to hire a sufficient number of nurses to provide such nursing care directly.

(B) Any waiver, which is in such form and containing such information as the Secretary may require and which is requested by an agency or organization under subparagraph (A) or (C), shall be deemed to be granted unless such request is denied by the Secretary within 60 days after the date such request is received by the Secretary. The granting of a waiver under subparagraph (A) or (C) shall not preclude the granting of any subsequent waiver request should such a waiver again become necessary.

(C) The Secretary may waive the requirements of paragraph (2)(A)(i) and (2)(A)(ii) for an agency or organization with respect to the services described in paragraph (1)(B) and, with respect to dietary counseling, paragraph (1)(H), if such agency or organization—

(i) is located in an area which is not an urbanized area (as defined by the Bureau of Census), and

(ii) demonstrates to the satisfaction of the Secretary that the agency or organization has been unable, despite diligent efforts, to recruit appropriate personnel.

(ee) Discharge planning process

(1) A discharge planning process of a hospital shall be considered sufficient if it is applicable to services furnished by the hospital to individuals entitled to benefits under this subchapter and if it meets the guidelines and standards established by the Secretary under paragraph (2).

(2) The Secretary shall develop guidelines and standards for the discharge planning process in order to ensure a timely and smooth transition to the most appropriate type of and setting for post-hospital or rehabilitative care. The guidelines and standards shall include the following:

(A) The hospital must identify, at an early stage of hospitalization, those patients who are likely to suffer adverse health consequences upon discharge in the absence of adequate discharge planning.

(B) Hospitals must provide a discharge planning evaluation for patients identified under subparagraph (A) and for other patients upon the request of the patient, patient's representative, or patient's physician.

(C) Any discharge planning evaluation must be made on a timely basis to ensure that appropriate arrangements for post-hospital care will be made before discharge and to avoid unnecessary delays in discharge.

(D) A discharge planning evaluation must include an evaluation of a patient's likely need for appropriate post-hospital services, including hospice services, and the availability of those services, including the availability of home health services through individuals and entities that participate in the program under this subchapter and that serve the area in which the patient resides and that request to be listed by the hospital as available.

(E) The discharge planning evaluation must be included in the patient's medical record for use in establishing an appropriate discharge plan and the results of the evaluation must be discussed with the patient (or the patient's representative).

(F) Upon the request of a patient's physician, the hospital must arrange for the development and initial implementation of a discharge plan for the patient.

(G) Any discharge planning evaluation or discharge plan required under this paragraph must be developed by, or under the supervision of, a registered professional nurse, social worker, or other appropriately qualified personnel.

(H) Consistent with section 1395a of this title, the discharge plan shall—

   (i) not specify or otherwise limit the qualified provider which may provide post-hospital home health services, and

   (ii) identify (in a form and manner specified by the Secretary) any entity to whom the individual is referred in which the hospital has a disclosable financial interest (as specified by the Secretary consistent with section 1395cc(a)(1)(S) of this title) or which has such an interest in the hospital.

(3) With respect to a discharge plan for an individual who is enrolled with a Medicare + Choice organization under a Medicare + Choice plan and is furnished inpatient hospital services by a hospital under a contract with the organization

   (A) the discharge planning evaluation under paragraph (2)(D) is not required to include information on the availability of home health services through individuals and entities which do not have a contract with the organization; and

   (B) notwithstanding subparagraph (H)(i), the plan may specify or limit the provider (or providers) of post-hospital home health services or other post-hospital services under the plan.

(ff) Partial hospitalization services

(1) The term "partial hospitalization services" means the items and services described in paragraph (2) prescribed by a physician and provided under a program described in paragraph (3) under the supervision of a physician pursuant to an individualized, written plan of treatment established and periodically reviewed by a physician (in consultation with appropriate staff participating in such program), which plan sets forth the physician's diagnosis, the type, amount, frequency, and duration of the items and services provided under the plan, and the goals for treatment under the plan.

(2) The items and services described in this paragraph are—

   (A) individual and group therapy with physicians or psychologists (or other mental health professionals to the extent authorized under State law),

   (B) occupational therapy requiring the skills of a qualified occupational therapist,

(C) services of social workers, trained psychiatric nurses, and other staff trained to work with psychiatric patients,

(D) drugs and biologicals furnished for therapeutic purposes (which cannot, as determined in accordance with regulations, be self-administered),

(E) individualized activity therapies that are not primarily recreational or diversionary,

(F) family counseling (the primary purpose of which is treatment of the individual's condition),

(G) patient training and education (to the extent that training and educational activities are closely and clearly related to individual's care and treatment),

(H) diagnostic services, and

(I) such other items and services as the Secretary may provide (but in no event to include meals and transportation);

that are reasonable and necessary for the diagnosis or active treatment of the individual's condition, reasonably expected to improve or maintain the individual's condition and functional level and to prevent relapse or hospitalization, and furnished pursuant to such guidelines relating to frequency and duration of services as the Secretary shall by regulation establish (taking into account accepted norms of medical practice and the reasonable expectation of patient improvement).

(3)(A) A program described in this paragraph is a program which is furnished by a hospital to its outpatients or by a community mental health center (as defined in subparagraph (B)), and which is a distinct and organized intensive ambulatory treatment service offering less than 24-hour-daily care.

(B) For purposes of subparagraph (A), the term "community mental health center" means an entity that—

(i)(I) provides the mental health services described in section 300x-2(c)(1) of this title; or

(II) in the case of an entity operating in a State that by law precludes the entity from providing itself the service described in subparagraph (E) of such section, provides for such service by contract with an approved organization or entity (as determined by the Secretary);

(ii) meets applicable licensing or certification requirements for community mental health centers in the State in which it is located; and

(iii) meets such additional conditions as the Secretary shall specify to ensure

(I) the health and safety of individuals being furnished such services,

(**II**) the effective and efficient furnishing of such services, and

(**III**) the compliance of such entity with the criteria described in section 300x–31(c)(1) of this title.

(**gg**) Certified nurse-midwife services

(**1**) The term "certified nurse-midwife services" means such services furnished by a certified nurse-midwife (as defined in paragraph (2)) and such services and supplies furnished as an incident to the nurse-midwife's service which the certified nurse-midwife is legally authorized to perform under State law (or the State regulatory mechanism provided by State law) as would otherwise be covered if furnished by a physician or as an incident to a physicians' service.

(**2**) The term "certified nurse-midwife" means a registered nurse who has successfully completed a program of study and clinical experience meeting guidelines prescribed by the Secretary, or has been certified by an organization recognized by the Secretary.

(**hh**) Clinical social worker; clinical social worker services

(**1**) The term "clinical social worker" means an individual who—

(**A**) possesses a master's or doctor's degree in social work;

(**B**) after obtaining such degree has performed at least 2 years of supervised clinical social work; and

(**C**)(**i**) is licensed or certified as a clinical social worker by the State in which the services are performed, or

(**ii**) in the case of an individual in a State which does not provide for licensure or certification—

(**I**) has completed at least 2 years or 3,000 hours of post-master's degree supervised clinical social work practice under the supervision of a master's level social worker in an appropriate setting (as determined by the Secretary), and

(**II**) meets such other criteria as the Secretary establishes.

(**2**) The term "clinical social worker services" means services performed by a clinical social worker (as defined in paragraph (1)) for the diagnosis and treatment of mental illnesses (other than services furnished to an inpatient of a hospital and other than services furnished to an inpatient of a skilled nursing facility which the facility is required to provide as a requirement for participation) which the clinical social worker is legally authorized to perform under State law (or the State regulatory mechanism provided by State law) of the State in which such services are performed as would otherwise be covered if furnished by a physician or as an incident to a physician's professional service.

(**ii**) Qualified psychologist services

The term "qualified psychologist services" means such services and such services and supplies furnished as an incident to his service furnished by a clinical psychologist (as defined by the Secretary) which the psychologist is legally authorized to perform under State law (or the State regulatory mechanism provided by State law) as would otherwise be covered if furnished by a physician or as an incident to a physician's service.

(jj) Screening mammography

The term "screening mammography" means a radiologic procedure provided to a woman for the purpose of early detection of breast cancer and includes a physician's interpretation of the results of the procedure.

(kk) Covered osteoporosis drug

The term "covered osteoporosis drug" means an injectable drug approved for the treatment of post-menopausal osteoporosis provided to an individual by a home health agency if, in accordance with regulations promulgated by the Secretary—

(1) the individual's attending physician certifies that the individual has suffered a bone fracture related to post-menopausal osteoporosis and that the individual is unable to learn the skills needed to self-administer such drug or is otherwise physically or mentally incapable of self-administering such drug; and

(2) the individual is confined to the individual's home (except when receiving items and services referred to in subsection (m)(7) of this section).

(ll) Speech-language pathology services; audiology services

(1) The term "speech-language pathology services" means such speech, language, and related function assessment and rehabilitation services furnished by a qualified speech-language pathologist as the speech-language pathologist is legally authorized to perform under State law (or the State regulatory mechanism provided by State law) as would otherwise be covered if furnished by a physician.

(2) The term "audiology services" means such hearing and balance assessment services furnished by a qualified audiologist as the audiologist is legally authorized to perform under State law (or the State regulatory mechanism provided by State law), as would otherwise be covered if furnished by a physician.

(3) In this subsection:

(A) The term "qualified speech-language pathologist" means an individual with a master's or doctoral degree in speech-language pathology who—

(i) is licensed as a speech-language pathologist by the State in which the individual furnishes such services, or

(ii) in the case of an individual who furnishes services in a State which does not license speech-language pathologists, has successfully completed 350 clock hours of supervised clinical practicum (or is in the process of accumulating such supervised clinical experience), performed not less than 9 months of supervised full-time speech-language pathology services after obtaining a master's or doctoral degree in speech-language pathology or a related field, and successfully completed a national examination in speech-language pathology approved by the Secretary.

(B) The term "qualified audiologist" means an individual with a master's or doctoral degree in audiology who—

(i) is licensed as an audiologist by the State in which the individual furnishes such services, or

(ii) in the case of an individual who furnishes services in a State which does not license audiologists, has successfully completed 350 clock hours of supervised clinical practicum (or is in the process of accumulating such supervised clinical experience), performed not less than 9 months of supervised full-time audiology services after obtaining a master's or doctoral degree in audiology or a related field, and successfully completed a national examination in audiology approved by the Secretary.

(mm) Critical access hospital; critical access hospital services

(1) The term "critical access hospital" means a facility certified by the Secretary as a critical access hospital under section 1395i–4(e) of this title.

(2) The term "inpatient critical access hospital services" means items and services, furnished to an inpatient of a critical access hospital by such facility, that would be inpatient hospital services if furnished to an inpatient of a hospital by a hospital.

(3) The term "outpatient critical access hospital services" means medical and other health services furnished by a critical access hospital on an outpatient basis.

(nn) Screening pap smear; screening pelvic exam

(1) The term "screening pap smear" means a diagnostic laboratory test consisting of a routine exfoliative cytology test (Papanicolaou test) provided to a woman for the purpose of early detection of cervical or vaginal cancer and includes a physician's interpretation of the results of the test, if the individual involved has not had such a test during the preceding 2 years, or during the preceding year in the case of a woman described in paragraph (3).

(2) The term "screening pelvic exam" means a pelvic examination provided to a woman if the woman involved has not had such an examination during the preceding 2 years, or during the preceding year in the case of a woman described in paragraph (3), and includes a clinical breast examination.

(3) A woman described in this paragraph is a woman who—

(A) is of childbearing age and has had a test described in this subsection during any of the preceding 3 years that indicated the presence of cervical or vaginal cancer or other abnormality; or

(B) is at high risk of developing cervical or vaginal cancer (as determined pursuant to factors identified by the Secretary).

(oo) Prostate cancer screening tests

(1) The term "prostate cancer screening test" means a test that consists of any (or all) of the procedures described in paragraph (2) provided for the purpose of early detection of prostate cancer to a man over 50 years of age who has not had such a test during the preceding year.

(2) The procedures described in this paragraph are as follows:

(A) A digital rectal examination.

(B) A prostate-specific antigen blood test.

(C) For years beginning after 2002, such other procedures as the Secretary finds appropriate for the purpose of early detection of prostate cancer, taking into account changes in technology and standards of medical practice, availability, effectiveness, costs, and such other factors as the Secretary considers appropriate.

(pp) Colorectal cancer screening tests

(1) The term "colorectal cancer screening test" means any of the following procedures furnished to an individual for the purpose of early detection of colorectal cancer:

(A) Screening fecal-occult blood test.

(B) Screening flexible sigmoidoscopy.

(C) Screening colonoscopy.

(D) Such other tests or procedures, and modifications to tests and procedures under this subsection, with such frequency and payment limits, as the Secretary determines appropriate, in consultation with appropriate organizations.

(2) An "individual at high risk for colorectal cancer" is an individual who, because of family history, prior experience of cancer or precursor neoplastic polyps, a history of chronic digestive disease condition (including inflammatory bowel disease, Crohn's Disease, or ulcerative colitis), the presence of any appropriate recognized gene markers for colorectal cancer, or other predisposing factors, faces a high risk for colorectal cancer.

(qq) Diabetes outpatient self-management training services

(1) The term "diabetes outpatient self-management training services" means educational and training services furnished (at such times as the Secretary determines appropriate) to an individual with diabetes by a certified provider (as described in paragraph (2)(A)) in an outpatient setting by an individual or entity who meets the quality standards described in paragraph (2)(B), but only if the physician who is managing the individual's diabetic condition certifies that such services are needed under a comprehensive plan of care related to the individual's diabetic condition to ensure therapy compliance or to provide the individual with necessary skills and knowledge (including skills related to the self-administration of injectable drugs) to participate in the management of the individual's condition.

(2) In paragraph (1)—

(A) a "certified provider" is a physician, or other individual or entity designated by the Secretary, that, in addition to providing diabetes outpatient self-management training services, provides other items or services for which payment may be made under this subchapter; and

(B) a physician, or such other individual or entity, meets the quality standards described in this paragraph if the physician, or individual or entity, meets quality standards established by the Secretary, except that the physician or other individual or entity shall be deemed to have met such standards if the physician or other individual or entity meets applicable standards originally established by the National Diabetes Advisory Board and subsequently revised by organizations who participated in the establishment of standards by such Board, or is recognized by an organization that represents individuals (including individuals under this subchapter) with diabetes as meeting standards for furnishing the services.

(rr) Bone mass measurement

(1) The term "bone mass measurement" means a radiologic or radioisotopic procedure or other procedure approved by the Food and Drug Administration performed on a qualified individual (as defined in paragraph (2)) for the purpose of identifying bone mass or detecting bone loss or determining bone quality, and includes a physician's interpretation of the results of the procedure.

(2) For purposes of this subsection, the term "qualified individual" means an individual who is (in accordance with regulations prescribed by the Secretary)—

(A) an estrogen-deficient woman at clinical risk for osteoporosis;

(B) an individual with vertebral abnormalities;

(C) an individual receiving long-term glucocorticoid steroid therapy;

(D) an individual with primary hyperparathyroidism; or

(E) an individual being monitored to assess the response to or efficacy of an approved osteoporosis drug therapy.

(3) The Secretary shall establish such standards regarding the frequency with which a qualified individual shall be eligible to be provided benefits for bone mass measurement under this subchapter.

(ss) Religious nonmedical health care institution SSRH31(1)

(1) The term "religious nonmedical health care institution" means an institution that—

(A) is described in subsection (c)(3) of section 501 of Title 26 and is exempt from taxes under subsection (a) of such section;

(B) is lawfully operated under all applicable Federal, State, and local laws and regulations;

(C) provides only nonmedical nursing items and services exclusively to patients who choose to rely solely upon a religious method of healing and for whom the acceptance of medical health services would be inconsistent with their religious beliefs;

(D) provides such nonmedical items and services exclusively through nonmedical nursing personnel who are experienced in caring for the physical needs of such patients;

(E) provides such nonmedical items and services to inpatients on a 24–hour basis;

(F) on the basis of its religious beliefs, does not provide through its personnel or otherwise medical items and services (including any medical screening, examination, diagnosis, prognosis, treatment, or the administration of drugs) for its patients;

(G)(i) is not owned by, under common ownership with, or has an ownership interest in, a provider of medical treatment or services;

(ii) is not affiliated with—

(I) a provider of medical treatment or services, or

(II) an individual who has an ownership interest in a provider of medical treatment or services;

(H) has in effect a utilization review plan which—

(i) provides for the review of admissions to the institution, of the duration of stays therein, of cases of continuous extended duration, and of the items and services furnished by the institution,

(ii) requires that such reviews be made by an appropriate committee of the institution that includes the individuals responsible for overall administration and for supervision of nursing personnel at the institution,

(iii) provides that records be maintained of the meetings, decisions, and actions of such committee, and (**iv**) meets such other requirements as the Secretary finds necessary to establish an effective utilization review plan;

(**I**) provides the Secretary with such information as the Secretary may require to implement section 1391i–5 of this title, including information relating to quality of care and coverage determinations; and

(**J**) meets such other requirements as the Secretary finds necessary in the interest of the health and safety of individuals who are furnished services in the institution.

(**2**) To the extent that the Secretary finds that the accreditation of an institution by a State, regional, or national agency or association provides reasonable assurances that any or all of the requirements of paragraph (1) are met or exceeded, the Secretary may treat such institution as meeting the condition or conditions with respect to which the Secretary made such finding.

(**3**)(**A**)(**i**) In administering this subsection and section 1395i–5 of this title, the Secretary shall not require any patient of a religious nonmedical health care institution to undergo medical screening, examination, diagnosis, prognosis, or treatment or to accept any other medical health care service, if such patient (or legal representative of the patient) objects thereto on religious grounds.

(**ii**) Clause (i) shall not be construed as preventing the Secretary from requiring under section 1395i–5(a)(2) of this title the provision of sufficient information regarding an individual's condition as a condition for receipt of benefits under part A of this subchapter for services provided in such an institution.

(**B**)(**i**) In administering this subsection and section 1395i–5 of this title, the Secretary shall not subject a religious nonmedical health care institution or its personnel to any medical supervision, regulation, or control, insofar as such supervision, regulation, or control would be contrary to the religious beliefs observed by the institution or such personnel.

(**ii**) Clause (i) shall not be construed as preventing the Secretary from reviewing items and services billed by the institution to the extent the Secretary determines such review to be necessary to determine whether such items and services were not covered under part A of this subchapter, are excessive, or are fraudulent.

(**4**)(**A**) For purposes of paragraph (1)(G)(i), an ownership interest of less than 5 percent shall not be taken into account.

(**B**) For purposes of paragraph (1)(G)(ii), none of the following shall be considered to create an affiliation:

(**i**) An individual serving as an uncompensated director, trustee, officer, or other member of the governing body of a religious nonmedical health care institution.

(ii) An individual who is a director, trustee, officer, employee, or staff member of a religious nonmedical health care institution having a family relationship with an individual who is affiliated with (or has an ownership interest in) a provider of medical treatment or services.

(iii) An individual or entity furnishing goods or services as a vendor to both providers of medical treatment or services and religious nonmedical health care institutions.

(tt) Post-institutional home health services; home health spell of illness

(1) The term "post-institutional home health services" means home health services furnished to an individual—

(A) after discharge from a hospital or rural primary care hospital in which the individual was an inpatient for not less than 3 consecutive days before such discharge if such home health services were initiated within 14 days after the date of such discharge; or

(B) after discharge from a skilled nursing facility in which the individual was provided post-hospital extended care services if such home health services were initiated within 14 days after the date of such discharge.

(2) The term "home health spell of illness" with respect to any individual means a period of consecutive days—

(A) beginning with the first day (not included in a previous home health spell of illness)

(i) on which such individual is furnished post-institutional home health services, and

(ii) which occurs in a month for which the individual is entitled to benefits under part A of this subchapter, and

(B) ending with the close of the first period of 60 consecutive days thereafter on each of which the individual is neither an inpatient of a hospital or critical access hospital nor an inpatient of a facility described in section 1395i–3(a)(1) of this title or subsection (y)(1) of this section nor provided home health services.

(uu) Screening for glaucoma

The term "screening for glaucoma" means a dilated eye examination with an intraocular pressure measurement, and a direct ophthalmoscopy or a slit-lamp biomicroscopic examination for the early detection of glaucoma which is furnished by or under the direct supervision of an optometrist or ophthalmologist who is legally authorized to furnish such services under State law (or the State regulatory mechanism provided by State law) of the State in which the services are furnished, as would otherwise be covered if furnished by a physician or as an incident to a physician's professional service, if the individual involved has not had such an examination in the preceding year.

(vv) Medical nutrition therapy services; registered dietitian or nutrition professional

(1) The term "medical nutrition therapy services" means nutritional diagnostic, therapy, and counseling services for the purpose of disease management which are furnished by a registered dietitian or nutrition professional (as defined in paragraph (2)) pursuant to a referral by a physician (as defined in subsection (r)(1)).

(2) Subject to paragraph (3), the term "registered dietitian or nutrition professional" means an individual who

(A) holds a baccalaureate or higher degree granted by a regionally accredited college or university in the United States (or an equivalent foreign degree) with completion of the academic requirements of a program in nutrition or dietetics, as accredited by an appropriate national accreditation organization recognized by the Secretary for this purpose;

(B) has completed at least 900 hours of supervised dietetics practice under the supervision of a registered dietitian or nutrition professional; and

(C)(i) is licensed or certified as a dietitian or nutrition professional by the State in which the services are performed; or

(ii) in the case of an individual in a State that does not provide for such licensure or certification, meets such other criteria as the Secretary establishes.

(3) Subparagraphs (A) and (B) of paragraph (2) shall not apply in the case of an individual who, as of December 21, 2000, is licensed or certified as a dietitian or nutrition professional by the State in which medical nutrition therapy services are performed.

§ 1395y. Exclusions from coverage and medicare as secondary payer

(a) Items or services specifically excluded

Notwithstanding any other provision of this subchapter, no payment may be made under part A or part B of this subchapter for any expenses incurred for items or services—

(1)(A) which, except for items and services described in a succeeding paragraph, are not reasonable and necessary for the diagnosis or treatment of illness or injury or to improve the functioning of a malformed body member,

(B) in the case of items and services described in section 1395x(s)(10) of this title, which are not reasonable and necessary for the prevention of illness,

(C) in the case of hospice care, which are not reasonable and necessary for the palliation or management of terminal illness,

(D) in the case of clinical care items and services provided with the concurrence of the Secretary and with respect to research and experimentation conducted by, or under contract with, the Medicare Payment Advisory Commission or the Secretary, which are not reasonable and necessary to carry out the purposes of section 1395ww(e)(6) of this title,

(E) in the case of research conducted pursuant to section 1320b–12 of this title, which is not reasonable and necessary to carry out the purposes of that section,

(F) in the case of screening mammography, which is performed more frequently than is covered under section 1395m(c)(2) of this title or which is not conducted by a facility described in section 1395m(c)(1)(B) of this title, in the case of screening pap smear and screening pelvic exam, which is performed more frequently than is provided under section 1395x(nn) of this title, and, in the case of screening for glaucoma, which is performed more frequently than is provided under section 1395x(uu) of this title,

(G) in the case of prostate cancer screening tests (as defined in section 1395x(oo) of this title), which are performed more frequently than is covered under such section,

(H) in the case of colorectal cancer screening tests, which are performed more frequently than is covered under section 1395m(d) of this title, and

(I) the frequency and duration of home health services which are in excess of normative guidelines that the Secretary shall establish by regulation;

(2) for which the individual furnished such items or services has no legal obligation to pay, and which no other person (by reason of such individual's membership in a prepayment plan or otherwise) has a legal obligation to provide or pay for, except in the case of Federally qualified health center services;

(3) which are paid for directly or indirectly by a governmental entity (other than under this chapter and other than under a health benefits or insurance plan established for employees of such an entity), except in the case of rural health clinic services, as defined in section 1395x(aa)(1) of this title, in the case of Federally qualified health center services, as defined in section 1395x(aa)(3) of this title, in the case of services for which payment may be made under section 1395qq(e) of this title, and in such other cases as the Secretary may specify;

(4) which are not provided within the United States (except for inpatient hospital services furnished outside the United States under the

627

conditions described in section 1395f(f) of this title and, subject to such conditions, limitations, and requirements as are provided under or pursuant to this subchapter, physicians' services and ambulance services furnished an individual in conjunction with such inpatient hospital services but only for the period during which such inpatient hospital services were furnished);

(5) which are required as a result of war, or of an act of war, occurring after the effective date of such individual's current coverage under such part;

(6) which constitute personal comfort items (except, in the case of hospice care, as is otherwise permitted under paragraph (1)(C));

(7) where such expenses are for routine physical checkups, eyeglasses (other than eyewear described in section 1395x(s)(8) of this title) or eye examinations for the purpose of prescribing, fitting, or changing eyeglasses, procedures performed (during the course of any eye examination) to determine the refractive state of the eyes, hearing aids or examinations therefor, or immunizations (except as otherwise allowed under section 1395x(s)(10) of this title and subparagraph (B), (F), (G), or (H) of paragraph (1);

(8) where such expenses are for orthopedic shoes or other supportive devices for the feet, other than shoes furnished pursuant to section 1395x(s)(12) of this title;

(9) where such expenses are for custodial care (except, in the case of hospice care, as is otherwise permitted under paragraph (1)(C));

(10) where such expenses are for cosmetic surgery or are incurred in connection therewith, except as required for the prompt repair of accidental injury or for improvement of the functioning of a malformed body member;

(11) where such expenses constitute charges imposed by immediate relatives of such individual or members of his household;

(12) where such expenses are for services in connection with the care, treatment, filling, removal, or replacement of teeth or structures directly supporting teeth, except that payment may be made under part A of this subchapter in the case of inpatient hospital services in connection with the provision of such dental services if the individual, because of his underlying medical condition and clinical status or because of the severity of the dental procedure, requires hospitalization in connection with the provision of such services;

(13) where such expenses are for—

(A) the treatment of flat foot conditions and the prescription of supportive devices therefor,

(B) the treatment of subluxations of the foot, or

(C) routine foot care (including the cutting or removal of corns or calluses, the trimming of nails, and other routine hygienic care);

(14) which are other than physicians' services (as defined in regulations promulgated specifically for purposes of this paragraph), services described by section 1395x(s)(2)(K) of this title, certified nurse-midwife services, qualified psychologist services, and services of a certified registered nurse anesthetist, and which are furnished to an individual who is a patient of a hospital or critical access hospital by an entity other than the hospital or critical access hospital, unless the services are furnished under arrangements (as defined in section 1395x(w)(1) of this title) with the entity made by the hospital or critical access hospital;

(15)(A) which are for services of an assistant at surgery in a cataract operation (including subsequent insertion of an intraocular lens) unless, before the surgery is performed, the appropriate utilization and quality control peer review organization (under part B of subchapter XI of this chapter) or a carrier under section 1395u of this title has approved of the use of such an assistant in the surgical procedure based on the existence of a complicating medical condition, or

(B) which are for services of an assistant at surgery to which section 1395w–4(i)(2)(B) of this title applies;

(16) in the case in which funds may not be used for such items and services under the Assisted Suicide Funding Restriction Act of 1997 [*42 U.S.C.A. § 14401* et seq.];

(17) where the expenses are for an item or service furnished in a competitive acquisition area (as established by the Secretary under section 1395w–3(a) of this title) by an entity other than an entity with which the Secretary has entered into a contract under section 1395w–3(b) of this title for the furnishing of such an item or service in that area, unless the Secretary finds that the expenses were incurred in a case of urgent need, or in other circumstances specified by the Secretary;

(18) which are covered skilled nursing facility services described in section 1395yy(e)(2)(A)(i) of this title and which are furnished to an individual who is a resident of a skilled nursing facility during a period in which the resident is provided covered post-hospital extended care services (or, for services described in section 1395x(s)(2)(D) of this title, which are furnished to such an individual without regard to such period), by an entity other than the skilled nursing facility, unless the services are furnished under arrangements (as defined in section 1395x(w)(1) of this title) with the entity made by the skilled nursing facility;

(19) which are for items or services which are furnished pursuant to a private contract described in section 1395a(b) of this title;

(20) in the case of outpatient occupational therapy services or outpatient physical therapy services furnished as an incident to a physician's professional services (as described in section 1395x(s)(2)(A) of this title), that do not meet the standards and conditions (other than any licensing requirement specified by the Secretary) under the second sentence of section 1395x(p) of this title (or under such sentence through the operation of section 1395x(g) of this title) as such standards and conditions would apply to such therapy services if furnished by a therapist; or

(21) where such expenses are for home health services (including medical supplies described in section 1395x(m)(5) of this title, but excluding durable medical equipment to the extent provided for in such section) furnished to an individual who is under a plan of care of the home health agency if the claim for payment for such services is not submitted by the agency.

Paragraph (7) shall not apply to Federally qualified health center services described in section 1395x(aa)(3)(B) of this title.

In making a national coverage determination (as defined in paragraph (1)(B) of section 1395ff(f) of this title) the Secretary shall ensure that the public is afforded notice and opportunity to comment prior to implementation by the Secretary of the determination; meetings of advisory committees established under section 1314(f) of this title with respect to the determination are made on the record; in making the determination, the Secretary has considered applicable information (including clinical experience and medical, technical, and scientific evidence) with respect to the subject matter of the determination; and in the determination, provide a clear statement of the basis for the determination (including responses to comments received from the public), the assumptions underlying that basis, and make available to the public the data (other than proprietary data) considered in making the determination.

(b) Medicare as secondary payer

(1) Requirements of group health plans

(A) Working aged under group health plans

(i) In general

A group health plan—

(I) may not take into account that an individual (or the individual's spouse) who is covered under the plan by virtue of the individual's current employment status with an employer is entitled to benefits under this subchapter under section 426(a) of this title, and

(II) shall provide that any individual age 65 or older (and the spouse age 65 or older of any individual) who has current employment status with an employer shall be entitled to the same benefits under the plan under the same conditions as any such individual (or spouse) under age 65.

(ii) Exclusion of group health plan of a small employer

Clause (i) shall not apply to a group health plan unless the plan is a plan of, or contributed to by, an employer that has 20 or more employees for each working day in each of 20 or more calendar weeks in the current calendar year or the preceding calendar year.

(iii) Exception for small employers in multiemployer or multiple employer group health plans

Clause (i) also shall not apply with respect to individuals enrolled in a multiemployer or multiple employer group health plan if the coverage of the individuals under the plan is by virtue of current employment status with an employer that does not have 20 or more individuals in current employment status for each working day in each of 20 or more calendar weeks in the current calendar year and the preceding calendar year; except that the exception provided in this clause shall only apply if the plan elects treatment under this clause.

(iv) Exception for individuals with end stage renal disease

Subparagraph (C) shall apply instead of clause (i) to an item or service furnished in a month to an individual if for the month the individual is, or (without regard to entitlement under section 426 of this title) would upon application be, entitled to benefits under section 426–1 of this title.

(v) "Group health plan" defined

In this subparagraph, and subparagraph (C), the term "group health plan" has the meaning given such term in section 5000(b)(1) of Title 26, without regard to section 5000(d) of Title 26.

(B) Disabled individuals in large group health plans

(i) In general

A large group health plan (as defined in clause (iii)) may not take into account that an individual (or a member of the individual's family) who is covered under the plan by virtue of the individual's current employment status with an employer is entitled to benefits under this subchapter under section 426(b) of this title.

(ii) Exception for individuals with end stage renal disease

Subparagraph (C) shall apply instead of clause (i) to an item or service furnished in a month to an individual if for the month the individual is, or (without regard to entitlement under section 426 of this title) would upon application be, entitled to benefits under section 426–1 of this title.

631

(iii) "Large group health plan" defined

In this subparagraph, the term "large group health plan" has the meaning given such term in section 5000(b)(2) of Title 26, without regard to section 5000(d) of Title 26.

(C) Individuals with end stage renal disease

A group health plan (as defined in subparagraph (A)(v))—

(i) may not take into account that an individual is entitled to or eligible for benefits under this subchapter under section 426–1 of this title during the 12–month period which begins with the first month in which the individual becomes entitled to benefits under part A under the provisions of section 426–1 of this title, or, if earlier, the first month in which the individual would have been entitled to benefits under such part under the provisions of section 426–1 of this title if the individual had filed an application for such benefits; and

(ii) may not differentiate in the benefits it provides between individuals having end stage renal disease and other individuals covered by such plan on the basis of the existence of end stage renal disease, the need for renal dialysis, or in any other manner;

except that clause (ii) shall not prohibit a plan from paying benefits secondary to this subchapter when an individual is entitled to or eligible for benefits under this subchapter under section 426–1 of this title after the end of the 12–month period described in clause (i). Effective for items and services furnished on or after February 1, 1991, and before August 5, 1997, (with respect to periods beginning on or after February 1, 1990), this subparagraph shall be applied by substituting "18–month" for "12–month" each place it appears. Effective for items and services furnished on or after August 5, 1997, (with respect to periods beginning on or after the date that is 18 months prior to such date), clauses (i) and (ii) shall be applied by substituting "30–month" for "12–month" each place it appears.

(D) Treatment of certain members of religious orders

In this subsection, an individual shall not be considered to be employed, or an employee, with respect to the performance of services as a member of a religious order which are considered employment only by virtue of an election made by the religious order under section 3121(r) of Title 26.

(E) General provisions

For purposes of this subsection:

(i) Aggregation rules

(I) All employers treated as a single employer under subsection (a) or (b) of section 52 of Title 26 shall be treated as a single employer.

(II) All employees of the members of an affiliated service group (as defined in section 414(m) of Title 26) shall be treated as employed by a single employer.

(III) Leased employees (as defined in section 414(n)(2) of Title 26) shall be treated as employees of the person for whom they perform services to the extent they are so treated under section 414(n) of Title 26.

In applying sections of Title 26 under this clause, the Secretary shall rely upon regulations and decisions of the Secretary of the Treasury respecting such sections.

(ii) Current employment status defined

An individual has "current employment status" with an employer if the individual is an employee, is the employer, or is associated with the employer in a business relationship.

(iii) Treatment of self-employed persons as employers

The term "employer" includes a self-employed person.

(F) Limitation on beneficiary liability

An individual who is entitled to benefits under this title and is furnished an item or service for which such benefits are incorrectly paid is not liable for repayment of such benefits under this paragraph unless payment of such benefits was made to the individual.

(2) Medicare secondary payer

(A) In general

Payment under this subchapter may not be made, except as provided in subparagraph (B), with respect to any item or service to the extent that—

(i) payment has been made, or can reasonably be expected to be made, with respect to the item or service as required under paragraph (1), or

(ii) payment has been made or can reasonably be expected to be made promptly (as determined in accordance with regulations) under a workmen's compensation law or plan of the United States or a State or under an automobile or liability insurance policy or plan (including a self-insured plan) or under no fault insurance.

In this subsection, the term "primary plan" means a group health plan or large group health plan, to the extent that clause (i) applies, and a workmen's compensation law or plan, an automobile or liability insurance policy or plan (including a self-insured plan) or no fault insurance, to the extent that clause (ii) applies.

(B) Repayment required

(i) Primary plans

Any payment under this subchapter with respect to any item or service to which subparagraph (A) applies shall be conditioned on reimbursement to the appropriate Trust Fund established by this subchapter when notice or other information is received that payment for such item or service has been or could be made under such subparagraph. If reimbursement is not made to the appropriate Trust Fund before the expiration of the 60–day period that begins on the date such notice or other information is received, the Secretary may charge interest (beginning with the date on which the notice or other information is received) on the amount of the reimbursement until reimbursement is made (at a rate determined by the Secretary in accordance with regulations of the Secretary of the Treasury applicable to charges for late payments).

(ii) Action by United States

In order to recover payment under this subchapter for such an item or service, the United States may bring an action against any entity which is required or responsible (directly, as a third-party administrator, or otherwise) to make payment with respect to such item or service (or any portion thereof) under a primary plan (and may, in accordance with paragraph (3)(A) collect double damages against that entity), or against any other entity (including any physician or provider) that has received payment from that entity with respect to the item or service, and may join or intervene in any action related to the events that gave rise to the need for the item or service. The United States may not recover from a third-party administrator under this clause in cases where the third-party administrator would not be able to recover the amount at issue from the employer or group health plan and is not employed by or under contract with the employer or group health plan at the time the action for recovery is initiated by the United States or for whom it provides administrative services due to the insolvency or bankruptcy of the employer or plan.

(iii) Subrogation rights

The United States shall be subrogated (to the extent of payment made under this subchapter for such an item or service) to any right under this subsection of an individual or any other entity to payment with respect to such item or service under a primary plan.

(iv) Waiver of rights

The Secretary may waive (in whole or in part) the provisions of this subparagraph in the case of an individual claim if the Secretary determines that the waiver is in the best interests of the program established under this subchapter.

(v) Claims-filing period

Notwithstanding any other time limits that may exist for filing a claim under an employer group health plan, the United States may seek to recover conditional payments in accordance with this subparagraph where the request for payment is submitted to the entity required or responsible under this subsection to pay with respect to the item or service (or any portion thereof) under a primary plan within the 3–year period beginning on the date on which the item or service was furnished.

(C) Treatment of questionnaires

The Secretary may not fail to make payment under subparagraph (A) solely on the ground that an individual failed to complete a questionnaire concerning the existence of a primary plan.

(3) Enforcement

(A) Private cause of action

There is established a private cause of action for damages (which shall be in an amount double the amount otherwise provided) in the case of a primary plan which fails to provide for primary payment (or appropriate reimbursement) in accordance with such paragraphs (1) and (2)(A).

(B) Reference to excise tax with respect to nonconforming group health plans

For provision imposing an excise tax with respect to nonconforming group health plans, see section 5000 of Title 26.

(C) Prohibition of financial incentives not to enroll in a group health plan or a large group health plan

It is unlawful for an employer or other entity to offer any financial or other incentive for an individual entitled to benefits under this subchapter not to enroll (or to terminate enrollment) under a group health plan or a large group health plan which would (in the case of such enrollment) be a primary plan (as defined in paragraph (2)(A)). Any entity that violates the previous sentence is subject to a civil money penalty of not to exceed $5,000 for each such violation. The provisions of section 1320a–7a of this title (other than subsections (a) and (b)) shall apply to a civil money penalty under the previous sentence in the same manner as such provisions apply to a penalty or proceeding under section 1320a–7a(a) of this title.

(4) Coordination of benefits

Where payment for an item or service by a primary plan is less than the amount of the charge for such item or service and is not payment in full, payment may be made under this subchapter (without regard to deductibles and coinsurance under this subchapter) for the remainder of such charge, but—

(A) payment under this subchapter may not exceed an amount which would be payable under this subchapter for such item or service if paragraph (2)(A) did not apply; and

(B) payment under this subchapter, when combined with the amount payable under the primary plan, may not exceed—

(i) in the case of an item or service payment for which is determined under this subchapter on the basis of reasonable cost (or other cost-related basis) or under section 1395ww of this title, the amount which would be payable under this subchapter on such basis, and

(ii) in the case of an item or service for which payment is authorized under this subchapter on another basis—

(I) the amount which would be payable under the primary plan (without regard to deductibles and coinsurance under such plan), or

(II) the reasonable charge or other amount which would be payable under this subchapter (without regard to deductibles and coinsurance under this subchapter),

whichever is greater.

(5) Identification of secondary payer situations

(A) Requesting matching information

(i) Commissioner of Social Security

The Commissioner of Social Security shall, not less often than annually, transmit to the Secretary of the Treasury a list of the names and TINs of medicare beneficiaries (as defined in section 6103(*l*)(12) of Title 26) and request that the Secretary disclose to the Commissioner the information described in subparagraph (A) of such section.

(ii) Administrator

The Administrator of the Health Care Financing Administration shall request, not less often than annually, the Commissioner of the Social Security Administration to disclose to the Administrator the information described in subparagraph (B) of section 6103(*l*)(12) of Title 26.

(B) Disclosure to fiscal intermediaries and carriers

In addition to any other information provided under this subchapter to fiscal intermediaries and carriers, the Administrator shall disclose to such intermediaries and carriers (or to such a single intermediary or carrier as the Secretary may designate) the information received under subparagraph (A) for purposes of carrying out this subsection.

(C) Contacting employers

(i) In general

With respect to each individual (in this subparagraph referred to as an "employee") who was furnished a written statement under section 6051 of Title 26 by a qualified employer (as defined in section 6103(*l*)(12)(E)(iii) of such title), as disclosed under subparagraph (B), the appropriate fiscal intermediary or carrier shall contact the employer in order to determine during what period the employee or employee's spouse may be (or have been) covered under a group health plan of the employer and the nature of the coverage that is or was provided under the plan (including the name, address, and identifying number of the plan).

(ii) Employer response

Within 30 days of the date of receipt of the inquiry, the employer shall notify the intermediary or carrier making the inquiry as to the determinations described in clause (i). An employer (other than a Federal or other governmental entity) who willfully or repeatedly fails to provide timely and accurate notice in accordance with the previous sentence shall be subject to a civil money penalty of not to exceed $1,000 for each individual with respect to which such an inquiry is made. The provisions of section 1320a–7a of this title (other than subsections (a) and (b)) shall apply to a civil money penalty under the previous sentence in the same manner as such provisions apply to a penalty or proceeding under section 1320a–7a(a) of this title.

(D) Obtaining information from beneficiaries

Before an individual applies for benefits under part A of this subchapter or enrolls under part B of this subchapter, the Administrator shall mail the individual a questionnaire to obtain information on whether the individual is covered under a primary plan and the nature of the coverage provided under the plan, including the name, address, and identifying number of the plan.

(6) Screening requirements for providers and suppliers

(A) In general

Notwithstanding any other provision of this subchapter, no payment may be made for any item or service furnished under part B of this subchapter unless the entity furnishing such item or service completes (to the best of its knowledge and on the basis of information obtained from the individual to whom the item or service is furnished) the portion of the claim form relating to the availability of other health benefit plans.

(B) Penalties

An entity that knowingly, willfully, and repeatedly fails to complete a claim form in accordance with subparagraph (A) or provides inaccurate information relating to the availability of other health benefit plans on a claim form under such subparagraph shall be subject to a civil money penalty of not to exceed $2,000 for each such incident. The provisions of section 1320a–7a of this title (other than subsections (a) and (b)) shall apply to a civil money penalty under the previous sentence in the same manner as such provisions apply to a penalty or proceeding under section 1320a–7a(a) of this title.

(c) Drug products

No payment may be made under part B of this subchapter for any expenses incurred for—

    (1) a drug product—

        (A) which is described in section 107(c)(3) of the Drug Amendments of 1962,

        (B) which may be dispensed only upon prescription,

        (C) for which the Secretary has issued a notice of an opportunity for a hearing under subsection (e) of section 355 of Title 21 on a proposed order of the Secretary to withdraw approval of an application for such drug product under such section because the Secretary has determined that the drug is less than effective for all conditions of use prescribed, recommended, or suggested in its labeling, and

        (D) for which the Secretary has not determined there is a compelling justification for its medical need; and

    (2) any other drug product—

        (A) which is identical, related, or similar (as determined in accordance with *section 310.6 of title 21 of the Code of Federal Regulations*) to a drug product described in paragraph (1), and

        (B) for which the Secretary has not determined there is a compelling justification for its medical need,

until such time as the Secretary withdraws such proposed order.

(d) Repealed. *Pub.L. 100–93, § 8(c)(1)(A)*, Aug. 18, 1987, 101 Stat. 692

(e) Item or service by excluded individual or entity or at direction of excluded physician; limitation of liability of beneficiaries with respect to services furnished by excluded individuals and entities

    (1) No payment may be made under this subchapter with respect to any item or service (other than an emergency item or service, not including items or services furnished in an emergency room of a hospital) furnished—

        (A) by an individual or entity during the period when such individual or entity is excluded pursuant to section 1320a–7, 1320a–7a, 1320c–5, or 1395u(j)(2) of this title from participation in the program under this subchapter; or

(B) at the medical direction or on the prescription of a physician during the period when he is excluded pursuant to section 1320a–7, 1320a–7a, 1320c–5, or 1395u(j)(2) of this title from participation in the program under this subchapter and when the person furnishing such item or service knew or had reason to know of the exclusion (after a reasonable time period after reasonable notice has been furnished to the person).

(2) Where an individual eligible for benefits under this subchapter submits a claim for payment for items or services furnished by an individual or entity excluded from participation in the programs under this subchapter, pursuant to section 1320a–7, 1320a–7a, 1320c–5, 1320c–9 (as in effect on September 2, 1982), 1395u(j)(2), 1395y(d) (as in effect on August 18, 1987), or 1395cc of this title, and such beneficiary did not know or have reason to know that such individual or entity was so excluded, then, to the extent permitted by this subchapter, and notwithstanding such exclusion, payment shall be made for such items or services. In each such case the Secretary shall notify the beneficiary of the exclusion of the individual or entity furnishing the items or services. Payment shall not be made for items or services furnished by an excluded individual or entity to a beneficiary after a reasonable time (as determined by the Secretary in regulations) after the Secretary has notified the beneficiary of the exclusion of that individual or entity.

(f) Utilization guidelines for provision of home health services

The Secretary shall establish utilization guidelines for the determination of whether or not payment may be made, consistent with paragraph (1)(A) of subsection (a) of this section, under part A or part B of this subchapter for expenses incurred with respect to the provision of home health services, and shall provide for the implementation of such guidelines through a process of selective postpayment coverage review by intermediaries or otherwise.

(g) Contracts with utilization and quality control peer review organizations

The Secretary shall, in making the determinations under paragraphs (1) and (9) of subsection (a) of this section, and for the purposes of promoting the effective, efficient, and economical delivery of health care services, and of promoting the quality of services of the type for which payment may be made under this subchapter, enter into contracts with utilization and quality control peer review organizations pursuant to part B of subchapter XI of this chapter.

(h) Repealed. *Pub.L. 104–224, § 1*, Oct. 2, 1996, 110 Stat. 3031

(i) Awards and contracts for original research and experimentation of new and existing medical procedures; conditions

In order to supplement the activities of the Medicare Payment Advisory Commission under section 1395ww(e) of this title in assessing the safety, efficacy, and cost-effectiveness of new and existing medical procedures, the

639

Secretary may carry out, or award grants or contracts for, original research and experimentation of the type described in clause (ii) of section 1395ww(e)(6)(E) of this title with respect to such a procedure if the Secretary finds that—

  (1) such procedure is not of sufficient commercial value to justify research and experimentation by a commercial organization;

  (2) research and experimentation with respect to such procedure is not of a type that may appropriately be carried out by an institute, division, or bureau of the National Institutes of Health; and

  (3) such procedure has the potential to be more cost-effective in the treatment of a condition than procedures currently in use with respect to such condition.

§ 1395z. Consultation with State agencies and other organizations to develop conditions of participation for providers of services

In carrying out his functions, relating to determination of conditions of participation by providers of services, under subsections (e)(9), (f)(4), (j)(15), (o)(6), (cc)(2)(I), and (dd)(2), and (mm)(1) of section 1395x of this title, or by ambulatory surgical centers under section 1395k(a)(2)(F)(i) of this title, the Secretary shall consult with appropriate State agencies and recognized national listing or accrediting bodies, and may consult with appropriate local agencies. Such conditions prescribed under any of such subsections may be varied for different areas or different classes of institutions or agencies and may, at the request of a State, provide higher requirements for such State than for other States; except that, in the case of any State or political subdivision of a State which imposes higher requirements on institutions as a condition to the purchase of services (or of certain specified services) in such institutions under a State plan approved under subchapter I, XVI, or XIX of this chapter, the Secretary shall impose like requirements as a condition to the payment for services (or for the services specified by the State or subdivision) in such institutions in such State or subdivision.

§ 1395aa. Agreements with States

  (a) Use of State agencies to determine compliance by providers of services with conditions of participation

The Secretary shall make an agreement with any State which is able and willing to do so under which the services of the State health agency or other appropriate State agency (or the appropriate local agencies) will be utilized by him for the purpose of determining whether an institution therein is a hospital or skilled nursing facility, or whether an agency therein is a home health agency, or whether an agency is a hospice program or whether a facility therein is a rural health clinic as defined in section 1395x(aa)(2) of this title, a critical access hospital, as defined in section 1395x(mm)(1) of this title, or a comprehensive outpatient rehabilitation facility as defined in section 1395x(cc)(2) of this title, or whether a laboratory meets the requirements of paragraphs (16) and (17) of section 1395x(s) of this title, or whether a clinic, rehabilitation agency or public health agency meets the requirements of subparagraph (A) or (B), as the case may be, of section 1395x(p)(4) of this title, or whether an ambulatory surgical center meets the standards specified under section 1395k(a)(2)(F)(i) of this title. To the extent that the Secretary finds it appropriate, an institution or agency which such a State (or local) agency certifies is a hospital, skilled nursing facility, rural health clinic, comprehensive outpatient rehabilitation facility, home health agency, or hospice program (as those terms are defined in section 1395x of this title) may be treated as such by the Secretary. Any State agency which has such an agreement may (subject to approval of the Secretary) furnish to a skilled nursing facility, after proper request by such facility, such specialized consultative services (which such agency is able and willing to furnish in a manner satisfactory to the Secretary) as such facility may need to meet one or more of the conditions specified in section 1395i–3(a) of this title. Any such services furnished by a State agency shall be deemed to have been furnished pursuant to such agreement. Within 90 days following the completion of each survey of any health care facility, ambulatory surgical center, rural health clinic, comprehensive outpatient rehabilitation facility, laboratory, clinic, agency, or organization by the appropriate State or local agency described in the first sentence of this subsection, the Secretary shall make public in readily available form and place, and require (in the case of skilled nursing facilities) the posting in a place readily accessible to patients (and patients' representatives), the pertinent findings of each such survey relating to the compliance of each such health care facility, ambulatory surgical center, rural health clinic, comprehensive outpatient rehabilitation facility, laboratory, clinic, agency, or organization with

> **(1)** the statutory conditions of participation imposed under this subchapter and

> **(2)** the major additional conditions which the Secretary finds necessary in the interest of health and safety of individuals who are furnished care or services by any such health care facility, ambulatory surgical center, rural health clinic, comprehensive outpatient rehabilitation facility, laboratory, clinic, agency, or organization.

Any agreement under this subsection shall provide for the appropriate State or local agency to maintain a toll-free hotline

> **(1)** to collect, maintain, and continually update information on home health agencies located in the State or locality that are certified to participate in the program established under this subchapter (which information shall include any significant deficiencies found with respect to patient care in the most recent certification survey conducted by a State agency or accreditation survey conducted by a private accreditation agency under section 1395bb of this title with respect to the home health agency, when that survey was completed, whether corrective actions have been taken or are planned, and the sanctions, if any, imposed under this subchapter with respect to the agency) and

(2) to receive complaints (and answer questions) with respect to home health agencies in the State or locality. Any such agreement shall provide for such State or local agency to maintain a unit for investigating such complaints that possesses enforcement authority and has access to survey and certification reports, information gathered by any private accreditation agency utilized by the Secretary under section 1395bb of this title, and consumer medical records (but only with the consent of the consumer or his or her legal representative).

(b) Payment in advance or by way of reimbursement to State for performance of functions of subsection (a)

The Secretary shall pay any such State, in advance or by way of reimbursement, as may be provided in the agreement with it (and may make adjustments in such payments on account of overpayments or underpayments previously made), for the reasonable cost of performing the functions specified in subsection (a) of this section, and for the Federal Hospital Insurance Trust Fund's fair share of the costs attributable to the planning and other efforts directed toward coordination of activities in carrying out its agreement and other activities related to the provision of services similar to those for which payment may be made under part A of this subchapter, or related to the facilities and personnel required for the provision of such services, or related to improving the quality of such services.

(c) Use of State or local agencies to survey provider entities

The Secretary is authorized to enter into an agreement with any State under which the appropriate State or local agency which performs the certification function described in subsection (a) of this section will survey, on a selective sample basis (or where the Secretary finds that a survey is appropriate because of substantial allegations of the existence of a significant deficiency or deficiencies which would, if found to be present, adversely affect health and safety of patients), provider entities that, pursuant to subsection (a) or (b)(1) of section 1395bb of this title, are treated as meeting the conditions or requirements of this subchapter. The Secretary shall pay for such services in the manner prescribed in subsection (b) of this section.

(d) Fulfillment of requirements by States

The Secretary may not enter an agreement under this section with a State with respect to determining whether an institution therein is a skilled nursing facility unless the State meets the requirements specified in section 1395i–3(e) of this title and section 1395i–3(g) of this title and the establishment of remedies under section 1395i–3(h)(2)(B) and 1395i–3(h)(2)(C) of this title (relating to establishment and application of remedies).

(e) Prohibition of user fees for survey and certification

Notwithstanding any other provision of law, the Secretary may not impose, or require a State to impose, any fee on any facility or entity subject to a determination under subsection (a) of this section, or any renal dialysis facility subject to the requirements of section 1395rr(b)(1) of this title, for any such determination or any survey relating to determining the compliance of such facility or entity with any requirement of this subchapter (other than any fee relating to section 263a of this title).

§ 1395bb.   Effect of accreditation

(a) In general

Except as provided in subsection (b) of this section and the second sentence of section 1395z of this title, if—

(1) an institution is accredited as a hospital by the Joint Commission on Accreditation of Hospitals, and

(2)(A) such institution authorizes the Commission to release to the Secretary upon his request (or such State agency as the Secretary may designate) a copy of the most current accreditation survey of such institution made by such Commission, together with any other information directly related to the survey as the Secretary may require (including corrective action plans),

(B) such Commission releases such a copy and any such information to the Secretary, then, such institution shall be deemed to meet the requirements of the numbered paragraphs of section 1395x(e) of this title; except—

(3) paragraph (6) thereof, and

(4) any standard, promulgated by the Secretary pursuant to paragraph (9) thereof, which is higher than the requirements prescribed for accreditation by such Commission.

If such Commission, as a condition for accreditation of a hospital, requires a utilization review plan (or imposes another requirement which serves substantially the same purpose), requires a discharge planning process (or imposes another requirement which serves substantially the same purpose), or imposes a standard which the Secretary determines is at least equivalent to the standard promulgated by the Secretary as described in paragraph (4) of this subsection, the Secretary is authorized to find that all institutions so accredited by such Commission comply also with clause (A) or (B) of section 1395x(e)(6) of this title or the standard described in such paragraph (4), as the case may be.

(b) American Osteopathic Association or other national accreditation body

(1) In addition, if the Secretary finds that accreditation of a provider entity (as defined in paragraph (4)) by the American Osteopathic Association or any other national accreditation body demonstrates that all of the applicable conditions or requirements of this subchapter (other than the requirements of section 1395m(j) of this section or the conditions and requirements under section 1395rr(b) of this title) are met or exceeded—

(A) in the case of a provider entity not described in paragraph (3)(B), the Secretary shall treat such entity as meeting those conditions or requirements with respect to which the Secretary made such finding; or

(B) in the case of a provider entity described in paragraph (3)(B), the Secretary may treat such entity as meeting those conditions or requirements with respect to which the Secretary made such finding.

(2) In making such a finding, the Secretary shall consider, among other factors with respect to a national accreditation body, its requirements for accreditation, its survey procedures, its ability to provide adequate resources for conducting required surveys and supplying information for use in enforcement activities, its monitoring procedures for provider entities found out of compliance with the conditions or requirements, and its ability to provide the Secretary with necessary data for validation.

(3)(A) Except as provided in subparagraph (B), not later than 60 days after the date of receipt of a written request for a finding under paragraph (1) (with any documentation necessary to make a determination on the request), the Secretary shall publish a notice identifying the national accreditation body making the request, describing the nature of the request, and providing a period of at least 30 days for the public to comment on the request. The Secretary shall approve or deny a request for such a finding, and shall publish notice of such approval or denial, not later than 210 days after the date of receipt of the request (with such documentation). Such an approval shall be effective with respect to accreditation determinations made on or after such effective date (which may not be later than the date of publication of the approval) as the Secretary specifies in the publication notice.

(B) The 210–day and 60–day deadlines specified in subparagraph (A) shall not apply in the case of any request for a finding with respect to accreditation of a provider entity to which the conditions and requirements of section 1395i–3 and 1395x(j) of this title apply.

(4) For purposes of this section, the term "provider entity" means a provider of services, supplier, facility, clinic, agency, or laboratory.

(c) Disclosure of accreditation survey

The Secretary may not disclose any accreditation survey (other than a survey with respect to a home health agency) made and released to him by the Joint Commission on Accreditation of Hospitals, the American Osteopathic Association, or any other national accreditation body, of an entity accredited by such body, except that the Secretary may disclose such a survey and information related to such a survey to the extent such survey and information relate to an enforcement action taken by the Secretary.

(d) Deficiencies

Notwithstanding any other provision of this subchapter, if the Secretary finds that a provider entity has significant deficiencies (as defined in regulations pertaining to health and safety), the entity shall, after the date of notice of such finding to the entity and for such period as may be prescribed in regulations, be deemed not to meet the conditions or requirements the entity has been treated as meeting pursuant to subsection (a) or (b)(1) of this section.

(e) State or local accreditation

For provisions relating to validation surveys of entities that are treated as meeting applicable conditions or requirements of this subchapter pursuant to subsection (a) or (b)(1) of this section, see section 1395aa(c) of this title.

§ 1395cc. Agreements with providers of services

(a) Filing of agreements; eligibility for payment; charges with respect to items and services

(1) Any provider of services (except a fund designated for purposes of section 1395f(g) and section 1395n(e) of this title) shall be qualified to participate under this subchapter and shall be eligible for payments under this subchapter if it files with the Secretary an agreement—

(A)(i) not to charge, except as provided in paragraph (2), any individual or any other person for items or services for which such individual is entitled to have payment made under this subchapter (or for which he would be so entitled if such provider of services had complied with the procedural and other requirements under or pursuant to this subchapter or for which such provider is paid pursuant to the provisions of section 1395f(e) of this title), and (ii) not to impose any charge that is prohibited under section 1396a(n)(3) of this title,

(B) not to charge any individual or any other person for items or services for which such individual is not entitled to have payment made under this subchapter because payment for expenses incurred for such items or services may not be made by reason of the provisions of paragraph (1) or (9) of section 1395y(a) of this title, but only if (i) such individual was without fault in incurring such expenses and (ii) the Secretary's determination that such payment may not be made for such items and services was made after the third year following the year in which notice of such payment was sent to such individual; except that the Secretary may reduce such three-year period to not less than one year if he finds such reduction is consistent with the objectives of this subchapter,

(C) to make adequate provision for return (or other disposition, in accordance with regulations) of any moneys incorrectly collected from such individual or other person,

(D) to promptly notify the Secretary of its employment of an individual who, at any time during the year preceding such employment, was employed in a managerial, accounting, auditing, or similar capacity (as determined by the Secretary by regulation) by an agency or organization which serves as a fiscal intermediary or carrier (for

purposes of part A or part B, or both, of this subchapter) with respect
to the provider,

(E) to release data with respect to patients of such provider
upon request to an organization having a contract with the Secretary
under part B of subchapter XI of this chapter as may be necessary (i)
to allow such organization to carry out its functions under such
contract, or (ii) to allow such organization to carry out similar review
functions under any contract the organization may have with a
private or public agency paying for health care in the same area with
respect to patients who authorize release of such data for such
purposes,

(F)(i) in the case of hospitals which provide inpatient hospital
services for which payment may be made under subsection (b), (c), or
(d) of section 1395ww of this title, to maintain an agreement with a
professional standards review organization (if there is such an organization in existence in the area in which the hospital is located) or
with a utilization and quality control peer review organization which
has a contract with the Secretary under part B of subchapter XI of
this chapter for the area in which the hospital is located, under which
the organization will perform functions under that part with respect
to the review of the validity of diagnostic information provided by
such hospital, the completeness, adequacy, and quality of care provided, the appropriateness of admissions and discharges, and the appropriateness of care provided for which additional payments are sought
under section 1395ww(d)(5) of this title, with respect to inpatient
hospital services for which payment may be made under part A of
this subchapter (and for purposes of payment under this subchapter,
the cost of such agreement to the hospital shall be considered a cost
incurred by such hospital in providing inpatient services under part
A of this subchapter, and (I) shall be paid directly by the Secretary to
such organization on behalf of such hospital in accordance with a
rate per review established by the Secretary, (II) shall be transferred
from the Federal Hospital Insurance Trust Fund, without regard to
amounts appropriated in advance in appropriation Acts, in the same
manner as transfers are made for payment for services provided
directly to beneficiaries, and (III) shall not be less in the aggregate
for a fiscal year than the aggregate amount expended in fiscal year
1988 for direct and administrative costs (adjusted for inflation and
for any direct or administrative costs incurred as a result of review
functions added with respect to a subsequent fiscal year) of such
reviews),

(ii) in the case of hospitals, critical access hospitals, skilled
nursing facilities, and home health agencies, to maintain an
agreement with a utilization and quality control peer review
organization (which has a contract with the Secretary under part
B of subchapter XI of this chapter for the area in which the

hospital, facility, or agency is located) to perform the functions described in paragraph (3)(A),

(G) in the case of hospitals which provide inpatient hospital services for which payment may be made under subsection (b) or (d) of section 1395ww of this title, not to charge any individual or any other person for inpatient hospital services for which such individual would be entitled to have payment made under part A of this subchapter but for a denial or reduction of payments under section 1395ww(f)(2) of this title,

(H)(i) in the case of hospitals which provide services for which payment may be made under this subchapter and in the case of rural primary care hospitals which provide rural primary care hospital services, to have all items and services (other than physicians' services as defined in regulations for purposes of section 1395y(a)(14) of this title, and other than services described by section 1395x(s)(2)(K) of this title, certified nurse-midwife services, qualified psychologist services, and services of a certified registered nurse anesthetist) (I) that are furnished to an individual who is a patient of the hospital, and (II) for which the individual is entitled to have payment made under this subchapter, furnished by the hospital or otherwise under arrangements (as defined in section 1395x(w)(1) of this title)made by the hospital,

(ii) in the case of skilled nursing facilities which provide covered skilled nursing facility services—

(I) that are furnished to an individual who is a resident of the skilled nursing facility during a period in which the resident is provided covered post-hospital extended care services (or, for services described in section 1395x(s)(2)(D) of this title, that are furnished to such an individual without regard to such period), and

(II) for which the individual is entitled to have payment made under this subchapter, to have items and services (other than services described in section 1395yy(e)(2)(A)(ii) of this title) furnished by the skilled nursing facility or otherwise under arrangements (as defined in section 1395x(w)(1) of this title) made by the skilled nursing facility,

(I) in the case of a hospital or critical access hospital—

(i) to adopt and enforce a policy to ensure compliance with the requirements of section 1395dd of this title and to meet the requirements of such section,

(ii) to maintain medical and other records related to individuals transferred to or from the hospital for a period of five years from the date of the transfer, and

(iii) to maintain a list of physicians who are on call for duty after the initial examination to provide treatment necessary to stabilize an individual with an emergency medical condition,

(J) in the case of hospitals which provide inpatient hospital services for which payment may be made under this subchapter, to be a participating provider of medical care under any health plan contracted for under section 1079 or 1086 of Title 10, or under section 1713 of Title 38, in accordance with admission practices, payment methodology, and amounts as prescribed under joint regulations issued by the Secretary and by the Secretaries of Defense and Transportation, in implementation of sections 1079 and 1086 of Title 10,

(K) not to charge any individual or any other person for items or services for which payment under this subchapter is denied under section 1320c–3(a)(2) of this title by reason of a determination under section 1320c–3(a)(1)(B) of this title,

(L) in the case of hospitals which provide inpatient hospital services for which payment may be made under this subchapter, to be a participating provider of medical care under section 1703 of Title 38, in accordance with such admission practices, and such payment methodology and amounts, as are prescribed under joint regulations issued by the Secretary and by the Secretary of Veterans Affairs in implementation of such section,

(M) in the case of hospitals, to provide to each individual who is entitled to benefits under part A of this subchapter (or to a person acting on the individual's behalf), at or about the time of the individual's admission as an inpatient to the hospital, a written statement (containing such language as the Secretary prescribes consistent with this paragraph) which explains—

(i) the individual's rights to benefits for inpatient hospital services and for post-hospital services under this subchapter,

(ii) the circumstances under which such an individual will and will not be liable for charges for continued stay in the hospital,

(iii) the individual's right to appeal denials of benefits for continued inpatient hospital services, including the practical steps to initiate such an appeal, and

(iv) the individual's liability for payment for services if such a denial of benefits is upheld on appeal,

and which provides such additional information as the Secretary may specify,

(N) in the case of hospitals and critical access hospitals—

(i) to make available to its patients the directory or directories of participating physicians (published under section 1395u(h)(4) of this title) for the area served by the hospital or critical access hospital,

(ii) if hospital personnel (including staff of any emergency or outpatient department) refer a patient to a nonparticipating physician for further medical care on an outpatient basis, the personnel must inform the patient that the physician is a nonparticipating physician and, whenever practicable, must identify at least one qualified participating physician who is listed in such a directory and from whom the patient may receive the necessary services,

(iii) to post conspicuously in any emergency department a sign (in a form specified by the Secretary) specifying rights of individuals under section 1395dd of this title with respect to examination and treatment for emergency medical conditions and women in labor, and

(iv) to post conspicuously (in a form specified by the Secretary) information indicating whether or not the hospital participates in the medicaid program under a State plan approved under subchapter XIX of this chapter,

(O) to accept as payment in full for services that are covered under this subchapter (less any payments under sections 1395ww(d)(11) and 1395ww(h)(3)(D) of this title) and are furnished to any individual enrolled with a Medicare + Choice organization under part C of this subchapter or with an eligible organization (i) with a risk-sharing contract under section 1395mm of this title, under section 1395mm(i)(2)(A) of this title (as in effect before February 1, 1985), under section 1395b–1(a) of this title, or under section 222(a) of the Social Security Amendments of 1972, and (ii) which does not have a contract establishing payment amounts for services furnished to members of the organization the amounts that would be made as a payment in full under this subchapter if the individuals were not so enrolled,

(P) in the case of home health agencies which provide home health services to individuals entitled to benefits under this subchapter who require catheters, catheter supplies, ostomy bags, and supplies related to ostomy care (described in section 1395x(m)(5) of this title), to offer to furnish such supplies to such an individual as part of their furnishing of home health services,

(Q) in the case of hospitals, skilled nursing facilities, home health agencies, and hospice programs, to comply with the requirement of subsection (f) of this section (relating to maintaining written policies and procedures respecting advance directives),

(R) to contract only with a health care clearinghouse (as defined in section 1320d of this title) that meets each standard and implementation specification adopted or established under part C of subchapter XI of this chapter on or after the date on which the health care clearinghouse is required to comply with the standard or specification, and

(S) in the case of a hospital that has a financial interest (as specified by the Secretary in regulations) in an entity to which individuals are referred as described in section 1395x(ee)(2)(H)(ii), or in which such an entity has such a financial interest, or in which another entity has such a financial interest (directly or indirectly) with such hospital and such an entity, to maintain and disclose to the Secretary (in a form and manner specified by the Secretary) information on—

(i) the nature of such financial interest,

(ii) the number of individuals who were discharged from the hospital and who were identified as requiring home health services, and

(iii) the percentage of such individuals who received such services from such provider (or another such provider).

In the case of a hospital which has an agreement in effect with an organization described in subparagraph (F), which organization's contract with the Secretary under part B of subchapter XI of this chapter is terminated on or after October 1, 1984, the hospital shall not be determined to be out of compliance with the requirement of such subparagraph during the six month period beginning on the date of the termination of that contract.

(2)(A) A provider of services may charge such individual or other person (i) the amount of any deduction or coinsurance amount imposed pursuant to section 1395e(a)(1), (a)(3), or (a)(4), section 1395l(b), or section 1395x(y)(3) of this title with respect to such items and services (not in excess of the amount customarily charged for such items and services by such provider), and (ii) an amount equal to 20 per centum of the reasonable charges for such items and services (not in excess of 20 per centum of the amount customarily charged for such items and services by such provider) for which payment is made under part B of this subchapter or which are durable medical equipment furnished as home health services (but in the case of items and services furnished to individuals with end-stage renal disease, an amount equal to 20 percent of the estimated amounts for such items and services calculated on the basis established by the Secretary). In the case of items and services described in section 1395l(c) of this title, clause (ii) of the preceding sentence shall be applied by substituting for 20 percent the proportion which is appropriate under such section. A provider of services may not impose a charge under clause (ii) of the first sentence of this subparagraph with respect to items and services described in section 1395x(s)(10)(A) of this title, and with respect to clinical diagnostic laboratory tests for which payment is made under part B of this subchapter. Notwithstanding the first sentence of this subparagraph, a home health agency may charge such an individual or person, with respect to covered items subject to payment under section 1395m(a) of this title, the amount of any deduction imposed under section 1395l(b) of this title and 20 percent of the payment basis described in section 1395m(a)(1)(B) of this title. In the case of items and services for which payment is made under part B of this subchapter under the prospective payment system established under section 1395l(t) of this title, clause (ii) of the first sentence shall be applied by substituting for 20 percent of the reasonable charge, the applicable copayment amount established under section 1395l(t)(5) of this title. In the case of services described in section 1395l(a)(8) of this title or 1395l(a)(9) of this title for which payment is made under part B of this subchapter under section 1395m(k) of this title, clause (ii) of the first sentence shall be applied by substituting for 20 percent of the reasonable charge for such services 20 percent of the lesser of the actual charge or the applicable fee schedule amount (as defined in such section) for such services.

(B) Where a provider of services has furnished, at the request of such individual, items or services which are in excess of or more expensive than the items or services with respect to which payment may be made under this subchapter, such provider of services may also charge such individual or other person for such more expensive items or services to the extent that the amount customarily charged by it for the items or services furnished at such request exceeds the amount customarily charged by it for the items or services with respect to which payment may be made under this subchapter.

(C) A provider of services may in accordance with its customary practice also appropriately charge any such individual for any whole blood (or equivalent quantities of packed red blood cells, as defined under regulations) furnished him with respect to which a deductible is imposed under section 1395e(a)(2) of this title, except that (i) any excess of such charge over the cost to such provider for the blood (or equivalent quantities of packed red blood cells, as so defined) shall be deducted from any payment to such provider under this subchapter, (ii) no such charge may be imposed for the cost of administration of such blood (or equivalent quantities of packed red blood cells, as so defined), and (iii) such charge may not be made to the extent such blood (or equivalent quantities of packed red blood cells, as so defined) has been replaced on behalf of such individual or arrangements have been made for its replacement on his behalf. For purposes of this subparagraph, whole blood (or equivalent quantities of packed red blood cells, as so defined) furnished an individual shall be deemed replaced when the provider of services is given one pint of blood for each pint of blood (or equivalent quantities of packed red blood cells, as so defined) furnished such individual with respect to which a deduction is imposed under section 1395e(a)(2) of this title.

(D) Where a provider of services customarily furnishes items or services which are in excess of or more expensive than the items or services with respect to which payment may be made under this subchapter, such provider, notwithstanding the preceding provisions of this paragraph, may not, under the authority of subparagraph (B)(ii) of this paragraph, charge any individual or other person any amount for such items or services in excess of the amount of the payment which may otherwise be made for such items or services under this subchapter if the admitting physician has a direct or indirect financial interest in such provider.

(3)(A) Under the agreement required under paragraph (1)(F)(ii), the peer review organization must perform functions (other than those covered under an agreement under paragraph (1)(F)(i)) under the third sentence of section 1320c-3(a)(4)(A) of this title and under section 1320c-3(a)(14) of this title with respect to services, furnished by the hospital, rural primary care hospital, facility, or agency involved, for which payment may be made under this subchapter.

(B) For purposes of payment under this subchapter, the cost of such an agreement to the hospital, critical access hospital, facility, or agency shall be considered a cost incurred by such hospital, rural primary care hospital, facility, or agency in providing covered services under this subchapter and shall be paid directly by the Secretary to the peer review organization on behalf of such hospital, critical access hospital, facility, or agency in accordance with a schedule established by the Secretary.

(C) Such payments—

(i) shall be transferred in appropriate proportions from the Federal Hospital Insurance Trust Fund and from the Federal Supplementary Medical Insurance Trust Fund, without regard to amounts appropriated in advance in appropriation Acts, in the same manner as transfers are made for payment for services provided directly to beneficiaries, and

(ii) shall not be less in the aggregate for a fiscal year—

(I) in the case of hospitals, than the amount specified in paragraph (1)(F)(i)(III), and

(II) in the case of facilities, critical access hospitals, and agencies, than the amounts the Secretary determines to be sufficient to cover the costs of such organizations' conducting the activities described in subparagraph (A) with respect to such facilities, critical access hospitals, or agencies under part B of subchapter XI of this chapter.

(b) Termination or nonrenewal of agreements

(1) A provider of services may terminate an agreement with the Secretary under this section at such time and upon such notice to the Secretary and the public as may be provided in regulations, except that notice of more than six months shall not be required.

(2) The Secretary may refuse to enter into an agreement under this section or, upon such reasonable notice to the provider and the public as may be specified in regulations, may refuse to renew or may terminate such an agreement after the Secretary—

(A) has determined that the provider fails to comply substantially with the provisions of the agreement, with the provisions of this subchapter and regulations thereunder, or with a corrective action required under section 1395ww(f)(2)(B) of this title,

(B) has determined that the provider fails substantially to meet the applicable provisions of section 1395x of this title,

(C) has excluded the provider from participation in a program under this subchapter pursuant to section 1320a–7 or section 1320a–7a of this title, or

(D) has ascertained that the provider has been convicted of a felony under Federal or State law for an offense which the Secretary determines is detrimental to the best interests of the program or program beneficiaries.

(3) A termination of an agreement or a refusal to renew an agreement under this subsection shall become effective on the same date and in the same manner as an exclusion from participation under the programs under this subchapter becomes effective under section 1320a–7(c) of this title.

(c) Refiling after termination or nonrenewal; notice of termination or nonrenewal

(1) Where the Secretary has terminated or has refused to renew an agreement under this subchapter with a provider of services, such provider may not file another agreement under this subchapter unless the Secretary finds that the reason for the termination or nonrenewal has been removed and that there is reasonable assurance that it will not recur.

(2) Where the Secretary has terminated or has refused to renew an agreement under this subchapter with a provider of services, the Secretary shall promptly notify each State agency which administers or supervises the administration of a State plan approved under subchapter XIX of this chapter of such termination or nonrenewal.

(d) Decision to withhold payment for failure to review long-stay cases

If the Secretary finds that there is a substantial failure to make timely review in accordance with section 1395x(k) of this title of long-stay cases in a hospital, he may, in lieu of terminating his agreement with such hospital, decide that, with respect to any individual admitted to such hospital after a subsequent date specified by him, no payment shall be made under this subchapter for inpatient hospital services (including inpatient psychiatric hospital services) after the 20th day of a continuous period of such services. Such decision may be made effective only after such notice to the hospital and to the public, as may be prescribed by regulations, and its effectiveness shall terminate when the Secretary finds that the reason therefor has been removed and that there is reasonable assurance that it will not recur. The Secretary shall not make any such decision except after reasonable notice and opportunity for hearing to the institution or agency affected thereby.

(e) "Provider of services" defined

For purposes of this section, the term "provider of services" shall include—

(1) a clinic, rehabilitation agency, or public health agency if, in the case of a clinic or rehabilitation agency, such clinic or agency meets the requirements of section 1395x(p)(4)(A) of this title (or meets the requirements of such section through the operation of section 1395x(g) of this title), or if, in the case of a public health agency, such agency meets the requirements of section 1395x(p)(4)(B) of this title (or meets the requirements of such section through the operation of section 1395x(g) of this title), but only with respect to the furnishing of outpatient physical therapy services (as therein defined) or (through the operation of section 1395x(g) of this title) with respect to the furnishing of outpatient occupational therapy services; and

(2) a community mental health center (as defined in section 1395x(ff)(3)(B) of this title), but only with respect to the furnishing of partial hospitalization services (as described in section 1395x(ff)(1) of this title).

(f) Maintenance of written policies and procedures

(1) For purposes of subsection (a)(1)(Q) of this section and sections 1395i-3(c)(2)(E), 1395l(s), 1395w–25(i), 1395mm(c)(8), and 1395bbb(a)(6) of this title, the requirement of this subsection is that a provider of services, Medicare + Choice organization, or prepaid or eligible organization (as the case may be) maintain written policies and procedures with respect to all adult individuals receiving medical care by or through the provider or organization—

(A) to provide written information to each such individual concerning—

(i) an individual's rights under State law (whether statutory or as recognized by the courts of the State) to make decisions concerning such medical care, including the right to accept or refuse medical or surgical treatment and the right to formulate advance directives (as defined in paragraph (3)), and

654

(ii) the written policies of the provider or organization respecting the implementation of such rights;

(B) to document in a prominent part of the individual's current medical record whether or not the individual has executed an advance directive;

(C) not to condition the provision of care or otherwise discriminate against an individual based on whether or not the individual has executed an advance directive;

(D) to ensure compliance with requirements of State law (whether statutory or as recognized by the courts of the State) respecting advance directives at facilities of the provider or organization; and

(E) to provide (individually or with others) for education for staff and the community on issues concerning advance directives.

Subparagraph (C) shall not be construed as requiring the provision of care which conflicts with an advance directive.

(2) The written information described in paragraph (1)(A) shall be provided to an adult individual—

(A) in the case of a hospital, at the time of the individual's admission as an inpatient,

(B) in the case of a skilled nursing facility, at the time of the individual's admission as a resident,

(C) in the case of a home health agency, in advance of the individual coming under the care of the agency,

(D) in the case of a hospice program, at the time of initial receipt of hospice care by the individual from the program, and

(E) in the case of an eligible organization (as defined in section 1395mm(b) of this title) or an organization provided payments under section 1395l(a)(1)(A) of this title or a Medicare + Choice organization, at the time of enrollment of the individual with the organization.

(3) In this subsection, the term "advance directive" means a written instruction, such as a living will or durable power of attorney for health care, recognized under State law (whether statutory or as recognized by the courts of the State) and relating to the provision of such care when the individual is incapacitated.

(4) For construction relating to this subsection, see section 14406 of this title (relating to clarification respecting assisted suicide, euthanasia, and mercy killing).

(g) Penalties for improper billing

Except as permitted under subsection (a)(2) of this section, any person who knowingly and willfully presents, or causes to be presented, a bill or request for payment inconsistent with an arrangement under subsection (a)(1)(H) of this section or in violation of the requirement for such an arrangement, is subject to a civil money penalty of not to exceed $2,000. The provisions of section 1320a–7a of this title (other than subsections (a) and (b)) shall apply to a civil money penalty under the previous sentence in the same manner as such provisions apply to a penalty or proceeding under section 1320a–7a(a) of this title.

(h) Dissatisfaction with determination of Secretary; appeal by institutions or agencies; single notice and hearing

(1) Except as provided in paragraph (2), an institution or agency dissatisfied with a determination by the Secretary that it is not a provider of services or with a determination described in subsection (b)(2) of this section shall be entitled to a hearing thereon by the Secretary (after reasonable notice) to the same extent as is provided in section 405(b) of this title, and to judicial review of the Secretary's final decision after such hearing as is provided in section 405(g) of this title, except that, in so applying such sections and in applying section 405(l) of this title thereto, any reference therein to the Commissioner of Social Security or the Social Security Administration shall be considered a reference to the Secretary or the Department of Health and Human Services, respectively".

(2) An institution or agency is not entitled to separate notice and opportunity for a hearing under both section 1320a–7 of this title and this section with respect to a determination or determinations based on the same underlying facts and issues.

(i) Intermediate sanctions for psychiatric hospitals

(1) If the Secretary determines that a psychiatric hospital which has an agreement in effect under this section no longer meets the requirements for a psychiatric hospital under this subchapter and further finds that the hospital's deficiencies—

(A) immediately jeopardize the health and safety of its patients, the Secretary shall terminate such agreement; or

(B) do not immediately jeopardize the health and safety of its patients, the Secretary may terminate such agreement, or provide that no payment will be made under this subchapter with respect to any individual admitted to such hospital after the effective date of the finding, or both.

(2) If a psychiatric hospital, found to have deficiencies described in paragraph (1)(B), has not complied with the requirements of this subchapter—

(A) within 3 months after the date the hospital is found to be out of compliance with such requirements, the Secretary shall provide that no payment will be made under this subchapter with respect to any individual admitted to such hospital after the end of such 3–month period, or

(B) within 6 months after the date the hospital is found to be out of compliance with such requirements, no payment may be made under this subchapter with respect to any individual in the hospital until the Secretary finds that the hospital is in compliance with the requirements of this subchapter.

§ 1395dd. Examination and treatment for emergency medical condition and women in labor

[See Emergency Medical Treatment and Labor Act (EMTALA) page ___].

§ 1395ff. Determinations of Secretary

(a) Entitlement to and amount of benefits

The determination of whether an individual is entitled to benefits under part A or part B of this subchapter, and the determination of the amount of benefits under part A or part B of this subchapter, and any other determination with respect to a claim for benefits under part A of this subchapter or a claim for benefits with respect to home health services under part B of this subchapter shall be made by the Secretary in accordance with regulations prescribed by him.

(b) Appeal by individuals; provider representation of beneficiaries

(1) Any individual dissatisfied with any determination under subsection (a) of this section as to—

(A) whether he meets the conditions of section 426 or section 426a of this title, or

(B) whether he is eligible to enroll and has enrolled pursuant to the provisions of part B of this subchapter or section 1395i–2 of this title,

(C) the amount of benefits under part A or part B of this subchapter (including a determination where such amount is determined to be zero), or

(D) any other denial (other than under part B of subchapter XI of this chapter) of a claim for benefits under part A of this subchapter or a claim for benefits with respect to home health services under part B of this subchapter,

shall be entitled to a hearing thereon by the Secretary to the same extent as is provided in section 405(b) of this title and to judicial review of the Secretary's final decision after such hearing as is provided in section 405(g) of this title, except that, in so applying such sections and in applying section 405(*l*) of this title thereto, any reference therein to the Commissioner of Social Security or the Social Security Administration shall be considered a reference to the Secretary or the Department of Health and Human Services, respectively. Sections 406(a), 1302, and 1395hh of this title shall not be construed as authorizing the Secretary to prohibit an individual from being represented under this subsection by a person that furnishes or supplies the individual, directly or indirectly, with services or items solely on the basis that the person furnishes or supplies the individual with such a service or item. Any person that furnishes services or items to an individual may not represent an individual under this subsection with respect to the issue described in section 1395pp(a)(2) of this title unless the person has waived any rights for payment from the beneficiary with respect to the services or items involved in the appeal. If a person furnishes services or items to an individual and represents the individual under this subsection, the person may not impose any financial liability on such individual in connection with such representation.

(2) Notwithstanding paragraph (1)(C) and (1)(D), in the case of a claim arising—

(A) under part A of this subchapter, a hearing shall not be available to an individual under paragraph (1)(C) and (1)(D) if the amount in controversy is less than $100 and judicial review shall not be available to the individual under that paragraph if the amount in controversy is less than $1,000; or

(B) under part B of this subchapter, a hearing shall not be available to an individual under paragraph (1)(C) and (1)(D) if the amount in controversy is less than $500 (or $100 in the case of home health services) and judicial review shall not be available to the individual under that paragraph if the aggregate amount in controversy is less than $1,000.

In determining the amount in controversy, the Secretary, under regulations, shall allow two or more claims to be aggregated if the claims involve the delivery of similar or related services to the same individual or involve common issues of law and fact arising from services furnished to two or more individuals.

(3) Review of any national coverage determination under section 1395y(a)(1) of this title respecting whether or not a particular type or class of items or services is covered under this subchapter shall be subject to the following limitations:

(A) Such a determination shall not be reviewed by any administrative law judge.

(B) Such a determination shall not be held unlawful or set aside on the ground that a requirement of section 553 of Title 5 or section 1395hh(b) of this title, relating to publication in the Federal Register or opportunity for public comment, was not satisfied.

(C) In any case in which a court determines that the record is incomplete or otherwise lacks adequate information to support the validity of the determination, it shall remand the matter to the

Secretary for additional proceedings to supplement the record and the court may not determine that an item or service is covered except upon review of the supplemented record.

(4) A regulation or instruction which relates to a method for determining the amount of payment under part B of this subchapter and which was initially issued before January 1, 1981, shall not be subject to judicial review.

(5) In an administrative hearing pursuant to paragraph (1), where the moving party alleges that there are no material issues of fact in dispute, the administrative law judge shall make an expedited determination as to whether any such facts are in dispute and, if not, shall determine the case expeditiously.

§ 1395gg. Overpayment on behalf of individuals and settlement of claims for benefits on behalf of deceased individuals

(a) Payments to providers of services or other person regarded as payment to individuals

Any payment under this subchapter to any provider of services or other person with respect to any items or services furnished any individual shall be regarded as a payment to such individual.

(b) Incorrect payments on behalf of individuals; payment adjustment

Where—

(1) more than the correct amount is paid under this subchapter to a provider of services or other person for items or services furnished an individual and the Secretary determines (A) that, within such period as he may specify, the excess over the correct amount cannot be recouped from such provider of services or other person, or (B) that such provider of services or other person was without fault with respect to the payment of such excess over the correct amount, or

(2) any payment has been made under section 1395f(e) of this title to a provider of services or other person for items or services furnished an individual,

proper adjustments shall be made, under regulations prescribed (after consultation with the Railroad Retirement Board) by the Secretary, by decreasing subsequent payments—

(3) to which such individual is entitled under subchapter II of this chapter or under the Railroad Retirement Act of 1974 [45 U.S.C.A. § 231 et seq.], as the case may be, or

(4) if such individual dies before such adjustment has been completed, to which any other individual is entitled under subchapter II of this chapter or under the Railroad Retirement Act of 1974 [45 U.S.C.A. § 231 et seq.], as the case may be, with respect to the wages and self-employment income or the compensation constituting the basis of the benefits of such deceased individual under subchapter II of this chapter.

As soon as practicable after any adjustment under paragraph (3) or (4) is determined to be necessary, the Secretary, for purposes of this section, section 1395i(g) of this title, and section 1395t(f) of this title, shall certify (to the Railroad Retirement Board if the adjustment is to be made by decreasing subsequent payments under the Railroad Retirement Act of 1974 [45 U.S.C.A. § 231 et seq.]) the amount of the overpayment as to which the adjustment is to be made. For purposes of clause (B) of paragraph (1), such provider of services or such other person shall, in the absence of evidence to the contrary, be deemed to be without fault if the Secretary's determination that more than such correct amount was paid was made subsequent to the third year following the year in which notice was sent to such individual that such amount had been paid; except that the Secretary may reduce such three-year period to not less than one year if he finds such reduction is consistent with the objectives of this subchapter.

(c) Exception to subsection (b) payment adjustment

There shall be no adjustment as provided in subsection (b) of this section (nor shall there be recovery) in any case where the incorrect payment has been made (including payments under section 1395f(e) of this title) with respect to an individual who is without fault or where the adjustment (or recovery) would be made by decreasing payments to which another person who is without fault is entitled as provided in subsection (b)(4) of this section, if such adjustment (or recovery) would defeat the purposes of subchapter II or subchapter XVIII of this chapter or would be against equity and good conscience. Adjustment or recovery of an incorrect payment (or only such part of an incorrect payment as the Secretary determines to be inconsistent with the purposes of this subchapter) against an individual who is without fault shall be deemed to be against equity and good conscience if (A) the incorrect payment was made for expenses incurred for items or services for which payment may not be made under this subchapter by reason of the provisions of paragraph (1) or (9) of section 1395y(a) of this title and (B) if the Secretary's determination that such payment was incorrect was made subsequent to the third year following the year in which notice of such payment was sent to such individual; except that the Secretary may reduce such three-year period to not less than one year if he finds such reduction is consistent with the objectives of this subchapter.

(d) Liability of certifying or disbursing officer for failure to recoup

No certifying or disbursing officer shall be held liable for any amount certified or paid by him to any provider of services or other person where the adjustment or recovery of such amount is waived under subsection (c) of this section or where adjustment under subsection (b) of this section is not completed prior to the death of all persons against whose benefits such adjustment is authorized.

(e) Settlement of claims for benefits under this subchapter on behalf of deceased individuals

If an individual, who received services for which payment may be made to such individual under this subchapter, dies, and payment for such services was made (other than under this subchapter), and the individual died before any payment due him under this subchapter with respect to such services was completed, payment of the amount due (including the amount of any unnegotiated checks) shall be made—

(1) if the payment for such services was made (before or after such individual's death) by a person other than the deceased individual, to the person or persons determined by the Secretary under regulations to have paid for such services, or if the payment for such services was made by the deceased individual before his death, to the legal representative of the estate of such deceased individual, if any;

(2) if there is no person who meets the requirements of paragraph (1), to the person, if any, who is determined by the Secretary to be the surviving spouse of the deceased individual and who was either living in the same household with the deceased at the time of his death or was, for the month in which the deceased individual died, entitled to a monthly benefit on the basis of the same wages and self-employment income as was the deceased individual;

(3) if there is no person who meets the requirements of paragraph (1) or (2), or if the person who meets such requirements dies before the payment due him under this subchapter is completed, to the child or children, if any, of the deceased individual who were, for the month in which the deceased individual died, entitled to monthly benefits on the basis of the same wages and self-employment income as was the deceased individual (and, in case there is more than one such child, in equal parts to each such child);

(4) if there is no person who meets the requirements of paragraph (1), (2), or (3), or if each person who meets such requirements dies before the payment due him under this subchapter is completed, to the parent or parents, if any, of the deceased individual who were, for the month in which the deceased individual died, entitled to monthly benefits on the basis of the same wages and self-employment income as was the deceased individual (and, in case there is more than one such parent, in equal parts to each such parent);

(5) if there is no person who meets the requirements of paragraph (1), (2), (3), or (4), or if each person who meets such requirements dies before the payment due him under this subchapter is completed, to the person, if any, determined by the Secretary to be the surviving spouse of the deceased individual;

(6) if there is no person who meets the requirements of paragraph (1), (2), (3), (4), or (5), or if each person who meets such requirements dies before the payment due him under this subchapter is completed, to the person or persons, if any, determined by the Secretary to be the child or children of the deceased individual (and, in case there is more than one such child, in equal parts to each such child);

(7) if there is no person who meets the requirements of paragraph (1), (2), (3), (4), (5), or (6), or if each person who meets such requirements dies before the payment due him under this subchapter is completed, to the parent or parents, if any, of the deceased individual (and, in case there is more than one such parent, in equal parts to each such parent); or

(8) if there is no person who meets the requirements of paragraph (1), (2), (3), (4), (5), (6), or (7), or if each person who meets such requirements dies before the payment due him under this subchapter is completed, to the legal representatives of the estate of the deceased individual, if any.

(f) Settlement of claims for section 1395k benefits on behalf of deceased individuals

If an individual who received medical and other health services for which payment may be made under section 1395k(a)(1) of this title dies, and no assignment of the right to payment for such services was made by such individual before his death, and payment for such services has not been made—

(1) if the person or persons who furnished the services agree to the terms of assignment specified in section 1395u(b)(3)(B)(ii) of this title with respect to the services, payment for such services shall be made to such person or persons, and

(2) if the person or persons who furnished the services do not agree to the terms of assignment specified in section 1395u(b)(3)(B)(ii) of this title with respect to the services, payment for such services shall be made on the basis of an itemized bill to the person who has agreed to assume the legal obligation to make payment for such services and files a request for payment (with such accompanying evidence of such legal obligation as may be required in regulations),

but only in such amount and subject to such conditions as would be applicable if the individual who received the services had not died.

(g) Refund of premiums for deceased individuals

If an individual, who is enrolled under section 1395i–2(c) of this title or under section 1395p of this title, dies, and premiums with respect to such enrollment have been received with respect to such individual for any month after the month of his death, such premiums shall be refunded to the person or persons determined by the Secretary under regulations to have paid such premiums or if payment for such premiums was made by the deceased individual before his death, to the legal representative of the estate of such deceased individual, if any. If there is no person who meets the requirements of the preceding sentence such premiums shall be refunded to the person or persons in the priorities specified in paragraphs (2) through (7) of subsection (e) of this section.

§ 1395hh. Regulations

(a) Authority to prescribe regulations; ineffectiveness of substantive rules not promulgated by regulation

(1) The Secretary shall prescribe such regulations as may be necessary to carry out the administration of the insurance programs under this subchapter. When used in this subchapter, the term "regulations" means, unless the context otherwise requires, regulations prescribed by the Secretary.

(2) No rule, requirement, or other statement of policy (other than a national coverage determination) that establishes or changes a substantive legal standard governing the scope of benefits, the payment for services, or the eligibility of individuals, entities, or organizations to furnish or receive services or benefits under this subchapter shall take effect unless it is promulgated by the Secretary by regulation under paragraph (1).

(b) Notice of proposed regulations; public comment

(1) Except as provided in paragraph (2), before issuing in final form any regulation under subsection (a) of this section, the Secretary shall provide for notice of the proposed regulation in the Federal Register and a period of not less than 60 days for public comment thereon.

(2) Paragraph (1) shall not apply where—

(A) a statute specifically permits a regulation to be issued in interim final form or otherwise with a shorter period for public comment,

(B) a statute establishes a specific deadline for the implementation of a provision and the deadline is less than 150 days after the date of the enactment of the statute in which the deadline is contained, or

(C) subsection (b) of section 553 of Title 5 does not apply pursuant to subparagraph (B) of such subsection.

(c) Publication of certain rules; public inspection; changes in data collection and retrieval

(1) The Secretary shall publish in the Federal Register, not less frequently than every 3 months, a list of all manual instructions, interpretative rules, statements of policy, and guidelines of general applicability which—

(A) are promulgated to carry out this subchapter, but

(B) are not published pursuant to subsection (a)(1) of this section and have not been previously published in a list under this subsection.

663

(2) Effective June 1, 1988, each fiscal intermediary and carrier administering claims for extended care, post-hospital extended care, home health care, and durable medical equipment benefits under this subchapter shall make available to the public all interpretative materials, guidelines, and clarifications of policies which relate to payments for such benefits.

(3) The Secretary shall to the extent feasible make such changes in automated data collection and retrieval by the Secretary and fiscal intermediaries with agreements under section 1395h of this title as are necessary to make easily accessible for the Secretary and other appropriate parties a data base which fairly and accurately reflects the provision of extended care, post-hospital extended care and home health care benefits pursuant to this subchapter, including such categories as benefit denials, results of appeals, and other relevant factors, and selectable by such categories and by fiscal intermediary, service provider, and region.

§ 1395mm. Payments to health maintenance organizations and competitive medical plans

(a) Rates and adjustments

(1)(A) The Secretary shall annually determine, and shall announce (in a manner intended to provide notice to interested parties) not later than September 7 before the calendar year concerned—

> **(i)** a per capita rate of payment for each class of individuals who are enrolled under this section with an eligible organization which has entered into a risk-sharing contract and who are entitled to benefits under part A of this subchapter and enrolled under part B of this subchapter, and

> **(ii)** a per capita rate of payment for each class of individuals who are so enrolled with such an organization and who are enrolled under part B of this subchapter only.

For purposes of this section, the term "risk-sharing contract" means a contract entered into under subsection (g) of this section and the term "reasonable cost reimbursement contract" means a contract entered into under subsection (h) of this section.

> **(B)** The Secretary shall define appropriate classes of members, based on age, disability status, and such other factors as the Secretary determines to be appropriate, so as to ensure actuarial equivalence. The Secretary may add to, modify, or substitute for such classes, if such changes will improve the determination of actuarial equivalence.

> **(C)** The annual per capita rate of payment for each such class shall be equal to 95 percent of the adjusted average per capita cost (as defined in paragraph (4)) for that class.

(D) In the case of an eligible organization with a risk-sharing contract, the Secretary shall make monthly payments in advance and in accordance with the rate determined under subparagraph (C) and except as provided in subsection (g)(2) of this section, to the organization for each individual enrolled with the organization under this section.

(E)(i) The amount of payment under this paragraph may be retroactively adjusted to take into account any difference between the actual number of individuals enrolled in the plan under this section and the number of such individuals estimated to be so enrolled in determining the amount of the advance payment.

(ii)(I) Subject to subclause (II), the Secretary may make retroactive adjustments under clause (i) to take into account individuals enrolled during the period beginning on the date on which the individual enrolls with an eligible organization (which has a risk-sharing contract under this section) under a health benefit plan operated, sponsored, or contributed to by the individual's employer or former employer (or the employer or former employer of the individual's spouse) and ending on the date on which the individual is enrolled in the plan under this section, except that for purposes of making such retroactive adjustments under this clause, such period may not exceed 90 days.

(II) No adjustment may be made under subclause (I) with respect to any individual who does not certify that the organization provided the individual with the explanation described in subsection (c)(3)(E) of this section at the time the individual enrolled with the organization.

(F)(i) At least 45 days before making the announcement under subparagraph (A) for a year (beginning with the announcement for 1991), the Secretary shall provide for notice to eligible organizations of proposed changes to be made in the methodology or benefit coverage assumptions from the methodology and assumptions used in the previous announcement and shall provide such organizations an opportunity to comment on such proposed changes.

(ii) In each announcement made under subparagraph (A) for a year (beginning with the announcement for 1991), the Secretary shall include an explanation of the assumptions (including any benefit coverage assumptions) and changes in methodology used in the announcement in sufficient detail so that eligible organizations can compute per capita rates of payment for classes of individuals located in each county (or equivalent area) which is in whole or in part within the service area of such an organization.

(2) With respect to any eligible organization which has entered into a reasonable cost reimbursement contract, payments shall be made to such plan in accordance with subsection (h)(2) of this section rather than paragraph (1).

(3) Subject to subsections (c)(2)(B)(ii) and (c)(7) of this section, payments under a contract to an eligible organization under paragraph (1) or (2) shall be instead of the amounts which (in the absence of the contract) would be otherwise payable, pursuant to sections 1395f(b) and 1395l(a) of this title, for services furnished by or through the organization to individuals enrolled with the organization under this section.

(4) For purposes of this section, the term "adjusted average per capita cost" means the average per capita amount that the Secretary estimates in advance (on the basis of actual experience, or retrospective actuarial equivalent based upon an adequate sample and other information and data, in a geographic area served by an eligible organization or in a similar area, with appropriate adjustments to assure actuarial equivalence) would be payable in any contract year for services covered under parts A and B of this subchapter, or part B only, and types of expenses otherwise reimbursable under parts A and B of this subchapter, or part B only (including administrative costs incurred by organizations described in sections 1395h and 1395u of this title), if the services were to be furnished by other than an eligible organization or, in the case of services covered only under section 1395x(s)(2)(H) of this title, if the services were to be furnished by a physician or as an incident to a physician's service.

(5) The payment to an eligible organization under this section for individuals enrolled under this section with the organization and entitled to benefits under part A of this subchapter and enrolled under part B of this subchapter shall be made from the Federal Hospital Insurance Trust Fund and the Federal Supplementary Medical Insurance Trust Fund. The portion of that payment to the organization for a month to be paid by each trust fund shall be determined as follows:

    (A) In regard to expenditures by eligible organizations having risk-sharing contracts, the allocation shall be determined each year by the Secretary based on the relative weight that benefits from each fund contribute to the adjusted average per capita cost.

    (B) In regard to expenditures by eligible organizations operating under a reasonable cost reimbursement contract, the initial allocation shall be based on the plan's most recent budget, such allocation to be adjusted, as needed, after cost settlement to reflect the distribution of actual expenditures.

The remainder of that payment shall be paid by the former trust fund.

(6) Subject to subsections (c)(2)(B)(ii) and (c)(7) of this section, if an individual is enrolled under this section with an eligible organization having a risk-sharing contract, only the eligible organization shall be entitled to receive payments from the Secretary under this subchapter for services furnished to the individual.

(b) Definitions; requirements

For purposes of this section, the term "eligible organization" means a public or private entity (which may be a health maintenance organization or a competitive medical plan), organized under the laws of any State, which—

(1) is a qualified health maintenance organization (as defined in section 300e-9(d) of this title), or

(2) meets the following requirements:

(A) The entity provides to enrolled members at least the following health care services:

(i) Physicians' services performed by physicians (as defined in section 1395x(r)(1) of this title).

(ii) Inpatient hospital services.

(iii) Laboratory, X-ray, emergency, and preventive services.

(iv) Out-of-area coverage.

(B) The entity is compensated (except for deductibles, coinsurance, and copayments) for the provision of health care services to enrolled members by a payment which is paid on a periodic basis without regard to the date the health care services are provided and which is fixed without regard to the frequency, extent, or kind of health care service actually provided to a member.

(C) The entity provides physicians' services primarily

(i) directly through physicians who are either employees or partners of such organization, or

(ii) through contracts with individual physicians or one or more groups of physicians (organized on a group practice or individual practice basis).

(D) The entity assumes full financial risk on a prospective basis for the provision of the health care services listed in subparagraph (A), except that such entity may—

(i) obtain insurance or make other arrangements for the cost of providing to any enrolled member health care services listed in subparagraph (A) the aggregate value of which exceeds $5,000 in any year,

(ii) obtain insurance or make other arrangements for the cost of health care service listed in subparagraph (A) provided to its enrolled members other than through the entity because medical necessity required their provision before they could be secured through the entity,

(iii) obtain insurance or make other arrangements for not more than 90 percent of the amount by which its costs for any of its fiscal years exceed 115 percent of its income for such fiscal year, and

(iv) make arrangements with physicians or other health professionals, health care institutions, or any combination of such individuals or institutions to assume all or part of the financial risk on a prospective basis for the provision of basic health services by the physicians or other health professionals or through the institutions.

(E) The entity has made adequate provision against the risk of insolvency, which provision is satisfactory to the Secretary.

Paragraph (2)(A)(ii) shall not apply to an entity which had contracted with a single State agency administering a State plan approved under subchapter XIX of this chapter for the provision of services (other than inpatient hospital services) to individuals eligible for such services under such State plan on a prepaid risk basis prior to 1970.

(c) Enrollment in plan; duties of organization to enrollees

(1) The Secretary may not enter into a contract under this section with an eligible organization unless it meets the requirements of this subsection and subsection (e) of this section with respect to members enrolled under this section.

(2)(A) The organization must provide to members enrolled under this section, through providers and other persons that meet the applicable requirements of this subchapter and part A of subchapter XI of this chapter—

(i) only those services covered under parts A and B of this subchapter, for those members entitled to benefits under part A of this subchapter and enrolled under part B of this subchapter, or

(ii) only those services covered under part B of this subchapter, for those members enrolled only under such part,

which are available to individuals residing in the geographic area served by the organization, except that

(I) the organization may provide such members with such additional health care services as the members may elect, at their option, to have covered, and

(II) in the case of an organization with a risk-sharing contract, the organization may provide such members with such additional health care services as the Secretary may approve. The Secretary shall approve any such additional health care services which the organization proposes to offer to such members, unless the Secretary determines that including such additional services will substantially discourage enrollment by covered individuals with the organization.

(B) If there is a national coverage determination made in the period beginning on the date of an announcement under subsection (a)(1)(A) of this section and ending on the date of the next announcement under such subsection that the Secretary projects will result in a significant change in the costs to the organization of providing the benefits that are the subject of such national coverage determination and that was not incorporated in the determination of the per capita rate of payment included in the announcement made at the beginning of such period—

(i) such determination shall not apply to risk-sharing contracts under this section until the first contract year that begins after the end of such period; and

(ii) if such coverage determination provides for coverage of additional benefits or under additional circumstances, subsection (a)(3) of this section shall not apply to payment for such additional benefits or benefits provided under such additional circumstances until the first contract year that begins after the end of such period,

unless otherwise required by law.

(3)(A)(i) Each eligible organization must have an open enrollment period, for the enrollment of individuals under this section, of at least 30 days duration every year and including the period or periods specified under clause (ii), and must provide that at any time during which enrollments are accepted, the organization will accept up to the limits of its capacity (as determined by the Secretary) and without restrictions, except as may be authorized in regulations, individuals who are eligible to enroll under subsection (d) of this section in the order in which they apply for enrollment, unless to do so would result in failure to meet the requirements of subsection (f) of this section or would result in the enrollment of enrollees substantially nonrepresentative, as determined in accordance with regulations of the Secretary, of the population in the geographic area served by the organization.

(ii)(I) If a risk-sharing contract under this section is not renewed or is otherwise terminated, eligible organizations with risk-sharing contracts under this section and serving a part of the same service area as under the terminated contract are required to have an open enrollment period for individuals who were enrolled under the terminated contract as of the date of notice of such termination. If a risk-sharing contract under this section is renewed in a manner that discontinues coverage for individuals residing in part of the service area, eligible organizations with risk-sharing contracts under this section and enrolling individuals residing in that part of the service area are required to have an open enrollment period for individuals residing in the part of the service area who were enrolled under the contract as of the date of notice of such discontinued coverage.

(II) The open enrollment periods required under subclause (I) shall be for 30 days and shall begin 30 days after the date that the Secretary provides notice of such requirement.

(III) Enrollment under this clause shall be effective 30 days after the end of the open enrollment period, or, if the Secretary determines that such date is not feasible, such other date as the Secretary specifies.

(B) An individual may enroll under this section with an eligible organization in such manner as may be prescribed in regulations and may terminate his enrollment with the eligible organization as of the beginning of the first calendar month following the date on which the request is made for such termination (or, in the case of financial insolvency of the organization, as may be prescribed by regulations) or, in the case of such an organization with a reasonable cost reimbursement contract, as may be prescribed by regulations. In the case of an individual's termination of enrollment, the organization shall provide the individual with a copy of the written request for termination of enrollment and a written explanation of the period (ending on the effective date of the termination) during which the individual continues to be enrolled with the organization and may not receive benefits under this subchapter other than through the organization.

(C) The Secretary may prescribe the procedures and conditions under which an eligible organization that has entered into a contract with the Secretary under this subsection may inform individuals eligible to enroll under this section with the organization about the organization, or may enroll such individuals with the organization. No brochures, application forms, or other promotional or informational material may be distributed by an organization to (or for the use of) individuals eligible to enroll with the organization under this section unless

(i) at least 45 days before its distribution, the organization has submitted the material to the Secretary for review and

(ii) the Secretary has not disapproved the distribution of the material. The Secretary shall review all such material submitted and shall disapprove such material if the Secretary determines, in the Secretary's discretion, that the material is materially inaccurate or misleading or otherwise makes a material misrepresentation.

(D) The organization must provide assurances to the Secretary that it will not expel or refuse to re-enroll any such individual because of the individual's health status or requirements for health care services, and that it will notify each such individual of such fact at the time of the individual's enrollment.

(E) Each eligible organization shall provide each enrollee, at the time of enrollment and not less frequently than annually thereafter, an explanation of the enrollee's rights under this section, including an explanation of—

(i) the enrollee's rights to benefits from the organization,

(ii) the restrictions on payments under this subchapter for services furnished other than by or through the organization,

(iii) out-of-area coverage provided by the organization,

(iv) the organization's coverage of emergency services and urgently needed care, and

(v) appeal rights of enrollees.

(F) Each eligible organization that provides items and services pursuant to a contract under this section shall provide assurances to the Secretary that in the event the organization ceases to provide such items and services, the organization shall provide or arrange for supplemental coverage of benefits under this subchapter related to a pre-existing condition with respect to any exclusion period, to all individuals enrolled with the entity who receive benefits under this subchapter, for the lesser of six months or the duration of such period.

(G)(i) Each eligible organization having a risk-sharing contract under this section shall notify individuals eligible to enroll with the organization under this section and individuals enrolled with the organization under this section that—

(I) the organization is authorized by law to terminate or refuse to renew the contract, and

(II) termination or nonrenewal of the contract may result in termination of the enrollments of individuals enrolled with the organization under this section.

(ii) The notice required by clause (i) shall be included in—

(I) any marketing materials described in subparagraph (C) that are distributed by an eligible organization to individuals eligible to enroll under this section with the organization, and

(II) any explanation provided to enrollees by the organization pursuant to subparagraph (E).

(4) The organization must—

(A) make the services described in paragraph (2) (and such other health care services as such individuals have contracted for)

(i) available and accessible to each such individual, within the area served by the organization, with reasonable promptness and in a manner which assures continuity, and

(ii) when medically necessary, available and accessible twenty-four hours a day and seven days a week, and

(B) provide for reimbursement with respect to services which are described in subparagraph (A) and which are provided to such an individual other than through the organization, if

(i) the services were medically necessary and immediately required because of an unforeseen illness, injury, or condition and

671

(ii) it was not reasonable given the circumstances to obtain the services through the organization.

(5)(A) The organization must provide meaningful procedures for hearing and resolving grievances between the organization (including any entity or individual through which the organization provides health care services) and members enrolled with the organization under this section.

(B) A member enrolled with an eligible organization under this section who is dissatisfied by reason of his failure to receive any health service to which he believes he is entitled and at no greater charge than he believes he is required to pay is entitled, if the amount in controversy is $100 or more, to a hearing before the Secretary to the same extent as is provided in section 405(b) of this title, and in any such hearing the Secretary shall make the eligible organization a party. If the amount in controversy is $1,000 or more, the individual or eligible organization shall, upon notifying the other party, be entitled to judicial review of the Secretary's final decision as provided in section 405(g) of this title, and both the individual and the eligible organization shall be entitled to be parties to that judicial review. In applying sections 405(b) and 405(g) of this title as provided in this subparagraph, and in applying section 405(l) of this title thereto, any reference therein to the Commissioner of Social Security or the Social Security Administration shall be considered a reference to the Secretary or the Department of Health and Human Services, respectively.

(6) The organization must have arrangements, established in accordance with regulations of the Secretary, for an ongoing quality assurance program for health care services it provides to such individuals, which program

(A) stresses health outcomes and

(B) provides review by physicians and other health care professionals of the process followed in the provision of such health care services.

(7) A risk-sharing contract under this section shall provide that in the case of an individual who is receiving inpatient hospital services from a subsection (d) hospital (as defined in section 1395ww(d)(1)(B) of this title) as of the effective date of the individual's—

(A) enrollment with an eligible organization under this section—

(i) payment for such services until the date of the individual's discharge shall be made under this subchapter as if the individual were not enrolled with the organization,

(ii) the organization shall not be financially responsible for payment for such services until the date after the date of the individual's discharge, and

(iii) the organization shall nonetheless be paid the full amount otherwise payable to the organization under this section; or

(B) termination of enrollment with an eligible organization under this section—

(i) the organization shall be financially responsible for payment for such services after such date and until the date of the individual's discharge,

(ii) payment for such services during the stay shall not be made under section 1395ww(d) of this title, and

(iii) the organization shall not receive any payment with respect to the individual under this section during the period the individual is not enrolled.

(8) A contract under this section shall provide that the eligible organization shall meet the requirement of section 1395cc(f) of this title (relating to maintaining written policies and procedures respecting advance directives).

(d) Right to enroll with contracting organization in geographic area

Subject to the provisions of subsection (c)(3) of this section, every individual entitled to benefits under part A of this subchapter and enrolled under part B of this subchapter or enrolled under part B of this subchapter only (other than an individual medically determined to have end-stage renal disease) shall be eligible to enroll under this section with any eligible organization with which the Secretary has entered into a contract under this section and which serves the geographic area in which the individual resides.

(e) Limitation on charges; election of coverage; "adjusted community rate" defined; workmen's compensation and insurance benefits

(1) In no case may—

(A) the portion of an eligible organization's premium rate and the actuarial value of its deductibles, coinsurance, and copayments charged (with respect to services covered under parts A and B of this subchapter) to individuals who are enrolled under this section with the organization and who are entitled to benefits under part A of this subchapter and enrolled under part B of this subchapter, or

(B) the portion of its premium rate and the actuarial value of its deductibles, coinsurance, and copayments charged (with respect to services covered under part B of this subchapter) to individuals who are enrolled under this section with the organization and enrolled under part B of this subchapter only exceed the actuarial value of the coinsurance and deductibles that would be applicable on the average to individuals enrolled under this section with the organization (or, if the Secretary finds that adequate data are not available to determine that actuarial value, the actuarial value of the coinsurance and

673

deductibles applicable on the average to individuals in the area, in the State, or in the United States, eligible to enroll under this section with the organization, or other appropriate data) and entitled to benefits under part A of this subchapter and enrolled under part B of this subchapter, or enrolled under part B only, respectively, if they were not members of an eligible organization.

(2) If the eligible organization provides to its members enrolled under this section services in addition to services covered under parts A and B of this subchapter, election of coverage for such additional services (unless such services have been approved by the Secretary under subsection (c)(2) of this section) shall be optional for such members and such organization shall furnish such members with information on the portion of its premium rate or other charges applicable to such additional services. In no case may the sum of—

(A) the portion of such organization's premium rate charged, with respect to such additional services, to members enrolled under this section, and

(B) the actuarial value of its deductibles, coinsurance, and co-payments charged, with respect to such services to such members exceed the adjusted community rate for such services.

(3) For purposes of this section, the term "adjusted community rate" for a service or services means, at the election of an eligible organization, either—

(A) the rate of payment for that service or services which the Secretary annually determines would apply to a member enrolled under this section with an eligible organization if the rate of payment were determined under a "community rating system" (as defined in section 300e–1(8) of this title, other than subparagraph (C)), or

(B) such portion of the weighted aggregate premium, which the Secretary annually estimates would apply to a member enrolled under this section with the eligible organization, as the Secretary annually estimates is attributable to that service or services,

but adjusted for differences between the utilization characteristics of the members enrolled with the eligible organization under this section and the utilization characteristics of the other members of the organization (or, if the Secretary finds that adequate data are not available to adjust for those differences, the differences between the utilization characteristics of members in other eligible organizations, or individuals in the area, in the State, or in the United States, eligible to enroll under this section with an eligible organization and the utilization characteristics of the rest of the population in the area, in the State, or in the United States, respectively).

(4) Notwithstanding any other provision of law, the eligible organization may (in the case of the provision of services to a member enrolled under this section for an illness or injury for which the member is entitled to benefits under a workmen's compensation law or plan of the United States or a State, under an automobile or liability insurance policy or plan, including a self-insured plan, or under no fault insurance) charge or authorize the provider of such services to charge, in accordance with the charges allowed under such law or policy—

(A) the insurance carrier, employer, or other entity which under such law, plan, or policy is to pay for the provision of such services, or

(B) such member to the extent that the member has been paid under such law, plan, or policy for such services.

(f) Membership requirements

(1) For contract periods beginning before January 1, 1999, each eligible organization with which the Secretary enters into a contract under this section shall have, for the duration of such contract, an enrolled membership at least one-half of which consists of individuals who are not entitled to benefits under this subchapter.

(2) Subject to paragraph (4), the Secretary may modify or waive the requirement imposed by paragraph (1) only—

(A) to the extent that more than 50 percent of the population of the area served by the organization consists of individuals who are entitled to benefits under this subchapter or under a State plan approved under subchapter XIX of this chapter, or

(B) in the case of an eligible organization that is owned and operated by a governmental entity, only with respect to a period of three years beginning on the date the organization first enters into a contract under this section, and only if the organization has taken and is making reasonable efforts to enroll individuals who are not entitled to benefits under this subchapter or under a State plan approved under subchapter XIX of this chapter.

(3) If the Secretary determines that an eligible organization has failed to comply with the requirements of this subsection, the Secretary may provide for the suspension of enrollment of individuals under this section or of payment to the organization under this section for individuals newly enrolled with the organization, after the date the Secretary notifies the organization of such noncompliance.

(4) Effective for contract periods beginning after December 31, 1996, the Secretary may waive or modify the requirement imposed by paragraph (1) to the extent the Secretary finds that it is in the public interest.

(g) Risk-sharing contract

(1) The Secretary may enter a risk-sharing contract with any eligible organization, as defined in subsection (b) of this section, which has at least 5,000 members, except that the Secretary may enter into such a

contract with an eligible organization that has fewer members if the organization primarily serves members residing outside of urbanized areas.

(2) Each risk-sharing contract shall provide that—

(A) if the adjusted community rate, as defined in subsection (e)(3) of this section, for services under parts A and B of this subchapter (as reduced for the actuarial value of the coinsurance and deductibles under those parts) for members enrolled under this section with the organization and entitled to benefits under part A of this subchapter and enrolled in part B of this subchapter, or

(B) if the adjusted community rate for services under part B of this subchapter (as reduced for the actuarial value of the coinsurance and deductibles under that part) for members enrolled under this section with the organization and entitled to benefits under part B of this subchapter only

is less than the average of the per capita rates of payment to be made under subsection (a)(1) of this section at the beginning of an annual contract period for members enrolled under this section with the organization and entitled to benefits under part A of this subchapter and enrolled in part B of this subchapter, or enrolled in part B of this subchapter only, respectively, the eligible organization shall provide to members enrolled under a risk-sharing contract under this section with the organization and entitled to benefits under part A of this subchapter and enrolled in part B of this subchapter, or enrolled in part B of this subchapter only, respectively, the additional benefits described in paragraph (3) which are selected by the eligible organization and which the Secretary finds are at least equal in value to the difference between that average per capita payment and the adjusted community rate (as so reduced); except that this paragraph shall not apply with respect to any organization which elects to receive a lesser payment to the extent that there is no longer a difference between the average per capita payment and adjusted community rate (as so reduced) and except that an organization (with the approval of the Secretary) may provide that a part of the value of such additional benefits be withheld and reserved by the Secretary as provided in paragraph (5). If the Secretary finds that there is insufficient enrollment experience to determine an average of the per capita rates of payment to be made under subsection (a)(1) of this section at the beginning of a contract period, the Secretary may determine such an average based on the enrollment experience of other contracts entered into under this section.

(3) The additional benefits referred to in paragraph (2) are—

(A) the reduction of the premium rate or other charges made with respect to services furnished by the organization to members enrolled under this section, or

(B) the provision of additional health benefits, or both.

(4) Repealed. *Pub.L. 100–203, Title IV, § 4012(b)*, Dec. 22, 1987, 101 Stat. 1330–61

(5) An organization having a risk-sharing contract under this section may (with the approval of the Secretary) provide that a part of the value of additional benefits otherwise required to be provided by reason of paragraph (2) be withheld and reserved in the Federal Hospital Insurance Trust Fund and in the Federal Supplementary Medical Insurance Trust Fund (in such proportions as the Secretary determines to be appropriate) by the Secretary for subsequent annual contract periods, to the extent required to stabilize and prevent undue fluctuations in the additional benefits offered in those subsequent periods by the organization in accordance with paragraph (3). Any of such value of additional benefits which is not provided to members of the organization in accordance with paragraph (3) prior to the end of such period, shall revert for the use of such trust funds.

(6)(A) A risk-sharing contract under this section shall require the eligible organization to provide prompt payment (consistent with the provisions of sections 1395h(c)(2) and 1395u(c)(2) of this title) of claims submitted for services and supplies furnished to individuals pursuant to such contract, if the services or supplies are not furnished under a contract between the organization and the provider or supplier.

(B) In the case of an eligible organization which the Secretary determines, after notice and opportunity for a hearing, has failed to make payments of amounts in compliance with subparagraph (A), the Secretary may provide for direct payment of the amounts owed to providers and suppliers for such covered services furnished to individuals enrolled under this section under the contract. If the Secretary provides for such direct payments, the Secretary shall provide for an appropriate reduction in the amount of payments otherwise made to the organization under this section to reflect the amount of the Secretary's payments (and costs incurred by the Secretary in making such payments).

(h) Reasonable cost reimbursement contract; requirements

(1) If—

(A) the Secretary is not satisfied that an eligible organization has the capacity to bear the risk of potential losses under a risk-sharing contract under this section, or

(B) the eligible organization so elects or has an insufficient number of members to be eligible to enter into a risk-sharing contract under subsection (g)(1) of this section,

the Secretary may, if he is otherwise satisfied that the eligible organization is able to perform its contractual obligations effectively and efficiently, enter into a contract with such organization pursuant to which such organization is reimbursed on the basis of its reasonable cost (as defined in section 1395x(v) of this title) in the manner prescribed in paragraph (3).

(2) A reasonable cost reimbursement contract under this subsection may, at the option of such organization, provide that the Secretary—

(A) will reimburse hospitals and skilled nursing facilities either for the reasonable cost (as determined under section 1395x(v) of this title) or for payment amounts determined in accordance with section 1395ww of this title, as applicable, of services furnished to individuals enrolled with such organization pursuant to subsection (d) of this section, and

(B) will deduct the amount of such reimbursement from payment which would otherwise be made to such organization.

If such an eligible organization pays a hospital or skilled nursing facility directly, the amount paid shall not exceed the reasonable cost of the services (as determined under section 1395x(v) of this title) or the amount determined under section 1395ww of this title, as applicable, unless such organization demonstrates to the satisfaction of the Secretary that such excess payments are justified on the basis of advantages gained by the organization.

(3) Payments made to an organization with a reasonable cost reimbursement contract shall be subject to appropriate retroactive corrective adjustment at the end of each contract year so as to assure that such organization is paid for the reasonable cost actually incurred (excluding any part of incurred cost found to be unnecessary in the efficient delivery of health services) or the amounts otherwise determined under section 1395ww of this title for the types of expenses otherwise reimbursable under this subchapter for providing services covered under this subchapter to individuals described in subsection (a)(1) of this section.

(4) Any reasonable cost reimbursement contract with an eligible organization under this subsection shall provide that the Secretary shall require, at such time following the expiration of each accounting period of the eligible organization (and in such form and in such detail) as he may prescribe—

(A) that the organization report to him in an independently certified financial statement its per capita incurred cost based on the types of components of expenses otherwise reimbursable under this subchapter for providing services described in subsection (a)(1) of this section, including therein, in accordance with accounting procedures prescribed by the Secretary, its methods of allocating costs between individuals enrolled under this section and other individuals enrolled with such organization;

(B) that failure to report such information as may be required may be deemed to constitute evidence of likely overpayment on the basis of which appropriate collection action may be taken;

(C) that in any case in which an eligible organization is related to another organization by common ownership or control, a consolidated financial statement shall be filed and that the allowable costs for such organization may not include costs for the types of expense otherwise reimbursable under this subchapter, in excess of those which would be determined to be reasonable in accordance with regulations (providing for limiting reimbursement to costs rather than charges to the eligible organization by related organizations and owners) issued by the Secretary; and

(D) that in any case in which compensation is paid by an eligible organization substantially in excess of what is normally paid for similar services by similar practitioners (regardless of method of compensation), such compensation may as appropriate be considered to constitute a distribution of profits.

(5)(A) After the date of the enactment of this paragraph, the Secretary may not enter into a reasonable cost reimbursement contract under this subsection (if the contract is not in effect as of such date), except for a contract with an eligible organization which, immediately previous to entering into such contract, had an agreement in effect under section 1395l(a)(1)(A) of this title.

(B) Subject to subparagraph (C), the Secretary shall approve an application for a modification to a reasonable cost contract under this section in order to expand the service area of such contract if—

(i) such application is submitted to the Secretary on or before September 1, 2003; and

(ii) the Secretary determines that the organization with the contract continues to meet the requirements applicable to such organizations and contracts under this section.

(C) The Secretary may not extend or renew a reasonable cost reimbursement contract under this subsection for any period beyond December 31, 2004.

(i) Duration, termination, effective date, and terms of contract; powers and duties of Secretary

(1) Each contract under this section shall be for a term of at least one year, as determined by the Secretary, and may be made automatically renewable from term to term in the absence of notice by either party of intention to terminate at the end of the current term; except that in accordance with procedures established under paragraph (9), the Secretary may at any time terminate any such contract or may impose the intermediate sanctions described in paragraph (6)(B) or (6)(C) (whichever is applicable) on the eligible organization if the Secretary determines that the organization—

(A) has failed substantially to carry out the contract;

(B) is carrying out the contract in a manner substantially inconsistent with the efficient and effective administration of this section; or

(C) no longer substantially meets the applicable conditions of subsections (b), (c), (e), and (f) of this section.

(2) The effective date of any contract executed pursuant to this section shall be specified in the contract.

(3) Each contract under this section—

(A) shall provide that the Secretary, or any person or organization designated by him—

(i) shall have the right to inspect or otherwise evaluate

(I) the quality, appropriateness, and timeliness of services performed under the contract and

(II) the facilities of the organization when there is reasonable evidence of some need for such inspection, and

(ii) shall have the right to audit and inspect any books and records of the eligible organization that pertain

(I) to the ability of the organization to bear the risk of potential financial losses, or

(II) to services performed or determinations of amounts payable under the contract;

(B) shall require the organization with a risk-sharing contract to provide (and pay for) written notice in advance of the contract's termination, as well as a description of alternatives for obtaining benefits under this subchapter, to each individual enrolled under this section with the organization; and

(C)(i) shall require the organization to comply with subsections (a) and (c) of section 300e–17 of this title (relating to disclosure of certain financial information) and with the requirement of section 300e(c)(8) of this title (relating to liability arrangements to protect members);

(ii) shall require the organization to provide and supply information (described in section 1395cc(b)(2)(C)(ii) of this title) in the manner such information is required to be provided or supplied under that section;

(iii) shall require the organization to notify the Secretary of loans and other special financial arrangements which are made between the organization and subcontractors, affiliates, and related parties; and

(D) shall contain such other terms and conditions not inconsistent with this section (including requiring the organization to provide the Secretary with such information) as the Secretary may find necessary and appropriate.

(4) The Secretary may not enter into a risk-sharing contract with an eligible organization if a previous risk-sharing contract with that organization under this section was terminated at the request of the organization within the preceding five-year period, except in circumstances which warrant special consideration, as determined by the Secretary.

(5) The authority vested in the Secretary by this section may be performed without regard to such provisions of law or regulations relating to the making, performance, amendment, or modification of contracts of the United States as the Secretary may determine to be inconsistent with the furtherance of the purpose of this subchapter.

(6)(A) If the Secretary determines that an eligible organization with a contract under this section—

> **(i)** fails substantially to provide medically necessary items and services that are required (under law or under the contract) to be provided to an individual covered under the contract, if the failure has adversely affected (or has substantial likelihood of adversely affecting) the individual;

> **(ii)** imposes premiums on individuals enrolled under this section in excess of the premiums permitted;

> **(iii)** acts to expel or to refuse to re-enroll an individual in violation of the provisions of this section;

> **(iv)** engages in any practice that would reasonably be expected to have the effect of denying or discouraging enrollment (except as permitted by this section) by eligible individuals with the organization whose medical condition or history indicates a need for substantial future medical services;

> **(v)** misrepresents or falsifies information that is furnished—

>> **(I)** to the Secretary under this section, or

>> **(II)** to an individual or to any other entity under this section;

> **(vi)** fails to comply with the requirements of subsection (g)(6)(A) or paragraph (8) of this section; or

> **(vii)** in the case of a risk-sharing contract, employs or contracts with any individual or entity that is excluded from participation under this subchapter under section 1320a–7 or 1320a–7a of this title for the provision of health care, utilization review, medical social work, or administrative services or employs or contracts with any entity for the provision (directly or indirectly) through such an excluded individual or entity of such services;

the Secretary may provide, in addition to any other remedies authorized by law, for any of the remedies described in subparagraph (B).

(B) The remedies described in this subparagraph are—

(i) civil money penalties of not more than $25,000 for each determination under subparagraph (A) or, with respect to a determination under clause (iv) or (v)(I) of such subparagraph, of not more than $100,000 for each such determination, plus, with respect to a determination under subparagraph (A)(ii), double the excess amount charged in violation of such subparagraph (and the excess amount charged shall be deducted from the penalty and returned to the individual concerned), and plus, with respect to a determination under subparagraph (A)(iv), $15,000 for each individual not enrolled as a result of the practice involved,

(ii) suspension of enrollment of individuals under this section after the date the Secretary notifies the organization of a determination under subparagraph (A) and until the Secretary is satisfied that the basis for such determination has been corrected and is not likely to recur, or

(iii) suspension of payment to the organization under this section for individuals enrolled after the date the Secretary notifies the organization of a determination under subparagraph (A) and until the Secretary is satisfied that the basis for such determination has been corrected and is not likely to recur.

(C) In the case of an eligible organization for which the Secretary makes a determination under paragraph (1), the basis of which is not described in subparagraph (A), the Secretary may apply the following intermediate sanctions:

(i) Civil money penalties of not more than $25,000 for each determination under paragraph (1) if the deficiency that is the basis of the determination has directly adversely affected (or has the substantial likelihood of adversely affecting) an individual covered under the organization's contract.

(ii) Civil money penalties of not more than $10,000 for each week beginning after the initiation of procedures by the Secretary under paragraph (9) during which the deficiency that is the basis of a determination under paragraph (1) exists.

(iii) Suspension of enrollment of individuals under this section after the date the Secretary notifies the organization of a determination under paragraph (1) and until the Secretary is satisfied that the deficiency that is the basis for the determination has been corrected and is not likely to recur.

(D) The provisions of section 1320a–7a of this title (other than subsections (a) and (b)) shall apply to a civil money penalty under subparagraph (B)(i) or (C)(i) in the same manner as such provisions apply to a civil money penalty or proceeding under section 1320a–7(a) of this title.

(7)(A) Each risk-sharing contract with an eligible organization under this section shall provide that the organization will maintain a written agreement with a utilization and quality control peer review organization (which has a contract with the Secretary under part B of subchapter XI of this chapter for the area in which the eligible organization is located) or with an entity selected by the Secretary under section 1320c–3(a)(4)(C) of this title under which the review organization will perform functions under section 1320c-3(a)(4)(B) of this title and section 1320c–3(a)(14) of this title (other than those performed under contracts described in section 1395cc(a)(1)(F) of this title) with respect to services, furnished by the eligible organization, for which payment may be made under this subchapter.

(B) For purposes of payment under this subchapter, the cost of such agreement to the eligible organization shall be considered a cost incurred by a provider of services in providing covered services under this subchapter and shall be paid directly by the Secretary to the review organization on behalf of such eligible organization in accordance with a schedule established by the Secretary.

(C) Such payments—

(i) shall be transferred in appropriate proportions from the Federal Hospital Insurance Trust Fund and from the Supplementary Medical Insurance Trust Fund, without regard to amounts appropriated in advance in appropriation Acts, in the same manner as transfers are made for payment for services provided directly to beneficiaries, and

(ii) shall not be less in the aggregate for such organizations for a fiscal year than the amounts the Secretary determines to be sufficient to cover the costs of such organizations' conducting activities described in subparagraph (A) with respect to such eligible organizations under part B of subchapter XI of this chapter.

(8)(A) Each contract with an eligible organization under this section shall provide that the organization may not operate any physician incentive plan (as defined in subparagraph (B)) unless the following requirements are met:

(i) No specific payment is made directly or indirectly under the plan to a physician or physician group as an inducement to reduce or limit medically necessary services provided with respect to a specific individual enrolled with the organization.

(ii) If the plan places a physician or physician group at substantial financial risk (as determined by the Secretary) for services not provided by the physician or physician group, the organization—

(I) provides stop-loss protection for the physician or group that is adequate and appropriate, based on standards developed by the Secretary that take into account the number of physicians placed at such substantial financial risk in the group or under the plan and the number of individuals enrolled with the organization who receive services from the physician or the physician group, and

(II) conducts periodic surveys of both individuals enrolled and individuals previously enrolled with the organization to determine the degree of access of such individuals to services provided by the organization and satisfaction with the quality of such services.

(iii) The organization provides the Secretary with descriptive information regarding the plan, sufficient to permit the Secretary to determine whether the plan is in compliance with the requirements of this subparagraph.

(B) In this paragraph, the term "physician incentive plan" means any compensation arrangement between an eligible organization and a physician or physician group that may directly or indirectly have the effect of reducing or limiting services provided with respect to individuals enrolled with the organization.

(9) The Secretary may terminate a contract with an eligible organization under this section or may impose the intermediate sanctions described in paragraph (6) on the organization in accordance with formal investigation and compliance procedures established by the Secretary under which—

(A) the Secretary first provides the organization with the reasonable opportunity to develop and implement a corrective action plan to correct the deficiencies that were the basis of the Secretary's determination under paragraph (1) and the organization fails to develop or implement such a plan;

(B) in deciding whether to impose sanctions, the Secretary considers aggravating factors such as whether an organization has a history of deficiencies or has not taken action to correct deficiencies the Secretary has brought to the organization's attention;

(C) there are no unreasonable or unnecessary delays between the finding of a deficiency and the imposition of sanctions; and

(D) the Secretary provides the organization with reasonable notice and opportunity for hearing (including the right to appeal an initial decision) before imposing any sanction or terminating the contract.

(j) Payment in full and limitation on actual charges; physicians, providers of services, or renal dialysis facilities not under contract with organization

(1)(A) In the case of physicians' services or renal dialysis services described in paragraph (2) which are furnished by a participating physician or provider of services or renal dialysis facility to an individual enrolled with an eligible organization under this section and enrolled under part B of this subchapter, the applicable participation agreement is deemed to provide that the physician or provider of services or renal dialysis facility will accept as payment in full from the eligible organization the amount that would be payable to the physician or provider of services or renal dialysis facility under part B of this subchapter and from the individual under such part, if the individual were not enrolled with an eligible organization under this section.

(B) In the case of physicians' services described in paragraph (2) which are furnished by a nonparticipating physician, the limitations on actual charges for such services otherwise applicable under part B of this subchapter (to services furnished by individuals not enrolled with an eligible organization under this section) shall apply in the same manner as such limitations apply to services furnished to individuals not enrolled with such an organization.

(2) The physicians' services or renal dialysis services described in this paragraph are physicians' services or renal dialysis services which are furnished to an enrollee of an eligible organization under this section by a physician, provider of services, or renal dialysis facility who is not under a contract with the organization.

(k) Risk-sharing contracts

(1) Except as provided in paragraph (2)—

(A) on or after the date standards for Medicare + Choice organizations and plans are first established under section 1395w–26(b)(1) of this title, the Secretary shall not enter into any risk-sharing contract under this section with an eligible organization; and

(B) for any contract year beginning on or after January 1, 1999, the Secretary shall not renew any such contract.

(2) An individual who is enrolled in part B only and is enrolled in an eligible organization with a risk-sharing contract under this section on December 31, 1998, may continue enrollment in such organization in accordance with regulations described in section 1395w–26(b)(1) of this title.

(3) Notwithstanding subsection (a), the Secretary shall provide that payment amounts under risk-sharing contracts under this section for months in a year (beginning with January 1998) shall be computed—

(A) with respect to individuals entitled to benefits under both parts A and B of this subchapter, by substituting payment rates

685

under section 1395w–25(a) of this title for the payment rates otherwise established under section 1395mm of this title, and

(B) with respect to individuals only entitled to benefits under part B of this subchapter, by substituting an appropriate proportion of such rates (reflecting the relative proportion of payments under this subchapter attributable to such part) for the payment rates otherwise established under subsection (a) of this section.

(4) The following requirements shall apply to eligible organizations with risk-sharing contracts under this section in the same manner as they apply to Medicare + Choice organizations under part C of this subchapter:

(A) Data collection requirements under section 1395w–23(a)(3)(B) of this title.

(B) Restrictions on imposition of premium taxes under section 1395w–24(g) of this title in relating to payments to such organizations under this section.

(C) The requirement to accept enrollment of new enrollees during November 1998 under section 1395w–21(e)(6) of this title.

(D) Payments under section 1395w–27(e)(2) of this title.

§ 1395nn.   Limitation on certain physician referrals

[See Stark Law page ___]

§ 1395oo.   Provider Reimbursement Review Board

(a) Establishment

Any provider of services which has filed a required cost report within the time specified in regulations may obtain a hearing with respect to such cost report by a Provider Reimbursement Review Board (hereinafter referred to as the "Board") which shall be established by the Secretary in accordance with subsection (h) of this section and (except as provided in subsection (g)(2) of this section) any hospital which receives payments in amounts computed under subsection (b) or (d) of section 1395ww of this title and which has submitted such reports within such time as the Secretary may require in order to make payment under such section may obtain a hearing with respect to such payment by the Board, if—

(1) such provider—

(A)(i) is dissatisfied with a final determination of the organization serving as its fiscal intermediary pursuant to section 1395h of this title as to the amount of total program reimbursement due the provider for the items and services furnished to individuals for which payment may be made under this subchapter for the period covered by such report, or

(ii) is dissatisfied with a final determination of the Secretary as to the amount of the payment under subsection (b) or (d) of section 1395ww of this title,

(B) has not received such final determination from such intermediary on a timely basis after filing such report, where such report complied with the rules and regulations of the Secretary relating to such report, or

(C) has not received such final determination on a timely basis after filing a supplementary cost report, where such cost report did not so comply and such supplementary cost report did so comply,

(2) the amount in controversy is $10,000 or more, and

(3) such provider files a request for a hearing within 180 days after notice of the intermediary's final determination under paragraph (1)(A)(i), or with respect to appeals under paragraph (1)(A)(ii), 180 days after notice of the Secretary's final determination, or with respect to appeals pursuant to paragraph (1)(B) or (C), within 180 days after notice of such determination would have been received if such determination had been made on a timely basis.

(b) Appeals by groups

The provisions of subsection (a) of this section shall apply to any group of providers of services if each provider of services in such group would, upon the filing of an appeal (but without regard to the $10,000 limitation), be entitled to such a hearing, but only if the matters in controversy involve a common question of fact or interpretation of law or regulations and the amount in controversy is, in the aggregate, $50,000 or more.

(c) Right to counsel; rules of evidence

At such hearing, the provider of services shall have the right to be represented by counsel, to introduce evidence, and to examine and cross-examine witnesses. Evidence may be received at any such hearing even though inadmissible under rules of evidence applicable to court procedure.

(d) Decisions of Board

A decision by the Board shall be based upon the record made at such hearing, which shall include the evidence considered by the intermediary and such other evidence as may be obtained or received by the Board, and shall be supported by substantial evidence when the record is viewed as a whole. The Board shall have the power to affirm, modify, or reverse a final determination of the fiscal intermediary with respect to a cost report and to make any other revisions on matters covered by such cost report (including revisions adverse to the provider of services) even though such matters were not considered by the intermediary in making such final determination.

(e) Rules and regulations

The Board shall have full power and authority to make rules and establish procedures, not inconsistent with the provisions of this subchapter or regulations of the Secretary, which are necessary or appropriate to carry out the provisions of this section. In the course of any hearing the Board may administer oaths and affirmations. The provisions of subsections (d) and (e) of section 405 of this title with respect to subpenas shall apply to the Board to the same extent as they apply to the Secretary with respect to subchapter II of this chapter.

(f) Finality of decision; judicial review; determinations of Board authority; jurisdiction; venue; interest on amount in controversy

(1) A decision of the Board shall be final unless the Secretary, on his own motion, and within 60 days after the provider of services is notified of the Board's decision, reverses, affirms, or modifies the Board's decision. Providers shall have the right to obtain judicial review of any final decision of the Board, or of any reversal, affirmance, or modification by the Secretary, by a civil action commenced within 60 days of the date on which notice of any final decision by the Board or of any reversal, affirmance, or modification by the Secretary is received. Providers shall also have the right to obtain judicial review of any action of the fiscal intermediary which involves a question of law or regulations relevant to the matters in controversy whenever the Board determines (on its own motion or at the request of a provider of services as described in the following sentence) that it is without authority to decide the question, by a civil action commenced within sixty days of the date on which notification of such determination is received. If a provider of services may obtain a hearing under subsection (a) of this section and has filed a request for such a hearing, such provider may file a request for a determination by the Board of its authority to decide the question of law or regulations relevant to the matters in controversy (accompanied by such documents and materials as the Board shall require for purposes of rendering such determination). The Board shall render such determination in writing within thirty days after the Board receives the request and such accompanying documents and materials, and the determination shall be considered a final decision and not subject to review by the Secretary. If the Board fails to render such determination within such period, the provider may bring a civil action (within sixty days of the end of such period) with respect to the matter in controversy contained in such request for a hearing. Such action shall be brought in the district court of the United States for the judicial district in which the provider is located (or, in an action brought jointly by several providers, the judicial district in which the greatest number of such providers are located) or in the District Court for the District of Columbia and shall be tried pursuant to the applicable provisions under chapter 7 of Title 5 notwithstanding any other provisions in section 405 of this title. Any appeal to the Board or action for judicial review by providers which are under common ownership or control or which have obtained a hearing under subsection (b) of this section must be brought by such providers as a group with respect to any matter involving an issue common to such providers.

(2) Where a provider seeks judicial review pursuant to paragraph (1), the amount in controversy shall be subject to annual interest beginning on the first day of the first month beginning after the 180–day period as determined pursuant to subsection (a)(3) of this section and equal to the rate of interest on obligations issued for purchase by the Federal Hospital Insurance Trust Fund for the month in which the civil action authorized under paragraph (1) is commenced, to be awarded by the reviewing court in favor of the prevailing party.

(3) No interest awarded pursuant to paragraph (2) shall be deemed income or cost for the purposes of determining reimbursement due providers under this chapter.

(g) Certain findings not reviewable

(1) The finding of a fiscal intermediary that no payment may be made under this subchapter for any expenses incurred for items or services furnished to an individual because such items or services are listed in section 1395y of this title shall not be reviewed by the Board, or by any court pursuant to an action brought under subsection (f) of this section.

(2) The determinations and other decisions described in section 1395ww(d)(7) of this title shall not be reviewed by the Board or by any court pursuant to an action brought under subsection (f) of this section or otherwise.

(h) Composition and compensation

The Board shall be composed of five members appointed by the Secretary without regard to the provisions of Title 5 governing appointments in the competitive services. Two of such members shall be representative of providers of services. All of the members of the Board shall be persons knowledgeable in the field of payment of providers of services, and at least one of them shall be a certified public accountant. Members of the Board shall be entitled to receive compensation at rates fixed by the Secretary, but not exceeding the rate specified (at the time the service involved is rendered by such members) for grade GS–18 in section 5332 of Title 5. The term of office shall be three years, except that the Secretary shall appoint the initial members of the Board for shorter terms to the extent necessary to permit staggered terms of office.

(i) Technical and clerical assistance

The Board is authorized to engage such technical assistance as may be required to carry out its functions, and the Secretary shall, in addition, make available to the Board such secretarial, clerical, and other assistance as the Board may require to carry out its functions.

(j) "Provider of services" defined

In this section, the term "provider of services" includes a rural health clinic and a Federally qualified health center.

§ 1395pp. Limitation on liability where claims are disallowed

(a) Conditions prerequisite to payment for items and services notwithstanding determination of disallowance

Where—

(1) a determination is made that, by reason of section 1395y(a)(1) or (9) of this title or by reason of a coverage denial described in subsection (g) of this section, payment may not be made under part A or part B of this subchapter for any expenses incurred for items or services furnished an individual by a provider of services or by another person pursuant to an assignment under section 1395u(b)(3)(B)(ii) of this title, and

(2) both such individual and such provider of services or such other person, as the case may be, did not know, and could not reasonably have been expected to know, that payment would not be made for such items or services under such part A or part B of this subchapter,

then to the extent permitted by this subchapter, payment shall, notwithstanding such determination, be made for such items or services (and for such period of time as the Secretary finds will carry out the objectives of this subchapter), as though section 1395y(a)(1) and section 1395y(a)(9) of this title did not apply and as though the coverage denial described in subsection (g) of this section had not occurred. In each such case the Secretary shall notify both such individual and such provider of services or such other person, as the case may be, of the conditions under which payment for such items or services was made and in the case of comparable situations arising thereafter with respect to such individual or such provider or such other person, each shall, by reason of such notice (or similar notices provided before the enactment of this section), be deemed to have knowledge that payment cannot be made for such items or services or reasonably comparable items or services. Any provider or other person furnishing items or services for which payment may not be made by reason of section 1395y(a)(1) or (9) of this title or by reason of a coverage denial described in subsection (g) of this section shall be deemed to have knowledge that payment cannot be made for such items or services if the claim relating to such items or services involves a case, provider or other person furnishing services, procedure, or test, with respect to which such provider or other person has been notified by the Secretary (including notification by a utilization and quality control peer review organization) that a pattern of inappropriate utilization has occurred in the past, and such provider or other person has been allowed a reasonable time to correct such inappropriate utilization.

(b) Knowledge of person or provider that payment could not be made; indemnification of individual

In any case in which the provisions of paragraphs (1) and (2) of subsection (a) of this section are met, except that such provider or such other person, as the case may be, knew, or could be expected to know, that payment for such services or items could not be made under such part A or part B of this subchapter, then the Secretary shall, upon proper application filed within such time as may be prescribed in regulations, indemnify the individual (referred to in such paragraphs) for any payments received from such individual by such provider or such other person, as the case may be, for such items or services. Any payments made by the Secretary as indemnification shall be deemed to have been made to such provider or such other person, as the case may be, and shall be treated as overpayments, recoverable from such provider or such other person, as the case may be, under applicable provisions of law. In each such case the Secretary shall notify such individual of the conditions under which indemnification is made and in the case of comparable situations arising thereafter with respect to such individual, he shall, by reason of such notice (or similar notices provided before the enactment of this section), be deemed to have knowledge that payment cannot be made for such items or services. No item or service for which an individual is indemnified under this subsection shall be taken into account in applying any limitation on the amount of items and services for which payment may be made to or on behalf of the individual under this subchapter.

(c) Knowledge of both provider and individual to whom items or services were furnished that payment could not be made

No payments shall be made under this subchapter in any cases in which the provisions of paragraph (1) of subsection (a) of this section are met, but both the individual to whom the items or services were furnished and the provider of service or other person, as the case may be, who furnished the items or services knew, or could reasonably have been expected to know, that payment could not be made for items or services under part A or part B of this subchapter by reason of section 1395y(a)(1) or (a)(9) of this title or by reason of a coverage denial described in subsection (g) of this section.

(d) Exercise of rights

In any case arising under subsection (b) of this section (but without regard to whether payments have been made by the individual to the provider or other person) or subsection (c) of this section, the provider or other person shall have the same rights that an individual has under sections 1395ff(b) and 1395u(b)(3)(C) of this title (as may be applicable) when the amount of benefit or payments is in controversy, except that such rights may, under prescribed regulations, be exercised by such provider or other person only after the Secretary determines that the individual will not exercise such rights under such sections.

(e) Payment where beneficiary not at fault

Where payment for inpatient hospital services or extended care services may not be made under part A of this subchapter on behalf of an individual entitled to benefits under such part solely because of an unintentional, inadvertent, or erroneous action with respect to the transfer of such individual from a hospital or skilled nursing facility that meets the requirements of section 1395x(e) or (j) of this title by such a provider of services acting in good

691

faith in accordance with the advice of a utilization review committee, quality control and peer review organization, or fiscal intermediary, or on the basis of a clearly erroneous administrative decision by a provider of services, the Secretary shall take such action with respect to the payment of such benefits as he determines may be necessary to correct the effects of such unintentional, inadvertent, or erroneous action.

(f) Presumption with respect to coverage denial; rebuttal; requirements; "fiscal intermediary" defined

(1) A home health agency which meets the applicable requirements of paragraphs (3) and (4) shall be presumed to meet the requirement of subsection (a)(2) of this section.

(2) The presumption of paragraph (1) with respect to specific services may be rebutted by actual or imputed knowledge of the facts described in subsection (a)(2) of this section, including any of the following:

(A) Notice by the fiscal intermediary of the fact that payment may not be made under this subchapter with respect to the services.

(B) It is clear and obvious that the provider should have known at the time the services were furnished that they were excluded from coverage.

(3) The requirements of this paragraph are as follows:

(A) The agency complies with requirements of the Secretary under this subchapter respecting timely submittal of bills for payment and medical documentation.

(B) The agency program has reasonable procedures to notify promptly each patient (and the patient's physician) where it is determined that a patient is being or will be furnished items or services which are excluded from coverage under this subchapter.

(4)(A) The requirement of this paragraph is that, on the basis of bills submitted by a home health agency during the previous quarter, the rate of denial of bills for the agency by reason of a coverage denial described in subsection (g) of this section does not exceed 2.5 percent, computed based on visits for home health services billed.

(B) For purposes of determining the rate of denial of bills for a home health agency under subparagraph (A), a bill shall not be considered to be denied until the expiration of the 60–day period that begins on the date such bill is denied by the fiscal intermediary, or, with respect to such a denial for which the agency requests reconsideration, until the fiscal intermediary issues a decision denying payment for such bill.

(5) In this subsection, the term "fiscal intermediary" means, with respect to a home health agency, an agency or organization with an agreement under section 1395h of this title with respect to the agency.

(6) The Secretary shall monitor the proportion of denied bills submitted by home health agencies for which reconsideration is requested, and shall notify Congress if the proportion of denials reversed upon reconsideration increases significantly.

(g) Coverage denial defined

The coverage denial described in this subsection is—

(1) with respect to the provision of home health services to an individual, a failure to meet the requirements of section 1395f(a)(2)(C) of this title or section 1395n(a)(2)(A) of this title in that the individual—

(A) is or was not confined to his home, or

(B) does or did not need skilled nursing care on an intermittent basis; and

(2) with respect to the provision of hospice care to an individual, a determination that the individual is not terminally ill.

(h) Supplier responsibility for items furnished on assignment basis

If a supplier of medical equipment and supplies (as defined in section 1395m(j)(5) of this title)—

(1) furnishes an item or service to a beneficiary for which no payment may be made by reason of section 1395m(j)(1) of this title;

(2) furnishes an item or service to a beneficiary for which payment is denied in advance under section 1395m(a)(15) of this title; or

(3) furnishes an item or service to a beneficiary for which no payment may be made by reason of section 1395(a)(17)(B) of this title,

any expenses incurred for items and services furnished to an individual by such a supplier on an assignment-related basis shall be the responsibility of such supplier. The individual shall have no financial responsibility for such expenses and the supplier shall refund on a timely basis to the individual (and shall be liable to the individual for) any amounts collected from the individual for such items or services. The provisions of section 1395m(a)(18) of this title shall apply to refunds required under the previous sentence in the same manner as such provisions apply to refunds under such section.

§ 1395rr.   End stage renal disease program

(a) Type, duration, and scope of benefits

The benefits provided by parts A and B of this subchapter shall include benefits for individuals who have been determined to have end stage renal disease as provided in section 426–1 of this title, and benefits for kidney donors as provided in subsection (d) of this section. Notwithstanding any other provision of this subchapter, the type, duration, and scope of the benefit provided by parts A and B of this subchapter with respect to individuals who have been determined to have end stage renal disease and who are entitled to such benefits without regard to section 426–1 of this title shall in no case be less than the type, duration, and scope of the benefits so provided for individuals entitled to such benefits solely by reason of that section.

(b) Payments with respect to services; dialysis; regulations; physicians' services; target reimbursement rates; home dialysis supplies and equipment; self-care home dialysis support services; self-care dialysis units; hepatitis B vaccine

(1) Payments under this subchapter with respect to services, in addition to services for which payment would otherwise be made under this subchapter, furnished to individuals who have been determined to have end stage renal disease shall include (A) payments on behalf of such individuals to providers of services and renal dialysis facilities which meet such requirements as the Secretary shall by regulation prescribe for institutional dialysis services and supplies (including self-dialysis services in a self-care dialysis unit maintained by the provider or facility), transplantation services, self-care home dialysis support services which are furnished by the provider or facility, and routine professional services performed by a physician during a maintenance dialysis episode if payments for his other professional services furnished to an individual who has end stage renal disease are made on the basis specified in paragraph (3)(A) of this subsection, (B), payments to or on behalf of such individuals for home dialysis supplies and equipment, and (C) payments to a supplier of home dialysis supplies and equipment that is not a provider of services, a renal dialysis facility, or a physician for self-administered erythropoietin as described in section 1395x(s)(2)(P) of this title if the Secretary finds that the patient receiving such drug from such a supplier can safely and effectively administer the drug (in accordance with the applicable methods and standards established by the Secretary pursuant to such section). The requirements prescribed by the Secretary under subparagraph (A) shall include requirements for a minimum utilization rate for transplantations.

(2)(A) With respect to payments for dialysis services furnished by providers of services and renal dialysis facilities to individuals determined to have end stage renal disease for which payments may be made under part B of this subchapter, such payments (unless otherwise provided in this section) shall be equal to 80 percent of the amounts determined in accordance with subparagraph (B); and with respect to payments for services for which payments may be made under part A of this subchapter, the amounts of such payments (which amounts shall not exceed, in respect to costs in procuring organs attributable to payments made to an organ procurement agency or histocompatibility laboratory, the costs incurred by that agency or laboratory) shall be determined in accordance with section 1395x(v) of this title or section 1395ww of this title (if applicable). Payments shall be made to a renal dialysis facility only if it agrees to accept such payments as payment in full for covered services, except for payment by the individual of 20 percent of the estimated amounts for such services calculated on the basis established by the

694

Secretary under subparagraph (B) and the deductible amount imposed by section 1395l(b) of this title.

(B) The Secretary shall prescribe in regulations any methods and procedures to (i) determine the costs incurred by providers of services and renal dialysis facilities in furnishing covered services to individuals determined to have end stage renal disease, and (ii) determine, on a cost-related basis or other economical and equitable basis (including any basis authorized under section 1395x(v) of this title) and consistent with any regulations promulgated under paragraph (7), the amounts of payments to be made for part B services furnished by such providers and facilities to such individuals.

(C) Such regulations, in the case of services furnished by proprietary providers and facilities (other than hospital outpatient departments) may include, if the Secretary finds it feasible and appropriate, provision for recognition of a reasonable rate of return on equity capital, providing such rate of return does not exceed the rate of return stipulated in section 1395x(v)(1)(B) of this title.

(D) For purposes of section 1395oo of this title, a renal dialysis facility shall be treated as a provider of services.

(3) With respect to payments for physicians' services furnished to individuals determined to have end stage renal disease, the Secretary shall pay 80 percent of the amounts calculated for such services—

(A) on a reasonable charge basis (but may, in such case, make payment on the basis of the prevailing charges of other physicians for comparable services or, for services furnished on or after January 1, 1992, on the basis described in section 1395w–4 of this title) except that payment may not be made under this subparagraph for routine services furnished during a maintenance dialysis episode, or

(B) on a comprehensive monthly fee or other basis (which effectively encourages the efficient delivery of dialysis services and provides incentives for the increased use of home dialysis) for an aggregate of services provided over a period of time (as defined in regulations).

(4)(A) Pursuant to agreements with approved providers of services and renal dialysis facilities, the Secretary may make payments to such providers and facilities for the cost of home dialysis supplies and equipment and self-care home dialysis support services furnished to patients whose self-care home dialysis is under the direct supervision of such provider or facility, on the basis of a target reimbursement rate (as defined in paragraph (6)) or on the basis of a method established under paragraph (7).

(B) The Secretary shall make payments to a supplier of home dialysis supplies and equipment furnished to a patient whose self-care home dialysis is not under the direct supervision of an approved provider of services or renal dialysis facility only in accordance with a written agreement under which—

>   **(i)** the patient certifies that the supplier is the sole provider of such supplies and equipment to the patient,

>   **(ii)** the supplier agrees to receive payment for the cost of such supplies and equipment only on an assignment-related basis, and

>   **(iii)** the supplier certifies that it has entered into a written agreement with an approved provider of services or renal dialysis facility under which such provider or facility agrees to furnish to such patient all self-care home dialysis support services and all other necessary dialysis services and supplies, including institutional dialysis services and supplies and emergency services.

(5) An agreement under paragraph (4) shall require, in accordance with regulations prescribed by the Secretary, that the provider or facility will—

>   **(A)** assume full responsibility for directly obtaining or arranging for the provision of—

>>   **(i)** such medically necessary dialysis equipment as is prescribed by the attending physician;

>>   **(ii)** dialysis equipment maintenance and repair services;

>>   **(iii)** the purchase and delivery of all necessary medical supplies; and

>>   **(iv)** where necessary, the services of trained home dialysis aides;

>   **(B)** perform all such administrative functions and maintain such information and records as the Secretary may require to verify the transactions and arrangements described in subparagraph (A);

>   **(C)** submit such cost reports, data, and information as the Secretary may require with respect to the costs incurred for equipment, supplies, and services furnished to the facility's home dialysis patient population; and

>   **(D)** provide for full access for the Secretary to all such records, data, and information as he may require to perform his functions under this section.

(6) The Secretary shall establish, for each calendar year, commencing with January 1, 1979, a target reimbursement rate for home dialysis which shall be adjusted for regional variations in the cost of providing home dialysis. In establishing such a rate, the Secretary shall include—

>   **(A)** the Secretary's estimate of the cost of providing medically necessary home dialysis supplies and equipment;

(B) an allowance, in an amount determined by the Secretary, to cover the cost of providing personnel to aid in home dialysis; and

(C) an allowance, in an amount determined by the Secretary, to cover administrative costs and to provide an incentive for the efficient delivery of home dialysis;

but in no event (except as may be provided in regulations under paragraph (7)) shall such target rate exceed 75 percent of the national average payment, adjusted for regional variations, for maintenance dialysis services furnished in approved providers and facilities during the preceding fiscal year. Any such target rate so established shall be utilized, without renegotiation of the rate, throughout the calendar year for which it is established. During the last quarter of each calendar year, the Secretary shall establish a home dialysis target reimbursement rate for the next calendar year based on the most recent data available to the Secretary at the time. In establishing any rate under this paragraph, the Secretary may utilize a competitive-bid procedure, a prenegotiated rate procedure, or any other procedure (including methods established under paragraph (7)) which the Secretary determines is appropriate and feasible in order to carry out this paragraph in an effective and efficient manner.

(7) The Secretary shall provide by regulation for a method (or methods) for determining prospectively the amounts of payments to be made for dialysis services furnished by providers of services and renal dialysis facilities to individuals in a facility and to such individuals at home. Such method (or methods) shall provide for the prospective determination of a rate (or rates) for each mode of care based on a single composite weighted formula (which takes into account the mix of patients who receive dialysis services at a facility or at home and the relative costs of providing such services in such settings) for hospital-based facilities and such a single composite weighted formula for other renal dialysis facilities, or based on such other method or combination of methods which differentiate between hospital-based facilities and other renal dialysis facilities and which the Secretary determines, after detailed analysis, will more effectively encourage the more efficient delivery of dialysis services and will provide greater incentives for increased use of home dialysis than through the single composite weighted formulas. The amount of a payment made under any method other than a method based on a single composite weighted formula may not exceed the amount (or, in the case of continuous cycling peritoneal dialysis, 130 percent of the amount) of the median payment that would have been made under the formula for hospital-based facilities. The Secretary shall provide for such exceptions to such methods as may be warranted by unusual circumstances (including the special circumstances of sole facilities located in isolated, rural areas and of pediatric facilities). Each application for such an exception shall be deemed to be approved unless the Secretary disapproves it by not later than 60 working days after the date the application is filed. The Secretary may provide that such method will serve in lieu of any target reimbursement rate that would otherwise be established under paragraph (6). The Secretary shall reduce the amount of each composite rate payment under this paragraph for each treatment by 50 cents (subject to such adjustments as may be required to reflect modes of dialysis other than hemodialysis) and provide for payment of such amount to the organizations (designated under subsection (c)(1)(A) of this section) for such organizations' necessary and proper administrative costs incurred in carrying out the responsibilities described in subsection (c)(2) of this section. The Secretary shall provide that amounts paid under the previous sentence shall be distributed to the organizations described in subsection (c)(1)(A) of this section to ensure equitable treatment of all such network organizations. The Secretary in distributing any such payments to network organizations shall take into account—

    (A) the geographic size of the network area;

    (B) the number of providers of end stage renal disease services in the network area;

    (C) the number of individuals who are entitled to end stage renal disease services in the network area; and

    (D) the proportion of the aggregate administrative funds collected in the network area.

The Secretary shall increase the amount of each composite rate payment for dialysis services furnished during 2000 by 1.2 percent above such composite rate payment amounts for such services furnished on December 31, 1999, and for such services furnished on or after January 1, 2001, by 2.4 percent above such composite rate payment amounts for such services furnished on December 31, 2000.

(8) For purposes of this subchapter, the term "home dialysis supplies and equipment" means medically necessary supplies and equipment (including supportive equipment) required by an individual suffering from end stage renal disease in connection with renal dialysis carried out in his home (as defined in regulations), including obtaining, installing, and maintaining such equipment.

(9) For purposes of this subchapter, the term "self-care home dialysis support services", to the extent permitted in regulation, means—

    (A) periodic monitoring of the patient's home adaptation, including visits by qualified provider or facility personnel (as defined in regulations), so long as this is done in accordance with a plan prepared and periodically reviewed by a professional team (as defined in regulations) including the individual's physician;

    (B) installation and maintenance of dialysis equipment;

    (C) testing and appropriate treatment of the water; and

    (D) such additional supportive services as the Secretary finds appropriate and desirable.

(10) For purposes of this subchapter, the term "self-care dialysis unit" means a renal dialysis facility or a distinct part of such facility or of a provider of services, which has been approved by the Secretary to make self-dialysis services, as defined by the Secretary in regulations, available to individuals who have been trained for self-dialysis. A self-care dialysis unit must, at a minimum, furnish the services, equipment and supplies needed for self-care dialysis, have patient-staff ratios which are appropriate to self-dialysis (allowing for such appropriate lesser degree of ongoing medical supervision and assistance of ancillary personnel than is required for full care maintenance dialysis), and meet such other requirements as the Secretary may prescribe with respect to the quality and cost-effectiveness of services.

(11)(A) Hepatitis B vaccine and its administration, when provided to a patient determined to have end stage renal disease, shall not be included as dialysis services for purposes of payment under any prospective payment amount or comprehensive fee established under this section. Payment for such vaccine and its administration shall be made separately in accordance with section 1395l of this title.

(B) Erythropoietin, when provided to a patient determined to have end stage renal disease, shall not be included as a dialysis service for purposes of payment under any prospective payment amount or comprehensive fee established under this section, and payment for such item shall be made separately—

(i) in the case of erythropoietin provided by a physician, in accordance with section 1395l of this title; and

(ii) in the case of erythropoietin provided by a provider of services, renal dialysis facility, or other supplier of home dialysis supplies and equipment—

(I) for erythropoietin provided during 1994, in an amount equal to $10 per thousand units (rounded to the nearest 100 units), and

(II) for erythropoietin provided during a subsequent year, in an amount determined to be appropriate by the Secretary, except that such amount may not exceed the amount determined under this clause for the previous year increased by the percentage increase (if any) in the implicit price deflator for gross national product (as published by the Department of Commerce) for the second quarter of the preceding year over the implicit price deflator for the second quarter of the second preceding year.

(C) The amount payable to a supplier of home dialysis supplies and equipment that is not a provider of services, a renal dialysis facility, or a physician for erythropoietin shall be determined in the same manner as the amount payable to a renal dialysis facility for such item.

(c) Renal disease network areas; coordinating councils, executive committees, and medical review boards; national end stage renal disease medical information system; functions of network organizations

(1)(A)(i) For the purpose of assuring effective and efficient administration of the benefits provided under this section, the Secretary shall, in accordance with such criteria as he finds necessary to assure the performance of the responsibilities and functions specified in paragraph (2)—

(I) establish at least 17 end stage renal disease network areas, and

(II) for each such area, designate a network administrative organization which, in accordance with regulations of the Secretary, shall establish (aa) a network council of renal dialysis and transplant facilities located in the area and (bb) a medical review board, which has a membership including at least one patient representative and physicians, nurses, and social workers engaged in treatment relating to end stage renal disease.

The Secretary shall publish in the Federal Register a description of the geographic area that he determines, after consultation with appropriate professional and patient organizations, constitutes each network area and the criteria on the basis of which such determination is made.

(ii)(I) In order to determine whether the Secretary should enter into, continue, or terminate an agreement with a network administrative organization designated for an area established under clause (i), the Secretary shall develop and publish in the Federal Register standards, criteria, and procedures to evaluate an applicant organization's capabilities to perform (and, in the case of an organization with which such an agreement is in effect, actual performance of) the responsibilities described in paragraph (2). The Secretary shall evaluate each applicant based on quality and scope of services and may not accord more than 20 percent of the weight of the evaluation to the element of price.

(II) An agreement with a network administrative organization may be terminated by the Secretary only if he finds, after applying such standards and criteria, that the organization has failed to perform its prescribed responsibilities effectively and efficiently. If such an agreement is to be terminated, the Secretary shall select a successor to the agreement on the basis of competitive bidding and in a manner that provides an orderly transition.

(B) At least one patient representative shall serve as a member of each network council and each medical review board.

(C) The Secretary shall, in regulations, prescribe requirements with respect to membership in network organizations by individuals (and the relatives of such individuals) (i) who have an ownership or control interest in a facility or provider which furnishes services referred to in section 1395x(s)(2)(F) of this title, or (ii) who have received remuneration from any such facility or provider in excess of such amounts as constitute reasonable compensation for services (including time and effort relative to the provision of professional medical services) or goods supplied to such facility or provider; and such requirements shall provide for the definition, disclosure, and, to the maximum extent consistent with effective administration, prevention of potential or actual financial or professional conflicts of interest with respect to decisions concerning the appropriateness, nature, or site of patient care.

(2) The network organizations of each network shall be responsible, in addition to such other duties and functions as may be prescribed by the Secretary, for—

(A) encouraging, consistent with sound medical practice, the use of those treatment settings most compatible with the successful rehabilitation of the patient and the participation of patients, providers of services, and renal disease facilities in vocational rehabilitation programs;

(B) developing criteria and standards relating to the quality and appropriateness of patient care and with respect to working with patients, facilities, and providers in encouraging participation in vocational rehabilitation programs; and network goals with respect to the placement of patients in self-care settings and undergoing or preparing for transplantation;

(C) evaluating the procedure by which facilities and providers in the network assess the appropriateness of patients for proposed treatment modalities;

(D) implementing a procedure for evaluating and resolving patient grievances;

(E) conducting on-site reviews of facilities and providers as necessary (as determined by a medical review board or the Secretary), utilizing standards of care established by the network organization to assure proper medical care;

(F) collecting, validating, and analyzing such data as are necessary to prepare the reports required by subparagraph (H) and to assure the maintenance of the registry established under paragraph (7);

(G) identifying facilities and providers that are not cooperating toward meeting network goals and assisting such facilities and providers in developing appropriate plans for correction and reporting to

701

the Secretary on facilities and providers that are not providing appropriate medical care; and

(H) submitting an annual report to the Secretary on July 1 of each year which shall include a full statement of the network's goals, data on the network's performance in meeting its goals (including data on the comparative performance of facilities and providers with respect to the identification and placement of suitable candidates in self-care settings and transplantation and encouraging participation in vocational rehabilitation programs), identification of those facilities that have consistently failed to cooperate with network goals, and recommendations with respect to the need for additional or alternative services or facilities in the network in order to meet the network goals, including self-dialysis training, transplantation, and organ procurement facilities.

(3) Where the Secretary determines, on the basis of the data contained in the network's annual report and such other relevant data as may be available to him, that a facility or provider has consistently failed to cooperate with network plans and goals or to follow the recommendations of the medical review board, he may terminate or withhold certification of such facility or provider (for purposes of payment for services furnished to individuals with end stage renal disease) until he determines that such provider or facility is making reasonable and appropriate efforts to cooperate with the network's plans and goals. If the Secretary determines that the facility's or provider's failure to cooperate with network plans and goals does not jeopardize patient health or safety or justify termination of certification, he may instead, after reasonable notice to the provider or facility and to the public, impose such other sanctions as he determines to be appropriate, which sanctions may include denial of reimbursement with respect to some or all patients admitted to the facility after the date of notice to the facility or provider, and graduated reduction in reimbursement for all patients.

(4) The Secretary shall, in determining whether to certify additional facilities or expansion of existing facilities within a network, take into account the network's goals and performance as reflected in the network's annual report.

(5) The Secretary, after consultation with appropriate professional and planning organizations, shall provide such guidelines with respect to the planning and delivery of renal disease services as are necessary to assist network organizations in their development of their respective networks' goals to promote the optimum use of self-dialysis and transplantation by suitable candidates for such modalities.

(6) It is the intent of the Congress that the maximum practical number of patients who are medically, socially, and psychologically suitable candidates for home dialysis or transplantation should be so treated and that the maximum practical number of patients who are suitable candidates for vocational rehabilitation services be given access to such services and encouraged to return to gainful employment. The Secretary shall consult with appropriate professional and network organizations and consider available evidence relating to developments in research, treatment methods, and technology for home dialysis and transplantation.

(7) The Secretary shall establish a national end stage renal disease registry the purpose of which shall be to assemble and analyze the data reported by network organizations, transplant centers, and other sources on all end stage renal disease patients in a manner that will permit—

(A) the preparation of the annual report to the Congress required under subsection (g) of this section;

(B) an identification of the economic impact, cost-effectiveness, and medical efficacy of alternative modalities of treatment;

(C) an evaluation with respect to the most appropriate allocation of resources for the treatment and research into the cause of end stage renal disease;

(D) the determination of patient mortality and morbidity rates, and trends in such rates, and other indices of quality of care; and

(E) such other analyses relating to the treatment and management of end stage renal disease as will assist the Congress in evaluating the end stage renal disease program under this section.

The Secretary shall provide for such coordination of data collection activities, and such consolidation of existing end stage renal disease data systems, as is necessary to achieve the purpose of such registry, shall determine the appropriate location of the registry, and shall provide for the appointment of a professional advisory group to assist the Secretary in the formulation of policies and procedures relevant to the management of such registry.

(8) The provisions of sections 1320c–6 and 1320c–9 of this title shall apply with respect to network administrative organizations (including such organizations as medical review boards) with which the Secretary has entered into agreements under this subsection.

(d) Donors of kidney for transplant surgery

Notwithstanding any provision to the contrary in section 426 of this title any individual who donates a kidney for transplant surgery shall be entitled to benefits under parts A and B of this subchapter with respect to such donation. Reimbursement for the reasonable expenses incurred by such an individual with respect to a kidney donation shall be made (without regard to the deductible, premium, and coinsurance provisions of this subchapter), in such manner as may be prescribed by the Secretary in regulations, for all reasonable preparatory, operation, and postoperation recovery expenses associated with such donation, including but not limited to the expenses for which payment could be made if he were an eligible individual for purposes of parts

A and B of this subchapter without regard to this subsection. Payments for postoperation recovery expenses shall be limited to the actual period of recovery.

(e) Reimbursement of providers, facilities, and nonprofit entities for costs of artificial kidney and automated dialysis peritoneal machines for home dialysis

(1) Notwithstanding any other provision of this subchapter, the Secretary may, pursuant to agreements with approved providers of services, renal dialysis facilities, and nonprofit entities which the Secretary finds can furnish equipment economically and efficiently, reimburse such providers, facilities, and nonprofit entities (without regard to the deductible and coinsurance provisions of this subchapter) for the reasonable cost of the purchase, installation, maintenance and reconditioning for subsequent use of artificial kidney and automated dialysis peritoneal machines (including supportive equipment) which are to be used exclusively by entitled individuals dialyzing at home.

(2) An agreement under this subsection shall require that the provider, facility, or other entity will—

(A) make the equipment available for use only by entitled individuals dialyzing at home;

(B) recondition the equipment, as needed, for reuse by such individuals throughout the useful life of the equipment, including modification of the equipment consistent with advances in research and technology;

(C) provide for full access for the Secretary to all records and information relating to the purchase, maintenance, and use of the equipment; and

(D) submit such reports, data, and information as the Secretary may require with respect to the cost, management, and use of the equipment.

(3) For purposes of this section, the term "supportive equipment" includes blood pumps, heparin pumps, bubble detectors, other alarm systems, and such other items as the Secretary may determine are medically necessary.

(f) Experiments, studies, and pilot projects

(1) The Secretary shall initiate and carry out, at selected locations in the United States, pilot projects under which financial assistance in the purchase of new or used durable medical equipment for renal dialysis is provided to individuals suffering from end stage renal disease at the time home dialysis is begun, with provision for a trial period to assure successful adaptation to home dialysis before the actual purchase of such equipment.

(2) The Secretary shall conduct experiments to evaluate methods for reducing the costs of the end stage renal disease program. Such experiments shall include (without being limited to) reimbursement for nurses and dialysis technicians to assist with home dialysis, and reimbursement to family members assisting with home dialysis.

(3) The Secretary shall conduct experiments to evaluate methods of dietary control for reducing the costs of the end stage renal disease program, including (without being limited to) the use of protein-controlled products to delay the necessity for, or reduce the frequency of, dialysis in the treatment of end stage renal disease.

(4) The Secretary shall conduct a comprehensive study of methods for increasing public participation in kidney donation and other organ donation programs.

(5) The Secretary shall conduct a full and complete study of the reimbursement of physicians for services furnished to patients with end stage renal disease under this subchapter, giving particular attention to the range of payments to physicians for such services, the average amounts of such payments, and the number of hours devoted to furnishing such services to patients at home, in renal disease facilities, in hospitals, and elsewhere.

(6) The Secretary shall conduct a study of the number of patients with end stage renal disease who are not eligible for benefits with respect to such disease under this subchapter (by reason of this section or otherwise), and of the economic impact of such noneligibility of such individuals. Such study shall include consideration of mechanisms whereby governmental and other health plans might be instituted or modified to permit the purchase of actuarially sound coverage for the costs of end stage renal disease.

(7)(A) The Secretary shall establish protocols on standards and conditions for the reuse of dialyzer filters for those facilities and providers which voluntarily elect to reuse such filters.

(B) With respect to dialysis services furnished on or after January 1, 1988 (or July 1, 1988, with respect to protocols that relate to the reuse of bloodlines), no dialysis facility may reuse dialysis supplies (other than dialyzer filters) unless the Secretary has established a protocol with respect to the reuse of such supplies and the facility follows the protocol so established.

(C) The Secretary shall incorporate protocols established under this paragraph, and the requirement of subparagraph (B), into the requirements for facilities prescribed under subsection (b)(1)(A) of this section and failure to follow such a protocol or requirement subjects such a facility to denial of participation in the program established under this section and to denial of payment for dialysis treatment not furnished in compliance with such a protocol or in violation of such requirement.

705

(8) The Secretary shall submit to the Congress no later than October 1, 1979, a full report on the experiments conducted under paragraphs (1), (2), (3), and (7), and the studies under paragraphs (4), (5), (6), and (7). Such report shall include any recommendations for legislative changes which the Secretary finds necessary or desirable as a result of such experiments and studies.

(g) Conditional approval of dialysis facilities; restriction-of-payments notice to public and facility; notice and hearing; judicial review

(1) In any case where the Secretary—

(A) finds that a renal dialysis facility is not in substantial compliance with requirements for such facilities prescribed under subsection (b)(1)(A) of this section,

(B) finds that the facility's deficiencies do not immediately jeopardize the health and safety of patients, and

(C) has given the facility a reasonable opportunity to correct its deficiencies,

the Secretary may, in lieu of terminating approval of the facility, determine that payment under this subchapter shall be made to the facility only for services furnished to individuals who were patients of the facility before the effective date of the notice.

(2) The Secretary's decision to restrict payments under this subsection shall be made effective only after such notice to the public and to the facility as may be prescribed in regulations, and shall remain in effect until (A) the Secretary finds that the facility is in substantial compliance with the requirements under subsection (b)(1)(A) of this section, or (B) the Secretary terminates the agreement under this subchapter with the facility.

(3) A facility dissatisfied with a determination by the Secretary under paragraph (1) shall be entitled to a hearing thereon by the Secretary (after reasonable notice) to the same extent as is provided in section 405(b) of this title, and to judicial review of the Secretary's final decision after such hearing as is provided in section 405(g) of this title, except that, in so applying such sections and in applying section 405(*l*) of this title thereto, any reference therein to the Commissioner of Social Security or the Social Security Administration shall be considered a reference to the Secretary or the Department of Health and Human Services, respectively.

§ 1395ww. Payments to hospitals for inpatient hospital services

(a) Determination of costs for inpatient hospital services; limitations; exemptions; "operating costs of inpatient hospital services" defined

(1)(A)(i) The Secretary, in determining the amount of the payments that may be made under this subchapter with respect to operating costs of inpatient hospital services (as defined in paragraph (4)) shall not recognize as reasonable (in the efficient delivery of health services) costs for the provision of such services by a hospital for a cost reporting period to the extent such costs exceed the applicable percentage (as determined under clause (ii)) of the average of such costs for all hospitals in the same grouping as such hospital for comparable time periods.

(ii) For purposes of clause (i), the applicable percentage for hospital cost reporting periods beginning—

(I) on or after October 1, 1982, and before October 1, 1983, is 120 percent;

(II) on or after October 1, 1983, and before October 1, 1984, is 115 percent; and

(III) on or after October 1, 1984, is 110 percent.

(B)(i) For purposes of subparagraph (A) the Secretary shall establish case mix indexes for all short-term hospitals, and shall set limits for each hospital based upon the general mix of types of medical cases with respect to which such hospital provides services for which payment may be made under this subchapter.

(ii) The Secretary shall set such limits for a cost reporting period of a hospital—

(I) by updating available data for a previous period to the immediate preceding cost reporting period by the estimated average rate of change of hospital costs industry-wide, and

(II) by projecting for the cost reporting period by the applicable percentage increase (as defined in subsection (b)(3)(B) of this section).

(C) The limitation established under subparagraph (A) for any hospital shall in no event be lower than the allowable operating costs of inpatient hospital services (as defined in paragraph (4)) recognized under this subchapter for such hospital for such hospital's last cost reporting period prior to the hospital's first cost reporting period for which this section is in effect.

(D) Subparagraph (A) shall not apply to cost reporting periods beginning on or after October 1, 1983.

(2) The Secretary shall provide for such exemptions from, and exceptions and adjustments to, the limitation established under paragraph (1)(A) as he deems appropriate, including those which he deems necessary to take into account—

(A) the special needs of sole community hospitals, of new hospitals, of risk based health maintenance organizations, and of hospitals

707

which provide atypical services or essential community services, and to take into account extraordinary circumstances beyond the hospital's control, medical and paramedical education costs, significantly fluctuating population in the service area of the hospital, and unusual labor costs,

(B) the special needs of psychiatric hospitals and of public or other hospitals that serve a significantly disproportionate number of patients who have low income or are entitled to benefits under part A of this subchapter, and

(C) a decrease in the inpatient hospital services that a hospital provides and that are customarily provided directly by similar hospitals which results in a significant distortion in the operating costs of inpatient hospital services.

(3) The limitation established under paragraph (1)(A) shall not apply with respect to any hospital which—

(A) is located outside of a standard metropolitan statistical area, and

(B)(i) has less than 50 beds, and

(ii) was in operation and had less than 50 beds on September 3, 1982.

(4) For purposes of this section, the term "operating costs of inpatient hospital services" includes all routine operating costs, ancillary service operating costs, and special care unit operating costs with respect to inpatient hospital services as such costs are determined on an average per admission or per discharge basis (as determined by the Secretary), and includes the costs of all services for which payment may be made under this subchapter that are provided by the hospital (or by an entity wholly owned or operated by the hospital) to the patient during the 3 days (or, in the case of a hospital that is not a subsection (d) hospital, during the 1 day) immediately preceding the date of the patient's admission if such services are diagnostic services (including clinical diagnostic laboratory tests) or are other services related to the admission (as defined by the Secretary). Such term does not include costs of approved educational activities, a return on equity capital, or, other capital-related costs (as defined by the Secretary for periods before October 1, 1987), or costs with respect to administering blood clotting factors to individuals with hemophilia.

(b) Computation of payment; definitions; exemptions; adjustments

(1) Notwithstanding section 1395f(b) of this title but subject to the provisions of section 1395e of this title, if the operating costs of inpatient hospital services (as defined in subsection (a)(4) of this section) of a hospital (other than a subsection (d) hospital, as defined in subsection (d)(1)(B) of this section and other than a rehabilitation facility described in subsection (j)(i) of this section) for a cost reporting period subject to this paragraph—

(A) are less than or equal to the target amount (as defined in paragraph (3)) for that hospital for that period, the amount of the payment with respect to such operating costs payable under part A of this subchapter on a per discharge or per admission basis (as the case may be) shall be equal to the amount of such operating costs, plus—

(i) 15 percent of the amount by which the target amount exceeds the amount of the operating costs, or

(ii) 2 percent of the target amount,

whichever is less;

(B) are greater than the target amount but do not exceed 110 percent of the target amount, the amount of the payment with respect to those operating costs payable under part A on a per discharge basis shall equal the target amount; or

(C) are greater than 110 percent of the target amount, the amount of the payment with respect to such operating costs payable under part A of this subchapter on a per discharge or per admission basis (as the case may be) shall be equal to (i) the target amount, plus (ii) in the case of cost reporting periods beginning on or after October 1, 1991, an additional amount equal to 50 percent of the amount by which the operating costs exceed 110 percent of the target amount (except that such additional amount may not exceed 10 percent of the target amount) after any exceptions or adjustments are made to such target amount for the cost reporting period;

plus the amount, if any, provided under paragraph (2), except that in no case may the amount payable under this subchapter (other than on the basis of a DRG prospective payment rate determined under subsection (d) of this section) with respect to operating costs of inpatient hospital services exceed the maximum amount payable with respect to such costs pursuant to subsection (a) of this section.

(2)(A) Except as provided in subparagraph (E), in addition to the payment computed under paragraph (1), in the case of an eligible hospital (described in subparagraph (B)), for a cost reporting period beginning on or after October 1, 1997, the amount of payment on a per discharge basis under paragraph (1) shall be increased by the lesser of—

(i) 50 percent of the amount by which the operating costs are less than the expected costs (as defined in subparagraph (D)) for the period; or

(ii) 1 percent of the target amount for the period.

(B) For purposes of this paragraph, an "eligible hospital" means with respect to a cost reporting period, a hospital—

(i) that has received payments under this subsection for at least 3 full cost reporting periods before that cost reporting period, and

(ii) whose operating costs for the period are less than the least of its target amount, its trended costs (as defined in subparagraph (C)), or its expected costs (as defined in subparagraph (D)) for the period.

(C) For purposes of subparagraph (B)(ii), the term "trended costs" means for a hospital cost reporting period ending in a fiscal year—

(i) in the case of a hospital for which its cost reporting period ending in fiscal year 1996 was its third or subsequent full cost reporting period for which it receives payments under this subsection, the lesser of the operating costs or target amount for that hospital for its cost reporting period ending in fiscal year 1996, or

(ii) in the case of any other hospital, the operating costs for that hospital for its third full cost reporting period for which it receives payments under this subsection,

increased (in a compounded manner) for each succeeding fiscal year (through the fiscal year involved) by the market basket percentage increase for the fiscal year.

(D) For purposes of this paragraph, the term "expected costs", with respect to the cost reporting period ending in a fiscal year, means the lesser of the operating costs of inpatient hospital services or target amount per discharge for the previous cost reporting period updated by the market basket percentage increase (as defined in paragraph (3)(B)(iii)) for the fiscal year.

(E)(i) In the case of an eligible hospital that is a hospital or unit that is within a class of hospital described in clause (ii) with a 12–month cost reporting period beginning before the enactment of this subparagraph, in determining the amount of the increase under subparagraph (A), the Secretary shall substitute for the percentage of the target amount applicable under subparagraph (A)(ii)—

(I) for a cost reporting period beginning on or after October 1, 2000, and before September 30, 2001, 1.5 percent; and

(II) for a cost reporting period beginning on or after October 1, 2001, and before September 30, 2002, 2 percent.

(ii) For purposes of clause (i), each of the following shall be treated as a separate class of hospital:

(I) Hospitals described in clause (i) of subsection (d)(1)(B) and psychiatric units described in the matter following clause (v) of such subsection.

(II) Hospitals described in clause (iv) of such subsection.

(3)(A) Except as provided in subparagraph (C) and succeeding subparagraphs, and in paragraph (7)(A)(ii), for purposes of this subsection, the term "target amount" means, with respect to a hospital for a particular 12–month cost reporting period—

(i) in the case of the first such reporting period for which this subsection is in effect, the allowable operating costs of inpatient hospital services (as defined in subsection (a)(4) of this section) recognized under this subchapter for such hospital for the preceding 12–month cost reporting period, and

(ii) in the case of a later reporting period, the target amount for the preceding 12–month cost reporting period,

increased by the applicable percentage increase under subparagraph (B) for that particular cost reporting period.

(B)(i) For purposes of subsection (d) of this section and subsection (j) of this section for discharges occurring during a fiscal year, the "applicable percentage increase" shall be—

(I) for fiscal year 1986, 1/2 percent,

(II) for fiscal year 1987, 1.15 percent,

(III) for fiscal year 1988, 3.0 percent for hospitals located in a rural area, 1.5 percent for hospitals located in a large urban area (as defined in subsection (d)(2)(D) of this section), and 1.0 percent for hospitals located in other urban areas,

(IV) for fiscal year 1989, the market basket percentage increase minus 1.5 percentage points for hospitals located in a rural area, the market basket percentage increase minus 2.0 percentage points for hospitals located in a large urban area, and the market basket percentage increase minus 2.5 percentage points for hospitals located in other urban areas,

(V) for fiscal year 1990, the market basket percentage increase plus 4.22 percentage points for hospitals located in a rural area, the market basket percentage increase plus 0.12 percentage points for hospitals located in a large urban area, and the market basket percentage increase minus 0.53 percentage points for hospitals located in other urban areas,

(VI) for fiscal year 1991, the market basket percentage increase minus 2.0 percentage points for hospitals in a large urban or other urban area, and the market basket percentage increase minus 0.7 percentage point for hospitals located in a rural area,

(VII) for fiscal year 1992, the market basket percentage increase minus 1.6 percentage points for hospitals in a large urban or other urban area, and the market basket percentage increase minus 0.6 percentage point for hospitals located in a rural area,

(VIII) for fiscal year 1993, the market basket percentage increase minus 1.55 percentage point for hospitals in a large urban or other urban area, and the market basket percentage increase minus 0.55 for hospitals located in a rural area,

(IX) for fiscal year 1994, the market basket percentage increase minus 2.5 percentage points for hospitals located in a large urban or other urban area, and the market basket percentage increase minus 1.0 percentage point for hospitals located in a rural area,

(X) for fiscal year 1995, the market basket percentage increase minus 2.5 percentage points for hospitals located in a large urban or other urban area, and such percentage increase for hospitals located in a rural area as will provide for the average standardized amount determined under subsection (d)(3)(A) of this section for hospitals located in a rural area being equal to such average standardized amount for hospitals located in an urban area (other than a large urban area),

(XI) for fiscal year 1996, the market basket percentage increase minus 2.0 percentage points for hospitals in all areas,

(XII) for fiscal year 1997, the market basket percentage increase minus 0.5 percentage point for hospitals in all areas,

(XIII) for fiscal year 1998, 0 percent,

(XIV) for fiscal year 1999, the market basket percentage increase minus 1.9 percentage points for hospitals in all areas,

(XV) for fiscal year 2000, the market basket percentage increase minus 1.8 percentage points for hospitals in all areas,

(XVI) for fiscal year 2001, the market basket percentage increase for hospitals in all areas,

712

(XVII) for fiscal year 2002, the market basket percentage increase minus 0.55 percentage points for hospitals in all areas,

(XVIII) for fiscal year 2003, the market basket percentage increase minus 0.55 percentage points for hospitals in all areas, and

(XIX) for fiscal year 2004 and each subsequent fiscal year, the market basket percentage increase for hospitals in all areas.

(ii) For purposes of subparagraphs (A) and (E), the "applicable percentage increase" for 12-month cost reporting periods beginning during—

(I) fiscal year 1986, is 0.5 percent,

(II) fiscal year 1987, is 1.15 percent,

(III) fiscal year 1988, is the market basket percentage increase minus 2.0 percentage points,

(IV) a subsequent fiscal year ending on or before September 30, 1993, is the market basket percentage increase,

(V) fiscal years 1994 through 1997, is the market basket percentage increase minus the applicable reduction (as defined in clause (v)(II)), or in the case of a hospital for a fiscal year for which the hospital's update adjustment percentage (as defined in clause (v)(I)) is at least 10 percent, the market basket percentage increase,

(VI) for fiscal year 1998, is 0 percent,

(VII) for fiscal years 1999 through 2002, is the applicable update factor specified under clause (vi) for the fiscal year, and

(VIII) subsequent fiscal years is the market basket percentage increase.

(iii) For purposes of this subparagraph, the term "market basket percentage increase" means, with respect to cost reporting periods and discharges occurring in a fiscal year, the percentage, estimated by the Secretary before the beginning of the period or fiscal year, by which the cost of the mix of goods and services (including personnel costs but excluding nonoperating costs) comprising routine, ancillary, and special care unit inpatient hospital services, based on an index of appropriately weighted indicators of changes in wages and prices which are representative of the mix of goods and services included in such inpatient hospital services, for the period or fiscal year will exceed the cost of such mix of goods and services for the preceding 12-month cost reporting period or fiscal year.

713

(iv) For purposes of subparagraphs (C) and (D), the "applicable percentage increase" is—

(I) for 12–month cost reporting periods beginning during fiscal years 1986 through 1993, the applicable percentage increase specified in clause (ii),

(II) for fiscal year 1994, the market basket percentage increase minus 2.3 percentage points (adjusted to exclude any portion of a cost reporting period beginning during fiscal year 1993 for which the applicable percentage increase is determined under subparagraph (I)),

(III) for fiscal year 1995, the market basket percentage increase minus 2.2 percentage points, and

(IV) for fiscal year 1996 and each subsequent fiscal year, the applicable percentage increase under clause (i).

(v) For purposes of clause (ii)(V)—

(I) a hospital's "update adjustment percentage" for a fiscal year is the percentage by which the hospital's allowable operating costs of inpatient hospital services recognized under this subchapter for the cost reporting period beginning in fiscal year 1990 exceeds the hospital's target amount (as determined under subparagraph (A)) for such cost reporting period, increased for each fiscal year (beginning with fiscal year 1994) by the sum of any of the hospital's applicable reductions under subclause (V) for previous fiscal years; and

(II) the "applicable reduction" with respect to a hospital for a fiscal year is the lesser of 1 percentage point or the percentage point difference between 10 percent and the hospital's update adjustment percentage for the fiscal year.

(vi) For purposes of clause (ii)(VII) for a fiscal year, if a hospital's allowable operating costs of inpatient hospital services recognized under this subchapter for the most recent cost reporting period for which information is available—

(I) is equal to, or exceeds, 110 percent of the hospital's target amount (as determined under subparagraph (A)) for such cost reporting period, the applicable update factor specified under this clause is the market basket percentage;

(II) exceeds 100 percent, but is less than 110 percent, of such target amount for the hospital, the applicable update factor specified under this clause is 0 percent or, if greater, the market basket percentage minus 0.25 percentage points for each percentage point by which such allowable operating costs (expressed as a percentage of such target amount) is less than 110 percent of such target amount;

(III) is equal to, or less than 100 percent, but exceeds 2/3 of such target amount for the hospital, the applicable update factor specified under this clause is 0 percent or, if greater, the market basket percentage minus 2.5 percentage points; or

(IV) does not exceed 2/3 of such target amount for the hospital, the applicable update factor specified under this clause is 0 percent.

(C) In the case of a hospital that is a sole community hospital (as defined in subsection (d)(5)(D)(iii) of this section) subject to subparagraph (I), the term "target amount" means—

(i) with respect to the first 12–month cost reporting period in which this subparagraph is applied to the hospital—

(I) the allowable operating costs of inpatient hospital services (as defined in subsection (a)(4) of this section) recognized under this subchapter for the hospital for the 12–month cost reporting period (in this subparagraph referred to as the "base cost reporting period") preceding the first cost reporting period for which this subsection was in effect with respect to such hospital, increased (in a compounded manner) by—

(II) the applicable percentage increases applied to such hospital under this paragraph for cost reporting periods after the base cost reporting period and up to and including such first 12–month cost reporting period,

(ii) with respect to a later cost reporting period beginning before fiscal year 1994, the target amount for the preceding 12–month cost reporting period, increased by the applicable percentage increase under subparagraph (B)(iv) for discharges occurring in the fiscal year in which that later cost reporting period begins,

(iii) with respect to discharges occurring in fiscal year 1994, the target amount for the cost reporting period beginning in fiscal year 1993 increased by the applicable percentage increase under subparagraph (B)(iv), or

(iv) with respect to discharges occurring in fiscal year 1995 and each subsequent fiscal year, the target amount for the preceding year increased by the applicable percentage increase under subparagraph (B)(iv).

There shall be substituted for the base cost reporting period described in clause (i) a hospital's cost reporting period (if any) beginning during fiscal year 1987 if such substitution results in an increase in the target amount for the hospital.

(D) For cost reporting periods ending on or before September 30, 1994, and for discharges beginning on or after October 1, 1997,

715

and before October 1, 2006, in the case of a hospital that is a medicare-dependent, small rural hospital (as defined in subsection (d)(5)(G) of this section), the term "target amount" means—

> (i) with respect to the first 12–month cost reporting period in which this subparagraph is applied to the hospital—

>> (I) the allowable operating costs of inpatient hospital services (as defined in subsection (a)(4) of this section) recognized under this subchapter for the hospital for the 12–month cost reporting period (in this subparagraph referred to as the "base cost reporting period") preceding the first cost reporting period for which this subsection was in effect with respect to such hospital, increased (in a compounded manner) by—

>> (II) the applicable percentage increases applied to such hospital under this paragraph for cost reporting periods after the base cost reporting period and up to and including such first 12–month cost reporting period, or

> (ii) with respect to a later cost reporting period beginning before fiscal year 1994, the target amount for the preceding 12–month cost reporting period, increased by the applicable percentage increase under subparagraph (B)(iv) for discharges occurring in the fiscal year in which that later cost reporting period begins,

> (iii) with respect to discharges occurring in fiscal year 1994, the target amount for the cost reporting period beginning in fiscal year 1993 increased by the applicable percentage increase under subparagraph (B)(iv), and

> (iv) with respect to discharges occurring during fiscal year 1998 through fiscal year 2005, the target amount for the preceding year increased by the applicable percentage increase under subparagraph (B)(iv).

There shall be substituted for the base cost reporting period described in clause (i) a hospital's cost reporting period (if any) beginning during fiscal year 1987 if such substitution results in an increase in the target amount for the hospital.

> (E) In the case of a hospital described in clause (v) of subsection (d)(1)(B) of this section, the term "target amount" means—

>> (i) with respect to the first 12–month cost reporting period in which this subparagraph is applied to the hospital—

>>> (I) the allowable operating costs of inpatient hospital services (as defined in subsection (a)(4) of this section) recognized under this subchapter for the hospital for the 12–month cost reporting period (in this subparagraph referred to as the "base cost reporting period") preceding the first cost reporting period for which this subsection was in effect

with respect to such hospital, increased (in a compounded manner) by—

(II) the sum of the applicable percentage increases applied to such hospital under this paragraph for cost reporting periods after the base cost reporting period and up to and including such first 12–month cost reporting period, or

(ii) with respect to a later cost reporting period, the target amount for the preceding 12–month cost reporting period, increased by the applicable percentage increase under subparagraph (B)(ii) for that later cost reporting period.

There shall be substituted for the base cost reporting period described in clause (i) a hospital's cost reporting period (if any) beginning during fiscal year 1987 if such substitution results in an increase in the target amount for the hospital.

(F)(i) In the case of a hospital (or unit described in the matter following clause (v) of subsection (d)(1)(B) of this section) that received payment under this subsection for inpatient hospital services furnished during cost reporting periods beginning before October 1, 1990, that is within a class of hospital described in clause (iii), and that elects (in a form and manner determined by the Secretary) this subparagraph to apply to the hospital, the target amount for the hospital's 12–month cost reporting period beginning during fiscal year 1998 is equal to the average described in clause (ii).

(ii) The average described in this clause for a hospital or unit shall be determined by the Secretary as follows:

(I) The Secretary shall determine the allowable operating costs for inpatient hospital services for the hospital or unit for each of the 5 cost reporting periods for which the Secretary has the most recent settled cost reports as of August 5, 1997.

(II) The Secretary shall increase the amount determined under subclause (I) for each cost reporting period by the applicable percentage increase under subparagraph (B)(ii) for each subsequent cost reporting period up to the cost reporting period described in clause (i).

(III) The Secretary shall identify among such 5 cost reporting periods the cost reporting periods for which the amount determined under subclause (II) is the highest, and the lowest.

(IV) The Secretary shall compute the averages of the amounts determined under subclause (II) for the 3 cost reporting periods not identified under subclause (III).

(iii) For purposes of this subparagraph, each of the following shall be treated as a separate class of hospital:

(I) Hospitals described in clause (i) of subsection (d)(1)(B) of this section and psychiatric units described in the matter following clause (v) of such subsection.

(II) Hospitals described in clause (ii) of such subsection and rehabilitation units described in the matter following clause (v) of such subsection.

(III) Hospitals described in clause (iii) of such subsection.

(IV) Hospitals described in clause (iv) of such subsection.

(V) Hospitals described in clause (v) of such subsection.

(G)(i) In the case of a qualified long-term care hospital (as defined in clause (ii)) that elects (in a form and manner determined by the Secretary) this subparagraph to apply to the hospital, the target amount for the hospital's 12–month cost reporting period beginning during fiscal year 1998 is equal to the allowable operating costs of inpatient hospital services (as defined in subsection (a)(4) of this section) recognized under this title for the hospital for the 12–month cost reporting period beginning during fiscal year 1996, increased by the applicable percentage increase for the cost reporting period beginning during fiscal year 1997.

(ii) In clause (i), a "qualified long-term care hospital" means, with respect to a cost reporting period, a hospital described in clause (iv) of subsection (d)(1)(B) of this section during each of the 2 cost reporting periods for which the Secretary has the most recent settled cost reports as of August 5, 1997—

(I) the hospital's allowable operating costs of inpatient hospital services recognized under this subchapter exceeded 115 percent of the hospital's target amount, and

(II) the hospital would have a disproportionate patient percentage of at least 70 percent (as determined by the Secretary under subsection (d)(5)(F)(vi) of this section) if the hospital were a subsection (d) hospital.

(H)(i) In the case of a hospital or unit that is within a class of hospital described in clause (iv), for a cost reporting period beginning during fiscal years 1998 through 2002, the target amount for such a hospital or unit may not exceed the amount as updated up to or for such cost reporting period under clause (ii).

(ii)(I) In the case of a hospital or unit that is within a class of hospital described in clause (iv), the Secretary shall estimate the 75th percentile of the target amounts for such hospitals within such class for cost reporting periods ending during fiscal year 1996, as adjusted under clause (iii).

718

(II) The Secretary shall update the amount determined under subclause (I), for each cost reporting period after the cost reporting period described in such subclause and up to the first cost reporting period beginning on or after October 1, 1997, by a factor equal to the market basket percentage increase.

(III) For cost reporting periods beginning during each of fiscal years 1999 through 2002, subject to subparagraph (J), the Secretary shall update such amount by a factor equal to the market basket percentage increase.

(iii) In applying clause (ii)(I) in the case of a hospital or unit, the Secretary shall provide for an appropriate adjustment to the labor-related portion of the amount determined under such subparagraph to take into account differences between average wage-related costs in the area of the hospital and the national average of such costs within the same class of hospital.

(iv) For purposes of this subparagraph, each of the following shall be treated as a separate class of hospital:

(I) Hospitals described in clause (i) of subsection (d)(1)(B) of this section and psychiatric units described in the matter following clause (v) of such subsection.

(II) Hospitals described in clause (ii) of such subsection and rehabilitation units described in the matter following clause (v) of such subsection.

(III) Hospitals described in clause (iv) of such subsection.

(I)(i) For cost reporting periods beginning on or after october 1, 2000, in the case of a sole community hospital there shall be substituted for the amount otherwise determined under subsection (d)(5)(D)(i), if such substitution results in a greater amount of payment under this section for the hospital—

(I) with respect to discharges occurring in fiscal year 2001, 75 percent of the the amount otherwise applicable to the hospital under subsection (d)(5)(D)(i) (referred to in this clause as the "subsection (d)(5)(D)(i) amount") and 25 percent of the rebased target amount (as defined in clause (ii));

(II) with respect to discharges occurring in fiscal year 2002, 50 percent of the subsection (d)(5)(D)(i) amount and 50 percent of the rebased target amount;

(III) with respect to discharges occurring in fiscal year 2003, 25 percent of the subsection (d)(5)(D)(i) amount and 75 percent of the rebased target amount; and

719

(IV) with respect to discharges occurring after fiscal year 2003, 100 percent of the rebased target amount.

(ii) For purposes of this subparagraph, the "rebased target amount" has the meaning given the term "target amount" in subparagraph (C) except that—

(I) there shall be substituted for the base cost reporting period the 12–month cost reporting period beginning during fiscal year 1996;

(II) any reference in subparagraph (C)(i) to the "first cost reporting period" described in such subparagraph is deemed a reference to the first cost reporting period beginning on or after October 1, 2000; and

(III) applicable increase percentage shall only be applied under subparagraph (C)(iv) for discharges occurring in fiscal years beginning with fiscal year 2002.

(J) For cost reporting periods beginning during fiscal year 2001, for a hospital described in subsection (d)(1)(b)(iv)—

(i) the limiting or cap amount otherwise determined under subparagraph (H) shall be increased by 2 percent; and

(ii) the target amount otherwise determined under subparagraph (A) shall be increased by 25 percent (subject to the limiting or cap amount determined under subparagraph (H), as increased by clause (i)).

(4)(A)(i) The Secretary shall provide for an exception and adjustment to (and in the case of a hospital described in subsection (d)(1)(B)(iii) of this section, may provide an exemption from), the method under this subsection for determining the amount of payment to a hospital where events beyond the hospital's control or extraordinary circumstances, including changes in the case mix of such hospital, create a distortion in the increase in costs for a cost reporting period (including any distortion in the costs for the base period against which such increase is measured). The Secretary may provide for such other exemptions from, and exceptions and adjustments to, such method as the Secretary deems appropriate, including the assignment of a new base period which is more representative, as determined by the Secretary, of the reasonable and necessary cost of inpatient services and including those which he deems necessary to take into account a decrease in the inpatient hospital services that a hospital provides and that are customarily provided directly by similar hospitals which results in a significant distortion in the operating costs of inpatient hospital services. The Secretary shall announce a decision on any request for an exemption, exception, or adjustment under this paragraph not later than 180 days after receiving a completed application from the intermediary for such exemption, exception, or adjustment, and shall include in such decision a detailed explanation of the grounds on which such request was approved or denied.

(ii) The payment reductions under paragraph (3)(B)(ii)(V) shall not be considered by the Secretary in making adjustments pursuant to clause (i). In making such reductions, the Secretary shall treat the applicable update factor described in paragraph (3)(B)(vi) for a fiscal year as being equal to the market basket percentage for that year.

(B) In determining under subparagraph (A) whether to assign a new base period which is more representative of the reasonable and necessary cost to a hospital of providing inpatient services, the Secretary shall take into consideration—

(i) changes in applicable technologies and medical practices, or differences in the severity of illness among patients, that increase the hospital's costs;

(ii) whether increases in wages and wage-related costs for hospitals located in the geographic area in which the hospital is located exceed the average of the increases in such costs paid by hospitals in the United States; and

(iii) such other factors as the Secretary considers appropriate in determining increases in the hospital's costs of providing inpatient services.

(C) Paragraph (1) shall not apply to payment of hospitals which is otherwise determined under paragraph (3) of section 1395f(b) of this title.

(5) In the case of any hospital having any cost reporting period of other than a 12–month period, the Secretary shall determine the 12–month period which shall be used for purposes of this section.

(6) In the case of any hospital which becomes subject to the taxes under section 3111 of Title 26, with respect to any or all of its employees, for part or all of a cost reporting period, and was not subject to such taxes with respect to any or all of its employees for all or part of the 12–month base cost reporting period referred to in subsection (b)(3)(A)(i) of this section, the Secretary shall provide for an adjustment by increasing the base period amount described in such subsection for such hospital by an amount equal to the amount of such taxes which would have been paid or accrued by such hospital for such base period if such hospital had been subject to such taxes for all of such base period with respect to all its employees, minus the amount of any such taxes actually paid or accrued for such base period.

(7)(A) Notwithstanding paragraph (1), in the case of a hospital or unit that is within a class of hospital described in subparagraph (B) which first receives payments under this section on or after October 1, 1997—

(i) for each of the first 2 cost reporting periods for which the hospital has a settled cost report, the amount of the payment with respect to operating costs described in paragraph (1) under part A on a per discharge or per admission basis (as the case may be) is equal to the lesser of—

(I) the amount of operating costs for such respective period, or

(II) 110 percent of the national median (as estimated by the Secretary) of the target amount for hospitals in the same class as the hospital for cost reporting periods ending during fiscal year 1996, updated by the hospital market basket increase percentage to the fiscal year in which the hospital first received payments under this section, as adjusted under subparagraph (C); and

(ii) for purposes of computing the target amount for the subsequent cost reporting period, the target amount for the preceding cost reporting period is equal to the amount determined under clause (i) for such preceding period.

(B) For purposes of this paragraph, each of the following shall be treated as a separate class of hospital:

(i) Hospitals described in clause (i) of subsection (d)(1)(B) of this section and psychiatric units described in the matter following clause (v) of such subsection.

(ii) Hospitals described in clause (ii) of such subsection and rehabilitation units described in the matter following clause (v) of such subsection.

(iii) Hospitals described in clause (iv) of such subsection.

(C) In applying subparagraph (A)(i)(II) in the case of a hospital or unit, the Secretary shall provide for an appropriate adjustment to the labor-related portion of the amount determined under such subparagraph to take into account differences between average wage-related costs in the area of the hospital and the national average of such costs within the same class of hospital.

(c) Payment in accordance with State hospital reimbursement control system; amount of payment; discontinuance of payments

(1) The Secretary may provide, in his discretion, that payment with respect to services provided by a hospital in a State may be made in accordance with a hospital reimbursement control system in a State, rather than in accordance with the other provisions of this title, if the chief executive officer of the State requests such treatment and if—

(A) the Secretary determines that the system, if approved under this subsection, will apply

(i) to substantially all non-Federal acute care hospitals (as defined by the Secretary) in the State and

(ii) to the review of at least 75 percent of all revenues or expenses in the State for inpatient hospital services and of revenues or expenses for inpatient hospital services provided under the State's plan approved under subchapter XIX of this chapter;

(B) the Secretary has been provided satisfactory assurances as to the equitable treatment under the system of all entities (including Federal and State programs) that pay hospitals for inpatient hospital services, of hospital employees, and of hospital patients;

(C) the Secretary has been provided satisfactory assurances that under the system, over 36–month periods (the first such period beginning with the first month in which this subsection applies to that system in the State), the amount of payments made under this subchapter under such system will not exceed the amount of payments which would otherwise have been made under this subchapter not using such system;

(D) the Secretary determines that the system will not preclude an eligible organization (as defined in section 1395mm(b) of this title) from negotiating directly with hospitals with respect to the organization's rate of payment for inpatient hospital services; and

(E) the Secretary determines that the system requires hospitals to meet the requirement of section 1395cc(a)(1)(G) of this title and the system provides for the exclusion of certain costs in accordance with section 1395y(a)(14) of this title (except for such waivers thereof as the Secretary provides by regulation).

The Secretary cannot deny the application of a State under this subsection on the ground that the State's hospital reimbursement control system is based on a payment methodology other than on the basis of a diagnosis-related group or on the ground that the amount of payments made under this subchapter under such system must be less than the amount of payments which would otherwise have been made under this subchapter not using such system. If the Secretary determines that the conditions described in subparagraph (C) are based on maintaining payment amounts at no more than a specified percentage increase above the payment amounts in a base period, the State has the option of applying such test (for inpatient hospital services under part A of this subchapter) on an aggregate payment basis or on the basis of the amount of payment per inpatient discharge or admission. If the Secretary determines that the conditions described in subparagraph (C) are based on maintaining aggregate payment amounts below a national average percentage increase in total payments under part A of this subchapter for inpatient hospital services, the Secretary cannot deny the application of a State under this subsection on the ground that the State's rate of increase in such payments for such services must be less than such national average rate of increase.

(2) In determining under paragraph (1)(C) the amount of payment which would otherwise have been made under this subchapter for a State, the Secretary may provide for appropriate adjustment of such amount to take into account previous reductions effected in the amount of payments made under this subchapter in the State due to the operation of the hospital reimbursement control system in the State if the system has resulted in an aggregate rate of increase in operating costs of inpatient hospital services (as defined in subsection (a)(4) of this section) under this subchapter for hospitals in the State which is less than the aggregate rate of increase in such costs under this subchapter for hospitals in the United States.

(3) The Secretary shall discontinue payments under a system described in paragraph (1) if the Secretary—

(A) determines that the system no longer meets the requirements of subparagraphs (A), (D), and (E) of paragraph (1) and, if applicable, the requirements of paragraph (5), or

(B) has reason to believe that the assurances described in subparagraph (B) or (C) of paragraph (1) (or, if applicable, in paragraph (5)) are not being (or will not be) met.

(4) The Secretary shall approve the request of a State under paragraph (1) with respect to a hospital reimbursement control system if—

(A) the requirements of subparagraphs (A), (B), (C), (D), and (E) of paragraph (1) have been met with respect to the system, and

(B) with respect to that system a waiver of certain requirements of this subchapter has been approved on or before (and which is in effect as of) April 20, 1983, pursuant to section 1395b–1(a) of this title or section 222(a) of the Social Security Amendments of 1972.

With respect to a State system described in this paragraph, the Secretary shall judge the effectiveness of such system on the basis of its rate of increase or inflation in inpatient hospital payments for individuals under this subchapter, as compared to the national rate of increase or inflation for such payments, with the State retaining the option to have the test applied on the basis of the aggregate payments under the State system as compared to aggregate payments which would have been made under the national system since October 1, 1984, to the most recent date for which annual data are available.

(5) The Secretary shall approve the request of a State under paragraph (1) with respect to a hospital reimbursement control system if—

(A) the requirements of subparagraphs (A), (B), (C), (D), and (E) of paragraph (1) have been met with respect to the system;

(B) the Secretary determines that the system—

(i) is operated directly by the State or by an entity designated pursuant to State law,

(ii) provides for payment of hospitals covered under the system under a methodology (which sets forth exceptions and adjustments, as well as any method for changes in the methodology) by which rates or amounts to be paid for hospital services during a specified period are established under the system prior to the defined rate period, and

(iii) hospitals covered under the system will make such reports (in lieu of cost and other reports, identified by the Secretary, otherwise required under this subchapter) as the Secretary may require in order to properly monitor assurances provided under this subsection;

(C) the State has provided the Secretary with satisfactory assurances that operation of the system will not result in any change in hospital admission practices which result in—

(i) a significant reduction in the proportion of patients (receiving hospital services covered under the system) who have no third-party coverage and who are unable to pay for hospital services,

(ii) a significant reduction in the proportion of individuals admitted to hospitals for inpatient hospital services for which payment is (or is likely to be) less than the anticipated charges for or costs of such services,

(iii) the refusal to admit patients who would be expected to require unusually costly or prolonged treatment for reasons other than those related to the appropriateness of the care available at the hospital, or

(iv) the refusal to provide emergency services to any person who is in need of emergency services if the hospital provides such services;

(D) any change by the State in the system which has the effect of materially reducing payments to hospitals can only take effect upon 60 days notice to the Secretary and to the hospitals the payment to which is likely to be materially affected by the change; and

(E) the State has provided the Secretary with satisfactory assurances that in the development of the system the State has consulted with local governmental officials concerning the impact of the system on public hospitals.

The Secretary shall respond to requests of States under this paragraph within 60 days of the date the request is submitted to the Secretary.

(6) If the Secretary determines that the assurances described in paragraph (1)(C) have not been met with respect to any 36–month period, the Secretary may reduce payments under this subchapter to hospitals

under the system in an amount equal to the amount by which the payment under this subchapter under such system for such period exceeded the amount of payments which would otherwise have been made under this subchapter not using such system.

(7) In the case of a State which made a request under paragraph (5) before December 31, 1984, for the approval of a State hospital reimbursement control system and which request was approved—

(A) in applying paragraphs (1)(C) and (6), a reference to a "36–month period" is deemed a reference to a "48–month period", and

(B) in order to allow the State the opportunity to provide the assurances described in paragraph (1)(C) for a 48–month period, the Secretary may not discontinue payments under the system, under the authority of paragraph (3)(A) because the Secretary has reason to believe that such assurances are not being (or will not be) met, before July 1, 1986.

(d) Inpatient hospital service payments on basis of prospective rates; Medicare Geographic Classification Review Board

(1)(A) Notwithstanding section 1395f(b) of this title but subject to the provisions of section 1395e of this title, the amount of the payment with respect to the operating costs of inpatient hospital services (as defined in subsection (a)(4) of this section) of a subsection (d) hospital (as defined in subparagraph (B)) for inpatient hospital discharges in a cost reporting period or in a fiscal year—

(i) beginning on or after October 1, 1983, and before October 1, 1984, is equal to the sum of—

(I) the target percentage (as defined in subparagraph (C)) of the hospital's target amount for the cost reporting period (as defined in subsection (b)(3)(A) of this section, but determined without the application of subsection (a) of this section), and

(II) the DRG percentage (as defined in subparagraph (C)) of the regional adjusted DRG prospective payment rate determined under paragraph (2) for such discharges;

(ii) beginning on or after October 1, 1984, and before October 1, 1987, is equal to the sum of—

(I) the target percentage (as defined in subparagraph (C)) of the hospital's target amount for the cost reporting period (as defined in subsection (b)(3)(A) of this section, but determined without the application of subsection (a) of this section), and

(II) the DRG percentage (as defined in subparagraph (C)) of the applicable combined adjusted DRG prospective payment rate determined under subparagraph (D) for such discharges; or

(iii) beginning on or after April 1, 1988, is equal to—

(I) the national adjusted DRG prospective payment rate determined under paragraph (3) for such discharges, or

(II) for discharges occurring during a fiscal year ending on or before September 30, 1996, the sum of 85 percent of the national adjusted DRG prospective payment rate determined under paragraph (3) for such discharges and 15 percent of the regional adjusted DRG prospective payment rate determined under such paragraph, but only if the average standardized amount (described in clause (i)(I) or clause (ii)(I) of paragraph (3)(D)) for hospitals within the region of, and in the same large urban or other area (or, for discharges occurring during a fiscal year ending on or before September 30, 1994, the same large urban or other area) as, the hospital is greater than the average standardized amount (described in the respective clause) for hospitals within the United States in that type of area for discharges occurring during such fiscal year.

(B) As used in this section, the term "subsection (d) hospital" means a hospital located in one of the fifty States or the District of Columbia other than—

(i) a psychiatric hospital (as defined in section 1395x(f) of this title),

(ii) a rehabilitation hospital (as defined by the Secretary),

(iii) a hospital whose inpatients are predominantly individuals under 18 years of age,

(iv)(I) a hospital which has an average inpatient length of stay (as determined by the Secretary) of greater than 25 days, or

(II) a hospital that first received payment under this subsection in 1986 which has an average inpatient length of stay (as determined by the Secretary) of greater than 20 days and that has 80 percent or more of its annual medicare inpatient discharges with a principal diagnosis that reflects a finding of neoplastic disease in the 12–month cost reporting period ending in fiscal year 1997, or

(v)(I) a hospital that the Secretary has classified, at any time on or before December 31, 1990, (or, in the case of a hospital that, as of December 19, 1989, is located in a State operating a demonstration project under section 1395f(b) of this title, on or before December 31, 1991) for purposes of applying exceptions and adjustments to payment amounts under this subsection, as a hospital involved extensively in treatment for or research on cancer,

(II) a hospital that was recognized as a comprehensive cancer center or clinical cancer research center by the National Cancer Institute of the National Institutes of Health as of April 20, 1983, that is located in a State which, as of December 19, 1989, was not operating a demonstration project under section 1395f(b) of this title, that applied and was denied, on or before December 31, 1990, for classification as a hospital involved extensively in treatment for or research on cancer under this clause (as in effect on the day before August 5, 1997), that as of August 5, 1997, is licensed for less than 50 acute care beds, and that demonstrates for the 4–year period ending on December 31, 1996, that at least 50 percent of its total discharges have a principal finding of neoplastic disease, as defined in subparagraph (E), or

(III) a hospital that was recognized as a clinical cancer research center by the National Cancer Institute of the National Institutes of Health as of February 18, 1998, that has never been reimbursed for inpatient hospital services pursuant to a reimbursement system under a demonstration project under section 1395f(b) of this title, that is a freestanding facility organized primarily for treatment of and research on cancer and is not a unit of another hospital, that as of December 21, 2000, is licensed for 162 acute care beds, and that demonstrates for the 4–year period ending on June 30, 1999, that at least 50 percent of its total discharges have a principal finding of neoplastic disease, as defined in subparagraph (E);

and, in accordance with regulations of the Secretary, does not include a psychiatric or rehabilitation unit of the hospital which is a distinct part of the hospital (as defined by the Secretary). A hospital that was classified by the Secretary on or before September 30, 1995, as a hospital described in clause (iv) shall continue to be so classified notwithstanding that it is located in the same building as, or on the same campus as, another hospital.

(C) For purposes of this subsection, for cost reporting periods beginning—

(i) on or after October 1, 1983, and before October 1, 1984, the "target percentage" is 75 percent and the "DRG percentage" is 25 percent;

(ii) on or after October 1, 1984, and before October 1, 1985, the "target percentage" is 50 percent and the "DRG percentage" is 50 percent;

(iii) on or after October 1, 1985, and before October 1, 1986, the "target percentage" is 45 percent and the "DRG percentage" is 55 percent; and

(iv) on or after October 1, 1986, and before October 1, 1987, the "target percentage" is 25 percent and the "DRG percentage" is 75 percent.

(D) For purposes of subparagraph (A)(ii)(II), the "applicable combined adjusted DRG prospective payment rate" for discharges occurring—

(i) on or after October 1, 1984, and before October 1, 1986, is a combined rate consisting of 25 percent of the national adjusted DRG prospective payment rate, and 75 percent of the regional adjusted DRG prospective payment rate, determined under paragraph (3) for such discharges; and

(ii) on or after October 1, 1986, and before October 1, 1987, is a combined rate consisting of 50 percent of the national adjusted DRG prospective payment rate, and 50 percent of the regional adjusted DRG prospective payment rate, determined under paragraph (3) for such discharges.

(E) For purposes of subclauses (II) and (III) of subparagraph (B)(v) only, the term "principal finding of neoplastic disease" means the condition established after study to be chiefly responsible for occasioning the admission of a patient to a hospital, except that only discharges with ICD–9–CM principal diagnosis codes of 140 through 239, V58.0, V58.1, V66.1, V66.2, or 990 will be considered to reflect such a principal diagnosis.

(2) The Secretary shall determine a national adjusted DRG prospective payment rate, for each inpatient hospital discharge in fiscal year 1984 involving inpatient hospital services of a subsection (d) hospital in the United States, and shall determine a regional adjusted DRG prospective payment rate for such discharges in each region, for which payment may be made under part A of this subchapter. Each such rate shall be determined for hospitals located in urban or rural areas within the United States or within each such region, respectively, as follows:

(A) The Secretary shall determine the allowable operating costs per discharge of inpatient hospital services for the hospital for the most recent cost reporting period for which data are available.

(B) The Secretary shall update each amount determined under subparagraph (A) for fiscal year 1984 by—

(i) updating for fiscal year 1983 by the estimated average rate of change of hospital costs industry-wide between the cost reporting period used under such subparagraph and fiscal year 1983 and the most recent case-mix data available, and

(ii) projecting for fiscal year 1984 by the applicable percentage increase (as defined in subsection (b)(3)(B) of this section) for fiscal year 1984.

(C) The Secretary shall standardize the amount updated under subparagraph (B) for each hospital by—

(i) excluding an estimate of indirect medical education costs (taking into account, for discharges occurring after September 30, 1986, the amendments made by section 9104(a) of the Medicare and Medicaid Budget Reconciliation Amendments of 1985), except that the Secretary shall not take into account any reduction in the amount of additional payments under paragraph (5)(B)(ii) resulting from the amendment made by section 4621(a)(1) of the Balanced Budget Act of 1997, or any additional payments under such paragraph resulting from the application of section 111 of the Medicare, Medicaid, and S CHIP Balanced Budget Refinement Act of 1999 or of section 302 of the Medicare, Medicaid, and S CHIP Benefits Improvement and Protection Act of 2000.

(ii) adjusting for variations among hospitals by area in the average hospital wage level,

(iii) adjusting for variations in case mix among hospitals, and

(iv) for discharges occurring on or after October 1, 1986, excluding an estimate of the additional payments to certain hospitals to be made under paragraph (5)(F), except that the Secretary shall not exclude additional payments under such paragraph made as a result of the enactment of section 6003(c) of the Omnibus Budget Reconciliation Act of 1989, the enactment of section 4002(b) of the Omnibus Budget Reconciliation Act of 1990, or the enactment of section 303 of the Medicare, Medicaid, and S CHIP Benefits Improvement and Protection Act of 2000.

(D) The Secretary shall compute an average of the standardized amounts determined under subparagraph (C) for the United States and for each region—

(i) for all subsection (d) hospitals located in an urban area within the United States or that region, respectively, and

(ii) for all subsection (d) hospitals located in a rural area within the United States or that region, respectively.

For purposes of this subsection, the term "region" means one of the nine census divisions, comprising the fifty States and the District of Columbia, established by the Bureau of the Census for statistical and reporting purposes; the term "urban area" means an area within a Metropolitan Statistical Area (as defined by the Office of Management and Budget) or within such similar area as the Secretary has recognized under subsection (a) of this section by regulation; the term "large urban area" means, with respect to a fiscal year, such an urban area which the Secretary determines (in the publications described in subsection (e)(5) of this section before the fiscal year) has a population of more than 1,000,000 (as determined by the Secretary based on the most recent available population data published by the Bureau of the Census); and the term "rural area" means any area outside such an area or similar area. A hospital located in a Metropolitan Statistical Area shall be deemed to be located in the region in which the largest number of the hospitals in the same Metropolitan Statistical Area are located, or, at the option of the Secretary, the region in which the majority of the inpatient discharges (with respect to which payments are made under this subchapter) from hospitals in the same Metropolitan Statistical Area are made.

(E) The Secretary shall reduce each of the average standardized amounts determined under subparagraph (D) by a proportion equal to the proportion (estimated by the Secretary) of the amount of payments under this subsection based on DRG prospective payment rates which are additional payments described in paragraph (5)(A) (relating to outlier payments).

(F) The Secretary shall adjust each of such average standardized amounts as may be required under subsection (e)(1)(B) of this section for that fiscal year.

(G) For each discharge classified within a diagnosis-related group, the Secretary shall establish a national DRG prospective payment rate and shall establish a regional DRG prospective payment rate for each region, each of which is equal—

    (i) for hospitals located in an urban area in the United States or that region (respectively), to the product of—

        (I) the average standardized amount (computed under subparagraph (D), reduced under subparagraph (E), and adjusted under subparagraph (F)) for hospitals located in an urban area in the United States or that region, and

        (II) the weighting factor (determined under paragraph (4)(B)) for that diagnosis-related group; and

    (ii) for hospitals located in a rural area in the United States or that region (respectively), to the product of—

        (I) the average standardized amount (computed under subparagraph (D), reduced under subparagraph (E), and adjusted under subparagraph (F)) for hospitals located in a rural area in the United States or that region, and

        (II) the weighting factor (determined under paragraph (4)(B)) for that diagnosis-related group.

(H) The Secretary shall adjust the proportion, (as estimated by the Secretary from time to time) of hospitals' costs which are attributable to wages and wage-related costs, of the national and regional DRG prospective payment rates computed under subparagraph (G) for area differences in hospital wage levels by a factor (established by the Secretary) reflecting the relative hospital wage level in the geographic area of the hospital compared to the national average hospital wage level.

(3) The Secretary shall determine a national adjusted DRG prospective payment rate, for each inpatient hospital discharge in a fiscal year after fiscal year 1984 involving inpatient hospital services of a subsection (d) hospital in the United States, and shall determine a regional adjusted DRG prospective payment rate for such discharges in each region for which payment may be made under part A of this subchapter. Each such rate shall be determined for hospitals located in large urban, other urban, or rural areas within the United States and within each such region, respectively, as follows:

(A)(i) For discharges occurring in a fiscal year beginning before October 1, 1987, the Secretary shall compute an average standardized amount for hospitals located in an urban area and for hospitals located in a rural area within the United States and for hospitals located in an urban area and for hospitals located in a rural area within each region, equal to the respective average standardized amount computed for the previous fiscal year under paragraph (2)(D) or under this subparagraph, increased for the fiscal year involved by the applicable percentage increase under subsection (b)(3)(B) of this section. With respect to discharges occurring on or after October 1, 1987, the Secretary shall compute urban and rural averages on the basis of discharge weighting rather than hospital weighting, making appropriate adjustments to ensure that computation on such basis does not result in total payments under this section that are greater or less than the total payments that would have been made under this section but for this sentence, and making appropriate changes in the manner of determining the reductions under subparagraph (C)(ii).

(ii) For discharges occurring in a fiscal year beginning on or after October 1, 1987, and ending on or before September 30, 1994, the Secretary shall compute an average standardized amount for hospitals located in a large urban area, for hospitals located in a rural area, and for hospitals located in other urban areas, within the United States and within each region, equal to the respective average standardized amount computed for the previous fiscal year under this subparagraph increased by the applicable percentage increase under subsection (b)(3)(B)(i) of this section with respect to hospitals located in the respective areas for the fiscal year involved.

(iii) For discharges occurring in the fiscal year beginning on October 1, 1994, the average standardized amount for hospitals located in a rural area shall be equal to the average standardized amount for hospitals located in an other urban area. For discharges occurring on or after October 1, 1994, the Secretary shall adjust the ratio of the labor portion to non-labor portion of each average standardized amount to equal such ratio for the national average of all standardized amounts.

(iv) For discharges occurring in a fiscal year beginning on or after October 1, 1995, the Secretary shall compute an average standardized amount for hospitals located in a large urban area and for hospitals located in other areas within the United States and within each region equal to the respective average standardized amount computed for the previous fiscal year under this subparagraph increased by the applicable percentage increase under subsection (b)(3)(B)(i) of this section with respect to hospitals located in the respective areas for the fiscal year involved.

(v) Average standardized amounts computed under this paragraph shall be adjusted to reflect the most recent case-mix data available.

(B) The Secretary shall reduce each of the average standardized amounts determined under subparagraph (A) by a factor equal to the proportion of payments under this subsection (as estimated by the Secretary) based on DRG prospective payment amounts which are additional payments described in paragraph (5)(A) (relating to outlier payments).

(C)(i) For discharges occurring in fiscal year 1985, the Secretary shall adjust each of such average standardized amounts as may be required under subsection (e)(1)(B) of this section for that fiscal year.

(ii) For discharges occurring after September 30, 1986, the Secretary shall further reduce each of the average standardized amounts (in a proportion which takes into account the differing effects of the standardization effected under paragraph (2)(C)(i) so as to provide for a reduction in the total of the payments (attributable to this paragraph) made for discharges occurring on or after October 1, 1986, of an amount equal to the estimated reduction in the payment amounts under paragraph (5)(B) that would have resulted from the enactment of the amendments made by section 9104 of the Medicare and Medicaid Budget Reconciliation Amendments of 1985 and by section 4003(a)(1) of the Omnibus Budget Reconciliation Act of 1987 if the factor described in clause (ii)(II) of paragraph (5)(B) (determined without regard to amendments made by the Omnibus Budget Reconciliation Act of 1990) were applied for discharges occurring on or

733

after such date instead of the factor described in clause (ii) of that paragraph.

(D) For each discharge classified within a diagnosis-related group, the Secretary shall establish for the fiscal year a national DRG prospective payment rate and shall establish a regional DRG prospective payment rate for each region, each of which is equal—

(i) for hospitals located in a large urban area in the United States or that region (respectively), to the product of—

(I) the average standardized amount (computed under subparagraph (A), reduced under subparagraph (B), and adjusted or reduced under subparagraph (C)) for the fiscal year for hospitals located in such a large urban area in the United States or that region, and

(II) the weighting factor (determined under paragraph (4)(B)) for that diagnosis-related group; and

(ii) for hospitals located in other areas in the United States or that region (respectively), to the product of—

(I) the average standardized amount (computed under subparagraph (A), reduced under subparagraph (B), and adjusted or reduced under subparagraph (C)) for the fiscal year for hospitals located in other areas in the United States or that region, and

(II) the weighting factor (determined under paragraph (4)(B)) for that diagnosis-related group.

(E) The Secretary shall adjust the proportion, (as estimated by the Secretary from time to time) of hospitals' costs which are attributable to wages and wage-related costs, of the DRG prospective payment rates computed under subparagraph (D) for area differences in hospital wage levels by a factor (established by the Secretary) reflecting the relative hospital wage level in the geographic area of the hospital compared to the national average hospital wage level. Not later than October 1, 1990, and October 1, 1993 (and at least every 12 months thereafter), the Secretary shall update the factor under the preceding sentence on the basis of a survey conducted by the Secretary (and updated as appropriate) of the wages and wage-related costs of subsection (d) hospitals in the United States. Not less often than once every 3 years the Secretary (through such survey or otherwise) shall measure the earnings and paid hours of employment by occupational category and shall exclude data with respect to the wages and wage-related costs incurred in furnishing skilled nursing facility services. Any adjustments or updates made under this subparagraph for a fiscal year (beginning with fiscal year 1991) shall be made in a manner that assures that the aggregate payments under this subsection in the fiscal year are not greater or less than those that would have been made in the year without such adjustment.

(4)(A) The Secretary shall establish a classification of inpatient hospital discharges by diagnosis-related groups and a methodology for classifying specific hospital discharges within these groups.

(B) For each such diagnosis-related group the Secretary shall assign an appropriate weighting factor which reflects the relative hospital resources used with respect to discharges classified within that group compared to discharges classified within other groups.

(C)(i) The Secretary shall adjust the classifications and weighting factors established under subparagraphs (A) and (B), for discharges in fiscal year 1988 and at least annually thereafter, to reflect changes in treatment patterns, technology (including a new medical service or technology under paragraph (5)(K)), and other factors which may change the relative use of hospital resources.

(ii) For discharges in fiscal year 1990, the Secretary shall reduce the weighting factor for each diagnosis-related group by 1.22 percent.

(iii) Any such adjustment under clause (i) for discharges in a fiscal year (beginning with fiscal year 1991) shall be made in a manner that assures that the aggregate payments under this subsection for discharges in the fiscal year are not greater or less than those that would have been made for discharges in the year without such adjustment.

(iv) The Secretary shall include recommendations with respect to adjustments to weighting factors under clause (i) in the annual report to Congress required under subsection (e)(3)(B) of this section.

(5)(A)(i) For discharges occurring during fiscal years ending on or before September 30, 1997, the Secretary shall provide for an additional payment for a subsection (d) hospital for any discharge in a diagnosis-related group, the length of stay of which exceeds the mean length of stay for discharges within that group by a fixed number of days, or exceeds such mean length of stay by some fixed number of standard deviations, whichever is the fewer number of days.

(ii) For cases which are not included in clause (i), a subsection (d) hospital may request additional payments in any case where charges, adjusted to cost, exceed a fixed multiple of the applicable DRG prospective payment rate, or exceed such other fixed dollar amount, whichever is greater, or, for discharges in fiscal years beginning on or after October 1, 1994, exceed the sum of the applicable DRG prospective payment rate plus any amounts payable under subparagraphs (B) and (F) plus a fixed dollar amount determined by the Secretary.

(iii) The amount of such additional payment under clauses (i) and (ii) shall be determined by the Secretary and shall (except as payments under clause (i) are required to be reduced to take into account the requirements of clause (v)) approximate the marginal cost of care beyond the cutoff point applicable under clause (i) or (ii).

(iv) The total amount of the additional payments made under this subparagraph for discharges in a fiscal year may not be less than 5 percent nor more than 6 percent of the total payments projected or estimated to be made based on DRG prospective payment rates for discharges in that year.

(v) The Secretary shall provide that—

(I) the day outlier percentage for fiscal year 1995 shall be 75 percent of the day outlier percentage for fiscal year 1994;

(II) the day outlier percentage for fiscal year 1996 shall be 50 percent of the day outlier percentage for fiscal year 1994; and

(III) the day outlier percentage for fiscal year 1997 shall be 25 percent of the day outlier percentage for fiscal year 1994.

(vi) For purposes of this subparagraph, the term "day outlier percentage" means, for a fiscal year, the percentage of the total additional payments made by the Secretary under this subparagraph for discharges in that fiscal year which are additional payments under clause (i).

(B) The Secretary shall provide for an additional payment amount for subsection (d) hospitals with indirect costs of medical education, in an amount computed in the same manner as the adjustment for such costs under regulations (in effect as of January 1, 1983) under subsection (a)(2) of this section, except as follows:

(i) The amount of such additional payment shall be determined by multiplying (I) the sum of the amount determined under paragraph (1)(A)(ii)(II) (or, if applicable, the amount determined under paragraph (1)(A)(iii)) and, for cases qualifying for additional payments under subparagraph (A)(i), the amount paid to the hospital under subparagraph (A), by (II) the indirect teaching adjustment factor described in clause (ii).

(ii) For purposes of clause (i)(II), the indirect teaching adjustment factor is equal to $c \times (((1 + r) \text{ to the } n^{th} \text{ power}) - 1)$, where "r" is the ratio of the hospital's full-time equivalent interns and residents to beds and "n" equals . 405. For discharges occurring—

(I) on or after October 1, 1988, and before October 1, 1997, "c" is equal to 1.89;

(II) during fiscal year 1998, "c" is equal to 1.72;

(III) during fiscal year 1999, "c" is equal to 1.6;

(IV) during fiscal year 2000, "c" is equal to 1.47;

(V) during fiscal year 2001, "c" is equal to 1.54;

(VI) during fiscal year 2002, "c" is equal to 1.6; and

(VII) on or after October 1, 2002, "c" is equal to 1.35.

(iii) In determining such adjustment the Secretary shall not distinguish between those interns and residents who are employees of a hospital and those interns and residents who furnish services to a hospital but are not employees of such hospital.

(iv) Effective for discharges occurring on or after October 1, 1997, all the time spent by an intern or resident in patient care activities under an approved medical residency training program at an entity in a nonhospital setting shall be counted towards the determination of full-time equivalency if the hospital incurs all, or substantially all, of the costs for the training program in that setting.

(v) In determining the adjustment with respect to a hospital for discharges occurring on or after October 1, 1997, the total number of full-time equivalent interns and residents in the fields of allopathic and osteopathic medicine in either a hospital or nonhospital setting may not exceed the number (or, 130 percent of such number in the case of a hospital located in a rural area) of such full-time equivalent interns and residents in the hospital with respect to the hospital's most recent cost reporting period ending on or before December 31, 1996. Rules similar to the rules of subsection (h)(4)(F)(ii) shall apply for purposes of this clause.

(vi) For purposes of clause (ii)—

(I) "r" may not exceed the ratio of the number of interns and residents, subject to the limit under clause (v), with respect to the hospital for its most recent cost reporting period to the hospital's available beds (as defined by the Secretary) during that cost reporting period, and

(II) for the hospital's cost reporting periods beginning on or after October 1, 1997, subject to the limits described in clauses (iv) and (v), the total number of full-time equivalent residents for payment purposes shall equal the average of the actual full-time equivalent resident count for the cost reporting period and the preceding two cost reporting periods.

737

In the case of the first cost reporting period beginning on or after October 1, 1997, subclause (II) shall be applied by using the average for such period and the preceding cost reporting period.

(vii) If any cost reporting period beginning on or after October 1, 1997, is not equal to twelve months, the Secretary shall make appropriate modifications to ensure that the average full-time equivalent residency count pursuant to subclause (II) of clause (vi) is based on the equivalent of full twelve-month cost reporting periods.

(viii) Rules similar to the rules of subsection (h)(4)(H) shall apply for purposes of clauses (v) and (vi).

(C)(i) The Secretary shall provide for such exceptions and adjustments to the payment amounts established under this subsection (other than under paragraph (9)) as the Secretary deems appropriate to take into account the special needs of regional and national referral centers (including those hospitals of 275 or more beds located in rural areas). A hospital which is classified as a rural hospital may appeal to the Secretary to be classified as a rural referral center under this clause on the basis of criteria (established by the Secretary) which shall allow the hospital to demonstrate that it should be so reclassified by reason of certain of its operating characteristics being similar to those of a typical urban hospital located in the same census region and which shall not require a rural osteopathic hospital to have more than 3,000 discharges in a year in order to be classified as a rural referral center. Such characteristics may include wages, scope of services, service area, and the mix of medical specialties. The Secretary shall publish the criteria not later than August 17, 1984, for implementation by October 1, 1984. An appeal allowed under this clause must be submitted to the Secretary (in such form and manner as the Secretary may prescribe) during the quarter before the first quarter of the hospital's cost reporting period (or, in the case of a cost reporting period beginning during October 1984, during the first quarter of that period), and the Secretary must make a final determination with respect to such appeal within 60 days after the date the appeal was submitted. Any payment adjustments necessitated by a reclassification based upon the appeal shall be effective at the beginning of such cost reporting period.

(ii) The Secretary shall provide, under clause (i), for the classification of a rural hospital as a regional referral center if the hospital has a case mix index equal to or greater than the median case mix index for hospitals (other than hospitals with approved teaching programs) located in an urban area in the same region (as defined in paragraph (2)(D)), has at least 5,000 discharges a year or, if less, the median number of discharges in urban hospitals in the region in which the hospital is located (or, in the case of a rural osteopathic hospital, meets the criterion established by the Secretary under clause (i) with respect to the annual number of discharges for such hospitals), and meets any other criteria established by the Secretary under clause (i).

(D)(i) For any cost reporting period beginning on or after April 1, 1990, with respect to a subsection (d) hospital which is a sole community hospital, payment under paragraph (1)(A) shall be—

> **(I)** an amount based on 100 percent of the hospital's target amount for the cost reporting period, as defined in subsection (b)(3)(C) of this section, or

> **(II)** the amount determined under paragraph (1)(A)(iii),

whichever results in greater payment to the hospital.

(ii) In the case of a sole community hospital that experiences, in a cost reporting period compared to the previous cost reporting period, a decrease of more than 5 percent in its total number of inpatient cases due to circumstances beyond its control, the Secretary shall provide for such adjustment to the payment amounts under this subsection (other than under paragraph (9)) as may be necessary to fully compensate the hospital for the fixed costs it incurs in the period in providing inpatient hospital services, including the reasonable cost of maintaining necessary core staff and services.

(iii) For purposes of this subchapter, the term "sole community hospital" means any hospital—

> **(I)** that the Secretary determines is located more than 35 road miles from another hospital,

> **(II)** that, by reason of factors such as the time required for an individual to travel to the nearest alternative source of appropriate inpatient care (in accordance with standards promulgated by the Secretary), location, weather conditions, travel conditions, or absence of other like hospitals (as determined by the Secretary), is the sole source of inpatient hospital services reasonably available to individuals in a geographic area who are entitled to benefits under part A of this subchapter, or

> **(III)** that is located in a rural area and designated by the Secretary as an essential access community hospital under section 1395i–4(i)(1) of this title as in effect on September 30, 1997.

(iv) The Secretary shall promulgate a standard for determining whether a hospital meets the criteria for classification as a sole community hospital under clause (iii)(II) because of the time required for an individual to travel to the nearest alternative source of appropriate inpatient care.

(v) If the Secretary determines that, in the case of a hospital located in a rural area and designated by the Secretary as an essential access community hospital under section 1395i–4(i)(1) of this title as in effect on September 30, 1997, the hospital has incurred increases in reasonable costs during a cost reporting period as a result of becoming a member of a rural health network (as defined in section 1395i–4(d) of this title) in the State in which it is located, and in incurring such increases, the hospital will increase its costs for subsequent cost reporting periods, the Secretary shall increase the hospital's target amount under subsection (b)(3)(C) of this section to account for such incurred increases.

(E)(i) The Secretary shall estimate the amount of reimbursement made for services described in section 1395y(a)(14) of this title with respect to which payment was made under part B of this subchapter in the base reporting periods referred to in paragraph (2)(A) and with respect to which payment is no longer being made.

(ii) The Secretary shall provide for an adjustment to the payment for subsection (d) hospitals in each fiscal year so as appropriately to reflect the net amount described in clause (i).

(F)(i) For discharges occurring on or after May 1, 1986, the Secretary shall provide, in accordance with this subparagraph, for an additional payment amount for each subsection (d) hospital which—

(I) serves a significantly disproportionate number of low-income patients (as defined in clause (v)), or

(II) is located in an urban area, has 100 or more beds, and can demonstrate that its net inpatient care revenues (excluding any of such revenues attributable to this subchapter or State plans approved under subchapter XIX of this chapter), during the cost reporting period in which the discharges occur, for indigent care from State and local government sources exceed 30 percent of its total of such net inpatient care revenues during the period.

(ii) Subject to clause (ix), the amount of such payment for each discharge shall be determined by multiplying (I) the sum of the amount determined under paragraph (1)(A)(ii)(II) (or, if applicable, the amount determined under paragraph (1)(A)(iii)) and, for cases qualifying for additional payment under subparagraph (A)(i), the amount paid to the hospital under subparagraph (A) for that discharge, by (II) the disproportionate share adjustment percentage established under clause (iii) or (iv) for the cost reporting period in which the discharge occurs.

(iii) The disproportionate share adjustment percentage for a cost reporting period for a hospital described in clause (i)(II) is equal to 35 percent.

(iv) The disproportionate share adjustment percentage for a cost reporting period for a hospital that is not described in clause (i)(II) and that—

(I) is located in an urban area and has 100 or more beds or is described in the second sentence of clause (v), is equal to the percent determined in accordance with the applicable formula described in clause (vii);

(II) is located in an urban area and has less than 100 beds, is equal to 5 percent or, for discharges occurring on or after April 1, 2001, is equal to the percent determined in accordance with clause (xiii);

(III) is located in a rural area and is not described in subclause (IV) or (V) or in the second sentence of clause (v), is equal to 4 percent or, for discharges occurring on or after April 1, 2001, is equal to the percent determined in accordance with clause (xii);

(IV) is located in a rural area, is classified as a rural referral center under subparagraph (C), and is classified as a sole community hospital under subparagraph (D), is equal to 10 percent or, if greater, the percent determined in accordance with the applicable formula described in clause (viii) or, for discharges occurring on or after April 1, 2001, the greater of the percentages determined under clause (x) or (xi);

(V) is located in a rural area, is classified as a rural referral center under subparagraph (C), and is not classified as a sole community hospital under subparagraph (D), is equal to the percent determined in accordance with the applicable formula described in clause (viii) or, for discharges occurring on or after April 1, 2001, is equal to the percent determined in accordance with clause (xi); or

(VI) is located in a rural area, is classified as a sole community hospital under subparagraph (D), and is not classified as a rural referral center under subparagraph (C), is 10 percent or, for discharges occurring on or after April 1, 2001, is equal to the percent determined in accordance with clause (x).

(v) In this subparagraph, a hospital "serves a significantly disproportionate number of low income patients" for a cost reporting period if the hospital has a disproportionate patient percentage (as defined in clause (vi)) for that period which equals, or exceeds—

(I) 15 percent, if the hospital is located in an urban area and has 100 or more beds,

(II) 30 percent (or 15 percent, for discharges occurring on or after April 1, 2001), if the hospital is located in a rural area and has more than 100 beds, or is located in a rural area and is classified as a sole community hospital under subparagraph (D),

(III) 40 percent (or 15 percent, for discharges occurring on or after April 1, 2001), if the hospital is located in an urban area and has less than 100 beds, or

(IV) 45 percent (or 15 percent, for discharges occurring on or after April 1, 2001), if the hospital is located in a rural area and is not described in subclause (II).

A hospital located in a rural area and with 500 or more beds also "serves a significantly disproportionate number of low income patients" for a cost reporting period if the hospital has a disproportionate patient percentage (as defined in clause (vi)) for that period which equals or exceeds a percentage specified by the Secretary.

(vi) In this subparagraph, the term "disproportionate patient percentage" means, with respect to a cost reporting period of a hospital, the sum of—

(I) the fraction (expressed as a percentage), the numerator of which is the number of such hospital's patient days for such period which were made up of patients who (for such days) were entitled to benefits under part A of this subchapter and were entitled to supplementary security income benefits (excluding any State supplementation) under subchapter XVI of this chapter, and the denominator of which is the number of such hospital's patient days for such fiscal year which were made up of patients who (for such days) were entitled to benefits under part A of this subchapter, and

(II) the fraction (expressed as a percentage), the numerator of which is the number of the hospital's patient days for such period which consist of patients who (for such days) were eligible for medical assistance under a State plan approved under subchapter XIX of this chapter, but who were not entitled to benefits under part A of this subchapter, and the denominator of which is the total number of the hospital's patient days for such period.

(vii) The formula used to determine the disproportionate share adjustment percentage for a cost reporting period for a hospital described in clause (iv)(I) is—

(I) in the case of such a hospital with a disproportionate patient percentage (as defined in clause (vi)) greater than 20.2—

(a) for discharges occurring on or after April 1, 1990, and on or before December 31, 1990, (P–20.2)(.65)+5.62,

(b) for discharges occurring on or after January 1, 1991, and on or before September 30, 1993, (P–20.2)(.7)+5.62,

(c) for discharges occurring on or after October 1, 1993, and on or before September 30, 1994, (P–20.2)(.8)+5.88, and

(d) for discharges occurring on or after October 1, 1994, (P–20.2)(.825)+ 5.88; or

(II) in the case of any other such hospital—

(a) for discharges occurring on or after April 1, 1990, and on or before December 31, 1990, (P–15)(.6)+2.5,

(b) for discharges occurring on or after January 1, 1991, and on or before September 30, 1993, (P–15)(.6)+2.5,

(c) for discharges occurring on or after October 1, 1993, (P–15)(.65)+2.5,

where "P" is the hospital's disproportionate patient percentage (as defined in clause (vi)).

(viii) The formula used to determine the disproportionate share adjustment percentage for a cost reporting period for a hospital described in clause (iv)(IV) or (iv)(V) is the percentage determined in accordance with the following formula: (P–30)(.6)+4.0, where "P" is the hospital's disproportionate patient percentage (as defined in clause (vi)).

(ix) In the case of discharges occurring—

(I) during fiscal year 1998, the additional payment amount otherwise determined under clause (ii) shall be reduced by 1 percent;

(II) during fiscal year 1999, such additional payment amount shall be reduced by 2 percent;

(III) during fiscal years 2000 and 2001, such additional payment amount shall be reduced by 3 percent and 2 percent, respectively;

(IV) during fiscal year 2002, such additional payment amount shall be reduced by 3 percent; and

743

(V) during fiscal year 2003 and each subsequent fiscal year, such additional payment amount shall be reduced by 0 percent.

(x) For purposes of clause (iv)(VI) (relating to sole community hospitals), in the case of a hospital for a cost reporting period with a disproportionate patient percentage (as defined in clause (vi)) that—

(I) is less than 19.3, the disproportionate share adjustment percentage is determined in accordance with the following formula: $(P–15)(.65)+2.5$;

(II) is equal to or exceeds 19.3, but is less than 30.0, such adjustment percentage is equal to 5.25 percent; or

(III) is equal to or exceeds 30, such adjustment percentage is equal to 10 percent,

where "P" is the hospital's disproportionate patient percentage (as defined in clause (vi)).

(xi) For purposes of clause (iv)(V) (relating to rural referral centers), in the case of a hospital for a cost reporting period with a disproportionate patient percentage (as defined in clause (vi)) that—

(I) is less than 19.3, the disproportionate share adjustment percentage is determined in accordance with the following formula: $(P–15)(.65)+2.5$;

(II) is equal to or exceeds 19.3, but is less than 30.0, such adjustment percentage is equal to 5.25 percent; or

(III) is equal to or exceeds 30, such adjustment percentage is determined in accordance with the following formula: $(P–30)(.6)+5.25$,

where "P" is the hospital's disproportionate patient percentage (as defined in clause (vi)).

(xii) For purposes of clause (iv)(III) (relating to small rural hospitals generally), in the case of a hospital for a cost reporting period with a disproportionate patient percentage (as defined in clause (vi)) that—

(I) is less than 19.3, the disproportionate share adjustment percentage is determined in accordance with the following formula: $(P–15)(.65)+2.5$; or

(II) is equal to or exceeds 19.3, such adjustment percentage is equal to 5.25 percent,

where "P" is the hospital's disproportionate patient percentage (as defined in clause (vi)).

744

(xiii) For purposes of clause (iv)(II) (relating to urban hospitals with less than 100 beds), in the case of a hospital for a cost reporting period with a disproportionate patient percentage (as defined in clause (vi)) that—

    (I) is less than 19.3, the disproportionate share adjustment percentage is determined in accordance with the following formula: (P–15)(.65) + 2.5; or

    (II) is equal to or exceeds 19.3, such adjustment percentage is equal to 5.25 percent,

where "P" is the hospital's disproportionate patient percentage (as defined in clause (vi)).

(G)(i) For any cost reporting period beginning on or after April 1, 1990, and before October 1, 1994, or discharges occurring on or after October 1, 1997, and before October 1, 2006, in the case of a subsection (d) hospital which is a medicare-dependent, small rural hospital, payment under paragraph (1)(A) shall be equal to the sum of the amount determined under clause (ii) and the amount determined under paragraph (1)(A)(iii).

    (I) an amount based on 100 percent of the hospital's target amount for the cost reporting period, as defined in subsection (b)(3)(D) of this section, or

    (II) the amount determined under paragraph (1)(A)(iii),

whichever results in the greater payment to the hospital.

(ii) The amount determined under this clause is—

    (I) for discharges occurring during the 36–month period beginning with the first day of the cost reporting period that begins on or after April 1, 1990, the amount by which the hospital's target amount for the cost reporting period (as defined in subsection (b)(3)(D) of this section) exceeds the amount determined under paragraph (1)(A)(iii); and

    (II) for discharges occurring during any subsequent cost reporting period (or portion thereof) and before October 1, 1994, or discharges occurring on or after October 1, 1997, and before October 1, 2006, 50 percent of the amount by which the hospital's target amount for the cost reporting period (as defined in subsection (b)(3)(D) of this section) exceeds the amount determined under paragraph (1)(A)(iii).

(iii) In the case of a medicare dependent, small rural hospital that experiences, in a cost reporting period compared to the previous cost reporting period, a decrease of more than 5 percent in its total number of inpatient cases due to circumstances beyond its control, the Secretary shall provide for such adjustment to the payment amounts under this subsection (other than

745

under paragraph (9)) as may be necessary to fully compensate the hospital for the fixed costs it incurs in the period in providing inpatient hospital services, including the reasonable cost of maintaining necessary core staff and services.

(iv) The term "medicare-dependent, small rural hospital" means, with respect to any cost reporting period to which clause (i) applies, any hospital—

    (I) located in a rural area,

    (II) that has not more than 100 beds,

    (III) that is not classified as a sole community hospital under subparagraph (D), and

    (IV) for which not less than 60 percent of its inpatient days or discharges during the cost reporting period beginning in fiscal year 1987, or 2 of the 3 most recently audited cost reporting periods for which the Secretary has a settled cost report, were attributable to inpatients entitled to benefits under part A of this subchapter.

(H) The Secretary may provide for such adjustments to the payment amounts under this subsection as the Secretary deems appropriate to take into account the unique circumstances of hospitals located in Alaska and Hawaii.

(I)(i) The Secretary shall provide by regulation for such other exceptions and adjustments to such payment amounts under this subsection as the Secretary deems appropriate.

(ii) In making adjustments under clause (i) for transfer cases (as defined by the Secretary) in a fiscal year, not taking in account the effect of subparagraph (J), the Secretary may make adjustments to each of the average standardized amounts determined under paragraph (3) to assure that the aggregate payments made under this subsection for such fiscal year are not greater or lesser than those that would have otherwise been made in such fiscal year.

(J)(i) The Secretary shall treat the term "transfer case" (as defined in subparagraph (I)(ii)) as including the case of a qualified discharge (as defined in clause (ii)), which is classified within a diagnosis-related group described in clause (iii), and which occurs on or after October 1, 1998. In the case of a qualified discharge for which a substantial portion of the costs of care are incurred in the early days of the inpatient stay (as defined by the Secretary), in no case may the payment amount otherwise provided under this subsection exceed an amount equal to the sum of—

    (I) 50 percent of the amount of payment under this subsection for transfer cases (as established under subparagraph (I)(i)), and

(II) 50 percent of the amount of payment which would have been made under this subsection with respect to the qualified discharge if no transfer were involved.

(i) For purposes of clause (i), subject to clause (iii), the term "qualified discharge" means a discharge classified with a diagnosis-related group (described in clause (iii)) of an individual from a subsection (d) hospital, if upon such discharge the individual—

(I) is admitted as an inpatient to a hospital or hospital unit that is not a subsection (d) hospital for the provision of inpatient hospital services;

(II) is admitted to a skilled nursing facility;

(III) is provided home health services from a home health agency, if such services relate to the condition or diagnosis for which such individual received inpatient hospital services from the subsection (d) hospital, and if such services are provided within an appropriate period (as determined by the Secretary); or

(IV) for discharges occurring on or after October 1, 2000, the individual receives post discharge services described in clause (iv)(I).

(iii) Subject to clause (iv), a diagnosis-related group described in this clause is—

(I) 1 of 10 diagnosis-related groups selected by the Secretary based upon a high volume of discharges classified within such groups and a disproportionate use of post discharge services described in clause (ii); and

(II) a diagnosis-related group specified by the Secretary under clause (iv)(II).

(iv) The Secretary shall include in the proposed rule published under subsection (e)(5)(A) for fiscal year 2001, a description of the effect of this subparagraph. The Secretary may include in the proposed rule (and in the final rule published under paragraph (6)) for fiscal year 2001 or a subsequent fiscal year, a description of—

(I) post-discharge services not described in subclauses (I), (II), and (III) of clause (ii), the receipt of which results in a qualified discharge; and

(II) diagnosis-related groups described in clause (iii)(I) in addition to the 10 selected under such clause.

(K)(i) Effective for discharges beginning on or after October 1, 2001, the Secretary shall establish a mechanism to recognize the costs of new medical services and technologies under the payment system established under this subsection. Such mechanism shall be established after notice and opportunity for public comment (in the publications required by subsection (e)(5) for a fiscal year or otherwise).

(ii) The mechanism established pursuant to clause (i) shall—

(I) apply to a new medical service or technology if, based on the estimated costs incurred with respect to discharges involving such service or technology, the DRG prospective payment rate otherwise applicable to such discharges under this subsection is inadequate;

(II) provide for the collection of data with respect to the costs of a new medical service or technology described in subclause (I) for a period of not less than two years and not more than three years beginning on the date on which an inpatient hospital code is issued with respect to the service or technology;

(III) subject to paragraph (4)(C)(iii), provide for additional payment to be made under this subsection with respect to discharges involving a new medical service or technology described in subclause (I) that occur during the period described in subclause (II) in an amount that adequately reflects the estimated average cost of such service or technology; and

(IV) provide that discharges involving such a service or technology that occur after the close of the period described in subclause (II) will be classified within a new or existing diagnosis-related group with a weighting factor under paragraph (4)(B) that is derived from cost data collected with respect to discharges occurring during such period.

(iii) For purposes of clause (ii)(II), the term "inpatient hospital code" means any code that is used with respect to inpatient hospital services for which payment may be made under this subsection and includes an alphanumeric code issued under the International Classification of Diseases, 9th Revision, Clinical Modification ("ICD–9–CM") and its subsequent revisions.

(iv) For purposes of clause (ii)(III), the term "additional payment" means, with respect to a discharge for a new medical service or technology described in clause (ii)(I), an amount that exceeds the prospective payment rate otherwise applicable under this subsection to discharges involving such service or technology that would be made but for this subparagraph.

(v) The requirement under clause (ii)(III) for an additional payment may be satisfied by means of a new-technology group (described in subparagraph (L)), an add-on payment, a payment adjustment, or any other similar mechanism for increasing the amount otherwise payable with respect to a discharge under this subsection. The Secretary may not establish a separate fee schedule for such additional payment for such services and technologies, by utilizing a methodology established under subsection (a) or (h) of section 1395m of this title to determine the amount of such additional payment, or by other similar mechanisms or methodologies.

(vi) For purposes of this subparagraph and subparagraph (L), a medical service or technology will be considered a "new medical service or technology" if the service or technology meets criteria established by the Secretary after notice and an opportunity for public comment.

(L)(i) In establishing the mechanism under subparagraph (K), the Secretary may establish new-technology groups into which a new medical service or technology will be classified if, based on the estimated average costs incurred with respect to discharges involving such service or technology, the DRG prospective payment rate otherwise applicable to such discharges under this subsection is inadequate.

(ii) Such groups—

(I) shall not be based on the costs associated with a specific new medical service or technology; but

(II) shall, in combination with the applicable standardized amounts and the weighting factors assigned to such groups under paragraph (4)(B), reflect such cost cohorts as the Secretary determines are appropriate for all new medical services and technologies that are likely to be provided as inpatient hospital services in a fiscal year.

(iii) The methodology for classifying specific hospital discharges within a diagnosis-related group under paragraph (4)(A) or a new-technology group shall provide that a specific hospital discharge may not be classified within both a diagnosis-related group and a new-technology group.

(6) The Secretary shall provide for publication in the Federal Register, on or before the August 1 before each fiscal year (beginning with fiscal year 1984), of a description of the methodology and data used in computing the adjusted DRG prospective payment rates under this subsection, including any adjustments required under subsection (e)(1)(B) of this section.

(7) There shall be no administrative or judicial review under section 1395oo of this title or otherwise of—

(A) the determination of the requirement, or the proportional amount, of any adjustment effected pursuant to subsection (e)(1) of this section, and

(B) the establishment of diagnosis-related groups, of the methodology for the classification of discharges within such groups, and of the appropriate weighting factors thereof under paragraph (4).

(8)(A) In the case of any hospital which is located in an area which is, at any time after April 20, 1983, reclassified from an urban to a rural area, payments to such hospital for the first two cost reporting periods for which such reclassification is effective shall be made as follows:

(i) For the first such cost reporting period, payment shall be equal to the amount payable to such hospital for such reporting period on the basis of the rural classification, plus an amount equal to two-thirds of the amount (if any) by which—

(I) the amount which would have been payable to such hospital for such reporting period on the basis of an urban classification, exceeds

(II) the amount payable to such hospital for such reporting period on the basis of the rural classification.

(ii) For the second such cost reporting period, payment shall be equal to the amount payable to such hospital for such reporting period on the basis of the rural classification, plus an amount equal to one-third of the amount (if any) by which—

(I) the amount which would have been payable to such hospital for such reporting period on the basis of an urban classification, exceeds

(II) the amount payable to such hospital for such reporting period on the basis of the rural classification.

(B)(i) For purposes of this subsection, the Secretary shall treat a hospital located in a rural county adjacent to one or more urban areas as being located in the urban metropolitan statistical area to which the greatest number of workers in the county commute, if the rural county would otherwise be considered part of an urban area, under the standards for designating Metropolitan Statistical Areas (and for designating New England County Metropolitan Areas) described in clause (ii), if the commuting rates used in determining outlying counties (or, for New England, similar recognized areas) were determined on the basis of the aggregate number of resident workers who commute to (and, if applicable under the standards, from) the central county or counties of all contiguous Metropolitan Statistical Areas (or New England County Metropolitan Areas).

(ii) The standards described in this clause for cost reporting periods beginning in a fiscal year

(I) before fiscal year 2003, are the standards published in the Federal Register on January 3, 1980, or, at the election of the hospital with respect to fiscal years 2001 and 2002, standards so published on March 30, 1990; and

(II) after fiscal year 2002, are the standards published in the Federal Register by the Director of the Office of Management and Budget based on the most recent available decennial population data.

Subparagraphs (C) and (D) shall not apply with respect to the application of subclause (I)

(C)(i) If the application of subparagraph (B) or a decision of the Medicare Geographic Classification Review Board or the Secretary under paragraph (10), by treating hospitals located in a rural county or counties as being located in an urban area, or by treating hospitals located in one urban area as being located in another urban area—

(I) reduces the wage index for that urban area (as applied under this subsection) by 1 percentage point or less, the Secretary, in calculating such wage index under this subsection, shall exclude those hospitals so treated, or

(II) reduces the wage index for that urban area by more than 1 percentage point (as applied under this subsection), the Secretary shall calculate and apply such wage index under this subsection separately to hospitals located in such urban area (excluding all the hospitals so treated) and to the hospitals so treated (as if such hospitals were located in such urban area).

(ii) If the application of subparagraph (B) or a decision of the Medicare Geographic Classification Review Board or the Secretary under paragraph (10), by treating hospitals located in a rural county or counties as not being located in the rural area in a State, reduces the wage index for that rural area (as applied under this subsection), the Secretary shall calculate and apply such wage index under this subsection as if the hospitals so treated had not been excluded from calculation of the wage index for that rural area.

(iii) The application of subparagraph (B) or a decision of the Medicare Geographic Classification Review Board or the Secretary under paragraph (10) may not result in the reduction of any county's wage index to a level below the wage index for rural areas in the State in which the county is located.

(iv) The application of subparagraph (B) or a decision of the Medicare Geographic Classification Review Board or of the Secretary under paragraph (10) may not result in a reduction in an urban area's wage index if—

(I) the urban area has a wage index below the wage index for rural areas in the State in which it is located; or

751

(II) the urban area is located in a State that is composed of a single urban area.

(v) This subparagraph shall apply with respect to discharges occurring in a fiscal year only if the Secretary uses a method for making adjustments to the DRG prospective payment rate for area differences in hospital wage levels under paragraph (3)(E) for the fiscal year that is based on the use of Metropolitan Statistical Area classifications.

(D) The Secretary shall make a proportional adjustment in the standardized amounts determined under paragraph (3) to assure that the provisions of subparagraphs (B) and (C) or a decision of the Medicare Geographic Classification Review Board or the Secretary under paragraph (10) do not result in aggregate payments under this section that are greater or less than those that would otherwise be made.

(E)(i) For purposes of this subsection, not later than 60 days after the receipt of an application (in a form and manner determined by the Secretary) from a subsection (d) hospital described in clause (ii), the Secretary shall treat the hospital as being located in the rural area (as defined in paragraph (2)(D)) of the State in which the hospital is located.

(ii) For purposes of clause (i), a subsection (d) hospital described in this clause is a subsection (d) hospital that is located in an urban area (as defined in paragraph (2)(D)) and satisfies any of the following criteria:

(I) The hospital is located in a rural census tract of a metropolitan statistical area (as determined under the most recent modification of the Goldsmith Modification, originally published in the Federal Register on February 27, 1992 (57 Fed. Reg. 6725)).

(II) The hospital is located in an area designated by any law or regulation of such State as a rural area (or is designated by such State as a rural hospital).

(III) The hospital would qualify as a rural, regional, or national referral center under paragraph (5)(C) or as a sole community hospital under paragraph (5)(D) if the hospital were located in a rural area.

(IV) The hospital meets such other criteria as the Secretary may specify.

(9)(A) Notwithstanding section 1395f(b) of this title, but subject to the provisions of section 1395e of this title, the amount of the payment with respect to the operating costs of inpatient hospital services of a subsection (d) Puerto Rico hospital for inpatient hospital discharges is equal to the sum of—

    (i) for discharges beginning on or after October 1, 1997, 50 percent (and for discharges between October 1, 1987, and September 30, 1997, 75 percent) of the Puerto Rico adjusted DRG prospective payment rate (determined under subparagraph (B) or (C)) for such discharges, and

    (ii) for discharges beginning in a fiscal year beginning on or after October 1, 1997, 50 percent (and for discharges between October 1, 1987, and September 30, 1997, 25 percent) of the discharge-weighted average of—

        (I) the national adjusted DRG prospective payment rate (determined under paragraph (3)(D)) for hospitals located in a large urban area,

        (II) such rate for hospitals located in other urban areas, and

        (III) such rate for hospitals located in a rural area,

for such discharges, adjusted in the manner provided in paragraph (3)(E) for different area wage levels. As used in this section, the term "subsection (d) Puerto Rico hospital" means a hospital that is located in Puerto Rico and that would be a subsection (d) hospital (as defined in paragraph (1)(B)) if it were located in one of the fifty States.

    (B) The Secretary shall determine a Puerto Rico adjusted DRG prospective payment rate, for each inpatient hospital discharge in fiscal year 1988 involving inpatient hospital services of a subsection (d) Puerto Rico hospital for which payment may be made under part A of this subchapter. Such rate shall be determined for such hospitals located in urban or rural areas within Puerto Rico, as follows:

    (i) The Secretary shall determine the target amount (as defined in subsection (b)(3)(A) of this section) for the hospital for the cost reporting period beginning in fiscal year 1987 and increase such amount by prorating the applicable percentage increase (as defined in subsection (b)(3)(B) of this section) to update the amount to the midpoint in fiscal year 1988.

    (ii) The Secretary shall standardize the amount determined under clause (i) for each hospital by—

        (I) excluding an estimate of indirect medical education costs,

        (II) adjusting for variations among hospitals by area in the average hospital wage level,

        (III) adjusting for variations in case mix among hospitals, and

(IV) excluding an estimate of the additional payments to certain subsection (d) Puerto Rico hospitals to be made under subparagraph (D)(iii) (relating to disproportionate share payments).

(iii) The Secretary shall compute a discharge weighted average of the standardized amounts determined under clause (ii) for all hospitals located in an urban area and for all hospitals located in a rural area (as such terms are defined in paragraph (2)(D)).

(iv) The Secretary shall reduce the average standardized amount by a proportion equal to the proportion (estimated by the Secretary) of the amount of payments under this paragraph which are additional payments described in subparagraph (D)(i) (relating to outlier payments).

(v) For each discharge classified within a diagnosis-related group for hospitals located in an urban or rural area, respectively, the Secretary shall establish a Puerto Rico DRG prospective payment rate equal to the product of—

(I) the average standardized amount (computed under clause (iii) and reduced under clause (iv)) for hospitals located in an urban or rural area, respectively, and

(II) the weighting factor (determined under paragraph (4)(B)) for that diagnosis-related group.

(vi) The Secretary shall adjust the proportion (as estimated by the Secretary from time to time) of hospitals' costs which are attributable to wages and wage-related costs, of the Puerto Rico DRG prospective payment rate computed under clause (v) for area differences in hospital wage levels by a factor (established by the Secretary) reflecting the relative hospital wage level in the geographic area of the hospital compared to the Puerto Rican average hospital wage level.

(C) The Secretary shall determine a Puerto Rico adjusted DRG prospective payment rate, for each inpatient hospital discharge after fiscal year 1988 involving inpatient hospital services of a subsection (d) Puerto Rico hospital for which payment may be made under part A of this subchapter. Such rate shall be determined for hospitals located in urban or rural areas within Puerto Rico as follows:

(i) The Secretary shall compute an average standardized amount for hospitals located in an urban area and for hospitals located in a rural area equal to the respective average standardized amount computed for the previous fiscal year under subparagraph (B)(iii) or under this clause, increased for fiscal year 1989 by the applicable percentage increase under subsection (b)(3)(B) of this section, and adjusted for subsequent fiscal years in accordance with the final determination of the Secretary under subsection (e)(4) of this section, and adjusted to reflect the most recent case-mix data available.

(ii) The Secretary shall reduce each of the average standardized amounts by a proportion equal to the proportion (estimated by the Secretary) of the amount of payments under this paragraph which are additional payments described in subparagraph (D)(i) (relating to outlier payments).

(iii) For each discharge classified within a diagnosis-related group for hospitals located in an urban or rural area, respectively, the Secretary shall establish a Puerto Rico DRG prospective payment rate equal to the product of—

(I) The average standardized amount (computed under clause (i) and reduced under clause (ii)) for hospitals located in an urban or rural area, respectively, and

(II) the weighting factor (determined under paragraph (4)(B)) for that diagnosis-related group.

(iv) The Secretary shall adjust the proportion (as estimated by the Secretary from time to time) of hospitals' costs which are attributable to wages and wage-related costs, of the Puerto Rico DRG prospective payment rate computed under clause (iii) for area differences in hospital wage levels by a factor (established by the Secretary) reflecting the relative hospital wage level in the geographic area of the hospital compared to the Puerto Rico average hospital wage level. The second and third sentences of paragraph (3)(E) shall apply to subsection (d) Puerto Rico hospitals under this clause in the same manner as they apply to subsection (d) hospitals under such paragraph and, for purposes of this clause, any reference in such paragraph to a subsection (d) hospital is deemed a reference to a subsection (d) Puerto Rico hospital.

(D) The following provisions of paragraph (5) shall apply to subsection (d) Puerto Rico hospitals receiving payment under this paragraph in the same manner and to the extent as they apply to subsection (d) hospitals receiving payment under this subsection:

(i) Subparagraph (A) (relating to outlier payments).

(ii) Subparagraph (B) (relating to payments for indirect medical education costs), except that for this purpose the sum of the amount determined under subparagraph (A) of this paragraph and the amount paid to the hospital under clause (i) of this subparagraph shall be substituted for the sum referred to in paragraph (5)(B)(i)(I).

(iii) Subparagraph (F) (relating to disproportionate share payments), except that for this purpose the sum described in clause (ii) of this subparagraph shall be substituted for the sum referred to in paragraph (5)(F)(ii)(I).

(iv) Subparagraph (H) (relating to exceptions and adjustments).

(10)(A) There is hereby established the Medicare Geographic Classification Review Board (hereinafter in this paragraph referred to as the "Board").

(B)(i) The Board shall be composed of 5 members appointed by the Secretary without regard to the provisions of Title 5, governing appointments in the competitive service. Two of such members shall be representative of subsection (d) hospitals located in a rural area under paragraph (2)(D). At least 1 member shall be knowledgeable in the field of analyzing costs with respect to the provision of inpatient hospital services.

(ii) The Secretary shall make initial appointments to the Board as provided in this paragraph within 180 days after December 19, 1989.

(C)(i) The Board shall consider the application of any subsection (d) hospital requesting that the Secretary change the hospital's geographic classification for purposes of determining for a fiscal year—

(I) the hospital's average standardized amount under paragraph (2)(D), or

(II) the factor used to adjust the DRG prospective payment rate for area differences in hospital wage levels that applies to such hospital under paragraph (3)(E).

(ii) A hospital requesting a change in geographic classification under clause (i) for a fiscal year shall submit its application to the Board not later than the first day of the 13-month period ending on September 30 of the preceding fiscal year.

(iii)(I) The Board shall render a decision on an application submitted under clause (i) not later than 180 days after the deadline referred to in clause (ii).

(II) Appeal of decisions of the Board shall be subject to the provisions of section 557b of Title 5. The Secretary shall issue a decision on such an appeal not later than 90 days after the date on which the appeal is filed. The decision of the Secretary shall be final and shall not be subject to judicial review.

(D)(i) The Secretary shall publish guidelines to be utilized by the Board in rendering decisions on applications submitted under this paragraph, and shall include in such guidelines the following:

(I) Guidelines for comparing wages, taking into account (to the extent the Secretary determines appropriate) occupational mix, in the area in which the hospital is classified and the area in which the hospital is applying to be classified.

(II) Guidelines for determining whether the county in which the hospital is located should be treated as being a part of a particular Metropolitan Statistical Area.

(III) Guidelines for considering information provided by an applicant with respect to the effects of the hospital's geographic classification on access to inpatient hospital services by medicare beneficiaries.

(IV) Guidelines for considering the appropriateness of the criteria used to define New England County Metropolitan Areas.

(ii) Notwithstanding clause (i), if the Secretary uses a method for making adjustments to the DRG prospective payment rate for area differences in hospital wage levels under paragraph (3)(E) that is not based on the use of Metropolitan Statistical Area classifications, the Secretary may revise the guidelines published under clause (i) to the extent such guidelines are used to determine the appropriateness of the geographic area in which the hospital is determined to be located for purposes of making such adjustments.

(iii) Under the guidelines published by the Secretary under clause (i), in the case of a hospital which has ever been classified by the Secretary as a rural referral center under paragraph (5)(C), the Board may not reject the application of the hospital under this paragraph on the basis of any comparison between the average hourly wage of the hospital and the average hourly wage of hospitals in the area in which it is located.

(iv) The Secretary shall publish the guidelines described in clause (i) by July 1, 1990.

(v) Any decision of the Board to reclassify a subsection (d) hospital for purposes of the adjustment factor described in subparagraph (C)(i)(II) for fiscal year 2001 or any fiscal year thereafter shall be effective for a period of 3 fiscal years, except that the Secretary shall establish procedures under which a subsection (d) hospital may elect to terminate such reclassification before the end of such period.

(vi) Such guidelines shall provide that, in making decisions on applications for reclassification for the purposes described in clause (v) for fiscal year 2003 and any succeeding fiscal year, the board shall base any comparison of the average hourly wage for the hospital with the average hourly wage for hospitals in an area on—

(I) an average of the average hourly wage amount for the hospital from the most recently published hospital wage survey data of the Secretary (as of the date on which the hospital applies for reclassification) and such amount from each of the two immediately preceding surveys; and

(II) an average of the average hourly wage amount for hospitals in such area from the most recently published hospital wage survey data of the Secretary (as of the date on which the hospital applies for reclassification) and such amount from each of the two immediately preceding surveys.

(E)(i) The Board shall have full power and authority to make rules and establish procedures, not inconsistent with the provisions of this subchapter or regulations of the Secretary, which are necessary or appropriate to carry out the provisions of this paragraph. In the course of any hearing the Board may administer oaths and affirmations. The provisions of subsections (d) and (e) of section 405 of this title with respect to subpenas shall apply to the Board to the same extent as such provisions apply to the Secretary with respect to subchapter II of this chapter.

(ii) The Board is authorized to engage such technical assistance and to receive such information as may be required to carry out its functions, and the Secretary shall, in addition, make available to the Board such secretarial, clerical, and other assistance as the Board may require to carry out its functions.

(F)(i) Each member of the Board who is not an officer or employee of the Federal Government shall be compensated at a rate equal to the daily equivalent of the annual rate of basic pay prescribed for grade GS–18 of the General Schedule under section 5332 of Title 5 for each day (including travel time) during which such member is engaged in the performance of the duties of the Board. Each member of the Board who is an officer or employee of the United States shall serve without compensation in addition to that received for service as an officer or employee of the United States.

(ii) Members of the Board shall be allowed travel expenses, including per diem in lieu of subsistence, at rates authorized for employees of agencies under subchapter I of chapter 57 of Title 5, while away from their homes or regular places of business in the performance of services for the Board.

(11) Additional payments for managed care enrollees

(A) In general

For portions of cost reporting periods occurring on or after January 1, 1998, the Secretary shall provide for an additional payment amount for each applicable discharge of any subsection (d) of this section hospital that has an approved medical residency training program.

(B) Applicable discharge

For purposes of this paragraph, the term "applicable discharge" means the discharge of any individual who is enrolled under a risk-sharing contract with an eligible organization under section 1395mm and who is entitled to benefits under part A of this subchapter or any individual who is enrolled with a Medicare + Choice organization under part C of this subchapter.

(C) Determination of amount

The amount of the payment under this paragraph with respect to any applicable discharge shall be equal to the applicable percentage (as defined in subsection (h)(3)(D)(ii)) of the estimated average per discharge amount that would otherwise have been paid under paragraph (5)(B) if the individuals had not been enrolled as described in subparagraph (B).

(D) Special rule for hospitals under reimbursement system

The Secretary shall establish rules for the application of this paragraph to a hospital reimbursed under a reimbursement system authorized under section 1395f(b)(3) of this title in the same manner as it would apply to the hospital if it were not reimbursed under such section.

(e) Proportional adjustments in applicable percentage increases; Prospective Payment Assessment Commission

(1)(A) For cost reporting periods of hospitals beginning in fiscal year 1984 or fiscal year 1985, the Secretary shall provide for such proportional adjustment in the applicable percentage increase (otherwise applicable to the periods under subsection (b)(3)(B) of this section) as may be necessary to assure that—

    (i) the aggregate payment amounts otherwise provided under subsection (d)(1)(A)(i)(I) of this section for that fiscal year for operating costs of inpatient hospital services of hospitals (excluding payments made under section 1395cc(a)(1)(F) of this title),

are not greater or less than—

    (ii) the target percentage (as defined in subsection (d)(1)(C) of this section) of the payment amounts which would have been payable for such services for those same hospitals for that fiscal year under this section under the law as in effect before April 20, 1983 (excluding payments made under section 1395cc(a)(1)(F) of this title);

except that the adjustment made under this subparagraph shall apply only to subsection (d) hospitals and shall not apply for purposes of making computations under subsection (d)(2)(B)(ii) of this section or subsection (d)(3)(A) of this section.

(B) For discharges occurring in fiscal year 1984 or fiscal year 1985, the Secretary shall provide under subsections (d)(2)(F) and (d)(3)(C) of this section for such equal proportional adjustment in each of the average standardized amounts otherwise computed for that fiscal year as may be necessary to assure that—

(i) the aggregate payment amounts otherwise provided under subsection (d)(1)(A)(i)(II) and (d)(5) of this section for that fiscal year for operating costs of inpatient hospital services of hospitals (excluding payments made under section 1395cc(a)(1)(F) of this title),

are not greater or less than—

(ii) the DRG percentage (as defined in subsection (d)(1)(C) of this section) of the payment amounts which would have been payable for such services for those same hospitals for that fiscal year under this section under the law as in effect before April 20, 1983 (excluding payments made under section 1395cc(a)(1)(F) of this title).

(C) For discharges occurring in fiscal year 1988, the Secretary shall provide for such equal proportional adjustment in each of the average standardized amounts otherwise computed under subsection (d)(3) of this section for that fiscal year as may be necessary to assure that—

(i) the aggregate payment amounts otherwise provided under subsections (d)(1)(A)(iii), (d)(5), and (d)(9) of this section for that fiscal year for operating costs of inpatient hospital services of subsection (d) hospitals and subsection (d) Puerto Rico hospitals,

are not greater or less than—

(ii) the payment amounts that would have been payable for such services for those same hospitals for that fiscal year but for the enactment of the amendments made by section 9304 of the Omnibus Budget Reconciliation Act of 1986.

(2) Repealed. Pub.L. 105–33, Title IV, § 4022(b)(1)(A)(i), Aug. 5, 1997, 111 Stat. 354

(3) The Secretary, not later than April 1, 1987, for fiscal year 1988 and not later than March 1 before the beginning of each fiscal year (beginning with fiscal year 1989), shall report to the Congress the Secretary's initial estimate of the percentage change that the Secretary will recommend under paragraph (4) with respect to that fiscal year.

(4)(A) Taking into consideration the recommendations of the Commission, the Secretary shall recommend for each fiscal year (beginning with fiscal year 1988) an appropriate change factor for inpatient hospital services for discharges in that fiscal year which will take into account amounts necessary for the efficient and effective delivery of medically appropriate and necessary care of high quality. The appropriate change factor may be different for all large urban subsection (d) hospitals, other urban subsection (d) hospitals, urban subsection (d) Puerto Rico hospitals, rural subsection (d) hospitals, and rural subsection (d) Puerto Rico hospitals, and all other hospitals and units not paid under subsection (d) of this section, and may vary among such other hospitals and units.

(B) In addition to the recommendation made under subparagraph (A), the Secretary shall, taking into consideration the recommendations of the Commission under paragraph (2)(B), recommend for each fiscal year (beginning with fiscal year 1992) other appropriate changes in each existing reimbursement policy under this subchapter under which payments to an institution are based upon prospectively determined rates.

(5) The Secretary shall cause to have published in the Federal Register, not later than—

(A) the April 1 before each fiscal year (beginning with fiscal year 1986), the Secretary's proposed recommendations under paragraph (4) for that fiscal year for public comment, and

(B) the August 1 before such fiscal year after such consideration of public comment on the proposal as is feasible in the time available, the Secretary's final recommendations under such paragraph for that year.

The Secretary shall include in the publication referred to in subparagraph (A) for a fiscal year the report of the Commission's recommendations submitted under paragraph (3) for that fiscal year. To the extent that the Secretary's recommendations under paragraph (4) differ from the Commission's recommendations for that fiscal year, the Secretary shall include in the publication referred to in subparagraph (A) an explanation of the Secretary's grounds for not following the Commission's recommendations.

(6) Repealed. Pub.L. 105–33, Title IV, § 4022(b)(1)(A)(i), Aug. 5, 1997, 111 Stat. 354

(f) Reporting of costs of hospitals receiving payments on basis of prospective rates

(1)(A) The Secretary shall maintain a system for the reporting of costs of hospitals receiving payments computed under subsection (d) of this section.

(B)(i) Subject to clause (ii), the Secretary shall place into effect a standardized electronic cost reporting format for hospitals under this subchapter.

(ii) The Secretary may delay or waive the implementation of such format in particular instances where such implementation would result in financial hardship (in particular with respect to hospitals with a small percentage of inpatients entitled to benefits under this subchapter).

(2) If the Secretary determines, based upon information supplied by a utilization and quality control peer review organization under part B of subchapter XI of this chapter, that a hospital, in order to circumvent the payment method established under subsection (b) or (d) of this section, has taken an action that results in the admission of individuals entitled to benefits under part A unnecessarily, unnecessary multiple admissions of the same such individuals, or other inappropriate medical or other practices with respect to such individuals, the Secretary may—

(A) deny payment (in whole or in part) under part A of this subchapter with respect to inpatient hospital services provided with respect to such an unnecessary admission (or subsequent admission of the same individual), or

(B) require the hospital to take other corrective action necessary to prevent or correct the inappropriate practice.

(3) The provisions of subsections (c) through (g) of section 1320a–7 of this title shall apply to determinations made under paragraph (2) in the same manner as they apply to exclusions effected under section 1320a–7(b)(13) of this title.

(g) Prospective payment for capital-related costs; return on equity capital for hospitals

(1)(A) Notwithstanding section 1395x(v) of this title, instead of any amounts that are otherwise payable under this subchapter with respect to the reasonable costs of subsection (d) hospitals and subsection (d) Puerto Rico hospitals for capital-related costs of inpatient hospital services, the Secretary shall, for hospital cost reporting periods beginning on or after October 1, 1991, provide for payments for such costs in accordance with a prospective payment system established by the Secretary. Aggregate payments made under subsection (d) of this section and this subsection during fiscal years 1992 through 1995 shall be reduced in a manner that results in a reduction (as estimated by the Secretary) in the amount of such payments equal to a 10 percent reduction in the amount of payments attributable to capital-related costs that would otherwise have been made during such fiscal year had the amount of such payments been based on reasonable costs (as defined in section 1395x(v) of this title). For discharges occurring after September 30, 1993, the Secretary shall reduce by 7.4 percent the unadjusted standard Federal capital payment rate (as described in 42 CFR 412.308(c), as in effect on August 10, 1993) and shall (for hospital cost reporting periods beginning on or after October 1, 1993) redetermine which payment methodology is applied to the hospital under such system to take into account such reduction. In addition to the reduction described in the preceding sentence, for discharges occurring on or after October 1, 1997, the Secretary shall apply the budget neutrality adjustment factor used to determine the Federal capital payment rate in effect on September 30, 1995 (as described in section 412.352 of title 42 of the Code of Federal Regulations), to (i) the unadjusted standard Federal capital payment rate (as described in section 412.308(c) of that title, as in effect on September 30, 1997), and (ii) the unadjusted hospital-specific rate (as described in section 412.328(e)(1) of that title, as in effect on September 30, 1997), and, for discharges occurring on or after October 1, 1997, and before October 1, 2002, reduce the rates described in clauses (i) and (ii) by 2.1 percent.

(B) Such system—

(i) shall provide for (I) a payment on a per discharge basis, and (II) an appropriate weighting of such payment amount as relates to the classification of the discharge;

(ii) may provide for an adjustment to take into account variations in the relative costs of capital and construction for the different types of facilities or areas in which they are located;

(iii) may provide for such exceptions (including appropriate exceptions to reflect capital obligations) as the Secretary determines to be appropriate, and

(iv) may provide for suitable adjustment to reflect hospital occupancy rate.

(C) In this paragraph, the term "capital-related costs" has the meaning given such term by the Secretary under subsection (a)(4) of this section as of September 30, 1987, and does not include a return on equity capital.

(2)(A) The Secretary shall provide that the amount which is allowable, with respect to reasonable costs of inpatient hospital services for which payment may be made under this subchapter, for a return on equity capital for hospitals shall, for cost reporting periods beginning on or after April 20, 1983, be equal to amounts otherwise allowable under regulations in effect on March 1, 1983, except that the rate of return to be recognized shall be equal to the applicable percentage (described in subparagraph (B)) of the average of the rates of interest, for each of the months any part of which is included in the reporting period, on obligations issued for purchase by the Federal Hospital Insurance Trust Fund.

(B) In this paragraph, the "applicable percentage" is—

(i) 75 percent, for cost reporting periods beginning during fiscal year 1987,

(ii) 50 percent, for cost reporting periods beginning during fiscal year 1988, (**iii**) 25 percent, for cost reporting periods beginning during fiscal year 1989, and

(**iv**) 0 percent, for cost reporting periods beginning on or after October 1, 1989.

(**3**)(**A**) Except as provided in subparagraph (B), in determining the amount of the payments that may be made under this subchapter with respect to all the capital-related costs of inpatient hospital services of a subsection (d) hospital and a subsection (d) Puerto Rico hospital, the Secretary shall reduce the amounts of such payments otherwise established under this subchapter by—

(**i**) 3.5 percent for payments attributable to portions of cost reporting periods occurring during fiscal year 1987,

(**ii**) 7 percent for payments attributable to portions of cost reporting periods or discharges (as the case may be) occurring during fiscal year 1988 on or after October 1, 1987, and before January 1, 1988,

(**iii**) 12 percent for payments attributable to portions of cost reporting periods or discharges (as the case may be) in fiscal year 1988, occurring on or after January 1, 1988,

(**iv**) 15 percent for payments attributable to portions of cost reporting periods or discharges (as the case may be) occurring during fiscal year 1989, and

(**v**) 15 percent for payments attributable to portions of cost reporting periods or discharges (as the case may be) occurring during the period beginning January 1, 1990, and ending September 30, 1991.

(**B**) Subparagraph (A) shall not apply to payments with respect to the capital-related costs of any hospital that is a sole community hospital (as defined in subsection (d)(5)(D)(iii) of this section or a critical access hospital (as defined in section 1395x(mm)(1) of this title)).

(**4**) In determining the amount of the payments that are attributable to portions of cost reporting periods occurring during fiscal years 1998 through 2002 and that may be made under this subchapter with respect to capital-related costs of inpatient hospital services of a hospital which is described in clause (i), (ii), or (iv) of subsection (d)(1)(B) of this section or a unit described in the matter after clause (v) of such subsection, the Secretary shall reduce the amounts of such payments otherwise determined under this title by 15 percent.

(**h**) Payments for direct graduate medical education costs

(**1**) Substitution of special payment rules

Notwithstanding section 1395x(v) of this title, instead of any amounts that are otherwise payable under this subchapter with respect to the reasonable costs of hospitals for direct graduate medical education costs, the Secretary shall provide for payments for such costs in accordance with paragraph (3) of this subsection. In providing for such payments, the Secretary shall provide for an allocation of such payments between part A and part B of this subchapter (and the trust funds established under the respective parts) as reasonably reflects the proportion of direct graduate medical education costs of hospitals associated with the provision of services under each respective part.

(2) Determination of hospital-specific approved FTE resident amounts

The Secretary shall determine, for each hospital with an approved medical residency training program, an approved FTE resident amount for each cost reporting period beginning on or after July 1, 1985, as follows:

(A) Determining allowable average cost per FTE resident in a hospital's base period

The Secretary shall determine, for the hospital's cost reporting period that began during fiscal year 1984, the average amount recognized as reasonable under this subchapter for direct graduate medical education costs of the hospital for each full-time-equivalent resident.

(B) Updating to the first cost reporting period

(i) In general

The Secretary shall update each average amount determined under subparagraph (A) by the percentage increase in the consumer price index during the 12–month cost reporting period described in such subparagraph.

(ii) Exception

The Secretary shall not perform an update under clause (i) in the case of a hospital if the hospital's reporting period, described in subparagraph (A), began on or after July 1, 1984, and before October 1, 1984.

(C) Amount for first cost reporting period

For the first cost reporting period of the hospital beginning on or after July 1, 1985, the approved FTE resident amount for the hospital is equal to the amount determined under subparagraph (B) increased by 1 percent.

(D) Amount for subsequent cost reporting periods

(i) In general

Except as provided in a subsequent clause, for each subsequent cost reporting period, the approved FTE resident amount for the hospital is equal to the approved FTE resident amount

765

determined under this paragraph for the previous cost reporting period updated, through the midpoint of the period, by projecting the estimated percentage change in the consumer price index during the 12–month period ending at that midpoint, with appropriate adjustments to reflect previous under-or over-estimations under this subparagraph in the projected percentage change in the consumer price index.

(ii) Freeze in update for fiscal years 1994 and 1995

For cost reporting periods beginning during fiscal year 1994 or fiscal year 1995, the approved FTE resident amount for a hospital shall not be updated under clause (i) for a resident who is not a primary care resident (as defined in paragraph (5)(H)) or a resident enrolled in an approved medical residency training program in obstetrics and gynecology.

(iii) Floor for locality adjusted national average per resident amount

The approved FTE resident amount for a hospital for the cost reporting period beginning during fiscal year 2001 shall not be less than 70 percent, and for the cost reporting period beginning during fiscal year 2002 shall not be less than 85 percent, of the locality adjusted national average per resident amount computed under subparagraph (E) for the hospital and period.

(v) Adjustment in rate of increase for hospitals with FTE approved amount above 140 percent of locality adjusted national average per resident amount

(I) Freeze for fiscal years 2001 and 2002

For a cost reporting period beginning during fiscal year 2001 or fiscal year 2002, if the approved FTE resident amount for a hospital for the preceding cost reporting period exceeds 140 percent of the locality adjusted national average per resident amount computed under subparagraph (E) for that hospital and period, subject to subclause (III), the approved FTE resident amount for the period involved shall be the same as the approved FTE resident amount for the hospital for such preceding cost reporting period.

(II) 2 percent decrease in update for fiscal years 2003, 2004, and 2005

For a cost reporting period beginning during fiscal year 2003, fiscal year 2004, or fiscal year 2005, if the approved FTE resident amount for a hospital for the preceding cost reporting period exceeds 140 percent of the locality adjusted national average per resident amount computed under subparagraph (E) for that hospital and preceding period, the approved FTE resident amount for the period involved shall be updated in the manner described in subparagraph (D)(i) except that, subject to subclause (III), the consumer price index applied for a 12–month period shall be reduced (but not below zero) by 2 percentage points.

(III) No adjustment below 140 percent

In no case shall subclause (I) or (II) reduce an approved FTE resident amount for a hospital for a cost reporting period below 140 percent of the locality adjusted national average per resident amount computed under subparagraph (E) for such hospital and period.

(E) Determination of locality adjusted national average per resident amount

The Secretary shall determine a locality adjusted national average per resident amount with respect to a cost reporting period of a hospital beginning during a fiscal year as follows:

(i) Determining hospital single per resident amount

The Secretary shall compute for each hospital operating an approved graduate medical education program a single per resident amount equal to the average (weighted by number of full-time equivalent residents, as determined under paragraph (4)) of the primary care per resident amount and the non-primary care per resident amount computed under paragraph (2) for cost reporting periods ending during fiscal year 1997.

(ii) Standardizing per resident amounts

The Secretary shall compute a standardized per resident amount for each such hospital by dividing the single per resident amount computed under clause (i) by an average of the 3 geographic index values (weighted by the national average weight for each of the work, practice expense, and malpractice components) as applied under section 1395w–4(e) of this title for 1999 for the fee schedule area in which the hospital is located.

(iii) Computing of weighted average

The Secretary shall compute the average of the standardized per resident amounts computed under clause (ii) for such hospitals, with the amount for each hospital weighted by the average number of full-time equivalent residents at such hospital (as determined under paragraph (4)).

(iv) Computing national average per resident amount

The Secretary shall compute the national average per resident amount, for a hospital's cost reporting period that begins during fiscal year 2001, equal to the weighted average computed under clause (iii) increased by the estimated percentage increase in the consumer price index for all urban consumers during the period beginning with the month that represents the midpoint of the cost reporting periods described in clause (i) and ending with the midpoint of the hospital's cost reporting period that begins during fiscal year 2001.

(v) Adjusting for locality

The Secretary shall compute the product of—

    (I) the national average per resident amount computed under clause (iv) for the hospital, and

    (II) the geographic index value average (described and applied under clause (ii)) for the fee schedule area in which the hospital is located.

(vi) Computing locality adjusted amount

The locality adjusted national per resident amount for a hospital for—

    (I) the cost reporting period beginning during fiscal year 2001 is the product computed under clause (v); or

    (II) each subsequent cost reporting period is equal to the locality adjusted national per resident amount for the hospital for the previous cost reporting period (as determined under this clause) updated, through the midpoint of the period, by projecting the estimated percentage change in the consumer price index for all urban consumers during the 12–month period ending at that midpoint.

(F) Treatment of certain hospitals

In the case of a hospital that did not have an approved medical residency training program or was not participating in the program under this subchapter for a cost reporting period beginning during fiscal year 1984, the Secretary shall, for the first such period for which it has such a residency training program and is participating under this subchapter, provide for such approved FTE resident amount as the Secretary determines to be appropriate, based on approved FTE resident amounts for comparable programs.

(3) Hospital payment amount per resident

(A) In general

The payment amount, for a hospital cost reporting period beginning on or after July 1, 1985, is equal to the product of—

    (i) the aggregate approved amount (as defined in subparagraph (B)) for that period, and

    (ii) the hospital's medicare patient load (as defined in subparagraph (C)) for that period.

(B) Aggregate approved amount

As used in subparagraph (A), the term "aggregate approved amount" means, for a hospital cost reporting period, the product of—

    (i) the hospital's approved FTE resident amount (determined under paragraph (2)) for that period, and

    (ii) the weighted average number of full-time-equivalent residents (as determined under paragraph (4)) in the hospital's approved medical residency training programs in that period.

The Secretary shall reduce the aggregate approved amount to the extent payment is made under subsection (k) of this section for residents included in the hospital's count of full-time equivalent residents.

(C) Medicare patient load

As used in subparagraph (A), the term "medicare patient load" means, with respect to a hospital's cost reporting period, the fraction of the total number of inpatient-bed-days (as established by the Secretary) during the period which are attributable to patients with respect to whom payment may be made under part A of this subchapter.

(D) Payment for managed care enrollees

    (i) In general

For portions of cost reporting periods occurring on or after January 1, 1998, the Secretary shall provide for an additional payment amount under this subsection for services furnished to individuals who are enrolled under a risk-sharing contract with an eligible organization under section 1395mm of this title and who are entitled to part A of this subchapter or with a Medicare + Choice organization under part C of this subchapter. The amount of such a payment shall equal, subject to clause (iii) the applicable percentage of the product of—

    (I) the aggregate approved amount (as defined in subparagraph (B)) for that period; and

    (II) the fraction of the total number of inpatient-bed days (as established by the Secretary) during the period which are attributable to such enrolled individuals.

    (ii) Applicable percentage

For purposes of clause (i), the applicable percentage is—

    (I) 20 percent in 1998,

    (II) 40 percent in 1999,

    (III) 60 percent in 2000, and

    (IV) 80 percent in 2001, and

    (V) 100 percent in 2002 and subsequent years.

(iii) Proportional reduction for nursing and allied health education

The Secretary shall estimate a proportional adjustment in payments to all hospitals determined under clauses (i) and (ii) for portions of cost reporting periods beginning in a year (beginning with 2000) such that the proportional adjustment reduces payments in an amount for such year equal to the total additional payment amounts for nursing and allied health education determined under subsection (l) for portions of cost reporting periods occurring in that year.

(iv) Special rule for hospitals under reimbursement system

The Secretary shall establish rules for the application of this subparagraph to a hospital reimbursed under a reimbursement system authorized under section 1395f(b)(3) of this title in the same manner as it would apply to the hospital if it were not reimbursed under such section.

(4) Determination of full-time-equivalent residents

(A) Rules

The Secretary shall establish rules consistent with this paragraph for the computation of the number of full-time-equivalent residents in an approved medical residency training program.

(B) Adjustment for part-year or part-time residents

Such rules shall take into account individuals who serve as residents for only a portion of a period with a hospital or simultaneously with more than one hospital.

(C) Weighting factors for certain residents

Subject to subparagraph (D), such rules shall provide, in calculating the number of full-time-equivalent residents in an approved residency program—

(i) before July 1, 1986, for each resident the weighting factor is 1.00,

(ii) on or after July 1, 1986, for a resident who is in the resident's initial residency period (as defined in paragraph (5)(F)), the weighting factor is 1.00,

(iii) on or after July 1, 1986, and before July 1, 1987, for a resident who is not in the resident's initial residency period (as defined in paragraph (5)(F)), the weighting factor is .75, and

(iv) on or after July 1, 1987, for a resident who is not in the resident's initial residency period (as defined in paragraph (5)(F)), the weighting factor is .50.

(D) Foreign medical graduates required to pass FMGEMS examination

(i) In general

Except as provided in clause (ii), such rules shall provide that, in the case of an individual who is a foreign medical graduate (as defined in paragraph (5)(D)), the individual shall not be counted as a resident on or after July 1, 1986, unless—

    (I) the individual has passed the FMGEMS examination (as defined in paragraph (5)(E)), or

    (II) the individual has previously received certification from, or has previously passed the examination of, the Educational Commission for Foreign Medical Graduates.

(ii) Transition for current FMGS

On or after July 1, 1986, but before July 1, 1987, in the case of a foreign medical graduate who—

    (I) has served as a resident before July 1, 1986, and is serving as a resident after that date, but

    (II) has not passed the FMGEMS examination or a previous examination of the Educational Commission for Foreign Medical Graduates before July 1, 1986,

the individual shall be counted as a resident at a rate equal to one-half of the rate at which the individual would otherwise be counted.

(E) Counting time spent in outpatient settings

Such rules shall provide that only time spent in activities relating to patient care shall be counted and that all the time so spent by a resident under an approved medical residency training program shall be counted towards the determination of full-time equivalency, without regard to the setting in which the activities are performed, if the hospital incurs all, or substantially all, of the costs for the training program in that setting.

(F) Limitation on number of residents in allopathic and osteopathic medicine

(i) In general

Such rules shall provide that for purposes of a cost reporting period beginning on or after October 1, 1997, the total number of full-time equivalent residents before application of weighting factors (as determined under this paragraph) with respect to a hospital's approved medical residency training program in the fields of allopathic medicine and osteopathic medicine may not exceed the number (or, 130 percent of such number in the case of a hospital located in a rural area) of such full-time equivalent residents for the hospital's most recent cost reporting period ending on or before December 31, 1996.

(ii) Counting primary care residents on certain approved leaves of absence in base year FTE count

(I) In general

In determining the number of such full-time equivalent residents for a hospital's most recent cost reporting period ending on or before December 31, 1996, for purposes of clause (i), the Secretary shall count an individual to the extent that the individual would have been counted as a primary care resident for such period but for the fact that the individual, as determined by the Secretary, was on maternity or disability leave or a similar approved leave of absence.

(II) Limitation to 3 FTE residents for any hospital

The total number of individuals counted under subclause (I) for a hospital may not exceed 3 full-time equivalent residents.

(G) Counting interns and residents for FY 1998 and subsequent years

(i) In general

For cost reporting periods beginning during fiscal years beginning on or after October 1, 1997, subject to the limit described in subparagraph (F), the total number of full-time equivalent residents for determining a hospital's graduate medical education payment shall equal the average of the actual full-time equivalent resident counts for the cost reporting period and the preceding two cost reporting periods.

(ii) Adjustment for short periods

If any cost reporting period beginning on or after October 1, 1997, is not equal to twelve months, the Secretary shall make appropriate modifications to ensure that the average full-time equivalent resident counts pursuant to clause (i) are based on the equivalent of full twelve-month cost reporting periods.

(iii) Transition rule for 1998

In the case of a hospital's first cost reporting period beginning on or after October 1, 1997, clause (i) shall be applied by using the average for such period and the preceding cost reporting period.

(H) Special rules for application of subparagraphs (F) and (G)

(i) New facilities

The Secretary shall, consistent with the principles of subparagraphs (F) and (G), prescribe rules for the application of such subparagraphs in the case of medical residency training programs established on or after January 1, 1995. In promulgating such rules for purposes of subparagraph (F), the Secretary shall give special consideration to facilities that meet the needs of underserved rural areas.

(ii) Aggregation

The Secretary may prescribe rules which allow institutions which are members of the same affiliated group (as defined by the Secretary) to elect to apply the limitation of subparagraph (F) on an aggregate basis.

(iii) Data collection

The Secretary may require any entity that operates a medical residency training program and to which subparagraphs (F) and (G) apply to submit to the Secretary such additional information as the Secretary considers necessary to carry out such subparagraphs.

(iv) Nonrural hospitals operating training programs in rural areas

In the case of a hospital that is not located in a rural area but establishes separately accredited approved medical residency training programs (or rural tracks) in an rural area or has an accredited training program with an integrated rural track, the Secretary shall adjust the limitation under subparagraph (F) in an appropriate manner insofar as it applies to such programs in such rural areas in order to encourage the training of physicians in rural areas.

(5) Definitions and special rules

As used in this subsection:

(A) Approved medical residency training program

The term "approved medical residency training program" means a residency or other postgraduate medical training program participation in which may be counted toward certification in a specialty or subspecialty and includes formal postgraduate training programs in geriatric medicine approved by the Secretary.

(B) Consumer price index

The term "consumer price index" refers to the Consumer Price Index for All Urban Consumers (United States city average), as published by the Secretary of Commerce.

(C) Direct graduate medical education costs

The term "direct graduate medical education costs" means direct costs of approved educational activities for approved medical residency training programs.

(D) Foreign medical graduate

The term "foreign medical graduate" means a resident who is not a graduate of—

(i) a school of medicine accredited by the Liaison Committee on Medical Education of the American Medical Association and the Association of American Medical Colleges (or approved by such Committee as meeting the standards necessary for such accreditation),

(ii) a school of osteopathy accredited by the American Osteopathic Association, or approved by such Association as meeting the standards necessary for such accreditation, or

(iii) a school of dentistry or podiatry which is accredited (or meets the standards for accreditation) by an organization recognized by the Secretary for such purpose.

(E) FMGEMS examination

The term "FMGEMS examination" means parts I and II of the Foreign Medical Graduate Examination in the Medical Sciences or any successor examination recognized by the Secretary for this purpose.

(F) Initial residency period

The term "initial residency period" means the period of board eligibility, except that—

(i) except as provided in clause (ii), in no case shall the initial period of residency exceed an aggregate period of formal training of more than five years for any individual, and

(ii) a period, of not more than two years, during which an individual is in a geriatric residency or fellowship program or a preventive medicine residency or fellowship program which meets such criteria as the Secretary may establish, shall be treated as part of the initial residency period, but shall not be counted against any limitation on the initial residency period.

Subject to subparagraph (G)(v), the initial residency period shall be determined, with respect to a resident, as of the time the resident enters the residency training program.

(G) Period of board eligibility

(i) General rule

Subject to clauses (ii), (iii), (iv), and (v) the term "period of board eligibility" means, for a resident, the minimum number of years of formal training necessary to satisfy the requirements for initial board eligibility in the particular specialty for which the resident is training.

(ii) Application of 1985–1986 Directory

Except as provided in clause (iii), the period of board eligibility shall be such period specified in the 1985–1986 Directory of

Residency Training Programs published by the Accreditation Council on Graduate Medical Education.

(iii) Changes in period of board eligibility

On or after July 1, 1989, if the Accreditation Council on Graduate Medical Education, in its Directory of Residency Training Programs—

(I) increases the minimum number of years of formal training necessary to satisfy the requirements for a specialty, above the period specified in its 1985–1986 Directory, the Secretary may increase the period of board eligibility for that specialty, but not to exceed the period of board eligibility specified in that later Directory, or

(II) decreases the minimum number of years of formal training necessary to satisfy the requirements for a specialty, below the period specified in its 1985–1986 Directory, the Secretary may decrease the period of board eligibility for that specialty, but not below the period of board eligibility specified in that later Directory.

(iv) Special rule for certain primary care combined residency programs

(I) In the case of a resident enrolled in a combined medical residency training program in which all of the individual programs (that are combined) are for training a primary care resident (as defined in subparagraph (H)), the period of board eligibility shall be the minimum number of years of formal training required to satisfy the requirements for initial board eligibility in the longest of the individual programs plus one additional year.

(II) A resident enrolled in a combined medical residency training program that includes an obstetrics and gynecology program shall qualify for the period of board eligibility under subclause (I) if the other programs such resident combines with such obstetrics and gynecology program are for training a primary care resident.

(v) Child neurology training programs

In the case of a resident enrolled in a child neurology residency training program, the period of board eligibility and the initial residency period shall be the period of board eligibility for pediatrics plus 2 years.

(H) Primary care resident

The term "primary care resident" means a resident enrolled in an approved medical residency training program in family medicine, general internal medicine, general pediatrics, preventive medicine, geriatric medicine, or osteopathic general practice.

(I) Resident

The term "resident" includes an intern or other participant in an approved medical residency training program.

(J) Adjustments for certain family practice residency programs

(i) In general

In the case of an approved medical residency training program (meeting the requirements of clause (ii)) of a hospital which received funds from the United States, a State, or a political subdivision of a State or an instrumentality of such a State or political subdivision (other than payments under this subchapter or a State plan under subchapter XIX of this chapter) for the program during the cost reporting period that began during fiscal year 1984, the Secretary shall—

(I) provide for an average amount under paragraph (2)(A) that takes into account the Secretary's estimate of the amount that would have been recognized as reasonable under this subchapter if the hospital had not received such funds, and

(II) reduce the payment amount otherwise provided under this subsection in an amount equal to the proportion of such program funds received during the cost reporting period involved that is allocable to this subchapter.

(ii) Additional requirements

A hospital's approved medical residency program meets the requirements of this clause if—

(I) the program is limited to training for family and community medicine;

(II) the program is the only approved medical residency program of the hospital; and

(III) the average amount determined under paragraph (2)(A) for the hospital (as determined without regard to the increase in such amount described in clause (i)(I)) does not exceed $10,000.

(6) Incentive payment under plans for voluntary reduction in number of residents

(A) In general

In the case of a voluntary residency reduction plan for which an application is approved under subparagraph (B), subject to subparagraph (F), each hospital which is part of the qualifying entity

776

submitting the plan shall be paid an applicable hold harmless percentage (as specified in subparagraph (E)) of the sum of—

(i) the amount (if any) by which—

(I) the amount of payment which would have been made under this subsection if there had been a 5–percent reduction in the number of full-time equivalent residents in the approved medical education training programs of the hospital as of June 30, 1997, exceeds

(II) the amount of payment which is made under this subsection, taking into account the reduction in such number effected under the reduction plan; and

(ii) the amount of the reduction in payment under subsection (d)(5)(B) of this section for the hospital that is attributable to the reduction in number of residents effected under the plan below 95 percent of the number of full-time equivalent residents in such programs of the hospital as of June 30, 1997.

The determination of the amounts under clauses (i) and (ii) for any year shall be made on the basis of the provisions of this title in effect on the application deadline date for the first calendar year to which the reduction plan applies.

(B) Approval of plan applications

The Secretary may not approve the application of an qualifying entity unless—

(i) the application is submitted in a form and manner specified by the Secretary and by not later than November 1, 1999,

(ii) the application provides for the operation of a plan for the reduction in the number of full-time equivalent residents in the approved medical residency training programs of the entity consistent with the requirements of subparagraph (D);

(iii) the entity elects in the application the period of residency training years (not greater than 5) over which the reduction will occur;

(iv) the entity will not reduce the proportion of its residents in primary care (to the total number of residents) below such proportion as in effect as of the applicable time described in subparagraph (D)(v); and

(v) the Secretary determines that the application and the entity and such plan meet such other requirements as the Secretary specifies in regulations.

(C) Qualifying entity

For purposes of this paragraph, any of the following may be a qualifying entity:

(i) Individual hospitals operating one or more approved medical residency training programs.

(ii) Two or more hospitals that operate such programs and apply for treatment under this paragraph as a single qualifying entity.

(iii) A qualifying consortium (as described in section 1394ww note of this title).

(D) Residency reduction requirements

(i) Individual hospital applicants

In the case of a qualifying entity described in subparagraph (C)(i), the number of full-time equivalent residents in all the approved medical residency training programs operated by or through the entity shall be reduced as follows:

(I) If the base number of residents exceeds 750 residents, by a number equal to at least 20 percent of such base number.

(II) Subject to subclause (IV), if the base number of residents exceeds 600 but is less than 750 residents, by 150 residents.

(III) Subject to subclause (IV), if the base number of residents does not exceed 600 residents, by a number equal to at least 25 percent of such base number.

(IV) In the case of a qualifying entity which is described in clause (v) and which elects treatment under this subclause, by a number equal to at least 20 percent of the base number.

(ii) Joint applicants

In the case of a qualifying entity described in subparagraph (C)(ii), the number of full-time equivalent residents in the aggregate for all the approved medical residency training programs operated by or through the entity shall be reduced as follows:

(I) Subject to subclause (II), by a number equal to at least 25 percent of the base number.

(II) In the case of such a qualifying entity which is described in clause (v) and which elects treatment under this subclause, by a number equal to at least 20 percent of the base number.

(iii) Consortia

In the case of a qualifying entity described in subparagraph (C)(iii), the number of full-time equivalent residents in the aggregate for all the approved medical residency training programs operated by or through the entity shall be reduced by a number equal to at least 20 percent of the base number.

(iv) Manner of reduction

The reductions specified under the preceding provisions of this subparagraph for a qualifying entity shall be below the base number of residents for that entity and shall be fully effective not later than the 5th residency training year in which the application under subparagraph (B) is effective.

(v) Entities providing assurance of increase in primary care residents

An entity is described in this clause if—

(I) the base number of residents for the entity is less than 750 or the entity is described in subparagraph (C)(ii); and

(II) the entity represents in its application under subparagraph (B) that it will increase the number of full-time equivalent residents in primary care by at least 20 percent (from such number included in the base number of residents) by not later than the 5th residency training year in which the application under subparagraph (B) is effective.

If a qualifying entity fails to comply with the representation described in subclause (II) by the end of such 5th residency training year, the entity shall be subject to repayment of all amounts paid under this paragraph, in accordance with procedures established to carry out subparagraph (F).

(vi) Base number of residents defined—

For purposes of this paragraph, the term "base number of residents" means, with respect to a qualifying entity (or its participating hospitals) operating approved medical residency training programs, the number of full-time equivalent residents in such programs (before application of weighting factors) of the entity as of the most recent residency training year ending before June 30, 1997, or, if less, for any subsequent residency training year that ends before the date the entity makes application under this paragraph.

(E) Applicable hold harmless percentage

For purposes of subparagraph (A), the "applicable hold harmless percentage" for the—

(i) first and second residency training years in which the reduction plan is in effect, 100 percent,

(ii) third such year, 75 percent,

779

(iii) fourth such year, 50 percent, and

(iv) fifth such year, 25 percent.

(F) Penalty for noncompliance

(i) In general

No payment may be made under this paragraph to a hospital for a residency training year if the hospital has failed to reduce the number of full-time equivalent residents (in the manner required under subparagraph (D)) to the number agreed to by the Secretary and the qualifying entity in approving the application under this paragraph with respect to such year.

(ii) Increase in number of residents in subsequent years

If payments are made under this paragraph to a hospital, and if the hospital increases the number of full-time equivalent residents above the number of such residents permitted under the reduction plan as of the completion of the plan, then, as specified by the Secretary, the entity is liable for repayment to the Secretary of the total amounts paid under this paragraph to the entity.

(G) Treatment of rotating residents

In applying this paragraph, the Secretary shall establish rules regarding the counting of residents who are assigned to institutions the medical residency training programs in which are not covered under approved applications under this paragraph.

(i) Avoiding duplicative payments to hospitals participating in rural demonstration programs.

The Secretary shall reduce any payment amounts otherwise determined under this section to the extent necessary to avoid duplication of any payment made under section 4005(e) of the Omnibus Budget Reconciliation Act of 1987.

(j) Prospective payment for inpatient rehabilitation services

(1) Payment during transition period

(A) In general

Notwithstanding section 1395f(b) of this title, but subject to the provisions of section 1395e of this title, the amount of the payment with respect to the operating and capital costs of inpatient hospital services of a rehabilitation hospital or a rehabilitation unit (in this subsection referred to as a "rehabilitation facility"), other than a facility making an election under subparagraph (F) in a cost reporting period beginning on or after October 1, 2000, and before October 1, 2002, is equal to the sum of—

(i) the TEFRA percentage (as defined in subparagraph (C)) of the amount that would have been paid under part A of this subchapter with respect to such costs if this subsection did not apply, and

(ii) the prospective payment percentage (as defined in subparagraph (C)) of the product of (I) the per unit payment rate established under this subsection for the fiscal year in which the payment unit of service occurs, and (II) the number of such payment units occurring in the cost reporting period.

(B) Fully implemented system

Notwithstanding section 1395f(b) of this title, but subject to the provisions of section 1395e of this title, the amount of the payment with respect to the operating and capital costs of inpatient hospital services of a rehabilitation facility for a payment unit in a cost reporting period beginning on or after October 1, 2002, or, in the case of a facility making an election under subparagraph (F), for any cost reporting period described in such subparagraph, is equal to the per unit payment rate established under this subsection for the fiscal year in which the payment unit of service occurs.

(C) TEFRA and prospective payment percentages specified

For purposes of subparagraph (A), for a cost reporting period beginning—

(i) on or after October 1, 2000, and before October 1, 2001, the "TEFRA percentage" is 66 2/3 percent and the 'prospective payment percentage' is 33 1/3 percent; and

(ii) on or after October 1, 2001, and before October 1, 2002, the "TEFRA percentage" is 33 1/3 percent and the "prospective payment percentage" is 66 2/3 percent.

(D) Payment unit

For purposes of this subsection, the term "payment unit" means a discharge.

(E) Construction relating to transfer authority

Nothing in this subsection shall be construed as preventing the Secretary from providing for an adjustment to payments to take into account the early transfer of a patient from a rehabilitation facility to another site of care.

(F) Election to apply full prospective payment system

A rehabilitation facility may elect, not later than 30 days before its first cost reporting period for which the payment methodology under this subsection applies to the facility, to have payment made to the facility under this subsection under the provisions of subparagraph (B) (rather than subparagraph (A)) for each cost reporting period to which such payment methodology applies.

(2) Patient case mix groups

(A) Establishment

The Secretary shall establish—

(i) classes of patient discharges of rehabilitation facilities by functional-related groups (each in this subsection referred to as a 'case mix group'), based on impairment, age, comorbidities, and functional capability of the patient and such other factors as the Secretary deems appropriate to improve the explanatory power of functional independence measure-function related groups; and

(ii) a method of classifying specific patients in rehabilitation facilities within these groups.

(B) Weighting factors

For each case mix group the Secretary shall assign an appropriate weighting which reflects the relative facility resources used with respect to patients classified within that group compared to patients classified within other groups.

(C) Adjustments for case mix

(i) In general

The Secretary shall from time to time adjust the classifications and weighting factors established under this paragraph as appropriate to reflect changes in treatment patterns, technology, case mix, number of payment units for which payment is made under this subchapter, and other factors which may affect the relative use of resources. Such adjustments shall be made in a manner so that changes in aggregate payments under the classification system are a result of real changes and are not a result of changes in coding that are unrelated to real changes in case mix.

(ii) Adjustment

Insofar as the Secretary determines that such adjustments for a previous fiscal year (or estimates that such adjustments for a future fiscal year) did (or are likely to) result in a change in aggregate payments under the classification system during the fiscal year that are a result of changes in the coding or classification of patients that do not reflect real changes in case mix, the Secretary shall adjust the per payment unit payment rate for subsequent years so as to eliminate the effect of such coding or classification changes.

(D) Data collection

The Secretary is authorized to require rehabilitation facilities that provide inpatient hospital services to submit such data as the Secretary deems necessary to establish and administer the prospective payment system under this subsection.

(3) Payment rate

(A) In general

The Secretary shall determine a prospective payment rate for each payment unit for which such rehabilitation facility is entitled to receive payment under this subchapter. Subject to subparagraph (B), such rate for payment units occurring during a fiscal year shall be based on the average payment per payment unit under this title for inpatient operating and capital costs of rehabilitation facilities using the most recent data available (as estimated by the Secretary as of the date of establishment of the system) adjusted—

(i) by updating such per-payment-unit amount to the fiscal year involved by the weighted average of the applicable percentage increases provided under subsection (b)(3)(B)(ii) of this section (for cost reporting periods beginning during the fiscal year) covering the period from the midpoint of the period for such data through the midpoint of fiscal year 2000 and by an increase factor (described in subparagraph (C)) specified by the Secretary for subsequent fiscal years up to the fiscal year involved;

(ii) by reducing such rates by a factor equal to the proportion of payments under this subsection (as estimated by the Secretary) based on prospective payment amounts which are additional payments described in paragraph (4) (relating to outlier and related payments);

(iii) for variations among rehabilitation facilities by area under paragraph (6);

(iv) by the weighting factors established under paragraph (2)(B); and

(v) by such other factors as the Secretary determines are necessary to properly reflect variations in necessary costs of treatment among rehabilitation facilities.

(B) Budget neutral rates

The Secretary shall establish the prospective payment amounts under this subsection for payment units during fiscal years 2001 and 2002 at levels such that, in the Secretary's estimation, the amount of total payments under this subsection for such fiscal years (including any payment adjustments pursuant to paragraphs (4) and (6) but not taking into account any payment adjustment resulting from an election permitted under paragraph (1)(F)) shall be equal to 98 percent for fiscal year 2001 and 100 percent for fiscal year 2002 of the amount of payments that would have been made under this subchapter during the fiscal years for operating and capital costs of rehabilitation facilities had this subsection not been enacted. In establishing such payment amounts, the Secretary shall consider the effects of the prospective payment system established under this subsection on the total number of payment units from rehabilitation facilities and other factors described in subparagraph (A).

(C) Increase factor

For purposes of this subsection for payment units in each fiscal year (beginning with fiscal year 2001), the Secretary shall establish an increase factor. Such factor shall be based on an appropriate percentage increase in a market basket of goods and services comprising services for which payment is made under this subsection, which may be the market basket percentage increase described in subsection (b)(3)(B)(iii) of this section.

(4) Outlier and special payments

(A) Outliers

(i) In general

The Secretary may provide for an additional payment to a rehabilitation facility for patients in a case mix group, based upon the patient being classified as an outlier based on an unusual length of stay, costs, or other factors specified by the Secretary.

(ii) Payment based on marginal cost of care

The amount of such additional payment under clause (i) shall be determined by the Secretary and shall approximate the marginal cost of care beyond the cutoff point applicable under clause (i).

(iii) Total payments

The total amount of the additional payments made under this subparagraph for payment units in a fiscal year may not exceed 5 percent of the total payments projected or estimated to be made based on prospective payment rates for payment units in that year.

(B) Adjustment

The Secretary may provide for such adjustments to the payment amounts under this subsection as the Secretary deems appropriate to take into account the unique circumstances of rehabilitation facilities located in Alaska and Hawaii.

(5) Publication

The Secretary shall provide for publication in the Federal Register, on or before August 1 before each fiscal year (beginning with fiscal year 2001), of the classification and weighting factors for case mix groups under paragraph (2) for such fiscal year and a description of the methodology and data used in computing the prospective payment rates under this subsection for that fiscal year.

(6) Area wage adjustment

The Secretary shall adjust the proportion (as estimated by the Secretary from time to time) of rehabilitation facilities' costs which are attributable to wages and wage-related costs, of the prospective payment rates computed under paragraph (3) for area differences in wage levels by a factor (established by the Secretary) reflecting the relative hospital wage level in the geographic area of the rehabilitation facility compared to the national average wage level for such facilities. Not later than October 1, 2001 (and at least every 36 months thereafter), the Secretary shall update the factor under the preceding sentence on the basis of information available to the Secretary (and updated as appropriate) of the wages and wage-related costs incurred in furnishing rehabilitation services. Any adjustments or updates made under this paragraph for a fiscal year shall be made in a manner that assures that the aggregated payments under this subsection in the fiscal year are not greater or less than those that would have been made in the year without such adjustment.

(7) Limitation on review

There shall be no administrative or judicial review under section 1395ff of this title, 1395oo of this title, or otherwise of the establishment of—

> **(A)** case mix groups, of the methodology for the classification of patients within such groups, and of the appropriate weighting factors thereof under paragraph (2),

> **(B)** the prospective payment rates under paragraph (3),

> **(C)** outlier and special payments under paragraph (4), and

> **(D)** area wage adjustments under paragraph (6).

(k) Payment to nonhospital providers

(1) In general

For cost reporting periods beginning on or after October 1, 1997, the Secretary may establish rules for payment to qualified nonhospital providers for their direct costs of medical education, if those costs are incurred in the operation of an approved medical residency training program described in subsection (h) of this section. Such rules shall specify the amounts, form, and manner in which such payments will be made and the portion of such payments that will be made from each of the trust funds under this subchapter.

(2) Qualified nonhospital providers

For purposes of this subsection, the term "qualified nonhospital providers" means—

> **(A)** a Federally qualified health center, as defined in section 1395x(aa)(4) of this title;

> **(B)** a rural health clinic, as defined in section 1395x(aa)(2) of this title;

(C) Medicare + Choice organizations; and

(D) such other providers (other than hospitals) as the Secretary determines to be appropriate.

(l) Payment for nursing and allied health education for managed care enrollees

(1) In general

For portions of cost reporting periods occurring in a year (beginning with 2000), the Secretary shall provide for an additional payment amount for any hospital that receives payments for the costs of approved educational activities for nurse and allied health professional training under section 1395x(v)(1) of this title.

(2) Payment amount

The additional payment amount under this subsection for each hospital for portions of cost reporting periods occurring in a year shall be an amount specified by the Secretary in a manner consistent with the following:

(A) Determination of managed care enrollee payment ratio for graduate medical education payments

The Secretary shall estimate the ratio of payments for all hospitals for portions of cost reporting periods occurring in the year under subsection (h)(3)(D) to total direct graduate medical education payments estimated for such portions of periods under subsection (h)(3).

(B) Application to fee-for-service nursing and allied health education payments

Such ratio shall be applied to the Secretary's estimate of total payments for nursing and allied health education determined under section 1395x(v) of this title for portions of cost reporting periods occurring in the year to determine a total amount of additional payments for nursing and allied health education to be distributed to hospitals under this subsection for portions of cost reporting periods occurring in the year; except that in no case shall such total amount exceed $60,000,000 in any year.

(C) Application to hospital

The amount of payment under this subsection to a hospital for portions of cost reporting periods occurring in a year is equal to the total amount of payments determined under subparagraph (B) for the year multiplied by the ratio of—

(i) the product of (I) the Secretary's estimate of the ratio of the amount of payments made under section 1395x(v) of this title to the hospital for nursing and allied health education activities for the hospital's cost reporting period ending in the second preceding fiscal year, to the hospital's total inpatient days for such period, and (II) the total number of inpatient days (as established by the Secretary) for such period which are attributable to services furnished to individuals who are enrolled under a risk sharing contract with an eligible organization under section 1395mm of this title and who are entitled to benefits under part A of this subchapter or who are enrolled with a Medicare + Choice organization under part C of this subchapter; to

(ii) the sum of the products determined under clause (i) for such cost reporting periods.

B. PEER REVIEW OF UTILIZATION AND QUALITY

§ 1320c. Purpose

The purpose of this part is to establish the contracting process which the Secretary must follow pursuant to the requirements of section 1395y(g) of this title, including the definition of the utilization and quality control peer review organizations with which the Secretary shall contract, the functions such peer review organizations are to perform, the confidentiality of medical records, and related administrative matters to facilitate the carrying out of the purposes of this part.

§ 1320c–1. "Utilization and quality control peer review organization" defined

The term "utilization and quality control peer review organization" means an entity which—

(1)(A) is composed of a substantial number of the licensed doctors of medicine and osteopathy engaged in the practice of medicine or surgery in the area and who are representative of the practicing physicians in the area, designated by the Secretary under section 1320c–2 of this title, with respect to which the entity shall perform services under this part, or (B) has available to it, by arrangement or otherwise, the services of a sufficient number of licensed doctors of medicine or osteopathy engaged in the practice of medicine or surgery in such area to assure that adequate peer review of the services provided by the various medical specialties and subspecialties can be assured;

(2) is able, in the judgment of the Secretary, to perform review functions required under section 1320c–3 of this title in a manner consistent with the efficient and effective administration of this part and to perform reviews of the pattern of quality of care in an area of medical practice where actual performance is measured against objective criteria which define acceptable and adequate practice; and

(3) has at least one individual who is a representative of consumers on its governing body.

§ 1320c–2. Contracts with utilization and quality control peer review organizations

(a) Establishment and consolidation of geographic areas

(1) The Secretary shall establish throughout the United States geographic areas with respect to which contracts under this part will be made. In establishing such areas, the Secretary shall use the same areas as established under section 1320c–1 of this title as in effect immediately prior to September 3, 1982, but subject to the provisions of paragraph (2).

(2) As soon as practicable after September 3, 1982, the Secretary shall consolidate such geographic areas, taking into account the following criteria:

(A) Each State shall generally be designated as a geographic area for purposes of paragraph (1).

(B) The Secretary shall establish local or regional areas rather than State areas only where the volume of review activity or other relevant factors (as determined by the Secretary) warrant such an establishment, and the Secretary determines that review activity can be carried out with equal or greater efficiency by establishing such local or regional areas. In applying this subparagraph the Secretary shall take into account the number of hospital admissions within each State for which payment may be made under subchapter XVIII of this chapter or a State plan approved under subchapter XIX of this chapter, with any State having fewer than 180,000 such admissions annually being established as a single statewide area, and no local or regional area being established which has fewer than 60,000 total hospital admissions (including public and private pay patients) under review annually, unless the Secretary determines that other relevant factors warrant otherwise.

(C) No local or regional area shall be designated which is not a self-contained medical service area, having a full spectrum of services, including medical specialists' services.

(b) Organizations entitled to contract with Secretary

(1) The Secretary shall enter into a contract with a utilization and quality control peer review organization for each area established under subsection (a) of this section if a qualified organization is available in such area and such organization and the Secretary have negotiated a proposed contract which the Secretary determines will be carried out by such organization in a manner consistent with the efficient and effective administration of this part. If more than one such qualified organization meets the requirements of the preceding sentence, priority shall be given to any such organization which is described in section 1320c–1(1)(A) of this title.

(2)(A) Prior to November 15, 1984, the Secretary shall not enter into a contract under this part with any entity which is, or is affiliated with (through management, ownership, or common control), an entity (other than a self-insured employer) which directly or indirectly makes payments to any practitioner or provider whose health care services are reviewed by such entity or would be reviewed by such entity if it entered into a contract with the Secretary under this part. For purposes of this paragraph, an entity shall not be considered to be affiliated with another entity which makes payments (directly or indirectly) to any practitioner or provider, by reason of management, ownership, or common control, if the management, ownership, or common control consists only of members of the governing board being affiliated (through management, ownership, or common control) with a health maintenance organization or competitive medical plan which is an "eligible organization" as defined in section 1395mm(b) of this title.

(B) If, after November 14, 1984, the Secretary determines that there is no other entity available for an area with which the Secretary can enter into a contract under this part, the Secretary may then enter into a contract under this part with an entity described in subparagraph (A) for such area if such entity otherwise meets the requirements of this part.

(3)(A) The Secretary shall not enter into a contract under this part with any entity which is, or is affiliated with (through management, ownership, or common control), a health care facility, or association of such facilities, within the area served by such entity or which would be served by such entity if it entered into a contract with the Secretary under this part.

(B) For purposes of subparagraph (A), an entity shall not be considered to be affiliated with a health care facility or association of facilities by reason of management, ownership, or common control if the management, ownership, or common control consists only of not more than 20 percent of the members of the governing board of the entity being affiliated (through management, ownership, or common control) with one or more of such facilities or associations.

(c) Terms of contract

Each contract with an organization under this section shall provide that—

(1) the organization shall perform the functions set forth in section 1320c-3(a) of this title, or may subcontract for the performance of all or some of such functions (and for purposes of paragraphs (2) and (3) of subsection (b) of this section, a subcontract under this paragraph shall not constitute an affiliation with the subcontractor);

(2) the Secretary shall have the right to evaluate the quality and effectiveness of the organization in carrying out the functions specified in the contract;

(3) the contract shall be for an initial term of three years and shall be renewable on a triennial basis thereafter;

(4) if the Secretary intends not to renew a contract, he shall notify the organization of his decision at least 90 days prior to the expiration of the contract term, and shall provide the organization an opportunity to present data, interpretations of data, and other information pertinent to its performance under the contract, which shall be reviewed in a timely manner by the Secretary;

(5) the organization may terminate the contract upon 90 days notice to the Secretary;

(6) the Secretary may terminate the contract prior to the expiration of the contract term upon 90 days notice to the organization if the Secretary determines that—

(A) the organization does not substantially meet the requirements of section 1320c–1 of this title; or

(B) the organization has failed substantially to carry out the contract or is carrying out the contract in a manner inconsistent with the efficient and effective administration of this part, but only after such organization has had an opportunity to submit data and have such data reviewed by the panel established under subsection (d) of this section;

(7) the Secretary shall include in the contract negotiated objectives against which the organization's performance will be judged, and negotiated specifications for use of regional norms, or modifications thereof based on national norms, for performing review functions under the contract; and

(8) reimbursement shall be made to the organization on a monthly basis, with payments for any month being made not later than 15 days after the close of such month.

In evaluating the performance of utilization and quality control peer review organizations under contracts under this part, the Secretary shall place emphasis on the performance of such organizations in educating providers and practitioners (particularly those in rural areas) concerning the review process and criteria being applied by the organization.

(d) Review prior to termination of contract; modification and termination; reviewing panel

(1) Prior to making any termination under subsection (c)(6)(B) of this section, the Secretary must provide the organization with an opportunity to provide data, interpretations of data, and other information pertinent to its performance under the contract. Such data and other information shall be reviewed in a timely manner by a panel appointed by the Secretary, and the panel shall submit a report of its findings to the Secretary in a timely manner. The Secretary shall make a copy of the report available to the organization.

(2) The Secretary may accept or not accept the findings of the panel. After the panel has submitted a report with respect to an organization, the Secretary may, with the concurrence of the organization, amend the contract to modify the scope of the functions to be carried out by the organization, or in any other manner. The Secretary may terminate a contract under the authority of subsection (c)(6)(B) of this section upon 90 days notice after the panel has submitted a report, or earlier if the organization so agrees.

(3) A panel appointed by the Secretary under this subsection shall consist of not more than five individuals, each of whom shall be a member

791

of a utilization and quality control peer review organization having a contract with the Secretary under this part. While serving on such panel individuals shall be paid at a per diem rate not to exceed the current per diem equivalent at the time that service on the panel is rendered for grade GS–18 under section 5332 of Title 5. Appointments shall be made without regard to Title 5.

(4) During the period after the Secretary has given notice of intent to terminate a contract, and prior to the time that the Secretary enters into a contract with another utilization and quality control peer review organization, the Secretary may transfer review responsibilities of the organization under the contract being terminated to another utilization and quality control peer review organization, or to an intermediary or carrier having an agreement under section 1395h of this title or a contract under section 1395u of this title.

(e) Authority of Secretary

(1) Except as provided in paragraph (2), contracting authority of the Secretary under this section may be carried out without regard to any provision of law relating to the making, performance, amendment, or modification of contracts of the United States as the Secretary may determine to be inconsistent with the purposes of this part. The Secretary may use different contracting methods with respect to different geographical areas.

(2) If a peer review organization with a contract under this section is required to carry out a review function in addition to any function required to be carried out at the time the Secretary entered into or renewed the contract with the organization, the Secretary shall, before requiring such organization to carry out such additional function, negotiate the necessary contractual modifications, including modifications that provide for an appropriate adjustment (in light of the cost of such additional function) to the amount of reimbursement made to the organization.

(f) Termination not subject to judicial review

Any determination by the Secretary to terminate or not to renew a contract under this section shall not be subject to judicial review.

(g) Timely provision of hospital data to peer review organizations

The Secretary shall provide that fiscal intermediaries furnish to peer review organizations, each month on a timely basis, data necessary to initiate the review process under section 1320c–3(a) of this title on a timely basis. If the Secretary determines that a fiscal intermediary is unable to furnish such data on a timely basis, the Secretary shall require the hospital to do so.

(h) Publication of new policy or procedure and general criteria and standards for evaluation; performance comparison report

(1) The Secretary shall publish in the Federal Register any new policy or procedure adopted by the Secretary that affects substantially the performance of contract obligations under this section not less than 30 days before the date on which such policy or procedure is to take effect. This paragraph shall not apply to the extent it is inconsistent with a statutory deadline.

(2) The Secretary shall publish in the Federal Register the general criteria and standards used for evaluating the efficient and effective performance of contract obligations under this section and shall provide opportunity for public comment with respect to such criteria and standards.

(3) The Secretary shall regularly furnish each peer review organization with a contract under this section with a report that documents the performance of the organization in relation to the performance of other such organizations.

(i) Preference in contracting with in-State organizations

(1) Notwithstanding any other provision of this section, the Secretary shall not renew a contract with any organization that is not an in-State organization (as defined in paragraph (3)) unless the Secretary has first complied with the requirements of paragraph (2).

(2)(A) Not later than six months before the date on which a contract period ends with respect to an organization that is not an in-State organization, the Secretary shall publish in the Federal Register—

(i) the date on which such period ends; and

(ii) the period of time in which an in-State organization may submit a proposal for the contract ending on such date.

(B) If one or more qualified in-State organizations submits a proposal within the period of time specified under subparagraph (A)(ii), the Secretary shall not automatically renew the current contract on a noncompetitive basis, but shall provide for competition for the contract in the same manner as a new contract under subsection (b) of this section.

(3) For purposes of this subsection, an in-State organization is an organization that has its primary place of business in the State in which review will be conducted (or, which is owned by a parent corporation the headquarters of which is located in such State).

§ 1320c–3.   Functions of peer review organizations

(a) Review of professional activities; determination of payment; determination of review authority; consultation with professional health care practitioners; standards of health care; other duties

Any utilization and quality control peer review organization entering into a contract with the Secretary under this part must perform the following functions:

(1) The organization shall review some or all of the professional activities in the area, subject to the terms of the contract and subject to the requirements of subsection (d) of this section, of physicians and other health care practitioners and institutional and noninstitutional providers of health care services in the provision of health care services and items for which payment may be made (in whole or in part) under subchapter XVIII of this chapter (including where payment is made for such services to eligible organizations pursuant to contracts under section 1395mm of this title) for the purpose of determining whether—

(A) such services and items are or were reasonable and medically necessary and whether such services and items are not allowable under subsection (a)(1) or (a)(9) of section 1395y of this title;

(B) the quality of such services meets professionally recognized standards of health care; and

(C) in case such services and items are proposed to be provided in a hospital or other health care facility on an inpatient basis, such services and items could, consistent with the provision of appropriate medical care, be effectively provided more economically on an outpatient basis or in an inpatient health care facility of a different type.

If the organization performs such reviews with respect to a type of health care practitioner other than medical doctors, the organization shall establish procedures for the involvement of health care practitioners of that type in such reviews.

(2) The organization shall determine, on the basis of the review carried out under subparagraphs (A), (B), and (C) of paragraph (1), whether payment shall be made for services under subchapter XVIII of this chapter. Such determination shall constitute the conclusive determination on those issues for purposes of payment under subchapter XVIII of this chapter, except that payment may be made if—

(A) such payment is allowed by reason of section 1395pp of this title;

(B) in the case of inpatient hospital services or extended care services, the peer review organization determines that additional time is required in order to arrange for postdischarge care, but payment may be continued under this subparagraph for not more than two days, but only in the case where the provider of such services did not know and could not reasonably have been expected to know (as determined under section 1395pp of this title) that payment would not otherwise be made for such services under subchapter XVIII of this chapter prior to notification by the organization under paragraph (3);

(C) such determination is changed as the result of any hearing or review of the determination under section 1320c–4 of this title; or

(D) such payment is authorized under section 1395x(v)(1)(G) of this title.

The organization shall identify cases for which payment should not be made by reason of paragraph (1)(B) only through the use of criteria developed pursuant to guidelines established by the Secretary.

(3)(A) Subject to subparagraphs (B) and (D), whenever the organization makes a determination that any health care services or items furnished or to be furnished to a patient by any practitioner or provider are disapproved, the organization shall promptly notify such patient and the agency or organization responsible for the payment of claims under subchapter XVIII of this chapter of such determination.

(B) The notification under subparagraph (A) with respect to services or items disapproved by reason of subparagraph (A) or (C) of paragraph (1) shall not occur until 20 days after the date that the organization has—

    (i) made a preliminary notification to such practitioner or provider of such proposed determination, and

    (ii) provided such practitioner or provider an opportunity for discussion and review of the proposed determination.

(C) The discussion and review conducted under subparagraph (B)(ii) shall not affect the rights of a practitioner or provider to a formal reconsideration of a determination under this part (as provided under section 1320c–4 of this title).

(D) The notification under subparagraph (A) with respect to services or items disapproved by reason of paragraph (1)(B) shall not occur until after—

    (i) the organization has notified the practitioner or provider involved of the determination and of the practitioner's or provider's right to a formal reconsideration of the determination under section 1320c–4 of this title, and

    (ii) if the provider or practitioner requests such a reconsideration, the organization has made such a reconsideration.

If a provider or practitioner is provided a reconsideration, such reconsideration shall be in lieu of any subsequent reconsideration to which the provider or practitioner may be otherwise entitled under section 1320c–4 of this title, but shall not affect the right of a beneficiary from seeking reconsideration under such section of the organization's determination (after any reconsideration requested by the provider or physician under clause (ii)).

(E)(i) In the case of services and items provided by a physician that were disapproved by reason of paragraph (1)(B), the notice to the patient shall state the following: "In the judgment of the peer review organization, the medical care received was not acceptable under the medicare program. The reasons for the denial have been discussed with your physician.''

   (ii) In the case of services or items provided by an entity or practitioner other than a physician, the Secretary may substitute the entity or practitioner which provided the services or items for the term "physician" in the notice described in clause (i).

(4)(A) The organization shall, after consultation with the Secretary, determine the types and kinds of cases (whether by type of health care or diagnosis involved, or whether in terms of other relevant criteria relating to the provision of health care services) with respect to which such organization will, in order to most effectively carry out the purposes of this part, exercise review authority under the contract. The organization shall notify the Secretary periodically with respect to such determinations. Each peer review organization shall provide that a reasonable proportion of its activities are involved with reviewing, under paragraph (1)(B), the quality of services and that a reasonable allocation of such activities is made among the different cases and settings (including post-acute-care settings, ambulatory settings, and health maintenance organizations). In establishing such allocation, the organization shall consider (i) whether there is reason to believe that there is a particular need for reviews of particular cases or settings because of previous problems regarding quality of care, (ii) the cost of such reviews and the likely yield of such reviews in terms of number and seriousness of quality of care problems likely to be discovered as a result of such reviews, and (iii) the availability and adequacy of alternative quality review and assurance mechanisms.

   (B) The contract of each organization shall provide for the review of services (including both inpatient and outpatient services) provided by eligible organizations pursuant to a risk-sharing contract under section 1395mm of this title (or that is subject to review under section 1395ss(t)(3) of this title) for the purpose of determining whether the quality of such services meets professionally recognized standards of health care, including whether appropriate health care services have not been provided or have been provided in inappropriate settings and whether individuals enrolled with an eligible organization have adequate access to health care services provided by or through such organization (as determined, in part, by a survey of individuals enrolled with the organization who have not yet used the organization to receive such services). The contract of each organization shall also provide that with respect to health care provided by a health maintenance organization or competitive medical plan under section 1395mm of this title, the organization shall maintain a beneficiary outreach program designed to apprise individuals receiving care under such section of the role of the peer review system, of the rights of the individual under such system, and of the method and purposes for contacting the organization. The previous two sentences shall not apply with respect to a contract year if another entity has been awarded a contract under subparagraph (C). Under the contract the level of effort expended by the organization on reviews under this subparagraph shall be equivalent, on a per enrollee basis, to the level of effort expended by the organization on utilization and quality reviews performed with respect to individuals not enrolled with an eligible organization.

(C) The Secretary may provide, by contract under competitive procurement procedures on a State-by-State basis in up to 25 States, for the review described in subparagraph (B) by an appropriate entity (which may be a peer review organization described in that subparagraph). In selecting among States in which to conduct such competitive procurement procedures, the Secretary may not select States which, as a group, have more than 50 percent of the total number of individuals enrolled with eligible organizations under section 1395mm of this title. Under a contract with an entity under this subparagraph—

(i) the entity must be, or must meet all the requirements under section 1320c–1 of this title to be, a utilization and quality control peer review organization (other than the ability to perform review functions under this section that are not described in subparagraph (B)),

(ii) the contract must meet the requirement of section 1320c–2(b)(3) of this title, and

(iii) the level of effort expended under the contract shall be, to the extent practicable, not less than the level of effort that would otherwise be required under the third sentence of subparagraph (B) if this subparagraph did not apply.

(5) The organization shall consult with nurses and other professional health care practitioners (other than physicians described in section 1395x(r)(1) of this title) and with representatives of institutional and noninstitutional providers of health care services, with respect to the organization's responsibility for the review under paragraph (1) of the professional activities of such practitioners and providers.

(6)(A) The organization shall, consistent with the provisions of its contract under this part, apply professionally developed norms of care, diagnosis, and treatment based upon typical patterns of practice within the geographic area served by the organization as principal points of evaluation and review, taking into consideration national norms where appropriate. Such norms with respect to treatment for particular illnesses or health conditions shall include—

(i) the types and extent of the health care services which, taking into account differing, but acceptable, modes of treatment and methods of organizing and delivering care, are considered within the range of appropriate diagnosis and treatment of such

797

illness or health condition, consistent with professionally recognized and accepted patterns of care; and

(ii) the type of health care facility which is considered, consistent with such standards, to be the type in which health care services which are medically appropriate for such illness or condition can most economically be provided.

As a component of the norms described in clause (i) or (ii), the organization shall take into account the special problems associated with delivering care in remote rural areas, the availability of service alternatives to inpatient hospitalization, and other appropriate factors (such as the distance from a patient's residence to the site of care, family support, availability of proximate alternative sites of care, and the patient's ability to carry out necessary or prescribed self-care regimens) that could adversely affect the safety or effectiveness of treatment provided on an outpatient basis.

(B) The organization shall—

(i) offer to provide, several times each year, for a physician representing the organization to meet (at a hospital or at a regional meeting) with medical and administrative staff of each hospital (the services of which are reviewed by the organization) respecting the organization's review of the hospital's services for which payment may be made under subchapter XVIII of this chapter, and

(ii) publish (not less often than annually) and distribute to providers and practitioners whose services are subject to review a report that describes the organization's findings with respect to the types of cases in which the organization has frequently determined that (I) inappropriate or unnecessary care has been provided, (II) services were rendered in an inappropriate setting, or (III) services did not meet professionally recognized standards of health care.

(7) The organization, to the extent necessary and appropriate to the performance of the contract, shall—

(A)(i) make arrangements to utilize the services of persons who are practitioners of, or specialists in, the various areas of medicine (including dentistry, optometry, and podiatry), or other types of health care, which persons shall, to the maximum extent practicable, be individuals engaged in the practice of their profession within the area served by such organization; and

(ii) in the case of psychiatric and physical rehabilitation services, make arrangements to ensure that (to the extent possible) initial review of such services be made by a physician who is trained in psychiatry or physical rehabilitation (as appropriate).

(B) undertake such professional inquiries either before or after, or both before and after, the provision of services with respect to which such organization has a responsibility for review which in the judgment of such organization will facilitate its activities;

(C) examine the pertinent records of any practitioner or provider of health care services providing services with respect to which such organization has a responsibility for review under paragraph (1); and

(D) inspect the facilities in which care is rendered or services are provided (which are located in such area) of any practitioner or provider of health care services providing services with respect to which such organization has a responsibility for review under paragraph (1).

(8) The organization shall perform such duties and functions and assume such responsibilities and comply with such other requirements as may be required by this part or under regulations of the Secretary promulgated to carry out the provisions of this part or as may be required to carry out section 1395y(a)(15) of this title.

(9)(A) The organization shall collect such information relevant to its functions, and keep and maintain such records, in such form as the Secretary may require to carry out the purposes of this part, and shall permit access to and use of any such information and records as the Secretary may require for such purposes, subject to the provisions of section 1320c–9 of this title.

(B) If the organization finds, after reasonable notice to and opportunity for discussion with the physician or practitioner concerned, that the physician or practitioner has furnished services in violation of section 1320c–5(a) of this title and the organization determines that the physician or practitioner should enter into a corrective action plan under section 1320c–5(b)(1) of this title, the organization shall notify the State board or boards responsible for the licensing or disciplining of the physician or practitioner of its finding and of any action taken as a result of the finding.

(10) The organization shall coordinate activities, including information exchanges, which are consistent with economical and efficient operation of programs among appropriate public and private agencies or organizations including—

(A) agencies under contract pursuant to sections 1395h and 1395u of this title;

(B) other peer review organizations having contracts under this part; and

(C) other public or private review organizations as may be appropriate.

799

(11) The organization shall make available its facilities and resources for contracting with private and public entities paying for health care in its area for review, as feasible and appropriate, of services reimbursed by such entities.

(12) Repealed. Pub.L. 103–432, Title I, § 156(a)(2)(A)(i), Oct. 31, 1994, 108 Stat. 4440

(13) Notwithstanding paragraph (4), the organization shall perform the review described in paragraph (1) with respect to early readmission cases to determine if the previous inpatient hospital services and the post-hospital services met professionally recognized standards of health care. Such reviews may be performed on a sample basis if the organization and the Secretary determine it to be appropriate. In this paragraph, an "early readmission case" is a case in which an individual, after discharge from a hospital, is readmitted to a hospital less than 31 days after the date of the most recent previous discharge.

(14) The organization shall conduct an appropriate review of all written complaints about the quality of services (for which payment may otherwise be made under subchapter XVIII of this chapter) not meeting professionally recognized standards of health care, if the complaint is filed with the organization by an individual entitled to benefits for such services under such subchapter (or a person acting on the individual's behalf). The organization shall inform the individual (or representative) of the organization's final disposition of the complaint. Before the organization concludes that the quality of services does not meet professionally recognized standards of health care, the organization must provide the practitioner or person concerned with reasonable notice and opportunity for discussion.

(15) During each year of the contract entered into under section 1320c–2(b) of this title, the organization shall perform significant on-site review activities, including on-site review in at least 20 percent of the rural hospitals in the organization's area.

(16) The organization shall provide for a review and report to the Secretary when requested by the Secretary under section 1395dd(d)(3) of this title. The organization shall provide reasonable notice of the review to the physician and hospital involved. Within the time period permitted by the Secretary, the organization shall provide a reasonable opportunity for discussion with the physician and hospital involved, and an opportunity for the physician and hospital to submit additional information, before issuing its report to the Secretary under such section.

(b) Review by physicians; physician's family defined

(1) No physician shall be permitted to review—

(A) health care services provided to a patient if he was directly responsible for providing such services; or

(B) health care services provided in or by an institution, organization, or agency, if he or any member of his family has, directly or indirectly, a significant financial interest in such institution, organization, or agency.

(2) For purposes of this subsection, a physician's family includes only his spouse (other than a spouse who is legally separated from him under a decree of divorce or separate maintenance), children (including legally adopted children), grandchildren, parents, and grandparents.

(c) Utilization of services of physicians to make final determinations of denial decisions with respect to professional conduct of other physicians

No utilization and quality control peer review organization shall utilize the services of any individual who is not a duly licensed doctor of medicine, osteopathy, dentistry, optometry, or podiatry to make final determinations of denial decisions in accordance with its duties and functions under this part with respect to the professional conduct of any other duly licensed doctor of medicine, osteopathy, dentistry, optometry, or podiatry or any act performed by any duly licensed doctor of medicine, osteopathy, dentistry, optometry, or podiatry in the exercise of his profession.

(d) Review of ambulatory surgical procedures

Each contract under this part shall require that the utilization and quality control peer review organization's review responsibility pursuant to subsection (a)(1) of this section will include review of all ambulatory surgical procedures specified pursuant to section 1395l (i)(1)(A) of this title which are performed in the area, or, at the discretion of the Secretary a sample of such procedures.

(e) Review of hospital denial notices

(1) If—

(A) a hospital has determined that a patient no longer requires inpatient hospital care, and

(B) the attending physician has agreed with the hospital's determination,

the hospital may provide the patient (or the patient's representative) with a notice (meeting conditions prescribed by the Secretary under section 1395pp of this title) of the determination.

(2) If—

(A) a hospital has determined that a patient no longer requires inpatient hospital care, but

(B) the attending physician has not agreed with the hospital's determination,

the hospital may request the appropriate peer review organization to review under subsection (a) of this section the validity of the hospital's determination. If the hospital requests such a review, it shall also notify the patient that the review has been requested.

(3)(A) If a patient (or a patient's representative)—

(i) has received a notice under paragraph (1), and

(ii) requests the appropriate peer review organization to review the determination,

then, the organization shall conduct a review under subsection (a) of this section of the validity of the hospital's determination and shall provide notice (by telephone and in writing) to the patient or representative and the hospital and attending physician involved of the results of the review. Such review shall be conducted regardless of whether or not the hospital will charge for continued hospital care or whether or not the patient will be liable for payment for such continued care.

(B) If a patient (or a patient's representative) requests a review under subparagraph (A) while the patient is still an inpatient in the hospital and not later than noon of the first working day after the date the patient receives the notice under paragraph (1), then—

(i) the hospital shall provide to the appropriate peer review organization the records required to review the determination by the close of business of such first working day, and

(ii) the peer review organization must provide the notice under subparagraph (A) by not later than one full working day after the date the organization has received the request and such records.

(4) If—

(A) a request is made under paragraph (3)(A) not later than noon of the first working day after the date the patient (or patient's representative) receives the notice under paragraph (1), and

(B) the conditions described in section 1395pp(a)(2) of this title with respect to the patient or representative are met,

the hospital may not charge the patient for inpatient hospital services furnished before noon of the day after the date the patient or representative receives notice of the peer review organization's decision.

(5) In any review conducted under paragraph (2) or (3), the organization shall solicit the views of the patient involved (or the patient's representative).

(f) Identification of methods for identifying cases of substandard care

The Secretary, in consultation with appropriate experts, shall identify methods that would be available to assist peer review organizations (under subsection (a)(4) of this section) in identifying those cases which are more likely than others to be associated with a quality of services which does not meet professionally recognized standards of health care.

§ 1320c–4. Right to hearing and judicial review

Any beneficiary who is entitled to benefits under subchapter XVIII of this chapter, and, subject to section 1320c–3(a)(3)(D) of this title, any practitioner or provider, who is dissatisfied with a determination made by a contracting peer review organization in conducting its review responsibilities under this part, shall be entitled to a reconsideration of such determination by the reviewing organization. Where the reconsideration is adverse to the beneficiary and where the matter in controversy is $200 or more, such beneficiary shall be entitled to a hearing by the Secretary (to the same extent as beneficiaries under subchapter II of this chapter are entitled to a hearing by the Commissioner of Social Security under section 405(b) of this title). For purposes of the preceding sentence, subsection (*l*) of section 405 of this title shall apply, except that any reference in such subsection to the Commissioner of Social Security or the Social Security Administration shall be deemed a reference to the Secretary or the Department of Health and Human Services, respectively. Where the amount in controversy is $2,000 or more, such beneficiary shall be entitled to judicial review of any final decision relating to a reconsideration described in this subsection.

§ 1320c–5. Obligations of health care practitioners and providers of health care services; sanctions and penalties; hearings and review

(a) Assurances regarding services and items ordered or provided by practitioner or provider

It shall be the obligation of any health care practitioner and any other person (including a hospital or other health care facility, organization, or agency) who provides health care services for which payment may be made (in whole or in part) under this chapter, to assure, to the extent of his authority that services or items ordered or provided by such practitioner or person to beneficiaries and recipients under this chapter—

(1) will be provided economically and only when, and to the extent, medically necessary;

(2) will be of a quality which meets professionally recognized standards of health care; and

(3) will be supported by evidence of medical necessity and quality in such form and fashion and at such time as may reasonably be required by a reviewing peer review organization in the exercise of its duties and responsibilities.

(b) Sanctions and penalties; hearings and review

(1) If after reasonable notice and opportunity for discussion with the practitioner or person concerned, and, if appropriate, after the practitioner or person has been given a reasonable opportunity to enter into and complete a corrective action plan (which may include remedial education) agreed to by the organization, and has failed successfully to complete such plan, any organization having a contract with the Secretary under this part determines that such practitioner or person has—

(A) failed in a substantial number of cases substantially to comply with any obligation imposed on him under subsection (a) of this section, or

(B) grossly and flagrantly violated any such obligation in one or more instances,

such organization shall submit a report and recommendations to the Secretary. If the Secretary agrees with such determination, the Secretary (in addition to any other sanction provided under law) may exclude (permanently or for such period as the Secretary may prescribe, except that such period may not be less than 1 year) such practitioner or person from eligibility to provide services under this chapter on a reimbursable basis. If the Secretary fails to act upon the recommendations submitted to him by such organization within 120 days after such submission, such practitioner or person shall be excluded from eligibility to provide services on a reimbursable basis until such time as the Secretary determines otherwise.

(2) A determination made by the Secretary under this subsection to exclude a practitioner or person shall be effective on the same date and in the same manner as an exclusion from participation under the programs under this chapter becomes effective under section 1320a–7(c) of this title, and shall (subject to the minimum period specified in the second sentence of paragraph (1)) remain in effect until the Secretary finds and gives reasonable notice to the public that the basis for such determination has been removed and that there is reasonable assurance that it will not recur.

(3) In lieu of the sanction authorized by paragraph (1), the Secretary may require that (as a condition to the continued eligibility of such practitioner or person to provide such health care services on a reimbursable basis) such practitioner or person pays to the United States, in case such acts or conduct involved the provision or ordering by such practitioner or person of health care services which were medically improper or unnecessary, an amount not in excess of up to $10,000 for each instance of the medically improper or unnecessary services so provided. Such amount may be deducted from any sums owing by the United States (or any instrumentality thereof) to the practitioner or person from whom such amount is claimed.

(4) Any practitioner or person furnishing services described in paragraph (1) who is dissatisfied with a determination made by the Secretary under this subsection shall be entitled to reasonable notice and opportunity for a hearing thereon by the Secretary to the same extent as is provided in section 405(b) of this title, and to judicial review of the Secretary's final decision after such hearing as is provided in section 405(g) of this title.

(5) Before the Secretary may effect an exclusion under paragraph (2) in the case of a provider or practitioner located in a rural health professional shortage area or in a county with a population of less than 70,000, the provider or practitioner adversely affected by the determination is entitled to a hearing before an administrative law judge (described in section 405(b) of this title) respecting whether the provider or practitioner should be able to continue furnishing services to individuals entitled to benefits under this chapter, pending completion of the administrative review procedure under paragraph (4). If the judge does not determine, by a preponderance of the evidence, that the provider or practitioner will pose a serious risk to such individuals if permitted to continue furnishing such services, the Secretary shall not effect the exclusion under paragraph (2) until the provider or practitioner has been provided reasonable notice and opportunity for an administrative hearing thereon under paragraph (4).

(6) When the Secretary effects an exclusion of a physician under paragraph (2), the Secretary shall notify the State board responsible for the licensing of the physician of the exclusion.

(c) Enlistment of support of other organizations to assure practitioner's or provider's compliance with obligations

It shall be the duty of each utilization and quality control peer review organization to use such authority or influence it may possess as a professional organization, and to enlist the support of any other professional or governmental organization having influence or authority over health care practitioners and any other person (including a hospital or other health care facility, organization, or agency) providing health care services in the area served by such review organization, in assuring that each practitioner or person (referred to in subsection (a) of this section) providing health care services in such area shall comply with all obligations imposed on him under subsection (a) of this section.

§ 1320c–6. Limitation on liability

(a) Providers of information to organizations having a contract with Secretary

Notwithstanding any other provision of law, no person providing information to any organization having a contract with the Secretary under this part shall be held, by reason of having provided such information, to have violated any criminal law, or to be civilly liable under any law of the United States or of any State (or political subdivision thereof) unless—

(1) such information is unrelated to the performance of the contract of such organization; or

(2) such information is false and the person providing it knew, or had reason to believe, that such information was false.

(b) Employees and fiduciaries of organizations having contracts with Secretary

No organization having a contract with the Secretary under this part and no person who is employed by, or who has a fiduciary relationship with, any such organization or who furnishes professional services to such organization, shall be held by reason of the performance of any duty, function, or activity required or authorized pursuant to this part or to a valid contract entered into under this part, to have violated any criminal law, or to be civilly liable under any law of the United States or of any State (or political subdivision thereof) provided due care was exercised in the performance of such duty, function, or activity.

(c) Physicians and providers

No doctor of medicine or osteopathy and no provider (including directors, trustees, employees, or officials thereof) of health care services shall be civilly liable to any person under any law of the United States or of any State (or political subdivision thereof) on account of any action taken by him in compliance with or reliance upon professionally developed norms of care and treatment applied by an organization under contract pursuant to section 1320c–2 of this title operating in the area where such doctor of medicine or osteopathy or provider took such action; but only if—

> **(1)** he takes such action in the exercise of his profession as a doctor of medicine or osteopathy or in the exercise of his functions as a provider of health care services; and

> **(2)** he exercised due care in all professional conduct taken or directed by him and reasonably related to, and resulting from, the actions taken in compliance with or reliance upon such professionally accepted norms of care and treatment.

(d) Reimbursement by Secretary for expenses incurred in defense of legal proceedings

The Secretary shall make payment to an organization under contract with him pursuant to this part, or to any member or employee thereof, or to any person who furnishes legal counsel or services to such organization, in an amount equal to the reasonable amount of the expenses incurred, as determined by the Secretary, in connection with the defense of any suit, action, or proceeding brought against such organization, member, or employee related to the performance of any duty or function under such contract by such organization, member, or employee.

§ 1320c–7. Application of this part to certain State programs receiving Federal financial assistance

(a) State plan provision that functions of peer review organizations may be performed by contract with such organization

A State plan approved under subchapter XIX of this chapter may provide that the functions specified in section 1320c–3 of this title may be performed in an area by contract with a utilization and quality control peer review organization that has entered into a contract with the Secretary in accordance with the provisions of section 1395y(g) of this title.

(b) Federal share of expenditures

In the event a State enters into a contract in accordance with subsection (a) of this section, the Federal share of the expenditures made to the contracting organization for its costs in the performance of its functions under the State plan shall be 75 percent (as provided in section 1396b(a)(3)(C) of this title).

§ 1320c–8. Authorization for use of certain funds to administer provisions of this part

Expenses incurred in the administration of the contracts described in section 1395y(g) of this title shall be payable from—

(1) funds in the Federal Hospital Insurance Trust Fund; and

(2) funds in the Federal Supplementary Medical Insurance Trust Fund,

in such amounts from each of such Trust Funds as the Secretary shall deem to be fair and equitable after taking into consideration the expenses attributable to the administration of this part with respect to each of such programs. The Secretary shall make such transfers of moneys between such Trust Funds as may be appropriate to settle accounts between them in cases where expenses properly payable from one such Trust Fund have been paid from the other such Trust Fund.

§ 1320c–9. Prohibition against disclosure of information

(a) Freedom of Information Act inapplicable; exceptions to nondisclosure

An organization, in carrying out its functions under a contract entered into under this part, shall not be a Federal agency for purposes of the provisions of section 552 of Title 5 (commonly referred to as the Freedom of Information Act). Any data or information acquired by any such organization in the exercise of its duties and functions shall be held in confidence and shall not be disclosed to any person except—

(1) to the extent that may be necessary to carry out the purposes of this part,

(2) in such cases and under such circumstances as the Secretary shall by regulations provide to assure adequate protection of the rights and interests of patients, health care practitioners, or providers of health care, or

(3) in accordance with subsection (b) of this section.

(b) Disclosure of information permitted

An organization having a contract with the Secretary under this part shall provide in accordance with procedures and safeguards established by the Secretary, data and information—

(1) which may identify specific providers or practitioners as may be necessary—

(A) to assist Federal and State agencies recognized by the Secretary as having responsibility for identifying and investigating cases or patterns of fraud or abuse, which data and information shall be provided by the peer review organization to any such agency at the request of such agency relating to a specific case or pattern;

(B) to assist appropriate Federal and State agencies recognized by the Secretary as having responsibility for identifying cases or patterns involving risks to the public health, which data and information shall be provided by the peer review organization to any such agency—

(i) at the discretion of the peer review organization, at the request of such agency relating to a specific case or pattern with respect to which such agency has made a finding, or has a reasonable belief, that there may be a substantial risk to the public health, or

(ii) upon a finding by, or the reasonable belief of, the peer review organization that there may be a substantial risk to the public health;

(C) to assist appropriate State agencies recognized by the Secretary as having responsibility for licensing or certification of providers or practitioners or to assist national accreditation bodies acting pursuant to section 1395bb of this title in accrediting providers for purposes of meeting the conditions described in subchapter XVIII of this chapter, which data and information shall be provided by the peer review organization to any such agency or body at the request of such agency or body relating to a specific case or to a possible pattern of substandard care, but only to the extent that such data and information are required by the agency or body to carry out its respective function which is within the jurisdiction of the agency or body under State law or under section 1395bb of this title; and

(D) to provide notice in accordance with section 1320c–3(a)(9)(B) of this title;

(2) to assist the Secretary, and such Federal and State agencies recognized by the Secretary as having health planning or related responsibilities under Federal or State law (including health systems agencies and State health planning and development agencies), in carrying out appropriate health care planning and related activities, which data and information shall be provided in such format and manner as may be prescribed by the Secretary or agreed upon by the responsible Federal and State agencies and such organization, and shall be in the form of aggregate statistical data (without explicitly identifying any individual) on a geographic, institutional, or other basis reflecting the volume and frequency of services furnished, as well as the demographic characteristics of the population subject to review by such organization.

The penalty provided in subsection (c) of this section shall not apply to the disclosure of any information received under this subsection, except that such penalty shall apply to the disclosure (by the agency receiving such information) of any such information described in paragraph (1) unless such disclosure is made in a judicial, administrative, or other formal legal proceeding resulting from an investigation conducted by the agency receiving the information. An organization may require payment of a reasonable fee for providing information under this subsection in response to a request for such information.

(c) Penalties

It shall be unlawful for any person to disclose any such information described in subsection (a) of this section other than for the purposes provided in subsections (a) and (b) of this section, and any person violating the provisions of this section shall, upon conviction, be fined not more than $1,000, and imprisoned for not more than 6 months, or both, and shall be required to pay the costs of prosecution.

(d) Subpoena and discovery proceedings regarding patient records

No patient record in the possession of an organization having a contract with the Secretary under this part shall be subject to subpoena or discovery proceedings in a civil action. No document or other information produced by such an organization in connection with its deliberations in making determinations under section 1320c–3(a)(1)(B) or 1320c–5(a)(2) of this title shall be subject to subpoena or discovery in any administrative or civil proceeding; except that such an organization shall provide, upon request of a practitioner or other person adversely affected by such a determination, a summary of the organization's findings and conclusions in making the determination.

(e) Organizations with contracts

For purposes of this section and section 1320c–6 of this title, the term "organization with a contract with the Secretary under this part" includes an entity with a contract with the Secretary under section 1320c–3(a)(4)(C) of this title.

§ 1320c–10.   Annual reports

The Secretary shall submit to the Congress not later than April 1 of each year, a full and complete report on the administration, impact, and cost of the program under this part during the preceding fiscal year, including data and information on—

    (1) the number, status, and service areas of all utilization and quality control peer review organizations participating in the program;

(2) the number of health care institutions and practitioners whose services are subject to review by such organizations, and the number of beneficiaries and recipients who received services subject to such review during such year;

(3) the various methods of reimbursement utilized in contracts under this part, and the relative efficiency of each such method of reimbursement;

(4) the imposition of penalties and sanctions under this subchapter for violations of law and for failure to comply with the obligations imposed by this part;

(5) the total costs incurred under subchapters XVIII and XIX of this chapter in the implementation and operation of all procedures required by such subchapters for the review of services to determine their medical necessity, appropriateness of use, and quality; and

(6) descriptions of the criteria upon which decisions are made, and the selection and relative weights of such criteria.

C. MEDICAID 42 U.S.C.A. § 1396

Table of Contents

GRANTS TO STATES FOR MEDICAL ASSISTANCE PROGRAMS

§ 1396 APPROPRIATIONS

i) Termination of certification for participation of and suspension of State of payments to intermediate care facilities for the mentally retarded.

j) Waiver or modification of 42 USCS §§ 1396 et seq. requirements with respect to medical assistance program in American Samoa.

k) [Deleted]

l) Description of group.

m) Description of individuals.

n) Payment amounts.

o) Certain benefits disregarded for purposes of determining post-eligibility contributions.

p) Exclusion power of State; exclusion as prerequisite for medical assistance payments; "exclude" defined.

q) Minimum monthly personal needs allowance deduction; "institutionalized individual or couple" defined.

r) Disregarding payments for certain medical expenses by institutionalized individuals.

s) Adjustment in payment for hospital services furnished to low-income children under the age of 6 years.

t) Limitation on payments to States for expenditures attributable to taxes.

u) Qualified COBRA continuation beneficiaries.

v) State agency disability and blindness determinations for medical assistance eligibility.

w) Maintenance of written policies and procedures respecting advance directives.

x) Physician identifier system; establishment.

y) Intermediate sanctions for psychiatric hospitals.

z) TB-infected individuals; TB-related services.

aa) Certain individuals with breast or cervical cancer.

bb) Payment for services provided by federally-qualified health centers and rural health clinics.

§ 1396b. *Payment To States*

a) Computation of amount.

b) Quarterly expenditures beginning after December 31, 1969.

c) Treatment of educationally-related services.

d) Estimates of State entitlement; installments; adjustments to reflect overpayments or underpayments; time for recovery or adjustment; uncollectable or discharged debts; obligated appropriations; disputed claims.

e) Transition costs of closures or conversions permitted.

f) Limitation on Federal participation in medical assistance.

g) Decrease in Federal medical assistance percentage of amounts paid for services furnished under State plan after June 30, 1973.

h) [Repealed]

i) Payment for organ transplants; item or service furnished by excluded individual, entity, or physicians; other restrictions.

j) Adjustment of amount.

k) Technical assistance to States.

l) [Repealed]

m) "Health maintenance organization" defined; duties and functions of Secretary; payments to States; provisional determination of status by State.

n) [Repealed]

o) Restrictions on authorized payments to States.

p) Assignment of rights of payment; incentive payments for enforcement and collection.

q) "State medicaid fraud control unit" defined.

r) Mechanized claims processing and information retrieval systems; operational, etc., requirements.

s) Limitations on certain physician referrals.

t) [Repealed]

u) Limitation of Federal financial participation in erroneous medical assistance expenditures.

v) Medical assistance to aliens not lawfully admitted for permanent residence.

w) Prohibition on use of voluntary contributions, and limitation on the use of provider-specific taxes to obtain Federal financial participation under Medicaid.

§ 1396c.   *Operation Of State Plans*

§ 1396d.   *Definitions*

a) Medical assistance.

b) Federal medical assistance percentage; State percentage; Indian health care percentage.

c) Nursing facility.

d) Intermediate care facility for mentally retarded.

§ **1396j.** *Indian Health Service Facilities*

   a) Eligibility for reimbursement for medical assistance.

   b) Facilities deemed to meet requirements upon submission of acceptable plan for achieving compliance.

   c) Agreement to reimburse State agency for providing care and services.

   d) Direct billing by Alaska Native and American Indian organizations.

§ **1396k.** *Assignment, Enforcement, And Collection Of Rights Of Payments For Medical Care; Establishment Of Procedures Pursuant To State Plan; Amounts Retained By State*

§ **1396l.** *Hospital Providers Of Nursing Facility Services.*

§ **1396m.** *Withholding Of Federal Share Of Payments For Certain Medicare Providers [omitted from this edited version]*

§ **1396n.** *Compliance With State Plan And Payment Provisions*

   a) Activities deemed as compliance.

   b) Waivers to promote cost-effectiveness and efficiency.

   c) Waiver respecting medical assistance requirement in State plan; scope, etc.; "habilitation services" defined; imposition of certain regulatory limits prohibited; computation of expenditures for certain disabled patients; coordinated services; substitution of participants.

   d) Home and community-based services for elderly.

   e) Waiver for children infected with AIDS or drug dependent at birth.

   f) Monitor of implementation of waivers; termination of waiver for noncompliance; time limitation for action on requests for plan approval, amendments, or waivers.

   g) Optional targeted case management services.

   h) Period of waivers; continuations.

§ **1396o.** *Use Of Enrollment Fees, Premiums, Deductions, Cost Sharing, And Similar Charges*

   a) Imposition of certain charges under the plan in the case of Individuals described in § 1396a(a)(10)(A) or (E)(i).

   b) Imposition of certain charges under the plan in the case of Individuals other than those described in § 1396a(a)(10)(A) or (E).

   c) Imposition of monthly premium; persons affected; amount; Prepayment; failure to pay; use of funds from other programs.

d) Premiums for qualified disabled and working individuals described in § 1396d(s).

e) Prohibition of denial of services on basis of individuals' inability to pay certain charges.

f) Charges imposed under waiver authority of Secretary.

g) State authority to impose income-related premiums and cost-sharing.

§ 1396p.   *Liens, Adjustments And Recoveries, And Transfers Of Assets*

a) Imposition of lien against the property of an individual on Account of medical assistance rendered to him under a State plan.

b) Adjustment or recovery of medical assistance correctly paid under a State plan.

c) Taking into account certain transfers of assets

d) Treatment of trust amounts

e) Definitions

§ 1396q.   *Application of Provisions of Title II Relating To Subpoenas [omitted from this edited version]*

§ 1396r.   *Requirements For Nursing Facilities*

a) "Nursing facility" defined.

b) Requirements relating to provision of services.

c) Requirements relating to residents' rights. [Nursing Home Residents Bill of Rights]

1) General rights
2) Transfer and discharge rights
3) Access and visitation rights
4) Equal access to quality care
5) Admissions policy
6) Protection of resident funds
7) Limitations on charges in case of medicaid eligible individual
8) Posting of survey results

d) Requirements relating to administration and other matters.

e) State requirements relating to nursing facility requirements.

f) Responsibilities of Secretary relating to nursing facility requirements.

g) Survey and certification process.

h) Enforcement process.

i) Construction

§ 1396r–1. *Presumptive Eligibility For Pregnant Women*

  a) Ambulatory prenatal care.

  b) Definitions.

  c) Duties of State agency, qualified providers, and presumptively eligible pregnant women.

  d) Ambulatory prenatal care as medical assistance.

§ 1396r–1a. *Presumptive Eligibility For Children*

  a) In general.

  b) Definitions; regulations.

  c) Application for medical assistance; procedure upon determination of presumptive eligibility.

  d) Treatment of medical assistance.

§ 1396r–1b. *Presumptive Eligibility For Certain Breast Or Cervical Cancer Patients*

  a) State option.
  b) Definitions.
  c) Administration.
  d) Payment.

§ 1396r–2. *Information Concerning Sanctions Taken By State Licensing Authorities Against Health Care Practitioners And Providers*

  a) Information reporting requirement; access to documents.
  b) Form of information.
  c) Confidentiality of information provided.
  d) Appropriate coordination.

§ 1396r–3. *Correction And Reduction Plans For Intermediate Care Facilities for the Mentally Retarded* [omitted from this edited version]

§ 1396r–4. *Adjustment In Payment For Inpatient Hospital Services Furnished By Disproportionate Share Hospitals*

  a) Implementation of requirement. [omitted from this edited version]

  b) Hospitals deemed disproportionate share.

  c) Payment adjustment.

  d) Requirements to qualify as disproportionate share hospital.

  e) Special rule. [omitted from this edited version]

  f) Limitation on Federal financial participation. [omitted from this edited version]

g) Limit on amount of payment to hospital.

h) Limitation on certain State DSH expenditures. [omitted from this edited version]

i) Requirement for direct payment.

§ 1396r–5. *Treatment Of Income And Resources For Certain Institutionalized Spouses*

a) Special treatment for institutionalized spouses.

b) Rules for treatment of income.

c) Rules for treatment of resources.

d) Protecting income for community spouse.

e) Notice and fair hearing.

f) Permitting transfer of resources to community spouse.

g) Indexing dollar amounts.

i) Definitions.

§ 1396r–6. *Extension Of Eligibility For Medical Assistance*

a) Initial 6–month extension.

b) Additional 6–month extension.

c) Applicability in States and territories.

d) General disqualification for fraud.

e) Caretaker relative defined.

f) Sunset.

§ 1396r–7. *[Repealed]*

§ 1396r–8. *Payment For Covered Outpatient Drugs*

a) Requirement for rebate agreement.

b) Terms of rebate agreement.

c) Determination of amount of rebate.

d) Limitations on coverage of drugs.

e) Treatment of pharmacy reimbursement limits.

[f)] Establishment of upper payment limits.

g) Drug use review.

h) Electronic claims management.

i) Annual report.

j) Exemption of organized health care settings.

k) Definitions.

§ 1396s. *Program For Distribution Of Pediatric Vaccines*

a) Establishment of program.

b) Vaccine-eligible children.

c) Program-registered providers.

d) Negotiation of contracts with manufacturers.

e) Use of pediatric vaccines list.

f) Requirement of State maintenance of immunization laws.

g) Definitions.

§ 1396t. *Home And Community Care For Functionally Disabled Elderly Individuals*

a) "Home and community care" defined.

b) "Functionally disabled elderly individual" defined.

c) Determinations of functional disability.

d) Individual community care plan (ICCP).

e) Ceiling on payment amounts and maintenance of effort.

f) Minimum requirements for home and community care.

g) Minimum requirements for small community care settings.

h) Minimum requirements for large community care settings.

i) Survey and certification process.

j) Enforcement process for providers of community care.

k) Secretarial responsibilities.

l) Waiver of statewideness.

m) Limitation on amount of expenditures as medical assistance.

§ 1396u. *Community Supported Living Arrangements Services*

a) Community supported living arrangements services.

b) "Developmentally disabled individual" defined.

c) Criteria for selection of participating States.

d) Quality assurance.

e) Maintenance of effort.

f) Excluded services.

g) Waiver of requirements.

h) Minimum protections.

i) Treatment of funds.

j) Limitation on amounts of expenditures as medical assistance.

§ 1396u–1. *Assuring Coverage For Certain Low–Income Families* [omitted from this edited version; summary of contents included here for reference]

a) References to title IV–A are references to pre-welfare-reform provisions.

b) Application of pre-welfare-reform eligibility criteria.

c) Treatment for purposes of transitional coverage provisions.

d) Waivers.

e) State option to use 1 application form.

f) Additional rules of construction.

g) Relation to other provisions.

Medicaid Statute, 42 USCA § 1396a

§ 1396a.   State plans for medical assistance

(a) Contents

A State plan for medical assistance must—

(1) provide that it shall be in effect in all political subdivisions of the State, and, if administered by them, be mandatory upon them;

(2) provide for financial participation by the State equal to not less than 40 per centum of the non-Federal share of the expenditures under the plan with respect to which payments under section 1396b of this title are authorized by this subchapter; and, effective July 1, 1969, provide for financial participation by the State equal to all of such non-Federal share or provide for distribution of funds from Federal or State sources, for carrying out the State plan, on an equalization or other basis which will assure that the lack of adequate funds from local sources will not result in lowering the amount, duration, scope, or quality of care and services available under the plan;

(3) provide for granting an opportunity for a fair hearing before the State agency to any individual whose claim for medical assistance under the plan is denied or is not acted upon with reasonable promptness;

(4) provide

(A) such methods of administration (including methods relating to the establishment and maintenance of personnel standards on a merit basis, except that the Secretary shall exercise no authority with respect to the selection, tenure of office, and compensation of any individual employed in accordance with such methods, and including provision for utilization of professional medical personnel in the administration and, where administered locally, supervision of administration of the plan) as are found by the Secretary to be necessary for the proper and efficient operation of the plan,

(B) for the training and effective use of paid subprofessional staff, with particular emphasis on the full-time or part-time employment of recipients and other persons of low income, as community service aides, in the administration of the plan and for the use of nonpaid or partially paid volunteers in a social service volunteer program in providing services to applicants and recipients and in assisting any advisory committees established by the State agency,

(C) that each State or local officer, employee, or independent contractor who is responsible for the expenditure of substantial amounts of funds under the State plan, each individual who formerly was such an officer, employee, or contractor and each partner of such an officer, employee, or contractor shall be prohibited from committing any act, in relation to any activity under the plan, the commission of which, in connection with any activity concerning the United States Government, by an officer or employee of the United States Government, an individual who was such an officer or employee, or a partner of such an officer or employee is prohibited by section 207 or 208 of Title 18, and

(D) that each State or local officer, employee, or independent contractor who is responsible for selecting, awarding, or otherwise obtaining items and services under the State plan shall be subject to safeguards against conflicts of interest that are at least as stringent as the safeguards that apply under section 27 of the Office of Federal Procurement Policy Act *(41 U.S.C. § 423)* to persons described in subsection (a)(2) of such section of that Act;

(5) either provide for the establishment or designation of a single State agency to administer or to supervise the administration of the plan; or provide for the establishment or designation of a single State agency to administer or to supervise the administration of the plan, except that the determination of eligibility for medical assistance under the plan shall be made by the State or local agency administering the State plan approved under subchapter I or XVI of this chapter (insofar as it relates to the aged) if the State is eligible to participate in the State plan program established under subchapter XVI of this chapter, or by the agency or agencies administering the supplemental security income program established under subchapter XVI or the State plan approved under part A of subchapter IV of this chapter if the State is not eligible to participate in the State plan program established under subchapter XVI of this chapter;

(6) provide that the State agency will make such reports, in such form and containing such information, as the Secretary may from time to time require, and comply with such provisions as the Secretary may from time to time find necessary to assure the correctness and verification of such reports;

(7) provide safeguards which restrict the use or disclosure of information concerning applicants and recipients to purposes directly connected with the administration of the plan;

(8) provide that all individuals wishing to make application for medical assistance under the plan shall have opportunity to do so, and that such assistance shall be furnished with reasonable promptness to all eligible individuals;

(9) provide—

(A) that the State health agency, or other appropriate State medical agency (whichever is utilized by the Secretary for the purpose specified in the first sentence of section 1395aa(a) of this title), shall be responsible for establishing and maintaining health standards for private or public institutions in which recipients of medical assistance under the plan may receive care or services,

(B) for the establishment or designation of a State authority or authorities which shall be responsible for establishing and maintaining standards, other than those relating to health, for such institutions, and

(C) that any laboratory services paid for under such plan must be provided by a laboratory which meets the applicable requirements of section 1395x(e)(9) of this title or paragraphs (16) and (17) of section 1395x(s) of this title, or, in the case of a laboratory which is in a rural health clinic, of section 1395x(aa)(2)(G) of this title;

821

(10) provide—

(A) for making medical assistance available, including at least the care and services listed in paragraphs (1) through (5), (17) and (21) of section 1396d(a) of this title, to—

(i) all individuals—

(I) who are receiving aid or assistance under any plan of the State approved under subchapter I, X, XIV, or XVI of this chapter, or part A or part E of subchapter IV of this chapter (including individuals eligible under this subchapter by reason of section 602(a)(37), 606(h), or 673(b) of this title, or considered by the State to be receiving such aid as authorized under section 682(e)(6) of this title),

(II) with respect to whom supplemental security income benefits are being paid under subchapter XVI of this chapter (or were being paid as of the date of the enactment of section 211(a) of the Personal Responsibility and Work Opportunity Reconciliation Act of 1996 (P.L. 104–193)) and would continue to be paid but for the enactment of that section or who are qualified severely impaired individuals (as defined in section 1396d(q) of this title),

(III) who are qualified pregnant women or children as defined in section 1396d(n) of this title,

(IV) who are described in subparagraph (A) or (B) of subsection $(l)(1)$ of this section and whose family income does not exceed the minimum income level the State is required to establish under subsection $(l)(2)(A)$ of this section for such a family;

(V) who are qualified family members as defined in section 1396d(m)(1) of this title;

(VI) who are described in subparagraph (C) of subsection $(l)(1)$ of this section and whose family income does not exceed the income level the State is required to establish under subsection $(l)(2)(B)$ of this section for such a family, or

(VII) who are described in subparagraph (D) of subsection $(l)(1)$ of this section and whose family income does not exceed the income level the State is required to establish under subsection $(l)(2)(C)$ of this section for such a family;

(ii) at the option of the State, to any group or groups of individuals described in section 1396d(a) of this title (or, in the case of individuals described in section 1396d(a)(i) of this title, to any reasonable categories of such individuals) who are not individuals described in clause (i) of this subparagraph but—

(I) who meet the income and resources requirements of the appropriate State plan described in clause (i) or the supplemental security income program (as the case may be),

(II) who would meet the income and resources requirements of the appropriate State plan described in clause (i) if their work-related child care costs were paid from their earnings rather than by a State agency as a service expenditure,

(III) who would be eligible to receive aid under the appropriate State plan described in clause (i) if coverage under such plan was as broad as allowed under Federal law,

(IV) with respect to whom there is being paid, or who are eligible, or would be eligible if they were not in a medical institution, to have paid with respect to them, aid or assistance under the appropriate State plan described in clause (i), supplemental security income benefits under subchapter XVI of this chapter, or a State supplementary payment;

(V) who are in a medical institution for a period of not less than 30 consecutive days (with eligibility by reason of this subclause beginning on the first day of such period), who meet the resource requirements of the appropriate State plan described in clause (i) or the supplemental security income program, and whose income does not exceed a separate income standard established by the State which is consistent with the limit established under section 1396b(f)(4)(C) of this title,

(VI) who would be eligible under the State plan under this subchapter if they were in a medical institution, with respect to whom there has been a determination that but for the provision of home or community-based services described in subsection (c), (d), or (e) of section 1396n of this title they would require the level of care provided in a hospital, nursing facility or intermediate care facility for the mentally retarded the cost of which could be reimbursed under the State plan, and who will receive home or community-based services pursuant to a waiver granted by the Secretary under subsection (c), (d), or (e) of section 1396n of this title,

(VII) who would be eligible under the State plan under this subchapter if they were in a medical institution, who are terminally ill, and who will receive hospice care pursuant to a voluntary election described in section 1396d(*o*) of this title;

(VIII) who is a child described in section 1396d(a)(i) of this title—

    (aa) for whom there is in effect an adoption assistance agreement (other than an agreement under part E of subchapter IV of this chapter) between the State and an adoptive parent or parents,

    (bb) who the State agency responsible for adoption assistance has determined cannot be placed with adoptive parents without medical assistance because such child has special needs for medical or rehabilitative care, and

    (cc) who was eligible for medical assistance under the State plan prior to the adoption assistance agreement being entered into, or who would have been eligible for medical assistance at such time if the eligibility standards and methodologies of the State's foster care program under part E of subchapter IV of this chapter were applied rather than the eligibility standards and methodologies of the State's aid to families with dependent children program under part A of subchapter IV of this chapter;

(IX) who are described in subsection (*l*)(1) of this section and are not described in clause (i)(IV), clause (i)(VI), or clause (i)(VII);

(X) who are described in subsection (m)(1) of this section;

(XI) who receive only an optional State supplementary payment based on need and paid on a regular basis, equal to the difference between the individual's countable income and the income standard used to determine eligibility for such supplementary payment (with countable income being the income remaining after deductions as established by the State pursuant to standards that may be more restrictive than the standards for supplementary security income benefits under subchapter XVI of this chapter), which are available to all individuals in the State (but which may be based on different income standards by political subdivision according to cost of living differences), and which are paid by a State that does not have an agreement with the Commissioner of Social Security under section 1382e or 1383c of this title;

(XII) who are described in subsection (z)(1) of this section (relating to certain TB-infected individuals);

(XIII) who are in families whose income is less than 250 percent of the income official poverty line (as defined by the Office of Management and Budget, and revised annually in accordance with section 9902(2) of this title) applicable to a family of the size involved, and who but for earnings in excess of the limit established under section 1396d(q)(2)(B) of this title, would be considered to be receiving supplemental security income (subject, notwithstanding section 1396o of this title, to payment of premiums or other cost-sharing charges (set on a sliding scale based on income) that the State may determine);

(XIV) who are optional targeted low-income children described in section 1396d(u)(2)(B) of this title; or

(XV) who, but for earnings in excess of the limit established under section 1905(q)(2)(B) [§ 1396d(q)(2)(B)], would be considered to be receiving supplemental security income, who is at least 16, but less than 65, years of age, and whose assets, resources, and earned or unearned income (or both) do not exceed such limitations (if any) as the State may establish;

(XVI) who are employed individuals with a medically improved disability described in section 1905(v)(1) [§ 1396d(v)(1)] and whose assets, resources, and earned or unearned income (or both) do not exceed such limitations (if any) as the State may establish, but only if the State provides medical assistance to individuals described in subclause (XV);

(XVII) who are independent foster care adolescents (as defined in section 1905(w)(1) [§ 1396d(w)(1)]), or who are within any reasonable categories of such adolescents specified by the State; or

(XVIII) who are described in subsection (aa) (relating to certain breast or cervical cancer patients);

(B) that the medical assistance made available to any individual described in subparagraph (A)—

(i) shall not be less in amount, duration, or scope than the medical assistance made available to any other such individual, and

(ii) shall not be less in amount, duration, or scope than the medical assistance made available to individuals not described in subparagraph (A);

(C) that if medical assistance is included for any group of individuals described in section 1396d(a) of this title who are not described in subparagraph (A) or (E), then—

(i) the plan must include a description of

(I) the criteria for determining eligibility of individuals in the group for such medical assistance,

(II) the amount, duration, and scope of medical assistance made available to individuals in the group, and

(III) the single standard to be employed in determining income and resource eligibility for all such groups, and the methodology to be employed in determining such eligibility, which shall be no more restrictive than the methodology which would be employed under the supplemental security income program in the case of groups consisting of aged, blind, or disabled individuals in a State in which such program is in effect, and which shall be no more restrictive than the methodology which would be employed under the appropriate State plan (described in subparagraph (A)(i)) to which such group is most closely categorically related in the case of other groups;

(ii) the plan must make available medical assistance—

(I) to individuals under the age of 18 who (but for income and resources) would be eligible for medical assistance as an individual described in subparagraph (A)(i), and

(II) to pregnant women, during the course of their pregnancy, who (but for income and resources) would be eligible for medical assistance as an individual described in subparagraph (A);

(iii) such medical assistance must include

(I) with respect to children under 18 and individuals entitled to institutional services, ambulatory services, and

(II) with respect to pregnant women, prenatal care and delivery services; and

(iv) if such medical assistance includes services in institutions for mental diseases or in an intermediate care facility for the mentally retarded (or both) for any such group, it also must include for all groups covered at least the care and services listed in paragraphs (1) through (5) and (17) of section 1396d(a) of this title or the care and services listed in any 7 of the paragraphs numbered (1) through (24) of such section;

(D) for the inclusion of home health services for any individual who, under the State plan, is entitled to nursing facility services; and

(E)(i) but, for making medical assistance available for medicare cost-sharing (as defined in section 1905(p)(3) [§ 1396d(p)(3)]) for qualified medicare beneficiaries described in section 1905(p)(1) [§ 1396d(p)(1)];

(ii) for making medical assistance available for payment of medicare cost-sharing described in section 1905(p)(3)(A)(i)

[§ 1396d(p)(3)(A)(i)] for qualified disabled and working individuals described in section 1905(s) [§ 1396d(s)];

(iii) for making medical assistance available for medicare cost sharing described in section 1905(p)(3)(A)(ii) [§ 1396d(p)(3)(A)(ii)] subject to section 1905(p)(4) [§ 1396d(p)(4)], for individuals who would be qualified medicare beneficiaries described in section 1905(p)(1) [§ 1396d(p)(1)] but for the fact that their income exceeds the income level established by the State under section 1905(p)(2) [§ 1396d(p)(2)] but is less than 110 percent in 1993 and 1994, and 120 percent in 1995 and years thereafter of the official poverty line (referred to in such section) for a family of the size involved; * * *

(F) at the option of a State, for making medical assistance available for COBRA premiums (as defined in subsection (u)(2) of this section) for qualified COBRA continuation beneficiaries described in subsection (u)(1) of this section; and

(G) that, in applying eligibility criteria of the supplemental security income program under subchapter XVI of this chapter [*42 U.S.C.A. § 1381* et seq.] for purposes of determining eligibility for medical assistance under the State plan of an individual who is not receiving supplemental security income, the State will disregard the provisions of subsections (c) and (e) of section 1382b of this title;except that

(I) the making available of the services described in paragraph (4), (14), or (16) of section 1396d(a) of this title to individuals meeting the age requirements prescribed therein shall not, by reason of this paragraph (10), require the making available of any such services, or the making available of such services of the same amount, duration, and scope, to individuals of any other ages,

(II) the making available of supplementary medical insurance benefits under part B of subchapter XVIII of this chapter to individuals eligible therefor (either pursuant to an agreement entered into under section 1395v of this title or by reason of the payment of premiums under such subchapter by the State agency on behalf of such individuals), or provision for meeting part or all of the cost of deductibles, cost sharing, or similar charges under part B of subchapter XVIII of this chapter for individuals eligible for benefits under such part, shall not, by reason of this paragraph (10), require the making available of any such benefits, or the making available of services of the same amount, duration, and scope, to any other individuals,

(III) the making available of medical assistance equal in amount, duration, and scope to the medical assistance made available to individuals described in clause (A) to any classification of individuals approved by the Secretary with respect to whom there is being paid, or who are eligible, or would be eligible if they were not in a medical institution, to have paid with respect to them, a State supplementary payment shall not, by reason of this paragraph (10), require the making available of any such assistance, or the making available of such assistance of the same amount, duration, and scope, to any other individuals not described in clause (A),

(IV) the imposition of a deductible, cost sharing, or similar charge for any item or service furnished to an individual not eligible for the exemption under section 1396o(a)(2) or (b)(2) of this title shall not require the imposition of a deductible, cost sharing, or similar charge for the same item or service furnished to an individual who is eligible for such exemption,

(V) the making available to pregnant women covered under the plan of services relating to pregnancy (including prenatal, delivery, and postpartum services) or to any other condition which may complicate pregnancy shall not, by reason of this paragraph (10), require the making available of such services, or the making available of such services of the same amount, duration, and scope, to any other individuals, provided such services are made available (in the same amount, duration, and scope) to all pregnant women covered under the State plan,

(VI) with respect to the making available of medical assistance for hospice care to terminally ill individuals who have made a voluntary election described in section 1396d(*o*) of this title to receive hospice care instead of medical assistance for certain other services, such assistance may not be made available in an amount, duration, or scope less than that provided under subchapter XVIII of this chapter, and the making available of such assistance shall not, by reason of this paragraph (10), require the making available of medical assistance for hospice care to other individuals or the making available of medical assistance for services waived by such terminally ill individuals,

(VII) the medical assistance made available to an individual described in subsection (*l*)(1)(A) of this section who is eligible for medical assistance only because of subparagraph (A)(i)(IV) or (A)(ii)(IX) shall be limited to medical assistance for services related to pregnancy (including prenatal, delivery, postpartum, and family planning services) and to other conditions which may complicate pregnancy,

(VIII) the medical assistance made available to a qualified medicare beneficiary described in section 1396d(p)(1) of this title who is only entitled to medical assistance because the individual is such a beneficiary shall be limited to medical assistance for medicare cost-sharing (described in section 1396d(p)(3) of this title), subject to the provisions of subsection (n) of this section and section 1396o(b) of this title,

(IX) the making available of respiratory care services in accordance with subsection (e)(9) of this section shall not, by reason of this paragraph (10), require the making available of such services, or the making available of such services of the same amount, duration, and scope, to any individuals not included under subsection (e)(9)(A) of this section, provided such services are made available (in the same amount, duration, and scope) to all individuals described in such subsection,

(X) if the plan provides for any fixed durational limit on medical assistance for inpatient hospital services (whether or not such a limit varies by medical condition or diagnosis), the plan must establish exceptions to such a limit for medically necessary inpatient hospital services furnished with respect to individuals under one year of age in a hospital defined under the State plan, pursuant to section 1396r–4(a)(1)(A) of this title, as a disproportionate share hospital and subparagraph (B) (relating to comparability) shall not be construed as requiring such an exception for other individuals, services, or hospitals,

(XI) the making available of medical assistance to cover the costs of premiums, deductibles, coinsurance, and other cost-sharing obligations for certain individuals for private health coverage as described in section 1396e of this title shall not, by reason of paragraph (10), require the making available of any such benefits or the making available of services of the same amount, duration, and scope of such private coverage to any other individuals,

(XII) the medical assistance made available to an individual described in subsection (u)(1) of this section who is eligible for medical assistance only because of subparagraph (F) shall be limited to medical assistance for COBRA continuation premiums (as defined in subsection (u)(2) of this section), and

(XIII) the medical assistance made available to an individual described in subsection (z)(1) of this section who is eligible for medical assistance only because of subparagraph

829

(A)(ii)(XII) shall be limited to medical assistance for TB-related services (described in subsection (z)(2) of this section);

(11)(A) provide for entering into cooperative arrangements with the State agencies responsible for administering or supervising the administration of health services and vocational rehabilitation services in the State looking toward maximum utilization of such services in the provision of medical assistance under the plan,

(B) provide, to the extent prescribed by the Secretary, for entering into agreements, with any agency, institution, or organization receiving payments under (or through an allotment under) subchapter V of this chapter,

(i) providing for utilizing such agency, institution, or organization in furnishing care and services which are available under such subchapter or allotment and which are included in the State plan approved under this section

(ii) making such provision as may be appropriate for reimbursing such agency, institution, or organization for the cost of any such care and services furnished any individual for which payment would otherwise be made to the State with respect to the individual under section 1396b of this title, and

(iii) providing for coordination of information and education on pediatric vaccinations and delivery of immunization services, and

(C) provide for coordination of the operations under this subchapter, including the provision of information and education on pediatric vaccinations and the delivery of immunization services, with the State's operations under the special supplemental nutrition program for women, infants, and children under section 1786 of this title;

(12) provide that, in determining whether an individual is blind, there shall be an examination by a physician skilled in the diseases of the eye or by an optometrist, whichever the individual may select;

(13) provide—

(A) for a public process for determination of rates of payment under the plan for hospital services, nursing facility services, and services of intermediate care facilities for the mentally retarded under which—

(i) proposed rates, the methodologies underlying the establishment of such rates, and justifications for the proposed rates are published,

(ii) providers, beneficiaries and their representatives, and other concerned State residents are given a reasonable opportunity for review and comment on the proposed rates, methodologies, and justifications,

(iii) final rates, the methodologies underlying the establishment of such rates, and justifications for such final rates are published, and

(iv) in the case of hospitals, such rates take into account (in a manner consistent with section 1923) the situation of hospitals which serve a disproportionate number of low-income patients with special needs;

(B) for payment for hospice care in amounts no lower than the amounts, using the same methodology, used under part A of subchapter XVIII of this chapter and for payment of amounts under section 1396d(o)(3) of this title; except that in the case of hospice care which is furnished to an individual who is a resident of a nursing facility or intermediate care facility for the mentally retarded, and who would be eligible under the plan for nursing facility services or services in an intermediate care facility for the mentally retarded if he had not elected to receive hospice care, there shall be paid an additional amount, to take into account the room and board furnished by the facility, equal to at least 95 percent of the rate that would have been paid by the State under the plan for facility services in that facility for that individual; and

(C)(i) for payment for services described in clause (B) or (C) of section 1396d(a)(2) of this title under the plan of 100 percent (or 95 percent for services furnished during fiscal year 2000, fiscal year 2001, or fiscal year 2002, 90 percent for services furnished during fiscal year 2003, or 85 percent for services furnished during fiscal year 2004) of costs which are reasonable and related to the cost of furnishing such services or based on such other tests of reasonableness, as the Secretary prescribes in regulations under section 1395l(a)(3) of this title, or, in the case of services to which those regulations do not apply, on the same methodology used under section 1395l(a)(3) of this title and

(ii) in carrying out clause (i) in the case of services furnished by a Federally-qualified health center or a rural health clinic pursuant to a contract between the center and an organization under section 1396b(m) of this title, for payment to the center or clinic at least quarterly by the State of a supplemental payment equal to the amount (if any) by which the amount determined under clause (i) exceeds the amount of the payments provided under such contract;

(14) provide that enrollment fees, premiums, or similar charges, and deductions, cost sharing, or similar charges, may be imposed only as provided in section 1396o of this title;

(15) Repealed.

(16) provide for inclusion, to the extent required by regulations prescribed by the Secretary, of provisions (conforming to such regulations) with respect to the furnishing of medical assistance under the plan to individuals who are residents of the State but are absent therefrom;

(17) except as provided in subsections (l)(3), (m)(3), and (m)(4) of this section, include reasonable standards (which shall be comparable for all groups and may, in accordance with standards prescribed by the Secretary, differ with respect to income levels, but only in the case of applicants or recipients of assistance under the plan who are not receiving aid or assistance under any plan of the State approved under subchapter I, X, XIV, or XVI, or part A of subchapter IV of this chapter, and with respect to whom supplemental security income benefits are not being paid under subchapter XVI of this chapter, based on the variations between shelter costs in urban areas and in rural areas) for determining eligibility for and the extent of medical assistance under the plan which

(A) are consistent with the objectives of this subchapter,

(B) provide for taking into account only such income and resources as are, as determined in accordance with standards prescribed by the Secretary, available to the applicant or recipient and (in the case of any applicant or recipient who would, except for income and resources, be eligible for aid or assistance in the form of money payments under any plan of the State approved under subchapter I, X, XIV, or XVI, or part A of subchapter IV, or to have paid with respect to him supplemental security income benefits under subchapter XVI of this chapter) as would not be disregarded (or set aside for future needs) in determining his eligibility for such aid, assistance, or benefits,

(C) provide for reasonable evaluation of any such income or resources, and

(D) do not take into account the financial responsibility of any individual for any applicant or recipient of assistance under the plan unless such applicant or recipient is such individual's spouse or such individual's child who is under age 21 or (with respect to States eligible to participate in the State program established under subchapter XVI of this chapter), is blind or permanently and totally disabled, or is blind or disabled as defined in section 1382c of this title (with respect to States which are not eligible to participate in such program); and provide for flexibility in the application of such standards with respect to income by taking into account, except to the extent prescribed by the Secretary, the costs (whether in the form of insurance premiums, payments made to the State under section 1396b(f)(2)(B) of this title, or otherwise and regardless of whether such costs are reimbursed under another public program of the State or political subdivision thereof) incurred for medical care or for any other type of remedial care recognized under State law;

(18) comply with the provisions of section 1396p of this title with respect to liens, adjustments and recoveries of medical assistance correctly paid, transfers of assets, and treatment of certain trusts;

(19) provide such safeguards as may be necessary to assure that eligibility for care and services under the plan will be determined, and such care and services will be provided, in a manner consistent with simplicity of administration and the best interests of the recipients;

(20) if the State plan includes medical assistance in behalf of individuals 65 years of age or older who are patients in institutions for mental diseases—

(A) provide for having in effect such agreements or other arrangements with State authorities concerned with mental diseases, and, where appropriate, with such institutions, as may be necessary for carrying out the State plan, including arrangements for joint planning and for development of alternate methods of care, arrangements providing assurance of immediate readmittance to institutions where needed for individuals under alternate plans of care, and arrangements providing for access to patients and facilities, for furnishing information, and for making reports;

(B) provide for an individual plan for each such patient to assure that the institutional care provided to him is in his best interests, including, to that end, assurances that there will be initial and periodic review of his medical and other needs, that he will be given appropriate medical treatment within the institution, and that there will be a periodic determination of his need for continued treatment in the institution; and

(C) provide for the development of alternate plans of care, making maximum utilization of available resources, for recipients 65 years of age or older who would otherwise need care in such institutions, including appropriate medical treatment and other aid or assistance; for services referred to in section 303(a)(4)(A)(i) and (ii) or section 1383(a)(4)(A)(i) and (ii) of this title which are appropriate for such recipients and for such patients; and for methods of administration necessary to assure that the responsibilities of the State agency under the State plan with respect to such recipients and such patients will be effectively carried out;

(21) if the State plan includes medical assistance in behalf of individuals 65 years of age or older who are patients in public institutions for mental diseases, show that the State is making satisfactory progress toward developing and implementing a comprehensive mental health program, including provision for utilization of community mental health centers, nursing facilities, and other alternatives to care in public institutions for mental diseases;

(22) include descriptions of

(A) the kinds and numbers of professional medical personnel and supporting staff that will be used in the administration of the plan and of the responsibilities they will have,

(B) the standards, for private or public institutions in which recipients of medical assistance under the plan may receive care or services, that will be utilized by the State authority or authorities responsible for establishing and maintaining such standards,

(C) the cooperative arrangements with State health agencies and State vocational rehabilitation agencies entered into with a view to maximum utilization of and coordination of the provision of medical assistance with the services administered or supervised by such agencies, and

(D) other standards and methods that the State will use to assure that medical or remedial care and services provided to recipients of medical assistance are of high quality;

(23) provide that

(A) any individual eligible for medical assistance (including drugs) may obtain such assistance from any institution, agency, community pharmacy, or person, qualified to perform the service or services required (including an organization which provides such services, or arranges for their availability, on a prepayment basis), who undertakes to provide him such services, and

(B) an enrollment of an individual eligible for medical assistance in a primary care case-management system (described in section 1396n(b)(1) of this title), a medicaid managed care organization, or a similar entity shall not restrict the choice of the qualified person from whom the individual may receive services under section 1396d(a)(4)(C) of this title, except as provided in subsection (g) of this section and in section 1396n of this title, except that this paragraph shall not apply in the case of Puerto Rico, the Virgin Islands, and Guam, and except that nothing in this paragraph shall be construed as requiring a State to provide medical assistance for such services furnished by a person or entity convicted of a felony under Federal or State law for an offense which the State agency determines is inconsistent with the best interests of beneficiaries under the State plan;

(24) effective July 1, 1969, provide for consultative services by health agencies and other appropriate agencies of the State to hospitals, nursing facilities, home health agencies, clinics, laboratories, and such other institutions as the Secretary may specify in order to assist them

(A) to qualify for payments under this chapter,

(B) to establish and maintain such fiscal records as may be necessary for the proper and efficient administration of this chapter, and

(C) to provide information needed to determine payments due under this chapter on account of care and services furnished to individuals;

(25) provide—

(A) that the State or local agency administering such plan will take all reasonable measures to ascertain the legal liability of third parties (including health insurers, group health plans (as defined in section 607(1) of the Employee Retirement Income Security Act of 1974 [*29 U.S.C.A. § 1167(1)]*), service benefit plans, and health maintenance organizations) to pay for care and services available under the plan, including—

(i) the collection of sufficient information (as specified by the Secretary in regulations) to enable the State to pursue claims against such third parties, with such information being collected at the time of any determination or redetermination of eligibility for medical assistance, and

(ii) the submission to the Secretary of a plan (subject to approval by the Secretary) for pursuing claims against such third parties, which plan shall be integrated with, and be monitored as a part of the Secretary's review of, the State's mechanized claims processing and information retrieval systems required under section 1396b(r) of this title;

(B) that in any case where such a legal liability is found to exist after medical assistance has been made available on behalf of the individual and where the amount of reimbursement the State can reasonably expect to recover exceeds the costs of such recovery, the State or local agency will seek reimbursement for such assistance to the extent of such legal liability;

(C) that in the case of an individual who is entitled to medical assistance under the State plan with respect to a service for which a third party is liable for payment, the person furnishing the service may not seek to collect from the individual (or any financially responsible relative or representative of that individual) payment of an amount for that service

(i) if the total of the amount of the liabilities of third parties for that service is at least equal to the amount payable for that service under the plan (disregarding section 1396o of this title), or

(ii) in an amount which exceeds the lesser of

(I) the amount which may be collected under section 1396o of this title, or

(II) the amount by which the amount payable for that service under the plan (disregarding section 1396o of this title), exceeds the total of the amount of the liabilities of third parties for that service;

(D) that a person who furnishes services and is participating under the plan may not refuse to furnish services to an individual (who is entitled to have payment made under the plan for the services the person furnishes) because of a third party's potential liability for payment for the service;

(E) that in the case of prenatal or preventive pediatric care (including early and periodic screening and diagnosis services under section 1396d(a)(4)(B) of this title) covered under the State plan, the State shall—

(i) make payment for such service in accordance with the usual payment schedule under such plan for such services without regard to the liability of a third party for payment for such services; and

(ii) seek reimbursement from such third party in accordance with subparagraph (B);

(F) that in the case of any services covered under such plan which are provided to an individual on whose behalf child support enforcement is being carried out by the State agency under part D of subchapter IV of this chapter, the State shall—

(i) make payment for such service in accordance with the usual payment schedule under such plan for such services without regard to any third-party liability for payment for such services, if such third-party liability is derived (through insurance or otherwise) from the parent whose obligation to pay support is being enforced by such agency, if payment has not been made by such third party within 30 days after such services are furnished; and

(ii) seek reimbursement from such third party in accordance with subparagraph (B);

(G) that the State prohibits any health insurer (including a group health plan, as defined in section 607(1) of the Employee Retirement Income Security Act of 1974 [*29 U.S.C.A. § 1167(1)*], a service benefit plan, and a health maintenance organization), in enrolling an individual or in making any payments for benefits to the individual or on the individual's behalf, from taking into account that the individual is eligible for or is provided medical assistance under a plan under this title for such State, or any other State; and

(H) that to the extent that payment has been made under the State plan for medical assistance in any case where a third party has a legal liability to make payment for such assistance, the State has in effect laws under which, to the extent that payment has been made under the State plan for medical assistance for health care items or services furnished to an individual, the State is considered to have acquired the rights of such individual to payment by any other party for such health care items or services;

(26) if the State plan includes medical assistance for inpatient mental hospital services, provide, with respect to each patient receiving such services, for a regular program of medical review (including medical evaluation) of his need for such services, and for a written plan of care;

(27) provide for agreements with every person or institution providing services under the State plan under which such person or institution agrees

(A) to keep such records as are necessary fully to disclose the extent of the services provided to individuals receiving assistance under the State plan, and

(B) to furnish the State agency or the Secretary with such information, regarding any payments claimed by such person or institution for providing services under the State plan, as the State agency or the Secretary may from time to time request;

(28) provide—

(A) that any nursing facility receiving payments under such plan must satisfy all the requirements of subsections (b) through (d) of section 1396r of this title as they apply to such facilities;

(B) for including in "nursing facility services" at least the items and services specified (or deemed to be specified) by the Secretary under section 1396r(f)(7) of this title and making available upon request a description of the items and services so included;

(C) for procedures to make available to the public the data and methodology used in establishing payment rates for nursing facilities under this subchapter; and

(D) for compliance (by the date specified in the respective sections) with the requirements of—

(i) section 1396r(e) of this title;

(ii) section 1396r(g) of this title (relating to responsibility for survey and certification of nursing facilities); and

(iii) sections 1396r(h)(2)(B) and 1396r(h)(2)(D) of this title (relating to establishment and application of remedies);

(29) include a State program which meets the requirements set forth in section 1396g of this title, for the licensing of administrators of nursing homes;

(30)(A) provide such methods and procedures relating to the utilization of, and the payment for, care and services available under the plan (including but not limited to utilization review plans as provided for in section 1396b(i)(4) of this title) as may be necessary to safeguard against unnecessary utilization of such care and services and to assure that payments are consistent with efficiency, economy, and quality of care and are sufficient to enlist enough providers so that care and services are available under the plan at least to the extent that such care and services are available to the general population in the geographic area; and

(B) provide, under the program described in subparagraph (A), that—

(i) each admission to a hospital, intermediate care facility for the mentally retarded, or hospital for mental diseases is reviewed or screened in accordance with criteria established by medical and other professional personnel who are not themselves directly responsible for the care of the patient involved, and who do not have a significant financial interest in any such institution and are not, except in the case of a hospital, employed by the institution providing the care involved, and

(ii) the information developed from such review or screening, along with the data obtained from prior reviews of the necessity for admission and continued stay of patients by such professional personnel, shall be used as the basis for establishing the size and composition of the sample of admissions to be subject to review and evaluation by such personnel, and any such sample may be of any size up to 100 percent of all admissions and must be of sufficient size to serve the purpose of

(I) identifying the patterns of care being provided and the changes occurring over time in such patterns so that the need for modification may be ascertained, and

(II) subjecting admissions to early or more extensive review where information indicates that such consideration is warranted to a hospital, intermediate care facility for the mentally retarded, or hospital for mental diseases;

(C) Repealed.

(31) with respect to services in an intermediate care facility for the mentally retarded (where the State plan includes medical assistance for such services) provide, with respect to each patient receiving such services, for a written plan of care, prior to admission to or authorization of benefits in such facility, in accordance with regulations of the Secretary, and for a regular program of independent professional review (including medical evaluation) which shall periodically review his need for such services;

(32) provide that no payment under the plan for any care or service provided to an individual shall be made to anyone other than such

individual or the person or institution providing such care or service, under an assignment or power of attorney or otherwise; except that—

(A) in the case of any care or service provided by a physician, dentist, or other individual practitioner, such payment may be made

(i) to the employer of such physician, dentist, or other practitioner if such physician, dentist, or practitioner is required as a condition of his employment to turn over his fee for such care or service to his employer, or

(ii) (where the care or service was provided in a hospital, clinic, or other facility) to the facility in which the care or service was provided if there is a contractual arrangement between such physician, dentist, or practitioner and such facility under which such facility submits the bill for such care or service;

(B) nothing in this paragraph shall be construed

(i) to prevent the making of such a payment in accordance with an assignment from the person or institution providing the care or service involved if such assignment is made to a governmental agency or entity or is established by or pursuant to the order of a court of competent jurisdiction, or

(ii) to preclude an agent of such person or institution from receiving any such payment if (but only if) such agent does so pursuant to an agency agreement under which the compensation to be paid to the agent for his services for or in connection with the billing or collection of payments due such person or institution under the plan is unrelated (directly or indirectly) to the amount of such payments or the billings therefor, and is not dependent upon the actual collection of any such payment;

(C) in the case of services furnished (during a period that does not exceed 14 continuous days in the case of an informal reciprocal arrangement or 90 continuous days (or such longer period as the Secretary may provide) in the case of an arrangement involving per diem or other fee-for-time compensation) by, or incident to the services of, one physician to the patients of another physician who submits the claim for such services, payment shall be made to the physician submitting the claim (as if the services were furnished by, or incident to, the physician's services), but only if the claim identifies (in a manner specified by the Secretary) the physician who furnished the services; and

(D) in the case of payment for a childhood vaccine administered before October 1, 1994, to individuals entitled to medical assistance under the State plan, the State plan may make payment directly to the manufacturer of the vaccine under a voluntary replacement program agreed to by the State pursuant to which the manufacturer

(i) supplies doses of the vaccine to providers administering the vaccine,

(ii) periodically replaces the supply of the vaccine, and

(iii) charges the State the manufacturer's price to the Centers for Disease Control and Prevention for the vaccine so administered (which price includes a reasonable amount to cover shipping and the handling of returns);

(33) provide—

(A) that the State health agency, or other appropriate State medical agency, shall be responsible for establishing a plan, consistent with regulations prescribed by the Secretary, for the review by appropriate professional health personnel of the appropriateness and quality of care and services furnished to recipients of medical assistance under the plan in order to provide guidance with respect thereto in the administration of the plan to the State agency established or designated pursuant to paragraph (5) and, where applicable, to the State agency described in the second sentence of this subsection; and

(B) that, except as provided in section 1396r(g) of this title, the State or local agency utilized by the Secretary for the purpose specified in the first sentence of section 1395aa(a) of this title, or, if such agency is not the State agency which is responsible for licensing health institutions, the State agency responsible for such licensing, will perform for the State agency administering or supervising the administration of the plan approved under this subchapter the function of determining whether institutions and agencies meet the requirements for participation in the program under such plan, except that, if the Secretary has cause to question the adequacy of such determinations, the Secretary is authorized to validate State determinations and, on that basis, make independent and binding determinations concerning the extent to which individual institutions and agencies meet the requirements for participation;

(34) provide that in the case of any individual who has been determined to be eligible for medical assistance under the plan, such assistance will be made available to him for care and services included under the plan and furnished in or after the third month before the month in which he made application (or application was made on his behalf in the case of a deceased individual) for such assistance if such individual was (or upon application would have been) eligible for such assistance at the time such care and services were furnished;

(35) provide that any disclosing entity (as defined in section 1320a–3(a)(2) of this title) receiving payments under such plan complies with the requirements of section 1320a–3 of this title;

(36) provide that within 90 days following the completion of each survey of any health care facility, laboratory, agency, clinic, or organization, by the appropriate State agency described in paragraph (9), such agency shall (in accordance with regulations of the Secretary) make public in readily available form and place the pertinent findings of each

such survey relating to the compliance of each such health care facility, laboratory, clinic, agency, or organization with

(A) the statutory conditions of participation imposed under this subchapter, and

(B) the major additional conditions which the Secretary finds necessary in the interest of health and safety of individuals who are furnished care or services by any such facility, laboratory, clinic, agency, or organization;

(37) provide for claims payment procedures which

(A) ensure that 90 per centum of claims for payment (for which no further written information or substantiation is required in order to make payment) made for services covered under the plan and furnished by health care practitioners through individual or group practices or through shared health facilities are paid within 30 days of the date of receipt of such claims and that 99 per centum of such claims are paid within 90 days of the date of receipt of such claims, and

(B) provide for procedures of prepayment and postpayment claims review, including review of appropriate data with respect to the recipient and provider of a service and the nature of the service for which payment is claimed, to ensure the proper and efficient payment of claims and management of the program;

(38) require that an entity (other than an individual practitioner or a group of practitioners) that furnishes, or arranges for the furnishing of, items or services under the plan, shall supply (within such period as may be specified in regulations by the Secretary or by the single State agency which administers or supervises the administration of the plan) upon request specifically addressed to such entity by the Secretary or such State agency, the information described in section 1320a–7(b)(9) of this title;

(39) provide that the State agency shall exclude any specified individual or entity from participation in the program under the State plan for the period specified by the Secretary, when required by him to do so pursuant to section 1320a–7 of this title or section 1320a–7a of this title, and provide that no payment may be made under the plan with respect to any item or service furnished by such individual or entity during such period;

(40) require each health services facility or organization which receives payments under the plan and of a type for which a uniform reporting system has been established under section 1320a(a) of this title to make reports to the Secretary of information described in such section in accordance with the uniform reporting system (established under such section) for that type of facility or organization;

(41) provide that whenever a provider of services or any other person is terminated, suspended, or otherwise sanctioned or prohibited from participating under the State plan, the State agency shall promptly notify the Secretary and, in the case of a physician and notwithstanding paragraph (7), the State medical licensing board of such action;

(42) provide that the records of any entity participating in the plan and providing services reimbursable on a cost-related basis will be audited as the Secretary determines to be necessary to insure that proper payments are made under the plan;

(43) provide for—

(A) informing all persons in the State who are under the age of 21 and who have been determined to be eligible for medical assistance including services described in section 1396d(a)(4)(B) of this title, of the availability of early and periodic screening, diagnostic, and treatment services as described in section 1396d(r) of this title and the need for age-appropriate immunizations against vaccine-preventable diseases,

(B) providing or arranging for the provision of such screening services in all cases where they are requested,

(C) arranging for (directly or through referral to appropriate agencies, organizations, or individuals) corrective treatment the need for which is disclosed by such child health screening services, and

(D) reporting to the Secretary (in a uniform form and manner established by the Secretary, by age group and by basis of eligibility for medical assistance, and by not later than April 1 after the end of each fiscal year, beginning with fiscal year 1990) the following information relating to early and periodic screening, diagnostic, and treatment services provided under the plan during each fiscal year:

(i) the number of children provided child health screening services,

(ii) the number of children referred for corrective treatment (the need for which is disclosed by such child health screening services),

(iii) the number of children receiving dental services, and

(iv) the State's results in attaining the participation goals set for the State under section 1396d(r) of this title;

(44) in each case for which payment for inpatient hospital services, services in an intermediate care facility for the mentally retarded, or inpatient mental hospital services is made under the State plan—

(A) a physician (or, in the case of skilled nursing facility services or intermediate care facility services, a physician, or a nurse practitioner or clinical nurse specialist who is not an employee of the facility but is working in collaboration with a physician) certifies at the time of admission, or, if later, the time the individual applies for medical assistance under the State plan (and a physician, a physician assistant under the supervision of a physician, or, in the case of skilled nursing facility services or intermediate care facility services, a physician, or a nurse practitioner or clinical nurse specialist who is not an employee of the facility but is working in collaboration with a physician, recertifies, where such services are furnished over a period of time, in such cases, at least as often as required under section 1396b(g)(6) of this title (or, in the case of services that are services provided in an intermediate care facility for the mentally retarded, every year), and accompanied by such supporting material, appropriate to the case involved, as may be provided in regulations of the Secretary), that such services are or were required to be given on an inpatient basis because the individual needs or needed such services, and

(B) such services were furnished under a plan established and periodically reviewed and evaluated by a physician, or, in the case of skilled nursing facility services or intermediate care facility services, a physician, or a nurse practitioner or clinical nurse specialist who is not an employee of the facility but is working in collaboration with a physician;

(45) provide for mandatory assignment of rights of payment for medical support and other medical care owed to recipients, in accordance with section 1396k of this title;

(46) provide that information is requested and exchanged for purposes of income and eligibility verification in accordance with a State system which meets the requirements of section 1320b–7 of this title;

(47) at the option of the State, provide for making ambulatory prenatal care available to pregnant women during a presumptive eligibility period in accordance with section 1396r–1 of this title and provide for making medical assistance for items and services described in subsection(a) of section 1396r–1a of this title available to children during a presumptive eligibility period in accordance with such section;

(48) provide a method of making cards evidencing eligibility for medical assistance available to an eligible individual who does not reside in a permanent dwelling or does not have a fixed home or mailing address;

(49) provide that the State will provide information and access to certain information respecting sanctions taken against health care practitioners and providers by State licensing authorities in accordance with section 1396r–2 of this title;

(50) provide, in accordance with subsection (q) of this section, for a monthly personal needs allowance for certain institutionalized individuals and couples;

(51) meet the requirements of section 1396r–5 of this title (relating to protection of community spouses);

(52) meet the requirements of section 1396r–6 of this title (relating to extension of eligibility for medical assistance);

(53) provide—

(A) for notifying in a timely manner all individuals in the State who are determined to be eligible for medical assistance and who are pregnant women, breastfeeding or postpartum women (as defined in section 1786 of this title), or children below the age of 5, of the availability of benefits furnished by the special supplemental nutrition program under such section, and

(B) for referring any such individual to the State agency responsible for administering such program;

(54) in the case of a State plan that provides medical assistance for covered outpatient drugs (as defined in section 1396r–8(k) of this title), comply with the applicable requirements of section 1396r–8 of this title;

(55) provide for receipt and initial processing of applications of individuals for medical assistance under subsection (a)(10)(A)(i)(IV), (a)(10)(A)(i)(VI), (a)(10)(A)(i)(VII), or (a)(10)(A)(ii)(IX) of this section—

(A) at locations which are other than those used for the receipt and processing of applications for aid under part A of subchapter IV of this chapter and which include facilities defined as disproportionate share hospitals under section 1396r–4(a)(1)(A) of this title and Federally-qualified health centers described in section 1396d(l)(2)(B) of this title, and

(B) using applications which are other than those used for applications for aid under such part;

(56) provide, in accordance with subsection (s) of this section, for adjusted payments for certain inpatient hospital services;

(57) provide that each hospital, nursing facility, provider of home health care or personal care services, hospice program, or medicaid managed care organization (as defined in section 1396b(m)(1)(A) of this title) receiving funds under the plan shall comply with the requirements of subsection (w) of this section;

(58) provide that the State, acting through a State agency, association, or other private nonprofit entity, develop a written description of the law of the State (whether statutory or as recognized by the courts of the State) concerning advance directives that would be distributed by providers or organizations under the requirements of subsection (w) of this section;

(59) maintain a list (updated not less often than monthly, and containing each physician's unique identifier provided under the system established under subsection (x) of this section) of all physicians who are certified to participate under the State plan;

(60) provide that the State agency shall provide assurances satisfactory to the Secretary that the State has in effect the laws relating to medical child support required under section 1396g–1 of this title;

(61) provide that the State must demonstrate that it operates a medicaid fraud and abuse control unit described in section 1396b(q) of this title that effectively carries out the functions and requirements described in such section, as determined in accordance with standards established by the Secretary, unless the State demonstrates to the satisfaction of the Secretary that the effective operation of such a unit in the State would not be cost-effective because minimal fraud exists in connection with the provision of covered services to eligible individuals under the State plan, and that beneficiaries under the plan will be protected from abuse and neglect in connection with the provision of medical assistance under the plan without the existence of such a unit;

(62) provide for a program for the distribution of pediatric vaccines to program-registered providers for the immunization of vaccine-eligible children in accordance with section 1396s of this title;

(63) provide for administration and determinations of eligibility with respect to individuals who are (or seek to be) eligible for medical assistance based on the application of section 1396u–1 of this title;

(64) provide, not later than 1 year after August 5, 1997, a mechanism to receive reports from beneficiaries and others and compile data concerning alleged instances of waste, fraud, and abuse relating to the operation of this subchapter; and

(65) provide that the State shall issue provider numbers for all suppliers of medical assistance consisting of durable medical equipment, as defined in section 1395x(n) of this title, and the State shall not issue or renew such a supplier number for any such supplier unless—

(A)(i) full and complete information as to the identity of each person with an ownership or control interest (as defined in section 1320a–3(a)(3) of this title) in the supplier or in any subcontractor (as defined by the Secretary in regulations) in which the supplier directly or indirectly has a 5 percent or more ownership interest; and

(ii) to the extent determined to be feasible under regulations of the Secretary, the name of any disclosing entity (as defined in section 1320a–3(a)(2) of this title) with respect to which a person with such an ownership or control interest in the supplier is a person with such an ownership or control interest in the disclosing entity; and

(B) a surety bond in a form specified by the Secretary under section 1395m(a)(16)(B) of this title and in an amount that is not less than $50,000 or such comparable surety bond as the Secretary may permit under the second sentence of such section.

Notwithstanding paragraph (5), if on January 1, 1965, and on the date on which a State submits its plan for approval under this subchapter, the State agency which administered or supervised the administration of the plan of such State approved under subchapter X of this chapter (or subchapter XVI of this chapter, insofar as it relates to the blind) was different from the State agency which administered or supervised the administration of the State plan approved under subchapter I of this chapter (or subchapter XVI of this chapter, insofar as it relates to the aged), the State agency which administered or supervised the administration of such plan approved under subchapter X of this chapter (or subchapter XVI of this chapter, insofar as it relates to the blind) may be designated to administer or supervise the administration of the portion of the State plan for medical assistance which relates to blind individuals and a different State agency may be established or designated to administer or supervise the administration of the rest of the State plan for medical assistance; and in such case the part of the plan which each such agency administers, or the administration of which each such agency supervises, shall be regarded as a separate plan for purposes of this subchapter (except for purposes of paragraph (10)). The provisions of paragraphs (9)(A), (31), and (33) and of section 1396b(i)(4) of this title shall not apply to a religious nonmedical health care institution (as defined in section 1395x(ss)(1) of this title).

For purposes of paragraph (10) any individual who, for the month of August 1972, was eligible for or receiving aid or assistance under a State plan approved under subchapter I, X, XIV, or XVI of this chapter, or part A of subchapter IV of this chapter and who for such month was entitled to monthly insurance benefits under subchapter II of this chapter shall for purposes of this subchapter only be deemed to be eligible for financial aid or assistance for any month thereafter if such individual would have been eligible for financial aid or assistance for such month had the increase in monthly insurance benefits under subchapter II of this chapter resulting from enactment of Public Law 92–336 not been applicable to such individual.

The requirement of clause (A) of paragraph (37) with respect to a State plan may be waived by the Secretary if he finds that the State has exercised good faith in trying to meet such requirement. For purposes of this subchapter, any child who meets the requirements of paragraph (1) or (2) of section 673(b) of this title shall be deemed to be a dependent child as defined in section 606 of this title and shall be deemed to be a recipient of aid to families with dependent children under part A of subchapter IV of this chapter in the State where such child resides. Notwithstanding paragraph (10)(B) or any other provision of this subsection, a State plan shall provide medical assistance with respect to an alien who is not lawfully admitted for permanent residence or otherwise permanently residing in the United States under color of law only in accordance with section 1396b(v) of this title.

(b) Approval by Secretary

The Secretary shall approve any plan which fulfills the conditions specified in subsection (a) of this section, except that he shall not approve any plan which imposes, as a condition of eligibility for medical assistance under the plan—

> **(1)** an age requirement of more than 65 years; or

> **(2)** any residence requirement which excludes any individual who resides in the State, regardless of whether or not the residence is maintained permanently or at a fixed address; or

> **(3)** any citizenship requirement which excludes any citizen of the United States.

(c) Lower payment levels or applying for benefits as condition of applying for, or receiving, medical assistance

Notwithstanding subsection (b) of this section, the Secretary shall not approve any State plan for medical assistance if the State requires individuals described in subsection (*l*)(1) of this section to apply for assistance under the State program funded under part A of subchapter IV of this chapter as a condition of applying for or receiving medical assistance under this subchapter.

(d) Performance of medical or utilization review functions

If a State contracts with an entity which meets the requirements of section 1320c–1 of this title, as determined by the Secretary, or a utilization and quality control peer review organization having a contract with the Secretary under part B of subchapter XI of this chapter for the performance of medical or utilization review functions required under this subchapter of a State plan with respect to specific services or providers (or services or providers in a geographic area of the State), such requirements shall be deemed to be met for those services or providers (or services or providers in that area) by delegation to an entity or organization under the contract of the State's authority to conduct such review activities if the contract provides for the performance of activities not inconsistent with part B of subchapter XI of this chapter and provides for such assurances of satisfactory performance by an entity or organization as the Secretary may prescribe.

(e) Continued eligibility of families determined ineligible because of income and resources or hours of work limitations of plan; individuals enrolled with health maintenance organizations; persons deemed recipients of supplemental security income or State supplemental payments; entitlement for certain newborns; postpartum eligibility for pregnant women

> **(1)(A)** Notwithstanding any other provision of this subchapter, effective January 1, 1974, subject to subparagraph (B) each State plan approved under this subchapter must provide that each family which was

847

receiving aid pursuant to a plan of the State approved under part A of subchapter IV of this chapter in at least 3 of the 6 months immediately preceding the month in which such family became ineligible for such aid because of increased hours of, or increased income from, employment, shall, while a member of such family is employed, remain eligible for assistance under the plan approved under this subchapter (as though the family was receiving aid under the plan approved under part A of subchapter IV of this chapter) for 4 calendar months beginning with the month in which such family became ineligible for aid under the plan approved under part A of subchapter IV of this chapter because of income and resources or hours of work limitations contained in such plan.

(B) Subparagraph (A) shall not apply with respect to families that cease to be eligible for aid under part A of subchapter IV of this chapter during the period beginning on April 1, 1990, and ending on September 30, 2001. During such period, for provisions relating to extension of eligibility for medical assistance for certain families who have received aid pursuant to a State plan approved under part A of subchapter IV of this chapter and have earned income, see section 1396r–6 of this title.

(2)(A) In the case of an individual who is enrolled with a medicaid managed care organization (as defined in section 1396b(m)(1)(A) of this title), with a primary care case manager (as defined in section 1396d(t) of this title), or with an eligible organization with a contract under section 1395mm of this title and who would (but for this paragraph) lose eligibility for benefits under this subchapter before the end of the minimum enrollment period (defined in subparagraph (B)), the State plan may provide, notwithstanding any other provision of this subchapter, that the individual shall be deemed to continue to be eligible for such benefits until the end of such minimum period, but, except for benefits furnished under section 1396d(a)(4)(C) of this title, only with respect to such benefits provided to the individual as an enrollee of such organization or entity or by or through the case manager.

(B) For purposes of subparagraph (A), the term "minimum enrollment period" means, with respect to an individual's enrollment with an organization or entity under a State plan, a period, established by the State, of not more than six months beginning on the date the individual's enrollment with the organization or entity becomes effective.

(3) At the option of the State, any individual who—

(A) is 18 years of age or younger and qualifies as a disabled individual under section 1382c(a) of this title;

(B) with respect to whom there has been a determination by the State that—

    (i) the individual requires a level of care provided in a hospital, nursing facility, or intermediate care facility for the mentally retarded,

    (ii) it is appropriate to provide such care for the individual outside such an institution, and

    (iii) the estimated amount which would be expended for medical assistance for the individual for such care outside an institution is not greater than the estimated amount which would otherwise be expended for medical assistance for the individual within an appropriate institution; and

(C) if the individual were in a medical institution, would be eligible for medical assistance under the State plan under this subchapter,

shall be deemed, for purposes of this subchapter only, to be an individual with respect to whom a supplemental security income payment, or State supplemental payment, respectively, is being paid under subchapter XVI of this chapter.

(4) A child born to a woman eligible for and receiving medical assistance under a State plan on the date of the child's birth shall be deemed to have applied for medical assistance and to have been found eligible for such assistance under such plan on the date of such birth and to remain eligible for such assistance for a period of one year so long as the child is a member of the woman's household and the woman remains (or would remain if pregnant) eligible for such assistance. During the period in which a child is deemed under the preceding sentence to be eligible for medical assistance, the medical assistance eligibility identification number of the mother shall also serve as the identification number of the child, and all claims shall be submitted and paid under such number (unless the State issues a separate identification number for the child before such period expires).

(5) A woman who, while pregnant, is eligible for, has applied for, and has received medical assistance under the State plan, shall continue to be eligible under the plan, as though she were pregnant, for all pregnancy-related and postpartum medical assistance under the plan, through the end of the month in which the 60–day period (beginning on the last day of her pregnancy) ends.

(6) In the case of a pregnant woman described in subsection (a)(10) of this section who, because of a change in income of the family of which she is a member, would not otherwise continue to be described in such subsection, the woman shall be deemed to continue to be an individual described in subsection (a)(10)(A)(i)(IV) of this section and subsection (*l*)(1)(A) of this section without regard to such change of income through the end of the month in which the 60–day period (beginning on the last day of her pregnancy) ends. The preceding sentence shall not apply in the case of a woman who has been provided ambulatory prenatal care

849

pursuant to section 1396r–1 of this title during a presumptive eligibility period and is then, in accordance with such section, determined to be ineligible for medical assistance under the State plan.

(7) In the case of an infant or child described in subparagraph (B), (C), or (D) of subsection (*l*)(1) of this section or paragraph (2) of section 1396d(n) of this title—

(A) who is receiving inpatient services for which medical assistance is provided on the date the infant or child attains the maximum age with respect to which coverage is provided under the State plan for such individuals, and

(B) who, but for attaining such age, would remain eligible for medical assistance under such subsection,

the infant or child shall continue to be treated as an individual described in such respective provision until the end of the stay for which the inpatient services are furnished.

(8) If an individual is determined to be a qualified medicare beneficiary (as defined in section 1396d(p)(1) of this title), such determination shall apply to services furnished after the end of the month in which the determination first occurs. For purposes of payment to a State under section 1396b(a) of this title, such determination shall be considered to be valid for an individual for a period of 12 months, except that a State may provide for such determinations more frequently, but not more frequently than once every 6 months for an individual.

(9)(A) At the option of the State, the plan may include as medical assistance respiratory care services for any individual who—

(i) is medically dependent on a ventilator for life support at least six hours per day;

(ii) has been so dependent for at least 30 consecutive days (or the maximum number of days authorized under the State plan, whichever is less) as an inpatient;

(iii) but for the availability of respiratory care services, would require respiratory care as an inpatient in a hospital, nursing facility, or intermediate care facility for the mentally retarded and would be eligible to have payment made for such inpatient care under the State plan;

(iv) has adequate social support services to be cared for at home; and

(v) wishes to be cared for at home.

(B) The requirements of subparagraph (A)(ii) may be satisfied by a continuous stay in one or more hospitals, nursing facilities, or intermediate care facilities for the mentally retarded.

(C) For purposes of this paragraph, respiratory care services means services provided on a part-time basis in the home of the individual by a respiratory therapist or other health care professional trained in respiratory therapy (as determined by the State), payment for which is not otherwise included within other items and services furnished to such individual as medical assistance under the plan.

(10)(A) The fact that an individual, child, or pregnant woman may be denied aid under part A of subchapter IV of this chapter pursuant to section 602(a)(43) of this title shall not be construed as denying (or permitting a State to deny) medical assistance under this subchapter to such individual, child, or woman who is eligible for assistance under this subchapter on a basis other than the receipt of aid under such part.

(B) If an individual, child, or pregnant woman is receiving aid under part A of subchapter IV of this chapter and such aid is terminated pursuant to section 602(a)(43) of this title, the State may not discontinue medical assistance under this subchapter for the individual, child, or woman until the State has determined that the individual, child, or woman is not eligible for assistance under this subchapter on a basis other than the receipt of aid under such part.

(11)(A) In the case of an individual who is enrolled with a group health plan under section 1396e of this title and who would (but for this paragraph) lose eligibility for benefits under this subchapter before the end of the minimum enrollment period (defined in subparagraph (B)), the State plan may provide, notwithstanding any other provision of this subchapter, that the individual shall be deemed to continue to be eligible for such benefits until the end of such minimum period, but only with respect to such benefits provided to the individual as an enrollee of such plan.

(B) For purposes of subparagraph (A), the term "minimum enrollment period" means, with respect to an individual's enrollment with a group health plan, a period established by the State, of not more than 6 months beginning on the date the individual's enrollment under the plan becomes effective.

(12) At the option of the State, the plan may provide that an individual who is under an age specified by the State (not to exceed 19 years of age) and who is determined to be eligible for benefits under a State plan approved under this title under subsection (a)(10)(A) of this section shall remain eligible for those benefits until the earlier of—

(A) the end of a period (not to exceed 12 months) following the determination; or

(B) the time that the individual exceeds that age.

(f) Effective date of State plan as determinative of duty of State to provide medical assistance to aged, blind, or disabled individuals

Notwithstanding any other provision of this subchapter, except as provided in subsection (e) of this section and section 1382h(b)(3) of this title and section 1396r–5 of this title, except with respect to qualified disabled and working individuals (described in section 1396d(s) of this title), and except with respect to qualified medicare beneficiaries, qualified severely impaired individuals, and individuals described in subsection (m)(1) of this section, no State not eligible to participate in the State plan program established under subchapter XVI of this chapter shall be required to provide medical assistance to any aged, blind, or disabled individual (within the meaning of subchapter XVI of this chapter) for any month unless such State would be (or would have been) required to provide medical assistance to such individual for such month had its plan for medical assistance approved under this subchapter and in effect on January 1, 1972, been in effect in such month, except that for this purpose any such individual shall be deemed eligible for medical assistance under such State plan if (in addition to meeting such other requirements as are or may be imposed under the State plan) the income of any such individual as determined in accordance with section 1396b(f) of this title (after deducting any supplemental security income payment and State supplementary payment made with respect to such individual, and incurred expenses for medical care as recognized under State law regardless of whether such expenses are reimbursed under another public program of the State or political subdivision thereof) is not in excess of the standard for medical assistance established under the State plan as in effect on January 1, 1972. In States which provide medical assistance to individuals pursuant to paragraph (10)(C) of subsection (a) of this section, an individual who is eligible for medical assistance by reason of the requirements of this section concerning the deduction of incurred medical expenses from income shall be considered an individual eligible for medical assistance under paragraph (10)(A) of that subsection if that individual is, or is eligible to be

(1) an individual with respect to whom there is payable a State supplementary payment on the basis of which similarly situated individuals are eligible to receive medical assistance equal in amount, duration, and scope to that provided to individuals eligible under paragraph (10)(A), or

(2) an eligible individual or eligible spouse, as defined in subchapter XVI of this chapter, with respect to whom supplemental security income benefits are payable; otherwise that individual shall be considered to be an individual eligible for medical assistance under paragraph (10)(C) of that subsection. In States which do not provide medical assistance to individuals pursuant to paragraph (10)(C) of that subsection, an individual who is eligible for medical assistance by reason of the requirements of this section concerning the deduction of incurred medical expenses from income shall be considered an individual eligible for medical assistance under paragraph (10)(A) of that subsection.

(g) Reduction of aid or assistance to providers of services attempting to collect from beneficiary in violation of third-party provisions

In addition to any other sanction available to a State, a State may provide for a reduction of any payment amount otherwise due with respect to a person who furnishes services under the plan in an amount equal to up to three times the amount of any payment sought to be collected by that person in violation of subsection (a)(25)(C) of this section.

(h) Payments for hospitals serving disproportionate number of low-income patients and for home and community care

Nothing in this subchapter (including subsections (a)(13) and (a)(30) of this section) shall be construed as authorizing the Secretary to limit the amount of payment that may be made under a plan under this subchapter for home and community care.

(i) Termination of certification for participation of and suspension of State payments to intermediate care facilities for the mentally retarded

(1) In addition to any other authority under State law, where a State determines that a intermediate care facility for the mentally retarded which is certified for participation under its plan no longer substantially meets the requirements for such a facility under this subchapter and further determines that the facility's deficiencies—

(A) immediately jeopardize the health and safety of its patients, the State shall provide for the termination of the facility's certification for participation under the plan and may provide, or

(B) do not immediately jeopardize the health and safety of its patients, the State may, in lieu of providing for terminating the facility's certification for participation under the plan, establish alternative remedies if the State demonstrates to the Secretary's satisfaction that the alternative remedies are effective in deterring noncompliance and correcting deficiencies, and may provide that no payment will be made under the State plan with respect to any individual admitted to such facility after a date specified by the State.

(2) The State shall not make such a decision with respect to a facility until the facility has had a reasonable opportunity, following the initial determination that it no longer substantially meets the requirements for such a facility under this subchapter, to correct its deficiencies, and, following this period, has been given reasonable notice and opportunity for a hearing.

(3) The State's decision to deny payment may be made effective only after such notice to the public and to the facility as may be provided for by the State, and its effectiveness shall terminate

(A) when the State finds that the facility is in substantial compliance (or is making good faith efforts to achieve substantial compliance) with the requirements for such a facility under this subchapter, or

(B) in the case described in paragraph (1)(B), with the end of the eleventh month following the month such decision is made effective, whichever occurs first. If a facility to which clause (B) of the previous sentence applies still fails to substantially meet the provisions of the respective section on the date specified in such clause, the State shall terminate such facility's certification for participation under the plan effective with the first day of the first month following the month specified in such clause.

(j) Waiver or modification of subchapter requirements with respect to medical assistance program in American Samoa

Notwithstanding any other requirement of this subchapter, the Secretary may waive or modify any requirement of this subchapter with respect to the medical assistance program in American Samoa and the Northern Mariana Islands, other than a waiver of the Federal medical assistance percentage, the limitation in section 1308(f) of this title, or the requirement that payment may be made for medical assistance only with respect to amounts expended by American Samoa or the Northern Mariana Islands for care and services described in a numbered paragraph of section 1396d(a) of this title.

(k) Repealed.

(l) Description of group

(1) Individuals described in this paragraph are—

(A) women during pregnancy (and during the 60–day period beginning on the last day of the pregnancy),

(B) infants under one year of age,

(C) children who have attained one year of age but have not attained 6 years of age, and

(D) children born after September 30, 1983 (or, at the option of a State, after any earlier date), who have attained 6 years of age but have not attained 19 years of age,

who are not described in any of subclauses (I) through (III) of subsection (a)(10)(A)(i) of this section and whose family income does not exceed the income level established by the State under paragraph (2) for a family size equal to the size of the family, including the woman, infant, or child.

(2)(A)(i) For purposes of paragraph (1) with respect to individuals described in subparagraph (A) or (B) of that paragraph, the State shall establish an income level which is a percentage (not less than the percentage provided under clause (ii) and not more than 185 percent) of the income official poverty line (as defined by the Office of Management and Budget, and revised annually in accordance with section 9902(2) of this title) applicable to a family of the size involved.

(ii) The percentage provided under this clause, with respect to eligibility for medical assistance on or after—

(I) July 1, 1989, is 75 percent, or, if greater, the percentage provided under clause (iii), and

(II) April 1, 1990, 133 percent, or, if greater, the percentage provided under clause (iv).

(iii) In the case of a State which, as of July 1, 1988, has elected to provide, and provides, medical assistance to individuals described in this subsection or has enacted legislation authorizing, or appropriating funds, to provide such assistance to such individuals before July 1, 1989, the percentage provided under clause (ii)(I) shall not be less than—

(I) the percentage specified by the State in an amendment to its State plan (whether approved or not) as of July 1, 1988, or

(II) if no such percentage is specified as of July 1, 1988, the percentage established under the State's authorizing legislation or provided for under the State's appropriations;

but in no case shall this clause require the percentage provided under clause (ii)(I) to exceed 100 percent.

(iv) In the case of a State which, as of December 19, 1989, has established under clause (i), or has enacted legislation authorizing, or appropriating funds, to provide for, a percentage (of the income official poverty line) that is greater than 133 percent, the percentage provided under clause (ii) for medical assistance on or after April 1, 1990, shall not be less than—

(I) the percentage specified by the State in an amendment to its State plan (whether approved or not) as of December 19, 1989, or

(II) if no such percentage is specified as of December 19, 1989, the percentage established under the State's authorizing legislation or provided for under the State's appropriations.

(B) For purposes of paragraph (1) with respect to individuals described in subparagraph (C) of such paragraph, the State shall establish an income level which is equal to 133 percent of the income official poverty line described in subparagraph (A) applicable to a family of the size involved.

(C) For purposes of paragraph (1) with respect to individuals described in subparagraph (D) of that paragraph, the State shall establish an income level which is equal to 100 percent of the income official poverty line described in subparagraph (A) applicable to a family of the size involved.

(3) Notwithstanding subsection (a)(17) of this section, for individuals who are eligible for medical assistance because of subsection (a)(10)(A)(i)(IV), (a)(10)(A)(i)(VI), (a)(10)(A)(i)(VII), or (a)(10)(A)(ii)(IX) of this section—

(A) application of a resource standard shall be at the option of the State;

(B) any resource standard or methodology that is applied with respect to an individual described in subparagraph (A) of paragraph

(1) may not be more restrictive than the resource standard or methodology that is applied under subchapter XVI of this chapter;

(C) any resource standard or methodology that is applied with respect to an individual described in subparagraph (B), (C), or (D) of paragraph (1) may not be more restrictive than the corresponding methodology that is applied under the State plan under part A of subchapter IV of this chapter;

(D) the income standard to be applied is the appropriate income standard established under paragraph (2); and

(E) family income shall be determined in accordance with the methodology employed under the State plan under part A or E of subchapter IV of this chapter (except to the extent such methodology is inconsistent with clause (D) of subsection (a)(17) of this section), and costs incurred for medical care or for any other type of remedial care shall not be taken into account.

Any different treatment provided under this paragraph for such individuals shall not, because of subsection (a)(17) of this section, require or permit such treatment for other individuals.

(4)(A) In the case of any State which is providing medical assistance to its residents under a waiver granted under section 1315 of this title, the Secretary shall require the State to provide medical assistance for pregnant women and infants under age 1 described in subsection (a)(10)(A)(i)(IV) of this section and for children described in subsection (a)(10)(A)(i)(VI) or subsection (a)(10)(A)(i)(VII) of this section in the same manner as the State would be required to provide such assistance for such individuals if the State had in effect a plan approved under this subchapter.

(B) In the case of a State which is not one of the 50 States or the District of Columbia, the State need not meet the requirement of subsection (a)(10)(A)(i)(IV), (a)(10)(A)(i)(VI), or (a)(10)(A)(i)(VII) of this section and, for purposes of paragraph (2)(A), the State may substitute for the percentage provided under clause (ii) of such paragraph any percentage.

(m) Description of individuals

(1) Individuals described in this paragraph are individuals—

(A) who are 65 years of age or older or are disabled individuals (as determined under section 1382c(a)(3) of this title),

(B) whose income (as determined under section 1382a of this title for purposes of the supplemental security income program, except as provided in paragraph 2(C)) does not exceed an income level established by the State consistent with paragraph (2)(A), and

(C) whose resources (as determined under section 1382b of this title for purposes of the supplemental security income program) do not exceed (except as provided in paragraph (2)(B)) the maximum amount of resources that an individual may have and obtain benefits under that program.

(2)(A) The income level established under paragraph (1)(B) may not exceed a percentage (not more than 100 percent) of the official poverty line (as defined by the Office of Management and Budget, and revised annually in accordance with section 9902(2) of this title) applicable to a family of the size involved.

(B) In the case of a State that provides medical assistance to individuals not described in subsection (a)(10)(A) of this section and at the State's option, the State may use under paragraph (1)(C) such resource level (which is higher than the level described in that paragraph) as may be applicable with respect to individuals described in paragraph (1)(A) who are not described in subsection (a)(10)(A) of this section.

(C) The provisions of section 1396d(p)(2)(D) of this title shall apply to determinations of income under this subsection in the same manner as they apply to determinations of income under section 1396d(p) of this title.

(3) Notwithstanding subsection (a)(17) of this section, for individuals described in paragraph (1) who are covered under the State plan by virtue of subsection (a)(10)(A)(ii)(X) of this section—

(A) the income standard to be applied is the income standard described in paragraph (1)(B), and

(B) except as provided in section 1382a(b)(4)(B)(ii) of this title, costs incurred for medical care or for any other type of remedial care shall not be taken into account in determining income.

Any different treatment provided under this paragraph for such individuals shall not, because of subsection (a)(17) of this section, require or permit such treatment for other individuals.

(4) Notwithstanding subsection (a)(17) of this section, for qualified medicare beneficiaries described in section 1396d(p)(1) of this title—

(A) the income standard to be applied is the income standard described in section 1396d(p)(1)(B) of this title, and

(B) except as provided in section 1382a(b)(4)(B)(ii) of this title, costs incurred for medical care or for any other type of remedial care shall not be taken into account in determining income.

Any different treatment provided under this paragraph for such individuals shall not, because of subsection (a)(17) of this section, require or permit such treatment for other individuals.

857

(*o*) Certain benefits disregarded for purposes of determining post-eligibility contributions

Notwithstanding any provision of subsection (a) of this section to the contrary, a State plan under this subchapter shall provide that any supplemental security income benefits paid by reason of subparagraph (E) or (G) of section 1382(e)(1) of this title to an individual who—

(1) is eligible for medical assistance under the plan, and

(2) is in a hospital, skilled nursing facility, or intermediate care facility at the time such benefits are paid,

will be disregarded for purposes of determining the amount of any post-eligibility contribution by the individual to the cost of the care and services provided by the hospital, skilled nursing facility, or intermediate care facility.

(p) Exclusion power of State; exclusion as prerequisite for medical assistance payments; "exclude" defined

(1) In addition to any other authority, a State may exclude any individual or entity for purposes of participating under the State plan under this subchapter for any reason for which the Secretary could exclude the individual or entity from participation in a program under subchapter XVIII of this chapter under section 1320a–7, 1320a–7a, or 1395cc(b)(2) of this title.

(2) In order for a State to receive payments for medical assistance under section 1396b(a) of this title, with respect to payments the State makes to a medicaid managed care organization (as defined in section 1396b(m) of this title) or to an entity furnishing services under a waiver approved under section 1396n(b)(1) of this title, the State must provide that it will exclude from participation, as such an organization or entity, any organization or entity that—

(A) could be excluded under section 1320a–7(b)(8) of this title (relating to owners and managing employees who have been convicted of certain crimes or received other sanctions),

(B) has, directly or indirectly, a substantial contractual relationship (as defined by the Secretary) with an individual or entity that is described in section 1320a–7(b)(8)(B) of this title, or

(C) employs or contracts with any individual or entity that is excluded from participation under this subchapter under section 1320a–7 or 1320a–7a of this title for the provision of health care, utilization review, medical social work, or administrative services or employs or contracts with any entity for the provision (directly or indirectly) through such an excluded individual or entity of such services.

(3) As used in this subsection, the term "exclude" includes the refusal to enter into or renew a participation agreement or the termination of such an agreement.

(q) Minimum monthly personal needs allowance deduction; "institutionalized individual or couple" defined

(1)(A) In order to meet the requirement of subsection (a)(50) of this section, the State plan must provide that, in the case of an institutionalized individual or couple described in subparagraph (B), in determining the amount of the individual's or couple's income to be applied monthly to payment for the cost of care in an institution, there shall be deducted from the monthly income (in addition to other allowances otherwise provided under the State plan) a monthly personal needs allowance—

    (i) which is reasonable in amount for clothing and other personal needs of the individual (or couple) while in an institution, and

    (ii) which is not less (and may be greater) than the minimum monthly personal needs allowance described in paragraph (2).

(B) In this subsection, the term "institutionalized individual or couple" means an individual or married couple—

    (i) who is an inpatient (or who are inpatients) in a medical institution or nursing facility for which payments are made under this subchapter throughout a month, and

    (ii) who is or are determined to be eligible for medical assistance under the State plan.

(2) The minimum monthly personal needs allowance described in this paragraph is $30 for an institutionalized individual and $60 for an institutionalized couple (if both are aged, blind, or disabled, and their incomes are considered available to each other in determining eligibility).

(r) Disregarding payments for certain medical expenses by institutionalized individuals

(1)(A) For purposes of sections 1396a(a)(17) and 1396r–5(d)(1)(D) of this title and for purposes of a waiver under section 1396n of this title, with respect to the post-eligibility treatment of income of individuals who are institutionalized or receiving home or community-based services under such a waiver the treatment described in subparagraph (B) shall apply, there shall be disregarded reparation payments made by the Federal Republic of Germany and, there shall be taken into account amounts for incurred expenses for medical or remedial care that are not subject to payment by a third party, including—

    (i) medicare and other health insurance premiums, deductibles, or coinsurance, and;

    (ii) necessary medical or remedial care recognized under State law but not covered under the State plan under this subchapter, subject to reasonable limits the State may establish on the amount of these expenses.

(B)(i) In the case of a veteran who does not have a spouse or a child, if the veteran—

(I) receives, after the veteran has been determined to be eligible for medical assistance under the State plan under this title, a veteran's pension in excess of $90 per month, and

(II) resides in a State veterans home with respect to which the Secretary of Veterans Affairs makes per diem payments for nursing home care pursuant to section 1741(a) of Title 38,

any such pension payment, including any payment made due to the need for aid and attendance, or for unreimbursed medical expenses, that is in excess of $90 per month shall be counted as income only for the purpose of applying such excess payment to the State veterans home's cost of providing nursing home care to the veteran.

(ii) The provisions of clause (i) shall apply with respect to a surviving spouse of a veteran who does not have a child in the same manner as they apply to a veteran described in such clause.

(2)(A) The methodology to be employed in determining income and resource eligibility for individuals under subsection (a)(10)(A)(i)(III), (a)(10)(A)(i)(IV), (a)(10)(A)(i)(VI), (a)(10)(A)(i)(VII), (a)(10)(A)(ii), (a)(10)(C)(i)(III), or (f) of this section or under section 1396d(p) of this title may be less restrictive, and shall be no more restrictive, than the methodology—

(i) in the case of groups consisting of aged, blind, or disabled individuals, under the supplemental security income program under subchapter XVI of this chapter, or

(ii) in the case of other groups, under the State plan most closely categorically related.

(B) For purposes of this subsection and subsection (a)(10) of this section, methodology is considered to be "no more restrictive" if, using the methodology, additional individuals may be eligible for medical assistance and no individuals who are otherwise eligible are made ineligible for such assistance.

(s) Adjustment in payment for hospital services furnished to low-income children under age of 6 years

In order to meet the requirements of subsection (a)(55) of this section, the State plan must provide that payments to hospitals under the plan for inpatient hospital services furnished to infants who have not attained the age of 1 year, and to children who have not attained the age of 6 years and who receive such services in a disproportionate share hospital described in section 1396r-4(b)(1) of this title, shall—

(1) if made on a prospective basis (whether per diem, per case, or otherwise) provide for an outlier adjustment in payment amounts for medically necessary inpatient hospital services involving exceptionally high costs or exceptionally long lengths of stay,

(2) not be limited by the imposition of day limits with respect to the delivery of such services to such individuals, and

(3) not be limited by the imposition of dollar limits (other than such limits resulting from prospective payments as adjusted pursuant to paragraph (1)) with respect to the delivery of such services to any such individual who has not attained their first birthday (or in the case of such an individual who is an inpatient on his first birthday until such individual is discharged).

(t) Limitation on payments to States for expenditures attributable to taxes

Nothing in this subchapter (including sections 1396b(a) and 1396d(a) of this title) shall be construed as authorizing the Secretary to deny or limit payments to a State for expenditures, for medical assistance for items or services, attributable to taxes of general applicability imposed with respect to the provision of such items or services.

(u) Qualified COBRA continuation beneficiaries

(1) Individuals described in this paragraph are individuals—

(A) who are entitled to elect COBRA continuation coverage (as defined in paragraph (3)).

(B) whose income (as determined under section 1382a of this title for purposes of the supplemental security income program) does not exceed 100 percent of the official poverty line (as defined by the Office of Management and Budget, and revised annually in accordance with section 9902(2) of this title) applicable to a family of the size involved,

(C) whose resources (as determined under section 1382b of this title for purposes of the supplemental security income program) do not exceed twice the maximum amount of resources that an individual may have and obtain benefits under that program, and

(D) with respect to whose enrollment for COBRA continuation coverage the State has determined that the savings in expenditures under this subchapter resulting from such enrollment is likely to exceed the amount of payments for COBRA premiums made.

(2) For purposes of subsection (a)(10)(F) of this section and this subsection, the term "COBRA premiums" means the applicable premium imposed with respect to COBRA continuation coverage.

(3) In this subsection, the term "COBRA continuation coverage" means coverage under a group health plan provided by an employer with 75 or more employees provided pursuant to title XXII of the Public

Health Service Act [*42 U.S.C.A. § 300bb–1* et seq.] section 4980B of Title 26, or title VI of the Employee Retirement Income Security Act of 1974 [*29 U.S.C.A. § 1161* et seq.]

(4) Notwithstanding subsection (a)(17) of this section, for individuals described in paragraph (1) who are covered under the State plan by virtue of subsection (a)(10)(A)(ii)(XI) of this section—

    (A) the income standard to be applied is the income standard described in paragraph (1)(B), and

    (B) except as provided in section 1382a(b)(4)(B)(ii) of this title, costs incurred for medical care or for any other type of remedial care shall not be taken into account in determining income.

Any different treatment provided under this paragraph for such individuals shall not, because of subsection (a)(10)(B) or (a)(17) of this section, require or permit such treatment for other individuals.

(v) State agency disability and blindness determinations for medical assistance eligibility

A State plan may provide for the making of determinations of disability or blindness for the purpose of determining eligibility for medical assistance under the State plan by the single State agency or its designee, and make medical assistance available to individuals whom it finds to be blind or disabled and who are determined otherwise eligible for such assistance during the period of time prior to which a final determination of disability or blindness is made by the Social Security Administration with respect to such an individual. In making such determinations, the State must apply the definitions of disability and blindness found in section 1382c(a) of this title.

(w) Maintenance of written policies and procedures respecting advance directives

    (1) For purposes of subsection (a)(57) of this section and sections 1396b(m)(1)(A) and 1396r(c)(2)(E) of this title, the requirement of this subsection is that a provider or organization (as the case may be) maintain written policies and procedures with respect to all adult individuals receiving medical care by or through the provider or organization—

        (A) to provide written information to each such individual concerning—

            (i) an individual's rights under State law (whether statutory or as recognized by the courts of the State) to make decisions concerning such medical care, including the right to accept or refuse medical or surgical treatment and the right to formulate advance directives (as defined in paragraph (3)), and

            (ii) the provider's or organization's written policies respecting the implementation of such rights;

        (B) to document in the individual's medical record whether or not the individual has executed an advance directive;

(C) not to condition the provision of care or otherwise discriminate against an individual based on whether or not the individual has executed an advance directive;

(D) to ensure compliance with requirements of State law (whether statutory or as recognized by the courts of the State) respecting advance directives; and

(E) to provide (individually or with others) for education for staff and the community on issues concerning advance directives.

Subparagraph (C) shall not be construed as requiring the provision of care which conflicts with an advance directive.

(2) The written information described in paragraph (1)(A) shall be provided to an adult individual—

(A) in the case of a hospital, at the time of the individual's admission as an inpatient,

(B) in the case of a nursing facility, at the time of the individual's admission as a resident,

(C) in the case of a provider of home health care or personal care services, in advance of the individual coming under the care of the provider,

(D) in the case of a hospice program, at the time of initial receipt of hospice care by the individual from the program, and

(E) in the case of a medicaid managed care organization, at the time of enrollment of the individual with the organization.

(3) Nothing in this section shall be construed to prohibit the application of a State law which allows for an objection on the basis of conscience for any health care provider or any agent of such provider which as a matter of conscience cannot implement an advance directive.

(4) In this subsection, the term "advance directive" means a written instruction, such as a living will or durable power of attorney for health care, recognized under State law (whether statutory or as recognized by the courts of the State) and relating to the provision of such care when the individual is incapacitated.

(5) For construction relating to this subsection, see section 14406 of this title (relating to clarification respecting assisted suicide, euthanasia, and mercy killing).

(x) Physician identifier system; establishment

The Secretary shall establish a system, for implementation by not later than July 1, 1991, which provides for a unique identifier for each physician who furnishes services for which payment may be made under a State plan approved under this subchapter.

(y) Intermediate sanctions for psychiatric hospitals

(1) In addition to any other authority under State law, where a State determines that a psychiatric hospital which is certified for participation under its plan no longer meets the requirements for a psychiatric hospital (referred to in section 1396d(h) of this title) and further finds that the hospital's deficiencies—

(A) immediately jeopardize the health and safety of its patients, the State shall terminate the hospital's participation under the State plan; or

(B) do not immediately jeopardize the health and safety of its patients, the State may terminate the hospital's participation under the State plan, or provide that no payment will be made under the State plan with respect to any individual admitted to such hospital after the effective date of the finding, or both.

(2) Except as provided in paragraph (3), if a psychiatric hospital described in paragraph (1)(B) has not complied with the requirements for a psychiatric hospital under this subchapter—

(A) within 3 months after the date the hospital is found to be out of compliance with such requirements, the State shall provide that no payment will be made under the State plan with respect to any individual admitted to such hospital after the end of such 3–month period, or

(B) within 6 months after the date the hospital is found to be out of compliance with such requirements, no Federal financial participation shall be provided under section 1396b(a) of this title with respect to further services provided in the hospital until the State finds that the hospital is in compliance with the requirements of this subchapter.

(3) The Secretary may continue payments, over a period of not longer than 6 months from the date the hospital is found to be out of compliance with such requirements, if—

(A) the State finds that it is more appropriate to take alternative action to assure compliance of the hospital with the requirements than to terminate the certification of the hospital,

(B) the State has submitted a plan and timetable for corrective action to the Secretary for approval and the Secretary approves the plan of corrective action, and

(C) the State agrees to repay to the Federal Government payments received under this paragraph if the corrective action is not taken in accordance with the approved plan and timetable.

(z) Optional coverage of TB-related services

(1) Individuals described in this paragraph are individuals not described in subsection (a)(10)(A)(i) of this section—

(A) who are infected with tuberculosis;

864

(B) whose income (as determined under the State plan under this subchapter with respect to disabled individuals) does not exceed the maximum amount of income a disabled individual described in subsection (a)(10)(A)(i) of this section may have and obtain medical assistance under the plan; and

(C) whose resources (as determined under the State plan under this subchapter with respect to disabled individuals) do not exceed the maximum amount of resources a disabled individual described in subsection (a)(10)(A)(i) of this section may have and obtain medical assistance under the plan.

(2) For purposes of subsection (a)(10) of this section, the term "TB-related services" means each of the following services relating to treatment of infection with tuberculosis:

(A) Prescribed drugs.

(B) Physicians' services and services described in section 1396d(a)(2) of this title.

(C) Laboratory and X-ray services (including services to confirm the presence of infection).

(D) Clinic services and Federally-qualified health center services.

(E) Case management services (as defined in section 1396n(g)(2) of this title).

(F) Services (other than room and board) designed to encourage completion of regimens of prescribed drugs by out-patients, including services to observe directly

    (aa) Certain individuals with breast or cervical cancer. Individuals described in this subsection are individuals who—

        (1) are not described in subsection (a)(10)(A)(i);

        (2) have not attained age 65;

        (3) have been screened for breast and cervical cancer under the Centers for Disease Control and Prevention breast and cervical cancer early detection program established under title XV of the Public Health Service Act (42 U.S.C.A. § 300k et seq.) in accordance with the requirements of section 1504 of that Act (42 U.S.C.A. § 300n) and need treatment for breast or cervical cancer; and

        (4) are not otherwise covered under creditable coverage, as defined in section 2701(c) of the Public Health Service Act (42 U.S.C.A. § 300gg(c)).

[bb](aa) Payment for services provided by federally-qualified health centers and rural health clinics

(1) In general. Beginning with fiscal year 2001 with respect to services furnished on or after January 1, 2001, and each succeeding fiscal year, the State plan shall provide for payment for services described in section 1905(a)(2)(C) [§ 1396d(a)(2)(C)] furnished by a Federally-qualified health center and services described in section 1905(a)(2)(B) [§ 1396(a)(2)(B)] furnished by a rural health clinic in accordance with the provisions of this subsection.

(2) Fiscal year 2001. Subject to paragraph (4), for services furnished on and after January 1, 2001, during fiscal year 2001, the State plan shall provide for payment for such services in an amount (calculated on a per visit basis) that is equal to 100 percent of the average of the costs of the center or clinic of furnishing such services during fiscal years 1999 and 2000 which are reasonable and related to the cost of furnishing such services, or based on such other tests of reasonableness as the Secretary prescribes in regulations under section 1833(a)(3) [42 USCS § 1395l(a)(3)], or, in the case of services to which such regulations do not apply, the same methodology used under section 1833(a)(3) [42 USCS § 1395l(a)(3)], adjusted to take into account any increase or decrease in the scope of such services furnished by the center or clinic during fiscal year 2001.

(3) Fiscal year 2002 and succeeding fiscal years. Subject to paragraph (4), for services furnished during fiscal year 2002 or a succeeding fiscal year, the State plan shall provide for payment for such services in an amount (calculated on a per visit basis) that is equal to the amount calculated for such services under this subsection for the preceding fiscal year—

(A) increased by the percentage increase in the MEI (as defined in section 1842(i)(3) [§ 1395u(i)(3)]) applicable to primary care services (as defined in section 1842(i)(4) [§ 1395u(i)(4)]) for that fiscal year; and

(B) adjusted to take into account any increase or decrease in the scope of such services furnished by the center or clinic during that fiscal year.

(4) Establishment of initial year payment amount for new centers or clinics. In any case in which an entity first qualifies as a Federally-qualified health center or rural health clinic after fiscal year 2000, the State plan shall provide for payment for services described in section 1905(a)(2)(C) [§ 1396d(a)(2)(C)] furnished by the center or services described in section 1905(a)(2)(B) [§ 1396d(a)(2)(B)] furnished by the clinic in the first fiscal year in which the center or clinic so qualifies in an amount (calculated on a per visit basis) that is equal to 100 percent of the costs of furnishing such services during such fiscal year based on the rates established under this subsection for the fiscal year for other such centers or clinics located in the same or adjacent area with a similar case load or, in the absence of such a center or clinic, in accordance with the regulations and methodology referred to in paragraph (2) or based on such other tests of reasonableness as the Secretary may specify. For each fiscal year following the fiscal year in which the entity first qualifies as a Federally-qualified health center or rural health clinic, the State plan shall provide for the payment amount to be calculated in accordance with paragraph (3).

(5) Administration in the case of managed care. (A) In general. In the case of services furnished by a Federally-qualified health center or rural health clinic pursuant to a contract between the center or clinic and a managed care entity (as defined in section 1932(a)(1)(B) [§ 1396u–2(a)(1)(B)]), the State plan shall provide for payment to the center or clinic by the State of a supplemental payment equal to the amount (if any) by which the amount determined under paragraphs (2), (3), and (4) of this subsection exceeds the amount of the payments provided under the contract.

(B) Payment schedule. The supplemental payment required under subparagraph (A) shall be made pursuant to a payment schedule agreed to by the State and the Federally-qualified health center or rural health clinic, but in no case less frequently than every 4 months.

(6) Alternative payment methodologies. Notwithstanding any other provision of this section, the State plan may provide for payment in any fiscal year to a Federally-qualified health center for services described in section 1905(a)(2)(C) [§ 1396d(a)(2)(C)] or to a rural health clinic for services described in section 1905(a)(2)(B) [§ 1396d(a)(2)(B)] in an amount which is determined under an alternative payment methodology that—

(A) is agreed to by the State and the center or clinic; and

(B) results in payment to the center or clinic of an amount which is at least equal to the amount otherwise required to be paid to the center or clinic under this section.

§ 1396b.   Payment to States.   [Payment process omitted]

* * *

(f) Limitation on Federal participation in medical assistance

(1)(A) Except as provided in paragraph (4), payment under the preceding provisions of this section shall not be made with respect to any amount expended as medical assistance in a calendar quarter, in any State, for any member of a family the annual income of which exceeds the applicable income limitation determined under this paragraph.

(B)(i) Except as provided in clause (ii) of this subparagraph, the applicable income limitation with respect to any family is the amount determined, in accordance with standards prescribed by the Secretary, to be equivalent to 133⅓ percent of the highest amount which would ordinarily be paid to a family of the same size without any income or resources, in the form of money payments, under the plan of the State approved under part A of title IV of this Act [§§ 601 et seq.]

(ii) If the Secretary finds that the operation of a uniform maximum limits payments to families of more than one size, he may adjust the amount otherwise determined under clause (i) to take account of families of different sizes.

(C) The total amount of any applicable income limitation determined under subparagraph (B) shall, if it is not a multiple of $100 or such other amount as the Secretary may prescribe, be rounded to the next higher multiple of $100 or such other amount, as the case may be.

(2)(A) In computing a family's income for purposes of paragraph (1), there shall be excluded any costs (whether in the form of insurance premiums or otherwise and regardless of whether such costs are reimbursed under another public program of the State or political subdivision thereof) incurred by such family for medical care or for any other type of remedial care recognized under State law or, (B) notwithstanding section 1916 [§ 1396o] at State option, an amount paid by such family, at the family's option, to the State, provided that the amount, when combined with costs incurred in prior months, is sufficient when excluded from the family's income to reduce such family's income below the applicable income limitation described in paragraph (1).   The amount of State expenditures for which medical assistance is available under subsection (a)(1) will be reduced by amounts paid to the State pursuant to this subparagraph.

(3) For purposes of paragraph (1)(B), in the case of a family consisting of only one individual, the "highest amount which would ordinarily be paid" to such family under the State's plan approved under part A of title IV of this Act [§§ 601 et seq.] shall be the amount determined by the State agency (on the basis of reasonable relationship to the amounts

868

payable under such plan to families consisting of two or more persons) to be the amount of the aid which would ordinarily be payable under such plan to a family (without any income or resources) consisting of one person if such plan provided for aid to such a family.

(4) The limitations on payment imposed by the preceding provisions of this subsection shall not apply with respect to any amount expended by a State as medical assistance for any individual described in section 1902(a)(10)(A)(i)(III),   1902(a)(10)(A)(i)(IV),   1902(a)(10)(A)(i)(V), 1902(a)(10)(A)(i)(VI),   1902(a)(10)(A)(i)(VII),   1902(a)(10)(A)(ii)(IX), 1902(a)(10)(A)(ii)(X),   1902(a)(10)(A)(ii)(XV),   1902(a)(10)(A)(ii)(XVI), 1902(a)(10)(A)(ii)(XVII),   1902(a)(10)(A)(ii)(XVIII), 1902(a)(10)(A)(ii)(XIII), 1902(a)(10)(A)(ii)(XIV), or 1905(p)(1) [42 USCS § 1396a(a)(10)(A)(i)(III), (IV), (V), (VI), (VII), (ii)(IX), (X), (XV), (XVI), (XVII), (XVIII), (XIII), (XIV), or 1396d(p)(1)] or for any individual—

(A) who is receiving aid or assistance under any plan of the State approved under title I, X, XIV or XVI, or part A of title IV [§§ 301 et seq., 1201 et seq., 1351 et seq., or 1381 et seq., or 601 et seq.], or with respect to whom supplemental security income benefits are being paid under title XVI [§§ 1381 et seq.], or

(B) who is not receiving such aid or assistance, and with respect to whom such benefits are not being paid, but (i) is eligible to receive such aid or assistance, or to have such benefits paid with respect to him, or (ii) would be eligible to receive such aid or assistance, or to have such benefits paid with respect to him if he were not in a medical institution, or

(C) with respect to whom there is being paid, or who is eligible, or would be eligible if he were not in a medical institution, to have paid with respect to him, a State supplementary payment and is eligible for medical assistance equal in amount, duration, and scope to the medical assistance made available to individuals described in section 1902(a)(10)(A) [§ 1396a(a)(10)(A)], or who is a PACE program eligible individual enrolled in a PACE program under section 1934 [§ 1396u–4], but only if the income of such individual (as determined under section 1612 [§ 1382a], but without regard to subsection (b) thereof) does not exceed 300 percent of the supplemental security income benefit rate established by section 1611(b)(1) [§ 1382(b)(1)],

at the time of the provision of the medical assistance giving rise to such expenditure.

(g) Decrease in Federal medical assistance percentage of amounts paid for services furnished under State plan after June 30, 1973

(1) Subject to paragraph (3), with respect to amounts paid for the following services furnished under the State plan after June 30, 1973 (other than services furnished pursuant to a contract with a health maintenance organization as defined in section 1876 [§ 1395mm] or which is a qualified health maintenance organization (as defined in section 1310(d) of the Public Health Service Act), the Federal medical assistance percentage shall be decreased as follows: After an individual has received inpatient hospital services or services in an intermediate care facility for the mentally retarded for 60 days or inpatient mental hospital services for 90 days (whether or not such days are consecutive), during any fiscal year, the Federal medical assistance percentage with respect to amounts paid for any such care furnished thereafter to such individual shall be decreased by a per centum thereof (determined under paragraph (5)) unless the State agency responsible for the administration of the plan makes a showing satisfactory to the Secretary that, with respect to each calendar quarter for which the State submits a request for payment at the full Federal medical assistance percentage for amounts paid for inpatient hospital services or services in an intermediate care facility for the mentally retarded furnished beyond 60 days (or inpatient mental hospital services furnished beyond 90 days), such State has an effective program of medical review of the care of patients in mental hospitals, and intermediate care facilities for the mentally retarded pursuant to paragraphs (26) and (31) of section 1902(a) [§ 1396a(a)(26) and (31)] whereby the professional management of each case is reviewed and evaluated at least annually by independent professional review teams. In determining the number of days on which an individual has received services described in this subsection, there shall not be counted any days with respect to which such individual is entitled to have payments made (in whole or in part) on his behalf under section 1812 [§ 1395d].

(2) The Secretary shall, as part of his validation procedures under this subsection, conduct timely sample onsite surveys of private and public institutions in which recipients of medical assistance may receive care and services under a State plan approved under this title [§§ 1396 et seq.], and his findings with respect to such surveys (as well as the showings of the State agency required under this subsection) shall be made available for public inspection.

* * *

(4)(A) The Secretary may not find the showing of a State, with respect to a calendar quarter under paragraph (1), to be satisfactory if the showing is submitted to the Secretary later than the 30th day after the last day of the calendar quarter, unless the State demonstrates to the satisfaction of the Secretary good cause for not meeting such deadline.

(B) The Secretary shall find a showing of a State, with respect to a calendar quarter under paragraph (1), to be satisfactory under such paragraph with respect to the requirement that the State conduct annual onsite inspections in mental hospitals and intermediate care facilities for the mentally retarded under paragraphs (26) and (31) of section 1902(a) [§ 1396a(a)(26) and (31)], if the showing demonstrates that the State has conducted such an onsite inspection during the 12-month period ending on the last date of the calendar quarter—

> **(i)** in each of not less than 98 per centum of the number of such hospitals and facilities requiring such inspection, and

> **(ii)** in every such hospital or facility which has 200 or more beds,

and that, with respect to such hospitals and facilities not inspected within such period, the State has exercised good faith and due diligence in attempting to conduct such inspection, or if the State demonstrates to the satisfaction of the Secretary that it would have made such a showing but for failings of a technical nature only.

(5) In the case of a State's unsatisfactory or invalid showing made with respect to a type of facility or institutional services in a calendar quarter, the per centum amount of the reduction of the State's Federal medical assistance percentage for that type of services under paragraph (1) is equal to 33⅓ per centum multiplied by a fraction, the denominator of which is equal to the total number of patients receiving that type of services in that quarter under the State plan in facilities or institutions for which a showing was required to be made under this subsection, and the numerator of which is equal to the number of such patients receiving such type of services in that quarter in those facilities or institutions for which a satisfactory and valid showing was not made for that calendar quarter.

(6)(A) Recertifications required under section 1902(a)(44) [§ 1396a(a)(44)] shall be conducted at least every 60 days in the case of inpatient hospital services.

> **(B)** Such recertifications in the case of services in an intermediate care facility for the mentally retarded shall be conducted at least—

>> **(i)** 60 days after the date of the initial certification,

>> **(ii)** 180 days after the date of the initial certification,

>> **(iii)** 12 months after the date of the initial certification,

>> **(iv)** 18 months after the date of the initial certification,

>> **(v)** 24 months after the date of the initial certification, and

>> **(vi)** every 12 months thereafter.

> **(C)** For purposes of determining compliance with the schedule established by this paragraph, a recertification shall be considered to have been done on a timely basis if it was performed not later than 10 days after the date the recertification was otherwise required and the State establishes good cause why the physician or other person making such recertification did not meet such schedule.

(h) [Repealed]

(i) Payment for organ transplants; item or service furnished by excluded individual, entity, or physicians; other restrictions. Payment under the preceding provisions of this section shall not be made—

(1) for organ transplant procedures unless the State plan provides for written standards respecting the coverage of such procedures and unless such standards provide that—

(A) similarly situated individuals are treated alike; and

(B) any restriction, on the facilities or practitioners which may provide such procedures, is consistent with the accessibility of high quality care to individuals eligible for the procedures under the State plan; or

(2) with respect to any amount expended for an item or service (other than an emergency item or service, not including items or services furnished in an emergency room of a hospital) furnished—

(A) under the plan by any individual or entity during any period when the individual or entity is excluded from participation * * * or

(B) at the medical direction or on the prescription of a physician, during the period when such physician is excluded from participation * * * and when the person furnishing such item or service knew or had reason to know of the exclusion (after a reasonable time period after reasonable notice has been furnished to the person); or

(3) with respect to any amount expended for inpatient hospital services furnished under the plan (other than amounts attributable to the special situation of a hospital which serves a disproportionate number of low income patients with special needs) to the extent that such amount exceeds the hospital's customary charges with respect to such services or (if such services are furnished under the plan by a public institution free of charge or at nominal charges to the public) exceeds an amount determined on the basis of those items (specified in regulations prescribed by the Secretary) included in the determination of such payment which the Secretary finds will provide fair compensation to such institution for such services; or

(4) with respect to any amount expended for care or services furnished under the plan by a hospital unless such hospital or skilled nursing facility has in effect a utilization review plan which meets the requirements imposed by section 1861(k) [§ 1395x(k)] for purposes of title XVIII [§§ 1395 et seq.]; and if such hospital has in effect such a utilization review plan for purposes of title XVIII [§§ 1395 et seq.], such plan shall serve as the plan required by this subsection (with the same standards and procedures and the same review committee or group) as a condition of payment under this title []; the Secretary is authorized to waive the requirements of this paragraph if the State agency demonstrates to his satisfaction that it has in operation utilization review procedures which are superior in their effectiveness to the procedures required under section 1861(k) [§ 1395x(k)]; or

(5) with respect to any amount expended for any drug product for which payment may not be made under part B of title XVIII [§§ 1395j et seq.] because of section 1862(c) [§ 1395y(c)]; or

(6) with respect to any amount expended for inpatient hospital tests (other than in emergency situations) not specifically ordered by the attending physician or other responsible practitioner; or

(7) with respect to any amount expended for clinical diagnostic laboratory tests performed by a physician, independent laboratory, or hospital, to the extent such amount exceeds the amount that would be recognized under section 1833(h) [§ 1395l(h)] for such tests performed for an individual enrolled under part B of title XVIII [§§ 1395j et seq.]; or

(8) with respect to any amount expended for medical assistance (A) for nursing facility services to reimburse (or otherwise compensate) a nursing facility for payment of a civil money penalty imposed under section 1919(h) [§ 1396r(h)] or (B) for home and community care to reimburse (or otherwise compensate) a provider of such care for payment of a civil money penalty imposed under this title or title XI [§§ 1396 et seq. or §§ 1301 et seq.] or for legal expenses in defense of an exclusion or civil money penalty under this title or title XI [§§ 1396 et seq. or §§ 1301 et seq.] if there is no reasonable legal ground for the provider's case; or

(9) [Deleted]

(10)(A) with respect to covered outpatient drugs unless there is a rebate agreement in effect under section 1927 [§ 1396r–8] with respect to such drugs or unless section 1927(a)(3) [§ 1396r–8(a)(3)] applies, and

> **(B)** with respect to any amount expended for an innovator multiple source drug (as defined in section 1927(k) [§ 1396r–8(k)]) dispensed on or after July 1, 1991, if, under applicable State law, a less expensive multiple source drug could have been dispensed, but only to the extent that such amount exceeds the upper payment limit for such multiple source drug; or

(11) with respect to any amount expended for physicians' services furnished on or after the first day of the first quarter beginning more than 60 days after the date of establishment of the physician identifier system under section 1902(x) [§ 1396a(x)], unless the claim for the services includes the unique physician identifier provided under such system; or

(12) [Deleted]

(13) with respect to any amount expended to reimburse (or otherwise compensate) a nursing facility for payment of legal expenses associated with any action initiated by the facility that is dismissed on the basis that no reasonable legal ground existed for the institution of such action; or

(14) with respect to any amount expended on administrative costs to carry out the program under section 1928 [§ 1396s]; or

(15) with respect to any amount expended for a single-antigen vaccine and its administration in any case in which the administration of a combined-antigen vaccine was medically appropriate (as determined by the Secretary); or

(16) with respect to any amount expended for which funds may not be used under the Assisted Suicide Funding Restriction Act of 1997; or

(17) with respect to any amount expended for roads, bridges, stadiums, or any other item or service not covered under a State plan under this title [§§ 1396 et seq.]; or

(18) with respect to any amount expended for home health care services provided by an agency or organization unless the agency or organization provides the State agency on a continuing basis a surety bond in a form specified by the Secretary under paragraph (7) of section 1861(*o*) [§ 1395x(*o*)] and in an amount that is not less than $50,000 or such comparable surety bond as the Secretary may permit under the last sentence of such section; or

(19) with respect to any amount expended on administrative costs to initiate or pursue litigation described in subsection (d)(3)(B); or

(20) with respect to amounts expended for medical assistance provided to an individual described in subclause (XV) or (XVI) of section 1902(a)(10)(A)(ii) [§ 1396a(a)(10)(A)(ii)] for a fiscal year unless the State demonstrates to the satisfaction of the Secretary that the level of State funds expended for such fiscal year for programs to enable working individuals with disabilities to work (other than for such medical assistance) is not less than the level expended for such programs during the most recent State fiscal year ending before the date of the enactment of this paragraph [enacted Dec. 17, 1999].

Nothing in paragraph (1) shall be construed as permitting a State to provide services under its plan under this title that are not reasonable in amount, duration, and scope to achieve their purpose. Paragraphs (1), (2), (16), (17), and (18) shall apply with respect to items or services furnished and amounts expended by or through a managed care entity (as defined in section 1932(a)(1)(B) [§ 1396u–2(a)(1)(B)]) in the same manner as such paragraphs apply to items or services furnished and amounts expended directly by the State.

* * *

(*l*) [Repealed]

(m) "Health maintenance organization" defined; duties and functions of Secretary; payments to States; provisional determination of status by State

(1)(A) The term "health maintenance organization" means a health maintenance organization, an eligible organization with a contract under section 1876 [§ 1395mm] or a Medicare + Choice organization with a contract under part C of title XVIII [§§ 1395w–21 et seq.], a provider sponsored organization, or any other public or private organization, which meets the requirement of section 1902(w) [§ 1396a(w)] and—

(i) makes services it provides to individuals eligible for benefits under this title [§§ 1396 et seq.] accessible to such individuals, within the area served by the organization, to the same extent as such services are made accessible to individuals (eligible for medical assistance under the State plan) not enrolled with the organization, and

(ii) has made adequate provision against the risk of insolvency, which provision is satisfactory to the State, meets the requirements of subparagraph (C)(i) (if applicable), and which assures that individuals eligible for benefits under this title [§§ 1396 et seq.] are in no case held liable for debts of the organization in case of the organization's insolvency.

An organization that is a qualified health maintenance organization (as defined in section 1310(d) of the Public Health Service Act) is deemed to meet the requirements of clauses (i) and (ii).

(B) The duties and functions of the Secretary, insofar as they involve making determinations as to whether an organization is a medicaid managed care organization within the meaning of subparagraph (A), shall be integrated with the administration of section 1312(a) and (b) of the Public Health Service Act [42 USCA § 300e–11(a) and (b)].

(C)(i) Subject to clause (ii), a provision meets the requirements of this subparagraph for an organization if the organization meets solvency standards established by the State for private health maintenance organizations or is licensed or certified by the State as a risk-bearing entity.

(ii) Clause (i) shall not apply to an organization if—

(I) the organization is not responsible for the provision (directly or through arrangements with providers of services) of inpatient hospital services and physicians' services;

(II) the organization is a public entity;

(III) the solvency of the organization is guaranteed by the State; or

(IV) the organization is (or is controlled by) one or more Federally-qualified health centers and meets solvency standards established by the State for such an organization.

For purposes of subclause (IV), the term "control" means the possession, whether direct or indirect, of the power to direct or cause the direction of the management and policies of the organization through membership, board representation, or an ownership interest equal to or greater than 50.1 percent.

(2)(A) Except as provided in subparagraphs (B), (C), and (G) no payment shall be made under this title [§§ 1396 et seq.] to a State with respect to expenditures incurred by it for payment (determined under a prepaid capitation basis or under any other risk basis) for services provided by any entity (including a health insuring organization) which is responsible for the provision (directly or through arrangements with providers of services) of inpatient hospital services and any other service described in paragraph (2), (3), (4), (5), or (7) of section 1905(a) [§ 1396d(a)(2)–(5), or (7)] or for the provision of any three or more of the services described in such paragraphs unless—

(i) the Secretary has determined that the entity is a medicaid managed care organization as defined in paragraph (1);

(ii) [Deleted]

(iii) such services are provided for the benefit of individuals eligible for benefits under this title in accordance with a contract between the State and the entity under which prepaid payments to the entity are made on an actuarially sound basis and under which the Secretary must provide prior approval for contracts providing for expenditures in excess of $1,000,000 for 1998 and, for a subsequent year, the amount established under this clause for the previous year increased by the percentage increase in the consumer price index for all urban consumers over the previous year;

(iv) such contract provides that the Secretary and the State (or any person or organization designated by either) shall have the right to audit and inspect any books and records of the entity (and of any subcontractor) that pertain (I) to the ability of the entity to bear the risk of potential financial losses, or (II) to services performed or determinations of amounts payable under the contract;

(v) such contract provides that in the entity's enrollment, reenrollment, or disenrollment of individuals who are eligible for benefits under this title [§§ 1396 et seq.] and eligible to enroll, reenroll, or disenroll with the entity pursuant to the contract, the entity will not discriminate among such individuals on the basis of their health status or requirements for health care services;

(vi) such contract (I) permits individuals who have elected under the plan to enroll with the entity for provision of such benefits to terminate such enrollment in accordance with section 1932(a)(4) [§ 1396u–2(a)(4)] [;] , and (II) provides for notification in accordance with such section of each such individual, at the time of the individual's enrollment, of such right to terminate such enrollment;

(vii) such contract provides that, in the case of medically necessary services which were provided (I) to an individual enrolled with the entity under the contract and entitled to benefits with respect to such services under the State's plan and (II) other than through the organization because the services were immediately required due to an unforeseen illness, injury, or condition, either the entity or the State provides for reimbursement with respect to those services, [;]

(viii) such contract provides for disclosure of information in accordance with section 1124 [§ 1320a–3] and paragraph (4) of this subsection;

(ix) such contract provides, in the case of an entity that has entered into a contract for the provision of services with a Federally-qualified health center or a rural health clinic, that the entity shall provide payment that is not less than the level and amount of payment which the entity would make for the services if the services were furnished by a provider which is not a Federally-qualified health center or a rural health clinic;

(x) any physician incentive plan that it operates meets the requirements described in section 1876(i)(8) [§ 1395mm(i)(8)];

(xi) such contract provides for maintenance of sufficient patient encounter data to identify the physician who delivers services to patients; and

(xii) such contract, and the entity complies with the applicable requirements of section 1932 [§ 1396u–2].

* * *

(4)(A) Each medicaid managed care organization which is not a qualified health maintenance organization (as defined in section 1310(d) of the Public Health Service Act) must report to the State and, upon request, to the Secretary, the Inspector General of the Department of Health and Human Services, and the Comptroller General a description of transactions between the organization and a party in interest (as defined in section 1318(b) of such Act [§ 300e–17(b)]), including the following transactions:

(i) Any sale or exchange, or leasing of any property between the organization and such a party.

(ii) Any furnishing for consideration of goods, services (including management services), or facilities between the organization and such a party, but not including salaries paid to employees for services provided in the normal course of their employment.

(iii) Any lending of money or other extension of credit between the organization and such a party.

The State or Secretary may require that information reported respecting an organization which controls, or is controlled by, or is under common control with, another entity be in the form of a consolidated financial statement for the organization and such entity.

(B) Each organization shall make the information reported pursuant to subparagraph (A) available to its enrollees upon reasonable request.

(5)(A) If the Secretary determines that an entity with a contract under this subsection—

(i) fails substantially to provide medically necessary items and services that are required (under law or under the contract) to be provided to an individual covered under the contract, if the failure has adversely affected (or has substantial likelihood of adversely affecting) the individual;

(ii) imposes premiums on individuals enrolled under this subsection in excess of the premiums permitted under this title [§§ 1396 et seq.];

(iii) acts to discriminate among individuals in violation of the provision of paragraph (2)(A)(v), including expulsion or refusal to re-enroll an individual or engaging in any practice that would reasonably be expected to have the effect of denying or discouraging enrollment (except as permitted by this subsection) by eligible individuals with the organization whose medical condition or history indicates a need for substantial future medical services;

(iv) misrepresents or falsifies information that is furnished—

(I) to the Secretary or the State under this subsection, or

(II) to an individual or to any other entity under this subsection, [;] or

(v) fails to comply with the requirements of section 1876(i)(8) [§ 1395mm(i)(8)],

the Secretary may provide, in addition to any other remedies available under law, for any of the remedies described in subparagraph (B).

(B) The remedies described in this subparagraph are—

(i) civil money penalties of not more than $25,000 for each determination under subparagraph (A), or, with respect to a determination under clause (iii) or (iv)(I) of such subparagraph, of not more than $100,000 for each such determination, plus, with respect to a determination under subparagraph (A)(ii), double the excess amount charged in violation of such subparagraph (and the excess amount charged shall be deducted from the penalty and returned to the individual concerned), and plus, with respect to a determination under subparagraph (A)(iii), $15,000 for each individual not enrolled as a result of a practice described in such subparagraph, or

(ii) denial of payment to the State for medical assistance furnished under the contract under this subsection for individuals enrolled after the date the Secretary notifies the organization of a determination under subparagraph (A) and until the Secretary is satisfied that the basis for such determination has been corrected and is not likely to recur.

The provisions of section 1128A [§ 1320a–7a] (other than subsections (a) and (b)) shall apply to a civil money penalty under clause (i) in the same manner as such provisions apply to a penalty or proceeding under section 1128A(a) [42 USCS § 1320a–7a(a)].

* * *

(*o*) Restrictions on authorized payments to States. Notwithstanding the preceding provisions of this section, no payment shall be made to a State under the preceding provisions of this section for expenditures for medical assistance provided for an individual under its State plan approved under this title [§§ 1396 et seq.] to the extent that a private insurer (as defined by the Secretary by regulation and including a group health plan (as defined in section 607(1) of the Employee Retirement Income Security Act of 1974 [29 USCS § 1167(1)]), a service benefit plan, and a health maintenance organization) would have been obligated to provide such assistance but for a provision of its insurance contract which has the effect of limiting or excluding such obligation because the individual is eligible for or is provided medical assistance under the plan.

(p) Assignment of rights of payment; incentive payments for enforcement and collection

(1) When a political subdivision of a State makes, for the State of which it is a political subdivision, or one State makes, for another State, the enforcement and collection of rights of support or payment assigned under section 1912 [§ 1396k], pursuant to a cooperative arrangement under such section (either within or outside of such State), there shall be paid to such political subdivision or such other State from amounts which would otherwise represent the Federal share of payments for medical assistance provided to the eligible individuals on whose behalf such enforcement and collection was made, an amount equal to 15 percent of any amount collected which is attributable to such rights of support or payment.

(2) Where more than one jurisdiction is involved in such enforcement or collection, the amount of the incentive payment determined under paragraph (1) shall be allocated among the jurisdictions in a manner to be prescribed by the Secretary.

(q) "State medicaid fraud control unit" defined. For the purposes of this section, the term "State medicaid fraud control unit" means a single identifiable entity of the State government which the Secretary certifies (and annually recertifies) as meeting the following requirements:

(1) The entity (A) is a unit of the office of the State Attorney General or of another department of State government which possesses statewide authority to prosecute individuals for criminal violations, (B) is in a State the constitution of which does not provide for the criminal prosecution of individuals by a statewide authority and has formal procedures, approved by the Secretary, that (i) assure its referral of suspected criminal violations relating to the program under this title [§§ 1396 et seq.] to the appropriate authority or authorities in the State for prosecution and (ii) assure its assistance of, and coordination with, such authority or authorities in such prosecutions, or (C) has a formal working relationship with the office of the State Attorney General and has formal procedures (including procedures for its referral of suspected criminal violations to such office) which are approved by the Secretary and which provide effective coordination of activities between the entity and such office with respect to the detection, investigation, and prosecution of suspected criminal violations relating to the program under this title [§§ 1396 et seq.].

(2) The entity is separate and distinct from the single State agency that administers or supervises the administration of the State plan under this title.

(3) The entity's function is conducting a statewide program for the investigation and prosecution of violations of all applicable State laws regarding any and all aspects of fraud in connection with (A) any aspect of the provision of medical assistance and the activities of providers of such assistance under the State plan under this title [§§ 1396 et seq.]; and (B) upon the approval of the Inspector General of the relevant Federal agency, any aspect of the provision of health care services and activities of providers of such services under any Federal health care program (as defined in section 1128B(f)(1) [§ 1320a–7(f)(1)]), if the suspected fraud or violation of law in such case or investigation is primarily related to the State plan under this title [42 USCS §§ 1396 et seq.].

(4)(A) The entity has—

    (i) procedures for reviewing complaints of abuse or neglect of patients in health care facilities which receive payments under the State plan under this title [§§ 1396 et seq.];

(ii) at the option of the entity, procedures for reviewing complaints of abuse or neglect of patients residing in board and care facilities; and

(iii) procedures for acting upon such complaints under the criminal laws of the State or for referring such complaints to other State agencies for action.

(B) For purposes of this paragraph, the term "board and care facility" means a residential setting which receives payment (regardless of whether such payment is made under the State plan under this title) from or on behalf of two or more unrelated adults who reside in such facility, and for whom one or both of the following is provided:

(i) Nursing care services provided by, or under the supervision of, a registered nurse, licensed practical nurse, or licensed nursing assistant.

(ii) A substantial amount of personal care services that assist residents with the activities of daily living, including personal hygiene, dressing, bathing, eating, toileting, ambulation, transfer, positioning, self-medication, body care, travel to medical services, essential shopping, meal preparation, laundry, and housework.

(5) The entity provides for the collection, or referral for collection to a single State agency, of overpayments that are made under the State plan or under any Federal health care program (as so defined) to health care facilities and that are discovered by the entity in carrying out its activities. All funds collected in accordance with this paragraph shall be credited exclusively to, and available for expenditure under, the Federal health care program (including the State plan under this title [§§ 1396 et seq.]) that was subject to the activity that was the basis for the collection.

(6) The entity employs such auditors, attorneys, investigators, and other necessary personnel and is organized in such a manner as is necessary to promote the effective and efficient conduct of the entity's activities.

(7) The entity submits to the Secretary an application and annual reports containing such information as the Secretary determines, by regulation, to be necessary to determine whether the entity meets the other requirements of this subsection.

* * *

(u) Limitation of Federal financial participation in erroneous medical assistance expenditures

(1)(A) Notwithstanding subsection (a)(1), if the ratio of a State's erroneous excess payments for medical assistance (as defined in subparagraph (D)) to its total expenditures for medical assistance under the State plan approved under this title [§§ 1396 et seq.] exceeds 0.03, for the period consisting of the third and fourth quarters of fiscal year 1983, or for any full fiscal year thereafter, then the Secretary shall make no payment for such period or fiscal year with respect to so much of such erroneous excess payments as exceeds such allowable error rate of 0.03.

(B) The Secretary may waive, in certain limited cases, all or part of the reduction required under subparagraph (A) with respect to any State if such State is unable to reach the allowable error rate for a period or fiscal year despite a good faith effort by such State.

(C) In estimating the amount to be paid to a State under subsection (d), the Secretary shall take into consideration the limitation on Federal financial participation imposed by subparagraph (A) and shall reduce the estimate he makes under subsection (d)(1), for purposes of payment to the State under subsection (d)(3), in light of any expected erroneous excess payments for medical assistance (estimated in accordance with such criteria, including sampling procedures, as he may prescribe and subject to subsequent adjustment, if necessary, under subsection (d)(2)).

(D)(i) For purposes of this subsection, the term "erroneous excess payments for medical assistance" means the total of—

(I) payments under the State plan with respect to ineligible individuals and families, and

(II) overpayments on behalf of eligible individuals and families by reason of error in determining the amount of expenditures for medical care required of an individual or family as a condition of eligibility.

(ii) In determining the amount of erroneous excess payments for medical assistance to an ineligible individual or family under clause (i)(I), if such ineligibility is the result of an error in determining the amount of the resources of such individual or family, the amount of the erroneous excess payment shall be the smaller of (I) the amount of the payment with respect to such individual or family, or (II) the difference between the actual amount of such resources and the allowable resource level established under the State plan.

(iii) In determining the amount of erroneous excess payments for medical assistance to an individual or family under clause (i)(II), the amount of the erroneous excess payment shall be the smaller of (I) the amount of the payment on behalf of the individual or family, or (II) the difference between the actual amount incurred for medical care by the individual or family and the amount which should have been incurred in order to establish eligibility for medical assistance.

(iv) In determining the amount of erroneous excess payments, there shall not be included any error resulting from a failure of an individual to cooperate or give correct information with respect to third-party liability as required under section 1912(a)(1)(C) [§ 1396k(a)(1)(C)] or 402(a)(26)(C) or with respect to payments made in violation of section 1906 [§ 1396e].

(v) In determining the amount of erroneous excess payments, there shall not be included any erroneous payments made for ambulatory prenatal care provided during a presumptive eligibility period (as defined in section 1920(b)(1) [§ 1396r–1(b)(1)]) for items and services described in subsection (a) of section 1920A [§ 1396r–1a] provided to a child during a presumptive eligibility period under such section, or for medical assistance provided to an individual described in subsection (a) of section 1920B [§ 1396r–1(b)] during a presumptive eligibility period under such section.

(E) For purposes of subparagraph (D), there shall be excluded, in determining both erroneous excess payments for medical assistance and total expenditures for medical assistance—

(i) payments with respect to any individual whose eligibility therefor was determined exclusively by the Secretary under an agreement pursuant to section 1634 [§ 1383c] and such other classes of individuals as the Secretary may by regulation prescribe whose eligibility was determined in part under such an agreement; and

(ii) payments made as the result of a technical error.

(2) The State agency administering the plan approved under this title shall, at such times and in such form as the Secretary may specify, provide information on the rates of erroneous excess payments made (or expected, with respect to future periods specified by the Secretary) in connection with its administration of such plan, together with any other data he requests that are reasonably necessary for him to carry out the provisions of this subsection.

(3)(A) If a State fails to cooperate with the Secretary in providing information necessary to carry out this subsection, the Secretary, directly or through contractual or such other arrangements as he may find appropriate, shall establish the error rates for that State on the basis of the best data reasonably available to him and in accordance with such techniques for sampling and estimating as he finds appropriate.

(B) In any case in which it is necessary for the Secretary to exercise his authority under subparagraph (A) to determine a State's error rates for a fiscal year, the amount that would otherwise be payable to such State under this title for quarters in such year shall be reduced by the costs incurred by the Secretary in making (directly or otherwise) such determination.

* * *

(v) Medical assistance to aliens not lawfully admitted for permanent residence

(1) Notwithstanding the preceding provisions of this section, except as provided in paragraph (2), no payment may be made to a State under this section for medical assistance furnished to an alien who is not lawfully admitted for permanent residence or otherwise permanently residing in the United States under color of law.

(2) Payment shall be made under this section for care and services that are furnished to an alien described in paragraph (1) only if—

(A) such care and services are necessary for the treatment of an emergency medical condition of the alien,

(B) such alien otherwise meets the eligibility requirements for medical assistance under the State plan approved under this title (other than the requirement of the receipt of aid or assistance under title IV [42 USCA §§ 601 et seq.], supplemental security income benefits under title XVI [42 USCA §§ 1381 et seq.], or a State supplementary payment), and

(C) such care and services are not related to an organ transplant procedure.

(3) For purposes of this subsection, the term "emergency medical condition" means a medical condition (including emergency labor and delivery) manifesting itself by acute symptoms of sufficient severity (including severe pain) such that the absence of immediate medical attention could reasonably be expected to result in—

(A) placing the patient's health in serious jeopardy,

(B) serious impairment to bodily functions, or

(C) serious dysfunction of any bodily organ or part.

(w) Prohibition on use of voluntary contributions, and limitation on the use of provider-specific taxes to obtain Federal financial participation under Medicaid

(1)(A) Notwithstanding the previous provisions of this section, for purposes of determining the amount to be paid to a State (as defined in paragraph (7)(D)) under subsection (a)(1) for quarters in any fiscal year, the total amount expended during such fiscal year as medical assistance under the State plan (as determined without regard to this subsection) shall be reduced by the sum of any revenues received by the State (or by a unit of local government in the State) during the fiscal year—

(i) from provider-related donations (as defined in paragraph (2)(A)), other than—

(I) bona fide provider-related donations (as defined in paragraph (2)(B)), and

884

(II) donations described in paragraph (2)(C);

(ii) from health care related taxes (as defined in paragraph (3)(A)), other than broad-based health care related taxes (as defined in paragraph (3)(B)); [or]

(iii) from a broad-based health care related tax, if there is in effect a hold harmless provision (described in paragraph (4)) with respect to the tax; * * *

(B) Notwithstanding the previous provisions of this section, for purposes of determining the amount to be paid to a State under subsection (a)(7) for all quarters in a Federal fiscal year (beginning with fiscal year 1993), the total amount expended during the fiscal year for administrative expenditures under the State plan (as determined without regard to this subsection) shall be reduced by the sum of any revenues received by the State (or by a unit of local government in the State) during such quarters from donations described in paragraph (2)(C), to the extent the amount of such donations exceeds 10 percent of the amounts expended under the State plan under this title during the fiscal year for purposes described in paragraphs (2), (3), (4), (6), and (7) of subsection (a).

(C)(i) Except as otherwise provided in clause (ii), subparagraph (A)(i) shall apply to donations received on or after January 1, 1992.

(ii) Subject to the limits described in clause (iii) and subparagraph (E), subparagraph (A)(i) shall not apply to donations received before the effective date specified in subparagraph (F) if such donations are received under programs in effect or as described in State plan amendments or related documents submitted to the Secretary by September 30, 1991, and applicable to State fiscal year 1992, as demonstrated by State plan amendments, written agreements, State budget documentation, or other documentary evidence in existence on that date.

(iii) In applying clause (ii) in the case of donations received in State fiscal year 1993, the maximum amount of such donations to which such clause may be applied may not exceed the total amount of such donations received in the corresponding period in State fiscal year 1992 (or not later than 5 days after the last day of the corresponding period).

(D)(i) Except as otherwise provided in clause (ii), subparagraphs (A)(ii) and (A)(iii) shall apply to taxes received on or after January 1, 1992.

(ii) Subparagraphs (A)(ii) and (A)(iii) shall not apply to impermissible taxes (as defined in clause (iii)) received before the effective date specified in subparagraph (F) to the extent the taxes (including the tax rate or base) were in effect, or the legislation or regulations imposing such taxes were enacted or adopted, as of November 22, 1991.

(iii) In this subparagraph and subparagraph (E), the term "impermissible tax" means a health care related tax for which a reduction may be made under clause (ii) or (iii) of subparagraph (A).

(E)(i) In no case may the total amount of donations and taxes permitted under the exception provided in subparagraphs (C)(ii) and (D)(ii) for the portion of State fiscal year 1992 occurring during calendar year 1992 exceed the limit under paragraph (5) minus the total amount of broad-based health care related taxes received in the portion of that fiscal year.

(ii) In no case may the total amount of donations and taxes permitted under the exception provided in subparagraphs (C)(ii) and (D)(ii) for State fiscal year 1993 exceed the limit under paragraph (5) minus the total amount of broad-based health care related taxes received in that fiscal year.

* * *

(2)(A) In this subsection (except as provided in paragraph (6)), the term "provider-related donation" means any donation or other voluntary payment (whether in cash or in kind) made (directly or indirectly) to a State or unit of local government by—

(i) a health care provider (as defined in paragraph (7)(B)),

(ii) an entity related to a health care provider (as defined in paragraph (7)(C)), or

(iii) an entity providing goods or services under the State plan for which payment is made to the State under paragraph (2), (3), (4), (6), or (7) of subsection (a).

(B) For purposes of paragraph (1)(A)(i)(I), the term "bona fide provider-related donation" means a provider-related donation that has no direct or indirect relationship (as determined by the Secretary) to payments made under this title to that provider, to providers furnishing the same class of items and services as that provider, or to any related entity, as established by the State to the satisfaction of the Secretary. The Secretary may by regulation specify types of provider-related donations described in the previous sentence that will be considered to be bona fide provider-related donations.

(C) For purposes of paragraph (1)(A)(i)(II), donations described in this subparagraph are funds expended by a hospital, clinic, or similar entity for the direct cost (including costs of training and of preparing and distributing outreach materials) of State or local agency personnel who are stationed at the hospital, clinic, or entity to determine the eligibility of individuals for medical assistance under this title and to provide outreach services to eligible or potentially eligible individuals.

(3)(A) In this subsection (except as provided in paragraph (6)), the term "health care related tax" means a tax (as defined in paragraph (7)(F)) that—

> **(i)** is related to health care items or services, or to the provision of, the authority to provide, or payment for, such items or services, or

> **(ii)** is not limited to such items or services but provides for treatment of individuals or entities that are providing or paying for such items or services that is different from the treatment provided to other individuals or entities.

In applying clause (i), a tax is considered to relate to health care items or services if at least 85 percent of the burden of such tax falls on health care providers.

(B) In this subsection, the term "broad-based health care related tax" means a health care related tax which is imposed with respect to a class of health care items or services (as described in paragraph (7)(A)) or with respect to providers of such items or services and which, except as provided in subparagraphs (D), (E), and (F)—

> **(i)** is imposed at least with respect to all items or services in the class furnished by all non-Federal, nonpublic providers in the State (or, in the case of a tax imposed by a unit of local government, the area over which the unit has jurisdiction) or is imposed with respect to all non-Federal, nonpublic providers in the class; and

> **(ii)** is imposed uniformly (in accordance with subparagraph (C)).

(C)(i) Subject to clause (ii), for purposes of subparagraph (B)(ii), a tax is considered to be imposed uniformly if—

> **(I)** in the case of a tax consisting of a licensing fee or similar tax on a class of health care items or services (or providers of such items or services), the amount of the tax imposed is the same for every provider providing items or services within the class;

> **(II)** in the case of a tax consisting of a licensing fee or similar tax imposed on a class of health care items or services (or providers of such services) on the basis of the number of beds (licensed or otherwise) of the provider, the amount of the tax is the same for each bed of each provider of such items or services in the class;

(III) in the case of a tax based on revenues or receipts with respect to a class of items or services (or providers of items or services) the tax is imposed at a uniform rate for all items and services (or providers of such items or services) in the class on all the gross revenues or receipts, or net operating revenues, relating to the provision of all such items or services (or all such providers) in the State (or, in the case of a tax imposed by a unit of local government within the State, in the area over which the unit has jurisdiction); or

(IV) in the case of any other tax, the State establishes to the satisfaction of the Secretary that the tax is imposed uniformly.

(ii) Subject to subparagraphs (D) and (E), a tax imposed with respect to a class of health care items and services is not considered to be imposed uniformly if the tax provides for any credits, exclusions, or deductions which have as their purpose or effect the return to providers of all or a portion of the tax paid in a manner that is inconsistent with subclauses (I) and (II) of subparagraph (E)(ii) or provides for a hold harmless provision described in paragraph (4).

(D) A tax imposed with respect to a class of health care items and services is considered to be imposed uniformly—

(i) notwithstanding that the tax is not imposed with respect to items or services (or the providers thereof) for which payment is made under a State plan under this title or title XVIII, or

(ii) in the case of a tax described in subparagraph (C)(i)(III), notwithstanding that the tax provides for exclusion (in whole or in part) of revenues or receipts from a State plan under this title or title XVIII.

(E)(i) A State may submit an application to the Secretary requesting that the Secretary treat a tax as a broad-based health care related tax, notwithstanding that the tax does not apply to all health care items or services in class (or all providers of such items and services), provides for a credit, deduction, or exclusion, is not applied uniformly, or otherwise does not meet the requirements of subparagraph (B) or (C). Permissible waivers may include exemptions for rural or sole-community providers.

(ii) The Secretary shall approve such an application if the State establishes to the satisfaction of the Secretary that—

(I) the net impact of the tax and associated expenditures under this title as proposed by the State is generally redistributive in nature, and

(II) the amount of the tax is not directly correlated to payments under this title for items or services with respect to which the tax is imposed.

The Secretary shall by regulation specify types of credits, exclusions, and deductions that will be considered to meet the requirements of this subparagraph.

(F) In no case shall a tax not qualify as a broad-based health care related tax under this paragraph because it does not apply to a hospital that is described in section 501(c)(3) of the Internal Revenue Code of 1986 [26 USCA § 501(c)(3)] and exempt from taxation under section 501(a) of such Code [26 USCA § 501(a)] and that does not accept payment under the State plan under this title or under title XVIII.

(4) For purposes of paragraph (1)(A)(iii), there is in effect a hold harmless provision with respect to a broad-based health care related tax imposed with respect to a class of items or services if the Secretary determines that any of the following applies:

(A) The State or other unit of government imposing the tax provides (directly or indirectly) for a payment (other than under this title) to taxpayers and the amount of such payment is positively correlated either to the amount of such tax or to the difference between the amount of the tax and the amount of payment under the State plan.

(B) All or any portion of the payment made under this title to the taxpayer varies based only upon the amount of the total tax paid.

(C) The State or other unit of government imposing the tax provides (directly or indirectly) for any payment, offset, or waiver that guarantees to hold taxpayers harmless for any portion of the costs of the tax.

The provisions of this paragraph shall not prevent use of the tax to reimburse health care providers in a class for expenditures under this title nor preclude States from relying on such reimbursement to justify or explain the tax in the legislative process.

(5)(A) For purposes of this subsection, the limit under this subparagraph with respect to a State is an amount equal to 25 percent (or, if greater, the State base percentage, as defined in subparagraph (B)) of the non-Federal share of the total amount expended under the State plan during a State fiscal year (or portion thereof), as it would be determined pursuant to paragraph (1)(A) without regard to paragraph (1)(A)(iv).

(B)(i) In subparagraph (A), the term "State base percentage" means, with respect to a State, an amount (expressed as a percentage) equal to—

(I) the total of the amount of health care related taxes (whether or not broad-based) and the amount of provider-related donations (whether or not bona fide) projected to be collected (in accordance with clause (ii)) during State fiscal year 1992, divided by

(II) the non-Federal share of the total amount estimated to be expended under the State plan during such State fiscal year.

(ii) For purposes of clause (i)(I), in the case of a tax that is not in effect throughout State fiscal year 1992 or the rate (or base) of which is increased during such fiscal year, the Secretary shall project the amount to be collected during such fiscal year as if the tax (or increase) were in effect during the entire State fiscal year.

(C)(i) The total amount of health care related taxes under subparagraph (B)(i)(I) shall be determined by the Secretary based on only those taxes (including the tax rate or base) which were in effect, or for which legislation or regulations imposing such taxes were enacted or adopted, as of November 22, 1991.

(ii) The amount of provider-related donations under subparagraph (B)(i)(I) shall be determined by the Secretary based on programs in effect on September 30, 1991, and applicable to State fiscal year 1992, as demonstrated by State plan amendments, written agreements, State budget documentation, or other documentary evidence in existence on that date.

(iii) The amount of expenditures described in subparagraph (B)(i)(II) shall be determined by the Secretary based on the best data available as of the date of the enactment of this subsection.

(6)(A) Notwithstanding the provisions of this subsection, the Secretary may not restrict States' use of funds where such funds are derived from State or local taxes (or funds appropriated to State university teaching hospitals) transferred from or certified by units of government within a State as the non-Federal share of expenditures under this title regardless of whether the unit of government is also a health care provider, except as provided in section 1902(a)(2) [§ 1396a(a)(2)], unless the transferred funds are derived by the unit of government from donations or taxes that would not otherwise be recognized as the non-Federal share under this section.

(B) For purposes of this subsection, funds the use of which the Secretary may not restrict under subparagraph (A) shall not be considered to be a provider-related donation or a health care related tax.

(7) For purposes of this subsection:

(A) Each of the following shall be considered a separate class of health care items and services:

(i) Inpatient hospital services.

(ii) Outpatient hospital services.

(iii) Nursing facility services (other than services of intermediate care facilities for the mentally retarded).

(iv) Services of intermediate care facilities for the mentally retarded.

(v) Physicians' services.

(vi) Home health care services.

(vii) Outpatient prescription drugs.

(viii) Services of a medicaid managed care organization with a contract under section 1903(m) [subsec. (m) of this section].

(ix) Such other classification of health care items and services consistent with this subparagraph as the Secretary may establish by regulation.

(B) The term "health care provider" means an individual or person that receives payments for the provision of health care items or services.

(C) An entity is considered to be "related" to a health care provider if the entity—

(i) is an organization, association, corporation or partnership formed by or on behalf of health care providers;

(ii) is a person with an ownership or control interest (as defined in section 1124(a)(3) [§ 1320a–3(a)(3)]) in the provider;

(iii) is the employee, spouse, parent, child, or sibling of the provider (or of a person described in clause (ii)); or

(iv) has a similar, close relationship (as defined in regulations) to the provider.

(D) The term "State" means only the 50 States and the District of Columbia but does not include any State whose entire program under this title is operated under a waiver granted under section 1115 [§ 1315].

(E) The "State fiscal year" means, with respect to a specified year, a State fiscal year ending in that specified year.

(F) The term "tax" includes any licensing fee, assessment, or other mandatory payment, but does not include payment of a criminal or civil fine or penalty (other than a fine or penalty imposed in lieu of or instead of a fee, assessment, or other mandatory payment).

(G) The term "unit of local government" means, with respect to a State, a city, county, special purpose district, or other governmental unit in the State.

* * *

§ 1396c.   Operation of State plans

If the Secretary, after reasonable notice and opportunity for hearing to the State agency administering or supervising the administration of the State plan approved under this subchapter, finds—

(1) that the plan has been so changed that it no longer complies with the provisions of section 1396a of this title; or

(2) that in the administration of the plan there is a failure to comply substantially with any such provision;

the Secretary shall notify such State agency that further payments will not be made to the State (or, in his discretion, that payments will be limited to categories under or parts of the State plan not affected by such failure), until the Secretary is satisfied that there will no longer be any such failure to comply. Until he is so satisfied he shall make no further payments to such State (or shall limit payments to categories under or parts of the State plan not affected by such failure).

§ 1396d.   Definitions

For purposes of this subchapter—

(a) Medical assistance

The term "medical assistance" means payment of part or all of the cost of the following care and services (if provided in or after the third month before the month in which the recipient makes application for assistance or, in the case of medicare cost-sharing with respect to a qualified medicare beneficiary described in subsection (p)(1) of this section, if provided after the month in which the individual becomes such a beneficiary) for individuals, and, with respect to physicians' or dentists' services, at the option of the State, to individuals (other than individuals with respect to whom there is being paid, or who are eligible, or would be eligible if they were not in a medical institution, to have paid with respect to them a State supplementary payment and are eligible for medical assistance equal in amount, duration, and scope to the medical assistance made available to individuals described in section 1396a(a)(10)(A) of this title) not receiving aid or assistance under any plan of the State approved under subchapter I, X, XIV, or XVI, or part A of subchapter IV, and with respect to whom supplemental security income benefits are not being paid under subchapter XVI of this chapter, who are—

(i) under the age of 21, or, at the option of the State, under the age of 20, 19, or 18 as the State may choose,

(ii) relatives specified in section 606(b)(1) of this title with whom a child is living if such child is (or would, if needy, be) a dependent child under part A of subchapter IV of this chapter,

(iii) 65 years of age or older,

(iv) blind, with respect to States eligible to participate in the State plan program established under subchapter XVI of this chapter,

(v) 18 years of age or older and permanently and totally disabled, with respect to States eligible to participate in the State plan program established under subchapter XVI of this chapter,

(vi) persons essential (as described in the second sentence of this subsection) to individuals receiving aid or assistance under State plans approved under subchapter I, X, XIV, or XVI of this chapter,

(vii) blind or disabled as defined in section 1382c of this title, with respect to States not eligible to participate in the State plan program established under subchapter XVI of this chapter,

(viii) pregnant women,

(ix) individuals provided extended benefits under section 1396r–6 of this title,

(x) individuals described in section 1396a(u)(1) of this title,

(xi) individuals described in section 1396a(z)(1) of this title,

(xii) employed individuals with a medically improved disability (as defined in subsection (v)), or

(xiii) individuals described in section 1396a(aa) of this title,

but whose income and resources are insufficient to meet all of such cost—

(1) inpatient hospital services (other than services in an institution for mental diseases);

(2)(A) outpatient hospital services,

(B) consistent with State law permitting such services, rural health clinic services (as defined in subsection (l)(1) of this section) and any other ambulatory services which are offered by a rural health clinic (as defined in subsection (l)(1) of this section) and which are otherwise included in the plan, and

(C) Federally-qualified health center services (as defined in subsection (l)(2) of this section) and any other ambulatory services offered by a Federally-qualified health center and which are otherwise included in the plan;

(3) other laboratory and X-ray services;

(4)(A) nursing facility services (other than services in an institution for mental diseases) for individuals 21 years of age or older;

(B) early and periodic screening, diagnostic, and treatment services (as defined in subsection (r) of this section) for individuals who are eligible under the plan and are under the age of 21; and

(C) family planning services and supplies furnished (directly or under arrangements with others) to individuals of child-bearing age (including minors who can be considered to be sexually active) who are eligible under the State plan and who desire such services and supplies;

(5)(A) physicians' services furnished by a physician (as defined in section 1395x(r)(1) of this title), whether furnished in the office, the patient's home, a hospital, or a nursing facility, or elsewhere, and

(B) medical and surgical services furnished by a dentist (described in section 1395x(r)(2) of this title) to the extent such services may be performed under State law either by a doctor of medicine or by a doctor of dental surgery or dental medicine and would be described in clause (A) if furnished by a physician (as defined in section 1395x(r)(1) of this title);

(6) medical care, or any other type of remedial care recognized under State law, furnished by licensed practitioners within the scope of their practice as defined by State law;

(7) home health care services;

(8) private duty nursing services;

(9) clinic services furnished by or under the direction of a physician, without regard to whether the clinic itself is administered by a physician, including such services furnished outside the clinic by clinic personnel to an eligible individual who does not reside in a permanent dwelling or does not have a fixed home or mailing address;

(10) dental services;

(11) physical therapy and related services;

(12) prescribed drugs, dentures, and prosthetic devices; and eyeglasses prescribed by a physician skilled in diseases of the eye or by an optometrist, whichever the individual may select;

(13) other diagnostic, screening, preventive, and rehabilitative services, including any medical or remedial services (provided in a facility, a home, or other setting) recommended by a physician or other licensed practitioner of the healing arts within the scope of their practice under State law, for the maximum reduction of physical or mental disability and restoration of an individual to the best possible functional level;

(14) inpatient hospital services and nursing facility services for individuals 65 years of age or over in an institution for mental diseases;

(15) services in an intermediate care facility for the mentally retarded (other than in an institution for mental diseases) for individuals who are determined, in accordance with section 1396a(a)(31) of this title, to be in need of such care;

(16) effective January 1, 1973, inpatient psychiatric hospital services for individuals under age 21, as defined in subsection (h) of this section;

(17) services furnished by a nurse-midwife (as defined in section 1395x(gg) of this title) which the nurse-midwife is legally authorized to perform under State law (or the State regulatory mechanism provided by State law), whether or not the nurse-midwife is under the supervision of, or associated with, a physician or other health care provider, and without regard to whether or not the services are performed in the area of management of the care of mothers and babies throughout the maternity cycle;

(18) hospice care (as defined in subsection (*o*) of this section);

(19) case-management services (as defined in section 1396n(g)(2) of this title) and TB-related services described in section 1396a(z)(2)(F) of this title;

(20) respiratory care services (as defined in section 1396a(e)(9)(C) of this title);

(21) services furnished by a certified pediatric nurse practitioner or certified family nurse practitioner (as defined by the Secretary) which the certified pediatric nurse practitioner or certified family nurse practitioner is legally authorized to perform under State law (or the State regulatory mechanism provided by State law), whether or not the certified pediatric nurse practitioner or certified family nurse practitioner is under the supervision of, or associated with, a physician or other health care provider;

(22) home and community care (to the extent allowed and as defined in section 1396t of this title) for functionally disabled elderly individuals; and

(23) community supported living arrangements services (to the extent allowed and as defined in section 1396u of this title);

(24) personal care services furnished to an individual who is not an inpatient or resident of a hospital, nursing facility, intermediate care facility for the mentally retarded, or institution for mental disease that are

(A) authorized for the individual by a physician in accordance with a plan of treatment or (at the option of the State) otherwise authorized for the individual in accordance with a service plan approved by the State,

(B) provided by an individual who is qualified to provide such services and who is not a member of the individual's family, and

(C) furnished in a home or other location;

(25) primary care case management services (as defined in subsection (t) of this section);

(26) services furnished under a PACE program under section 1396u–4 of this title to PACE program eligible individuals enrolled under the program under such section; and

895

(27) any other medical care, and any other type of remedial care recognized under State law, specified by the Secretary, except as otherwise provided in paragraph (16), such term does not include—

(A) any such payments with respect to care or services for any individual who is an inmate of a public institution (except as a patient in a medical institution); or

(B) any such payments with respect to care or services for any individual who has not attained 65 years of age and who is a patient in an institution for mental diseases.

For purposes of clause (vi) of the preceding sentence, a person shall be considered essential to another individual if such person is the spouse of and is living with such individual, the needs of such person are taken into account in determining the amount of aid or assistance furnished to such individual (under a State plan approved under subchapter I, X, XIV, or XVI of this chapter), and such person is determined, under such a State plan, to be essential to the well-being of such individual. The payment described in the first sentence may include expenditures for medicare cost-sharing and for premiums under part B of subchapter XVIII of this chapter for individuals who are eligible for medical assistance under the plan and (A) are receiving aid or assistance under any plan of the State approved under subchapters I, X, XIV, or XVI of this chapter, or part A of subchapter IV of this chapter, or with respect to whom supplemental security income benefits are being paid under subchapter XVI of this chapter, or (B) with respect to whom there is being paid a State supplementary payment and are eligible for medical assistance equal in amount, duration, and scope to the medical assistance made available to individuals described in section 1396a(a)(10)(A) of this title, and, except in the case of individuals 65 years of age or older and disabled individuals entitled to health insurance benefits under subchapter XVIII of this chapter who are not enrolled under part B of subchapter XVIII of this chapter, other insurance premiums for medical or any other type of remedial care or the cost thereof. No service (including counseling) shall be excluded from the definition of "medical assistance" solely because it is provided as a treatment service for alcoholism or drug dependency.

(b) Federal medical assistance percentage; State percentage; Indian health care percentage

Subject to section 1396u–3 of this title, the term "Federal medical assistance percentage" for any State shall be 100 per centum less the State percentage; and the State percentage shall be that percentage which bears the same ratio to 45 per centum as the square of the per capita income of such State bears to the square of the per capita income of the continental United States (including Alaska) and Hawaii; except that

(1) the Federal medical assistance percentage shall in no case be less than 50 per centum or more than 83 per centum,

(2) the Federal medical assistance percentage for Puerto Rico, the Virgin Islands, Guam, the Northern Mariana Islands, and American Samoa shall be 50 per centum,

(3) for purposes of this subchapter and subchapter XXI of this chapter, the Federal medical assistance percentage for the District of Columbia shall be 70 percent. The Federal medical assistance percentage for any State shall be determined and promulgated in accordance with the provisions of section 1301(a)(8)(B) of this title. Notwithstanding the first sentence of this section, the Federal medical assistance percentage shall be 100 per centum with respect to amounts expended as medical assistance for services which are received through an Indian Health Service facility whether operated by the Indian Health Service or by an Indian tribe or tribal organization (as defined in section 1603 of Title 25). Notwithstanding the first sentence of this subsection, in the case of a State plan that meets the condition described in subsection (u)(1) of this section, with respect to expenditures (other than expenditures under section 1396r–4 of this title) described in subsection (u)(2)(A) of this section or subsection (u)(3) of this section for the State for a fiscal year, and that do not exceed the amount of the State's available allotment under section 1397dd of this title, the Federal medical assistance percentage is equal to the enhanced FMAP described in section 1397ee(b) of this title, and

(4) the Federal medical assistance percentage shall be equal to the enhanced FMAP described in section 1397ee(b) of this title with respect to medical assistance provided to individuals who are eligible for such assistance only on the basis of section 1396a(a)(10)(A)(ii)(XVIII) of this title.

(c) Nursing facility

For definition of the term "nursing facility", see section 1396r(a) of this title.

(d) Intermediate care facility for mentally retarded

The term "intermediate care facility for the mentally retarded" means an institution (or distinct part thereof) for the mentally retarded or persons with related conditions if—

(1) the primary purpose of such institution (or distinct part thereof) is to provide health or rehabilitative services for mentally retarded individuals and the institution meets such standards as may be prescribed by the Secretary;

(2) the mentally retarded individual with respect to whom a request for payment is made under a plan approved under this subchapter is receiving active treatment under such a program; and

(3) in the case of a public institution, the State or political subdivision responsible for the operation of such institution has agreed that the non-Federal expenditures in any calendar quarter prior to January 1,

1975, with respect to services furnished to patients in such institution (or distinct part thereof) in the State will not, because of payments made under this subchapter, be reduced below the average amount expended for such services in such institution in the four quarters immediately preceding the quarter in which the State in which such institution is located elected to make such services available under its plan approved under this subchapter.

(e) Physicians' services

In the case of any State the State plan of which (as approved under this subchapter)—

(1) does not provide for the payment of services (other than services covered under section 1396a(a)(12) of this title) provided by an optometrist; but

(2) at a prior period did provide for the payment of services referred to in paragraph (1);

the term "physicians' services" (as used in subsection (a)(5) of this section) shall include services of the type which an optometrist is legally authorized to perform where the State plan specifically provides that the term "physicians' services", as employed in such plan, includes services of the type which an optometrist is legally authorized to perform, and shall be reimbursed whether furnished by a physician or an optometrist.

(f) Nursing facility services

For purposes of this subchapter, the term "nursing facility services" means services which are or were required to be given an individual who needs or needed on a daily basis nursing care (provided directly by or requiring the supervision of nursing personnel) or other rehabilitation services which as a practical matter can only be provided in a nursing facility on an inpatient basis.

(g) Chiropractors' services

If the State plan includes provision of chiropractors' services, such services include only—

(1) services provided by a chiropractor

(A) who is licensed as such by the State and

(B) who meets uniform minimum standards promulgated by the Secretary under section 1395x(r)(5) of this title; and

(2) services which consist of treatment by means of manual manipulation of the spine which the chiropractor is legally authorized to perform by the State.

(h) Inpatient psychiatric hospital services for individuals under age 21

(1) For purposes of paragraph (16) of subsection (a) of this section, the term "inpatient psychiatric hospital services for individuals under age 21" includes only—

(A) inpatient services which are provided in an institution (or distinct part thereof) which is a psychiatric hospital as defined in section 1395x(f) of this title or in another inpatient setting that the Secretary has specified in regulations;

(B) inpatient services which, in the case of any individual

(i) involve active treatment which meets such standards as may be prescribed in regulations by the Secretary, and

(ii) a team, consisting of physicians and other personnel qualified to make determinations with respect to mental health conditions and the treatment thereof, has determined are necessary on an inpatient basis and can reasonably be expected to improve the condition, by reason of which such services are necessary, to the extent that eventually such services will no longer be necessary; and

(C) inpatient services which, in the case of any individual, are provided prior to

(i) the date such individual attains age 21, or

(ii) in the case of an individual who was receiving such services in the period immediately preceding the date on which he attained age 21,

(I) the date such individual no longer requires such services, or

(II) if earlier, the date such individual attains age 22;

(2) Such term does not include services provided during any calendar quarter under the State plan of any State if the total amount of the funds expended, during such quarter, by the State (and the political subdivisions thereof) from non-Federal funds for inpatient services included under paragraph (1), and for active psychiatric care and treatment provided on an outpatient basis for eligible mentally ill children, is less than the average quarterly amount of the funds expended, during the 4–quarter period ending December 31, 1971, by the State (and the political subdivisions thereof) from non-Federal funds for such services.

(i) Institution for mental diseases

The term "institution for mental diseases" means a hospital, nursing facility, or other institution of more than 16 beds, that is primarily engaged in providing diagnosis, treatment, or care of persons with mental diseases, including medical attention, nursing care, and related services.

(j) State supplementary payment

The term "State supplementary payment" means any cash payment made by a State on a regular basis to an individual who is receiving supplemental security income benefits under subchapter XVI of this chapter or who would but for his income be eligible to receive such benefits, as assistance based on need in supplementation of such benefits (as determined by the Commissioner of Social Security), but only to the extent that such payments are made with respect to an individual with respect to whom supplemental security income benefits are payable under subchapter XVI of this chapter, or would but for his income be payable under that subchapter.

(k) Supplemental security income benefits

Increased supplemental security income benefits payable pursuant to *section 211 of Public Law 93–66* shall not be considered supplemental security income benefits payable under subchapter XVI of this chapter.

(l) Rural health clinics

(1) The terms "rural health clinic services" and "rural health clinic" have the meanings given such terms in section 1395x(aa) of this title, except that

(A) clause (ii) of section 1395x(aa)(2) of this title shall not apply to such terms, and

(B) the physician arrangement required under section 1395x(aa)(2)(B) of this title shall only apply with respect to rural health clinic services and, with respect to other ambulatory care services, the physician arrangement required shall be only such as may be required under the State plan for those services.

(2)(A) The term "Federally-qualified health center services" means services of the type described in subparagraphs (A) through (C) of section 1395x(aa)(1) of this title when furnished to an individual as a patient of a Federally-qualified health center and, for this purpose, any reference to a rural health clinic or a physician described in section 1395x(aa)(2)(B) of this title is deemed a reference to a Federally-qualified health center or a physician at the center, respectively.

(B) The term "Federally-qualified health center" means an entity which—

(i) is receiving a grant under section 254b of this title,

(ii)(I) is receiving funding from such a grant under a contract with the recipient of such a grant, and

(II) meets the requirements to receive a grant under section 254b of this title,

(iii) based on the recommendation of the Health Resources and Services Administration within the Public Health Service, is determined by the Secretary to meet the requirements for receiving such a grant, including requirements of the Secretary that an entity may not be owned, controlled, or operated by another entity, or

(iv) was treated by the Secretary, for purposes of part B of subchapter XVIII of this chapter, as a comprehensive Federally funded health center as of January 1, 1990;

and includes an outpatient health program or facility operated by a tribe or tribal organization under the Indian Self–Determination Act (*Public Law 93–638*) [*25 U.S.C.A. § 450f* et seq.] or by an urban Indian organization receiving funds under title V of the Indian Health Care Improvement Act [*25 U.S.C.A. § 1651* et seq.] for the provision of primary health services. In applying clause (ii), the Secretary may waive any requirement referred to in such clause for up to 2 years for good cause shown.

(m) Qualified family member

(1) Subject to paragraph (2), the term "qualified family member" means an individual (other than a qualified pregnant woman or child, as defined in subsection (n) of this section) who is a member of a family that would be receiving aid under the State plan under part A of subchapter IV of this chapter pursuant to section 607 of this title if the State had not exercised the option under section 607(b)(2)(B)(i) of this title.

(2) No individual shall be a qualified family member for any period after September 30, 1998.

(n) Qualified pregnant woman or child

The term "qualified pregnant woman or child" means—

(1) a pregnant woman who—

(A) would be eligible for aid to families with dependent children under part A of subchapter IV of this chapter (or would be eligible for such aid if coverage under the State plan under part A of subchapter IV of this chapter included aid to families with dependent children of unemployed parents pursuant to section 607 of this title) if her child had been born and was living with her in the month such aid would be paid, and such pregnancy has been medically verified;

(B) is a member of a family which would be eligible for aid under the State plan under part A of subchapter IV of this chapter pursuant to section 607 of this title if the plan required the payment of aid pursuant to such section; or

(C) otherwise meets the income and resources requirements of a State plan under part A of subchapter IV of this chapter; and

(2) a child who has not attained the age of 19, who was born after September 30, 1983 (or such earlier date as the State may designate), and who meets the income and resources requirements of the State plan under part A of subchapter IV of this chapter.

(*o*) Optional hospice benefits

(1)(A) Subject to subparagraph (B), the term "hospice care" means the care described in section 1395x(dd)(1) of this title furnished by a hospice program (as defined in section 1395x(dd)(2) of this title) to a terminally ill individual who has voluntarily elected (in accordance with paragraph (2)) to have payment made for hospice care instead of having payment made for certain benefits described in section 1395d(d)(2)(A) of this title and for which payment may otherwise be made under subchapter XVIII of this chapter and intermediate care facility services under the plan. For purposes of such election, hospice care may be provided to an individual while such individual is a resident of a skilled nursing facility or intermediate care facility, but the only payment made under the State plan shall be for the hospice care.

(B) For purposes of this subchapter, with respect to the definition of hospice program under section 1395x(dd)(2) of this title, the Secretary may allow an agency or organization to make the assurance under subparagraph (A)(iii) of such section without taking into account any individual who is afflicted with acquired immune deficiency syndrome (AIDS).

(2) An individual's voluntary election under this subsection—

(A) shall be made in accordance with procedures that are established by the State and that are consistent with the procedures established under section 1395d(d)(2) of this title;

(B) shall be for such a period or periods (which need not be the same periods described in section 1395d(d)(1) of this title) as the State may establish; and

(C) may be revoked at any time without a showing of cause and may be modified so as to change the hospice program with respect to which a previous election was made.

(3) In the case of an individual—

(A) who is residing in a nursing facility or intermediate care facility for the mentally retarded and is receiving medical assistance for services in such facility under the plan,

(B) who is entitled to benefits under part A of subchapter XVIII of this chapter and has elected, under section 1395d(d) of this title, to receive hospice care under such part, and

(C) with respect to whom the hospice program under such subchapter and the nursing facility or intermediate care facility for the mentally retarded have entered into a written agreement under which the program takes full responsibility for the professional management of the individual's hospice care and the facility agrees to provide room and board to the individual,

instead of any payment otherwise made under the plan with respect to the facility's services, the State shall provide for payment to the hospice program of an amount equal to the additional amount determined in section 1396a(a)(13)(B) of this title and, if the individual is an individual described in section 1396a(a)(10)(A) of this title, shall provide for payment of any coinsurance amounts imposed under section 1395e(a)(4) of this title.

(p) Qualified medicare beneficiary; medicare cost-sharing

(1) The term "qualified medicare beneficiary" means an individual—

(A) who is entitled to hospital insurance benefits under part A of title XVIII [§§ 1395c et seq.] (including an individual entitled to such benefits pursuant to an enrollment under section 1818 [§ 1395i–2], but not including an individual entitled to such benefits only pursuant to an enrollment under section 1818A [§ 1395i–2a]),

(B) whose income (as determined under section 1612 [§ 1382a]) for purposes of the supplemental security income program, except as provided in paragraph (2)(D) does not exceed an income level established by the State consistent with paragraph (2), and

(C) whose resources (as determined under section 1613 [§ 1382b] for purposes of the supplemental security income program) do not exceed twice the maximum amount of resources that an individual may have and obtain benefits under that program.

(2)(A) The income level established under paragraph (1)(B) shall be at least the percent provided under subparagraph (B) (but not more than 100 percent) of the official poverty line (as defined by the Office of Management and Budget, and revised annually in accordance with section 673(2) of the Omnibus Budget Reconciliation Act of 1981) applicable to a family of the size involved.

(B) Except as provided in subparagraph (C), the percent provided under this clause, with respect to eligibility for medical assistance on or after—

* * *

(iii) January 1, 1991, is 100 per cent.

(C) In the case of a State which has elected treatment under section 1902(f) [§ 1396a(f)] and which, as of January 1, 1987, used an income standard for individuals age 65 or older which was more restrictive than the income standard established under the supplemental security income program under title XVI [§§ 1381 et seq.], the percent provided under subparagraph (B), with respect to eligibility for medical assistance on or after—

* * *

(iv) January 1, 1992, is 100 percent.

(D)(i) In determining under this subsection the income of an individual who is entitled to monthly insurance benefits under title II [§§ 401 et seq.] for a transition month (as defined in clause (ii)) in a year, such income shall not include any amounts attributable to an increase in the level of monthly insurance benefits payable under such title which have occurred pursuant to section 215(i) [§ 415(i)] for benefits payable for months beginning with December of the previous year.

 (ii) For purposes of clause (i), the term "transition month" means each month in a year through the month following the month in which the annual revision of the official poverty line, referred to in subparagraph (A), is published.

(3) The term "medicare cost-sharing" means (subject to section 1902(n)(2) [§ 1396a(n)(2)]) the following costs incurred with respect to a qualified medicare beneficiary, without regard to whether the costs incurred were for items and services for which medical assistance is otherwise available under the plan:

 (A)(i) premiums under section 1818 or 1818A [§ 1395i–2 or 1395i–2a], and

 (ii) premiums under section 1839 [§ 1395r], [.]

 (B) Coinsurance under title XVIII (including coinsurance described in section 1813 [§ 1395e]).

 (C) Deductibles established under title XVIII (including those described in section 1813 and section 1833(b) [§§ 1395e and 1395l(b)]).

 (D) The difference between the amount that is paid under section 1833(a) [§ 1395l(a)] and the amount that would be paid under such section if any reference to "80 percent" therein were deemed a reference to "100 percent".

Such term also may include, at the option of a State, premiums for enrollment of a qualified medicare beneficiary with an eligible organization under section 1876 [§ 1395mm].

 (4) Notwithstanding any other provision of this title, in the case of a State (other than the 50 States and the District of Columbia)—

 (A) the requirement stated in section 1902(a)(10)(E) [§ 1396a(a)(10)(E)] shall be optional, and

 (B) for purposes of paragraph (2), the State may substitute for the percent provided under subparagraph (B) [of such paragraph] or [section] 1902(a)(10)(E)(iii) [§ 1396a(a)(10)(E)(iii)] [of such paragraph] any percent.

In the case of any State which is providing medical assistance to its residents under a waiver granted under section 1115 [§ 1315], the Secretary shall require the State to meet the requirement of section 1902(a)(10)(E) [§ 1396a(a)(10)(E)] in the same manner as the State would be required to meet such requirement if the State had in effect a plan approved under this title.

* * *

(q) Qualified severely impaired individual

The term "qualified severely impaired individual" means an individual under age 65—

(1) who for the month preceding the first month to which this subsection applies to such individual—

(A) received

(i) a payment of supplemental security income benefits under section 1382(b) of this title on the basis of blindness or disability,

(ii) a supplementary payment under section 1382e of this title or under *section 212 of Public Law 93–66* on such basis,

(iii) a payment of monthly benefits under section 1382h(a) of this title, or (iv) a supplementary payment under section 1382e(c)(3) of this title, and

(B) was eligible for medical assistance under the State plan approved under this subchapter; and

(2) with respect to whom the Commissioner of Social Security determines that—

(A) the individual continues to be blind or continues to have the disabling physical or mental impairment on the basis of which he was found to be under a disability and, except for his earnings, continues to meet all non-disability-related requirements for eligibility for benefits under subchapter XVI of this chapter,

(B) the income of such individual would not, except for his earnings, be equal to or in excess of the amount which would cause him to be ineligible for payments under section 1382(b) of this title (if he were otherwise eligible for such payments),

(C) the lack of eligibility for benefits under this subchapter would seriously inhibit his ability to continue or obtain employment, and

(D) the individual's earnings are not sufficient to allow him to provide for himself a reasonable equivalent of the benefits under subchapter XVI of this chapter (including any federally administered State supplementary payments), this subchapter, and publicly funded attendant care services (including personal care assistance) that would be available to him in the absence of such earnings.

In the case of an individual who is eligible for medical assistance pursuant to section 1382h(b) of this title in June, 1987, the individual shall be a qualified severely impaired individual for so long as such individual meets the requirements of paragraph (2).

(r) Early and periodic screening, diagnostic, and treatment services

The term "early and periodic screening, diagnostic, and treatment services" means the following items and services:

(1) Screening services—

(A) which are provided—

(i) at intervals which meet reasonable standards of medical and dental practice, as determined by the State after consultation with recognized medical and dental organizations involved in child health care and, with respect to immunizations under subparagraph (B)(iii), in accordance with the schedule referred to in section 1396s(c)(2)(B)(i) of this title for pediatric vaccines, and

(ii) at such other intervals, indicated as medically necessary, to determine the existence of certain physical or mental illnesses or conditions; and

(B) which shall at a minimum include—

(i) a comprehensive health and developmental history (including assessment of both physical and mental health development),

(ii) a comprehensive unclothed physical exam,

(iii) appropriate immunizations (according to the schedule referred to in section 1396s(c)(2)(B)(i) of this title for pediatric vaccines) according to age and health history,

(iv) laboratory tests (including lead blood level assessment appropriate for age and risk factors), and

(v) health education (including anticipatory guidance).

(2) Vision services—

(A) which are provided—

(i) at intervals which meet reasonable standards of medical practice, as determined by the State after consultation with recognized medical organizations involved in child health care, and

(ii) at such other intervals, indicated as medically necessary, to determine the existence of a suspected illness or condition; and

(B) which shall at a minimum include diagnosis and treatment for defects in vision, including eyeglasses.

(3) Dental services—

(A) which are provided—

(i) at intervals which meet reasonable standards of dental practice, as determined by the State after consultation with recognized dental organizations involved in child health care, and

(ii) at such other intervals, indicated as medically necessary, to determine the existence of a suspected illness or condition; and

(B) which shall at a minimum include relief of pain and infections, restoration of teeth, and maintenance of dental health.

(4) Hearing services—

(A) which are provided—

(i) at intervals which meet reasonable standards of medical practice, as determined by the State after consultation with recognized medical organizations involved in child health care, and

(ii) at such other intervals, indicated as medically necessary, to determine the existence of a suspected illness or condition; and

(B) which shall at a minimum include diagnosis and treatment for defects in hearing, including hearing aids.

(5) Such other necessary health care, diagnostic services, treatment, and other measures described in subsection (a) of this section to correct or ameliorate defects and physical and mental illnesses and conditions discovered by the screening services, whether or not such services are covered under the State plan.

Nothing in this subchapter shall be construed as limiting providers of early and periodic screening, diagnostic, and treatment services to providers who are qualified to provide all of the items and services described in the previous sentence or as preventing a provider that is qualified under the plan to furnish one or more (but not all) of such items or services from being qualified to provide such items and services as part of early and periodic screening, diagnostic, and treatment services. The Secretary shall, not later than July 1, 1990, and every 12 months thereafter, develop and set annual participation goals for each State for participation of individuals who are covered under the State plan under this subchapter in early and periodic screening, diagnostic, and treatment services.

(s) Qualified disabled and working individual

The term "qualified disabled and working individual" means an individual—

(1) who is entitled to enroll for hospital insurance benefits under part A of subchapter XVIII of this chapter under section 1395i–2a of this title;

(2) whose income (as determined under section 1382a of this title for purposes of the supplemental security income program) does not exceed 200 percent of the official poverty line (as defined by the Office of Management and Budget and revised annually in accordance with section 9902(2) of this title) applicable to a family of the size involved;

(3) whose resources (as determined under section 1382b of this title for purposes of the supplemental security income program) do not exceed twice the maximum amount of resources that an individual or a couple (in the case of an individual with a spouse) may have and obtain benefits for supplemental security income benefits under subchapter XVI of this chapter; and

(4) who is not otherwise eligible for medical assistance under this subchapter.

(t) "Primary care case management services", "primary care case manager", "primary care case management contract", and "primary care" defined

(1) The term "primary care case management services" means case-management related services (including locating, coordinating, and monitoring of health care services) provided by a primary care case manager under a primary care case management contract.

(2) The term "primary care case manager" means any of the following that provides services of the type described in paragraph (1) under a contract referred to in such paragraph:

(A) A physician, a physician group practice, or an entity employing or having other arrangements with physicians to provide such services.

(B) At State option—

(i) a nurse practitioner (as described in subsection (a)(21) of this section);

(ii) a certified nurse-midwife (as defined in section 1395x(gg) of this title); or

(iii) a physician assistant (as defined in section 1395x(aa)(5) of this title).

(3) The term "primary care case management contract" means a contract between a primary care case manager and a State under which the manager undertakes to locate, coordinate, and monitor covered primary care (and such other covered services as may be specified under the contract) to all individuals enrolled with the manager, and which—

(A) provides for reasonable and adequate hours of operation, including 24–hour availability of information, referral, and treatment with respect to medical emergencies;

(B) restricts enrollment to individuals residing sufficiently near a service delivery site of the manager to be able to reach that site within a reasonable time using available and affordable modes of transportation;

(C) provides for arrangements with, or referrals to, sufficient numbers of physicians and other appropriate health care professionals to ensure that services under the contract can be furnished to enrollees promptly and without compromise to quality of care;

(D) prohibits discrimination on the basis of health status or requirements for health care services in enrollment, disenrollment, or reenrollment of individuals eligible for medical assistance under this subchapter;

(E) provides for a right for an enrollee to terminate enrollment in accordance with section 1396u–2(a)(4) of this title; and

(F) complies with the other applicable provisions of section 1396u–2 of this title.

(4) For purposes of this subsection, the term "primary care" includes all health care services customarily provided in accordance with State licensure and certification laws and regulations, and all laboratory services customarily provided by or through, a general practitioner, family medicine physician, internal medicine physician, obstetrician/gynecologist, or pediatrician.

(u) Conditions for State plans

(1) The conditions described in this paragraph for a State plan are as follows:

(A) The State is complying with the requirement of section 1397ee(d)(1) of this title.

(B) The plan provides for such reporting of information about expenditures and payments attributable to the operation of this subsection as the Secretary deems necessary in order to carry out the fourth sentence of subsection (b) of this section.

(2)(A) For purposes of subsection (b) of this section, the expenditures described in this subparagraph are expenditures for medical assistance for optional targeted low-income children described in subparagraph (B).

(B) For purposes of this paragraph, the term "optional targeted low-income child" means a targeted low-income child as defined in section 1397jj(b)(1) of this title (determined without regard to that portion of subparagraph (C) of such section concerning eligibility for medical assistance under this subchapter) who would not qualify for medical assistance under the State plan under this subchapter as in effect on March 31, 1997 (but taking into account the expansion of age of eligibility effected through the operation of section 1396a(*l*)(1)(D)) of this title.

* * *

(3) For purposes of subsection (b) of this section, the expenditures described in this paragraph are expenditures for medical assistance for children who are born before October 1, 1983, and who would be described in section 1396a(*l*)(1)(D) of this title if they had been born on or after such date, and who are not eligible for such assistance under the

State plan under this subchapter based on such State plan as in effect as of March 31, 1997.

(4) The limitations on payment under subsections (f) and (g) of section 1308 of this title shall not apply to Federal payments made under section 1396b(a)(1) of this title based on an enhanced FMAP described in section 1397ee(b) of this title.

(v) Employed individuals with a medically improved disability

(1) The term "employed individual with a medically improved disability" means an individual who

    (A) is at least 16, but less than 65, years of age;

    (B) is employed (as defined in paragraph (2));

    (C) ceases to be eligible for medical assistance under section 1396a(a)(10)(A)(ii)(XV) of this title because the individual, by reason of medical improvement, is determined at the time of a regularly scheduled continuing disability review to no longer be eligible for benefits under section 423(d) or 1382c(a)(3) of this title; and

    (D) continues to have a severe medically determinable impairment, as determined under regulations of the Secretary.

(2) For purposes of paragraph (1), an individual is considered to be "employed" if the individual

    (A) is earning at least the applicable minimum wage requirement under section 206 of Title 29 and working at least 40 hours per month; or

    (B) is engaged in a work effort that meets substantial and reasonable threshold criteria for hours of work, wages, or other measures, as defined by the State and approved by the Secretary.

(w) Independent foster care adolescent

(1) For purposes of this subchapter, the term "independent foster care adolescent" means an individual—

    (A) who is under 21 years of age;

    (B) who, on the individual's 18th birthday, was in foster care under the responsibility of a State; and

    (C) whose assets, resources, and income do not exceed such levels (if any) as the State may establish consistent with paragraph (2).

(2) The levels established by a State under paragraph (1)(C) may not be less than the corresponding levels applied by the State under section 1396u–1(b) of this title.

(3) A State may limit the eligibility of independent foster care adolescents under section 1396a(a)(10)(A)(ii)(XVII) of this title to those individuals with respect to whom foster care maintenance payments or independent living services were furnished under a program funded under part E of subchapter IV of this chapter [*42 U.S.C.A. § 670* et seq.] before the date the individuals attained 18 years of age.

§ 1396e. Enrollment of individuals under group health plans

(a) Requirements of each State plan; guidelines

Each State plan—

(1) may implement guidelines established by the Secretary, consistent with subsection (b) of this section, to identify those cases in which enrollment of an individual otherwise entitled to medical assistance under this subchapter in a group health plan (in which the individual is otherwise eligible to be enrolled) is cost-effective (as defined in subsection (e)(2) of this section);

(2) may require, in case of an individual so identified and as a condition of the individual being or remaining eligible for medical assistance under this subchapter and subject to subsection (b)(2) of this section, notwithstanding any other provision of this subchapter, that the individual (or in the case of a child, the child's parent) apply for enrollment in the group health plan; and

(3) in the case of such enrollment (except as provided in subsection (c)(1)(B) of this section), shall provide for payment of all enrollee premiums for such enrollment and all deductibles, coinsurance, and other cost-sharing obligations for items and services otherwise covered under the State plan under this subchapter (exceeding the amount otherwise permitted under section 1396o of this title), and shall treat coverage under the group health plan as a third party liability (under section 1396a(a)(25) of this title).

(b) Timing of enrollment; failure to enroll

(1) In establishing guidelines under subsection (a)(1) of this section, the Secretary shall take into account that an individual may only be eligible to enroll in group health plans at limited times and only if other individuals (not entitled to medical assistance under the plan) are also enrolled in the plan simultaneously.

(2) If a parent of a child fails to enroll the child in a group health plan in accordance with subsection (a)(2) of this section, such failure shall not affect the child's eligibility for benefits under this subchapter.

(c) Premiums considered payments for medical assistance; eligibility

(1)(A) In the case of payments of premiums, deductibles, coinsurance, and other cost-sharing obligations under this section shall be considered, for purposes of section 1396b(a) of this title, to be payments for medical assistance.

(B) If all members of a family are not eligible for medical assistance under this subchapter and enrollment of the members so eligible in a group health plan is not possible without also enrolling members not so eligible—

> **(i)** payment of premiums for enrollment of such other members shall be treated as payments for medical assistance for eligible individuals, if it would be cost-effective (taking into account payment of all such premiums), but

> **(ii)** payment of deductibles, coinsurance, and other cost-sharing obligations for such other members shall not be treated as payments for medical assistance for eligible individuals.

(2) The fact that an individual is enrolled in a group health plan under this section shall not change the individual's eligibility for benefits under the State plan, except insofar as section 1396a(a)(25) of this title provides that payment for such benefits shall first be made by such plan.

(d) [Repealed.]

(e) Definitions

In this section:

(1) The term "group health plan" has the meaning given such term in section 5000(b)(1) of Title 26, and includes the provision of continuation coverage by such a plan pursuant to subchapter XX of chapter 6A of this title, section 4980B of Title 26, or title VI of the Employee Retirement Income Security Act of 1974.

(2) The term "cost-effective" means, as established by the Secretary, that the reduction in expenditures under this subchapter with respect to an individual who is enrolled in a group health plan is likely to be greater than the additional expenditures for premiums and cost-sharing required under this section with respect to such enrollment.

§ 1396f. Observance of religious beliefs

Nothing in this subchapter shall be construed to require any State which has a plan approved under this subchapter to compel any person to undergo any medical screening, examination, diagnosis, or treatment or to accept any other health care or services provided under such plan for any purpose (other than for the purpose of discovering and preventing the spread of infection or contagious disease or for the purpose of protecting environmental health), if such person objects (or, in case such person is a child, his parent or guardian objects) thereto on religious grounds.

* * *

§ 1396g–1. Required laws relating to medical child support

(a) In general. The laws relating to medical child support, which a State is required to have in effect under section 1902(a)(60) [§ 1396a(a)(60)], are as follows:

(1) A law that prohibits an insurer from denying enrollment of a child under the health coverage of the child's parent on the ground that—

(A) the child was born out of wedlock,

(B) the child is not claimed as a dependent on the parent's Federal income tax return, or

(C) the child does not reside with the parent or in the insurer's service area.

(2) In any case in which a parent is required by a court or administrative order to provide health coverage for a child and the parent is eligible for family health coverage through an insurer, a law that requires such insurer—

(A) to permit such parent to enroll under such family coverage any such child who is otherwise eligible for such coverage (without regard to any enrollment season restrictions);

(B) if such a parent is enrolled but fails to make application to obtain coverage of such child, to enroll such child under such family coverage upon application by the child's other parent or by the State agency administering the program under this title or part D of title IV; and

(C) not to disenroll (or eliminate coverage of) such a child unless the insurer is provided satisfactory written evidence that—

(i) such court or administrative order is no longer in effect, or

(ii) the child is or will be enrolled in comparable health coverage through another insurer which will take effect not later than the effective date of such disenrollment.

(3) In any case in which a parent is required by a court or administrative order to provide health coverage for a child and the parent is eligible for family health coverage through an employer doing business in the State, a law that requires such employer—

(A) to permit such parent to enroll under such family coverage any such child who is otherwise eligible for such coverage (without regard to any enrollment season restrictions);

(B) if such a parent is enrolled but fails to make application to obtain coverage of such child, to enroll such child under such family coverage upon application by the child's other parent or by the State agency administering the program under this title or part D of title IV; and

(C) not to disenroll (or eliminate coverage of) any such child unless—

(i) the employer is provided satisfactory written evidence that—

(I) such court or administrative order is no longer in effect, or

913

(II) the child is or will be enrolled in comparable health coverage which will take effect not later than the effective date of such disenrollment, or

(ii) the employer has eliminated family health coverage for all of its employees; and

(D) to withhold from such employee's compensation the employee's share (if any) of premiums for health coverage (except that the amount so withheld may not exceed the maximum amount permitted to be withheld under section 303(b) of the Consumer Credit Protection Act [15 USCA § 1673(b)]), and to pay such share of premiums to the insurer, except that the Secretary may provide by regulation for appropriate circumstances under which an employer may withhold less than such employee's share of such premiums.

(4) A law that prohibits an insurer from imposing requirements on a State agency, which has been assigned the rights of an individual eligible for medical assistance under this title and covered for health benefits from the insurer, that are different from requirements applicable to an agent or assignee of any other individual so covered.

(5) A law that requires an insurer, in any case in which a child has health coverage through the insurer of a noncustodial parent—

(A) to provide such information to the custodial parent as may be necessary for the child to obtain benefits through such coverage;

(B) to permit the custodial parent (or provider, with the custodial parent's approval) to submit claims for covered services without the approval of the noncustodial parent; and

(C) to make payment on claims submitted in accordance with subparagraph (B) directly to such custodial parent, the provider, or the State agency.

(6) A law that permits the State agency under this title to garnish the wages, salary, or other employment income of, and requires withholding amounts from State tax refunds to, any person who—

(A) is required by court or administrative order to provide coverage of the costs of health services to a child who is eligible for medical assistance under this title,

(B) has received payment from a third party for the costs of such services to such child, but

(C) has not used such payments to reimburse, as appropriate, either the other parent or guardian of such child or the provider of such services,

to the extent necessary to reimburse the State agency for expenditures for such costs under its plan under this title [42 USCS §§ 1396 et seq.], but any claims for current or past-due child support shall take priority over any such claims for the costs of such services.

(b) "Insurer" defined. For purposes of this section, the term "insurer" includes a group health plan, as defined in section 607(1) of the Employee Retirement Income Security Act of 1974 [29 USCA § 1167(1)], a health maintenance organization, and an entity offering a service benefit plan.

* * *

§ 1396i. Certification and approval of rural health clinics and intermediate care facilities for the mentally retarded

(a)(1) Whenever the Secretary certifies a facility in a State to be qualified as a rural health clinic under title XVIII, such facility shall be deemed to meet the standards for certification as a rural health clinic for purposes of providing rural health clinic services under this title.

(2) The Secretary shall notify the State agency administering the medical assistance plan of his approval or disapproval of any facility in that State which has applied for certification by him as a qualified rural health clinic.

(b)(1) The Secretary may cancel approval of any intermediate care facility for the mentally retarded at any time if he finds on the basis of a determination made by him as provided in section 1902(a)(33)(B) [§ 1396a(a)(33)(B)] that a facility fails to meet the requirements contained in section 1902(a)(31) or section 1905(d) [§ 1396a(a)(31) or 1396d(d)], or if he finds grounds for termination of his agreement with the facility pursuant to section 1866(b) [§ 1395cc(b)]. In that event the Secretary shall notify the State agency and the intermediate care facility for the mentally retarded that approval of eligibility of the facility to participate in the programs established by this title and title XVIII shall be terminated at a time specified by the Secretary. The approval of eligibility of any such facility to participate in such programs may not be reinstated unless the Secretary finds that the reason for termination has been removed and there is reasonable assurance that it will not recur.

(2) Any intermediate care facility for the mentally retarded which is dissatisfied with a determination by the Secretary that it no longer qualifies as a [an] intermediate care facility for the mentally retarded for purposes of this title, shall be entitled to a hearing by the Secretary to the same extent as is provided in section 205(b) [42 USCA § 405(b)] and to judicial review of the Secretary's final decision after such hearing as is provided in section 205(g) [42 USCA § 405(g)], except that, in so applying such sections and in applying section 205(*l*) [42 USCA § 405(*l*)] thereto, any reference therein to the Commissioner of Social Security or the Social Security Administration shall be considered a reference to the Secretary or the Department of Health and Human Services, respectively. Any agreement between such facility and the State agency shall remain in effect until the period for filing a request for a hearing has expired or, if a request has been filed, until a decision has been made by the Secretary; except that the agreement shall not be extended if the Secretary makes a written determination, specifying the reasons therefor, that the continuation of provider status constitutes an immediate and serious threat to the health and safety of patients, and the Secretary certifies that the facility has been notified of its deficiencies and has failed to correct them.

* * *

§ 1396j. Indian health service facilities

(a) Eligibility for reimbursement for medical assistance

A facility of the Indian Health Service (including a hospital, nursing facility, or any other type of facility which provides services of a type otherwise covered under the State plan), whether operated by such Service or by an Indian tribe or tribal organization (as those terms are defined in section 1603 of Title 25), shall be eligible for reimbursement for medical assistance provided under a State plan if and for so long as it meets all of the conditions and requirements which are applicable generally to such facilities under this subchapter.

(b) Facilities deemed to meet requirements upon submission of acceptable plan for achieving compliance

Notwithstanding subsection (a) of this section, a facility of the Indian Health Service (including a hospital, nursing facility, or any other type of facility which provides services of a type otherwise covered under the State plan) which does not meet all of the conditions and requirements of this title which are applicable generally to such facility, but which submits to the Secretary within six months after September 30, 1976, an acceptable plan for achieving compliance with such conditions and requirements, shall be deemed to meet such conditions and requirements (and to be eligible for reimbursement under this subchapter), without regard to the extent of its actual compliance with such conditions and requirements, during the first twelve months after the month in which such plan is submitted.

(c) Agreement to reimburse State agency for providing care and services

The Secretary is authorized to enter into agreements with the State agency for the purpose of reimbursing such agency for health care and services provided in Indian Health Service facilities to Indians who are eligible for medical assistance under the State plan.

(d) Direct billing for payment under medicare, medicaid, and other third party payors

For provisions relating to the authority of certain Indian tribes, tribal organizations, and Alaska Native health organizations to elect to directly bill for, and receive payment for, health care services provided by a hospital or clinic of such tribes or organizations and for which payment may be made under this subchapter, see section 1645 of Title 25.

§ 1396k. Assignment, enforcement, and collection of rights of payments for medical care; establishment of procedures pursuant to State plan; amounts retained by State

(a) For the purpose of assisting in the collection of medical support payments and other payments for medical care owed to recipients of medical assistance under the State plan approved under this subchapter, a State plan for medical assistance shall—

(1) provide that, as a condition of eligibility for medical assistance under the State plan to an individual who has the legal capacity to execute an assignment for himself, the individual is required—

(A) to assign the State any rights, of the individual or of any other person who is eligible for medical assistance under this subchapter and on whose behalf the individual has the legal authority to execute an assignment of such rights, to support (specified as support for the purpose of medical care by a court or administrative order) and to payment for medical care from any third party;

(B) to cooperate with the State

(i) in establishing the paternity of such person (referred to in subparagraph (A)) if the person is a child born out of wedlock, and

(ii) in obtaining support and payments (described in subparagraph (A)) for himself and for such person, unless (in either case) the individual is described in section 1396a(*l*)(1)(A) of this title or the individual is found to have good cause for refusing to cooperate as determined by the State agency in accordance with standards prescribed by the Secretary, which standards shall take into consideration the best interests of the individuals involved; and

(C) to cooperate with the State in identifying, and providing information to assist the State in pursuing, any third party who may be liable to pay for care and services available under the plan, unless such individual has good cause for refusing to cooperate as determined by the State agency in accordance with standards prescribed by the Secretary, which standards shall take into consideration the best interests of the individuals involved; and

(2) provide for entering into cooperative arrangements (including financial arrangements), with any appropriate agency of any State (including, with respect to the enforcement and collection of rights of payment for medical care by or through a parent, with a State's agency established or designated under section 654(3) of this title) and with

917

appropriate courts and law enforcement officials, to assist the agency or agencies administering the State plan with respect to

(A) the enforcement and collection of rights to support or payment assigned under this section and

(B) any other matters of common concern.

(b) Such part of any amount collected by the State under an assignment made under the provisions of this section shall be retained by the State as is necessary to reimburse it for medical assistance payments made on behalf of an individual with respect to whom such assignment was executed (with appropriate reimbursement of the Federal Government to the extent of its participation in the financing of such medical assistance), and the remainder of such amount collected shall be paid to such individual.

§ 1396l. Hospital providers of nursing facility services

(a) Notwithstanding any other provision of this subchapter, payment may be made, in accordance with this section, under a State plan approved under this subchapter for nursing facility services furnished by a hospital which has in effect an agreement under section 1395tt of this title and which, with respect to the provision of such services, meets the requirements of subsections (b) through (d) of section 1396r of this title.

(b)(1) Except as provided in paragraph (3), payment to any such hospital, for any nursing facility services furnished pursuant to subsection (a) of this section, shall be at a rate equal to the average rate per patient-day paid for routine services during the previous calendar year under the State plan to nursing facilities, respectively, located in the State in which the hospital is located. The reasonable cost of ancillary services shall be determined in the same manner as the reasonable cost of ancillary services provided for inpatient hospital services.

(2) With respect to any period for which a hospital has an agreement under section 1395tt of this title, in order to allocate routine costs between hospital and long-term care services, the total reimbursement for routine services due from all classes of long-term care patients (including subchapter XVIII of this chapter, this subchapter, and private pay patients) shall be subtracted from the hospital total routine costs before calculations are made to determine reimbursement for routine hospital services under the State plan.

(3) Payment to all such hospitals, for any nursing facility services furnished pursuant to subsection (a) of this section, may be made at a payment rate established by the State in accordance with the requirements of section 1396a(a)(13)(A) of this title.

* * *

§ 1396n. Compliance with State plan and payment provisions

(a) Activities deemed as compliance

A State shall not be deemed to be out of compliance with the requirements of paragraphs (1), (10), or (23) of section 1396a(a) of this title solely by reason of the fact that the State (or any political subdivision thereof)—

> **(1)** has entered into—

>> **(A)** a contract with an organization which has agreed to provide care and services in addition to those offered under the State plan to individuals eligible for medical assistance who reside in the geographic area served by such organization and who elect to obtain such care and services from such organization, or by reason of the fact that the plan provides for payment for rural health clinic services only if those services are provided by a rural health clinic; or

>> **(B)** arrangements through a competitive bidding process or otherwise for the purchase of laboratory services referred to in section 1396d(a)(3) of this title or medical devices if the Secretary has found that—

>>> **(i)** adequate services or devices will be available under such arrangements, and

>>> **(ii)** any such laboratory services will be provided only through laboratories—

>>>> **(I)** which meet the applicable requirements of section 1395x(e)(9) of this title or paragraphs (16) and (17) of section 1395x(s) of this title, and such additional requirements as the Secretary may require, and

>>>> **(II)** no more than 75 percent of whose charges for such services are for services provided to individuals who are entitled to benefits under this subchapter or under part A or part B of subchapter XVIII of this chapter; or

> **(2)** restricts for a reasonable period of time the provider or providers from which an individual (eligible for medical assistance for items or services under the State plan) can receive such items or services, if—

>> **(A)** the State has found, after notice and opportunity for a hearing (in accordance with procedures established by the State), that the individual has utilized such items or services at a frequency or amount not medically necessary (as determined in accordance with utilization guidelines established by the State), and

>> **(B)** under such restriction, individuals eligible for medical assistance for such services have reasonable access (taking into account geographic location and reasonable travel time) to such services of adequate quality.

919

(b) Waivers to promote cost-effectiveness and efficiency

The Secretary, to the extent he finds it to be cost-effective and efficient and not inconsistent with the purposes of this subchapter, may waive such requirements of section 1396a of this title (other than subsection (s) of this section) (other than sections 1396a(a)(15), 1396a(aa), and 1396a(a)(10)(A) of this title insofar as it requires provision of the care and services described in section 1396d(a)(2)(C) of this title) as may be necessary for a State—

    (1) to implement a primary care case-management system or a specialty physician services arrangement which restricts the provider from (or through) whom an individual (eligible for medical assistance under this subchapter) can obtain medical care services (other than in emergency circumstances), if such restriction does not substantially impair access to such services of adequate quality where medically necessary,

    (2) to allow a locality to act as a central broker in assisting individuals (eligible for medical assistance under this subchapter) in selecting among competing health care plans, if such restriction does not substantially impair access to services of adequate quality where medically necessary,

    (3) to share (through provision of additional services) with recipients of medical assistance under the State plan cost savings resulting from use by the recipient of more cost-effective medical care, and

    (4) to restrict the provider from (or through) whom an individual (eligible for medical assistance under this subchapter) can obtain services (other than in emergency circumstances) to providers or practitioners who undertake to provide such services and who meet, accept, and comply with the reimbursement, quality, and utilization standards under the State plan, which standards shall be consistent with the requirements of section 1396r–4 of this title and are consistent with access, quality, and efficient and economic provision of covered care and services, if such restriction does not discriminate among classes of providers on grounds unrelated to their demonstrated effectiveness and efficiency in providing those services and if providers under such restriction are paid on a timely basis in the same manner as health care practitioners must be paid under section 1396a(a)(37)(A) of this title.

No waiver under this subsection may restrict the choice of the individual in receiving services under section 1396d(a)(4)(C) of this title.

(c) Waiver respecting medical assistance requirement in State plan: scope, etc.; "habilitation services" defined; imposition of certain regulatory limits prohibited; computation of expenditures for certain disabled patients; coordinated services; substitution of participants

    (1) The Secretary may by waiver provide that a State plan approved under this subchapter may include as "medical assistance" under such plan payment for part or all of the cost of home or community-based services (other than room and board) approved by the Secretary which are provided pursuant to a written plan of care to individuals with respect to whom there has been a determination that but for the provision of such services the individuals would require the level of care provided in a hospital or a nursing facility or intermediate care facility for the mentally retarded the cost of which could be reimbursed under the State plan. For purposes of this subsection, the term "room and board" shall not include an amount established under a method determined by the State to reflect the portion of costs of rent and food attributable to an unrelated personal caregiver who is residing in the same household with an individual who, but for the assistance of such caregiver, would require admission to a hospital, nursing facility, or intermediate care facility for the mentally retarded.

(2) A waiver shall not be granted under this subsection unless the State provides assurances satisfactory to the Secretary that—

(A) necessary safeguards (including adequate standards for provider participation) have been taken to protect the health and welfare of individuals provided services under the waiver and to assure financial accountability for funds expended with respect to such services;

(B) the State will provide, with respect to individuals who—

(i) are entitled to medical assistance for inpatient hospital services, nursing facility services, or services in an intermediate care facility for the mentally retarded under the State plan,

(ii) may require such services, and

(iii) may be eligible for such home or community-based care under such waiver,

for an evaluation of the need for inpatient hospital services, nursing facility services, or services in an intermediate care facility for the mentally retarded;

(C) such individuals who are determined to be likely to require the level of care provided in a hospital, nursing facility, or intermediate care facility for the mentally retarded are informed of the feasible alternatives, if available under the waiver, at the choice of such individuals, to the provision of inpatient hospital services, nursing facility services, or services in an intermediate care facility for the mentally retarded;

(D) under such waiver the average per capita expenditure estimated by the State in any fiscal year for medical assistance provided with respect to such individuals does not exceed 100 percent of the average per capita expenditure that the State reasonably estimates would have been made in that fiscal year for expenditures under the State plan for such individuals if the waiver had not been granted; and

(E) the State will provide to the Secretary annually, consistent with a data collection plan designed by the Secretary, information on the impact of the waiver granted under this subsection on the type and amount of medical assistance provided under the State plan and on the health and welfare of recipients.

(3) A waiver granted under this subsection may include a waiver of the requirements of section 1396a(a)(1) of this title (relating to statewideness), section 1396a(a)(10)(B) of this title (relating to comparability), and section 1396a(a)(10)(C)(i)(III) of this title (relating to income and resource rules applicable in the community). A waiver under this subsection shall be for an initial term of three years and, upon the request of a State, shall be extended for additional five-year periods unless the Secretary determines that for the previous waiver period the assurances provided under paragraph (2) have not been met. A waiver may provide, with respect to post-eligibility treatment of income of all individuals receiving services under that waiver, that the maximum amount of the individual's income which may be disregarded for any month for the maintenance needs of the individual may be an amount greater than the maximum allowed for that purpose under regulations in effect on July 1, 1985.

(4) A waiver granted under this subsection may, consistent with paragraph (2)—

(A) limit the individuals provided benefits under such waiver to individuals with respect to whom the State has determined that there is a reasonable expectation that the amount of medical assistance provided with respect to the individual under such waiver will not exceed the amount of such medical assistance provided for such individual if the waiver did not apply, and

(B) provide medical assistance to individuals (to the extent consistent with written plans of care, which are subject to the approval of the State) for case management services, homemaker/home health aide services and personal care services, adult day health services, habilitation services, respite care, and such other services requested by the State as the Secretary may approve and for day treatment or other partial hospitalization services, psychosocial rehabilitation services, and clinic services (whether or not furnished in a facility) for individuals with chronic mental illness.

Except as provided under paragraph (2)(D), the Secretary may not restrict the number of hours or days of respite care in any period which a State may provide under a waiver under this subsection.

(5) For purposes of paragraph (4)(B), the term ''habilitation services''—

(A) means services designed to assist individuals in acquiring, retaining, and improving the self-help, socialization, and adaptive skills necessary to reside successfully in home and community based settings; and

(B) includes (except as provided in subparagraph (C)) prevocational, educational, and supported employment services; but

(C) does not include—

(i) special education and related services (as defined in paragraphs (16) and (17) of section 1401(a) of Title 20), which otherwise are available to the individual through a local educational agency; and

(ii) vocational rehabilitation services which otherwise are available to the individual through a program funded under section 730 of Title 29.

(6) The Secretary may not require, as a condition of approval of a waiver under this section under paragraph (2)(D), that the actual total expenditures for home and community-based services under the waiver (and a claim for Federal financial participation in expenditures for the services) cannot exceed the approved estimates for these services. The Secretary may not deny Federal financial payment with respect to services under such a waiver on the ground that, in order to comply with paragraph (2)(D), a State has failed to comply with such a requirement.

(7)(A) In making estimates under paragraph (2)(D) in the case of a waiver that applies only to individuals with a particular illness or condition who are inpatients in, or who would require the level of care provided in, hospitals, nursing facilities, or intermediate care facilities for the mentally retarded, the State may determine the average per capita expenditure that would have been made in a fiscal year for those individuals under the State plan separately from the expenditures for other individuals who are inpatients in, or who would require the level of care provided in, those respective facilities.

(B) In making estimates under paragraph (2)(D) in the case of a waiver that applies only to individuals with developmental disabilities who are inpatients in a nursing facility and whom the State has determined, on the basis of an evaluation under paragraph (2)(B), to need the level of services provided by an intermediate care facility for the mentally retarded, the State may determine the average per capita expenditures that would have been made in a fiscal year for those individuals under the State plan on the basis of the average per capita expenditures under the State plan for services to individuals who are inpatients in an intermediate care facility for the mentally retarded, without regard to the availability of beds for such inpatients.

(C) In making estimates under paragraph (2)(D) in the case of a waiver to the extent that it applies to individuals with mental retardation or a related condition who are resident in an intermediate care facility for the mentally retarded the participation of which under the State plan is terminated, the State may determine the average per capita expenditures that would have been made in a fiscal year for those individuals without regard to any such termination.

(8) The State agency administering the plan under this subchapter may, whenever appropriate, enter into cooperative arrangements with the State agency responsible for administering the program for children with special health care needs under subchapter V of this chapter in order to assure improved access to coordinated services to meet the needs of such children.

(9) In the case of any waiver under this subsection which contains a limit on the number of individuals who shall receive home or community-based services, the State may substitute additional individuals to receive such services to replace any individuals who die or become ineligible for services under the State plan.

(10) The Secretary shall not limit to fewer than 200 the number of individuals in the State who may receive home and community-based services under a waiver under this subsection.

(d) Home and community-based services for elderly

(1) Subject to paragraph (2), the Secretary shall grant a waiver to provide that a State plan approved under this subchapter shall include as "medical assistance" under such plan payment for part or all of the cost of home or community-based services (other than room and board) which are provided pursuant to a written plan of care to individuals 65 years of age or older with respect to whom there has been a determination that but for the provision of such services the individuals would be likely to require the level of care provided in a skilled nursing facility or intermediate care facility the cost of which could be reimbursed under the State plan. For purposes of this subsection, the term "room and board" shall not include an amount established under a method determined by the State to reflect the portion of costs of rent and food attributable to an unrelated personal caregiver who is residing in the same household with an individual who, but for the assistance of such caregiver, would require admission to a hospital, nursing facility, or intermediate care facility for the mentally retarded.

(2) A waiver shall not be granted under this subsection unless the State provides assurances satisfactory to the Secretary that—

    (A) necessary safeguards (including adequate standards for provider participation) have been taken to protect the health and welfare of individuals provided services under the waiver and to assure financial accountability for funds expended with respect to such services;

    (B) with respect to individuals 65 years of age or older who—

        (i) are entitled to medical assistance for skilled nursing or intermediate care facility services under the State plan,

        (ii) may require such services, and

(iii) may be eligible for such home or community-based services under such waiver,

the State will provide for an evaluation of the need for such skilled nursing facility or intermediate care facility services; and

(C) such individuals who are determined to be likely to require the level of care provided in a skilled nursing facility or intermediate care facility are informed of the feasible alternatives to the provision of skilled nursing facility or intermediate care facility services, which such individuals may choose if available under the waiver.

Each State with a waiver under this subsection shall provide to the Secretary annually, consistent with a reasonable data collection plan designed by the Secretary, information on the impact of the waiver granted under this subsection on the type and amount of medical assistance provided under the State plan and on the health and welfare of recipients.

(3) A waiver granted under this subsection may include a waiver of the requirements of section 1396a(a)(1) of this title (relating to statewideness), section 1396a(a)(10)(B) of this title (relating to comparability), and section 1396a(a)(10)(C)(i)(III) of this title (relating to income and resource rules applicable in the community). Subject to a termination by the State (with notice to the Secretary) at any time, a waiver under this subsection shall be for an initial term of 3 years and, upon the request of a State, shall be extended for additional 5–year periods unless the Secretary determines that for the previous waiver period the assurances provided under paragraph (2) have not been met. A waiver may provide, with respect to post-eligibility treatment of income of all individuals receiving services under the waiver, that the maximum amount of the individual's income which may be disregarded for any month is equal to the amount that may be allowed for that purpose under a waiver under subsection (c) of this section.

(4) A waiver under this subsection may, consistent with paragraph (2), provide medical assistance to individuals for case management services, homemaker/home health aide services and personal care services, adult day health services, respite care, and other medical and social services that can contribute to the health and well-being of individuals and their ability to reside in a community-based care setting.

(5)(A) In the case of a State having a waiver approved under this subsection, notwithstanding any other provision of section 1396b of this title to the contrary, the total amount expended by the State for medical assistance with respect to skilled nursing facility services, intermediate care facility services, and home and community-based services under the State plan for individuals 65 years of age or older during a waiver year under this subsection may not exceed the projected amount determined under subparagraph (B).

(B) For purposes of subparagraph (A), the projected amount under this subparagraph is the sum of the following:

(i) The aggregate amount of the State's medical assistance under this subchapter for skilled nursing facility services and intermediate care facility services furnished to individuals who have attained the age of 65 for the base year increased by a percentage which is equal to the lesser of 7 percent times the number of years (rounded to the nearest quarter of a year) beginning after the base year and ending at the end of the waiver year involved or the sum of—

(I) the percentage increase (based on an appropriate market-basket index representing the costs of elements of such services) between the beginning of the base year and the beginning of the waiver year involved, plus

(II) the percentage increase between the beginning of the base year and the beginning of the waiver year involved in the number of residents in the State who have attained the age of 65, plus

(III) 2 percent for each year (rounded to the nearest quarter of a year) beginning after the base year and ending at the end of the waiver year.

(ii) The aggregate amount of the State's medical assistance under this subchapter for home and community-based services for individuals who have attained the age of 65 for the base year increased by a percentage which is equal to the lesser of 7 percent times the number of years (rounded to the nearest quarter of a year) beginning after the base year and ending at the end of the waiver year involved or the sum of—

(I) the percentage increase (based on an appropriate market-basket index representing the costs of elements of such services) between the beginning of the base year and the beginning of the waiver year involved, plus

(II) the percentage increase between the beginning of the base year and the beginning of the waiver year involved in the number of residents in the State who have attained the age of 65, plus

(III) 2 percent for each year (rounded to the nearest quarter of a year) beginning after the base year and ending at the end of the waiver year.

(iii) The Secretary shall develop and promulgate by regulation (by not later than October 1, 1989)—

(I) a method, based on an index of appropriately weighted indicators of changes in the wages and prices of the mix of goods and services which comprise both skilled nursing facility services and intermediate care facility services (regardless of the source of payment for such services), for projecting the percentage increase for purposes of clause (i)(I);

(II) a method, based on an index of appropriately weighted indicators of changes in the wages and prices of the mix of goods and services which comprise home and community-based services (regardless of the source of payment for such services), for projecting the percentage increase for purposes of clause (ii)(I); and

(III) a method for projecting, on a State specific basis, the percentage increase in the number of residents in each State who are over 65 years of age for any period.

The Secretary shall develop (by not later than October 1, 1989) a method for projecting, on a State-specific basis, the percentage increase in the number of residents in each State who are over 65 years of age for any period. Effective on and after the date the Secretary promulgates the regulation under clause (iii), any reference in this subparagraph to the "lesser of 7 percent" shall be deemed to be a reference to the "greater of 7 percent".

(iv) If there is enacted after December 22, 1987, an Act which amends this subchapter whose provisions become effective on or after such date and which results in an increase in the aggregate amount of medical assistance under this subchapter for nursing facility services and home and community-based services for individuals who have attained the age of 65 years, the Secretary, at the request of a State with a waiver under this subsection for a waiver year or years and in close consultation with the State, shall adjust the projected amount computed under this subparagraph for the waiver year or years to take into account such increase.

(C) In this paragraph:

(i) The term "home and community-based services" includes services described in sections 1396d(a)(7) and 1396d(a)(8) of this title, services described in subsection (c)(4)(B) of this section, services described in paragraph (4), and personal care services.

(ii)(I) Subject to subclause (II), the term "base year" means the most recent year (ending before December 22, 1987) for which actual final expenditures under this subchapter have been reported to, and accepted by, the Secretary.

(II) For purposes of subparagraph (C), in the case of a State that does not report expenditures on the basis of the age categories described in such subparagraph for a year ending before December 22, 1987, the term "base year" means fiscal year 1989.

(iii) The term "intermediate care facility services" does not include services furnished in an institution certified in accordance with section 1396d(d) of this title.

(6)(A) A determination by the Secretary to deny a request for a waiver (or extension of waiver) under this subsection shall be subject to review to the extent provided under section 1316(b) of this title.

(B) Notwithstanding any other provision of this chapter, if the Secretary denies a request of the State for an extension of a waiver under this subsection, any waiver under this subsection in effect on the date such request is made shall remain in effect for a period of not less than 90 days after the date on which the Secretary denies such request (or, if the State seeks review of such determination in accordance with subparagraph (A), the date on which a final determination is made with respect to such review).

(e) Waiver for children infected with AIDS or drug dependent at birth

(1)(A) Subject to paragraph (2), the Secretary shall grant a waiver to provide that a State plan approved under this subchapter shall include as "medical assistance" under such plan payment for part or all of the cost of nursing care, respite care, physicians' services, prescribed drugs, medical devices and supplies, transportation services, and such other services requested by the State as the Secretary may approve which are provided pursuant to a written plan of care to a child described in subparagraph (B) with respect to whom there has been a determination that but for the provision of such services the infants would be likely to require the level of care provided in a hospital or nursing facility the cost of which could be reimbursed under the State plan.

(B) Children described in this subparagraph are individuals under 5 years of age who—

(i) at the time of birth were infected with (or tested positively for) the etiologic agent for acquired immune deficiency syndrome (AIDS),

(ii) have such syndrome, or

(iii) at the time of birth were dependent on heroin, cocaine, or phencyclidine,

and with respect to whom adoption or foster care assistance is (or will be) made available under part E of subchapter IV of this chapter.

(2) A waiver shall not be granted under this subsection unless the State provides assurances satisfactory to the Secretary that—

(A) necessary safeguards (including adequate standards for provider participation) have been taken to protect the health and welfare of individuals provided services under the waiver and to assure financial accountability for funds expended with respect to such services;

(B) under such waiver the average per capita expenditure estimated by the State in any fiscal year for medical assistance provided with respect to such individuals does not exceed 100 percent of the average per capita expenditure that the State reasonably estimates would have been made in that fiscal year for expenditures under the State plan for such individuals if the waiver had not been granted; and

(C) the State will provide to the Secretary annually, consistent with a data collection plan designed by the Secretary, information on the impact of the waiver granted under this subsection on the type and amount of medical assistance provided under the State plan and on the health and welfare of recipients.

(3) A waiver granted under this subsection may include a waiver of the requirements of section 1396a(a)(1) of this title (relating to statewideness) and section 1396a(a)(10)(B) of this title (relating to comparability). A waiver under this subsection shall be for an initial term of 3 years and, upon the request of a State, shall be extended for additional five-year periods unless the Secretary determines that for the previous waiver period the assurances provided under paragraph (2) have not been met.

(4) The provisions of paragraph (6) of subsection (d) of this section shall apply to this subsection in the same manner as it applies to subsection (d) of this section.

(f) Monitor of implementation of waivers; termination of waiver for noncompliance; time limitation for action on requests for plan approval, amendments, or waivers

(1) The Secretary shall monitor the implementation of waivers granted under this section to assure that the requirements for such waiver are being met and shall, after notice and opportunity for a hearing, terminate any such waiver where he finds noncompliance has occurred.

(2) A request to the Secretary from a State for approval of a proposed State plan or plan amendment or a waiver of a requirement of this subchapter submitted by the State pursuant to a provision of this subchapter shall be deemed granted unless the Secretary, within 90 days after the date of its submission to the Secretary, either denies such request in writing or informs the State agency in writing with respect to any additional information which is needed in order to make a final determination with respect to the request. After the date the Secretary receives such additional information, the request shall be deemed granted unless the Secretary, within 90 days of such date, denies such request.

(g) Optional targeted case management services

(1) A State may provide, as medical assistance, case management services under the plan without regard to the requirements of section 1396a(a)(1) of this title and section 1396a(a)(10)(B) of this title. The provision of case management services under this subsection shall not restrict the choice of the individual to receive medical assistance in violation of section 1396a(a)(23) of this title. A State may limit the provision of case management services under this subsection to individuals with acquired immune deficiency syndrome (AIDS), or with AIDS-related conditions, or with either, or to individuals described in section 1396a(z)(1)(A) of this title and a State may limit the provision of case management services under this subsection to individuals with chronic mental illness. The State may limit the case managers available with respect to case management services for eligible individuals with developmental disabilities or with chronic mental illness in order to ensure that the case managers for such individuals are capable of ensuring that such individuals receive needed services.

(2) For purposes of this subsection, the term "case management services" means services which will assist individuals eligible under the plan in gaining access to needed medical, social, educational, and other services.

(h) Period of waivers; continuations

No waiver under this section (other than a waiver under subsection (c), (d), or (e) of this section) may extend over a period of longer than two years unless the State requests continuation of such waiver, and such request shall be deemed granted unless the Secretary, within 90 days after the date of its submission to the Secretary, either denies such request in writing or informs the State agency in writing with respect to any additional information which is needed in order to make a final determination with respect to the request. After the date the Secretary receives such additional information, the request shall be deemed granted unless the Secretary, within 90 days of such date, denies such request.

§ 1396o. Use of enrollment fees, premiums, deductions, cost sharing, and similar charges

(a) Imposition of certain charges under plan in case of individuals described in section 1396a(a)(10)(A) or (E)(i)

Subject to subsection (g), the State plan shall provide that in the case of individuals described in subparagraph (A) or (E)(i) of section 1396a(a)(10) of this title who are eligible under the plan—

(1) no enrollment fee, premium, or similar charge will be imposed under the plan (except for a premium imposed under subsection (c) of this section);

(2) no deduction, cost sharing or similar charge will be imposed under the plan with respect to—

(A) services furnished to individuals under 18 years of age (and, at the option of the State, individuals under 21, 20, or 19 years of age, or any reasonable category of individuals 18 years of age or over),

(B) services furnished to pregnant women, if such services relate to the pregnancy or to any other medical condition which may complicate the pregnancy (or, at the option of the State, any services furnished to pregnant women),

(C) services furnished to any individual who is an inpatient in a hospital, nursing facility, intermediate care facility for the mentally retarded, or other medical institution, if such individual is required, as a condition of receiving services in such institution under the State plan, to spend for costs of medical care all but a minimal amount of his income required for personal needs,

(D) emergency services (as defined by the Secretary), family planning services and supplies described in section 1396d(a)(4)(C) of this title, or

(E) services furnished to an individual who is receiving hospice care (as defined in section 1396d(o) of this title); and

(3) any deduction, cost sharing, or similar charge imposed under the plan with respect to other such individuals or other care and services will be nominal in amount (as determined by the Secretary in regulations which shall, if the definition of "nominal" under the regulations in effect on July 1, 1982 is changed, take into account the level of cash assistance provided in such State and such other criteria as the Secretary determines to be appropriate); except that a deduction, cost-sharing, or similar charge of up to twice the nominal amount established for outpatient services may be imposed by a State under a waiver granted by the Secretary for services received at a hospital emergency room if the services are not emergency services (referred to in paragraph (2)(D)) and the State has established to the satisfaction of the Secretary that individuals eligible for services under the plan have actually available and accessible to them alternative sources of nonemergency, outpatient services.

(b) Imposition of certain charges under plan in case of individuals other than those described in section 1396a(a)(10)(A) or (E)

The State plan shall provide that in the case of individuals other than those described in subparagraph (A) or (E) of section 1396a(a)(10) of this title who are eligible under the plan—

(1) there may be imposed an enrollment fee, premium, or similar charge, which (as determined in accordance with standards prescribed by the Secretary) is related to the individual's income,

(2) no deduction, cost sharing, or similar charge will be imposed under the plan with respect to—

(A) services furnished to individuals under 18 years of age (and, at the option of the State, individuals under 21, 20, or 19 years of age, or any reasonable category of individuals 18 years of age or over),

(B) services furnished to pregnant women, if such services relate to the pregnancy or to any other medical condition which may complicate the pregnancy (or, at the option of the State, any services furnished to pregnant women),

(C) services furnished to any individual who is an inpatient in a hospital, nursing facility, intermediate care facility for the mentally retarded, or other medical institution, if such individual is required, as a condition of receiving services in such institution under the State plan, to spend for costs of medical care all but a minimal amount of his income required for personal needs,

(D) emergency services (as defined by the Secretary), family planning services and supplies described in section 1396d(a)(4)(C) of this title, or

(E) services furnished to an individual who is receiving hospice care (as defined in section 1396d(*o*) of this title); and

(3) any deduction, cost sharing, or similar charge imposed under the plan with respect to other such individuals or other care and services will be nominal in amount (as determined by the Secretary in regulations which shall, if the definition of "nominal" under the regulations in effect on July 1, 1982 is changed, take into account the level of cash assistance provided in such State and such other criteria as the Secretary determines to be appropriate); except that a deduction, cost-sharing, or similar charge of up to twice the nominal amount established for outpatient services may be imposed by a State under a waiver granted by the Secretary for services received at a hospital emergency room if the services are not emergency services (referred to in paragraph (2)(D)) and the State has established to the satisfaction of the Secretary that individuals eligible for services under the plan have actually available and accessible to them alternative sources of nonemergency, outpatient services.

(c) Imposition of monthly premium; persons affected; amount; prepayment; failure to pay; use of funds from other programs

(1) The State plan of a State may at the option of the State provide for imposing a monthly premium (in an amount that does not exceed the limit established under paragraph (2)) with respect to an individual described in subparagraph (A) or (B) of section 1396a(*l*)(1) of this title who is receiving medical assistance on the basis of section 1396a(a)(10)(A)(ii)(IX) of this title and whose family income (as determined in accordance with the methodology specified in section 1396a(*l*)(3) of this title) equals or exceeds 150 percent of the income official poverty line (as defined by the Office of Management and Budget, and revised annually in accordance with section 9902(2) of this title) applicable to a family of the size involved.

(2) In no case may the amount of any premium imposed under paragraph (1) exceed 10 percent of the amount by which the family income (less expenses for the care of a dependent child) of an individual exceeds 150 percent of the line described in paragraph (1).

(3) A State shall not require prepayment of a premium imposed pursuant to paragraph (1) and shall not terminate eligibility of an individual for medical assistance under this subchapter on the basis of failure to pay any such premium until such failure continues for a period of not less than 60 days. The State may waive payment of any such premium in any case where the State determines that requiring such payment would create an undue hardship.

(4) A State may permit State or local funds available under other programs to be used for payment of a premium imposed under paragraph (1). Payment of a premium with such funds shall not be counted as income to the individual with respect to whom such payment is made.

(d) Premiums for qualified disabled and working individuals described in section 1396d(s)

With respect to a qualified disabled and working individual described in section 1396d(s) of this title whose income (as determined under paragraph (3) of that section) exceeds 150 percent of the official poverty line referred to in that paragraph, the State plan of a State may provide for the charging of a premium (expressed as a percentage of the medicare cost-sharing described in section 1396d(p)(3)(A)(i) of this title provided with respect to the individual) according to a sliding scale under which such percentage increases from 0 percent to 100 percent, in reasonable increments (as determined by the Secretary), as the individual's income increases from 150 percent of such poverty line to 200 percent of such poverty line.

(e) Prohibition of denial of services on basis of individual's inability to pay certain charges

The State plan shall require that no provider participating under the State plan may deny care or services to an individual eligible for such care or services under the plan on account of such individual's inability to pay a deduction, cost sharing, or similar charge. The requirements of this subsection shall not extinguish the liability of the individual to whom the care or services were furnished for payment of the deduction, cost sharing, or similar charge.

(f) Charges imposed under waiver authority of Secretary

No deduction, cost sharing, or similar charge may be imposed under any waiver authority of the Secretary, except as provided in subsections (a)(3) and (b)(3) of this section, unless such waiver is for a demonstration project which the Secretary finds after public notice and opportunity for comment—

(1) will test a unique and previously untested use of copayments,

(2) is limited to a period of not more than two years,

(3) will provide benefits to recipients of medical assistance which can reasonably be expected to be equivalent to the risks to the recipients,

(4) is based on a reasonable hypothesis which the demonstration is designed to test in a methodologically sound manner, including the use of control groups of similar recipients of medical assistance in the area, and

(5) is voluntary, or makes provision for assumption of liability for preventable damage to the health of recipients of medical assistance resulting from involuntary participation.

(g) State authority to impose income-related premiums and cost sharing

With respect to individuals provided medical assistance only under subclause (xv) or (xvi) of section 1396a(a)(10)(a)(ii) of this title—

(1) a State may (in a uniform manner for individuals described in either such subclause)—

(A) require such individuals to pay premiums or other cost-sharing charges set on a sliding scale based on income that the State may determine; and

(B) require payment of 100 percent of such premiums for such year in the case of such an individual who has income for a year that exceeds 250 percent of the income official poverty line (referred to in subsection (c)(1)) applicable to a family of the size involved, except that in the case of such an individual who has income for a year that does not exceed 450 percent of such poverty line, such requirement may only apply to the extent such premiums do not exceed 7.5 percent of such income; and

(2) such State shall require payment of 100 percent of such premiums for a year by such an individual whose adjusted gross income (as defined in section 62 of the Internal Revenue Code of 1986) for such year exceeds $75,000, except that a State may choose to subsidize such premiums by using State funds which may not be federally matched under this title.

In the case of any calendar year beginning after 2000, the dollar amount specified in paragraph (2) shall be increased in accordance with the provisions of section 415(i)(2)(A)(ii) of this title.

* * *

§ 1396p. Liens, adjustments and recoveries, and transfers of assets

(a) Imposition of lien against the property of an individual on account of medical assistance rendered to him under a State plan

(1) No lien may be imposed against the property of any individual prior to his death on account of medical assistance paid or to be paid on his behalf under the State plan, except—

(A) pursuant to the judgment of a court on account of benefits incorrectly paid on behalf of such individual, or

(B) in the case of the real property of an individual—

(i) who is an inpatient in a nursing facility, intermediate care facility for the mentally retarded, or other medical institution, if such individual is required, as a condition of receiving services in such institution under the State plan, to spend for costs of medical care all but a minimal amount of his income required for personal needs, and

(ii) with respect to whom the State determines, after notice and opportunity for a hearing (in accordance with procedures established by the State), that he cannot reasonably be expected to be discharged from the medical institution and to return home,

except as provided in paragraph (2).

(2) No lien may be imposed under paragraph (1)(B) on such individual's home if—

(A) the spouse of such individual,

(B) such individual's child who is under age 21, or (with respect to States eligible to participate in the State program established under title XVI [§§ 1381 et seq.]) is blind or permanently and totally disabled, or (with respect to States which are not eligible to participate in such program) is blind or disabled as defined in section 1614 [§ 1382c], or

(C) a sibling of such individual (who has an equity interest in such home and who was residing in such individual's home for a period of at least one year immediately before the date of the individual's admission to the medical institution),

is lawfully residing in such home.

(3) Any lien imposed with respect to an individual pursuant to paragraph (1)(B) shall dissolve upon that individual's discharge from the medical institution and return home.

(b) Adjustment or recovery of medical assistance correctly paid under a State plan

(1) No adjustment or recovery of any medical assistance correctly paid on behalf of an individual under the State plan may be made, except that the State shall seek adjustment or recovery of any medical assistance correctly paid on behalf of an individual under the State plan in the case of the following individuals:

(A) In the case of an individual described in subsection (a)(1)(B), the State shall seek adjustment or recovery from the individual's

935

estate or upon sale of the property subject to a lien imposed on account of medical assistance paid on behalf of the individual.

(B) In the case of an individual who was 55 years of age or older when the individual received such medical assistance, the State shall seek adjustment or recovery from the individual's estate, but only for medical assistance consisting of—

    (i) nursing facility services, home and community-based services, and related hospital and prescription drug services, or

    (ii) at the option of the State, any items or services under the State plan.

(C)(i) In the case of an individual who has received (or is entitled to receive) benefits under a long-term care insurance policy in connection with which assets or resources are disregarded in the manner described in clause (ii), except as provided in such clause, the State shall seek adjustment or recovery from the individual's estate on account of medical assistance paid on behalf of the individual for nursing facility and other long-term care services.

    (ii) Clause (i) shall not apply in the case of an individual who received medical assistance under a State plan of a State which had a State plan amendment approved as of May 14, 1993, which provided for the disregard of any assets or resources—

        (I) to the extent that payments are made under a long-term care insurance policy; or

        (II) because an individual has received (or is entitled to receive) benefits under a long-term care insurance policy.

(2) Any adjustment or recovery under paragraph (1) may be made only after the death of the individual's surviving spouse, if any, and only at a time—

(A) when he has no surviving child who is under age 21, or (with respect to States eligible to participate in the State program established under title XVI [§§ 1381 et seq.]) is blind or permanently and totally disabled, or (with respect to States which are not eligible to participate in such program) is blind or disabled as defined in section 1614 [§ 1382c]; and

(B) in the case of a lien on an individual's home under subsection (a)(1)(B), when—

    (i) no sibling of the individual (who was residing in the individual's home for a period of at least one year immediately before the date of the individual's admission to the medical institution), and

(ii) no son or daughter of the individual (who was residing in the individual's home for a period of at least two years immediately before the date of the individual's admission to the medical institution, and who establishes to the satisfaction of the State that he or she provided care to such individual which permitted such individual to reside at home rather than in an institution),

is lawfully residing in such home who has lawfully resided in such home on a continuous basis since the date of the individual's admission to the medical institution.

(3) The State agency shall establish procedures (in accordance with standards specified by the Secretary) under which the agency shall waive the application of this subsection (other than paragraph (1)(C)) if such application would work an undue hardship as determined on the basis of criteria established by the Secretary.

(4) For purposes of this subsection, the term "estate", with respect to a deceased individual—

(A) shall include all real and personal property and other assets included within the individual's estate, as defined for purposes of State probate law; and

(B) may include, at the option of the State (and shall include, in the case of an individual to whom paragraph (1)(C)(i) applies), any other real and personal property and other assets in which the individual had any legal title or interest at the time of death (to the extent of such interest), including such assets conveyed to a survivor, heir, or assign of the deceased individual through joint tenancy, tenancy in common, survivorship, life estate, living trust, or other arrangement.

(c) Taking into account certain transfers of assets

(1)(A) In order to meet the requirements of this subsection for purposes of section 1902(a)(18) [§ 1396a(a)(18)], the State plan must provide that if an institutionalized individual or the spouse of such an individual (or, at the option of a State, a noninstitutionalized individual or the spouse of such an individual) disposes of assets for less than fair market value on or after the look-back date specified in subparagraph (B)(i), the individual is ineligible for medical assistance for services described in subparagraph (C)(i) (or, in the case of a noninstitutionalized individual, for the services described in subparagraph (C)(ii)) during the period beginning on the date specified in subparagraph (D) and equal to the number of months specified in subparagraph (E).

(B)(i) The look-back date specified in this subparagraph is a date that is 36 months (or, in the case of payments from a trust or portions of a trust that are treated as assets disposed of by the individual pursuant to paragraph (3)(A)(iii) or (3)(B)(ii) of subsection (d), 60 months) before the date specified in clause (ii).

(ii) The date specified in this clause, with respect to—

(I) an institutionalized individual is the first date as of which the individual both is an institutionalized individual and has applied for medical assistance under the State plan, or

(II) a noninstitutionalized individual is the date on which the individual applies for medical assistance under the State plan or, if later, the date on which the individual disposes of assets for less than fair market value.

(C)(i) The services described in this subparagraph with respect to an institutionalized individual are the following:

(I) Nursing facility services.

(II) A level of care in any institution equivalent to that of nursing facility services.

(III) Home or community-based services furnished under a waiver granted under subsection (c) or (d) of section 1915 [§ 1396n(c) or (d)].

(ii) The services described in this subparagraph with respect to a noninstitutionalized individual are services (not including any services described in clause (i)) that are described in paragraph (7), (22), or (24) of section 1905(a) [§ 1396d(a)(7), (22), or (24)], and, at the option of a State, other long-term care services for which medical assistance is otherwise available under the State plan to individuals requiring long-term care.

(D) The date specified in this subparagraph is the first day of the first month during or after which assets have been transferred for less than fair market value and which does not occur in any other periods of ineligibility under this subsection.

(E)(i) With respect to an institutionalized individual, the number of months of ineligibility under this subparagraph for an individual shall be equal to—

(I) the total, cumulative uncompensated value of all assets transferred by the individual (or individual's spouse) on or after the look-back date specified in subparagraph (B)(i), divided by

(II) the average monthly cost to a private patient of nursing facility services in the State (or, at the option of the State, in the community in which the individual is institutionalized) at the time of application.

(ii) With respect to a noninstitutionalized individual, the number of months of ineligibility under this subparagraph for an individual shall not be greater than a number equal to—

(I) the total, cumulative uncompensated value of all assets transferred by the individual (or individual's spouse) on or after the look-back date specified in subparagraph (B)(i), divided by

(II) the average monthly cost to a private patient of nursing facility services in the State (or, at the option of the State, in the community in which the individual is institutionalized) at the time of application.

(iii) The number of months of ineligibility otherwise determined under clause (i) or (ii) with respect to the disposal of an asset shall be reduced—

(I) in the case of periods of ineligibility determined under clause (i), by the number of months of ineligibility applicable to the individual under clause (ii) as a result of such disposal, and

(II) in the case of periods of ineligibility determined under clause (ii), by the number of months of ineligibility applicable to the individual under clause (i) as a result of such disposal.

(2) An individual shall not be ineligible for medical assistance by reason of paragraph (1) to the extent that—

(A) the assets transferred were a home and title to the home was transferred to—

(i) the spouse of such individual;

(ii) a child of such individual who (I) is under age 21, or (II) (with respect to States eligible to participate in the State program established under title XVI [§§ 1381 et seq.]) is blind or permanently and totally disabled, or (with respect to States which are not eligible to participate in such program) is blind or disabled as defined in section 1614 [§ 1382c];

(iii) a sibling of such individual who has an equity interest in such home and who was residing in such individual's home for a period of at least one year immediately before the date the individual becomes an institutionalized individual; or

(iv) a son or daughter of such individual (other than a child described in clause (ii)) who was residing in such individual's home for a period of at least two years immediately before the date the individual becomes an institutionalized individual, and who (as determined by the State) provided care to such individual which permitted such individual to reside at home rather than in such an institution or facility;

(B) the assets—

(i) were transferred to the individual's spouse or to another for the sole benefit of the individual's spouse,

(ii) were transferred from the individual's spouse to another for the sole benefit of the individual's spouse,

(iii) were transferred to, or to a trust (including a trust described in subsection (d)(4)) established solely for the benefit of, the individual's child described in subparagraph (A)(ii)(II), or

(iv) were transferred to a trust (including a trust described in subsection (d)(4)) established solely for the benefit of an individual under 65 years of age who is disabled (as defined in section 1614(a)(3)) [§ 1382c(a)(3)];

(C) a satisfactory showing is made to the State (in accordance with regulations promulgated by the Secretary) that (i) the individual intended to dispose of the assets either at fair market value, or for other valuable consideration, (ii) the assets were transferred exclusively for a purpose other than to qualify for medical assistance, or (iii) all assets transferred for less than fair market value have been returned to the individual; or

(D) the State determines, under procedures established by the State (in accordance with standards specified by the Secretary), that the denial of eligibility would work an undue hardship as determined on the basis of criteria established by the Secretary; [.]

(3) For purposes of this subsection, in the case of an asset held by an individual in common with another person or persons in a joint tenancy, tenancy in common, or similar arrangement, the asset (or the affected portion of such asset) shall be considered to be transferred by such individual when any action is taken, either by such individual or by any other person, that reduces or eliminates such individual's ownership or control of such asset.

(4) A State (including a State which has elected treatment under section 1902(f) [§ 1396a(f)]) may not provide for any period of ineligibility for an individual due to transfer of resources for less than fair market value except in accordance with this subsection. In the case of a transfer by the spouse of an individual which results in a period of ineligibility for medical assistance under a State plan for such individual, a State shall, using a reasonable methodology (as specified by the Secretary), apportion such period of ineligibility (or any portion of such period) among the individual and the individual's spouse if the spouse otherwise becomes eligible for medical assistance under the State plan.

(5) In this subsection, the term "resources" has the meaning given such term in section 1613 [§ 1382b], without regard to the exclusion described in subsection (a)(1) thereof.

(d) Treatment of trust amounts

(1) For purposes of determining an individual's eligibility for, or amount of, benefits under a State plan under this title [§§ 1396 et seq.], subject to paragraph (4), the rules specified in paragraph (3) shall apply to a trust established by such individual.

(2)(A) For purposes of this subsection, an individual shall be considered to have established a trust if assets of the individual were used to form all or part of the corpus of the trust and if any of the following individuals established such trust other than by will:

    (i) The individual.

    (ii) The individual's spouse.

    (iii) A person, including a court or administrative body, with legal authority to act in place of or on behalf of the individual or the individual's spouse.

    (iv) A person, including any court or administrative body, acting at the direction or upon the request of the individual or the individual's spouse.

(B) In the case of a trust the corpus of which includes assets of an individual (as determined under subparagraph (A)) and assets of any other person or persons, the provisions of this subsection shall apply to the portion of the trust attributable to the assets of the individual.

(C) Subject to paragraph (4), this subsection shall apply without regard to—

    (i) the purposes for which a trust is established,

    (ii) whether the trustees have or exercise any discretion under the trust,

    (iii) any restrictions on when or whether distributions may be made from the trust, or

    (iv) any restrictions on the use of distributions from the trust.

(3)(A) In the case of a revocable trust—

    (i) the corpus of the trust shall be considered resources available to the individual,

    (ii) payments from the trust to or for the benefit of the individual shall be considered income of the individual, and

(iii) any other payments from the trust shall be considered assets disposed of by the individual for purposes of subsection (c).

(B) In the case of an irrevocable trust—

(i) if there are any circumstances under which payment from the trust could be made to or for the benefit of the individual, the portion of the corpus from which, or the income on the corpus from which, payment to the individual could be made shall be considered resources available to the individual, and payments from that portion of the corpus or income—

(I) to or for the benefit of the individual, shall be considered income of the individual, and

(II) for any other purpose, shall be considered a transfer of assets by the individual subject to subsection (c); and

(ii) any portion of the trust from which, or any income on the corpus from which, no payment could under any circumstances be made to the individual shall be considered, as of the date of establishment of the trust (or, if later, the date on which payment to the individual was foreclosed) to be assets disposed by the individual for purposes of subsection (c), and the value of the trust shall be determined for purposes of such subsection by including the amount of any payments made from such portion of the trust after such date.

(4) This subsection shall not apply to any of the following trusts:

(A) A trust containing the assets of an individual under age 65 who is disabled (as defined in section 1614(a)(3) [§ 1382c(a)(3)]) and which is established for the benefit of such individual by a parent, grandparent, legal guardian of the individual, or a court if the State will receive all amounts remaining in the trust upon the death of such individual up to an amount equal to the total medical assistance paid on behalf of the individual under a State plan under this title [42 USCS §§ 1396 et seq.].

(B) A trust established in a State for the benefit of an individual if—

(i) the trust is composed only of pension, Social Security, and other income to the individual (and accumulated income in the trust),

(ii) the State will receive all amounts remaining in the trust upon the death of such individual up to an amount equal to the total medical assistance paid on behalf of the individual under a State plan under this title [42 USCS §§ 1396 et seq.], and

(iii) the State makes medical assistance available to individuals described in section 1902(a)(10)(A)(ii)(V)

[§ 1396a(a)(10)(A)(ii)(V)], but does not make such assistance available to individuals for nursing facility services under section 1902(a)(10)(C) [§ 1396a(a)(10)(C)].

(C) A trust containing the assets of an individual who is disabled (as defined in section 1614(a)(3)) [§ 1382c(a)(3)] that meets the following conditions:

(i) The trust is established and managed by a non-profit association.

(ii) A separate account is maintained for each beneficiary of the trust, but, for purposes of investment and management of funds, the trust pools these accounts.

(iii) Accounts in the trust are established solely for the benefit of individuals who are disabled (as defined in section 1614(a)(3)) [§ 1382c(a)(3)] by the parent, grandparent, or legal guardian of such individuals, by such individuals, or by a court.

(iv) To the extent that amounts remaining in the beneficiary's account upon the death of the beneficiary are not retained by the trust, the trust pays to the State from such remaining amounts in the account an amount equal to the total amount of medical assistance paid on behalf of the beneficiary under the State plan under this title [§§ 1396 et seq.].

(5) The State agency shall establish procedures (in accordance with standards specified by the Secretary) under which the agency waives the application of this subsection with respect to an individual if the individual establishes that such application would work an undue hardship on the individual as determined on the basis of criteria established by the Secretary.

(6) The term "trust" includes any legal instrument or device that is similar to a trust but includes an annuity only to such extent and in such manner as the Secretary specifies.

(e) Definitions. In this section, the following definitions shall apply:

(1) The term "assets", with respect to an individual, includes all income and resources of the individual and of the individual's spouse, including any income or resources which the individual or such individual's spouse is entitled to but does not receive because of action—

(A) by the individual or such individual's spouse,

(B) by a person, including a court or administrative body, with legal authority to act in place of or on behalf of the individual or such individual's spouse, or

(C) by any person, including any court or administrative body, acting at the direction or upon the request of the individual or such individual's spouse.

(2) The term "income" has the meaning given such term in section 1612 [42 USCA § 1382a].

(3) The term "institutionalized individual" means an individual who is an inpatient in a nursing facility, who is an inpatient in a medical institution and with respect to whom payment is made based on a level of care provided in a nursing facility, or who is described in section 1902(a)(10)(A)(ii)(VI) [§ 1396a(a)(10)(A)(ii)(VI)].

(4) The term "noninstitutionalized individual" means an individual receiving any of the services specified in subsection (c)(1)(C)(ii).

(5) The term "resources" has the meaning given such term in section 1613 [42 USCA § 1382b], without regard (in the case of an institutionalized individual) to the exclusion described in subsection (a)(1) of such section.

* * *

§ 1396r. Requirements for nursing facilities

(a) "Nursing facility" defined

In this subchapter, the term "nursing facility" means an institution (or a distinct part of an institution) which—

(1) is primarily engaged in providing to residents—

(A) skilled nursing care and related services for residents who require medical or nursing care,

(B) rehabilitation services for the rehabilitation of injured, disabled, or sick persons, or

(C) on a regular basis, health-related care and services to individuals who because of their mental or physical condition require care and services (above the level of room and board) which can be made available to them only through institutional facilities,

and is not primarily for the care and treatment of mental diseases;

(2) has in effect a transfer agreement (meeting the requirements of section 1395x(*l*) of this title) with one or more hospitals having agreements in effect under section 1395cc of this title; and

(3) meets the requirements for a nursing facility described in subsections (b), (c), and (d) of this section.

Such term also includes any facility which is located in a State on an Indian reservation and is certified by the Secretary as meeting the requirements of paragraph (1) and subsections (b), (c), and (d) of this section.

(b) Requirements relating to provision of services

(1) Quality of life

(A) In general

A nursing facility must care for its residents in such a manner and in such an environment as will promote maintenance or enhancement of the quality of life of each resident.

(B) Quality assessment and assurance

A nursing facility must maintain a quality assessment and assurance committee, consisting of the director of nursing services, a physician designated by the facility, and at least 3 other members of the facility's staff, which (i) meets at least quarterly to identify issues with respect to which quality assessment and assurance activities are necessary and (ii) develops and implements appropriate plans of action to correct identified quality deficiencies. A State or the Secretary may not require disclosure of the records of such committee except insofar as such disclosure is related to the compliance of such committee with the requirements of this subparagraph.

(2) Scope of services and activities under plan of care

A nursing facility must provide services and activities to attain or maintain the highest practicable physical, mental, and psychosocial well-being of each resident in accordance with a written plan of care which—

(A) describes the medical, nursing, and psychosocial needs of the resident and how such needs will be met;

(B) is initially prepared, with the participation to the extent practicable of the resident or the resident's family or legal representative, by a team which includes the resident's attending physician and a registered professional nurse with responsibility for the resident; and

(C) is periodically reviewed and revised by such team after each assessment under paragraph (3).

(3) Residents' assessment

(A) Requirement

A nursing facility must conduct a comprehensive, accurate, standardized, reproducible assessment of each resident's functional capacity, which assessment—

(i) describes the resident's capability to perform daily life functions and significant impairments in functional capacity;

(ii) is based on a uniform minimum data set specified by the Secretary under subsection (f)(6)(A) of this section;

(iii) uses an instrument which is specified by the State under subsection (e)(5) of this section; and

(iv) includes the identification of medical problems.

(B) Certification

(i) In general

Each such assessment must be conducted or coordinated (with the appropriate participation of health professionals) by a registered professional nurse who signs and certifies the completion of the assessment. Each individual who completes a portion of such an assessment shall sign and certify as to the accuracy of that portion of the assessment.

(ii) Penalty for falsification

(I) An individual who willfully and knowingly certifies under clause (i) a material and false statement in a resident assessment is subject to a civil money penalty of not more than $1,000 with respect to each assessment.

(II) An individual who willfully and knowingly causes another individual to certify under clause (i) a material and false statement in a resident assessment is subject to a civil money penalty of not more than $5,000 with respect to each assessment.

(III) The provisions of section 1320a–7a of this title (other than subsections (a) and (b)) shall apply to a civil money penalty under this clause in the same manner as such provisions apply to a penalty or proceeding under section 1320a–7a(a) of this title.

(iii) Use of independent assessors

If a State determines, under a survey under subsection (g) of this section or otherwise, that there has been a knowing and willful certification of false assessments under this paragraph, the State may require (for a period specified by the State) that resident assessments under this paragraph be conducted and certified by individuals who are independent of the facility and who are approved by the State.

(C) Frequency

(i) In general

Such an assessment must be conducted—

(I) promptly upon (but no later than 14 days after the date of) admission for each individual admitted on or after October 1, 1990, and by not later than October 1, 1991, for each resident of the facility on that date;

(II) promptly after a significant change in the resident's physical or mental condition; and

(III) in no case less often than once every 12 months.

(ii) Resident review

The nursing facility must examine each resident no less frequently than once every 3 months and, as appropriate, revise the resident's assessment to assure the continuing accuracy of the assessment.

(D) Use

The results of such an assessment shall be used in developing, reviewing, and revising the resident's plan of care under paragraph (2).

(E) Coordination

Such assessments shall be coordinated with any State-required preadmission screening program to the maximum extent practicable in order to avoid duplicative testing and effort. In addition, a nursing facility shall notify the State mental health authority or State mental retardation or developmental disability authority, as applicable, promptly after a significant change in the physical or mental condition of a resident who is mentally ill or mentally retarded.

(F) Requirements relating to preadmission screening for mentally ill and mentally retarded individuals

Except as provided in clauses (ii) and (iii) of subsection (e)(7)(A) of this section, a nursing facility must not admit, on or after January 1, 1989, any new resident who—

    (i) is mentally ill (as defined in subsection (e)(7)(G)(i) of this section) unless the State mental health authority has determined (based on an independent physical and mental evaluation performed by a person or entity other than the State mental health authority) prior to admission that, because of the physical and mental condition of the individual, the individual requires the level of services provided by a nursing facility, and, if the individual requires such level of services, whether the individual requires specialized services for mental illness, or

    (ii) is mentally retarded (as defined in subsection (e)(7)(G)(ii) of this section) unless the State mental retardation or developmental disability authority has determined prior to admission that, because of the physical and mental condition of the individual, the individual requires the level of services provided by a nursing facility, and, if the individual requires such level of services, whether the individual requires specialized services for mental retardation.

A State mental health authority and a State mental retardation or developmental disability authority may not delegate (by subcontract or otherwise) their responsibilities under this subparagraph to a nursing facility (or to an entity that has a direct or indirect affiliation or relationship with such a facility).

(4) Provision of services and activities

(A) In general

To the extent needed to fulfill all plans of care described in paragraph (2), a nursing facility must provide (or arrange for the provision of)—

(i) nursing and related services and specialized rehabilitative services to attain or maintain the highest practicable physical, mental, and psychosocial well-being of each resident;

(ii) medically-related social services to attain or maintain the highest practicable physical, mental, and psychosocial well-being of each resident;

(iii) pharmaceutical services (including procedures that assure the accurate acquiring, receiving, dispensing, and administering of all drugs and biologicals) to meet the needs of each resident;

(iv) dietary services that assure that the meals meet the daily nutritional and special dietary needs of each resident;

(v) an on-going program, directed by a qualified professional, of activities designed to meet the interests and the physical, mental, and psychosocial well-being of each resident;

(vi) routine dental services (to the extent covered under the State plan) and emergency dental services to meet the needs of each resident; and

(vii) treatment and services required by mentally ill and mentally retarded residents not otherwise provided or arranged for (or required to be provided or arranged for) by the State.

The services provided or arranged by the facility must meet professional standards of quality.

(B) Qualified persons providing services

Services described in clauses (i), (ii), (iii), (iv), and (vi) of subparagraph (A) must be provided by qualified persons in accordance with each resident's written plan of care.

(C) Required nursing care; facility waivers

(i) General requirements

With respect to nursing facility services provided on or after October 1, 1990, a nursing facility—

(I) except as provided in clause (ii), must provide 24–hour licensed nursing services which are sufficient to meet the nursing needs of its residents, and

(II) except as provided in clause (ii), must use the services of a registered professional nurse for at least 8 consecutive hours a day, 7 days a week.

(ii) Waiver by State

To the extent that a facility is unable to meet the requirements of clause (i), a State may waive such requirements with respect to the facility if—

(I) the facility demonstrates to the satisfaction of the State that the facility has been unable, despite diligent efforts (including offering wages at the community prevailing rate for nursing facilities), to recruit appropriate personnel,

(II) the State determines that a waiver of the requirement will not endanger the health or safety of individuals staying in the facility,

(III) the State finds that, for any such periods in which licensed nursing services are not available, a registered professional nurse or a physician is obligated to respond immediately to telephone calls from the facility,

(IV) the State agency granting a waiver of such requirements provides notice of the waiver to the State long-term care ombudsman (established under section 307(a)(12) of the Older Americans Act of 1965 [*42 U.S.C.A. § 3027(a)(12)]*) and the protection and advocacy system in the State for the mentally ill and the mentally retarded, and

(V) the nursing facility that is granted such a waiver by a State notifies residents of the facility (or, where appropriate, the guardians or legal representatives of such residents) and members of their immediate families of the waiver.

A waiver under this clause shall be subject to annual review and to the review of the Secretary and subject to clause (iii) shall be accepted by the Secretary for purposes of this subchapter to the same extent as is the State's certification of the facility. In granting or renewing a waiver, a State may require the facility to use other qualified, licensed personnel.

(iii) Assumption of waiver authority by Secretary

If the Secretary determines that a State has shown a clear pattern and practice of allowing waivers in the absence of diligent efforts by facilities to meet the staffing requirements, the Secretary shall assume and exercise the authority of the State to grant waivers.

(5) Required training of nurse aides

(A) In general

(i) Except as provided in clause (ii), a nursing facility must not use on a full-time basis any individual as a nurse aide in the facility on or after October 1, 1990, for more than 4 months unless the individual—

(I) has completed a training and competency evaluation program, or a competency evaluation program, approved by the State under subsection (e)(1)(A) of this section, and

(II) is competent to provide nursing or nursing-related services.

(ii) A nursing facility must not use on a temporary, per diem, leased, or on any other basis other than as a permanent employee any individual as a nurse aide in the facility on or after January 1, 1991, unless the individual meets the requirements described in clause (i).

(B) Offering competency evaluation programs for current employees

A nursing facility must provide, for individuals used as a nurse aide by the facility as of January 1, 1990, for a competency evaluation program approved by the State under subsection (e)(1) of this section and such preparation as may be necessary for the individual to complete such a program by October 1, 1990.

(C) Competency

The nursing facility must not permit an individual, other than in a training and competency evaluation program approved by the State, to serve as a nurse aide or provide services of a type for which the individual has not demonstrated competency and must not use such an individual as a nurse aide unless the facility has inquired of any State registry established under subsection (e)(2)(A) of this section that the facility believes will include information concerning the individual.

(D) Re-training required

For purposes of subparagraph (A), if, since an individual's most recent completion of a training and competency evaluation program, there has been a continuous period of 24 consecutive months during none of which the individual performed nursing or nursing-related services for monetary compensation, such individual shall complete a new training and competency evaluation program or a new competency evaluation program.

(E) Regular in-service education

The nursing facility must provide such regular performance review and regular in-service education as assures that individuals used as nurse aides are competent to perform services as nurse aides, including training for individuals providing nursing and nursing-related services to residents with cognitive impairments.

(F) Nurse aide defined

In this paragraph, the term "nurse aide" means any individual providing nursing or nursing-related services to residents in a nursing facility, but does not include an individual—

(i) who is a licensed health professional (as defined in subparagraph (G)) or a registered dietician, or

(ii) who volunteers to provide such services without monetary compensation.

(G) Licensed health professional defined

In this paragraph, the term "licensed health professional" means a physician, physician assistant, nurse practitioner, physical, speech, or occupational therapist, physical or occupational therapy assistant, registered professional nurse, licensed practical nurse, or licensed or certified social worker.

(6) Physician supervision and clinical records

A nursing facility must—

(A) require that the health care of every resident be provided under the supervision of a physician (or, at the option of a State, under the supervision of a nurse practitioner, clinical nurse specialist, or physician assistant who is not an employee of the facility but who is working in collaboration with a physician);

(B) provide for having a physician available to furnish necessary medical care in case of emergency; and

(C) maintain clinical records on all residents, which records include the plans of care (described in paragraph (2)) and the residents' assessments (described in paragraph (3)), as well as the results of any pre-admission screening conducted under subsection (e)(7) of this section.

(7) Required social services

In the case of a nursing facility with more than 120 beds, the facility must have at least one social worker (with at least a bachelor's degree in social work or similar professional qualifications) employed full-time to provide or assure the provision of social services.

(c) Requirements relating to residents' rights [Nursing home residents' bill of rights]

(1) General rights

(A) Specified rights

A nursing facility must protect and promote the rights of each resident, including each of the following rights:

(i) Free choice

The right to choose a personal attending physician, to be fully informed in advance about care and treatment, to be fully informed in advance of any changes in care or treatment that may affect the resident's well-being, and (except with respect to a resident adjudged incompetent) to participate in planning care and treatment or changes in care and treatment.

(ii) Free from restraints

The right to be free from physical or mental abuse, corporal punishment, involuntary seclusion, and any physical or chemical restraints imposed for purposes of discipline or convenience and not required to treat the resident's medical symptoms. Restraints may only be imposed—

> **(I)** to ensure the physical safety of the resident or other residents, and

> **(II)** only upon the written order of a physician that specifies the duration and circumstances under which the restraints are to be used (except in emergency circumstances specified by the Secretary until such an order could reasonably be obtained).

(iii) Privacy

The right to privacy with regard to accommodations, medical treatment, written and telephonic communications, visits, and meetings of family and of resident groups.

(iv) Confidentiality

The right to confidentiality of personal and clinical records and to access to current clinical records of the resident upon request by the resident or the resident's legal representative, within 24 hours (excluding hours occurring during a weekend or holiday) after making such a request.

(v) Accommodation of needs

The right—

> **(I)** to reside and receive services with reasonable accommodation of individual needs and preferences, except where the health or safety of the individual or other residents would be endangered, and

> **(II)** to receive notice before the room or roommate of the resident in the facility is changed.

(vi) Grievances

The right to voice grievances with respect to treatment or care that is (or fails to be) furnished, without discrimination or reprisal for voicing the grievances and the right to prompt efforts by the facility to resolve grievances the resident may have, including those with respect to the behavior of other residents.

(vii) Participation in resident and family groups

The right of the resident to organize and participate in resident groups in the facility and the right of the resident's family to meet in the facility with the families of other residents in the facility.

(viii) Participation in other activities

The right of the resident to participate in social, religious, and community activities that do not interfere with the rights of other residents in the facility.

(ix) Examination of survey results

The right to examine, upon reasonable request, the results of the most recent survey of the facility conducted by the Secretary or a State with respect to the facility and any plan of correction in effect with respect to the facility.

(x) Refusal of certain transfers

The right to refuse a transfer to another room within the facility, if a purpose of the transfer is to relocate the resident from a portion of the facility that is not a skilled nursing facility (for purposes of subchapter XVIII of this chapter) to a portion of the facility that is such a skilled nursing facility.

(xi) Other rights

Any other right established by the Secretary.

Clause (iii) shall not be construed as requiring the provision of a private room. A resident's exercise of a right to refuse transfer under clause (x) shall not affect the resident's eligibility or entitlement to medical assistance under this subchapter or a State's entitlement to Federal medical assistance under this subchapter with respect to services furnished to such a resident.

(B) Notice of rights

A nursing facility must—

(i) inform each resident, orally and in writing at the time of admission to the facility, of the resident's legal rights during the stay at the facility and of the requirements and procedures for establishing eligibility for medical assistance under this subchapter, including the right to request an assessment under section 1396r–5(c)(1)(B) of this title;

(ii) make available to each resident, upon reasonable request, a written statement of such rights (which statement is updated upon changes in such rights) including the notice (if any) of the State developed under subsection (e)(6) of this section;

953

(iii) inform each resident who is entitled to medical assistance under this subchapter—

(I) at the time of admission to the facility or, if later, at the time the resident becomes eligible for such assistance, of the items and services (including those specified under section 1396a(a)(28)(B) of this title) that are included in nursing facility services under the State plan and for which the resident may not be charged (except as permitted in section 1396o of this title), and of those other items and services that the facility offers and for which the resident may be charged and the amount of the charges for such items and services, and

(II) of changes in the items and services described in subclause (I) and of changes in the charges imposed for items and services described in that subclause; and

(iv) inform each other resident, in writing before or at the time of admission and periodically during the resident's stay, of services available in the facility and of related charges for such services, including any charges for services not covered under subchapter XVIII of this chapter or by the facility's basic per diem charge.

The written description of legal rights under this subparagraph shall include a description of the protection of personal funds under paragraph (6) and a statement that a resident may file a complaint with a State survey and certification agency respecting resident abuse and neglect and misappropriation of resident property in the facility.

(C) Rights of incompetent residents

In the case of a resident adjudged incompetent under the laws of a State, the rights of the resident under this subchapter shall devolve upon, and, to the extent judged necessary by a court of competent jurisdiction, be exercised by, the person appointed under State law to act on the resident's behalf.

(D) Use of psychopharmacologic drugs

Psychopharmacologic drugs may be administered only on the orders of a physician and only as part of a plan (included in the written plan of care described in paragraph (2)) designed to eliminate or modify the symptoms for which the drugs are prescribed and only if, at least annually an independent, external consultant reviews the appropriateness of the drug plan of each resident receiving such drugs.

(2) Transfer and discharge rights

(A) In general

A nursing facility must permit each resident to remain in the facility and must not transfer or discharge the resident from the facility unless—

(i) the transfer or discharge is necessary to meet the resident's welfare and the resident's welfare cannot be met in the facility;

(ii) the transfer or discharge is appropriate because the resident's health has improved sufficiently so the resident no longer needs the services provided by the facility;

(iii) the safety of individuals in the facility is endangered;

(iv) the health of individuals in the facility would otherwise be endangered;

(v) the resident has failed, after reasonable and appropriate notice, to pay (or to have paid under this subchapter or subchapter XVIII of this chapter on the resident's behalf) for a stay at the facility; or

(vi) the facility ceases to operate.

In each of the cases described in clauses (i) through (iv), the basis for the transfer or discharge must be documented in the resident's clinical record. In the cases described in clauses (i) and (ii), the documentation must be made by the resident's physician, and in the case described in clause (iv) the documentation must be made by a physician. For purposes of clause (v), in the case of a resident who becomes eligible for assistance under this subchapter after admission to the facility, only charges which may be imposed under this subchapter shall be considered to be allowable.

(B) Pre-transfer and pre-discharge notice

(i) In general

Before effecting a transfer or discharge of a resident, a nursing facility must—

(I) notify the resident (and, if known, an immediate family member of the resident or legal representative) of the transfer or discharge and the reasons therefor,

(II) record the reasons in the resident's clinical record (including any documentation required under subparagraph (A)), and

(III) include in the notice the items described in clause (iii).

(ii) Timing of notice

The notice under clause (i)(I) must be made at least 30 days in advance of the resident's transfer or discharge except—

(I) in a case described in clause (iii) or (iv) of subparagraph (A);

955

(II) in a case described in clause (ii) of subparagraph (A), where the resident's health improves sufficiently to allow a more immediate transfer or discharge;

(III) in a case described in clause (i) of subparagraph (A), where a more immediate transfer or discharge is necessitated by the resident's urgent medical needs; or

(IV) in a case where a resident has not resided in the facility for 30 days.

In the case of such exceptions, notice must be given as many days before the date of the transfer or discharge as is practicable.

(iii) Items included in notice

Each notice under clause (i) must include—

(I) for transfers or discharges effected on or after October 1, 1989, notice of the resident's right to appeal the transfer or discharge under the State process established under subsection (e)(3) of this section;

(II) the name, mailing address, and telephone number of the State long-term care ombudsman (established under title III or VII of the Older Americans Act of 1965 [*42 U.S.C.A. § 3021* et seq. or 3058 et seq.] in accordance with section 712 of the Act [*42 U.S.C.A. § 3058g]*);

(III) in the case of residents with developmental disabilities, the mailing address and telephone number of the agency responsible for the protection and advocacy system for developmentally disabled individuals established under subtitle C of the Developmental Disabilities Assistance and Bill of Rights Act of 2000 [42 U.S.C.A. § 15041 et seq.]; and

(IV) in the case of mentally ill residents (as defined in subsection (e)(7)(G)(i) of this section), the mailing address and telephone number of the agency responsible for the protection and advocacy system for mentally ill individuals established under the Protection and Advocacy for Mentally Ill Individuals Act [*42 U.S.C.A. § 10801* et seq.].

(C) Orientation

A nursing facility must provide sufficient preparation and orientation to residents to ensure safe and orderly transfer or discharge from the facility.

(D) Notice on bed-hold policy and readmission

(i) Notice before transfer

Before a resident of a nursing facility is transferred for hospitalization or therapeutic leave, a nursing facility must provide written information to the resident and an immediate family member or legal representative concerning—

(I) the provisions of the State plan under this subchapter regarding the period (if any) during which the resident will be permitted under the State plan to return and resume residence in the facility, and

(II) the policies of the facility regarding such a period, which policies must be consistent with clause (iii).

(ii) Notice upon transfer

At the time of transfer of a resident to a hospital or for therapeutic leave, a nursing facility must provide written notice to the resident and an immediate family member or legal representative of the duration of any period described in clause (i).

(iii) Permitting resident to return

A nursing facility must establish and follow a written policy under which a resident—

(I) who is eligible for medical assistance for nursing facility services under a State plan,

(II) who is transferred from the facility for hospitalization or therapeutic leave, and

(III) whose hospitalization or therapeutic leave exceeds a period paid for under the State plan for the holding of a bed in the facility for the resident,

will be permitted to be readmitted to the facility immediately upon the first availability of a bed in a semiprivate room in the facility if, at the time of readmission, the resident requires the services provided by the facility.

(E) Information respecting advance directives

A nursing facility must comply with the requirement of section 1396a(w) of this title (relating to maintaining written policies and procedures respecting advance directives).

(F) Continuing rights in case of voluntary withdrawal from participation

(i) In general

In the case of a nursing facility that voluntarily withdraws from participation in a State plan under this subchapter but continues to provide services of the type provided by nursing facilities—

(I) the facility's voluntary withdrawal from participation is not an acceptable basis for the transfer or discharge of residents of the facility who were residing in the facility on the day before the effective date of the withdrawal (including those residents who were not entitled to medical assistance as of such day);

(II) the provisions of this section continue to apply to such residents until the date of their discharge from the facility; and

(III) in the case of each individual who begins residence in the facility after the effective date of such withdrawal, the facility shall provide notice orally and in a prominent manner in writing on a separate page at the time the individual begins residence of the information described in clause (ii) and shall obtain from each such individual at such time an acknowledgment of receipt of such information that is in writing, signed by the individual, and separate from other documents signed by such individual.

Nothing in this subparagraph shall be construed as affecting any requirement of a participation agreement that a nursing facility provide advance notice to the State or the Secretary, or both, of its intention to terminate the agreement.

(ii) Information for new residents

The information described in this clause for a resident is the following:

(I) The facility is not participating in the program under this subchapter with respect to that resident.

(II) The facility may transfer or discharge the resident from the facility at such time as the resident is unable to pay the charges of the facility, even though the resident may have become eligible for medical assistance for nursing facility services under this subchapter.

(iii) Continuation of payments and oversight authority

Notwithstanding any other provision of this subchapter, with respect to the residents described in clause (i)(I), a participation agreement of a facility described in clause (i) is deemed to continue in effect under such plan after the effective date of the facility's voluntary withdrawal from participation under the State plan for purposes of—

(I) receiving payments under the State plan for nursing facility services provided to such residents;

(II) maintaining compliance with all applicable requirements of this subchapter; and

(III) continuing to apply the survey, certification, and enforcement authority provided under subsections (g) and (h) (including involuntary termination of a participation agreement deemed continued under this clause).

(iv) No application to new residents

This paragraph (other than subclause (III) of clause (i)) shall not apply to an individual who begins residence in a facility on or after the effective date of the withdrawal from participation under this subparagraph.

(3) Access and visitation rights

A nursing facility must—

(A) permit immediate access to any resident by any representative of the Secretary, by any representative of the State, by an ombudsman or agency described in subclause (II), (III), or (IV) of paragraph (2)(B)(iii), or by the resident's individual physician;

(B) permit immediate access to a resident, subject to the resident's right to deny or withdraw consent at any time, by immediate family or other relatives of the resident;

(C) permit immediate access to a resident, subject to reasonable restrictions and the resident's right to deny or withdraw consent at any time, by others who are visiting with the consent of the resident;

(D) permit reasonable access to a resident by any entity or individual that provides health, social, legal, or other services to the resident, subject to the resident's right to deny or withdraw consent at any time; and

(E) permit representatives of the State ombudsman (described in paragraph (2)(B)(iii)(II)), with the permission of the resident (or the resident's legal representative) and consistent with State law, to examine a resident's clinical records.

(4) Equal access to quality care

(A) In general

A nursing facility must establish and maintain identical policies and practices regarding transfer, discharge, and the provision of services required under the State plan for all individuals regardless of source of payment.

(B) Construction

(i) Nothing prohibiting any charges for non-medicaid patients

Subparagraph (A) shall not be construed as prohibiting a nursing facility from charging any amount for services furnished, consistent with the notice in paragraph (1)(B) describing such charges.

(ii) No additional services required

Subparagraph (A) shall not be construed as requiring a State to offer additional services on behalf of a resident than are otherwise provided under the State plan.

959

(5) Admissions policy

(A) Admission

With respect to admissions practices, a nursing facility must—

(i)(I) not require individuals applying to reside or residing in the facility to waive their rights to benefits under this subchapter or subchapter XVIII of this chapter,

(II) not require oral or written assurance that such individuals are not eligible for, or will not apply for, benefits under this subchapter or subchapter XVIII of this chapter, and

(III) prominently display in the facility written information, and provide to such individuals oral and written information, about how to apply for and use such benefits and how to receive refunds for previous payments covered by such benefits;

(ii) not require a third party guarantee of payment to the facility as a condition of admission (or expedited admission) to, or continued stay in, the facility; and

(iii) in the case of an individual who is entitled to medical assistance for nursing facility services, not charge, solicit, accept, or receive, in addition to any amount otherwise required to be paid under the State plan under this subchapter, any gift, money, donation, or other consideration as a precondition of admitting (or expediting the admission of) the individual to the facility or as a requirement for the individual's continued stay in the facility.

(B) Construction

(i) No preemption of stricter standards

Subparagraph (A) shall not be construed as preventing States or political subdivisions therein from prohibiting, under State or local law, the discrimination against individuals who are entitled to medical assistance under the State plan with respect to admissions practices of nursing facilities.

(ii) Contracts with legal representatives

Subparagraph (A)(ii) shall not be construed as preventing a facility from requiring an individual, who has legal access to a resident's income or resources available to pay for care in the facility, to sign a contract (without incurring personal financial liability) to provide payment from the resident's income or resources for such care.

(iii) Charges for additional services requested

Subparagraph (A)(iii) shall not be construed as preventing a facility from charging a resident, eligible for medical assistance under the State plan, for items or services the resident has requested and received and that are not specified in the State plan as included in the term "nursing facility services".

(iv) Bona fide contributions

Subparagraph (A)(iii) shall not be construed as prohibiting a nursing facility from soliciting, accepting, or receiving a charitable, religious, or philanthropic contribution from an organization or from a person unrelated to the resident (or potential resident), but only to the extent that such contribution is not a condition of admission, expediting admission, or continued stay in the facility.

(6) Protection of resident funds

(A) In general

The nursing facility—

(i) may not require residents to deposit their personal funds with the facility, and

(ii) upon the written authorization of the resident, must hold, safeguard, and account for such personal funds under a system established and maintained by the facility in accordance with this paragraph.

(B) Management of personal funds

Upon written authorization of a resident under subparagraph (A)(ii), the facility must manage and account for the personal funds of the resident deposited with the facility as follows:

(i) Deposit

The facility must deposit any amount of personal funds in excess of $50 with respect to a resident in an interest bearing account (or accounts) that is separate from any of the facility's operating accounts and credits all interest earned on such separate account to such account. With respect to any other personal funds, the facility must maintain such funds in a non-interest bearing account or petty cash fund.

(ii) Accounting and records

The facility must assure a full and complete separate accounting of each such resident's personal funds, maintain a written record of all financial transactions involving the personal funds of a resident deposited with the facility, and afford the resident (or a legal representative of the resident) reasonable access to such record.

(iii) Notice of certain balances

The facility must notify each resident receiving medical assistance under the State plan under this subchapter when the amount in the resident's account reaches $200 less than the dollar amount determined under section 1382(a)(3)(B) of this title and the fact that if the amount in the account (in addition to the value of the resident's other nonexempt resources) reaches the amount determined under such section the resident may lose eligibility for such medical assistance or for benefits under subchapter XVI of this chapter.

(iv) Conveyance upon death

Upon the death of a resident with such an account, the facility must convey promptly the resident's personal funds (and a final accounting of such funds) to the individual administering the resident's estate.

(C) Assurance of financial security

The facility must purchase a surety bond, or otherwise provide assurance satisfactory to the Secretary, to assure the security of all personal funds of residents deposited with the facility.

(D) Limitation on charges to personal funds

The facility may not impose a charge against the personal funds of a resident for any item or service for which payment is made under this subchapter or subchapter XVIII of this chapter.

(7) Limitation on charges in case of medicaid-eligible individuals

(A) In general

A nursing facility may not impose charges, for certain medicaid-eligible individuals for nursing facility services covered by the State under its plan under this subchapter, that exceed the payment amounts established by the State for such services under this subchapter.

(B) "Certain medicaid-eligible individual" defined

In subparagraph (A), the term "certain medicaid-eligible individual" means an individual who is entitled to medical assistance for nursing facility services in the facility under this subchapter but with respect to whom such benefits are not being paid because, in determining the amount of the individual's income to be applied monthly to payment for the costs of such services, the amount of such income exceeds the payment amounts established by the State for such services under this subchapter.

(8) Posting of survey results

A nursing facility must post in a place readily accessible to residents, and family members and legal representatives of residents, the results of the most recent survey of the facility conducted under subsection (g) of this section.

(d) Requirements relating to administration and other matters

(1) Administration

(A) In general

A nursing facility must be administered in a manner that enables it to use its resources effectively and efficiently to attain or maintain the highest practicable physical, mental, and psychosocial well-being of each resident (consistent with requirements established under subsection (f)(5) of this section).

(B) Required notices

If a change occurs in—

(i) the persons with an ownership or control interest (as defined in section 1320a–3(a)(3) of this title) in the facility,

(ii) the persons who are officers, directors, agents, or managing employees (as defined in section 1320a–5(b) of this title) of the facility,

(iii) the corporation, association, or other company responsible for the management of the facility, or

(iv) the individual who is the administrator or director of nursing of the facility,

the nursing facility must provide notice to the State agency responsible for the licensing of the facility, at the time of the change, of the change and of the identity of each new person, company, or individual described in the respective clause.

(C) Nursing facility administrator

The administrator of a nursing facility must meet standards established by the Secretary under subsection (f)(4) of this section.

(2) Licensing and life safety code

(A) Licensing

A nursing facility must be licensed under applicable State and local law.

(B) Life Safety Code

A nursing facility must meet such provisions of such edition (as specified by the Secretary in regulation) of the Life Safety Code of the National Fire Protection Association as are applicable to nursing homes; except that—

(i) the Secretary may waive, for such periods as he deems appropriate, specific provisions of such Code which if rigidly applied would result in unreasonable hardship upon a facility, but only if such waiver would not adversely affect the health and safety of residents or personnel, and

(ii) the provisions of such Code shall not apply in any State if the Secretary finds that in such State there is in effect a fire and safety code, imposed by State law, which adequately protects residents of and personnel in nursing facilities.

(3) Sanitary and infection control and physical environment

A nursing facility must—

(A) establish and maintain an infection control program designed to provide a safe, sanitary, and comfortable environment in which residents reside and to help prevent the development and transmission of disease and infection, and

(B) be designed, constructed, equipped, and maintained in a manner to protect the health and safety of residents, personnel, and the general public.

(4) Miscellaneous

(A) Compliance with Federal, State, and local laws and professional standards

A nursing facility must operate and provide services in compliance with all applicable Federal, State, and local laws and regulations (including the requirements of section 1320a–3 of this title) and with accepted professional standards and principles which apply to professionals providing services in such a facility.

(B) Other

A nursing facility must meet such other requirements relating to the health and safety of residents or relating to the physical facilities thereof as the Secretary may find necessary.

(e) State requirements relating to nursing facility requirements

As a condition of approval of its plan under this subchapter, a State must provide for the following:

(1) Specification and review of nurse aide training and competency evaluation programs and of nurse aide competency evaluation programs

The State must—

(A) by not later than January 1, 1989, specify those training and competency evaluation programs, and those competency evaluation programs, that the State approves for purposes of subsection (b)(5) of this section and that meet the requirements established under subsection (f)(2) of this section, and

(B) by not later than January 1, 1990, provide for the review and reapproval of such programs, at a frequency and using a methodology consistent with the requirements established under subsection (f)(2)(A)(iii) of this section.

The failure of the Secretary to establish requirements under subsection (f)(2) of this section shall not relieve any State of its responsibility under this paragraph.

(2) Nurse aide registry

(A) In general

By not later than January 1, 1989, the State shall establish and maintain a registry of all individuals who have satisfactorily completed a nurse aide training and competency evaluation program, or a nurse aide competency evaluation program, approved under paragraph (1) in the State, or any individual described in subsection (f)(2)(B)(ii) of this section or in subparagraph (B), (C), or (D) of section 6901(b)(4) of the Omnibus Budget Reconciliation Act of 1989.

(B) Information in registry

The registry under subparagraph (A) shall provide (in accordance with regulations of the Secretary) for the inclusion of specific documented findings by a State under subsection (g)(1)(C) of this section of resident neglect or abuse or misappropriation of resident property involving an individual listed in the registry, as well as any brief statement of the individual disputing the findings. The State shall make available to the public information in the registry. In the case of inquiries to the registry concerning an individual listed in the registry, any information disclosed concerning such a finding shall also include disclosure of any such statement in the registry relating to the finding or a clear and accurate summary of such a statement.

(C) Prohibition against charges

A State may not impose any charges on a nurse aide relating to the registry established and maintained under subparagraph (A).

(3) State appeals process for transfers and discharges

The State, for transfers and discharges from nursing facilities effected on or after October 1, 1989, must provide for a fair mechanism, meeting the guidelines established under subsection (f)(3) of this section, for hearing appeals on transfers and discharges of residents of such facilities; but the failure of the Secretary to establish such guidelines under such subsection shall not relieve any State of its responsibility under this paragraph.

(4) Nursing facility administrator standards

By not later than July 1, 1989, the State must have implemented and enforced the nursing facility administrator standards developed under subsection (f)(4) of this section respecting the qualification of administrators of nursing facilities.

(5) Specification of resident assessment instrument

Effective July 1, 1990, the State shall specify the instrument to be used by nursing facilities in the State in complying with the requirement of subsection (b)(3)(A)(iii) of this section. Such instrument shall be—

    (A) one of the instruments designated under subsection (f)(6)(B) of this section, or

    (B) an instrument which the Secretary has approved as being consistent with the minimum data set of core elements, common definitions, and utilization guidelines specified by the Secretary under subsection (f)(6)(A) of this section.

(6) Notice of medicaid rights

Each State, as a condition of approval of its plan under this subchapter, effective April 1, 1988, must develop (and periodically update) a written notice of the rights and obligations of residents of nursing facilities (and spouses of such residents) under this subchapter.

    (7) State requirements for preadmission screening and resident review

    (A) Preadmission screening

      (i) In general

      Effective January 1, 1989, the State must have in effect a preadmission screening program, for making determinations (using any criteria developed under subsection (f)(8) of this section) described in subsection (b)(3)(F) of this section for mentally ill and mentally retarded individuals (as defined in subparagraph (G)) who are admitted to nursing facilities on or after January 1, 1989. The failure of the Secretary to develop minimum criteria under subsection (f)(8) of this section shall not relieve any State of its responsibility to have a preadmission screening program under this subparagraph or to perform resident reviews under subparagraph (B).

      (ii) Clarification with respect to certain readmissions

      The preadmission screening program under clause (i) need not provide for determinations in the case of the readmission to a nursing facility of an individual who, after being admitted to the nursing facility, was transferred for care in a hospital.

      (iii) Exception for certain hospital discharges

      The preadmission screening program under clause (i) shall not apply to the admission to a nursing facility of an individual—

        (I) who is admitted to the facility directly from a hospital after receiving acute inpatient care at the hospital,

        (II) who requires nursing facility services for the condition for which the individual received care in the hospital, and

(III) whose attending physician has certified, before admission to the facility, that the individual is likely to require less than 30 days of nursing facility services.

(B) State requirement for resident review

(i) For mentally ill residents

As of April 1, 1990, in the case of each resident of a nursing facility who is mentally ill, the State mental health authority must review and determine (using any criteria developed under subsection (f)(8) of this section and based on an independent physical and mental evaluation performed by a person or entity other than the State mental health authority)—

(I) whether or not the resident, because of the resident's physical and mental condition, requires the level of services provided by a nursing facility or requires the level of services of an inpatient psychiatric hospital for individuals under age 21 (as described in section 1396d(h) of this title) or of an institution for mental diseases providing medical assistance to individuals 65 years of age or older; and

(II) whether or not the resident requires specialized services for mental illness.

(ii) For mentally retarded residents

As of April 1, 1990, in the case of each resident of a nursing facility who is mentally retarded, the State mental retardation or developmental disability authority must review and determine (using any criteria developed under subsection (f)(8) of this section)—

(I) whether or not the resident, because of the resident's physical and mental condition, requires the level of services provided by a nursing facility or requires the level of services of an intermediate care facility described under section 1396d(d) of this title; and

(II) whether or not the resident requires specialized services for mental retardation.

(iii) Review required upon change in resident's condition

A review and determination under clause (i) or (ii) must be conducted promptly after a nursing facility has notified the State mental health authority or State mental retardation or developmental disability authority, as applicable, under subsection (b)(3)(E) of this section with respect to a mentally ill or mentally retarded resident, that there has been a significant change in the resident's physical or mental condition.

967

(iv) Prohibition of delegation

A State mental health authority, a State mental retardation or developmental disability authority, and a State may not delegate (by subcontract or otherwise) their responsibilities under this subparagraph to a nursing facility (or to an entity that has a direct or indirect affiliation or relationship with such a facility).

(C) Response to preadmission screening and resident review

As of April 1, 1990, the State must meet the following requirements:

(i) Long-term residents not requiring nursing facility services, but requiring specialized services

In the case of a resident who is determined, under subparagraph (B), not to require the level of services provided by a nursing facility, but to require specialized services for mental illness or mental retardation, and who has continuously resided in a nursing facility for at least 30 months before the date of the determination, the State must, in consultation with the resident's family or legal representative and care-givers—

(I) inform the resident of the institutional and noninstitutional alternatives covered under the State plan for the resident,

(II) offer the resident the choice of remaining in the facility or of receiving covered services in an alternative appropriate institutional or noninstitutional setting,

(III) clarify the effect on eligibility for services under the State plan if the resident chooses to leave the facility (including its effect on readmission to the facility), and

(IV) regardless of the resident's choice, provide for (or arrange for the provision of) such specialized services for the mental illness or mental retardation.

A State shall not be denied payment under this subchapter for nursing facility services for a resident described in this clause because the resident does not require the level of services provided by such a facility, if the resident chooses to remain in such a facility.

(ii) Other residents not requiring nursing facility services, but requiring specialized services

In the case of a resident who is determined, under subparagraph (B), not to require the level of services provided by a nursing facility, but to require specialized services for mental illness or mental retardation, and who has not continuously resided in a nursing facility for at least 30 months before the date of the determination, the State must, in consultation with the resident's family or legal representative and care-givers—

(I) arrange for the safe and orderly discharge of the resident from the facility, consistent with the requirements of subsection (c)(2) of this section,

(II) prepare and orient the resident for such discharge, and

(III) provide for (or arrange for the provision of) such specialized services for the mental illness or mental retardation.

(iii) Residents not requiring nursing facility services and not requiring specialized services

In the case of a resident who is determined, under subparagraph (B), not to require the level of services provided by a nursing facility and not to require specialized services for mental illness or mental retardation, the State must—

(I) arrange for the safe and orderly discharge of the resident from the facility, consistent with the requirements of subsection (c)(2) of this section, and

(II) prepare and orient the resident for such discharge.

(iv) Annual report

Each State shall report to the Secretary annually concerning the number and disposition of residents described in each of clauses (ii) and (iii).

(D) Denial of payment

(i) For failure to conduct preadmission screening or review

No payment may be made under section 1996b(a) of this title with respect to nursing facility services furnished to an individual for whom a determination is required under subsection (b)(3)(F) of this section or subparagraph (B) but for whom the determination is not made.

(ii) For certain residents not requiring nursing facility level of services

No payment may be made under section 1396b(a) of this title with respect to nursing facility services furnished to an individual (other than an individual described in subparagraph (C)(i)) who does not require the level of services provided by a nursing facility.

(E) Permitting alternative disposition plans

With respect to residents of a nursing facility who are mentally retarded or mentally ill and who are determined under subparagraph (B) not to require the level of services of such a facility, but who require specialized services for mental illness or mental retardation, a State and the nursing facility shall be considered to be in compliance with the requirements of subparagraphs (A) through (C) of this paragraph if, before April 1, 1989, the State and the Secretary have entered into an agreement relating to the disposition of such residents of the facility and the State is in compliance with such agreement. Such an agreement may provide for the disposition of the residents after the date specified in subparagraph (C). The State may revise such an agreement, subject to the approval of the Secretary, before October 1, 1991, but only if, under the revised agreement, all residents subject to the agreement who do not require the level of services of such a facility are discharged from the facility by not later than April 1, 1994.

(F) Appeals procedures

Each State, as a condition of approval of its plan under this subchapter, effective January 1, 1989, must have in effect an appeals process for individuals adversely affected by determinations under subparagraph (A) or (B).

(G) Definitions

In this paragraph and in subsection (b)(3)(F) of this section:

(i) An individual is considered to be "mentally ill" if the individual has serious mental illness (as defined by the Secretary in consultation with the National Institute of Mental Health) and does not have a primary diagnosis of dementia (including Alzheimer's disease or a related disorder) or a diagnosis (other than a primary diagnosis) of dementia and a primary diagnosis that is not a serious mental illness.

(ii) An individual is considered to be "mentally retarded" if the individual is mentally retarded or a person with a related condition (as described in section 1396d(d) of this title).

(iii) The term "specialized services" has the meaning given such term by the Secretary in regulations, but does not include, in the case of a resident of a nursing facility, services within the scope of services which the facility must provide or arrange for its residents under subsection (b)(4) of this section.

(f) Responsibilities of Secretary relating to nursing facility requirements

(1) General responsibility

It is the duty and responsibility of the Secretary to assure that requirements which govern the provision of care in nursing facilities under State plans approved under this subchapter, and the enforcement of such requirements, are adequate to protect the health, safety, welfare, and rights of residents and to promote the effective and efficient use of public moneys.

970

(2) Requirements for nurse aide training and competency evaluation programs and for nurse aide competency evaluation programs

(A) In general

For purposes of subsections (b)(5) and (e)(1)(A) of this section, the Secretary shall establish, by not later than September 1, 1988—

(i) requirements for the approval of nurse aide training and competency evaluation programs, including requirements relating to (I) the areas to be covered in such a program (including at least basic nursing skills, personal care skills, recognition of mental health and social service needs, care of cognitively impaired residents, basic restorative services, and residents' rights) and content of the curriculum, (II) minimum hours of initial and ongoing training and retraining (including not less than 75 hours in the case of initial training), (III) qualifications of instructors, and (IV) procedures for determination of competency;

(ii) requirements for the approval of nurse aide competency evaluation programs, including requirement relating to the areas to be covered in such a program, including at least basic nursing skills, personal care skills, recognition of mental health and social service needs, care of cognitively impaired residents, basic restorative services, and residents' rights, and procedures for determination of competency;

(iii) requirements respecting the minimum frequency and methodology to be used by a State in reviewing such programs' compliance with the requirements for such programs; and

(iv) requirements, under both such programs, that—

(I) provide procedures for determining competency that permit a nurse aide, at the nurse aide's option, to establish competency through procedures or methods other than the passing of a written examination and to have the competency evaluation conducted at the nursing facility at which the aide is (or will be) employed (unless the facility is described in subparagraph (B)(iii)(I)),

(II) prohibit the imposition on a nurse aide who is employed by (or who has received an offer of employment from) a facility on the date on which the aide begins either such program of any charges (including any charges for textbooks and other required course materials and any charges for the competency evaluation) for either such program, and

(III) in the case of a nurse aide not described in subclause (II) who is employed by (or who has received an offer of employment from) a facility not later than 12 months after completing either such program, the State shall provide for the reimbursement of costs incurred in completing such program on a prorata basis during the period in which the nurse aide is so employed.

(B) Approval of certain programs

Such requirements—

(i) may permit approval of programs offered by or in facilities, as well as outside facilities (including employee organizations), and of programs in effect on December 22, 1987;

(ii) shall permit a State to find that an individual who has completed (before July 1, 1989) a nurse aide training and competency evaluation program shall be deemed to have completed such a program approved under subsection (b)(5) of this section if the State determines that, at the time the program was offered, the program met the requirements for approval under such paragraph; and

(iii) subject to subparagraph (C), shall prohibit approval of such a program—

(I) offered by or in a nursing facility which, within the previous 2 years—

(a) has operated under a waiver under subsection (b)(4)(C)(ii) of this section that was granted on the basis of a demonstration that the facility is unable to provide the nursing care required under subsection (b)(4)(C)(i) of this section for a period in excess of 48 hours during a week;

(b) has been subject to an extended (or partial extended) survey under section 1395i–3(g)(2)(B)(i) of this title or subsection (g)(2)(B)(i) of this section; or

(c) has been assessed a civil money penalty described in section 1395i–3(h)(2)(B)(ii) of this title or subsection (h)(2)(A)(ii) of this section of not less than $5,000, or has been subject to a remedy described in subsection (h)(1)(B)(i) of this section, clauses (i), (iii), or (iv) of subsection (h)(2)(A) of this section, clauses (i) or (iii) of section 1395i–3(h)(2)(B) of this title, or section 1395i–3(h)(4) of this title, or

(II) offered by or in a nursing facility unless the State makes the determination, upon an individual's completion of the program, that the individual is competent to provide nursing and nursing-related services in nursing facilities.

A State may not delegate (through subcontract or otherwise) its responsibility under clause (iii)(II) to the nursing facility.

(C) Waiver authorized

Clause (iii)(I) of subparagraph (B) shall not apply to a program offered in (but not by) a nursing facility (or skilled nursing facility for purposes of subchapter XVIII of this chapter) in a State if the State—

(i) determines that there is no other such program offered within a reasonable distance of the facility,

(ii) assures, through an oversight effort, that an adequate environment exists for operating the program in the facility, and

(iii) provides notice of such determination and assurances to the State long-term care ombudsman.

(3) Federal guidelines for State appeals process for transfers and discharges

For purposes of subsections (c)(2)(B)(iii) and (e)(3) of this section, by not later than October 1, 1988, the Secretary shall establish guidelines for minimum standards which State appeals processes under subsection (e)(3) of this section must meet to provide a fair mechanism for hearing appeals on transfers and discharges of residents from nursing facilities.

(4) Secretarial standards qualification of administrators

For purposes of subsections (d)(1)(C) and (e)(4) of this section, the Secretary shall develop, by not later than March 1, 1988, standards to be applied in assuring the qualifications of administrators of nursing facilities.

(5) Criteria for administration

The Secretary shall establish criteria for assessing a nursing facility's compliance with the requirement of subsection (d)(1) of this section with respect to—

(A) its governing body and management,

(B) agreements with hospitals regarding transfers of residents to and from the hospitals and to and from other nursing facilities,

(C) disaster preparedness,

(D) direction of medical care by a physician,

(E) laboratory and radiological services,

(F) clinical records, and

(G) resident and advocate participation.

(6) Specification of resident assessment data set and instruments

The Secretary shall—

(A) not later than January 1, 1989, specify a minimum data set of core elements and common definitions for use by nursing facilities in conducting the assessments required under subsection (b)(3) of this section, and establish guidelines for utilization of the data set; and

(B) by not later than April 1, 1990, designate one or more instruments which are consistent with the specification made under subparagraph (A) and which a State may specify under subsection (e)(5)(A) of this section for use by nursing facilities in complying with the requirements of subsection (b)(3)(A)(iii) of this section.

(7) List of items and services furnished in nursing facilities not chargeable to the personal funds of a resident

(A) Regulations required

Pursuant to the requirement of section 21(b) of the Medicare–Medicaid Anti-Fraud and Abuse Amendments of 1977, the Secretary shall issue regulations, on or before the first day of the seventh month to begin after December 22, 1987, that define those costs which may be charged to the personal funds of residents in nursing facilities who are individuals receiving medical assistance with respect to nursing facility services under this subchapter and those costs which are to be included in the payment amount under this subchapter for nursing facility services.

(B) Rule if failure to publish regulations

If the Secretary does not issue the regulations under subparagraph (A) on or before the date required in that subparagraph, in the case of a resident of a nursing facility who is eligible to receive benefits for nursing facility services under this subchapter, for purposes of section 1396a(a)(28)(B) of this title, the Secretary shall be deemed to have promulgated regulations under this paragraph which provide that the costs which may not be charged to the personal funds of such resident (and for which payment is considered to be made under this subchapter) include, at a minimum, the costs for routine personal hygiene items and services furnished by the facility.

(8) Federal minimum criteria and monitoring for preadmission screening and resident review

(A) Minimum criteria

The Secretary shall develop, by not later than October 1, 1988, minimum criteria for States to use in making determinations under subsections (b)(3)(F) and (e)(7)(B) of this section and in permitting individuals adversely affected to appeal such determinations, and shall notify the States of such criteria.

(B) Monitoring compliance

The Secretary shall review, in a sufficient number of cases to allow reasonable inferences, each State's compliance with the requirements of subsection (e)(7)(C)(ii) of this section (relating to discharge and placement for active treatment of certain residents).

(9) Criteria for monitoring State waivers

The Secretary shall develop, by not later than October 1, 1988, criteria and procedures for monitoring State performances and granting waivers pursuant to subsection (b)(4)(C)(ii) of this section.

(g) Survey and certification process

(1) State and Federal responsibility

(A) In general

Under each State plan under this subchapter, the State shall be responsible for certifying, in accordance with surveys conducted under paragraph (2), the compliance of nursing facilities (other than facilities of the State) with the requirements of subsections (b), (c), and (d) of this section. The Secretary shall be responsible for certifying, in accordance with surveys conducted under paragraph (2), the compliance of State nursing facilities with the requirements of such subsections.

(B) Educational program

Each State shall conduct periodic educational programs for the staff and residents (and their representatives) of nursing facilities in order to present current regulations, procedures, and policies under this section.

(C) Investigation of allegations of resident neglect and abuse and misappropriation of resident property

The State shall provide, through the agency responsible for surveys and certification of nursing facilities under this subsection, for a process for the receipt and timely review and investigation of allegations of neglect and abuse and misappropriation of resident property by a nurse aide of a resident in a nursing facility or by another individual used by the facility in providing services to such a resident. The State shall, after notice to the individual involved and a reasonable opportunity for a hearing for the individual to rebut allegations, make a finding as to the accuracy of the allegations. If the State finds that a nurse aide has neglected or abused a resident or misappropriated resident property in a facility, the State shall notify the nurse aide and the registry of such finding. If the State finds that any other individual used by the facility has neglected or abused a resident or misappropriated resident property in a facility, the State shall notify the appropriate licensure authority. A State shall not make a finding that an individual has neglected a resident if the individual demonstrates that such neglect was caused by factors beyond the control of the individual.

(D) Removal of name from nurse aide registry

(i) In general

In the case of a finding of neglect under subparagraph (C), the State shall establish a procedure to permit a nurse aide to petition the State to have his or her name removed from the registry upon a determination by the State that—

 (I) the employment and personal history of the nurse aide does not reflect a pattern of abusive behavior or neglect; and

 (II) the neglect involved in the original finding was a singular occurrence.

(ii) Timing of determination

In no case shall a determination on a petition submitted under clause (i) be made prior to the expiration of the 1–year period beginning on the date on which the name of the petitioner was added to the registry under subparagraph (C).

(E) Construction

The failure of the Secretary to issue regulations to carry out this subsection shall not relieve a State of its responsibility under this subsection.

(2) Surveys

 (A) Annual standard survey

 (i) In general

Each nursing facility shall be subject to a standard survey, to be conducted without any prior notice to the facility. Any individual who notifies (or causes to be notified) a nursing facility of the time or date on which such a survey is scheduled to be conducted is subject to a civil money penalty of not to exceed $2,000. The provisions of section 1320a–7a of this title (other than subsections (a) and (b)) shall apply to a civil money penalty under the previous sentence in the same manner as such provisions apply to a penalty or proceeding under section 1320a–7a(a) of this title. The Secretary shall review each State's procedures for scheduling and conduct of standard surveys to assure that the State has taken all reasonable steps to avoid giving notice of such a survey through the scheduling procedures and the conduct of the surveys themselves.

 (ii) Contents

Each standard survey shall include, for a case-mix stratified sample of residents—

 (I) a survey of the quality of care furnished, as measured by indicators of medical, nursing, and rehabilitative care, dietary and nutrition services, activities and social participation, and sanitation, infection control, and the physical environment,

(II) written plans of care provided under subsection (b)(2) of this section and an audit of the residents' assessments under subsection (b)(3) of this section to determine the accuracy of such assessments and the adequacy of such plans of care, and

(III) a review of compliance with residents' rights under subsection (c) of this section.

(iii) Frequency

(I) In general

Each nursing facility shall be subject to a standard survey not later than 15 months after the date of the previous standard survey conducted under this subparagraph. The statewide average interval between standard surveys of a nursing facility shall not exceed 12 months.

(II) Special surveys

If not otherwise conducted under subclause (I), a standard survey (or an abbreviated standard survey) may be conducted within 2 months of any change of ownership, administration, management of a nursing facility, or director of nursing in order to determine whether the change has resulted in any decline in the quality of care furnished in the facility.

(B) Extended surveys

(i) In general

Each nursing facility which is found, under a standard survey, to have provided substandard quality of care shall be subject to an extended survey. Any other facility may, at the Secretary's or State's discretion, be subject to such an extended survey (or a partial extended survey).

(ii) Timing

The extended survey shall be conducted immediately after the standard survey (or, if not practicable, not later than 2 weeks after the date of completion of the standard survey).

(iii) Contents

In such an extended survey, the survey team shall review and identify the policies and procedures which produced such substandard quality of care and shall determine whether the facility has complied with all the requirements described in subsections (b), (c), and (d) of this section. Such review shall include an expansion of the size of the sample of residents' assessments reviewed and a review of the staffing, of in-service training, and, if appropriate, of contracts with consultants.

(iv) Construction

Nothing in this paragraph shall be construed as requiring an extended or partial extended survey as a prerequisite to imposing a sanction against a facility under subsection (h) of this section on the basis of findings in a standard survey.

(C) Survey protocol

Standard and extended surveys shall be conducted—

(i) based upon a protocol which the Secretary has developed, tested, and validated by not later than January 1, 1990, and

(ii) by individuals, of a survey team, who meet such minimum qualifications as the Secretary establishes by not later than such date.

The failure of the Secretary to develop, test, or validate such protocols or to establish such minimum qualifications shall not relieve any State of its responsibility (or the Secretary of the Secretary's responsibility) to conduct surveys under this subsection.

(D) Consistency of surveys

Each State shall implement programs to measure and reduce inconsistency in the application of survey results among surveyors.

(E) Survey teams

(i) In general

Surveys under this subsection shall be conducted by a multidisciplinary team of professionals (including a registered professional nurse).

(ii) Prohibition of conflicts of interest

A State may not use as a member of a survey team under this subsection an individual who is serving (or has served within the previous 2 years) as a member of the staff of, or as a consultant to, the facility surveyed respecting compliance with the requirements of subsections (b), (c), and (d) of this section, or who has a personal or familial financial interest in the facility being surveyed.

(iii) Training

The Secretary shall provide for the comprehensive training of State and Federal surveyors in the conduct of standard and extended surveys under this subsection, including the auditing of resident assessments and plans of care. No individual shall serve as a member of a survey team unless the individual has successfully completed a training and testing program in survey and certification techniques that has been approved by the Secretary.

(3) Validation surveys

(A) In general

The Secretary shall conduct onsite surveys of a representative sample of nursing facilities in each State, within 2 months of the date of surveys conducted under paragraph (2) by the State, in a sufficient number to allow inferences about the adequacies of each State's surveys conducted under paragraph (2). In conducting such surveys, the Secretary shall use the same survey protocols as the State is required to use under paragraph (2). If the State has determined that an individual nursing facility meets the requirements of subsections (b), (c), and (d) of this section, but the Secretary determines that the facility does not meet such requirements, the Secretary's determination as to the facility's noncompliance with such requirements is binding and supersedes that of the State survey.

(B) Scope

With respect to each State, the Secretary shall conduct surveys under subparagraph (A) each year with respect to at least 5 percent of the number of nursing facilities surveyed by the State in the year, but in no case less than 5 nursing facilities in the State.

(C) Reduction in administrative costs for substandard performance

If the Secretary finds, on the basis of such surveys, that a State has failed to perform surveys as required under paragraph (2) or that a State's survey and certification performance otherwise is not adequate, the Secretary may provide for the training of survey teams in the State and shall provide for a reduction of the payment otherwise made to the State under section 1396b(a)(2)(D) of this title with respect to a quarter equal to 33 percent multiplied by a fraction, the denominator of which is equal to the total number of residents in nursing facilities surveyed by the Secretary that quarter and the numerator of which is equal to the total number of residents in nursing facilities which were found pursuant to such surveys to be not in compliance with any of the requirements of subsections (b), (c), and (d) of this section. A State that is dissatisfied with the Secretary's findings under this subparagraph may obtain reconsideration and review of the findings under section 1316 of this title in the same manner as a State may seek reconsideration and review under that section of the Secretary's determination under section 1316(a)(1) of this title.

(D) Special surveys of compliance

Where the Secretary has reason to question the compliance of a nursing facility with any of the requirements of subsections (b), (c), and (d) of this section, the Secretary may conduct a survey of the facility and, on the basis of that survey, make independent and binding determinations concerning the extent to which the nursing facility meets such requirements.

(4) Investigation of complaints and monitoring nursing facility compliance

Each State shall maintain procedures and adequate staff to—

(A) investigate complaints of violations of requirements by nursing facilities, and

(B) monitor, on-site, on a regular, as needed basis, a nursing facility's compliance with the requirements of subsections (b), (c), and (d) of this section, if—

(i) the facility has been found not to be in compliance with such requirements and is in the process of correcting deficiencies to achieve such compliance;

(ii) the facility was previously found not to be in compliance with such requirements, has corrected deficiencies to achieve such compliance, and verification of continued compliance is indicated; or

(iii) the State has reason to question the compliance of the facility with such requirements.

A State may maintain and utilize a specialized team (including an attorney, an auditor, and appropriate health care professionals) for the purpose of identifying, surveying, gathering and preserving evidence, and carrying out appropriate enforcement actions against substandard nursing facilities.

(5) Disclosure of results of inspections and activities

(A) Public information

Each State, and the Secretary, shall make available to the public—

(i) information respecting all surveys and certifications made respecting nursing facilities, including statements of deficiencies, within 14 calendar days after such information is made available to those facilities, and approved plans of correction,

(ii) copies of cost reports of such facilities filed under this subchapter or under subchapter XVIII of this chapter,

(iii) copies of statements of ownership under section 1320a–3 of this title, and

(iv) information disclosed under section 1320a–5 of this title.

(B) Notice to ombudsman

Each State shall notify the State long-term care ombudsman of the State's findings of noncompliance with any of the requirements of subsections (b), (c), and (d) of this section, or of any adverse action taken against a nursing facility under paragraphs (1), (2), or (3) of subsection (h) of this section, with respect to a nursing facility in the State.

(C) Notice to physicians and nursing facility administrator licensing board

If a State finds that a nursing facility has provided substandard quality of care, the State shall notify—

    (i) the attending physician of each resident with respect to which such finding is made, and

    (ii) any State board responsible for the licensing of the nursing facility administrator of the facility.

(D) Access to fraud control units

Each State shall provide its State medicaid fraud and abuse control unit (established under section 1396b(q) of this title) with access to all information of the State agency responsible for surveys and certifications under this subsection.

(h) Enforcement process

(1) In general

If a State finds, on the basis of a standard, extended, or partial extended survey under subsection (g)(2) of this section or otherwise, that a nursing facility no longer meets a requirement of subsection (b), (c), or (d) of this section, and further finds that the facility's deficiencies—

    (A) immediately jeopardize the health or safety of its residents, the State shall take immediate action to remove the jeopardy and correct the deficiencies through the remedy specified in paragraph (2)(A)(iii), or terminate the facility's participation under the State plan and may provide, in addition, for one or more of the other remedies described in paragraph (2); or

    (B) do not immediately jeopardize the health or safety of its residents, the State may—

        (i) terminate the facility's participation under the State plan,

        (ii) provide for one or more of the remedies described in paragraph (2), or

        (iii) do both.

Nothing in this paragraph shall be construed as restricting the remedies available to a State to remedy a nursing facility's deficiencies. If a State finds that a nursing facility meets the requirements of subsections (b), (c), and (d) of this section, but, as of a previous period, did not meet such requirements, the State may provide for a civil money penalty under paragraph (2)(A)(ii) for the days in which it finds that the facility was not in compliance with such requirements.

(2) Specified remedies

(A) Listing

Except as provided in subparagraph (B)(ii), each State shall establish by law (whether statute or regulation) at least the following remedies:

(i) Denial of payment under the State plan with respect to any individual admitted to the nursing facility involved after such notice to the public and to the facility as may be provided for by the State.

(ii) A civil money penalty assessed and collected, with interest, for each day in which the facility is or was out of compliance with a requirement of subsection (b), (c), or (d) of this section. Funds collected by a State as a result of imposition of such a penalty (or as a result of the imposition by the State of a civil money penalty for activities described in subsections (b)(3)(B)(ii)(I), (b)(3)(B)(ii)(II), or (g)(2)(A)(i) of this section) shall be applied to the protection of the health or property of residents of nursing facilities that the State or the Secretary finds deficient, including payment for the costs of relocation of residents to other facilities, maintenance of operation of a facility pending correction of deficiencies or closure, and reimbursement of residents for personal funds lost.

(iii) The appointment of temporary management to oversee the operation of the facility and to assure the health and safety of the facility's residents, where there is a need for temporary management while—

(I) there is an orderly closure of the facility, or

(II) improvements are made in order to bring the facility into compliance with all the requirements of subsections (b), (c), and (d) of this section.

The temporary management under this clause shall not be terminated under subclause (II) until the State has determined that the facility has the management capability to ensure continued compliance with all the requirements of subsections (b), (c), and (d) of this section.

(iv) The authority, in the case of an emergency, to close the facility, to transfer residents in that facility to other facilities, or both.

The State also shall specify criteria, as to when and how each of such remedies is to be applied, the amounts of any fines, and the severity of each of these remedies, to be used in the imposition of such remedies. Such criteria shall be designed so as to minimize the time between the identification of violations and final imposition of the remedies and shall provide for the imposition of incrementally more

982

severe fines for repeated or uncorrected deficiencies. In addition, the State may provide for other specified remedies, such as directed plans of correction.

(B) Deadline and guidance

(i) Except as provided in clause (ii), as a condition for approval of a State plan for calendar quarters beginning on or after October 1, 1989, each State shall establish the remedies described in clauses (i) through (iv) of subparagraph (A) by not later than October 1, 1989. The Secretary shall provide, through regulations by not later than October 1, 1988, guidance to States in establishing such remedies; but the failure of the Secretary to provide such guidance shall not relieve a State of the responsibility for establishing such remedies.

(ii) A State may establish alternative remedies (other than termination of participation) other than those described in clauses (i) through (iv) of subparagraph (A), if the State demonstrates to the Secretary's satisfaction that the alternative remedies are as effective in deterring noncompliance and correcting deficiencies as those described in subparagraph (A).

(C) Assuring prompt compliance

If a nursing facility has not complied with any of the requirements of subsections (b), (c), and (d) of this section, within 3 months after the date the facility is found to be out of compliance with such requirements, the State shall impose the remedy described in subparagraph (A)(i) for all individuals who are admitted to the facility after such date.

(D) Repeated noncompliance

In the case of a nursing facility which, on 3 consecutive standard surveys conducted under subsection (g)(2) of this section, has been found to have provided substandard quality of care, the State shall (regardless of what other remedies are provided)—

(i) impose the remedy described in subparagraph (A)(i), and

(ii) monitor the facility under subsection (g)(4)(B) of this section,

until the facility has demonstrated, to the satisfaction of the State, that it is in compliance with the requirements of subsections (b), (c), and (d) of this section, and that it will remain in compliance with such requirements.

(E) Funding

The reasonable expenditures of a State to provide for temporary management and other expenses associated with implementing the remedies described in clauses (iii) and (iv) of subparagraph (A) shall be considered, for purposes of section 1396b(a)(7) of this title, to be necessary for the proper and efficient administration of the State plan.

(F) Incentives for high quality care

In addition to the remedies specified in this paragraph, a State may establish a program to reward, through public recognition, incentive payments, or both, nursing facilities that provide the highest quality care to residents who are entitled to medical assistance under this subchapter. For purposes of section 1396b(a)(7) of this title, proper expenses incurred by a State in carrying out such a program shall be considered to be expenses necessary for the proper and efficient administration of the State plan under this subchapter.

(3) Secretarial authority

(A) For State nursing facilities

With respect to a State nursing facility, the Secretary shall have the authority and duties of a State under this subsection, including the authority to impose remedies described in clauses (i), (ii), and (iii) of paragraph (2)(A).

(B) Other nursing facilities

With respect to any other nursing facility in a State, if the Secretary finds that a nursing facility no longer meets a requirement of subsection (b), (c), (d), or (e) of this section, and further finds that the facility's deficiencies—

    (i) immediately jeopardize the health or safety of its residents, the Secretary shall take immediate action to remove the jeopardy and correct the deficiencies through the remedy specified in subparagraph (C)(iii), or terminate the facility's participation under the State plan and may provide, in addition, for one or more of the other remedies described in subparagraph (C); or

    (ii) do not immediately jeopardize the health or safety of its residents, the Secretary may impose any of the remedies described in subparagraph (C).

Nothing in this subparagraph shall be construed as restricting the remedies available to the Secretary to remedy a nursing facility's deficiencies. If the Secretary finds that a nursing facility meets such requirements but, as of a previous period, did not meet such requirements, the Secretary may provide for a civil money penalty under subparagraph (C)(ii) for the days on which he finds that the facility was not in compliance with such requirements.

(C) Specified remedies

The Secretary may take the following actions with respect to a finding that a facility has not met an applicable requirement:

    (i) Denial of payment

    The Secretary may deny any further payments to the State for medical assistance furnished by the facility to all individuals in the facility or to individuals admitted to the facility after the effective date of the finding.

(ii) Authority with respect to civil money penalties

The Secretary may impose a civil money penalty in an amount not to exceed $10,000 for each day of noncompliance. The provisions of section 1320a–7a of this title (other than subsections (a) and (b)) shall apply to a civil money penalty under the previous sentence in the same manner as such provisions apply to a penalty or proceeding under section 1320a–7a(a) of this title.

(iii) Appointment of temporary management

In consultation with the State, the Secretary may appoint temporary management to oversee the operation of the facility and to assure the health and safety of the facility's residents, where there is a need for temporary management while—

(I) there is an orderly closure of the facility, or

(II) improvements are made in order to bring the facility into compliance with all the requirements of subsections (b), (c), and (d) of this section.

The temporary management under this clause shall not be terminated under subclause (II) until the Secretary has determined that the facility has the management capability to ensure continued compliance with all the requirements of subsections (b), (c), and (d) of this section.

The Secretary shall specify criteria, as to when and how each of such remedies is to be applied, the amounts of any fines, and the severity of each of these remedies, to be used in the imposition of such remedies. Such criteria shall be designed so as to minimize the time between the identification of violations and final imposition of the remedies and shall provide for the imposition of incrementally more severe fines for repeated or uncorrected deficiencies. In addition, the Secretary may provide for other specified remedies, such as directed plans of correction.

(D) Continuation of payments pending remediation

The Secretary may continue payments, over a period of not longer than 6 months after the effective date of the findings, under this subchapter with respect to a nursing facility not in compliance with a requirement of subsection (b), (c), or (d) of this section, if—

(i) the State survey agency finds that it is more appropriate to take alternative action to assure compliance of the facility with the requirements than to terminate the certification of the facility, and

(ii) the State has submitted a plan and timetable for corrective action to the Secretary for approval and the Secretary approves the plan of corrective action.

The Secretary shall establish guidelines for approval of corrective actions requested by States under this subparagraph.

(4) Effective period of denial of payment

A finding to deny payment under this subsection shall terminate when the State or Secretary (or both, as the case may be) finds that the facility is in substantial compliance with all the requirements of subsections (b), (c), and (d) of this section.

(5) Immediate termination of participation for facility where State or Secretary finds noncompliance and immediate jeopardy

If either the State or the Secretary finds that a nursing facility has not met a requirement of subsection (b), (c), or (d) of this section, and finds that the failure immediately jeopardizes the health or safety of its residents, the State or the Secretary, respectively shall notify the other of such finding, and the State or the Secretary, respectively, shall take immediate action to remove the jeopardy and correct the deficiencies through the remedy specified in paragraph (2)(A)(iii) or (3)(C)(iii), or terminate the facility's participation under the State plan. If the facility's participation in the State plan is terminated by either the State or the Secretary, the State shall provide for the safe and orderly transfer of the residents eligible under the State plan consistent with the requirements of subsection (c)(2) of this section.

(6) Special rules where State and Secretary do not agree on finding of noncompliance

(A) State finding of noncompliance and no Secretarial finding of noncompliance

If the Secretary finds that a nursing facility has met all the requirements of subsections (b), (c), and (d) of this section, but a State finds that the facility has not met such requirements and the failure does not immediately jeopardize the health or safety of its residents, the State's findings shall control and the remedies imposed by the State shall be applied.

(B) Secretarial finding of noncompliance and no State finding of noncompliance

If the Secretary finds that a nursing facility has not met all the requirements of subsections (b), (c), and (d) of this section, and that the failure does not immediately jeopardize the health or safety of its residents, but the State has not made such a finding, the Secretary—

(i) may impose any remedies specified in paragraph (3)(C) with respect to the facility, and

(ii) shall (pending any termination by the Secretary) permit continuation of payments in accordance with paragraph (3)(D).

(7) Special rules for timing of termination of participation where remedies overlap

If both the Secretary and the State find that a nursing facility has not met all the requirements of subsections (b), (c), and (d) of this section, and neither finds that the failure immediately jeopardizes the health or safety of its residents—

(A)(i) if both find that the facility's participation under the State plan should be terminated, the State's timing of any termination shall control so long as the termination date does not occur later than 6 months after the date of the finding to terminate;

(ii) if the Secretary, but not the State, finds that the facility's participation under the State plan should be terminated, the Secretary shall (pending any termination by the Secretary) permit continuation of payments in accordance with paragraph (3)(D); or

(iii) if the State, but not the Secretary, finds that the facility's participation under the State plan should be terminated, the State's decision to terminate, and timing of such termination, shall control; and

(B)(i) if the Secretary or the State, but not both, establishes one or more remedies which are additional or alternative to the remedy of terminating the facility's participation under the State plan, such additional or alternative remedies shall also be applied, or

(ii) if both the Secretary and the State establish one or more remedies which are additional or alternative to the remedy of terminating the facility's participation under the State plan, only the additional or alternative remedies of the Secretary shall apply.

(8) Construction

The remedies provided under this subsection are in addition to those otherwise available under State or Federal law and shall not be construed as limiting such other remedies, including any remedy available to an individual at common law. The remedies described in clauses (i), (iii), and (iv) of paragraph (2)(A) may be imposed during the pendency of any hearing. The provisions of this subsection shall apply to a nursing facility (or portion thereof) notwithstanding that the facility (or portion thereof) also is a skilled nursing facility for purposes of subchapter XVIII of this chapter.

(9) Sharing of information

Notwithstanding any other provision of law, all information concerning nursing facilities required by this section to be filed with the Secretary or a State agency shall be made available by such facilities to Federal or State employees for purposes consistent with the effective administration of programs established under this subchapter and subchapter XVIII of this chapter, including investigations by State medicaid fraud control units.

(i) Construction

Where requirements or obligations under this section are identical to those provided under section 1395i–3 of this title, the fulfillment of those requirements or obligations under section 1395i–3 of this title shall be considered to be the fulfillment of the corresponding requirements or obligations under this section.

§ 1396r–1. Presumptive eligibility for pregnant women

(a) Ambulatory prenatal care

A State plan approved under section 1396a of this title may provide for making ambulatory prenatal care available to a pregnant woman during a presumptive eligibility period.

(b) Definitions

For purposes of this section—

(1) the term "presumptive eligibility period" means, with respect to a pregnant woman, the period that—

(A) begins with the date on which a qualified provider determines, on the basis of preliminary information, that the family income of the woman does not exceed the applicable income level of eligibility under the State plan, and

(B) ends with (and includes) the earlier of—

(i) the day on which a determination is made with respect to the eligibility of the woman for medical assistance under the State plan, or

(ii) in the case of a woman who does not file an application by the last day of the month following the month during which the provider makes the determination referred to in subparagraph (A), such last day; and

(2) the term "qualified provider" means any provider that—

(A) is eligible for payments under a State plan approved under this subchapter,

(B) provides services of the type described in subparagraph (A) or (B) of section 1396d(a)(2) of this title or in section 1396d(a)(9) of this title,

(C) is determined by the State agency to be capable of making determinations of the type described in paragraph (1)(A), and

(D)(i) receives funds under—

    (I) section 254b or 254c of this title,

    (II) subchapter V of this chapter, or

    (III) title V of the Indian Health Care Improvement Act [*25 U.S.C.A. § 1651* et seq.];

(ii) participates in a program established under—

    (I) section 1786 of this title, or

    (II) section 4(a) of the Agriculture and Consumer Protection Act of 1973;

(iii) participates in a State perinatal program; or

(iv) is the Indian Health Service or is a health program or facility operated by a tribe or tribal organization under the Indian Self-Determination Act (*Public Law 93–638*) [*25 U.S.C.A. § 450f* et seq.].

(c) Duties of State agency, qualified providers, and presumptively eligible pregnant women

(1) The State agency shall provide qualified providers with—

(A) such forms as are necessary for a pregnant woman to make application for medical assistance under the State plan, and

(B) information on how to assist such women in completing and filing such forms.

(2) A qualified provider that determines under subsection (b)(1)(A) of this section that a pregnant woman is presumptively eligible for medical assistance under a State plan shall—

(A) notify the State agency of the determination within 5 working days after the date on which determination is made, and

(B) inform the woman at the time the determination is made that she is required to make application for medical assistance under the State plan by no later than the last day of the month following the month during which the determination is made.

(3) A pregnant woman who is determined by a qualified provider to be presumptively eligible for medical assistance under a State plan shall make application for medical assistance under such plan by no later than the last day of the month following the month during which the determination is made which application may be the application used for the receipt of medical assistance by individuals described in section 1396a(*l*)(1)(A) of this title.

(d) Ambulatory prenatal care as medical assistance

Notwithstanding any other provision of this subchapter, ambulatory prenatal care that—

(1) is furnished to a pregnant woman—

(A) during a presumptive eligibility period,

(B) by a provider that is eligible for payments under the State plan; and

(2) is included in the care and services covered by a State plan;

shall be treated as medical assistance provided by such plan for purposes of section 1396b of this title.

§ 1396r–1a. Presumptive eligibility for children

(a) A State plan approved under section 1396a of this title may provide for making medical assistance with respect to health care items and services covered under the State plan available to a child during a presumptive eligibility period.

(b) For purposes of this section:

(1) The term "child" means an individual under 19 years of age.

(2) The term "presumptive eligibility period" means, with respect to a child, the period that—

(A) begins with the date on which a qualified entity determines, on the basis of preliminary information, that the family income of the child does not exceed the applicable income level of eligibility under the State plan, and

(B) ends with (and includes) the earlier of—

(i) the day on which a determination is made with respect to the eligibility of the child for medical assistance under the State plan, or

(ii) in the case of a child on whose behalf an application is not filed by the last day of the month following the month during which the entity makes the determination referred to in subparagraph (A), such last day.

(3)(A) Subject to subparagraph (B), the term "qualified entity" means any entity that—

(i)(I) is eligible for payments under a State plan approved under this subchapter and provides items and services described in subsection (a) of this section,

(II) is authorized to determine eligibility of a child to participate in a Head Start program under the Head Start Act (*42 U.S.C. 9831* et seq.), eligibility of a child to receive child care services for which financial assistance is provided under the Child Care and Development Block Grant Act of 1990 (*42 U.S.C. 9858* et seq.), eligibility of an infant or child to receive assistance under the special supplemental nutrition program for women, infants, and children (WIC) under section 1786 of this title, eligibility of a child for medical assistance under the State plan under this subchapter, or eligibility of a child for child health assistance under the program funded under subchapter XXI of this chapter,

(III) is an elementary school or secondary school, as such terms are defined in section 8801 of Title 20, an elementary or secondary school operated or supported by the Bureau of Indian Affairs, a State or tribal child support enforcement agency, an organization that is providing emergency food and shelter under a grant under the Stewart B. McKinney Homeless Assistance Act, or a State or tribal office or entity involved in enrollment in the program under this subchapter, under part A of subchapter IV of this chapter, under subchapter XXI of this chapter, or that determines eligibility for any assistance or benefits provided under any program of public or assisted housing that receives Federal funds, including the program under Section 8 or any other section of the United States Housing Act of 1937 (*42 U.S.C. 1437* et seq.) or under the Native American Housing Assistance and Self-Determination Act of 1996 (*25 U.S.C. 4101* et seq.), or

(IV) any other entity the State so deems, as approved by the Secretary; and

(ii) is determined by the State agency to be capable of making determinations of the type described in paragraph (2).

(B) The Secretary may issue regulations further limiting those entities that may become qualified entities in order to prevent fraud and abuse and for other reasons.

(C) Nothing in this section shall be construed as preventing a State from limiting the classes of entities that may become qualified entities, consistent with any limitations imposed under subparagraph (B).

(c)(1) The State agency shall provide qualified entities with—

(A) such forms as are necessary for an application to be made on behalf of a child for medical assistance under the State plan, and

(B) information on how to assist parents, guardians, and other persons in completing and filing such forms.

(2) A qualified entity that determines under subsection (b)(2) of this section that a child is presumptively eligible for medical assistance under a State plan shall—

(A) notify the State agency of the determination within 5 working days after the date on which determination is made, and

(B) inform the parent or custodian of the child at the time the determination is made that an application for medical assistance under the State plan is required to be made by not later than the last day of the month following the month during which the determination is made.

(3) In the case of a child who is determined by a qualified entity to be presumptively eligible for medical assistance under a State plan, the parent, guardian, or other person shall make application on behalf of the child for medical assistance under such plan by not later than the last day of the month following the month during which the determination is made, which application may be the application used for the receipt of medical assistance by individuals described in section 1396a(*l*)(1) of this title.

(d) Notwithstanding any other provision of this subchapter, medical assistance for items and services described in subsection (a) of this section that—

(1) are furnished to a child—

(A) during a presumptive eligibility period,

(B) by an entity that is eligible for payments under the State plan; and

(2) are included in the care and services covered by a State plan;

shall be treated as medical assistance provided by such plan for purposes of section 1396b of this section.

§ 1396r–1b. Presumptive eligibility for certain breast or cervical cancer patients

(a) State option

A State plan approved under section 1396a of this title may provide for making medical assistance available to an individual described in section 1396a(aa) of this title (relating to certain breast or cervical cancer patients) during a presumptive eligibility period.

(b) Definitions

For purposes of this section:

(1) Presumptive eligibility period

The term "presumptive eligibility period" means, with respect to an individual described in subsection (a), the period that—

(A) begins with the date on which a qualified entity determines, on the basis of preliminary information, that the individual is described in section 1396a(aa) of this title; and

(B) ends with (and includes) the earlier of—

(i) the day on which a determination is made with respect to the eligibility of such individual for services under the State plan; or

(ii) in the case of such an individual who does not file an application by the last day of the month following the month during which the entity makes the determination referred to in subparagraph (A), such last day.

(2) Qualified entity

(A) In general

Subject to subparagraph (B), the term "qualified entity" means any entity that—

(i) is eligible for payments under a State plan approved under this subchapter; and

(ii) is determined by the State agency to be capable of making determinations of the type described in paragraph (1)(A).

(B) Regulations

The Secretary may issue regulations further limiting those entities that may become qualified entities in order to prevent fraud and abuse and for other reasons.

(C) Rule of construction

Nothing in this paragraph shall be construed as preventing a State from limiting the classes of entities that may become qualified entities, consistent with any limitations imposed under subparagraph (B).

(c) Administration

(1) In general

The State agency shall provide qualified entities with—

(A) such forms as are necessary for an application to be made by an individual described in subsection (a) for medical assistance under the State plan; and

(B) information on how to assist such individuals in completing and filing such forms.

(2) Notification requirements

A qualified entity that determines under subsection (b)(1)(A) that an individual described in subsection (a) is presumptively eligible for medical assistance under a State plan shall—

(A) notify the State agency of the determination within 5 working days after the date on which determination is made; and

(B) inform such individual at the time the determination is made that an application for medical assistance under the State plan is required to be made by not later than the last day of the month following the month during which the determination is made.

(3) Application for medical assistance

In the case of an individual described in subsection (a) who is determined by a qualified entity to be presumptively eligible for medical assistance under a State plan, the individual shall apply for medical assistance under such plan by not later than the last day of the month following the month during which the determination is made.

(d) Payment

Notwithstanding any other provision of this subchapter, medical assistance that—

(1) is furnished to an individual described in subsection (a)—

(A) during a presumptive eligibility period;

(B) by a entity that is eligible for payments under the State plan; and

(2) is included in the care and services covered by the State plan,

shall be treated as medical assistance provided by such plan for purposes of clause (4) of the first sentence of section 1396d(b) of this title.

* * *

§ 1396r–2. Information concerning sanctions taken by State licensing authorities against health care practitioners and providers

(a) Information reporting requirement; access to documents. The requirement referred to in section 1902(a)(49) [§ 1396a(a)(49)] is that the State must provide for the following:

(1) Information reporting system. The State must have in effect a system of reporting the following information with respect to formal proceedings (as defined by the Secretary in regulations) concluded against a health care practitioner or entity by any authority of the State (or of a political subdivision thereof) responsible for the licensing of health care practitioners (or any peer review organization or private accreditation entity reviewing the services provided by health care practitioners) or entities:

(A) Any adverse action taken by such licensing authority as a result of the proceeding, including any revocation or suspension of a license (and the length of any such suspension), reprimand, censure, or probation.

(B) Any dismissal or closure of the proceedings by reason of the practitioner or entity surrendering the license or leaving the State or jurisdiction.

(C) Any other loss of the license of the practitioner or entity, whether by operation of law, voluntary surrender, or otherwise.

(D) Any negative action or finding by such authority, organization, or entity regarding the practitioner or entity.

(2) Access to documents. The State must provide the Secretary (or an entity designated by the Secretary) with access to such documents of the authority described in paragraph (1) as may be necessary for the Secretary to determine the facts and circumstances concerning the actions and determinations described in such paragraph for the purpose of carrying out this Act.

(b) Form of information. The information described in subsection (a)(1) shall be provided to the Secretary (or to an appropriate private or public agency, under suitable arrangements made by the Secretary with respect to receipt, storage, protection of confidentiality, and dissemination of information) in such a form and manner as the Secretary determines to be appropriate in order to provide for activities of the Secretary under this Act and in order to provide, directly or through suitable arrangements made by the Secretary, information—

(1) to agencies administering Federal health care programs, including private entities administering such programs under contract,

(2) to licensing authorities described in subsection (a)(1),

(3) to State agencies administering or supervising the administration of State health care programs (as defined in section 1128(h) [§ 1320a–7(h)]),

(4) to utilization and quality control peer review organizations described in part B of title XI [§§ 1320c et seq.] and to appropriate entities with contracts under section 1154(a)(4)(C) [§ 1320c–3(a)(4)(C)] with respect to eligible organizations reviewed under the contracts,

(5) to State medicaid fraud control units (as defined in section 1903(q) [42 USCS § 1396b(q)]),

(6) to hospitals and other health care entities (as defined in section 431 of the Health Care Quality Improvement Act of 1986 [§ 11151]), with respect to physicians or other licensed health care practitioners that have entered (or may be entering) into an employment or affiliation relationship with, or have applied for clinical privileges or appointments to the medical staff of, such hospitals or other health care entities (and such information shall be deemed to be disclosed pursuant to section 427 [§ 11137] of, and be subject to the provisions of, that Act [§§ 11101 et seq.]),

(7) to the Attorney General and such other law enforcement officials as the Secretary deems appropriate, and

(8) upon request, to the Comptroller General,

in order for such authorities to determine the fitness of individuals to provide health care services, to protect the health and safety of individuals receiving health care through such programs, and to protect the fiscal integrity of such programs.

(c) Confidentiality of information provided. The Secretary shall provide for suitable safeguards for the confidentiality of the information furnished under subsection (a). Nothing in this subsection shall prevent the disclosure of such information by a party which is otherwise authorized, under applicable State law, to make such disclosure.

(d) Appropriate coordination. The Secretary shall provide for the maximum appropriate coordination in the implementation of subsection (a) of this section and section 422 of the Health Care Quality Improvement Act of 1986 [§ 11132].

* * *

§ 1396r–4. Adjustment in payment for inpatient hospital services furnished by disproportionate share hospitals

(a) Implementation of requirement [omitted from this edited version]

* * *

(b) Hospitals deemed disproportionate share

(1) For purposes of subsection (a)(1) of this section, a hospital which meets the requirements of subsection (d) of this section is deemed to be a disproportionate share hospital if—

(A) the hospital's medicaid inpatient utilization rate (as defined in paragraph (2)) is at least one standard deviation above the mean medicaid inpatient utilization rate for hospitals receiving medicaid payments in the State; or

(B) the hospital's low-income utilization rate (as defined in paragraph (3)) exceeds 25 percent.

(2) For purposes of paragraph (1)(A), the term "medicaid inpatient utilization rate" means, for a hospital, a fraction (expressed as a percentage), the numerator of which is the hospital's number of inpatient days attributable to patients who (for such days) were eligible for medical assistance under a State plan approved under this subchapter in a period (regardless of whether such patients receive medical assistance on a fee-for-service basis or through a managed care entity), and the denominator of which is the total number of the hospital's inpatient days in that period. In this paragraph, the term "inpatient day" includes each day in which an individual (including a newborn) is an inpatient in the hospital, whether or not the individual is in a specialized ward and whether or not the individual remains in the hospital for lack of suitable placement elsewhere.

(3) For purposes of paragraph (1)(B), the term "low-income utilization rate" means, for a hospital, the sum of—

(A) the fraction (expressed as a percentage)—

(i) the numerator of which is the sum (for a period) of (I) the total revenues paid the hospital for patient services under a State plan under this subchapter (regardless of whether the services were furnished on a fee-for-service basis or through a managed care entity) and (II) the amount of the cash subsidies for patient services received directly from State and local governments, and

(ii) the denominator of which is the total amount of revenues of the hospital for patient services (including the amount of such cash subsidies) in the period; and

(B) a fraction (expressed as a percentage)—

(i) the numerator of which is the total amount of the hospital's charges for inpatient hospital services which are attributable to charity care in a period, less the portion of any cash subsidies described in clause (i)(II) of subparagraph (A) in the period reasonably attributable to inpatient hospital services, and

(ii) the denominator of which is the total amount of the hospital's charges for inpatient hospital services in the hospital in the period.

The numerator under subparagraph (B)(i) shall not include contractual allowances and discounts (other than for indigent patients not eligible for medical assistance under a State plan approved under this subchapter).

(4) The Secretary may not restrict a State's authority to designate hospitals as disproportionate share hospitals under this section. The previous sentence shall not be construed to affect the authority of the Secretary to reduce payments pursuant to section 1396b(w)(1)(A)(iii) of this title if the Secretary determines that, as a result of such designations, there is in effect a hold harmless provision described in section 1396b(w)(4) of this title.

(c) Payment adjustment

Subject to subsections (f) and (g) of this section, in order to be consistent with this subsection, a payment adjustment for a disproportionate share hospital must either—

(1) be in an amount equal to at least the product of (A) the amount paid under the State plan to the hospital for operating costs for inpatient hospital services (of the kind described in section 1395ww(a)(4) of this title), and (B) the hospital's disproportionate share adjustment percentage (established under section 1395ww(d)(5)(F)(iv) of this title);

(2) provide for a minimum specified additional payment amount (or increased percentage payment) and (without regard to whether the hospital is described in subparagraph (A) or (B) of subsection (b)(1) of this section) for an increase in such a payment amount (or percentage payment) in proportion to the percentage by which the hospital's medicaid utilization rate (as defined in subsection (b)(2) of this section) exceeds one standard deviation above the mean medicaid inpatient utilization rate for hospitals receiving medicaid payments in the State or the hospital's low-income utilization rate (as defined in subsection (b)(3) of this section); or

(3) provide for a minimum specified additional payment amount (or increased percentage payment) that varies according to type of hospital under a methodology that—

> **(A)** applies equally to all hospitals of each type; and

> **(B)** results in an adjustment for each type of hospital that is reasonably related to the costs, volume, or proportion of services provided to patients eligible for medical assistance under a State plan approved under this subchapter or to low-income patients,

except that, for purposes of paragraphs (1)(B) and (2)(A) of subsection (a) of this section, the payment adjustment for a disproportionate share hospital is consistent with this subsection if the appropriate increase in the rate or amount of payment is equal to at least one-third of the increase otherwise applicable under this subsection (in the case of such paragraph (1)(B)) and at least two-thirds of such increase (in the case of such paragraph (2)(A)). In the case of a hospital described in subsection (d)(2)(A)(i) of this section (relating to children's hospitals), in computing the hospital's disproportionate share adjustment percentage for purposes of paragraph (1)(B) of this subsection, the disproportionate patient percentage (defined in section 1395ww(d)(5)(F)(vi) of this title) shall be computed by substituting for the fraction described in subclause (I) of such section the fraction described in subclause (II) of that section. If a State elects in a State plan amendment under subsection (a) of this section to provide the payment adjustment described in paragraph (2), the State must include in the amendment a detailed description of the specific methodology to be used in determining the specified additional payment amount (or increased percentage payment) to be made to each hospital qualifying for such a payment adjustment and must publish at least annually the name of each hospital qualifying for such a payment adjustment and the amount of such payment adjustment made for each such hospital.

(d) Requirements to qualify as disproportionate share hospital

(1) Except as provided in paragraph (2), no hospital may be defined or deemed as a disproportionate share hospital under a State plan under this subchapter or under subsection (b) of this section unless the hospital has at least 2 obstetricians who have staff privileges at the hospital and who have agreed to provide obstetric services to individuals who are entitled to medical assistance for such services under such State plan.

(2)(A) Paragraph (1) shall not apply to a hospital—

> **(i)** the inpatients of which are predominantly individuals under 18 years of age; or

> **(ii)** which does not offer nonemergency obstetric services to the general population as of December 22, 1987.

(B) In the case of a hospital located in a rural area (as defined for purposes of section 1395ww of this title), in paragraph (1) the term "obstetrician" includes any physician with staff privileges at the hospital to perform nonemergency obstetric procedures.

(3) No hospital may be defined or deemed as a disproportionate share hospital under a State plan under this subchapter or under subsection (b) or (e) of this section unless the hospital has a medicaid inpatient utilization rate (as defined in subsection (b)(2) of this section) of not less than 1 percent.

* * *

(f) Limitation on Federal financial participation

(1) In general.   Payment under section 1903(a) [§ 1396b(a)] shall not be made to a State with respect to any payment adjustment made under this section for hospitals in a State for quarters in a fiscal year in excess of the disproportionate share hospital (in this subsection referred to as "DSH") allotment for the State for the fiscal year, as specified in paragraphs (2) and (3).

(2) State DSH allotments for fiscal years 1998 through 2002.   Subject to paragraph (4), the DSH allotment for a State for each fiscal year during the period beginning with fiscal year 1998 and ending with fiscal year 2002 is determined in accordance with the following table:

(3) State DSH allotments for fiscal year 2003 and thereafter.   (A) In general.   The DSH allotment for any State for fiscal year 2003 and each succeeding fiscal year is equal to the DSH allotment for the State for the preceding fiscal year under paragraph (2) or this paragraph, increased, subject to subparagraph (B) and paragraph (5), by the percentage change in the consumer price index for all urban consumers (all items; U.S. city average), for the previous fiscal year.

(B) Limitation.   The DSH allotment for a State shall not be increased under subparagraph (A) for a fiscal year to the extent that such an increase would result in the DSH allotment for the year exceeding the greater of—

> **(i)** the DSH allotment for the previous year, or

> **(ii)** 12 percent of the total amount of expenditures under the State plan for medical assistance during the fiscal year.

999

(4) Special rule for fiscal years 2001 and 2002.

(A) In general. Notwithstanding paragraph (2), the DSH allotment for any State for—

(i) fiscal year 2001, shall be the DSH allotment determined under paragraph (2) for fiscal year 2000 increased, subject to subparagraph (B) and paragraph (5), by the percentage change in the consumer price index for all urban consumers (all items; U.S. city average) for fiscal year 2000; and

(ii) fiscal year 2002, shall be the DSH allotment determined under clause (i) increased, subject to subparagraph (B) and paragraph (5), by the percentage change in the consumer price index for all urban consumers (all items; U.S. city average) for fiscal year 2001.

(B) Limitation. Subparagraph (B) of paragraph (3) shall apply to subparagraph (A) of this paragraph in the same manner as that subparagraph (B) applies to paragraph (3)(A).

(C) No application to allotments after fiscal year 2002. The DSH allotment for any State for fiscal year 2003 or any succeeding fiscal year shall be determined under paragraph (3) without regard to the DSH allotments determined under subparagraph (A) of this paragraph.

(5) Special rule for extremely low DSH States. In the case of a State in which the total expenditures under the State plan (including Federal and State shares) for disproportionate share hospital adjustments under this section for fiscal year 1999, as reported to the Administrator of the Health Care Financing Administration as of August 31, 2000, is greater than 0 but less than 1 percent of the State's total amount of expenditures under the State plan for medical assistance during the fiscal year, the DSH allotment for fiscal year 2001 shall be increased to 1 percent of the State's total amount of expenditures under such plan for such assistance during such fiscal year. In subsequent fiscal years, such increased allotment is subject to an increase for inflation as provided in paragraph (3)(A).

(6) Definition of State. In this subsection, the term "State" means the 50 States and the District of Columbia.

(g) Limit on amount of payment to hospital

(1) Amount of adjustment subject to uncompensated costs

(A) In general. A payment adjustment during a fiscal year shall not be considered to be consistent with subsection (c) with respect to a hospital if the payment adjustment exceeds the costs incurred during the year of furnishing hospital services (as determined by the Secretary and net of payments under this title [42 USCS §§ 1396 et seq.], other than under this section, and by uninsured patients) by the hospital to individuals who either are eligible for medical assistance under the State plan or have no health insurance (or other source of third party coverage) for services provided during the year. For purposes of the preceding sentence, payments made to a hospital for services provided to indigent patients made by a State or a unit of local government within a State shall not be considered to be a source of third party payment.

(B) Limit to public hospitals during transition period.   With respect to payment adjustments during a State fiscal year that begins before January 1, 1995, subparagraph (A) shall apply only to hospitals owned or operated by a State (or by an instrumentality or a unit of government within a State).

(C) Modifications for private hospitals.   With respect to hospitals that are not owned or operated by a State (or by an instrumentality or a unit of government within a State), the Secretary may make such modifications to the manner in which the limitation on payment adjustments is applied to such hospitals as the Secretary considers appropriate.

(2) Additional amount during transition period for certain hospitals with high disproportionate share.   (A) In general.   In the case of a hospital with high disproportionate share (as defined in subparagraph (B)), a payment adjustment during a State fiscal year that begins before January 1, 1995, shall be considered consistent with subsection (c) if the payment adjustment does not exceed 200 percent of the costs of furnishing hospital services described in paragraph (1)(A) during the year, but only if the Governor of the State certifies to the satisfaction of the Secretary that the hospital's applicable minimum amount is used for health services during the year.   In determining the amount that is used for such services during a year, there shall be excluded any amounts received under the Public Health Service Act [§§ 201 et seq.], title V [§§ 701 et seq.], title XVIII, or from third party payors (not including the State plan under this title) that are used for providing such services during the year.

(B) Hospitals with high disproportionate share defined.   In subparagraph (A), a hospital is a "hospital with high disproportionate share" if—

(i) the hospital is owned or operated by a State (or by an instrumentality or a unit of government within a State); and

(ii) the hospital—

(I) meets the requirement described in subsection (b)(1)(A), or

(II) has the largest number of inpatient days attributable to individuals entitled to benefits under the State plan of any hospital in such State for the previous State fiscal year.

(C) Applicable minimum amount defined. In subparagraph (A), the "applicable minimum amount" for a hospital for a fiscal year is equal to the difference between the amount of the hospital's payment adjustment for the fiscal year and the costs to the hospital of furnishing hospital services described in paragraph (1)(A) during the fiscal year.

* * *

(i) Requirement for direct payment

(1) In general. No payment may be made under section 1903(a)(1) [42 USCS § 1396b(a)(1)] with respect to a payment adjustment made under this section, for services furnished by a hospital on or after October 1, 1997, with respect to individuals eligible for medical assistance under the State plan who are enrolled with a managed care entity (as defined in section 1932(a)(1)(B) [42 USCS § 1396u–2(a)(1)(B)]) or under any other managed care arrangement unless a payment, equal to the amount of the payment adjustment—

(A) is made directly to the hospital by the State; and

(B) is not used to determine the amount of a prepaid capitation payment under the State plan to the entity or arrangement with respect to such individuals.

(2) Exception for current arrangements. Paragraph (1) shall not apply to a payment adjustment provided pursuant to a payment arrangement in effect on July 1, 1997.

* * *

§ 1396r–5. Treatment of income and resources for certain institutionalized spouses

(a) Special treatment for institutionalized spouses

(1) Supersedes other provisions

In determining the eligibility for medical assistance of an institutionalized spouse (as defined in subsection (h)(1) of this section), the provisions of this section supersede any other provision of this subchapter (including sections 1396a(a)(17) and 1396a(f) of this title) which is inconsistent with them.

(2) No comparable treatment required

Any different treatment provided under this section for institutionalized spouses shall not, by reason of paragraph (10) or (17) of section 1396a(a) of this title, require such treatment for other individuals.

(3) Does not affect certain determinations

Except as this section specifically provides, this section does not apply to—

(A) the determination of what constitutes income or resources, or

(B) the methodology and standards for determining and evaluating income and resources.

(4) Application in certain States and territories

(A) Application in States operating under demonstration projects

In the case of any State which is providing medical assistance to its residents under a waiver granted under section 1315 of this title, the Secretary shall require the State to meet the requirements of this section in the same manner as the State would be required to meet such requirement if the State had in effect a plan approved under this subchapter.

(B) No application in commonwealths and territories

This section shall only apply to a State that is one of the 50 States or the District of Columbia.

(5) Application to individuals receiving services under PACE programs

This section applies to individuals receiving institutional or noninstitutional services under a PACE demonstration waiver program (as defined in section 1396u–4(a)(7) of this title) or under a PACE program under section 1936u–4 or 1395eee of this title.

(b) Rules for treatment of income

(1) Separate treatment of income

During any month in which an institutionalized spouse is in the institution, except as provided in paragraph (2), no income of the community spouse shall be deemed available to the institutionalized spouse.

(2) Attribution of income

In determining the income of an institutionalized spouse or community spouse for purposes of the post-eligibility income determination described in subsection (d) of this section, except as otherwise provided in this section and regardless of any State laws relating to community property or the division of marital property, the following rules apply:

(A) Non-trust property

Subject to subparagraphs (C) and (D), in the case of income not from a trust, unless the instrument providing the income otherwise specifically provides—

(i) if payment of income is made solely in the name of the institutionalized spouse or the community spouse, the income shall be considered available only to that respective spouse;

(ii) if payment of income is made in the names of the institutionalized spouse and the community spouse, one-half of the income shall be considered available to each of them; and

(iii) if payment of income is made in the names of the institutionalized spouse or the community spouse, or both, and to another person or persons, the income shall be considered available to each spouse in proportion to the spouse's interest (or, if payment is made with respect to both spouses and no such interest is specified, one-half of the joint interest shall be considered available to each spouse).

(B) Trust property

In the case of a trust—

(i) except as provided in clause (ii), income shall be attributed in accordance with the provisions of this subchapter (including sections 1396a(a)(17) and 1396p(d) of this title), and

(ii) income shall be considered available to each spouse as provided in the trust, or, in the absence of a specific provision in the trust—

(I) if payment of income is made solely to the institutionalized spouse or the community spouse, the income shall be considered available only to that respective spouse;

(II) if payment of income is made to both the institutionalized spouse and the community spouse, one-half of the income shall be considered available to each of them; and

(III) if payment of income is made to the institutionalized spouse or the community spouse, or both, and to another person or persons, the income shall be considered available to each spouse in proportion to the spouse's interest (or, if payment is made with respect to both spouses and no such interest is specified, one-half of the joint interest shall be considered available to each spouse).

(C) Property with no instrument

In the case of income not from a trust in which there is no instrument establishing ownership, subject to subparagraph (D), one-half of the income shall be considered to be available to the institutionalized spouse and one-half to the community spouse.

(D) Rebutting ownership

The rules of subparagraphs (A) and (C) are superseded to the extent that an institutionalized spouse can establish, by a preponderance of the evidence, that the ownership interests in income are other than as provided under such subparagraphs.

(c) Rules for treatment of resources

(1) Computation of spousal share at time of institutionalization

(A) Total joint resources

There shall be computed (as of the beginning of the first continuous period of institutionalization (beginning on or after September 30, 1989) of the institutionalized spouse)—

(i) the total value of the resources to the extent either the institutionalized spouse or the community spouse has an ownership interest, and

(ii) a spousal share which is equal to 1/2 of such total value.

(B) Assessment

At the request of an institutionalized spouse or community spouse, at the beginning of the first continuous period of institutionalization (beginning on or after September 30, 1989) of the institutionalized spouse and upon the receipt of relevant documentation of resources, the State shall promptly assess and document the total value described in subparagraph (A)(i) and shall provide a copy of such assessment and documentation to each spouse and shall retain a copy of the assessment for use under this section. If the request is not part of an application for medical assistance under this subchapter, the State may, at its option as a condition of providing the assessment, require payment of a fee not exceeding the reasonable expenses of providing and documenting the assessment. At the time of providing the copy of the assessment, the State shall include a notice indicating that the spouse will have a right to a fair hearing under subsection (e)(2) of this section.

(2) Attribution of resources at time of initial eligibility determination

In determining the resources of an institutionalized spouse at the time of application for benefits under this subchapter, regardless of any State laws relating to community property or the division of marital property—

(A) except as provided in subparagraph (B), all the resources held by either the institutionalized spouse, community spouse, or both, shall be considered to be available to the institutionalized spouse, and

(B) resources shall be considered to be available to an institutionalized spouse, but only to the extent that the amount of such resources exceeds the amount computed under subsection (f)(2)(A) of this section (as of the time of application for benefits).

(3) Assignment of support rights

The institutionalized spouse shall not be ineligible by reason of resources determined under paragraph (2) to be available for the cost of care where—

(A) the institutionalized spouse has assigned to the State any rights to support from the community spouse;

(B) the institutionalized spouse lacks the ability to execute an assignment due to physical or mental impairment but the State has the right to bring a support proceeding against a community spouse without such assignment; or

(C) the State determines that denial of eligibility would work an undue hardship.

(4) Separate treatment of resources after eligibility for benefits established

During the continuous period in which an institutionalized spouse is in an institution and after the month in which an institutionalized spouse is determined to be eligible for benefits under this subchapter, no resources of the community spouse shall be deemed available to the institutionalized spouse.

(5) Resources defined

In this section, the term "resources" does not include—

(A) resources excluded under subsection (a) or (d) of section 1382b of this title, and

(B) resources that would be excluded under section 1382b(a)(2)(A) of this title but for the limitation on total value described in such section.

(d) Protecting income for community spouse

(1) Allowances to be offset from income of institutionalized spouse

After an institutionalized spouse is determined or redetermined to be eligible for medical assistance, in determining the amount of the spouse's income that is to be applied monthly to payment for the costs of care in the institution, there shall be deducted from the spouse's monthly income the following amounts in the following order:

(A) A personal needs allowance (described in section 1396a(q)(1) of this title), in an amount not less than the amount specified in section 1396a(q)(2) of this title.

(B) A community spouse monthly income allowance (as defined in paragraph (2)), but only to the extent income of the institutionalized spouse is made available to (or for the benefit of) the community spouse.

(C) A family allowance, for each family member, equal to at least 1/3 of the amount by which the amount described in paragraph (3)(A)(i) exceeds the amount of the monthly income of that family member.

(D) Amounts for incurred expenses for medical or remedial care for the institutionalized spouse (as provided under section 1396a(r) of this title).

In subparagraph (C), the term "family member" only includes minor or dependent children, dependent parents, or dependent siblings of the institutionalized or community spouse who are residing with the community spouse.

(2) Community spouse monthly income allowance defined

In this section (except as provided in paragraph (5)), the "community spouse monthly income allowance" for a community spouse is an amount by which—

(A) except as provided in subsection (e) of this section, the minimum monthly maintenance needs allowance (established under and in accordance with paragraph (3)) for the spouse, exceeds

(B) the amount of monthly income otherwise available to the community spouse (determined without regard to such an allowance).

(3) Establishment of minimum monthly maintenance needs allowance

(A) In general

Each State shall establish a minimum monthly maintenance needs allowance for each community spouse which, subject to subparagraph (C), is equal to or exceeds—

(i) the applicable percent (described in subparagraph (B)) of 1/12 of the income official poverty line (defined by the Office of Management and Budget and revised annually in accordance with section 9902(2) of this title) for a family unit of 2 members; plus

(ii) an excess shelter allowance (as defined in paragraph (4)).

A revision of the official poverty line referred to in clause (i) shall apply to medical assistance furnished during and after the second calendar quarter that begins after the date of publication of the revision.

(B) Applicable percent

For purposes of subparagraph (A)(i), the "applicable percent" described in this paragraph, effective as of—

* * *

(iii) July 1, 1992, is 150 percent.

(C) Cap on minimum monthly maintenance needs allowance

The minimum monthly maintenance needs allowance established under subparagraph (A) may not exceed $1,500 (subject to adjustment under subsections (e) and (g) of this section).

(4) Excess shelter allowance defined

In paragraph (3)(A)(ii), the term "excess shelter allowance" means, for a community spouse, the amount by which the sum of—

(A) the spouse's expenses for rent or mortgage payment (including principal and interest), taxes and insurance and, in the case of a condominium or cooperative, required maintenance charge, for the community spouse's principal residence, and

(B) the standard utility allowance (used by the State under section 2014(e) of Title 7) or, if the State does not use such an allowance, the spouse's actual utility expenses,

exceeds 30 percent of the amount described in paragraph (3)(A)(i), except that, in the case of a condominium or cooperative, for which a maintenance charge is included under subparagraph (A), any allowance under subparagraph (B) shall be reduced to the extent the maintenance charge includes utility expenses.

(5) Court ordered support

If a court has entered an order against an institutionalized spouse for monthly income for the support of the community spouse, the community spouse monthly income allowance for the spouse shall be not less than the amount of the monthly income so ordered.

(e) Notice and fair hearing

(1) Notice

Upon—

(A) a determination of eligibility for medical assistance of an institutionalized spouse, or

(B) a request by either the institutionalized spouse, or the community spouse, or a representative acting on behalf of either spouse,

each State shall notify both spouses (in the case described in subparagraph (A)) or the spouse making the request (in the case described in subparagraph (B)) of the amount of the community spouse monthly income allowance (described in subsection (d)(1)(B) of this section), of the amount of any family allowances (described in subsection (d)(1)(C) of this section), of the method for computing the amount of the community spouse resources allowance permitted under subsection (f) of this section, and of the spouse's right to a fair hearing under this subsection respecting ownership or availability of income or resources, and the determination of the community spouse monthly income or resource allowance.

1008

(2) Fair hearing

(A) In general

If either the institutionalized spouse or the community spouse is dissatisfied with a determination of—

    (i) the community spouse monthly income allowance;

    (ii) the amount of monthly income otherwise available to the community spouse (as applied under subsection (d)(2)(B) of this section);

    (iii) the computation of the spousal share of resources under subsection (c)(1) of this section;

    (iv) the attribution of resources under subsection (c)(2) of this section; or

    (v) the determination of the community spouse resource allowance (as defined in subsection (f)(2) of this section);

such spouse is entitled to a fair hearing described in section 1396a(a)(3) of this title with respect to such determination if an application for benefits under this subchapter has been made on behalf of the institutionalized spouse. Any such hearing respecting the determination of the community spouse resource allowance shall be held within 30 days of the date of the request for the hearing.

(B) Revision of minimum monthly maintenance needs allowance

If either such spouse establishes that the community spouse needs income, above the level otherwise provided by the minimum monthly maintenance needs allowance, due to exceptional circumstances resulting in significant financial duress, there shall be substituted, for the minimum monthly maintenance needs allowance in subsection (d)(2)(A) of this section, an amount adequate to provide such additional income as is necessary.

(C) Revision of community spouse resource allowance

If either such spouse establishes that the community spouse resource allowance (in relation to the amount of income generated by such an allowance) is inadequate to raise the community spouse's income to the minimum monthly maintenance needs allowance, there shall be substituted, for the community spouse resource allowance under subsection (f)(2) of this section, an amount adequate to provide such a minimum monthly maintenance needs allowance.

(f) Permitting transfer of resources to community spouse

(1) In general

An institutionalized spouse may, without regard to section 1396p(c)(1) of this title, transfer an amount equal to the community spouse resource allowance (as defined in paragraph (2)), but only to the extent the resources of the institutionalized spouse are transferred to (or for the sole benefit of) the community spouse. The transfer under the preceding sentence shall be made as soon as practicable after the date of the initial determination of eligibility, taking into account such time as may be necessary to obtain a court order under paragraph (3).

(2) Community spouse resource allowance defined

In paragraph (1), the "community spouse resource allowance" for a community spouse is an amount (if any) by which—

(A) the greatest of—

(i) $12,000 (subject to adjustment under subsection (g) of this section), or, if greater (but not to exceed the amount specified in clause (ii)(II)) an amount specified under the State plan,

(ii) the lesser of (I) the spousal share computed under subsection (c)(1) of this section, or (II) $60,000 (subject to adjustment under subsection (g) of this section),

(iii) the amount established under subsection (e)(2) of this section; or

(iv) the amount transferred under a court order under paragraph (3);

exceeds

(B) the amount of the resources otherwise available to the community spouse (determined without regard to such an allowance).

(3) Transfers under court orders

If a court has entered an order against an institutionalized spouse for the support of the community spouse, section 1396p of this title shall not apply to amounts of resources transferred pursuant to such order for the support of the spouse or a family member (as defined in subsection (d)(1) of this section).

(g) Indexing dollar amounts

For services furnished during a calendar year after 1989, the dollar amounts specified in subsections (d)(3)(C), (f)(2)(A)(i), and (f)(2)(A)(ii)(II) of this section shall be increased by the same percentage as the percentage increase in the consumer price index for all urban consumers (all items; U.S. city average) between September 1988 and the September before the calendar year involved.

(h) Definitions

In this section:

(1) The term "institutionalized spouse" means an individual who—

(A) is in a medical institution or nursing facility or who (at the option of the State) is described in section 1396a(a)(10)(A)(ii)(VI) of this title, and

(B) is married to a spouse who is not in a medical institution or nursing facility;

but does not include any such individual who is not likely to meet the requirements of subparagraph (A) for at least 30 consecutive days.

(2) The term "community spouse" means the spouse of an institutionalized spouse

§ 1396r–6. Extension of eligibility for medical assistance

(a) Initial 6–month extension

(1) Requirement

Notwithstanding any other provision of this subchapter, each State plan approved under this subchapter must provide that each family which was receiving aid pursuant to a plan of the State approved under part A of subchapter IV of this chapter in at least 3 of the 6 months immediately preceding the month in which such family becomes ineligible for such aid, because of hours of, or income from, employment of the caretaker relative (as defined in subsection (e) of this section) or because of section 602(a)(8)(B)(ii)(II) of this title (providing for a time-limited earned income disregard), shall, subject to paragraph (3) and without any reapplication for benefits under the plan, remain eligible for assistance under the plan approved under this subchapter during the immediately succeeding 6–month period in accordance with this subsection.

(2) Notice of benefits

Each State, in the notice of termination of aid under part A of subchapter IV of this chapter sent to a family meeting the requirements of paragraph (1)—

(A) shall notify the family of its right to extended medical assistance under this subsection and include in the notice a description of the reporting requirement of subsection (b)(2)(B)(i) of this section and of the circumstances (described in paragraph (3)) under which such extension may be terminated; and

(B) shall include a card or other evidence of the family's entitlement to assistance under this subchapter for the period provided in this subsection.

(3) Termination of extension

(A) No dependent child

Subject to subparagraphs (B) and (C), extension of assistance during the 6–month period described in paragraph (1) to a family shall terminate (during such period) at the close of the first month in which the family ceases to include a child, whether or not the child is (or would if needy be) a dependent child under part A of subchapter IV of this chapter.

(B) Notice before termination

No termination of assistance shall become effective under subparagraph (A) until the State has provided the family with notice of the grounds for the termination.

(C) Continuation in certain cases until redetermination

With respect to a child who would cease to receive medical assistance because of subparagraph (A) but who may be eligible for assistance under the State plan because the child is described in clause (i) of section 1396d(a) of this title or clause (i)(IV), (i)(VI), (i)(VII), or (ii)(IX) of section 1396a(a)(10)(A) of this title, the State may not discontinue such assistance under such subparagraph until the State has determined that the child is not eligible for assistance under the plan.

(4) Scope of coverage

(A) In general

Subject to subparagraph (B), during the 6–month extension period under this subsection, the amount, duration, and scope of medical assistance made available with respect to a family shall be the same as if the family were still receiving aid under the plan approved under part A of subchapter IV of this chapter.

(B) State Medicaid "wrap-around" option

A State, at its option, may pay a family's expenses for premiums, deductibles, coinsurance, and similar costs for health insurance or other health coverage offered by an employer of the caretaker relative or by an employer of the absent parent of a dependent child. In the case of such coverage offered by an employer of the caretaker relative—

    (i) the State may require the caretaker relative, as a condition of extension of coverage under this subsection for the caretaker and the caretaker's family, to make application for such employer coverage, but only if—

        (I) the caretaker relative is not required to make financial contributions for such coverage (whether through payroll deduction, payment of deductibles, coinsurance, or similar costs, or otherwise), and

        (II) the State provides, directly or otherwise, for payment of any of the premium amount, deductible, coinsurance, or similar expense that the employee is otherwise required to pay; and

    (ii) the State shall treat the coverage under such an employer plan as a third party liability (under section 1396a(a)(25) of this title).

Payments for premiums, deductibles, coinsurance, and similar expenses under this subparagraph shall be considered, for purposes of section 1396b(a) of this title, to be payments for medical assistance.

(b) Additional 6–month extension

(1) Requirement

Notwithstanding any other provision of this subchapter, each State plan approved under this subchapter shall provide that the State shall offer to each family, which has received assistance during the entire 6–month period under subsection (a) of this section and which meets the requirement of paragraph (2)(B)(i), in the last month of the period the option of extending coverage under this subsection for the succeeding 6–month period, subject to paragraph (3).

(2) Notice and reporting requirements

(A) Notices

(i) Notice during initial extension period of option and requirements

Each State, during the 3rd and 6th month of any extended assistance furnished to a family under subsection (a) of this section, shall notify the family of the family's option for additional extended assistance under this subsection. Each such notice shall include (I) in the 3rd month notice, a statement of the reporting requirement under subparagraph (B)(i), and, in the 6th month notice, a statement of the reporting requirement under subparagraph (B)(ii), (II) a statement as to whether any premiums are required for such additional extended assistance, and (III) a description of other out-of-pocket expenses, benefits, reporting and payment procedures, and any pre-existing condition limitations, waiting periods, or other coverage limitations imposed under any alternative coverage options offered under paragraph (4)(D). The 6th month notice under this subparagraph shall describe the amount of any premium required of a particular family for each of the first 3 months of additional extended assistance under this subsection.

(ii) Notice during additional extension period of reporting requirements and premiums

Each State, during the 3rd month of any additional extended assistance furnished to a family under this subsection, shall notify the family of the reporting requirement under subparagraph (B)(ii) and a statement of the amount of any premium required for such extended assistance for the succeeding 3 months.

(B) Reporting requirements

(i) During initial extension period

Each State shall require (as a condition for additional extended assistance under this subsection) that a family receiving extended assistance under subsection (a) of this section report to the State, not later than the 21st day of the 4th month in the period of extended assistance under subsection (a) of this section, on the family's gross monthly earnings and on the family's costs for such child care as is necessary for the employment of the caretaker relative in each of the first 3 months of that period. A State may permit such additional extended assistance under this subsection notwithstanding a failure to report under this clause if the family has established, to the satisfaction of the State, good cause for the failure to report on a timely basis.

(ii) During additional extension period

Each State shall require that a family receiving extended assistance under this subsection report to the State, not later than the 21st day of the 1st month and of the 4th month in the period of additional extended assistance under this subsection, on the family's gross monthly earnings and on the family's costs for such child care as is necessary for the employment of the caretaker relative in each of the 3 preceding months.

(iii) Clarification on frequency of reporting

A State may not require that a family receiving extended assistance under this subsection or subsection (a) report more frequently than as required under clause (i) or (ii).

(3) Termination of extension

(A) In general

Subject to subparagraphs (B) and (C), extension of assistance during the 6-month period described in paragraph (1) to a family shall terminate (during the period) as follows:

(i) No dependent child

The extension shall terminate at the close of the first month in which the family ceases to include a child, whether or not the child is (or would if needy be) a dependent child under part A of subchapter IV of this chapter.

(ii) Failure to pay any premium

If the family fails to pay any premium for a month under paragraph (5) by the 21st day of the following month, the extension shall terminate at the close of that following month, unless the family has established, to the satisfaction of the State, good cause for the failure to pay such premium on a timely basis.

(iii) Quarterly income reporting and test

The extension under this subsection shall terminate at the close of the 1st or 4th month of the 6-month period if—

(I) the family fails to report to the State, by the 21st day of such month, the information required under paragraph (2)(B)(ii), unless the family has established, to the satisfaction of the State, good cause for the failure to report on a timely basis;

(II) the caretaker relative had no earnings in one or more of the previous 3 months, unless such lack of any earnings was due to an involuntary loss of employment, illness, or other good cause, established to the satisfaction of the State; or

(III) the State determines that the family's average gross monthly earnings (less such costs for such child care as is necessary for the employment of the caretaker relative) during the immediately preceding 3–month period exceed 185 percent of the official poverty line (as defined by the Office of Management and Budget, and revised annually in accordance with section 9902(2) of this title) applicable to a family of the size involved.

Information described in clause (iii)(I) shall be subject to the restrictions on use and disclosure of information provided under section 602(a)(9) of this title. Instead of terminating a family's extension under clause (iii)(I), a State, at its option, may provide for suspension of the extension until the month after the month in which the family reports information required under paragraph (2)(B)(ii), but only if the family's extension has not otherwise been terminated under subclause (II) or (III) of clause (iii). The State shall make determinations under clause (iii)(III) for a family each time a report under paragraph (2)(B)(ii) for the family is received.

(B) Notice before termination

No termination of assistance shall become effective under subparagraph (A) until the State has provided the family with notice of the grounds for the termination, which notice shall include (in the case of termination under subparagraph (A)(iii)(II), relating to no continued earnings) a description of how the family may reestablish eligibility for medical assistance under the State plan. No such termination shall be effective earlier than 10 days after the date of mailing of such notice.

(C) Continuation in certain cases until redetermination

(i) Dependent children

With respect to a child who would cease to receive medical assistance because of subparagraph (A)(i) but who may be eligible for assistance under the State plan because the child is described in clause (i) of section 1396d(a) of this title or clause (i)(IV), (i)(VI), (i)(VII), or (ii)(IX) of section 1396a(a)(10)(A) of this title, the State may not discontinue such assistance under such subparagraph until the State has determined that the child is not eligible for assistance under the plan.

(ii) Medically needy

With respect to an individual who would cease to receive medical assistance because of clause (ii) or (iii) of subparagraph (A) but who may be eligible for assistance under the State plan because the individual is within a category of person for which medical assistance under the State plan is available under section 1396a(a)(10)(C) of this title (relating to medically needy individuals), the State may not discontinue such assistance under such subparagraph until the State has determined that the individual is not eligible for assistance under the plan.

(4) Coverage

(A) In general

During the extension period under this subsection—

(i) the State plan shall offer to each family medical assistance which (subject to subparagraphs (B) and (C)) is the same amount, duration, and scope as would be made available to the family if it were still receiving aid under the plan approved under part A of subchapter IV of this chapter; and

(ii) the State plan may offer alternative coverage described in subparagraph (D).

(B) Elimination of most non-acute care benefits

At a State's option and notwithstanding any other provision of this subchapter, a State may choose not to provide medical assistance under this subsection with respect to any (or all) of the items and services described in paragraphs (4)(A), (6), (7), (8), (11), (13), (14), (15), (16), (18), (20), and (21) of section 1396d(a) of this title.

(C) State medicaid "wrap-around" option

At a State's option, the State may elect to apply the option described in subsection (a)(4)(B) of this section (relating to "wrap-around" coverage) for families electing medical assistance under this subsection in the same manner as such option applies to families provided extended eligibility for medical assistance under subsection (a) of this section.

(D) Alternative assistance

At a State's option, the State may offer families a choice of health care coverage under one or more of the following, instead of the medical assistance otherwise made available under this subsection:

(i) Enrollment in family option of employer plan

Enrollment of the caretaker relative and dependent children in a family option of the group health plan offered to the caretaker relative.

(ii) Enrollment in family option of State employee plan

Enrollment of the caretaker relative and dependent children in a family option within the options of the group health plan or plans offered by the State to State employees.

(iii) Enrollment in State uninsured plan

Enrollment of the caretaker relative and dependent children in a basic State health plan offered by the State to individuals in the State (or areas of the State) otherwise unable to obtain health insurance coverage.

(iv) Enrollment in medicaid managed care organization

Enrollment of the caretaker relative and dependent children in a medicaid managed care organization (as defined in section 1396b(m)(1)(A) of this title). The option of enrollment under this clause is in addition to, and not in lieu of, any enrollment option that the State might offer under subparagraph (A)(i) with respect to receiving services through a medicaid managed care organization in accordance with section 1396b(m) of this title and the applicable requirements of section 1396u–2 of this title.

If a State elects to offer an option to enroll a family under this subparagraph, the State shall pay any premiums and other costs for such enrollment imposed on the family and may pay deductibles and coinsurance imposed on the family. A State's payment of premiums for the enrollment of families under this subparagraph (not including any premiums otherwise payable by an employer and less the amount of premiums collected from such families under paragraph (5)) and payment of any deductibles and coinsurance shall be considered, for purposes of section 1396b(a)(1) of this title, to be payments for medical assistance.

(E) Prohibition on cost-sharing for maternity and preventive pediatric care

(i) In general

If a State offers any alternative option under subparagraph (D) for families, under each such option the State must assure that care described in clause (ii) is available without charge to the families through—

(I) payment of any deductibles, coinsurance, and other cost-sharing respecting such care, or

(II) providing coverage under the State plan for such care without any cost-sharing, or any combination of such mechanisms.

(ii) Care described

The care described in this clause consists of—

(I) services related to pregnancy (including prenatal, delivery, and post partum services), and

(II) ambulatory preventive pediatric care (including ambulatory early and periodic screening, diagnosis, and treatment services under section 1396d(a)(4)(B) of this title) for each child who meets the age and date of birth requirements to be a qualified child under section 1396d(n)(2) of this title.

(5) Premium

(A) Permitted

Notwithstanding any other provision of this subchapter (including section 1396o, of this title), a State may impose a premium for a family for additional extended coverage under this subsection for a premium payment period (as defined in subparagraph (D)(i)), but only if the family's average gross monthly earnings (less the average monthly costs for such child care as is necessary for the employment of the caretaker relative) for the premium base period exceed 100 percent of the official poverty line (as defined by the Office of Management and Budget, and revised annually in accordance with section 9902(2) of this title) applicable to a family of the size involved.

(B) Level may vary by option offered

The level of such premium may vary, for the same family, for each option offered by a State under paragraph (4)(D).

(C) Limit on premium

In no case may the amount of any premium under this paragraph for a family for a month in either of the premium payment periods described in subparagraph (D)(i) exceed 3 percent of the family's average gross monthly earnings (less the average monthly costs for such child care as is necessary for the employment of the caretaker relative) during the premium base period (as defined in subparagraph (D)(ii)).

(D) Definitions

In this paragraph:

(i) A "premium payment period" described in this clause is a 3–month period beginning with the 1st or 4th month of the 6–month additional extension period provided under this subsection.

(ii) The term "premium base period" means, with respect to a particular premium payment period, the period of 3 consecutive months the last of which is 4 months before the beginning of that premium payment period.

(c) Applicability in States and territories

(1) States operating under demonstration projects

In the case of any State which is providing medical assistance to its residents under a waiver granted under section 1315(a) of this title, the Secretary shall require the State to meet the requirements of this section in the same manner as the State would be required to meet such requirement if the State had in effect a plan approved under this subchapter.

(2) Inapplicability in commonwealths and territories

The provisions of this section shall only apply to the 50 States and the District of Columbia.

(d) General disqualification for fraud

(1) Ineligibility for aid

This section shall not apply to an individual who is a member of a family which has received aid under part A of subchapter IV of this chapter if the State makes a finding that, at any time during the last 6 months in which the family was receiving such aid before otherwise being provided extended eligibility under this section, the individual was ineligible for such aid because of fraud.

(2) General disqualifications

For additional provisions relating to fraud and program abuse, see sections 1320a–7, 1320a–7a, and 1320a–7b of this title.

(e) "Caretaker relative" defined

In this section, the term "caretaker relative" has the meaning of such term as used in part A of subchapter IV of this chapter.

(f) Sunset

This section shall not apply with respect to families that cease to be eligible for aid under part A of subchapter IV of this chapter after September 30, 2002.

* * *

1396r–8. Payment for covered outpatient drugs

(a) Requirement for rebate agreement

(1) In general

In order for payment to be available under section 1396b(a) of this title for covered outpatient drugs of a manufacturer, the manufacturer must have entered into and have in effect a rebate agreement described in subsection (b) of this section with the Secretary, on behalf of States (except that, the Secretary may authorize a State to enter directly into agreements with a manufacturer), and must meet the requirements of paragraph (5) (with respect to drugs purchased by a covered entity on or after the first day of the first month that begins after November 4, 1992) and paragraph (6). Any agreement between a State and a manufacturer prior to April 1, 1991, shall be deemed to have been entered into on January 1, 1991, and payment to such manufacturer shall be retroactively calculated as if the agreement between the manufacturer and the State had been entered into on January 1, 1991. If a manufacturer has not entered into such an agreement before March 1, 1991, such an agreement, subsequently entered into, shall become effective as of the date on which the agreement is entered into or, at State option, on any date thereafter on or before the first day of the calendar quarter that begins more than 60 days after the date the agreement is entered into.

* * *

(3) Authorizing payment for drugs not covered under rebate agreements

Paragraph (1), and section 1396b(i)(10)(A) of this title, shall not apply to the dispensing of a single source drug or innovator multiple source drug if (A)(i) the State has made a determination that the availability of the drug is essential to the health of beneficiaries under the State plan for medical assistance; (ii) such drug has been given a rating of 1–A by the Food and Drug Administration; and (iii)(I) the physician has obtained approval for use of the drug in advance of its dispensing in accordance with a prior authorization program described in subsection (d) of this section, or (II) the Secretary has reviewed and approved the State's determination under subparagraph (A); or (B) the Secretary determines that in the first calendar quarter of 1991, there were extenuating circumstances.

(4) Effect on existing agreements

In the case of a rebate agreement in effect between a State and a manufacturer on November 5, 1990, such agreement, for the initial agreement period specified therein, shall be considered to be a rebate agreement in compliance with this section with respect to that State, if the State agrees to report to the Secretary any rebates paid pursuant to the agreement and such agreement provides for a minimum aggregate rebate of 10 percent of the State's total expenditures under the State plan for coverage of the manufacturer's drugs under this subchapter. If, after the initial agreement period, the State establishes to the satisfaction of the Secretary that an agreement in effect on November 5, 1990, provides for rebates that are at least as large as the rebates otherwise required under this section, and the State agrees to report any rebates under the agreement to the Secretary, the agreement shall be considered to be a rebate agreement in compliance with the section for the renewal periods of such agreement.

(5) Limitation on prices of drugs purchased by covered entities

(A) Agreement with Secretary

A manufacturer meets the requirements of this paragraph if the manufacturer has entered into an agreement with the Secretary that meets the requirements of section 256b of this title with respect to covered outpatient drugs purchased by a covered entity on or after the first day of the first month that begins after November 4, 1992.

(B) Covered entity defined

In this subsection, the term "covered entity" means an entity described in section 256b(a)(4) of this title.

(C) Establishment of alternative mechanism to ensure against duplicate discounts or rebates

If the Secretary does not establish a mechanism under section 256b(a)(5)(A) of this title within 12 months of November 4, 1992, the following requirements shall apply:

(i) Entities

Each covered entity shall inform the single State agency under section 1396a(a)(5) of this title when it is seeking reimbursement from the State plan for medical assistance described in section 1396d(a)(12) of this title with respect to a unit of any covered outpatient drug which is subject to an agreement under section 256b(a) of this title.

(ii) State agency

Each such single State agency shall provide a means by which a covered entity shall indicate on any drug reimbursement claims form (or format, where electronic claims management is used) that a unit of the drug that is the subject of the form is subject to an agreement under section 256b of this title, and not submit to any manufacturer a claim for a rebate payment under subsection (b) of this section with respect to such a drug.

(D) Effect of subsequent amendments

In determining whether an agreement under subparagraph (A) meets the requirements of section 256b of this title, the Secretary shall not take into account any amendments to such section that are enacted after November 4, 1992.

(E) Determination of compliance

A manufacturer is deemed to meet the requirements of this paragraph if the manufacturer establishes to the satisfaction of the Secretary that the manufacturer would comply (and has offered to comply) with the provisions of section 256b of this title (as in effect immediately after November 4, 1992) and would have entered into an agreement under such section (as such section was in effect at such time), but for a legislative change in such section after November 4, 1992.

* * *

(b) Terms of rebate agreement

(1) Periodic rebates

(A) In general. A rebate agreement under this subsection shall require the manufacturer to provide, to each State plan approved under this title, a rebate for a rebate period in an amount specified in subsection (c) for covered outpatient drugs of the manufacturer dispensed after December 31, 1990, for which payment was made under the State plan for such period. Such rebate shall be paid by the manufacturer not later than 30 days after the date of receipt of the information described in paragraph (2) for the period involved.

(B) Offset against medical assistance. Amounts received by a State under this section (or under an agreement authorized by the Secretary under subsection (a)(1) or an agreement described in subsection (a)(4)) in any quarter shall be considered to be a reduction in the amount expended under the State plan in the quarter for medical assistance for purposes of section 1903(a)(1) [§ 1396b(a)(1)].

(2) State provision of information

(A) State responsibility. Each State agency under this title shall report to each manufacturer not later than 60 days after the end of each rebate period and in a form consistent with a standard reporting format established by the Secretary, information on the total number of units of each dosage form and strength and package size of each covered outpatient drug dispensed after December 31, 1990, for which payment was made under the plan during the period, and shall promptly transmit a copy of such report to the Secretary.

(B) Audits. A manufacturer may audit the information provided (or required to be provided) under subparagraph (A). Adjustments to rebates shall be made to the extent that information indicates that utilization was greater or less than the amount previously specified.

(3) Manufacturer provision of price information

(A) In general. Each manufacturer with an agreement in effect under this section shall report to the Secretary—

(i) not later than 30 days after the last day of each rebate period under the agreement (beginning on or after January 1, 1991), on the average manufacturer price (as defined in subsection (k)(1)) and, (for single source drugs and innovator multiple source drugs), the manufacturer's best price (as defined in subsection (c)(2)(B)) for covered outpatient drugs for the rebate period under the agreement, and

(ii) not later than 30 days after the date of entering into an agreement under this section on the average manufacturer price (as defined in subsection (k)(1)) as of October 1, 1990[,] for each of the manufacturer's covered outpatient drugs.

(B) Verification surveys of average manufacturer price. The Secretary may survey wholesalers and manufacturers that directly distribute their covered outpatient drugs, when necessary, to verify manufacturer prices reported under subparagraph (A). The Secretary may impose a civil monetary penalty in an amount not to exceed $100,000 on a wholesaler, manufacturer, or direct seller, if the wholesaler, manufacturer, or direct seller of a covered outpatient drug refuses a request for information about charges or prices by the Secretary in connection with a survey under this subparagraph or knowingly provides false information. The provisions of section 1128A [§ 1320a-7a] (other than subsections (a) (with respect to amounts of penalties or additional assessments) and (b)) shall apply to a civil money penalty under this subparagraph in the same manner as such provisions apply to a penalty or proceeding under section 1128A(a) [§ 1320a–7a(a)].

(C) Penalties

(i) Failure to provide timely information. In the case of a manufacturer with an agreement under this section that fails to provide information required under subparagraph (A) on a timely basis, the amount of the penalty shall be increased by $10,000 for each day in which such information has not been provided and such amount shall be paid to the Treasury, and, if such information is not reported within 90 days of the deadline imposed, the agreement shall be suspended for services furnished after the end of the 90-day period and until the date such information is reported (but in no case shall such suspension be for a period of less than 30 days).

(ii) False information. Any manufacturer with an agreement under this section that knowingly provides false information is subject to a civil money penalty in an amount not to exceed $100,000 for each item of false information. Such civil money penalties are in addition to other penalties as may be prescribed by law. The provisions of section 1128A [42 USCS § 1320a–7a] (other than subsections (a) and (b)) shall apply to a civil money penalty under this subparagraph in the same manner as such provisions apply to a penalty or proceeding under section 1128A(a) [§ 1320a–7a(a)].

(D) Confidentiality of information. Notwithstanding any other provision of law, information disclosed by manufacturers or wholesalers under this paragraph or under an agreement with the Secretary of Veterans Affairs described in subsection (a)(6)(A)(ii) is confidential and shall not be disclosed by the Secretary or the Secretary of Veterans Affairs or a State agency (or contractor therewith) in a form which discloses the identity of a specific manufacturer or wholesaler, prices charged for drugs by such manufacturer or wholesaler, except—

(i) as the Secretary determines to be necessary to carry out this section,

(ii) to permit the Comptroller General to review the information provided, and

(iii) to permit the Director of the Congressional Budget Office to review the information provided.

(4) Length of agreement

(A) In general. A rebate agreement shall be effective for an initial period of not less than 1 year and shall be automatically renewed for a period of not less than one year unless terminated under subparagraph (B).

(B) Termination

(i) By the Secretary. The Secretary may provide for termination of a rebate agreement for violation of the requirements of the agreement or other good cause shown. Such termination shall not be effective earlier than 60 days after the date of notice of such termination. The Secretary shall provide, upon request, a manufacturer with a hearing concerning such a termination, but such hearing shall not delay the effective date of the termination.

(ii) By a manufacturer. A manufacturer may terminate a rebate agreement under this section for any reason. Any such termination shall not be effective until the calendar quarter beginning at least 60 days after the date the manufacturer provides notice to the Secretary.

(iii) Effectiveness of termination. Any termination under this subparagraph shall not affect rebates due under the agreement before the effective date of its termination.

(iv) Notice to States. In the case of a termination under this subparagraph, the Secretary shall provide notice of such termination to the States within not less than 30 days before the effective date of such termination.

(v) Application to terminations of other agreements. The provisions of this subparagraph shall apply to the terminations of agreements described in section 340B(a)(1) of the Public

Health Service Act [§ 256b(a)(1)] and master agreements described in section 8126(a) of title 38, United States Code.

(C) Delay before reentry. In the case of any rebate agreement with a manufacturer under this section which is terminated, another such agreement with the manufacturer (or a successor manufacturer) may not be entered into until a period of 1 calendar quarter has elapsed since the date of the termination, unless the Secretary finds good cause for an earlier reinstatement of such an agreement.

(c) Determination of amount of rebate

(1) Basic rebate for single source drugs and innovator multiple source drugs

(A) In general. Except as provided in paragraph (2), the amount of the rebate specified in this subsection for a rebate period (as defined in subsection (k)(8)) with respect to each dosage form and strength of a single source drug or an innovator multiple source drug shall be equal to the product of—

(i) the total number of units of each dosage form and strength paid for under the State plan in the rebate period (as reported by the State); and

(ii) subject to subparagraph (B)(ii), the greater of—

(I) the difference between the average manufacturer price and the best price (as defined in subparagraph (C)) for the dosage form and strength of the drug, or

(II) the minimum rebate percentage (specified in subparagraph (B)(i)) of such average manufacturer price,

for the rebate period.

(B) Range of rebates required

(i) Minimum rebate percentage. For purposes of subparagraph (A)(ii)(II), the "minimum rebate percentage" for rebate periods beginning—

* * *

(V) after December 31, 1995, is 15.1 percent.

(ii) Temporary limitation on maximum rebate amount. In no case shall the amount applied under subparagraph (A)(ii) for a rebate period beginning—

* * *

(II) after December 31, 1991, and before January 1, 1993, exceed 50 percent of the average manufacturer price.

(C) Best price defined. For purposes of this section—

(i) In general. The term "best price" means, with respect to a single source drug or innovator multiple source drug of a manufacturer, the lowest price available from the manufacturer during the rebate period to any wholesaler, retailer, provider, health maintenance organization, nonprofit entity, or governmental entity within the United States, excluding—

(I) any prices charged on or after October 1, 1992, to the Indian Health Service, the Department of Veterans Affairs, a State home receiving funds under section 1741 of title 38, United States Code, the Department of Defense, the Public Health Service, or a covered entity described in subsection (a)(5)(B);

(II) any prices charged under the Federal Supply Schedule of the General Services Administration;

(III) any prices used under a State pharmaceutical assistance program; and

(IV) any depot prices and single award contract prices, as defined by the Secretary, of any agency of the Federal Government.

(ii) Special rules. The term "best price"—

(I) shall be inclusive of cash discounts, free goods that are contingent on any purchase requirement, volume discounts, and rebates (other than rebates under this section);

(II) shall be determined without regard to special packaging, labeling, or identifiers on the dosage form or product or package; and

(III) shall not take into account prices that are merely nominal in amount.

(2) Additional rebate for single source and innovator multiple source drugs.

(A) In general. The amount of the rebate specified in this subsection for a rebate period, with respect to each dosage form and strength of a single source drug or an innovator multiple source drug, shall be increased by an amount equal to the product of—

(i) the total number of units of such dosage form and strength dispensed after December 31, 1990, for which payment was made under the State plan for the rebate period; and

(ii) the amount (if any) by which—

(I) the average manufacturer price for the dosage form and strength of the drug for the period, exceeds

(II) the average manufacturer price for such dosage form and strength for the calendar quarter beginning July 1,

1990 (without regard to whether or not the drug has been sold or transferred to an entity, including a division or subsidiary of the manufacturer, after the first day of such quarter), increased by the percentage by which the consumer price index for all urban consumers (United States city average) for the month before the month in which the rebate period begins exceeds such index for September 1990.

(B) Treatment of subsequently approved drugs. In the case of a covered outpatient drug approved by the Food and Drug Administration after October 1, 1990, clause (ii)(II) of subparagraph (A) shall be applied by substituting "the first full calendar quarter after the day on which the drug was first marketed" for "the calendar quarter beginning July 1, 1990" and "the month prior to the first month of the first full calendar quarter after the day on which the drug was first marketed" for "September 1990".

(3) Rebate for other drugs

(A) In general. The amount of the rebate paid to a State for a rebate period with respect to each dosage form and strength of covered outpatient drugs (other than single source drugs and innovator multiple source drugs) shall be equal to the product of—

    (i) the applicable percentage (as described in subparagraph (B)) of the average manufacturer price for the dosage form and strength for the rebate period, and

    (ii) the total number of units of such dosage form and strength dispensed after December 31, 1990, for which payment was made under the State plan for the rebate period.

(B) Applicable percentage defined. For purposes of subparagraph (A)(i), the "applicable percentage" for rebate periods beginning—

* * *

    (ii) after December 31, 1993, is 11 percent.

(d) Limitations on coverage of drugs

(1) Permissible restrictions

(A) A State may subject to prior authorization any covered outpatient drug. Any such prior authorization program shall comply with the requirements of paragraph (5).

(B) A State may exclude or otherwise restrict coverage of a covered outpatient drug if—

    (i) the prescribed use is not for a medically accepted indication (as defined in subsection (k)(6));

    (ii) the drug is contained in the list referred to in paragraph (2);

1027

(iii) the drug is subject to such restrictions pursuant to an agreement between a manufacturer and a State authorized by the Secretary under subsection (a)(1) or in effect pursuant to subsection (a)(4); or

(iv) the State has excluded coverage of the drug from its formulary established in accordance with paragraph (4).

(2) List of drugs subject to restriction. The following drugs or classes of drugs, or their medical uses, may be excluded from coverage or otherwise restricted:

(A) Agents when used for anorexia, weight loss, or weight gain.

(B) Agents when used to promote fertility.

(C) Agents when used for cosmetic purposes or hair growth.

(D) Agents when used for the symptomatic relief of cough and colds.

(E) Agents when used to promote smoking cessation.

(F) Prescription vitamins and mineral products, except prenatal vitamins and fluoride preparations.

(G) Nonprescription drugs.

(H) Covered outpatient drugs which the manufacturer seeks to require as a condition of sale that associated tests or monitoring services be purchased exclusively from the manufacturer or its designee.

(I) Barbiturates.

(J) Benzodiazepines.

(3) Update of drug listings. The Secretary shall, by regulation, periodically update the list of drugs or classes of drugs described in paragraph (2) or their medical uses, which the Secretary has determined, based on data collected by surveillance and utilization review programs of State medical assistance programs, to be subject to clinical abuse or inappropriate use.

(4) Requirements for formularies. A State may establish a formulary if the formulary meets the following requirements:

(A) The formulary is developed by a committee consisting of physicians, pharmacists, and other appropriate individuals appointed by the Governor of the State (or, at the option of the State, the State's drug use review board established under subsection (g)(3)).

(B) Except as provided in subparagraph (C), the formulary includes the covered outpatient drugs of any manufacturer which has entered into and complies with an agreement under subsection (a) (other than any drug excluded from coverage or otherwise restricted under paragraph (2)).

(C) A covered outpatient drug may be excluded with respect to the treatment of a specific disease or condition for an identified population (if any) only if, based on the drug's labeling (or, in the case of a drug the prescribed use of which is not approved under the Federal Food, Drug, and Cosmetic Act [21 USCA §§ 301 et seq.] but is a medically accepted indication, based on information from the appropriate compendia described in subsection (k)(6)), the excluded drug does not have a significant, clinically meaningful therapeutic advantage in terms of safety, effectiveness, or clinical outcome of such treatment for such population over other drugs included in the formulary and there is a written explanation (available to the public) of the basis for the exclusion.

(D) The State plan permits coverage of a drug excluded from the formulary (other than any drug excluded from coverage or otherwise restricted under paragraph (2)) pursuant to a prior authorization program that is consistent with paragraph (5).

(E) The formulary meets such other requirements as the Secretary may impose in order to achieve program savings consistent with protecting the health of program beneficiaries.

A prior authorization program established by a State under paragraph (5) is not a formulary subject to the requirements of this paragraph.

(5) Requirements of prior authorization programs. A State plan under this title may require, as a condition of coverage or payment for a covered outpatient drug for which Federal financial participation is available in accordance with this section, with respect to drugs dispensed on or after July 1, 1991, the approval of the drug before its dispensing for any medically accepted indication (as defined in subsection (k)(6)) only if the system providing for such approval—

(A) provides response by telephone or other telecommunication device within 24 hours of a request for prior authorization; and

(B) except with respect to the drugs on the list referred to in paragraph (2), provides for the dispensing of at least 72-hour supply of a covered outpatient prescription drug in an emergency situation (as defined by the Secretary).

(6) Other permissible restrictions. A State may impose limitations, with respect to all such drugs in a therapeutic class, on the minimum or maximum quantities per prescription or on the number of refills, if such limitations are necessary to discourage waste, and may address instances of fraud or abuse by individuals in any manner authorized under this Act.

* * *

[(f)] Establishment of upper payment limits. HCFA shall establish a Federal upper reimbursement limit for each multiple source drug for which the FDA has rated three or more products therapeutically and additional formulations are rated as such and shall use only such formulations when determining any such upper limit.

(g) Drug use review

(1) In general

(A) In order to meet the requirement of section 1903(i)(10)(B) [§ 1396b(i)(10)(B)], a State shall provide, by not later than January 1, 1993, for a drug use review program described in paragraph (2) for covered outpatient drugs in order to assure that prescriptions (i) are appropriate, (ii) are medically necessary, and (iii) are not likely to result in adverse medical results. The program shall be designed to educate physicians and pharmacists to identify and reduce the frequency of patterns of fraud, abuse, gross overuse, or inappropriate or medically unnecessary care, among physicians, pharmacists, and patients, or associated with specific drugs or groups of drugs, as well as potential and actual severe adverse reactions to drugs including education on therapeutic appropriateness, overutilization and underutilization, appropriate use of generic products, therapeutic duplication, drug-disease contraindications, drug-drug interactions, incorrect drug dosage or duration of drug treatment, drug-allergy interactions, and clinical abuse/misuse.

(B) The program shall assess date on drug use against predetermined standards, consistent with the following:

(i) compendia which shall consist of the following:

(I) American Hospital Formulary Service Drug Information;

(II) United States Pharmacopeia-Drug Information;

(III) the DRUGDEX Information System; and

(IV) American Medical Association Drug Evaluations; and

(ii) the peer-reviewed medical literature.

(C) The Secretary, under the procedures established in section 1903 [§ 1396b], shall pay to each State an amount equal to 75 per centum of so much of the sums expended by the State plan during calendar years 1991 through 1993 as the Secretary determines is attributable to the statewide adoption of a drug use review program which conforms to the requirements of this subsection.

(D) States shall not be required to perform additional drug use reviews with respect to drugs dispensed to residents of nursing facilities which are in compliance with the drug regimen review procedures prescribed by the Secretary for such facilities in regulations implementing section 1919 [§ 1396r], currently at section 483.60 of title 42, Code of Federal Regulations.

(2) Description of program. Each drug use review program shall meet the following requirements for covered outpatient drugs:

(A) Prospective drug review

(i) The State plan shall provide for a review of drug therapy before each prescription is filled or delivered to an individual receiving benefits under this title [§§ 1396 et seq.], typically at the point-of-sale or point of distribution. The review shall include screening for potential drug therapy problems due to therapeutic duplication, drug-disease contraindications, drug-drug interactions (including serious interactions with nonprescription or over-the-counter drugs), incorrect drug dosage or duration of drug treatment, drug-allergy interactions, and clinical abuse/misuse. Each State shall use the compendia and literature referred to in paragraph (1)(B) as its source of standards for such review.

(ii) As part of the State's prospective drug use review program under this subparagraph applicable State law shall establish standards for counseling of individuals receiving benefits under this title [§§ 1396 et seq.] by pharmacists which includes at least the following:

(I) The pharmacist must offer to discuss with each individual receiving benefits under this title [§§ 1396 et seq.] or caregiver of such individual (in person, whenever practicable, or through access to a telephone service which is toll-free for long-distance calls) who presents a prescription, matters which in the exercise of the pharmacist's professional judgment (consistent with State law respecting the provision of such information), the pharmacist deems significant including the following:

(aa) The name and description of the medication.

(bb) The route, dosage form, dosage, route of administration, and duration of drug therapy.

(cc) Special directions and precautions for preparation, administration and use by the patient.

(dd) Common severe side or adverse effects or interactions and therapeutic contraindications that may be encountered, including their avoidance, and the action required if they occur.

(ee) Techniques for self-monitoring drug therapy.

(ff) Proper storage.

(gg) Prescription refill information.

(hh) Action to be taken in the event of a missed dose.

(II) A reasonable effort must be made by the pharmacist to obtain, record, and maintain at least the following information regarding individuals receiving benefits under this title [42 USCS §§ 1396 et seq.]:

(aa) Name, address, telephone number, date of birth (or age) and gender.

(bb) Individual history where significant, including disease state or states, known allergies and drug reactions, and a comprehensive list of medications and relevant devices.

(cc) Pharmacist comments relevant to the individual's drug therapy.

Nothing in this clause shall be construed as requiring a pharmacist to provide consultation when an individual receiving benefits under this title [42 USCS §§ 1396 et seq.] or caregiver of such individual refuses such consultation.

(B) Retrospective drug use review. The program shall provide, through its mechanized drug claims processing and information retrieval systems (approved by the Secretary under section 1903(r) [§ 1396b(r)]) or otherwise, for the ongoing periodic examination of claims data and other records in order to identify patterns of fraud, abuse, gross overuse, or inappropriate or medically unnecessary care, among physicians, pharmacists and individuals receiving benefits under this title [§§ 1396 et seq.], or associated with specific drugs or groups of drugs.

(C) Application of standards. The program shall, on an ongoing basis, assess data on drug use against explicit predetermined standards (using the compendia and literature referred to in subsection [paragraph] (1)(B) as the source of standards for such assessment) including but not limited to monitoring for therapeutic appropriateness, overutilization and underutilization, appropriate use of generic products, therapeutic duplication, drug-disease contraindications, drug-drug interactions, incorrect drug dosage or duration of drug treatment, and clinical abuse/misuse and, as necessary, introduce remedial strategies, in order to improve the quality of care and to conserve program funds or personal expenditures.

(D) Educational program. The program shall, through its State drug use review board established under paragraph (3), either directly or through contracts with accredited health care educational institutions, State medical societies or State pharmacists associations/societies or other organizations as specified by the State, and using data provided by the State drug use review board on common drug therapy problems, provide for active and ongoing educational outreach programs (including the activities described in paragraph (3)(C)(iii) of this subsection) to educate practitioners on common drug therapy problems with the aim of improving prescribing or dispensing practices.

(3) State drug use review board.

(A) Establishment.   Each State shall provide for the establishment of a drug use review board (hereinafter referred to as the "DUR Board") either directly or through a contract with a private organization.

(B) Membership.   The membership of the DUR Board shall include health care professionals who have recognized knowledge and expertise in one or more of the following:

(i) The clinically appropriate prescribing of covered outpatient drugs.

(ii) The clinically appropriate dispensing and monitoring of covered outpatient drugs.

(iii) Drug use review, evaluation, and intervention.

(iv) Medical quality assurance.   The membership of the DUR Board shall be made up at least 1/3 but no more than 51 percent licensed and actively practicing physicians and at least 1/3 [* * *] licensed and actively practicing pharmacists.

(C) Activities.   The activities of the DUR Board shall include but not be limited to the following:

(i) Retrospective DUR as defined in section [paragraph] (2)(B).

(ii) Application of standards as defined in section [paragraph] (2)(C).

(iii) Ongoing interventions for physicians and pharmacists, targeted toward therapy problems or individuals identified in the course of retrospective drug use reviews performed under this subsection.   Intervention programs shall include, in appropriate instances, at least:

(I) information dissemination sufficient to ensure the ready availability to physicians and pharmacists in the State of information concerning its duties, powers, and basis for its standards;

(II) written, oral, or electronic reminders containing patient-specific or drug-specific (or both) information and suggested changes in prescribing or dispensing practices, communicated in a manner designed to ensure the privacy of patient-related information;

(III) use of face-to-face discussions between health care professionals who are experts in rational drug therapy and selected prescribers and pharmacists who have been targeted for educational intervention, including discussion of optimal prescribing, dispensing, or pharmacy care practices, and follow-up face-to-face discussions; and

(IV) intensified review or monitoring of selected prescribers or dispensers.

The Board shall re-evaluate interventions after an appropriate period of time to determine if the intervention improved the quality of drug therapy, to evaluate the success of the interventions and make modifications as necessary.

(D) Annual report. Each State shall require the DUR Board to prepare a report on an annual basis. The State shall submit a report on an annual basis to the Secretary which shall include a description of the activities of the Board, including the nature and scope of the prospective and retrospective drug use review programs, a summary of the interventions used, an assessment of the impact of these educational interventions on quality of care, and an estimate of the cost savings generated as a result of such program. The Secretary shall utilize such report in evaluating the effectiveness of each State's drug use review program.

(h) Electronic claims management

(1) In general. In accordance with chapter 35 of title 44, United States Code [44 USCS §§ 3501 et seq.] (relating to coordination of Federal information policy), the Secretary shall encourage each State agency to establish, as its principal means of processing claims for covered outpatient drugs under this title [42 USCS §§ 1396 et seq.], a point-of-sale electronic claims management system, for the purpose of performing on-line, real time eligibility verifications, claims data capture, adjudication of claims, and assisting pharmacists (and other authorized persons) in applying for and receiving payment.

(2) Encouragement. In order to carry out paragraph (1)—

(A) for calendar quarters during fiscal years 1991 and 1992, expenditures under the State plan attributable to development of a system described in paragraph (1) shall receive Federal financial participation under section 1903(a)(3)(A)(i) [§ 1396b(a)(3)(A)(i)] (at a matching rate of 90 percent) if the State acquires, through applicable competitive procurement process in the State, the most cost-effective telecommunications network and automatic data processing services and equipment; and

(B) the Secretary may permit, in the procurement described in subparagraph (A) in the application of part 433 of title 42, Code of Federal Regulations, and parts 95, 205, and 307 of title 45, Code of Federal Regulations, the substitution of the State's request for proposal in competitive procurement for advance planning and implementation documents otherwise required.

(i) Annual report

(1) In general. Not later than May 1 of each year the Secretary shall transmit to the Committee on Finance of the Senate, the Committee on Energy and Commerce of the House of Representatives, and the Committees on Aging of the Senate and the House of Representatives a report on the operation of this section in the preceding fiscal year.

(2) Details. Each report shall include information on—

(A) ingredient costs paid under this title for single source drugs, multiple source drugs, and nonprescription covered outpatient drugs;

(B) the total value of rebates received and number of manufacturers providing such rebates;

(C) how the size of such rebates compare with the size or [of] rebates offered to other purchasers of covered outpatient drugs;

(D) the effect of inflation on the value of rebates required under this section;

(E) trends in prices paid under this title for covered outpatient drugs; and

(F) Federal and State administrative costs associated with compliance with the provisions of this title.

(j) Exemption of organized health care settings

(1) Covered outpatient drugs dispensed by health maintenance organizations, including medicaid managed care organizations that contract under section 1903(m) [§ 1396b(m)], are not subject to the requirements of this section.

(2) The State plan shall provide that a hospital (providing medical assistance under such plan) that dispenses covered outpatient drugs using drug formulary systems, and bills the plan no more than the hospital's purchasing costs for covered outpatient drugs (as determined under the State plan) shall not be subject to the requirements of this section.

(3) Nothing in this subsection shall be construed as providing that amounts for covered outpatient drugs paid by the institutions described in this subsection should not be taken into account for purposes of determining the best price as described in subsection (c).

(k) Definitions. In this section—

(1) Average manufacturer price. The term "average manufacturer price" means, with respect to a covered outpatient drug of a manufacturer for a rebate period, the average price paid to the manufacturer for the drug in the United States by wholesalers for drugs distributed to the retail pharmacy class of trade, after deducting customary prompt pay discounts.

1035

(2) Covered outpatient drug. Subject to the exceptions in paragraph (3), the term "covered outpatient drug" means—

(A) of those drugs which are treated as prescribed drugs for purposes of section 1905(a)(12) [§ 1396d(a)(12)], a drug which may be dispensed only upon prescription (except as provided in paragraph (5)), and—

(i) which is approved for safety and effectiveness as a prescription drug under section 505 or 507 of the Federal Food, Drug, and Cosmetic Act [21 USCA § 355 or former 357] or which is approved under section 505(j) of such Act [21 USCA § 355(j)];

(ii)(I) which was commercially used or sold in the United States before the date of the enactment of the Drug Amendments of 1962 [enacted Oct. 10, 1962] or which is identical, similar, or related (within the meaning of section 310.6(b)(1) of title 21 of the Code of Federal Regulations) to such a drug, and (II) which has not been the subject of a final determination by the Secretary that it is a "new drug" (within the meaning of section 201(p) of the Federal Food, Drug, and Cosmetic Act [21 USCA § 321(p)]) or an action brought by the Secretary under section 301, 302(a), or 304(a) of such Act [21 USCA § 331, 332(a), or 334(a)] to enforce section 502(f) or 505(a) of such Act [21 USCA § 352(f) or 355(a)]; or

(iii)(I) which is described in section 107(c)(3) of the Drug Amendments of 1962 [21 USCA § 321] and for which the Secretary has determined there is a compelling justification for its medical need, or is identical, similar, or related (within the meaning of section 310.6(b)(1) of title 21 of the Code of Federal Regulations) to such a drug, and (II) for which the Secretary has not issued a notice of an opportunity for a hearing under section 505(e) of the Federal Food, Drug, and Cosmetic Act [21 USCA § 355(e)] on a proposed order of the Secretary to withdraw approval of an application for such drug under such section because the Secretary has determined that the drug is less than effective for some or all conditions of use prescribed, recommended, or suggested in its labeling; and

(B) a biological product, other than a vaccine which—

(i) may only be dispensed upon prescription,

(ii) is licensed under section 351 of the Public Health Service Act [42 USCA § 262], and

(iii) is produced at an establishment licensed under such section to produce such product; and

(C) insulin certified under section 506 of the Federal Food, Drug, and Cosmetic Act [42 USCA § 356].

(3) Limiting definition. The term "covered outpatient drug" does not include any drug, biological product, or insulin provided as part of, or as incident to and in the same setting as, any of the following (and for which payment may be made under this title as part of payment for the following and not as direct reimbursement for the drug):

    (A) Inpatient hospital services.

    (B) Hospice services.

    (C) Dental services, except that drugs for which the State plan authorizes direct reimbursement to the dispensing dentist are covered outpatient drugs.

    (D) Physicians' services.

    (E) Outpatient hospital services.

    (F) Nursing facility services and services provided by an intermediate care facility for the mentally retarded.

    (G) Other laboratory and x-ray services.

    (H) Renal dialysis.

Such term also does not include any such drug or product for which a National Drug Code number is not required by the Food and Drug Administration or a drug or biological [product] used for a medical indication which is not a medically accepted indication. Any drug, biological product, or insulin excluded from the definition of such term as a result of this paragraph shall be treated as a covered outpatient drug for purposes of determining the best price (as defined in subsection (c)(1)(C)) for such drug, biological product, or insulin.

    (4) Nonprescription drugs. If a State plan for medical assistance under this title includes coverage of prescribed drugs as described in section 1905(a)(12) [§ 1396d(a)(12)] and permits coverage of drugs which may be sold without a prescription (commonly referred to as "over-the-counter" drugs), if they are prescribed by a physician (or other person authorized to prescribe under State law), such a drug shall be regarded as a covered outpatient drug.

    (5) Manufacturer. The term "manufacturer" means any entity which is engaged in—

        (A) the production, preparation, propagation, compounding, conversion, or processing of prescription drug products, either directly or indirectly by extraction from substances of natural origin, or independently by means of chemical synthesis, or by a combination of extraction and chemical synthesis, or

        (B) in the packaging, repackaging, labeling, relabeling, or distribution of prescription drug products.

Such term does not include a wholesale distributor of drugs or a retail pharmacy licensed under State law.

    (6) Medically accepted indication. The term "medically accepted indication" means any use for a covered outpatient drug which is approved under the Federal Food, Drug, and Cosmetic Act or the use of which is supported by one or more citations included or approved for inclusion in any of the compendia described in subsection (g)(1)(B)(i).

(7) Multiple source drug; innovator multiple source drug; noninnovator multiple source drug; single source drug.

(A) Defined.

(i) Multiple source drug. The term "multiple source drug" means, with respect to a rebate period, a covered outpatient drug (not including any drug described in paragraph (5)) for which there are 2 or more drug products which—

(I) are rated as therapeutically equivalent (under the Food and Drug Administration's most recent publication of "Approved Drug Products with Therapeutic Equivalence Evaluations"),

(II) except as provided in subparagraph (B), are pharmaceutically equivalent and bioequivalent, as defined in subparagraph (C) and as determined by the Food and Drug Administration, and

(III) are sold or marketed in the State during the period.

(ii) Innovator multiple source drug. The term "innovator multiple source drug" means a multiple source drug that was originally marketed under an original new drug application approved by the Food and Drug Administration.

(iii) Noninnovator multiple source drug. The term "noninnovator multiple source drug" means a multiple source drug that is not an innovator multiple source drug.

(iv) Single source drug. The term "single source drug" means a covered outpatient drug which is produced or distributed under an original new drug application approved by the Food and Drug Administration, including a drug product marketed by any cross-licensed producers or distributors operating under the new drug application.

(B) Exception. Subparagraph (A)(i)(II) shall not apply if the Food and Drug Administration changes by regulation the requirement that, for purposes of the publication described in subparagraph (A)(i)(I), in order for drug products to rated as therapeutically equivalent, they must be pharmaceutically equivalent and bioequivalent, as defined in subparagraph (C).

(C) Definitions. For purposes of this paragraph—

(i) drug products are pharmaceutically equivalent if the products contain identical amounts of the same active drug ingredient in the same dosage form and meet compendial or other applicable standards of strength, quality, purity, and identity;

    (ii) drugs are bioequivalent if they do not present a known or potential bioequivalence problem, or, if they do present such a problem, they are shown to meet an appropriate standard of bioequivalence; and

    (iii) a drug product is considered to be sold or marketed in a State if it appears in a published national listing of average wholesale prices selected by the Secretary, provided that the listed product is generally available to the public through retail pharmacies in that State.

(8) Rebate period. The term "rebate period" means, with respect to an agreement under subsection (a), a calendar quarter or other period specified by the Secretary with respect to the payment of rebates under such agreement.

(9) State agency. The term "State agency" means the agency designated under section 1902(a)(5) [1396a(a)(5)] to administer or supervise the administration of the State plan for medical assistance.

* * *

§ 1396s.   Program for distribution of pediatric vaccines

(a) Establishment of program

    (1) In general

In order to meet the requirement of section 1396a(a)(62) of this title, each State shall establish a pediatric vaccine distribution program (which may be administered by the State department of health), consistent with the requirements of this section, under which—

    (A) each vaccine-eligible child (as defined in subsection (b) of this section), in receiving an immunization with a qualified pediatric vaccine (as defined in subsection (h)(8) of this section) from a program-registered provider (as defined in subsection (c) of this section) on or after October 1, 1994, is entitled to receive the immunization without charge for the cost of such vaccine; and

    (B)(i) each program-registered provider who administers such a pediatric vaccine to a vaccine-eligible child on or after such date is entitled to receive such vaccine under the program without charge either for the vaccine or its delivery to the provider, and (ii) no vaccine is distributed under the program to a provider unless the provider is a program-registered provider.

    (2) Delivery of sufficient quantities of pediatric vaccines to immunize federally vaccine-eligible children

    (A) In general

The Secretary shall provide under subsection (d) of this section for the purchase and delivery on behalf of each State meeting the requirement of section 1396a(a)(62) of this title (or, with respect to vaccines administered by an Indian tribe or tribal organization to Indian children, directly to the tribe or organization), without charge to the State, of such quantities of qualified pediatric vaccines as may be necessary for the administration of such vaccines to all federally vaccine-eligible children in the State on or after October 1, 1994. This paragraph constitutes budget authority in advance of appropriations Acts, and represents the obligation of the Federal Government to provide for the purchase and delivery to States of the vaccines (or payment under subparagraph (C)) in accordance with this paragraph.

(B) Special rules where vaccine is unavailable

To the extent that a sufficient quantity of a vaccine is not available for purchase or delivery under subsection (d) of this section, the Secretary shall provide for the purchase and delivery of the available vaccine in accordance with priorities established by the Secretary, with priority given to federally vaccine-eligible children unless the Secretary finds there are other public health considerations.

(C) Special rules where State is a manufacturer

(i) Payments in lieu of vaccines

In the case of a State that manufactures a pediatric vaccine the Secretary, instead of providing the vaccine on behalf of a State under subparagraph (A), shall provide to the State an amount equal to the value of the quantity of such vaccine that otherwise would have been delivered on behalf of the State under such subparagraph, but only if the State agrees that such payments will only be used for purposes relating to pediatric immunizations.

(ii) Determination of value

In determining the amount to pay a State under clause (i) with respect to a pediatric vaccine, the value of the quantity of vaccine shall be determined on the basis of the price in effect for the qualified pediatric vaccine under contracts under subsection (d) of this section. If more than 1 such contract is in effect, the Secretary shall determine such value on the basis of the average of the prices under the contracts, after weighting each such price in relation to the quantity of vaccine under the contract involved.

(b) Vaccine-eligible children

For purposes of this section:

(1) In general

The term "vaccine-eligible child" means a child who is a federally vaccine-eligible child (as defined in paragraph (2)) or a State vaccine-eligible child (as defined in paragraph (3)).

(2) Federally vaccine-eligible child

(A) In general

The term "federally vaccine-eligible child" means any of the following children:

(i) A medicaid-eligible child.

(ii) A child who is not insured.

(iii) A child who

(I) is administered a qualified pediatric vaccine by a federally-qualified health center (as defined in section 1396d(l)(2)(B) of this title) or a rural health clinic (as defined in section 1396d(l)(1) of this title), and (II) is not insured with respect to the vaccine.

(iv) A child who is an Indian (as defined in subsection (h)(3) of this section).

(B) Definitions

In subparagraph (A):

(i) The term "medicaid-eligible" means, with respect to a child, a child who is entitled to medical assistance under a state plan approved under this subchapter.

(ii) The term "insured" means, with respect to a child—

(I) for purposes of subparagraph (A)(ii), that the child is enrolled under, and entitled to benefits under, a health insurance policy or plan, including a group health plan, a prepaid health plan, or an employee welfare benefit plan under the Employee Retirement Income Security Act of 1974 [*29 U.S.C.A. § 1001* et seq.]; and

(II) for purposes of subparagraph (A)(iii)(II) with respect to a pediatric vaccine, that the child is entitled to benefits under such a health insurance policy or plan, but such benefits are not available with respect to the cost of the pediatric vaccine.

(3) State vaccine-eligible child

The term "State vaccine-eligible child" means, with respect to a State and a qualified pediatric vaccine, a child who is within a class of children for which the State is purchasing the vaccine pursuant to subsection (d)(4)(B) of this section.

(c) Program-registered providers

(1) Defined

In this section, except as otherwise provided, the term "program-registered provider" means, with respect to a State, any health care provider that—

(A) is licensed or otherwise authorized for administration of pediatric vaccines under the law of the State in which the administration occurs (subject to section 254f(e) of this title), without regard to whether or not the provider participates in the plan under this subchapter;

(B) submits to the State an executed provider agreement described in paragraph (2); and

(C) has not been found, by the Secretary or the State, to have violated such agreement or other applicable requirements established by the Secretary or the State consistent with this section.

(2) Provider agreement

A provider agreement for a provider under this paragraph is an agreement (in such form and manner as the Secretary may require) that the provider agrees as follows:

(A)(i) Before administering a qualified pediatric vaccine to a child, the provider will ask a parent of the child such questions as are necessary to determine whether the child is a vaccine-eligible child, but the provider need not independently verify the answers to such questions.

(ii) The provider will, for a period of time specified by the Secretary, maintain records of responses made to the questions.

(iii) The provider will, upon request, make such records available to the State and to the Secretary, subject to section 1396a(a)(7) of this title.

(B)(i) Subject to clause (ii), the provider will comply with the schedule, regarding the appropriate periodicity, dosage, and contraindications applicable to pediatric vaccines, that is established and periodically reviewed and, as appropriate, revised by the advisory committee referred to in subsection (e) of this section, except in such cases as, in the provider's medical judgment subject to accepted medical practice, such compliance is medically inappropriate.

(ii) The provider will provide pediatric vaccines in compliance with applicable State law, including any such law relating to any religious or other exemption.

(C)(i) In administering a qualified pediatric vaccine to a vaccine-eligible child, the provider will not impose a charge for the cost of the vaccine. A program-registered provider is not required under this section to administer such a vaccine to each child for whom an immunization with the vaccine is sought from the provider.

(ii) The provider may impose a fee for the administration of a qualified pediatric vaccine so long as the fee in the case of a federally vaccine-eligible child does not exceed the costs of such administration (as determined by the Secretary based on actual regional costs for such administration).

(iii) The provider will not deny administration of a qualified pediatric vaccine to a vaccine-eligible child due to the inability of the child's parent to pay an administration fee.

* * *

(3) Encouraging involvement of providers. Each program under this section shall provide, in accordance with criteria established by the Secretary—

(A) for encouraging the following to become program-registered providers: private health care providers, the Indian Health Service, health care providers that receive funds under title V of the Indian Health Care Improvement Act [25 USCA §§ 1651 et seq.], and health programs or facilities operated by Indian tribes or tribal organizations; and

(B) for identifying, with respect to any population of vaccine-eligible children a substantial portion of whose parents have a limited ability to speak the English language, those program-registered providers who are able to communicate with the population involved in the language and cultural context that is most appropriate.

(4) State requirements. Except as the Secretary may permit in order to prevent fraud and abuse and for related purposes, a State may not impose additional qualifications or conditions, in addition to the requirements of paragraph (1), in order that a provider qualify as a program-registered provider under this section. This subsection does not limit the exercise of State authority under section 1915(b) [§ 1396n(b)].

(d) Negotiation of contracts with manufacturers

(1) In general. For the purpose of meeting obligations under this section, the Secretary shall negotiate and enter into contracts with manufacturers of pediatric vaccines consistent with the requirements of this subsection and, to the maximum extent practicable, consolidate such contracting with any other contracting activities conducted by the Secretary to purchase vaccines. The Secretary may enter into such contracts under which the Federal Government is obligated to make outlays, the budget authority for which is not provided for in advance in appropriations Acts, for the purchase and delivery of pediatric vaccines under subsection (a)(2)(A).

(2) Authority to decline contracts. The Secretary may decline to enter into such contracts and may modify or extend such contracts.

(3) Contract price

(A) In general. The Secretary, in negotiating the prices at which pediatric vaccines will be purchased and delivered from a manufacturer under this subsection, shall take into account quantities of vaccines to be purchased by States under the option under paragraph (4)(B).

(B) Negotiation of discounted price for current vaccines. With respect to contracts entered into under this subsection for a pediatric vaccine for which the Centers for Disease Control and Prevention has a contract in effect under section 317(j)(1) of the Public Health Service Act [§ 247b(j)(1)] as of May 1, 1993, no price for the purchase of such vaccine for vaccine-eligible children shall be agreed to by the Secretary under this subsection if the price per dose of such vaccine (including delivery costs and any applicable excise tax established under section 4131 of the Internal Revenue Code of 1986 [§ 4131]) exceeds the price per dose for the vaccine in effect under such a contract as of such date increased by the percentage increase in the consumer price index for all urban consumers (all items; United States city average) from May 1993 to the month before the month in which such contract is entered into.

(C) Negotiation of discounted price for new vaccines. With respect to contracts entered into for a pediatric vaccine not described in subparagraph (B), the price for the purchase of such vaccine shall be a discounted price negotiated by the Secretary that may be established without regard to such subparagraph.

(4) Quantities and terms of delivery. Under such contracts—

(A) the Secretary shall provide, consistent with paragraph (6), for the purchase and delivery on behalf of States (and tribes and tribal organizations) of quantities of pediatric vaccines for federally vaccine-eligible children; and

(B) each State, at the option of the State, shall be permitted to obtain additional quantities of pediatric vaccines (subject to amounts specified to the Secretary by the State in advance of negotiations) through purchasing the vaccines from the manufacturers at the applicable price negotiated by the Secretary consistent with paragraph (3), if (i) the State agrees that the vaccines will be used to provide immunizations only for children who are not federally vaccine-eligible children and (ii) the State provides to the Secretary such information (at a time and manner specified by the Secretary, including in advance of negotiations under paragraph (1)) as the Secretary determines to be necessary, to provide for quantities of pediatric vaccines for the State to purchase pursuant to this subsection and to determine annually the percentage of the vaccine market that is purchased pursuant to this section and this subparagraph.

The Secretary shall enter into the initial negotiations under the preceding sentence not later than 180 days after the date of the enactment of the Omnibus Budget Reconciliation Act of 1993 [enacted Aug. 10. 1993].

(5) Charges for shipping and handling. The Secretary may enter into a contract referred to in paragraph (1) only if the manufacturer involved agrees to submit to the Secretary such reports as the Secretary determines to be appropriate to assure compliance with the contract and if, with respect to a State program under this section that does not provide for the direct delivery of qualified pediatric vaccines, the manufacturer involved agrees that the manufacturer will provide for the delivery of the vaccines on behalf of the State in accordance with such program and will not impose any charges for the costs of such delivery (except to the extent such costs are provided for in the price established under paragraph (3)).

(6) Assuring adequate supply of vaccines. The Secretary, in negotiations under paragraph (1), shall negotiate for quantities of pediatric vaccines such that an adequate supply of such vaccines will be maintained to meet unanticipated needs for the vaccines. For purposes of the preceding sentence, the Secretary shall negotiate for a 6-month supply of vaccines in addition to the quantity that the Secretary otherwise would provide for in such negotiations. In carrying out this paragraph, the Secretary shall consider the potential for outbreaks of the diseases with respect to which the vaccines have been developed.

(7) Multiple suppliers. In the case of the pediatric vaccine involved, the Secretary shall, as appropriate, enter into a contract referred to in paragraph (1) with each manufacturer of the vaccine that meets the terms and conditions of the Secretary for an award of such a contract (including terms and conditions regarding safety and quality). With respect to multiple contracts entered into pursuant to this paragraph, the Secretary may have in effect different prices under each of such contracts and, with respect to a purchase by States pursuant to paragraph (4)(B), the Secretary shall determine which of such contracts will be applicable to the purchase.

* * *

(e) Use of pediatric vaccines list

The Secretary shall use, for the purpose of the purchase, delivery, and administration of pediatric vaccines under this section, the list established (and periodically reviewed and as appropriate revised) by the Advisory Committee on Immunization Practices (an advisory committee established by the Secretary, acting through the Director of the Centers for Disease Control and Prevention).

(f) Requirement of state maintenance of immunization laws

In the case of a State that had in effect as of May 1, 1993, a law that requires some or all health insurance policies or plans to provide some coverage with respect to a pediatric vaccine, a State program under this section does not comply with the requirements of this section unless the State certifies to the Secretary that the State has not modified or repealed such law in a manner that reduces the amount of coverage so required.

(g) Termination

This section, and the requirement of section 1396a(a)(62) of this title, shall cease to be in effect beginning on such date as may be prescribed in Federal law providing for immunization services for all children as part of a broad-based reform of the national health care system.

(h) Definitions

For purposes of this section:

(1) The term "child" means an individual 18 years of age or younger.

(2) The term "immunization" means an immunization against a vaccine-preventable disease.

(3) The terms "Indian", "Indian tribe" and "tribal organization" have the meanings given such terms in section 4 of the Indian Health Care Improvement Act [*25 U.S.C.A. § 1603*].

(4) The term "manufacturer" means any corporation, organization, or institution, whether public or private (including Federal, State, and local departments, agencies, and instrumentalities), which manufactures, imports, processes, or distributes under its label any pediatric vaccine. The term "manufacture" means to manufacture, import, process, or distribute a vaccine.

(5) The term "parent" includes, with respect to a child, an individual who qualifies as a legal guardian under State law.

(6) The term "pediatric vaccine" means a vaccine included on the list under subsection (e) of this section.

(7) The term "program-registered provider" has the meaning given such term in subsection (c) of this section.

(8) The term "qualified pediatric vaccine" means a pediatric vaccine with respect to which a contract is in effect under subsection (d) of this section.

(9) The terms "vaccine-eligible child", "federally vaccine-eligible child", and "State vaccine-eligible child" have the meaning given such terms in subsection (b) of this section.

§ 1396t. Home and community care for functionally disabled elderly individuals

(a) "Home and community care" defined

In this subchapter, the term "home and community care" means one or more of the following services furnished to an individual who has been determined, after an assessment under subsection (c) of this section, to be a functionally disabled elderly individual, furnished in accordance with an individual community care plan (established and periodically reviewed and revised by a qualified community care case manager under subsection (d) of this section):

(1) Homemaker/home health aide services.

(2) Chore services.

(3) Personal care services.

(4) Nursing care services provided by, or under the supervision of, a registered nurse.

(5) Respite care.

(6) Training for family members in managing the individual.

(7) Adult day care.

(8) In the case of an individual with chronic mental illness, day treatment or other partial hospitalization, psychosocial rehabilitation services, and clinic services (whether or not furnished in a facility).

(9) Such other home and community-based services (other than room and board) as the Secretary may approve.

(b) "Functionally disabled elderly individual" defined

(1) In general

In this subchapter, the term "functionally disabled elderly individual" means an individual who—

(A) is 65 years of age or older,

(B) is determined to be a functionally disabled individual under subsection (c) of this section, and

(C) subject to section 1396a(f) of this title (as applied consistent with section 1396a(r)(2) of this title), is receiving supplemental security income benefits under subchapter XVI of this chapter (or under a State plan approved under subchapter XVI of this chapter or, at the option of the State, is described in section 1396a(a)(10)(C) of this title.

(2) Treatment of certain individuals previously covered under a waiver

(A) In the case of a State which—

(i) at the time of its election to provide coverage for home and community care under this section has a waiver approved under section 1396n(c) of this title or 1396n(d) of this title with respect to individuals 65 years of age or older, and

(ii) subsequently discontinues such waiver, individuals who were eligible for benefits under the waiver as of the date of its discontinuance and who would, but for income or resources, be eligible for medical assistance for home and community care under the plan shall, notwithstanding any other provision of this subchapter, be deemed a functionally disabled elderly individual for so long as the individual would have remained eligible for medical assistance under such waiver.

(B) In the case of a State which used a health insuring organization before January 1, 1986, and which, as of December 31, 1990, had in effect a waiver under section 1315 of this title that provides under the State plan under this subchapter for personal care services for functionally disabled individuals, the term "functionally disabled elderly individual" may include, at the option of the State, an individual who—

> **(i)** is 65 years of age or older or is disabled (as determined under the supplemental security income program under subchapter XVI of this chapter);

> **(ii)** is determined to meet the test of functional disability applied under the waiver as of such date; and

> **(iii)** meets the resource requirement and income standard that apply in the State to individuals described in section 1396a(a)(10)(A)(ii)(V) of this title.

(3) Use of projected income

In applying section 1396b(f)(1) of this title in determining the eligibility of an individual (described in section 1396a(a)(10)(C) of this title) for medical assistance for home and community care, a State may, at its option, provide for the determination of the individual's anticipated medical expenses (to be deducted from income) over a period of up to 6 months.

(c) Determinations of functional disability

(1) In general

In this section, an individual is "functionally disabled" if the individual—

> **(A)** is unable to perform without substantial assistance from another individual at least 2 of the following 3 activities of daily living: toileting, transferring, and eating; or

> **(B)** has a primary or secondary diagnosis of Alzheimer's disease and is

>> **(i)** unable to perform without substantial human assistance (including verbal reminding or physical cueing) or supervision at least 2 of the following 5 activities of daily living: bathing, dressing, toileting, transferring, and eating; or

>> **(ii)** cognitively impaired so as to require substantial supervision from another individual because he or she engages in

inappropriate behaviors that pose serious health or safety hazards to himself or herself or others.

(2) Assessments of functional disability

(A) Requests for assessments

If a State has elected to provide home and community care under this section, upon the request of an individual who is 65 years of age or older and who meets the requirements of subsection (b)(1)(C) of this section (or another person on such individual's behalf), the State shall provide for a comprehensive functional assessment under this subparagraph which—

(i) is used to determine whether or not the individual is functionally disabled,

(ii) is based on a uniform minimum data set specified by the Secretary under subparagraph (C)(i), and

(iii) uses an instrument which has been specified by the State under subparagraph (B).

No fee may be charged for such an assessment.

(B) Specification of assessment instrument

The State shall specify the instrument to be used in the State in complying with the requirement of subparagraph (A)(iii) which instrument shall be—

(i) one of the instruments designated under subparagraph (C)(ii); or

(ii) an instrument which the Secretary has approved as being consistent with the minimum data set of core elements, common definitions, and utilization guidelines specified by the Secretary in subparagraph (C)(i).

(C) Specification of assessment data set and instruments

The Secretary shall—

(i) not later than July 1, 1991—

(I) specify a minimum data set of core elements and common definitions for use in conducting the assessments required under subparagraph (A); and

(II) establish guidelines for use of the data set; and

(ii) by not later than July 1, 1991, designate one or more instruments which are consistent with the specification made under subparagraph (A) and which a State may specify under subparagraph (B) for use in complying with the requirements of subparagraph (A).

1049

(D) Periodic review

Each individual who qualifies as a functionally disabled elderly individual shall have the individual's assessment periodically reviewed and revised not less often than once every 12 months.

(E) Conduct of assessment by interdisciplinary teams

An assessment under subparagraph (A) and a review under subparagraph (D) must be conducted by an interdisciplinary team designated by the State. The Secretary shall permit a State to provide for assessments and reviews through teams under contracts—

    (i) with public organizations; or

    (ii) with nonpublic organizations which do not provide home and community care or nursing facility services and do not have a direct or indirect ownership or control interest in, or direct or indirect affiliation or relationship with, an entity that provides, community care or nursing facility services.

(F) Contents of assessment

The interdisciplinary team must—

    (i) identify in each such assessment or review each individual's functional disabilities and need for home and community care, including information about the individual's health status, home and community environment, and informal support system; and

    (ii) based on such assessment or review, determine whether the individual is (or continues to be) functionally disabled.

The results of such an assessment or review shall be used in establishing, reviewing, and revising the individual's ICCP under subsection (d)(1) of this section.

(G) Appeal procedures

Each State which elects to provide home and community care under this section must have in effect an appeals process for individuals adversely affected by determinations under subparagraph (F).

(d) Individual community care plan (ICCP)

(1) Individual community care plan defined

In this section, the terms "individual community care plan" and "ICCP" mean, with respect to a functionally disabled elderly individual, a written plan which—

    (A) is established, and is periodically reviewed and revised, by a qualified case manager after a face-to-face interview with the individual or primary caregiver and based upon the most recent comprehensive functional assessment of such individual conducted under subsection (c)(2) of this section;

    (B) specifies, within any amount, duration, and scope limitations imposed on home and community care provided under the State plan, the home and community care to be provided to such individual under the plan, and indicates the individual's preferences for the types and providers of services; and

(C) may specify other services required by such individual.

An ICCP may also designate the specific providers (qualified to provide home and community care under the State plan) which will provide the home and community care described in subparagraph (B). Nothing in this section shall be construed as authorizing an ICCP or the State to restrict the specific persons or individuals (who are competent to provide home and community care under the State plan) who will provide the home and community care described in subparagraph (B).

(2) Qualified community care case manager defined

In this section, the term "qualified community care case manager" means a nonprofit or public agency or organization which—

(A) has experience or has been trained in establishing, and in periodically reviewing and revising, individual community care plans and in the provision of case management services to the elderly;

(B) is responsible for (i) assuring that home and community care covered under the State plan and specified in the ICCP is being provided, (ii) visiting each individual's home or community setting where care is being provided not less often than once every 90 days, and (iii) informing the elderly individual or primary caregiver on how to contact the case manager if service providers fail to properly provide services or other similar problems occur;

(C) in the case of a nonpublic agency, does not provide home and community care or nursing facility services and does not have a direct or indirect ownership or control interest in, or direct or indirect affiliation or relationship with, an entity that provides, home and community care or nursing facility services;

(D) has procedures for assuring the quality of case management services that includes a peer review process;

(E) completes the ICCP in a timely manner and reviews and discusses new and revised ICCPs with elderly individuals or primary caregivers; and

(F) meets such other standards, established by the Secretary, as to assure that—

 (i) such a manager is competent to perform case management functions;

 (ii) individuals whose home and community care they manage are not at risk of financial exploitation due to such a manager; and

 (iii) meets such other standards as the State may establish.

The Secretary may waive the requirement of subparagraph (C) in the case of a nonprofit agency located in a rural area.

(3) Appeals process

Each State which elects to provide home and community care under this section must have in effect an appeals process for individuals who disagree with the ICCP established.

(e) Ceiling on payment amounts and maintenance of effort

(1) Ceiling on payment amounts

Payments may not be made under section 1396b(a) of this title to a State for home and community care provided under this section in a quarter to the extent that the medical assistance for such care in the quarter exceeds 50 percent of the product of—

(A) the average number of individuals in the quarter receiving such care under this section;

(B) the average per diem rate of payment which the Secretary has determined (before the beginning of the quarter) will be payable under subchapter XVIII of this chapter (without regard to coinsurance) for extended care services to be provided in the State during such quarter; and

(C) the number of days in such quarter.

(2) Maintenance of effort

(A) Annual reports

As a condition for the receipt of payment under section 1396b(a) of this section with respect to medical assistance provided by a State for home and community care (other than a waiver under section 1396n(c) of this title and other than home health care services described in section 1396d(a)(7) of this title and personal care services specified under regulations under section 1396d(a)(23) of this title), the State shall report to the Secretary, with respect to each Federal fiscal year (beginning with fiscal year 1990) and in a format developed or approved by the Secretary, the amount of funds obligated by the State with respect to the provision of home and community care to the functionally disabled elderly in that fiscal year.

(B) Reduction in payment if failure to maintain effort

If the amount reported under subparagraph (A) by a State with respect to a fiscal year is less than the amount reported under subparagraph (A) with respect to fiscal year 1989, the Secretary shall provide for a reduction in payments to the State under section 1396b(a) of this title in an amount equal to the difference between the amounts so reported.

(f) Minimum requirements for home and community care

(1) Requirements

Home and Community care provided under this section must meet such requirements for individuals' rights and quality as are published or developed by the Secretary under subsection (k) of this section. Such requirements shall include—

   (A) the requirement that individuals providing care are competent to provide such care; and

   (B) the rights specified in paragraph (2).

(2) Specified rights

The rights specified in this paragraph are as follows:

   (A) The right to be fully informed in advance, orally and in writing, of the care to be provided, to be fully informed in advance of any changes in care to be provided, and (except with respect to an individual determined incompetent) to participate in planning care or changes in care.

   (B) The right to voice grievances with respect to services that are (or fail to be) furnished without discrimination or reprisal for voicing grievances, and to be told how to complain to State and local authorities.

   (C) The right to confidentiality of personal and clinical records.

   (D) The right to privacy and to have one's property treated with respect.

   (E) The right to refuse all or part of any care and to be informed of the likely consequences of such refusal.

   (F) The right to education or training for oneself and for members of one's family or household on the management of care.

   (G) The right to be free from physical or mental abuse, corporal punishment, and any physical or chemical restraints imposed for purposes of discipline or convenience and not included in an individual's ICCP.

   (H) The right to be fully informed orally and in writing of the individual's rights.

   (I) Guidelines for such minimum compensation for individuals providing such care as will assure the availability and continuity of competent individuals to provide such care for functionally disabled individuals who have functional disabilities of varying levels of severity.

   (J) Any other rights established by the Secretary.

(g) Minimum requirements for small community care settings

(1) Small community care settings defined

In this section, the term "small community care setting" means—

   (A) a nonresidential setting that serves more than 2 and less than 8 individuals; or

(B) a residential setting in which more than 2 and less than 8 unrelated adults reside and in which personal services (other than merely board) are provided in conjunction with residing in the setting.

(2) Minimum requirements

A small community care setting in which community care is provided under this section must—

(A) meet such requirements as are published or developed by the Secretary under subsection (k) of this section;

(B) meet the requirements of paragraphs (1)(A), (1)(C), (1)(D), (3), and (6) of section 1396r(c) of this title, to the extent applicable to such a setting;

(C) inform each individual receiving community care under this section in the setting, orally and in writing at the time the individual first receives community care in the setting, of the individual's legal rights with respect to such a setting and the care provided in the setting;

(D) meet any applicable State or local requirements regarding certification or licensure;

(E) meet any applicable State and local zoning, building, and housing codes, and State and local fire and safety regulations; and

(F) be designed, constructed, equipped, and maintained in a manner to protect the health and safety of residents.

(h) Minimum requirements for large community care settings

(1) Large community care setting defined

In this section, the term "large community care setting" means—

(A) a nonresidential setting in which more than 8 individuals are served; or

(B) a residential setting in which more than 8 unrelated adults reside and in which personal services are provided in conjunction with residing in the setting in which home and community care under this section is provided.

(2) Minimum requirements

A large community care setting in which community care is provided under this section must—

(A) meet such requirements as are published or developed by the Secretary under subsection (k) of this section;

(B) meet the requirements of paragraphs (1)(A), (1)(C), (1)(D), (3), and (6) of section 1396r(c) of this title, to the extent applicable to such a setting;

(C) inform each individual receiving community care under this section in the setting, orally and in writing at the time the individual first receives home and community care in the setting, of the individual's legal rights with respect to such a setting and the care provided in the setting; and

(D) meet the requirements of paragraphs (2) and (3) of section 1396r(d) (relating to administration and other matters) in the same manner as such requirements apply to nursing facilities under such section; except that, in applying the requirement of section 1396r(d)(2) of this title (relating to life safety code), the Secretary shall provide for the application of such life safety requirements (if any) that are appropriate to the setting.

(3) Disclosure of ownership and control interests and exclusion of repeated violators

A community care setting—

(A) must disclose persons with an ownership or control interest (including such persons as defined in section 1320a–3(a)(3) of this title) in the setting; and

(B) may not have, as a person with an ownership or control interest in the setting, any individual or person who has been excluded from participation in the program under this subchapter or who has had such an ownership or control interest in one or more community care settings which have been found repeatedly to be substandard or to have failed to meet the requirements of paragraph (2).

(i) Survey and certification process

(1) Certifications

(A) Responsibilities of the State

Under each State plan under this subchapter, the State shall be responsible for certifying the compliance of providers of home and community care and community care settings with the applicable requirements of subsections (f), (g) and (h) of this section. The failure of the Secretary to issue regulations to carry out this subsection shall not relieve a State of its responsibility under this subsection.

(B) Responsibilities of the Secretary

The Secretary shall be responsible for certifying the compliance of State providers of home and community care, and of State community care settings in which such care is provided, with the requirements of subsections (f), (g) and (h) of this section.

(C) Frequency of certifications

Certification of providers and settings under this subsection shall occur no less frequently than once every 12 months.

(2) Reviews of providers

(A) In general

The certification under this subsection with respect to a provider of home or community care must be based on a periodic review of the provider's performance in providing the care required under ICCP's in accordance with the requirements of subsection (f) of this section.

(B) Special reviews of compliance

Where the Secretary has reason to question the compliance of a provider of home or community care with any of the requirements of subsection (f) of this section, the Secretary may conduct a review of the provider and, on the basis of that review, make independent and binding determinations concerning the extent to which the provider meets such requirements.

(3) Surveys of community care settings

(A) In general

The certification under this subsection with respect to community care settings must be based on a survey. Such survey for such a setting must be conducted without prior notice to the setting. Any individual who notifies (or causes to be notified) a community care setting of the time or date on which such a survey is scheduled to be conducted is subject to a civil money penalty of not to exceed $2,000. The provisions of section 1320a–7a of this title (other than subsections (a) and (b)) shall apply to a civil money penalty under the previous sentence in the same manner as such provisions apply to a penalty or proceeding under section 1320a–7a(a) of this title. The Secretary shall review each State's procedures for scheduling and conducting such surveys to assure that the State has taken all reasonable steps to avoid giving notice of such a survey through the scheduling procedures and the conduct of the surveys themselves.

(B) Survey protocol

Surveys under this paragraph shall be conducted based upon a protocol which the Secretary has provided for under subsection (k) of this section.

(C) Prohibition of conflict of interest in survey team membership

A State and the Secretary may not use as a member of a survey team under this paragraph an individual who is serving (or has served within the previous 2 years) as a member of the staff of, or as a consultant to, the community care setting being surveyed (or the person responsible for such setting) respecting compliance with the requirements of subsection (g) or (h) of this section or who has a personal or familial financial interest in the setting being surveyed.

(D) Validation surveys of community care settings

The Secretary shall conduct onsite surveys of a representative sample of community care settings in each State, within 2 months of the date of surveys conducted under subparagraph (A) by the State, in a sufficient number to allow inferences about the adequacies of each State's surveys conducted under subparagraph (A). In conducting such surveys, the Secretary shall use the same survey protocols as the State is required to use under subparagraph (B). If the State has determined that an individual setting meets the requirements of subsection (g) of this section, but the Secretary determines that the setting does not meet such requirements, the Secretary's determination as to the setting's noncompliance with such requirements is binding and supersedes that of the State survey.

(E) Special surveys of compliance

Where the Secretary has reason to question the compliance of a community care setting with any of the requirements of subsection (g) or (h) of this section, the Secretary may conduct a survey of the setting and, on the basis of that survey, make independent and binding determinations concerning the extent to which the setting meets such requirements.

(4) Investigation of complaints and monitoring of providers and settings

Each State and the Secretary shall maintain procedures and adequate staff to investigate complaints of violations of applicable requirements imposed on providers of community care or on community care settings under subsections (f), (g) and (h) of this section.

(5) Investigation of allegations of individual neglect and abuse and misappropriation of individual property

The State shall provide, through the agency responsible for surveys and certification of providers of home or community care and community care settings under this subsection, for a process for the receipt, review, and investigation of allegations of individual neglect and abuse (including injuries of unknown source) by individuals providing such care or in such setting and of misappropriation of individual property by such individuals. The State shall, after notice to the individual involved and a reasonable opportunity for hearing for the individual to rebut allegations, make a finding as to the accuracy of the allegations. If the State finds that an individual has neglected or abused an individual receiving community care or misappropriated such individual's property, the State shall notify the individual against whom the finding is made. A State shall not make a finding that a person has neglected an individual receiving community care if the person demonstrates that such neglect was caused by factors beyond the control of the person. The State shall provide for public disclosure of findings under this paragraph upon request and for inclusion, in any such disclosure of such findings, of any brief statement (or of a clear and accurate summary thereof) of the individual disputing such findings.

(6) Disclosure of results of inspections and activities

(A) Public information

Each State, and the Secretary, shall make available to the public—

(i) information respecting all surveys, reviews, and certifications made under this subsection respecting providers of home or community care and community care settings, including statements of deficiencies,

(ii) copies of cost reports (if any) of such providers and settings filed under this subchapter,

(iii) copies of statements of ownership under section 1320a–3 of this title, and

(iv) information disclosed under section 1320a–5 of this title.

(B) Notices of substandard care

If a State finds that—

(i) a provider of home or community care has provided care of substandard quality with respect to an individual, the State shall make a reasonable effort to notify promptly

(I) an immediate family member of each such individual and

(II) individuals receiving home or community care from that provider under this subchapter, or

(ii) a community care setting is substandard, the State shall make a reasonable effort to notify promptly

(I) individuals receiving community care in that setting, and

(II) immediate family members of such individuals.

(C) Access to fraud control units

Each State shall provide its State medicaid fraud and abuse control unit (established under section 1396b(q) of this title) with access to all information of the State agency responsible for surveys, reviews, and certifications under this subsection.

(j) Enforcement process for providers of community care

(1) State authority

(A) In general

If a State finds, on the basis of a review under subsection (i)(2) of this section or otherwise, that a provider of home or community care no longer meets the requirements of this section, the State may terminate the provider's participation under the State plan and may provide in addition for a civil money penalty. Nothing in this subparagraph shall be construed as restricting the remedies available to a State to remedy a provider's deficiencies. If the State finds that a provider meets such requirements but, as of a previous period, did not meet such requirements, the State may provide for a civil money penalty under paragraph (2)(A) for the period during which it finds that the provider was not in compliance with such requirements.

(B) Civil money penalty

(i) In general

Each State shall establish by law (whether statute or regulation) at least the following remedy: A civil money penalty assessed and collected, with interest, for each day in which the provider is or was out of compliance with a requirement of this section. Funds collected by a State as a result of imposition of such a penalty (or as a result of the imposition by the State of a civil money penalty under subsection (i)(3)(A) of this section) may be applied to reimbursement of individuals for personal funds lost due to a failure of home or community care providers to meet the requirements of this section. The State also shall specify criteria, as to when and how this remedy is to be applied and the amounts of any penalties. Such criteria shall be designed so as to minimize the time between the identification of violations and final imposition of the penalties and shall provide for the imposition of incrementally more severe penalties for repeated or uncorrected deficiencies.

(ii) Deadline and guidance

Each State which elects to provide home and community care under this section must establish the civil money penalty remedy described in clause (i) applicable to all providers of community care covered under this section. The Secretary shall provide, through regulations or otherwise by not later than July 1, 1990, guidance to States in establishing such remedy; but the failure of the Secretary to provide such guidance shall not relieve a State of the responsibility for establishing such remedy.

(2) Secretarial authority

(A) For State providers

With respect to a State provider of home or community care, the Secretary shall have the authority and duties of a State under this subsection, except that the civil money penalty remedy described in subparagraph (C) shall be substituted for the civil money remedy described in paragraph (1)(B)(i).

(B) Other providers

With respect to any other provider of home or community care in a State, if the Secretary finds that a provider no longer meets a requirement of this section, the Secretary may terminate the provider's participation under the State plan and may provide, in addition, for a civil money penalty under subparagraph (C). If the Secretary finds that a provider meets such requirements but, as of a previous period, did not meet such requirements, the Secretary may provide for a civil money penalty under subparagraph (C) for the period during which the Secretary finds that the provider was not in compliance with such requirements.

(C) Civil money penalty

If the Secretary finds on the basis of a review under subsection (i)(2) of this section or otherwise that a home or community care provider no longer meets the requirements of this section, the Secretary shall impose a civil money penalty in an amount not to exceed $10,000 for each day of noncompliance. The provisions of section 1320a–7a of this title (other than subsections (a) and (b)) shall apply to a civil money penalty under the previous sentence in the same manner as such provisions apply to a penalty or proceeding under section 1320a–7a(a) of this title. The Secretary shall specify criteria, as to when and how this remedy is to be applied and the amounts of any penalties. Such criteria shall be designed so as to minimize the time between the identification of violations and final imposition of the penalties and shall provide for the imposition of incrementally more severe penalties for repeated or uncorrected deficiencies.

(*l*) Waiver of Statewideness

States may waive the requirement of section 1396a(a)(1) of this title (related to Statewideness) for a program of home and community care under this section.

(m) Limitation on amount of expenditures as medical assistance

(1) Limitation on amount

* * *

(2) Assurance of entitlement to service

A State which receives Federal medical assistance for expenditures for home and community care under this section must provide home and community care specified under the Individual Community Care Plan under subsection (d) of this section to individuals described in subsection (b) of this section for the duration of the election period, without regard to the amount of funds available to the State under paragraph (1). For purposes of this paragraph, an election period is the period of 4 or more calendar quarters elected by the State, and approved by the Secretary, for the provision of home and community care under this section.

(3) Limitation on eligibility

The State may limit eligibility for home and community care under this section during an election period under paragraph (2) to reasonable classifications (based on age, degree of functional disability, and need for services).

(4) Allocation of medical assistance

The Secretary shall establish a limitation on the amount of Federal medical assistance available to any State during the State's election period under paragraph (2). The limitation under this paragraph shall take into account the limitation under paragraph (1) and the number of elderly individuals age 65 or over residing in such State in relation to the number of such elderly individuals in the United States during 1990. For purposes of the previous sentence, elderly individuals shall, to the maximum extent practicable, be low-income elderly individuals.

* * *

§ 1396u. Community supported living arrangements services

(a) Community supported living arrangements services. In this title, the term "community supported living arrangements services" means one or more of the following services meeting the requirements of subsection (h) provided in a State eligible to provide services under this section (as defined in subsection (d)) to assist a developmentally disabled individual (as defined in subsection (b)) in activities of daily living necessary to permit such individual to live in the individual's own home, apartment, family home, or rental unit furnished in a community supported living arrangement setting:

(1) Personal assistance.

(2) Training and habilitation services (necessary to assist the individual in achieving increased integration, independence and productivity).

(3) 24-hour emergency assistance (as defined by the Secretary).

(4) Assistive technology.

(5) Adaptive equipment.

(6) Other services (as approved by the Secretary, except those services described in subsection (g)).

(7) Support services necessary to aid an individual to participate in community activities.

(b) "Developmentally disabled individual" defined. In this title the term[,] "developmentally disabled individual" means an individual who as defined by the Secretary is described within the term "mental retardation and related conditions" as defined in regulations as in effect on July 1, 1990, and who is residing with the individual's family or legal guardian in such individual's own home in which no more than 3 other recipients of services under this section are residing and without regard to whether or not such individual is at risk of institutionalization (as defined by the Secretary).

(c) Criteria for selection of participating States. The Secretary shall develop criteria to review the applications of States submitted under this section to provide community supported living arrangement services. The Secretary shall provide in such criteria that during the first 5 years of the provision of services under this section that no less than 2 and no more than 8 States shall be allowed to receive Federal financial participation for providing the services described in this section.

(d) Quality assurance. A State selected by the Secretary to provide services under this section shall in order to continue to receive Federal financial participation for providing services under this section be required to establish and maintain a quality assurance program, that provides that—

(1) the State will certify and survey providers of services under this section (such surveys to be unannounced and average at least 1 a year);

(2) the State will adopt standards for survey and certification that include—

(A) minimum qualifications and training requirements for provider staff;

(B) financial operating standards; and

(C) a consumer grievance process;

(3) the State will provide a system that allows for monitoring boards consisting of providers, family members, consumers, and neighbors;

(4) the State will establish reporting procedures to make available information to the public;

(5) the State will provide ongoing monitoring of the health and well-being of each recipient;

(6) the State will provide the services defined in subsection (a) in accordance with an individual support plan (as defined by the Secretary in regulations); and

(7) the State plan amendment under this section shall be reviewed by the State Council on Developmental Disabilities established under section 125 of the Developmental Disabilities Assistance and Bill of Rights Act of 2000 [42 USCA § 15025] and the protection and advocacy system established under subtitle C [of title I] of that Act [42 USCA §§ 15041 et seq.].

The Secretary shall not approve a quality assurance plan under this subsection and allow a State to continue to receive Federal financial participation under this section unless the State provides for public hearings on the plan prior to adoption and implementation of its plan under this subsection.

(e) Maintenance of effort. States selected by the Secretary to receive Federal financial participation to provide services under this section shall maintain current levels of spending for such services in order to be eligible to continue to receive Federal financial participation for the provision of such services under this section.

(f) Excluded services. No Federal financial participation shall be allowed for the provision of the following services under this section:

(1) Room and board.

(2) Cost of prevocational, vocational and supported employment.

(g) Waiver of requirements. The Secretary may waive such provisions of this title [42 USCS §§ 1396 et seq.] as necessary to carry out the provisions of this section including the following requirements of this title

(1) comparability of amount, duration, and scope of services; and

(2) statewideness.

(h) Minimum protections.

(1) Publication of interim and final requirements.

(A) In general. The Secretary shall publish, by July 1, 1991, a regulation (that shall be effective on an interim basis pending the promulgation of final regulations), and by October 1, 1992, a final regulation, that sets forth interim and final requirements, respectively, consistent with subparagraph (B), to protect the health, safety, and welfare of individuals receiving community supported living arrangements services.

(B) Minimum protections. Interim and final requirements under subparagraph (A) shall assure, through methods other than reliance on State licensure processes or the State quality assurance programs under subsection (d), that—

(i) individuals receiving community supported living arrangements services are protected from neglect, physical and sexual abuse, and financial exploitation;

(ii) a provider of community supported living arrangements services may not use individuals who have been convicted of child or client abuse, neglect, or mistreatment or of a felony involving physical harm to an individual and shall take all reasonable steps to determine whether applicants for employment by the provider have histories indicating involvement in child or client abuse, neglect, or mistreatment or a criminal record involving physical harm to an individual;

(iii) individuals or entities delivering such services are not unjustly enriched as a result of abusive financial arrangements (such as owner lease-backs); and

1063

(iv) individuals or entities delivering such services to clients, or relatives of such individuals, are prohibited from being named beneficiaries of life insurance policies purchased by (or on behalf of) such clients.

(2) Specified remedies. If the Secretary finds that a provider has not met an applicable requirement under subsection (h), the Secretary shall impose a civil money penalty in an amount not to exceed $10,000 for each day of noncompliance. The provisions of section 1128A (other than subsections (a) and (b)) shall apply to a civil money penalty under the previous sentence in the same manner as such provisions apply to a penalty or proceeding under section 1128A(a) [42 USCA § 1320a–7a(a)].

(i) Treatment of funds. Any funds expended under this section for medical assistance shall be in addition to funds expended for any existing services covered under the State plan, including any waiver services for which an individual receiving services under this program is already eligible.

* * *

§ 1396u–2. Provisions relating to managed care

(a) State option to use managed care

(1) Use of medicaid managed care organizations and primary care case managers

(A) In general

Subject to the succeeding provisions of this section, and notwithstanding paragraph (1), (10)(B), or (23)(A) of section 1396a(a) of this title, a State—

(i) may require an individual who is eligible for medical assistance under the State plan under this subchapter to enroll with a managed care entity as a condition of receiving such assistance (and, with respect to assistance furnished by or under arrangements with such entity, to receive such assistance through the entity), if—

(I) the entity and the contract with the State meet the applicable requirements of this section and section 1396b(m) or section 1396d(t) of this title, and

(II) the requirements described in the succeeding paragraphs of this subsection are met; and

(ii) may restrict the number of provider agreements with managed care entities under the State plan if such restriction does not substantially impair access to services.

(B) Definition of managed care entity

In this section, the term "managed care entity" means—

(i) a medicaid managed care organization, as defined in section 1396b(m)(1)(A) of this title, that provides or arranges for services for enrollees under a contract pursuant to section 1396b(m) of this title; and

(ii) a primary care case manager, as defined in section 1396d(t)(2) of this title.

(2) Special rules

(A) Exemption of certain children with special needs

A State may not require under paragraph (1) the enrollment in a managed care entity of an individual under 19 years of age who—

(i) is eligible for supplemental security income under subchapter XVI of this chapter;

(ii) is described in section 701(a)(1)(D) of this title;

(iii) is described in section 1396a(e)(3) of this title;

(iv) is receiving foster care or adoption assistance under part E of subchapter IV of this chapter; or

(v) is in foster care or otherwise in an out-of-home placement.

(3) Choice of coverage

(A) In general

A State must permit an individual to choose a managed care entity from not less than two such entities that meet the applicable requirements of this section, and of section 1396b(m) or section 1396d(t) of this title.

(B) State option

At the option of the State, a State shall be considered to meet the requirements of subparagraph (A) in the case of an individual residing in a rural area, if the State requires the individual to enroll with a managed care entity if such entity—

(i) permits the individual to receive such assistance through not less than two physicians or case managers (to the extent that at least two physicians or case managers are available to provide such assistance in the area), and

(ii) permits the individual to obtain such assistance from any other provider in appropriate circumstances (as established by the State under regulations of the Secretary).

(C) Treatment of certain county-operated health insuring organizations

A State shall be considered to meet the requirement of subparagraph (A) if—

(i) the managed care entity in which the individual is enrolled is a health-insuring organization which—

(I) first became operational prior to January 1, 1986, or

(II) is described in section 9517(c)(3) of the Omnibus Budget Reconciliation Act of 1985 (as added by section 4734(2) of the Omnibus Budget Reconciliation Act of 1990) [*42 U.S.C.A. § 1396*], and

(ii) the individual is given a choice between at least two providers within such entity.

(4) Process for enrollment and termination and change of enrollment

As conditions under paragraph (1)(A)—

(A) In general

The State, enrollment broker (if any), and managed care entity shall permit an individual eligible for medical assistance under the State plan under this subchapter who is enrolled with the entity under this subchapter to terminate (or change) such enrollment—

(i) for cause at any time (consistent with section 1396b(m)(2)(A)(vi) of this title), and

(ii) without cause—

(I) during the 90–day period beginning on the date the individual receives notice of such enrollment, and

(II) at least every 12 months thereafter.

(B) Notice of termination rights

The State shall provide for notice to each such individual of the opportunity to terminate (or change) enrollment under such conditions. Such notice shall be provided at least 60 days before each annual enrollment opportunity described in subparagraph (A)(ii)(II).

(C) Enrollment priorities

In carrying out paragraph (1)(A), the State shall establish a method for establishing enrollment priorities in the case of a managed care entity that does not have sufficient capacity to enroll all such individuals seeking enrollment under which individuals already enrolled with the entity are given priority in continuing enrollment with the entity.

(D) Default enrollment process

In carrying out paragraph (1)(A), the State shall establish a default enrollment process—

(i) under which any such individual who does not enroll with a managed care entity during the enrollment period specified by the State shall be enrolled by the State with such an entity which has not been found to be out of substantial compliance with the applicable requirements of this section and of section 1396b(m) or section 1396d(t) of this title; and

(ii) that takes into consideration—

(I) maintaining existing provider-individual relationships or relationships with providers that have traditionally served beneficiaries under this subchapter; and

(II) if maintaining such provider relationships is not possible, the equitable distribution of such individuals among qualified managed care entities available to enroll such individuals, consistent with the enrollment capacities of the entities.

(5) Provision of information

(A) Information in easily understood form

Each State, enrollment broker, or managed care entity shall provide all enrollment notices and informational and instructional materials relating to such an entity under this subchapter in a manner and form which may be easily understood by enrollees and potential enrollees of the entity who are eligible for medical assistance under the State plan under this subchapter.

(B) Information to enrollees and potential enrollees

Each managed care entity that is a medicaid managed care organization shall, upon request, make available to enrollees and potential enrollees in the organization's service area information concerning the following:

(i) Providers

The identity, locations, qualifications, and availability of health care providers that participate with the organization.

(ii) Enrollee rights and responsibilities

The rights and responsibilities of enrollees.

(iii) Grievance and appeal procedures

The procedures available to an enrollee and a health care provider to challenge or appeal the failure of the organization to cover a service.

(iv) Information on covered items and services

All items and services that are available to enrollees under the contract between the State and the organization that are covered either directly or through a method of referral and prior authorization. Each managed care entity that is a primary care case manager shall, upon request, make available to enrollees and potential enrollees in the organization's service area the information described in clause (iii).

1067

(C) Comparative information

A State that requires individuals to enroll with managed care entities under paragraph (1)(A) shall annually (and upon request) provide, directly or through the managed care entity, to such individuals a list identifying the managed care entities that are (or will be) available and information (presented in a comparative, chart-like form) relating to the following for each such entity offered:

(i) Benefits and cost-sharing

The benefits covered and cost-sharing imposed by the entity.

(ii) Service area

The service area of the entity.

(iii) Quality and performance

To the extent available, quality and performance indicators for the benefits under the entity.

(D) Information on benefits not covered under managed care arrangement

A State, directly or through managed care entities, shall, on or before an individual enrolls with such an entity under this subchapter, inform the enrollee in a written and prominent manner of any benefits to which the enrollee may be entitled to under this subchapter but which are not made available to the enrollee through the entity. Such information shall include information on where and how such enrollees may access benefits not made available to the enrollee through the entity.

(b) Beneficiary protections

(1) Specification of benefits

Each contract with a managed care entity under section 1396b(m) of this title or under section 1396d(t)(3) of this title shall specify the benefits the provision (or arrangement) for which the entity is responsible.

(2) Assuring coverage to emergency services

(A) In general

Each contract with a medicaid managed care organization under section 1396b(m) of this title and each contract with a primary care case manager under section 1396d(t)(3) of this title shall require the organization or manager—

(i) to provide coverage for emergency services (as defined in subparagraph (B)) without regard to prior authorization or the emergency care provider's contractual relationship with the organization or manager, and

(ii) to comply with guidelines established under section 1395w–22 of this title (respecting coordination of post-stabilization care) in the same manner as such guidelines apply to Medicare + Choice plans offered under part C of subchapter XVII of this chapter.

The requirement under clause (ii) shall first apply 30 days after the date of promulgation of the guidelines referred to in such clause.

(B) "Emergency services" defined

In subparagraph (A)(i), the term "emergency services" means, with respect to an individual enrolled with an organization, covered inpatient and outpatient services that—

(i) are furnished by a provider that is qualified to furnish such services under this subchapter, and

(ii) are needed to evaluate or stabilize an emergency medical condition (as defined in subparagraph (C)).

(C) "Emergency medical condition" defined

In subparagraph (B)(ii), the term "emergency medical condition" means a medical condition manifesting itself by acute symptoms of sufficient severity (including severe pain) such that a prudent layperson, who possesses an average knowledge of health and medicine, could reasonably expect the absence of immediate medical attention to result in—

(i) placing the health of the individual (or, with respect to a pregnant woman, the health of the woman or her unborn child) in serious jeopardy,

(ii) serious impairment to bodily functions, or

(iii) serious dysfunction of any bodily organ or part.

(3) Protection of enrollee-provider communications

(A) In general

Subject to subparagraphs (B) and (C), under a contract under section 1396b(m) of this title a medicaid managed care organization (in relation to an individual enrolled under the contract) shall not prohibit or otherwise restrict a covered health care professional (as defined in subparagraph (D)) from advising such an individual who is a patient of the professional about the health status of the individual or medical care or treatment for the individual's condition or disease, regardless of whether benefits for such care or treatment are provided under the contract, if the professional is acting within the lawful scope of practice.

(B) Construction

Subparagraph (A) shall not be construed as requiring a medicaid managed care organization to provide, reimburse for, or provide coverage of, a counseling or referral service if the organization—

(i) objects to the provision of such service on moral or religious grounds; and

(ii) in the manner and through the written instrumentalities such organization deems appropriate, makes available information on its policies regarding such service to prospective enrollees before or during enrollment and to enrollees within 90 days after the date that the organization adopts a change in policy regarding such a counseling or referral service.

Nothing in this subparagraph shall be construed to affect disclosure requirements under State law or under the Employee Retirement Income Security Act of 1974 [*29 U.S.C.A. § 1001* et seq.].

(C) "Health care professional" defined

For purposes of this paragraph, the term "health care professional" means a physician (as defined in section 1395x(r) of this title) or other health care professional if coverage for the professional's services is provided under the contract referred to in subparagraph (A) for the services of the professional. Such term includes a podiatrist, optometrist, chiropractor, psychologist, dentist, physician assistant, physical or occupational therapist and therapy assistant, speech-language pathologist, audiologist, registered or licensed practical nurse (including nurse practitioner, clinical nurse specialist, certified registered nurse anesthetist, and certified nurse-midwife), licensed certified social worker, registered respiratory therapist, and certified respiratory therapy technician.

(4) Grievance procedures

Each medicaid managed care organization shall establish an internal grievance procedure under which an enrollee who is eligible for medical assistance under the State plan under this subchapter, or a provider on behalf of such an enrollee, may challenge the denial of coverage of or payment for such assistance.

(5) Demonstration of adequate capacity and services

Each medicaid managed care organization shall provide the State and the Secretary with adequate assurances (in a time and manner determined by the Secretary) that the organization, with respect to a service area, has the capacity to serve the expected enrollment in such service area, including assurances that the organization—

(A) offers an appropriate range of services and access to preventive and primary care services for the population expected to be enrolled in such service area, and

(B) maintains a sufficient number, mix, and geographic distribution of providers of services.

(6) Protecting enrollees against liability for payment

Each medicaid managed care organization shall provide that an individual eligible for medical assistance under the State plan under this subchapter who is enrolled with the organization may not be held liable—

(A) for the debts of the organization, in the event of the organization's insolvency,

(B) for services provided to the individual—

(i) in the event of the organization failing to receive payment from the State for such services; or

(ii) in the event of a health care provider with a contractual, referral, or other arrangement with the organization failing to receive payment from the State or the organization for such services, or

(C) for payments to a provider that furnishes covered services under a contractual, referral, or other arrangement with the organization in excess of the amount that would be owed by the individual if the organization had directly provided the services.

(7) Antidiscrimination

A medicaid managed care organization shall not discriminate with respect to participation, reimbursement, or indemnification as to any provider who is acting within the scope of the provider's license or certification under applicable State law, solely on the basis of such license or certification. This paragraph shall not be construed to prohibit an organization from including providers only to the extent necessary to meet the needs of the organization's enrollees or from establishing any measure designed to maintain quality and control costs consistent with the responsibilities of the organization.

(8) Compliance with certain maternity and mental health requirements

Each medicaid managed care organization shall comply with the requirements of subpart 3 of part A of subchapter XXV of chapter 6A of this title insofar as such requirements apply and are effective with respect to a health insurance issuer that offers group health insurance coverage.

(c) Quality assurance standards

(1) Quality assessment and improvement strategy

(A) In general

If a State provides for contracts with medicaid managed care organizations under section 1396b(m) of this title, the State shall develop and implement a quality assessment and improvement strategy consistent with this paragraph. Such strategy shall include the following:

(i) Access standards

Standards for access to care so that covered services are available within reasonable timeframes and in a manner that ensures continuity of care and adequate primary care and specialized services capacity.

(ii) Other measures

Examination of other aspects of care and service directly related to the improvement of quality of care (including grievance procedures and marketing and information standards).

(iii) Monitoring procedures

Procedures for monitoring and evaluating the quality and appropriateness of care and services to enrollees that reflect the full spectrum of populations enrolled under the contract and that includes requirements for provision of quality assurance data to the State using the data and information set that the Secretary has specified for use under part C of subchapter XVIII of this chapter or such alternative data as the Secretary approves, in consultation with the State.

(iv) Periodic review

Regular, periodic examinations of the scope and content of the strategy.

(B) Standards

The strategy developed under subparagraph (A) shall be consistent with standards that the Secretary first establishes within 1 year after August 5, 1997. Such standards shall not preempt any State standards that are more stringent than such standards. Guidelines relating to quality assurance that are applied under section 1396n(b)(2) of this title shall apply under this subsection until the effective date of standards for quality assurance established under this subparagraph.

(C) Monitoring

The Secretary shall monitor the development and implementation of strategies under subparagraph (A).

(D) Consultation

The Secretary shall conduct activities under subparagraphs (B) and (C) in consultation with the States.

(2) External independent review of managed care activities

(A) Review of contracts

(i) In general

Each contract under section 1396b(m) of this title with a medicaid managed care organization shall provide for an annual (as appropriate) external independent review conducted by a qualified independent entity of the quality outcomes and timeliness of, and access to, the items and services for which the organization is responsible under the contract. The requirement for such a review shall not apply until after the date that the Secretary establishes the identification method described in clause (ii).

(ii) Qualifications of reviewer

The Secretary, in consultation with the States, shall establish a method for the identification of entities that are qualified to conduct reviews under clause (i).

(iii) Use of protocols

The Secretary, in coordination with the National Governors' Association, shall contract with an independent quality review organization (such as the National Committee for Quality Assurance) to develop the protocols to be used in external independent reviews conducted under this paragraph on and after January 1, 1999.

(iv) Availability of results

The results of each external independent review conducted under this subparagraph shall be available to participating health care providers, enrollees, and potential enrollees of the organization, except that the results may not be made available in a manner that discloses the identity of any individual patient.

(B) Nonduplication of accreditation

A State may provide that, in the case of a medicaid managed care organization that is accredited by a private independent entity (such as those described in section 1395w–22(e)(4) of this title) or that has an external review conducted under section 1395w–22(e)(3) of this title, the external review activities conducted under subparagraph (A) with respect to the organization shall not be duplicative of review activities conducted as part of the accreditation process or the external review conducted under such section.

(C) Deemed compliance for medicare managed care organizations

At the option of a State, the requirements of subparagraph (A) shall not apply with respect to a medicaid managed care organization if the organization is an eligible organization with a contract in effect under section 1395mm of this title or a Medicare + Choice organization with a contract in effect under part C of subchapter XVIII of this chapter [*42 U.S.C.A. § 1395w–21* et seq.] and the organization has had a contract in effect under section 1396b(m) of this title at least during the previous 2–year period.

(d) Protections against fraud and abuse

(1) Prohibiting affiliations with individuals debarred by Federal agencies

(A) In general

A managed care entity may not knowingly—

(i) have a person described in subparagraph (C) as a director, officer, partner, or person with beneficial ownership of more than 5 percent of the entity's equity, or

(ii) have an employment, consulting, or other agreement with a person described in such subparagraph for the provision of items and services that are significant and material to the entity's obligations under its contract with the State.

(B) Effect of noncompliance

If a State finds that a managed care entity is not in compliance with clause (i) or (ii) of subparagraph (A), the State—

(i) shall notify the Secretary of such noncompliance;

(ii) may continue an existing agreement with the entity unless the Secretary (in consultation with the Inspector General of the Department of Health and Human Services) directs otherwise; and

(iii) may not renew or otherwise extend the duration of an existing agreement with the entity unless the Secretary (in consultation with the Inspector General of the Department of Health and Human Services) provides to the State and to Congress a written statement describing compelling reasons that exist for renewing or extending the agreement.

(C) Persons described

A person is described in this subparagraph if such person—

(i) is debarred, suspended, or otherwise excluded from participating in procurement activities under the Federal Acquisition Regulation or from participating in nonprocurement activities under regulations issued pursuant to Executive Order No. 12549 or under guidelines implementing such order; or

(ii) is an affiliate (as defined in such Regulation) of a person described in clause (i).

(2) Restrictions on marketing

(A) Distribution of materials

(i) In general

A managed care entity, with respect to activities under this subchapter, may not distribute directly or through any agent or independent contractor marketing materials within any State—

(I) without the prior approval of the State, and

(II) that contain false or materially misleading information.

The requirement of subclause (I) shall not apply with respect to a State until such date as the Secretary specifies in consultation with such State.

(ii) Consultation in review of market materials

In the process of reviewing and approving such materials, the State shall provide for consultation with a medical care advisory committee.

(B) Service market

A managed care entity shall distribute marketing materials to the entire service area of such entity covered under the contract under section 1396b(m) or section 1396d(t)(3) of this title.

(C) Prohibition of tie-ins

A managed care entity, or any agency of such entity, may not seek to influence an individual's enrollment with the entity in conjunction with the sale of any other insurance.

(D) Prohibiting marketing fraud

Each managed care entity shall comply with such procedures and conditions as the Secretary prescribes in order to ensure that, before an individual is enrolled with the entity, the individual is provided accurate oral and written information sufficient to make an informed decision whether or not to enroll.

(E) Prohibition of "cold-call" marketing

Each managed care entity shall not, directly or indirectly, conduct door-to-door, telephonic, or other "cold-call" marketing of enrollment under this subchapter.

(3) State conflict-of-interest safeguards in medicaid risk contracting

A medicaid managed care organization may not enter into a contract with any State under section 1396b(m) of this title unless the State has in effect conflict-of-interest safeguards with respect to officers and employees of the State with responsibilities relating to contracts with such organizations or to the default enrollment process described in subsection (a)(4)(C)(ii) of this section that are at least as effective as the Federal safeguards provided under section 27 of the Office of Federal Procurement Policy Act [41 U.S.C.A. § 423], against conflicts of interest that apply with respect to Federal procurement officials with comparable responsibilities with respect to such contracts.

(4) Use of unique physician identifier for participating physicians

Each medicaid managed care organization shall require each physician providing services to enrollees eligible for medical assistance under the State plan under this title to have a unique identifier in accordance with the system established under section 1320d–2(b) of this title.

(e) Sanctions for noncompliance

(1) Use of intermediate sanctions by the State to enforce requirements

(A) In general

A State may not enter into or renew a contract under section 1396b(m) of this title unless the State has established intermediate sanctions, which may include any of the types described in paragraph (2), other than the termination of a contract with a medicaid managed care organization, which the State may impose against a medicaid managed care organization with such a contract, if the organization—

(i) fails substantially to provide medically necessary items and services that are required (under law or under such organization's contract with the State) to be provided to an enrollee covered under the contract;

(ii) imposes premiums or charges on enrollees in excess of the premiums or charges permitted under this subchapter;

(iii) acts to discriminate among enrollees on the basis of their health status or requirements for health care services, including expulsion or refusal to reenroll an individual, except as permitted by this subchapter, or engaging in any practice that would reasonably be expected to have the effect of denying or discouraging enrollment with the organization by eligible individuals whose medical condition or history indicates a need for substantial future medical services;

(iv) misrepresents or falsifies information that is furnished—

(I) to the Secretary or the State under this subchapter; or

(II) to an enrollee, potential enrollee, or a health care provider under such subchapter; or

(v) fails to comply with the applicable requirements of section 1396b(m)(2)(A)(x) of this title.

The State may also impose such intermediate sanction against a managed care entity if the State determines that the entity distributed directly or through any agent or independent contractor marketing materials in violation of subsection (d)(2)(A)(i)(II) of this section.

(B) Rule of construction

Clause (i) of subparagraph (A) shall not apply to the provision of abortion services, except that a State may impose a sanction on any medicaid managed care organization that has a contract to provide abortion services if the organization does not provide such services as provided for under the contract.

(2) Intermediate sanctions

The sanctions described in this paragraph are as follows:

(A) Civil money penalties as follows:

(i) Except as provided in clause (ii), (iii), or (iv), not more than $25,000 for each determination under paragraph (1)(A).

(ii) With respect to a determination under clause (iii) or (iv)(I) of paragraph (1)(A), not more than $100,000 for each such determination.

(iii) With respect to a determination under paragraph (1)(A)(ii), double the excess amount charged in violation of such subsection (and the excess amount charged shall be deducted from the penalty and returned to the individual concerned).

(iv) Subject to clause (ii), with respect to a determination under paragraph (1)(A)(iii), $15,000 for each individual not enrolled as a result of a practice described in such subsection.

(B) The appointment of temporary management—

(i) to oversee the operation of the medicaid managed care organization upon a finding by the State that there is continued egregious behavior by the organization or there is a substantial risk to the health of enrollees; or

(ii) to assure the health of the organization's enrollees, if there is a need for temporary management while—

(I) there is an orderly termination or reorganization of the organization; or

(II) improvements are made to remedy the violations found under paragraph (1),

except that temporary management under this subparagraph may not be terminated until the State has determined that the medicaid managed care organization has the capability to ensure that the violations shall not recur.

(C) Permitting individuals enrolled with the managed care entity to terminate enrollment without cause, and notifying such individuals of such right to terminate enrollment.

(D) Suspension or default of all enrollment of individuals under this subchapter after the date the Secretary or the State notifies the entity of a determination of a violation of any requirement of section 1396b(m) of this title or this section.

1077

(E) Suspension of payment to the entity under this subchapter for individuals enrolled after the date the Secretary or State notifies the entity of such a determination and until the Secretary or State is satisfied that the basis for such determination has been corrected and is not likely to recur.

(3) Treatment of chronic substandard entities

In the case of a medicaid managed care organization which has repeatedly failed to meet the requirements of section 1396b(m) of this title and this section, the State shall (regardless of what other sanctions are provided) impose the sanctions described in subparagraphs (B) and (C) of paragraph (2).

(4) Authority to terminate contract

(A) In general

In the case of a managed care entity which has failed to meet the requirements of this part or a contract under section 1396b(m) or 1396d(t)(3) of this title, the State shall have the authority to terminate such contract with the entity and to enroll such entity's enrollees with other managed care entities (or to permit such enrollees to receive medical assistance under the State plan under this subchapter other than through a managed care entity).

(B) Availability of hearing prior to termination of contract

A State may not terminate a contract with a managed care entity under subparagraph (A) unless the entity is provided with a hearing prior to the termination.

(C) Notice and right to disenroll in cases of termination hearing

A State may—

(i) notify individuals enrolled with a managed care entity which is the subject of a hearing to terminate the entity's contract with the State of the hearing, and

(ii) in the case of such an entity, permit such enrollees to disenroll immediately with the entity without cause.

(5) Other protections for managed care entities against sanctions imposed by State

Before imposing any sanction against a managed care entity other than termination of the entity's contract, the State shall provide the entity with notice and such other due process protections as the State may provide, except that a State may not provide a managed care entity with a pre-termination hearing before imposing the sanction described in paragraph (2)(B).

(f) Timeliness of payment

A contract under section 1396b(m) of this title with a medicaid managed care organization shall provide that the organization shall make payment to health care providers for items and services which are subject to the contract and that are furnished to individuals eligible for medical assistance under the State plan under this subchapter who are enrolled with the organization on a timely basis consistent with the claims payment procedures described in section 1396a(a)(37)(A) of this title, unless the health care provider and the organization agree to an alternate payment schedule.

* * *

§ 1396u–3. State coverage of medicare cost-sharing for additional low-income medicare beneficiaries

(a) In general. A State plan under this title shall provide, under section 1902(a)(10)(E)(iv) [§ 1396a(a)(10)(E)(iv)] and subject to the succeeding provisions of this section and through a plan amendment, for medical assistance for payment of the cost of medicare cost-sharing described in such section on behalf of all individuals described in such section (in this section referred to as "qualifying individuals") who are selected to receive such assistance under subsection (b).

(b) Selection of qualifying individuals. A State shall select qualifying individuals, and provide such individuals with assistance, under this section consistent with the following:

(1) All qualifying individuals may apply. The State shall permit all qualifying individuals to apply for assistance during a calendar year.

(2) Selection on first-come, first-served basis.

(A) In general. For each calendar year (beginning with 1998), from (and to the extent of) the amount of the allocation under subsection (c) for the State for the fiscal year ending in such calendar year, the State shall select qualifying individuals who apply for the assistance in the order in which they apply.

(B) Carryover. For calendar years after 1998, the State shall give preference to individuals who were provided such assistance (or other assistance described in section 1902(a)(10)(E) [§ 1396a(a)(10(E)]) in the last month of the previous year and who continue to be (or become) qualifying individuals.

(3) Limit on number of individuals based on allocation. The State shall limit the number of qualifying individuals selected with respect to assistance in a calendar year so that the aggregate amount of such assistance provided to such individuals in such year is estimated to be equal to (but not exceed) the State's allocation under subsection (c) for the fiscal year ending in such calendar year.

(4) Receipt of assistance during duration of year. If a qualifying individual is selected to receive assistance under this section for a month in a year, the individual is entitled to receive such assistance for the remainder of the year if the individual continues to be a qualifying individual. The fact that an individual is selected to receive assistance under this section at any time during a year does not entitle the individual to continued assistance for any succeeding year.

(c) Allocation.

(1) Total allocation. The total amount available for allocation under this section for—

* * *

(E) fiscal year 2002 is $400,000,000.

(2) Allocation to States. The Secretary shall provide for the allocation of the total amount described in paragraph (1) for a fiscal year, among the States that executed a plan amendment in accordance with subsection (a), based upon the Secretary's estimate of the ratio of—

(A) an amount equal to the sum of—

(i) twice the total number of individuals described in section 1902(a)(10)(E)(iv)(I) [§ 1396a(a)(10)(E)(iv)(I)] in the State, and

(ii) the total number of individuals described in section 1902(a)(10)(E)(iv)(II) [§ 1396a(a)(10)(E)(iv)(II)] in the State; to

(B) the sum of the amounts computed under subparagraph (A) for all eligible States.

(d) Applicable FMAP. With respect to assistance described in section 1902(a)(10)(E)(iv) [§ 1902a(a)(10)(E)(iv)] furnished in a State for calendar quarters in a calendar year—

(1) to the extent that such assistance does not exceed the State's allocation under subsection (c) for the fiscal year ending in the calendar year, the Federal medical assistance percentage shall be equal to 100 percent; and

(2) to the extent that such assistance exceeds such allocation, the Federal medical assistance percentage is 0 percent.

(e) Limitation on entitlement. Except as specifically provided under this section, nothing in this title shall be construed as establishing any entitlement of individuals described in section 1902(a)(10)(E)(iv) [§ 1396a(a)(10)(E)(iv)] to assistance described in such section.

(f) Coverage of costs through Part B of the medicare program. For each fiscal year, the Secretary shall provide for the transfer from the Federal Supplementary Medical Insurance Trust Fund under section 1841 [§ 1395t] to the appropriate account in the Treasury that provides for payments under section 1903(a) [§ 1396b(a)] with respect to medical assistance provided under this section, of an amount equivalent to the total of the amount of payments made under such section that is attributable to this section and such transfer shall be treated as an expenditure from such Trust Fund for purposes of section 1839 [§ 1395r].

§ 1396u–4. Program of all-inclusive care for the elderly (PACE)

(a) State option

(1) In general. A State may elect to provide medical assistance under this section with respect to PACE program services to PACE program eligible individuals who are eligible for medical assistance under the State plan and who are enrolled in a PACE program under a PACE program agreement. Such individuals need not be eligible for benefits under part A [§§ 1395c et seq.], or enrolled under part B [§§ 1395j et seq.], of title XVIII to be eligible to enroll under this section. In the case of an individual enrolled with a PACE program pursuant to such an election—

(A) the individual shall receive benefits under the plan solely through such program, and

(B) the PACE provider shall receive payment in accordance with the PACE program agreement for provision of such benefits.

A State may establish a numerical limit on the number of individuals who may be enrolled in a PACE program under a PACE program agreement.

(2) PACE program defined. For purposes of this section, the term "PACE program" means a program of all-inclusive care for the elderly that meets the following requirements:

(A) Operation. The entity operating the program is a PACE provider (as defined in paragraph (3)).

(B) Comprehensive benefits. The program provides comprehensive health care services to PACE program eligible individuals in accordance with the PACE program agreement and regulations under this section.

(C) Transition. In the case of an individual who is enrolled under the program under this section and whose enrollment ceases for any reason (including that the individual no longer qualifies as a PACE program eligible individual, the termination of a PACE program agreement, or otherwise), the program provides assistance to the individual in obtaining necessary transitional care through appropriate referrals and making the individual's medical records available to new providers.

(3) PACE provider defined.

(A) In general. For purposes of this section, the term "PACE provider" means an entity that—

(i) subject to subparagraph (B), is (or is a distinct part of) a public entity or a private, nonprofit entity organized for charitable purposes under section 501(c)(3) of the Internal Revenue Code of 1986 [26 USCA § 501(c)(3)], and

(ii) has entered into a PACE program agreement with respect to its operation of a PACE program.

(B) Treatment of private, for-profit providers. Clause (i) of subparagraph (A) shall not apply—

(i) to entities subject to a demonstration project waiver under subsection (h); and

(ii) after the date the report under section 4804(b) of the Balanced Budget Act of 1997 [§ 1395eee note] is submitted, unless the Secretary determines that any of the findings described in subparagraph (A), (B), (C), or (D) of paragraph (2) of such section are true.

(4) PACE program agreement defined. For purposes of this section, the term "PACE program agreement" means, with respect to a PACE provider, an agreement, consistent with this section, section 1894 [42 USCA § 1395eee] (if applicable), and regulations promulgated to carry out such sections, among the PACE provider, the Secretary, and a State administering agency for the operation of a PACE program by the provider under such sections.

(5) PACE program eligible individual defined. For purposes of this section, the term "PACE program eligible individual" means, with respect to a PACE program, an individual who—

(A) is 55 years of age or older;

(B) subject to subsection (c)(4), is determined under subsection (c) to require the level of care required under the State medicaid plan for coverage of nursing facility services;

(C) resides in the service area of the PACE program; and

(D) meets such other eligibility conditions as may be imposed under the PACE program agreement for the program under subsection (e)(2)(A)(ii).

(6) PACE protocol. For purposes of this section, the term "PACE protocol" means the Protocol for the Program of All-inclusive Care for the Elderly (PACE), as published by On Lok, Inc., as of April 14, 1995, or any successor protocol that may be agreed upon between the Secretary and On Lok, Inc.

* * *

(8) State administering agency defined. For purposes of this section, the term "State administering agency" means, with respect to the operation of a PACE program in a State, the agency of that State (which may be the single agency responsible for administration of the State plan under this title [42 USCS §§ 1396 et seq.] in the State) responsible for administering PACE program agreements under this section and section 1894 [§ 1395eee] in the State.

(9) Trial period defined.

(A) In general. For purposes of this section, the term "trial period" means, with respect to a PACE program operated by a PACE provider under a PACE program agreement, the first 3 contract years under such agreement with respect to such program.

(B) Treatment of entities previously operating pace demonstration waiver programs. Each contract year (including a year occurring before the effective date of this section) during which an entity has operated a PACE demonstration waiver program shall be counted under subparagraph (A) as a contract year during which the entity operated a PACE program as a PACE provider under a PACE program agreement.

(10) Regulations. For purposes of this section, the term "regulations" refers to interim final or final regulations promulgated under subsection (f) to carry out this section and section 1894 [§ 1395eee].

(b) Scope of benefits; beneficiary safeguards.

(1) In general. Under a PACE program agreement, a PACE provider shall—

(A) provide to PACE program eligible individuals, regardless of source of payment and directly or under contracts with other entities, at a minimum—

(i) all items and services covered under title XVIII (for individuals enrolled under section 1894 [§ 1395eee]) and all items and services covered under this title [42 USCS §§ 1396 et seq.], but without any limitation or condition as to amount, duration, or scope and without application of deductibles, copayments, coinsurance, or other cost-sharing that would otherwise apply under such title or this title, respectively; and

(ii) all additional items and services specified in regulations, based upon those required under the PACE protocol;

(B) provide such enrollees access to necessary covered items and services 24 hours per day, every day of the year;

(C) provide services to such enrollees through a comprehensive, multidisciplinary health and social services delivery system which integrates acute and long-term care services pursuant to regulations; and

(D) specify the covered items and services that will not be provided directly by the entity, and to arrange for delivery of those items and services through contracts meeting the requirements of regulations.

(2) Quality assurance; patient safeguards. The PACE program agreement shall require the PACE provider to have in effect at a minimum—

(A) a written plan of quality assurance and improvement, and procedures implementing such plan, in accordance with regulations, and

(B) written safeguards of the rights of enrolled participants (including a patient bill of rights and procedures for grievances and appeals) in accordance with regulations and with other requirements of this title and Federal and State law designed for the protection of patients.

(c) Eligibility determinations.

(1) In general. The determination of—

(A) whether an individual is a PACE program eligible individual shall be made under and in accordance with the PACE program agreement, and

(B) who is entitled to medical assistance under this title shall be made (or who is not so entitled, may be made) by the State administering agency.

(2) Condition. An individual is not a PACE program eligible individual (with respect to payment under this section) unless the individual's health status has been determined by the Secretary or the State administering agency, in accordance with regulations, to be comparable to the health status of individuals who have participated in the PACE demonstration waiver programs. Such determination shall be based upon information on health status and related indicators (such as medical diagnoses and measures of activities of daily living, instrumental activities of daily living, and cognitive impairment) that are part of a uniform minimum data set collected by PACE providers on potential eligible individuals.

(3) Annual eligibility recertifications

(A) In general. Subject to subparagraph (B), the determination described in subsection (a)(5)(B) for an individual shall be reevaluated at least annually.

(B) Exception. The requirement of annual reevaluation under subparagraph (A) may be waived during a period in accordance with regulations in those cases in which the State administering agency determines that there is no reasonable expectation of improvement or significant change in an individual's condition during the period because of the severity of chronic condition, or degree of impairment of functional capacity of the individual involved.

(4) Continuation of eligibility. An individual who is a PACE program eligible individual may be deemed to continue to be such an individual notwithstanding a determination that the individual no longer meets the requirement of subsection (a)(5)(B) if, in accordance with regulations, in the absence of continued coverage under a PACE program the individual reasonably would be expected to meet such requirement within the succeeding 6-month period.

(5) Enrollment; disenrollment.

(A) Voluntary disenrollment at any time. The enrollment and disenrollment of PACE program eligible individuals in a PACE program shall be pursuant to regulations and the PACE program agreement and shall permit enrollees to voluntarily disenroll without cause at any time.

(B) Limitations on disenrollment.

(i) In general. Regulations promulgated by the Secretary under this section and section 1894 [§ 1395eee], and the PACE program agreement, shall provide that the PACE program may not disenroll a PACE program eligible individual except—

(I) for nonpayment of premiums (if applicable) on a timely basis; or

(II) for engaging in disruptive or threatening behavior, as defined in such regulations (developed in close consultation with State administering agencies).

(ii) No disenrollment for noncompliant behavior. Except as allowed under regulations promulgated to carry out clause (i)(II), a PACE program may not disenroll a PACE program eligible individual on the ground that the individual has engaged in noncompliant behavior if such behavior is related to a mental or physical condition of the individual. For purposes of the preceding sentence, the term "noncompliant behavior" includes repeated noncompliance with medical advice and repeated failure to appear for appointments.

(iii) Timely review of proposed nonvoluntary disenrollment. A proposed disenrollment, other than a voluntary disenrollment, shall be subject to timely review and final determination by the Secretary or by the State administering agency (as applicable), prior to the proposed disenrollment becoming effective.

(d) Payments to PACE providers on a capitated basis.

(1) In general. In the case of a PACE provider with a PACE program agreement under this section, except as provided in this subsection or by regulations, the State shall make prospective monthly payments of a capitation amount for each PACE program eligible individual enrolled under the agreement under this section.

(2) Capitation amount. The capitation amount to be applied under this subsection for a provider for a contract year shall be an amount specified in the PACE program agreement for the year. Such amount shall be an amount, specified under the PACE agreement, which is less than the amount that would otherwise have been made under the State

plan if the individuals were not so enrolled and shall be adjusted to take into account the comparative frailty of PACE enrollees and such other factors as the Secretary determines to be appropriate. The payment under this section shall be in addition to any payment made under section 1894 [§ 1395eee] for individuals who are enrolled in a PACE program under such section.

(e) PACE program agreement

    (1) Requirement

        (A) In general. The Secretary, in close cooperation with the State administering agency, shall establish procedures for entering into, extending, and terminating PACE program agreements for the operation of PACE programs by entities that meet the requirements for a PACE provider under this section, section 1894 [§ 1395eee], and regulations.

        (B) Numerical limitation

            (i) In general. The Secretary shall not permit the number of PACE providers with which agreements are in effect under this section or under section 9412(b) of the Omnibus Budget Reconciliation Act of 1986 to exceed—

                (I) 40 as of the date of the enactment of this section [enacted Aug. 5, 1997], or

                (II) as of each succeeding anniversary of such date, the numerical limitation under this subparagraph for the preceding year plus 20.

    Subclause (II) shall apply without regard to the actual number of agreements in effect as of a previous anniversary date.

            (ii) Treatment of certain private, for-profit providers. The numerical limitation in clause (i) shall not apply to a PACE provider that—

                (I) is operating under a demonstration project waiver under subsection (h), or

                (II) was operating under such a waiver and subsequently qualifies for PACE provider status pursuant to subsection (a)(3)(B)(ii).

    (2) Service area and eligibility

        (A) In general. A PACE program agreement for a PACE program—

            (i) shall designate the service area of the program;

            (ii) may provide additional requirements for individuals to qualify as PACE program eligible individuals with respect to the program;

(iii) shall be effective for a contract year, but may be extended for additional contract years in the absence of a notice by a party to terminate, and is subject to termination by the Secretary and the State administering agency at any time for cause (as provided under the agreement);

(iv) shall require a PACE provider to meet all applicable State and local laws and requirements; and

(v) shall contain such additional terms and conditions as the parties may agree to, so long as such terms and conditions are consistent with this section and regulations.

(B) Service area overlap. In designating a service area under a PACE program agreement under subparagraph (A)(i), the Secretary (in consultation with the State administering agency) may exclude from designation an area that is already covered under another PACE program agreement, in order to avoid unnecessary duplication of services and avoid impairing the financial and service viability of an existing program.

(3) Data collection; development of outcome measures.

(A) Data collection.

(i) In general. Under a PACE program agreement, the PACE provider shall—

(I) collect data;

(II) maintain, and afford the Secretary and the State administering agency access to, the records relating to the program, including pertinent financial, medical, and personnel records; and

(III) submit to the Secretary and the State administering agency such reports as the Secretary finds (in consultation with State administering agencies) necessary to monitor the operation, cost, and effectiveness of the PACE program.

(ii) Requirements during trial period. During the first 3 years of operation of a PACE program (either under this section or under a PACE demonstration waiver program), the PACE provider shall provide such additional data as the Secretary specifies in regulations in order to perform the oversight required under paragraph (4)(A).

(B) Development of outcome measures. Under a PACE program agreement, the PACE provider, the Secretary, and the State administering agency shall jointly cooperate in the development and implementation of health status and quality of life outcome measures with respect to PACE program eligible individuals.

(4) Oversight

(A) Annual, close oversight during trial period. During the trial period (as defined in subsection (a)(9)) with respect to a PACE program operated by a PACE provider, the Secretary (in cooperation with the State administering agency) shall conduct a comprehensive annual review of the operation of the PACE program by the provider in order to assure compliance with the requirements of this section and regulations. Such a review shall include—

(i) an onsite visit to the program site;

(ii) comprehensive assessment of a provider's fiscal soundness;

(iii) comprehensive assessment of the provider's capacity to provide all PACE services to all enrolled participants;

(iv) detailed analysis of the entity's substantial compliance with all significant requirements of this section and regulations; and

(v) any other elements the Secretary or the State administering agency considers necessary or appropriate.

(B) Continuing oversight. After the trial period, the Secretary (in cooperation with the State administering agency) shall continue to conduct such review of the operation of PACE providers and PACE programs as may be appropriate, taking into account the performance level of a provider and compliance of a provider with all significant requirements of this section and regulations.

(C) Disclosure. The results of reviews under this paragraph shall be reported promptly to the PACE provider, along with any recommendations for changes to the provider's program, and shall be made available to the public upon request.

(5) Termination of pace provider agreements

(A) In general. Under regulations—

(i) the Secretary or a State administering agency may terminate a PACE program agreement for cause, and

(ii) a PACE provider may terminate such an agreement after appropriate notice to the Secretary, the State administering agency, and enrollees.

(B) Causes for termination. In accordance with regulations establishing procedures for termination of PACE program agreements, the Secretary or a State administering agency may terminate a PACE program agreement with a PACE provider for, among other reasons, the fact that—

(i) the Secretary or State administering agency determines that—

(I) there are significant deficiencies in the quality of care provided to enrolled participants; or

(II) the provider has failed to comply substantially with conditions for a program or provider under this section or section 1894 [42 USCS § 1395eee]; and

(ii) the entity has failed to develop and successfully initiate, within 30 days of the date of the receipt of written notice of such a determination, a plan to correct the deficiencies, or has failed to continue implementation of such a plan.

(C) Termination and transition procedures. An entity whose PACE provider agreement is terminated under this paragraph shall implement the transition procedures required under subsection (a)(2)(C).

(6) Secretary's oversight; enforcement authority

(A) In general. Under regulations, if the Secretary determines (after consultation with the State administering agency) that a PACE provider is failing substantially to comply with the requirements of this section and regulations, the Secretary (and the State administering agency) may take any or all of the following actions:

(i) Condition the continuation of the PACE program agreement upon timely execution of a corrective action plan.

(ii) Withhold some or all further payments under the PACE program agreement under this section or section 1894 [42 USCS § 1395eee] with respect to PACE program services furnished by such provider until the deficiencies have been corrected.

(iii) Terminate such agreement.

(B) Application of intermediate sanctions. Under regulations, the Secretary may provide for the application against a PACE provider of remedies described in section 1857(g)(2) [§ 1395w–27(g)(2)] * * *

(7) Procedures for termination or imposition of sanctions. Under regulations, the provisions of section 1857(h) [§ 1395w–27(h)] (or for periods before January 1, 1999, section 1876(i)(9) [§ 1395mm(i)(9)]) shall apply to termination and sanctions respecting a PACE program agreement and PACE provider under this subsection in the same manner as they apply to a termination and sanctions with respect to a contract and a Medicare + Choice organization under part C of title XVIII [§§ 1395w–21 et seq.] (or for such periods an eligible organization under section 1876 [§ 1395mm]).

(8) Timely consideration of applications for pace program provider status. In considering an application for PACE provider program status, the application shall be deemed approved unless the Secretary, within 90 days after the date of the submission of the application to the Secretary, either denies such request in writing or informs the applicant in writing with respect to any additional information that is needed in order to make a final determination with respect to the application. After the date the Secretary receives such additional information, the application shall be deemed approved unless the Secretary, within 90 days of such date, denies such request.

(f) Regulations

(1) In general. The Secretary shall issue interim final or final regulations to carry out this section and section 1894 [§ 1395eee].

(2) Use of pace protocol

(A) In general. In issuing such regulations, the Secretary shall, to the extent consistent with the provisions of this section, incorporate the requirements applied to PACE demonstration waiver programs under the PACE protocol.

(B) Flexibility. In order to provide for reasonable flexibility in adapting the PACE service delivery model to the needs of particular organizations (such as those in rural areas or those that may determine it appropriate to use nonstaff physicians according to State licensing law requirements) under this section and section 1894 [§ 1395eee], the Secretary (in close consultation with State administering agencies) may modify or waive provisions of the PACE protocol so long as any such modification or waiver is not inconsistent with and would not impair the essential elements, objectives, and requirements of this section, but may not modify or waive any of the following provisions:

(i) The focus on frail elderly qualifying individuals who require the level of care provided in a nursing facility.

(ii) The delivery of comprehensive, integrated acute and long-term care services.

(iii) The interdisciplinary team approach to care management and service delivery.

(iv) Capitated, integrated financing that allows the provider to pool payments received from public and private programs and individuals.

(v) The assumption by the provider of full financial risk.

(C) Continuation of modifications or waivers of operational requirements under demonstration status. If a PACE program operating under demonstration authority has contractual or other operating arrangements which are not otherwise recognized in regulation and which were in effect on July 1[,] 2000, the Secretary (in close consultation with, and with the concurrence of, the State administering agency) shall permit any such program to continue such arrangements so long as such arrangements are found by the Secretary and

1090

the State to be reasonably consistent with the objectives of the PACE program.

(3) Application of certain additional beneficiary and program protections.

(A) In general. In issuing such regulations and subject to subparagraph (B), the Secretary may apply with respect to PACE programs, providers, and agreements such requirements of part C of title XVIII [§§ 1395w–21 et seq.] (or, for periods before January 1, 1999, section 1876 [42 USCS § 1395mm]) and sections 1903(m) and 1932 [§§ 1396b(m), 1396u–2] relating to protection of beneficiaries and program integrity as would apply to Medicare + Choice organizations under such part C (or for such periods eligible organizations under risk-sharing contracts under section 1876 [§ 1395mm]) and to medicaid managed care organizations under prepaid capitation agreements under section 1903(m) [§§ 1396b(m)].

(B) Considerations. In issuing such regulations, the Secretary shall—

(i) take into account the differences between populations served and benefits provided under this section and under part C of title XVIII [§§ 1395w–21 et seq.] (or, for periods before January 1, 1999, section 1876 [42 USCS § 1395mm]) and section 1903(m) [§§ 1396b(m)];

(ii) not include any requirement that conflicts with carrying out PACE programs under this section; and

(iii) not include any requirement restricting the proportion of enrollees who are eligible for benefits under this title or title XVIII.

(4) Construction. Nothing in this subsection shall be construed as preventing the Secretary from including in regulations provisions to ensure the health and safety of individuals enrolled in a PACE program under this section that are in addition to those otherwise provided under paragraphs (2) and (3).

(g) Waivers of requirements. With respect to carrying out a PACE program under this section, the following requirements of this title (and regulations relating to such requirements) shall not apply:

(1) Section 1902(a)(1) [§ 1396a(a)(1)], relating to any requirement that PACE programs or PACE program services be provided in all areas of a State.

(2) Section 1902(a)(10) [§ 1396a(a)(10)], insofar as such section relates to comparability of services among different population groups.

(3) Sections 1902(a)(23) and 1915(b)(4) [§ 1396a(a)(23), 1396n(b)(4)], relating to freedom of choice of providers under a PACE program.

(4) Section 1903(m)(2)(A) [§ 1396b(m)(2)(A)], insofar as it restricts a PACE provider from receiving prepaid capitation payments.

(5) Such other provisions of this title that, as added or amended by the Balanced Budget Act of 1997, the Secretary determines are inapplicable to carrying out a PACE program under this section.

(h) Demonstration project for for-profit entities

(1) In general. In order to demonstrate the operation of a PACE program by a private, for-profit entity, the Secretary (in close consultation with State administering agencies) shall grant waivers from the requirement under subsection (a)(3) that a PACE provider may not be a for-profit, private entity.

(2) Similar terms and conditions

(A) In general. Except as provided under subparagraph (B), and paragraph (1), the terms and conditions for operation of a PACE program by a provider under this subsection shall be the same as those for PACE providers that are nonprofit, private organizations.

(B) Numerical limitation. The number of programs for which waivers are granted under this subsection shall not exceed 10. Programs with waivers granted under this subsection shall not be counted against the numerical limitation specified in subsection (e)(1)(B).

(i) Post-eligibility treatment of income. A State may provide for post-eligibility treatment of income for individuals enrolled in PACE programs under this section in the same manner as a State treats post-eligibility income for individuals receiving services under a waiver under section 1915(c) [§ 1396n(c)].

* * *

D. STATE CHILDREN'S HEALTH INSURANCE PROGRAM: 42 U.S.C. SECTIONS 1397aa– 1397jj

Analysis

§ 1397ii. Miscellaneous provisions
§ 1397jj. Definitions

---

§ 1397aa.   Purpose; State child health plans

(a) Purpose

The purpose of this subchapter is to provide funds to States to enable them to initiate and expand the provision of child health assistance to uninsured, low-income children in an effective and efficient manner that is coordinated with other sources of health benefits coverage for children. Such assistance shall be provided primarily for obtaining health benefits coverage through—

    (1) obtaining coverage that meets the requirements of section 1397cc of this title, or

    (2) providing benefits under the State's medicaid plan under subchapter XIX of this chapter, or a combination of both.

(b) State child health plan required

A State is not eligible for payment under section 1397ee of this title unless the State has submitted to the Secretary under section 1397ff of this title a plan that—

    (1) sets forth how the State intends to use the funds provided under this subchapter to provide child health assistance to needy children consistent with the provisions of this subchapter, and

    (2) has been approved under section 1397ff of this title.

(c) State entitlement

This subchapter constitutes budget authority in advance of appropriations Acts and represents the obligation of the Federal Government to provide for the payment to States of amounts provided under section 1397dd of this title.

(d) Effective date

No State is eligible for payments under section 1397ee of this title for child health assistance for coverage provided for periods beginning before October 1, 1997.

§ 1397bb.   General contents of State child health plan; eligibility; outreach

(a) General background and description

A State child health plan shall include a description, consistent with the requirements of this subchapter, of—

    (1) the extent to which, and manner in which, children in the State, including targeted low-income children and other classes of children

1093

classified by income and other relevant factors, currently have creditable health coverage (as defined in section 1397jj(c)(2) of this title);

(2) current State efforts to provide or obtain creditable health coverage for uncovered children, including the steps the State is taking to identify and enroll all uncovered children who are eligible to participate in public health insurance programs and health insurance programs that involve public-private partnerships;

(3) how the plan is designed to be coordinated with such efforts to increase coverage of children under creditable health coverage;

(4) the child health assistance provided under the plan for targeted low-income children, including the proposed methods of delivery, and utilization control systems;

(5) eligibility standards consistent with subsection (b) of this section;

(6) outreach activities consistent with subsection (c) of this section; and

(7) methods (including monitoring) used—

(A) to assure the quality and appropriateness of care, particularly with respect to well-baby care, well-child care, and immunizations provided under the plan, and

(B) to assure access to covered services, including emergency services.

(b) General description of eligibility standards and methodology

(1) Eligibility standards

(A) In general

The plan shall include a description of the standards used to determine the eligibility of targeted low-income children for child health assistance under the plan. Such standards may include (to the extent consistent with this subchapter) those relating to the geographic areas to be served by the plan, age, income and resources (including any standards relating to spenddowns and disposition of resources), residency, disability status (so long as any standard relating to such status does not restrict eligibility), access to or coverage under other health coverage, and duration of eligibility. Such standards may not discriminate on the basis of diagnosis.

(B) Limitations on eligibility standards

Such eligibility standards–

(i) shall, within any defined group of covered targeted low-income children, not cover such children with higher family income without covering children with a lower family income, and

(ii) may not deny eligibility based on a child having a preexisting medical condition.

(2) Methodology

The plan shall include a description of methods of establishing and continuing eligibility and enrollment.

(3) Eligibility screening; coordination with other health coverage programs

The plan shall include a description of procedures to be used to ensure—

(A) through both intake and followup screening, that only targeted low-income children are furnished child health assistance under the State child health plan;

(B) that children found through the screening to be eligible for medical assistance under the State medicaid plan under subchapter XIX of this chapter are enrolled for such assistance under such plan;

(C) that the insurance provided under the State child health plan does not substitute for coverage under group health plans;

(D) the provision of child health assistance to targeted low-income children in the State who are Indians (as defined in section 1603(c) of title 25); and

(E) coordination with other public and private programs providing creditable coverage for low-income children.

(4) Nonentitlement

Nothing in this subchapter shall be construed as providing an individual with an entitlement to child health assistance under a State child health plan.

(c) Outreach and coordination

A State child health plan shall include a description of the procedures to be used by the State to accomplish the following:

(1) Outreach

Outreach to families of children likely to be eligible for child health assistance under the plan or under other public or private health coverage programs to inform these families of the availability of, and to assist them in enrolling their children in, such a program.

(2) Coordination with other health insurance programs Coordination of the administration of the State program under this subchapter with other public and private health insurance programs.

§ 1397cc.   Coverage requirements for children's health insurance

(a) Required scope of health insurance coverage

The child health assistance provided to a targeted low-income child under the plan in the form described in paragraph (1) of section 1397aa(a) of this title shall consist, consistent with subsection (c)(5) of this section, of any of the following:

(1) Benchmark coverage

Health benefits coverage that is equivalent to the benefits coverage in a benchmark benefit package described in subsection (b) of this section.

(2) Benchmark-equivalent coverage

Health benefits coverage that meets the following requirements:

(A) Inclusion of basic services

The coverage includes benefits for items and services within each of the categories of basic services described in subsection (c)(1) of this section.

(B) Aggregate actuarial value equivalent to benchmark package

The coverage has an aggregate actuarial value that is at least actuarially equivalent to one of the benchmark benefit packages.

(C) Substantial actuarial value for additional services included in benchmark package. With respect to each of the categories of additional services described in subsection (c)(2) of this section for which coverage is provided under the benchmark benefit package used under subparagraph (B), the coverage has an actuarial value that is equal to at least 75 percent of the actuarial value of the coverage of that category of services in such package.

(3) Existing comprehensive State-based coverage Health benefits coverage under an existing comprehensive State-based program, described in subsection (d)(1) of this section.

(4) Secretary-approved coverage

Any other health benefits coverage that the Secretary determines, upon application by a State, provides appropriate coverage for the population of targeted low-income children proposed to be provided such coverage.

(b) Benchmark benefit packages

The benchmark benefit packages are as follows:

(1) FEHBP-equivalent children's health insurance coverage

The standard Blue Cross/Blue Shield preferred provider option service benefit plan, described in and offered under section 8903(1) of title 5.

(2) State employee coverage

A health benefits coverage plan that is offered and generally available to State employees in the State involved.

(3) Coverage offered through HMO

The health insurance coverage plan that—

(A) is offered by a health maintenance organization (as defined in section 2791(b)(3) of the Public Health Service Act (42 U.S.C. 300gg–91(b)(3))), and

(B) has the largest insured commercial, non-medicaid enrollment of covered lives of such coverage plans offered by such a health maintenance organization in the State involved.

(c) Categories of services; determination of actuarial value of coverage

(1) Categories of basic services

For purposes of this section, the categories of basic services described in this paragraph are as follows:

(A) Inpatient and outpatient hospital services.

(B) Physicians' surgical and medical services.

(C) Laboratory and x-ray services.

(D) Well-baby and well-child care, including age-appropriate immunizations.

(2) Categories of additional services

For purposes of this section, the categories of additional services described in this paragraph are as follows:

(A) Coverage of prescription drugs.

(B) Mental health services.

(C) Vision services.

(D) Hearing services.

(3) Treatment of other categories

Nothing in this subsection shall be construed as preventing a State child health plan from providing coverage of benefits that are not within a category of services described in paragraph (1) or (2).

(4) Determination of actuarial value

The actuarial value of coverage of benchmark benefit packages, coverage offered under the State child health plan, and coverage of any categories of additional services under benchmark benefit packages and under coverage offered by such a plan, shall be set forth in an actuarial opinion in an actuarial report that has been prepared—

(A) by an individual who is a member of the American Academy of Actuaries;

(B) using generally accepted actuarial principles and methodologies;

(C) using a standardized set of utilization and price factors;

(D) using a standardized population that is representative of privately insured children of the age of children who are expected to be covered under the State child health plan;

1097

(E) applying the same principles and factors in comparing the value of different coverage (or categories of services);

(F) without taking into account any differences in coverage based on the method of delivery or means of cost control or utilization used; and

(G) taking into account the ability of a State to reduce benefits by taking into account the increase in actuarial value of benefits coverage offered under the State child health plan that results from the limitations on cost sharing under such coverage.

The actuary preparing the opinion shall select and specify in the memorandum the standardized set and population to be used under subparagraphs (C) and (D).

(5) Construction on prohibited coverage

Nothing in this section shall be construed as requiring any health benefits coverage offered under the plan to provide coverage for items or services for which payment is prohibited under this subchapter, notwithstanding that any benchmark benefit package includes coverage for such an item or service.

(d) Description of existing comprehensive State-based coverage

(1) In general

A program described in this paragraph is a child health coverage program that—

(A) includes coverage of a range of benefits;

(B) is administered or overseen by the State and receives funds from the State;

(C) is offered in New York, Florida, or Pennsylvania; and

(D) was offered as of August 5, 1997.

(2) Modifications

A State may modify a program described in paragraph (1) from time to time so long as it continues to meet the requirement of subparagraph (A) and does not reduce the actuarial value of the coverage under the program below the lower of—

(A) the actuarial value of the coverage under the program as of August 5, 1997, or

(B) the actuarial value described in subsection (a)(2)(B) of this section, evaluated as of the time of the modification.

(e) Cost-sharing

(1) Description; general conditions

(A) Description

A State child health plan shall include a description, consistent with this subsection, of the amount (if any) of premiums, deductibles, coinsurance, and other cost sharing imposed. Any such charges shall be imposed pursuant to a public schedule.

(B) Protection for lower income children

The State child health plan may only vary premiums, deductibles, coinsurance, and other cost sharing based on the family income of targeted low-income children in a manner that does not favor children from families with higher income over children from families with lower income.

(2) No cost sharing on benefits for preventive services

The State child health plan may not impose deductibles, coinsurance, or other cost sharing with respect to benefits for services within the category of services described in subsection (c)(1)(D) of this section.

(3) Limitations on premiums and cost-sharing

(A) Children in families with income below 150 percent of poverty line

In the case of a targeted low-income child whose family income is at or below 150 percent of the poverty line, the State child health plan may not impose—

(i) an enrollment fee, premium, or similar charge that exceeds the maximum monthly charge permitted consistent with standards established to carry out section 1396o(b)(1) of this title (with respect to individuals described in such section); and

(ii) a deductible, cost sharing, or similar charge that exceeds an amount that is nominal (as determined consistent with regulations referred to in section 1396o(a)(3) of this title, with such appropriate adjustment for inflation or other reasons as the Secretary determines to be reasonable).

(B) Other children

For children not described in subparagraph (A), subject to paragraphs (1)(B) and (2), any premiums, deductibles, cost sharing or similar charges imposed under the State child health plan may be imposed on a sliding scale related to income, except that the total annual aggregate cost-sharing with respect to all targeted low-income children in a family under this subchapter may not exceed 5 percent of such family's income for the year involved.

(4) Relation to medicaid requirements

Nothing in this subsection shall be construed as affecting the rules relating to the use of enrollment fees, premiums, deductions, cost sharing, and similar charges in the case of targeted low-income children who are provided child health assistance in the form of coverage under a medicaid program under section 1397aa(a)(2) of this title.

(f) Application of certain requirements

(1) Restriction on application of preexisting condition exclusions

(A) In general

Subject to subparagraph (B), the State child health plan shall not permit the imposition of any preexisting condition exclusion for covered benefits under the plan.

(B) Group health plans and group health insurance coverage

If the State child health plan provides for benefits through payment for, or a contract with, a group health plan or group health insurance coverage, the plan may permit the imposition of a preexisting condition exclusion but only insofar as it is permitted under the applicable provisions of part 7 of subtitle B of title I of the Employee Retirement Income Security Act of 1974 [29 U.S.C.A. § 1181 et seq.] and title XXVII of the Public Health Service Act [42 U.S.C.A. § 300gg et seq.].

(2) Compliance with other requirements

Coverage offered under this section shall comply with the requirements of subpart 2 of part A of title XXVII of the Public Health Service Act [42 U.S.C.A. § 300gg–4 et seq.] insofar as such requirements apply with respect to a health insurance issuer that offers group health insurance coverage.

§ 1397dd. Allotments

(a) Appropriation; total allotment

For the purpose of providing allotments to States under this section, there is appropriated, out of any money in the Treasury not otherwise appropriated—

(1) for fiscal year 1998, $4,295,000,000;

(2) for fiscal year 1999, $4,275,000,000;

(3) for fiscal year 2000, $4,275,000,000;

(4) for fiscal year 2001, $4,275,000,000;

(5) for fiscal year 2002, $3,150,000,000;

(6) for fiscal year 2003, $3,150,000,000;

(7) for fiscal year 2004, $3,150,000,000;

(8) for fiscal year 2005, $4,050,000,000;

(9) for fiscal year 2006, $4,050,000,000; and

(10) for fiscal year 2007, $5,000,000,000.

(b) Allotments to 50 States and District of Columbia

(1) In general

Subject to paragraph (4) and subsection (d) of this section, of the amount available for allotment under subsection (a) of this section for a fiscal year, reduced by the amount of allotments made under subsection (c) of this section (determined without regard to paragraph (4) thereof) for the fiscal year, the Secretary shall allot to each State (other than a State described in such subsection) with a State child health plan approved under this subchapter the same proportion as the ratio of—

(A) the product of (i) the number of children described in paragraph (2) for the State for the fiscal year and (ii) the State cost factor for that State (established under paragraph (3)); to

(B) the sum of the products computed under subparagraph (A).

(2) Number of children

(A) In general

The number of children described in this paragraph for a State for—

(i) each of fiscal years 1998 through 2000 is equal to the number of low-income children in the State with no health insurance coverage for the fiscal year;

(ii) fiscal year 2001 is equal to—

(I) 75 percent of the number of low-income children in the State for the fiscal year with no health insurance coverage, plus

(II) 25 percent of the number of low-income children in the State for the fiscal year; and

(iii) each succeeding fiscal year is equal to—

(I) 50 percent of the number of low-income children in the State for the fiscal year with no health insurance coverage, plus

(II) 50 percent of the number of low-income children in the State for the fiscal year.

(B) Determination of number of children

For purposes of subparagraph (A), a determination of the number of low-income children (and of such children who have no health insurance coverage) for a State for a fiscal year shall be made on the basis of the arithmetic average of the number of such children, as reported and defined in the 3 most recent March supplements to the Current Population Survey of the Bureau of the Census before the beginning of the fiscal year.

(3) Adjustment for geographic variations in health costs

(A) In general

For purposes of paragraph (1)(A)(ii), the "State cost factor" for a State for a fiscal year equal to the sum of—

    (i) 0.15, and

    (ii) 0.85 multiplied by the ratio of—

        (I) the annual average wages per employee for the State for such year (as determined under subparagraph (B)), to

        (II) the annual average wages per employee for the 50 States and the District of Columbia.

(B) Annual average wages per employee

For purposes of subparagraph (A), the "annual average wages per employee" for a State, or for all the States, for a fiscal year is equal to the average of the annual wages per employee for the State or for the 50 States and the District of Columbia for employees in the health services industry (SIC code 8000), as reported by the Bureau of Labor Statistics of the Department of Labor for each of the most recent 3 years before the beginning of the fiscal year involved.

(4) Floor for States

In no case shall the amount of the allotment under this subsection for one of the 50 States or the District of Columbia for a year be less than $2,000,000. To the extent that the application of the previous sentence results in an increase in the allotment to a State above the amount otherwise provided, the allotments for the other States and the District of Columbia under this subsection shall be reduced in a pro rata manner (but not below $2,000,000) so that the total of such allotments in a fiscal year does not exceed the amount otherwise provided for allotment under paragraph (1) for that fiscal year.

(c) Allotments to territories [omitted]

* * *

(d) Certain medicaid expenditures counted against individual State allotments

The amount of the allotment otherwise provided to a State under subsection (b) or (c) of this section for a fiscal year shall be reduced by the sum of—

    (1) the amount (if any) of the payments made to that State under section 1396b(a) of this title for expenditures claimed by the State during such fiscal year that is attributable to the provision of medical assistance to a child during a presumptive eligibility period under section 1396r–1a of this title, and

    (2) the amount (if any) of the payments made to that State under section 1396b(a) of this title for expenditures claimed by the State during such fiscal year that is attributable to the provision of medical assistance to a child for which payment is made under section 1396b(a)(1) of this title on the basis of an enhanced FMAP under the fourth sentence of section 1396d(b) of this title.

(e) 3–year availability of amounts allotted

Amounts allotted to a State pursuant to this section for a fiscal year shall remain available for expenditure by the State through the end of the second succeeding fiscal year; except that amounts reallotted to a State under subsection (f) of this section shall be available for expenditure by the State through the end of the fiscal year in which they are reallotted.

(f) Procedure for redistribution of unused allotments

The Secretary shall determine an appropriate procedure for redistribution of allotments from States that were provided allotments under this section for a fiscal year but that do not expend all of the amount of such allotments during the period in which such allotments are available for expenditure under subsection (e) of this section, to States that have fully expended the amount of their allotments under this section.

§ 1397ee. Payments to States

(a) In general

Subject to the succeeding provisions of this section, the Secretary shall pay to each State with a plan approved under this subchapter, from its allotment under section 1397dd of this title (taking into account any adjustment under section 1397dd(d) of this title), an amount for each quarter equal to the enhanced FMAP of expenditures in the quarter—

(1) for child health assistance under the plan for targeted low-income children in the form of providing health benefits coverage that meets the requirements of section 1397cc of this title; and

(2) only to the extent permitted consistent with subsection (c) of this section—

(A) for payment for other child health assistance for targeted low-income children;

(B) for expenditures for health services initiatives under the plan for improving the health of children (including targeted low-income children and other low-income children);

(C) for expenditures for outreach activities as provided in section 1397bb(c)(1) of this title under the plan; and

(D) for other reasonable costs incurred by the State to administer the plan.

(b) Enhanced FMAP

For purposes of subsection (a) of this section, the "enhanced FMAP", for a State for a fiscal year, is equal to the Federal medical assistance percentage (as defined in the first sentence of section 1396d(b) of this title) for the State increased by a number of percentage points equal to 30 percent of the number of percentage points by which (1) such Federal medical assistance percentage for the State, is less than (2) 100 percent; but in no case shall the enhanced FMAP for a State exceed 85 percent.

(c) Limitation on certain payments for certain expenditures

(1) General limitations

Funds provided to a State under this subchapter shall only be used to carry out the purposes of this subchapter (as described in section 1397aa of this title), and any health insurance coverage provided with such funds may include coverage of abortion only if necessary to save the life of the mother or if the pregnancy is the result of an act of rape or incest.

(2) Limitation on expenditures not used for medicaid or health insurance assistance

(A) In general

Except as provided in this paragraph, payment shall not be made under subsection (a) of this section for expenditures for items described in subsection (a) of this section (other than paragraph (1)) for a fiscal year to the extent the total of such expenditures (for which payment is made under such subsection) exceeds 10 percent of the sum of—

(i) the total of such expenditures for such fiscal year, and

(ii) the total expenditures for medical assistance by the State under subchapter XIX of this chapter for which Federal payments made under section 1396b(a)(1) of this title are based on an enhanced FMAP described in subsection (b) of this section for such fiscal year.

(B) Waiver authorized for cost-effective alternative

The limitation under subparagraph (A) on expenditures for items described in subsection (a)(2) of this section shall not apply to the extent that a State establishes to the satisfaction of the Secretary that—

(i) coverage provided to targeted low-income children through such expenditures meets the requirements of section 1397cc of this title;

(ii) the cost of such coverage is not greater, on an average per child basis, than the cost of coverage that would otherwise be provided under section 1397cc of this title; and

(iii) such coverage is provided through the use of a community-based health delivery system, such as through contracts with health centers receiving funds under section 254b of this title or with hospitals such as those that receive disproportionate share payment adjustments under section 1395ww(d)(5)(F) or 1396r–4 of this title.

(3) Waiver for purchase of family coverage Payment may be made to a State under subsection (a)(1) of this section for the purchase of family coverage under a group health plan or health insurance coverage that includes coverage of targeted low-income children only if the State establishes to the satisfaction of the Secretary that—

(A) purchase of such coverage is cost-effective relative to the amounts that the State would have paid to obtain comparable coverage only of the targeted low-income children involved, and

(B) such coverage shall not be provided if it would otherwise substitute for health insurance coverage that would be provided to such children but for the purchase of family coverage.

(4) Use of non-Federal funds for State matching requirement

Amounts provided by the Federal Government, or services assisted or subsidized to any significant extent by the Federal Government, may not be included in determining the amount of non-Federal contributions required under subsection (a) of this section.

(5) Offset of receipts attributable to premiums and other cost-sharing

For purposes of subsection (a) of this section, the amount of the expenditures under the plan shall be reduced by the amount of any premiums and other cost-sharing received by the State.

(6) Prevention of duplicative payments

(A) Other health plans

No payment shall be made to a State under this section for expenditures for child health assistance provided for a targeted low-income child under its plan to the extent that a private insurer (as defined by the Secretary by regulation and including a group health plan (as defined in section 1167(1) of title 29), a service benefit plan, and a health maintenance organization) would have been obligated to provide such assistance but for a provision of its insurance contract which has the effect of limiting or excluding such obligation because the individual is eligible for or is provided child health assistance under the plan.

(B) Other Federal governmental programs

Except as otherwise provided by law, no payment shall be made to a State under this section for expenditures for child health assistance provided for a targeted low-income child under its plan to the extent that payment has been made or can reasonably be expected to be made promptly (as determined in accordance with regulations) under any other federally operated or financed health care insurance program, other than an insurance program operated or financed by the Indian Health Service, as identified by the Secretary.

1105

For purposes of this paragraph, rules similar to the rules for overpayments under section 1396b(d)(2) of this title shall apply.

(7) Limitation on payment for abortions

(A) In general

Payment shall not be made to a State under this section for any amount expended under the State plan to pay for any abortion or to assist in the purchase, in whole or in part, of health benefit coverage that includes coverage of abortion.

(B) Exception

Subparagraph (A) shall not apply to an abortion only if necessary to save the life of the mother or if the pregnancy is the result of an act of rape or incest.

(C) Rule of construction

Nothing in this section shall be construed as affecting the expenditure by a State, locality, or private person or entity of State, local, or private funds (other than funds expended under the State plan) for any abortion or for health benefits coverage that includes coverage of abortion.

(d) Maintenance of effort

(1) In medicaid eligibility standards

No payment may be made under subsection (a) of this section with respect to child health assistance provided under a State child health plan if the State adopts income and resource standards and methodologies for purposes of determining a child's eligibility for medical assistance under the State plan under subchapter XIX of this chapter that are more restrictive than those applied as of June 1, 1997.

(2) In amounts of payment expended for certain State-funded health insurance programs for children

(A) In general

The amount of the allotment for a State in a fiscal year (beginning with fiscal year 1999) shall be reduced by the amount by which—

(i) the total of the State children's health insurance expenditures in the preceding fiscal year, is less than

(ii) the total of such expenditures in fiscal year 1996.

(B) State children's health insurance expenditures

The term "State children's health insurance expenditures" means the following:

(i) The State share of expenditures under this subchapter.

(ii) The State share of expenditures under subchapter XIX of this chapter that are attributable to an enhanced FMAP under section 1396d(u) of this title.

(iii) State expenditures under health benefits coverage under an existing comprehensive State-based program, described [in] section 1397cc(d) of this title.

(e) Advance payment; retrospective adjustment

The Secretary may make payments under this section for each quarter on the basis of advance estimates of expenditures submitted by the State and such other investigation as the Secretary may find necessary, and may reduce or increase the payments as necessary to adjust for any overpayment or underpayment for prior quarters.

(f) Flexibility in submittal of claims

Nothing in this section or subsections (e) and (f) of section 1397dd of this title shall be construed as preventing a State from claiming as expenditures in the quarter expenditures that were incurred in a previous quarter.

§ 1397ff.   Process for submission, approval, and amendment of State child health plans

(a) Initial plan

(1) In general

As a condition of receiving payment under section 1397ee of this title, a State shall submit to the Secretary a State child health plan that meets the applicable requirements of this subchapter.

(2) Approval

Except as the Secretary may provide under subsection (e) of this section, a State plan submitted under paragraph (1)—

(A) shall be approved for purposes of this subchapter, and

(B) shall be effective beginning with a calendar quarter that is specified in the plan, but in no case earlier than October 1, 1997.

(b) Plan amendments

(1) In general

A State may amend, in whole or in part, its State child health plan at any time through transmittal of a plan amendment.

(2) Approval

Except as the Secretary may provide under subsection (e) of this section, an amendment to a State plan submitted under paragraph (1)—

(A) shall be approved for purposes of this subchapter, and

(B) shall be effective as provided in paragraph (3).

(3) Effective dates for amendments

(A) In general

Subject to the succeeding provisions of this paragraph, an amendment to a State plan shall take effect on one or more effective dates specified in the amendment.

(B) Amendments relating to eligibility or benefits

(i) Notice requirement

Any plan amendment that eliminates or restricts eligibility or benefits under the plan may not take effect unless the State certifies that it has provided prior public notice of the change, in a form and manner provided under applicable State law.

(ii) Timely transmittal

Any plan amendment that eliminates or restricts eligibility or benefits under the plan shall not be effective for longer than a 60–day period unless the amendment has been transmitted to the Secretary before the end of such period.

(C) Other amendments

Any plan amendment that is not described in subparagraph (B) and that becomes effective in a State fiscal year may not remain in effect after the end of such fiscal year (or, if later, the end of the 90–day period on which it becomes effective) unless the amendment has been transmitted to the Secretary.

(c) Disapproval of plans and plan amendments

(1) Prompt review of plan submittals

The Secretary shall promptly review State plans and plan amendments submitted under this section to determine if they substantially comply with the requirements of this subchapter.

(2) 90–day approval deadlines

A State plan or plan amendment is considered approved unless the Secretary notifies the State in writing, within 90 days after receipt of the plan or amendment, that the plan or amendment is disapproved (and the reasons for disapproval) or that specified additional information is needed.

(3) Correction

In the case of a disapproval of a plan or plan amendment, the Secretary shall provide a State with a reasonable opportunity for correction before taking financial sanctions against the State on the basis of such disapproval.

(d) Program operation

(1) In general

The State shall conduct the program in accordance with the plan (and any amendments) approved under subsection (c) of this section and with the requirements of this subchapter.

(2) Violations

The Secretary shall establish a process for enforcing requirements under this subchapter. Such process shall provide for the withholding of funds in the case of substantial noncompliance with such requirements. In the case of an enforcement action against a State under this paragraph, the Secretary shall provide a State with a reasonable opportunity for correction before taking financial sanctions against the State on the basis of such an action.

(e) Continued approval

An approved State child health plan shall continue in effect unless and until the State amends the plan under subsection (b) of this section or the Secretary finds, under subsection (d) of this section, substantial noncompliance of the plan with the requirements of this subchapter.

§ 1397gg.   Strategic objectives and performance goals; plan administration

(a) Strategic objectives and performance goals

(1) Description

A State child health plan shall include a description of—

(A) the strategic objectives,

(B) the performance goals, and

(C) the performance measures, the State has established for providing child health assistance to targeted low-income children under the plan and otherwise for maximizing health benefits coverage for other low-income children and children generally in the State.

(2) Strategic objectives

Such plan shall identify specific strategic objectives relating to increasing the extent of creditable health coverage among targeted low-income children and other low-income children.

(3) Performance goals

Such plan shall specify one or more performance goals for each such strategic objective so identified.

(4) Performance measures

Such plan shall describe how performance under the plan will be—

(A) measured through objective, independently verifiable means, and

(B) compared against performance goals, in order to determine the State's performance under this subchapter.

(b) Records, reports, audits, and evaluation

(1) Data collection, records, and reports

A State child health plan shall include an assurance that the State will collect the data, maintain the records, and furnish the reports to the Secretary, at the times and in the standardized format the Secretary may require in order to enable the Secretary to monitor State program administration and compliance and to evaluate and compare the effectiveness of State plans under this subchapter.

(2) State assessment and study

A State child health plan shall include a description of the State's plan for the annual assessments and reports under section 1397hh(a) of this title and the evaluation required by section 1397hh(b) of this title.

(3) Audits

A State child health plan shall include an assurance that the State will afford the Secretary access to any records or information relating to the plan for the purposes of review or audit.

(c) Program development process

A State child health plan shall include a description of the process used to involve the public in the design and implementation of the plan and the method for ensuring ongoing public involvement.

(d) Program budget

A State child health plan shall include a description of the budget for the plan. The description shall be updated periodically as necessary and shall include details on the planned use of funds and the sources of the non-Federal share of plan expenditures, including any requirements for cost-sharing by beneficiaries.

(e) Application of certain general provisions

The following sections of this chapter shall apply to States under this subchapter in the same manner as they apply to a State under subchapter XIX of this chapter:

(1) Subchapter XIX provisions

(A) Section 1396a(a)(4)(C) of this title (relating to conflict of interest standards).

(B) Paragraphs (2), (16), and (17) of section 1396b(i) of this title (relating to limitations on payment).

(C) Section 1396b(w) of this title (relating to limitations on provider taxes and donations).

(2) Subchapter XI provisions

(A) Section 1315 of this title (relating to waiver authority).

(B) Section 1316 of this title (relating to administrative and judicial review), but only insofar as consistent with this subchapter.

(C) Section 1320a–3 of this title (relating to disclosure of ownership and related information).

(D) Section 1320a–5 of this title (relating to disclosure of information about certain convicted individuals).

(E) Section 1320a–7a of this title (relating to civil monetary penalties).

(F) Section 1320a–7b(d) of this title (relating to criminal penalties for certain additional charges).

(G) Section 1320b–2 of this title (relating to periods within which claims must be filed).

§ 1397hh. Annual reports; evaluations

(a) Annual report

The State shall—

(1) assess the operation of the State plan under this subchapter in each fiscal year, including the progress made in reducing the number of uncovered low-income children; and

(2) report to the Secretary, by January 1 following the end of the fiscal year, on the result of the assessment.

(b) State evaluations

(1) In general

By March 31, 2000, each State that has a State child health plan shall submit to the Secretary an evaluation that includes each of the following:

(A) An assessment of the effectiveness of the State plan in increasing the number of children with creditable health coverage.

(B) A description and analysis of the effectiveness of elements of the State plan, including—

(i) the characteristics of the children and families assisted under the State plan including age of the children, family income, and the assisted child's access to or coverage by other health insurance prior to the State plan and after eligibility for the State plan ends,

(ii) the quality of health coverage provided including the types of benefits provided,

(iii) the amount and level (including payment of part or all of any premium) of assistance provided by the State,

(iv) the service area of the State plan,

(v) the time limits for coverage of a child under the State plan,

(vi) the State's choice of health benefits coverage and other methods used for providing child health assistance, and

(vii) the sources of non-Federal funding used in the State plan.

(C) An assessment of the effectiveness of other public and private programs in the State in increasing the availability of affordable quality individual and family health insurance for children.

(D) A review and assessment of State activities to coordinate the plan under this subchapter with other public and private programs providing health care and health care financing, including medicaid and maternal and child health services.

(E) An analysis of changes and trends in the State that affect the provision of accessible, affordable, quality health insurance and health care to children.

(F) A description of any plans the State has for improving the availability of health insurance and health care for children.

(G) Recommendations for improving the program under this subchapter.

(H) Any other matters the State and the Secretary consider appropriate.

(2) Report of the Secretary

The Secretary shall submit to Congress and make available to the public by December 31, 2001, a report based on the evaluations submitted by States under paragraph (1), containing any conclusions and recommendations the Secretary considers appropriate.

§ 1397ii. Miscellaneous provisions

(a) Relation to other laws

(1) HIPAA

Health benefits coverage provided under section 1397aa(a)(1) of this title (and coverage provided under a waiver under section 1397ee(c)(2)(B) of this title) shall be treated as creditable coverage for purposes of part 7 of subtitle B of title II of the Employee Retirement Income Security Act of 1974, title XXVII of the Public Health Service Act (42 U.S.C.A. § 300gg et seq.), and subtitle K of the Internal Revenue Code of 1986.

(2) ERISA

Nothing in this subchapter shall be construed as affecting or modifying section 514 of the Employee Retirement Income Security Act of 1974 (29 U.S.C.A. § 1144) with respect to a group health plan (as defined in section 2791(a)(1) of the Public Health Service Act (42 U.S.C.A. § 300gg–91(a)(1))[)].

* * *

§ 1397jj.   Definitions

(a) Child health assistance

For purposes of this subchapter, the term "child health assistance" means payment for part or all of the cost of health benefits coverage for targeted low-income children that includes any of the following (and includes, in the case described in section 1397ee(a)(2)(A) of this title, payment for part or all of the cost of providing any of the following), as specified under the State plan:

(1) Inpatient hospital services.

(2) Outpatient hospital services.

(3) Physician services.

(4) Surgical services.

(5) Clinic services (including health center services) and other ambulatory health care services.

(6) Prescription drugs and biologicals and the administration of such drugs and biologicals, only if such drugs and biologicals are not furnished for the purpose of causing, or assisting in causing, the death, suicide, euthanasia, or mercy killing of a person.

(7) Over-the-counter medications.

(8) Laboratory and radiological services.

(9) Prenatal care and prepregnancy family planning services and supplies.

(10) Inpatient mental health services, other than services described in paragraph (18) but including services furnished in a State-operated mental hospital and including residential or other 24–hour therapeutically planned structured services.

(11) Outpatient mental health services, other than services described in paragraph (19) but including services furnished in a State-operated mental hospital and including community-based services.

(12) Durable medical equipment and other medically-related or remedial devices (such as prosthetic devices, implants, eyeglasses, hearing aids, dental devices, and adaptive devices).

(13) Disposable medical supplies.

(14) Home and community-based health care services and related supportive services (such as home health nursing services, home health aide services, personal care, assistance with activities of daily living, chore services, day care services, respite care services, training for family members, and minor modifications to the home).

(15) Nursing care services (such as nurse practitioner services, nurse midwife services, advanced practice nurse services, private duty nursing care, pediatric nurse services, and respiratory care services) in a home, school, or other setting.

(16) Abortion only if necessary to save the life of the mother or if the pregnancy is the result of an act of rape or incest.

(17) Dental services.

(18) Inpatient substance abuse treatment services and residential substance abuse treatment services.

(19) Outpatient substance abuse treatment services.

(20) Case management services.

(21) Care coordination services.

(22) Physical therapy, occupational therapy, and services for individuals with speech, hearing, and language disorders.

(23) Hospice care.

(24) Any other medical, diagnostic, screening, preventive, restorative, remedial, therapeutic, or rehabilitative services (whether in a facility, home, school, or other setting) if recognized by State law and only if the service is—

    (A) prescribed by or furnished by a physician or other licensed or registered practitioner within the scope of practice as defined by State law,

    (B) performed under the general supervision or at the direction of a physician, or

    (C) furnished by a health care facility that is operated by a State or local government or is licensed under State law and operating within the scope of the license.

(25) Premiums for private health care insurance coverage.

(26) Medical transportation.

(27) Enabling services (such as transportation, translation, and outreach services) only if designed to increase the accessibility of primary and preventive health care services for eligible low-income individuals.

(28) Any other health care services or items specified by the Secretary and not excluded under this section.

(b) "Targeted low-income child" defined

For purposes of this subchapter—

(1) In general

Subject to paragraph (2), the term "targeted low-income child" means a child—

    (A) who has been determined eligible by the State for child health assistance under the State plan;

    (B)(i) who is a low-income child, or

  (ii) is a child—

   (I) whose family income (as determined under the State child health plan) exceeds the medicaid applicable income level (as defined in paragraph (4)), but does not exceed 50 percentage points above the medicaid applicable income level;

   (II) whose family income (as so determined) does not exceed the medicaid applicable income level (as defined in paragraph (4) but determined as if "June 1, 1997" were substituted for "March 31, 1997"); or

   (III) who resides in a State that does not have a medicaid applicable income level (as defined in paragraph (4)); and

  (C) who is not found to be eligible for medical assistance under subchapter XIX of this chapter or covered under a group health plan or under health insurance coverage (as such terms are defined in section 300gg–91 of this title).

(2) Children excluded

Such term does not include—

  (A) a child who is an inmate of a public institution or a patient in an institution for mental diseases; or

  (B) a child who is a member of a family that is eligible for health benefits coverage under a State health benefits plan on the basis of a family member's employment with a public agency in the State.

(3) Special rule

A child shall not be considered to be described in paragraph (1)(C) notwithstanding that the child is covered under a health insurance coverage program that has been in operation since before July 1, 1997, and that is offered by a State which receives no Federal funds for the program's operation.

(4) Medicaid applicable income level

The term "medicaid applicable income level" means, with respect to a child, the effective income level (expressed as a percent of the poverty line) that has been specified under the State plan under subchapter XIX of this chapter (including under a waiver authorized by the Secretary or under section 1396a(r)(2) of this title), as of March 31, 1997, for the child to be eligible for medical assistance under section 1396a(l)(2) or 1396d(n)(2) of this title (as selected by a State) for the age of such child.

(c) Additional definitions

For purposes of this subchapter:

 (1) Child

The term "child" means an individual under 19 years of age.

(2) Creditable health coverage

The term "creditable health coverage" has the meaning given the term "creditable coverage" under section 300gg(c) of this title and includes coverage that meets the requirements of section 1397cc of this title provided to a targeted low-income child under this subchapter or under a waiver approved under section 1397ee(c)(2)(B) of this title (relating to a direct service waiver).

(3) Group health plan; health insurance coverage; etc.

The terms "group health plan", "group health insurance coverage", and "health insurance coverage" have the meanings given such terms in section 300gg–91 of this title.

(4) Low-income child

The term "low-income child" means a child whose family income is at or below 200 percent of the poverty line for a family of the size involved.

(5) Poverty line defined

The term "poverty line" has the meaning given such term in section 9902(2) of this title, including any revision required by such section.

(6) Preexisting condition exclusion

The term "preexisting condition exclusion" has the meaning given such term in section 300gg(b)(1)(A) of this title.

(7) State child health plan; plan

Unless the context otherwise requires, the terms "State child health plan" and "plan" mean a State child health plan approved under section 1397ff of this title.

(8) Uncovered child

The term "uncovered child" means a child that does not have creditable health coverage.

PART THREE: PRESERVING THE QUALITY OF HEALTH CARE AND PROTECTING PATIENT DECISION-MAKING

VI. DEVELOPING NEW DRUGS AND DEVICES AND REGULATION OF RESEARCH INVOLVING HUMAN SUBJECTS

A. BASIC DEPARTMENT OF HEALTH AND HUMAN SERVICES POLICY FOR PROTECTION OF HUMAN RESEARCH SUBJECTS: 45 C.F.R. PART 46

§ 46.101 To what does this policy apply?

(a) Except as provided in paragraph (b) of this section, this policy applies to all research involving human subjects conducted, supported or otherwise subject to regulation by any federal department or agency which takes appropriate administrative action to make the policy applicable to such research. This includes research conducted by federal civilian employees or military personnel, except that each department or agency head may adopt such procedural modifications as may be appropriate from an administrative standpoint. It also includes research conducted, supported, or otherwise subject to regulation by the federal government outside the United States.

(1) Research that is conducted or supported by a federal department or agency, whether or not it is regulated as defined in § 46.102(e) must comply with all sections of this policy.

(2) Research that is neither conducted nor supported by a federal department or agency but is subject to regulation as defined in § 46.102(e) must be reviewed and approved, in compliance with § 46.101 & § 46.102 and § 46.107 through § 46.117 of this policy, by an institutional review board (IRB) that operates in accordance with the pertinent requirements of this policy.

(b) Unless otherwise required by department or agency heads, research activities in which the only involvement of human subjects will be in one or more of the following categories are exempt from this policy:

(1) Research conducted in established or commonly accepted educational settings, involving normal educational practices, such as (i)

1117

research on regular and special education instructional strategies, or (ii) research on the effectiveness of or the comparison among instructional techniques, curricula, or classroom management methods.

(2) Research involving the use of educational tests (cognitive, diagnostic, aptitude, achievement), survey procedures, interview procedures or observation of public behavior, unless:

(i) Information obtained is recorded in such a manner that human subjects can be identified, directly or through identifiers linked to the subjects; and

(ii) any disclosure of the human subjects' responses outside the research could reasonably place the subjects at risk of criminal or civil liability or be damaging to the subjects' financial standing, employability, or reputation.

(3) Research involving the use of educational tests (cognitive, diagnostic, aptitude, achievement), survey procedures, interview procedures, or observation of public behavior that is not exempt under paragraph (b)(2) of this section, if:

(i) The human subjects are elected or appointed public officials or candidates for public office; or

(ii) federal statute(s) require(s) without exception that the confidentiality of the personally identifiable information will be maintained throughout the research and thereafter.

(4) Research, involving the collection or study of existing data, documents, records, pathological specimens, or diagnostic specimens, if these sources are publicly available or if the information is recorded by the investigator in such a manner that subjects cannot be identified, directly or through identifiers linked to the subjects.

(5) Research and demonstration projects which are conducted by or subject to the approval of department or agency heads, and which are designed to study, evaluate, or otherwise examine:

(i) Public benefit or service program;

(ii) procedures for obtaining benefits or services under those programs;

(iii) possible changes in or alternatives to those programs or procedures; or

(iv) possible changes in methods or levels of payment for benefits or services under those programs.

(6) Taste and food quality evaluation and consumer acceptance studies.

* * *

(c) Department or agency heads retain final judgment as to whether a particular activity is covered by this policy.

(d) Department or agency heads may require that specific research activities or classes of research activities conducted, supported, or otherwise subject to regulation by the department or agency but not otherwise covered by this policy, comply with some or all of the requirements of this policy.

* * *

(f) This policy does not affect any state or local laws or regulations which may otherwise be applicable and which provide additional protections for human subjects.

(g) This policy does not affect any foreign laws or regulations which may otherwise be applicable and which provide additional protections to human subjects of research.

(h) When research covered by this policy takes place in foreign countries, procedures normally followed in the foreign countries to protect human subjects may differ from those set forth in this policy. [An example is a foreign institution which complies with guidelines consistent with the World Medical Assembly Declaration (Declaration of Helsinki amended 1989) issued either by sovereign states or by an organization whose function for the protection of human research subjects is internationally recognized.] In these circumstances, if a department or agency head determines that the procedures prescribed by the institution afford protections that are at least equivalent to those provided in this policy, the department or agency head may approve the substitution of the foreign procedures in lieu of the procedural requirements provided in this policy.

* * *

(i) Unless otherwise required by law, department or agency heads may waive the applicability of some or all of the provisions of this policy to specific research activities or classes of research activities otherwise covered by this policy.

* * *

§ 46.102 Definitions

(a) Department or agency head means the head of any federal department or agency and any other office or employee of any department or agency to whom authority has been delegated.

(b) Institution means any public or private entity or agency (including federal, state, and other agencies).

(c) Legally authorized representative means an individual or judicial or other body authorized under applicable law to consent on behalf of a prospective subject to the subject's participation in the procedure(s) involved in the research.

(d) Research means a systematic investigation, including research development, testing and evaluation, designed to develop or contribute to generalizable knowledge. Activities which meet this definition constitute research for purposes of this policy, whether or not they are conducted or supported under a program which is considered research for other purposes. For example, some demonstration and service programs may include research activities.

(e) Research subject to regulation and similar terms are intended to encompass those research activities for which a federal department or agency has specific responsibility for regulating as a research activity, (for example, Investigational New Drug requirements administered by the Food and Drug Administration).

* * *

(f) Human subject means a living individual about whom an investigator (whether professional or student) conducting research obtains

   (1) Data through intervention or interaction with the individual, or

   (2) Identifiable private information. Intervention includes both physical procedures by which data are gathered (for example, venipuncture) or manipulations of the subject or the subject's environment that are performed for research purposes. Interaction includes communication or interpersonal contact between investigator and subject. Private information includes information about behavior that occurs in a context in which an individual can reasonably expect that no observation or recording is taking place, and information which has been provided for specific purposes by an individual and which the individual can reasonably expect will not be made public (for example, a medical record). Private information must be individually identifiable (i.e., the identity of the subject is or may readily be ascertained by the investigator or associated with the information) in order for obtaining the information to constitute research involving human subjects.

(g) IRB means an institutional review board established in accord with and for the purposes expressed in this policy.

(h) IRB approval means the determination of the IRB that the research has been reviewed and may be conducted at an institution within the constraints set forth by the IRB and by other institutional and federal requirements.

(i) Minimal risk means that the probability and magnitude of harm or discomfort anticipated in the research are not greater in and of themselves than those ordinarily encountered in daily life or during the performance of routine physical or psychological examinations or tests.

* * *

§ 46.107   IRB membership

   (a) Each IRB shall have at least five members, with varying backgrounds to promote complete and adequate review of research activities commonly conducted by the institution. The IRB shall be sufficiently qualified through the experience and expertise of its members, and the diversity of the members, including consideration of race, gender, and cultural backgrounds and sensitivity to such issues as community attitudes, to promote respect for its advice and counsel in safeguarding the rights and welfare of human subjects. In addition to possessing the professional competence necessary to review specific research activities, the IRB shall be able to ascertain the acceptability of proposed research in terms of institutional commitments and regulations, applicable law, and standards of professional conduct and practice. The IRB shall therefore include persons knowledgeable in these areas. If an IRB regularly reviews research that involves a vulnerable category of subjects, such as children, prisoners, pregnant women, or handicapped or mentally disabled persons, consideration shall be given to the inclusion of one or more individuals who are knowledgeable about and experienced in working with these subjects.

(b) Every nondiscriminatory effort will be made to ensure that no IRB consists entirely of men or entirely of women, including the institution's consideration of qualified persons of both sexes, so long as no selection is made to the IRB on the basis of gender. No IRB may consist entirely of members of one profession.

(c) Each IRB shall include at least one member whose primary concerns are in scientific areas and at least one member whose primary concerns are in nonscientific areas.

(d) Each IRB shall include at least one member who is not otherwise affiliated with the institution and who is not part of the immediate family of a person who is affiliated with the institution.

(e) No IRB may have a member participate in the IRB's initial or continuing review of any project in which the member has a conflicting interest, except to provide information requested by the IRB.

(f) An IRB may, in its discretion, invite individuals with competence in special areas to assist in the review of issues which require expertise beyond or in addition to that available on the IRB. These individuals may not vote with the IRB.

§ 46.108   IRB functions and operations

In order to fulfill the requirements of this policy each IRB shall:

* * *

(b) Except when an expedited review procedure is used (see § 46.110), review proposed research at convened meetings at which a majority of the members of the IRB are present, including at least one member whose primary concerns are in nonscientific areas. In order for the research to be approved, it shall receive the approval of a majority of those members present at the meeting.

§ 46.109   IRB review of research

(a) An IRB shall review and have authority to approve, require modification in (to secure approval), or disapprove all research activities covered by this policy.

(b) An IRB shall require that information given to subjects as part of informed consent is in accordance with § 46.116. The IRB may require that information, in addition to that specifically mentioned in § 46.116, be given to the subjects when the IRB's judgment the information would meaningfully add to the protection of the rights and welfare of subjects.

(c) An IRB shall require documentation of informed consent or may waive documentation in accordance with § 46.117.

(d) An IRB shall notify investigators and the institution in writing of its decision to approve or disapprove the proposed research activity, or of modifications required to secure IRB approval of the research activity. If the IRB decides to disapprove a research activity, it shall include in its written notification a statement of the reasons for its decision and give the investigator an opportunity to respond in person or in writing.

(e) An IRB shall conduct continuing review of research covered by this policy at intervals appropriate to the degree of risk, but not less than one per year, and shall have authority to observe or have a third party observe the consent process and the research.

§ 46.110   Expedited review procedures for certain kinds of research involving no more than minimal risk, and for minor changes in approved research

* * *

(b) An IRB may use the expedited review procedure to review either or both of the following:

(1) Some or all of the research appearing on the list [published by the DHHS in the Federal Register] and found by the reviewer(s) to involve no more than minimal risk.

(2) Minor changes in previously approved research during the period (of one year or less) for which approval is authorized.

Under an expedited review procedure, the review may be carried out by the IRB chairperson or by one or more experienced reviewers designated by the chairperson from among members of the IRB. In reviewing the research, the reviewers may exercise all of the authorities of the IRB except that the reviewers may not disapprove the research. A research activity may de disapproved only after review in accordance with the non-expedited procedure set forth in § 46.108(b).

(c) Each IRB which uses an expedited review procedure shall adopt a method for keeping all members advised of research proposals which have been approved under the procedure.

(d) The department or agency head may restrict, suspend, terminate, or choose not to authorize an institution's or IRB's use of the expedited review procedure.

§ 46.111 Criteria for IRB approval of research

(a) In order to approve research covered by this policy the IRB shall determine that all of the following requirements are satisfied:

(1) Risks to subjects are minimized:

(i) By using procedures which are consistent with sound research design and which do not unnecessarily expose subjects to risk, and

(ii) whenever appropriate, by using procedures already being performed on the subjects for diagnostic or treatment purposes.

(2) Risks to subjects are reasonable in relation to anticipated benefits, if any, to subjects, and the importance of the knowledge that may reasonable be expected to result. In evaluating risks and benefits, the IRB should consider only those risks and benefits that may result from the research (as distinguished from risks and benefits of therapies subjects would receive even if not participating in the research). The IRB should not consider possible long-range effects of applying knowledge gained in the research (for example, the possible effects of the research on public policy) as among those research risks that fall within the purview of its responsibility.

(3) Selection of subjects is equitable. In making this assessment the IRB should take into account the purposes of the research and the setting in which the research will be conducted and should be particularly cognizant of the special problems or research involving vulnerable populations, such as children, prisoners, pregnant women, mentally disabled persons, or economically or educationally disadvantaged persons.

(4) Informed consent will be sought from each prospective subject or the subject's legally authorized representative, in accordance with, and to the extent required by § 46.116.

(5) Informed consent will be appropriately documented, in accordance with, and to the extent required by § 46.117.

(6) When appropriate, the research plan makes adequate provision for monitoring the data collected to ensure the safety of subjects.

(7) When appropriate, there are adequate provisions to protect the privacy of subjects and to maintain the confidentiality of data.

(b) When some or all of the subjects are likely to be vulnerable to coercion or undue influence, such as children, prisoners, pregnant women, mentally disabled persons, or economically or educationally disadvantaged persons, additional safeguards have been included in the study to protect the rights and welfare of these subjects.

§ 46.112   Review by institution

Research covered by this policy that has been approved by the IRB may be subject to further appropriate review and approval or disapproval by officials of the institution. However, those officials may not approve the research if it has not been approved by an IRB.

§ 46.113   Suspension or termination of IRB approval of research

An IRB shall have authority to suspend or terminate approval of research that is not being conducted in accordance with the IRB's requirements or that has been associated with unexpected serious harm to subjects. Any suspension or termination of approval shall include a statement of the reasons for the IRB's action and shall be reported promptly to the investigator, appropriate institutional officials, and the department head and agency * * *.

§ 46.114   Cooperative research

Cooperative research projects are those projects covered by this policy which involve more than one institution. In the conduct of cooperative research projects, each institution is responsible for safeguarding the rights and welfare of human subjects and for complying with this policy. With the approval of the department or agency head, an institution participating in a cooperative project may enter into a joint review arrangement, rely upon the review of another qualified IRB, or make similar arrangements for avoiding duplication of effort.

* * *

§ 46.116   General requirements for informed consent

Except as provided elsewhere in this policy, no investigator may involve a human being as a subject in research covered by this policy unless the investigator has obtained the legally effective informed consent of the subject or the subject's legally authorized representative. An investigator shall seek such consent only under circumstances that provide the prospective subject or the representative sufficient opportunity to consider whether or not to participate and that minimize the possibility of coercion or undue influence. The information that is given to the subject or the representative shall be in language understandable to the subject or the representative. No informed consent, whether oral or written, may include any exculpatory language through which the subject or the representative is made to waive or appear to waive any of the subject's legal rights, or releases or appears to release the investigator, the sponsor, the institution or its agents from liability for negligence.

(a) Basic elements of informed consent. Except as provided in paragraph (c) or (d) of this section, in seeking informed consent the following information shall be provided to each subject:

(1) A statement that the study involves research, an explanation of the purposes of the research and the expected duration of the subject's participation, a description of the procedures to be followed, and identification of any procedures which are experimental;

(2) A description of any reasonably foreseeable risks or discomforts to the subject;

(3) A description of any benefits to the subject or to others which may reasonably be expected from the research;

(4) A disclosure of appropriate alternative procedures or courses of treatment, if any, that might be advantageous to the subject;

(5) a statement describing the extent, if any, to which confidentiality of records identifying the subject will be maintained;

(6) For research involving more than minimal risk, an explanation as to whether any compensation and an explanation as to whether any medical treatments are available if injury occurs and, if so, what they consist of, or where further information may be obtained;

(7) An explanation of whom to contact for answers to pertinent questions about the research and research subjects' rights, to whom to contact in the event of a research-related injury to the subject; and

(8) A statement that participation is voluntary, refusal to participate will involve no penalty or loss of benefits to which the subject is otherwise entitled, and the subject may discontinue participation at any time without penalty or loss of benefits to which the subject is otherwise entitled.

(b) Additional elements of informed consent. When appropriate, one or more of the following elements of information shall also be provided to each subject;

(1) A statement that the particular treatment or procedure may involve risks to the subject (or to the embryo or fetus, if the subject is or may become pregnant) which are currently unforeseeable;

(2) Anticipated circumstances under which the subject's participation may be terminated by the investigator without regard to the subject's consent;

(3) Any additional costs to the subject that may result from participation in the research;

1125

(4) The consequences of a subject's decision to withdraw from the research and procedures for orderly termination of participation by the subject;

(5) A statement that significant new findings developed during the course of the research which may relate to the subject's willingness to continue participation will be provided to the subject; and

(6) The approximate number of subjects involved in the study.

(c) An IRB may approve a consent procedure which does not include, or which alters, some or all of the elements of informed consent set forth above, or waive the requirements to obtain information consent provided the IRB finds and documents that:

(1) The research or demonstration project is to be conducted by or subject to the approval of state or local government officials and is designed to study, evaluate, or otherwise examine:

(i) Public benefit of service programs;

(ii) procedures for obtaining benefits or services under those programs;

(iii) possible changes in or alternatives to those programs or procedures; or

(iv) possible changes in methods or levels of payment for benefits or services under those programs; and

(2) The research could not practicably be carried out without the waiver or alteration.

(d) An IRB may approve a consent procedure which does not include, or which alters, some or all of the elements of informed consent set forth in this actions, or waive the requirements to obtain informed consent provided the IRB finds and documents that:

(1) The research involves no more than minimal risks to the subjects;

(2) The waiver or alteration will not adversely affect the rights and welfare of the subjects;

(3) The research could not practicably be carried out without the waiver or alteration; and

(4) Whenever appropriate, the subjects will be provided with additional pertinent information after participation.

(e) The informed consent requirements in this policy are not intended to preempt any applicable federal, state, or local laws which require additional information to be disclosed in order for informed consent to be legally effective.

(f) Nothing in this policy is intended to limit the authority of a physician to provide emergency medical care, to the extent the physician is permitted to do so under applicable federal, state, or local law.

§ 46.117   Documentation of informed consent

(a) Except as provided in paragraph (c) of this section, informed consent shall be documented by the use of a written consent form approved by the IRB and signed by the subject or the subject's legally authorized representative. A copy shall be given to the person signing the form.

(b) Except as provided in paragraph (c) of this section, the consent form may be either of the following:

(1) A written consent document that embodies the elements of informed consent required by § 46.116. This form may be read to the subject or the subject's legally authorized representative, but in any event, the investigator shall give either the subject or the representative adequate opportunity to read it before it is signed; or

(2) A short form written consent document stating that the elements of informed consent required by § 46.116 have been presented orally to the subject or the subject's legally authorized representative. When this method is used, there shall be a witness to the oral presentation. Also, the IRB shall approve a written summary or the representative. Only the short form itself is to be signed by the subject or the representative. However, the witness shall sign both the short form and a copy of the summary, and the person actually obtaining consent shall sign a copy of the summary. A copy of the summary shall be given to the subject or the representative, in addition to a copy of the short form.

(c) An IRB may waive the requirement for the investigator to obtain a signed consent form for some or all subjects if it finds either:

(1) That the only record linking the subject and the research would be the consent document and the principal risk would be potential harm resulting from a breach of confidentiality. Each subject will be asked whether the subject wants documentation linking the subject with the research, and the subject's wishes will govern; or

(2) That the research presents no more than minimal risk of harm to subjects and involves no procedures for which consent is normally required outside of the research context.

In cases in which the documentation requirement is waived, the IRB may require the investigator to provide subjects with a written statement regarding the research.

* * *

§ 46.122   Use of Federal funds

Federal funds administered by a department or agency may not be expended for research involving human subjects unless the requirements of this policy have been satisfied.

* * *

§ 46.124   Conditions

With respect to any research project or any class of research projects the department or agency head may impose additional conditions prior to or at the time of approval when in the judgment of the department or agency head additional conditions are necessary for the protection of human subjects.

B.   FEDERAL FOOD, DRUG AND COSMETIC ACT: 21 U.S.C.A. § 355

§ 355.   New drugs

(a) Necessity of effective approval of application.

No person shall introduce or deliver for introduction into interstate commerce any new drug, unless an approval of an application filed pursuant to subsection (b) or (j) of this section is effective with respect to such drug.

(b) Filing application; contents.

(1) Any person may file with the Secretary an application with respect to any drug subject to the provisions of subsection (a) of this section. Such person shall submit to the Secretary as a part of the application

    (A) full reports of investigations which have been made to show whether or not such drug is safe for use and whether such drug is effective in use;

    (B) a full list of the articles used as components of such drug;

    (C) a full statement of the composition of such drug;

    (D) a full description of the methods used in, and the facilities and controls used for, the manufacture, processing, and packing of such drug;

    (E) such samples of such drug and of the articles used as components thereof as the Secretary may require; and

    (F) specimens of the labeling proposed to be used for such drug. The applicant shall file with the application the patent number and the expiration date of any patent which claims the drug for which the applicant submitted the application or which claims a method of using such drug and with respect to which a claim of patent infringement could reasonably be asserted if a person not licensed by the owner engaged in the manufacture, use, or sale of the drug. If an application is filed under this subsection for a drug and a patent which claims such drug or a method of using such drug is issued after the filing date but before approval of the application, the applicant shall amend the application to include the information required by the preceding sentence. Upon approval of the application, the Secretary shall publish information submitted under the two preceding sentences. The Secretary shall, in consultation with the Director of the National Institutes of Health and with representatives of the drug manufacturing industry, review and develop guidance, as appropriate, on the inclusion of women and minorities in clinical trials required by clause (A).

(2) An application submitted under paragraph (1) for a drug for which the investigations described in clause (A) of such paragraph and relied upon by the applicant for approval of the application were not conducted by or for the applicant and for which the applicant has not obtained a right of reference or use from the person by or for whom the investigations were conducted shall also include—

> **(A)** a certification, in the opinion of the applicant and to the best of his knowledge, with respect to each patent which claims the drug for which such investigations were conducted or which claims a use for such drug for which the applicant is seeking approval under this subsection and for which information is required to be filed under paragraph (1) or subsection (c) of this section—

>> **(i)** that such patent information has not been filed,

>> **(ii)** that such patent has expired,

>> **(iii)** of the date on which such patent will expire, or

>> **(iv)** that such patent is invalid or will not be infringed by the manufacture, use, or sale of the new drug for which the application is submitted; and

> **(B)** if with respect to the drug for which investigations described in paragraph (1)(A) were conducted information was filed under paragraph (1) or subsection (c) of this section for a method of use patent which does not claim a use for which the applicant is seeking approval under this subsection, a statement that the method of use patent does not claim such a use.

(3)(A) An applicant who makes a certification described in paragraph (2)(A)(iv) shall include in the application a statement that the applicant will give the notice required by subparagraph (B) to—

> **(i)** each owner of the patent which is the subject of the certification or the representative of such owner designated to receive such notice, and

> **(ii)** the holder of the approved application under subsection (b) of this section for the drug which is claimed by the patent or a use of which is claimed by the patent or the representative of such holder designated to receive such notice.

(B) The notice referred to in subparagraph (A) shall state that an application has been submitted under this subsection for the drug with respect to which the certification is made to obtain approval to engage in the commercial manufacture, use, or sale of the drug before the expiration of the patent referred to in the certification. Such notice shall include a detailed statement of the factual and legal basis of the applicant's opinion that the patent is not valid or will not be infringed.

(C) If an application is amended to include a certification described in paragraph (2)(A)(iv), the notice required by subparagraph (B) shall be given when the amended application is submitted.

(4)(A) The Secretary shall issue guidance for the individuals who review applications submitted under paragraph (1) or under section 262 of Title 42, which shall relate to promptness in conducting the review, technical excellence, lack of bias and conflict of interest, and knowledge of regulatory and scientific standards, and which shall apply equally to all individuals who review such applications.

(B) The Secretary shall meet with a sponsor of an investigation or an applicant for approval for a drug under this subsection or section 262 of Title 42 if the sponsor or applicant makes a reasonable written request for a meeting for the purpose of reaching agreement on the design and size of clinical trials intended to form the primary basis of an effectiveness claim. The sponsor or applicant shall provide information necessary for discussion and agreement on the design and size of the clinical trials. Minutes of any such meeting shall be prepared by the Secretary and made available to the sponsor or applicant upon request.

(C) Any agreement regarding the parameters of the design and size of clinical trials of a new drug under this paragraph that is reached between the Secretary and a sponsor or applicant shall be reduced to writing and made part of the administrative record by the Secretary. Such agreement shall not be changed after the testing begins, except—

(i) with the written agreement of the sponsor or applicant; or

(ii) pursuant to a decision, made in accordance with subparagraph (D) by the director of the reviewing division, that a substantial scientific issue essential to determining the safety or effectiveness of the drug has been identified after the testing has begun.

(D) A decision under subparagraph (C)(ii) by the director shall be in writing and the Secretary shall provide to the sponsor or applicant an opportunity for a meeting at which the director and the sponsor or applicant will be present and at which the director will document the scientific issue involved.

(E) The written decisions of the reviewing division shall be binding upon, and may not directly or indirectly be changed by, the field or compliance division personnel unless such field or compliance division personnel demonstrate to the reviewing division why such decision should be modified.

(F) No action by the reviewing division may be delayed because of the unavailability of information from or action by field personnel unless the reviewing division determines that a delay is necessary to assure the marketing of a safe and effective drug.

(G) For purposes of this paragraph, the reviewing division is the division responsible for the review of an application for approval of a drug under this subsection or section 262 of Title 42 (including all scientific and medical matters, chemistry, manufacturing, and controls).

(c) Period for approval of application; period for, notice, and expedition of hearing; period for issuance of order

(1) Within one hundred and eighty days after the filing of an application under subsection (b) of this section, or such additional period as may be agreed upon by the Secretary and the applicant, the Secretary shall either—

(A) Approve the application if he then finds that none of the grounds for denying approval specified in subsection (d) of this section applies, or

(B) Give the applicant notice of an opportunity for a hearing before the Secretary under subsection (d) of this section on the question whether such application is approvable. If the applicant elects to accept the opportunity for hearing by written request within thirty days after such notice, such hearing shall commence not more than ninety days after the expiration of such thirty days unless the Secretary and the applicant otherwise agree. Any such hearing shall thereafter be conducted on an expedited basis and the Secretary's order thereon shall be issued within ninety days after the date fixed by the Secretary for filing final briefs.

(2) If the patent information described in subsection (b) of this section could not be filed with the submission of an application under subsection (b) of this section because the application was filed before the patent information was required under subsection (b) of this section or a patent was issued after the application was approved under such subsection, the holder of an approved application shall file with the Secretary the patent number and the expiration date of any patent which claims the drug for which the application was submitted or which claims a method of using such drug and with respect to which a claim of patent infringement could reasonably be asserted if a person not licensed by the owner engaged in the manufacture, use, or sale of the drug. If the holder of an approved application could not file patent information under subsection (b) of this section because it was not required at the time the application was approved, the holder shall file such information under this subsection not later than thirty days after September 24, 1984, and if the holder of an approved application could not file patent information under subsection (b) of this section because no patent had been issued when an application was filed or approved, the holder shall file such information under this subsection not later than thirty days after the date the patent involved is issued. Upon the submission of patent information under this subsection, the Secretary shall publish it.

(3) The approval of an application filed under subsection (b) of this section which contains a certification required by paragraph (2) of such subsection shall be made effective on the last applicable date determined under the following:

(A) If the applicant only made a certification described in clause (i) or (ii) of subsection (b)(2)(A) of this section or in both such clauses, the approval may be made effective immediately.

(B) If the applicant made a certification described in clause (iii) of subsection (b)(2)(A) of this section, the approval may be made effective on the date certified under clause (iii).

(C) If the applicant made a certification described in clause (iv) of subsection (b)(2)(A) of this section, the approval shall be made effective immediately unless an action is brought for infringement of a patent which is the subject of the certification before the expiration of forty-five days from the date the notice provided under paragraph (3)(B) is received. If such an action is brought before the expiration of such days, the approval may be made effective upon the expiration of the thirty-month period beginning on the date of the receipt of the notice provided under paragraph (3)(B) or such shorter or longer period as the court may order because either party to the action failed to reasonably cooperate in expediting the action, except that—

(i) if before the expiration of such period the court decides that such patent is invalid or not infringed, the approval may be made effective on the date of the court decision,

(ii) if before the expiration of such period the court decides that such patent has been infringed, the approval may be made effective on such date as the court orders under section 271(e)(4)(A) of Title 35, or

(iii) if before the expiration of such period the court grants a preliminary injunction prohibiting the applicant from engaging in the commercial manufacture or sale of the drug until the court decides the issues of patent validity and infringement and if the court decides that such patent is invalid or not infringed, the approval shall be made effective on the date of such court decision.

In such an action, each of the parties shall reasonably cooperate in expediting the action. Until the expiration of forty-five days from the date the notice made under paragraph (3)(B) is received, no action may be brought under section 2201 of Title 28 for a declaratory judgment with respect to the patent. Any action brought under such section 2201 shall be brought in the judicial district where the defendant has its principal place of business or a regular and established place of business.

(D)(i) If an application (other than an abbreviated new drug application) submitted under subsection (b) of this section for a drug, no active ingredient (including any ester or salt of the active ingredient) of which has been approved in any other application under subsection (b) of this section, was approved during the period beginning January 1, 1982, and ending on September 24, 1984, the Secretary may not make the approval of another application for a drug for which the investigations described in clause (A) of subsection (b)(1) of this section and relied upon by the applicant for approval of the application were not conducted by or for the applicant and for which the applicant has not obtained a right of reference or use from the person by or for whom the investigations were conducted effective before the expiration of ten years from the date of the approval of the application previously approved under subsection (b) of this section.

(ii) If an application submitted under subsection (b) of this section for a drug, no active ingredient (including any ester or salt of the active ingredient) of which has been approved in any other application under subsection (b) of this section, is approved after September 24, 1984, no application which refers to the drug for which the subsection (b) application was submitted and for which the investigations described in clause (A) of subsection (b)(1) of this section and relied upon by the applicant for approval of the application were not conducted by or for the applicant and for which the applicant has not obtained a right of reference or use from the person by or for whom the investigations were conducted may be submitted under subsection (b) of this section before the expiration of five years from the date of the approval of the application under subsection (b) of this section, except that such an application may be submitted under subsection (b) of this section after the expiration of four years from the date of the approval of the subsection (b) application if it contains a certification of patent invalidity or noninfringement described in clause (iv) of subsection (b)(2)(A) of this section. The approval of such an application shall be made effective in accordance with this paragraph except that, if an action for patent infringement is commenced during the one-year period beginning forty-eight months after the date of the approval of the subsection (b) application, the thirty-month period referred to in subparagraph (C) shall be extended by such amount of time (if any) which is required for seven and one-half years to have elapsed from the date of approval of the subsection (b) application.

(iii) If an application submitted under subsection (b) of this section for a drug, which includes an active ingredient (including any ester or salt of the active ingredient) that has been approved in another application approved under subsection (b) of this section, is approved after September 24, 1984, and if such application contains reports of new clinical investigations (other than bioavailability studies) essential to the approval of the application and conducted or sponsored by the applicant, the Secretary may not make the approval of an application submitted under subsection (b) of this section for the conditions of approval of such drug in the approved subsection (b) application effective before the expiration of three years from the date of the approval of the application under subsection (b) of this section if the investigations described in clause (A) of subsection (b)(1) of this section and relied upon by the applicant for approval of the application were not conducted by or for the applicant and if the applicant has not obtained a right of reference or use from the person by or for whom the investigations were conducted.

(iv) If a supplement to an application approved under subsection (b) of this section is approved after September 24, 1984, and the supplement contains reports of new clinical investigations (other than bioavailability studies) essential to the approval of the supplement and conducted or sponsored by the person submitting the supplement, the Secretary may not make the approval of an application submitted under subsection (b) of this section for a change approved in the supplement effective before the expiration of three years from the date of the approval of the supplement under subsection (b) of this section if the investigations described in clause (A) of subsection (b)(1) of this section and relied upon by the applicant for approval of the application were not conducted by or for the applicant and if the applicant has not obtained a right of reference or use from the person by or for whom the investigations were conducted.

(v) If an application (or supplement to an application) submitted under subsection (b) of this section for a drug, which includes an active ingredient (including any ester or salt of the active ingredient) that has been approved in another application under subsection (b) of this section, was approved during the period beginning January 1, 1982, and ending on September 24, 1984, the Secretary may not make the approval of an application submitted under this subsection and for which the investigations described in clause (A) of subsection (b)(1) of this section and relied upon by the applicant for approval of the application were not conducted by or for the applicant and for which the applicant has not obtained a right of reference or use from the person by or for whom the investigations were conducted and which refers to the drug for which the subsection (b) application was submitted effective before the expiration of two years from September 24, 1984.

(4) A drug manufactured in a pilot or other small facility may be used to demonstrate the safety and effectiveness of the drug and to obtain approval for the drug prior to manufacture of the drug in a larger facility, unless the Secretary makes a determination that a full scale production facility is necessary to ensure the safety or effectiveness of the drug.

(d) Grounds for refusing application; approval of application; "substantial evidence" defined

If the Secretary finds, after due notice to the applicant in accordance with subsection (c) of this section and giving him an opportunity for a hearing, in accordance with said subsection, that

(1) the investigations, reports of which are required to be submitted to the Secretary pursuant to subsection (b) of this section, do not include adequate tests by all methods reasonably applicable to show whether or not such drug is safe for use under the conditions prescribed, recommended, or suggested in the proposed labeling thereof;

(2) the results of such tests show that such drug is unsafe for use under such conditions or do not show that such drug is safe for use under such conditions;

(3) the methods used in, and the facilities and controls used for, the manufacture, processing, and packing of such drug are inadequate to preserve its identity, strength, quality, and purity;

(4) upon the basis of the information submitted to him as part of the application, or upon the basis of any other information before him with respect to such drug, he has insufficient information to determine whether such drug is safe for use under such conditions; or

(5) evaluated on the basis of the information submitted to him as part of the application and any other information before him with respect to such drug, there is a lack of substantial evidence that the drug will have the effect it purports or is represented to have under the conditions of use prescribed, recommended, or suggested in the proposed labeling thereof; or

(6) the application failed to contain the patent information prescribed by subsection (b) of this section; or

(7) based on a fair evaluation of all material facts, such labeling is false or misleading in any particular; he shall issue an order refusing to approve the application. If, after such notice and opportunity for hearing, the Secretary finds that clauses (1) through (6) do not apply, he shall issue an order approving the application. As used in this subsection and subsection (e) of this section, the term "substantial evidence" means

1135

evidence consisting of adequate and well-controlled investigations, including clinical investigations, by experts qualified by scientific training and experience to evaluate the effectiveness of the drug involved, on the basis of which it could fairly and responsibly be concluded by such experts that the drug will have the effect it purports or is represented to have under the conditions of use prescribed, recommended, or suggested in the labeling or proposed labeling thereof. If the Secretary determines, based on relevant science, that data from one adequate and well-controlled clinical investigation and confirmatory evidence (obtained prior to or after such investigation) are sufficient to establish effectiveness, the Secretary may consider such data and evidence to constitute substantial evidence for purposes of the preceding sentence.

(e) Withdrawal of approval; grounds; immediate suspension upon finding imminent hazard to public health

The Secretary shall, after due notice and opportunity for hearing to the applicant, withdraw approval of an application with respect to any drug under this section if the Secretary finds

(1) that clinical or other experience, tests, or other scientific data show that such drug is unsafe for use under the conditions of use upon the basis of which the application was approved;

(2) that new evidence of clinical experience, not contained in such application or not available to the Secretary until after such application was approved, or tests by new methods, or tests by methods not deemed reasonably applicable when such application was approved, evaluated together with the evidence available to the Secretary when the application was approved, shows that such drug is not shown to be safe for use under the conditions of use upon the basis of which the application was approved; or

(3) on the basis of new information before him with respect to such drug, evaluated together with the evidence available to him when the application was approved, that there is a lack of substantial evidence that the drug will have the effect it purports or is represented to have under the conditions of use prescribed, recommended, or suggested in the labeling thereof; or

(4) the patent information prescribed by subsection (c) of this section was not filed within thirty days after the receipt of written notice from the Secretary specifying the failure to file such information; or

(5) that the at the application contains any untrue statement of a material fact: Provided, That if the Secretary (or in his absence the officer acting as Secretary) finds that there is an imminent hazard to the public health, he may suspend the approval of such application immediately, and give the applicant prompt notice of his action and afford the applicant the opportunity for an expedited hearing under this subsection; but the authority conferred by this proviso to suspend the approval of an application shall not be delegated. The Secretary may also, after due notice and opportunity for hearing to the applicant, withdraw the approval of an application submitted under subsection (b) or (j) of this section with respect to any drug under this section if the Secretary finds (1) that the applicant has failed to establish a system for maintaining required records, or has repeatedly or deliberately failed to maintain such records or to make required reports, in accordance with a regulation or order under subsection (k) of this section or to comply with the notice requirements of section 360(k)(2) of this title, or the applicant has refused to permit access to, or copying or verification of, such records as required by paragraph (2) of such subsection; or (2) that on the basis of new information before him, evaluated together with the evidence before him when the application was approved, the methods used in, or the facilities and controls used for, the manufacture, processing, and packing of such drug are inadequate to assure and preserve its identity, strength, quality, and purity and were not made adequate within a reasonable time after receipt of written notice from the Secretary specifying the matter complained of; or (3) that on the basis of new information before him, evaluated together with the evidence before him when the application was approved, the labeling of such drug, based on a fair evaluation of all material facts, is false or misleading in any particular and was not corrected within a reasonable time after receipt of written notice from the Secretary specifying the matter complained of. Any order under this subsection shall state the findings upon which it is based.

(f) Revocation of order refusing, withdrawing or suspending approval of application

Whenever the Secretary finds that the facts so require, he shall revoke any previous order under subsection (d) or (e) of this section refusing, withdrawing, or suspending approval of an application and shall approve such application or reinstate such approval, as may be appropriate.

(g) Service of orders

Orders of the Secretary issued under this section shall be served

(1) in person by any officer or employee of the Department designated by the Secretary or

(2) by mailing the order by registered mail or by certified mail addressed to the applicant or respondent at his last-known address in the records of the Secretary.

(h) Appeal from order

An appeal may be taken by the applicant from an order of the Secretary refusing or withdrawing approval of an application under this section. Such appeal shall be taken by filing in the United States court of appeals for the circuit wherein such applicant resides or has his principal place of business, or in the United States Court of Appeals for the District of Columbia Circuit, within sixty days after the entry of such order, a written petition praying that the order of the Secretary be set aside. A copy of such petition shall be

1137

forthwith transmitted by the clerk of the court to the Secretary, or any officer designated by him for that purpose, and thereupon the Secretary shall certify and file in the court the record upon which the order complained of was entered, as provided in section 2112 of Title 28. Upon the filing of such petition such court shall have exclusive jurisdiction to affirm or set aside such order, except that until the filing of the record the Secretary may modify or set aside his order. No objection to the order of the Secretary shall be considered by the court unless such objection shall have been urged before the Secretary or unless there were reasonable grounds for failure so to do. The finding of the Secretary as to the facts, if supported by substantial evidence, shall be conclusive. If any person shall apply to the court for leave to adduce additional evidence, and shall show to the satisfaction of the court that such additional evidence is material and that there were reasonable grounds for failure to adduce such evidence in the proceeding before the Secretary, the court may order such additional evidence to be taken before the Secretary and to be adduced upon the hearing in such manner and upon such terms and conditions as to the court may seem proper. The Secretary may modify his findings as to the facts by reason of the additional evidence so taken, and he shall file with the court such modified findings which, if supported by substantial evidence, shall be conclusive, and his recommendation, if any, for the setting aside of the original order. The judgment of the court affirming or setting aside any such order of the Secretary shall be final, subject to review by the Supreme Court of the United States upon certiorari or certification as provided in section 1254 of Title 28. The commencement of proceedings under this subsection shall not, unless specifically ordered by the court to the contrary, operate as a stay of the Secretary's order.

(i) Exemptions of drugs for research; discretionary and mandatory conditions; direct reports to Secretary

(1) The Secretary shall promulgate regulations for exempting from the operation of the foregoing subsections of this section drugs intended solely for investigational use by experts qualified by scientific training and experience to investigate the safety and effectiveness of drugs. Such regulations may, within the discretion of the Secretary, among other conditions relating to the protection of the public health, provide for conditioning such exemption upon—

(A) the submission to the Secretary, before any clinical testing of a new drug is undertaken, of reports, by the manufacturer or the sponsor of the investigation of such drug, of preclinical tests (including tests on animals) of such drug adequate to justify the proposed clinical testing;

(B) the manufacturer or the sponsor of the investigation of a new drug proposed to be distributed to investigators for clinical testing obtaining a signed agreement from each of such investigators that patients to whom the drug is administered will be under his personal supervision, or under the supervision of investigators responsible to him, and that he will not supply such drug to any other investigator, or to clinics, for administration to human beings; and

(C) the establishment and maintenance of such records, and the making of such reports to the Secretary, by the manufacturer or the sponsor of the investigation of such drug, of data (including but not limited to analytical reports by investigators) obtained as the result of such investigational use of such drug, as the Secretary finds will enable him to evaluate the safety and effectiveness of such drug in the event of the filing of an application pursuant to subsection (b) of this section.

(2) Subject to paragraph (3), a clinical investigation of a new drug may begin 30 days after the Secretary has received from the manufacturer or sponsor of the investigation a submission containing such information about the drug and the clinical investigation, including—

(A) information on design of the investigation and adequate reports of basic information, certified by the applicant to be accurate reports, necessary to assess the safety of the drug for use in clinical investigation; and

(B) adequate information on the chemistry and manufacturing of the drug, controls available for the drug, and primary data tabulations from animal or human studies.

(3)(A) At any time, the Secretary may prohibit the sponsor of an investigation from conducting the investigation (referred to in this paragraph as a "clinical hold") if the Secretary makes a determination described in subparagraph (B). The Secretary shall specify the basis for the clinical hold, including the specific information available to the Secretary which served as the basis for such clinical hold, and confirm such determination in writing.

(B) For purposes of subparagraph (A), a determination described in this subparagraph with respect to a clinical hold is that—

(i) the drug involved represents an unreasonable risk to the safety of the persons who are the subjects of the clinical investigation, taking into account the qualifications of the clinical investigators, information about the drug, the design of the clinical investigation, the condition for which the drug is to be investigated, and the health status of the subjects involved; or

(ii) the clinical hold should be issued for such other reasons as the Secretary may by regulation establish (including reasons established by regulation before November 21, 1997).

(C) Any written request to the Secretary from the sponsor of an investigation that a clinical hold be removed shall receive a decision, in writing and specifying the reasons therefor, within 30 days after receipt of such request. Any such request shall include sufficient information to support the removal of such clinical hold.

(4) Regulations under paragraph (1) shall provide that such exemption shall be conditioned upon the manufacturer, or the sponsor of the investigation, requiring that experts using such drugs for investigational purposes certify to such manufacturer or sponsor that they will inform any human beings to whom such drugs, or any controls used in connection therewith, are being administered, or their representatives, that such drugs are being used for investigational purposes and will obtain the consent of such human beings or their representatives, except where it is not feasible or it is contrary to the best interests of such human beings. Nothing in this subsection shall be construed to require any clinical investigator to submit directly to the Secretary reports on the investigational use of drugs.

(j) Abbreviated new drug applications

(1) Any person may file with the Secretary an abbreviated application for the approval of a new drug.

(2)(A) An abbreviated application for a new drug shall contain—

(i) information to show that the conditions of use prescribed, recommended, or suggested in the labeling proposed for the new drug have been previously approved for a drug listed under paragraph (7) (hereinafter in this subsection referred to as a "listed drug");

(ii)(I) if the listed drug referred to in clause (i) has only one active ingredient, information to show that the active ingredient of the new drug is the same as that of the listed drug;

(II) if the listed drug referred to in clause (i) has more than one active ingredient, information to show that the active ingredients of the new drug are the same as those of the listed drug, or

(III) if the listed drug referred to in clause (i) has more than one active ingredient and if one of the active ingredients of the new drug is different and the application is filed pursuant to the approval of a petition filed under subparagraph (C), information to show that the other active ingredients of the new drug are the same as the active ingredients of the listed drug, information to show that the different active ingredient is an active ingredient of a listed drug or of a drug which does not meet the requirements of section 321(p) of this title, and such other information respecting the different active ingredient with respect to which the petition was filed as the Secretary may require;

(iii) information to show that the route of administration, the dosage form, and the strength of the new drug are the same as those of the listed drug referred to in clause (i) or, if the route of administration, the dosage form, or the strength of the new drug is different and the application is filed pursuant to the approval of a petition filed under subparagraph (C), such information respecting the route of administration, dosage form, or strength with respect to which the petition was filed as the Secretary may require;

   (iv) information to show that the new drug is bioequivalent to the listed drug referred to in clause (i), except that if the application is filed pursuant to the approval of a petition filed under subparagraph (C), information to show that the active ingredients of the new drug are of the same pharmacological or therapeutic class as those of the listed drug referred to in clause (i) and the new drug can be expected to have the same therapeutic effect as the listed drug when administered to patients for a condition of use referred to in clause (i);

   (v) information to show that the labeling proposed for the new drug is the same as the labeling approved for the listed drug referred to in clause (i) except for changes required because of differences approved under a petition filed under subparagraph (C) or because the new drug and the listed drug are produced or distributed by different manufacturers;

   (vi) the items specified in clauses (B) through (F) of subsection (b)(1) of this section;

   (vii) a certification, in the opinion of the applicant and to the best of his knowledge, with respect to each patent which claims the listed drug referred to in clause (i) or which claims a use for such listed drug for which the applicant is seeking approval under this subsection and for which information is required to be filed under subsection (b) or (c) of this section—

   (I) that such patent information has not been filed,

   (II) that such patent has expired,

   (III) of the date on which such patent will expire, or

   (IV) that such patent is invalid or will not be infringed by the manufacture, use, or sale of the new drug for which the application is submitted; and

   (viii) if with respect to the listed drug referred to in clause (i) information was filed under subsection (b) or (c) of this section for a method of use patent which does not claim a use for which the applicant is seeking approval under this subsection, a statement that the method of use patent does not claim such a use.

The Secretary may not require that an abbreviated application contain information in addition to that required by clauses (i) through (viii).

(B)(i) An applicant who makes a certification described in subparagraph (A)(vii)(IV) shall include in the application a statement that the applicant will give the notice required by clause (ii) to—

(I) each owner of the patent which is the subject of the certification or the representative of such owner designated to receive such notice, and

(II) the holder of the approved application under subsection (b) of this section for the drug which is claimed by the patent or a use of which is claimed by the patent or the representative of such holder designated to receive such notice.

(ii) The notice referred to in clause (i) shall state that an application, which contains data from bioavailability or bioequivalence studies, has been submitted under this subsection for the drug with respect to which the certification is made to obtain approval to engage in the commercial manufacture, use, or sale of such drug before the expiration of the patent referred to in the certification. Such notice shall include a detailed statement of the factual and legal basis of the applicant's opinion that the patent is not valid or will not be infringed.

(iii) If an application is amended to include a certification described in subparagraph (A)(vii)(IV), the notice required by clause (ii) shall be given when the amended application is submitted.

(C) If a person wants to submit an abbreviated application for a new drug which has a different active ingredient or whose route of administration, dosage form, or strength differ from that of a listed drug, such person shall submit a petition to the Secretary seeking permission to file such an application. The Secretary shall approve or disapprove a petition submitted under this subparagraph within ninety days of the date the petition is submitted. The Secretary shall approve such a petition unless the Secretary finds—

(i) that investigations must be conducted to show the safety and effectiveness of the drug or of any of its active ingredients, the route of administration, the dosage form, or strength which differ from the listed drug; or

(ii) that any drug with a different active ingredient may not be adequately evaluated for approval as safe and effective on the basis of the information required to be submitted in an abbreviated application.

(3)(A) The Secretary shall issue guidance for the individuals who review applications submitted under paragraph (1), which shall relate to promptness in conducting the review, technical excellence, lack of bias and conflict of interest, and knowledge of regulatory and scientific standards, and which shall apply equally to all individuals who review such applications.

(B) The Secretary shall meet with a sponsor of an investigation or an applicant for approval for a drug under this subsection if the sponsor or applicant makes a reasonable written request for a meeting for the purpose of reaching agreement on the design and size of bioavailability and bioequivalence studies needed for approval of such application. The sponsor or applicant shall provide information necessary for discussion and agreement on the design and size of such studies. Minutes of any such meeting shall be prepared by the Secretary and made available to the sponsor or applicant.

(C) Any agreement regarding the parameters of design and size of bioavailability and bioequivalence studies of a drug under this paragraph that is reached between the Secretary and a sponsor or applicant shall be reduced to writing and made part of the administrative record by the Secretary. Such agreement shall not be changed after the testing begins, except—

    (i) with the written agreement of the sponsor or applicant; or

    (ii) pursuant to a decision, made in accordance with subparagraph (D) by the director of the reviewing division, that a substantial scientific issue essential to determining the safety or effectiveness of the drug has been identified after the testing has begun.

(D) A decision under subparagraph (C)(ii) by the director shall be in writing and the Secretary shall provide to the sponsor or applicant an opportunity for a meeting at which the director and the sponsor or applicant will be present and at which the director will document the scientific issue involved.

(E) The written decisions of the reviewing division shall be binding upon, and may not directly or indirectly be changed by, the field or compliance office personnel unless such field or compliance office personnel demonstrate to the reviewing division why such decision should be modified.

(F) No action by the reviewing division may be delayed because of the unavailability of information from or action by field personnel unless the reviewing division determines that a delay is necessary to assure the marketing of a safe and effective drug.

(G) For purposes of this paragraph, the reviewing division is the division responsible for the review of an application for approval of a drug under this subsection (including scientific matters, chemistry, manufacturing, and controls).

(4) Subject to paragraph (5), the Secretary shall approve an application for a drug unless the Secretary finds—

(A) the methods used in, or the facilities and controls used for, the manufacture, processing, and packing of the drug are inadequate to assure and preserve its identity, strength, quality, and purity;

(B) information submitted with the application is insufficient to show that each of the proposed conditions of use have been previously approved for the listed drug referred to in the application;

(C)(i) if the listed drug has only one active ingredient, information submitted with the application is insufficient to show that the active ingredient is the same as that of the listed drug;

(ii) if the listed drug has more than one active ingredient, information submitted with the application is insufficient to show that the active ingredients are the same as the active ingredients of the listed drug, or

(iii) if the listed drug has more than one active ingredient and if the application is for a drug which has an active ingredient different from the listed drug, information submitted with the application is insufficient to show—

(I) that the other active ingredients are the same as the active ingredients of the listed drug, or

(II) that the different active ingredient is an active ingredient of a listed drug or a drug which does not meet the requirements of section 321(p) of this title,

or no petition to file an application for the drug with the different ingredient was approved under paragraph (2)(C);

(D)(i) if the application is for a drug whose route of administration, dosage form, or strength of the drug is the same as the route of administration, dosage form, or strength of the listed drug referred to in the application, information submitted in the application is insufficient to show that the route of administration, dosage form, or strength is the same as that of the listed drug, or

(ii) if the application is for a drug whose route of administration, dosage form, or strength of the drug is different from that of the listed drug referred to in the application, no petition to file an application for the drug with the different route of administration, dosage form, or strength was approved under paragraph (2)(C);

(E) if the application was filed pursuant to the approval of a petition under paragraph (2)(C), the application did not contain the information required by the Secretary respecting the active ingredient, route of administration, dosage form, or strength which is not the same;

(F) information submitted in the application is insufficient to show that the drug is bioequivalent to the listed drug referred to in

1144

the application or, if the application was filed pursuant to a petition approved under paragraph (2)(C), information submitted in the application is insufficient to show that the active ingredients of the new drug are of the same pharmacological or therapeutic class as those of the listed drug referred to in paragraph (2)(A)(i) and that the new drug can be expected to have the same therapeutic effect as the listed drug when administered to patients for a condition of use referred to in such paragraph;

(G) information submitted in the application is insufficient to show that the labeling proposed for the drug is the same as the labeling approved for the listed drug referred to in the application except for changes required because of differences approved under a petition filed under paragraph (2)(C) or because the drug and the listed drug are produced or distributed by different manufacturers;

(H) information submitted in the application or any other information available to the Secretary shows that

(i) the inactive ingredients of the drug are unsafe for use under the conditions prescribed, recommended, or suggested in the labeling proposed for the drug, or

(ii) the composition of the drug is unsafe under such conditions because of the type or quantity of inactive ingredients included or the manner in which the inactive ingredients are included;

(I) the approval under subsection (c) of this section of the listed drug referred to in the application under this subsection has been withdrawn or suspended for grounds described in the first sentence of subsection (e) of this section, the Secretary has published a notice of opportunity for hearing to withdraw approval of the listed drug under subsection (c) of this section for grounds described in the first sentence of subsection (e) of this section, the approval under this subsection of the listed drug referred to in the application under this subsection has been withdrawn or suspended under paragraph (6), or the Secretary has determined that the listed drug has been withdrawn from sale for safety or effectiveness reasons;

(J) the application does not meet any other requirement of paragraph (2)(A); or

(K) the application contains an untrue statement of material fact.

(5)(A) Within one hundred and eighty days of the initial receipt of an application under paragraph (2) or within such additional period as may be agreed upon by the Secretary and the applicant, the Secretary shall approve or disapprove the application.

(B) The approval of an application submitted under paragraph (2) shall be made effective on the last applicable date determined under the following:

(i) If the applicant only made a certification described in subclause (I) or (II) of paragraph (2)(A)(vii) or in both such subclauses, the approval may be made effective immediately.

(ii) If the applicant made a certification described in subclause (III) of paragraph (2)(A)(vii), the approval may be made effective on the date certified under subclause (III).

(iii) If the applicant made a certification described in subclause (IV) of paragraph (2)(A)(vii), the approval shall be made effective immediately unless an action is brought for infringement of a patent which is the subject of the certification before the expiration of forty-five days from the date the notice provided under paragraph (2)(B)(i) is received. If such an action is brought before the expiration of such days, the approval shall be made effective upon the expiration of the thirty-month period beginning on the date of the receipt of the notice provided under paragraph (2)(B)(i) or such shorter or longer period as the court may order because either party to the action failed to reasonably cooperate in expediting the action, except that—

(I) if before the expiration of such period the court decides that such patent is invalid or not infringed, the approval shall be made effective on the date of the court decision,

(II) if before the expiration of such period the court decides that such patent has been infringed, the approval shall be made effective on such date as the court orders under section 271(e)(4)(A) of Title 35, or

(III) if before the expiration of such period the court grants a preliminary injunction prohibiting the applicant from engaging in the commercial manufacture or sale of the drug until the court decides the issues of patent validity and infringement and if the court decides that such patent is invalid or not infringed, the approval shall be made effective on the date of such court decision.

In such an action, each of the parties shall reasonably cooperate in expediting the action. Until the expiration of forty-five days from the date the notice made under paragraph (2)(B)(i) is received, no action may be brought under section 2201 of Title 28, for a declaratory judgment with respect to the patent. Any action brought under section 2201 shall be brought in the judicial district where the defendant has its principal place of business or a regular and established place of business.

(iv) If the application contains a certification described in subclause (IV) of paragraph (2)(A)(vii) and is for a drug for which a previous application has been submitted under this subsection continuing such a certification, the application shall be made effective not earlier than one hundred and eighty days after—

(I) the date the Secretary receives notice from the applicant under the previous application of the first commercial marketing of the drug under the previous application, or

(II) the date of a decision of a court in an action described in clause (iii) holding the patent which is the subject of the certification to be invalid or not infringed,

whichever is earlier.

(C) If the Secretary decides to disapprove an application, the Secretary shall give the applicant notice of an opportunity for a hearing before the Secretary on the question of whether such application is approvable. If the applicant elects to accept the opportunity for hearing by written request within thirty days after such notice, such hearing shall commence not more than ninety days after the expiration of such thirty days unless the Secretary and the applicant otherwise agree. Any such hearing shall thereafter be conducted on an expedited basis and the Secretary's order thereon shall be issued within ninety days after the date fixed by the Secretary for filing final briefs.

(D)(i) If an application (other than an abbreviated new drug application) submitted under subsection (b) of this section for a drug, no active ingredient (including any ester or salt of the active ingredient) of which has been approved in any other application under subsection (b) of this section, was approved during the period beginning January 1, 1982, and ending on September 24, 1984, the Secretary may not make the approval of an application submitted under this subsection which refers to the drug for which the subsection (b) application was submitted effective before the expiration of ten years from the date of the approval of the application under subsection (b) of this section.

(ii) If an application submitted under subsection (b) of this section for a drug, no active ingredient (including any ester or salt of the active ingredient) of which has been approved in any other application under subsection (b) of this section, is approved after September 24, 1984, no application may be submitted under this subsection which refers to the drug for which the subsection (b) application was submitted before the expiration of five years from the date of the approval of the application under subsection (b) of this section, except that such an application may be submitted under this subsection after the expiration of

1147

four years from the date of the approval of the subsection (b) application if it contains a certification of patent invalidity or noninfringement described in subclause (IV) of paragraph (2)(A)(vii). The approval of such an application shall be made effective in accordance with subparagraph (B) except that, if an action for patent infringement is commenced during the one-year period beginning forty-eight months after the date of the approval of the subsection (b) application, the thirty-month period referred to in subparagraph (B)(iii) shall be extended by such amount of time (if any) which is required for seven and one-half years to have elapsed from the date of approval of the subsection (b) application.

(iii) If an application submitted under subsection (b) of this section for a drug, which includes an active ingredient (including any ester or salt of the active ingredient) that has been approved in another application approved under subsection (b) of this section, is approved after September 24, 1984, and if such application contains reports of new clinical investigations (other than bioavailability studies) essential to the approval of the application and conducted or sponsored by the applicant, the Secretary may not make the approval of an application submitted under this subsection for the conditions of approval of such drug in the subsection (b) application effective before the expiration of three years from the date of the approval of the application under subsection (b) of this section for such drug.

(iv) If a supplement to an application approved under subsection (b) of this section is approved after September 24, 1984, and the supplement contains reports of new clinical investigations (other than bioavailability studies) essential to the approval of the supplement and conducted or sponsored by the person submitting the supplement, the Secretary may not make the approval of an application submitted under this subsection for a change approved in the supplement effective before the expiration of three years from the date of the approval of the supplement under subsection (b) of this section.

(v) If an application (or supplement to an application) submitted under subsection (b) of this section for a drug, which includes an active ingredient (including any ester or salt of the active ingredient) that has been approved in another application under subsection (b) of this section, was approved during the period beginning January 1, 1982, and ending on September 24, 1984, the Secretary may not make the approval of an application submitted under this subsection which refers to the drug for which the subsection (b) application was submitted or which refers to a change approved in a supplement to the subsection (b) application effective before the expiration of two years from September 24, 1984.

(6) If a drug approved under this subsection refers in its approved application to a drug the approval of which was withdrawn or suspended for grounds described in the first sentence of subsection (e) of this section or was withdrawn or suspended under this paragraph or which, as determined by the Secretary, has been withdrawn from sale for safety or effectiveness reasons, the approval of the drug under this subsection shall be withdrawn or suspended—

(A) for the same period as the withdrawal or suspension under subsection (e) of this section or this paragraph, or

(B) if the listed drug has been withdrawn from sale, for the period of withdrawal from sale or, if earlier, the period ending on the date the Secretary determines that the withdrawal from sale is not for safety or effectiveness reasons.

(7)(A)(i) Within sixty days of September 24, 1984, the Secretary shall publish and make available to the public—

(I) a list in alphabetical order of the official and proprietary name of each drug which has been approved for safety and effectiveness under subsection (c) of this section before September 24, 1984;

(II) the date of approval if the drug is approved after 1981 and the number of the application which was approved; and

(III) whether in vitro or in vivo bioequivalence studies, or both such studies, are required for applications filed under this subsection which will refer to the drug published.

(ii) Every thirty days after the publication of the first list under clause (i) the Secretary shall revise the list to include each drug which has been approved for safety and effectiveness under subsection (c) of this section or approved under this subsection during the thirty-day period.

(iii) When patent information submitted under subsection (b) or (c) of this section respecting a drug included on the list is to be published by the Secretary, the Secretary shall, in revisions made under clause (ii), include such information for such drug.

(B) A drug approved for safety and effectiveness under subsection (c) of this section or approved under this subsection shall, for purposes of this subsection, be considered to have been published under subparagraph (A) on the date of its approval or September 24, 1984, whichever is later.

(C) If the approval of a drug was withdrawn or suspended for grounds described in the first sentence of subsection (e) of this section or was withdrawn or suspended under paragraph (6) or if the Secretary determines that a drug has been withdrawn from sale for safety or effectiveness reasons, it may not be published in the list under subparagraph (A) or, if the withdrawal or suspension occurred after its publication in such list, it shall be immediately removed from such list—

(i) for the same period as the withdrawal or suspension under subsection (e) of this section or paragraph (6), or

(ii) if the listed drug has been withdrawn from sale, for the period of withdrawal from sale or, if earlier, the period ending on the date the Secretary determines that the withdrawal from sale is not for safety or effectiveness reasons.

A notice of the removal shall be published in the Federal Register.

(8) For purposes of this subsection:

(A) The term "bioavailability" means the rate and extent to which the active ingredient or therapeutic ingredient is absorbed from a drug and becomes available at the site of drug action.

(B) A drug shall be considered to be bioequivalent to a listed drug if—

(i) the rate and extent of absorption of the drug do not show a significant difference from the rate and extent of absorption of the listed drug when administered at the same molar dose of the therapeutic ingredient under similar experimental conditions in either a single dose or multiple doses; or

(ii) the extent of absorption of the drug does not show a significant difference from the extent of absorption of the listed drug when administered at the same molar dose of the therapeutic ingredient under similar experimental conditions in either a single dose or multiple doses and the difference from the listed drug in the rate of absorption of the drug is intentional, is reflected in its proposed labeling, is not essential to the attainment of effective body drug concentrations on chronic use, and is considered medically insignificant for the drug.

(9) The Secretary shall, with respect to each application submitted under this subsection, maintain a record of—

(A) the name of the applicant,

(B) the name of the drug covered by the application,

(C) the name of each person to whom the review of the chemistry of the application was assigned and the date of such assignment, and

(D) the name of each person to whom the bioequivalence review for such application was assigned and the date of such assignment.

The information the Secretary is required to maintain under this paragraph with respect to an application submitted under this subsection shall be made available to the public after the approval of such application.

(k) Records and reports; required information; regulations and orders; access to records

(1) In the case of any drug for which an approval of an application filed under subsection (b) or (j) of this section is in effect, the applicant shall establish and maintain such records, and make such reports to the Secretary, of data relating to clinical experience and other data or information, received or otherwise obtained by such applicant with respect to such drug, as the Secretary may by general regulation, or by order with respect to such application, prescribe on the basis of a finding that such records and reports are necessary in order to enable the Secretary to determine, or facilitate a determination, whether there is or may be ground for invoking subsection (e) of this section. Regulations and orders issued under this subsection and under subsection (i) of this section shall have due regard for the professional ethics of the medical profession and the interests of patients and shall provide, where the Secretary deems it to be appropriate, for the examination, upon request, by the persons to whom such regulations or orders are applicable, of similar information received or otherwise obtained by the Secretary.

(2) Every person required under this section to maintain records, and every person in charge or custody thereof, shall, upon request of an officer or employee designated by the Secretary, permit such officer or employee at all reasonable times to have access to and copy and verify such records.

(l) Public disclosure of safety and effectiveness data

Safety and effectiveness data and information which has been submitted in an application under subsection (b) of this section for a drug and which has not previously been disclosed to the public shall be made available to the public, upon request, unless extraordinary circumstances are shown—

(1) if no work is being or will be undertaken to have the application approved,

(2) if the Secretary has determined that the application is not approvable and all legal appeals have been exhausted,

(3) if approval of the application under subsection (c) of this section is withdrawn and all legal appeals have been exhausted,

(4) if the Secretary has determined that such drug is not a new drug, or

(5) upon the effective date of the approval of the first application under subsection (j) of this section which refers to such drug or upon the date upon which the approval of an application under subsection (j) of this section which refers to such drug could be made effective if such an application had been submitted.

(m) "Patent" defined

For purposes of this section, the term "patent" means a patent issued by the United States Patent and Trademark Office.

(n) Scientific advisory panels

(1) For the purpose of providing expert scientific advice and recommendations to the Secretary regarding a clinical investigation of a drug or the approval for marketing of a drug under *section 355* of this title or section 262 of Title 42, the Secretary shall establish panels of experts or use panels of experts established before November 21, 1997, or both.

(2) The Secretary may delegate the appointment and oversight authority granted under section 394 of this title to a director of a center or successor entity within the Food and Drug Administration.

(3) The Secretary shall make appointments to each panel established under paragraph (1) so that each panel shall consist of—

(A) members who are qualified by training and experience to evaluate the safety and effectiveness of the drugs to be referred to the panel and who, to the extent feasible, possess skill and experience in the development, manufacture, or utilization of such drugs;

(B) members with diverse expertise in such fields as clinical and administrative medicine, pharmacy, pharmacology, pharmacoeconomics, biological and physical sciences, and other related professions;

(C) a representative of consumer interests, and a representative of interests of the drug manufacturing industry not directly affected by the matter to be brought before the panel; and

(D) two or more members who are specialists or have other expertise in the particular disease or condition for which the drug under review is proposed to be indicated.

Scientific, trade, and consumer organizations shall be afforded an opportunity to nominate individuals for appointment to the panels. No individual who is in the regular full-time employ of the United States and engaged in the administration of this chapter may be a voting member of any panel. The Secretary shall designate one of the members of each panel to serve as chairman thereof.

(4) Each member of a panel shall publicly disclose all conflicts of interest that member may have with the work to be undertaken by the panel. No member of a panel may vote on any matter where the member or the immediate family of such member could gain financially from the advice given to the Secretary. The Secretary may grant a waiver of any conflict of interest requirement upon public disclosure of such conflict of interest if such waiver is necessary to afford the panel essential expertise,

except that the Secretary may not grant a waiver for a member of a panel when the member's own scientific work is involved.

(5) The Secretary shall, as appropriate, provide education and training to each new panel member before such member participates in a panel's activities, including education regarding requirements under this Act and related regulations of the Secretary, and the administrative processes and procedures related to panel meetings.

(6) Panel members (other than officers or employees of the United States), while attending meetings or conferences of a panel or otherwise engaged in its business, shall be entitled to receive compensation for each day so engaged, including traveltime, at rates to be fixed by the Secretary, but not to exceed the daily equivalent of the rate in effect for positions classified above grade GS–15 of the General Schedule. While serving away from their homes or regular places of business, panel members may be allowed travel expenses (including per diem in lieu of subsistence) as authorized by section 5703 of Title 5, for persons in the Government service employed intermittently.

(7) The Secretary shall ensure that scientific advisory panels meet regularly and at appropriate intervals so that any matter to be reviewed by such a panel can be presented to the panel not more than 60 days after the matter is ready for such review. Meetings of the panel may be held using electronic communication to convene the meetings.

(8) Within 90 days after a scientific advisory panel makes recommendations on any matter under its review, the Food and Drug Administration official responsible for the matter shall review the conclusions and recommendations of the panel, and notify the affected persons of the final decision on the matter, or of the reasons that no such decision has been reached. Each such final decision shall be documented including the rationale for the decision.

§ 355a. Pediatric studies of drugs

(a) Market exclusivity for new drugs

If, prior to approval of an application that is submitted under section 355(b)(1) of this title, the Secretary determines that information relating to the use of a new drug in the pediatric population may produce health benefits in that population, the Secretary makes a written request for pediatric studies (which shall include a timeframe for completing such studies), and such studies are completed within any such timeframe and the reports thereof submitted in accordance with subsection (d)(2) of this section or accepted in accordance with subsection (d)(3) of this section—

(1)(A)(i) the period referred to in subsection (c)(3)(D)(ii) of section 355 of this title, and in subsection (j)(4)(D)(ii) of such section, is deemed to be five years and six months rather than five years, and the references in subsections (c)(3)(D)(ii) and (j)(4)(D)(ii) of such section to four years, to forty-eight months, and to seven and one-half years are deemed to be four and one-half years, fifty-four months, and eight years, respectively; or

(ii) the period referred to in clauses (iii) and (iv) of subsection (c)(3)(D) of such section, and in clauses (iii) and (iv) of subsection (j)(4)(D) of such section, is deemed to be three years and six months rather than three years; and

(B) if the drug is designated under section 360bb of this title for a rare disease or condition, the period referred to in section 360cc of this title is deemed to be seven years and six months rather than seven years; and

(2)(A) if the drug is the subject of—

(i) a listed patent for which a certification has been submitted under subsection (b)(2)(A)(ii) or (j)(2)(A)(vii)(II) of section 355 of this title and for which pediatric studies were submitted prior to the expiration of the patent (including any patent extensions); or

(ii) a listed patent for which a certification has been submitted under subsections (b)(2)(A)(iii) or (j)(2)(A)(vii)(III) of section 355 of this title,

the period during which an application may not be approved under section 355(c)(3) or section 355(j)(4)(B) of this title shall be extended by a period of six months after the date the patent expires (including any patent extensions); or

(B) if the drug is the subject of a listed patent for which a certification has been submitted under subsection (b)(2)(A)(iv) or (j)(2)(A)(vii)(IV) of section 355 of this title, and in the patent infringement litigation resulting from the certification the court determines that the patent is valid and would be infringed, the period during which an application may not be approved under section 355(c)(3) or section 355(j)(4)(B) of this title shall be extended by a period of six months after the date the patent expires (including any patent extensions).

(b) Secretary to develop list of drugs for which additional pediatric information may be beneficial

Not later than 180 days after November 21, 1997, the Secretary, after consultation with experts in pediatric research shall develop, prioritize, and publish an initial list of approved drugs for which additional pediatric information may produce health benefits in the pediatric population. The Secretary shall annually update the list.

(c) Market exclusivity for already-marketed drugs

If the Secretary makes a written request to the holder of an approved application under section 355(b)(1) of this title for pediatric studies (which shall include a timeframe for completing such studies) concerning a drug identified in the list described in subsection (b) of this section, the holder agrees to the request, the studies are completed within any such timeframe, and the reports thereof are submitted in accordance with subsection (d)(2) of this section or accepted in accordance with subsection (d)(3) of this section—

(1)(A)(i) the period referred to in subsection (c)(3)(D)(ii) of section 355 of this title, and in subsection (j)(4)(D)(ii) of such section, is deemed to be five years and six months rather than five years, and the references in subsections (c)(3)(D)(ii) and (j)(4)(D)(ii) of such section to four years, to forty-eight months, and to seven and one-half years are deemed to be four and one-half years, fifty-four months, and eight years, respectively; or

(ii) the period referred to in clauses (iii) and (iv) of subsection (c)(3)(D) of such section, and in clauses (iii) and (iv) of subsection (j)(4)(D) of such section, is deemed to be three years and six months rather than three years; and

(B) if the drug is designated under section 360bb of this title for a rare disease or condition, the period referred to in section 360cc(a) of this title is deemed to be seven years and six months rather than seven years; and

(2)(A) if the drug is the subject of—

(i) a listed patent for which a certification has been submitted under subsection (b)(2)(A)(ii) or (j)(2)(A)(vii)(II) of section 355 of this title and for which pediatric studies were submitted prior to the expiration of the patent (including any patent extensions); or

(ii) a listed patent for which a certification has been submitted under subsection (b)(2)(A)(iii) or (j)(2)(A)(vii)(III) of section 355 of this title, the period during which an application may not be approved under section 355(c)(3) or section 355(j)(4)(B) of this title shall be extended by a period of six months after the date the patent expires (including any patent extensions); or

(B) if the drug is the subject of a listed patent for which a certification has been submitted under subsection (b)(2)(A)(iv) or (j)(2)(A)(vii)(IV) of section 355 of this title, and in the patent infringement litigation resulting from the certification the court determines that the patent is valid and would be infringed, the period during which an application may not be approved under section 355(c)(3) or section 355(j)(4)(B) of this title shall be extended by a period of six months after the date the patent expires (including any patent extensions).

(d) Conduct of pediatric studies

(1) Agreement for studies

The Secretary may, pursuant to a written request from the Secretary under subsection (a) or (c) of this section, after consultation with—

(A) the sponsor of an application for an investigational new drug under section 355(i) of this title;

(B) the sponsor of an application for a new drug under section 355(b)(1) of this title; or

(C) the holder of an approved application for a drug under section 355(b)(1) of this title,

agree with the sponsor or holder for the conduct of pediatric studies for such drug. Such agreement shall be in writing and shall include a timeframe for such studies.

(2) Written protocols to meet the studies requirement

If the sponsor or holder and the Secretary agree upon written protocols for the studies, the studies requirement of subsection (a) or (c) of this section is satisfied upon the completion of the studies and submission of the reports thereof in accordance with the original written request and the written agreement referred to in paragraph (1). Not later than 60 days after the submission of the report of the studies, the Secretary shall determine if such studies were or were not conducted in accordance with the original written request and the written agreement and reported in accordance with the requirements of the Secretary for filing and so notify the sponsor or holder.

(3) Other methods to meet the studies requirement

If the sponsor or holder and the Secretary have not agreed in writing on the protocols for the studies, the studies requirement of subsection (a) or (c) of this section is satisfied when such studies have been completed and the reports accepted by the Secretary. Not later than 90 days after the submission of the reports of the studies, the Secretary shall accept or reject such reports and so notify the sponsor or holder. The Secretary's only responsibility in accepting or rejecting the reports shall be to determine, within the 90 days, whether the studies fairly respond to the written request, have been conducted in accordance with commonly accepted scientific principles and protocols, and have been reported in accordance with the requirements of the Secretary for filing.

(e) Delay of effective date for certain application

If the Secretary determines that the acceptance or approval of an application under section 355(b)(2) or 355(j) of this title for a new drug may occur after submission of reports of pediatric studies under this section, which were submitted prior to the expiration of the patent (including any patent extension) or the applicable period under clauses (ii) through (iv) of section 355(c)(3)(D) of this title or clauses (ii) through (iv) of section 355(j)(4)(D) of this title, but before the Secretary has determined whether the requirements of subsection (d) of this section have been satisfied, the Secretary shall delay the acceptance or approval under section 355(b)(2) or 355(j) of this title until the determination under subsection (d) of this section is made, but any such delay shall not exceed 90 days. In the event that requirements of this section are satisfied, the applicable six-month period under subsection (a) or (c) of this section shall be deemed to have been running during the period of delay.

(f) Notice of determinations on studies requirement

The Secretary shall publish a notice of any determination that the requirements of subsection (d) of this section have been met and that submissions and approvals under subsection (b)(2) or (j) of section 355 of this title for a drug will be subject to the provisions of this section.

(g) Definitions

As used in this section, the term "pediatric studies" or "studies" means at least one clinical investigation (that, at the Secretary's discretion, may include pharmacokinetic studies) in pediatric age groups in which a drug is anticipated to be used.

(h) Limitations

A drug to which the six-month period under subsection (a) or (b) of this section has already been applied—

    (1) may receive an additional six-month period under subsection (c)(1)(A)(ii) of this section for a supplemental application if all other requirements under this section are satisfied, except that such a drug may not receive any additional such period under subsection (c)(2) of this section; and

    (2) may not receive any additional such period under subsection (c)(1)(B) of this section.

(i) Relationship to regulations

Notwithstanding any other provision of law, if any pediatric study is required pursuant to regulations promulgated by the Secretary and such study meets the completeness, timeliness, and other requirements of this section, such study shall be deemed to satisfy the requirement for market exclusivity pursuant to this section.

(j) Sunset

A drug may not receive any six-month period under subsection (a) or (c) of this section unless the application for the drug under section 355(b)(1) of this section is submitted on or before January 1, 2002. After January 1, 2002, a drug shall receive a six-month period under subsection (c) of this section if—

    (1) the drug was in commercial distribution as of November 21, 1997;

    (2) the drug was included by the Secretary on the list under subsection (b) of this section as of January 1, 2002;

    (3) the Secretary determines that there is a continuing need for information relating to the use of the drug in the pediatric population and that the drug may provide health benefits in that population; and

    (4) all requirements of this section are met.

(k) Report

The Secretary shall conduct a study and report to Congress not later than January 1, 2001, based on the experience under the program established under this section. The study and report shall examine all relevant issues, including—

(1) the effectiveness of the program in improving information about important pediatric uses for approved drugs;

(2) the adequacy of the incentive provided under this section;

(3) the economic impact of the program on taxpayers and consumers, including the impact of the lack of lower cost generic drugs on patients, including on lower income patients; and

(4) any suggestions for modification that the Secretary determines to be appropriate.

§ 356. Fast track products

(a) Designation of drug as a fast track product.—

(1) In general

The Secretary shall, at the request of the sponsor of a new drug, facilitate the development and expedite the review of such drug if it is intended for the treatment of a serious or life-threatening condition and it demonstrates the potential to address unmet medical needs for such a condition. (In this section, such a drug is referred to as a "fast track product".)

(2) Request for designation

The sponsor of a new drug may request the Secretary to designate the drug as a fast track product. A request for the designation may be made concurrently with, or at any time after, submission of an application for the investigation of the drug under section 355(i) or section 360hh(a)(3) of this title.

(3) Designation

Within 60 calendar days after the receipt of a request under paragraph (2), the Secretary shall determine whether the drug that is the subject of the request meets the criteria described in paragraph (1). If the Secretary finds that the drug meets the criteria, the Secretary shall designate the drug as a fast track product and shall take such actions as are appropriate to expedite the development and review of the application for approval of such product.

(b) Approval of application for a fast track product

(1) In general

The Secretary may approve an application for approval of a fast track product under section 355(c) or section 360hh of this title upon a determination that the product has an effect on a clinical endpoint or on a surrogate endpoint that is reasonably likely to predict clinical benefit.

(2) Limitation

Approval of a fast track product under this subsection may be subject to the requirements—

(A) that the sponsor conduct appropriate post-approval studies to validate the surrogate endpoint or otherwise confirm the effect on the clinical endpoint; and

(B) that the sponsor submit copies of all promotional materials related to the fast track product during the preapproval review period and, following approval and for such period thereafter as the Secretary determines to be appropriate, at least 30 days prior to dissemination of the materials.

(3) Expedited withdrawal of approval

The Secretary may withdraw approval of a fast track product using expedited procedures (as prescribed by the Secretary in regulations which shall include an opportunity for an informal hearing) if—

(A) the sponsor fails to conduct any required post-approval study of the fast track drug with due diligence;

(B) a post-approval study of the fast track product fails to verify clinical benefit of the product;

(C) other evidence demonstrates that the fast track product is not safe or effective under the conditions of use; or

(D) the sponsor disseminates false or misleading promotional materials with respect to the product.

(c) Review of incomplete applications for approval of a fast track product

(1) In general

If the Secretary determines, after preliminary evaluation of clinical data submitted by the sponsor, that a fast track product may be effective, the Secretary shall evaluate for filing, and may commence review of portions of, an application for the approval of the product before the sponsor submits a complete application. The Secretary shall commence such review only if the applicant—

(A) provides a schedule for submission of information necessary to make the application complete; and

(B) pays any fee that may be required under section 379h of this title.

(2) Exception

Any time period for review of human drug applications that has been agreed to by the Secretary and that has been set forth in goals identified in letters of the Secretary (relating to the use of fees collected under section 379h of this title to expedite the drug development process and the review of human drug applications) shall not apply to an application submitted under paragraph (1) until the date on which the application is complete.

(d) Awareness efforts

The Secretary shall—

(1) develop and disseminate to physicians, patient organizations, pharmaceutical and biotechnology companies, and other appropriate persons a description of the provisions of this section applicable to fast track products; and

(2) establish a program to encourage the development of surrogate endpoints that are reasonably likely to predict clinical benefit for serious or life-threatening conditions for which there exist significant unmet medical needs.

§ 356a. **Manufacturing changes**

(a) In general

With respect to a drug for which there is in effect an approved application under section 355 or 360b of this title or a license under section 262 of Title 42, a change from the manufacturing process approved pursuant to such application or license may be made, and the drug as made with the change may be distributed, if—

(1) the holder of the approved application or license (referred to in this section as a "holder") has validated the effects of the change in accordance with subsection (b) of this section; and

(2)(A) in the case of a major manufacturing change, the holder has complied with the requirements of subsection (c) of this section; or

(B) in the case of a change that is not a major manufacturing change, the holder complies with the applicable requirements of subsection (d) of this section.

(b) Validation of effects of changes

For purposes of subsection (a)(1) of this section, a drug made with a manufacturing change (whether a major manufacturing change or otherwise) may be distributed only if, before distribution of the drug as so made, the holder involved validates the effects of the change on the identity, strength, quality, purity, and potency of the drug as the identity, strength, quality, purity, and potency may relate to the safety or effectiveness of the drug.

(c) Major manufacturing changes

(1) Requirement of supplemental application

For purposes of subsection (a)(2)(A) of this section, a drug made with a major manufacturing change may be distributed only if, before the distribution of the drug as so made, the holder involved submits to the

Secretary a supplemental application for such change and the Secretary approves the application. The application shall contain such information as the Secretary determines to be appropriate, and shall include the information developed under subsection (b) of this section by the holder in validating the effects of the change.

(2) Changes qualifying as major changes

For purposes of subsection (a)(2)(A) of this section, a major manufacturing change is a manufacturing change that is determined by the Secretary to have substantial potential to adversely affect the identity, strength, quality, purity, or potency of the drug as they may relate to the safety or effectiveness of a drug. Such a change includes a change that—

(A) is made in the qualitative or quantitative formulation of the drug involved or in the specifications in the approved application or license referred to in subsection (a) of this section for the drug (unless exempted by the Secretary by regulation or guidance from the requirements of this subsection);

(B) is determined by the Secretary by regulation or guidance to require completion of an appropriate clinical study demonstrating equivalence of the drug to the drug as manufactured without the change; or

(C) is another type of change determined by the Secretary by regulation or guidance to have a substantial potential to adversely affect the safety or effectiveness of the drug.

(d) Other manufacturing changes

(1) In general

For purposes of subsection (a)(2)(B) of this section, the Secretary may regulate drugs made with manufacturing changes that are not major manufacturing changes as follows:

(A) The Secretary may in accordance with paragraph (2) authorize holders to distribute such drugs without submitting a supplemental application for such changes.

(B) The Secretary may in accordance with paragraph (3) require that, prior to the distribution of such drugs, holders submit to the Secretary supplemental applications for such changes.

(C) The Secretary may establish categories of such changes and designate categories to which subparagraph (A) applies and categories to which subparagraph (B) applies.

(2) Changes not requiring supplemental application

(A) Submission of report

A holder making a manufacturing change to which paragraph (1)(A) applies shall submit to the Secretary a report on the change, which shall contain such information as the Secretary determines to

1161

be appropriate, and which shall include the information developed under subsection (b) of this section by the holder in validating the effects of the change. The report shall be submitted by such date as the Secretary may specify.

(B) Authority regarding annual reports

In the case of a holder that during a single year makes more than one manufacturing change to which paragraph (1)(A) applies, the Secretary may in carrying out subparagraph (A) authorize the holder to comply with such subparagraph by submitting a single report for the year that provides the information required in such subparagraph for all the changes made by the holder during the year.

(3) Changes requiring supplemental application

(A) Submission of supplemental application

The supplemental application required under paragraph (1)(B) for a manufacturing change shall contain such information as the Secretary determines to be appropriate, which shall include the information developed under subsection (b) of this section by the holder in validating the effects of the change.

(B) Authority for distribution

In the case of a manufacturing change to which paragraph (1)(B) applies:

(i) The holder involved may commence distribution of the drug involved 30 days after the Secretary receives the supplemental application under such paragraph, unless the Secretary notifies the holder within such 30–day period that prior approval of the application is required before distribution may be commenced.

(ii) The Secretary may designate a category of such changes for the purpose of providing that, in the case of a change that is in such category, the holder involved may commence distribution of the drug involved upon the receipt by the Secretary of a supplemental application for the change.

(iii) If the Secretary disapproves the supplemental application, the Secretary may order the manufacturer to cease the distribution of the drugs that have been made with the manufacturing change.

§ 356b. **Reports of postmarketing studies**

(a) Submission

(1) In general

A sponsor of a drug that has entered into an agreement with the Secretary to conduct a postmarketing study of a drug shall submit to the Secretary, within 1 year after the approval of such drug and annually thereafter until the study is completed or terminated, a report of the progress of the study or the reasons for the failure of the sponsor to conduct the study. The report shall be submitted in such form as is prescribed by the Secretary in regulations issued by the Secretary.

(2) Agreements prior to effective date

Any agreement entered into between the Secretary and a sponsor of a drug, prior to November 21, 1997, to conduct a postmarketing study of a drug shall be subject to the requirements of paragraph (1). An initial report for such an agreement shall be submitted within 6 months after the date of the issuance of the regulations under paragraph (1).

(b) Consideration of information as public information

Any information pertaining to a report described in subsection (a) of this section shall be considered to be public information to the extent that the information is necessary—

(1) to identify the sponsor; and

(2) to establish the status of a study described in subsection (a) of this section and the reasons, if any, for any failure to carry out the study.

(c) Status of studies and reports

The Secretary shall annually develop and publish in the Federal Register a report that provides information on the status of the postmarketing studies—

(1) that sponsors have entered into agreements to conduct; and

(2) for which reports have been submitted under subsection (a)(1) of this section.

§ 356c. **Discontinuance of a life saving product**

(a) In general

A manufacturer that is the sole manufacturer of a drug—

(1) that is—

(A) life-supporting;

(B) life-sustaining; or

(C) intended for use in the prevention of a debilitating disease or condition;

(2) for which an application has been approved under section 355(b) or 355(j) of this title; and

(3) that is not a product that was originally derived from human tissue and was replaced by a recombinant product,

shall notify the Secretary of a discontinuance of the manufacture of the drug at least 6 months prior to the date of the discontinuance.

(b) Reduction in notification period

The notification period required under subsection (a) of this section for a manufacturer may be reduced if the manufacturer certifies to the Secretary that good cause exists for the reduction, such as a situation in which—

(1) a public health problem may result from continuation of the manufacturing for the 6–month period;

(2) a biomaterials shortage prevents the continuation of the manufacturing for the 6–month period;

(3) a liability problem may exist for the manufacturer if the manufacturing is continued for the 6–month period;

(4) continuation of the manufacturing for the 6–month period may cause substantial economic hardship for the manufacturer;

(5) the manufacturer has filed for bankruptcy under chapter 7 or 11 of Title 11 [*11 U.S.C.A. § 701* et seq. or § 1101 et seq.]; or

(6) the manufacturer can continue the distribution of the drug involved for 6 months.

(c) Distribution

To the maximum extent practicable, the Secretary shall distribute information on the discontinuation of the drugs described in subsection (a) of this section to appropriate physician and patient organizations.

* * *

§ 360c. Classification of devices intended for human use

(a) Classes of devices

(1) There are established the following classes of devices intended for human use:

(A) Class I, General Controls.—

(i) A device for which the controls authorized by or under section 351, 352, 360, 360f, 360h, 360i, or 360j of this title or any combination of such sections are sufficient to provide reasonable assurance of the safety and effectiveness of the device.

(ii) A device for which insufficient information exists to determine that the controls referred to in clause (i) are sufficient to provide reasonable assurance of the safety and effectiveness of the device or to establish special controls to provide such assurance, but because it—

(I) is not purported or represented to be for a use in supporting or sustaining human life or for a use which is of substantial importance in preventing impairment of human health, and

(II) does not present a potential unreasonable risk of illness or injury, is to be regulated by the controls referred to in clause (i).

(B) Class II, Special Controls.—

A device which cannot be classified as a class I device because the general controls by themselves are insufficient to provide reasonable assurance of the safety and effectiveness of the device, and for which there is sufficient information to establish special controls to provide such assurance, including the promulgation of performance standards, postmarket surveillance, patient registries, development and dissemination of guidelines (including guidelines for the submission of clinical data in premarket notification submissions in accordance with section 360(k) of this title), recommendations, and other appropriate actions as the Secretary deems necessary to provide such assurance. For a device that is purported or represented to be for a use in supporting or sustaining human life, the Secretary shall examine and identify the special controls, if any, that are necessary to provide adequate assurance of safety and effectiveness and describe how such controls provide such assurance.

(C) Class III, Premarket Approval.—

A device which because—

(i) it

(I) cannot be classified as a class I device because insufficient information exists to determine that the application of general controls are sufficient to provide reasonable assurance of the safety and effectiveness of the device, and

(II) cannot be classified as a class II device because insufficient information exists to determine that the special controls described in subparagraph (B) would provide reasonable assurance of its safety and effectiveness, and

(ii)(I) is purported or represented to be for a use in supporting or sustaining human life or for a use which is of substantial importance in preventing impairment of human health, or

(II) presents a potential unreasonable risk of illness or injury,

is to be subject, in accordance with section 360e of this title, to premarket approval to provide reasonable assurance of its safety and effectiveness.

If there is not sufficient information to establish a performance standard for a device to provide reasonable assurance of its safety and effectiveness, the Secretary may conduct such activities as may be necessary to develop or obtain such information.

(2) For purposes of this section and sections 360d and 360e of this title, the safety and effectiveness of a device are to be determined—

(A) with respect to the persons for whose use the device is represented or intended,

(B) with respect to the conditions of use prescribed, recommended, or suggested in the labeling of the device, and

(C) weighing any probable benefit to health from the use of the device against any probable risk of injury or illness from such use.

(3)(A) Except as authorized by subparagraph (B), the effectiveness of a device is, for purposes of this section and sections 360d and 360e of this title, to be determined, in accordance with regulations promulgated by the Secretary, on the basis of well-controlled investigations, including 1 or more clinical investigations where appropriate, by experts qualified by training and experience to evaluate the effectiveness of the device, from which investigations it can fairly and responsibly be concluded by qualified experts that the device will have the effect it purports or is represented to have under the conditions of use prescribed, recommended, or suggested in the labeling of the device.

(B) If the Secretary determines that there exists valid scientific evidence (other than evidence derived from investigations described in subparagraph (A))—

(i) which is sufficient to determine the effectiveness of a device, and

(ii) from which it can fairly and responsibly be concluded by qualified experts that the device will have the effect it purports or is represented to have under the conditions of use prescribed, recommended, or suggested in the labeling of the device,

then, for purposes of this section and sections 360d and 360e of this title, the Secretary may authorize the effectiveness of the device to be determined on the basis of such evidence.

(C) In making a determination of a reasonable assurance of the effectiveness of a device for which an application under section 360e of this title has been submitted, the Secretary shall consider whether the extent of data that otherwise would be required for approval of the application with respect to effectiveness can be reduced through reliance on postmarket controls.

(D)(i) The Secretary, upon the written request of any person intending to submit an application under section 360e of this title, shall meet with such person to determine the type of valid scientific evidence (within the meaning of subparagraphs (A) and (B)) that will be necessary to demonstrate for purposes of approval of an application the effectiveness of a device for the conditions of use proposed by such person. The written request shall include a detailed description of the device, a detailed description of the proposed conditions of use of the device, a proposed plan for determining whether there is a reasonable assurance of effectiveness, and, if available, information

1166

regarding the expected performance from the device. Within 30 days after such meeting, the Secretary shall specify in writing the type of valid scientific evidence that will provide a reasonable assurance that a device is effective under the conditions of use proposed by such person.

(ii) Any clinical data, including one or more well-controlled investigations, specified in writing by the Secretary for demonstrating a reasonable assurance of device effectiveness shall be specified as result of a determination by the Secretary that such data are necessary to establish device effectiveness. The Secretary shall consider, in consultation with the applicant, the least burdensome appropriate means of evaluating device effectiveness that would have a reasonable likelihood of resulting in approval.

(iii) The determination of the Secretary with respect to the specification of valid scientific evidence under clauses (i) and (ii) shall be binding upon the Secretary, unless such determination by the Secretary could be contrary to the public health.

(b) Classification panels

(1) For purposes of—

(A) determining which devices intended for human use should be subject to the requirements of general controls, performance standards, or premarket approval, and

(B) providing notice to the manufacturers and importers of such devices to enable them to prepare for the application of such requirements to devices manufactured or imported by them,

the Secretary shall classify all such devices (other than devices classified by subsection (f) of this section) into the classes established by subsection (a) of this section. For the purpose of securing recommendations with respect to the classification of devices, the Secretary shall establish panels of experts or use panels of experts established before May 28, 1976, or both. Section 14 of the Federal Advisory Committee Act shall not apply to the duration of a panel established under this paragraph.

(2) The Secretary shall appoint to each panel established under paragraph (1) persons who are qualified by training and experience to evaluate the safety and effectiveness of the devices to be referred to the panel and who, to the extent feasible, possess skill in the use of, or experience in the development, manufacture, or utilization of, such devices. The Secretary shall make appointments to each panel so that each panel shall consist of members with adequately diversified expertise in such fields as clinical and administrative medicine, engineering, biological and physical sciences, and other related professions. In addition, each panel shall include as nonvoting members a representative of consumer interests and a representative of interests of the device manufacturing industry. Scientific, trade, and consumer organizations shall be afforded

an opportunity to nominate individuals for appointment to the panels. No individual who is in the regular full-time employ of the United States and engaged in the administration of this chapter may be a member of any panel. The Secretary shall designate one of the members of each panel to serve as chairman thereof.

(3) Panel members (other than officers or employees of the United States), while attending meetings or conferences of a panel or otherwise engaged in its business, shall be entitled to receive compensation at rates to be fixed by the Secretary, but not at rates exceeding the daily equivalent of the rate in effect for grade GS–18 of the General Schedule, for each day so engaged, including traveltime; and while so serving away from their homes or regular places of business each member may be allowed travel expenses (including per diem in lieu of subsistence) as authorized by section 5703 of Title 5, for persons in the Government service employed intermittently.

(4) The Secretary shall furnish each panel with adequate clerical and other necessary assistance.

(5) Classification panels covering each type of device shall be scheduled to meet at such times as may be appropriate for the Secretary to meet applicable statutory deadlines.

(6)(A) Any person whose device is specifically the subject of review by a classification panel shall have—

(i) the same access to data and information submitted to a classification panel (except for data and information that are not available for public disclosure under section 552 of Title 5) as the Secretary;

(ii) the opportunity to submit, for review by a classification panel, information that is based on the data or information provided in the application submitted under section 360e of this title by the person, which information shall be submitted to the Secretary for prompt transmittal to the classification panel; and

(iii) the same opportunity as the Secretary to participate in meetings of the panel.

(B) Any meetings of a classification panel shall provide adequate time for initial presentations and for response to any differing views by persons whose devices are specifically the subject of a classification panel review, and shall encourage free and open participation by all interested persons.

(7) After receiving from a classification panel the conclusions and recommendations of the panel on a matter that the panel has reviewed, the Secretary shall review the conclusions and recommendations, shall make a final decision on the matter in accordance with section 360e(d)(2) of this title, and shall notify the affected persons of the decision in writing

and, if the decision differs from the conclusions and recommendations of the panel, shall include the reasons for the difference.

(8) A classification panel under this subsection shall not be subject to the annual chartering and annual report requirements of the Federal Advisory Committee Act.

(c) Classification panel organization and operation

(1) The Secretary shall organize the panels according to the various fields of clinical medicine and fundamental sciences in which devices intended for human use are used. The Secretary shall refer a device to be classified under this section to an appropriate panel established or authorized to be used under subsection (b) of this section for its review and for its recommendation respecting the classification of the device. The Secretary shall by regulation prescribe the procedure to be followed by the panels in making their reviews and recommendations. In making their reviews of devices, the panels, to the maximum extent practicable, shall provide an opportunity for interested persons to submit data and views on the classification of the devices.

(2)(A) Upon completion of a panel's review of a device referred to it under paragraph (1), the panel shall, subject to subparagraphs (B) and (C), submit to the Secretary its recommendation for the classification of the device. Any such recommendation shall

> **(i)** contain

>> **(I)** a summary of the reasons for the recommendation,

>> **(II)** a summary of the data upon which the recommendation is based, and

>> **(III)** an identification of the risks to health (if any) presented by the device with respect to which the recommendation is made, and

> **(ii)** to the extent practicable, include a recommendation for the assignment of a priority for the application of the requirements of section 360d or 360e of this title to a device recommended to be classified in class II or class III.

(B) A recommendation of a panel for the classification of a device in class I shall include a recommendation as to whether the device should be exempted from the requirements of section 360, 360i, or 360j(f) of this title.

(C) In the case of a device which has been referred under paragraph (1) to a panel, and which—

> **(i)** is intended to be implanted in the human body or is purported or represented to be for a use in supporting or sustaining human life, and

(ii)(I) has been introduced or delivered for introduction into interstate commerce for commercial distribution before May 28, 1976, or

(II) is within a type of device which was so introduced or delivered before such date and is substantially equivalent to another device within that type,

such panel shall recommend to the Secretary that the device be classified in class III unless the panel determines that classification of the device in such class is not necessary to provide reasonable assurance of its safety and effectiveness. If a panel does not recommend that such a device be classified in class III, it shall in its recommendation to the Secretary for the classification of the device set forth the reasons for not recommending classification of the device in such class.

(3) The panels shall submit to the Secretary within one year of the date funds are first appropriated for the implementation of this section their recommendations respecting all devices of a type introduced or delivered for introduction into interstate commerce for commercial distribution before May 28, 1976.

(d) Panel recommendation; publication; priorities

(1) Upon receipt of a recommendation from a panel respecting a device, the Secretary shall publish in the Federal Register the panel's recommendation and a proposed regulation classifying such device and shall provide interested persons an opportunity to submit comments on such recommendation and the proposed regulation. After reviewing such comments, the Secretary shall, subject to paragraph (2), by regulation classify such device.

(2)(A) A regulation under paragraph (1) classifying a device in class I shall prescribe which, if any, of the requirements of section 360, 360i, or 360j(f) of this title shall not apply to the device. A regulation which makes a requirement of section 360, 360i, or 360j(f) of this title inapplicable to a device shall be accompanied by a statement of the reasons of the Secretary for making such requirement inapplicable.

(B) A device described in subsection (c)(2)(C) of this section shall be classified in class III unless the Secretary determines that classification of the device in such class is not necessary to provide reasonable assurance of its safety and effectiveness. A proposed regulation under paragraph (1) classifying such a device in a class other than class III shall be accompanied by a full statement of the reasons of the Secretary (and supporting documentation and data) for not classifying such device in such class and an identification of the risks to health (if any) presented by such device.

(3) In the case of devices classified in class II and devices classified under this subsection in class III and described in section 360e(b)(1) of this title the Secretary may establish priorities which, in his discretion, shall be used in applying sections 360d and 360e of this title, as appropriate, to such devices.

(e) Classification changes

(1) Based on new information respecting a device, the Secretary may, upon his own initiative or upon petition of an interested person, by regulation

    (A) change such device's classification, and

    (B) revoke, because of the change in classification, any regulation or requirement in effect under section 360d or 360e of this title with respect to such device. In the promulgation of such a regulation respecting a device's classification, the Secretary may secure from the panel to which the device was last referred pursuant to subsection (c) of this section a recommendation respecting the proposed change in the device's classification and shall publish in the Federal Register any recommendation submitted to the Secretary by the panel respecting such change. A regulation under this subsection changing the classification of a device from class III to class II may provide that such classification shall not take effect until the effective date of a performance standard established under section 360d of this title for such device.

(2) By regulation promulgated under paragraph (1), the Secretary may change the classification of a device from class III—

    (A) to class II if the Secretary determines that special controls would provide reasonable assurance of the safety and effectiveness of the device and that general controls would not provide reasonable assurance of the safety and effectiveness of the device, or

    (B) to class I if the Secretary determines that general controls would provide reasonable assurance of the safety and effectiveness of the device.

(f) Initial classification and reclassification of certain devices

(1) Any device intended for human use which was not introduced or delivered for introduction into interstate commerce for commercial distribution before May 28, 1976, is classified in class III unless—

    (A) the device—

        (i) is within a type of device

            (I) which was introduced or delivered for introduction into interstate commerce for commercial distribution before such date and which is to be classified pursuant to subsection (b) of this section, or

            (II) which was not so introduced or delivered before such date and has been classified in class I or II, and

(ii) is substantially equivalent to another device within such type, or

(B) the Secretary in response to a petition submitted under paragraph (3) has classified such device in class I or II.

A device classified in class III under this paragraph shall be classified in that class until the effective date of an order of the Secretary under paragraph (2) or (3) classifying the device in class I or II.

(2)(A) Any person who submits a report under section 360(k) of this title for a type of device that has not been previously classified under this chapter, and that is classified into class III under paragraph (1), may request, within 30 days after receiving written notice of such a classification, the Secretary to classify the device under the criteria set forth in subparagraphs (A) through (C) of subsection (a)(1) of this section. The person may, in the request, recommend to the Secretary a classification for the device. Any such request shall describe the device and provide detailed information and reasons for the recommended classification.

(B)(i) Not later than 60 days after the date of the submission of the request under subparagraph (A), the Secretary shall by written order classify the device involved. Such classification shall be the initial classification of the device for purposes of paragraph (1) and any device classified under this paragraph shall be a predicate device for determining substantial equivalence under paragraph (1).

(ii) A device that remains in class III under this subparagraph shall be deemed to be adulterated within the meaning of section 351(f)(1)(B) of this title until approved under section 360e of this title or exempted from such approval under section 360j(g) of this title.

(C) Within 30 days after the issuance of an order classifying a device under this paragraph, the Secretary shall publish a notice in the Federal Register announcing such classification.

(3)(A) The Secretary may initiate the reclassification of a device classified into class III under paragraph (1) of this subsection or the manufacturer or importer of a device classified under paragraph (1) may petition the Secretary (in such form and manner as he shall prescribe) for the issuance of an order classifying the device in class I or class II. Within thirty days of the filing of such a petition, the Secretary shall notify the petitioner of any deficiencies in the petition which prevent the Secretary from making a decision on the petition.

(B)(i) Upon determining that a petition does not contain any deficiency which prevents the Secretary from making a decision on the petition, the Secretary may for good cause shown refer the petition to an appropriate panel established or authorized to be used under subsection (b) of this section. A panel to which such a petition has been referred shall not later than ninety days after the referral of

1172

the petition make a recommendation to the Secretary respecting approval or denial of the petition. Any such recommendation shall contain

(I) a summary of the reasons for the recommendation,

(II) a summary of the data upon which the recommendation is based, and

(III) an identification of the risks to health (if any) presented by the device with respect to which the petition was filed. In the case of a petition for a device which is intended to be implanted in the human body or which is purported or represented to be for a use in supporting or sustaining human life, the panel shall recommend that the petition be denied unless the panel determines that the classification in class III of the device is not necessary to provide reasonable assurance of its safety and effectiveness. If the panel recommends that such petition be approved, it shall in its recommendation to the Secretary set forth its reasons for such recommendation.

(ii) The requirements of paragraphs (1) and (2) of subsection (c) of this section (relating to opportunities for submission of data and views and recommendations respecting priorities and exemptions from sections 360, 360i, and 360j(f) of this title) shall apply with respect to consideration by panels of petitions submitted under subparagraph (A).

(C)(i) Within ninety days from the date the Secretary receives the recommendation of a panel respecting a petition (but not later than 210 days after the filing of such petition) the Secretary shall by order deny or approve the petition. If the Secretary approves the petition, the Secretary shall order the classification of the device into class I or class II in accordance with the criteria prescribed by subsection (a)(1)(A) or (a)(1)(B) of this section. In the case of a petition for a device which is intended to be implanted in the human body or which is purported or represented to be for a use in supporting or sustaining human life, the Secretary shall deny the petition unless the Secretary determines that the classification in class III of the device is not necessary to provide reasonable assurance of its safety and effectiveness. An order approving such petition shall be accompanied by a full statement of the reasons of the Secretary (and supporting documentation and data) for approving the petition and an identification of the risks to health (if any) presented by the device to which such order applies.

(ii) The requirements of paragraphs (1) and (2)(A) of subsection (d) of this section (relating to publication of recommendations, opportunity for submission of comments, and exemption from sections 360, 360i, and 360j(f) of this title) shall apply with respect to action by the Secretary on petitions submitted under subparagraph (A).

(4) If a manufacturer reports to the Secretary under section 360(k) of this title that a device is substantially equivalent to another device—

(A) which the Secretary has classified as a class III device under subsection (b) of this section,

(B) which was introduced or delivered for introduction into interstate commerce for commercial distribution before December 1, 1990, and

(C) for which no final regulation requiring premarket approval has been promulgated under section 360e(b) of this title,

the manufacturer shall certify to the Secretary that the manufacturer has conducted a reasonable search of all information known or otherwise available to the manufacturer respecting such other device and has included in the report under section 360(k) of this title a summary of and a citation to all adverse safety and effectiveness data respecting such other device and respecting the device for which the section 360(k) report is being made and which has not been submitted to the Secretary under section 360i of this title. The Secretary may require the manufacturer to submit the adverse safety and effectiveness data described in the report.

(5) The Secretary may not withhold a determination of the initial classification of a device under paragraph (1) because of a failure to comply with any provision of this chapter unrelated to a substantial equivalence decision, including a finding that the facility in which the device is manufactured is not in compliance with good manufacturing requirements as set forth in regulations of the Secretary under section 360j(f) of this title (other than a finding that there is a substantial likelihood that the failure to comply with such regulations will potentially present a serious risk to human health).

(g) Information

Within sixty days of the receipt of a written request of any person for information respecting the class in which a device has been classified or the requirements applicable to a device under this chapter, the Secretary shall provide such person a written statement of the classification (if any) of such device and the requirements of this chapter applicable to the device.

(h) Definitions

For purposes of this section and sections 351, 360, 360d, 360e, 360f, 360i, and 360j of this title

(1) a reference to "general controls" is a reference to the controls authorized by or under sections 351, 352, 360, 360f, 360h, 360i, and 360j of this title,

(2) a reference to "class I", "class II", or "class III" is a reference to a class of medical devices described in subparagraph (A), (B), or (C) of subsection (a)(1) of this section, and

(3) a reference to a "panel under section 360c of this title" is a reference to a panel established or authorized to be used under this section.

(i) Substantial equivalence

(1)(A) For purposes of determinations of substantial equivalence under subsection (f) of this section and section 360j(*l*) of this title, the term "substantially equivalent" or "substantial equivalence" means, with respect to a device being compared to a predicate device, that the device has the same intended use as the predicate device and that the Secretary by order has found that the device—

    (i) has the same technological characteristics as the predicate device, or

    (ii)(I) has different technological characteristics and the information submitted that the device is substantially equivalent to the predicate device contains information, including appropriate clinical or scientific data if deemed necessary by the Secretary or a person accredited under section 360m of this title, that demonstrates that the device is as safe and effective as a legally marketed device, and

        (II) does not raise different questions of safety and effectiveness than the predicate device.

(B) For purposes of subparagraph (A), the term "different technological characteristics" means, with respect to a device being compared to a predicate device, that there is a significant change in the materials, design, energy source, or other features of the device from those of the predicate device.

(C) To facilitate reviews of reports submitted to the Secretary under section 360(k) of this title, the Secretary shall consider the extent to which reliance on postmarket controls may expedite the classification of devices under subsection (f)(1) of this section.

(D) Whenever the Secretary requests information to demonstrate that devices with differing technological characteristics are substantially equivalent, the Secretary shall only request information that is necessary to making substantial equivalence determinations. In making such request, the Secretary shall consider the least burdensome means of demonstrating substantial equivalence and request information accordingly.

(E)(i) Any determination by the Secretary of the intended use of a device shall be based upon the proposed labeling submitted in a report for the device under section 360(k) of this title. However, when determining that a device can be found substantially equivalent

1175

to a legally marketed device, the director of the organizational unit responsible for regulating devices (in this subparagraph referred to as the "Director") may require a statement in labeling that provides appropriate information regarding a use of the device not identified in the proposed labeling if, after providing an opportunity for consultation with the person who submitted such report, the Director determines and states in writing—

(I) that there is a reasonable likelihood that the device will be used for an intended use not identified in the proposed labeling for the device; and

(II) that such use could cause harm.

(ii) Such determination shall—

(I) be provided to the person who submitted the report within 10 days from the date of the notification of the Director's concerns regarding the proposed labeling;

(II) specify the limitations on the use of the device not included in the proposed labeling; and

(III) find the device substantially equivalent if the requirements of subparagraph (A) are met and if the labeling for such device conforms to the limitations specified in subclause (II).

(iii) The responsibilities of the Director under this subparagraph may not be delegated.

(iv) This subparagraph has no legal effect after the expiration of the five-year period beginning on November 21, 1997.

(F) Not later than 270 days after November 21, 1997, the Secretary shall issue guidance specifying the general principles that the Secretary will consider in determining when a specific intended use of a device is not reasonably included within a general use of such device for purposes of a determination of substantial equivalence under subsection (f) of this section or section 360j(*l*) of this title.

(2) A device may not be found to be substantially equivalent to a predicate device that has been removed from the market at the initiative of the Secretary or that has been determined to be misbranded or adulterated by a judicial order.

(3)(A) As part of a submission under section 360(k) of this title respecting a device, the person required to file a premarket notification under such section shall provide an adequate summary of any information respecting safety and effectiveness or state that such information will be made available upon request by any person.

(B) Any summary under subparagraph (A) respecting a device shall contain detailed information regarding data concerning adverse health effects and shall be made available to the public by the Secretary within 30 days of the issuance of a determination that such device is substantially equivalent to another device.

§ 360d. Performance standards

(a) Reasonable assurance of safe and effective performance; periodic evaluation

(1) The special controls required by section 360c(a)(1)(B) of this title shall include performance standards for a class II device if the Secretary determines that a performance standard is necessary to provide reasonable assurance of the safety and effectiveness of the device. A class III device may also be considered a class II device for purposes of establishing a standard for the device under subsection (b) of this section if the device has been reclassified as a class II device under a regulation under section 360c(e) of this title but such regulation provides that the reclassification is not to take effect until the effective date of such a standard for the device.

(2) A performance standard established under subsection (b) of this section for a device—

(A) shall include provisions to provide reasonable assurance of its safe and effective performance;

(B) shall, where necessary to provide reasonable assurance of its safe and effective performance, include—

(i) provisions respecting the construction, components, ingredients, and properties of the device and its compatibility with power systems and connections to such systems,

(ii) provisions for the testing (on a sample basis or, if necessary, on an individual basis) of the device or, if it is determined that no other more practicable means are available to the Secretary to assure the conformity of the device to the standard, provisions for the testing (on a sample basis or, if necessary, on an individual basis) by the Secretary or by another person at the direction of the Secretary,

(iii) provisions for the measurement of the performance characteristics of the device,

(iv) provisions requiring that the results of each or of certain of the tests of the device required to be made under clause (ii) show that the device is in conformity with the portions of the standard for which the test or tests were required, and

(v) a provision requiring that the sale and distribution of the device be restricted but only to the extent that the sale and distribution of a device may be restricted under a regulation under section 360j(e) of this title; and

(**C**) shall, where appropriate, require the use and prescribe the form and content of labeling for the proper installation, maintenance, operation, and use of the device.

(**3**) The Secretary shall provide for periodic evaluation of performance standards established under subsection (b) of this section to determine if such standards should be changed to reflect new medical, scientific, or other technological data.

(**4**) In carrying out his duties under this subsection and subsection (b) of this section, the Secretary shall, to the maximum extent practicable—

(**A**) use personnel, facilities, and other technical support available in other Federal agencies,

(**B**) consult with other Federal agencies concerned with standard-setting and other nationally or internationally recognized standard-setting entities, and

(**C**) invite appropriate participation, through joint or other conferences, workshops, or other means, by informed persons representative of scientific, professional, industry, or consumer organizations who in his judgment can make a significant contribution.

(**b**) Establishment of a standard

(**1**)(**A**) The Secretary shall publish in the Federal Register a notice of proposed rulemaking for the establishment, amendment, or revocation of any performance standard for a device.

(**B**) A notice of proposed rulemaking for the establishment or amendment of a performance standard for a device shall—

(**i**) set forth a finding with supporting justification that the performance standard is appropriate and necessary to provide reasonable assurance of the safety and effectiveness of the device,

(**ii**) set forth proposed findings with respect to the risk of illness or injury that the performance standard is intended to reduce or eliminate,

(**iii**) invite interested persons to submit to the Secretary, within 30 days of the publication of the notice, requests for changes in the classification of the device pursuant to section 360c(e) of this title based on new information relevant to the classification, and

(**iv**) invite interested persons to submit an existing performance standard for the device, including a draft or proposed performance standard, for consideration by the Secretary.

(**C**) A notice of proposed rulemaking for the revocation of a performance standard shall set forth a finding with supporting justification that the performance standard is no longer necessary to provide reasonable assurance of the safety and effectiveness of a device.

(D) The Secretary shall provide for a comment period of not less than 60 days.

(2) If, after publication of a notice in accordance with paragraph (1), the Secretary receives a request for a change in the classification of the device, the Secretary shall, within 60 days of the publication of the notice, after consultation with the appropriate panel under section 360c of this title, either deny the request or give notice of an intent to initiate such change under section 360c(e) of this title.

(3)(A) After the expiration of the period for comment on a notice of proposed rulemaking published under paragraph (1) respecting a performance standard and after consideration of such comments and any report from an advisory committee under paragraph (5), the Secretary shall (i) promulgate a regulation establishing a performance standard and publish in the Federal Register findings on the matters referred to in paragraph (1), or (ii) publish a notice terminating the proceeding for the development of the standard together with the reasons for such termination. If a notice of termination is published, the Secretary shall (unless such notice is issued because the device is a banned device under section 360f of this title) initiate a proceeding under section 360c(e) of this title to reclassify the device subject to the proceeding terminated by such notice.

(B) A regulation establishing a performance standard shall set forth the date of dates upon which the standard shall take effect, but no such regulation may take effect before one year after the date of its publication unless

    (i) the Secretary determines that an earlier effective date is necessary for the protection of the public health and safety, or

    (ii) such standard has been established for a device which, effective upon the effective date of the standard, has been reclassified from class III to class II. Such date or dates shall be established so as to minimize, consistent with the public health and safety, economic loss to, and disruption or dislocation of, domestic and international trade.

(4)(A) The Secretary, upon his own initiative or upon petition of an interested person may by regulation, promulgated in accordance with the requirements of paragraphs (1), (2), and (3)(B) of this subsection, amend or revoke a performance standard.

(B) The Secretary may declare a proposed amendment of a performance standard to be effective on and after its publication in the Federal Register and until the effective date of any final action taken on such amendment if he determines that making it so effective is in the public interest. A proposed amendment of a performance standard made so effective under the preceding sentence may not prohibit, during the period in which it is so effective, the introduction or delivery for introduction into interstate commerce of a device which conforms to such standard without the change or changes provided by such proposed amendment.

(5)(A) The Secretary—

 (i) may on his own initiative refer a proposed regulation for the establishment, amendment, or revocation of a performance standard, or

 (ii) shall, upon the request of an interested person which demonstrates good cause for referral and which is made before the expiration of the period for submission of comments on such proposed regulation refer such proposed regulation,

to an advisory committee of experts, established pursuant to subparagraph (B), for a report and recommendation with respect to any matter involved in the proposed regulation which requires the exercise of scientific judgment. If a proposed regulation is referred under this subparagraph to an advisory committee, the Secretary shall provide the advisory committee with the data and information on which such proposed regulation is based. The advisory committee shall, within sixty days of the referral of a proposed regulation and after independent study of the data and information furnished to it by the Secretary and other data and information before it, submit to the Secretary a report and recommendation respecting such regulation, together with all underlying data and information and a statement of the reason or basis for the recommendation. A copy of such report and recommendation shall be made public by the Secretary.

(B) The Secretary shall establish advisory committees (which may not be panels under section 360c of this title) to receive referrals under subparagraph (A). The Secretary shall appoint as members of any such advisory committee persons qualified in the subject matter to be referred to the committee and of appropriately diversified professional background, except that the Secretary may not appoint to such a committee any individual who is in the regular full-time employ of the United States and engaged in the administration of this chapter. Each such committee shall include as nonvoting members a representative of consumer interests and a representative of interests of the device manufacturing industry. Members of an advisory committee who are not officers or employees of the United States, while attending conferences or meetings of their committee or otherwise serving at the request of the Secretary, shall be entitled to receive compensation at rates to be fixed by the Secretary, which rates may not exceed the daily equivalent of the rate in effect for grade GS–18 of the General Schedule, for each day (including travel-time) they are so engaged; and while so serving away from their homes or regular places of business each member may be allowed travel expenses, including per diem in lieu of subsistence, as authorized by section 5703 of Title 5 for persons in the Government service employed intermittently. The Secretary shall designate one of the members of each advisory committee to serve as chairman thereof. The Secretary shall furnish each advisory committee with clerical and other assistance, and shall by regulation prescribe the procedures to be followed by each such committee in acting on referrals made under subparagraph (A).

(c) Recognition of a standard

(1)(A) In addition to establishing a performance standard under this section, the Secretary shall, by publication in the Federal Register, recognize all or part of an appropriate standard established by a nationally or internationally recognized standard development organization for which a person may submit a declaration of conformity in order to meet a premarket submission requirement or other requirement under this chapter to which such standard is applicable.

(B) If a person elects to use a standard recognized by the Secretary under subparagraph (A) to meet the requirements described in such subparagraph, the person shall provide a declaration of conformity to the Secretary that certifies that the device is in conformity with such standard. A person may elect to use data, or information, other than data required by a standard recognized under subparagraph (A) to meet any requirement regarding devices under this chapter.

(2) The Secretary may withdraw such recognition of a standard through publication of a notice in the Federal Register if the Secretary determines that the standard is no longer appropriate for meeting a requirement regarding devices under this chapter.

(3)(A) Subject to subparagraph (B), the Secretary shall accept a declaration of conformity that a device is in conformity with a standard recognized under paragraph (1) unless the Secretary finds—

(i) that the data or information submitted to support such declaration does not demonstrate that the device is in conformity with the standard identified in the declaration of conformity; or

(ii) that the standard identified in the declaration of conformity is not applicable to the particular device under review.

(B) The Secretary may request, at any time, the data or information relied on by the person to make a declaration of conformity with respect to a standard recognized under paragraph (1).

(C) A person making a declaration of conformity with respect to a standard recognized under paragraph (1) shall maintain the data and information demonstrating conformity of the device to the standard for a period of two years after the date of the classification or approval of the device by the Secretary or a period equal to the expected design life of the device, whichever is longer.

§ 360e. Premarket approval

(a) General requirement

A class III device—

(1) which is subject to a regulation promulgated under subsection (b) of this section; or

(2) which is a class III device because of section 360c(f) of this title,

is required to have, unless exempt under section 360j(g) of this title, an approval under this section of an application for premarket approval.

(b) Regulation to require premarket approval

(1) In the case of a class III device which—

(A) was introduced or delivered for introduction into interstate commerce for commercial distribution before May 28, 1976; or

(B) is

(i) of a type so introduced or delivered, and (ii) is substantially equivalent to another device within that type,

the Secretary shall by regulation, promulgated in accordance with this subsection, require that such device have an approval under this section of an application for premarket approval.

(2)(A) A proceeding for the promulgation of a regulation under paragraph (1) respecting a device shall be initiated by the publication in the Federal Register of a notice of proposed rulemaking. Such notice shall contain—

(i) the proposed regulation;

(ii) proposed findings with respect to the degree of risk of illness or injury designed to be eliminated or reduced by requiring the device to have an approved application for premarket approval and the benefit to the public from use of the device;

(iii) opportunity for the submission of comments on the proposed regulation and the proposed findings; and

(iv) opportunity to request a change in the classification of the device based on new information relevant to the classification of the device.

(B) If, within fifteen days after publication of a notice under subparagraph (A), the Secretary receives a request for a change in the classification of a device, he shall, within sixty days of the publication of such notice and after consultation with the appropriate panel under section 360c of this title, by order published in the Federal Register, either deny the request for change in classification or give notice of his intent to initiate such a change under section 360c(e) of this title.

(3) After the expiration of the period for comment on a proposed regulation and proposed findings published under paragraph (2) and after consideration of comments submitted on such proposed regulation and findings, the Secretary shall (A) promulgate such regulation and publish in the Federal Register findings on the matters referred to in paragraph (2)(A)(ii), or (B) publish a notice terminating the proceeding for the promulgation of the regulation together with the reasons for such termination. If a notice of termination is published, the Secretary shall (unless such notice is issued because the device is a banned device under section 360f of this title) initiate a proceeding under section 360c(e) of this title to reclassify the device subject to the proceeding terminated by such notice.

(4) The Secretary, upon his own initiative or upon petition of an interested person, may by regulation amend or revoke any regulation promulgated under this subsection. A regulation to amend or revoke a regulation under this subsection shall be promulgated in accordance with the requirements prescribed by this subsection for the promulgation of the regulation to be amended or revoked.

(c) Application for premarket approval

(1) Any person may file with the Secretary an application for premarket approval for a class III device. Such an application for a device shall contain—

(A) full reports of all information, published or known to or which should reasonably be known to the applicant, concerning investigations which have been made to show whether or not such device is safe and effective;

(B) a full statement of the components, ingredients, and properties and of the principle or principles of operation, of such device;

(C) a full description of the methods used in, and the facilities and controls used for, the manufacture, processing, and, when relevant, packing and installation of, such device;

(D) an identifying reference to any performance standard under section 360d of this title which would be applicable to any aspect of such device if it were a class II device, and either adequate information to show that such aspect of such device fully meets such performance standard or adequate information to justify any deviation from such standard;

(E) such samples of such device and of components thereof as the Secretary may reasonably require, except that where the submission of such samples is impracticable or unduly burdensome, the requirement of this subparagraph may be met by the submission of complete information concerning the location of one or more such devices readily available for examination and testing;

(F) specimens of the labeling proposed to be used for such device; and

(G) such other information relevant to the subject matter of the application as the Secretary, with the concurrence of the appropriate panel under section 360c of this title, may require.

(2) Upon receipt of an application meeting the requirements set forth in paragraph (1), the Secretary—

(A) may on the Secretary's own initiative, or

(B) shall, upon the request of an applicant unless the Secretary finds that the information in the application which would be reviewed by a panel substantially duplicates information which has previously been reviewed by a panel appointed under section 360c of this title,

refer such application to the appropriate panel under section 360c of this title for study and for submission (within such period as he may establish) of a report and recommendation respecting approval of the application, together with all underlying data and the reasons or basis for the recommendation.

(d) Action on application for premarket approval

(1)(A) As promptly as possible, but in no event later than one hundred and eighty days after the receipt of an application under subsection (c) of this section (except as provided in section 360j(*l*)(3)(D)(ii) of this title or unless, in accordance with subparagraph (B)(i), an additional period as agreed upon by the Secretary and the applicant), the Secretary, after considering the report and recommendation submitted under paragraph (2) of such subsection, shall—

(i) issue an order approving the application if he finds that none of the grounds for denying approval specified in paragraph (2) of this subsection applies; or

(ii) deny approval of the application if he finds (and sets forth the basis for such finding as part of or accompanying such denial) that one or more grounds for denial specified in paragraph (2) of this subsection apply.

In making the determination whether to approve or deny the application, the Secretary shall rely on the conditions of use included in the proposed labeling as the basis for determining whether or not there is a reasonable assurance of safety and effectiveness, if the proposed labeling is neither false nor misleading. In determining whether or not such labeling is false or misleading, the Secretary shall fairly evaluate all material facts pertinent to the proposed labeling.

(B)(i) The Secretary may not enter into an agreement to extend the period in which to take action with respect to an application submitted for a device subject to a regulation promulgated under subsection (b) of this section unless he finds that the continued availability of the device is necessary for the public health.

(ii) An order approving an application for a device may require as a condition to such approval that the sale and distribution of the device be restricted but only to the extent that the sale and distribution of a device may be restricted under a regulation under section 360j(e) of this title.

(iii) The Secretary shall accept and review statistically valid and reliable data and any other information from investigations conducted under the authority of regulations required by section 360j(g) of this title to make a determination of whether there is a reasonable assurance of safety and effectiveness of a device subject to a pending application under this section if—

(I) the data or information is derived from investigations of an earlier version of the device, the device has been modified during or after the investigations (but prior to submission of an application under subsection (c) of this section) and such a modification of the device does not constitute a significant change in the design or in the basic principles of operation of the device that would invalidate the data or information; or

(II) the data or information relates to a device approved under this section, is available for use under this chapter, and is relevant to the design and intended use of the device for which the application is pending.

(2) The Secretary shall deny approval of an application for a device if, upon the basis of the information submitted to the Secretary as part of the application and any other information before him with respect to such device, the Secretary finds that—

(A) there is a lack of a showing of reasonable assurance that such device is safe under the conditions of use prescribed, recommended, or suggested in the proposed labeling thereof;

(B) there is a lack of a showing of reasonable assurance that the device is effective under the conditions of use prescribed, recommended, or suggested in the proposed labeling thereof;

(C) the methods used in, or the facilities or controls used for, the manufacture, processing, packing, or installation of such device do not conform to the requirements of section 360j(f) of this title;

(D) based on a fair evaluation of all material facts, the proposed labeling is false or misleading in any particular; or

1185

(E) such device is not shown to conform in all respects to a performance standard in effect under section 360d of this title compliance with which is a condition to approval of the application and there is a lack of adequate information to justify the deviation from such standard.

Any denial of an application shall, insofar as the Secretary determines to be practicable, be accompanied by a statement informing the applicant of the measures required to place such application in approvable form (which measures may include further research by the applicant in accordance with one or more protocols prescribed by the Secretary).

(3)(A)(i) The Secretary shall, upon the written request of an applicant, meet with the applicant, not later than 100 days after the receipt of an application that has been filed as complete under subsection (c) of this section, to discuss the review status of the application.

(ii) The Secretary shall, in writing and prior to the meeting, provide to the applicant a description of any deficiencies in the application that, at that point, have been identified by the Secretary based on an interim review of the entire application and identify the information that is required to correct those deficiencies.

(iii) The Secretary shall notify the applicant promptly of—

(I) any additional deficiency identified in the application, or

(II) any additional information required to achieve completion of the review and final action on the application,

that was not described as a deficiency in the written description provided by the Secretary under clause (ii).

(B) The Secretary and the applicant may, by mutual consent, establish a different schedule for a meeting required under this paragraph.

(4) An applicant whose application has been denied approval may, by petition filed on or before the thirtieth day after the date upon which he receives notice of such denial, obtain review thereof in accordance with either paragraph (1) or (2) of subsection (g) of this section, and any interested person may obtain review, in accordance with paragraph (1) or (2) of subsection (g) of this section, of an order of the Secretary approving an application.

(5) In order to provide for more effective treatment or diagnosis of life-threatening or irreversibly debilitating human diseases or conditions, the Secretary shall provide review priority for devices—

(A) representing breakthrough technologies,

(B) for which no approved alternatives exist,

(C) which offer significant advantages over existing approved alternatives, or

(D) the availability of which is in the best interest of the patients.

(6)(A)(i) A supplemental application shall be required for any change to a device subject to an approved application under this subsection that affects safety or effectiveness, unless such change is a modification in a manufacturing procedure or method of manufacturing and the holder of the approved application submits a written notice to the Secretary that describes in detail the change, summarizes the data or information supporting the change, and informs the Secretary that the change has been made under the requirements of section 360j(f) of this title.

(ii) The holder of an approved application who submits a notice under clause (i) with respect to a manufacturing change of a device may distribute the device 30 days after the date on which the Secretary receives the notice, unless the Secretary within such 30–day period notifies the holder that the notice is not adequate and describes such further information or action that is required for acceptance of such change. If the Secretary notifies the holder that a supplemental application is required, the Secretary shall review the supplement within 135 days after the receipt of the supplement. The time used by the Secretary to review the notice of the manufacturing change shall be deducted from the 135–day review period if the notice meets appropriate content requirements for premarket approval supplements.

(B)(i) Subject to clause (ii), in reviewing a supplement to an approved application, for an incremental change to the design of a device that affects safety or effectiveness, the Secretary shall approve such supplement if—

(I) nonclinical data demonstrate that the design modification creates the intended additional capacity, function, or performance of the device; and

(II) clinical data from the approved application and any supplement to the approved application provide a reasonable assurance of safety and effectiveness for the changed device.

(ii) The Secretary may require, when necessary, additional clinical data to evaluate the design modification of the device to provide a reasonable assurance of safety and effectiveness.

(e) Withdrawal and temporary suspension of approval of application

(1) The Secretary shall, upon obtaining, where appropriate, advice on scientific matters from a panel or panels under section 360c of this title, and after due notice and opportunity for informal hearing to the

holder of an approved application for a device, issue an order withdrawing approval of the application if the Secretary finds—

(A) that such device is unsafe or ineffective under the conditions of use prescribed, recommended, or suggested in the labeling thereof;

(B) on the basis of new information before him with respect to such device, evaluated together with the evidence available to him when the application was approved, that there is a lack of a showing of reasonable assurance that the device is safe or effective under the conditions of use prescribed, recommended, or suggested in the labeling thereof;

(C) that the application contained or was accompanied by an untrue statement of a material fact;

(D) that the applicant (i) has failed to establish a system for maintaining records, or has repeatedly or deliberately failed to maintain records or to make reports, required by an applicable regulation under section 360i(a) of this title, (ii) has refused to permit access to, or copying or verification of, such records as required by section 374 of this title, or (iii) has not complied with the requirements of section 360 of this title;

(E) on the basis of new information before him with respect to such device, evaluated together with the evidence before him when the application was approved, that the methods used in, or the facilities and controls used for, the manufacture, processing, packing, or installation of such device do not conform with the requirements of section 360j(f) of this title and were not brought into conformity with such requirements within a reasonable time after receipt of written notice from the Secretary of nonconformity;

(F) on the basis of new information before him, evaluated together with the evidence before him when the application was approved, that the labeling of such device, based on a fair evaluation of all material facts, is false or misleading in any particular and was not corrected within a reasonable time after receipt of written notice from the Secretary of such fact; or

(G) on the basis of new information before him, evaluated together with the evidence before him when the application was approved, that such device is not shown to conform in all respects to a performance standard which is in effect under section 360d of this title compliance with which was a condition to approval of the application and that there is a lack of adequate information to justify the deviation from such standard.

(2) The holder of an application subject to an order issued under paragraph (1) withdrawing approval of the application may, by petition filed on or before the thirtieth day after the date upon which he receives notice of such withdrawal, obtain review thereof in accordance with either paragraph (1) or (2) of subsection (g) of this section.

(3) If, after providing an opportunity for an informal hearing, the Secretary determines there is reasonable probability that the continuation of distribution of a device under an approved application would cause serious, adverse health consequences or death, the Secretary shall by order temporarily suspend the approval of the application approved under this section. If the Secretary issues such an order, the Secretary shall proceed expeditiously under paragraph (1) to withdraw such application.

(f) Product development protocol

(1) In the case of a class III device which is required to have an approval of an application submitted under subsection (c) of this section, such device shall be considered as having such an approval if a notice of completion of testing conducted in accordance with a product development protocol approved under paragraph (4) has been declared completed under paragraph (6).

(2) Any person may submit to the Secretary a proposed product development protocol with respect to a device. Such a protocol shall be accompanied by data supporting it. If, within thirty days of the receipt of such a protocol, the Secretary determines that it appears to be appropriate to apply the requirements of this subsection to the device with respect to which the protocol is submitted, the Secretary—

    (A) may, at the initiative of the Secretary, refer the proposed protocol to the appropriate panel under section 360c of this title for its recommendation respecting approval of the protocol; or

    (B) shall so refer such protocol upon the request of the submitter, unless the Secretary finds that the proposed protocol and accompanying data which would be reviewed by such panel substantially duplicate a product development protocol and accompanying data which have previously been reviewed by such a panel.

(3) A proposed product development protocol for a device may be approved only if—

    (A) the Secretary determines that it is appropriate to apply the requirements of this subsection to the device in lieu of the requirement of approval of an application submitted under subsection (c) of this section; and

    (B) the Secretary determines that the proposed protocol provides—

        (i) a description of the device and the changes which may be made in the device,

(ii) a description of the preclinical trials (if any) of the device and a specification of

(I) the results from such trials to be required before the commencement of clinical trials of the device, and

(II) any permissible variations in preclinical trials and the results therefrom,

(iii) a description of the clinical trials (if any) of the device and a specification of

(I) the results from such trials to be required before the filing of a notice of completion of the requirements of the protocol, and

(II) any permissible variations in such trials and the results therefrom,

(iv) a description of the methods to be used in, and the facilities and controls to be used for, the manufacture, processing, and, when relevant, packing and installation of the device,

(v) an identifying reference to any performance standard under section 360d of this title to be applicable to any aspect of such device,

(vi) if appropriate, specimens of the labeling proposed to be used for such device,

(vii) such other information relevant to the subject matter of the protocol as the Secretary, with the concurrence of the appropriate panel or panels under section 360c of this title, may require, and

(viii) a requirement for submission of progress reports and, when completed, records of the trials conducted under the protocol which records are adequate to show compliance with the protocol.

(4) The Secretary shall approve or disapprove a proposed product development protocol submitted under paragraph (2) within one hundred and twenty days of its receipt unless an additional period is agreed upon by the Secretary and the person who submitted the protocol. Approval of a protocol or denial of approval of a protocol is final agency action subject to judicial review under chapter 7 of Title 5.

(5) At any time after a product development protocol for a device has been approved pursuant to paragraph (4), the person for whom the protocol was approved may submit a notice of completion—

(A) stating

(i) his determination that the requirements of the protocol have been fulfilled and that, to the best of his knowledge, there is no reason bearing on safety or effectiveness why the notice of completion should not become effective, and

(ii) the data and other information upon which such determination was made, and

(B) setting forth the results of the trials required by the protocol and all the information required by subsection (c)(1) of this section.

(6)(A) The Secretary may, after providing the person who has an approved protocol an opportunity for an informal hearing and at any time prior to receipt of notice of completion of such protocol, issue a final order to revoke such protocol if he finds that—

    (i) such person has failed substantially to comply with the requirements of the protocol,

    (ii) the results of the trials obtained under the protocol differ so substantially from the results required by the protocol that further trials cannot be justified, or

    (iii) the results of the trials conducted under the protocol or available new information do not demonstrate that the device tested under the protocol does not present an unreasonable risk to health and safety.

(B) After the receipt of a notice of completion of an approved protocol the Secretary shall, within the ninety-day period beginning on the date such notice is received, by order either declare the protocol completed or declare it not completed. An order declaring a protocol not completed may take effect only after the Secretary has provided the person who has the protocol opportunity for an informal hearing on the order. Such an order may be issued only if the Secretary finds—

    (i) such person has failed substantially to comply with the requirements of the protocol,

    (ii) the results of the trials obtained under the protocol differ substantially from the results required by the protocol, or

    (iii) there is a lack of a showing of reasonable assurance of the safety and effectiveness of the device under the conditions of use prescribed, recommended, or suggested in the proposed labeling thereof.

(C) A final order issued under subparagraph (A) or (B) shall be in writing and shall contain the reasons to support the conclusions thereof.

(7) At any time after a notice of completion has become effective, the Secretary may issue an order (after due notice and opportunity for an informal hearing to the person for whom the notice is effective) revoking the approval of a device provided by a notice of completion which has become effective as provided in subparagraph (B) if he finds that any of the grounds listed in subparagraphs (A) through (G) of subsection (e)(1) of this section apply. Each reference in such subparagraphs to an applica-

tion shall be considered for purposes of this paragraph as a reference to a protocol and the notice of completion of such protocol, and each reference to the time when an application was approved shall be considered for purposes of this paragraph as a reference to the time when a notice of completion took effect.

(8) A person who has an approved protocol subject to an order issued under paragraph (6)(A) revoking such protocol, a person who has an approved protocol with respect to which an order under paragraph (6)(B) was issued declaring that the protocol had not been completed, or a person subject to an order issued under paragraph (7) revoking the approval of a device may, by petition filed on or before the thirtieth day after the date upon which he receives notice of such order, obtain review thereof in accordance with either paragraph (1) or (2) of subsection (g) of this section.

(g) Review

(1) Upon petition for review of—

(A) an order under subsection (d) of this section approving or denying approval of an application or an order under subsection (e) of this section withdrawing approval of an application, or

(B) an order under subsection (f)(6)(A) of this section revoking an approved protocol, under subsection (f)(6)(B) of this section declaring that an approved protocol has not been completed, or under subsection (f)(7) of this section revoking the approval of a device,

the Secretary shall, unless he finds the petition to be without good cause or unless a petition for review of such order has been submitted under paragraph (2), hold a hearing, in accordance with section 554 of Title 5, on the order. The panel or panels which considered the application, protocol, or device subject to such order shall designate a member to appear and testify at any such hearing upon request of the Secretary, the petitioner, or the officer conducting the hearing, but this requirement does not preclude any other member of the panel or panels from appearing and testifying at any such hearing. Upon completion of such hearing and after considering the record established in such hearing, the Secretary shall issue an order either affirming the order subject to the hearing or reversing such order and, as appropriate, approving or denying approval of the application, reinstating the application's approval, approving the protocol, or placing in effect a notice of completion.

(2)(A) Upon petition for review of—

(i) an order under subsection (d) of this section approving or denying approval of an application or an order under subsection (e) of this section withdrawing approval of an application, or

(ii) an order under subsection (f)(6)(A) of this section revoking an approved protocol, under subsection (f)(6)(B) of this section declaring that an approved protocol has not been completed, or under subsection (f)(7) of this section revoking the approval of a device,

the Secretary shall refer the application or protocol subject to the order and the basis for the order to an advisory committee of experts established pursuant to subparagraph (B) for a report and recommendation with respect to the order. The advisory committee shall, after independent study of the data and information furnished to it by the Secretary and other data and information before it, submit to the Secretary a report and recommendation, together with all underlying data and information and a statement of the reasons or basis for the recommendation. A copy of such report shall be promptly supplied by the Secretary to any person who petitioned for such referral to the advisory committee.

(B) The Secretary shall establish advisory committees (which may not be panels under section 360c of this title) to receive referrals under subparagraph (A). The Secretary shall appoint as members of any such advisory committee persons qualified in the subject matter to be referred to the committee and of appropriately diversified professional backgrounds, except that the Secretary may not appoint to such a committee any individual who is in the regular full-time employ of the United States and engaged in the administration of this chapter. Members of an advisory committee (other than officers or employees of the United States), while attending conferences or meetings of their committee or otherwise serving at the request of the Secretary, shall be entitled to receive compensation at rates to be fixed by the Secretary, which rates may not exceed the daily equivalent for grade GS–18 of the General Schedule for each day (including traveltime) they are so engaged; and while so serving away from their homes or regular places of business each member may be allowed travel expenses, including per diem in lieu of subsistence, as authorized by section 5703 of Title 5 for persons in the Government service employed intermittently. The Secretary shall designate the chairman of an advisory committee from its members. The Secretary shall furnish each advisory committee with clerical and other assistance, and shall by regulation prescribe the procedures to be followed by each such committee in acting on referrals made under subparagraph (A).

(C) The Secretary shall make public the report and recommendation made by an advisory committee with respect to an application and shall by order, stating the reasons therefor, either affirm the order referred to the advisory committee or reverse such order and, if appropriate, approve or deny approval of the application, reinstate the application's approval, approve the protocol, or place in effect a notice of completion.

1193

(h) Service of orders

Orders of the Secretary under this section shall be served (1) in person by any officer or employee of the department designated by the Secretary, or (2) by mailing the order by registered mail or certified mail addressed to the applicant at his last known address in the records of the Secretary.

(i) Revision

(1) Before December 1, 1995, the Secretary shall by order require manufacturers of devices, which were introduced or delivered for introduction into interstate commerce for commercial distribution before May 28, 1976, and which are subject to revision of classification under paragraph (2), to submit to the Secretary a summary of and citation to any information known or otherwise available to the manufacturer respecting such devices, including adverse safety or effectiveness information which has not been submitted under section 360i of this title. The Secretary may require the manufacturer to submit the adverse safety or effectiveness data for which a summary and citation were submitted, if such data are available to the manufacturer.

(2) After the issuance of an order under paragraph (1) but before December 1, 1995, the Secretary shall publish a regulation in the Federal Register for each device—

(A) which the Secretary has classified as a class III device, and

(B) for which no final regulation has been promulgated under subsection (b) of this section,

revising the classification of the device so that the device is classified into class I or class II, unless the regulation requires the device to remain in class III. In determining whether to revise the classification of a device or to require a device to remain in class III, the Secretary shall apply the criteria set forth in section 360c(a) of this title. Before the publication of a regulation requiring a device to remain in class III or revising its classification, the Secretary shall publish a proposed regulation respecting the classification of a device under this paragraph and provide reasonable opportunity for the submission of comments on any such regulation. No regulation requiring a device to remain in class III or revising its classification may take effect before the expiration of 90 days from the date of its publication in the Federal Register as a proposed regulation.

(3) The Secretary shall, as promptly as is reasonably achievable, but not later than 12 months after the effective date of the regulation requiring a device to remain in class III, establish a schedule for the promulgation of a subsection (b) of this section regulation for each device which is subject to the regulation requiring the device to remain in class III.

§ 360f. Banned devices

(a) General rule

Whenever the Secretary finds, on the basis of all available data and information that—

(1) a device intended for human use presents substantial deception or an unreasonable and substantial risk of illness or injury; and

(2) in the case of substantial deception or an unreasonable and substantial risk of illness or injury which the Secretary determined could be corrected or eliminated by labeling or change in labeling and with respect to which the Secretary provided written notice to the manufacturer specifying the deception or risk of illness or injury, the labeling or change in labeling to correct the deception or eliminate or reduce such risk, and the period within which such labeling or change in labeling was to be done, such labeling or change in labeling was not done within such period;

he may initiate a proceeding to promulgate a regulation to make such device a banned device.

(b) Special effective date

The Secretary may declare a proposed regulation under subsection (a) of this section to be effective upon its publication in the Federal Register and until the effective date of any final action taken respecting such regulation if

(1) he determines, on the basis of all available data and information, that the deception or risk of illness or injury associated with the use of the device which is subject to the regulation presents an unreasonable, direct, and substantial danger to the health of individuals, and

(2) before the date of the publication of such regulation, the Secretary notifies the manufacturer of such device that such regulation is to be made so effective. If the Secretary makes a proposed regulation so effective, he shall, as expeditiously as possible, give interested persons prompt notice of his action under this subsection, provide reasonable opportunity for an informal hearing on the proposed regulation, and either affirm, modify, or revoke such proposed regulation.

§ 360g.   Judicial review

(a) Petition; record

Not later than thirty days after—

(1) the promulgation of a regulation under section 360c of this title classifying a device in class I or changing the classification of a device to class I or an order under subsection (f)(2) of such section reclassifying a device or denying a petition for reclassification of a device,

(2) the promulgation of a regulation under section 360d of this title establishing, amending, or revoking a performance standard for a device,

(3) the issuance of an order under section 360d(b)(2) or 360e(b)(2)(B) of this title denying a request for reclassification of a device,

(4) the promulgation of a regulation under paragraph (3) of section 360e(b) of this title requiring a device to have an approval of a premarket application, a regulation under paragraph (4) of that section amending or revoking a regulation under paragraph (3), or an order pursuant to section 360e(g)(1) or 360e(g)(2)(C) of this title,

(5) the promulgation of a regulation under section 360f of this title (other than a proposed regulation made effective under subsection (b) of such section upon the regulation's publication) making a device a banned device,

(6) the issuance of an order under section 360j(f)(2) of this title,

(7) an order under section 360j(g)(4) of this title disapproving an application for an exemption of a device for investigational use or an order under section 360j(g)(5) of this title withdrawing such an exemption for a device,

(8) an order pursuant to section 360c(i) of this title, or

(9) a regulation under section 360e(i)(2) or 360j(*l*)(5)(B) of this title,

(10) Repealed. *Pub.L. 105–115, Title II, § 216(a)(2)(C)*, Nov. 21, 1997, 111 Stat. 2349

any person adversely affected by such regulation or order may file a petition with the United States Court of Appeals for the District of Columbia or for the circuit wherein such person resides or has his principal place of business for judicial review of such regulation or order. A copy of the petition shall be transmitted by the clerk of the court to the Secretary or other officer designated by him for that purpose. The Secretary shall file in the court the record of the proceedings on which the Secretary based his regulation or order as provided in section 2112 of Title 28. For purposes of this section, the term "record" means all notices and other matter published in the Federal Register with respect to the regulation or order reviewed, all information submitted to the Secretary with respect to such regulation or order, proceedings of any panel or advisory committee with respect to such regulation or order, any hearing held with respect to such regulation or order, and any other information identified by the Secretary, in the administrative proceeding held with respect to such regulation or order, as being relevant to such regulation or order.

(b) Additional data, views, and arguments

If the petitioner applies to the court for leave to adduce additional data, views, or arguments respecting the regulation or order being reviewed and shows to the satisfaction of the court that such additional data, views, or arguments are material and that there were reasonable grounds for the petitioner's failure to adduce such data, views, or arguments in the proceedings before the Secretary, the court may order the Secretary to provide additional opportunity for the oral presentation of data, views, or arguments and for written submissions. The Secretary may modify his findings, or make new findings by reason of the additional data, views, or arguments so taken and shall file with the court such modified or new findings, and his recommendation, if any, for the modification or setting aside of the regulation or order being reviewed, with the return of such additional data, views, or arguments.

(c) Standard for review

Upon the filing of the petition under subsection (a) of this section for judicial review of a regulation or order, the court shall have jurisdiction to review the regulation or order in accordance with chapter 7 of Title 5 and to grant appropriate relief, including interim relief, as provided in such chapter. A regulation described in paragraph (2) or (5) of subsection (a) of this section and an order issued after the review provided by section 360e(g) of this title shall not be affirmed if it is found to be unsupported by substantial evidence on the record taken as a whole.

(d) Finality of judgments

The judgment of the court affirming or setting aside, in whole or in part, any regulation or order shall be final, subject to review by the Supreme Court of the United States upon certiorari or certification, as provided in section 1254 of Title 28.

(e) Remedies

The remedies provided for in this section shall be in addition to and not in lieu of any other remedies provided by law.

(f) Statement of reasons

To facilitate judicial review under this section or under any other provision of law of a regulation or order issued under section 360c, 360d, 360e, 360f, 360h, 360i, 360j, or 360k of this title each such regulation or order shall contain a statement of the reasons for its issuance and the basis, in the record of the proceedings held in connection with its issuance, for its issuance.

§ 360h.   Notification and other remedies

(a) Notification

If the Secretary determines that—

    (1) a device intended for human use which is introduced or delivered for introduction into interstate commerce for commercial distribution presents an unreasonable risk of substantial harm to the public health, and

    (2) notification under this subsection is necessary to eliminate the unreasonable risk of such harm and no more practicable means is available under the provisions of this chapter (other than this section) to eliminate such risk,

the Secretary may issue such order as may be necessary to assure that adequate notification is provided in an appropriate form, by the persons and means best suited under the circumstances involved, to all health professionals who prescribe or use the device and to any other person (including manufacturers, importers, distributors, retailers, and device users) who should properly receive such notification in order to eliminate such risk. An order under this subsection shall require that the individuals subject to the risk with respect to which the order is to be issued be included in the persons to be notified of the risk unless the Secretary determines that notice to such individuals would present a greater danger to the health of such individuals than no such notification. If the Secretary makes such a determination with respect to such individuals, the order shall require that the health professionals who prescribe or use the device provide for the notification of the individuals whom the health professionals treated with the device of the risk presented by the device and of any action which may be taken by or on behalf of such individuals to eliminate or reduce such risk. Before issuing an order under this subsection, the Secretary shall consult with the persons who are to give notice under the order.

(b) Repair, replacement, or refund

(1)(A) If, after affording opportunity for an informal hearing, the Secretary determines that—

> **(i)** a device intended for human use which is introduced or delivered for introduction into interstate commerce for commercial distribution presents an unreasonable risk of substantial harm to the public health,

> **(ii)** there are reasonable grounds to believe that the device was not properly designed or manufactured with reference to the state of the art as it existed at the time of its design or manufacture,

> **(iii)** there are reasonable grounds to believe that the unreasonable risk was not caused by failure of a person other than a manufacturer, importer, distributor, or retailer of the device to exercise due care in the installation, maintenance, repair, or use of the device, and

> **(iv)** the notification authorized by subsection (a) of this section would not by itself be sufficient to eliminate the unreasonable risk and action described in paragraph (2) of this subsection is necessary to eliminate such risk,

the Secretary may order the manufacturer, importer, or any distributor of such device, or any combination of such persons, to submit to him within a reasonable time a plan for taking one or more of the actions described in paragraph (2). An order issued under the preceding sentence which is directed to more than one person shall specify which person may decide which action shall be taken under such plan and the person specified shall be the person who the Secretary determines bears the principal, ultimate financial responsibility for action taken under the plan unless the Secretary cannot determine who bears such responsibility or the Secretary determines that the protection of the public health requires that such decision be made by a person (including a device user or health professional) other than the person he determines bears such responsibility.

(B) The Secretary shall approve a plan submitted pursuant to an order issued under subparagraph (A) unless he determines (after affording opportunity for an informal hearing) that the action or actions to be taken under the plan or the manner in which such action or actions are to be taken under the plan will not assure that the unreasonable risk with respect to which such order was issued will be eliminated. If the Secretary disapproves a plan, he shall order a revised plan to be submitted to him within a reasonable time. If the Secretary determines (after affording opportunity for an informal hearing) that the revised plan is unsatisfactory or if no revised plan or no initial plan has been submitted to the Secretary within the prescribed time, the Secretary shall

> **(i)** prescribe a plan to be carried out by the person or persons to whom the order issued under subparagraph (A) was directed, or

> **(ii)** after affording an opportunity for an informal hearing, by order prescribe a plan to be carried out by a person who is a manufacturer, importer, distributor, or retailer of the device with respect to which the order was issued but to whom the order under subparagraph (A) was not directed.

(2) The actions which may be taken under a plan submitted under an order issued under paragraph (1) are as follows:

(A) To repair the device so that it does not present the unreasonable risk of substantial harm with respect to which the order under paragraph (1) was issued.

(B) To replace the device with a like or equivalent device which is in conformity with all applicable requirements of this chapter.

(C) To refund the purchase price of the device (less a reasonable allowance for use if such device has been in the possession of the device user for one year or more—

> **(i)** at the time of notification ordered under subsection (a) of this section, or

> **(ii)** at the time the device user receives actual notice of the unreasonable risk with respect to which the order was issued under paragraph (1).

whichever first occurs).

(3) No charge shall be made to any person (other than a manufacturer, importer, distributor or retailer) for availing himself of any remedy, described in paragraph (2) and provided under an order issued under paragraph (1), and the person subject to the order shall reimburse each person (other than a manufacturer, importer, distributor, or retailer) who is entitled to such a remedy for any reasonable and foreseeable expenses actually incurred by such person in availing himself of such remedy.

(c) Reimbursement

An order issued under subsection (b) of this section with respect to a device may require any person who is a manufacturer, importer, distributor, or retailer of the device to reimburse any other person who is a manufacturer, importer, distributor, or retailer of such device for such other person's expenses actually incurred in connection with carrying out the order if the Secretary determines such reimbursement is required for the protection of the public health. Any such requirement shall not affect any rights or obligations under any contract to which the person receiving reimbursement or the person making such reimbursement is a party.

(d) Effect on other liability

Compliance with an order issued under this section shall not relieve any person from liability under Federal or State law. In awarding damages for economic loss in an action brought for the enforcement of any such liability, the value to the plaintiff in such action of any remedy provided him under such order shall be taken into account.

(e) Recall authority

(1) If the Secretary finds that there is a reasonable probability that a device intended for human use would cause serious, adverse health consequences or death, the Secretary shall issue an order requiring the appropriate person (including the manufacturers, importers, distributors, or retailers of the device)—

(A) to immediately cease distribution of such device, and

(B) to immediately notify health professionals and device user facilities of the order and to instruct such professionals and facilities to cease use of such device.

The order shall provide the person subject to the order with an opportunity for an informal hearing, to be held not later than 10 days after the date of the issuance of the order, on the actions required by the order and on whether the order should be amended to require a recall of such device. If, after providing an opportunity for such a hearing, the Secretary determines that inadequate grounds exist to support the actions required by the order, the Secretary shall vacate the order.

(2)(A) If, after providing an opportunity for an informal hearing under paragraph (1), the Secretary determines that the order should be amended to include a recall of the device with respect to which the order was issued, the Secretary shall, except as provided in subparagraphs (B) and (C), amend the order to require a recall. The Secretary shall specify a timetable in which the device recall will occur and shall require periodic reports to the Secretary describing the progress of the recall.

(B) An amended order under subparagraph (A)—

(i) shall—

(I) not include recall of a device from individuals, and

(II) not include recall of a device from device user facilities if the Secretary determines that the risk of recalling such device from the facilities presents a greater health risk than the health risk of not recalling the device from use, and

(ii) shall provide for notice to individuals subject to the risks associated with the use of such device.

In providing the notice required by clause (ii), the Secretary may use the assistance of health professionals who prescribed or used such a device for individuals. If a significant number of such individuals cannot be identified, the Secretary shall notify such individuals pursuant to section 375(b) of this title.

(3) The remedy provided by this subsection shall be in addition to remedies provided by subsections (a), (b), and (c) of this section.

* * *

§ 360aa. Recommendations for investigations of drugs for rare diseases or conditions

(a) Request by sponsor; response by Secretary

The sponsor of a drug for a disease or condition which is rare in the States may request the Secretary to provide written recommendations for the non-clinical and clinical investigations which must be conducted with the drug before—

(1) it may be approved for such disease or condition under section 355 of this title, or

(2) if the drug is a biological product, it may be licensed for such disease or condition under section 262 of Title 42.

(3) Redesignated (2)

If the Secretary has reason to believe that a drug for which a request is made under this section is a drug for a disease or condition which is rare in the States, the Secretary shall provide the person making the request written recommendations for the non-clinical and clinical investigations which the Secretary believes, on the basis of information available to the Secretary at the time of the request under this section, would be necessary for approval of such drug for such disease or condition under section 355 of this title, or licensing of such drug for such disease or condition under section 262 of Title 42.

(b) Regulations

The Secretary shall by regulation promulgate procedures for the implementation of subsection (a) of this section.

§ 360bb. Designation of drugs for rare diseases or conditions

(a) Request by sponsor; preconditions; "rare disease or condition" defined

(1) The manufacturer or the sponsor of a drug may request the Secretary to designate the drug as a drug for a rare disease or condition. A request for designation of a drug shall be made before the submission of an application under section 355(b) of this title for the drug, or the submission of an application for licensing of the drug under section 262 of Title 42. If the Secretary finds that a drug for which a request is submitted under this subsection is being or will be investigated for a rare disease or condition and—

(A) if an application for such drug is approved under section 355 of this title, or

(B) if a license for such drug is issued under section 262 of Title 42,

(C) Redesignated (B)

the approval, certification, or license would be for use for such disease or condition, the Secretary shall designate the drug as a drug for such disease or condition. A request for a designation of a drug under this subsection shall contain the consent of the applicant to notice being given by the Secretary under subsection (b) of this section respecting the designation of the drug.

(2) For purposes of paragraph (1), the term "rare disease or condition" means any disease or condition which (A) affects less than 200,000 persons in the United States, or (B) affects more than 200,000 in the United States and for which there is no reasonable expectation that the cost of developing and making available in the United States a drug for such disease or condition will be recovered from sales in the United States of such drug. Determinations under the preceding sentence with respect to any drug shall be made on the basis of the facts and circumstances as of the date the request for designation of the drug under this subsection is made.

(b) Notification of discontinuance of drug or application as condition

A designation of a drug under subsection (a) of this section shall be subject to the condition that—

(1) if an application was approved for the drug under section 355(b) of this title, or a license was issued for the drug under section 262 of Title 42, the manufacturer of the drug will notify the Secretary of any

discontinuance of the production of the drug at least one year before discontinuance, and

(2) if an application has not been approved for the drug under section 355(b) of this title, or a license has not been issued for the drug under section 262 of Title 42, and if preclinical investigations or investigations under section 355(i) of this title are being conducted with the drug, the manufacturer or sponsor of the drug will notify the Secretary of any decision to discontinue active pursuit of approval of an application under section 355(b) of this title, or approval of a license under section 262 of Title 42.

(c) Notice to public

Notice respecting the designation of a drug under subsection (a) of this section shall be made available to the public.

(d) Regulations

The Secretary shall by regulation promulgate procedures for the implementation of subsection (a) of this section.

§ 360cc.   Protection for drugs for rare diseases or conditions

(a) Exclusive approval, certification, or license

Except as provided in subsection (b) of this section, if the Secretary—

(1) approves an application filed pursuant to section 355 of this title, or

(2) issues a license under section 262 of Title 42

(3) Redesignated (2)

for a drug designated under section 360bb of this title for a rare disease or condition, the Secretary may not approve another application under section 355 of this title, or issue another license under section 262 of Title 42 for such drug for such disease or condition for a person who is not the holder of such approved application, of such certification, or of such license until the expiration of seven years from the date of the approval of the approved application, the issuance of the certification, or the issuance of the license. Section 355(c)(2) of this title does not apply to the refusal to approve an application under the preceding sentence.

(b) Exceptions

If an application filed pursuant to section 355 of this title is approved for a drug designated under section 360bb of this title for a rare disease or condition, or if a license is issued under section 262 of Title 42 for such a drug, the Secretary may, during the seven-year period beginning on the date of the application approval, or of the issuance of the license, approve another application under section 355 of this title, or issue a license under section 262 of Title 42, for such drug for such disease or condition for a person who is not the holder of such approved application, or of such license if—

(1) the Secretary finds, after providing the holder notice and opportunity for the submission of views, that in such period the holder of the approved application, or of the license cannot assure the availability of sufficient quantities of the drug to meet the needs of persons with the disease or condition for which the drug was designated; or

(2) such holder provides the Secretary in writing the consent of such holder for the approval of other applications, or the issuance of other licenses before the expiration of such seven-year period.

§ 360dd. Open protocols for investigations of drugs for rare diseases or conditions

If a drug is designated under section 360bb of this title as a drug for a rare disease or condition and if notice of a claimed exemption under section 355(i) of this title or regulations issued thereunder is filed for such drug, the Secretary shall encourage the sponsor of such drug to design protocols for clinical investigations of the drug which may be conducted under the exemption to permit the addition to the investigations of persons with the disease or condition who need the drug to treat the disease or condition and who cannot be satisfactorily treated by available alternative drugs.

§ 360ee. Grants and contracts for development of drugs for rare diseases and conditions

(a) Authority of Secretary

The Secretary may make grants to and enter into contracts with public and private entities and individuals to assist in

(1) defraying the costs of qualified testing expenses incurred in connection with the development of drugs for rare diseases and conditions,

(2) defraying the costs of developing medical devices for rare diseases or conditions, and

(3) defraying the costs of developing medical foods for rare diseases or conditions.

(b) Definitions

For purposes of subsection (a) of this section:

(1) The term "qualified testing" means—

(A) human clinical testing—

(i) which is carried out under an exemption for a drug for a rare disease or condition under section 355(i) of this title (or regulations issued under such section); and

1204

(ii) which occurs after the date such drug is designated under section 360bb of this title and before the date on which an application with respect to such drug is submitted under section 355(b) of this title or under section 262 of Title 42; and

(B) preclinical testing involving a drug for a rare disease or condition which occurs after the date such drug is designated under section 360bb of this title and before the date on which an application with respect to such drug is submitted under section 355(b) of this title or under section 262 of Title 42.

(2) The term "rare disease or condition" means (1) in the case of a drug, any disease or condition which

(A) affects less than 200,000 persons in the United States, or

(B) affects more than 200,000 in the United States and for which there is no reasonable expectation that the cost of developing and making available in the United States a drug for such disease or condition will be recovered from sales in the United States of such drug, (2) in the case of a medical device, any disease or condition that occurs so infrequently in the United States that there is no reasonable expectation that a medical device for such disease or condition will be developed without assistance under subsection (a) of this section, and (3) in the case of a medical food, any disease or condition that occurs so infrequently in the United States that there is no reasonable expectation that a medical food for such disease or condition will be developed without assistance under subsection (a) of this section. Determinations under the preceding sentence with respect to any drug shall be made on the basis of the facts and circumstances as of the date the request for designation of the drug under section 360bb of this title is made.

(3) The term "medical food" means a food which is formulated to be consumed or administered enterally under the supervision of a physician and which is intended for the specific dietary management of a disease or condition for which distinctive nutritional requirements, based on recognized scientific principles, are established by medical evaluation.

(c) Authorization of appropriations

For grants and contracts under subsection (a) of this section there are authorized to be appropriated $10,000,000 for fiscal year 1988, $12,000,000 for fiscal year 1989, $14,000,000 for fiscal year 1990.

* * *

§ 360aaa-1. Information authorized to be disseminated

(a) Authorized information

A manufacturer may disseminate information under section 360aaa of this title on a new use only if the information—

(1) is in the form of an unabridged—

(A) reprint or copy of an article, peer-reviewed by experts qualified by scientific training or experience to evaluate the safety or effectiveness of the drug or device involved, which was published in a scientific or medical journal (as defined in section 360aaa–5(5) of this title), which is about a clinical investigation with respect to the drug or device, and which would be considered to be scientifically sound by such experts; or

(B) reference publication, described in subsection (b) of this section, that includes information about a clinical investigation with respect to the drug or device that would be considered to be scientifically sound by experts qualified by scientific training or experience to evaluate the safety or effectiveness of the drug or device that is the subject of such a clinical investigation; and

(2) is not false or misleading and would not pose a significant risk to the public health.

(b) Reference publication

A reference publication referred to in subsection (a)(1)(B) of this section is a publication that—

(1) has not been written, edited, excerpted, or published specifically for, or at the request of, a manufacturer of a drug or device;

(2) has not been edited or significantly influenced by such a manufacturer;

(3) is not solely distributed through such a manufacturer but is generally available in bookstores or other distribution channels where medical textbooks are sold;

(4) does not focus on any particular drug or device of a manufacturer that disseminates information under section 360aaa of this title and does not have a primary focus on new uses of drugs or devices that are marketed or under investigation by a manufacturer supporting the dissemination of information; and

(5) presents materials that are not false or misleading.

* * *

§ 360aaa–2. Establishment of list of articles and publications disseminated and list of providers that received articles and reference publications

(a) In general

A manufacturer may disseminate information under section 360aaa of this title on a new use only if the manufacturer prepares and submits to the Secretary biannually—

(1) a list containing the titles of the articles and reference publications relating to the new use of drugs or devices that were disseminated

by the manufacturer to a person described in section 360aaa(a) of this title for the 6-month period preceding the date on which the manufacturer submits the list to the Secretary; and

(2) a list that identifies the categories of providers (as described in section 360aaa(a) of this title) that received the articles and reference publications for the 6-month period described in paragraph (1).

(b) Records

A manufacturer that disseminates information under section 360aaa of this title shall keep records that may be used by the manufacturer when, pursuant to section 360aaa-4 of this title, such manufacturer is required to take corrective action and shall be made available to the Secretary, upon request, for purposes of ensuring or taking corrective action pursuant to such section. Such records, at the Secretary's discretion, may identify the recipient of information provided pursuant to section 360aaa of this title or the categories of such recipients.

* * *

§ 360aaa-3.   Requirement regarding submission of supplemental application for new use; exemption from requirement

(a) In general

A manufacturer may disseminate information under section 360aaa of this title on a new use only if—

(1)(A) the manufacturer has submitted to the Secretary a supplemental application for such use; or

(B) the manufacturer meets the condition described in subsection (b) or (c) of this section (relating to a certification that the manufacturer will submit such an application); or

(2) there is in effect for the manufacturer an exemption under subsection (d) of this section from the requirement of paragraph (1).

(b) Certification on supplemental application; condition in case of completed studies

For purposes of subsection (a)(1)(B) of this section, a manufacturer may disseminate information on a new use if the manufacturer has submitted to the Secretary an application containing a certification that—

(1) the studies needed for the submission of a supplemental application for the new use have been completed; and

(2) the supplemental application will be submitted to the Secretary not later than 6 months after the date of the initial dissemination of information under section 360aaa of this title.

(c) Certification on supplemental application; condition in case of planned studies

(1) In general

For purposes of subsection (a)(1)(B) of this section, a manufacturer may disseminate information on a new use if—

(A) the manufacturer has submitted to the Secretary an application containing—

(i) a proposed protocol and schedule for conducting the studies needed for the submission of a supplemental application for the new use; and

(ii) a certification that the supplemental application will be submitted to the Secretary not later than 36 months after the date of the initial dissemination of information under section 360aaa of this title (or, as applicable, not later than such date as the Secretary may specify pursuant to an extension under paragraph (3)); and

(B) the Secretary has determined that the proposed protocol is adequate and that the schedule for completing such studies is reasonable.

(2) Progress reports on studies

A manufacturer that submits to the Secretary an application under paragraph (1) shall submit to the Secretary periodic reports describing the status of the studies involved.

(3) Extension of time regarding planned studies

The period of 36 months authorized in paragraph (1)(A)(ii) for the completion of studies may be extended by the Secretary if—

(A) the Secretary determines that the studies needed to submit such an application cannot be completed and submitted within 36 months; or

(B) the manufacturer involved submits to the Secretary a written request for the extension and the Secretary determines that the manufacturer has acted with due diligence to conduct the studies in a timely manner, except that an extension under this subparagraph may not be provided for more than 24 additional months.

(d) Exemption from requirement of supplemental application

(1) In general

For purposes of subsection (a)(2) of this section, a manufacturer may disseminate information on a new use if—

(A) the manufacturer has submitted to the Secretary an application for an exemption from meeting the requirement of subsection (a)(1) of this section; and

(B)(i) the Secretary has approved the application in accordance with paragraph (2); or

(ii) the application is deemed under paragraph (3)(A) to have been approved (unless such approval is terminated pursuant to paragraph (3)(B)).

(2) Conditions for approval

The Secretary may approve an application under paragraph (1) for an exemption if the Secretary makes a determination described in subparagraph (A) or (B), as follows:

(A) The Secretary makes a determination that, for reasons defined by the Secretary, it would be economically prohibitive with respect to such drug or device for the manufacturer to incur the costs necessary for the submission of a supplemental application. In making such determination, the Secretary shall consider (in addition to any other considerations the Secretary finds appropriate)—

(i) the lack of the availability under law of any period during which the manufacturer would have exclusive marketing rights with respect to the new use involved; and

(ii) the size of the population expected to benefit from approval of the supplemental application.

(B) The Secretary makes a determination that, for reasons defined by the Secretary, it would be unethical to conduct the studies necessary for the supplemental application. In making such determination, the Secretary shall consider (in addition to any other considerations the Secretary finds appropriate) whether the new use involved is the standard of medical care for a health condition.

(3) Time for consideration of application; deemed approval

(A) In general

The Secretary shall approve or deny an application under paragraph (1) for an exemption not later than 60 days after the receipt of the application. If the Secretary does not comply with the preceding sentence, the application is deemed to be approved.

(B) Termination of deemed approval

If pursuant to a deemed approval under subparagraph (A) a manufacturer disseminates written information under section 360aaa of this title on a new use, the Secretary may at any time terminate such approval and under section 360aaa–4(b)(3) of this title order the manufacturer to cease disseminating the information.

(e) Requirements regarding applications

Applications under this section shall be submitted in the form and manner prescribed by the Secretary.

§ 360aaa–4. Corrective actions; cessation of dissemination

(a) Postdissemination data regarding safety and effectiveness

(1) Corrective actions

With respect to data received by the Secretary after the dissemination of information under section 360aaa of this title by a manufacturer has begun (whether received pursuant to paragraph (2) or otherwise), if the Secretary determines that the data indicate that the new use involved may not be effective or may present a significant risk to public health, the Secretary shall, after consultation with the manufacturer, take such action regarding the dissemination of the information as the Secretary determines to be appropriate for the protection of the public health, which may include ordering that the manufacturer cease the dissemination of the information.

(2) Responsibilities of manufacturers to submit data

After a manufacturer disseminates information under section 360aaa of this title, the manufacturer shall submit to the Secretary a notification of any additional knowledge of the manufacturer on clinical research or other data that relate to the safety or effectiveness of the new use involved. If the manufacturer is in possession of the data, the notification shall include the data. The Secretary shall by regulation establish the scope of the responsibilities of manufacturers under this paragraph, including such limits on the responsibilities as the Secretary determines to be appropriate.

(b) Cessation of dissemination

(1) Failure of manufacturer to comply with requirements

The Secretary may order a manufacturer to cease the dissemination of information pursuant to section 360aaa of this title if the Secretary determines that the information being disseminated does not comply with the requirements established in this subchapter. Such an order may be issued only after the Secretary has provided notice to the manufacturer of the intent of the Secretary to issue the order and (unless paragraph (2)(B) applies) has provided an opportunity for a meeting with respect to such intent. If the failure of the manufacturer constitutes a minor violation of this subchapter, the Secretary shall delay issuing the order and provide to the manufacturer an opportunity to correct the violation.

(2) Supplemental applications

The Secretary may order a manufacturer to cease the dissemination of information pursuant to section 360aaa of this title if—

(A) in the case of a manufacturer that has submitted a supplemental application for a new use pursuant to section 360aaa–3(a)(1) of this title, the Secretary determines that the supplemental application does not contain adequate information for approval of the new use for which the application was submitted;

(B) in the case of a manufacturer that has submitted a certification under section 360aaa–3(b) of this title, the manufacturer has not, within the 6–month period involved, submitted the supplemental application referred to in the certification; or

(C) in the case of a manufacturer that has submitted a certification under section 360aaa–3(c) of this title but has not yet submitted the supplemental application referred to in the certification, the Secretary determines, after an informal hearing, that the manufacturer is not acting with due diligence to complete the studies involved.

(3) Termination of deemed approval of exemption regarding supplemental applications

If under section 360aaa–3(d)(3) of this title the Secretary terminates a deemed approval of an exemption, the Secretary may order the manufacturer involved to cease disseminating the information. A manufacturer shall comply with an order under the preceding sentence not later than 60 days after the receipt of the order.

(c) Corrective actions by manufacturers

(1) In general

In any case in which under this section the Secretary orders a manufacturer to cease disseminating information, the Secretary may order the manufacturer to take action to correct the information that has been disseminated, except as provided in paragraph (2).

(2) Termination of deemed approval of exemption regarding supplemental applications

In the case of an order under subsection (b)(3) of this section to cease disseminating information, the Secretary may not order the manufacturer involved to take action to correct the information that has been disseminated unless the Secretary determines that the new use described in the information would pose a significant risk to the public health.

§ 360aaa–5. Definitions

For purposes of this subchapter:

(1) The term "health care practitioner" means a physician, or other individual who is a provider of health care, who is licensed under the law of a State to prescribe drugs or devices.

(2) The terms "health insurance issuer" and "group health plan" have the meaning given such terms under section 300gg–91 of Title 42.

(3) The term "manufacturer" means a person who manufactures a drug or device, or who is licensed by such person to distribute or market the drug or device.

(4) The term "new use"—

(A) with respect to a drug, means a use that is not included in the labeling of the approved drug; and

(B) with respect to a device, means a use that is not included in the labeling for the approved or cleared device.

(5) The term "scientific or medical journal" means a scientific or medical publication—

(A) that is published by an organization—

(i) that has an editorial board;

(ii) that utilizes experts, who have demonstrated expertise in the subject of an article under review by the organization and who are independent of the organization, to review and objectively select, reject, or provide comments about proposed articles; and

(iii) that has a publicly stated policy, to which the organization adheres, of full disclosure of any conflict of interest or biases for all authors or contributors involved with the journal or organization;

(B) whose articles are peer-reviewed and published in accordance with the regular peer-review procedures of the organization;

(C) that is generally recognized to be of national scope and reputation;

(D) that is indexed in the Index Medicus of the National Library of Medicine of the National Institutes of Health; and

(E) that is not in the form of a special supplement that has been funded in whole or in part by one or more manufacturers.

§ 360aaa–6. Rules of construction

(a) Unsolicited request

Nothing in section 360aaa of this title shall be construed as prohibiting a manufacturer from disseminating information in response to an unsolicited request from a health care practitioner.

(b) Dissemination of information on drugs or devices not evidence of intended use

Notwithstanding subsection (a), (f), or (o) of section 352 of this title, or any other provision of law, the dissemination of information relating to a new use of a drug or device, in accordance with section 360aaa of this title, shall not be construed by the Secretary as evidence of a new intended use of the drug or device that is different from the intended use of the drug or device set forth in the official labeling of the drug or device. Such dissemination shall not be considered by the Secretary as labeling, adulteration, or misbranding of the drug or device.

(c) Patent protection

Nothing in section 360aaa of this title shall affect patent rights in any manner.

(d) Authorization for dissemination of articles and fees for reprints of articles

Nothing in section 360aaa of this title shall be construed as prohibiting an entity that publishes a scientific journal (as defined in section 360aaa–5(5) of this title) from requiring authorization from the entity to disseminate an article published by such entity or charging fees for the purchase of reprints of published articles from such entity.

§ 360bbb.   Expanded access to unapproved therapies and diagnostics

(a) Emergency situations

The Secretary may, under appropriate conditions determined by the Secretary, authorize the shipment of investigational drugs or investigational devices for the diagnosis, monitoring, or treatment of a serious disease or condition in emergency situations.

(b) Individual patient access to investigational products intended for serious diseases

Any person, acting through a physician licensed in accordance with State law, may request from a manufacturer or distributor, and any manufacturer or distributor may, after complying with the provisions of this subsection, provide to such physician an investigational drug or investigational device for the diagnosis, monitoring, or treatment of a serious disease or condition if—

(1) the licensed physician determines that the person has no comparable or satisfactory alternative therapy available to diagnose, monitor, or treat the disease or condition involved, and that the probable risk to the person from the investigational drug or investigational device is not greater than the probable risk from the disease or condition;

(2) the Secretary determines that there is sufficient evidence of safety and effectiveness to support the use of the investigational drug or investigational device in the case described in paragraph (1);

(3) the Secretary determines that provision of the investigational drug or investigational device will not interfere with the initiation, conduct, or completion of clinical investigations to support marketing approval; and

(4) the sponsor, or clinical investigator, of the investigational drug or investigational device submits to the Secretary a clinical protocol consistent with the provisions of section 355(i) or 360j(g) of this title, including any regulations promulgated under section 355(i) or 360j(g), describing the use of the investigational drug or investigational device in a single patient or a small group of patients.

(c) Treatment investigational new drug applications and treatment investigational device exemptions

Upon submission by a sponsor or a physician of a protocol intended to provide widespread access to an investigational drug or investigational device for eligible patients (referred to in this subsection as an 'expanded access protocol'), the Secretary shall permit such investigational drug or investigational device to be made available for expanded access under a treatment investigational new drug application or treatment investigational device exemption if the Secretary determines that—

(1) under the treatment investigational new drug application or treatment investigational device exemption, the investigational drug or investigational device is intended for use in the diagnosis, monitoring, or treatment of a serious or immediately life-threatening disease or condition;

(2) there is no comparable or satisfactory alternative therapy available to diagnose, monitor, or treat that stage of disease or condition in the population of patients to which the investigational drug or investigational device is intended to be administered;

(3)(A) the investigational drug or investigational device is under investigation in a controlled clinical trial for the use described in paragraph (1) under an investigational drug application in effect under section 355(i) of this title or investigational device exemption in effect under section 360j(g) of this title; or

(B) all clinical trials necessary for approval of that use of the investigational drug or investigational device have been completed;

(4) the sponsor of the controlled clinical trials is actively pursuing marketing approval of the investigational drug or investigational device for the use described in paragraph (1) with due diligence;

(5) in the case of an investigational drug or investigational device described in paragraph (3)(A), the provision of the investigational drug or investigational device will not interfere with the enrollment of patients in ongoing clinical investigations under section 355(i) or 360j(g) of this title;

(6) in the case of serious diseases, there is sufficient evidence of safety and effectiveness to support the use described in paragraph (1); and

(7) in the case of immediately life-threatening diseases, the available scientific evidence, taken as a whole, provides a reasonable basis to conclude that the investigational drug or investigational device may be effective for its intended use and would not expose patients to an unreasonable and significant risk of illness or injury.

A protocol submitted under this subsection shall be subject to the provisions of section 355(i) or 360j(g) of this title, including regulations promulgated under section 355(i) or 360j(g) of this title. The Secretary may inform national, State, and local medical associations and societies, voluntary health associations, and other appropriate persons about the availability of an investigational drug or investigational device under expanded access protocols submitted under this subsection. The information provided by the Secretary, in accordance with the preceding sentence, shall be the same type of information that is required by section 282(j)(3) of Title 42.

(d) Termination

The Secretary may, at any time, with respect to a sponsor, physician, manufacturer, or distributor described in this section, terminate expanded access provided under this section for an investigational drug or investigational device if the requirements under this section are no longer met.

(e) Definitions

In this section, the terms "investigational drug", "investigational device", "treatment investigational new drug application", and "treatment investigational device exemption" shall have the meanings given the terms in regulations prescribed by the Secretary.

§ 360bbb–1. Dispute resolution

If, regarding an obligation concerning drugs or devices under this chapter or section 262 of Title 42, there is a scientific controversy between the Secretary and a person who is a sponsor, applicant, or manufacturer and no specific provision of the chapter involved, including a regulation promulgated under such chapter, provides a right of review of the matter in controversy, the Secretary shall, by regulation, establish a procedure under which such sponsor, applicant, or manufacturer may request a review of such controversy, including a review by an appropriate scientific advisory panel described in section 355(n) of this title or an advisory committee described in section 360e(g)(2)(B) of this title. Any such review shall take place in a timely manner. The Secretary shall promulgate such regulations within 1 year after November 21, 1997.

§ 360bbb–2. Classification of products

(a) Request

A person who submits an application or submission (including a petition, notification, and any other similar form of request) under this Act for a product, may submit a request to the Secretary respecting the classification of the product as a drug, biological product, device, or a combination product subject to section 353(g) of this title or respecting the component of the Food and Drug Administration that will regulate the product. In submitting the request, the person shall recommend a classification for the product, or a component to regulate the product, as appropriate.

(b) Statement

Not later than 60 days after the receipt of the request described in subsection (a) of this section, the Secretary shall determine the classification of the product under subsection (a) of this section, or the component of the

Food and Drug Administration that will regulate the product, and shall provide to the person a written statement that identifies such classification or such component, and the reasons for such determination. The Secretary may not modify such statement except with the written consent of the person, or for public health reasons based on scientific evidence.

(c) Inaction of secretary

If the Secretary does not provide the statement within the 60–day period described in subsection (b) of this section, the recommendation made by the person under subsection (a) of this section shall be considered to be a final determination by the Secretary of such classification of the product, or the component of the Food and Drug Administration that will regulate the product, as applicable, and may not be modified by the Secretary except with the written consent of the person, or for public health reasons based on scientific evidence.

* * *

VII. HIPAA PRIVACY REGULATIONS

Analysis

TITLE 45—PUBLIC WELFARE

SUBTITLE A—DEPARTMENT OF HEALTH AND HUMAN SERVICES

SUBCHAPTER C—ADMINISTRATIVE DATA STANDARDS AND RELATED REQUIREMENTS

PART 160—GENERAL ADMINISTRATIVE REQUIREMENTS

SUBPART A—GENERAL PROVISIONS

SUBPART B—PREEMPTION OF STATE LAW

SUBPART C—COMPLIANCE AND ENFORCEMENT

PART 162—ADMINISTRATIVE REQUIREMENTS (omitted from this edited version of the regulations)

PART 164—SECURITY AND PRIVACY

SUBPART A—GENERAL PROVISIONS

SUBPART E—PRIVACY OF INDIVIDUALLY IDENTIFIABLE HEALTH INFORMATION

CODE OF FEDERAL REGULATIONS

TITLE 45—PUBLIC WELFARE

SUBTITLE A, SUBCHAPTER C

PART 160, GENERAL ADMINISTRATIVE REQUIREMENTS

Subpart A—General Provisions

§ 160.101 Statutory basis and purpose

The requirements of this subchapter implement sections 1171 through 1179 of the Social Security Act (the Act), as added by section 262 of Public Law 104–191, and section 264 of Public Law 104–191.

§ 160.102 Applicability

(a) Except as otherwise provided, the standards, requirements, and implementation specifications adopted under this subchapter apply to the following entities:

(1) A health plan.

(2) A health care clearinghouse.

(3) A health care provider who transmits any health information in electronic form in connection with a transaction covered by this subchapter.

(b) To the extent required under the Social Security Act, 42 U.S.C. 1320a–7c(a)(5), nothing in this subchapter shall be construed to diminish the authority of any Inspector General, including such authority as provided in the Inspector General Act of 1978, as amended (5 U.S.C. App.).

§ 160.103 Definitions.

Except as otherwise provided, the following definitions apply to this subchapter:

Act means the Social Security Act.

ANSI stands for the American National Standards Institute.

Business associate:

(1) Except as provided in paragraph (2) of this definition, business associate means, with respect to a covered entity, a person who:

(i) On behalf of such covered entity or of an organized health care arrangement (as defined in § 164.501 of this subchapter) in which the covered entity participates, but other than in the capacity

1219

of a member of the workforce of such covered entity or arrangement, performs, or assists in the performance of:

(A) A function or activity involving the use or disclosure of individually identifiable health information, including claims processing or administration, data analysis, processing or administration, utilization review, quality assurance, billing, benefit management, practice management, and repricing; or

(B) Any other function or activity regulated by this subchapter; or

(ii) Provides, other than in the capacity of a member of the workforce of such covered entity, legal, actuarial, accounting, consulting, data aggregation (as defined in § 164.501 of this subchapter), management, administrative, accreditation, or financial services to or for such covered entity, or to or for an organized health care arrangement in which the covered entity participates, where the provision of the service involves the disclosure of individually identifiable health information from such covered entity or arrangement, or from another business associate of such covered entity or arrangement, to the person.

(2) A covered entity participating in an organized health care arrangement that performs a function or activity as described by paragraph (1)(i) of this definition for or on behalf of such organized health care arrangement, or that provides a service as described in paragraph (1)(ii) of this definition to or for such organized health care arrangement, does not, simply through the performance of such function or activity or the provision of such service, become a business associate of other covered entities participating in such organized health care arrangement.

(3) A covered entity may be a business associate of another covered entity.

CMS stands for Centers for Medicare & Medicaid Services within the Department of Health and Human Services.

Compliance date means the date by which a covered entity must comply with a standard, implementation specification, requirement, or modification adopted under this subchapter.

Covered entity means:

(1) A health plan.

(2) A health care clearinghouse.

(3) A health care provider who transmits any health information in electronic form in connection with a transaction covered by this subchapter.

EIN stands for the employer identification number assigned by the Internal Revenue Service, U.S. Department of the Treasury. The EIN is the taxpayer identifying number of an individual or other entity (whether or not an employer) assigned under one of the following:

(1) 26 U.S.C. 6011(b), which is the portion of the Internal Revenue Code dealing with identifying the taxpayer in tax returns and statements, or corresponding provisions of prior law.

(2) 26 U.S.C. 6109, which is the portion of the Internal Revenue Code dealing with identifying numbers in tax returns, statements, and other required documents.

Employer is defined as it is in 26 U.S.C. 3401(d).

Group health plan (also see definition of health plan in this section) means an employee welfare benefit plan (as defined in section 3(1) of the Employee Retirement Income and Security Act of 1974 (ERISA), 29 U.S.C. 1002(1)), including insured and self-insured plans, to the extent that the plan provides medical care (as defined in section 2791(a)(2) of the Public Health Service Act (PHS Act), 42 U.S.C. 300gg–91(a)(2)), including items and services paid for as medical care, to employees or their dependents directly or through insurance, reimbursement, or otherwise, that:

(1) Has 50 or more participants (as defined in section 3(7) of ERISA, 29 U.S.C. 1002(7)); or

(2) Is administered by an entity other than the employer that established and maintains the plan.

HHS stands for the Department of Health and Human Services.

Health care means care, services, or supplies related to the health of an individual. Health care includes, but is not limited to, the following:

(1) Preventive, diagnostic, therapeutic, rehabilitative, maintenance, or palliative care, and counseling, service, assessment, or procedure with respect to the physical or mental condition, or functional status, of an individual or that affects the structure or function of the body; and

(2) Sale or dispensing of a drug, device, equipment, or other item in accordance with a prescription.

Health care clearinghouse means a public or private entity, including a billing service, repricing company, community health management information system or community health information system, and "value-added" networks and switches, that does either of the following functions:

(1) Processes or facilitates the processing of health information received from another entity in a nonstandard format or containing nonstandard data content into standard data elements or a standard transaction.

(2) Receives a standard transaction from another entity and processes or facilitates the processing of health information into nonstandard format or nonstandard data content for the receiving entity.

Health care provider means a provider of services (as defined in section 1861(u) of the Act, 42 U.S.C. 1395x(u)), a provider of medical or health services (as defined in section 1861(s) of the Act, 42 U.S.C. 1395x(s)), and any other person or organization who furnishes, bills, or is paid for health care in the normal course of business.

Health information means any information, whether oral or recorded in any form or medium, that:

(1) Is created or received by a health care provider, health plan, public health authority, employer, life insurer, school or university, or health care clearinghouse; and

(2) Relates to the past, present, or future physical or mental health or condition of an individual; the provision of health care to an individual; or the past, present, or future payment for the provision of health care to an individual.

Health insurance issuer (as defined in section 2791(b)(2) of the PHS Act, 42 U.S.C. 300gg–91(b)(2) and used in the definition of health plan in this section) means an insurance company, insurance service, or insurance organization (including an HMO) that is licensed to engage in the business of insurance in a State and is subject to State law that regulates insurance. Such term does not include a group health plan.

Health maintenance organization (HMO) (as defined in section 2791(b)(3) of the PHS Act, 42 U.S.C. 300gg–91(b)(3) and used in the definition of health plan in this section) means a federally qualified HMO, an organization recognized as an HMO under State law, or a similar organization regulated for solvency under State law in the same manner and to the same extent as such an HMO.

Health plan means an individual or group plan that provides, or pays the cost of, medical care (as defined in section 2791(a)(2) of the PHS Act, 42 U.S.C. 300gg–91(a)(2)).

(1) Health plan includes the following, singly or in combination:

(i) A group health plan, as defined in this section.

(ii) A health insurance issuer, as defined in this section.

(iii) An HMO, as defined in this section.

(iv) Part A or Part B of the Medicare program under title XVIII of the Act.

(v) The Medicaid program under title XIX of the Act, 42 U.S.C. 1396, et seq.

(vi) An issuer of a Medicare supplemental policy (as defined in section 1882(g)(1) of the Act, 42 U.S.C. 1395ss(g)(1)).

(vii) An issuer of a long-term care policy, excluding a nursing home fixed-indemnity policy.

(viii) An employee welfare benefit plan or any other arrangement that is established or maintained for the purpose of offering or providing health benefits to the employees of two or more employers.

(ix) The health care program for active military personnel under title 10 of the United States Code.

(x) The veterans health care program under 38 U.S.C. chapter 17.

(xi) The Civilian Health and Medical Program of the Uniformed Services (CHAMPUS) (as defined in 10 U.S.C. 1072(4)).

(xii) The Indian Health Service program under the Indian Health Care Improvement Act, 25 U.S.C. 1601, et seq.

(xiii) The Federal Employees Health Benefits Program under 5 U.S.C. 8902, et seq.

(xiv) An approved State child health plan under title XXI of the Act, providing benefits for child health assistance that meet the requirements of section 2103 of the Act, 42 U.S.C. 1397, et seq.

(xv) The Medicare + Choice program under Part C of title XVIII of the Act, 42 U.S.C. 1395w–21 through 1395w–28.

(xvi) A high risk pool that is a mechanism established under State law to provide health insurance coverage or comparable coverage to eligible individuals.

(xvii) Any other individual or group plan, or combination of individual or group plans, that provides or pays for the cost of medical care (as defined in section 2791(a)(2) of the PHS Act, 42 U.S.C. 300gg–91(a)(2)).

(2) Health plan excludes:

(i) Any policy, plan, or program to the extent that it provides, or pays for the cost of, excepted benefits that are listed in section 2791(c)(1) of the PHS Act, 42 U.S.C. 300gg–91(c)(1); and

(ii) A government-funded program (other than one listed in paragraph (1)(i)–(xvi) of this definition):

(A) Whose principal purpose is other than providing, or paying the cost of, health care; or

(B) Whose principal activity is:

(1) The direct provision of health care to persons; or

(2) The making of grants to fund the direct provision of health care to persons.

Implementation specification means specific requirements or instructions for implementing a standard.

Individually identifiable health information is information that is a subset of health information, including demographic information collected from an individual, and:

(1) Is created or received by a health care provider, health plan, employer, or health care clearinghouse; and

(2) Relates to the past, present, or future physical or mental health or condition of an individual; the provision of health care to an individual; or the past, present, or future payment for the provision of health care to an individual; and

(i) That identifies the individual; or

(ii) With respect to which there is a reasonable basis to believe the information can be used to identify the individual.

Modify or modification refers to a change adopted by the Secretary, through regulation, to a standard or an implementation specification.

Secretary means the Secretary of Health and Human Services or any other officer or employee of HHS to whom the authority involved has been delegated.

Small health plan means a health plan with annual receipts of $5 million or less.

Standard means a rule, condition, or requirement:

(1) Describing the following information for products, systems, services or practices:

(i) Classification of components.

(ii) Specification of materials, performance, or operations; or

(iii) Delineation of procedures; or

(2) With respect to the privacy of individually identifiable health information.

Standard setting organization (SSO) means an organization accredited by the American National Standards Institute that develops and maintains standards for information transactions or data elements, or any other standard that is necessary for, or will facilitate the implementation of, this part.

State refers to one of the following:

(1) For a health plan established or regulated by Federal law, State has the meaning set forth in the applicable section of the United States Code for such health plan.

(2) For all other purposes, State means any of the several States, the District of Columbia, the Commonwealth of Puerto Rico, the Virgin Islands, and Guam.

Trading partner agreement means an agreement related to the exchange of information in electronic transactions, whether the agreement is distinct or part of a larger agreement, between each party to the agreement. (For example, a trading partner agreement may specify, among other things, the duties and responsibilities of each party to the agreement in conducting a standard transaction.)

Transaction means the transmission of information between two parties to carry out financial or administrative activities related to health care. It includes the following types of information transmissions:

(1) Health care claims or equivalent encounter information.

(2) Health care payment and remittance advice.

(3) Coordination of benefits.

(4) Health care claim status.

(5) Enrollment and disenrollment in a health plan.

(6) Eligibility for a health plan.

(7) Health plan premium payments.

(8) Referral certification and authorization.

(9) First report of injury.

(10) Health claims attachments.

(11) Other transactions that the Secretary may prescribe by regulation.

Workforce means employees, volunteers, trainees, and other persons whose conduct, in the performance of work for a covered entity, is under the direct control of such entity, whether or not they are paid by the covered entity.

§ 160.104 Modifications.

(a) Except as provided in paragraph (b) of this section, the Secretary may adopt a modification to a standard or implementation specification adopted under this subchapter no more frequently than once every 12 months.

(b) The Secretary may adopt a modification at any time during the first year after the standard or implementation specification is initially adopted, if the Secretary determines that the modification is necessary to permit compliance with the standard or implementation specification.

(c) The Secretary will establish the compliance date for any standard or implementation specification modified under this section.

(1) The compliance date for a modification is no earlier than 180 days after the effective date of the final rule in which the Secretary adopts the modification.

(2) The Secretary may consider the extent of the modification and the time needed to comply with the modification in determining the compliance date for the modification.

(3) The Secretary may extend the compliance date for small health plans, as the Secretary determines is appropriate.

Subpart B—Preemption of State Law

§ 160.201   Applicability.

The provisions of this subpart implement section 1178 of the Act, as added by section 262 of Public Law 104–191.

§ 160.202   Definitions.

For purposes of this subpart, the following terms have the following meanings:

Contrary, when used to compare a provision of State law to a standard, requirement, or implementation specification adopted under this subchapter, means:

(1) A covered entity would find it impossible to comply with both the State and federal requirements; or

(2) The provision of State law stands as an obstacle to the accomplishment and execution of the full purposes and objectives of part C of title XI of the Act or section 264 of Pub. L. 104–191, as applicable.

More stringent means, in the context of a comparison of a provision of State law and a standard, requirement, or implementation specification adopted under subpart E of part 164 of this subchapter, a State law that meets one or more of the following criteria:

(1) With respect to a use or disclosure, the law prohibits or restricts a use or disclosure in circumstances under which such use or disclosure otherwise would be permitted under this subchapter, except if the disclosure is:

(i) Required by the Secretary in connection with determining whether a covered entity is in compliance with this subchapter; or

(ii) To the individual who is the subject of the individually identifiable health information.

(2) With respect to the rights of an individual, who is the subject of the individually identifiable health information, regarding access to or amendment of individually identifiable health information, permits greater rights of access or amendment, as applicable.

(3) With respect to information to be provided to an individual who is the subject of the individually identifiable health information about a use, a disclosure, rights, and remedies, provides the greater amount of information.

(4) With respect to the form, substance, or the need for express legal permission from an individual, who is the subject of the individually identifiable health information, for use or disclosure of individually identifiable health information, provides requirements that narrow the scope or duration, increase the privacy protections afforded (such as by expand-

ing the criteria for), or reduce the coercive effect of the circumstances surrounding the express legal permission, as applicable.

(5) With respect to recordkeeping or requirements relating to accounting of disclosures, provides for the retention or reporting of more detailed information or for a longer duration.

(6) With respect to any other matter, provides greater privacy protection for the individual who is the subject of the individually identifiable health information.

Relates to the privacy of individually identifiable health information means, with respect to a State law, that the State law has the specific purpose of protecting the privacy of health information or affects the privacy of health information in a direct, clear, and substantial way.

State law means a constitution, statute, regulation, rule, common law, or other State action having the force and effect of law.

§ 160.203   General rule and exceptions.

A standard, requirement, or implementation specification adopted under this subchapter that is contrary to a provision of State law preempts the provision of State law. This general rule applies, except if one or more of the following conditions is met:

(a) A determination is made by the Secretary under § 160.204 that the provision of State law:

   (1) Is necessary:

      (i) To prevent fraud and abuse related to the provision of or payment for health care;

      (ii) To ensure appropriate State regulation of insurance and health plans to the extent expressly authorized by statute or regulation;

      (iii) For State reporting on health care delivery or costs; or

      (iv) For purposes of serving a compelling need related to public health, safety, or welfare, and, if a standard, requirement, or implementation specification under part 164 of this subchapter is at issue, if the Secretary determines that the intrusion into privacy is warranted when balanced against the need to be served; or

   (2) Has as its principal purpose the regulation of the manufacture, registration, distribution, dispensing, or other control of any controlled substances (as defined in 21 U.S.C. 802), or that is deemed a controlled substance by State law.

(b) The provision of State law relates to the privacy of individually identifiable health information and is more stringent than a standard, requirement, or implementation specification adopted under subpart E of part 164 of this subchapter.

(c) The provision of State law, including State procedures established under such law, as applicable, provides for the reporting of disease or injury, child abuse, birth, or death, or for the conduct of public health surveillance, investigation, or intervention.

(d) The provision of State law requires a health plan to report, or to provide access to, information for the purpose of management audits, financial audits, program monitoring and evaluation, or the licensure or certification of facilities or individuals.

§ 160.204 Process for requesting exception determinations.

(a) A request to except a provision of State law from preemption under § 160.203(a) may be submitted to the Secretary. A request by a State must be submitted through its chief elected official, or his or her designee. The request must be in writing and include the following information:

(1) The State law for which the exception is requested;

(2) The particular standard, requirement, or implementation specification for which the exception is requested;

(3) The part of the standard or other provision that will not be implemented based on the exception or the additional data to be collected based on the exception, as appropriate;

(4) How health care providers, health plans, and other entities would be affected by the exception;

(5) The reasons why the State law should not be preempted by the federal standard, requirement, or implementation specification, including how the State law meets one or more of the criteria at § 160.203(a); and

(6) Any other information the Secretary may request in order to make the determination.

(b) Requests for exception under this section must be submitted to the Secretary at an address that will be published in the Federal Register. Until the Secretary's determination is made, the standard, requirement, or implementation specification under this subchapter remains in effect.

(c) The Secretary's determination under this section will be made on the basis of the extent to which the information provided and other factors demonstrate that one or more of the criteria at § 160.203(a) has been met.

§ 160.205 Duration of effectiveness of exception determinations.

An exception granted under this subpart remains in effect until:

(a) Either the State law or the federal standard, requirement, or implementation specification that provided the basis for the exception is materially changed such that the ground for the exception no longer exists; or

(b) The Secretary revokes the exception, based on a determination that the ground supporting the need for the exception no longer exists.

Subpart C—Compliance and Enforcement

§ 160.300   Applicability.

This subpart applies to actions by the Secretary, covered entities, and others with respect to ascertaining the compliance by covered entities with and the enforcement of the applicable requirements of this part 160 and the applicable standards, requirements, and implementation specifications of subpart E of part 164 of this subchapter.

§ 160.302   Definitions.

As used in this subpart, terms defined in § 164.501 of this subchapter have the same meanings given to them in that section.

§ 160.304   Principles for achieving compliance.

(a) Cooperation. The Secretary will, to the extent practicable, seek the cooperation of covered entities in obtaining compliance with the applicable requirements of this part 160 and the applicable standards, requirements, and implementation specifications of subpart E of part 164 of this subchapter.

(b) Assistance. The Secretary may provide technical assistance to covered entities to help them comply voluntarily with the applicable requirements of this part 160 or the applicable standards, requirements, and implementation specifications of subpart E of part 164 of this subchapter.

§ 160.306   Complaints to the Secretary.

(a) Right to file a complaint. A person who believes a covered entity is not complying with the applicable requirements of this part 160 or the applicable standards, requirements, and implementation specifications of subpart E of part 164 of this subchapter may file a complaint with the Secretary.

(b) Requirements for filing complaints. Complaints under this section must meet the following requirements:

    (1) A complaint must be filed in writing, either on paper or electronically.

    (2) A complaint must name the entity that is the subject of the complaint and describe the acts or omissions believed to be in violation of the applicable requirements of this part 160 or the applicable standards, requirements, and implementation specifications of subpart E of part 164 of this subchapter.

    (3) A complaint must be filed within 180 days of when the complainant knew or should have known that the act or omission complained of occurred, unless this time limit is waived by the Secretary for good cause shown.

(4) The Secretary may prescribe additional procedures for the filing of complaints, as well as the place and manner of filing, by notice in the Federal Register.

(c) Investigation. The Secretary may investigate complaints filed under this section. Such investigation may include a review of the pertinent policies, procedures, or practices of the covered entity and of the circumstances regarding any alleged acts or omissions concerning compliance.

§ 160.308 Compliance reviews.

The Secretary may conduct compliance reviews to determine whether covered entities are complying with the applicable requirements of this part 160 and the applicable standards, requirements, and implementation specifications of subpart E of part 164 of this subchapter.

§ 160.310 Responsibilities of covered entities.

(a) Provide records and compliance reports. A covered entity must keep such records and submit such compliance reports, in such time and manner and containing such information, as the Secretary may determine to be necessary to enable the Secretary to ascertain whether the covered entity has complied or is complying with the applicable requirements of this part 160 and the applicable standards, requirements, and implementation specifications of subpart E of part 164 of this subchapter.

(b) Cooperate with complaint investigations and compliance reviews. A covered entity must cooperate with the Secretary, if the Secretary undertakes an investigation or compliance review of the policies, procedures, or practices of a covered entity to determine whether it is complying with the applicable requirements of this part 160 and the standards, requirements, and implementation specifications of subpart E of part 164 of this subchapter.

(c) Permit access to information.

(1) A covered entity must permit access by the Secretary during normal business hours to its facilities, books, records, accounts, and other sources of information, including protected health information, that are pertinent to ascertaining compliance with the applicable requirements of this part 160 and the applicable standards, requirements, and implementation specifications of subpart E of part 164 of this subchapter. If the Secretary determines that exigent circumstances exist, such as when documents may be hidden or destroyed, a covered entity must permit access by the Secretary at any time and without notice.

(2) If any information required of a covered entity under this section is in the exclusive possession of any other agency, institution, or person and the other agency, institution, or person fails or refuses to furnish the information, the covered entity must so certify and set forth what efforts it has made to obtain the information.

(3) Protected health information obtained by the Secretary in connection with an investigation or compliance review under this subpart will not be disclosed by the Secretary, except if necessary for ascertaining or enforcing compliance with the applicable requirements of this part 160 and the applicable standards, requirements, and implementation specifications of subpart E of part 164 of this subchapter, or if otherwise required by law.

§ 160.312 Secretarial action regarding complaints and compliance reviews.

(a) Resolution where noncompliance is indicated.

(1) If an investigation pursuant to § 160.306 or a compliance review pursuant to § 160.308 indicates a failure to comply, the Secretary will so inform the covered entity and, if the matter arose from a complaint, the complainant, in writing and attempt to resolve the matter by informal means whenever possible.

(2) If the Secretary finds the covered entity is not in compliance and determines that the matter cannot be resolved by informal means, the Secretary may issue to the covered entity and, if the matter arose from a complaint, to the complainant written findings documenting the noncompliance.

(b) Resolution when no violation is found. If, after an investigation or compliance review, the Secretary determines that further action is not warranted, the Secretary will so inform the covered entity and, if the matter arose from a complaint, the complainant in writing.

PART 162—ADMINISTRATIVE REQUIREMENTS
(omitted from this edited version of the regulations)

PART 164—SECURITY AND PRIVACY

PART A—GENERAL PROVISIONS

§ 164.102 Statutory basis.

The provisions of this part are adopted pursuant to the Secretary's authority to prescribe standards, requirements, and implementation specifications under part C of title XI of the Act and section 264 of Public Law 104–191.

§ 164.104 Applicability.

Except as otherwise provided, the provisions of this part apply to covered entities: health plans, health care clearinghouses, and health care providers who transmit health information in electronic form in connection with any transaction referred to in section 1173(a)(1) of the Act.

§ 164.106   Relationship to other parts.

In complying with the requirements of this part, covered entities are required to comply with the applicable provisions of parts 160 and 162 of this subchapter.

PART E—PRIVACY OF INDIVIDUALLY IDENTIFIABLE HEALTH INFORMATION

§ 164.500   Applicability.

(a) Except as otherwise provided herein, the standards, requirements, and implementation specifications of this subpart apply to covered entities with respect to protected health information.

(b) Health care clearinghouses must comply with the standards, requirements, and implementation specifications as follows:

(1) When a health care clearinghouse creates or receives protected health information as a business associate of another covered entity, the clearinghouse must comply with:

(i) Section 164.500 relating to applicability;

(ii) Section 164.501 relating to definitions;

(iii) Section 164.502 relating to uses and disclosures of protected health information, except that a clearinghouse is prohibited from using or disclosing protected health information other than as permitted in the business associate contract under which it created or received the protected health information;

(iv) Section 164.504 relating to the organizational requirements for covered entities, including the designation of health care components of a covered entity;

(v) Section 164.512 relating to uses and disclosures for which individual authorization or an opportunity to agree or object is not required, except that a clearinghouse is prohibited from using or disclosing protected health information other than as permitted in the business associate contract under which it created or received the protected health information;

(vi) Section 164.532 relating to transition requirements; and

(vii) Section 164.534 relating to compliance dates for initial implementation of the privacy standards.

(2) When a health care clearinghouse creates or receives protected health information other than as a business associate of a covered entity, the clearinghouse must comply with all of the standards, requirements, and implementation specifications of this subpart.

(c) The standards, requirements, and implementation specifications of this subpart do not apply to the Department of Defense or to any other federal agency, or non-governmental organization acting on its behalf, when providing health care to overseas foreign national beneficiaries.

§ 164.501 Definitions.

As used in this subpart, the following terms have the following meanings:

Correctional institution means any penal or correctional facility, jail, reformatory, detention center, work farm, halfway house, or residential community program center operated by, or under contract to, the United States, a State, a territory, a political subdivision of a State or territory, or an Indian tribe, for the confinement or rehabilitation of persons charged with or convicted of a criminal offense or other persons held in lawful custody. Other persons held in lawful custody includes juvenile offenders adjudicated delinquent, aliens detained awaiting deportation, persons committed to mental institutions through the criminal justice system, witnesses, or others awaiting charges or trial.

Covered functions means those functions of a covered entity the performance of which makes the entity a health plan, health care provider, or health care clearinghouse.

Data aggregation means, with respect to protected health information created or received by a business associate in its capacity as the business associate of a covered entity, the combining of such protected health information by the business associate with the protected health information received by the business associate in its capacity as a business associate of another covered entity, to permit data analyses that relate to the health care operations of the respective covered entities.

Designated record set means:

(1) A group of records maintained by or for a covered entity that is:

(i) The medical records and billing records about individuals maintained by or for a covered health care provider;

(ii) The enrollment, payment, claims adjudication, and case or medical management record systems maintained by or for a health plan; or

(iii) Used, in whole or in part, by or for the covered entity to make decisions about individuals.

(2) For purposes of this paragraph, the term record means any item, collection, or grouping of information that includes protected health information and is maintained, collected, used, or disseminated by or for a covered entity.

Direct treatment relationship means a treatment relationship between an individual and a health care provider that is not an indirect treatment relationship.

Disclosure means the release, transfer, provision of access to, or divulging in any other manner of information outside the entity holding the information.

Health care operations means any of the following activities of the covered entity to the extent that the activities are related to covered functions:

(1) Conducting quality assessment and improvement activities, including outcomes evaluation and development of clinical guidelines, provided that the obtaining of generalizable knowledge is not the primary purpose of any studies resulting from such activities; population-based activities relating to improving health or reducing health care costs, protocol development, case management and care coordination, contacting of health care providers and patients with information about treatment alternatives; and related functions that do not include treatment;

(2) Reviewing the competence or qualifications of health care professionals, evaluating practitioner and provider performance, health plan performance, conducting training programs in which students, trainees, or practitioners in areas of health care learn under supervision to practice or improve their skills as health care providers, training of non-health care professionals, accreditation, certification, licensing, or credentialing activities;

(3) Underwriting, premium rating, and other activities relating to the creation, renewal or replacement of a contract of health insurance or health benefits, and ceding, securing, or placing a contract for reinsurance of risk relating to claims for health care (including stop-loss insurance and excess of loss insurance), provided that the requirements of § 164.514(g) are met, if applicable;

(4) Conducting or arranging for medical review, legal services, and auditing functions, including fraud and abuse detection and compliance programs;

(5) Business planning and development, such as conducting cost-management and planning-related analyses related to managing and operating the entity, including formulary development and administration, development or improvement of methods of payment or coverage policies; and

(6) Business management and general administrative activities of the entity, including, but not limited to:

(i) Management activities relating to implementation of and compliance with the requirements of this subchapter;

(ii) Customer service, including the provision of data analyses for policy holders, plan sponsors, or other customers, provided that protected health information is not disclosed to such policy holder, plan sponsor, or customer.

(iii) Resolution of internal grievances;

(iv) The sale, transfer, merger, or consolidation of all or part of the covered entity with another covered entity, or an entity that following such activity will become a covered entity and due diligence related to such activity; and

(v) Consistent with the applicable requirements of § 164.514, creating de-identified health information or a limited data set, and fundraising for the benefit of the covered entity.

Health oversight agency means an agency or authority of the United States, a State, a territory, a political subdivision of a State or territory, or an Indian tribe, or a person or entity acting under a grant of authority from or contract with such public agency, including the employees or agents of such public agency or its contractors or persons or entities to whom it has granted authority, that is authorized by law to oversee the health care system (whether public or private) or government programs in which health information is necessary to determine eligibility or compliance, or to enforce civil rights laws for which health information is relevant.

Indirect treatment relationship means a relationship between an individual and a health care provider in which:

(1) The health care provider delivers health care to the individual based on the orders of another health care provider; and

(2) The health care provider typically provides services or products, or reports the diagnosis or results associated with the health care, directly to another health care provider, who provides the services or products or reports to the individual.

Individual means the person who is the subject of protected health information.

Inmate means a person incarcerated in or otherwise confined to a correctional institution.

Law enforcement official means an officer or employee of any agency or authority of the United States, a State, a territory, a political subdivision of a State or territory, or an Indian tribe, who is empowered by law to:

(1) Investigate or conduct an official inquiry into a potential violation of law; or

(2) Prosecute or otherwise conduct a criminal, civil, or administrative proceeding arising from an alleged violation of law.

Marketing means:

(1) To make a communication about a product or service that encourages recipients of the communication to purchase or use the product or service, unless the communication is made:

(i) To describe a health-related product or service (or payment for such product or service) that is provided by, or included in a plan of benefits of, the covered entity making the communication, including communications about: the entities participating in a health care provider network or health plan network; replacement of, or enhancements to, a health plan; and health-related products or services available only to a health plan enrollee that add value to, but are not part of, a plan of benefits.

(ii) For treatment of the individual; or

(iii) For case management or care coordination for the individual, or to direct or recommend alternative treatments, therapies, health care providers, or settings of care to the individual.

(2) An arrangement between a covered entity and any other entity whereby the covered entity discloses protected health information to the other entity, in exchange for direct or indirect remuneration, for the other entity or its affiliate to make a communication about its own product or service that encourages recipients of the communication to purchase or use that product or service.

Organized health care arrangement means:

(1) A clinically integrated care setting in which individuals typically receive health care from more than one health care provider;

(2) An organized system of health care in which more than one covered entity participates, and in which the participating covered entities:

(i) Hold themselves out to the public as participating in a joint arrangement; and

(ii) Participate in joint activities that include at least one of the following:

(A) Utilization review, in which health care decisions by participating covered entities are reviewed by other participating covered entities or by a third party on their behalf;

(B) Quality assessment and improvement activities, in which treatment provided by participating covered entities is assessed by other participating covered entities or by a third party on their behalf; or

(C) Payment activities, if the financial risk for delivering health care is shared, in part or in whole, by participating covered entities through the joint arrangement and if protected health information created or received by a covered entity is reviewed by other participating covered entities or by a third party on their behalf for the purpose of administering the sharing of financial risk.

(3) A group health plan and a health insurance issuer or HMO with respect to such group health plan, but only with respect to protected health information created or received by such health insurance issuer or HMO that relates to individuals who are or who have been participants or beneficiaries in such group health plan;

(4) A group health plan and one or more other group health plans each of which are maintained by the same plan sponsor; or

(5) The group health plans described in paragraph (4) of this definition and health insurance issuers or HMOs with respect to such group health plans, but only with respect to protected health information created or received by such health insurance issuers or HMOs that relates to individuals who are or have been participants or beneficiaries in any of such group health plans.

Payment means:

(1) The activities undertaken by:

(i) A health plan to obtain premiums or to determine or fulfill its responsibility for coverage and provision of benefits under the health plan; or

(ii) A health care provider or health plan to obtain or provide reimbursement for the provision of health care; and

(2) The activities in paragraph (1) of this definition relate to the individual to whom health care is provided and include, but are not limited to:

(i) Determinations of eligibility or coverage (including coordination of benefits or the determination of cost sharing amounts), and adjudication or subrogation of health benefit claims;

(ii) Risk adjusting amounts due based on enrollee health status and demographic characteristics;

(iii) Billing, claims management, collection activities, obtaining payment under a contract for reinsurance (including stop-loss insurance and excess of loss insurance), and related health care data processing;

(iv) Review of health care services with respect to medical necessity, coverage under a health plan, appropriateness of care, or justification of charges;

(v) Utilization review activities, including precertification and preauthorization of services, concurrent and retrospective review of services; and

(vi) Disclosure to consumer reporting agencies of any of the following protected health information relating to collection of premiums or reimbursement:

(A) Name and address;

(B) Date of birth;

(C) Social security number;

(D) Payment history;

(E) Account number; and

1237

(F) Name and address of the health care provider and/or health plan.

Plan sponsor is defined as defined at section 3(16)(B) of ERISA, 29 U.S.C. 1002(16)(B).

Protected health information means individually identifiable health information:

(1) Except as provided in paragraph (2) of this definition, that is:

(i) Transmitted by electronic media;

(ii) Maintained in any medium described in the definition of electronic media at § 162.103 of this subchapter; or

(iii) Transmitted or maintained in any other form or medium.

(2) Protected health information excludes individually identifiable health information in:

(i) Education records covered by the Family Educational Rights and Privacy Act, as amended, 20 U.S.C. 1232g;

(ii) Records described at 20 U.S.C. 1232g(a)(4)(B)(iv); and

(iii) Employment records held by a covered entity in its role as employer.

Psychotherapy notes means notes recorded (in any medium) by a health care provider who is a mental health professional documenting or analyzing the contents of conversation during a private counseling session or a group, joint, or family counseling session and that are separated from the rest of the individual's medical record. Psychotherapy notes excludes medication prescription and monitoring, counseling session start and stop times, the modalities and frequencies of treatment furnished, results of clinical tests, and any summary of the following items: Diagnosis, functional status, the treatment plan, symptoms, prognosis, and progress to date.

Public health authority means an agency or authority of the United States, a State, a territory, a political subdivision of a State or territory, or an Indian tribe, or a person or entity acting under a grant of authority from or contract with such public agency, including the employees or agents of such public agency or its contractors or persons or entities to whom it has granted authority, that is responsible for public health matters as part of its official mandate.

Required by law means a mandate contained in law that compels an entity to make a use or disclosure of protected health information and that is enforceable in a court of law. Required by law includes, but is not limited to, court orders and court-ordered warrants; subpoenas or summons issued by a court, grand jury, a governmental or tribal inspector general, or an administrative body authorized to require the production of information; a civil or an authorized investigative demand; Medicare conditions of participation with respect to health care providers participating in the program; and statutes or regulations that require the production of information, including statutes or regulations that require such information if payment is sought under a government program providing public benefits.

Research means a systematic investigation, including research development, testing, and evaluation, designed to develop or contribute to generalizable knowledge.

Treatment means the provision, coordination, or management of health care and related services by one or more health care providers, including the coordination or management of health care by a health care provider with a third party; consultation between health care providers relating to a patient; or the referral of a patient for health care from one health care provider to another.

Use means, with respect to individually identifiable health information, the sharing, employment, application, utilization, examination, or analysis of such information within an entity that maintains such information.

§ 164.502   Uses and disclosures of protected health information: general rules.

(a) Standard. A covered entity may not use or disclose protected health information, except as permitted or required by this subpart or by subpart C of part 160 of this subchapter.

(1) Permitted uses and disclosures. A covered entity is permitted to use or disclose protected health information as follows:

(i) To the individual;

(ii) For treatment, payment, or health care operations, as permitted by and in compliance with § 164.506;

(iii) Incident to a use or disclosure otherwise permitted or required by this subpart, provided that the covered entity has complied with the applicable requirements of § 164.502(b), § 164.514(d), and § 164.530(c) with respect to such otherwise permitted or required use or disclosure;

(iv) Pursuant to and in compliance with a valid authorization under § 164.508;

(v) Pursuant to an agreement under, or as otherwise permitted by, § 164.510; and

(vi) As permitted by and in compliance with this section, § 164.512, or § 164.514(e), (f), or (g).

(2) Required disclosures. A covered entity is required to disclose protected health information:

(i) To an individual, when requested under, and required by § 164.524 or § 164.528; and

(ii) When required by the Secretary under subpart C of part 160 of this subchapter to investigate or determine the covered entity's compliance with this subpart.

(b) Standard: Minimum necessary.

(1) Minimum necessary applies. When using or disclosing protected health information or when requesting protected health information from another covered entity, a covered entity must make reasonable efforts to limit protected health information to the minimum necessary to accomplish the intended purpose of the use, disclosure, or request.

(2) Minimum necessary does not apply. This requirement does not apply to:

(i) Disclosures to or requests by a health care provider for treatment;

(ii) Uses or disclosures made to the individual, as permitted under paragraph (a)(1)(i) of this section or as required by paragraph (a)(2)(i) of this section;

(iii) Uses or disclosures made pursuant to an authorization under § 164.508;

(iv) Disclosures made to the Secretary in accordance with subpart C of part 160 of this subchapter;

(v) Uses or disclosures that are required by law, as described by § 164.512(a); and

(vi) Uses or disclosures that are required for compliance with applicable requirements of this subchapter.

(c) Standard: Uses and disclosures of protected health information subject to an agreed upon restriction. A covered entity that has agreed to a restriction pursuant to § 164.522(a)(1) may not use or disclose the protected health information covered by the restriction in violation of such restriction, except as otherwise provided in § 164.522(a).

(d) Standard: Uses and disclosures of de-identified protected health information.

(1) Uses and disclosures to create de-identified information. A covered entity may use protected health information to create information that is not individually identifiable health information or disclose protected health information only to a business associate for such purpose, whether or not the de-identified information is to be used by the covered entity.

(2) Uses and disclosures of de-identified information. Health information that meets the standard and implementation specifications for de-identification under § 164.514(a) and (b) is considered not to be individually identifiable health information, i.e., de-identified. The requirements of this subpart do not apply to information that has been de-identified in accordance with the applicable requirements of § 164.514, provided that:

(i) Disclosure of a code or other means of record identification designed to enable coded or otherwise de-identified information to be re-identified constitutes disclosure of protected health information; and

(ii) If de-identified information is re-identified, a covered entity may use or disclose such re-identified information only as permitted or required by this subpart.

(e)(1) Standard: Disclosures to business associates.

(i) A covered entity may disclose protected health information to a business associate and may allow a business associate to create or receive protected health information on its behalf, if the covered entity obtains satisfactory assurance that the business associate will appropriately safeguard the information.

(ii) This standard does not apply:

(A) With respect to disclosures by a covered entity to a health care provider concerning the treatment of the individual;

(B) With respect to disclosures by a group health plan or a health insurance issuer or HMO with respect to a group health plan to the plan sponsor, to the extent that the requirements of § 164.504(f) apply and are met; or

(C) With respect to uses or disclosures by a health plan that is a government program providing public benefits, if eligibility for, or enrollment in, the health plan is determined by an agency other than the agency administering the health plan, or if the protected health information used to determine enrollment or eligibility in the health plan is collected by an agency other than the agency administering the health plan, and such activity is authorized by law, with respect to the collection and sharing of individually identifiable health information for the performance of such functions by the health plan and the agency other than the agency administering the health plan.

(iii) A covered entity that violates the satisfactory assurances it provided as a business associate of another covered entity will be in noncompliance with the standards, implementation specifications, and requirements of this paragraph and § 164.504(e).

(2) Implementation specification: documentation. A covered entity must document the satisfactory assurances required by paragraph (e)(1) of this section through a written contract or other written agreement or arrangement with the business associate that meets the applicable requirements of § 164.504(e).

(f) Standard: Deceased individuals. A covered entity must comply with the requirements of this subpart with respect to the protected health information of a deceased individual.

(g)(1) Standard: Personal representatives. As specified in this paragraph, a covered entity must, except as provided in paragraphs (g)(3) and (g)(5) of this section, treat a personal representative as the individual for purposes of this subchapter.

(2) Implementation specification: adults and emancipated minors. If under applicable law a person has authority to act on behalf of an individual who is an adult or an emancipated minor in making decisions related to health care, a covered entity must treat such person as a personal representative under this subchapter, with respect to protected health information relevant to such personal representation.

(3)(i) Implementation specification: unemancipated minors. If under applicable law a parent, guardian, or other person acting in loco parentis has authority to act on behalf of an individual who is an unemancipated minor in making decisions related to health care, a covered entity must treat such person as a personal representative under this subchapter, with respect to protected health information relevant to such personal representation, except that such person may not be a personal representative of an unemancipated minor, and the minor has the authority to act as an individual, with respect to protected health information pertaining to a health care service, if:

(A) The minor consents to such health care service; no other consent to such health care service is required by law, regardless of whether the consent of another person has also been obtained; and the minor has not requested that such person be treated as the personal representative;

(B) The minor may lawfully obtain such health care service without the consent of a parent, guardian, or other person acting in loco parentis, and the minor, a court, or another person authorized by law consents to such health care service; or

(C) A parent, guardian, or other person acting in loco parentis assents to an agreement of confidentiality between a covered health care provider and the minor with respect to such health care service.

(ii) Notwithstanding the provisions of paragraph (g)(3)(i) of this section:

(A) If, and to the extent, permitted or required by an applicable provision of State or other law, including applicable case law, a covered entity may disclose, or provide access in accordance with § 164.524 to, protected health information about an unemancipated minor to a parent, guardian, or other person acting in loco parentis;

(B) If, and to the extent, prohibited by an applicable provision of State or other law, including applicable case law, a covered entity may not disclose, or provide access in accordance with § 164.524 to, protected health information about an un-emancipated minor to a parent, guardian, or other person acting in loco parentis; and

(C) Where the parent, guardian, or other person acting in loco parentis, is not the personal representative under paragraphs (g)(3)(i)(A), (B), or (C) of this section and where there is no applicable access provision under State or other law, including case law, a covered entity may provide or deny access under § 164.524 to a parent, guardian, or other person acting in loco parentis, if such action is consistent with State or other applicable law, provided that such decision must be made by a licensed health care professional, in the exercise of professional judgment.

(4) Implementation specification: Deceased individuals. If under applicable law an executor, administrator, or other person has authority to act on behalf of a deceased individual or of the individual's estate, a covered entity must treat such person as a personal representative under this subchapter, with respect to protected health information relevant to such personal representation.

(5) Implementation specification: Abuse, neglect, endangerment situations. Notwithstanding a State law or any requirement of this paragraph to the contrary, a covered entity may elect not to treat a person as the personal representative of an individual if:

(i) The covered entity has a reasonable belief that:

(A) The individual has been or may be subjected to domestic violence, abuse, or neglect by such person; or

(B) Treating such person as the personal representative could endanger the individual; and

(ii) The covered entity, in the exercise of professional judgment, decides that it is not in the best interest of the individual to treat the person as the individual's personal representative.

(h) Standard: Confidential communications. A covered health care provider or health plan must comply with the applicable requirements of § 164.522(b) in communicating protected health information.

(i) Standard: Uses and disclosures consistent with notice. A covered entity that is required by § 164.520 to have a notice may not use or disclose protected health information in a manner inconsistent with such notice. A covered entity that is required by § 164.520(b)(1)(iii) to include a specific statement in its notice if it intends to engage in an activity listed in § 164.520(b)(1)(iii)(A)–(C), may not use or disclose protected health information for such activities, unless the required statement is included in the notice.

(j) Standard: Disclosures by whistleblowers and workforce member crime victims.

(1) Disclosures by whistleblowers. A covered entity is not considered to have violated the requirements of this subpart if a member of its workforce or a business associate discloses protected health information, provided that:

(i) The workforce member or business associate believes in good faith that the covered entity has engaged in conduct that is unlawful or otherwise violates professional or clinical standards, or that the care, services, or conditions provided by the covered entity potentially endangers one or more patients, workers, or the public; and

(ii) The disclosure is to:

(A) A health oversight agency or public health authority authorized by law to investigate or otherwise oversee the relevant conduct or conditions of the covered entity or to an appropriate health care accreditation organization for the purpose of reporting the allegation of failure to meet professional standards or misconduct by the covered entity; or

(B) An attorney retained by or on behalf of the workforce member or business associate for the purpose of determining the legal options of the workforce member or business associate with regard to the conduct described in paragraph (j)(1)(i) of this section.

(2) Disclosures by workforce members who are victims of a crime. A covered entity is not considered to have violated the requirements of this subpart if a member of its workforce who is the victim of a criminal act discloses protected health information to a law enforcement official, provided that:

(i) The protected health information disclosed is about the suspected perpetrator of the criminal act; and

(ii) The protected health information disclosed is limited to the information listed in § 164.512(f)(2)(i).

§ 164.504 Uses and disclosures: Organizational requirements.

(a) Definitions. As used in this section:

Common control exists if an entity has the power, directly or indirectly, significantly to influence or direct the actions or policies of another entity.

Common ownership exists if an entity or entities possess an ownership or equity interest of 5 percent or more in another entity.

Health care component means a component or combination of components of a hybrid entity designated by the hybrid entity in accordance with paragraph (c)(3)(iii) of this section.

Hybrid entity means a single legal entity:

(1) That is a covered entity;

(2) Whose business activities include both covered and non-covered functions; and

(3) That designates health care components in accordance with paragraph (c)(3)(iii) of this section.

Plan administration functions means administration functions performed by the plan sponsor of a group health plan on behalf of the group health plan and excludes functions performed by the plan sponsor in connection with any other benefit or benefit plan of the plan sponsor.

Summary health information means information, that may be individually identifiable health information, and:

(1) That summarizes the claims history, claims expenses, or type of claims experienced by individuals for whom a plan sponsor has provided health benefits under a group health plan; and

(2) From which the information described at § 164.514(b)(2)(i) has been deleted, except that the geographic information described in § 164.514(b)(2)(i)(B) need only be aggregated to the level of a five digit zip code.

(b) Standard: Health care component. If a covered entity is a hybrid entity, the requirements of this subpart, other than the requirements of this section, apply only to the health care component(s) of the entity, as specified in this section.

(c)(1) Implementation specification: Application of other provisions. In applying a provision of this subpart, other than this section, to a hybrid entity:

(i) A reference in such provision to a "covered entity" refers to a health care component of the covered entity;

(ii) A reference in such provision to a "health plan," "covered health care provider," or "health care clearinghouse" refers to a health care component of the covered entity if such health care component performs the functions of a health plan, health care provider, or health care clearinghouse, as applicable; and

(iii) A reference in such provision to "protected health information" refers to protected health information that is created or received by or on behalf of the health care component of the covered entity.

(2) Implementation specifications: Safeguard requirements. The covered entity that is a hybrid entity must ensure that a health care component of the entity complies with the applicable requirements of this subpart. In particular, and without limiting this requirement, such covered entity must ensure that:

(i) Its health care component does not disclose protected health information to another component of the covered entity in circumstances in which this subpart would prohibit such disclosure if the health care component and the other component were separate and distinct legal entities;

(ii) A component that is described by paragraph (c)(3)(iii)(B) of this section does not use or disclose protected health information that it creates or receives from or on behalf of the health care component in a way prohibited by this subpart; and

(iii) If a person performs duties for both the health care component in the capacity of a member of the workforce of such component and for another component of the entity in the same capacity with respect to that component, such workforce member must not use or disclose protected health information created or received in the course of or incident to the member's work for the health care component in a way prohibited by this subpart.

(3) Implementation specifications: Responsibilities of the covered entity. A covered entity that is a hybrid entity has the following responsibilities:

(i) For purposes of subpart C of part 160 of this subchapter, pertaining to compliance and enforcement, the covered entity has the responsibility to comply with this subpart.

(ii) The covered entity has the responsibility for complying with § 164.530(i), pertaining to the implementation of policies and procedures to ensure compliance with this subpart, including the safeguard requirements in paragraph (c)(2) of this section.

(iii) The covered entity is responsible for designating the components that are part of one or more health care components of the covered entity and documenting the designation as required by § 164.530(j), provided that, if the covered entity designates a health care component or components, it must include any component that would meet the definition of covered entity if it were a separate legal entity. Health care component(s) also may include a component only to the extent that it performs:

(A) Covered functions; or

(B) Activities that would make such component a business associate of a component that performs covered functions if the two components were separate legal entities.

(d)(1) Standard: Affiliated covered entities. Legally separate covered entities that are affiliated may designate themselves as a single covered entity for purposes of this subpart.

(2) Implementation specifications: Requirements for designation of an affiliated covered entity.

(i) Legally separate covered entities may designate themselves (including any health care component of such covered entity) as a single affiliated covered entity, for purposes of this subpart, if all of the covered entities designated are under common ownership or control.

(ii) The designation of an affiliated covered entity must be documented and the documentation maintained as required by § 164.530(j).

(3) Implementation specifications: Safeguard requirements. An affiliated covered entity must ensure that:

(i) The affiliated covered entity's use and disclosure of protected health information comply with the applicable requirements of this subpart; and

(ii) If the affiliated covered entity combines the functions of a health plan, health care provider, or health care clearinghouse, the affiliated covered entity complies with paragraph (g) of this section.

(e)(1) Standard: Business associate contracts.

(i) The contract or other arrangement between the covered entity and the business associate required by § 164.502(e)(2) must meet the requirements of paragraph (e)(2) or (e)(3) of this section, as applicable.

(ii) A covered entity is not in compliance with the standards in § 164.502(e) and paragraph (e) of this section, if the covered entity knew of a pattern of activity or practice of the business associate that constituted a material breach or violation of the business associate's obligation under the contract or other arrangement, unless the covered entity took reasonable steps to cure the breach or end the violation, as applicable, and, if such steps were unsuccessful:

(A) Terminated the contract or arrangement, if feasible; or

(B) If termination is not feasible, reported the problem to the Secretary.

(2) Implementation specifications: Business associate contracts. A contract between the covered entity and a business associate must:

(i) Establish the permitted and required uses and disclosures of such information by the business associate. The contract may not authorize the business associate to use or further disclose the information in a manner that would violate the requirements of this subpart, if done by the covered entity, except that:

(A) The contract may permit the business associate to use and disclose protected health information for the proper management and administration of the business associate, as provided in paragraph (e)(4) of this section; and

(B) The contract may permit the business associate to provide data aggregation services relating to the health care operations of the covered entity.

(ii) Provide that the business associate will:

(A) Not use or further disclose the information other than as permitted or required by the contract or as required by law;

(B) Use appropriate safeguards to prevent use or disclosure of the information other than as provided for by its contract;

(C) Report to the covered entity any use or disclosure of the information not provided for by its contract of which it becomes aware;

(D) Ensure that any agents, including a subcontractor, to whom it provides protected health information received from, or created or received by the business associate on behalf of, the covered entity agrees to the same restrictions and conditions that apply to the business associate with respect to such information;

(E) Make available protected health information in accordance with § 164.524;

(F) Make available protected health information for amendment and incorporate any amendments to protected health information in accordance with § 164.526;

(G) Make available the information required to provide an accounting of disclosures in accordance with § 164.528;

(H) Make its internal practices, books, and records relating to the use and disclosure of protected health information received from, or created or received by the business associate on behalf of, the covered entity available to the Secretary for purposes of determining the covered entity's compliance with this subpart; and

(I) At termination of the contract, if feasible, return or destroy all protected health information received from, or created or received by the business associate on behalf of, the covered entity that the business associate still maintains in any form and retain no copies of such information or, if such return or destruction is not feasible, extend the protections of the contract to the information and limit further uses and disclosures to those purposes that make the return or destruction of the information infeasible.

(iii) Authorize termination of the contract by the covered entity, if the covered entity determines that the business associate has violated a material term of the contract.

(3) Implementation specifications: Other arrangements.

(i) If a covered entity and its business associate are both governmental entities:

(A) The covered entity may comply with paragraph (e) of this section by entering into a memorandum of understanding with the business associate that contains terms that accomplish the objectives of paragraph (e)(2) of this section.

(B) The covered entity may comply with paragraph (e) of this section, if other law (including regulations adopted by the covered entity or its business associate) contains requirements applicable to the business associate that accomplish the objectives of paragraph (e)(2) of this section.

(ii) If a business associate is required by law to perform a function or activity on behalf of a covered entity or to provide a service described in the definition of business associate in § 160.103 of this subchapter to a covered entity, such covered entity may disclose protected health information to the business associate to the extent necessary to comply with the legal mandate without meeting the requirements of this paragraph (e), provided that the covered entity attempts in good faith to obtain satisfactory assurances as required by paragraph (e)(3)(i) of this section, and, if such attempt fails, documents the attempt and the reasons that such assurances cannot be obtained.

(iii) The covered entity may omit from its other arrangements the termination authorization required by paragraph (e)(2)(iii) of this section, if such authorization is inconsistent with the statutory obligations of the covered entity or its business associate.

(4) Implementation specifications: Other requirements for contracts and other arrangements.

(i) The contract or other arrangement between the covered entity and the business associate may permit the business associate to use the information received by the business associate in its capacity as a business associate to the covered entity, if necessary:

(A) For the proper management and administration of the business associate; or

(B) To carry out the legal responsibilities of the business associate.

(ii) The contract or other arrangement between the covered entity and the business associate may permit the business associate to disclose the information received by the business associate in its capacity as a business associate for the purposes described in paragraph (e)(4)(i) of this section, if:

(A) The disclosure is required by law; or

(B)(1) The business associate obtains reasonable assurances from the person to whom the information is disclosed that it will be held confidentially and used or further disclosed only as required by law or for the purpose for which it was disclosed to the person; and

(2) The person notifies the business associate of any instances of which it is aware in which the confidentiality of the information has been breached.

(f)(1) Standard: Requirements for group health plans.

(i) Except as provided under paragraph (f)(1)(ii) or (iii) of this section or as otherwise authorized under § 164.508, a group health plan, in order to disclose protected health information to the plan sponsor or to provide for or permit the disclosure of protected health information to the plan sponsor by a health insurance issuer or HMO with respect to the group health plan, must ensure that the plan documents restrict uses and disclosures of such information by the plan sponsor consistent with the requirements of this subpart.

(ii) The group health plan, or a health insurance issuer or HMO with respect to the group health plan, may disclose summary health information to the plan sponsor, if the plan sponsor requests the summary health information for the purpose of:

(A) Obtaining premium bids from health plans for providing health insurance coverage under the group health plan; or

(B) Modifying, amending, or terminating the group health plan.

(iii) The group health plan, or a health insurance issuer or HMO with respect to the group health plan, may disclose to the plan sponsor information on whether the individual is participating in the group health plan, or is enrolled in or has disenrolled from a health insurance issuer or HMO offered by the plan.

(2) Implementation specifications: Requirements for plan documents. The plan documents of the group health plan must be amended to incorporate provisions to:

(i) Establish the permitted and required uses and disclosures of such information by the plan sponsor, provided that such permitted and required uses and disclosures may not be inconsistent with this subpart.

(ii) Provide that the group health plan will disclose protected health information to the plan sponsor only upon receipt of a certification by the plan sponsor that the plan documents have been amended to incorporate the following provisions and that the plan sponsor agrees to:

(A) Not use or further disclose the information other than as permitted or required by the plan documents or as required by law;

(B) Ensure that any agents, including a subcontractor, to whom it provides protected health information received from the group health plan agree to the same restrictions and conditions that apply to the plan sponsor with respect to such information;

(C) Not use or disclose the information for employment-related actions and decisions or in connection with any other benefit or employee benefit plan of the plan sponsor;

(D) Report to the group health plan any use or disclosure of the information that is inconsistent with the uses or disclosures provided for of which it becomes aware;

(E) Make available protected health information in accordance with § 164.524;

(F) Make available protected health information for amendment and incorporate any amendments to protected health information in accordance with § 164.526;

(G) Make available the information required to provide an accounting of disclosures in accordance with § 164.528;

(H) Make its internal practices, books, and records relating to the use and disclosure of protected health information received from the group health plan available to the Secretary for purposes of determining compliance by the group health plan with this subpart;

(I) If feasible, return or destroy all protected health information received from the group health plan that the sponsor still maintains in any form and retain no copies of such information when no longer needed for the purpose for which disclosure was made, except that, if such return or destruction is not feasible, limit further uses and disclosures to those purposes that make the return or destruction of the information infeasible; and

(J) Ensure that the adequate separation required in paragraph (f)(2)(iii) of this section is established.

(iii) Provide for adequate separation between the group health plan and the plan sponsor. The plan documents must:

(A) Describe those employees or classes of employees or other persons under the control of the plan sponsor to be given access to the protected health information to be disclosed, provided that any employee or person who receives protected health information relating to payment under, health care operations of, or other matters pertaining to the group health plan in the ordinary course of business must be included in such description;

(B) Restrict the access to and use by such employees and other persons described in paragraph (f)(2)(iii)(A) of this section to the plan administration functions that the plan sponsor performs for the group health plan; and

(C) Provide an effective mechanism for resolving any issues of noncompliance by persons described in paragraph (f)(2)(iii)(A) of this section with the plan document provisions required by this paragraph.

(3) Implementation specifications: Uses and disclosures. A group health plan may:

(i) Disclose protected health information to a plan sponsor to carry out plan administration functions that the plan sponsor performs only consistent with the provisions of paragraph (f)(2) of this section;

(ii) Not permit a health insurance issuer or HMO with respect to the group health plan to disclose protected health information to the plan sponsor except as permitted by this paragraph;

(iii) Not disclose and may not permit a health insurance issuer or HMO to disclose protected health information to a plan sponsor as otherwise permitted by this paragraph unless a statement required by § 164.520(b)(1)(iii)(C) is included in the appropriate notice; and (iv) Not disclose protected health information to the plan sponsor for the purpose of employment-related actions or decisions or in connection with any other benefit or employee benefit plan of the plan sponsor.

(g) Standard: Requirements for a covered entity with multiple covered functions.

(1) A covered entity that performs multiple covered functions that would make the entity any combination of a health plan, a covered health care provider, and a health care clearinghouse, must comply with the standards, requirements, and implementation specifications of this subpart, as applicable to the health plan, health care provider, or health care clearinghouse covered functions performed.

(2) A covered entity that performs multiple covered functions may use or disclose the protected health information of individuals who receive the covered entity's health plan or health care provider services, but not both, only for purposes related to the appropriate function being performed.

§ 164.506 Uses and disclosures to carry out treatment, payment, or health care operations.

(a) Standard: Permitted uses and disclosures. Except with respect to uses or disclosures that require an authorization under § 164.508(a)(2) and (3), a covered entity may use or disclose protected health information for treatment, payment, or health care operations as set forth in paragraph (c) of this section, provided that such use or disclosure is consistent with other applicable requirements of this subpart.

(b) Standard: Consent for uses and disclosures permitted.

(1) A covered entity may obtain consent of the individual to use or disclose protected health information to carry out treatment, payment, or health care operations.

(2) Consent, under paragraph (b) of this section, shall not be effective to permit a use or disclosure of protected health information when an authorization, under § 164.508, is required or when another condition must be met for such use or disclosure to be permissible under this subpart.

(c) Implementation specifications: Treatment, payment, or health care operations.

(1) A covered entity may use or disclose protected health information for its own treatment, payment, or health care operations.

(2) A covered entity may disclose protected health information for treatment activities of a health care provider.

(3) A covered entity may disclose protected health information to another covered entity or a health care provider for the payment activities of the entity that receives the information.

(4) A covered entity may disclose protected health information to another covered entity for health care operations activities of the entity that receives the information, if each entity either has or had a relationship with the individual who is the subject of the protected health information being requested, the protected health information pertains to such relationship, and the disclosure is:

(i) For a purpose listed in paragraph (1) or (2) of the definition of health care operations; or

(ii) For the purpose of health care fraud and abuse detection or compliance.

(5) A covered entity that participates in an organized health care arrangement may disclose protected health information about an individual to another covered entity that participates in the organized health care arrangement for any health care operations activities of the organized health care arrangement.

§ 164.508 Uses and disclosures for which an authorization is required.

(a) Standard: authorizations for uses and disclosures.—

(1) Authorization required: general rule. Except as otherwise permitted or required by this subchapter, a covered entity may not use or disclose protected health information without an authorization that is valid under this section. When a covered entity obtains or receives a valid authorization for its use or disclosure of protected health information, such use or disclosure must be consistent with such authorization.

(2) Authorization required: psychotherapy notes. Notwithstanding any provision of this subpart, other than the transition provisions in § 164.532, a covered entity must obtain an authorization for any use or disclosure of psychotherapy notes, except:

(i) To carry out the following treatment, payment, or health care operations:

(A) Use by the originator of the psychotherapy notes for treatment;

(B) Use or disclosure by the covered entity for its own training programs in which students, trainees, or practitioners in mental health learn under supervision to practice or improve their skills in group, joint, family, or individual counseling; or

(C) Use or disclosure by the covered entity to defend itself in a legal action or other proceeding brought by the individual; and

(ii) A use or disclosure that is required by § 164.502(a)(2)(ii) or permitted by § 164.512(a); § 164.512(d) with respect to the oversight of the originator of the psychotherapy notes; § 164.512(g)(1); or § 164.512(j)(1)(i).

(3) Authorization required: Marketing.

(i) Notwithstanding any provision of this subpart, other than the transition provisions in § 164.532, a covered entity must obtain an authorization for any use or disclosure of protected health information for marketing, except if the communication is in the form of:

(A) A face-to-face communication made by a covered entity to an individual; or

(B) A promotional gift of nominal value provided by the covered entity.

(ii) If the marketing involves direct or indirect remuneration to the covered entity from a third party, the authorization must state that such remuneration is involved.

(b) Implementation specifications: general requirements.—

(1) Valid authorizations.

(i) A valid authorization is a document that meets the requirements in paragraphs (a)(3)(ii), (c)(1), and (c)(2) of this section, as applicable.

(ii) A valid authorization may contain elements or information in addition to the elements required by this section, provided that such additional elements or information are not inconsistent with the elements required by this section.

(2) Defective authorizations. An authorization is not valid, if the document submitted has any of the following defects:

(**i**) The expiration date has passed or the expiration event is known by the covered entity to have occurred;

(**ii**) The authorization has not been filled out completely, with respect to an element described by paragraph (c) of this section, if applicable;

(**iii**) The authorization is known by the covered entity to have been revoked;

(**iv**) The authorization violates paragraph (b)(3) or (4) of this section, if applicable;

(**v**) Any material information in the authorization is known by the covered entity to be false.

(3) Compound authorizations. An authorization for use or disclosure of protected health information may not be combined with any other document to create a compound authorization, except as follows:

(**i**) An authorization for the use or disclosure of protected health information for a research study may be combined with any other type of written permission for the same research study, including another authorization for the use or disclosure of protected health information for such research or a consent to participate in such research;

(**ii**) An authorization for a use or disclosure of psychotherapy notes may only be combined with another authorization for a use or disclosure of psychotherapy notes;

(**iii**) An authorization under this section, other than an authorization for a use or disclosure of psychotherapy notes, may be combined with any other such authorization under this section, except when a covered entity has conditioned the provision of treatment, payment, enrollment in the health plan, or eligibility for benefits under paragraph (b)(4) of this section on the provision of one of the authorizations.

(4) Prohibition on conditioning of authorizations. A covered entity may not condition the provision to an individual of treatment, payment, enrollment in the health plan, or eligibility for benefits on the provision of an authorization, except:

(**i**) A covered health care provider may condition the provision of research-related treatment on provision of an authorization for the use or disclosure of protected health information for such research under this section;

(**ii**) A health plan may condition enrollment in the health plan or eligibility for benefits on provision of an authorization requested by the health plan prior to an individual's enrollment in the health plan, if:

(A) The authorization sought is for the health plan's eligibility or enrollment determinations relating to the individual or for its underwriting or risk rating determinations; and

(B) The authorization is not for a use or disclosure of psychotherapy notes under paragraph (a)(2) of this section; and

(iii) A covered entity may condition the provision of health care that is solely for the purpose of creating protected health information for disclosure to a third party on provision of an authorization for the disclosure of the protected health information to such third party.

(5) Revocation of authorizations. An individual may revoke an authorization provided under this section at any time, provided that the revocation is in writing, except to the extent that:

(i) The covered entity has taken action in reliance thereon; or

(ii) If the authorization was obtained as a condition of obtaining insurance coverage, other law provides the insurer with the right to contest a claim under the policy or the policy itself.

(6) Documentation. A covered entity must document and retain any signed authorization under this section as required by § 164.530(j).

(c) Implementation specifications: Core elements and requirements.—

(1) Core elements. A valid authorization under this section must contain at least the following elements:

(i) A description of the information to be used or disclosed that identifies the information in a specific and meaningful fashion.

(ii) The name or other specific identification of the person(s), or class of persons, authorized to make the requested use or disclosure.

(iii) The name or other specific identification of the person(s), or class of persons, to whom the covered entity may make the requested use or disclosure.

(iv) A description of each purpose of the requested use or disclosure. The statement "at the request of the individual" is a sufficient description of the purpose when an individual initiates the authorization and does not, or elects not to, provide a statement of the purpose.

(v) An expiration date or an expiration event that relates to the individual or the purpose of the use or disclosure. The statement "end of the research study," "none," or similar language is sufficient if the authorization is for a use or disclosure of protected health information for research, including for the creation and maintenance of a research database or research repository.

(vi) Signature of the individual and date. If the authorization is signed by a personal representative of the individual, a description of such representative's authority to act for the individual must also be provided.

(2) Required statements. In addition to the core elements, the authorization must contain statements adequate to place the individual on notice of all of the following:

(i) The individual's right to revoke the authorization in writing, and either:

(A) The exceptions to the right to revoke and a description of how the individual may revoke the authorization; or

(B) To the extent that the information in paragraph (c)(2)(i)(A) of this section is included in the notice required by § 164.520, a reference to the covered entity's notice.

(ii) The ability or inability to condition treatment, payment, enrollment or eligibility for benefits on the authorization, by stating either:

(A) The covered entity may not condition treatment, payment, enrollment or eligibility for benefits on whether the individual signs the authorization when the prohibition on conditioning of authorizations in paragraph (b)(4) of this section applies; or

(B) The consequences to the individual of a refusal to sign the authorization when, in accordance with paragraph (b)(4) of this section, the covered entity can condition treatment, enrollment in the health plan, or eligibility for benefits on failure to obtain such authorization.

(iii) The potential for information disclosed pursuant to the authorization to be subject to redisclosure by the recipient and no longer be protected by this subpart.

(3) Plain language requirement. The authorization must be written in plain language.

(4) Copy to the individual. If a covered entity seeks an authorization from an individual for a use or disclosure of protected health information, the covered entity must provide the individual with a copy of the signed authorization.

§ 164.510   Uses and disclosures requiring an opportunity for the individual to agree or to object.

A covered entity may use or disclose protected health information, provided that the individual is informed in advance of the use or disclosure and has the opportunity to agree to or prohibit or restrict the use or disclosure, in accordance with the applicable requirements of this section. The covered entity may orally inform the individual of and obtain the individual's oral agreement or objection to a use or disclosure permitted by this section.

(a) Standard: use and disclosure for facility directories.

(1) Permitted uses and disclosure. Except when an objection is expressed in accordance with paragraphs (a)(2) or (3) of this section, a covered health care provider may:

(i) Use the following protected health information to maintain a directory of individuals in its facility:

(A) The individual's name;

(B) The individual's location in the covered health care provider's facility;

(C) The individual's condition described in general terms that does not communicate specific medical information about the individual; and

(D) The individual's religious affiliation; and

(ii) Disclose for directory purposes such information:

(A) To members of the clergy; or

(B) Except for religious affiliation, to other persons who ask for the individual by name.

(2) Opportunity to object. A covered health care provider must inform an individual of the protected health information that it may include in a directory and the persons to whom it may disclose such information (including disclosures to clergy of information regarding religious affiliation) and provide the individual with the opportunity to restrict or prohibit some or all of the uses or disclosures permitted by paragraph (a)(1) of this section.

(3) Emergency circumstances.

(i) If the opportunity to object to uses or disclosures required by paragraph (a)(2) of this section cannot practicably be provided because of the individual's incapacity or an emergency treatment circumstance, a covered health care provider may use or disclose some or all of the protected health information permitted by paragraph (a)(1) of this section for the facility's directory, if such disclosure is:

(A) Consistent with a prior expressed preference of the individual, if any, that is known to the covered health care provider; and

(B) In the individual's best interest as determined by the covered health care provider, in the exercise of professional judgment.

(ii) The covered health care provider must inform the individual and provide an opportunity to object to uses or disclosures for directory purposes as required by paragraph (a)(2) of this section when it becomes practicable to do so.

(b) Standard: uses and disclosures for involvement in the individual's care and notification purposes.

(1) Permitted uses and disclosures.

(i) A covered entity may, in accordance with paragraphs (b)(2) or (3) of this section, disclose to a family member, other relative, or a close personal friend of the individual, or any other person identified by the individual, the protected health information directly relevant to such person's involvement with the individual's care or payment related to the individual's health care.

(ii) A covered entity may use or disclose protected health information to notify, or assist in the notification of (including identifying or locating), a family member, a personal representative of the individual, or another person responsible for the care of the individual of the individual's location, general condition, or death. Any such use or disclosure of protected health information for such notification purposes must be in accordance with paragraphs (b)(2), (3), or (4) of this section, as applicable.

(2) Uses and disclosures with the individual present. If the individual is present for, or otherwise available prior to, a use or disclosure permitted by paragraph (b)(1) of this section and has the capacity to make health care decisions, the covered entity may use or disclose the protected health information if it:

(i) Obtains the individual's agreement;

(ii) Provides the individual with the opportunity to object to the disclosure, and the individual does not express an objection; or

(iii) Reasonably infers from the circumstances, based the exercise of professional judgment, that the individual does not object to the disclosure.

(3) Limited uses and disclosures when the individual is not present. If the individual is not present, or the opportunity to agree or object to the use or disclosure cannot practicably be provided because of the individual's incapacity or an emergency circumstance, the covered entity may, in the exercise of professional judgment, determine whether the disclosure is in the best interests of the individual and, if so, disclose only the protected health information that is directly relevant to the person's involvement with the individual's health care. A covered entity may use professional judgment and its experience with common practice to make reasonable inferences of the individual's best interest in allowing a person to act on behalf of the individual to pick up filled prescriptions, medical supplies, X-rays, or other similar forms of protected health information.

(4) Use and disclosures for disaster relief purposes. A covered entity may use or disclose protected health information to a public or private entity authorized by law or by its charter to assist in disaster relief efforts, for the purpose of coordinating with such entities the uses or disclosures permitted by paragraph (b)(1)(ii) of this section. The requirements in paragraphs (b)(2) and (3) of this section apply to such uses and disclosure to the extent that the covered entity, in the exercise of professional judgment, determines that the requirements do not interfere with the ability to respond to the emergency circumstances.

§ 164.512 Uses and disclosures for which an authorization or opportunity to agree or object is not required.

A covered entity may use or disclose protected health information without the written authorization of the individual, as described in § 164.508, or the opportunity for the individual to agree or object as described in § 164.510, in the situations covered by this section, subject to the applicable requirements of this section. When the covered entity is required by this section to inform the individual of, or when the individual may agree to, a use or disclosure permitted by this section, the covered entity's information and the individual's agreement may be given orally.

(a) Standard: Uses and disclosures required by law.

(1) A covered entity may use or disclose protected health information to the extent that such use or disclosure is required by law and the use or disclosure complies with and is limited to the relevant requirements of such law.

(2) A covered entity must meet the requirements described in paragraph (c), (e), or (f) of this section for uses or disclosures required by law.

(b) Standard: uses and disclosures for public health activities.

(1) Permitted disclosures. A covered entity may disclose protected health information for the public health activities and purposes described in this paragraph to:

(i) A public health authority that is authorized by law to collect or receive such information for the purpose of preventing or controlling disease, injury, or disability, including, but not limited to, the reporting of disease, injury, vital events such as birth or death, and the conduct of public health surveillance, public health investigations, and public health interventions; or, at the direction of a public health authority, to an official of a foreign government agency that is acting in collaboration with a public health authority;

(ii) A public health authority or other appropriate government authority authorized by law to receive reports of child abuse or neglect;

(iii) A person subject to the jurisdiction of the Food and Drug Administration (FDA) with respect to an FDA-regulated product or activity for which that person has responsibility, for the purpose of activities related to the quality, safety or effectiveness of such FDA-regulated product or activity. Such purposes include:

(A) To collect or report adverse events (or similar activities with respect to food or dietary supplements), product defects or problems (including problems with the use or labeling of a product), or biological product deviations;

(B) To track FDA-regulated products;

(C) To enable product recalls, repairs, or replacement, or lookback (including locating and notifying individuals who have received products that have been recalled, withdrawn, or are the subject of lookback); or

(D) To conduct post marketing surveillance;

(iv) A person who may have been exposed to a communicable disease or may otherwise be at risk of contracting or spreading a disease or condition, if the covered entity or public health authority is authorized by law to notify such person as necessary in the conduct of a public health intervention or investigation; or

(v) An employer, about an individual who is a member of the workforce of the employer, if:

(A) The covered entity is a covered health care provider who is a member of the workforce of such employer or who provides health care to the individual at the request of the employer:

(1) To conduct an evaluation relating to medical surveillance of the workplace; or

(2) To evaluate whether the individual has a work-related illness or injury;

(B) The protected health information that is disclosed consists of findings concerning a work-related illness or injury or a workplace-related medical surveillance;

(C) The employer needs such findings in order to comply with its obligations, under 29 CFR parts 1904 through 1928, 30 CFR parts 50 through 90, or under state law having a similar purpose, to record such illness or injury or to carry out responsibilities for workplace medical surveillance; and

(D) The covered health care provider provides written notice to the individual that protected health information relating to the medical surveillance of the workplace and work-related illnesses and injuries is disclosed to the employer:

(1) By giving a copy of the notice to the individual at the time the health care is provided; or

(2) If the health care is provided on the work site of the employer, by posting the notice in a prominent place at the location where the health care is provided.

(3) Permitted uses. If the covered entity also is a public health authority, the covered entity is permitted to use protected health information in all cases in which it is permitted to disclose such information for public health activities under paragraph (b)(1) of this section.

(c) Standard: Disclosures about victims of abuse, neglect or domestic violence.

(1) Permitted disclosures. Except for reports of child abuse or neglect permitted by paragraph (b)(1)(ii) of this section, a covered entity may disclose protected health information about an individual whom the covered entity reasonably believes to be a victim of abuse, neglect, or domestic violence to a government authority, including a social service or protective services agency, authorized by law to receive reports of such abuse, neglect, or domestic violence:

(i) To the extent the disclosure is required by law and the disclosure complies with and is limited to the relevant requirements of such law;

(ii) If the individual agrees to the disclosure; or

(iii) To the extent the disclosure is expressly authorized by statute or regulation and:

(A) The covered entity, in the exercise of professional judgment, believes the disclosure is necessary to prevent serious harm to the individual or other potential victims; or

(B) If the individual is unable to agree because of incapacity, a law enforcement or other public official authorized to receive the report represents that the protected health information for which disclosure is sought is not intended to be used against the individual and that an immediate enforcement activity that depends upon the disclosure would be materially and adversely affected by waiting until the individual is able to agree to the disclosure.

(2) Informing the individual. A covered entity that makes a disclosure permitted by paragraph (c)(1) of this section must promptly inform the individual that such a report has been or will be made, except if:

(i) The covered entity, in the exercise of professional judgment, believes informing the individual would place the individual at risk of serious harm; or

(ii) The covered entity would be informing a personal representative, and the covered entity reasonably believes the personal representative is responsible for the abuse, neglect, or other injury, and that informing such person would not be in the best interests of the individual as determined by the covered entity, in the exercise of professional judgment.

(d) Standard: Uses and disclosures for health oversight activities.

(1) Permitted disclosures. A covered entity may disclose protected health information to a health oversight agency for oversight activities authorized by law, including audits; civil, administrative, or criminal investigations; inspections; licensure or disciplinary actions; civil, administrative, or criminal proceedings or actions; or other activities necessary for appropriate oversight of:

(i) The health care system;

(ii) Government benefit programs for which health information is relevant to beneficiary eligibility;

(iii) Entities subject to government regulatory programs for which health information is necessary for determining compliance with program standards; or

(iv) Entities subject to civil rights laws for which health information is necessary for determining compliance.

(2) Exception to health oversight activities. For the purpose of the disclosures permitted by paragraph (d)(1) of this section, a health oversight activity does not include an investigation or other activity in which the individual is the subject of the investigation or activity and such investigation or other activity does not arise out of and is not directly related to:

(i) The receipt of health care;

(ii) A claim for public benefits related to health; or

(iii) Qualification for, or receipt of, public benefits or services when a patient's health is integral to the claim for public benefits or services.

(3) Joint activities or investigations. Notwithstanding paragraph (d)(2) of this section, if a health oversight activity or investigation is conducted in conjunction with an oversight activity or investigation relating to a claim for public benefits not related to health, the joint activity or investigation is considered a health oversight activity for purposes of paragraph (d) of this section.

(4) Permitted uses. If a covered entity also is a health oversight agency, the covered entity may use protected health information for health oversight activities as permitted by paragraph (d) of this section.

(e) Standard: Disclosures for judicial and administrative proceedings.

(1) Permitted disclosures. A covered entity may disclose protected health information in the course of any judicial or administrative proceeding:

(i) In response to an order of a court or administrative tribunal, provided that the covered entity discloses only the protected health information expressly authorized by such order; or

(ii) In response to a subpoena, discovery request, or other lawful process, that is not accompanied by an order of a court or administrative tribunal, if:

(A) The covered entity receives satisfactory assurance, as described in paragraph (e)(1)(iii) of this section, from the party seeking the information that reasonable efforts have been made by such party to ensure that the individual who is the subject of the protected health information that has been requested has been given notice of the request; or

(B) The covered entity receives satisfactory assurance, as described in paragraph (e)(1)(iv) of this section, from the party seeking the information that reasonable efforts have been made by such party to secure a qualified protective order that meets the requirements of paragraph (e)(1)(v) of this section.

(iii) For the purposes of paragraph (e)(1)(ii)(A) of this section, a covered entity receives satisfactory assurances from a party seeking protecting health information if the covered entity receives from such party a written statement and accompanying documentation demonstrating that:

(A) The party requesting such information has made a good faith attempt to provide written notice to the individual (or, if the individual's location is unknown, to mail a notice to the individual's last known address);

(B) The notice included sufficient information about the litigation or proceeding in which the protected health information is requested to permit the individual to raise an objection to the court or administrative tribunal; and

(C) The time for the individual to raise objections to the court or administrative tribunal has elapsed, and:

(1) No objections were filed; or

(2) All objections filed by the individual have been resolved by the court or the administrative tribunal and the disclosures being sought are consistent with such resolution.

(iv) For the purposes of paragraph (e)(1)(ii)(B) of this section, a covered entity receives satisfactory assurances from a party seeking protected health information, if the covered entity receives from such party a written statement and accompanying documentation demonstrating that:

(A) The parties to the dispute giving rise to the request for information have agreed to a qualified protective order and have presented it to the court or administrative tribunal with jurisdiction over the dispute; or

(B) The party seeking the protected health information has requested a qualified protective order from such court or administrative tribunal.

(v) For purposes of paragraph (e)(1) of this section, a qualified protective order means, with respect to protected health information requested under paragraph (e)(1)(ii) of this section, an order of a court or of an administrative tribunal or a stipulation by the parties to the litigation or administrative proceeding that:

(A) Prohibits the parties from using or disclosing the protected health information for any purpose other than the litigation or proceeding for which such information was requested; and

(B) Requires the return to the covered entity or destruction of the protected health information (including all copies made) at the end of the litigation or proceeding.

(vi) Notwithstanding paragraph (e)(1)(ii) of this section, a covered entity may disclose protected health information in response to lawful process described in paragraph (e)(1)(ii) of this section without receiving satisfactory assurance under paragraph (e)(1)(ii)(A) or (B) of this section, if the covered entity makes reasonable efforts to provide notice to the individual sufficient to meet the requirements of paragraph (e)(1)(iii) of this section or to seek a qualified protective order sufficient to meet the requirements of paragraph (e)(1)(iv) of this section.

(2) Other uses and disclosures under this section. The provisions of this paragraph do not supersede other provisions of this section that otherwise permit or restrict uses or disclosures of protected health information.

(f) Standard: Disclosures for law enforcement purposes. A covered entity may disclose protected health information for a law enforcement purpose to a law enforcement official if the conditions in paragraphs (f)(1) through (f)(6) of this section are met, as applicable.

(1) Permitted disclosures: Pursuant to process and as otherwise required by law. A covered entity may disclose protected health information:

(i) As required by law including laws that require the reporting of certain types of wounds or other physical injuries, except for laws subject to paragraph (b)(1)(ii) or (c)(1)(i) of this section; or

(ii) In compliance with and as limited by the relevant requirements of:

(A) A court order or court-ordered warrant, or a subpoena or summons issued by a judicial officer;

(B) A grand jury subpoena; or

(C) An administrative request, including an administrative subpoena or summons, a civil or an authorized investigative demand, or similar process authorized under law, provided that:

(I) The information sought is relevant and material to a legitimate law enforcement inquiry;

(II) The request is specific and limited in scope to the extent reasonably practicable in light of the purpose for which the information is sought; and

(III) De-identified information could not reasonably be used.

(2) Permitted disclosures: Limited information for identification and location purposes. Except for disclosures required by law as permitted by paragraph (f)(1) of this section, a covered entity may disclose protected health information in response to a law enforcement official's request for such information for the purpose of identifying or locating a suspect, fugitive, material witness, or missing person, provided that:

(i) The covered entity may disclose only the following information:

(A) Name and address;

(B) Date and place of birth;

(C) Social security number;

(D) ABO blood type and rh factor;

(E) Type of injury;

(F) Date and time of treatment;

(G) Date and time of death, if applicable; and

(H) A description of distinguishing physical characteristics, including height, weight, gender, race, hair and eye color, presence or absence of facial hair (beard or moustache), scars, and tattoos.

(ii) Except as permitted by paragraph (f)(2)(i) of this section, the covered entity may not disclose for the purposes of identification or location under paragraph (f)(2) of this section any protected health information related to the individual's DNA or DNA analysis, dental records, or typing, samples or analysis of body fluids or tissue.

(3) Permitted disclosure: Victims of a crime. Except for disclosures required by law as permitted by paragraph (f)(1) of this section, a covered entity may disclose protected health information in response to a law enforcement official's request for such information about an individual who is or is suspected to be a victim of a crime, other than disclosures that are subject to paragraph (b) or (c) of this section, if:

(i) The individual agrees to the disclosure; or

(ii) The covered entity is unable to obtain the individual's agreement because of incapacity or other emergency circumstance, provided that:

(A) The law enforcement official represents that such information is needed to determine whether a violation of law by a person other than the victim has occurred, and such information is not intended to be used against the victim;

(B) The law enforcement official represents that immediate law enforcement activity that depends upon the disclosure would be materially and adversely affected by waiting until the individual is able to agree to the disclosure; and

(C) The disclosure is in the best interests of the individual as determined by the covered entity, in the exercise of professional judgment.

(4) Permitted disclosure: Decedents. A covered entity may disclose protected health information about an individual who has died to a law enforcement official for the purpose of alerting law enforcement of the death of the individual if the covered entity has a suspicion that such death may have resulted from criminal conduct.

(5) Permitted disclosure: Crime on premises. A covered entity may disclose to a law enforcement official protected health information that the covered entity believes in good faith constitutes evidence of criminal conduct that occurred on the premises of the covered entity.

(6) Permitted disclosure: Reporting crime in emergencies.

(i) A covered health care provider providing emergency health care in response to a medical emergency, other than such emergency on the premises of the covered health care provider, may disclose protected health information to a law enforcement official if such disclosure appears necessary to alert law enforcement to:

(A) The commission and nature of a crime;

(B) The location of such crime or of the victim(s) of such crime; and

(C) The identity, description, and location of the perpetrator of such crime.

(ii) If a covered health care provider believes that the medical emergency described in paragraph (f)(6)(i) of this section is the result of abuse, neglect, or domestic violence of the individual in need of emergency health care, paragraph (f)(6)(i) of this section does not apply and any disclosure to a law enforcement official for law enforcement purposes is subject to paragraph (c) of this section.

(g) Standard: Uses and disclosures about decedents.

(1) Coroners and medical examiners. A covered entity may disclose protected health information to a coroner or medical examiner for the

purpose of identifying a deceased person, determining a cause of death, or other duties as authorized by law. A covered entity that also performs the duties of a coroner or medical examiner may use protected health information for the purposes described in this paragraph.

(2) Funeral directors. A covered entity may disclose protected health information to funeral directors, consistent with applicable law, as necessary to carry out their duties with respect to the decedent. If necessary for funeral directors to carry out their duties, the covered entity may disclose the protected health information prior to, and in reasonable anticipation of, the individual's death.

(h) Standard: Uses and disclosures for cadaveric organ, eye or tissue donation purposes. A covered entity may use or disclose protected health information to organ procurement organizations or other entities engaged in the procurement, banking, or transplantation of cadaveric organs, eyes, or tissue for the purpose of facilitating organ, eye or tissue donation and transplantation.

(i) Standard: Uses and disclosures for research purposes.

(1) Permitted uses and disclosures. A covered entity may use or disclose protected health information for research, regardless of the source of funding of the research, provided that:

(i) Board approval of a waiver of authorization. The covered entity obtains documentation that an alteration to or waiver, in whole or in part, of the individual authorization required by § 164.508 for use or disclosure of protected health information has been approved by either:

(A) An Institutional Review Board (IRB), established in accordance with 7 CFR lc.107, 10 CFR 745.107, 14 CFR 1230.107, 15 CFR 27.107, 16 CFR 1028.107, 21 CFR 56.107, 22 CFR 225.107, 24 CFR 60.107, 28 CFR 46.107, 32 CFR 219.107, 34 CFR 97.107, 38 CFR 16.107, 40 CFR 26.107, 45 CFR 46.107, 45 CFR 690.107, or 49 CFR 11.107; or

(B) A privacy board that:

(I) Has members with varying backgrounds and appropriate professional competency as necessary to review the effect of the research protocol on the individual's privacy rights and related interests;

(II) Includes at least one member who is not affiliated with the covered entity, not affiliated with any entity conducting or sponsoring the research, and not related to any person who is affiliated with any of such entities; and

(III) Does not have any member participating in a review of any project in which the member has a conflict of interest.

(ii) Reviews preparatory to research. The covered entity obtains from the researcher representations that:

(A) Use or disclosure is sought solely to review protected health information as necessary to prepare a research protocol or for similar purposes preparatory to research;

(B) No protected health information is to be removed from the covered entity by the researcher in the course of the review; and

(C) The protected health information for which use or access is sought is necessary for the research purposes.

(iii) Research on decedent's information. The covered entity obtains from the researcher:

(A) Representation that the use or disclosure sought is solely for research on the protected health information of decedents;

(B) Documentation, at the request of the covered entity, of the death of such individuals; and

(C) Representation that the protected health information for which use or disclosure is sought is necessary for the research purposes.

(2) Documentation of waiver approval. For a use or disclosure to be permitted based on documentation of approval of an alteration or waiver, under paragraph (i)(1)(i) of this section, the documentation must include all of the following:

(i) Identification and date of action. A statement identifying the IRB or privacy board and the date on which the alteration or waiver of authorization was approved;

(ii) Waiver criteria. A statement that the IRB or privacy board has determined that the alteration or waiver, in whole or in part, of authorization satisfies the following criteria:

(A) The use or disclosure of protected health information involves no more than a minimal risk to the privacy of individuals, based on, at least, the presence of the following elements;

(I) An adequate plan to protect the identifiers from improper use and disclosure;

(II) An adequate plan to destroy the identifiers at the earliest opportunity consistent with conduct of the research, unless there is a health or research justification for retaining the identifiers or such retention is otherwise required by law; and

(III) Adequate written assurances that the protected health information will not be reused or disclosed to any other person or entity, except as required by law, for authorized oversight of the research study, or for other research for which the use or disclosure of protected health information would be permitted by this subpart;

(B) The research could not practicably be conducted without the waiver or alteration; and

(C) The research could not practicably be conducted without access to and use of the protected health information.

(iii) Protected health information needed. A brief description of the protected health information for which use or access has been determined to be necessary by the IRB or privacy board has determined, pursuant to paragraph (i)(2)(ii)(C) of this section;

(iv) Review and approval procedures. A statement that the alteration or waiver of authorization has been reviewed and approved under either normal or expedited review procedures, as follows:

(A) An IRB must follow the requirements of the Common Rule, including the normal review procedures (7 CFR 1c.108(b), 10 CFR 745.108(b), 14 CFR 1230.108(b), 15 CFR 27.108(b), 16 CFR 1028.108(b), 21 CFR 56.108(b), 22 CFR 225.108(b), 24 CFR 60.108(b), 28 CFR 46.108(b), 32 CFR 219.108(b), 34 CFR 97.108(b), 38 CFR 16.108(b), 40 CFR 26.108(b), 45 CFR 46.108(b), 45 CFR 690.108(b), or 49 CFR 11.108(b)) or the expedited review procedures (7 CFR 1c.110, 10 CFR 745.110, 14 CFR 1230.110, 15 CFR 27.110, 16 CFR 1028.110, 21 CFR 56.110, 22 CFR 225.110, 24 CFR 60.110, 28 CFR 46.110, 32 CFR 219.110, 34 CFR 97.110, 38 CFR 16.110, 40 CFR 26.110, 45 CFR 46.110, 45 CFR 690.110, or 49 CFR 11.110);

(B) A privacy board must review the proposed research at convened meetings at which a majority of the privacy board members are present, including at least one member who satisfies the criterion stated in paragraph (i)(1)(i)(B)(2) of this section, and the alteration or waiver of authorization must be approved by the majority of the privacy board members present at the meeting, unless the privacy board elects to use an expedited review procedure in accordance with paragraph (i)(2)(iv)(C) of this section;

(C) A privacy board may use an expedited review procedure if the research involves no more than minimal risk to the privacy of the individuals who are the subject of the protected health information for which use or disclosure is being sought. If the privacy board elects to use an expedited review procedure, the review and approval of the alteration or waiver of authorization may be carried out by the chair of the privacy board, or by one or more members of the privacy board as designated by the chair; and (**v**) *Required signature.* The documentation of the alteration or waiver of authorization must be signed by the chair or other member, as designated by the chair, of the IRB or the privacy board, as applicable.

(**j**) Standard: Uses and disclosures to avert a serious threat to health or safety.

(**1**) *Permitted disclosures.* A covered entity may, consistent with applicable law and standards of ethical conduct, use or disclose protected health information, if the covered entity, in good faith, believes the use or disclosure:

(**i**)(**A**) Is necessary to prevent or lessen a serious and imminent threat to the health or safety of a person or the public; and

(**B**) Is to a person or persons reasonably able to prevent or lessen the threat, including the target of the threat; or

(**ii**) Is necessary for law enforcement authorities to identify or apprehend an individual:

(**A**) Because of a statement by an individual admitting participation in a violent crime that the covered entity reasonably believes may have caused serious physical harm to the victim; or

(**B**) Where it appears from all the circumstances that the individual has escaped from a correctional institution or from lawful custody, as those terms are defined in § 164.501.

(**2**) *Use or disclosure not permitted.* A use or disclosure pursuant to paragraph (j)(1)(ii)(A) of this section may not be made if the information described in paragraph (j)(1)(ii)(A) of this section is learned by the covered entity:

(**i**) In the course of treatment to affect the propensity to commit the criminal conduct that is the basis for the disclosure under paragraph (j)(1)(ii)(A) of this section, or counseling or therapy; or

(**ii**) Through a request by the individual to initiate or to be referred for the treatment, counseling, or therapy described in paragraph (j)(2)(i) of this section.

(**3**) *Limit on information that may be disclosed.* A disclosure made pursuant to paragraph (j)(1)(ii)(A) of this section shall contain only the statement described in paragraph (j)(1)(ii)(A) of this section and the protected health information described in paragraph (f)(2)(i) of this section.

(**4**) *Presumption of good faith belief.* A covered entity that uses or discloses protected health information pursuant to paragraph (j)(1) of this section is presumed to have acted in good faith with regard to a belief described in paragraph (j)(1)(i) or (ii) of this section, if the belief is based upon the covered entity's actual knowledge or in reliance on a credible representation by a person with apparent knowledge or authority.

(k) Standard: Uses and disclosures for specialized government functions.

(1) Military and veterans activities.

(i) Armed Forces personnel. A covered entity may use and disclose the protected health information of individuals who are Armed Forces personnel for activities deemed necessary by appropriate military command authorities to assure the proper execution of the military mission, if the appropriate military authority has published by notice in the Federal Register the following information:

(A) Appropriate military command authorities; and

(B) The purposes for which the protected health information may be used or disclosed.

(ii) Separation or discharge from military service. A covered entity that is a component of the Departments of Defense or Transportation may disclose to the Department of Veterans Affairs (DVA) the protected health information of an individual who is a member of the Armed Forces upon the separation or discharge of the individual from military service for the purpose of a determination by DVA of the individual's eligibility for or entitlement to benefits under laws administered by the Secretary of Veterans Affairs.

(iii) Veterans. A covered entity that is a component of the Department of Veterans Affairs may use and disclose protected health information to components of the Department that determine eligibility for or entitlement to, or that provide, benefits under the laws administered by the Secretary of Veterans Affairs.

(iv) Foreign military personnel. A covered entity may use and disclose the protected health information of individuals who are foreign military personnel to their appropriate foreign military authority for the same purposes for which uses and disclosures are permitted for Armed Forces personnel under the notice published in the Federal Register pursuant to paragraph (k)(1)(i) of this section.

(2) National security and intelligence activities. A covered entity may disclose protected health information to authorized federal officials for the conduct of lawful intelligence, counter-intelligence, and other national security activities authorized by the National Security Act (50 U.S.C. 401, et seq.) and implementing authority (e.g., Executive Order 12333).

(3) Protective services for the President and others. A covered entity may disclose protected health information to authorized federal officials for the provision of protective services to the President or other persons authorized by 18 U.S.C. 3056, or to foreign heads of state or other persons authorized by 22 U.S.C. 2709(a)(3), or to for the conduct of investigations authorized by 18 U.S.C. 871 and 879.

(4) Medical suitability determinations. A covered entity that is a component of the Department of State may use protected health information to make medical suitability determinations and may disclose whether or not the individual was determined to be medically suitable to the officials in the Department of State who need access to such information for the following purposes:

(i) For the purpose of a required security clearance conducted pursuant to Executive Orders 10450 and 12698;

(ii) As necessary to determine worldwide availability or availability for mandatory service abroad under sections 101(a)(4) and 504 of the Foreign Service Act; or

(iii) For a family to accompany a Foreign Service member abroad, consistent with section 101(b)(5) and 904 of the Foreign Service Act.

(5) Correctional institutions and other law enforcement custodial situations.

(i) Permitted disclosures. A covered entity may disclose to a correctional institution or a law enforcement official having lawful custody of an inmate or other individual protected health information about such inmate or individual, if the correctional institution or such law enforcement official represents that such protected health information is necessary for:

(A) The provision of health care to such individuals;

(B) The health and safety of such individual or other inmates;

(C) The health and safety of the officers or employees of or others at the correctional institution;

(D) The health and safety of such individuals and officers or other persons responsible for the transporting of inmates or their transfer from one institution, facility, or setting to another;

(E) Law enforcement on the premises of the correctional institution; and

(F) The administration and maintenance of the safety, security, and good order of the correctional institution.

(ii) Permitted uses. A covered entity that is a correctional institution may use protected health information of individuals who are inmates for any purpose for which such protected health information may be disclosed.

(iii) No application after release. For the purposes of this provision, an individual is no longer an inmate when released on parole, probation, supervised release, or otherwise is no longer in lawful custody.

(6) Covered entities that are government programs providing public benefits.

(i) A health plan that is a government program providing public benefits may disclose protected health information relating to eligibility for or enrollment in the health plan to another agency administering a government program providing public benefits if the sharing of eligibility or enrollment information among such government agencies or the maintenance of such information in a single or combined data system accessible to all such government agencies is required or expressly authorized by statute or regulation.

(ii) A covered entity that is a government agency administering a government program providing public benefits may disclose protected health information relating to the program to another covered entity that is a government agency administering a government program providing public benefits if the programs serve the same or similar populations and the disclosure of protected health information is necessary to coordinate the covered functions of such programs or to improve administration and management relating to the covered functions of such programs.

(*l*) Standard: Disclosures for workers' compensation. A covered entity may disclose protected health information as authorized by and to the extent necessary to comply with laws relating to workers' compensation or other similar programs, established by law, that provide benefits for work-related injuries or illness without regard to fault.

§ 164.514 Other requirements relating to uses and disclosures of protected health information.

(a) Standard: de-identification of protected health information. Health information that does not identify an individual and with respect to which there is no reasonable basis to believe that the information can be used to identify an individual is not individually identifiable health information.

(b) Implementation specifications: requirements for de-identification of protected health information. A covered entity may determine that health information is not individually identifiable health information only if:

(1) A person with appropriate knowledge of and experience with generally accepted statistical and scientific principles and methods for rendering information not individually identifiable:

(i) Applying such principles and methods, determines that the risk is very small that the information could be used, alone or in combination with other reasonably available information, by an anticipated recipient to identify an individual who is a subject of the information; and

(ii) Documents the methods and results of the analysis that justify such determination; or

(2)(i) The following identifiers of the individual or of relatives, employers, or household members of the individual, are removed:

(A) Names;

(B) All geographic subdivisions smaller than a State, including street address, city, county, precinct, zip code, and their equivalent geocodes, except for the initial three digits of a zip code if, according to the current publicly available data from the Bureau of the Census:

(I) The geographic unit formed by combining all zip codes with the same three initial digits contains more than 20,000 people; and

(II) The initial three digits of a zip code for all such geographic units containing 20,000 or fewer people is changed to 000.

(C) All elements of dates (except year) for dates directly related to an individual, including birth date, admission date, discharge date, date of death; and all ages over 89 and all elements of dates (including year) indicative of such age, except that such ages and elements may be aggregated into a single category of age 90 or older;

(D) Telephone numbers;

(E) Fax numbers;

(F) Electronic mail addresses;

(G) Social security numbers;

(H) Medical record numbers;

(I) Health plan beneficiary numbers;

(J) Account numbers;

(K) Certificate/license numbers;

(L) Vehicle identifiers and serial numbers, including license plate numbers;

(M) Device identifiers and serial numbers;

(N) Web Universal Resource Locators (URLs);

(O) Internet Protocol (IP) address numbers;

(P) Biometric identifiers, including finger and voice prints;

(Q) Full face photographic images and any comparable images; and

(R) Any other unique identifying number, characteristic, or code, except as permitted by paragraph (c) of this section; and

(ii) The covered entity does not have actual knowledge that the information could be used alone or in combination with other information to identify an individual who is a subject of the information.

(c) Implementation specifications: re-identification. A covered entity may assign a code or other means of record identification to allow information de-identified under this section to be re-identified by the covered entity, provided that:

(1) Derivation. The code or other means of record identification is not derived from or related to information about the individual and is not otherwise capable of being translated so as to identify the individual; and

(2) Security. The covered entity does not use or disclose the code or other means of record identification for any other purpose, and does not disclose the mechanism for re-identification.

(d)(1) Standard: minimum necessary requirements. In order to comply with § 164.502(b) and this section, a covered entity must meet the requirements of paragraphs (d)(2) through (d)(5) of this section with respect to a request for, or the use and disclosure of, protected health information.

(2) Implementation specifications: minimum necessary uses of protected health information.

(i) A covered entity must identify:

(A) Those persons or classes of persons, as appropriate, in its workforce who need access to protected health information to carry out their duties; and

(B) For each such person or class of persons, the category or categories of protected health information to which access is needed and any conditions appropriate to such access.

(ii) A covered entity must make reasonable efforts to limit the access of such persons or classes identified in paragraph (d)(2)(i)(A) of this section to protected health information consistent with paragraph (d)(2)(i)(B) of this section.

(3) Implementation specification: Minimum necessary disclosures of protected health information.

(i) For any type of disclosure that it makes on a routine and recurring basis, a covered entity must implement policies and procedures (which may be standard protocols) that limit the protected health information disclosed to the amount reasonably necessary to achieve the purpose of the disclosure.

(ii) For all other disclosures, a covered entity must:

(A) Develop criteria designed to limit the protected health information disclosed to the information reasonably necessary to accomplish the purpose for which disclosure is sought; and

(B) Review requests for disclosure on an individual basis in accordance with such criteria.

(iii) A covered entity may rely, if such reliance is reasonable under the circumstances, on a requested disclosure as the minimum necessary for the stated purpose when:

(A) Making disclosures to public officials that are permitted under § 164.512, if the public official represents that the information requested is the minimum necessary for the stated purpose(s);

(B) The information is requested by another covered entity;

(C) The information is requested by a professional who is a member of its workforce or is a business associate of the covered entity for the purpose of providing professional services to the covered entity, if the professional represents that the information requested is the minimum necessary for the stated purpose(s); or

(D) Documentation or representations that comply with the applicable requirements of § 164.512(i) have been provided by a person requesting the information for research purposes.

(4) Implementation specifications: Minimum necessary requests for protected health information.

(i) A covered entity must limit any request for protected health information to that which is reasonably necessary to accomplish the purpose for which the request is made, when requesting such information from other covered entities.

(ii) For a request that is made on a routine and recurring basis, a covered entity must implement policies and procedures (which may be standard protocols) that limit the protected health information requested to the amount reasonably necessary to accomplish the purpose for which the request is made.

(iii) For all other requests, a covered entity must:

(A) Develop criteria designed to limit the request for protected health information to the information reasonably necessary to accomplish the purpose for which the request is made; and

(B) Review requests for disclosure on an individual basis in accordance with such criteria.

(5) Implementation specification: Other content requirement. For all uses, disclosures, or requests to which the requirements in paragraph (d) of this section apply, a covered entity may not use, disclose or request an entire medical record, except when the entire medical record is specifically justified as the amount that is reasonably necessary to accomplish the purpose of the use, disclosure, or request.

(e)(1) Standard: Limited data set. A covered entity may use or disclose a limited data set that meets the requirements of paragraphs (e)(2) and (e)(3) of this section, if the covered entity enters into a data use agreement with the limited data set recipient, in accordance with paragraph (e)(4) of this section.

(2) Implementation specification: Limited data set: A limited data set is protected health information that excludes the following direct identifiers of the individual or of relatives, employers, or household members of the individual:

(i) Names;

(ii) Postal address information, other than town or city, State, and zip code;

(iii) Telephone numbers;

(iv) Fax numbers;

(v) Electronic mail addresses;

(vi) Social security numbers;

(vii) Medical record numbers;

(viii) Health plan beneficiary numbers;

(ix) Account numbers;

(x) Certificate/license numbers;

(xi) Vehicle identifiers and serial numbers, including license plate numbers;

(xii) Device identifiers and serial numbers;

(xiii) Web Universal Resource Locators (URLs);

(xiv) Internet Protocol (IP) address numbers;

(xv) Biometric identifiers, including finger and voice prints; and

(xvi) Full face photographic images and any comparable images.

(3) Implementation specification: Permitted purposes for uses and disclosures.

(i) A covered entity may use or disclose a limited data set under paragraph (e)(1) of this section only for the purposes of research, public health, or health care operations.

(ii) A covered entity may use protected health information to create a limited data set that meets the requirements of paragraph (e)(2) of this section, or disclose protected health information only to a business associate for such purpose, whether or not the limited data set is to be used by the covered entity.

(4) Implementation specifications: Data use agreement.—

(i) Agreement required. A covered entity may use or disclose a limited data set under paragraph (e)(1) of this section only if the covered entity obtains satisfactory assurance, in the form of a data use agreement that meets the requirements of this section, that the limited data set recipient will only use or disclose the protected health information for limited purposes.

(ii) Contents. A data use agreement between the covered entity and the limited data set recipient must:

(A) Establish the permitted uses and disclosures of such information by the limited data set recipient, consistent with paragraph (e)(3) of this section. The data use agreement may not authorize the limited data set recipient to use or further disclose the information in a manner that would violate the requirements of this subpart, if done by the covered entity;

(B) Establish who is permitted to use or receive the limited data set; and

(C) Provide that the limited data set recipient will:

(I) Not use or further disclose the information other than as permitted by the data use agreement or as otherwise required by law;

(II) Use appropriate safeguards to prevent use or disclosure of the information other than as provided for by the data use agreement;

(III) Report to the covered entity any use or disclosure of the information not provided for by its data use agreement of which it becomes aware;

(IV) Ensure that any agents, including a subcontractor, to whom it provides the limited data set agrees to the same restrictions and conditions that apply to the limited data set recipient with respect to such information; and

(V) Not identify the information or contact the individuals.

(iii) Compliance.

(A) A covered entity is not in compliance with the standards in paragraph (e) of this section if the covered entity knew of a pattern of activity or practice of the limited data set recipient that constituted a material breach or violation of the data use agreement, unless the covered entity took reasonable steps to cure the breach or end the violation, as applicable, and, if such steps were unsuccessful:

(I) Discontinued disclosure of protected health information to the recipient; and

(II) Reported the problem to the Secretary.

(B) A covered entity that is a limited data set recipient and violates a data use agreement will be in noncompliance with the standards, implementation specifications, and requirements of paragraph (e) of this section.

(f)(1) Standard: Uses and disclosures for fundraising. A covered entity may use, or disclose to a business associate or to an institutionally related foundation, the following protected health information for the purpose of raising funds for its own benefit, without an authorization meeting the requirements of § 164.508:

(i) Demographic information relating to an individual; and

(ii) Dates of health care provided to an individual.

(2) Implementation specifications: Fundraising requirements.

(i) The covered entity may not use or disclose protected health information for fundraising purposes as otherwise permitted by paragraph (f)(1) of this section unless a statement required by § 164.520(b)(1)(iii)(B) is included in the covered entity's notice;

(ii) The covered entity must include in any fundraising materials it sends to an individual under this paragraph a description of how the individual may opt out of receiving any further fundraising communications.

(iii) The covered entity must make reasonable efforts to ensure that individuals who decide to opt out of receiving future fundraising communications are not sent such communications.

(g) Standard: Uses and disclosures for underwriting and related purposes. If a health plan receives protected health information for the purpose of underwriting, premium rating, or other activities relating to the creation, renewal, or replacement of a contract of health insurance or health benefits, and if such health insurance or health benefits are not placed with the health plan, such health plan may not use or disclose such protected health information for any other purpose, except as may be required by law.

(h)(1) Standard: Verification requirements. Prior to any disclosure permitted by this subpart, a covered entity must:

(i) Except with respect to disclosures under § 164.510, verify the identity of a person requesting protected health information and the authority of any such person to have access to protected health information under this subpart, if the identity or any such authority of such person is not known to the covered entity; and

(ii) Obtain any documentation, statements, or representations, whether oral or written, from the person requesting the protected health information when such documentation, statement, or representation is a condition of the disclosure under this subpart.

(2) Implementation specifications: Verification.

(i) Conditions on disclosures. If a disclosure is conditioned by this subpart on particular documentation, statements, or representations from the person requesting the protected health information, a covered entity may rely, if such reliance is reasonable under the circumstances, on documentation, statements, or representations that, on their face, meet the applicable requirements.

(A) The conditions in § 164.512(f)(1)(ii)(C) may be satisfied by the administrative subpoena or similar process or by a separate written statement that, on its face, demonstrates that the applicable requirements have been met.

(B) The documentation required by § 164.512(i)(2) may be satisfied by one or more written statements, provided that each is appropriately dated and signed in accordance with § 164.512(i)(2)(i) and (v).

(ii) Identity of public officials. A covered entity may rely, if such reliance is reasonable under the circumstances, on any of the following to verify identity when the disclosure of protected health information is to a public official or a person acting on behalf of the public official:

(A) If the request is made in person, presentation of an agency identification badge, other official credentials, or other proof of government status;

(B) If the request is in writing, the request is on the appropriate government letterhead; or

(C) If the disclosure is to a person acting on behalf of a public official, a written statement on appropriate government letterhead that the person is acting under the government's authority or other evidence or documentation of agency, such as a contract for services, memorandum of understanding, or purchase order, that establishes that the person is acting on behalf of the public official.

(iii) Authority of public officials. A covered entity may rely, if such reliance is reasonable under the circumstances, on any of the following to verify authority when the disclosure of protected health information is to a public official or a person acting on behalf of the public official:

(A) A written statement of the legal authority under which the information is requested, or, if a written statement would be impracticable, an oral statement of such legal authority;

(B) If a request is made pursuant to legal process, warrant, subpoena, order, or other legal process issued by a grand jury or a judicial or administrative tribunal is presumed to constitute legal authority.

(iv) Exercise of professional judgment. The verification requirements of this paragraph are met if the covered entity relies on the exercise of professional judgment in making a use or disclosure in accordance with § 164.510 or acts on a good faith belief in making a disclosure in accordance with § 164.512(j).

§ 164.520 Notice of privacy practices for protected health information.

(a) Standard: notice of privacy practices.

(1) Right to notice. Except as provided by paragraph (a)(2) or (3) of this section, an individual has a right to adequate notice of the uses and disclosures of protected health information that may be made by the covered entity, and of the individual's rights and the covered entity's legal duties with respect to protected health information.

(2) Exception for group health plans.

(i) An individual enrolled in a group health plan has a right to notice:

(A) From the group health plan, if, and to the extent that, such an individual does not receive health benefits under the group health plan through an insurance contract with a health insurance issuer or HMO; or

(B) From the health insurance issuer or HMO with respect to the group health plan through which such individuals receive their health benefits under the group health plan.

(ii) A group health plan that provides health benefits solely through an insurance contract with a health insurance issuer or HMO, and that creates or receives protected health information in addition to summary health information as defined in § 164.504(a) or information on whether the individual is participating in the group health plan, or is enrolled in or has disenrolled from a health insurance issuer or HMO offered by the plan, must:

(A) Maintain a notice under this section; and

(B) Provide such notice upon request to any person. The provisions of paragraph (c)(1) of this section do not apply to such group health plan.

(iii) A group health plan that provides health benefits solely through an insurance contract with a health insurance issuer or HMO, and does not create or receive protected health information other than summary health information as defined in § 164.504(a) or information on whether an individual is participating in the group health plan, or is enrolled in or has disenrolled from a health insurance issuer or HMO offered by the plan, is not required to maintain or provide a notice under this section.

(3) Exception for inmates. An inmate does not have a right to notice under this section, and the requirements of this section do not apply to a correctional institution that is a covered entity.

(b) Implementation specifications: content of notice.

(1) Required elements. The covered entity must provide a notice that is written in plain language and that contains the elements required by this paragraph.

(i) Header. The notice must contain the following statement as a header or otherwise prominently displayed: "THIS NOTICE DE-SCRIBES HOW MEDICAL INFORMATION ABOUT YOU MAY BE USED AND DISCLOSED AND HOW YOU CAN GET ACCESS TO THIS INFORMATION. PLEASE REVIEW IT CAREFULLY."

(ii) Uses and disclosures. The notice must contain:

(A) A description, including at least one example, of the types of uses and disclosures that the covered entity is permitted by this subpart to make for each of the following purposes: treatment, payment, and health care operations.

(B) A description of each of the other purposes for which the covered entity is permitted or required by this subpart to use or disclose protected health information without the individual's written authorization.

(C) If a use or disclosure for any purpose described in paragraphs (b)(1)(ii)(A) or (B) of this section is prohibited or materially limited by other applicable law, the description of such use or disclosure must reflect the more stringent law as defined in § 160.202 of this subchapter.

(D) For each purpose described in paragraph (b)(1)(ii)(A) or (B) of this section, the description must include sufficient detail to place the individual on notice of the uses and disclosures that are permitted or required by this subpart and other applicable law.

(E) A statement that other uses and disclosures will be made only with the individual's written authorization and that the individual may revoke such authorization as provided by § 164.508(b)(5).

(iii) Separate statements for certain uses or disclosures. If the covered entity intends to engage in any of the following activities, the description required by paragraph (b)(1)(ii)(A) of this section must include a separate statement, as applicable, that:

(A) The covered entity may contact the individual to provide appointment reminders or information about treatment alternatives or other health-related benefits and services that may be of interest to the individual;

(B) The covered entity may contact the individual to raise funds for the covered entity; or

(C) A group health plan, or a health insurance issuer or HMO with respect to a group health plan, may disclose protected health information to the sponsor of the plan.

(iv) Individual rights. The notice must contain a statement of the individual's rights with respect to protected health information and a brief description of how the individual may exercise these rights, as follows:

(A) The right to request restrictions on certain uses and disclosures of protected health information as provided by § 164.522(a), including a statement that the covered entity is not required to agree to a requested restriction;

(B) The right to receive confidential communications of protected health information as provided by § 164.522(b), as applicable;

(C) The right to inspect and copy protected health information as provided by § 164.524;

(D) The right to amend protected health information as provided by § 164.526;

(E) The right to receive an accounting of disclosures of protected health information as provided by § 164.528; and

(F) The right of an individual, including an individual who has agreed to receive the notice electronically in accordance with paragraph (c)(3) of this section, to obtain a paper copy of the notice from the covered entity upon request.

(v) Covered entity's duties. The notice must contain:

(A) A statement that the covered entity is required by law to maintain the privacy of protected health information and to provide individuals with notice of its legal duties and privacy practices with respect to protected health information;

(B) A statement that the covered entity is required to abide by the terms of the notice currently in effect; and

(C) For the covered entity to apply a change in a privacy practice that is described in the notice to protected health information that the covered entity created or received prior to issuing a revised notice, in accordance with § 164.530(i)(2)(ii), a statement that it reserves the right to change the terms of its notice and to make the new notice provisions effective for all protected health information that it maintains. The statement must also describe how it will provide individuals with a revised notice.

(vi) Complaints. The notice must contain a statement that individuals may complain to the covered entity and to the Secretary if they believe their privacy rights have been violated, a brief description of how the individual may file a complaint with the covered entity, and a statement that the individual will not be retaliated against for filing a complaint.

(vii) Contact. The notice must contain the name, or title, and telephone number of a person or office to contact for further information as required by § 164.530(a)(1)(ii).

(viii) Effective date. The notice must contain the date on which the notice is first in effect, which may not be earlier than the date on which the notice is printed or otherwise published.

(2) Optional elements.

(i) In addition to the information required by paragraph (b)(1) of this section, if a covered entity elects to limit the uses or disclosures that it is permitted to make under this subpart, the covered entity may describe its more limited uses or disclosures in its notice, provided that the covered entity may not include in its notice a limitation affecting its right to make a use or disclosure that is required by law or permitted by § 164.512(j)(1)(i).

(ii) For the covered entity to apply a change in its more limited uses and disclosures to protected health information created or received prior to issuing a revised notice, in accordance with § 164.530(i)(2)(ii), the notice must include the statements required by paragraph (b)(1)(v)(C) of this section.

(3) Revisions to the notice. The covered entity must promptly revise and distribute its notice whenever there is a material change to the uses or disclosures, the individual's rights, the covered entity's legal duties, or other privacy practices stated in the notice. Except when required by law, a material change to any term of the notice may not be implemented prior to the effective date of the notice in which such material change is reflected.

(c) Implementation specifications: Provision of notice. A covered entity must make the notice required by this section available on request to any person and to individuals as specified in paragraphs (c)(1) through (c)(3) of this section, as applicable.

(1) Specific requirements for health plans.

(i) A health plan must provide notice:

(A) No later than the compliance date for the health plan, to individuals then covered by the plan;

(B) Thereafter, at the time of enrollment, to individuals who are new enrollees; and

(C) Within 60 days of a material revision to the notice, to individuals then covered by the plan.

(ii) No less frequently than once every three years, the health plan must notify individuals then covered by the plan of the availability of the notice and how to obtain the notice.

(iii) The health plan satisfies the requirements of paragraph (c)(1) of this section if notice is provided to the named insured of a policy under which coverage is provided to the named insured and one or more dependents.

(iv) If a health plan has more than one notice, it satisfies the requirements of paragraph (c)(1) of this section by providing the notice that is relevant to the individual or other person requesting the notice.

(2) Specific requirements for certain covered health care providers. A covered health care provider that has a direct treatment relationship with an individual must:

(i) Provide the notice:

(A) No later than the date of the first service delivery, including service delivered electronically, to such individual after the compliance date for the covered health care provider; or

(B) In an emergency treatment situation, as soon as reasonably practicable after the emergency treatment situation.

(ii) Except in an emergency treatment situation, make a good faith effort to obtain a written acknowledgment of receipt of the notice provided in accordance with paragraph (c)(2)(i) of this section, and if not obtained, document its good faith efforts to obtain such acknowledgment and the reason why the acknowledgment was not obtained;

(iii) If the covered health care provider maintains a physical service delivery site:

(A) Have the notice available at the service delivery site for individuals to request to take with them; and

(B) Post the notice in a clear and prominent location where it is reasonable to expect individuals seeking service from the covered health care provider to be able to read the notice; and

(iv) Whenever the notice is revised, make the notice available upon request on or after the effective date of the revision and promptly comply with the requirements of paragraph (c)(2)(iii) of this section, if applicable.

(3) Specific requirements for electronic notice.

(i) A covered entity that maintains a web site that provides information about the covered entity's customer services or benefits must prominently post its notice on the web site and make the notice available electronically through the web site.

(ii) A covered entity may provide the notice required by this section to an individual by e-mail, if the individual agrees to electronic notice and such agreement has not been withdrawn. If the covered entity knows that the e-mail transmission has failed, a paper copy of the notice must be provided to the individual. Provision of electronic notice by the covered entity will satisfy the provision requirements of paragraph (c) of this section when timely made in accordance with paragraph (c)(1) or (2) of this section.

(iii) For purposes of paragraph (c)(2)(i) of this section, if the first service delivery to an individual is delivered electronically, the covered health care provider must provide electronic notice automatically and contemporaneously in response to the individual's first request for service. The requirements in paragraph (c)(2)(ii) of this section apply to electronic notice.

(iv) The individual who is the recipient of electronic notice retains the right to obtain a paper copy of the notice from a covered entity upon request.

(d) Implementation specifications: Joint notice by separate covered entities. Covered entities that participate in organized health care arrangements may comply with this section by a joint notice, provided that:

(1) The covered entities participating in the organized health care arrangement agree to abide by the terms of the notice with respect to protected health information created or received by the covered entity as part of its participation in the organized health care arrangement;

(2) The joint notice meets the implementation specifications in paragraph (b) of this section, except that the statements required by this section may be altered to reflect the fact that the notice covers more than one covered entity; and

(i) Describes with reasonable specificity the covered entities, or class of entities, to which the joint notice applies;

(ii) Describes with reasonable specificity the service delivery sites, or classes of service delivery sites, to which the joint notice applies; and

(iii) If applicable, states that the covered entities participating in the organized health care arrangement will share protected health information with each other, as necessary to carry out treatment, payment, or health care operations relating to the organized health care arrangement.

(3) The covered entities included in the joint notice must provide the notice to individuals in accordance with the applicable implementation specifications of paragraph (c) of this section. Provision of the joint notice to an individual by any one of the covered entities included in the joint notice will satisfy the provision requirement of paragraph (c) of this section with respect to all others covered by the joint notice.

(e) Implementation specifications: Documentation. A covered entity must document compliance with the notice requirements, as required by § 164.530(j), by retaining copies of the notices issued by the covered entity and, if applicable, any written acknowledgments of receipt of the notice or documentation of good faith efforts to obtain such written acknowledgment, in accordance with paragraph (c)(2)(ii) of this section.

§ 164.522 Rights to request privacy protection for protected health information.

(a)(1) Standard: Right of an individual to request restriction of uses and disclosures.

(i) A covered entity must permit an individual to request that the covered entity restrict:

(A) Uses or disclosures of protected health information about the individual to carry out treatment, payment, or health care operations; and

(B) Disclosures permitted under § 164.510(b).

(ii) A covered entity is not required to agree to a restriction.

(iii) A covered entity that agrees to a restriction under paragraph (a)(1)(i) of this section may not use or disclose protected health information in violation of such restriction, except that, if the individual who requested the restriction is in need of emergency treatment and the restricted protected health information is needed to provide the emergency treatment, the covered entity may use the restricted protected health information, or may disclose such information to a health care provider, to provide such treatment to the individual.

(iv) If restricted protected health information is disclosed to a health care provider for emergency treatment under paragraph (a)(1)(iii) of this section, the covered entity must request that such health care provider not further use or disclose the information.

(v) A restriction agreed to by a covered entity under paragraph (a) of this section, is not effective under this subpart to prevent uses or disclosures permitted or required under § § 164.502(a)(2)(ii), 164.510(a) or 164.512.

(2) Implementation specifications: Terminating a restriction. A covered entity may terminate its agreement to a restriction, if:

(i) The individual agrees to or requests the termination in writing;

(ii) The individual orally agrees to the termination and the oral agreement is documented; or

(iii) The covered entity informs the individual that it is terminating its agreement to a restriction, except that such termination is only effective with respect to protected health information created or received after it has so informed the individual.

(3) Implementation specification: Documentation. A covered entity that agrees to a restriction must document the restriction in accordance with § 164.530(j).

(b)(1) Standard: Confidential communications requirements.

(i) A covered health care provider must permit individuals to request and must accommodate reasonable requests by individuals to receive communications of protected health information from the covered health care provider by alternative means or at alternative locations.

(ii) A health plan must permit individuals to request and must accommodate reasonable requests by individuals to receive communications of protected health information from the health plan by alternative means or at alternative locations, if the individual clearly states that the disclosure of all or part of that information could endanger the individual.

(2) Implementation specifications: Conditions on providing confidential communications.

(i) A covered entity may require the individual to make a request for a confidential communication described in paragraph (b)(1) of this section in writing.

(ii) A covered entity may condition the provision of a reasonable accommodation on:

(A) When appropriate, information as to how payment, if any, will be handled; and

(B) Specification of an alternative address or other method of contact.

(iii) A covered health care provider may not require an explanation from the individual as to the basis for the request as a condition of providing communications on a confidential basis.

(iv) A health plan may require that a request contain a statement that disclosure of all or part of the information to which the request pertains could endanger the individual.

§ 164.524　Access of individuals to protected health information.

(a) Standard: Access to protected health information.

(1) Right of access. Except as otherwise provided in paragraph (a)(2) or (a)(3) of this section, an individual has a right of access to inspect and obtain a copy of protected health information about the individual in a designated record set, for as long as the protected health information is maintained in the designated record set, except for:

(i) Psychotherapy notes;

(ii) Information compiled in reasonable anticipation of, or for use in, a civil, criminal, or administrative action or proceeding; and

(iii) Protected health information maintained by a covered entity that is:

(A) Subject to the Clinical Laboratory Improvements Amendments of 1988, 42 U.S.C. 263a, to the extent the provision of access to the individual would be prohibited by law; or

(B) Exempt from the Clinical Laboratory Improvements Amendments of 1988, pursuant to 42 CFR 493.3(a)(2).

(2) Unreviewable grounds for denial. A covered entity may deny an individual access without providing the individual an opportunity for review, in the following circumstances.

(i) The protected health information is excepted from the right of access by paragraph (a)(1) of this section.

(ii) A covered entity that is a correctional institution or a covered health care provider acting under the direction of the correctional institution may deny, in whole or in part, an inmate's request to obtain a copy of protected health information, if obtaining such copy would jeopardize the health, safety, security, custody, or rehabilitation of the individual or of other inmates, or the safety of any officer, employee, or other person at the correctional institution or responsible for the transporting of the inmate.

(iii) An individual's access to protected health information created or obtained by a covered health care provider in the course of research that includes treatment may be temporarily suspended for as long as the research is in progress, provided that the individual has agreed to the denial of access when consenting to participate in the research that includes treatment, and the covered health care provider has informed the individual that the right of access will be reinstated upon completion of the research.

(iv) An individual's access to protected health information that is contained in records that are subject to the Privacy Act, 5 U.S.C. 552a, may be denied, if the denial of access under the Privacy Act would meet the requirements of that law.

(v) An individual's access may be denied if the protected health information was obtained from someone other than a health care provider under a promise of confidentiality and the access requested would be reasonably likely to reveal the source of the information.

(3) Reviewable grounds for denial. A covered entity may deny an individual access, provided that the individual is given a right to have

such denials reviewed, as required by paragraph (a)(4) of this section, in the following circumstances:

(i) A licensed health care professional has determined, in the exercise of professional judgment, that the access requested is reasonably likely to endanger the life or physical safety of the individual or another person;

(ii) The protected health information makes reference to another person (unless such other person is a health care provider) and a licensed health care professional has determined, in the exercise of professional judgment, that the access requested is reasonably likely to cause substantial harm to such other person; or

(iii) The request for access is made by the individual's personal representative and a licensed health care professional has determined, in the exercise of professional judgment, that the provision of access to such personal representative is reasonably likely to cause substantial harm to the individual or another person.

(4) Review of a denial of access. If access is denied on a ground permitted under paragraph (a)(3) of this section, the individual has the right to have the denial reviewed by a licensed health care professional who is designated by the covered entity to act as a reviewing official and who did not participate in the original decision to deny. The covered entity must provide or deny access in accordance with the determination of the reviewing official under paragraph (d)(4) of this section.

(b) Implementation specifications: requests for access and timely action.

(1) Individual's request for access. The covered entity must permit an individual to request access to inspect or to obtain a copy of the protected health information about the individual that is maintained in a designated record set. The covered entity may require individuals to make requests for access in writing, provided that it informs individuals of such a requirement.

(2) Timely action by the covered entity.

(i) Except as provided in paragraph (b)(2)(ii) of this section, the covered entity must act on a request for access no later than 30 days after receipt of the request as follows.

(A) If the covered entity grants the request, in whole or in part, it must inform the individual of the acceptance of the request and provide the access requested, in accordance with paragraph (c) of this section.

(B) If the covered entity denies the request, in whole or in part, it must provide the individual with a written denial, in accordance with paragraph (d) of this section.

(ii) If the request for access is for protected health information that is not maintained or accessible to the covered entity on-site, the covered entity must take an action required by paragraph (b)(2)(i) of this section by no later than 60 days from the receipt of such a request.

(iii) If the covered entity is unable to take an action required by paragraph (b)(2)(i)(A) or (B) of this section within the time required by paragraph (b)(2)(i) or (ii) of this section, as applicable, the covered entity may extend the time for such actions by no more than 30 days, provided that:

(A) The covered entity, within the time limit set by paragraph (b)(2)(i) or (ii) of this section, as applicable, provides the individual with a written statement of the reasons for the delay and the date by which the covered entity will complete its action on the request; and

(B) The covered entity may have only one such extension of time for action on a request for access.

(c) Implementation specifications: Provision of access. If the covered entity provides an individual with access, in whole or in part, to protected health information, the covered entity must comply with the following requirements.

(1) Providing the access requested. The covered entity must provide the access requested by individuals, including inspection or obtaining a copy, or both, of the protected health information about them in designated record sets. If the same protected health information that is the subject of a request for access is maintained in more than one designated record set or at more than one location, the covered entity need only produce the protected health information once in response to a request for access.

(2) Form of access requested.

(i) The covered entity must provide the individual with access to the protected health information in the form or format requested by the individual, if it is readily producible in such form or format; or, if not, in a readable hard copy form or such other form or format as agreed to by the covered entity and the individual.

(ii) The covered entity may provide the individual with a summary of the protected health information requested, in lieu of providing access to the protected health information or may provide an explanation of the protected health information to which access has been provided, if:

(A) The individual agrees in advance to such a summary or explanation; and

(B) The individual agrees in advance to the fees imposed, if any, by the covered entity for such summary or explanation.

(3) Time and manner of access. The covered entity must provide the access as requested by the individual in a timely manner as required by paragraph (b)(2) of this section, including arranging with the individual for a convenient time and place to inspect or obtain a copy of the protected health information, or mailing the copy of the protected health information at the individual's request. The covered entity may discuss the scope, format, and other aspects of the request for access with the individual as necessary to facilitate the timely provision of access.

(4) Fees. If the individual requests a copy of the protected health information or agrees to a summary or explanation of such information, the covered entity may impose a reasonable, cost-based fee, provided that the fee includes only the cost of:

(i) Copying, including the cost of supplies for and labor of copying, the protected health information requested by the individual;

(ii) Postage, when the individual has requested the copy, or the summary or explanation, be mailed; and

(iii) Preparing an explanation or summary of the protected health information, if agreed to by the individual as required by paragraph (c)(2)(ii) of this section.

(d) Implementation specifications: Denial of access. If the covered entity denies access, in whole or in part, to protected health information, the covered entity must comply with the following requirements.

(1) Making other information accessible. The covered entity must, to the extent possible, give the individual access to any other protected health information requested, after excluding the protected health information as to which the covered entity has a ground to deny access.

(2) Denial. The covered entity must provide a timely, written denial to the individual, in accordance with paragraph (b)(2) of this section. The denial must be in plain language and contain:

(i) The basis for the denial;

(ii) If applicable, a statement of the individual's review rights under paragraph (a)(4) of this section, including a description of how the individual may exercise such review rights; and

(iii) A description of how the individual may complain to the covered entity pursuant to the complaint procedures in § 164.530(d) or to the Secretary pursuant to the procedures in § 160.306. The description must include the name, or title, and telephone number of the contact person or office designated in § 164.530(a)(1)(ii).

(3) Other responsibility. If the covered entity does not maintain the protected health information that is the subject of the individual's request for access, and the covered entity knows where the requested information is maintained, the covered entity must inform the individual where to direct the request for access.

(4) Review of denial requested. If the individual has requested a review of a denial under paragraph (a)(4) of this section, the covered entity must designate a licensed health care professional, who was not directly involved in the denial to review the decision to deny access. The covered entity must promptly refer a request for review to such designated reviewing official. The designated reviewing official must determine, within a reasonable period of time, whether or not to deny the access requested based on the standards in paragraph (a)(3) of this section. The covered entity must promptly provide written notice to the individual of the determination of the designated reviewing official and take other action as required by this section to carry out the designated reviewing official's determination.

(e) Implementation specification: Documentation. A covered entity must document the following and retain the documentation as required by § 164.530(j):

(1) The designated record sets that are subject to access by individuals; and

(2) The titles of the persons or offices responsible for receiving and processing requests for access by individuals.

§ 164.526 Amendment of protected health information.

(a) Standard: Right to amend.

(1) Right to amend. An individual has the right to have a covered entity amend protected health information or a record about the individual in a designated record set for as long as the protected health information is maintained in the designated record set.

(2) Denial of amendment. A covered entity may deny an individual's request for amendment, if it determines that the protected health information or record that is the subject of the request:

(i) Was not created by the covered entity, unless the individual provides a reasonable basis to believe that the originator of protected health information is no longer available to act on the requested amendment;

(ii) Is not part of the designated record set;

(iii) Would not be available for inspection under § 164.524; or

(iv) Is accurate and complete.

(b) Implementation specifications: requests for amendment and timely action.

(1) Individual's request for amendment. The covered entity must permit an individual to request that the covered entity amend the protected health information maintained in the designated record set.

The covered entity may require individuals to make requests for amendment in writing and to provide a reason to support a requested amendment, provided that it informs individuals in advance of such requirements.

(2) Timely action by the covered entity.

(i) The covered entity must act on the individual's request for an amendment no later than 60 days after receipt of such a request, as follows.

(A) If the covered entity grants the requested amendment, in whole or in part, it must take the actions required by paragraphs (c)(1) and (2) of this section.

(B) If the covered entity denies the requested amendment, in whole or in part, it must provide the individual with a written denial, in accordance with paragraph (d)(1) of this section.

(ii) If the covered entity is unable to act on the amendment within the time required by paragraph (b)(2)(i) of this section, the covered entity may extend the time for such action by no more than 30 days, provided that:

(A) The covered entity, within the time limit set by paragraph (b)(2)(i) of this section, provides the individual with a written statement of the reasons for the delay and the date by which the covered entity will complete its action on the request; and

(B) The covered entity may have only one such extension of time for action on a request for an amendment.

(c) Implementation specifications: Accepting the amendment. If the covered entity accepts the requested amendment, in whole or in part, the covered entity must comply with the following requirements.

(1) Making the amendment. The covered entity must make the appropriate amendment to the protected health information or record that is the subject of the request for amendment by, at a minimum, identifying the records in the designated record set that are affected by the amendment and appending or otherwise providing a link to the location of the amendment.

(2) Informing the individual. In accordance with paragraph (b) of this section, the covered entity must timely inform the individual that the amendment is accepted and obtain the individual's identification of and agreement to have the covered entity notify the relevant persons with which the amendment needs to be shared in accordance with paragraph (c)(3) of this section.

(3) Informing others. The covered entity must make reasonable efforts to inform and provide the amendment within a reasonable time to:

(i) Persons identified by the individual as having received protected health information about the individual and needing the amendment; and

(ii) Persons, including business associates, that the covered entity knows have the protected health information that is the subject of the amendment and that may have relied, or could foreseeably rely, on such information to the detriment of the individual.

(d) Implementation specifications: Denying the amendment. If the covered entity denies the requested amendment, in whole or in part, the covered entity must comply with the following requirements.

(1) Denial. The covered entity must provide the individual with a timely, written denial, in accordance with paragraph (b)(2) of this section. The denial must use plain language and contain:

(i) The basis for the denial, in accordance with paragraph (a)(2) of this section;

(ii) The individual's right to submit a written statement disagreeing with the denial and how the individual may file such a statement;

(iii) A statement that, if the individual does not submit a statement of disagreement, the individual may request that the covered entity provide the individual's request for amendment and the denial with any future disclosures of the protected health information that is the subject of the amendment; and

(iv) A description of how the individual may complain to the covered entity pursuant to the complaint procedures established in § 164.530(d) or to the Secretary pursuant to the procedures established in § 160.306. The description must include the name, or title, and telephone number of the contact person or office designated in § 164.530(a)(1)(ii).

(2) Statement of disagreement. The covered entity must permit the individual to submit to the covered entity a written statement disagreeing with the denial of all or part of a requested amendment and the basis of such disagreement. The covered entity may reasonably limit the length of a statement of disagreement.

(3) Rebuttal statement. The covered entity may prepare a written rebuttal to the individual's statement of disagreement. Whenever such a rebuttal is prepared, the covered entity must provide a copy to the individual who submitted the statement of disagreement.

(4) Recordkeeping. The covered entity must, as appropriate, identify the record or protected health information in the designated record set that is the subject of the disputed amendment and append or otherwise link the individual's request for an amendment, the covered entity's denial of the request, the individual's statement of disagreement, if any, and the covered entity's rebuttal, if any, to the designated record set.

(5) Future disclosures.

(i) If a statement of disagreement has been submitted by the individual, the covered entity must include the material appended in accordance with paragraph (d)(4) of this section, or, at the election of the covered entity, an accurate summary of any such information, with any subsequent disclosure of the protected health information to which the disagreement relates.

(ii) If the individual has not submitted a written statement of disagreement, the covered entity must include the individual's request for amendment and its denial, or an accurate summary of such information, with any subsequent disclosure of the protected health information only if the individual has requested such action in accordance with paragraph (d)(1)(iii) of this section.

(iii) When a subsequent disclosure described in paragraph (d)(5)(i) or (ii) of this section is made using a standard transaction under part 162 of this subchapter that does not permit the additional material to be included with the disclosure, the covered entity may separately transmit the material required by paragraph (d)(5)(i) or (ii) of this section, as applicable, to the recipient of the standard transaction.

(e) Implementation specification: Actions on notices of amendment. A covered entity that is informed by another covered entity of an amendment to an individual's protected health information, in accordance with paragraph (c)(3) of this section, must amend the protected health information in designated record sets as provided by paragraph (c)(1) of this section.

(f) Implementation specification: Documentation. A covered entity must document the titles of the persons or offices responsible for receiving and processing requests for amendments by individuals and retain the documentation as required by § 164.530(j).

§ 164.528 Accounting of disclosures of protected health information.

(a) Standard: Right to an accounting of disclosures of protected health information.

(1) An individual has a right to receive an accounting of disclosures of protected health information made by a covered entity in the six years prior to the date on which the accounting is requested, except for disclosures:

(i) To carry out treatment, payment and health care operations as provided in § 164.506;

(ii) To individuals of protected health information about them as provided in § 164.502;

(iii) Incident to a use or disclosure otherwise permitted or required by this subpart, as provided in § 164.502;

(iv) Pursuant to an authorization as provided in § 164.508;

(v) For the facility's directory or to persons involved in the individual's care or other notification purposes as provided in § 164.510;

(vi) For national security or intelligence purposes as provided in § 164.512(k)(2);

(vii) To correctional institutions or law enforcement officials as provided in § 164.512(k)(5);

(viii) As part of a limited data set in accordance with § 164.514(e); or

(ix) That occurred prior to the compliance date for the covered entity.

(2)(i) The covered entity must temporarily suspend an individual's right to receive an accounting of disclosures to a health oversight agency or law enforcement official, as provided in § 164.512(d) or (f), respectively, for the time specified by such agency or official, if such agency or official provides the covered entity with a written statement that such an accounting to the individual would be reasonably likely to impede the agency's activities and specifying the time for which such a suspension is required.

(ii) If the agency or official statement in paragraph (a)(2)(i) of this section is made orally, the covered entity must:

(A) Document the statement, including the identity of the agency or official making the statement;

(B) Temporarily suspend the individual's right to an accounting of disclosures subject to the statement; and

(C) Limit the temporary suspension to no longer than 30 days from the date of the oral statement, unless a written statement pursuant to paragraph (a)(2)(i) of this section is submitted during that time.

(3) An individual may request an accounting of disclosures for a period of time less than six years from the date of the request.

(b) Implementation specifications: Content of the accounting. The covered entity must provide the individual with a written accounting that meets the following requirements.

(1) Except as otherwise provided by paragraph (a) of this section, the accounting must include disclosures of protected health information that occurred during the six years (or such shorter time period at the request of the individual as provided in paragraph (a)(3) of this section) prior to

the date of the request for an accounting, including disclosures to or by business associates of the covered entity.

(2) Except as otherwise provided by paragraphs (b)(3) or (b)(4) of this section, the accounting must include for each disclosure:

    (i) The date of the disclosure;

    (ii) The name of the entity or person who received the protected health information and, if known, the address of such entity or person;

    (iii) A brief description of the protected health information disclosed; and

    (iv) A brief statement of the purpose of the disclosure that reasonably informs the individual of the basis for the disclosure or, in lieu of such statement, a copy of a written request for a disclosure under § § 164.502(a)(2)(ii) or 164.512, if any.

(3) If, during the period covered by the accounting, the covered entity has made multiple disclosures of protected health information to the same person or entity for a single purpose under § § 164.502(a)(2)(ii) or 164.512, the accounting may, with respect to such multiple disclosures, provide:

    (i) The information required by paragraph (b)(2) of this section for the first disclosure during the accounting period;

    (ii) The frequency, periodicity, or number of the disclosures made during the accounting period; and

    (iii) The date of the last such disclosure during the accounting period.

(4)(i) If, during the period covered by the accounting, the covered entity has made disclosures of protected health information for a particular research purpose in accordance with § 164.512(i) for 50 or more individuals, the accounting may, with respect to such disclosures for which the protected health information about the individual may have been included, provide:

    (A) The name of the protocol or other research activity;

    (B) A description, in plain language, of the research protocol or other research activity, including the purpose of the research and the criteria for selecting particular records;

    (C) A brief description of the type of protected health information that was disclosed;

    (D) The date or period of time during which such disclosures occurred, or may have occurred, including the date of the last such disclosure during the accounting period;

(E) The name, address, and telephone number of the entity that sponsored the research and of the researcher to whom the information was disclosed; and

(F) A statement that the protected health information of the individual may or may not have been disclosed for a particular protocol or other research activity.

(ii) If the covered entity provides an accounting for research disclosures, in accordance with paragraph (b)(4) of this section, and if it is reasonably likely that the protected health information of the individual was disclosed for such research protocol or activity, the covered entity shall, at the request of the individual, assist in contacting the entity that sponsored the research and the researcher.

(c) Implementation specifications: Provision of the accounting.

(1) The covered entity must act on the individual's request for an accounting, no later than 60 days after receipt of such a request, as follows.

(i) The covered entity must provide the individual with the accounting requested; or

(ii) If the covered entity is unable to provide the accounting within the time required by paragraph (c)(1) of this section, the covered entity may extend the time to provide the accounting by no more than 30 days, provided that:

(A) The covered entity, within the time limit set by paragraph (c)(1) of this section, provides the individual with a written statement of the reasons for the delay and the date by which the covered entity will provide the accounting; and

(B) The covered entity may have only one such extension of time for action on a request for an accounting.

(2) The covered entity must provide the first accounting to an individual in any 12 month period without charge. The covered entity may impose a reasonable, cost-based fee for each subsequent request for an accounting by the same individual within the 12 month period, provided that the covered entity informs the individual in advance of the fee and provides the individual with an opportunity to withdraw or modify the request for a subsequent accounting in order to avoid or reduce the fee.

(d) Implementation specification: Documentation. A covered entity must document the following and retain the documentation as required by § 164.530(j):

(1) The information required to be included in an accounting under paragraph (b) of this section for disclosures of protected health information that are subject to an accounting under paragraph (a) of this section;

1300

(2) The written accounting that is provided to the individual under this section; and

(3) The titles of the persons or offices responsible for receiving and processing requests for an accounting by individuals.

§ 164.530 Administrative requirements.

(a)(1) Standard: Personnel designations.

(i) A covered entity must designate a privacy official who is responsible for the development and implementation of the policies and procedures of the entity.

(ii) A covered entity must designate a contact person or office who is responsible for receiving complaints under this section and who is able to provide further information about matters covered by the notice required by § 164.520.

(2) Implementation specification: Personnel designations. A covered entity must document the personnel designations in paragraph (a)(1) of this section as required by paragraph (j) of this section.

(b)(1) Standard: Training. A covered entity must train all members of its workforce on the policies and procedures with respect to protected health information required by this subpart, as necessary and appropriate for the members of the workforce to carry out their function within the covered entity.

(2) Implementation specifications: Training.

(i) A covered entity must provide training that meets the requirements of paragraph (b)(1) of this section, as follows:

(A) To each member of the covered entity's workforce by no later than the compliance date for the covered entity;

(B) Thereafter, to each new member of the workforce within a reasonable period of time after the person joins the covered entity's workforce; and

(C) To each member of the covered entity's workforce whose functions are affected by a material change in the policies or procedures required by this subpart, within a reasonable period of time after the material change becomes effective in accordance with paragraph (i) of this section.

(ii) A covered entity must document that the training as described in paragraph (b)(2)(i) of this section has been provided, as required by paragraph (j) of this section.

(c)(1) Standard: Safeguards. A covered entity must have in place appropriate administrative, technical, and physical safeguards to protect the privacy of protected health information.

(2)(i) Implementation specification: Safeguards. A covered entity must reasonably safeguard protected health information from any intentional or unintentional use or disclosure that is in violation of the standards, implementation specifications or other requirements of this subpart.

(ii) A covered entity must reasonably safeguard protected health information to limit incidental uses or disclosures made pursuant to an otherwise permitted or required use or disclosure.

(d)(1) Standard: Complaints to the covered entity. A covered entity must provide a process for individuals to make complaints concerning the covered entity's policies and procedures required by this subpart or its compliance with such policies and procedures or the requirements of this subpart.

(2) Implementation specification: Documentation of complaints. As required by paragraph (j) of this section, a covered entity must document all complaints received, and their disposition, if any.

(e)(1) Standard: Sanctions. A covered entity must have and apply appropriate sanctions against members of its workforce who fail to comply with the privacy policies and procedures of the covered entity or the requirements of this subpart. This standard does not apply to a member of the covered entity's workforce with respect to actions that are covered by and that meet the conditions of § 164.502(j) or paragraph (g)(2) of this section.

(2) Implementation specification: Documentation. As required by paragraph (j) of this section, a covered entity must document the sanctions that are applied, if any.

(f) Standard: Mitigation. A covered entity must mitigate, to the extent practicable, any harmful effect that is known to the covered entity of a use or disclosure of protected health information in violation of its policies and procedures or the requirements of this subpart by the covered entity or its business associate.

(g) Standard: Refraining from intimidating or retaliatory acts. A covered entity may not intimidate, threaten, coerce, discriminate against, or take other retaliatory action against:

(1) Individuals. Any individual for the exercise by the individual of any right under, or for participation by the individual in any process established by this subpart, including the filing of a complaint under this section;

(2) Individuals and others. Any individual or other person for:

(i) Filing of a complaint with the Secretary under subpart C of part 160 of this subchapter;

(ii) Testifying, assisting, or participating in an investigation, compliance review, proceeding, or hearing under Part C of Title XI; or

(iii) Opposing any act or practice made unlawful by this subpart, provided the individual or person has a good faith belief that the practice opposed is unlawful, and the manner of the opposition is reasonable and does not involve a disclosure of protected health information in violation of this subpart.

(h) Standard: Waiver of rights. A covered entity may not require individuals to waive their rights under § 160.306 of this subchapter or this subpart as a condition of the provision of treatment, payment, enrollment in a health plan, or eligibility for benefits.

(i)(1) Standard: Policies and procedures. A covered entity must implement policies and procedures with respect to protected health information that are designed to comply with the standards, implementation specifications, or other requirements of this subpart. The policies and procedures must be reasonably designed, taking into account the size of and the type of activities that relate to protected health information undertaken by the covered entity, to ensure such compliance. This standard is not to be construed to permit or excuse an action that violates any other standard, implementation specification, or other requirement of this subpart.

(2) Standard: Changes to policies or procedures.

(i) A covered entity must change its policies and procedures as necessary and appropriate to comply with changes in the law, including the standards, requirements, and implementation specifications of this subpart;

(ii) When a covered entity changes a privacy practice that is stated in the notice described in § 164.520, and makes corresponding changes to its policies and procedures, it may make the changes effective for protected health information that it created or received prior to the effective date of the notice revision, if the covered entity has, in accordance with § 164.520(b)(1)(v)(C), included in the notice a statement reserving its right to make such a change in its privacy practices; or

(iii) A covered entity may make any other changes to policies and procedures at any time, provided that the changes are documented and implemented in accordance with paragraph (i)(5) of this section.

(3) Implementation specification: Changes in law. Whenever there is a change in law that necessitates a change to the covered entity's policies or procedures, the covered entity must promptly document and implement the revised policy or procedure. If the change in law materially affects the content of the notice required by § 164.520, the covered entity must promptly make the appropriate revisions to the notice in accordance with § 164.520(b)(3). Nothing in this paragraph may be used by a covered entity to excuse a failure to comply with the law.

(4) Implementation specifications: Changes to privacy practices stated in the notice.

(i) To implement a change as provided by paragraph (i)(2)(ii) of this section, a covered entity must:

(A) Ensure that the policy or procedure, as revised to reflect a change in the covered entity's privacy practice as stated in its notice, complies with the standards, requirements, and implementation specifications of this subpart;

(B) Document the policy or procedure, as revised, as required by paragraph (j) of this section; and

(C) Revise the notice as required by § 164.520(b)(3) to state the changed practice and make the revised notice available as required by § 164.520(c). The covered entity may not implement a change to a policy or procedure prior to the effective date of the revised notice.

(ii) If a covered entity has not reserved its right under § 164.520(b)(1)(v)(C) to change a privacy practice that is stated in the notice, the covered entity is bound by the privacy practices as stated in the notice with respect to protected health information created or received while such notice is in effect. A covered entity may change a privacy practice that is stated in the notice, and the related policies and procedures, without having reserved the right to do so, provided that:

(A) Such change meets the implementation specifications in paragraphs (i)(4)(i)(A)–(C) of this section; and

(B) Such change is effective only with respect to protected health information created or received after the effective date of the notice.

(5) Implementation specification: Changes to other policies or procedures. A covered entity may change, at any time, a policy or procedure that does not materially affect the content of the notice required by § 164.520, provided that:

(i) The policy or procedure, as revised, complies with the standards, requirements, and implementation specifications of this subpart; and

(ii) Prior to the effective date of the change, the policy or procedure, as revised, is documented as required by paragraph (j) of this section.

(j)(1) Standard: Documentation. A covered entity must:

(i) Maintain the policies and procedures provided for in paragraph (i) of this section in written or electronic form;

(ii) If a communication is required by this subpart to be in writing, maintain such writing, or an electronic copy, as documentation; and

(iii) If an action, activity, or designation is required by this subpart to be documented, maintain a written or electronic record of such action, activity, or designation.

(2) Implementation specification: Retention period. A covered entity must retain the documentation required by paragraph (j)(1) of this section for six years from the date of its creation or the date when it last was in effect, whichever is later.

(k) Standard: Group health plans.

(1) A group health plan is not subject to the standards or implementation specifications in paragraphs (a) through (f) and (i) of this section, to the extent that:

(i) The group health plan provides health benefits solely through an insurance contract with a health insurance issuer or an HMO; and

(ii) The group health plan does not create or receive protected health information, except for:

(A) Summary health information as defined in § 164.504(a); or

(B) Information on whether the individual is participating in the group health plan, or is enrolled in or has disenrolled from a health insurance issuer or HMO offered by the plan.

(2) A group health plan described in paragraph (k)(1) of this section is subject to the standard and implementation specification in paragraph (j) of this section only with respect to plan documents amended in accordance with § 164.504(f).

§ 164.532   Transition provisions.

(a) Standard: Effect of prior authorizations. Notwithstanding § § 164.508 and 164.512(i), a covered entity may use or disclose protected health information, consistent with paragraphs (b) and (c) of this section, pursuant to an authorization or other express legal permission obtained from an individual permitting the use or disclosure of protected health information, informed consent of the individual to participate in research, or a waiver of informed consent by an IRB.

(b) Implementation specification: Effect of prior authorization for purposes other than research. Notwithstanding any provisions in § 164.508, a covered entity may use or disclose protected health information that it created or received prior to the applicable compliance date of this subpart pursuant to an authorization or other express legal permission obtained from an individual prior to the applicable compliance date of this subpart, provided that the authorization or other express legal permission specifically permits such use or disclosure and there is no agreed-to restriction in accordance with § 164.522(a).

(c) Implementation specification: Effect of prior permission for research. Notwithstanding any provisions in § § 164.508 and 164.512(i), a covered entity may, to the extent allowed by one of the following permissions, use or disclose, for research, protected health information that it created or received either before or after the applicable compliance date of this subpart, provided that there is no agreed-to restriction in accordance with § 164.522(a), and the covered entity has obtained, prior to the applicable compliance date, either:

(1) An authorization or other express legal permission from an individual to use or disclose protected health information for the research;

(2) The informed consent of the individual to participate in the research; or

(3) A waiver, by an IRB, of informed consent for the research, in accordance with 7 CFR 1c.116(d), 10 CFR 745.116(d), 14 CFR 1230.116(d), 15 CFR 27.116(d), 16 CFR 1028.116(d), 21 CFR 50.24, 22 CFR 225.116(d), 24 CFR 60.116(d), 28 CFR 46.116(d), 32 CFR 219.116(d), 34 CFR 97.116(d), 38 CFR 16.116(d), 40 CFR 26.116(d), 45 CFR 46.116(d), 45 CFR 690.116(d), or 49 CFR 11.116(d), provided that a covered entity must obtain authorization in accordance with § 164.508 if, after the compliance date, informed consent is sought from an individual participating in the research.

(d) Standard: Effect of prior contracts or other arrangements with business associates. Notwithstanding any other provisions of this subpart, a covered entity, other than a small health plan, may disclose protected health information to a business associate and may allow a business associate to create, receive, or use protected health information on its behalf pursuant to a written contract or other written arrangement with such business associate that does not comply with § § 164.502(e) and 164.504(e) consistent with the requirements, and only for such time, set forth in paragraph (e) of this section.

(e) Implementation specification: Deemed compliance.—

(1) Qualification. Notwithstanding other sections of this subpart, a covered entity, other than a small health plan, is deemed to be in compliance with the documentation and contract requirements of § § 164.502(e) and 164.504(e), with respect to a particular business associate relationship, for the time period set forth in paragraph (e)(2) of this section, if:

(i) Prior to October 15, 2002, such covered entity has entered into and is operating pursuant to a written contract or other written arrangement with a business associate for such business associate to perform functions or activities or provide services that make the entity a business associate; and

(ii) The contract or other arrangement is not renewed or modified from October 15, 2002, until the compliance date set forth in § 164.534.

(2) Limited deemed compliance period. A prior contract or other arrangement that meets the qualification requirements in paragraph (e) of this section, shall be deemed compliant until the earlier of:

(i) The date such contract or other arrangement is renewed or modified on or after the compliance date set forth in § 164.534; or

(ii) April 14, 2004.

(3) Covered entity responsibilities. Nothing in this section shall alter the requirements of a covered entity to comply with part 160, subpart C of this subchapter and § § 164.524, 164.526, 164.528, and 164.530(f) with respect to protected health information held by a business associate.

§ 164.534 Compliance dates for initial implementation of the privacy standards.

(a) Health care providers. A covered health care provider must comply with the applicable requirements of this subpart no later than April 14, 2003.

(b) Health plans. A health plan must comply with the applicable requirements of this subpart no later than the following as applicable:

(1) Health plans other than small health plans. April 14, 2003.

(2) Small health plans. April 14, 2004.

(c) Health clearinghouses. A health care clearinghouse must comply with the applicable requirements of this subpart no later than April 14, 2003.

VIII. STATE LICENSING OF HEALTH CARE PROFESSIONALS

A. ILLINOIS MEDICAL PRACTICE ACT, 225 ILL.COMP.STAT. § 60/1

§ 1. Short title

This Act shall be known and may be cited as the Medical Practice Act of 1987.

§ 2. Definitions

For purposes of this Act, the following definitions shall have the following meanings, except where the context requires otherwise:

1. "Act" means the Medical Practice Act of 1987.

2. "Department" means the Department of Professional Regulation.

3. "Director" means the Director of Professional Regulation.

4. "Disciplinary Action" means revocation, suspension, probation, supervision, practice modification, reprimand, required education, fines or any other action taken by the Department against a person holding a license.

5. "Disciplinary Board" means the Medical Disciplinary Board.

6. "Final Determination" means the governing body's final action taken under the procedure followed by a health care institution, or professional association or society, against any person licensed under the Act in accordance with the bylaws or rules and regulations of such health care institution, or professional association or society.

7. "Fund" means the Medical Disciplinary Fund.

8. "Impaired" means the inability to practice medicine with reasonable skill and safety due to physical or mental disabilities as evidenced by a written determination or written consent based on clinical evidence including deterioration through the aging process or loss of motor skill, or abuse of drugs or alcohol, of sufficient degree to diminish a person's ability to deliver competent patient care.

9. "Licensing Board" means the Medical Licensing Board.

10. "Physician" means a person licensed under the Medical Practice Act to practice medicine in all of its branches or a chiropractic physician licensed to treat human ailments without the use of drugs and without operative surgery.

11. "Professional Association" means an association or society of persons licensed under this Act, and operating within the State of Illinois, including but not limited to, medical societies, osteopathic organizations, and chiropractic organizations, but this term shall not be deemed to include hospital medical staffs.

12. "Program of Care, Counseling, or Treatment" means a written schedule of organized treatment, care, counseling, activities, or education, satisfactory to the Disciplinary Board, designed for the purpose of restoring an impaired person to a condition whereby the impaired person can practice medicine with reasonable skill and safety of a sufficient degree to deliver competent patient care.

§ 3. Licensure requirement

No person shall practice medicine, or any of its branches, or treat human ailments without the use of drugs and without operative surgery, without a valid, existing license to do so, except that a physician who holds an active license in another state or a second year resident enrolled in a residency program accredited by the Liaison Committee on Graduate Medical Education or the Bureau of Professional Education of the American Osteopathic Association may provide medical services to patients in Illinois during a bonafide emergency in immediate preparation for or during interstate transit.

§ 3.5. Unlicensed practice; violation; civil penalty

(a) Any person who practices, offers to practice, attempts to practice, or holds oneself out to practice as a physician without being licensed under this Act shall, in addition to any other penalty provided by law, pay a civil penalty to the Department in an amount not to exceed $5,000 for each offense as determined by the Department. The civil penalty shall be assessed by the Department after a hearing is held in accordance with the provisions set forth in this Act regarding the provision of a hearing for the discipline of a licensee.

(b) The Department has the authority and power to investigate any and all unlicensed activity.

(c) The civil penalty shall be paid within 60 days after the effective date of the order imposing the civil penalty. The order shall constitute a judgment and may be filed and execution had thereon in the same manner as any judgment from any court of record.

§ 4. Exemptions

(a) This Act does not apply to:

(1) persons lawfully carrying on their particular profession or business under any valid existing regulatory Act of this State;

(2) persons rendering gratuitous services in cases of emergency;

(3) persons treating human ailments by prayer or spiritual means as an exercise or enjoyment of religious freedom.

(b) Section 22 of this Act does not apply to persons who carry out or assist in the implementation of a court order effecting the provisions of Section 119–5 of the Code of Criminal Procedure of 1963.

§ 5. Service on committees; exemption from civil liabilities

Because the candid and conscientious evaluation of clinical practices is essential to the provision of adequate health care, it is the policy of this State to encourage peer review by health care providers. Therefore, while serving upon any committee whose purpose, directly or indirectly, is internal quality control or medical study to reduce morbidity or mortality, or for improving patient care or physician services within a hospital duly licensed under the Hospital Licensing Act, or within a professional association of persons licensed under this Act, or the improving or benefiting of patient care and treatment whether within a hospital or not, or for the purpose of professional discipline, any person serving on such committee, and any person providing service to such committees, shall not be liable for civil damages as a result of their acts, omissions, decisions, or any other conduct in connection with their duties on such committees, except those involving wilful or wanton misconduct.

Information considered shall be afforded the same status as is information concerning medical studies by Part 21 of Article VIII of the "Code of Civil Procedure", as now or hereafter amended.

§ 6. Exclusive State power or function

It is declared to be the public policy of this State, pursuant to paragraphs (h) and (i) of *Section 6 of Article VII of the Illinois Constitution of 1970*, that any power or function set forth in this Act to be exercised by the State is an exclusive State power or function. Such power or function shall not be exercised concurrently, either directly or indirectly, by any unit of local government, including home rule units, except as otherwise provided in this Act.

§ 7. Medical Disciplinary Board

(A) There is hereby created the Illinois State Medical Disciplinary Board (hereinafter referred to as the "Disciplinary Board"). The Disciplinary Board shall consist of 9 members, to be appointed by the Governor by and with the advice and consent of the Senate. All shall be residents of the State, not more than 5 of whom shall be members of the same political party. Five members shall be physicians licensed to practice medicine in all of its branches in Illinois possessing the degree of doctor of medicine. Two shall be members of the public, who shall not be engaged in any way, directly or indirectly, as providers of health care. The 2 public members shall act as nonvoting, ex-officio members and shall not be considered in determining the existence, or lack of existence, of a quorum for all purposes for which a quorum may be called pursuant to this Act. One member shall be a physician licensed to practice in Illinois possessing the degree of doctor of osteopathy or osteopathic medicine. One member shall be a physician licensed to practice in Illinois and possessing the degree of doctor of chiropractic.

(B) Members of the Disciplinary Board shall be appointed for terms of 4 years. Upon the expiration of the term of any member, their successor shall be appointed for a term of 4 years by the Governor by and with the advice and consent of the Senate. The Governor shall fill any vacancy for the remainder of the unexpired term by and with the advice and consent of the Senate. Upon recommendation of the Board, any member of the Disciplinary Board may be removed by the Governor for misfeasance, malfeasance, or wilful neglect of duty, after notice, and a public hearing, unless such notice and hearing shall be expressly waived in writing. Each member shall serve on the Disciplinary Board until their successor is appointed and qualified. No member of the Disciplinary Board shall serve more than 2 consecutive 4 year terms.

In making appointments the Governor shall attempt to insure that the various social and geographic regions of the State of Illinois are properly represented.

In making the designation of persons to act for the several professions represented on the Disciplinary Board, the Governor shall give due consideration to recommendations by members of the respective professions and by organizations therein.

(C) The Disciplinary Board shall annually elect one of its voting members as chairperson and one as vice chairperson. No officer shall be elected more than twice in succession to the same office. Each officer shall serve until their successor has been elected and qualified.

* * *

(E) Four voting members of the Disciplinary Board shall constitute a quorum. A vacancy in the membership of the Disciplinary Board shall not impair the right of a quorum to exercise all the rights and perform all the duties of the Disciplinary Board. Any action taken by the Disciplinary Board under this Act may be authorized by resolution at any regular or special meeting and each such resolution shall take effect immediately. The Disciplinary Board shall meet at least quarterly. The Disciplinary Board is empowered to adopt all rules and regulations necessary and incident to the powers granted to it under this Act.

(F) Each member, and member-officer, of the Disciplinary Board shall receive a per diem stipend as the Director of the Department, hereinafter referred to as the Director, shall determine. The Director shall also determine the per diem stipend that each ex-officio member shall receive. Each member shall be paid their necessary expenses while engaged in the performance of their duties.

(G) The Director shall select a Chief Medical Coordinator and a Deputy Medical Coordinator who shall not be members of the Disciplinary Board. Each medical coordinator shall be a physician licensed to practice medicine in all of its branches, and the Director shall set their rates of compensation. The Director shall assign one medical coordinator to a region composed of Cook County and such other counties as the Director may deem appropriate, and such medical coordinator shall locate their office in Chicago. The Director shall assign the remaining medical coordinator to a region composed of the balance of counties in the State, and such medical coordinator shall locate their office in Springfield. Each medical coordinator shall be the chief enforcement officer of this Act in their assigned region and shall serve at the will of the Disciplinary Board.

The Director shall employ, in conformity with the Personnel Code, not less than one full time investigator for every 5000 physicians licensed in the State. Each investigator shall be a college graduate with at least 2 years' investigative experience or one year advanced medical education. Upon the written request of the Disciplinary Board, the Director shall employ, in conformity with the Personnel Code, such other professional, technical, investigative, and clerical help, either on a full or part-time basis as the Disciplinary Board deems necessary for the proper performance of its duties.

(H) Upon the specific request of the Disciplinary Board, signed by either the chairman, vice chairman, or a medical coordinator of the Disciplinary Board, the Department of Human Services or the Department of State Police shall make available any and all information that they have in their possession regarding a particular case then under investigation by the Disciplinary Board.

(I) Members of the Disciplinary Board shall be immune from suit in any action based upon any disciplinary proceedings or other acts performed in good faith as members of the Disciplinary Board.

(J) The Disciplinary Board may compile and establish a statewide roster of physicians and other medical professionals, including the several medical specialties, of such physicians and medical professionals, who have agreed to serve from time to time as advisors to the medical coordinators. Such advisors shall assist the medical coordinators in their investigations and participation in complaints against physicians. Such advisors shall serve under contract and shall be reimbursed at a reasonable rate for the services provided, plus reasonable expenses incurred. While serving in this capacity, the advisor, for any act undertaken in good faith and in the conduct of their duties under this Section, shall be immune from civil suit.

§ 8. Medical Licensing Board

(A) There is hereby created a Medical Licensing Board (hereinafter referred to as the "Licensing Board"). The Licensing Board shall be composed of 7 members, to be appointed by the Governor by and with the advice and consent of the Senate; 5 of whom shall be reputable physicians licensed to practice medicine in all of its branches in Illinois, possessing the degree of doctor of medicine; one member shall be a reputable physician licensed in Illinois to practice medicine in all of its branches, possessing the degree of doctor of osteopathy or osteopathic medicine; and one member shall be a reputable physician licensed to practice in Illinois and possessing the degree of doctor of chiropractic. Of the 5 members holding the degree of doctor of medicine, one shall be a full-time or part-time teacher of professorial rank in the clinical department of an Illinois school of medicine.

(B) Members of the Licensing Board shall be appointed for terms of 4 years, and until their successors are appointed and qualified. Appointments to fill vacancies shall be made in the same manner as original appointments, for the unexpired portion of the vacated term. No more than 4 members of the Licensing Board shall be members of the same political party and all members shall be residents of this State. No member of the Licensing Board may be appointed to more than 2 successive 4 year terms. This limitation shall only apply to individuals appointed to the Licensing Board after the effective date of this Act.

(C) Members of the Licensing Board shall be immune from suit in any action based upon any licensing proceedings or other acts performed in good faith as members of the Licensing Board.

* * *

(E) The Licensing Board shall annually elect one of its members as chairperson and one as vice chairperson. No member shall be elected more than twice in succession to the same office. Each officer shall serve until their successor has been elected and qualified.

(F) None of the functions, powers or duties of the Department with respect to policies regarding licensure and examination under this Act, including the promulgation of such rules as may be necessary for the administration of this Act, shall be exercised by the Department except upon review of the Licensing Board.

(G) The Licensing Board shall receive the same compensation as the members of the Medical Disciplinary Board, which compensation shall be paid out of the Illinois State Medical Disciplinary Fund.

§ 9. Application for license

Each applicant for a license shall:

(A) Make application on blank forms prepared and furnished by the Department of Professional Regulation hereinafter referred to as the Department.

(B) Submit evidence satisfactory to the Department that the applicant:

(1) is of good moral character. In determining moral character under this Section, the Department may take into consideration whether the applicant has engaged in conduct or activities which would constitute grounds for discipline under this Act. The Department may also request the applicant to submit, and may consider as evidence of moral character, endorsements from 2 or 3 individuals licensed under this Act;

(2) has the preliminary and professional education required by this Act;

* * *

(4) is physically, mentally, and professionally capable of practicing medicine with reasonable judgment, skill, and safety. In determining physical, mental and professional capacity under this Section, the Medical Licensing Board may, upon a showing of a possible incapacity, compel any applicant to submit to a mental or physical examination, or both. The Licensing Board may condition or restrict any license, subject to the same terms and conditions as are provided for the Medical Disciplinary Board under Section 22 of this Act. Any such condition of a restricted license shall provide that the Chief Medical Coordinator or Deputy Medical Coordinator shall have the authority to review the subject physician's compliance with such conditions or restrictions, including, where appropriate, the physician's record of treatment and counseling regarding the impairment, to the extent permitted by applicable federal statutes and regulations safeguarding the confidentiality of medical records of patients.

In determining professional capacity under this Section any individual who has not been actively engaged in the practice of medicine or as a medical, osteopathic, or chiropractic student or who has not been engaged in a formal program of medical education during the 2 years immediately preceding their application may be required to complete such additional testing, training, or remedial education as the Licensing Board may deem necessary in order to establish the applicant's present capacity to practice medicine with reasonable judgment, skill, and safety.

(C) Designate specifically the name, location, and kind of professional school, college, or institution of which the applicant is a graduate and the category under which the applicant seeks, and will undertake, to practice.

(D) Pay to the Department at the time of application the required fees.

(E) Pursuant to Department rules, as required, pass an examination authorized by the Department to determine the applicant's fitness to receive a license.

(F) Complete the application process within 3 years from the date of application. If the process has not been completed within 3 years, the application shall be denied, application fees shall be forfeited, and the applicant must reapply and meet the requirements in effect at the time of reapplication.

§ 9.5. Social Security Number on license application

In addition to any other information required to be contained in the application, every application for an original, renewal, or restored license under this Act shall include the applicant's Social Security Number.

§ 9.7. Criminal background check

The Department shall require an applicant for a license under Section 19 of this Act to undergo a criminal background check. The Department shall adopt rules to implement this Section.

§ 10. Rules and regulations

The Department shall:

(A) Make rules for establishing reasonable minimum standards of educational requirements to be observed by medical, osteopathic and chiropractic colleges;

(B) Effectuate the policy of the State of Illinois that the quality of medical training is an appropriate concern in the recruiting, licensing, credentialing and participation in residency programs of physicians. However, it is inappropriate to discriminate against any physician because of national origin or geographic location of medical education;

(C) Formulate rules and regulations required for the administration of this Act.

§ 11. Minimum education standards

The minimum standards of professional education to be enforced by the Department in conducting examinations and issuing licenses shall be as follows:

(A) Practice of medicine. For the practice of medicine in all of its branches:

(1) For applications for licensure under subsection (D) of Section 19 of this Act:

(a) that the applicant is a graduate of a medical or osteopathic college in the United States, its territories or Canada, that the applicant has completed a 2 year course of instruction in a college of liberal arts, or its equivalent, and a course of instruction in a medical or osteopathic college approved by the Department or by a private, not for profit accrediting body approved by the Department, and in addition thereto, a course of postgraduate clinical training of not less than 12 months as approved by the Department; or

(b) that the applicant is a graduate of a medical or osteopathic college located outside the United States, its territories or Canada, and that the degree conferred is officially recognized by the country for the purposes of licensure, that the applicant has completed a 2 year course of instruction in a college of liberal arts or its equivalent, and a course of instruction in a medical or osteopathic college approved by the Department, which course shall have been not less than 132 weeks in duration and shall have been completed within a period of not less than 35 months, and, in addition thereto, has completed a course of postgraduate clinical training of not less than 12 months, as approved by the Department, and has complied with any other standards established by rule.

For the purposes of this subparagraph (b) an applicant is considered to be a graduate of a medical college if the degree which is conferred is officially recognized by that country for the purposes of receiving a license to practice medicine in all of its branches or a document is granted by the medical college which certifies the completion of all formal training requirements including any internship and social service; or

(c) that the applicant has studied medicine at a medical or osteopathic college located outside the United States, its territories, or Canada, that the applicant has completed a 2 year course of instruction in a college of liberal arts or its equivalent and all of the formal requirements of a foreign medical school except internship and social service, which course shall have been not less than 132 weeks in duration and shall have been completed within a period of not less than 35 months; that the applicant has submitted an application to a medical college accredited by the Liaison Committee on Medical Education and submitted to such evaluation procedures, including use of nationally recognized medical student tests or tests devised by the individual medical college, and that the applicant has satisfactorily completed one academic year of supervised clinical training under the direction of such medical college; and, in addition thereto has completed a course of postgraduate clinical training of not less than 12 months, as approved by the Department, and has complied with any other standards established by rule.

(d) Any clinical clerkships must have been completed in compliance with Section 10.3 of the Hospital Licensing Act, as amended.

(2) Effective January 1, 1988, for applications for licensure made subsequent to January 1, 1988, under Sections 9 or 17 of this Act by individuals not described in paragraph (3) of subsection (A) of Section 11 who graduated after December 31, 1984:

(a) that the applicant:

(i) graduated from a medical or osteopathic college officially recognized by the jurisdiction in which it is located for the purpose of receiving a license to practice medicine in all of its branches, and the applicant has completed, as defined by the Department, a 6 year postsecondary course of study comprising at least 2 academic years of study in the basic medical sciences; and 2 academic years of study in the clinical sciences, while enrolled in the medical college which conferred the degree, the core rotations of which must have been completed in clinical teaching facilities owned, operated or formally affiliated with the medical college which conferred the degree, or under contract in teaching facilities owned, operated or affiliated with another medical college which is officially recognized by the jurisdiction in which the medical school which conferred the degree is located; or

(ii) graduated from a medical or osteopathic college accredited by the Liaison Committee on Medical Education, the Committee on Accreditation of Canadian Medical Schools in conjunction with the Liaison Committee on Medical Education, or the Bureau of Professional Education of the American Osteopathic Association; and,

(iii) in addition thereto, has completed a course of postgraduate clinical training of not less than 24 months, as approved by the Department; or

(b) that the applicant has studied medicine at a medical or osteopathic college located outside the United States, its territories, or Canada, that the applicant, in addition to satisfying the requirements of subparagraph (a), except for the awarding of a degree, has completed all of the formal requirements of a foreign medical school except internship and social service and has submitted an application to a medical college accredited by the Liaison Committee on Medical Education and submitted to such evaluation procedures, including use of nationally recognized medical student tests or tests devised by the individual medical college, and that the applicant has satisfactorily completed one academic year of supervised clinical training under the direction of such medical college; and, in addition thereto, has completed a course of postgraduate clinical training of not less than 24 months, as approved by the Department, and has complied with any other standards established by rule.

* * *

(4) Any person granted a temporary license pursuant to Section 17 of this Act who shall satisfactorily complete a course of postgraduate clinical training and meet all of the requirements for licensure shall be granted a permanent license pursuant to Section 9.

(5) Notwithstanding any other provision of this Section an individual holding a temporary license under Section 17 of this Act shall be required to satisfy the undergraduate medical and post-graduate clinical training educational requirements in effect on the date of

their application for a temporary license, provided they apply for a license under Section 9 of this Act and satisfy all other requirements of this Section while their temporary license is in effect.

(B) Treating human ailments without drugs and without operative surgery.

For the practice of treating human ailments without the use of drugs and without operative surgery:

(1) For an applicant who was a resident student and who is a graduate after July 1, 1926, of a chiropractic college or institution, that such school, college or institution, at the time of the applicant's graduation required as a prerequisite to admission thereto a 4 year course of instruction in a high school, and, as a prerequisite to graduation therefrom, a course of instruction in the treatment of human ailments, of not less than 132 weeks in duration and which shall have been completed within a period of not less than 35 months except that as to students matriculating or entering upon a course of chiropractic study during the years 1940, 1941, 1942, 1943, 1944, 1945, 1946, and 1947, such elapsed time shall be not less than 32 months, such high school and such school, college or institution having been reputable and in good standing in the judgment of the Department.

(2) For an applicant who is a matriculant in a chiropractic college after September 1, 1969, that such applicant shall be required to complete a 2 year course of instruction in a liberal arts college or its equivalent and a course of instruction in a chiropractic college in the treatment of human ailments, such course, as a prerequisite to graduation therefrom, having been not less than 132 weeks in duration and shall have been completed within a period of not less than 35 months, such college of liberal arts and chiropractic college having been reputable and in good standing in the judgment of the Department.

(3) For an applicant who is a graduate of a United States chiropractic college after August 19, 1981, the college of the applicant must be fully accredited by the Commission on Accreditation of the Council on Chiropractic Education or its successor at the time of graduation. Such graduates shall be considered to have met the minimum requirements which shall be in addition to those requirements set forth in the rules and regulations promulgated by the Department.

(4) For an applicant who is a graduate of a chiropractic college in another country; that such chiropractic college be equivalent to the standards of education as set forth for chiropractic colleges located in the United States.

§ 12. Examinations

All examinations provided for by this Act shall be conducted under rules prescribed from time to time by the Department. Examinations shall be held not less frequently than 2 times every year, at times and places prescribed by the Department, of which applicants shall be notified by the Department in writing, and may be conducted wholly or in part in writing.

If an applicant neglects, fails without an approved excuse or refuses to take the next available examination offered for license under this Act, the fee paid by the applicant shall be forfeited and the application denied. If an applicant fails to pass an examination for a license under this Act within 3 years after filing their application, the application shall be denied. However, such applicant may thereafter make a new application for examination, accompanied by the required fee and satisfy the requirements then in existence for a license.

§ 13. Medical students

Candidates for the degree of doctor of medicine, doctor of osteopathy, or doctor of osteopathic medicine enrolled in a medical or osteopathic college, accredited by the Liaison Committee on Medical Education or the Bureau of Professional Education of the American Osteopathic Association, may practice under the direct, on-premises supervision of a physician who is licensed to practice medicine in all its branches in Illinois and who is a member of the faculty of an accredited medical or osteopathic college.

§ 14. Chiropractic students

Candidates for the degree of doctor of chiropractic enrolled in a chiropractic college, accredited by the Council on Chiropractic Education, may practice under the direct, on-premises supervision of a physician who is licensed to treat human ailments without the use of drugs and without operative surgery and who is a member of the faculty of an accredited chiropractic college.

§ 15. Physician licensed to practice without drugs and operative surgery; license for general practice

Any physician licensed under this Act to treat human ailments without the use of prescriptive drugs and operative surgery shall be permitted to take the examination for licensure as a physician to practice medicine in all its branches and shall receive a license to practice medicine in all of its branches if he or she shall successfully pass such examination, upon proof of having successfully completed in a medical college, osteopathic college or chiropractic college reputable and in good standing in the judgment of the Department, courses of instruction in materia medica, therapeutics, surgery, obstetrics, and theory and practice deemed by the Department to be equal to the courses of instruction required in those subjects for admission to the examination for a license to practice medicine in all of its branches, together with proof of having completed

(a) the 2 year course of instruction in a college of liberal arts, or its equivalent, required under this Act, and

(b) a course of postgraduate clinical training of not less than 24 months as approved by the Department.

§ 16. Ineligibility for examination

Any person who shall fail any examination for licensure as a medical doctor, doctor of osteopathy or osteopathic medicine, or doctor of chiropractic in this or any other jurisdiction a total of 5 times shall thereafter be ineligible for further examinations until such time as such person shall submit to the Department evidence of further formal professional study, as required by rule of the Department, in an accredited institution.

§ 17. Temporary license

Persons holding the degree of Doctor of Medicine, persons holding the degree of Doctor of Osteopathy or Doctor of Osteopathic Medicine, and persons holding the degree of Doctor of Chiropractic or persons who have satisfied the requirements therefor and are eligible to receive such degree from a medical, osteopathic, or chiropractic school, who wish to pursue programs of graduate or specialty training in this State, may receive without examination, in the discretion of the Department, a 3–year temporary license. In order to receive a 3–year temporary license hereunder, an applicant shall furnish satisfactory proof to the Department that the applicant:

(A) Is of good moral character. In determining moral character under this Section, the Department may take into consideration whether the applicant has engaged in conduct or activities which would constitute grounds for discipline under this Act. The Department may also request the applicant to submit, and may consider as evidence of moral character, endorsements from 2 or 3 individuals licensed under this Act;

(B) Has been accepted or appointed for specialty or residency training by a hospital situated in this State or a training program in hospitals or facilities maintained by the State of Illinois or affiliated training facilities which is approved by the Department for the purpose of such training under this Act. The applicant shall indicate the beginning and ending dates of the period for which the applicant has been accepted or appointed;

(C) Has or will satisfy the professional education requirements of Section 11 of this Act which are effective at the date of application except for postgraduate clinical training;

(D) Is physically, mentally, and professionally capable of practicing medicine or treating human ailments without the use of drugs or operative surgery with reasonable judgment, skill, and safety. In determining physical, mental and professional capacity under this Section, the Medical Licensing Board may, upon a showing of a possible incapacity, compel an applicant to submit to a mental or physical examination, or both, and may condition or restrict any temporary license, subject to the same terms and conditions as are provided for the Medical Disciplinary Board under Section 22 of this Act. Any such condition of restricted temporary license shall provide that the Chief Medical Coordinator or Deputy Medical Coordinator shall have the authority to review the subject physician's compliance with such conditions or restrictions, including, where appropriate, the physician's record of treatment and counseling regarding the impairment, to the extent permitted by applicable federal statutes and regulations safeguarding the confidentiality of medical records of patients.

Three-year temporary licenses issued pursuant to this Section shall be valid only for the period of time designated therein, and may be extended or renewed pursuant to the rules of the Department, and if a temporary license is thereafter extended, it shall not extend beyond completion of the residency program. The holder of a valid 3–year temporary license shall be entitled thereby to perform only such acts as may be prescribed by and incidental to their program of residency training; they shall not be entitled to otherwise engage in the practice of medicine in this State unless fully licensed in this State.

A 3–year temporary license may be revoked by the Department upon proof that the holder thereof has engaged in the practice of medicine in this State outside of the program of their residency or specialty training, or if the holder shall fail to supply the Department, within 10 days of its request, with information as to their current status and activities in their specialty training program.

§ 18.   Visiting professor, physician, or resident permits

(A) Visiting professor permit.

(1) A visiting professor permit shall entitle a person to practice medicine in all of its branches or to practice the treatment of human ailments without the use of drugs and without operative surgery provided:

(a) the person maintains an equivalent authorization to practice medicine in all of its branches or to practice the treatment of human ailments without the use of drugs and without operative surgery in good standing in their native licensing jurisdiction during the period of the visiting professor permit; and

(b) the person has received a faculty appointment to teach in a medical, osteopathic or chiropractic school in Illinois.

(2) Application for visiting professor permits shall be made to the Department, in writing, on forms prescribed by the Department and shall be accompanied by the required fee established by rule, which shall not be refundable. Any application shall require the information as, in the judgment of the Department, will enable the Department to pass on the qualifications of the applicant.

(3) A visiting professor permit shall be valid for one year from the date of issuance or until the time the faculty appointment is terminated, whichever occurs first, and may be renewed only once.

(4) The applicant may be required to appear before the Medical Licensing Board for an interview prior to, and as a requirement for, the issuance of the original permit and the renewal.

(5) Persons holding a permit under this Section shall only practice medicine in all of its branches or practice the treatment of human ailments without the use of drugs and without operative surgery in the State of Illinois in their official capacity under their contract.

(B) Visiting physician permit.

(1) The Department may, in its discretion, issue a temporary visiting physician permit, without examination, provided:

* * *

(b) that the person maintains an equivalent authorization to practice medicine in all of its branches or to practice the treatment of human ailments without the use of drugs and without operative surgery in good standing in his or her native licensing jurisdiction during the period of the temporary visiting physician permit;

(c) that the person has received an invitation or appointment to study, demonstrate, or perform a specific medical, osteopathic, chiropractic or clinical subject or technique in a medical, osteopathic, or chiropractic school, a hospital licensed under the Hospital Licensing Act, a hospital organized under the University of Illinois Hospital Act, or a facility operated pursuant to the Ambulatory Surgical Treatment Center Act; and

(d) that the temporary visiting physician permit shall only permit the holder to practice medicine in all of its branches or practice the treatment of human ailments without the use of drugs and without operative surgery within the scope of the medical, osteopathic, chiropractic, or clinical studies for which the holder was invited or appointed.

(2) The application for the temporary visiting physician permit shall be made to the Department, in writing, on forms prescribed by the Department, and shall be accompanied by the required fee established by rule, which shall not be refundable. The application shall require information that, in the judgment of the Department, will enable the Department to pass on the qualification of the applicant, and the necessity for the granting of a temporary visiting physician permit.

(3) A temporary visiting physician permit shall be valid for 180 days from the date of issuance or until the time the medical, osteopathic, chiropractic, or clinical studies are completed, whichever occurs first.

(4) The applicant for a temporary visiting physician permit may be required to appear before the Medical Licensing Board for an interview prior to, and as a requirement for, the issuance of a temporary visiting physician permit.

(5) A limited temporary visiting physician permit shall be issued to a physician licensed in another state who has been requested to perform emergency procedures in Illinois if he or she meets the requirements as established by rule.

(C) Visiting resident permit.

(1) The Department may, in its discretion, issue a temporary visiting resident permit, without examination, provided:

* * *

(b) that the person maintains an equivalent authorization to practice medicine in all of its branches or to practice the treatment of human ailments without the use of drugs and without operative surgery in good standing in his or her native licensing jurisdiction during the period of the temporary visiting resident permit;

(c) that the applicant is enrolled in a postgraduate clinical training program outside the State of Illinois that is approved by the Department;

(d) that the individual has been invited or appointed for a specific period of time to perform a portion of that post graduate clinical training program under the supervision of an Illinois licensed physician in an Illinois patient care clinic or facility that is affiliated with the out-of-State post graduate training program; and

(e) that the temporary visiting resident permit shall only permit the holder to practice medicine in all of its branches or practice the treatment of human ailments without the use of drugs and without operative surgery within the scope of the medical, osteopathic, chiropractic or clinical studies for which the holder was invited or appointed.

(2) The application for the temporary visiting resident permit shall be made to the Department, in writing, on forms prescribed by the Department, and shall be accompanied by the required fee established by rule. The application shall require information that, in the judgment of the Department, will enable the Department to pass on the qualifications of the applicant.

(3) A temporary visiting resident permit shall be valid for 180 days from the date of issuance or until the time the medical, osteopathic, chiropractic, or clinical studies are completed, whichever occurs first.

(4) The applicant for a temporary visiting resident permit may be required to appear before the Medical Licensing Board for an interview prior to, and as a requirement for, the issuance of a temporary visiting resident permit.

§ 19. Licensure without examination

The Department may, in its discretion, issue a license without examination to any person who is currently licensed to practice medicine in all of its branches, or to practice the treatment of human ailments without the use of drugs or operative surgery, in any other state, territory, country or province, upon the following conditions:

* * *

(B) That the applicant is of good moral character. In determining moral character under this Section, the Department may take into consideration whether the applicant has engaged in conduct or activities which would constitute grounds for discipline under this Act. The Department may also request the applicant to submit, and may consider as evidence of moral character, endorsements from 2 or 3 individuals licensed under this Act;

(C) That the applicant is physically, mentally and professionally capable of practicing medicine with reasonable judgment, skill and safety. In determining physical, mental and professional capacity under this Section the Medical Licensing Board may, upon a showing of a possible incapacity, compel an applicant to submit to a mental or physical examination, or both, and may condition or restrict any license, subject to the same terms and conditions as are provided for the Medical Disciplinary Board under Section 22 of this Act. The Medical Licensing Board or the Department may order the examining physician to present testimony concerning this mental or physical examination of the applicant. No information shall be excluded by reason of any common law or statutory privilege relating to communications between the applicant and the examining physician. Any condition of restricted license shall provide that the Chief Medical Coordinator or Deputy Medical Coordinator shall have the authority to review the subject physician's compliance with such conditions or restrictions, including, where appropriate, the physician's record of treatment and counseling regarding the impairment, to the extent permitted by applicable federal statutes and regulations safeguarding the confidentiality of medical records of patients.

(D) That if the applicant seeks to practice medicine in all of its branches:

    (1) if the applicant was licensed in another jurisdiction prior to January 1, 1988, that the applicant has satisfied the educational requirements of paragraph (1) of subsection (A) or paragraph (2) of subsection (A) of Section 11 of this Act; or

    (2) if the applicant was licensed in another jurisdiction after December 31, 1987, that the applicant has satisfied the educational requirements of paragraph (A)(2) of Section 11 of this Act; and

    (3) the requirements for a license to practice medicine in all of its branches in the particular state, territory, country or province in which the applicant is licensed are deemed by the Department to have been substantially equivalent to the requirements for a license to practice medicine in all of its branches in force in this State at the date of the applicant's license;

(E) That if the applicant seeks to treat human ailments without the use of drugs and without operative surgery:

    (1) the applicant is a graduate of a chiropractic school or college approved by the Department at the time of their graduation;

    (2) the requirements for the applicant's license to practice the treatment of human ailments without the use of drugs are deemed by the Department to have been substantially equivalent to the requirements for a license to practice in this State at the date of the applicant's license;

(F) That the Department may, in its discretion, issue a license, without examination, to any graduate of a medical or osteopathic college, reputable and in good standing in the judgment of the Department, who has passed an examination for admission to the United States Public Health Service, or who has passed any other examination deemed by the Department to have been at least equal in all substantial respects to the examination required for admission to any such medical corps;

(G) That applications for licenses without examination shall be filed with the Department, under oath, on forms prepared and furnished by the Department, and shall set forth, and applicants therefor shall supply such information respecting the life, education, professional practice, and moral character of applicants as the Department may require to be filed for its use;

(H) That the applicant undergo the criminal background check established under Section 9.7 of this Act.

In the exercise of its discretion under this Section, the Department is empowered to consider and evaluate each applicant on an individual basis. It may take into account, among other things, the extent to which there is or is not available to the Department, authentic and definitive information concerning the quality of medical education and clinical training which the applicant has had. Under no circumstances shall a license be issued under the provisions of this Section to any person who has previously taken and failed the written examination conducted by the Department for such license. In determining moral character, the Department may take into consideration whether the applicant has engaged in conduct or activities which would constitute grounds for discipline under this Act. The Department may also request the applicant to submit, and may consider as evidence of moral character, evidence from 2 or 3 individuals licensed under this Act. Applicants have 3 years from the date of application to complete the application process. If the process has not been completed within 3 years, the application shall be denied, the fees shall be forfeited, and the applicant must reapply and meet the requirements in effect at the time of reapplication.

§ 20. Continuing education

The Department shall promulgate rules of continuing education for persons licensed under this Act that require 150 hours of continuing education per license renewal cycle. These rules shall be consistent with requirements of relevant professional associations, speciality societies, or boards. The rules shall also address variances for illness or hardship. In establishing these rules, the Department shall consider educational requirements for medical staffs, requirements for specialty society board certification or for continuing education requirements as a condition of membership in societies representing the 2 categories of licensee under this Act. These rules shall assure that licensees are given the opportunity to participate in those programs sponsored by or through their professional associations or hospitals which are relevant to their practice. Each licensee is responsible for maintaining records of completion of continuing education and shall be prepared to produce the records when requested by the Department.

§ 21. License renewal; restoration; inactive status; disposition and collection of fees

(A) Renewal.

The expiration date and renewal period for each license issued under this Act shall be set by rule. The holder of a license may renew the license by paying the required fee. The holder of a license may also renew the license within 90 days after its expiration by complying with the requirements for renewal and payment of an additional fee. A license renewal within 90 days after expiration shall be effective retroactively to the expiration date.

The Department shall mail to each licensee under this Act, at his or her last known address, at least 60 days in advance of the expiration date of his or her license, a notice of that fact and an application for renewal form. No such license shall be deemed to have lapsed until 90 days after the expiration date and after such notice and application have been mailed by the Department as herein provided.

(B) Restoration.

Any licensee who has permitted his or her license to lapse or who has had his or her license on inactive status may have his or her license restored by making application to the Department and filing proof acceptable to the Department of his or her fitness to have the license restored, including evidence certifying to active practice in another jurisdiction satisfactory to the Department, proof of meeting the continuing education requirements for one renewal period, and by paying the required restoration fee.

If the licensee has not maintained an active practice in another jurisdiction satisfactory to the Department, the Licensing Board shall determine, by an evaluation program established by rule, the applicant's fitness to resume active status and may require the licensee to complete a period of evaluated clinical experience and may require successful completion of the practical examination.

However, any registrant whose license has expired while he or she has been engaged

    (a) in Federal Service on active duty with the Army of the United States, the United States Navy, the Marine Corps, the Air Force, the Coast Guard, the Public Health Service or the State Militia called into the service or training of the United States of America, or

    (b) in training or education under the supervision of the United States preliminary to induction into the military service,

may have his or her license reinstated or restored without paying any lapsed renewal fees, if within 2 years after honorable termination of such service, training, or education, he or she furnishes to the Department with satisfactory evidence to the effect that he or she has been so engaged and that his or her service, training, or education has been so terminated.

(C) Inactive licenses.

Any licensee who notifies the Department, in writing on forms prescribed by the Department, may elect to place his or her license on an inactive status and shall, subject to rules of the Department, be excused from payment of renewal fees until he or she notifies the Department in writing of his or her desire to resume active status.

Any licensee requesting restoration from inactive status shall be required to pay the current renewal fee, provide proof of meeting the continuing education requirements for the period of time the license is inactive not to exceed one renewal period, and shall be required to restore his or her license as provided in subsection (B).

Any licensee whose license is in an inactive status shall not practice in the State of Illinois.

(D) Disposition of monies collected.

All monies collected under this Act by the Department shall be deposited in the Illinois State Medical Disciplinary Fund in the State Treasury, and used only for the following purposes:

(a) by the Medical Disciplinary Board in the exercise of its powers and performance of its duties, as such use is made by the Department with full consideration of all recommendations of the Medical Disciplinary Board,

(b) for costs directly related to persons licensed under this Act, and

(c) for direct and allocable indirect costs related to the public purposes of the Department of Professional Regulation.

Moneys in the Fund may be transferred to the Professions Indirect Cost Fund as authorized under Section 2105–300 of the Department of Professional Regulation Law (*20 ILCS 2105/2105–300*).

All earnings received from investment of monies in the Illinois State Medical Disciplinary Fund shall be deposited in the Illinois State Medical Disciplinary Fund and shall be used for the same purposes as fees deposited in such Fund.

(E) Fees.

The following fees are nonrefundable.

(1) Applicants for any examination shall be required to pay, either to the Department or to the designated testing service, a fee covering the cost of determining the applicant's eligibility and providing the examination. Failure to appear for the examination on the scheduled date, at the time and place specified, after the applicant's application for examination has been received and acknowledged by the Department or the designated testing service, shall result in the forfeiture of the examination fee.

(2) The fee for a license under Section 9 of this Act is $300.

(3) The fee for a license under Section 19 of this Act is $300.

(4) The fee for the renewal of a license for a resident of Illinois shall be calculated at the rate of $100 per year, except for licensees who were issued a license within 12 months of the expiration date of the license, the fee for the renewal shall be $100. The fee for the renewal of a license for a nonresident shall be calculated at the rate of $200 per year, except for licensees who were issued a license within 12 months of the expiration date of the license, the fee for the renewal shall be $200.

(5) The fee for the restoration of a license other than from inactive status, is $100. In addition, payment of all lapsed renewal fees not to exceed $600 is required.

(6) The fee for a 3–year temporary license under Section 17 is $100.

(7) The fee for the issuance of a duplicate license, for the issuance of a replacement license for a license which has been lost or destroyed, or for the issuance of a license with a change of name or address other than during the renewal period is $20. No fee is required for name and address changes on Department records when no duplicate license is issued.

(8) The fee to be paid for a license record for any purpose is $20.

(9) The fee to be paid to have the scoring of an examination, administered by the Department, reviewed and verified, is $20 plus any fees charged by the applicable testing service.

(10) The fee to be paid by a licensee for a wall certificate showing his or her license shall be the actual cost of producing the certificate.

(11) The fee for a roster of persons licensed as physicians in this State shall be the actual cost of producing such a roster.

(F) Any person who delivers a check or other payment to the Department that is returned to the Department unpaid by the financial institution upon which it is drawn shall pay to the Department, in addition to the amount already owed to the Department, a fine of $50. If the check or other payment was for a renewal or issuance fee and that person practices without paying the renewal fee or issuance fee and the fine due, an additional fine of $100 shall be imposed. The fines imposed by this Section are in addition to any other discipline provided under this Act for unlicensed practice or practice on a nonrenewed license. The Department shall notify the person that payment of fees and fines shall be paid to the Department by certified check or money order within 30 calendar days of the notification. If, after the expiration of 30 days from the date of the notification, the person has failed to submit the necessary remittance, the Department shall automatically terminate the license or certificate or deny the application, without hearing. If, after termination or denial, the person seeks a license or certificate, he or she shall apply to the Department for restoration or issuance of the license or certificate and pay all fees and fines due to the Department. The Department may establish a fee for the processing of an application for restoration of a license or certificate to pay all expenses of processing this application. The Director may waive the fines due under this Section in individual cases where the Director finds that the fines would be unreasonable or unnecessarily burdensome.

§ 22.   Disciplinary action

(A) The Department may revoke, suspend, place on probationary status, or take any other disciplinary action as the Department may deem proper with regard to the license or visiting professor permit of any person issued under this Act to practice medicine, or to treat human ailments without the use of drugs and without operative surgery upon any of the following grounds:

(1) Performance of an elective abortion in any place, locale, facility, or institution other than:

(a) a facility licensed pursuant to the Ambulatory Surgical Treatment Center Act;

(b) an institution licensed under the Hospital Licensing Act; or

(c) an ambulatory surgical treatment center or hospitalization or care facility maintained by the State or any agency thereof, where such department or agency has authority under law to establish and enforce standards for the ambulatory surgical treatment centers, hospitalization, or care facilities under its management and control; or

(d) ambulatory surgical treatment centers, hospitalization or care facilities maintained by the Federal Government; or

(e) ambulatory surgical treatment centers, hospitalization or care facilities maintained by any university or college established under the laws of this State and supported principally by public funds raised by taxation.

(2) Performance of an abortion procedure in a wilful and wanton manner on a woman who was not pregnant at the time the abortion procedure was performed.

(3) The conviction of a felony in this or any other jurisdiction, except as otherwise provided in subsection B of this Section, whether or not related to practice under this Act, or the entry of a guilty or nolo contendere plea to a felony charge.

(4) Gross negligence in practice under this Act.

(5) Engaging in dishonorable, unethical or unprofessional conduct of a character likely to deceive, defraud or harm the public.

(6) Obtaining any fee by fraud, deceit, or misrepresentation.

(7) Habitual or excessive use or abuse of drugs defined in law as controlled substances, of alcohol, or of any other substances which results in the inability to practice with reasonable judgment, skill or safety.

(8) Practicing under a false or, except as provided by law, an assumed name.

(9) Fraud or misrepresentation in applying for, or procuring, a license under this Act or in connection with applying for renewal of a license under this Act.

(10) Making a false or misleading statement regarding their skill or the efficacy or value of the medicine, treatment, or remedy

prescribed by them at their direction in the treatment of any disease or other condition of the body or mind.

(11) Allowing another person or organization to use their license, procured under this Act, to practice.

(12) Disciplinary action of another state or jurisdiction against a license or other authorization to practice as a medical doctor, doctor of osteopathy, doctor of osteopathic medicine or doctor of chiropractic, a certified copy of the record of the action taken by the other state or jurisdiction being prima facie evidence thereof.

(13) Violation of any provision of this Act or of the Medical Practice Act prior to the repeal of that Act, or violation of the rules, or a final administrative action of the Director, after consideration of the recommendation of the Disciplinary Board.

(14) Dividing with anyone other than physicians with whom the licensee practices in a partnership, Professional Association, limited liability company, or Medical or Professional Corporation any fee, commission, rebate or other form of compensation for any professional services not actually and personally rendered. Nothing contained in this subsection prohibits persons holding valid and current licenses under this Act from practicing medicine in partnership under a partnership agreement, including a limited liability partnership, in a limited liability company under the Limited Liability Company Act, in a corporation authorized by the Medical Corporation Act, as an association authorized by the Professional Association Act, or in a corporation under the Professional Corporation Act or from pooling, sharing, dividing or apportioning the fees and monies received by them or by the partnership, corporation or association in accordance with the partnership agreement or the policies of the Board of Directors of the corporation or association. Nothing contained in this subsection prohibits 2 or more corporations authorized by the Medical Corporation Act, from forming a partnership or joint venture of such corporations, and providing medical, surgical and scientific research and knowledge by employees of these corporations if such employees are licensed under this Act, or from pooling, sharing, dividing, or apportioning the fees and monies received by the partnership or joint venture in accordance with the partnership or joint venture agreement. Nothing contained in this subsection shall abrogate the right of 2 or more persons, holding valid and current licenses under this Act, to each receive adequate compensation for concurrently rendering professional services to a patient and divide a fee; provided, the patient has full knowledge of the division, and, provided, that the division is made in proportion to the services performed and responsibility assumed by each.

(15) A finding by the Medical Disciplinary Board that the registrant after having his or her license placed on probationary status or subjected to conditions or restrictions violated the terms of the probation or failed to comply with such terms or conditions.

(16) Abandonment of a patient.

(17) Prescribing, selling, administering, distributing, giving or self-administering any drug classified as a controlled substance (designated product) or narcotic for other than medically accepted therapeutic purposes.

(18) Promotion of the sale of drugs, devices, appliances or goods provided for a patient in such manner as to exploit the patient for financial gain of the physician.

(19) Offering, undertaking or agreeing to cure or treat disease by a secret method, procedure, treatment or medicine, or the treating, operating or prescribing for any human condition by a method, means or procedure which the licensee refuses to divulge upon demand of the Department.

(20) Immoral conduct in the commission of any act including, but not limited to, commission of an act of sexual misconduct related to the licensee's practice.

(21) Wilfully making or filing false records or reports in his or her practice as a physician, including, but not limited to, false records to support claims against the medical assistance program of the Department of Public Aid under the Illinois Public Aid Code.

(22) Wilful omission to file or record, or wilfully impeding the filing or recording, or inducing another person to omit to file or record, medical reports as required by law, or wilfully failing to report an instance of suspected abuse or neglect as required by law.

(23) Being named as a perpetrator in an indicated report by the Department of Children and Family Services under the Abused and Neglected Child Reporting Act, and upon proof by clear and convincing evidence that the licensee has caused a child to be an abused child or neglected child as defined in the Abused and Neglected Child Reporting Act.

(24) Solicitation of professional patronage by any corporation, agents or persons, or profiting from those representing themselves to be agents of the licensee.

(25) Gross and wilful and continued overcharging for professional services, including filing false statements for collection of fees for which services are not rendered, including, but not limited to, filing such false statements for collection of monies for services not rendered from the medical assistance program of the Department of Public Aid under the Illinois Public Aid Code.

(26) A pattern of practice or other behavior which demonstrates incapacity or incompetence to practice under this Act.

(27) Mental illness or disability which results in the inability to practice under this Act with reasonable judgment, skill or safety.

(28) Physical illness, including, but not limited to, deterioration through the aging process, or loss of motor skill which results in a physician's inability to practice under this Act with reasonable judgment, skill or safety.

(29) Cheating on or attempt to subvert the licensing examinations administered under this Act.

(30) Wilfully or negligently violating the confidentiality between physician and patient except as required by law.

(31) The use of any false, fraudulent, or deceptive statement in any document connected with practice under this Act.

(32) Aiding and abetting an individual not licensed under this Act in the practice of a profession licensed under this Act.

(33) Violating state or federal laws or regulations relating to controlled substances.

(34) Failure to report to the Department any adverse final action taken against them by another licensing jurisdiction (any other state or any territory of the United States or any foreign state or country), by any peer review body, by any health care institution, by any professional society or association related to practice under this Act, by any governmental agency, by any law enforcement agency, or by any court for acts or conduct similar to acts or conduct which would constitute grounds for action as defined in this Section.

(35) Failure to report to the Department surrender of a license or authorization to practice as a medical doctor, a doctor of osteopathy, a doctor of osteopathic medicine, or doctor of chiropractic in another state or jurisdiction, or surrender of membership on any medical staff or in any medical or professional association or society, while under disciplinary investigation by any of those authorities or bodies, for acts or conduct similar to acts or conduct which would constitute grounds for action as defined in this Section.

(36) Failure to report to the Department any adverse judgment, settlement, or award arising from a liability claim related to acts or conduct similar to acts or conduct which would constitute grounds for action as defined in this Section.

(37) Failure to transfer copies of medical records as required by law.

(38) Failure to furnish the Department, its investigators or representatives, relevant information, legally requested by the Department after consultation with the Chief Medical Coordinator or the Deputy Medical Coordinator.

(39) Violating the Health Care Worker Self–Referral Act.

(40) Willful failure to provide notice when notice is required under the Parental Notice of Abortion Act of 1995.

(41) Failure to establish and maintain records of patient care and treatment as required by this law.

(42) Entering into an excessive number of written collaborative agreements with licensed advanced practice nurses resulting in an inability to adequately collaborate and provide medical direction.

(43) Repeated failure to adequately collaborate with or provide medical direction to a licensed advanced practice nurse.

All proceedings to suspend, revoke, place on probationary status, or take any other disciplinary action as the Department may deem proper, with regard to a license on any of the foregoing grounds, must be commenced within 3 years next after receipt by the Department of a complaint alleging the commission of or notice of the conviction order for any of the acts described herein. Except for the grounds numbered (8), (9) and (29), no action shall be commenced more than 5 years after the date of the incident or act alleged to have violated this Section. In the event of the settlement of any claim or cause of action in favor of the claimant or the reduction to final judgment of any civil action in favor of the plaintiff, such claim, cause of action or civil action being grounded on the allegation that a person licensed under this Act was negligent in providing care, the Department shall have an additional period of one year from the date of notification to the Department under Section 23 of this Act of such settlement or final judgment in which to investigate and commence formal disciplinary proceedings under Section 36 of this Act, except as otherwise provided by law. The time during which the holder of the license was outside the State of Illinois shall not be included within any period of time limiting the commencement of disciplinary action by the Department.

The entry of an order or judgment by any circuit court establishing that any person holding a license under this Act is a person in need of mental treatment operates as a suspension of that license. That person may resume their practice only upon the entry of a Departmental order based upon a finding by the Medical Disciplinary Board that they have been determined to be recovered from mental illness by the court and upon the Disciplinary Board's recommendation that they be permitted to resume their practice.

The Department may refuse to issue or take disciplinary action concerning the license of any person who fails to file a return, or to pay the tax, penalty or interest shown in a filed return, or to pay any final assessment of tax, penalty or interest, as required by any tax Act administered by the Illinois Department of Revenue, until such time as the requirements of any such tax Act are satisfied as determined by the Illinois Department of Revenue.

The Department, upon the recommendation of the Disciplinary Board, shall adopt rules which set forth standards to be used in determining:

>   **(a)** when a person will be deemed sufficiently rehabilitated to warrant the public trust;

>   **(b)** what constitutes dishonorable, unethical or unprofessional conduct of a character likely to deceive, defraud, or harm the public;

>   **(c)** what constitutes immoral conduct in the commission of any act, including, but not limited to, commission of an act of sexual misconduct related to the licensee's practice; and

>   **(d)** what constitutes gross negligence in the practice of medicine.

However, no such rule shall be admissible into evidence in any civil action except for review of a licensing or other disciplinary action under this Act.

In enforcing this Section, the Medical Disciplinary Board, upon a showing of a possible violation, may compel any individual licensed to practice under this Act, or who has applied for licensure or a permit pursuant to this Act, to submit to a mental or physical examination, or both, as required by and at the expense of the Department. The examining physician or physicians shall be those specifically designated by the Disciplinary Board. The Medical Disciplinary Board or the Department may order the examining physician to present testimony concerning this mental or physical examination of the licensee or applicant. No information shall be excluded by reason of any common law or statutory privilege relating to communication between the licensee or applicant and the examining physician. The individual to be examined may have, at his or her own expense, another physician of his or her choice present during all aspects of the examination. Failure of any individual to submit to mental or physical examination, when directed, shall be grounds for suspension of his or her license until such time as the individual submits to the examination if the Disciplinary Board finds, after notice and hearing, that the refusal to submit to the examination was without reasonable cause. If the Disciplinary Board finds a physician unable to practice because of the reasons set forth in this Section, the Disciplinary Board shall require such physician to submit to care, counseling, or treatment by physicians approved or designated by the Disciplinary Board, as a condition for continued, reinstated, or renewed licensure to practice. Any physician, whose license was granted pursuant to Sections 9, 17, or 19 of this Act, or, continued, reinstated, renewed, disciplined or supervised, subject to such terms, conditions or restrictions who shall fail to comply with such terms, conditions or restrictions, or to complete a required program of care, counseling, or treatment, as determined by the Chief Medical Coordinator or Deputy Medical Coordinators, shall be referred to the Director for a determination as to whether the licensee shall have their license suspended immediately, pending a hearing by the Disciplinary

Board. In instances in which the Director immediately suspends a license under this Section, a hearing upon such person's license must be convened by the Disciplinary Board within 15 days after such suspension and completed without appreciable delay. The Disciplinary Board shall have the authority to review the subject physician's record of treatment and counseling regarding the impairment, to the extent permitted by applicable federal statutes and regulations safeguarding the confidentiality of medical records.

An individual licensed under this Act, affected under this Section, shall be afforded an opportunity to demonstrate to the Disciplinary Board that they can resume practice in compliance with acceptable and prevailing standards under the provisions of their license.

The Department may promulgate rules for the imposition of fines in disciplinary cases, not to exceed $5,000 for each violation of this Act. Fines may be imposed in conjunction with other forms of disciplinary action, but shall not be the exclusive disposition of any disciplinary action arising out of conduct resulting in death or injury to a patient. Any funds collected from such fines shall be deposited in the Medical Disciplinary Fund.

(B) The Department shall revoke the license or visiting permit of any person issued under this Act to practice medicine or to treat human ailments without the use of drugs and without operative surgery, who has been convicted a second time of committing any felony under the Illinois Controlled Substances Act, or who has been convicted a second time of committing a Class 1 felony under Sections 8A–3 and 8A–6 of the Illinois Public Aid Code. A person whose license or visiting permit is revoked under this subsection B of Section 22 of this Act shall be prohibited from practicing medicine or treating human ailments without the use of drugs and without operative surgery.

(C) The Medical Disciplinary Board shall recommend to the Department civil penalties and any other appropriate discipline in disciplinary cases when the Board finds that a physician willfully performed an abortion with actual knowledge that the person upon whom the abortion has been performed is a minor or an incompetent person without notice as required under the Parental Notice of Abortion Act of 1995. Upon the Board's recommendation, the Department shall impose, for the first violation, a civil penalty of $1,000 and for a second or subsequent violation, a civil penalty of $5,000.

§ 23. Reports relating to professional conduct and capacity

(A) Entities required to report.

(1) Health care institutions.

The chief administrator or executive officer of any health care institution licensed by the Illinois Department of Public Health shall report to the Disciplinary Board when any person's clinical privileges are terminated or are restricted based on a final determination, in accordance with that institution's by-laws or rules and regulations, that a person has either committed an act or acts which may directly threaten patient care, and not of an administrative nature, or that a person may be mentally or physically disabled in such a manner as to endanger patients under that person's care. Such officer also shall report if a person accepts voluntary termination or restriction of clinical privileges in lieu of formal action based upon conduct related directly to patient care and not of an administrative nature, or in lieu of formal action seeking to determine whether a person may be mentally or physically disabled in such a manner as to endanger patients under that person's care. The Medical Disciplinary Board shall, by rule, provide for the reporting to it of all instances in which a person, licensed under this Act, who is impaired by reason of age, drug or alcohol abuse or physical or mental impairment, is under supervision and, where appropriate, is in a program of rehabilitation. Such reports shall be strictly confidential and may be reviewed and considered only by the members of the Disciplinary Board, or by authorized staff as provided by rules of the Disciplinary Board. Provisions shall be made for the periodic report of the status of any such person not less than twice annually in order that the Disciplinary Board shall have current information upon which to determine the status of any such person. Such initial and periodic reports of impaired physicians shall not be considered records within the meaning of The State Records Act and shall be disposed of, following a determination by the Disciplinary Board that such reports are no longer required, in a manner and at such time as the Disciplinary Board shall determine by rule. The filing of such reports shall be construed as the filing of a report for purposes of subsection (C) of this Section.

(2) Professional associations.

The President or chief executive officer of any association or society, of persons licensed under this Act, operating within this State shall report to the Disciplinary Board when the association or society renders a final determination that a person has committed unprofessional conduct related directly to patient care or that a person may be mentally or physically disabled in such a manner as to endanger patients under that person's care.

(3) Professional liability insurers.

Every insurance company which offers policies of professional liability insurance to persons licensed under this Act, or any other entity which seeks to indemnify the professional liability of a person licensed under this Act, shall report to the Disciplinary Board the settlement of any claim or cause of action, or final judgment rendered in any cause of action, which alleged negligence in the furnishing of medical care by such licensed person when such settlement or final judgment is in favor of the plaintiff.

(4) State's Attorneys.

The State's Attorney of each county shall report to the Disciplinary Board all instances in which a person licensed under this Act is convicted or otherwise found guilty of the commission of any felony. The State's Attorney of each county may report to the Disciplinary Board through a verified complaint any instance in which the State's Attorney believes that a physician has willfully violated the notice requirements of the Parental Notice of Abortion Act of 1995.

(5) State agencies.

All agencies, boards, commissions, departments, or other instrumentalities of the government of the State of Illinois shall report to the Disciplinary Board any instance arising in connection with the operations of such agency, including the administration of any law by such agency, in which a person licensed under this Act has either committed an act or acts which may be a violation of this Act or which may constitute unprofessional conduct related directly to patient care or which indicates that a person licensed under this Act may be mentally or physically disabled in such a manner as to endanger patients under that person's care.

(B) Mandatory reporting.

All reports required by items (34), (35), and (36) of subsection (A) of Section 22 and by Section 23 shall be submitted to the Disciplinary Board in a timely fashion. The reports shall be filed in writing within 60 days after a determination that a report is required under this Act. All reports shall contain the following information:

(1) The name, address and telephone number of the person making the report.

(2) The name, address and telephone number of the person who is the subject of the report.

(3) The name or other means of identification of any patient or patients whose treatment is a subject of the report, provided, however, no medical records may be revealed without the written consent of the patient or patients.

(4) A brief description of the facts which gave rise to the issuance of the report, including the dates of any occurrences deemed to necessitate the filing of the report.

(5) If court action is involved, the identity of the court in which the action is filed, along with the docket number and date of filing of the action.

(6) Any further pertinent information which the reporting party deems to be an aid in the evaluation of the report.

The Department shall have the right to inform patients of the right to provide written consent for the Department to obtain copies of hospital and medical records. The Disciplinary Board or Department may exercise the power under Section 38 of this Act to subpoena copies of hospital or medical records in mandatory report cases alleging death or permanent bodily injury when consent to obtain records is not provided by a patient or legal representative. Appropriate rules shall be adopted by the Department with the approval of the Disciplinary Board.

When the Department has received written reports concerning incidents required to be reported in items (34), (35), and (36) of subsection (A) of Section 22, the licensee's failure to report the incident to the Department under those items shall not be the sole grounds for disciplinary action.

Nothing contained in this Section shall act to in any way, waive or modify the confidentiality of medical reports and committee reports to the extent provided by law. Any information reported or disclosed shall be kept for the confidential use of the Disciplinary Board, the Medical Coordinators, the Disciplinary Board's attorneys, the medical investigative staff, and authorized clerical staff, as provided in this Act, and shall be afforded the same status as is provided information concerning medical studies in Part 21 of Article VIII of the Code of Civil Procedure.

(C) Immunity from prosecution.

Any individual or organization acting in good faith, and not in a wilful and wanton manner, in complying with this Act by providing any report or other information to the Disciplinary Board, or assisting in the investigation or preparation of such information, or by participating in proceedings of the Disciplinary Board, or by serving as a member of the Disciplinary Board, shall not, as a result of such actions, be subject to criminal prosecution or civil damages.

(D) Indemnification.

Members of the Disciplinary Board, the Medical Coordinators, the Disciplinary Board's attorneys, the medical investigative staff, physicians retained under contract to assist and advise the medical coordinators in the investigation, and authorized clerical staff shall be indemnified by the State for any actions occurring within the scope of services on the Disciplinary Board, done in good faith and not wilful and wanton in nature. The Attorney General shall defend all such actions unless he or she determines either that there would be a conflict of interest in such representation or that the actions complained of were not in good faith or were wilful and wanton.

Should the Attorney General decline representation, the member shall have the right to employ counsel of his or her choice, whose fees shall be provided by the State, after approval by the Attorney General, unless there is a determination by a court that the member's actions were not in good faith or were wilful and wanton.

The member must notify the Attorney General within 7 days of receipt of notice of the initiation of any action involving services of the Disciplinary Board. Failure to so notify the Attorney General shall constitute an absolute waiver of the right to a defense and indemnification.

The Attorney General shall determine within 7 days after receiving such notice, whether he or she will undertake to represent the member.

(E) Deliberations of Disciplinary Board

Upon the receipt of any report called for by this Act, other than those reports of impaired persons licensed under this Act required pursuant to the rules of the Disciplinary Board, the Disciplinary Board shall notify in writing, by certified mail, the person who is the subject of the report. Such notification shall be made within 30 days of receipt by the Disciplinary Board of the report.

The notification shall include a written notice setting forth the person's right to examine the report. Included in such notification shall be the address at which the file is maintained, the name of the custodian of the reports, and the telephone number at which the custodian may be reached. The person who is the subject of the report shall submit a written statement responding, clarifying, adding to, or proposing the amending of the report previously filed. The statement shall become a permanent part of the file and must be received by the Disciplinary Board no more than 60 days after the date on which the person was notified by the Disciplinary Board of the existence of the original report.

The Disciplinary Board shall review all reports received by it, together with any supporting information and responding statements submitted by persons who are the subject of reports. The review by the Disciplinary Board shall be in a timely manner but in no event, shall the Disciplinary Board's initial review of the material contained in each disciplinary file be less than 61 days nor more than 180 days after the receipt of the initial report by the Disciplinary Board.

When the Disciplinary Board makes its initial review of the materials contained within its disciplinary files, the Disciplinary Board shall, in writing, make a determination as to whether there are sufficient facts to warrant further investigation or action. Failure to make such determination within the time provided shall be deemed to be a determination that there are not sufficient facts to warrant further investigation or action.

Should the Disciplinary Board find that there are not sufficient facts to warrant further investigation, or action, the report shall be accepted for filing and the matter shall be deemed closed and so reported to the Director. The Director shall then have 30 days to accept the Medical

Disciplinary Board's decision or request further investigation. The Director shall inform the Board in writing of the decision to request further investigation, including the specific reasons for the decision. The individual or entity filing the original report or complaint and the person who is the subject of the report or complaint shall be notified in writing by the Director of any final action on their report or complaint.

(F) Summary reports.

The Disciplinary Board shall prepare, on a timely basis, but in no event less than one every other month, a summary report of final actions taken upon disciplinary files maintained by the Disciplinary Board. The summary reports shall be sent by the Disciplinary Board to every health care facility licensed by the Illinois Department of Public Health, every professional association and society of persons licensed under this Act functioning on a statewide basis in this State, the American Medical Association, the American Osteopathic Association, the American Chiropractic Association, all insurers providing professional liability insurance to persons licensed under this Act in the State of Illinois, the Federation of State Medical Licensing Boards, and the Illinois Pharmacists Association.

(G) Any violation of this Section shall be a Class A misdemeanor.

(H) If any such person violates the provisions of this Section an action may be brought in the name of the People of the State of Illinois, through the Attorney General of the State of Illinois, for an order enjoining such violation or for an order enforcing compliance with this Section. Upon filing of a verified petition in such court, the court may issue a temporary restraining order without notice or bond and may preliminarily or permanently enjoin such violation, and if it is established that such person has violated or is violating the injunction, the court may punish the offender for contempt of court. Proceedings under this paragraph shall be in addition to, and not in lieu of, all other remedies and penalties provided for by this Section.

§ 24. Report of violations; medical associations

Any physician licensed under this Act, the Illinois State Medical Society, the Illinois Association of Osteopathic Physicians and Surgeons, the Illinois Chiropractic Society, the Illinois Prairie State Chiropractic Association, or any component societies of any of these 4 groups, and any other person, may report to the Disciplinary Board any information the physician, association, society, or person may have that appears to show that a physician is or may be in violation of any of the provisions of Section 22 of this Act.

The Department may enter into agreements with the Illinois State Medical Society, the Illinois Association of Osteopathic Physicians and Surgeons, the Illinois Prairie State Chiropractic Association, or the Illinois Chiropractic Society to allow these organizations to assist the Disciplinary Board in the review of alleged violations of this Act. Subject to the approval of the Department, any organization party to such an agreement may subcontract with other individuals or organizations to assist in review.

Any physician, association, society, or person participating in good faith in the making of a report, under this Act or participating in or assisting with an investigation or review under this Section shall have immunity from any civil, criminal, or other liability that might result by reason of those actions.

The medical information in the custody of an entity under contract with the Department participating in an investigation or review shall be privileged and confidential to the same extent as are information and reports under the provisions of Part 21 of Article VIII of the Code of Civil Procedure.

For the purpose of any civil or criminal proceedings, the good faith of any physician, association, society or person shall be presumed. The Disciplinary Board may request the Illinois State Medical Society, the Illinois Association of Osteopathic Physicians and Surgeons, the Illinois Prairie State Chiropractic Association, or the Illinois Chiropractic Society to assist the Disciplinary Board in preparing for or conducting any medical competency examination as the Board may deem appropriate.

§ 25. Summary suspension

The Director of the Department may, upon receipt of a written communication from the Secretary of Human Services, the Director of Public Aid, or the Director of Public Health that continuation of practice of a person licensed under this Act constitutes an immediate danger to the public, and after consultation with the Chief Medical Coordinator or Deputy Medical Coordinator, immediately suspend the license of such person without a hearing. In instances in which the Director immediately suspends a license under this Section, a hearing upon such person's license must be convened by the Disciplinary Board within 15 days after such suspension and completed without appreciable delay. Such hearing is to be held to determine whether to recommend to the Director that the person's license be revoked, suspended, placed on probationary status or reinstated, or whether such person should be subject to other disciplinary action. In the hearing, the written communication and any other evidence submitted therewith may be introduced as evidence against such person; provided however, the person, or their counsel, shall have the opportunity to discredit, impeach and submit evidence rebutting such evidence.

§ 26. Advertising

(1) Any person licensed under this Act may advertise the availability of professional services in the public media or on the premises where such professional services are rendered. Such advertising shall be limited to the following information:

> (a) Publication of the person's name, title, office hours, address and telephone number;

    (b) Information pertaining to the person's areas of specialization, including appropriate board certification or limitation of professional practice;

    (c) Information on usual and customary fees for routine professional services offered, which information shall include, notification that fees may be adjusted due to complications or unforeseen circumstances;

    (d) Announcement of the opening of, change of, absence from, or return to business;

    (e) Announcement of additions to or deletions from professional licensed staff;

    (f) The issuance of business or appointment cards.

    (2) It is unlawful for any person licensed under this Act to use testimonials or claims of superior quality of care to entice the public. It shall be unlawful to advertise fee comparisons of available services with those of other persons licensed under this Act.

    (3) This Act does not authorize the advertising of professional services which the offeror of such services is not licensed to render. Nor shall the advertiser use statements which contain false, fraudulent, deceptive or misleading material or guarantees of success, statements which play upon the vanity or fears of the public, or statements which promote or produce unfair competition.

    (4) A licensee shall include in every advertisement for services regulated under this Act his or her title as it appears on the license or the initials authorized under this Act.

§ 27. Advertising violations; third party payments

    It is unlawful and punishable under Section 59 for any person licensed under this Act to knowingly advertise that the licensee will accept as payment for services rendered by assignment from any third party payor the amount the third party payor covers as payment in full, if the effect is to give the impression of eliminating the need of payment by the patient of any required deductible or copayment applicable in the patient's health benefit plan.

As used in this Section, "advertise" means solicitation by the licensee or through another by means of handbills, posters, circulars, motion pictures, radio, newspapers, television or in any other manner.

§ 28. Use of titles

    Nothing in this Act shall prohibit the use of the titles "Doctor of Medicine" or "M.D." by a person licensed in this State to practice medicine in all of its branches who has received a degree in medicine from a medical school or college, other than an osteopathic medical college, which satisfies the requirements of paragraph (a) of Section 11 of this Act, notwithstanding that such degree in medicine does not translate literally into "Doctor of Medicine" or "M.D.".

§ 29. Releases from liability prior to, or as a condition of treatment

Any contract or agreement signed by any person prior to, or as a condition of, such person receiving medical treatment in any form, which releases from liability any physician, hospital or other health care provider for any malfeasance, misfeasance or nonfeasance in the course of administering any medical treatment or service is void and against the public policy of the State of Illinois.

§ 30. Emergency care; civil liability

Exemption from civil liability for emergency care is as provided in the Good Samaritan Act.

§ 31. Liability exclusion; free medical clinic

Exemption from civil liability for medical services in a free clinic is as provided in the Good Samaritan Act.

§ 32. Practice by person licensed in another state pending examination

This Act does not prohibit the practice of medicine by a person who is licensed to practice medicine in all of its branches in any other state of the United States or the District of Columbia who has applied in writing to the Department, in form and substance satisfactory to the Department, for a license to practice medicine in all of its branches and has complied with all of the provisions of Section 19 except the passing of an examination which may be given under Section 19, until:

(a) the expiration of 9 months after the filing of such written application, or

(b) the decision of the Department that the applicant has failed to pass an examination within 9 months or failed without an approved excuse to take an examination conducted within 9 months by the Department, or

(c) the withdrawal of the application.

§ 33. Legend drugs; dispensing drugs or medications

Any person licensed under this Act to practice medicine in all of its branches shall be authorized to purchase legend drugs requiring an order of a person authorized to prescribe drugs, and to dispense such legend drugs in the regular course of practicing medicine. The dispensing of such legend drugs shall be the personal act of the person licensed under this Act and may not be delegated to any other person not licensed under this Act or the Pharmacy Practice Act of 1987 unless such delegated dispensing functions are under the direct supervision of the physician authorized to dispense legend drugs. Except when dispensing manufacturers' samples or other legend drugs in a maximum 72 hour supply, persons licensed under this Act shall maintain a book or file of prescriptions as required in the Pharmacy Practice Act of 1987. Any person licensed under this Act who dispenses any drug or medicine shall dispense such drug or medicine in good faith and shall affix to the box, bottle, vessel or package containing the same a label indicating

(a) the date on which such drug or medicine is dispensed;

(b) the name of the patient;

(c) the last name of the person dispensing such drug or medicine;

(d) the directions for use thereof; and

(e) the proprietary name or names or, if there are none, the established name or names of the drug or medicine, the dosage and quantity, except as otherwise authorized by regulation of the Department of Professional Regulation. The foregoing labeling requirements shall not apply to drugs or medicines in a package which bears a label of the manufacturer containing information describing its contents which is in compliance with requirements of the Federal Food, Drug, and Cosmetic Act and the Illinois Food, Drug, and Cosmetic Act. "Drug" and "medicine" have the meaning ascribed to them in the Pharmacy Practice Act of 1987, as now or hereafter amended; "good faith" has the meaning ascribed to it in subsection (v) of Section 102 of the "Illinois Controlled Substances Act", approved August 16, 1971, as amended.

Prior to dispensing a prescription to a patient, the physician shall offer a written prescription to the patient which the patient may elect to have filled by the physician or any licensed pharmacy.

A violation of any provision of this Section shall constitute a violation of this Act and shall be grounds for disciplinary action provided for in this Act.

§ 34.   Construction and administration of Act

The provisions of this Act shall not be so construed nor shall they be so administered as to discriminate against any type or category of physician or against any medical, osteopathic or chiropractic college.

§ 35.   Hearing officers

The Director shall have the authority to appoint an attorney duly licensed to practice law in the State of Illinois to serve as the hearing officer in any action to suspend, revoke, place on probationary status, or take any other disciplinary action with regard to a license. The hearing officer shall have full authority to conduct the hearing. The hearing officer shall report his findings and recommendations to the Disciplinary Board within 30 days of the receipt of the record. The Disciplinary Board shall have 60 days from receipt of the report to review the report of the hearing officer and present their findings of fact, conclusions of law and recommendations to the Director.

§ 36. Violations investigations

Upon the motion of either the Department or the Disciplinary Board or upon the verified complaint in writing of any person setting forth facts which, if proven, would constitute grounds for suspension or revocation under Section 22 of this Act, the Department shall investigate the actions of any person, so accused, who holds or represents that they hold a license. Such person is hereinafter called the accused.

The Department shall, before suspending, revoking, placing on probationary status, or taking any other disciplinary action as the Department may deem proper with regard to any license at least 30 days prior to the date set for the hearing, notify the accused in writing of any charges made and the time and place for a hearing of the charges before the Disciplinary Board, direct them to file their written answer thereto to the Disciplinary Board under oath within 20 days after the service on them of such notice and inform them that if they fail to file such answer default will be taken against them and their license may be suspended, revoked, placed on probationary status, or have other disciplinary action, including limiting the scope, nature or extent of their practice, as the Department may deem proper taken with regard thereto.

Where a physician has been found, upon complaint and investigation of the Department, and after hearing, to have performed an abortion procedure in a wilful and wanton manner upon a woman who was not pregnant at the time such abortion procedure was performed, the Department shall automatically revoke the license of such physician to practice medicine in Illinois.

Such written notice and any notice in such proceedings thereafter may be served by delivery of the same, personally, to the accused person, or by mailing the same by registered or certified mail to the address last theretofore specified by the accused in their last notification to the Department.

All information gathered by the Department during its investigation including information subpoenaed under Section 23 or 38 of this Act and the investigative file shall be kept for the confidential use of the Director, Disciplinary Board, the Medical Coordinators, persons employed by contract to advise the Medical Coordinator or the Department, the Disciplinary Board's attorneys, the medical investigative staff, and authorized clerical staff, as provided in this Act and shall be afforded the same status as is provided information concerning medical studies in Part 21 of Article VIII of the Code of Civil Procedure.

§ 37. Disciplinary actions

At the time and place fixed in the notice, the Disciplinary Board provided for in this Act shall proceed to hear the charges and both the accused person and the complainant shall be accorded ample opportunity to present in person, or by counsel, such statements, testimony, evidence and argument as may be pertinent to the charges or to any defense thereto. The Disciplinary Board may continue such hearing from time to time. If the Disciplinary Board is not sitting at the time and place fixed in the notice or at the time and place to which the hearing has been continued, the Department shall continue such hearing for a period not to exceed 30 days.

In case the accused person, after receiving notice, fails to file an answer, their license may, in the discretion of the Director, having received first the recommendation of the Disciplinary Board, be suspended, revoked or placed on probationary status, or the Director may take whatever disciplinary action as he or she may deem proper, including limiting the scope, nature, or extent of said person's practice, without a hearing, if the act or acts charged constitute sufficient grounds for such action under this Act.

The Disciplinary Board has the authority to recommend to the Director that probation be granted or that other disciplinary action, including the limitation of the scope, nature or extent of a person's practice, be taken as it deems proper. If disciplinary action, other than suspension or revocation, is taken the Disciplinary Board may recommend that the Director impose reasonable limitations and requirements upon the accused registrant to insure compliance with the terms of the probation or other disciplinary action including, but not limited to, regular reporting by the accused to the Department of their actions, placing themselves under the care of a qualified physician for treatment, or limiting their practice in such manner as the Director may require.

The Director, after consultation with the Chief Medical Coordinator or Deputy Medical Coordinator, may temporarily suspend the license of a physician without a hearing, simultaneously with the institution of proceedings for a hearing provided under this Section if the Director finds that evidence in his or her possession indicates that a physician's continuation in practice would constitute an immediate danger to the public. In the event that the Director suspends, temporarily, the license of a physician without a hearing, a hearing by the Disciplinary Board shall be held within 15 days after such suspension has occurred and shall be concluded without appreciable delay.

§ 38. Subpoenas; oaths; right of inspection

The Disciplinary Board or Department has power to subpoena and bring before it any person in this State and to take testimony either orally or by deposition, or both, with the same fees and mileage and in the same manner as is prescribed by law for judicial procedure in civil cases.

The Disciplinary Board, upon a determination that probable cause exists that a violation of one or more of the grounds for discipline listed in Section 22 has occurred or is occurring, may subpoena the medical and hospital records of individual patients of physicians licensed under this Act, provided, that prior to the submission of such records to the Disciplinary Board, all information indicating the identity of the patient shall be removed and deleted. Notwithstanding the foregoing, the Disciplinary Board and Department shall possess the power to subpoena copies of hospital or medical records in mandatory report cases under Section 23 alleging death or permanent bodily injury when consent to obtain records is not provided by a patient or legal representative. Prior to submission of the records to the Disciplinary Board, all information indicating the identity of the patient shall be removed and deleted. All medical records and other information received pursuant to subpoena shall be confidential and shall be afforded the same status as is proved information concerning medical studies in Part 21 of Article VIII of the Code of Civil Procedure. The use of such records shall be restricted to members of the Disciplinary Board, the medical coordinators, and appropriate staff of the Department of Professional Regulation designated by the Disciplinary Board for the purpose of determining the existence of one or more grounds for discipline of the physician as provided for by Section 22 of this Act. Any such review of individual patients' records shall be conducted by the Disciplinary Board in strict confidentiality, provided that such patient records shall be admissible in a disciplinary hearing, before the Disciplinary Board, when necessary to substantiate the grounds for discipline alleged against the physician licensed under this Act, and provided further, that nothing herein shall be deemed to supersede the provisions of Part 21 of Article VIII of the "Code of Civil Procedure", as now or hereafter amended, to the extent applicable.

The Director, and any member of the Disciplinary Board each have power to administer oaths at any hearing which the Disciplinary Board or Department is authorized by law to conduct.

The Disciplinary Board, upon a determination that probable cause exists that a violation of one or more of the grounds for discipline listed in Section 22 has occurred or is occurring on the business premises of a physician licensed under this Act, may issue an order authorizing an appropriately qualified investigator employed by the Department to enter upon the business premises with due consideration for patient care of the subject of the investigation so as to inspect the physical premises and equipment and furnishings therein. No such order shall include the right of inspection of business, medical, or personnel records located on the premises. For purposes of this Section, "business premises" is defined as the office or offices where the physician conducts the practice of medicine. Any such order shall expire and become void five business days after its issuance by the Disciplinary Board. The execution of any such order shall be valid only during the normal business hours of the facility or office to be inspected.

§ 39. Stenographer; transcript

The Department, at its expense, shall provide a stenographer to take down the testimony and preserve a record of all proceedings at the hearing of any case wherein a license may be revoked, suspended, placed on probationary status, or other disciplinary action taken with regard thereto. The notice of hearing, complaint and all other documents in the nature of pleadings and written motions filed in the proceedings, the transcript of testimony, the report of the Licensing Board and the orders of the Department constitute the record of the proceedings. The Department shall furnish a transcript of the record to any person interested in such hearing upon payment of the fee required under Section 2105–115 of the Department of Professional Regulation Law (*20 ILCS 2105/2105–115*).

§ 40.   Report of Disciplinary Board; orders; surrender of license; list of persons disciplined; protected files

The Disciplinary Board shall present to the Director a written report of its findings and recommendations. A copy of such report shall be served upon the accused person, either personally or by registered or certified mail. Within 20 days after such service, the accused person may present to the Department their motion, in writing, for a rehearing, which written motion shall specify the particular ground therefor. If the accused person orders and pays for a transcript of the record as provided in Section 39, the time elapsing thereafter and before such transcript is ready for delivery to them shall not be counted as part of such 20 days.

At the expiration of the time allowed for filing a motion for rehearing, the Director may take the action recommended by the Disciplinary Board. Upon the suspension, revocation, placement on probationary status, or the taking of any other disciplinary action, including the limiting of the scope, nature, or extent of one's practice, deemed proper by the Department, with regard to the license, certificate or visiting professor permit, the accused shall surrender their license to the Department, if ordered to do so by the Department, and upon their failure or refusal so to do, the Department may seize the same.

Each certificate of order of revocation, suspension, or other disciplinary action shall contain a brief, concise statement of the ground or grounds upon which the Department's action is based, as well as the specific terms and conditions of such action. This document shall be retained as a permanent record by the Disciplinary Board and the Director.

The Department shall at least annually publish a list of the names of all persons disciplined under this Act in the preceding 12 months. Such lists shall be mailed by the Department to any person in the State upon request.

In those instances where an order of revocation, suspension, or other disciplinary action has been rendered by virtue of a physician's physical illness, including, but not limited to, deterioration through the aging process, or loss of motor skill which results in a physician's inability to practice medicine with reasonable judgment, skill, or safety, the Department shall only permit this document, and the record of the hearing incident thereto, to be observed, inspected, viewed, or copied pursuant to court order.

§ 41.   Administrative review; certification of record

All final administrative decisions of the Department are subject to judicial review pursuant to the Administrative Review Law and its rules. The term "administrative decision" is defined as in Section 3–101 of the Code of Civil Procedure.

Proceedings for judicial review shall be commenced in the circuit court of the county in which the party applying for review resides; but if the party is not a resident of this State, the venue shall be in Sangamon County.

The Department shall not be required to certify any record to the court or file any answer in court or otherwise appear in any court in a judicial review proceeding, unless there is filed in the court, with the complaint, a receipt from the Department acknowledging payment of the costs of furnishing and certifying the record, which costs shall be computed at the rate of 20 cents per page of the record. Exhibits shall be certified without cost. Failure on the part of the plaintiff to file a receipt in court shall be grounds for dismissal of the action. During the pendency and hearing of any and all judicial proceedings incident to the disciplinary action the sanctions imposed upon the accused by the Department because of acts or omissions related to the delivery of direct patient care as specified in the Department's final administrative decision, shall as a matter of public policy remain in full force and effect in order to protect the public pending final resolution of any of the proceedings.

§ 42.   Order or certified copy; prima facie proof

An order of revocation, suspension, placing the license on probationary status, or other formal disciplinary action as the Department may deem proper, or a certified copy thereof, over the seal of the Department and purporting to be signed by the Director, is prima facie proof that:

(a) Such signature is the genuine signature of the Director;

(b) The Director is duly appointed and qualified; and

(c) The Disciplinary Board and the members thereof are qualified.

Such proof may be rebutted.

§ 43.   Restoration of license

At any time after the suspension, revocation, placing on probationary status, or taking disciplinary action with regard to any license, the Department may restore it to the accused person, or take any other action to reinstate the license to good standing, without examination, upon the written recommendation of the Disciplinary Board.

§ 44.   Departmental exercise of disciplinary functions, powers and duties; director's authority

None of the disciplinary functions, powers and duties enumerated in this Act shall be exercised by the Department except upon the action and report in writing of the Disciplinary Board.

In all instances, under this Act, in which the Disciplinary Board has rendered a recommendation to the Director with respect to a particular physician, the Director shall, in the event that he or she disagrees with or takes action contrary to the recommendation of the Disciplinary Board, file with the Disciplinary Board and the Secretary of State his or her specific written reasons of disagreement with the Disciplinary Board. Such reasons shall be filed within 30 days of the occurrence of the Director's contrary position having been taken.

The action and report in writing of a majority of the Disciplinary Board designated is sufficient authority upon which the Director may act.

Whenever the Director is satisfied that substantial justice has not been done either in an examination, or in a formal disciplinary action, or refusal to restore a license, he or she may order a reexamination or rehearing by the same or other examiners

§ 45. Confidential information

In all hearings conducted under this Act, information received, pursuant to law, relating to any information acquired by a physician in attending any patient in a professional character, necessary to enable them professionally to serve such patient, shall be deemed strictly confidential and shall only be made available either as part of the record of such hearing or otherwise:

(a) when such record is required, in its entirety, for purposes of judicial review pursuant to this Act; or

(b) upon the express, written consent of the patient, or in the case of their death or disability, of their personal representative.

§ 46. Orders of formal disciplinary action without reasonable basis in fact; liability of state

In the event that the Department's order of revocation, suspension, placing the licensee on probationary status, or other order of formal disciplinary action is without any reasonable basis in fact of any kind, then the State of Illinois shall be liable to the injured physician for those special damages they have suffered as a direct result of such order.

§ 47. Administrative Procedure Act

The Illinois Administrative Procedure Act is hereby expressly adopted and incorporated herein as if all of the provisions of that Act were included in this Act, except that the provision of subsection (d) of Section 10–65 of the Illinois Administrative Procedure Act that provides that at hearings the licensee has the right to show compliance with all lawful requirements for retention, continuation or renewal of the license is specifically excluded. For the purposes of this Act the notice required under Section 10–25 of the Illinois Administrative Procedure Act is deemed sufficient when mailed to the last known address of a party.

§ 48.   Existing licenses and certificates

All licenses and certificates heretofore legally issued by authority of law in this State permitting the holder thereof to practice medicine in all of its branches, or to treat human ailments without the use of drugs and operative surgery, and which are valid and in full force and effect on the taking effect of this Act, shall have the same force and effect, and be subject to the same authority of the Department to revoke or suspend them as licenses issued under this Act.

§ 49.   Persons without license holding themselves out to public as being engaged in diagnosis or treatment of ailments of human beings; penalty

If any person does any of the following and does not possess a valid license issued under this Act, that person shall be sentenced as provided in Section 59:

(i) holds himself or herself out to the public as being engaged in the diagnosis or treatment of physical or mental ailments or conditions including, but not limited to, deformities, diseases, disorders, or injuries of human beings;

(ii) suggests, recommends or prescribes any form of treatment for the palliation, relief or cure of any physical or mental ailment or condition of any person with the intention of receiving, either directly or indirectly, any fee, gift, or compensation whatever;

(iii) diagnoses or attempts to diagnose, operates upon, professes to heal, prescribes for, or otherwise treats any ailment or condition, or supposed ailment or condition, of another;

(iv) maintains an office for examination or treatment of persons afflicted, or alleged or supposed to be afflicted, by any ailment or condition;

(v) manipulates or adjusts osseous or articular structures; or

(vi) attaches the title Doctor, Physician, Surgeon, M.D., D.O. or D.C. or any other word or abbreviation to his or her name indicating that he or she is engaged in the treatment of human ailments or conditions as a business.

Whenever the Department has reason to believe that any person has violated this Section the Department may issue a rule to show cause why an order to cease and desist should not be entered against that person. The rule shall clearly set forth the grounds relied upon by the Department and shall provide a period of 7 days from the date of the rule to file an answer to the satisfaction of the Department. Failure to answer to the satisfaction of the Department shall cause an order to cease and desist to be issued immediately.

§ 49.5. Telemedicine

(a) The General Assembly finds and declares that because of technological advances and changing practice patterns the practice of medicine is occurring with increasing frequency across state lines and that certain technological advances in the practice of medicine are in the public interest. The General Assembly further finds and declares that the practice of medicine is a privilege and that the licensure by this State of practitioners outside this State engaging in medical practice within this State and the ability to discipline those practitioners is necessary for the protection of the public health, welfare, and safety.

(b) A person who engages in the practice of telemedicine without a license issued under this Act shall be subject to penalties provided in Section 59.

(c) For purposes of this Act, "telemedicine" means the performance of any of the activities listed in Section 49, including but not limited to rendering written or oral opinions concerning diagnosis or treatment of a patient in Illinois by a person located outside the State of Illinois as a result of transmission of individual patient data by telephonic, electronic, or other means of communication from within this State. "Telemedicine" does not include the following:

(1) periodic consultations between a person licensed under this Act and a person outside the State of Illinois;

(2) a second opinion provided to a person licensed under this Act; and

(3) diagnosis or treatment services provided to a patient in Illinois following care or treatment originally provided to the patient in the state in which the provider is licensed to practice medicine.

(d) Whenever the Department has reason to believe that a person has violated this Section, the Department may issue a rule to show cause why an order to cease and desist should not be entered against that person. The rule shall clearly set forth the grounds relied upon by the Department and shall provide a period of 7 days from the date of the rule to file an answer to the satisfaction of the Department. Failure to answer to the satisfaction of the Department shall cause an order to cease and desist to be issued immediately.

(e) An out-of-state person providing a service listed in Section 49 to a patient residing in Illinois through the practice of telemedicine submits himself or herself to the jurisdiction of the courts of this State.

§ 50. Practice of medicine without license; penalty

Any person who practices medicine in all of its branches or treats human ailments without the use of drugs or operative surgery including, but not limited to, treatment or diagnosis of any physical or mental ailments or conditions including, but not limited to, deformities, diseases, disorders, or injuries without a valid license under the laws of this State shall be sentenced as provided in Section 59.

§ 51. Treatment by use of drugs or surgery when only licensed to treat ailments without use of drugs or surgery; penalty

Any person who treats human ailments by the use of drugs or operative surgery and has only a license to treat human ailments without the use of drugs and without operative surgery, shall be sentenced as provided in Section 59.

§ 52. Unlicensed persons holding themselves out by signs, advertisements or writings, to treat human ailments without indicating system, method or kind of practice in which they are licensed; penalty

Any person, not licensed in this State to practice medicine in all of its branches, who holds themselves out by any sign or advertisement, or by a writing of any kind, to treat human ailments without therein attaching to their name a word or words indicating the system, method or kind of practice which they are licensed to pursue in this State, shall be sentenced as provided in Section 59.

§ 53. Receiving fees on representation of ability to permanently cure a manifestly incurable condition of sickness, disease or injury; penalty

Any person who obtains a fee, either directly or indirectly, either in money or in value, or in the form of a financial profit either as personal compensation or as compensation, charge, profit or gain for an employer, or any other person or persons, on the representation that they can permanently cure a manifestly incurable condition of sickness, disease or injury of any person, shall be sentenced as provided in Section 59.

§ 54. Practice under assumed name; impersonation; penalty

A person who holds himself or herself out to treat human ailments under a name other than his or her own, or by personation of any physician, shall be punished as provided in Section 59.

However, nothing in this Act shall be construed as prohibiting partnerships, limited liability companies, associations, or corporations in accordance with item (14) of subsection (A) of Section 22 of this Act.

§ 54.5.   Physician delegation of authority

(a) Physicians licensed to practice medicine in all its branches may delegate care and treatment responsibilities to a physician assistant under guidelines in accordance with the requirements of the Physician Assistant Practice Act of 1987. A physician licensed to practice medicine in all its branches may enter into supervising physician agreements with no more than 2 physician assistants.

(b) A physician licensed to practice medicine in all its branches in active clinical practice may collaborate with an advanced practice nurse in accordance with the requirements of Title 15 of the Nursing and Advanced Practice Nursing Act. Collaboration is for the purpose of providing medical direction, and no employment relationship is required. A written collaborative agreement shall conform to the requirements of Sections 15–15 and 15–20 of the Nursing and Advanced Practice Nursing Act. The written collaborative agreement shall be for services the collaborating physician generally provides to his or her patients in the normal course of clinical medical practice. Physician medical direction shall be adequate with respect to collaboration with certified nurse practitioners, certified nurse midwives, and clinical nurse specialists if a collaborating physician:

(1) participates in the joint formulation and joint approval of orders or guidelines with the advanced practice nurse and periodically reviews such orders and the services provided patients under such orders in accordance with accepted standards of medical practice and advanced practice nursing practice;

(2) is on site at least once a month to provide medical direction and consultation; and

(3) is available through telecommunications for consultation on medical problems, complications, or emergencies or patient referral.

(b–5) An anesthesiologist or physician licensed to practice medicine in all its branches may collaborate with a certified registered nurse anesthetist in accordance with Section 15–25 of the Nursing and Advanced Practice Nursing Act. Medical direction for a certified registered nurse anesthetist shall be adequate if:

(1) an anesthesiologist or a physician participates in the joint formulation and joint approval of orders or guidelines and periodically reviews such orders and the services provided patients under such orders; and

(2) for anesthesia services, the anesthesiologist or physician participates through discussion of and agreement with the anesthesia plan and is physically present and available on the premises during the delivery of anesthesia services for diagnosis, consultation, and treatment of emergency medical conditions. Anesthesia services in a hospital shall be conducted in accordance with Section 10.7 of the Hospital Licensing Act and in an ambulatory surgical treatment center in accordance with Section 6.5 of the Ambulatory Surgical Treatment Center Act.

(**b–10**) The anesthesiologist or operating physician must agree with the anesthesia plan prior to the delivery of services.

(**c**) The supervising physician shall have access to the medical records of all patients attended by a physician assistant. The collaborating physician shall have access to the medical records of all patients attended to by an advanced practice nurse.

(**d**) Nothing in this Act shall be construed to limit the delegation of tasks or duties by a physician licensed to practice medicine in all its branches to a licensed practical nurse, a registered professional nurse, or other personnel.

(**e**) A physician shall not be liable for the acts or omissions of a physician assistant or advanced practice nurse solely on the basis of having signed a supervision agreement or guidelines or a collaborative agreement, an order, a standing medical order, a standing delegation order, or other order or guideline authorizing a physician assistant or advanced practice nurse to perform acts, unless the physician has reason to believe the physician assistant or advanced practice nurse lacked the competency to perform the act or acts or commits willful and wanton misconduct.

§ 55. Treatment by system or method other than that for which licensed; penalty

Any person who holds themselves out to treat human ailments by any system or method of treatment other than that for which they hold a valid license shall be sentenced as provided in Section 59.

§ 56. Fraud in procurement or renewal of license; penalty

Any person who employs fraud or deception in applying for or securing a license under this Act, or in passing any examination therefor, shall be sentenced as provided by Section 59. Any person who employs fraud or misrepresentation in applying for, or procuring, a license under this Act or in connection with applying for renewal of a license under this Act, or cheating on or attempting to subvert the licensing examinations administered under this Act, shall be sentenced as provided by Section 59.

§ 57. Filing diploma or license of another; forgery

Any person who shall in connection with any application or examination before the Department file, or attempt to file, with the Department as their own, the diploma or license of another, shall be sentenced therefor as the law shall prescribe at the time for forgery.

§ 58. Perjury

Any person who shall wilfully swear or affirm falsely, or make or file any affidavit wilfully and corruptly, in filing or prosecuting their application for a license before the Department, or in submitting any complaint, evidence or testimony to the Department under the provisions of this Act, or under any rule or regulation of the Department, shall be sentenced therefor as the law shall prescribe at the time for perjury.

§ 59.   Violations; penalties

Any person who violates for the first time Section 49, 50, 51, 52, 53, 54, 55, or 56 of this Act is guilty of a Class 4 felony. Any person who violates for the first time Section 27 of this Act is guilty of a Class A misdemeanor.

Any person who has been previously convicted under Section 49, 50, 51, 52, 53, 54, 55, or 56 of this Act and who subsequently violates any of the Sections is guilty of a Class 3 felony. Any person who has been previously convicted under Section 27 of this Act and who subsequently violates Section 27 is guilty of a Class 4 felony. In addition, whenever any person is punished as a repeat offender under this Section, the Director of the Department shall proceed to obtain a permanent injunction against such person under Section 61 of this Act.

§ 60.   Fines; Professional Regulation Evidence Fund

All such fines shall be deposited in the Professional Regulation Evidence Fund.

§ 61.   Public nuisances; injunctions

The practice of medicine in all of its branches or the treatment of human ailments without the use of drugs and without operative surgery by any person not at that time holding a valid and current license under this Act to do so is hereby declared to be inimical to the public welfare and to constitute a public nuisance. The Director of the Department, the Attorney General of the State of Illinois, the State's Attorney of any County in the State, or any resident citizen may maintain an action in the name of the people of the State of Illinois, may apply for an injunction in the circuit court to enjoin any such person from engaging in such practice; and, upon the filing of a verified petition in such court, the court or any judge thereof, if satisfied by affidavit, or otherwise, that such person has been engaged in such practice without a valid and current license to do so, may issue a temporary restraining order or preliminary injunction without notice or bond, enjoining the defendant from any such further practice. A copy of the verified complaint shall be served upon the defendant and the proceedings shall thereafter be conducted as in other civil cases. If it be established that the defendant has been, or is engaged in any such unlawful practice, the court, or any judge thereof, may enter an order or judgment perpetually enjoining the defendant from further engaging in such practice. In all proceedings hereunder the court, in its discretion, may apportion the costs among the parties interested in the suit, including cost of filing complaint, service of process, witness fees and expenses, court reporter charges and reasonable attorneys fees. In case of violation of any injunction entered under the provisions of this Section, the court, or any judge thereof, may summarily try and punish the offender for contempt of court. Such injunction proceedings shall be in addition to, and not in lieu of, all penalties and other remedies in this Act provided.

§ 62. Proceedings to revoke or suspend license; effect of passage of Act

No proceedings to revoke or suspend any license shall abate by reason of the passage of this Act. The Department may revoke or suspend a license on account of any act or circumstance occurring before this Act shall take effect, if such act or circumstance is a ground for such revocation or suspension under the provisions of the law in effect at the time of such act or circumstance.

§ 63. Reinstatement of existing licenses

All certificates, permits, and licenses in effect on the date this amendatory Act of 1996 becomes a law, and issued pursuant to the Medical Practice Act of 1987, as amended, are reinstated for the balance of the term for which last issued. All rules in effect on the date this Act becomes law and promulgated pursuant to the Medical Practice Act of 1987, as amended, shall remain in full force and effect on the effective date of this amendatory Act of 1996 without being promulgated again by the Department, except to the extent any such rule or regulation is inconsistent with any provision of this Act.

B. ILLINOIS NURSING AND ADVANCED PRACTICE NURSING ACT, 225 ILL.COMP.STAT. § 65/5–1

§ 5–1. Short title

This Article may be cited as the Nursing and Advanced Practice Nursing Act, and throughout this Article, references to this Act shall mean this Article.

§ 5–5. Legislative purpose

The practice of professional and practical nursing in the State of Illinois is hereby declared to affect the public health, safety, and welfare and to be subject to regulation and control in the public interest. It is further declared to be a matter of public interest and concern that the practice of nursing, as defined in this Act, merit and receive the confidence of the public and that only qualified persons be authorized to so practice in the State of Illinois. This Act shall be liberally construed to best carry out these subjects and purposes.

§ 5–10. Definitions

Each of the following terms, when used in this Act, shall have the meaning ascribed to it in this Section, except where the context clearly indicates otherwise:

(a) "Department" means the Department of Professional Regulation.

(b) "Director" means the Director of Professional Regulation.

(c) "Board" means the Board of Nursing appointed by the Director.

(d) "Academic year" means the customary annual schedule of courses at a college, university, or approved school, customarily regarded as the school year as distinguished from the calendar year.

(e) "Approved program of professional nursing education" and "approved program of practical nursing education" are programs of professional or practical nursing, respectively, approved by the Department under the provisions of this Act.

(f) "Nursing Act Coordinator" means a registered professional nurse appointed by the Director to carry out the administrative policies of the Department.

(g) "Assistant Nursing Act Coordinator" means a registered professional nurse appointed by the Director to assist in carrying out the administrative policies of the Department.

(h) "Registered" is the equivalent of "licensed".

(i) "Practical nurse" or "licensed practical nurse" means a person who is licensed as a practical nurse under this Act and practices practical nursing as defined in paragraph (j) of this Section. Only a practical nurse licensed under this Act is entitled to use the title "licensed practical nurse" and the abbreviation "L.P.N.".

(j) "Practical nursing" means the performance of nursing acts requiring the basic nursing knowledge, judgement, and skill acquired by means of completion of an approved practical nursing education program. Practical nursing includes assisting in the nursing process as delegated by and under the direction of a registered professional nurse. The practical nurse may work under the direction of a licensed physician, dentist, podiatrist, or other health care professional determined by the Department.

(k) "Registered Nurse" or "Registered Professional Nurse" means a person who is licensed as a professional nurse under this Act and practices nursing as defined in paragraph (*l*) of this Section. Only a registered nurse licensed under this Act is entitled to use the titles "registered nurse" and "registered professional nurse" and the abbreviation, "R.N.".

(l) "Registered professional nursing practice" includes all nursing specialities and means the performance of any nursing act based upon professional knowledge, judgment, and skills acquired by means of completion of an approved registered professional nursing education program. A registered professional nurse provides nursing care emphasizing the importance of the whole and the interdependence of its parts through the nursing process to individuals, groups, families, or communities, that includes but is not limited to:

(1) the assessment of healthcare needs, nursing diagnosis, planning, implementation, and nursing evaluation;

(2) the promotion, maintenance, and restoration of health;

(3) counseling, patient education, health education, and patient advocacy;

(4) the administration of medications and treatments as prescribed by a physician licensed to practice medicine in all of its branches, a licensed dentist, a licensed podiatrist, or a licensed optometrist or as prescribed by a physician assistant in accordance with written guidelines required under the Physician Assistant Practice Act of 1987 or by an advanced practice nurse in accordance with a written collaborative agreement required under the Nursing and Advanced Practice Nursing Act;

(5) the coordination and management of the nursing plan of care;

(6) the delegation to and supervision of individuals who assist the registered professional nurse implementing the plan of care; and

(7) teaching and supervision of nursing students. The foregoing shall not be deemed to include those acts of medical diagnosis or prescription of therapeutic or corrective measures that are properly performed only by physicians licensed in the State of Illinois.

(m) "Current nursing practice update course" means a planned nursing education curriculum approved by the Department consisting of activities that have educational objectives, instructional methods, content or subject matter, clinical practice, and evaluation methods, related to basic review and updating content and specifically planned for those nurses previously licensed in the United States or its territories and preparing for reentry into nursing practice.

(n) "Professional assistance program for nurses" means a professional assistance program that meets criteria established by the Board of Nursing and approved by the Director, which provides a non-disciplinary treatment approach for nurses licensed under this Act whose ability to practice is compromised by alcohol or chemical substance addiction.

§ 5–15. Policy; application of Act

For the protection of life and the promotion of health, and the prevention of illness and communicable diseases, any person practicing or offering to practice professional and practical nursing in Illinois shall submit evidence that he or she is qualified to practice, and shall be licensed as provided under this Act. No person shall practice or offer to practice professional or practical nursing in Illinois or use any title, sign, card or device to indicate that such a person is practicing professional or practical nursing unless such person has been licensed under the provisions of this Act.

This Act does not prohibit the following:

(a) The practice of nursing in Federal employment in the discharge of the employee's duties by a person who is employed by the United States government or any bureau, division or agency thereof and is a legally qualified and licensed nurse of another state or territory and not in conflict with Sections 10–5, 10–30, and 10–45 of this Act.

(b) Nursing that is included in their program of study by students enrolled in programs of nursing or in current nurse practice update courses approved by the Department.

(c) The furnishing of nursing assistance in an emergency.

(d) The practice of nursing by a nurse who holds an active license in another state when providing services to patients in Illinois during a bonafide emergency or in immediate preparation for or during interstate transit.

(e) The incidental care of the sick by members of the family, domestic servants or housekeepers, or care of the sick where treatment is by prayer or spiritual means.

(f) Persons from being employed as nursing aides, attendants, orderlies, and other auxiliary workers in private homes, long term care facilities, nurseries, hospitals or other institutions.

(g) The practice of practical nursing by one who has applied in writing to the Department in form and substance satisfactory to the Department, for a license as a licensed practical nurse and who has complied with all the provisions under Section 10–30, except the passing of an examination to be eligible to receive such license, until: the decision of the Department that the applicant has failed to pass the next available examination authorized by the Department or has failed, without an approved excuse, to take the next available examination authorized by the Department or until the withdrawal of the application, but not to exceed 3 months. No applicant for licensure practicing under the provisions of this paragraph shall practice practical nursing except under the direct supervision of a registered professional nurse licensed under this Act or a licensed physician, dentist or podiatrist. In no instance shall any such applicant practice or be employed in any supervisory capacity.

(h) The practice of practical nursing by one who is a licensed practical nurse under the laws of another U.S. jurisdiction and has applied in writing to the Department, in form and substance satisfactory to the Department, for a license as a licensed practical nurse and who is qualified to receive such license under Section 10–30, until

(1) the expiration of 6 months after the filing of such written application,

(2) the withdrawal of such application, or

(3) the denial of such application by the Department.

(i) The practice of professional nursing by one who has applied in writing to the Department in form and substance satisfactory to the Department for a license as a registered professional nurse and has complied with all the provisions under Section 10–30 except the passing of an examination to be eligible to receive such license, until the decision of the Department that the applicant has failed to pass the next available examination authorized by the Department or has failed, without an approved excuse, to take the next available examination authorized by the Department or until the withdrawal of the application, but not to exceed 3 months. No applicant for licensure practicing under the provisions of this paragraph shall practice professional nursing except under the direct supervision of a registered professional nurse licensed under this Act. In no instance shall any such applicant practice or be employed in any supervisory capacity.

(j) The practice of professional nursing by one who is a registered professional nurse under the laws of another state, territory of the United States or country and has applied in writing to the Department, in form and substance satisfactory to the Department, for a license as a registered professional nurse and who is qualified to receive such license under Section 10–30, until

    (1) the expiration of 6 months after the filing of such written application,

    (2) the withdrawal of such application, or

    (3) the denial of such application by the Department.

(k) The practice of professional nursing that is included in a program of study by one who is a registered professional nurse under the laws of another state or territory of the United States or foreign country, territory or province and who is enrolled in a graduate nursing education program or a program for the completion of a baccalaureate nursing degree in this State, which includes clinical supervision by faculty as determined by the educational institution offering the program and the health care organization where the practice of nursing occurs. The educational institution will file with the Department each academic term a list of the names and origin of license of all professional nurses practicing nursing as part of their programs under this provision.

(l) Any person licensed in this State under any other Act from engaging in the practice for which she or he is licensed.

(m) Delegation to authorized direct care staff trained under Section 15.4 of the Mental Health and Developmental Disabilities Administrative Act.

An applicant for license practicing under the exceptions set forth in subparagraphs (g), (h), (i), and (j) of this Section shall use the title R.N. Lic. Pend. or L.P.N. Lic. Pend. respectively and no other.

* * *

§ 5–20.   Unlicensed practice; violation; civil penalty

(a) Any person who practices, offers to practice, attempts to practice, or holds oneself out to practice nursing without being licensed under this Act shall, in addition to any other penalty provided by law, pay a civil penalty to the Department in an amount not to exceed $5,000 for each offense as determined by the Department. The civil penalty shall be assessed by the Department after a hearing is held in accordance with the provisions set forth in this Act regarding the provision of a hearing for the discipline of a licensee.

(b) The Department has the authority and power to investigate any and all unlicensed activity.

(c) The civil penalty shall be paid within 60 days after the effective date of the order imposing the civil penalty. The order shall constitute a judgment and may be filed and execution had thereon in the same manner as any judgment from any court of record.

* * *

§ 5–22.   Social Security Number on license application

In addition to any other information required to be contained in the application, every application for an original, renewal, or restored license under this Act shall include the applicant's Social Security Number.

§ 5–23.   Criminal background check

After the effective date of this amendatory Act of the 91st General Assembly, the Department shall require an applicant for initial licensure under this Act to submit to a criminal background check as part of the qualification for licensure. If an applicant's criminal background check indicates criminal conviction, the applicant must further submit to a fingerprint-based criminal background check. The Department shall adopt rules to implement this Section.

§ 5–25.   Emergency care; civil liability

Exemption from civil liability for emergency care is as provided in the Good Samaritan Act.

§ 5–30.   Services rendered without compensation; civil liability

Exemption from civil liability for services rendered without compensation is as provided in the Good Samaritan Act.

§ 10–5.   Prohibited acts

No person shall:

(a) Practice professional nursing without a valid license as a registered professional nurse except as provided in paragraphs (i) and (j) of Section 5–15 of this Act;

(b) Practice practical nursing without a valid license as a licensed practical nurse; or practice practical nursing other than under the direction of a licensed physician, licensed dentist, or registered professional nurse; except as provided in paragraphs (g), (h), and (j) of Section 5–15 of this Act;

(c) Practice nursing under cover of any diploma, license, or record illegally or fraudulently obtained or signed or issued unlawfully or under fraudulent representation;

(d) Practice nursing during the time her or his license is suspended, revoked, expired or on inactive status;

(e) Use any words, abbreviations, figures, letters, title, sign, card, or device tending to imply that she or he is a registered professional nurse, including the titles or initials, "Registered Nurse," "Professional Nurse," "Registered Professional Nurse," "Certified Nurse," "Trained Nurse," "Graduate Nurse," "P.N.," or "R.N.," or "R.P.N." or similar titles or initials with intention of indicating practice without a valid license as a registered professional nurse;

(f) Use any words, abbreviations figures, letters, title, sign, card, or device tending to imply that she or he is a licensed practical nurse including the titles or initials "Practical Nurse," "Licensed Practical Nurse," "P.N.," or "L.P.N.," or similar titles or initials with intention of indicated practice as a licensed practical nurse without a valid license as a licensed practical nurse under this Act;

(f–5) Advertise services regulated under this Act without including in every advertisement his or her title as it appears on the license or the initials authorized under this Act;

(g) Obtain or furnish a license by or for money or any other thing of value other than the fees required by Section 20–35, or by any fraudulent representation or act;

(h) Make any wilfully false oath or affirmation required by this Act;

(i) Conduct a nursing education program preparing persons for licensure that has not been approved by the Department;

(j) Represent that any school or course is approved or accredited as a school or course for the education of registered professional nurses or licensed practical nurses unless such school or course is approved by the Department under the provisions of this Act;

(k) Attempt or offer to do any of the acts enumerated in this Section, or knowingly aid, abet, assist in the doing of any such acts or in the attempt or offer to do any of such acts;

(l) Seek employment as a registered professional nurse under the terms of paragraphs (i) and (j) of Section 5–15 of this Act without possessing a written authorization which has been issued by the Department or designated testing service and which evidences the filing of the written application referred to in paragraphs (i) and (j) of Section 5–15 of this Act;

(m) Seek employment as a licensed practical nurse under the terms of paragraphs (g) and (h) of Section 5–15 of this Act without possessing a written authorization which has been issued by the Department or designated testing service and which evidences the filing of the written application referred to in paragraphs (g) and (h) of Section 5–15 of this Act;

(n) Employ or utilize persons not licensed under this Act to practice professional nursing or practical nursing; and

(o) Otherwise intentionally violate any provision of this Act.

Any person, including a firm, association or corporation who violates any provision of this Section shall be guilty of a Class A misdemeanor.

§ 10–10.   Department powers and duties.

(a) The Department shall exercise the powers and duties prescribed by the Civil Administrative Code of Illinois for administration of licensing acts and shall exercise other powers and duties necessary for effectuating the purpose of this Act. None of the functions, powers, or duties of the Department with respect to licensure and examination shall be exercised by the Department except upon review by the Board. The Department shall adopt rules to implement, interpret, or make specific the provisions and purposes of this Act; however no such rules shall be adopted by the Department except upon review by the Board.

(b) The Department shall:

(1) prepare and maintain a list of approved programs of professional nursing education and programs of practical nursing education in this State, whose graduates, if they have the other necessary qualifications provided in this Act, shall be eligible to apply for a license to practice nursing in this State;

(2) promulgate rules defining what constitutes an approved program of professional nursing education and what constitutes an approved program of practical nursing education; and

(3) adopt rules for examination of candidates for licenses and for issuance of licenses authorizing candidates upon passing an examination to practice under this Act.

§ 10–15.   Nursing Act Coordinator

The Department shall obtain, pursuant to the Personnel Code, a Nursing Act Coordinator and assistants. The Nursing Coordinator and assistants shall be professional nurses licensed in this State and graduated from approved schools of nursing and each shall have been actively engaged in nursing education not less than one year prior to appointment. The Nursing Act

Coordinator shall hold at least a master's degree in nursing from an approved college or university and shall have at least 5 years experience since graduation in progressively responsible positions in nursing education. Each assistant shall hold at least a master's degree in nursing from an approved college or university and shall have at least 3 years experience since graduation in progressively responsible positions in nursing education. The Nursing Act Coordinator and assistants shall perform such administrative functions as may be delegated to them by the Director.

§ 10–25. Board

(a) The Director shall appoint the Board of Nursing which, beginning January 1, 2000, shall be composed of 7 registered professional nurses, 2 licensed practical nurses and one public member who shall also be a voting member and who is not a licensed health care provider. Two registered nurses shall hold at least a master's degree in nursing and be educators in professional nursing programs, one representing baccalaureate nursing education, one representing associate degree nursing education; one registered nurse shall hold at least a bachelor's degree with a major in nursing and be an educator in a licensed practical nursing program; one registered nurse shall hold a master's degree in nursing and shall represent nursing service administration; 2 registered nurses shall represent clinical nursing practice, one of whom shall have at least a master's degree in nursing; and, until January 1, 2000, 2 registered nurses shall represent advanced specialty practice. Each of the nurses shall have had a minimum of 5 years experience in nursing, 3 of which shall be in the area they represent on the Board and be actively engaged in the area of nursing they represent at the time of appointment and during their tenure on the Board. Members shall be appointed for a term of 3 years. No member shall be eligible for appointment to more than 2 consecutive terms and any appointment to fill a vacancy shall be for the unexpired portion of the term. In making Board appointments, the Director shall give consideration to recommendations submitted by nursing organizations. Consideration shall be given to equal geographic representation. The Board shall receive actual and necessary expenses incurred in the performance of their duties.

* * *

The Director may remove any member of the Board for misconduct, incapacity, or neglect of duty. The Director shall reduce to writing any causes for removal.

The Board shall meet annually to elect a chairperson and vice chairperson. The Board may hold such other meetings during the year as may be necessary to conduct its business. Six voting members of the Board shall constitute a quorum at any meeting. Any action taken by the Board must be on the affirmative vote of 6 members. Voting by proxy shall not be permitted.

The Board shall submit an annual report to the Director.

The members of the Board shall be immune from suit in any action based upon any disciplinary proceedings or other acts performed in good faith as members of the Board.

(b) The Board is authorized to:

(1) recommend the adoption and, from time to time, the revision of such rules that may be necessary to carry out the provisions of this Act;

(2) conduct hearings and disciplinary conferences upon charges calling for discipline of a licensee as provided in Section 10–45;

(3) report to the Department, upon completion of a hearing, the disciplinary actions recommended to be taken against persons violating this Act;

(4) recommend the approval, denial of approval, withdrawal of approval, or discipline of nursing education programs;

(5) participate in a national organization of state boards of nursing; and

(6) recommend a list of the registered nurses to serve as Nursing Act Coordinator and Assistant Nursing Act Coordinator, respectively.

§ 10–30. Qualifications for licensure

(a) Each applicant who successfully meets the requirements of this Section shall be entitled to licensure as a Registered Nurse or Licensed Practical Nurse, whichever is applicable.

(b) An applicant for licensure by examination to practice as a registered nurse or licensed practical nurse shall:

(1) submit a completed written application, on forms provided by the Department and fees as established by the Department;

(2) for registered nurse licensure, have completed an approved professional nursing education program of not less than 2 academic years and have graduated from the program; for licensed practical nurse licensure, have completed an approved practical nursing education program of not less than one academic year and have graduated from the program;

(3) have not violated the provisions of Section 10–45 of this Act. The Department may take into consideration any felony conviction of the applicant, but such a conviction shall not operate as an absolute bar to licensure;

(4) meet all other requirements as established by rule;

(5) pay, either to the Department or its designated testing service, a fee covering the cost of providing the examination. Failure to appear for the examination on the scheduled date at the time and place specified after the applicant's application for examination has been received and acknowledged by the Department or the designated testing service shall result in the forfeiture of the examination fee.

If an applicant neglects, fails, or refuses to take an examination or fails to pass an examination for a license under this Act within 3 years after filing the application, the application shall be denied. However, the applicant may make a new application accompanied by the required fee and provide evidence of meeting the requirements in force at the time of the new application.

An applicant shall have one year from the date of notification of successful completion of the examination to apply to the Department for a license. If an applicant fails to apply within one year, the applicant shall be required to again take and pass the examination unless licensed in another jurisdiction of the United States within one year of passing the examination.

(c) An applicant for licensure who is a registered professional nurse or a licensed practical nurse licensed by examination under the laws of another state or territory of the United States shall:

    (1) submit a completed written application, on forms supplied by the Department, and fees as established by the Department;

    (2) for registered nurse licensure, have completed an approved professional nursing education program of not less than 2 academic years and have graduated from the program; for licensed practical nurse licensure, have completed an approved practical nursing education program of not less than one academic year and have graduated from the program;

    (3) submit verification of licensure status directly from the United States jurisdiction of licensure;

    (4) have passed the examination authorized by the Department;

    (5) meet all other requirements as established by rule.

(d) All applicants for licensure pursuant to this Section who are graduates of nursing educational programs in a country other than the United States or its territories must submit to the Department certification of successful completion of the Commission of Graduates of Foreign Nursing Schools (CGFNS) examination. An applicant, who is unable to provide appropriate documentation to satisfy CGFNS of her or his educational qualifications for the CGFNS examination, shall be required to pass an examination to test competency in the English language which shall be prescribed by the Department, if the applicant is determined by the Board to be educationally prepared in nursing. The Board shall make appropriate inquiry into the reasons for any adverse determination by CGFNS before making its own decision.

An applicant licensed in another state or territory who is applying for licensure and has received her or his education in a country other than the United States or its territories shall be exempt from the completion of the Commission of Graduates of Foreign Nursing Schools (CGFNS) examination if the applicant meets all of the following requirements:

    (1) successful passage of the licensure examination authorized by the Department;

(2) holds an active, unencumbered license in another state; and

(3) has been actively practicing for a minimum of 2 years in another state.

(e) No applicant shall be issued a license as a registered nurse or practical nurse under this Section unless he or she has passed the examination authorized by the Department within 3 years of completion and graduation from an approved nursing education program, unless such applicant submits proof of successful completion of a Department-authorized remedial nursing education program or recompletion of an approved registered nursing program or licensed practical nursing program, as appropriate.

(f) Pending the issuance of a license under subsection (b) of this Section, the Department may grant an applicant a temporary license to practice nursing as a registered nurse or as a licensed practical nurse if the Department is satisfied that the applicant holds an active, unencumbered license in good standing in another jurisdiction. If the applicant holds more than one current active license, or one or more active temporary licenses from other jurisdictions, the Department shall not issue a temporary license until it is satisfied that each current active license held by the applicant is unencumbered. The temporary license, which shall be issued no later than 14 working days following receipt by the Department of an application for the temporary license, shall be granted upon the submission of the following to the Department:

(1) a signed and completed application for licensure under subsection (a) of this Section as a registered nurse or a licensed practical nurse;

(2) proof of a current, active license in at least one other jurisdiction and proof that each current active license or temporary license held by the applicant is unencumbered;

(3) a signed and completed application for a temporary license; and

(4) the required permit fee.

(g) The Department may refuse to issue an applicant a temporary license authorized pursuant to this Section if, within 14 working days following its receipt of an application for a temporary license, the Department determines that:

(1) the applicant has been convicted of a crime under the laws of a jurisdiction of the United States:

(i) which is a felony; or

(ii) which is a misdemeanor directly related to the practice of the profession, within the last 5 years;

(2) within the last 5 years the applicant has had a license or permit related to the practice of nursing revoked, suspended, or placed on probation by another jurisdiction, if at least one of the grounds for

revoking, suspending, or placing on probation is the same or substantially equivalent to grounds in Illinois; or

(3) it intends to deny licensure by endorsement.

For purposes of this Section, an "unencumbered license" means a license against which no disciplinary action has been taken or is pending and for which all fees and charges are paid and current.

(h) The Department may revoke a temporary license issued pursuant to this Section if:

(1) it determines that the applicant has been convicted of a crime under the law of any jurisdiction of the United States that is

(i) a felony or

(ii) a misdemeanor directly related to the practice of the profession, within the last 5 years;

(2) it determines that within the last 5 years the applicant has had a license or permit related to the practice of nursing revoked, suspended, or placed on probation by another jurisdiction, if at least one of the grounds for revoking, suspending, or placing on probation is the same or substantially equivalent to grounds in Illinois; or

(3) it determines that it intends to deny licensure by endorsement.

A temporary license or renewed temporary license shall expire

(i) upon issuance of an Illinois license or

(ii) upon notification that the Department intends to deny licensure by endorsement. A temporary license shall expire 6 months from the date of issuance. Further renewal may be granted by the Department in hardship cases, as defined by rule. However, a temporary license shall automatically expire upon issuance of the Illinois license or upon notification that the Department intends to deny licensure, whichever occurs first. No extensions shall be granted beyond the 6–month period unless approved by the Director. Notification by the Department under this Section shall be by certified or registered mail.

§ 10–35. Concurrent theory and clinical practice education requirements

The educational requirements of Section 10–30 relating to registered professional nursing and licensed practical nursing shall not be deemed to have been satisfied by the completion of any correspondence course or any program of nursing that does not require coordinated or concurrent theory and clinical practice. The Department may, upon recommendation of the Board, grant an Illinois license to those applicants who have received advanced graduate degrees in nursing from an approved program with concurrent theory and clinical practice or to those applicants who are currently licensed in another state and have been actively practicing clinical nursing for a minimum of 2 years.

§ 10–40. Endorsement

Upon payment of the required fee, an applicant who is a registered professional nurse or a licensed practical nurse educated and licensed under the laws of a foreign country, territory or province shall write and pass an examination conducted by the Department to determine her or his fitness for licensure as a registered professional nurse or a licensed practical nurse:

(a) whenever the requirements of such country, territory or province were at the date of license substantially equal to the requirements then in force in this State; and with respect to practical nursing, if prior to the enactment of this Act, substantially equal to the requirements of this Act at the time of its enactment; or

(b) whenever such requirements of another country, territory or province together with educational and professional qualifications, as distinguished from practical experience, of the applicant since obtaining a license as a registered professional nurse or a licensed practical nurse in such country, territory or province are substantially equal to the requirements in force in Illinois at the time of application for licensure as a registered nurse or a licensed practical nurse in Illinois.

The examination shall be the same as that required of other applicants for licensure by examination.

Applicants have 3 years from the date of application to complete the application process. If the process has not been completed in 3 years, the application shall be denied, the fee forfeited and the applicant must reapply and meet the requirements in effect at the time of reapplication.

§ 10–45. Grounds for disciplinary action

(a) The Department may, upon recommendation of the Board, refuse to issue or to renew, or may revoke, suspend, place on probation, reprimand, or take other disciplinary action as the Department may deem appropriate with regard to a license for any one or combination of the causes set forth in subsection (b) below. Fines up to $2,500 may be imposed in conjunction with other forms of disciplinary action for those violations that result in monetary gain for the licensee. Fines shall not be the exclusive disposition of any disciplinary action arising out of conduct resulting in death or injury to a patient. Fines shall not be assessed in disciplinary actions involving mental or physical illness or impairment. All fines collected under this Section shall be deposited in the Nursing Dedicated and Professional Fund.

(b) Grounds for disciplinary action include the following:

(1) Material deception in furnishing information to the Department.

(2) Material violations of any provision of this Act or violation of the rules of or final administrative action of the Director, after consideration of the recommendation of the Board.

(3) Conviction of any crime under the laws of any jurisdiction of the United States:

    (i) which is a felony; or

    (ii) which is a misdemeanor, an essential element of which is dishonesty, or

    (iii) of any crime which is directly related to the practice of the profession.

(4) A pattern of practice or other behavior which demonstrates incapacity or incompetency to practice under this Act.

(5) Knowingly aiding or assisting another person in violating any provision of this Act or rules.

(6) Failing, within 90 days, to provide a response to a request for information in response to a written request made by the Department by certified mail.

(7) Engaging in dishonorable, unethical or unprofessional conduct of a character likely to deceive, defraud or harm the public, as defined by rule.

(8) Unlawful sale or distribution of any drug, narcotic, or prescription device, or unlawful conversion of any drug, narcotic or prescription device.

(9) Habitual or excessive use or addiction to alcohol, narcotics, stimulants, or any other chemical agent or drug which results in a licensee's inability to practice with reasonable judgment, skill or safety.

(10) Discipline by another U.S. jurisdiction or foreign nation, if at least one of the grounds for the discipline is the same or substantially equivalent to those set forth in this Section.

(11) A finding that the licensee, after having her or his license placed on probationary status, has violated the terms of probation.

(12) Being named as a perpetrator in an indicated report by the Department of Children and Family Services and under the Abused and Neglected Child Reporting Act, and upon proof by clear and convincing evidence that the licensee has caused a child to be an abused child or neglected child as defined in the Abused and Neglected Child Reporting Act.

(13) Willful omission to file or record, or willfully impeding the filing or recording or inducing another person to omit to file or record medical reports as required by law or willfully failing to report an instance of suspected child abuse or neglect as required by the Abused and Neglected Child Reporting Act.

(14) Gross negligence in the practice of nursing.

(15) Holding oneself out to be practicing nursing under any name other than one's own.

(16) Fraud, deceit or misrepresentation in applying for or procuring a license under this Act or in connection with applying for renewal of a license under this Act.

(17) Allowing another person or organization to use the licensees' license to deceive the public.

(18) Willfully making or filing false records or reports in the licensee's practice, including but not limited to false records to support claims against the medical assistance program of the Department of Public Aid under the Illinois Public Aid Code.

(19) Attempting to subvert or cheat on a nurse licensing examination administered under this Act.

(20) Immoral conduct in the commission of an act, such as sexual abuse, sexual misconduct, or sexual exploitation, related to the licensee's practice.

(21) Willfully or negligently violating the confidentiality between nurse and patient except as required by law.

(22) Practicing under a false or assumed name, except as provided by law.

(23) The use of any false, fraudulent, or deceptive statement in any document connected with the licensee's practice.

(24) Directly or indirectly giving to or receiving from a person, firm, corporation, partnership, or association a fee, commission, rebate, or other form of compensation for professional services not actually or personally rendered.

(25) Failure of a licensee to report to the Department any adverse final action taken against such licensee by another licensing jurisdiction (any other jurisdiction of the United States or any foreign state or country), by any peer review body, by any health care institution, by any professional or nursing society or association, by any governmental agency, by any law enforcement agency, or by any court or a nursing liability claim related to acts or conduct similar to acts or conduct that would constitute grounds for action as defined in this Section.

(26) Failure of a licensee to report to the Department surrender by the licensee of a license or authorization to practice nursing in another state or jurisdiction, or current surrender by the licensee of membership on any nursing staff or in any nursing or professional association or society while under disciplinary investigation by any of those authorities or bodies for acts or conduct similar to acts or conduct that would constitute grounds for action as defined by this Section.

(27) A violation of the Health Care Worker Self–Referral Act.

(28) Physical illness, including but not limited to deterioration through the aging process or loss of motor skill, mental illness, or disability that results in the inability to practice the profession with reasonable judgment, skill, or safety.

(c) The determination by a circuit court that a licensee is subject to involuntary admission or judicial admission as provided in the Mental Health and Developmental Disabilities Code, as amended, operates as an automatic suspension. The suspension will end only upon a finding by a court that the patient is no longer subject to involuntary admission or judicial admission and issues an order so finding and discharging the patient; and upon the recommendation of the Board to the Director that the licensee be allowed to resume his or her practice.

(d) The Department may refuse to issue or may suspend the license of any person who fails to file a return, or to pay the tax, penalty or interest shown in a filed return, or to pay any final assessment of the tax, penalty, or interest as required by any tax Act administered by the Illinois Department of Revenue, until such time as the requirements of any such tax Act are satisfied.

(e) In enforcing this Section, the Department or Board upon a showing of a possible violation may compel an individual licensed to practice under this Act, or who has applied for licensure under this Act, to submit to a mental or physical examination, or both, as required by and at the expense of the Department. The Department or Board may order the examining physician to present testimony concerning the mental or physical examination of the licensee or applicant. No information shall be excluded by reason of any common law or statutory privilege relating to communications between the licensee or applicant and the examining physician. The examining physicians shall be specifically designated by the Board or Department. The individual to be examined may have, at his or her own expense, another physician of his or her choice present during all aspects of this examination. Failure of an individual to submit to a mental or physical examination, when directed, shall be grounds for suspension of his or her license until the individual submits to the examination if the Department finds, after notice and hearing, that the refusal to submit to the examination was without reasonable cause.

If the Department or Board finds an individual unable to practice because of the reasons set forth in this Section, the Department or Board may require that individual to submit to care, counseling, or treatment by physicians approved or designated by the Department or Board, as a condition, term, or restriction for continued, reinstated, or renewed licensure to practice; or, in lieu of care, counseling, or treatment, the Department may file, or the Board may recommend to the Department to file, a complaint to immediately suspend, revoke, or otherwise discipline the license of the individual. An individual whose license was granted, continued, reinstated, renewed, disciplined or supervised subject to such terms, conditions, or restrictions, and who fails to comply with such terms, conditions, or restrictions, shall be referred to the Director for a determination as to whether the individual shall have his or her license suspended immediately, pending a hearing by the Department.

In instances in which the Director immediately suspends a person's license under this Section, a hearing on that person's license must be convened by the Department within 15 days after the suspension and completed without appreciable delay. The Department and Board shall have the authority to review the subject individual's record of treatment and counseling regarding the impairment to the extent permitted by applicable federal statutes and regulations safeguarding the confidentiality of medical records.

An individual licensed under this Act and affected under this Section shall be afforded an opportunity to demonstrate to the Department or Board that he or she can resume practice in compliance with acceptable and prevailing standards under the provisions of his or her license.

§ 10–50.   Intoxication and drug abuse

(a) A professional assistance program for nurses shall be established by January 1, 1999.

(b) The Director shall appoint a task force to advise in the creation of the assistance program. The task force shall include members of the Department and professional nurses, and shall report its findings and recommendations to the Committee on Nursing.

(c) Any registered professional nurse who is an administrator or officer in any hospital, nursing home, other health care agency or facility, or nurse agency and has knowledge of any action or condition which reasonably indicates to her or him that a registered professional nurse or licensed practical nurse employed by or practicing nursing in such hospital, nursing home, other health care agency or facility, or nurse agency is habitually intoxicated or addicted to the use of habit-forming drugs to the extent that such intoxication or addiction adversely affects such nurse's professional performance, or unlawfully possesses, uses, distributes or converts habit-forming drugs belonging to the hospital, nursing home or other health care agency or facility for such nurse's own use, shall promptly file a written report thereof to the Department; provided however, an administrator or officer need not file the report if the nurse participates in a course of remedial professional counseling or medical treatment for substance abuse, as long as such nurse actively pursues such treatment under monitoring by the administrator or officer or by the hospital, nursing home, health care agency or facility, or nurse agency and the nurse continues to be employed by such hospital, nursing home, health care agency or facility, or nurse agency. The Department shall review all reports received by it in a timely manner. Its initial review shall be completed no later than 60 days after receipt of the report. Within this 60 day period, the Department shall, in writing, make a determination as to whether there are sufficient facts to warrant further investigation or action.

Should the Department find insufficient facts to warrant further investigation, or action, the report shall be accepted for filing and the matter shall be deemed closed and so reported.

Should the Department find sufficient facts to warrant further investigation, such investigation shall be completed within 60 days of the date of the determination of sufficient facts to warrant further investigation or action. Final action shall be determined no later than 30 days after the completion of the investigation. If there is a finding which verifies habitual intoxication or drug addiction which adversely affects professional performance or the unlawful possession, use, distribution or conversion of habit-forming drugs by the reported nurse, the Department may refuse to issue or renew or may suspend or revoke that nurse's license as a registered professional nurse or a licensed practical nurse.

Any of the aforementioned actions or a determination that there are insufficient facts to warrant further investigation or action shall be considered a final action. The nurse administrator or officer who filed the original report or complaint, and the nurse who is the subject of the report, shall be notified in writing by the Department within 15 days of any final action taken by the Department.

Each year on March 1, commencing with the effective date of this Act, the Department shall submit a report to the General Assembly. The report shall include the number of reports made under this Section to the Department during the previous year, the number of reports reviewed and found insufficient to warrant further investigation, the number of reports not completed and the reasons for incompletion. This report shall be made available also to nurses requesting the report.

Any person making a report under this Section or in good faith assisting another person in making such a report shall have immunity from any liability, either criminal or civil, that might result by reason of such action. For the purpose of any legal proceeding, criminal or civil, there shall be a rebuttable presumption that any person making a report under this Section or assisting another person in making such report was acting in good faith. All such reports and any information disclosed to or collected by the Department pursuant to this Section shall remain confidential records of the Department and shall not be disclosed nor be subject to any law or regulation of this State relating to freedom of information or public disclosure of records.

§ 15–5. Definitions

As used in this Title:

"APN Board" means the Advanced Practice Nursing Board.

"Advanced practice nurse" or "APN" means a person who:

(1) is licensed as a registered professional nurse under this Act;

(2) meets the requirements for licensure as an advanced practice nurse under Section 15–10;

(3) except as provided in Section 15–25, has a written collaborative agreement with a collaborating physician in the diagnosis of illness and management of wellness and other conditions as appropriate to the level and area of his or her practice in accordance with Section 15–15; and

(4) cares for patients

(A) by using advanced diagnostic skills, the results of diagnostic tests and procedures ordered by the advanced practice nurse, a physician assistant, a dentist, a podiatrist, or a physician, and professional judgment to initiate and coordinate the care of patients;

(B) by ordering diagnostic tests, prescribing medications and drugs in accordance with Section 15–20, and administering medications and drugs; and

(C) by using medical, therapeutic, and corrective measures to treat illness and improve health status. Categories include certified nurse midwife (CNM), certified nurse practitioner (CNP), certified registered nurse anesthetist (CRNA), or certified clinical nurse specialist (CNS).

"Collaborating physician" means a physician who works with an advanced practice nurse and provides medical direction as documented in a written collaborative agreement required under Section 15–15.

"Licensed hospital" means a hospital licensed under the Hospital Licensing Act or organized under the University of Illinois Hospital Act.

"Physician" means a person licensed to practice medicine in all its branches under the Medical Practice Act of 1987.

§ 15–10. Advanced practice nurse; qualifications; roster

(a) A person shall be qualified for licensure as an advanced practice nurse if that person:

(1) has applied in writing in form and substance satisfactory to the Department and has not violated a provision of this Act or the rules adopted under this Act. The Department may take into consideration any felony conviction of the applicant but a conviction shall not operate as an absolute bar to licensure;

(2) holds a current license to practice as a registered nurse in Illinois;

(3) has successfully completed requirements to practice as, and holds a current, national certification as, a nurse midwife, clinical nurse specialist, or nurse practitioner, or certified registered nurse anesthetist from the appropriate national certifying body as determined by rule of the Department;

(4) has paid the required fees as set by rule; and

(5) has successfully completed a post-basic advanced practice formal education program in the area of his or her nursing specialty.

(b) In addition to meeting the requirements of subsection (a), except item (5) of that subsection, beginning July 1, 2001 or 12 months after the adoption of final rules to implement this Section, whichever is sooner, applicants for initial licensure shall have a graduate degree appropriate for national certification in a clinical advanced practice nursing specialty.

(c) The Department shall provide by rule for APN licensure of registered professional nurses who

   (1) apply for licensure before July 1, 2001 and

   (2) submit evidence of completion of a program described in item (5) of subsection (a) or in subsection (b) and evidence of practice for at least 10 years as a nurse practitioner.

(d) The Department shall maintain a separate roster of advanced practice nurses licensed under this Title and their licenses shall indicate "Registered Nurse/Advanced Practice Nurse".

§ 15–15. Written collaborative agreements

(a) Except as provided in Section 15–25, no person shall engage in the practice of advanced practice nursing except when licensed under this Title and pursuant to a written collaborative agreement with a collaborating physician.

(b) A written collaborative agreement shall describe the working relationship of the advanced practice nurse with the collaborating physician and shall authorize the categories of care, treatment, or procedures to be performed by the advanced practice nurse. Collaboration does not require an employment relationship between the collaborating physician and advanced practice nurse. Collaboration means the relationship under which an advanced practice nurse works with a collaborating physician in an active clinical practice to deliver health care services in accordance with

   (i) the advanced practice nurse's training, education, and experience and

   (ii) medical direction as documented in a jointly developed written collaborative agreement.

The agreement shall be defined to promote the exercise of professional judgment by the advanced practice nurse commensurate with his or her education and experience. The services to be provided by the advanced practice nurse shall be services that the collaborating physician generally provides to his or her patients in the normal course of his or her clinical medical practice. The agreement need not describe the exact steps that an advanced practice nurse must take with respect to each specific condition, disease, or symptom but must specify which authorized procedures require a physician's presence as the procedures are being performed. The collaborative relationship under an agreement shall not be construed to require the personal presence of a physician at all times at the place where services are rendered. Methods of communication shall be available for consultation with the collaborating physician in person or by telecommunications in accordance with established written guidelines as set forth in the written agreement.

(c) Physician medical direction under an agreement shall be adequate if a collaborating physician:

    (1) participates in the joint formulation and joint approval of orders or guidelines with the APN and he or she periodically reviews such orders and the services provided patients under such orders in accordance with accepted standards of medical practice and advanced practice nursing practice;

    (2) is on site at least once a month to provide medical direction and consultation; and

    (3) is available through telecommunications for consultation on medical problems, complications, or emergencies or patient referral.

(d) A copy of the signed, written collaborative agreement must be available to the Department upon request from both the advanced practice nurse and the collaborating physician and shall be annually updated. An advanced practice nurse shall inform each collaborating physician of all collaborative agreements he or she has signed and provide a copy of these to any collaborating physician, upon request.

§ 15–20.   Prescriptive authority

(a) A collaborating physician may, but is not required to, delegate limited prescriptive authority to an advanced practice nurse as part of a written collaborative agreement. This authority may, but is not required to, include prescription and dispensing of legend drugs and legend controlled substances categorized as Schedule III, IV, or V controlled substances, as defined in Article II of the Illinois Controlled Substances Act.

(b) To prescribe Schedule III, IV, or V controlled substances under this Section, an advanced practice nurse must obtain a mid-level practitioner controlled substance license. Medication orders shall be reviewed periodically by the collaborating physician.

(c) The collaborating physician shall file with the Department notice of delegation of prescriptive authority and termination of such delegation, in accordance with rules of the Department. Upon receipt of this notice delegating authority to prescribe Schedule III, IV, or V controlled substances, the licensed advanced practice nurse shall be eligible to register for a mid-level practitioner controlled substance license under Section 303.05 of the Illinois Controlled Substances Act.

(d) Nothing in this Act shall be construed to limit the delegation of tasks or duties by a physician to a licensed practical nurse, a registered professional nurse, or other personnel.

§ 15–25. Certified registered nurse anesthetists

(a) A licensed certified registered nurse anesthetist may provide anesthesia services pursuant to the order of a licensed physician, licensed dentist, or licensed podiatrist in a licensed hospital, a licensed ambulatory surgical treatment center, or the office of a licensed physician, the office of a licensed dentist, or the office of a licensed podiatrist. For anesthesia services, an anesthesiologist, physician, dentist, or podiatrist shall participate through discussion of and agreement with the anesthesia plan and shall remain physically present and be available on the premises during the delivery of anesthesia services for diagnosis, consultation, and treatment of emergency medical conditions, unless hospital policy adopted pursuant to clause (B) of subdivision (3) of Section 10.7 of the Hospital Licensing Act or ambulatory surgical treatment center policy adopted pursuant to clause (B) of subdivision (3) of Section 6.5 of the Ambulatory Surgical Treatment Center Act provides otherwise.

(b) A certified registered nurse anesthetist who provides anesthesia services in a hospital shall do so in accordance with Section 10.7 of the Hospital Licensing Act and, in an ambulatory surgical treatment center, in accordance with Section 6.5 of the Ambulatory Surgical Treatment Center Act.

(c) A certified registered nurse anesthetist who provides anesthesia services in a physician office, dental office, or podiatric office shall enter into a written practice agreement with an anesthesiologist or the physician licensed to practice medicine in all its branches, the dentist, or the podiatrist performing the procedure. The agreement shall describe the working relationship of the certified registered nurse anesthetist and anesthesiologist, physician, dentist, or podiatrist and shall authorize the categories of care, treatment, or procedures to be performed by the certified registered nurse anesthetist. In a dentist's office, the certified registered nurse anesthetist may only provide those services the dentist is authorized to provide pursuant to the Illinois Dental Practice Act and rules. In a podiatrist's office, the certified registered nurse anesthetist may only provide those services the podiatrist is authorized to provide pursuant to the Podiatric Medical Practice Act of 1987 and rules. For anesthesia services, an anesthesiologist, physician, dentist, or podiatrist shall participate through discussion of and agreement with the anesthesia plan and shall remain physically present and be available on the premises during the delivery of anesthesia services for diagnosis, consultation, and treatment of emergency medical conditions.

(d) A certified registered nurse anesthetist is not required to possess prescriptive authority or a written collaborative agreement meeting the requirements of Section 15–15 to provide anesthesia services ordered by a licensed physician, dentist, or podiatrist. Certified registered nurse anesthetists are authorized to select, order, and administer drugs and apply the appropriate medical devices in the provision of anesthesia services under the anesthesia plan agreed with by the anesthesiologist or the physician in accordance with hospital alternative policy or the medical staff consulting committee policies of a licensed ambulatory surgical treatment center. In a physician's office, dentist's office, or podiatrist's office, the anesthesiologist, operating physician, operating dentist, or operating podiatrist shall agree with the anesthesia plan, in accordance with the written practice agreement.

(e) A certified registered nurse anesthetist may be delegated limited prescriptive authority under Section 15–20 in a written collaborative agreement meeting the requirements of Section 15–15.

§ 15–30.   Title.

(a) No person shall use any words, abbreviations, figures, letters, title, sign, card, or device tending to imply that he or she is an advanced practice nurse, including but not limited to using the titles or initials "Advanced Practice Nurse", "Certified Nurse Midwife", "Certified Nurse Practitioner", "Certified Registered Nurse Anesthetist", "Clinical Nurse Specialist", "A.P.N.", "C.N.M.", "C.N.P.", "C.R.N.A.", "C.N.S.", or similar titles or initials, with the intention of indicating practice as an advanced practice nurse without meeting the requirements of this Act. No advanced practice nurse shall use the title of doctor or associate with his or her name or any other term to indicate to other persons that he or she is qualified to engage in the general practice of medicine.

(b) An advanced practice nurse shall verbally identify himself or herself as an advanced practice nurse including specialty certification to each patient.

(c) Nothing in this Act shall be construed to relieve a physician of professional or legal responsibility for the care and treatment of persons attended by him or her or to relieve an advanced practice nurse of the professional or legal responsibility for the care and treatment of persons attended by him or her.

§ 15–35.   Advanced Practice Nursing Board

(a) There is hereby established an Advanced Practice Nursing Board, hereinafter referred to as the "APN Board". The APN Board shall review and make recommendations to the Department regarding matters relating to licensure and discipline of advanced practice nurses. The APN Board shall be composed of 9 members to be appointed by the Governor, 4 of whom shall be advanced practice nurses and 3 of whom shall be physicians licensed to practice medicine in all its branches. The 4 advanced practice nurses shall have collaborative agreements, except that any certified registered nurse anesthetist is not required to have a collaborative agreement. The 3 physicians shall have collaborative agreements, except that an anesthesiologist is not required to have a collaborative agreement. In making appointments to the APN Board, the Governor shall give due consideration to recommendations by statewide professional associations or societies representing nurses and physicians in Illinois. Two members, not employed or having any material interest in any health care field, shall represent the public. The chairperson of the APN Board shall be a member elected by a majority vote of the APN

Board. The APN Board shall meet and report to the Department quarterly and as advanced practice nurse issues arise.

Initial appointments to the APN Board shall be made within 90 days after the effective date of this amendatory Act of 1998. The terms of office of each of the original members shall be at staggered intervals. One physician and one advanced practice nurse shall serve one-year terms. One physician and one advanced practice nurse shall serve 2–year terms. One physician and one advanced practice nurse shall serve 3–year terms. One advanced practice nurse and the public members shall serve 4–year terms. Upon the expiration of the term of an initial member, his or her successor shall be appointed for a term of 4 years. No member shall serve more than 2 consecutive terms, excluding initial appointment terms. An appointment to fill a vacancy shall be for the unexpired portion of the term. Members of the APN Board shall be reimbursed for all authorized legitimate and necessary expenses incurred in attending the meetings of the APN Board. A majority of the APN Board members appointed shall constitute a quorum. A vacancy in the membership of the APN Board shall not impair the right of a quorum to perform all of the duties of the APN Board. A member of the APN Board shall have no liability in an action based upon a disciplinary proceeding or other activity performed in good faith as a member of the APN Board.

(b) Complaints received concerning advanced practice nurses shall be reviewed by the APN Board. Complaints received concerning collaborating physicians shall be reviewed by the Medical Disciplinary Board.

§ 15–40.   Advertising

(a) A person licensed under this Title may advertise the availability of professional services in the public media or on the premises where the professional services are rendered. The advertising shall be limited to the following information:

(1) publication of the person's name, title, office hours, address, and telephone number;

(2) information pertaining to the person's areas of specialization, including but not limited to appropriate board certification or limitation of professional practice;

(3) publication of the person's collaborating physician's name, title, and areas of specialization;

(4) information on usual and customary fees for routine professional services offered, which shall include notification that fees may be adjusted due to complications or unforeseen circumstances;

(5) announcements of the opening of, change of, absence from, or return to business;

(6) announcement of additions to or deletions from professional licensed staff; and

(7) the issuance of business or appointment cards.

(b) It is unlawful for a person licensed under this Title to use testimonials or claims of superior quality of care to entice the public. It shall be unlawful to advertise fee comparisons of available services with those of other licensed persons.

(c) This Title does not authorize the advertising of professional services that the offeror of the services is not licensed or authorized to render. Nor shall the advertiser use statements that contain false, fraudulent, deceptive, or misleading material or guarantees of success, statements that play upon the vanity or fears of the public, or statements that promote or produce unfair competition.

(d) It is unlawful and punishable under the penalty provisions of this Act for a person licensed under this Title to knowingly advertise that the licensee will accept as payment for services rendered by assignment from any third party payor the amount the third party payor covers as payment in full, if the effect is to give the impression of eliminating the need of payment by the patient of any required deductible or copayment applicable in the patient's health benefit plan.

(d–5) A licensee shall include in every advertisement for services regulated under this Act his or her title as it appears on the license or the initials authorized under this Act.

(e) As used in this Section, "advertise" means solicitation by the licensee or through another person or entity by means of handbills, posters, circulars, motion pictures, radio, newspapers, or television or any other manner.

§ 15–45. Continuing education

The Department shall adopt rules of continuing education for persons licensed under this Title that require 50 hours of continuing education per 2–year license renewal cycle. The rules shall not be inconsistent with requirements of relevant national certifying bodies or State or national professional associations. The rules shall also address variances for illness or hardship. The continuing education rules shall assure that licensees are given the opportunity to participate in programs sponsored by or through their State or national professional associations, hospitals, or other providers of continuing education. Each licensee is responsible for maintaining records of completion of continuing education and shall be prepared to produce the records when requested by the Department.

§ 15–50. Grounds for disciplinary action

(a) The Department may, upon the recommendation of the APN Board, refuse to issue or to renew, or may revoke, suspend, place on probation, censure or reprimand, or take other disciplinary action as the Department may deem appropriate with regard to a license issued under this Title, including the issuance of fines not to exceed $5,000 for each violation, for any one or combination of the grounds for discipline set forth in Section 10–45 of this Act or for any one or combination of the following causes:

(1) Gross negligence in the practice of advanced practice nursing.

(2) Exceeding the terms of a collaborative agreement or the prescriptive authority delegated to him or her by his or her collaborating physician or alternate collaborating physician in guidelines established under a written collaborative agreement.

(3) Making a false or misleading statement regarding his or her skill or the efficacy or value of the medicine, treatment, or remedy prescribed by him or her in the course of treatment.

(4) Prescribing, selling, administering, distributing, giving, or self-administering a drug classified as a controlled substance (designated product) or narcotic for other than medically accepted therapeutic purposes.

(5) Promotion of the sale of drugs, devices, appliances, or goods provided for a patient in a manner to exploit the patient for financial gain.

(6) Violating State or federal laws or regulations relating to controlled substances.

(7) Willfully or negligently violating the confidentiality between advanced practice nurse, collaborating physician, and patient, except as required by law.

(8) Failure of a licensee to report to the Department any adverse final action taken against such licensee by another licensing jurisdiction (any other jurisdiction of the United States or any foreign state or country), any peer review body, any health care institution, a professional or nursing or advanced practice nursing society or association, a governmental agency, a law enforcement agency, or a court or a liability claim relating to acts or conduct similar to acts or conduct that would constitute grounds for action as defined in this Section.

(9) Failure of a licensee to report to the Department surrender by the licensee of a license or authorization to practice nursing or advanced practice nursing in another state or jurisdiction, or current surrender by the licensee of membership on any nursing staff or organized health care professional staff or in any nursing, advanced practice nurse, or professional association or society while under disciplinary investigation by any of those authorities or bodies for acts or conduct similar to acts or conduct that would constitute grounds for action as defined in this Section.

(10) Failing, within 60 days, to provide information in response to a written request made by the Department.

(11) Failure to establish and maintain records of patient care and treatment as required by law.

(12) Any violation of any Section of this Title or Act.

When the Department has received written reports concerning incidents required to be reported in items (8) and (9), the licensee's failure to report the incident to the Department under those items shall not be the sole grounds for disciplinary action.

(b) The Department may refuse to issue or may suspend the license of any person who fails to file a return, to pay the tax, penalty, or interest shown in a filed return, or to pay any final assessment of the tax, penalty, or interest as required by a tax Act administered by the Department of Revenue, until the requirements of the tax Act are satisfied.

(c) In enforcing this Section, the Department or APN Board, upon a showing of a possible violation, may compel an individual licensed to practice under this Title, or who has applied for licensure under this Title, to submit to a mental or physical examination or both, as required by and at the expense of the Department. The Department or APN Board may order the examining physician to present testimony concerning the mental or physical examination of the licensee or applicant. No information shall be excluded by reason of any common law or statutory privilege relating to communications between the licensee or applicant and the examining physician. The examining physician shall be specifically designated by the APN Board or Department. The individual to be examined may have, at his or her own expense, another physician of his or her choice present during all aspects of this examination. Failure of an individual to submit to a mental or physical examination when directed shall be grounds for suspension of his or her license until the individual submits to the examination if the Department finds, after notice and hearing, that the refusal to submit to the examination was without reasonable cause.

If the Department or APN Board finds an individual unable to practice because of the reasons set forth in this Section, the Department or APN Board may require that individual to submit to care, counseling, or treatment by physicians approved or designated by the Department or APN Board as a condition, term, or restriction for continued, reinstated, or renewed licensure to practice; or, in lieu of care, counseling, or treatment, the Department may file, or the APN Board may recommend to the Department to file, a complaint to immediately suspend, revoke, or otherwise discipline the license of the individual. An individual whose license was granted, continued, reinstated, renewed, disciplined or supervised subject to terms, conditions, or restrictions, and who fails to comply with the terms, conditions, or restrictions, shall be referred to the Director for a determination as to whether the individual shall have his or her license suspended immediately, pending a hearing by the Department.

In instances in which the Director immediately suspends a person's license under this Section, a hearing on that person's license shall be convened by the Department within 15 days after the suspension and shall be completed without appreciable delay. The Department and APN Board shall have the authority to review the subject individual's record of treatment and counseling regarding the impairment to the extent permitted by applicable federal statutes and regulations safeguarding the confidentiality of medical records.

An individual licensed under this Title and affected under this Section shall be afforded an opportunity to demonstrate to the Department or APN Board that he or she can resume practice in compliance with acceptable and prevailing standards under the provisions of his or her license.

§ 15–55. Reports relating to professional conduct and capacity

(a) Entities Required to Report.

(1) Health Care Institutions. The chief administrator or executive officer of a health care institution licensed by the Department of Public Health, which provides the minimum due process set forth in Section 10.4 of the Hospital Licensing Act, shall report to the APN Board when a licensee's organized professional staff clinical privileges are terminated or are restricted based on a final determination, in accordance with that institution's bylaws or rules and regulations, that

(i) a person has either committed an act or acts that may directly threaten patient care and that are not of an administrative nature or

(ii) that a person may be mentally or physically disabled in a manner that may endanger patients under that person's care. The chief administrator or officer shall also report if a licensee accepts voluntary termination or restriction of clinical privileges in lieu of formal action based upon conduct related directly to patient care and not of an administrative nature, or in lieu of formal action seeking to determine whether a person may be mentally or physically disabled in a manner that may endanger patients under that person's care. The APN Board shall provide by rule for the reporting to it of all instances in which a person licensed under this Title, who is impaired by reason of age, drug, or alcohol abuse or physical or mental impairment, is under supervision and, where appropriate, is in a program of rehabilitation. Reports submitted under this subsection shall be strictly confidential and may be reviewed and considered only by the members of the APN Board or authorized staff as provided by rule of the APN Board. Provisions shall be made for the periodic report of the status of any such reported person not less than twice annually in order that the APN Board shall have current information upon which to determine the status of that person. Initial and periodic reports of impaired advanced practice nurses shall not be considered records within the meaning of the State Records Act and shall be disposed of, following a determination by the APN Board that such reports are no longer required, in a manner and at an appropriate time as the APN Board shall determine by rule. The filing of reports submitted under this subsection shall be construed as the filing of a report for purposes of subsection (c) of this Section.

(2) Professional Associations. The President or chief executive officer of an association or society of persons licensed under this Title, operating within this State, shall report to the APN Board when the association or society renders a final determination that a person licensed under this Title has committed unprofessional conduct related directly to patient care or that a person may be mentally or physically disabled in a manner that may endanger patients under the person's care.

(3) Professional Liability Insurers. Every insurance company that offers policies of professional liability insurance to persons licensed under this Title, or any other entity that seeks to indemnify the professional liability of a person licensed under this Title, shall report to the APN Board the settlement of any claim or cause of action, or final judgment rendered in any cause of action, that alleged negligence in the furnishing of patient care by the licensee when the settlement or final judgment is in favor of the plaintiff.

(4) State's Attorneys. The State's Attorney of each county shall report to the APN Board all instances in which a person licensed under this Title is convicted or otherwise found guilty of the commission of a felony.

(5) State Agencies. All agencies, boards, commissions, departments, or other instrumentalities of the government of this State shall report to the APN Board any instance arising in connection with the operations of the agency, including the administration of any law by the agency, in which a person licensed under this Title has either committed an act or acts that may constitute a violation of this Title, that may constitute unprofessional conduct related directly to patient care, or that indicates that a person licensed under this Title may be mentally or physically disabled in a manner that may endanger patients under that person's care.

(b) Mandatory Reporting.

All reports required under items (8) and (9) of subsection (a) of Section 15–50 and under this Section shall be submitted to the APN Board in a timely fashion. The reports shall be filed in writing within 60 days after a determination that a report is required under this Title. All reports shall contain the following information:

(1) The name, address, and telephone number of the person making the report.

(2) The name, address, and telephone number of the person who is the subject of the report.

(3) The name or other means of identification of any patient or patients whose treatment is a subject of the report, except that no medical records may be revealed without the written consent of the patient or patients.

(4) A brief description of the facts that gave rise to the issuance of the report, including but not limited to the dates of any occurrences deemed to necessitate the filing of the report.

(5) If court action is involved, the identity of the court in which the action is filed, the docket number, and date of filing of the action.

(6) Any further pertinent information that the reporting party deems to be an aid in the evaluation of the report.

Nothing contained in this Section shall be construed to in any way waive or modify the confidentiality of medical reports and committee reports to the extent provided by law. Any information reported or disclosed shall be kept for the confidential use of the APN Board, the APN Board's attorneys, the investigative staff, and authorized clerical staff and shall be afforded the same status as is provided information concerning medical studies in Part 21 of Article VIII of the Code of Civil Procedure.

(c) Immunity from Prosecution.

An individual or organization acting in good faith, and not in a wilful and wanton manner, in complying with this Title by providing a report or other information to the APN Board, by assisting in the investigation or preparation of a report or information, by participating in proceedings of the APN Board, or by serving as a member of the Board shall not, as a result of such actions, be subject to criminal prosecution or civil damages.

(d) Indemnification.

Members of the APN Board, the APN Board's attorneys, the investigative staff, advanced practice nurses or physicians retained under contract to assist and advise in the investigation, and authorized clerical staff shall be indemnified by the State for any actions

(i) occurring within the scope of services on the APN Board,

(ii) performed in good faith, and

(iii) not wilful and wanton in nature. The Attorney General shall defend all actions taken against those persons unless he or she determines either that there would be a conflict of interest in the representation or that the actions complained of were not performed in good faith or were wilful and wanton in nature. If the Attorney General declines representation, the member shall have the right to employ counsel of his or her choice, whose fees shall be provided by the State, after approval by the Attorney General, unless there is a determination by a court that the member's actions were not performed in good faith or were wilful and wanton in nature. The member shall notify the Attorney General within 7 days of receipt of notice of the initiation of an action involving services of the APN Board. Failure to so notify the Attorney General shall constitute an absolute waiver of the right to a defense and indemnification. The Attorney General shall determine within 7 days after receiving the notice whether he or she will undertake to represent the member.

(e) Deliberations of APN Board.

Upon the receipt of a report called for by this Title, other than those reports of impaired persons licensed under this Title required pursuant to the rules of the APN Board, the APN Board shall notify in writing by certified mail the person who is the subject of the report. The notification shall be made within 30 days of receipt by the APN Board of the report. The notification shall include a written notice setting forth the person's right to examine the report. Included in the notification shall be the address at which the file is maintained, the name of the custodian of the reports, and the telephone number at which the custodian may be reached. The person who is the subject of the report shall submit a written statement responding to, clarifying, adding to, or proposing to amend the report previously filed. The statement shall become a permanent part of the file and shall be received by the APN Board no more than 30 days after the date on which the person was notified of the existence of the original report. The APN Board shall review all reports received by it and any supporting information and responding statements submitted by persons who are the subject of reports. The review by the APN Board shall be in a timely manner but in no event shall the APN Board's initial review of the material contained in each disciplinary file be less than 61 days nor more than 180 days after the receipt of the initial report by the APN Board. When the APN Board makes its initial review of the materials contained within its disciplinary files, the APN Board shall, in writing, make a determination as to whether there are sufficient facts to warrant further investigation or action. Failure to make that determination within the time provided shall be deemed to be a determination that there are not sufficient facts to warrant further investigation or action. Should the APN Board find that there are not sufficient facts to warrant further investigation or action, the report shall be accepted for filing and the matter shall be deemed closed and so reported. The individual or entity filing the original report or complaint and the person who is the subject of the report or complaint shall be notified in writing by the APN Board of any final action on their report or complaint.

(f) Summary Reports.

The APN Board shall prepare, on a timely basis, but in no event less than one every other month, a summary report of final actions taken upon disciplinary files maintained by the APN Board. The summary reports shall be sent by the APN Board to every health care facility licensed by the Department of Public Health, every professional association and society of persons licensed under this Title functioning on a statewide basis in this State, all insurers providing professional liability insurance to persons licensed under this Title in this State, and the Illinois Pharmacists Association.

(g) Any violation of this Section shall constitute a Class A misdemeanor.

(h) If a person violates the provisions of this Section, an action may be brought in the name of the People of the State of Illinois, through the Attorney General of the State of Illinois, for an order enjoining the violation or for an order enforcing compliance with this Section. Upon filing of a verified petition in court, the court may issue a temporary restraining order without notice or bond and may preliminarily or permanently enjoin the violation, and if it is established that the person has violated or is violating the injunction, the court may punish the offender for contempt of court. Proceedings under this subsection shall be in addition to, and not in lieu of, all other remedies and penalties provided for by this Section.

§ 20–2. References to Board

References in this Title to the "Board" shall mean the Board of Nursing in the case of an administrative or enforcement matter concerning the practice of practical nursing or professional nursing, and shall mean the Advanced Practice Nursing Board in the case of an administrative or enforcement matter concerning the practice of advanced practice nursing.

§ 20–5. Expiration of license; renewal

The expiration date and renewal period for each license issued under this Act shall be set by rule. The holder of a license may renew the license during the month preceding the expiration date of the license by paying the required fee. It is the responsibility of the licensee to notify the Department in writing of a change of address.

§ 20–10. Restoration of license; temporary permit

(a) Any license issued under this Act that has expired or that is on inactive status may be restored by making application to the Department and filing proof of fitness acceptable to the Department as specified by rule, to have the license restored, and by paying the required restoration fee. Such proof of fitness may include evidence certifying to active lawful practice in another jurisdiction.

However, any license issued under this Act that expired while the licensee was

(1) in federal service on active duty with the Armed Forces of the United States, or the State Militia called into service or training, or

(2) in training or education under the supervision of the United States preliminary to induction into the military service, may have the license restored without paying any lapsed renewal fees if within 2 years after honorable termination of such service, training, or education, the applicant furnishes the Department with satisfactory evidence to the effect that the applicant has been so engaged and that the individual's service, training, or education has been so terminated.

Any licensee who shall engage in the practice of nursing or advanced practice nursing with a lapsed license or while on inactive status shall be considered to be practicing without a license which shall be grounds for discipline under Section 10–30 or Article 15, respectively.

(b) Pending restoration of a license under subsection (a) of this Section, the Department may grant an applicant a temporary license to practice nursing as a registered nurse or as a licensed practical nurse if the Department is satisfied that the applicant holds an active, unencumbered license in good standing in another jurisdiction. If the applicant holds more than one current active license, or one or more active temporary licenses from other jurisdictions, the Department shall not issue a temporary license until it is satisfied that each current active license held by the applicant is unencumbered. The temporary license, which shall be issued no later than 14 working days following receipt by the Department of an application for the license, shall be granted upon the submission of the following to the Department:

(1) a signed and completed application for restoration of licensure under this Section as a registered nurse or a licensed practical nurse;

(2) proof of

(i) a current, active license in at least one other jurisdiction and proof that each current, active license or temporary permit held by the applicant is unencumbered or

(ii) fitness to practice nursing in Illinois as specified by rule;

(3) a signed and completed application for a temporary permit; and

(4) the required permit fee.

(c) The Department may refuse to issue to an applicant a temporary permit authorized under this Section if, within 14 working days following its receipt of an application for a temporary permit, the Department determines that:

(1) the applicant has been convicted within the last 5 years of any crime under the laws of any jurisdiction of the United States that is

(i) a felony or

(ii) a misdemeanor directly related to the practice of the profession;

(2) within the last 5 years the applicant had a license or permit related to the practice of nursing revoked, suspended, or placed on probation by another jurisdiction if at least one of the grounds for revoking, suspending, or placing on probation is the same or substantially equivalent to grounds in Illinois; or

(3) it is determined by the Department that it intends to deny restoration of the license.

For purposes of this Section, an "unencumbered license" means any license against which no disciplinary action has been taken or is pending and for which all fees and charges are paid and current.

(d) The Department may revoke a temporary permit issued under this Section if:

(1) it determines that the applicant has been convicted within the last 5 years of any crime under the law of any jurisdiction of the United States that is

(i) a felony or

(ii) a misdemeanor directly related to the practice of the profession;

(2) within the last 5 years the applicant had a license or permit related to the practice of nursing revoked, suspended, or placed on probation by another jurisdiction, if at least one of the grounds for revoking, suspending, or placing on probation is the same or substantially equivalent to grounds in Illinois; or

(3) it is determined by the Department that it intends to deny restoration of the license.

A temporary permit or renewed temporary permit shall expire

(i) upon issuance of an Illinois license or

(ii) upon notification that the Department intends to deny restoration of licensure. A temporary permit shall expire 6 months from the date of issuance. Further renewal may be granted by the Department, in hardship cases, that shall automatically expire upon issuance of the Illinois license or upon notification that the Department intends to deny licensure, whichever occurs first. No extensions shall be granted beyond the 6 months period unless approved by the Director. Notification by the Department under this Section shall be by certified or registered mail.

§ 20–15. Inactive status

Any nurse who notifies the Department in writing on forms prescribed by the Department, may elect to place her or his license on inactive status and shall, subject to rules of the Department, be excused from payment of renewal fees until notice is given to the Department in writing of her or his intent to restore the license.

Any nurse requesting restoration from inactive status shall be required to pay the current renewal fee and shall be required to restore her or his license, as provided by rule of the Department.

Any nurse whose license is in an inactive status shall not practice nursing in the State of Illinois.

§ 20–25.   Returned checks; fines

Any person who delivers a check or other payment to the Department that is returned to the Department unpaid by the financial institution upon which it is drawn shall pay to the Department, in addition to the amount already owed to the Department, a fine of $50. If the check or other payment was for a renewal or issuance fee and that person practices without paying the renewal fee or issuance fee and the fine due, an additional fine of $100 shall be imposed. The fines imposed by this Section are in addition to any other discipline provided under this Act for unlicensed practice or practice on a non renewed license. The Department shall notify the person that payment of fees and fines shall be paid to the Department by certified check or money order within 30 calendar days of the notification. If, after the expiration of 30 days from the date of the notification, the person has failed to submit the necessary remittance, the Department shall automatically terminate the license or deny the application, without hearing. If, after termination or denial, the person seeks a license, he or she shall apply to the Department for restoration or issuance of the license and pay all fees and fines due to the Department. The Department may establish a fee for the processing of an application for restoration of a license to pay all expenses of processing this application. The Director may waive the fines due under this Section in individual cases where the Director finds that the fines would be unreasonable or unnecessarily burdensome.

§ 20–30.   Roster

The Department shall maintain a roster of the names and addresses of all licensees and of all persons whose licenses have been suspended or revoked. This roster shall be available upon written request and payment of the required fees.

§ 20–35.   Fees

(a) The Department shall provide by rule for a schedule of fees to be paid for licenses by all applicants.

(a–5) Except as provided in subsection (b), the fees for the administration and enforcement of this Act, including but not limited to original licensure, renewal, and restoration, shall be set by rule. The fees shall not be refundable.

(b) In addition, applicants for any examination as a Registered Professional Nurse or a Licensed Practical Nurse shall be required to pay, either to the Department or to the designated testing service, a fee covering the cost of providing the examination. Failure to appear for the examination on the scheduled date, at the time and place specified, after the applicant's application for examination has been received and acknowledged by the Department or the designated testing service, shall result in the forfeiture of the examination fee.

§ 20–40. Fund

There is hereby created within the State Treasury the Nursing Dedicated and Professional Fund. The monies in the Fund may be used by and at the direction of the Department for the administration and enforcement of this Act, including but not limited to:

(a) Distribution and publication of the Nursing and Advanced Practice Nursing Act and the rules at the time of renewal to all persons licensed by the Department under this Act.

(b) Employment of secretarial, nursing, administrative, enforcement, and other staff for the administration of this Act.

(c) Conducting a survey, as prescribed by rule of the Department, once every 4 years during the license renewal period.

(d) Conducting of training seminars for licensees under this Act relating to the obligations, responsibilities, enforcement and other provisions of the Act and its rules.

(e) Disposition of Fees:

* * *

(ii) All of the fees and fines collected pursuant to this Act shall be deposited in the Nursing Dedicated and Professional Fund.

(iii) For the fiscal year beginning July 1, 1988, the moneys deposited in the Nursing Dedicated and Professional Fund shall be appropriated to the Department for expenses of the Department and the Board in the administration of this Act. All earnings received from investment of moneys in the Nursing Dedicated and Professional Fund shall be deposited in the Nursing Dedicated and Professional Fund and shall be used for the same purposes as fees deposited in the Fund.

(iv) For the fiscal year beginning July 1, 1991 and for each fiscal year thereafter, either 10% of the moneys deposited in the Nursing Dedicated and Professional Fund each year, not including interest accumulated on such moneys, or any moneys deposited in the Fund in each year which are in excess of the amount appropriated in that year to meet ordinary and contingent expenses of the Board, whichever is less, shall be set aside and appropriated to the Illinois Department of Public Health for nursing scholarships awarded pursuant to the Nursing Education Scholarship Law.

(v) Moneys in the Fund may be transferred to the Professions Indirect Cost Fund as authorized under Section 2105–300 of the Department of Professional Regulation Law (*20 ILCS 2105/2105–300*).

§ 20–50.   Limitation on action

All proceedings to suspend, revoke, or take any other disciplinary action as the Department may deem proper, with regard to a license on any of the foregoing grounds may not be commenced later than 3 years next after the commission of any act which is a ground for discipline or a final conviction order for any of the acts described herein. In the event of the settlement of any claim or cause of action in favor of the claimant or the reduction to the final judgment of any civil action in favor of the plaintiff, such claim, cause of action or civil action being rounded on the allegation that a person licensed under this Act was negligent in providing care, the Department shall have an additional period of one year from the date of such settlement or final judgment in which to investigate and commence formal disciplinary proceedings under Section 25 of this Act, except as otherwise provided by law. The time during which the holder of the license was outside the State of Illinois shall not be included within any period of time limiting the commencement of disciplinary action by the Board.

§ 20–55.   Suspension for imminent danger

The Director of the Department may, upon receipt of a written communication from the Secretary of Human Services, the Director of Public Aid, or the Director of Public Health that continuation of practice of a person licensed under this Act constitutes an immediate danger to the public, immediately suspend the license of such person without a hearing. In instances in which the Director immediately suspends a license under this Section, a hearing upon such person's license must be convened by the Department within 30 days after such suspension and completed without appreciable delay, such hearing held to determine whether to recommend to the Director that the person's license be revoked, suspended, placed on probationary status or reinstated, or such person be subject to other disciplinary action. In such hearing, the written communication and any other evidence submitted therewith may be introduced as evidence against such person; provided, however, the person, or his or her counsel, shall have the opportunity to discredit or impeach and submit evidence rebutting such evidence.

§ 20–65.   Liability of State

In the event that the Department's order of revocation, suspension, placing the licensee on probationary status, or other order of formal disciplinary action is without any reasonable basis, then the State of Illinois shall be liable to the injured party for those special damages suffered as a direct result of such order.

§ 20–70.   Right to legal counsel

No action of a disciplinary nature that is predicated on charges alleging unethical or unprofessional conduct of a person who is a registered professional nurse or a licensed practical nurse and that can be reasonably expected to affect adversely that person's maintenance of her or his present, or her or his securing of future, employment as such a nurse may be taken by the Department, by any association, or by any person unless the person against whom such charges are made is afforded the right to be represented by legal counsel of her or his choosing and to present any witness, whether an attorney or otherwise to testify on matters relevant to such charges.

§ 20–75. Injunctive remedies

(a) If any person violates the provision of this Act, the Director may, in the name of the People of the State of Illinois, through the Attorney General of the State of Illinois, or the State's Attorney of any county in which the action is brought, petition for an order enjoining such violation or for an order enforcing compliance with this Act. Upon the filing of a verified petition in court, the court may issue a temporary restraining order, without notice or bond, and may preliminarily and permanently enjoin such violation, and if it is established that such person has violated or is violating the injunction, the court may punish the offender for contempt of court. Proceedings under this Section shall be in addition to, and not in lieu of, all other remedies and penalties provided by this Act.

(b) If any person shall practice as a nurse or hold herself or himself out as a nurse without being licensed under the provisions of this Act, then any licensed nurse, any interested party, or any person injured thereby may, in addition to the Director, petition for relief as provided in subsection (a) of this Section.

Whoever knowingly practices or offers to practice nursing in this State without a license for that purpose shall be guilty of a Class A misdemeanor and for each subsequent conviction, shall be guilty of a Class 4 felony. All criminal fines, monies, or other property collected or received by the Department under this Section or any other State or federal statute, including, but not limited to, property forfeited to the Department under Section 505 of the Illinois Controlled Substances Act, shall be deposited into the Professional Regulation Evidence Fund.

(c) Whenever in the opinion of the Department any person violates any provision of this Act, the Department may issue a rule to show cause why an order to cease and desist should not be entered against him. The rule shall clearly set forth the grounds relied upon by the Department and shall provide a period of 7 days from the date of the rule to file an answer to the satisfaction of the Department. Failure to answer to the satisfaction of the Department shall cause an order to cease and desist to be issued forthwith.

§ 20–80. Investigation; notice; hearing

Prior to bringing an action before the Board, the Department may investigate the actions of any applicant or of any person or persons holding or claiming to hold a license. The Department shall, before suspending, revoking, placing on probationary status, or taking any other disciplinary action as the

Department may deem proper with regard to any license, at least 30 days prior to the date set for the hearing, notify the accused in writing of any charges made and the time and place for a hearing of the charges before the Board, direct her or him to file a written answer thereto to the Board under oath within 20 days after the service of such notice and inform the licensee that if she or he fails to file such answer default will be taken against the licensee and such license may be suspended, revoked, placed on probationary status, or have other disciplinary action, including limiting the scope, nature or extent of her or his practice, as the Department may deem proper taken with regard thereto. Such written notice may be served by personal delivery or certified or registered mail to the respondent at the address of her or his last notification to the Department. At the time and place fixed in the notice, the Department shall proceed to hear the charges and the parties or their counsel shall be accorded ample opportunity to present such statements, testimony, evidence and argument as may be pertinent to the charges or to the defense to the charges. The Department may continue a hearing from time to time. In case the accused person, after receiving notice, fails to file an answer, her or his license may in the discretion of the Director, having received first the recommendation of the Board, be suspended, revoked, placed on probationary status, or the Director may take whatever disciplinary action as he or she may deem proper, including limiting the scope, nature, or extent of said person's practice, without a hearing, if the act or acts charged constitute sufficient grounds for such action under this Act.

§ 20–85. Stenographer; transcript

The Department, at its expense, shall provide a stenographer to take down the testimony and preserve a record of all proceedings at the hearing of any case wherein any disciplinary action is taken regarding a license. The notice of hearing, complaint and all other documents in the nature of pleadings and written motions filed in the proceedings, the transcript of testimony, the report of the Board and the orders of the Department shall be the record of the proceedings. The Department shall furnish a transcript of the record to any person interested in the hearing upon payment of the fee required under Section 2105–115 of the Department of Professional Regulation Law (*20 ILCS 2105/2105–115*).

§ 20–90. Compelled testimony and production of documents

Any circuit court may, upon application of the Department or designee or of the applicant or licensee against whom proceedings upon Section 20–80 of this Act are pending, enter an order requiring the attendance of witnesses and their testimony, and the production of documents, papers, files, books and records in connection with any hearing or investigation. The court may compel obedience to its order by proceedings for contempt.

§ 20–95.   Subpoena power; oaths

The Department shall have power to subpoena and bring before it any person in this State and to take testimony, either orally or by deposition or both, with the same fees and mileage and in the same manner as prescribed by law in judicial proceedings in civil cases in circuit courts of this State.

The Director and any member of the Board designated by the Director shall each have power to administer oaths to witnesses at any hearing which the Department is authorized to conduct under this Act, and any other oaths required or authorized to be administered by the Department under this Act.

§ 20–100.   Board report

At the conclusion of the hearing the Board shall present to the Director a written report of its findings of fact, conclusions of law, and recommendations. The report shall contain a finding whether or not the accused person violated this Act or failed to comply with the conditions required in this Act. The report shall specify the nature of the violation or failure to comply, and the Board shall make its recommendations to the Director.

The report of findings of fact, conclusions of law, and recommendation of the Board shall be the basis for the Department's order of refusal or for the granting of a license or permit unless the Director shall determine that the report is contrary to the manifest weight of the evidence, in which case the Director may issue an order in contravention of the report. The findings are not admissible in evidence against the person in a criminal prosecution brought for the violation of this Act, but the hearing and findings are not a bar to a criminal prosecution brought for the violation of this Act.

§ 20–105.   Hearing officer

The Director shall have the authority to appoint an attorney duly licensed to practice law in the State of Illinois to serve as the hearing officer in any action before the Board to revoke, suspend, place on probation, reprimand, fine, or take any other disciplinary action with regard to a license. The hearing officer shall have full authority to conduct the hearing. The Board shall have the right to have at least one member present at any hearing conducted by such hearing officer. There may be present at least one RN member of the Board at any such hearing or disciplinary conference. An LPN member or LPN educator may be present for hearings and disciplinary conferences of an LPN. The hearing officer shall report her or his findings and recommendations to the Board within 30 days of the receipt of the record. The Board shall have 90 days from receipt of the report to review the report of the hearing officer and present their findings of fact, conclusions of law and recommendations to the Director. If the Board fails to present its report within the 90–day period, the Director may issue an order based on the report of the hearing officer. However, if the Board does present its report within the specified 90 days, the Director's order shall be based upon the report of the Board.

§ 20–110. Motion for rehearing

In any case involving refusal to issue, renew, or the discipline of a license, a copy of the Board's report shall be served upon the respondent by the Department, either personally or as provided in this Act, for the service of the notice of hearing. Within 20 days after such service, the respondent may present to the Department a motion in writing for a rehearing, which motion shall specify the particular grounds for a rehearing. If no motion for rehearing is filed, then upon the expiration of the time then upon such denial the Director may enter an order in accordance with recommendations of the Board except as provided in Sections 20–100 and 20–105 of this Act. If the respondent shall order from the reporting service, and pay for a transcript of the record within the time for filing a motion for rehearing, the 20 day period within which such a motion may be filed shall commence upon the delivery of the transcript to the respondent.

§ 20–115. Order for rehearing

Whenever the Director is satisfied that substantial justice has not been done in the revocation, suspension, or refusal to issue or renew a license, the Director may order a hearing by the same or another hearing officer or the Board.

§ 20–120. Order of Director

An order regarding any disciplinary action or a certified copy thereof, over the seal of the Department and purporting to be signed by the Director, shall be prima facie evidence that:

(a) the signature is the genuine signature of the Director;

(b) the Director is duly appointed and qualified; and

(c) the Board and the Board members are qualified to act.

§ 20–125. Restoration after suspension or revocation

At any time after the suspension or revocation of any license, the Department may restore it to the accused person unless, after an investigation and a hearing, the Department determines that restoration is not in the public interest.

§ 20–130. Surrender of license

Upon revocation or suspension of any license, the licensee shall forthwith surrender the license to the Department and if the licensee fails to do so, the Department shall have the right to seize the license.

§ 20–135. Temporary suspension

The Director may temporarily suspend the license of a nurse without a hearing, simultaneously with the institution of proceedings for a hearing provided for in Section 20–80 of this Act, if the Director finds that evidence in his or her possession indicates that continuation in practice would constitute an imminent danger to the public. In the event that the Director suspends, temporarily, this license without a hearing, a hearing by the Department must be held within 30 days after the suspension has occurred, and be concluded without appreciable delay.

Proceedings for judicial review shall be commenced in the circuit court of the county in which the party applying for review resides; but if the party is not a resident of this State, the venue shall be in Sangamon County.

§ 20–140. Administrative Review Law

All final administrative decisions of the Department hereunder shall be subject to judicial review pursuant to the revisions of the Administrative Review Law, and all amendments and modifications thereof, and the rule adopted pursuant thereto. The term "administrative decision" is defined as in Section 3–101 of the Code of Civil Procedure.

§ 20–145. Certification of record

The Department shall not be required to certify any record to the Court or file any answer in court or otherwise appear in any court in a judicial review proceeding, unless there is filed in the court, with the complaint, a receipt from the Department acknowledging payment of the costs of furnishing and certifying the record. Failure on the part of the plaintiff to file such receipt in Court shall be grounds for dismissal of the action.

§ 20–150. Criminal penalties

Any person who is found to have violated any provision of this Act is guilty of a Class A misdemeanor. On conviction of a second or subsequent offense, the violator shall be guilty of a Class 4 felony.

* * *

§ 20–160. Illinois Administrative Procedure Act

The Illinois Administrative Procedure Act is hereby expressly adopted and incorporated herein as if all of the provisions of that Act were included in this Act, except that the provision of subsection (d) of Section 10–65 of the Illinois Administrative Procedure Act that provides that at hearings the licensee has the right to show compliance with all lawful requirements for retention, continuation or renewal of the license is specifically excluded. For the purposes of this Act, the notice required under Section 10–25 of the Illinois Administrative Procedure Act is deemed sufficient when mailed to the last known address of a party.

§ 20–165.   Home rule preemption

It is declared to be the public policy of this State, pursuant to paragraphs (h) of *Section 6 of Article VII of the Illinois Constitution of 1970*, that any power or function set forth in this Act to be exercised by the State is an exclusive State power or function. Such power or function shall not be exercised concurrently, either directly or indirectly, by any unit of local government, including home rule units, except as otherwise provided in this Act.

C. LICENSING OF ORIENTAL MEDICINE PRACTITIONERS, WEST'S NEVADA REVISED STATUTES ANNOTATED CHAPTER 634A

§ 634A.010.   Legislative declaration

The practice of Oriental medicine and any branch thereof is hereby declared to be a learned profession, affecting public safety and welfare and charged with the public interest, and therefore subject to protection and regulation by the state.

§ 634A.020.   Definitions

As used in this chapter, unless the context otherwise requires:

1. "Acupuncture" means the insertion of needles into the human body by piercing the skin of the body to control and regulate the flow and balance of energy in the body and to cure, relieve or palliate:

   (a) Any ailment or disease of the mind or body; or

   (b) Any wound, bodily injury or deformity.

2. "Board" means the state board of Oriental medicine.

3. "Doctor of acupuncture" means a person licensed under the provisions of this chapter to practice acupuncture.

4. "Doctor of Oriental medicine" means a person who is licensed under the provisions of this chapter to practice Oriental medicine.

5. "Herbal medicine" and "practice of herbal medicine" mean suggesting, recommending, prescribing or directing the use of herbs for the cure, relief or palliation of any ailment or disease of the mind or body, or for the cure or relief of any wound, bodily injury or deformity.

6. "Herbs" means plants or parts of plants valued for medicinal qualities.

7. "Licensed assistant in acupuncture" means a person who assists in the practice of acupuncture under the direct supervision of a person licensed under the provisions of this chapter to practice Oriental medicine or acupuncture.

8. "Oriental medicine" means that system of the healing art which places the chief emphasis on the flow and balance of energy in the body mechanism as being the most important single factor in maintaining the well-being of the organism in health and disease. The term includes the practice of acupuncture and herbal medicine and other services approved by the board.

§ 634A.030. Creation; number and appointment of members; oaths

1. The state board of Oriental medicine, consisting of five members appointed by the governor, is hereby created.

2. The governor shall appoint to the board:

(a) Three members who are licensed pursuant to this chapter.

(b) Two members who are representatives of the general public.

3. Each member of the board shall, before entering upon the duties of his office, take the oath of office prescribed by the constitution before someone qualified to administer oaths.

§ 634A.040. Qualifications of members

All members of the board shall be citizens of the United States and residents of the State of Nevada.

§ 634A.050. Compensation of members and employees

1. Each member of the board is entitled to receive:

(a) A salary of not more than $80 per day, as fixed by the board, while engaged in the business of the board; and

(b) A per diem allowance and travel expenses at a rate fixed by the board, while engaged in the business of the board. The rate must not exceed the rate provided for state officers and employees generally.

2. While engaged in the business of the board, each employee of the board is entitled to receive a per diem allowance and travel expenses at a rate fixed by the board. The rate must not exceed the rate provided for state officers and employees generally.

§ 634A.060. Officers

The board shall annually elect from its members a president, vice president and secretary-treasurer, and may fix and pay a salary to the secretary-treasurer.

§ 634A.070. Powers

The board may:

1. Employ attorneys, investigators and other professional consultants and clerical personnel necessary to discharge its duties. To conduct its

examinations, the board may call to its aid persons of established reputation and known ability in Oriental medicine.

2. Maintain offices in as many localities in the state as it finds necessary to carry out the provisions of this chapter.

3. Adopt regulations not inconsistent with the provisions of this chapter. The regulations may include a code of ethics regulating the professional conduct of licensees.

4. Compel the attendance of witnesses and the production of evidence by subpoena.

§ 634A.080. Duties

The board shall:

1. Hold meetings at least once a year and at any other time at the request of the president or the majority of the members;

2. Have and use a common seal;

3. Deposit in interest-bearing accounts in the State of Nevada all moneys received under the provisions of this chapter, which shall be used to defray the expenses of the board;

4. Operate on the basis of the fiscal year beginning July 1, and ending June 30; and

5. Keep a record of its proceedings which shall be open to the public at all times and which shall also contain the name and business address of every registered licensee in this state.

§ 634A.090. Approval of schools of Oriental medicine

1. A school or college of Oriental medicine may be established and maintained in this state only if:

   (a) Its establishment is approved by the board; and

   (b) Its curriculum is approved annually by the board for content and quality of instruction in accordance with the requirements of this chapter.

2. The board may prescribe the courses of study required for the respective degrees of doctor of acupuncture and doctor of Oriental medicine.

* * *

§ 634A.110. Application; fees

[Text of section effective until repeal of the federal law requiring states to establish procedures for restricting licenses for persons with child support arrearages or related procedural noncompliance]

1. An applicant for examination for a license to practice Oriental medicine or any branch thereof, shall:

   (a) Submit an application to the board on forms provided by the board;

(b) Submit satisfactory evidence that he is 21 years or older and meets the appropriate educational requirements;

(c) Pay a fee established by the board of not more than $1,000; and

(d) Pay any fees required by the board for an investigation of the applicant or for the services of a translator, if the translator is required to enable the applicant to take the examination.

2. An application submitted to the board pursuant to subsection 1 must include the social security number of the applicant.

§ 634A.115. Payment of child support: Statement by applicant for license; grounds for denial of license; duty of board

1. An applicant for the issuance or renewal of a license issued pursuant to this chapter shall submit to the board the statement prescribed by the welfare division of the department of human resources pursuant to *NRS 425.520.* The statement must be completed and signed by the applicant.

2. The board shall include the statement required pursuant to subsection 1 in:

(a) The application or any other forms that must be submitted for the issuance or renewal of the license; or

(b) A separate form prescribed by the board.

3. A license may not be issued or renewed by the board pursuant to this chapter if the applicant:

(a) Fails to submit the statement required pursuant to subsection 1; or

(b) Indicates on the statement submitted pursuant to subsection 1 that he is subject to a court order for the support of a child and is not in compliance with the order or a plan approved by the district attorney or other public agency enforcing the order for the repayment of the amount owed pursuant to the order.

4. If an applicant indicates on the statement submitted pursuant to subsection 1 that he is subject to a court order for the support of a child and is not in compliance with the order or a plan approved by the district attorney or other public agency enforcing the order for the repayment of the amount owed pursuant to the order, the board shall advise the applicant to contact the district attorney or other public agency enforcing the order to determine the actions that the applicant may take to satisfy the arrearage.

§ 634A.120. Examinations: Times; subjects covered

1. Examinations must be given at least once a year at a time and place fixed by the board.

2. Applicants for licenses to practice acupuncture or Oriental medicine or to practice as an assistant in acupuncture must be examined in the appropriate subjects as determined by the board.

* * *

§ 634A.140. Issuance of license to practice Oriental medicine or acupuncture

The board shall issue separate licenses to practice respectively Oriental medicine or acupuncture, as appropriate, where the applicant:

1. Has successfully completed a course of study of:

   (a) Four years in Oriental medicine; or

   (b) Three years in acupuncture at any college or school approved by the board which is located in any country, territory, province or state or has qualifications considered equivalent by the board;

2. Has practiced Oriental medicine, including acupuncture and herbal medicine for 6 years; and

3. Passes the examination of the board.

§ 634A.150. Issuance of license as assistant in acupuncture

The board shall issue a license for an assistant in acupuncture where the applicant:

1. Has successfully completed a course of study in acupuncture in any college or school approved by the board which is located in any country, territory, province or state requiring an attendance of 3 years or other qualifications deemed by the board to be equivalent to the course of study; and

2. Passes the examination of the board for assistant in acupuncture or has other qualifications deemed by the board to be the equivalent.

§ 634A.160. Display of licenses; annual registration fee; submission of statement; penalty for failure to pay fee or submit statement

[Text of section effective until repeal of the federal law requiring states to establish procedures for restricting licenses for persons with child support arrearages or related procedural noncompliance]

1. Every license must be displayed in the office, place of business or place of employment of the holder thereof.

2. Every person holding a license shall pay to the board on or before February 1 of each year, the annual registration fee required pursuant to subsection 4. The holder of a license shall submit with the registration fee the

statement required pursuant to *NRS 634A.115*. If the holder of a license fails to pay the registration fee or submit the statement, his license must be suspended. The license may be reinstated by payment of the required fee and submission of the statement within 90 days after February 1.

3. A license which is suspended for more than 3 months under the provisions of subsection 2 may be canceled by the board after 30 days' notice to the holder of the license.

4. The annual registration fees must be prescribed annually by the board and must not exceed $1,000.

§ 634A.160. Display of licenses; annual fee for registration; penalty for failure to pay fee

[Text of section effective upon repeal of the federal law requiring states to establish procedures for restricting licenses for persons with child support arrearages or related procedural noncompliance]

1. Every license must be displayed in the office, place of business or place of employment of the holder thereof.

2. Every person holding a license shall pay to the board on or before February 1 of each year, the annual registration fee required pursuant to subsection 4. If the holder of a license fails to pay the registration fee his license must be suspended. The license may be reinstated by payment of the required fee within 90 days after February 1.

3. A license which is suspended for more than 3 months under the provisions of subsection 2 may be canceled by the board after 30 days' notice to the holder of the license.

4. The annual registration fees must be prescribed annually by the board and must not exceed $1,000.

§ 634A.165. Issuance of temporary certificates for lecturing or educational seminars

1. The board may adopt regulations for the issuance of temporary certificates to persons not licensed pursuant to this chapter. A temporary certificate may be issued:

  (a) In connection with a bona fide educational seminar concerning Oriental medicine or acupuncture; or

  (b) For the purpose of authorizing a person to engage in lecturing on or teaching Oriental medicine or acupuncture in this state on a short-term basis.

2. The board may charge a fee for the issuance of a temporary certificate. The fee must not exceed an amount which adequately reimburses the board for costs incurred in:

  (a) Investigating an applicant under this section; and

(b) Monitoring a seminar, if the board deems that action necessary.

§ 634A.167.   Requirements for renewal; duty of board to require continuing education for renewal or reinstatement

[Text of section effective until repeal of the federal law requiring states to establish procedures for restricting licenses for persons with child support arrearages or related procedural noncompliance]

1.   To renew a license issued pursuant to this chapter, each person must, on or before February 1 of each year:

(a) Apply to the board for renewal;

(b) Submit the statement required pursuant to *NRS 634A.115*;

(c) Pay the annual fee for registration prescribed by the board; and

(d) Submit evidence to the board of his completion of the requirements for continuing education.

2.   The board shall, as a prerequisite for the renewal or reinstatement of a license, require each holder of a license to comply with the requirements for continuing education adopted by the board.

§ 634A.167.   Requirements for renewal; duty of board to require continuing education for renewal or reinstatement

[Text of section effective upon repeal of the federal law requiring states to establish procedures for restricting licenses for persons with child support arrearages or related procedural noncompliance]

1.   To renew a license issued pursuant to this chapter, each person must, on or before February 1 of each year:

(a) Apply to the board for renewal;

(b) Pay the annual fee for registration prescribed by the board; and

(c) Submit evidence to the board of his completion of the requirements for continuing education.

2.   The board shall, as a prerequisite for the renewal or reinstatement of a license, require each holder of a license to comply with the requirements for continuing education adopted by the board.

§ 634A.170.   Suspension, revocation or refusal of license: Grounds

The board may refuse to issue or may suspend or revoke any license for any one or any combination of the following causes:

1.   Conviction of:

(a) A felony;

(b) Any offense involving moral turpitude;

(c) A violation of any state or federal law regulating the possession, distribution or use of any controlled substance, as shown by a certified copy of the record of the court; or

(d) A violation of any of the provisions of *NRS 616D.200, 616D.220, 616D.240* or *616D.300* to *616D.440*, inclusive;

2. The obtaining of or any attempt to obtain a license or practice in the profession for money or any other thing of value, by fraudulent misrepresentations;

3. Gross or repeated malpractice, which may be evidenced by claims of malpractice settled against a practitioner;

4. Advertising by means of a knowingly false or deceptive statement;

5. Advertising, practicing or attempting to practice under a name other than one's own;

6. Habitual drunkenness or habitual addiction to the use of a controlled substance;

7. Using any false, fraudulent or forged statement or document, or engaging in any fraudulent, deceitful, dishonest or immoral practice in connection with the licensing requirements of this chapter;

8. Sustaining a physical or mental disability which renders further practice dangerous;

9. Engaging in any dishonorable, unethical or unprofessional conduct which may deceive, defraud or harm the public, or which is unbecoming a person licensed to practice under this chapter;

10. Using any false or fraudulent statement in connection with the practice of Oriental medicine or any branch thereof;

11. Violating or attempting to violate, or assisting or abetting the violation of, or conspiring to violate any provision of this chapter;

12. Being adjudicated incompetent or insane;

13. Advertising in an unethical or unprofessional manner;

14. Obtaining a fee or financial benefit for any person by the use of fraudulent diagnosis, therapy or treatment;

15. Willful disclosure of a privileged communication;

16. Failure of a licensee to designate the nature of his practice in the professional use of his name by the term doctor of Oriental medicine, doctor of acupuncture or acupuncture assistant, as the case may be;

17. Willful violation of the law relating to the health, safety or welfare of the public or of the regulations adopted by the state board of health;

18. Administering, dispensing or prescribing any controlled substance, except for the prevention, alleviation or cure of disease or for relief from suffering; and

19. Performing, assisting or advising in the injection of any liquid silicone substance into the human body.

§ 634A.175. Suspension of license for failure to pay child support or comply with certain subpoenas or warrants; reinstatement of license

1. If the board receives a copy of a court order issued pursuant to *NRS 425.540* that provides for the suspension of all professional, occupational and recreational licenses, certificates and permits issued to a person who is the holder of a license issued pursuant to this chapter, the board shall deem the license issued to that person to be suspended at the end of the 30th day after the date on which the court order was issued unless the board receives a letter issued to the holder of the license by the district attorney or other public agency pursuant to *NRS 425.550* stating that the holder of the license has complied with the subpoena or warrant or has satisfied the arrearage pursuant to *NRS 425.560*.

2. The board shall reinstate a license issued pursuant to this chapter that has been suspended by a district court pursuant to *NRS 425.540* if the board receives a letter issued by the district attorney or other public agency pursuant to *NRS 425.550* to the person whose license was suspended stating that the person whose license was suspended has complied with the subpoena or warrant or has satisfied the arrearage pursuant to *NRS 425.560*.

§ 634A.180. Suspension, revocation or refusal of license: Notice and hearing

The board shall not refuse to issue, refuse to renew, suspend or revoke any license for any of the causes enumerated in *NRS 634A.170*, unless the person accused has been given at least 20 days' notice in writing of the charge against him and a hearing by the board. If the board receives a report pursuant to subsection 5 of *NRS 228.420*, a hearing must be held within 30 days after receiving the report.

§ 634A.190. Licensees not subject to chapter 630 of NRS; reference to licensee as physician of Oriental medicine

1. Persons licensed pursuant to this chapter are not subject to the provisions of chapter 630 of NRS [Physicians and Assistants].

2. A person who is licensed pursuant to this chapter to practice Oriental medicine may refer to himself as a physician of Oriental medicine.

§ 634A.200. Applicability of chapter

1. This chapter does not apply to Oriental physicians who are called into this state for consultation.

2. This chapter does not prohibit:

(a) Gratuitous services of druggists or other persons in cases of emergency.

(b) The domestic administration of family remedies.

(c) Any person from assisting any person in the practice of the healing arts licensed under this chapter, except that such person may not insert needles into the skin or prescribe herbal medicine.

§ 634A.210. Reporting vital statistics

Doctors of Oriental medicine and doctors of acupuncture shall observe and are subject to all state and municipal regulations relative to reporting all births and deaths in all matters pertaining to the public health.

§ 634A.225. Seminars not in accordance with board's regulations prohibited; penalty

1. No seminar concerning Oriental medicine or acupuncture may be conducted in this state except in accordance with regulations prescribed by the board for bona fide educational seminars.

2. Any person who violates subsection 1 is guilty of a misdemeanor.

§ 634A.230. Practice without license prohibited; penalty

Any person who represents himself as a practitioner of Oriental medicine, or any branch thereof, or who engages in the practice of Oriental medicine, or any branch thereof, in this state without holding a valid license issued by the board is guilty of a gross misdemeanor.

§ 634A.240. Injunctive relief

1. The board may maintain in any court of competent jurisdiction a suit for an injunction against any person who violates any provision of this chapter.

2. Such an injunction:

(a) May be issued without proof of actual damage sustained by any person, this provision being understood to be a preventive as well as a punitive measure.

(b) Shall not relieve such person from any criminal prosecution for the violation.

§ 634A.250. Administrative fines; recovery of costs and attorney's fees by board

1. In addition to any other penalties prescribed by law, the board may, after notice and hearing, impose upon any person who violates any provision of this chapter or the regulations adopted pursuant thereto an administrative fine of not more than $2,500.

2. If discipline is imposed pursuant to this chapter, the costs of the proceeding, including investigative costs and attorney's fees, may be recovered by the board.

IX. STATE STATUTES RELATING TO MEDICAL MALPRACTICE

A. NEW MEXICO MEDICAL MALPRACTICE ACT, NMSA 41–5–1 ET SEQ.

§ 41–5–1. Short title

Chapter 41, Article 5 NMSA 1978 may be cited as the "Medical Malpractice Act".

§ 41–5–2. Purpose of act

The purpose of the Medical Malpractice Act [this article] is to promote the health and welfare of the people of New Mexico by making available professional liability insurance for health care providers in New Mexico.

§ 41–5–3. Definitions

As used in the Medical Malpractice Act [this article]:

A. "health care provider" means a person, corporation, organization, facility or institution licensed or certified by this state to provide health care or professional services as a doctor of medicine, hospital, outpatient health care facility, doctor of osteopathy, chiropractor, podiatrist, nurse anesthetist or physician's assistant;

B. "insurer" means an insurance company engaged in writing health care provider malpractice liability insurance in this state;

C. "malpractice claim" includes any cause of action arising in this state against a health care provider for medical treatment, lack of medical treatment or other claimed departure from accepted standards of health care which proximately results in injury to the patient, whether the patient's claim or cause of action sounds in tort or contract, and includes but is not limited to actions based on battery or wrongful death; "malpractice claim" does not include a cause of action arising out of the driving, flying or nonmedical acts involved in the operation, use or maintenance of a vehicular or aircraft ambulance;

D. "medical care and related benefits" means all reasonable medical, surgical, physical rehabilitation and custodial services and includes drugs, prosthetic devices and other similar materials reasonably necessary in the provision of such services;

E. "patient" means a natural person who received or should have received health care from a licensed health care provider, under a contract, express or implied; and

F.   "superintendent" means the superintendent of insurance of this state.

§ 41–5–4.   Ad damnum clause

A patient or his representative having a malpractice claim for bodily injury or death may file a complaint in any court of law having requisite jurisdiction and demand right of trial by jury. No dollar amount or figure shall be included in the demand in any complaint asserting a malpractice claim and filed after the effective date of this section, but the request shall be for such damages as are reasonable. This section shall not prevent a patient or his representative from alleging a requisite jurisdictional amount in a malpractice claim filed in a court requiring such an allegation.

§ 41–5–5   Qualifications

A.   To be qualified under the provisions of the Medical Malpractice Act [this article], a health care provider shall:

(1) establish its financial responsibility by filing proof with the superintendent that the health care provider is insured by a policy of malpractice liability insurance issued by an authorized insurer in the amount of at least two hundred thousand dollars ($200,000) per occurrence or for an individual health care provider, excluding hospitals and outpatient health care facilities, by having continuously on deposit the sum of six hundred thousand dollars ($600,000) in cash with the superintendent or such other like deposit as the superintendent may allow by rule or regulation; provided that in the absence of an additional deposit or policy as required by this subsection, the deposit or policy shall provide coverage for not more than three separate occurrences; and

(2) pay the surcharge assessed on health care providers by the superintendent pursuant to Section 41–5–25 NMSA 1978.

B.   For hospitals or outpatient health care facilities electing to be covered under the Medical Malpractice Act, the superintendent shall determine, based on a risk assessment of each hospital or outpatient health care facility, each hospital's or outpatient health care facility's base coverage or deposit and additional charges for the patient's compensation fund. The superintendent shall arrange for an actuarial study, as provided in Section 41–5–25 NMSA 1978.

C.   A health care provider not qualifying under this section shall not have the benefit of any of the provisions of the Medical Malpractice Act in the event of a malpractice claim against it.

§ 41–5–6.   Limitation of recovery

A.   Except for punitive damages and medical care and related benefits, the aggregate dollar amount recoverable by all persons for or arising from any injury or death to a patient as a result of malpractice shall not exceed six hundred thousand dollars ($600,000) per occurrence. In jury cases, the jury shall not be given any instructions dealing with this limitation.

B.   The value of accrued medical care and related benefits shall not be subject to the six hundred thousand dollar ($600,000) limitation.

C.   Monetary damages shall not be awarded for future medical expenses in malpractice claims.

D.   A health care provider's personal liability is limited to two hundred thousand dollars ($200,000) for monetary damages and medical care and related benefits as provided in Section 41–5–7 NMSA 1978. Any amount due from a judgment or settlement in excess of two hundred thousand dollars ($200,000) shall be paid from the patient's compensation fund, as provided in Section 41–5–25 NMSA 1978.

E.   For the purposes of Subsections A and B of this section, the six hundred thousand dollar ($600,000) aggregate amount recoverable by all persons for or arising from any injury or death to a patient as a result of malpractice shall apply only to malpractice occurring on or after April 1, 1995.

§ 41–5–7.   Future medical expenses

A.   In all malpractice claims where liability is established, the jury shall be given a special interrogatory asking if the patient is in need of future medical care and related benefits. No inquiry shall be made concerning the value of future medical care and related benefits, and evidence relating to the value of future medical care shall not be admissible. In actions upon malpractice claims tried to the court, where liability is found, the court's findings shall include a recitation that the patient is or is not in need of future medical care and related benefits.

B.   Except as provided in Section 41–5–10 NMSA 1978, once a judgment is entered in favor of a patient who is found to be in need of future medical care and related benefits or a settlement is reached between a patient and health care provider in which the provision of medical care and related benefits is agreed upon, and continuing as long as medical or surgical attention is reasonably necessary, the patient shall be furnished with all medical care and related benefits directly or indirectly made necessary by the health care provider's malpractice, subject to a semi-private room limitation in the event of hospitalization, unless the patient refuses to allow them to be so furnished.

C.   Awards of future medical care and related benefits shall not be subject to the six hundred thousand dollar ($600,000) limitation imposed in Section 41–5–6 NMSA 1978.

D.   Payment for medical care and related benefits shall be made as expenses are incurred.

E.   The health care provider shall be liable for all medical care and related benefit payments until the total payments made by or on behalf of it for monetary damages and medical care and related benefits combined equals two hundred thousand dollars ($200,000), after which the payments shall be made by the patient's compensation fund.

F.   This section shall not be construed to prevent a patient and a health care provider from entering into a settlement agreement whereby medical care and related benefits shall be provided for a limited period of time only or to a limited degree.

G.   The court in a supplemental proceeding shall estimate the value of the future medical care and related benefits reasonably due the patient on the basis of evidence presented to it. That figure shall not be included in any award or judgment but shall be included in the record as a separate court finding.

H.   A judgment of punitive damages against a health care provider shall be the personal liability of the health care provider. Punitive damages shall not be paid from the patient's compensation fund or from the proceeds of the health care provider's insurance contract unless the contract expressly provides coverage. Nothing in Section 41–5–6 NMSA 1978 precludes the award of punitive damages to a patient. Nothing in this subsection authorizes the imposition of liability for punitive damages on a derivative basis where that imposition would not be otherwise authorized by law.

§ 41–5–8.   Medical benefits prior to judgment

A health care provider named as a defendant in a malpractice claim, or named as a respondent in a proceeding before the medical review commission created in the Medical Malpractice Act [this article], shall have the option of paying for the patient's medical care and related benefits at any time prior to the entry of a judgment. Except as provided in Section 11 [41–5–11 NMSA 1978] of the Medical Malpractice Act, evidence of a health care provider's payment for such benefits shall not be admissible in the trial of the malpractice claim brought against it.

§ 41–5–9.   District court; continuing jurisdiction

A.   The district court from which final judgment issues shall have continuing jurisdiction in cases where medical care and related benefits are awarded pursuant to Section 7 [41–5–7 NMSA 1978].

B.   In all cases where the patient's continued need of such benefits, or the degree to which such benefits are needed is challenged at a point in time after a judgment is entered, the court, sitting without a jury, shall determine whether such need continues to exist and the extent of such need.

C.   Whenever a patient petitions the district court for an increase in medical care and related benefits, the petition shall be set down for hearing at the earliest possible time and takes precedence over all matters except older matters of the same character and motions for preliminary injunctions * * *.

D.   The health care provider shall have the burden of proving that the patient's need for benefits has subsided or abated, or that medical care and related benefits are not reasonably necessary, which it shall establish by clear and convincing evidence. The patient shall have the burden of proving that his need for medical care and related benefits has increased, which he shall establish by a preponderance of the evidence.

§ 41–5–10. Patient; future examinations and hearings

A. Any health care provider shall be entitled to have a physical examination of the patient by a physician of the health care provider's choice from time to time for the purpose of determining the patient's continued need of medical care and related benefits, subject to the following requirements:

(1) notice in writing shall be delivered to or served upon the patient specifying the time and place where it is intended to conduct the examination. Such notice must be given at least ten days prior to the time stated in the notice. Delivery by certified mail is permitted;

(2) such examination shall be by a physician qualified to practice medicine under the law of this state or of the state or county wherein the patient resides;

(3) the place at which such examination is to be conducted shall not involve an unreasonable amount of travel for the patient considering all the circumstances. It shall not be necessary for a patient who resides outside this state to come into this state for such an examination unless so ordered by the court;

(4) within thirty days after the examination, the patient shall be compensated by the party requesting the examination for all necessary and reasonable expenses incidental to submitting to the examination including the reasonable cost of travel, meals, lodging, loss of pay or other like direct expense;

(5) examinations may not be required more frequently than at six-month intervals; except that upon application to the court having jurisdiction of the claim and after reasonable cause shown therefor, examination within a shorter interval may be ordered. In considering such application, the court should exercise care to prevent harassment to the patient;

(6) the patient shall be entitled to have a physician or an attorney of his own choice or both present at such examination. The patient shall pay such physician or attorney himself; and

(7) the patient shall be promptly furnished with a copy of the report of the physical examination made by the physician making the examination on behalf of the health care provider.

B. If a patient fails or refuses to submit to examination in accordance with the notice and if the requirements of Subsection A of this section have been satisfied, the court may forfeit all medical care and related benefits which would accrue or become due to him except for such failure or refusal to submit to examination during the period that he willfully persists in such failure or refusal.

C. If any patient shall persist in any injurious practice which imperils, retards or impairs his recovery or increases his injury or refuses to submit to such medical or surgical treatment as is reasonably essential to promote his recovery, the court may in its discretion reduce or suspend his medical care and related benefits until the injurious practice is discontinued.

D. Any physician selected by the health care provider and paid by the health care provider who shall make or be present at an examination of the patient conducted in pursuance of this section may be required to testify as to the conduct thereof and the findings made. Communications made by the patient upon such examination to such physician or physicians shall not be considered privileged.

E. The health care provider or the custodian of the patient's compensation fund shall pay all reasonable legal fees, cost of medical examinations and the cost of the fees of medical expert witnesses in any proceeding in which the patient succeeds in raising his medical care and related benefits or in any unsuccessful proceeding brought by the health care provider or the patient's compensation fund custodian to reduce medical care and related benefits.

§ 41-5-11. Set-off of advance payments

A. Evidence of an advance payment is not admissible until there is a final judgment in favor of the patient, in which event the court shall reduce the judgment to the patient to the extent of the advance payment. In jury cases where there is a factual dispute concerning an alleged advance payment, all questions of fact relating to such an advance payment shall be resolved by the jury after it has reached its verdict. The advance payment shall inure to the exclusive benefit of the health care provider or a party making the payment in its behalf. In the event the advance payment exceeds the liability of the defendant or the insurer making it, the court shall order any adjustment necessary to equitably apportion the amount which each defendant is obligated to pay, exclusive of costs. In no case shall an advance payment in excess of an award be repayable by the person receiving it.

B. If a health care provider should elect to pay for medical care and related benefits at any time prior to the entry of a judgment, as provided in Section 8 [41-5-8 NMSA 1978] of the Medical Malpractice Act, and subsequently is found not to be liable, its legal and equitable right of recovery for all such payments shall not be foreclosed or prejudiced in any way.

§ 41-5-12. Claims for compensation not assignable

A patient's claim for compensation under the Medical Malpractice Act [this article] is not assignable.

§ 41–5–13. Limitations

No claim for malpractice arising out of an act of malpractice which occurred subsequent to the effective date of the Medical Malpractice may be brought against a health care provider unless filed within three years after the date that the act of malpractice occurred except that a minor under the full age of six years shall have until his ninth birthday in which to file. This subsection [section] applies to all persons regardless of minority or other legal disability.

§ 41–5–14. Medical review commission

A.   The New Mexico medical review commission is created. The function of the New Mexico medical review commission is to provide panels to review all malpractice claims against health care providers covered by the Medical Malpractice Act [this article].

B.   Those eligible to sit on a panel shall consist of health care providers licensed pursuant to New Mexico law and residing in New Mexico and the members of the state bar.

C.   Cases which a panel will consider include all cases involving any alleged act of malpractice occurring in New Mexico by health care providers qualified under the Medical Malpractice Act.

D.   An attorney shall submit a case for the consideration of a panel, prior to filing a complaint in any district court or other court sitting in New Mexico, by addressing an application, in writing, signed by the patient or his attorney, to the director of the medical review commission.

E.   The director of the medical review commission will be an attorney appointed by and serving at the pleasure of the chief justice of the New Mexico supreme court.

F.   The chief justice shall set the director's salary and report the same to the superintendent in his capacity as custodian of the patient's compensation fund.

§ 41–5–15. Commission decision required; application

A.   No malpractice action may be filed in any court against a qualifying health care provider before application is made to the medical review commission and its decision is rendered.

B.   This application shall contain the following:

(1) a brief statement of the facts of the case, naming the persons involved, the dates and the circumstances, so far as they are known, of the alleged act or acts of malpractice; and

(2) a statement authorizing the panel to obtain access to all medical and hospital records and information pertaining to the matter giving rise to the application, and, for the purposes of its consideration of the matter only, waiving any claim of privilege as to the contents of those records.

Nothing in that statement shall in any way be construed as waiving that privilege for any other purpose or in any other context, in or out of court.

§ 41–5–16. Application procedure

A. Upon receipt of an application for review, the commission's director or his delegate shall cause to be served a true copy of the application on the health care providers involved. Service shall be effected pursuant to New Mexico law. If the health care provider involved chooses to retain legal counsel, his attorney shall informally enter his appearance with the director.

B. The health care provider shall answer the application for review and in addition shall submit a statement authorizing the panel to obtain access to all medical and hospital records and information pertaining to the matter giving rise to the application, and, for the purposes of its consideration of the matter only, waiving any claim of privilege as to the contents of those records. Nothing in that statement shall in any way be construed as waiving that privilege for any other purpose or in any other context, in or out of court.

C. In instances where applications are received employing the theory of respondeat superior or some other derivative theory of recovery, the director shall forward such applications to the state professional societies, associations or licensing boards of both the individual health care provider whose alleged malpractice caused the application to be filed, and the health care provider named a respondent as employer, master or principal.

§ 41–5–17. Panel selection

A. Applications for review shall be promptly transmitted by the director to the directors of the health care provider's state professional society or association and the state bar association, who shall each select three panelists within thirty days from the date of transmittal of the application.

B. If no state professional society or association exists, or if the health care provider does not belong to such a society or association, the director shall transmit the application to the health care provider's state licensing board, which shall in turn select three persons from the health care provider's profession and, where applicable, to [two] persons specializing in the same field or discipline as the health care provider.

C. In cases where there are multiple defendants, the case against each health care provider may be reviewed by a separate panel, or a single combined panel may review the claim against all parties defendant, at the discretion of the director.

D. Three panel members from the health care provider's profession and three panel members from the state bar association shall sit in review in each case.

E. In those cases where the theory of respondeat superior or some other derivative theory of recovery is employed, two of the panel members shall be chosen from the individual health care provider's profession and one panel member shall be chosen from the profession of the health care provider named a respondent employer, master or principal.

F.   The director of the commission or his delegate, who shall be an attorney, shall sit on each panel and serve as chairman.

G.   Any member shall disqualify himself from consideration of any case in which, by virtue of his circumstances, he feels his presence on the panel would be inappropriate, considering the purpose of the panel. The director may excuse a proposed panelist from serving.

H.   Whenever a party shall make and file an affidavit that a panel member selected pursuant to this section cannot, according to the belief of the party making the affidavit, sit in review of the application with impartiality, that panel member shall proceed no further. Another panel member shall be selected by the health care provider's professional association, state licensing board or the state bar association, as the case may be. A party may not disqualify more than three proposed panel members in this manner in any single malpractice claim.

§ 41–5–19.   Hearing procedures

A.   At the time set for hearing, the attorney submitting the case for review shall be present and shall make a brief introduction of his case, including a resume of the facts constituting alleged professional malpractice which he is prepared to prove. The health care provider against whom the claim is brought and its attorney may be present and may make an introductory statement of its case.

B.   Both parties may call witnesses to testify before the panel, which witnesses shall be sworn. Medical texts, journals, studies and other documentary evidence relied upon by either party may be offered and admitted if relevant. Written statements of fact of treating health care providers may be reviewed. The monetary damages in any case shall not be a subject of inquiry or discussion.

C.   The hearing will be informal and no official transcript shall be made. Nothing contained in this paragraph shall preclude the taking of the testimony by the parties at their own expense.

D.   At the conclusion of the hearing, the panel may take the case under advisement or it may request that additional facts, records, witnesses or other information be obtained and presented to it at a supplemental hearing, which shall be set for a date and time certain, not longer than thirty days from the date of the original hearing unless the attorney bringing the matter for review shall in writing consent to a longer period.

E.   Any supplemental hearing shall be held in the same manner as the original hearing, and the parties concerned and their attorneys may be present.

§ 41-5-20. Panel deliberations and decision

A. The deliberations of the panel shall be and remain confidential. Upon consideration of all the relevant material, the panel shall decide only two questions:

(1) whether there is substantial evidence that the acts complained of occurred and that they constitute malpractice; and

(2) whether there is a reasonable medical probability that the patient was injured thereby.

B. All votes of the panel on the two questions for decision shall be by secret ballot. The decision shall be by a majority vote of those voting members of the panel who have sat on the entire case. The decision shall be communicated in writing to the parties and attorneys concerned and a copy thereof shall be retained in the permanent files of the commission.

C. The decision shall in every case be signed for the panel by the chairman, who shall vote only in the event the other members of the panel are evenly divided, and shall contain only the conclusions reached by a majority of its members and the number of members, if any, dissenting therefrom; provided, however, that if the vote is not unanimous, the majority may briefly explain the reasoning and basis for their conclusion, and the dissenters may likewise explain the reasons for disagreement.

D. The report of the medical review panel shall not be admissible as evidence in any action subsequently brought in a court of law. A copy of the report shall be sent to the health care provider's professional licensing board.

E. Panelists and witnesses shall have absolute immunity from civil liability for all communications, findings, opinions and conclusions made in the course and scope of duties prescribed by the Medical Malpractice Act [this article].

F. The panel's decisions shall be without administrative or judicial authority and shall not be binding on any party. The panel shall make no effort to settle or compromise any claim nor express any opinion on the monetary value of any claim.

§ 41-5-21. Director; rules of procedure

The director is authorized to adopt and publish rules of procedure necessary to implement and carry out the duties of the medical review commission. No rule shall be adopted, however, which requires a party to make a monetary payment as a condition to bringing a malpractice claim before the medical review panel.

§ 41-5-22. Tolling of statute of limitation

The running of the applicable limitation period in a malpractice claim shall be tolled upon submission of the case for the consideration of the panel and shall not commence to run again until thirty days after the panel's final decision is entered in the permanent files of the commission and a copy is served upon the claimant and his attorney by certified mail.

§ 41–5–23. Provision of expert witness

In any malpractice claim where the panel has determined that the acts complained of were or reasonably might constitute malpractice and that the patient was or may have been injured by the act, the panel, its members, the director and the professional association concerned will cooperate fully with the patient in retaining a physician qualified in the field of medicine involved, who will consult with, assist in trial preparation and testify on behalf of the patient, upon his payment of a reasonable fee to the same effect as if the physician had been engaged originally by the patient.

§ 41–5–24. Maintenance of records

The director shall maintain records of all proceedings before the medical review commission which shall include the nature of the acts or omissions complained of, a brief summary of the evidence presented, the decision of the panel and any majority or dissenting opinions filed. Such records shall not be made public and shall not be subject to subpoena but shall be used solely for the purpose of compiling statistical data and facilitating on-going studies of medical malpractice in New Mexico.

§ 41–5–25. Patient's compensation fund

A. There is created in the state treasury a "patient's compensation fund" to be collected and received by the superintendent for exclusive use for the purposes stated in the Medical Malpractice Act [Chapter 41, Article 5 NMSA 1978]. The fund and any income from it shall be held in trust, deposited in a segregated account, invested and reinvested by the superintendent with the prior approval of the state board of finance and shall not become a part of or revert to the general fund of this state. The fund and any income from the fund shall only be expended for the purposes of and to the extent provided in the Medical Malpractice Act. The superintendent shall have the authority to use fund money to purchase insurance for the fund and its obligations. The superintendent, as custodian of the patient's compensation fund, shall be notified by the health care provider or his insurer within thirty days of service on the health care provider of a complaint asserting a malpractice claim brought in a court in this state against the health care provider.

B. To create the patient's compensation fund, an annual surcharge shall be levied on all health care providers qualifying under Paragraph (1) of Subsection A of Section 41–5–5 NMSA 1978 in New Mexico. The surcharge shall be determined by the superintendent based upon sound actuarial principles, using data obtained from New Mexico experience if available. The surcharge shall be collected on the same basis as premiums by each insurer from the health care provider.

C. The surcharge with accrued interest shall be due and payable within thirty days after the premiums for malpractice liability insurance have been received by the insurer from the health care provider in New Mexico.

D. If the annual premium surcharge is collected but not paid within the time limit specified in Subsection C of this section, the certificate of authority of the insurer may be suspended until the annual premium surcharge is paid.

E. All expenses of collecting, protecting and administering the patient's compensation fund or of purchasing insurance for the fund shall be paid from the fund.

F. Claims payable pursuant to Laws 1976, Chapter 2, Section 30 shall be paid in accordance with the payment schedule constructed by the court. If the patient's compensation fund would be exhausted by payment of all claims allowed during a particular calendar year, then the amounts paid to each patient and other parties obtaining judgments shall be prorated, with each such party receiving an amount equal to the percentage his own payment schedule bears to the total of payment schedules outstanding and payable by the fund. Any amounts due and unpaid as a result of such proration shall be paid in the following calendar years. However, payments for medical care and related benefits shall be made before any payment made under Laws 1976, Chapter 2, Section 30.

G. Upon receipt of one of the proofs of authenticity listed in this subsection, reflecting a judgment for damages rendered pursuant to the Medical Malpractice Act [Chapter 41, Article 5 NMSA 1978], the superintendent shall issue or have issued warrants in accordance with the payment schedule constructed by the court and made a part of its final judgment. The only claim against the patient's compensation fund shall be a voucher or other appropriate request by the superintendent after he receives:

(1) a certified copy of a final judgment in excess of two hundred thousand dollars ($200,000) against a health care provider;

(2) a certified copy of a court-approved settlement or certification of settlement made prior to initiating suit, signed by both parties, in excess of two hundred thousand dollars ($200,000) against a health care provider; or

(3) a certified copy of a final judgment less than two hundred thousand dollars ($200,000) and an affidavit of a health care provider or its insurer attesting that payments made pursuant to Subsection E of Section 41-5-7 NMSA 1978, combined with the monetary recovery, exceed two hundred thousand dollars ($200,000).

H. The superintendent shall contract for an independent actuarial study of the patient's compensation fund to be performed not less than once every two years.

§ 41–5–26. Malpractice coverage

A. The filing of proof of financial responsibility with the superintendent, as provided in Section 41–5–5 NMSA 1978, shall constitute a conclusive and unqualified acceptance of the provisions of the Medical Malpractice Act [this article].

B. Any provision in a policy attempting to limit or modify the liability of the insurer contrary to the provisions of the Medical Malpractice Act is void.

C. Every policy issued under the Medical Malpractice Act is deemed to include the following provisions:

(1) the insurer assumes all obligations to pay an award imposed against its insured under the provisions of the Medical Malpractice Act; and

(2) any termination of a policy by an insurer shall not be effective unless written notice of such termination has been mailed by certified mail to both the insured and the superintendent at least ninety days prior to the date the cancellation is to become effective, except that an insurer may terminate a policy if a billed premium payment is thirty days past due upon ten days' prior written notice mailed by certified mail to the insured of the failure of the insured to pay premiums, and an insured may terminate his policy by written request to the insurer but the effective date of termination shall be not sooner than ten days after the receipt by the insurer of the written request to terminate. In all cases when a policy is terminated for failure of the insured to pay premiums or at the request of the insured, the insurer shall notify the superintendent in writing immediately of the effective date of termination of the policy. The insurer shall remain liable for all causes of action accruing prior to the effective date of the termination, unless otherwise barred by the provisions of the Medical Malpractice Act.

B. ILLINOIS STATUTES—MEDICAL MALPRACTICE—RES IPSA LOQUITUR, 735 ILCS 5/2–1113

In all cases of alleged medical or dental malpractice, where the plaintiff relies upon the doctrine of res ipsa loquitur, the court shall determine whether that doctrine applies. In making that determination, the court shall rely upon either the common knowledge of laymen, if it determines that to be adequate, or upon expert medical testimony, that the medical result complained of would not have ordinarily occurred in the absence of negligence on the part of the defendant. Proof of an unusual, unexpected or untoward medical result which ordinarily does not occur in the absence of negligence will suffice in the application of the doctrine.

C. ILLINOIS STATUTES—CONTINGENT FEES FOR ATTORNEYS IN MEDICAL MALPRACTICE ACTIONS, 735 ILCS 5/2–1114

(a) In all medical malpractice actions the total contingent fee for plaintiff's attorney or attorneys shall not exceed the following amounts:

33⅓% of the first $150,000 of the sum recovered;

25% of the next $850,000 of the sum recovered; and

20% of any amount recovered over $1,000,000 of the sum recovered.

(b) For purposes of determining any lump sum contingent fee, any future damages recoverable by the plaintiff in periodic installments shall be reduced to a lump sum value.

(c) The court may review contingent fee agreements for fairness. In special circumstances, where an attorney performs extraordinary services involving more than usual participation in time and effort the attorney may apply to the court for approval of additional compensation.

(d) As used in this Section, "contingent fee basis" includes any fee arrangement under which the compensation is to be determined in whole or in part on the result obtained.

D. ILLINOIS STATUTES—PUNITIVE DAMAGES NOT RECOVERABLE IN HEALING ART AND LEGAL MALPRACTICE CASES, 735 ILCS 5/2–1115

Punitive damages not recoverable in healing art and legal malpractice cases. In all cases, whether in tort, contract or otherwise, in which the plaintiff seeks damages by reason of legal, medical, hospital, or other healing art malpractice, no punitive, exemplary, vindictive or aggravated damages shall be allowed.

E. ILLINOIS STATUTES—HEALING ART MALPRACTICE REQUIREMENT [SPECIAL PLEADING AND CERTIFICATE REQUIREMENTS IN MEDICAL MALPRACTICE CASES], 735 ILCS 5/2–622

(a) In any action, whether in tort, contract or otherwise, in which the plaintiff seeks damages for injuries or death by reason of medical, hospital, or other healing art malpractice, the plaintiff's attorney or the plaintiff, if the plaintiff is proceeding pro se, shall file an affidavit, attached to the original and all copies of the complaint, declaring one of the following:

1. That the affiant has consulted and reviewed the facts of the case with a health professional who the affiant reasonably believes:

(i) is knowledgeable in the relevant issues involved in the particular action;

(ii) practices or has practiced within the last 6 years or teaches or has taught within the last 6 years in the same area of health care or medicine that is at issue in the particular action; and

(iii) is qualified by experience or demonstrated competence in the subject of the case; that the reviewing health professional has determined in a written report, after a review of the medical record and other relevant material involved in the particular action that there is a reasonable and meritorious cause for the filing of such action; and that the affiant has concluded on the basis of the reviewing health professional's review and consultation that there is a reasonable and meritorious cause for filing of such action. If the affidavit is filed as to a defendant who is a physician licensed to treat human ailments without the use of drugs or medicines and without operative surgery, a dentist, a podiatrist, a psychologist, or a naprapath, the written report must be from a health professional licensed in the same profession, with the same class of license, as the defendant. For affidavits filed as to all other defendants, the written report must be from a physician licensed to practice medicine in all its branches. In either event, the affidavit must identify the profession of the reviewing health professional. A copy of the written report, clearly identifying the plaintiff and the reasons for the reviewing health professional's determination that a reasonable and meritorious cause for the filing of the action exists, must be attached to the affidavit. The report shall include the name and the address of the health professional.

2. That the plaintiff has not previously voluntarily dismissed an action based upon the same or substantially the same acts, omissions, or occurrences and that the affiant was unable to obtain a consultation required by paragraph 1 because a statute of limitations would impair the action and the consultation required could not be obtained before the expiration of the statute of limitations. If an affidavit is executed pursuant to this paragraph, the certificate and written report required by paragraph 1 shall be filed within 90 days after the filing of the complaint. The defendant shall be excused from answering or otherwise pleading until 30 days after being served with a certificate required by paragraph 1.

3. That a request has been made by the plaintiff or his attorney for examination and copying of records pursuant to Part 20 of Article VIII of this Code and the party required to comply under those Sections has failed to produce such records within 60 days of the receipt of the request. If an affidavit is executed pursuant to this paragraph, the certificate and written report required by paragraph 1 shall be filed within 90 days following receipt of the requested records. All defendants except those whose failure to comply with Part 20 of Article VIII of this Code is the basis for an affidavit under this paragraph shall be excused from answering or otherwise pleading until 30 days after being served with the certificate required by paragraph 1.

(b) Where a certificate and written report are required pursuant to this Section a separate certificate and written report shall be filed as to each defendant who has been named in the complaint and shall be filed as to each defendant named at a later time.

(c) Where the plaintiff intends to rely on the doctrine of "res ipsa loquitur", as defined by Section 2–1113 of this Code [735 ILCS 5/2–1113], the certificate and written report must state that, in the opinion of the reviewing health professional, negligence has occurred in the course of medical treatment. The affiant shall certify upon filing of the complaint that he is relying on the doctrine of "res ipsa loquitur".

(d) When the attorney intends to rely on the doctrine of failure to inform of the consequences of the procedure, the attorney shall certify upon the filing of the complaint that the reviewing health professional has, after reviewing the medical record and other relevant materials involved in the particular action, concluded that a reasonable health professional would have informed the patient of the consequences of the procedure.

(e) Allegations and denials in the affidavit, made without reasonable cause and found to be untrue, shall subject the party pleading them or his attorney, or both, to the payment of reasonable expenses, actually incurred by the other party by reason of the untrue pleading, together with reasonable attorneys' fees to be summarily taxed by the court upon motion made within 30 days of the judgment or dismissal. In no event shall the award for attorneys' fees and expenses exceed those actually paid by the moving party, including the insurer, if any. In proceedings under this paragraph (e), the moving party shall have the right to depose and examine any and all reviewing health professionals who prepared reports used in conjunction with an affidavit required by this Section.

(f) A reviewing health professional who in good faith prepares a report used in conjunction with an affidavit required by this Section shall have civil immunity from liability which otherwise might result from the preparation of such report.

(g) The failure to file a certificate required by this Section shall be grounds for dismissal under Section 2–619 [735 ILCS 5/2–619].

* * *

F.   TEXAS GOOD SAMARITAN ACT, CIV.PRAC. & REM. § 74.001

§ 74.001.   Liability for Emergency Care

(a) A person who in good faith administers emergency care, including using an automated external defibrillator, at the scene of an emergency but not in a hospital or other health care facility or means of medical transport is not liable in civil damages for an act performed during the emergency unless the act is wilfully or wantonly negligent.

(b) This section does not apply to care administered:

    (1) for or in expectation of remuneration; or

    (2) by a person who was at the scene of the emergency because he or a person he represents as an agent was soliciting business or seeking to perform a service for remuneration.

(c) If the scene of an emergency is in a hospital or other health care facility or means of medical transport, a person who in good faith administers emergency care is not liable in civil damages for an act performed during the emergency unless the act is wilfully or wantonly negligent, provided that this subsection does not apply to care administered:

    (1) by a person who regularly administers care in a hospital emergency room unless such person is at the scene of the emergency for reasons wholly unrelated to the person's work in administering health care; or

    (2) by an admitting or attending physician of the patient or a treating physician associated by the admitting or attending physician of the patient in question.

(d) For purposes of Subsections (b)(1) and (c)(1), a person who would ordinarily receive or be entitled to receive a salary, fee, or other remuneration for administering care under such circumstances to the patient in question shall be deemed to be acting for or in expectation of remuneration even if the person waives or elects not to charge or receive remuneration on the occasion in question.

(e) This section does not apply to a person whose negligent act or omission was a producing cause of the emergency for which care is being administered.

§ 74.002. Unlicensed Medical Personnel

Persons not licensed in the healing arts who in good faith administer emergency care as emergency medical service personnel are not liable in civil damages for an act performed in administering the care unless the act is wilfully or wantonly negligent. This section applies without regard to whether the care is provided for or in expectation of remuneration.

G. TEXAS INFORMED CONSENT STATUTE, TEX.REV.CIV.STAT.ANN. ART. 4590i

§ 6.01 Definition

In this subchapter, "panel" means the Texas Medical Disclosure Panel.

§ 6.02 Theory of Recovery

In a suit against a physician or health care provider involving a health care liability claim that is based on the failure of the physician or health care provider to disclose or adequately to disclose the risks and hazards involved in the medical care or surgical procedure rendered by the physician or health care provider, the only theory on which recovery may be obtained is that of negligence in failing to disclose the risks or hazards that could have influenced a reasonable person in making a decision to give or withhold consent.

§ 6.03   Texas Medical Disclosure Panel

(a) The Texas Medical Disclosure Panel is created to determine which risks and hazards related to medical care and surgical procedures must be disclosed by health care providers or physicians to their patients or persons authorized to consent for their patients and to establish the general form and substance of such disclosure.

(b) The panel established herein is administratively attached to the Texas Department of Health. The Texas Department of Health, at the request of the panel, shall provide administrative assistance to the panel; and the Texas Department of Health and the panel shall coordinate administrative responsibilities in order to avoid unnecessary duplication of facilities and services. The Texas Department of Health, at the request of the panel, shall submit the panel's budget request to the legislature. The panel shall be subject, except where inconsistent, to the rules and procedures of the Texas Department of Health; however, the duties and responsibilities of the panel as set forth in the Medical Liability and Insurance Improvement Act of Texas, as amended (*Article 4590i, Vernon's Texas Civil Statutes*), shall be exercised solely by the panel and the board or Texas Department of Health shall have no authority or responsibility with respect to same.

(c) The panel is composed of nine members, with three members licensed to practice law in this state and six members licensed to practice medicine in this state. Members of the panel shall be selected by the Commissioner of Health.

(d) The commissioner shall select members of the panel according to the following schedule:

(1) one attorney and two physicians to serve a term of two years, which term shall begin on September 1, 1979, and expire on August 31, 1981, or until a successor is qualified;

(2) one attorney and two physicians to serve a term of four years, which terms shall begin September 1, 1979, and expire August 31, 1983, or until a successor is qualified;

(3) one attorney and two physicians to serve a term of six years, which term shall begin September 1, 1979, and expire on August 31, 1985, or until a successor is qualified.

Thereafter, at the expiration of the term of each member of the panel so appointed, the commissioner shall select a successor, and such successor shall serve for a term of six years, or until his successor is selected. Any member who is absent for three consecutive meetings without the consent of a majority of the panel present at each such meeting may be removed by the commissioner at the request of the panel submitted in writing and signed by the chairman. Upon the death, resignation, or removal of any member, the commissioner shall fill the vacancy by selection for the unexpired portion of the term.

(e) Members of the panel are not entitled to compensation for their services, but each panelist is entitled to reimbursement of any necessary expense incurred in the performance of his duties on the panel including necessary travel expenses.

(f) Meetings of the panel shall be held at the call of the chairman or on petition of at least three members of the panel.

(g) At the first meeting of the panel each year after its members assume their positions, the panelists shall select one of the panel members to serve as chairman and one of the panel members to serve as vice-chairman, and each such officer shall serve for a term of one year. The chairman shall preside at meetings of the panel, and in his absence, the vice-chairman shall preside.

(h) Employees of the Texas Department of Health shall serve as the staff for the panel.

§ 6.04 Duties of Panel

(a) To the extent feasible, the panel shall identify and make a thorough examination of all medical treatments and surgical procedures in which physicians and health care providers may be involved in order to determine which of those treatments and procedures do and do not require disclosure of the risks and hazards to the patient or person authorized to consent for the patient.

(b) The panel shall prepare separate lists of those medical treatments and surgical procedures that do and do not require disclosure and for those treatments and procedures that do require disclosure shall establish the degree of disclosure required and the form in which the disclosure will be made.

(c) Lists prepared under Subsection (b) of this section together with written explanations of the degree and form of disclosure shall be published in the Texas Register.

(d) At least annually, or at such other period the panel may determine from time to time, the panel will identify and examine any new medical treatments and surgical procedures that have been developed since its last determinations, shall assign them to the proper list, and shall establish the degree of disclosure required and the form in which the disclosure will be made. The panel will also examine such treatments and procedures for the purpose of revising lists previously published. These determinations shall be published in the Texas Register.

§ 6.05   Duty of Physician or Health Care Provider

Before a patient or a person authorized to consent for a patient gives consent to any medical care or surgical procedure that appears on the panel's list requiring disclosure, the physician or health care provider shall disclose to the patient, or person authorized to consent for the patient, the risks and hazards involved in that kind of care or procedure. A physician or health care provider shall be considered to have complied with the requirements of this section if disclosure is made as provided in Section 6.06 of this subchapter.

§ 6.06   Manner of Disclosure

Consent to medical care that appears on the panel's list requiring disclosure shall be considered effective under this subchapter if it is given in writing, signed by the patient or a person authorized to give the consent and by a competent witness, and if the written consent specifically states the risks and hazards that are involved in the medical care or surgical procedure in the form and to the degree required by the panel under Section 6.04 of this subchapter.

§ 6.07   Effect of Disclosure

(a) In a suit against a physician or health care provider involving a health care liability claim that is based on the negligent failure of the physician or health care provider to disclose or adequately to disclose the risks and hazards involved in the medical care or surgical procedure rendered by the physician or health care provider:

(1) both disclosure made as provided in Section 6.05 of this subchapter and failure to disclose based on inclusion of any medical care or surgical procedure on the panel's list for which disclosure is not required shall be admissible in evidence and shall create a rebuttable presumption that the requirements of Sections 6.05 and 6.06 of this subchapter have been complied with and this presumption shall be included in the charge to the jury; and

(2) failure to disclose the risks and hazards involved in any medical care or surgical procedure required to be disclosed under Sections 6.05 and 6.06 of this subchapter shall be admissible in evidence and shall create a rebuttable presumption of a negligent failure to conform to the duty of disclosure set forth in Sections 6.05 and 6.06 of this subchapter, and this presumption shall be included in the charge to the jury; but failure to disclose may be found not to be negligent if there was an emergency or if for some other reason it was not medically feasible to make a disclosure of the kind that would otherwise have been negligence.

(b) If medical care or surgical procedure is rendered with respect to which the panel has made no determination either way regarding a duty of disclosure, the physician or health care provider is under the duty otherwise imposed by law.

§ 6.08   Informed Consent for Hysterectomies

(a) The panel shall develop and prepare written materials to inform a patient or person authorized to consent for a patient of the risks and hazards of a hysterectomy.

(b) The materials shall be available in English, Spanish, and any other language the panel considers appropriate. The information must be presented in a manner understandable to a layperson.

(c) The materials must include:

(1) a notice that a decision made at any time to refuse to undergo a hysterectomy will not result in the withdrawal or withholding of any benefits provided by programs or projects receiving federal funds or otherwise affect the patient's right to future care or treatment;

(2) the name of the person providing and explaining the materials;

(3) a statement that the patient or person authorized to consent for the patient understands that the hysterectomy is permanent and nonreversible and that the patient will not be able to become pregnant or bear children if she undergoes a hysterectomy;

(4) a statement that the patient has the right to seek a consultation from a second physician;

(5) a statement that the patient or person authorized to consent for the patient has been informed that a hysterectomy is a removal of the uterus through an incision in the lower abdomen or vagina and that additional surgery may be necessary to remove or repair other organs, including an ovary, tube, appendix, bladder, rectum, or vagina;

(6) a description of the risks and hazards involved in the performance of the procedure; and

(7) a written statement to be signed by the patient or person authorized to consent for the patient indicating that the materials have been provided and explained to the patient or person authorized to consent for the patient and that the patient or person authorized to consent for the patient understands the nature and consequences of a hysterectomy.

(d) The physician or health care provider shall obtain informed consent under this section and Section 6.05 of this Act from the patient or person authorized to consent for the patient before performing a hysterectomy unless the hysterectomy is performed in a life-threatening situation in which the physician determines obtaining informed consent is not reasonably possible. If obtaining informed consent is not reasonably possible, the physician or health care provider shall include in the patient's medical records a written statement signed by the physician certifying the nature of the emergency.

(e) The panel may not prescribe materials under this section without first consulting with the Texas State Board of Medical Examiners.

X. FEDERAL AND STATE STATUTES RELATING TO HEALTHCARE DECISIONMAKING, DEATH AND DYING

A. UNIFORM HEALTH–CARE DECISIONS ACT (1993)

§ 1. Definitions

In this [Act]:

(1) "Advance health-care directive" means an individual instruction or a power of attorney for health care.

(2) "Agent" means an individual designated in a power of attorney for health care to make a health-care decision for the individual granting the power.

(3) "Capacity" means an individual's ability to understand the significant benefits, risks, and alternatives to proposed health care and to make and communicate a health-care decision.

(4) "Guardian" means a judicially appointed guardian or conservator having authority to make a health-care decision for an individual.

(5) "Health care" means any care, treatment, service, or procedure to maintain, diagnose, or otherwise affect an individual's physical or mental condition.

(6) "Health-care decision" means a decision made by an individual or the individual's agent, guardian, or surrogate, regarding the individual's health care, including:

(i) selection and discharge of health-care providers and institutions;

(ii) approval or disapproval of diagnostic tests, surgical procedures, programs of medication, and orders not to resuscitate; and

(iii) directions to provide, withhold, or withdraw artificial nutrition and hydration and all other forms of health care.

(7) "Health-care institution" means an institution, facility, or agency licensed, certified, or otherwise authorized or permitted by law to provide health care in the ordinary course of business.

(8) "Health-care provider" means an individual licensed, certified, or otherwise authorized or permitted by law to provide health care in the ordinary course of business or practice of a profession.

(9) "Individual instruction" means an individual's direction concerning a health-care decision for the individual.

(10) "Person" means an individual, corporation, business trust, estate, trust, partnership, association, joint venture, government, governmental subdivision, agency, or instrumentality, or any other legal or commercial entity.

(11) "Physician" means an individual authorized to practice medicine [or osteopathy] under [appropriate statute].

(12) "Power of attorney for health care" means the designation of an agent to make health-care decisions for the individual granting the power.

(13) "Primary physician" means a physician designated by an individual or the individual's agent, guardian, or surrogate, to have primary responsibility for the individual's health care or, in the absence of a designation or if the designated physician is not reasonably available, a physician who undertakes the responsibility.

(14) "Reasonably available" means readily able to be contacted without undue effort and willing and able to act in a timely manner considering the urgency of the patient's health-care needs.

(15) "State" means a State of the United States, the District of Columbia, the Commonwealth of Puerto Rico, or a territory or insular possession subject to the jurisdiction of the United States.

(16) "Supervising health-care provider" means the primary physician or, if there is no primary physician or the primary physician is not reasonably available, the health-care provider who has undertaken primary responsibility for an individual's health care.

(17) "Surrogate" means an individual, other than a patient's agent or guardian, authorized under this [Act] to make a health-care decision for the patient.

§ 2. Advance Health–Care Directives

(a) An adult or emancipated minor may give an individual instruction. The instruction may be oral or written. The instruction may be limited to take effect only if a specified condition arises.

(b) An adult or emancipated minor may execute a power of attorney for health care, which may authorize the agent to make any health-care decision the principal could have made while having capacity. The power must be in writing and signed by the principal. The power remains in effect notwithstanding the principal's later incapacity and may include individual instructions. Unless related to the principal by blood, marriage, or adoption, an agent may not be an owner, operator, or employee of [a residential long-term health-care institution] at which the principal is receiving care.

(c) Unless otherwise specified in a power of attorney for health care, the authority of an agent becomes effective only upon a determination that the principal lacks capacity, and ceases to be effective upon a determination that the principal has recovered capacity.

(d) Unless otherwise specified in a written advance health-care directive, a determination that an individual lacks or has recovered capacity, or that another condition exists that affects an individual instruction or the authority of an agent, must be made by the primary physician.

(e) An agent shall make a health-care decision in accordance with the principal's individual instructions, if any, and other wishes to the extent known to the agent. Otherwise, the agent shall make the decision in accordance with the agent's determination of the principal's best interest. In determining the principal's best interest, the agent shall consider the principal's personal values to the extent known to the agent.

(f) A health-care decision made by an agent for a principal is effective without judicial approval.

(g) A written advance health-care directive may include the individual's nomination of a guardian of the person.

(h) An advance health-care directive is valid for purposes of this [Act] if it complies with this [Act], regardless of when or where executed or communicated.

§ 3. Revocation of Advance Health–Care Directive

(a) An individual may revoke the designation of an agent only by a signed writing or by personally informing the supervising health-care provider.

(b) An individual may revoke all or part of an advance health-care directive, other than the designation of an agent, at any time and in any manner that communicates an intent to revoke.

(c) A health-care provider, agent, guardian, or surrogate who is informed of a revocation shall promptly communicate the fact of the revocation to the supervising health-care provider and to any health-care institution at which the patient is receiving care.

(d) A decree of annulment, divorce, dissolution of marriage, or legal separation revokes a previous designation of a spouse as agent unless otherwise specified in the decree or in a power of attorney for health care.

(e) An advance health-care directive that conflicts with an earlier advance health-care directive revokes the earlier directive to the extent of the conflict.

§ 4. Optional Form

The following form may, but need not, be used to create an advance health-care directive. The other sections of this [Act] govern the effect of this or any other writing used to create an advance health-care directive. An individual may complete or modify all or any part of the following form:

ADVANCE HEALTH–CARE DIRECTIVE

Explanation

You have the right to give instructions about your own health care. You also have the right to name someone else to make health-care decisions for you. This form lets you do either or both of these things. It also lets you express your wishes regarding donation of organs and the designation of your primary physician. If you use this form, you may complete or modify all or any part of it. You are free to use a different form.

Part 1 of this form is a power of attorney for health care. Part 1 lets you name another individual as agent to make health-care decisions for you if you become incapable of making your own decisions or if you want someone else to make those decisions for you now even though you are still capable. You may also name an alternate agent to act for you if your first choice is not willing, able, or reasonably available to make decisions for you. Unless related to you, your agent may not be an owner, operator, or employee of [a residential long-term health-care institution] at which you are receiving care.

Unless the form you sign limits the authority of your agent, your agent may make all health-care decisions for you. This form has a place for you to limit the authority of your agent. You need not limit the authority of your agent if you wish to rely on your agent for all health-care decisions that may have to be made. If you choose not to limit the authority of your agent, your agent will have the right to:

    (a) consent or refuse consent to any care, treatment, service, or procedure to maintain, diagnose, or otherwise affect a physical or mental condition;

    (b) select or discharge health-care providers and institutions;

    (c) approve or disapprove diagnostic tests, surgical procedures, programs of medication, and orders not to resuscitate; and

    (d) direct the provision, withholding, or withdrawal of artificial nutrition and hydration and all other forms of health care.

Part 2 of this form lets you give specific instructions about any aspect of your health care. Choices are provided for you to express your wishes regarding the provision, withholding, or withdrawal of treatment to keep you alive, including the provision of artificial nutrition and hydration, as well as the provision of pain relief. Space is also provided for you to add to the choices you have made or for you to write out any additional wishes.

Part 3 of this form lets you express an intention to donate your bodily organs and tissues following your death.

Part 4 of this form lets you designate a physician to have primary responsibility for your health care.

After completing this form, sign and date the form at the end. It is recommended but not required that you request two other individuals to sign as witnesses. Give a copy of the signed and completed form to your physician, to any other health-care providers you may have, to any health-care institution at which you are receiving care, and to any health-care agents you have named. You should talk to the person you have named as agent to make sure that he or she understands your wishes and is willing to take the responsibility.

You have the right to revoke this advance health-care directive or replace this form at any time.

PART 1

POWER OF ATTORNEY FOR HEALTH CARE

(1) DESIGNATION OF AGENT: I designate the following individual as my agent to make health-care decisions for me:

_____

(name of individual you choose as agent)

_____

(address) (city) (state) (zip code)

_____

(home phone) (work phone)

OPTIONAL: If I revoke my agent's authority or if my agent is not willing, able, or reasonably available to make a health-care decision for me, I designate as my first alternate agent:

_____

(name of individual you choose as first alternate agent)

_____

(address) (city) (state) (zip code)

_____

(home phone) (work phone)

OPTIONAL: If I revoke the authority of my agent and first alternate agent or if neither is willing, able, or reasonably available to make a health-care decision for me, I designate as my second alternate agent:

_____

(name of individual you choose as second alternate agent)

_____

(address) (city) (state) (zip code)

_____

(home phone) (work phone)

(2) AGENT'S AUTHORITY: My agent is authorized to make all health-care decisions for me, including decisions to provide, withhold, or withdraw artificial nutrition and hydration and all other forms of health care to keep me alive, except as I state here:

_____

_____

(add additional sheets if needed.)

1437

(3) WHEN AGENT'S AUTHORITY BECOMES EFFECTIVE: My agent's authority becomes effective when my primary physician determines that I am unable to make my own health-care decisions unless I mark the following box. If I mark this box [ ], my agent's authority to make health-care decisions for me takes effect immediately.

(4) AGENT'S OBLIGATION: My agent shall make health-care decisions for me in accordance with this power of attorney for health care, any instructions I give in Part 2 of this form, and my other wishes to the extent known to my agent. To the extent my wishes are unknown, my agent shall make health-care decisions for me in accordance with what my agent determines to be in my best interest. In determining my best interest, my agent shall consider my personal values to the extent known to my agent.

(5) NOMINATION OF GUARDIAN: If a guardian of my person needs to be appointed for me by a court, I nominate the agent designated in this form. If that agent is not willing, able, or reasonably available to act as guardian, I nominate the alternate agents whom I have named, in the order designated.

PART 2

INSTRUCTIONS FOR HEALTH CARE

If you are satisfied to allow your agent to determine what is best for you in making end-of-life decisions, you need not fill out this part of the form. If you do fill out this part of the form, you may strike any wording you do not want.

(6) END–OF–LIFE DECISIONS: I direct that my health-care providers and others involved in my care provide, withhold, or withdraw treatment in accordance with the choice I have marked below:

"[ ] **(a)** Choice Not To Prolong Life

I do not want my life to be prolonged if

(i) I have an incurable and irreversible condition that will result in my death within a relatively short time,

(ii) I become unconscious and, to a reasonable degree of medical certainty, I will not regain consciousness, or

(ii) the likely risks and burdens of treatment would outweigh the expected benefits, OR

"[ ] **(b)** Choice To Prolong Life

I want my life to be prolonged as long as possible within the limits of generally accepted health-care standards.

(7) ARTIFICIAL NUTRITION AND HYDRATION: Artificial nutrition and hydration must be provided, withheld, or withdrawn in accordance with the choice I have made in paragraph (6) unless I mark the following box. If I mark this box [ ], artificial nutrition and hydration must be provided regardless of my condition and regardless of the choice I have made in paragraph (6).

(8) RELIEF FROM PAIN: Except as I state in the following space, I direct that treatment for alleviation of pain or discomfort be provided at all times, even if it hastens my death:

_____

(9) OTHER WISHES: (If you do not agree with any of the optional choices above and wish to write your own, or if you wish to add to the instructions you have given above, you may do so here.) I direct that:

_____

(Add additional sheets if needed.)

PART 3

DONATION OF ORGANS AT DEATH

(OPTIONAL)

(10) Upon my death (mark applicable box)

[ ] **(a)** I give any needed organs, tissues, or parts, OR

[ ] **(b)** I give the following organs, tissues, or parts only

_____

(c) My gift is for the following purposes (strike any of the following you do not want)

(i) Transplant

(ii) Therapy

(iii) Research

(iv) Education

PART 4

PRIMARY PHYSICIAN

(OPTIONAL)

(11) I designate the following physician as my primary physician:

_____
(name of physician)

_____
(address) (city) (state) (zip code)

_____
(phone)

OPTIONAL: If the physician I have designated above is not willing, able, or reasonably available to act as my primary physician, I designate the following physician as my primary physician:

_____
(name of physician)

_____

(address) (city) (state) (zip code)

_____

(phone)

(12) EFFECT OF COPY: A copy of this form has the same effect as the original.

(13) SIGNATURES: Sign and date the form here:

_____   _____

(date)   (sign your name)

_____   _____

(address)   (print your name)

_____

(city) (state)

(OPTIONAL) SIGNATURES OF WITNESSES:

First witness   Second witness

_____   _____

(print name)   (print name)

_____   _____

(address)   (address)

_____   _____

(city)   (state) (city)   (state)

_____   _____

(signature of witness)   (signature of witness)

_____   _____

(date)   (date)

§ 5. Decisions by Surrogate

(a) A surrogate may make a health-care decision for a patient who is an adult or emancipated minor if the patient has been determined by the primary physician to lack capacity and no agent or guardian has been appointed or the agent or guardian is not reasonably available.

(b) An adult or emancipated minor may designate any individual to act as surrogate by personally informing the supervising health-care provider. In the absence of a designation, or if the designee is not reasonably available, any member of the following classes of the patient's family who is reasonably available, in descending order of priority, may act as surrogate:

    (1) the spouse, unless legally separated;

    (2) an adult child;

    (3) a parent; or

(4) an adult brother or sister.

(c) If none of the individuals eligible to act as surrogate under subsection (b) is reasonably available, an adult who has exhibited special care and concern for the patient, who is familiar with the patient's personal values, and who is reasonably available may act as surrogate.

(d) A surrogate shall communicate his or her assumption of authority as promptly as practicable to the members of the patient's family specified in subsection (b) who can be readily contacted.

(e) If more than one member of a class assumes authority to act as surrogate, and they do not agree on a health-care decision and the supervising health-care provider is so informed, the supervising health-care provider shall comply with the decision of a majority of the members of that class who have communicated their views to the provider. If the class is evenly divided concerning the health-care decision and the supervising health-care provider is so informed, that class and all individuals having lower priority are disqualified from making the decision.

(f) A surrogate shall make a health-care decision in accordance with the patient's individual instructions, if any, and other wishes to the extent known to the surrogate. Otherwise, the surrogate shall make the decision in accordance with the surrogate's determination of the patient's best interest. In determining the patient's best interest, the surrogate shall consider the patient's personal values to the extent known to the surrogate.

(g) A health-care decision made by a surrogate for a patient is effective without judicial approval.

(h) An individual at any time may disqualify another, including a member of the individual's family, from acting as the individual's surrogate by a signed writing or by personally informing the supervising health-care provider of the disqualification.

(i) Unless related to the patient by blood, marriage, or adoption, a surrogate may not be an owner, operator, or employee of [a residential long-term health-care institution] at which the patient is receiving care.

(j) A supervising health-care provider may require an individual claiming the right to act as surrogate for a patient to provide a written declaration under penalty of perjury stating facts and circumstances reasonably sufficient to establish the claimed authority.

§ 6. Decisions by Guardian

(a) A guardian shall comply with the ward's individual instructions and may not revoke the ward's advance health-care directive unless the appointing court expressly so authorizes.

(b) Absent a court order to the contrary, a health-care decision of an agent takes precedence over that of a guardian.

(c) A health-care decision made by a guardian for the ward is effective without judicial approval.

§ 7. Obligations of Health–Care Provider

(a) Before implementing a health-care decision made for a patient, a supervising health-care provider, if possible, shall promptly communicate to the patient the decision made and the identity of the person making the decision.

(b) A supervising health-care provider who knows of the existence of an advance health-care directive, a revocation of an advance health-care directive, or a designation or disqualification of a surrogate, shall promptly record its existence in the patient's health-care record and, if it is in writing, shall request a copy and if one is furnished shall arrange for its maintenance in the health-care record.

(c) A primary physician who makes or is informed of a determination that a patient lacks or has recovered capacity, or that another condition exists which affects an individual instruction or the authority of an agent, guardian, or surrogate, shall promptly record the determination in the patient's health-care record and communicate the determination to the patient, if possible, and to any person then authorized to make health-care decisions for the patient.

(d) Except as provided in subsections (e) and (f), a health-care provider or institution providing care to a patient shall:

(1) comply with an individual instruction of the patient and with a reasonable interpretation of that instruction made by a person then authorized to make health-care decisions for the patient; and

(2) comply with a health-care decision for the patient made by a person then authorized to make health-care decisions for the patient to the same extent as if the decision had been made by the patient while having capacity.

(e) A health-care provider may decline to comply with an individual instruction or health-care decision for reasons of conscience. A health-care institution may decline to comply with an individual instruction or health-care decision if the instruction or decision is contrary to a policy of the institution which is expressly based on reasons of conscience and if the policy was timely communicated to the patient or to a person then authorized to make health-care decisions for the patient.

(f) A health-care provider or institution may decline to comply with an individual instruction or health-care decision that requires medically ineffective health care or health care contrary to generally accepted health-care standards applicable to the health-care provider or institution.

(g) A health-care provider or institution that declines to comply with an individual instruction or health-care decision shall:

(1) promptly so inform the patient, if possible, and any person then authorized to make health-care decisions for the patient;

(2) provide continuing care to the patient until a transfer can be effected; and

(3) unless the patient or person then authorized to make health-care decisions for the patient refuses assistance, immediately make all reasonable efforts to assist in the transfer of the patient to another health-care provider or institution that is willing to comply with the instruction or decision.

(h) A health-care provider or institution may not require or prohibit the execution or revocation of an advance health-care directive as a condition for providing health care.

§ 8. Health–Care Information

Unless otherwise specified in an advance health-care directive, a person then authorized to make health-care decisions for a patient has the same rights as the patient to request, receive, examine, copy, and consent to the disclosure of medical or any other health-care information.

§ 9. Immunities

(a) A health-care provider or institution acting in good faith and in accordance with generally accepted health-care standards applicable to the health-care provider or institution is not subject to civil or criminal liability or to discipline for unprofessional conduct for:

(1) complying with a health-care decision of a person apparently having authority to make a health-care decision for a patient, including a decision to withhold or withdraw health care;

(2) declining to comply with a health-care decision of a person based on a belief that the person then lacked authority; or

(3) complying with an advance health-care directive and assuming that the directive was valid when made and has not been revoked or terminated.

(b) An individual acting as agent or surrogate under this [Act] is not subject to civil or criminal liability or to discipline for unprofessional conduct for health-care decisions made in good faith.

§ 10. Statutory Damages

(a) A health-care provider or institution that intentionally violates this [Act] is subject to liability to the aggrieved individual for damages of $[500] or actual damages resulting from the violation, whichever is greater, plus reasonable attorney's fees.

(b) A person who intentionally falsifies, forges, conceals, defaces, or obliterates an individual's advance health-care directive or a revocation of an advance health-care directive without the individual's consent, or who coerces or fraudulently induces an individual to give, revoke, or not to give an advance health-care directive, is subject to liability to that individual for damages of $[2,500] or actual damages resulting from the action, whichever is greater, plus reasonable attorney's fees.

§ 11. Capacity

(a) This [Act] does not affect the right of an individual to make health-care decisions while having capacity to do so.

(b) An individual is presumed to have capacity to make a health-care decision, to give or revoke an advance health-care directive, and to designate or disqualify a surrogate.

§ 12. Effect of Copy

A copy of a written advance health-care directive, revocation of an advance health-care directive, or designation or disqualification of a surrogate has the same effect as the original.

§ 13. Effect of [Act]

(a) This [Act] does not create a presumption concerning the intention of an individual who has not made or who has revoked an advance health-care directive.

(b) Death resulting from the withholding or withdrawal of health care in accordance with this [Act] does not for any purpose constitute a suicide or homicide or legally impair or invalidate a policy of insurance or an annuity providing a death benefit, notwithstanding any term of the policy or annuity to the contrary.

(c) This [Act] does not authorize mercy killing, assisted suicide, euthanasia, or the provision, withholding, or withdrawal of health care, to the extent prohibited by other statutes of this State.

(d) This [Act] does not authorize or require a health-care provider or institution to provide health care contrary to generally accepted health-care standards applicable to the health-care provider or institution.

(e) This [Act] does not authorize an agent or surrogate to consent to the admission of an individual to a mental health-care institution unless the individual's written advance health-care directive expressly so provides.

(f) This [Act] does not affect other statutes of this State governing treatment for mental illness of an individual involuntarily committed to a [mental health-care institution under appropriate statute].

§ 14. Judicial Relief

On petition of a patient, the patient's agent, guardian, or surrogate, a health-care provider or institution involved with the patient's care, or an individual described in Section 5(b) or (c), the [appropriate] court may enjoin or direct a health-care decision or order other equitable relief. A proceeding under this section is governed by [here insert appropriate reference to the rules of procedure or statutory provisions governing expedited proceedings and proceedings affecting incapacitated persons].

§ 15. Uniformity of Application and Construction

This [Act] shall be applied and construed to effectuate its general purpose to make uniform the law with respect to the subject matter of this [Act] among States enacting.

§ 16. Short Title

This [Act] may be cited as the Uniform Health–Care Decisions Act.

§ 17. Severability Clause

If any provision of this [Act] or its application to any person or circumstance is held invalid, the invalidity does not affect other provisions or applications of this [Act] which can be given effect without the invalid provision or application, and to this end the provisions of this [Act] are severable.

* * *

B. PATIENT SELF DETERMINATION ACT: 42 U.S.C.A. § 1395cc(f)

(1) For purposes of subsection (a)(1)(Q) of this section and sections 1395i–3(c)(2)(E), 1395l(s), 1395w–25(i), 1395mm(c)(8), and 1395bbb(a)(6) of this title, the requirement of this subsection is that a provider of services, Medicare + Choice organization, or prepaid or eligible organization (as the case may be) maintain written policies and procedures with respect to all adult individuals receiving medical care by or through the provider or organization—

(A) to provide written information to each such individual concerning—

(i) an individual's rights under State law (whether statutory or as recognized by the courts of the State) to make decisions concerning such medical care, including the right to accept or refuse medical or surgical treatment and the right to formulate advance directives (as defined in paragraph (3)), and

(ii) the written policies of the provider or organization respecting the implementation of such rights;

(B) to document in a prominent part of the individual's current medical record whether or not the individual has executed an advance directive;

(C) not to condition the provision of care or otherwise discriminate against an individual based on whether or not the individual has executed an advance directive;

(D) to ensure compliance with requirements of State law (whether statutory or as recognized by the courts of the State) respecting advance directives at facilities of the provider or organization; and

(E) to provide (individually or with others) for education for staff and the community on issues concerning advance directives.

Subparagraph (C) shall not be construed as requiring the provision of care which conflicts with an advance directive.

(2) The written information described in paragraph (1)(A) shall be provided to an adult individual—

(A) in the case of a hospital, at the time of the individual's admission as an inpatient,

(B) in the case of a skilled nursing facility, at the time of the individual's admission as a resident,

(C) in the case of a home health agency, in advance of the individual coming under the care of the agency,

(D) in the case of a hospice program, at the time of initial receipt of hospice care by the individual from the program, and

(E) in the case of an eligible organization (as defined in section 1395mm(b) of this title) or an organization provided payments under section 1395l(a)(1)(A) of this title or a Medicare + Choice organization, at the time of enrollment of the individual with the organization.

(3) In this subsection, the term "advance directive" means a written instruction, such as a living will or durable power of attorney for health care, recognized under State law (whether statutory or as recognized by the courts of the State) and relating to the provision of such care when the individual is incapacitated.

(4) For construction relating to this subsection, see section 14406 of this title (relating to clarification respecting assisted suicide, euthanasia, and mercy killing).

C. BABY DOE STATUTE: 42 U.S.C.A. § 5106

* * *

§ 5106g. Definitions

For purposes of this subchapter—

* * *

(6) the term "withholding of medically indicated treatment" means the failure to respond to the infant's life-threatening conditions by providing treatment (including appropriate nutrition, hydration, and medication) which, in the treating physician's or physicians' reasonable medical judgment, will be most likely to be effective in ameliorating or correcting all such conditions, except that the term does not include the failure to provide treatment (other than appropriate nutrition, hydration, or medication) to an infant when, in the treating physician's or physicians' reasonable medical judgment—

> **(A)** the infant is chronically and irreversibly comatose;
>
> **(B)** the provision of such treatment would—
>
>> **(i)** merely prolong dying;
>>
>> **(ii)** not be effective in ameliorating or correcting all of the infant's life-threatening conditions; or
>>
>> **(iii)** otherwise be futile in terms of the survival of the infant; or
>
> **(C)** the provision of such treatment would be virtually futile in terms of the survival of the infant and the treatment itself under such circumstances would be inhumane.

* * *

§ 5106i. Rule of Construction

(a) In general

Nothing in this subchapter and subchapters III and V of this chapter shall be construed—

> **(1)** as establishing a Federal requirement that a parent or legal guardian provide a child any medical service or treatment against the religious beliefs of the parent or legal guardian; and
>
> **(2)** to require that a State find, or to prohibit a State from finding, abuse or neglect in cases in which a parent or legal guardian relies solely or partially upon spiritual means rather than medical treatment, in accordance with the religious beliefs of the parent or legal guardian.

(b) State requirement

Notwithstanding subsection (a) of this section, a State shall, at a minimum, have in place authority under State law to permit the child protective services system of the State to pursue any legal remedies, including the authority to initiate legal proceedings in a court of competent jurisdiction, to provide medical care or treatment for a child when such care or treatment is necessary to prevent or remedy serious harm to the child, or to prevent the withholding of medically indicated treatment from children with life threatening conditions. Except with respect to the withholding of medically indicated treatments from disabled infants with life threatening conditions, case by case determinations concerning the exercise of the authority of this subsection shall be within the sole discretion of the State.

D. CALIFORNIA CHILD NEGLECT STATUTE (WITH SPIRITUAL HEALING EXCEPTION): CAL. PENAL CODE § 270

§ 270. Failure to provide; parent; punishment; effect of custody; evidence; applicability of section; artificial insemination; treatment by spiritual means

If a parent of a minor child willfully omits, without lawful excuse, to furnish necessary clothing, food, shelter or medical attendance, or other remedial care for his or her child, he or she is guilty of a misdemeanor punishable by a fine not exceeding two thousand dollars ($2,000), or by imprisonment in the county jail not exceeding one year, or by both such fine and imprisonment. If a court of competent jurisdiction has made a final adjudication in either a civil or a criminal action that a person is the parent of a minor child and the person has notice of such adjudication and he or she then willfully omits, without lawful excuse, to furnish necessary clothing, food, shelter, medical attendance or other remedial care for his or her child, this conduct is punishable by imprisonment in the county jail not exceeding one year or in a state prison for a determinate term of one year and one day, or by a fine not exceeding two thousand dollars ($2,000), or by both such fine and imprisonment. This statute shall not be construed so as to relieve such parent from the criminal liability defined herein for such omission merely because the other parent of such child is legally entitled to the custody of such child nor because the other parent of such child or any other person or organization voluntarily or involuntarily furnishes such necessary food, clothing, shelter or medical attendance or other remedial care for such child or undertakes to do so.

Proof of abandonment or desertion of a child by such parent, or the omission by such parent to furnish necessary food, clothing, shelter or medical attendance or other remedial care for his or her child is prima facie evidence that such abandonment or desertion or omission to furnish necessary food, clothing, shelter or medical attendance or other remedial care is willful and without lawful excuse.

The court, in determining the ability of the parent to support his or her child, shall consider all income, including social insurance benefits and gifts.

The provisions of this section are applicable whether the parents of such child are or were ever married or divorced, and regardless of any decree made in any divorce action relative to alimony or to the support of the child. A child conceived but not yet born is to be deemed an existing person insofar as this section is concerned.

The husband of a woman who bears a child as a result of artificial insemination shall be considered the father of that child for the purpose of this section, if he consented in writing to the artificial insemination.

If a parent provides a minor with treatment by spiritual means through prayer alone in accordance with the tenets and practices of a recognized church or religious denomination, by a duly accredited practitioner thereof, such treatment shall constitute "other remedial care", as used in this section.

E. UNIFORM DETERMINATION OF DEATH ACT: 12A U.L.A. 589 (1980)

§ 1. [Determination of Death]

An individual who has sustained either

(1) irreversible cessation of circulatory and respiratory functions, or

(2) irreversible cessation of all functions of the entire brain, including the brain stem, is dead. A determination of death must be made in accordance with accepted medical standards.

§ 2. [Uniformity of Construction Application]

This Act shall be applied and construed to effectuate its general purpose to make uniform the law with respect to the subject of this Act among states enacting it.

§ 3. [Short Title]

This Act may be cited as the Uniform Determination of Death Act.

F. OREGON DEATH WITH DIGNITY ACT: ORE.REV.STAT. 1953, 127.800 ET SEQ.

§ 127.800. Definitions

The following words and phrases, whenever used in *ORS 127.800* to *127.897*, have the following meanings:

(1) "Adult" means an individual who is 18 years of age or older.

(2) "Attending physician" means the physician who has primary responsibility for the care of the patient and treatment of the patient's terminal disease.

(3) "Capable" means that in the opinion of a court or in the opinion of the patient's attending physician or consulting physician, psychiatrist or psychologist, a patient has the ability to make and communicate health care decisions to health care providers, including communication through persons familiar with the patient's manner of communicating if those persons are available.

(4) "Consulting physician" means a physician who is qualified by specialty or experience to make a professional diagnosis and prognosis regarding the patient's disease.

(5) "Counseling" means one or more consultations as necessary between a state licensed psychiatrist or psychologist and a patient for the purpose of determining that the patient is capable and not suffering from a psychiatric or psychological disorder or depression causing impaired judgment.

(6) "Health care provider" means a person licensed, certified or otherwise authorized or permitted by the law of this state to administer health care or dispense medication in the ordinary course of business or practice of a profession, and includes a health care facility.

(7) "Informed decision" means a decision by a qualified patient, to request and obtain a prescription to end his or her life in a humane and dignified manner, that is based on an appreciation of the relevant facts and after being fully informed by the attending physician of:

(a) His or her medical diagnosis;

(b) His or her prognosis;

(c) The potential risks associated with taking the medication to be prescribed;

(d) The probable result of taking the medication to be prescribed; and

(e) The feasible alternatives, including, but not limited to, comfort care, hospice care and pain control.

(8) "Medically confirmed" means the medical opinion of the attending physician has been confirmed by a consulting physician who has examined the patient and the patient's relevant medical records.

(9) "Patient" means a person who is under the care of a physician.

(10) "Physician" means a doctor of medicine or osteopathy licensed to practice medicine by the Board of Medical Examiners for the State of Oregon.

(11) "Qualified patient" means a capable adult who is a resident of Oregon and has satisfied the requirements of ORS 127.800 to 127.897 in order to obtain a prescription for medication to end his or her life in a humane and dignified manner.

(12) "Terminal disease" means an incurable and irreversible disease that has been medically confirmed and will, within reasonable medical judgment, produce death within six months.

§ 127.805. Who may initiate a written request for medication

(1) An adult who is capable, is a resident of Oregon, and has been determined by the attending physician and consulting physician to be suffering from a terminal disease, and who has voluntarily expressed his or her wish to die, may make a written request for medication for the purpose of

ending his or her life in a humane and dignified manner in accordance with *ORS 127.800* to *127.897*.

(2) No person shall qualify under the provisions of *ORS 127.800* to *127.897* solely because of age or disability.

§ 127.810. Form of the written request

(1) A valid request for medication under *ORS 127.800* to *127.897* shall be in substantially the form described in *ORS 127.897*, signed and dated by the patient and witnessed by at least two individuals who, in the presence of the patient, attest that to the best of their knowledge and belief the patient is capable, acting voluntarily, and is not being coerced to sign the request.

(2) One of the witnesses shall be a person who is not:

(a) A relative of the patient by blood, marriage or adoption;

(b) A person who at the time the request is signed would be entitled to any portion of the estate of the qualified patient upon death under any will or by operation of law; or

(c) An owner, operator or employee of a health care facility where the qualified patient is receiving medical treatment or is a resident.

(3) The patient's attending physician at the time the request is signed shall not be a witness.

(4) If the patient is a patient in a long term care facility at the time the written request is made, one of the witnesses shall be an individual designated by the facility and having the qualifications specified by the Department of Human Services by rule.

§ 127.815. Attending physician responsibilities

(1) The attending physician shall:

(a) Make the initial determination of whether a patient has a terminal disease, is capable, and has made the request voluntarily;

(b) Request that the patient demonstrate Oregon residency pursuant to *ORS 127.860*;

(c) To ensure that the patient is making an informed decision, inform the patient of:

(A) His or her medical diagnosis;

(B) His or her prognosis;

(C) The potential risks associated with taking the medication to be prescribed;

(D) The probable result of taking the medication to be prescribed; and

(E) The feasible alternatives, including, but not limited to, comfort care, hospice care and pain control;

(d) Refer the patient to a consulting physician for medical confirmation of the diagnosis, and for a determination that the patient is capable and acting voluntarily;

(e) Refer the patient for counseling if appropriate pursuant to *ORS 127.825*;

(f) Recommend that the patient notify next of kin;

(g) Counsel the patient about the importance of having another person present when the patient takes the medication prescribed pursuant to *ORS 127.800* to *127.897* and of not taking the medication in a public place;

(h) Inform the patient that he or she has an opportunity to rescind the request at any time and in any manner, and offer the patient an opportunity to rescind at the end of the 15 day waiting period pursuant to *ORS 127.840*;

(i) Verify, immediately prior to writing the prescription for medication under *ORS 127.800* to *127.897*, that the patient is making an informed decision;

(j) Fulfill the medical record documentation requirements of *ORS 127.855*;

(k) Ensure that all appropriate steps are carried out in accordance with *ORS 127.800* to *127.897* prior to writing a prescription for medication to enable a qualified patient to end his or her life in a humane and dignified manner; and

(l)(A) Dispense medications directly, including ancillary medications intended to facilitate the desired effect to minimize the patient's discomfort, provided the attending physician is registered as a dispensing physician with the Board of Medical Examiners, has a current Drug Enforcement Administration certificate and complies with any applicable administrative rule; or

(B) With the patient's written consent:

(i) Contact a pharmacist and inform the pharmacist of the prescription; and

(ii) Deliver the written prescription personally or by mail to the pharmacist, who will dispense the medications to either the patient, the attending physician or an expressly identified agent of the patient.

(2) Notwithstanding any other provision of law, the attending physician may sign the patient's death certificate.

§ 127.820. Consulting physician confirmation

Before a patient is qualified under *ORS 127.800* to *127.897*, a consulting physician shall examine the patient and his or her relevant medical records and confirm, in writing, the attending physician's diagnosis that the patient is suffering from a terminal disease, and verify that the patient is capable, is acting voluntarily and has made an informed decision.

§ 127.825.   Counseling referral

If in the opinion of the attending physician or the consulting physician a patient may be suffering from a psychiatric or psychological disorder, or depression causing impaired judgment, either physician shall refer the patient for counseling. No medication to end a patient's life in a humane and dignified manner shall be prescribed until the person performing the counseling determines that the patient is not suffering from a psychiatric or psychological disorder, or depression causing impaired judgment.

§ 127.830.   Informed decision

No person shall receive a prescription for medication to end his or her life in a humane and dignified manner unless he or she has made an informed decision as defined in *ORS 127.800(7)*. Immediately prior to writing a prescription for medication under *ORS 127.800 to 127.897*, the attending physician shall verify that the patient is making an informed decision.

§ 127.835.   Family notification

The attending physician shall ask the patient to notify next of kin of his or her request for medication pursuant to *ORS 127.800 to 127.897*. A patient who declines or is unable to notify next of kin shall not have his or her request denied for that reason.

§ 127.840.   Written and oral requests

In order to receive a prescription for medication to end his or her life in a humane and dignified manner, a qualified patient shall have made an oral request and a written request, and reiterate the oral request to his or her attending physician no less than fifteen (15) days after making the initial oral request. At the time the qualified patient makes his or her second oral request, the attending physician shall offer the patient an opportunity to rescind the request.

§ 127.845.   Right to rescind request

A patient may rescind his or her request at any time and in any manner without regard to his or her mental state. No prescription for medication under *ORS 127.800 to 127.897* may be written without the attending physician offering the qualified patient an opportunity to rescind the request.

§ 127.850.   Waiting periods

No less than fifteen (15) days shall elapse between the patient's initial oral request and the writing of a prescription under *ORS 127.800 to 127.897*.

No less than 48 hours shall elapse between the patient's written request and the writing of a prescription under *ORS 127.800* to *127.897*.

§ 127.855. Medical record documentation requirements.

The following shall be documented or filed in the patient's medical record:

(1) All oral requests by a patient for medication to end his or her life in a humane and dignified manner;

(2) All written requests by a patient for medication to end his or her life in a humane and dignified manner;

(3) The attending physician's diagnosis and prognosis, determination that the patient is capable, acting voluntarily and has made an informed decision;

(4) The consulting physician's diagnosis and prognosis, and verification that the patient is capable, acting voluntarily and has made an informed decision;

(5) A report of the outcome and determinations made during counseling, if performed;

(6) The attending physician's offer to the patient to rescind his or her request at the time of the patient's second oral request pursuant to *ORS 127.840*; and

(7) A note by the attending physician indicating that all requirements under *ORS 127.800* to *127.897* have been met and indicating the steps taken to carry out the request, including a notation of the medication prescribed.

§ 127.860. Residency requirement

Only requests made by Oregon residents under *ORS 127.800* to *127.897* shall be granted. Factors demonstrating Oregon residency include but are not limited to:

(1) Possession of an Oregon driver license;

(2) Registration to vote in Oregon;

(3) Evidence that the person owns or leases property in Oregon; or

(4) Filing of an Oregon tax return for the most recent tax year.

§ 127.865. Reporting requirements

(1)(a) The Health Division shall annually review a sample of records maintained pursuant to *ORS 127.800* to *127.897*.

(b) The division shall require any health care provider upon dispensing medication pursuant to *ORS 127.800* to *127.897* to file a copy of the dispensing record with the division.

(2) The Health Division shall make rules to facilitate the collection of information regarding compliance with *ORS 127.800* to *127.897*. Except as otherwise required by law, the information collected shall not be a public record and may not be made available for inspection by the public.

(3) The division shall generate and make available to the public an annual statistical report of information collected under subsection (2) of this section.

§ 127.870. Effect on construction of wills, contracts and statutes

(1) No provision in a contract, will or other agreement, whether written or oral, to the extent the provision would affect whether a person may make or rescind a request for medication to end his or her life in a humane and dignified manner, shall be valid.

(2) No obligation owing under any currently existing contract shall be conditioned or affected by the making or rescinding of a request, by a person, for medication to end his or her life in a humane and dignified manner.

§ 127.875. Insurance or annuity policies

The sale, procurement, or issuance of any life, health, or accident insurance or annuity policy or the rate charged for any policy shall not be conditioned upon or affected by the making or rescinding of a request, by a person, for medication to end his or her life in a humane and dignified manner. Neither shall a qualified patient's act of ingesting medication to end his or her life in a humane and dignified manner have an effect upon a life, health, or accident insurance or annuity policy.

§ 127.880. Construction of Act

Nothing in *ORS 127.800* to *127.897* shall be construed to authorize a physician or any other person to end a patient's life by lethal injection, mercy killing or active euthanasia. Actions taken in accordance with *ORS 127.800* to *127.897* shall not, for any purpose, constitute suicide, assisted suicide, mercy killing or homicide, under the law.

§ 127.885. Immunities; basis for prohibiting health care provider from participation; notification; permissible sanctions

Except as provided in *ORS 127.890*:

(1) No person shall be subject to civil or criminal liability or professional disciplinary action for participating in good faith compliance with *ORS 127.800* to *127.897*. This includes being present when a qualified patient takes the prescribed medication to end his or her life in a humane and dignified manner.

1455

(2) No professional organization or association, or health care provider, may subject a person to censure, discipline, suspension, loss of license, loss of privileges, loss of membership or other penalty for participating or refusing to participate in good faith compliance with *ORS 127.800* to *127.897*.

(3) No request by a patient for or provision by an attending physician of medication in good faith compliance with the provisions of *ORS 127.800* to *127.897* shall constitute neglect for any purpose of law or provide the sole basis for the appointment of a guardian or conservator.

(4) No health care provider shall be under any duty, whether by contract, by statute or by any other legal requirement to participate in the provision to a qualified patient of medication to end his or her life in a humane and dignified manner. If a health care provider is unable or unwilling to carry out a patient's request under *ORS 127.800* to *127.897*, and the patient transfers his or her care to a new health care provider, the prior health care provider shall transfer, upon request, a copy of the patient's relevant medical records to the new health care provider.

(5)(a) Notwithstanding any other provision of law, a health care provider may prohibit another health care provider from participating in *ORS 127.800* to *127.897* on the premises of the prohibiting provider if the prohibiting provider has notified the health care provider of the prohibiting provider's policy regarding participating in *ORS 127.800* to *127.897*. Nothing in this paragraph prevents a health care provider from providing health care services to a patient that do not constitute participation in *ORS 127.800* to *127.897*.

(b) Notwithstanding the provisions of subsections (1) to (4) of this section, a health care provider may subject another health care provider to the sanctions stated in this paragraph if the sanctioning health care provider has notified the sanctioned provider prior to participation in *ORS 127.800* to *127.897* that it prohibits participation in *ORS 127.800* to *127.897*:

(A) Loss of privileges, loss of membership or other sanction provided pursuant to the medical staff bylaws, policies and procedures of the sanctioning health care provider if the sanctioned provider is a member of the sanctioning provider's medical staff and participates in *ORS 127.800* to *127.897* while on the health care facility premises, as defined in *ORS 442.015*, of the sanctioning health care provider, but not including the private medical office of a physician or other provider;

(B) Termination of lease or other property contract or other nonmonetary remedies provided by lease contract, not including loss or restriction of medical staff privileges or exclusion from a provider panel, if the sanctioned provider participates in *ORS 127.800* to *127.897* while on the premises of the sanctioning health care provider or on property that is owned by or under the direct control of the sanctioning health care provider; or

(C) Termination of contract or other nonmonetary remedies provided by contract if the sanctioned provider participates in *ORS 127.800* to *127.897* while acting in the course and scope of the sanctioned provider's capacity as an employee or independent contractor of the sanctioning health care provider. Nothing in this subparagraph shall be construed to prevent:

(i) A health care provider from participating in *ORS 127.800* to *127.897* while acting outside the course and scope of the provider's capacity as an employee or independent contractor; or

(ii) A patient from contracting with his or her attending physician and consulting physician to act outside the course and scope of the provider's capacity as an employee or independent contractor of the sanctioning health care provider.

(c) A health care provider that imposes sanctions pursuant to paragraph (b) of this subsection must follow all due process and other procedures the sanctioning health care provider may have that are related to the imposition of sanctions on another health care provider.

(d) For purposes of this subsection:

(A) "Notify" means a separate statement in writing to the health care provider specifically informing the health care provider prior to the provider's participation in *ORS 127.800* to *127.897* of the sanctioning health care provider's policy about participation in activities covered by *ORS 127.800* to *127.897*.

(B) "Participate in *ORS 127.800* to *127.897*" means to perform the duties of an attending physician pursuant to *ORS 127.815*, the consulting physician function pursuant to *ORS 127.820* or the counseling function pursuant to *ORS 127.825*. "Participate in *ORS 127.800* to *127.897*" does not include:

(i) Making an initial determination that a patient has a terminal disease and informing the patient of the medical prognosis;

(ii) Providing information about the Oregon Death with Dignity Act to a patient upon the request of the patient;

(iii) Providing a patient, upon the request of the patient, with a referral to another physician; or

(iv) A patient contracting with his or her attending physician and consulting physician to act outside of the course and scope of the provider's capacity as an employee or independent contractor of the sanctioning health care provider.

(6) Suspension or termination of staff membership or privileges under subsection (5) of this section is not reportable under *ORS 441.820*. Action taken pursuant to *ORS 127.810, 127.815, 127.820* or *127.825* shall not be the sole basis for a report of unprofessional or dishonorable conduct under *ORS 677.415 (2) or (3)*.

(7) No provision of *ORS 127.800* to *127.897* shall be construed to allow a lower standard of care for patients in the community where the patient is treated or a similar community.

§ 127.890. Liabilities

(1) A person who without authorization of the patient willfully alters or forges a request for medication or conceals or destroys a rescission of that request with the intent or effect of causing the patient's death shall be guilty of a Class A felony.

(2) A person who coerces or exerts undue influence on a patient to request medication for the purpose of ending the patient's life, or to destroy a rescission of such a request, shall be guilty of a Class A felony.

(3) Nothing in *ORS 127.800* to *127.897* limits further liability for civil damages resulting from other negligent conduct or intentional misconduct by any person.

(4) The penalties in *ORS 127.800* to *127.897* do not preclude criminal penalties applicable under other law for conduct which is inconsistent with the provisions of *ORS 127.800* to *127.897*.

§ 127.892. Claims by governmental entity for costs incurred

Any governmental entity that incurs costs resulting from a person terminating his or her life pursuant to the provisions of *ORS 127.800* to *127.897* in a public place shall have a claim against the estate of the person to recover such costs and reasonable attorney fees related to enforcing the claim.

§ 127.895. Severability

Any section of *ORS 127.800* to *127.897* being held invalid as to any person or circumstance shall not affect the application of any other section of *ORS 127.800* to *127.897* which can be given full effect without the invalid section or application.

§ 127.897. Form of the request

A request for a medication as authorized by *ORS 127.800* to *127.897* shall be in substantially the following form:

REQUEST FOR MEDICATION TO END MY LIFE IN A HUMANE AND DIGNIFIED MANNER

I, _____, am an adult of sound mind.

I am suffering from _____, which my attending physician has determined is a terminal disease and which has been medically confirmed by a consulting physician.

I have been fully informed of my diagnosis, prognosis, the nature of medication to be prescribed and potential associated risks, the expected result, and the feasible alternatives, including comfort care, hospice care and pain control.

I request that my attending physician prescribe medication that will end my life in a humane and dignified manner.

INITIAL ONE:

____ I have informed my family of my decision and taken their opinions into consideration.

____ I have decided not to inform my family of my decision.

____ I have no family to inform of my decision.

I understand that I have the right to rescind this request at any time.

I understand the full import of this request and I expect to die when I take the medication to be prescribed. I further understand that although most deaths occur within three hours, my death may take longer and my physician has counseled me about this possibility.

I make this request voluntarily and without reservation, and I accept full moral responsibility for my actions.

Signed: _____

Dated: _____

DECLARATION OF WITNESSES

We declare that the person signing this request:

(a) Is personally known to us or has provided proof of identity;

(b) Signed this request in our presence;

(c) Appears to be of sound mind and not under duress, fraud or undue influence;

(d) Is not a patient for whom either of us is attending physician.

_____ Witness 1/Date

_____ Witness 2/Date

NOTE: One witness shall not be a relative (by blood, marriage or adoption) of the person signing this request, shall not be entitled to any portion of the person's estate upon death and shall not own, operate or be employed at a health care facility where the person is a patient or resident. If the patient is an inpatient at a health care facility, one of the witnesses shall be an individual designated by the facility.

§ 127.995. Penalties

(1) It shall be a Class A felony for a person without authorization of the principal to willfully alter, forge, conceal or destroy an instrument, the reinstatement or revocation of an instrument or any other evidence or document reflecting the principal's desires and interests, with the intent and effect of causing a withholding or withdrawal of life-sustaining procedures or of artificially administered nutrition and hydration which hastens the death of the principal.

(2) Except as provided in subsection (1) of this section, it shall be a Class A misdemeanor for a person without authorization of the principal to willfully alter, forge, conceal or destroy an instrument, the reinstatement or revocation of an instrument, or any other evidence or document reflecting the principal's desires and interests with the intent or effect of affecting a health care decision.

G. KANSAS ASSISTED SUICIDE STATUTE: KAN. STAT. ANN. § 21–3406

§ 21–3406. Assisting suicide.

(a) Assisting suicide is:

(1) Knowingly by force or duress causing another person to commit or to attempt to commit suicide; or

(2) with the intent and purpose of assisting another person to commit or to attempt to commit suicide, knowingly either:

(A) Providing the physical means by which another person commits or attempts to commit suicide; or

(B) participating in a physical act by which another person commits or attempts to commit suicide.

(b) Assisting suicide under subsection (1) is a severity level 3, person felony. Assisting suicide under subsection (2) is a severity level 9, person felony.

XI. FEDERAL AND STATE STATUTES RELATING TO REPRODUCTIVE ISSUES

A. FREEDOM OF ACCESS TO CLINIC ENTRANCES ACT: 18 U.S.C.A. § 248

(a) Prohibited activities.—Whoever—

(1) by force or threat of force or by physical obstruction, intentionally injures, intimidates or interferes with or attempts to injure, intimidate or interfere with any person because that person is or has been, or in order to intimidate such person or any other person or any class of persons from, obtaining or providing reproductive health services;

(2) by force or threat of force or by physical obstruction, intentionally injures, intimidates or interferes with or attempts to injure, intimidate or interfere with any person lawfully exercising or seeking to exercise the First Amendment right of religious freedom at a place of religious worship; or

(3) intentionally damages or destroys the property of a facility, or attempts to do so, because such facility provides reproductive health services, or intentionally damages or destroys the property of a place of religious worship,

shall be subject to the penalties provided in subsection (b) and the civil remedies provided in subsection (c), except that a parent or legal guardian of a minor shall not be subject to any penalties or civil remedies under this section for such activities insofar as they are directed exclusively at that minor.

(b) Penalties.—Whoever violates this section shall—

(1) in the case of a first offense, be fined in accordance with this title, or imprisoned not more than one year, or both; and

(2) in the case of a second or subsequent offense after a prior conviction under this section, be fined in accordance with this title, or imprisoned not more than 3 years, or both;

except that for an offense involving exclusively a nonviolent physical obstruction, the fine shall be not more than $10,000 and the length of imprisonment shall be not more than six months, or both, for the first offense; and the fine shall, notwithstanding section 3571, be not more than $25,000 and the length of imprisonment shall be not more than 18 months, or both, for a subsequent offense; and except that if bodily injury results, the length of imprisonment shall be not more than 10 years, and if death results, it shall be for any term of years or for life.

(c) Civil remedies.—

(1) Right of action.—

(A) In general.—Any person aggrieved by reason of the conduct prohibited by subsection (a) may commence a civil action for the relief set forth in subparagraph (B), except that such an action may be brought under subsection (a)(1) only by a person involved in providing or seeking to provide, or obtaining or seeking to obtain, services in a facility that provides reproductive health services, and such an action may be brought under subsection (a)(2) only by a person lawfully exercising or seeking to exercise the First Amendment right of religious freedom at a place of religious worship or by the entity that owns or operates such place of religious worship.

(B) Relief.—In any action under subparagraph (A), the court may award appropriate relief, including temporary, preliminary or permanent injunctive relief and compensatory and punitive damages, as well as the costs of suit and reasonable fees for attorneys and expert witnesses. With respect to compensatory damages, the plaintiff may elect, at any time prior to the rendering of final judgment, to recover, in lieu of actual damages, an award of statutory damages in the amount of $5,000 per violation.

(2) Action by Attorney General of the United States.—

(A) In general.—If the Attorney General of the United States has reasonable cause to believe that any person or group of persons is being, has been, or may be injured by conduct constituting a violation of this section, the Attorney General may commence a civil action in any appropriate United States District Court.

(B) Relief.—In any action under subparagraph (A), the court may award appropriate relief, including temporary, preliminary or permanent injunctive relief, and compensatory damages to persons aggrieved as described in paragraph (1)(B). The court, to vindicate the public interest, may also assess a civil penalty against each respondent—

(i) in an amount not exceeding $10,000 for a nonviolent physical obstruction and $15,000 for other first violations; and

(ii) in an amount not exceeding $15,000 for a nonviolent physical obstruction and $25,000 for any other subsequent violation.

(3) Actions by State Attorneys General.—

(A) In general.—If the Attorney General of a State has reasonable cause to believe that any person or group of persons is being, has been, or may be injured by conduct constituting a violation of this section, such Attorney General may commence a civil action in the name of such State, as parens patriae on behalf of natural persons residing in such State, in any appropriate United States District Court.

(B) Relief.—In any action under subparagraph (A), the court may award appropriate relief, including temporary, preliminary or permanent injunctive relief, compensatory damages, and civil penalties as described in paragraph (2)(B).

(d) Rules of construction.—Nothing in this section shall be construed—

(1) to prohibit any expressive conduct (including peaceful picketing or other peaceful demonstration) protected from legal prohibition by the First Amendment to the Constitution;

(2) to create new remedies for interference with activities protected by the free speech or free exercise clauses of the First Amendment to the Constitution, occurring outside a facility, regardless of the point of view expressed, or to limit any existing legal remedies for such interference;

(3) to provide exclusive criminal penalties or civil remedies with respect to the conduct prohibited by this section, or to preempt State or local laws that may provide such penalties or remedies; or

(4) to interfere with the enforcement of State or local laws regulating the performance of abortions or other reproductive health services.

(e) Definitions.—As used in this section:

(1) Facility.—The term "facility" includes a hospital, clinic, physician's office, or other facility that provides reproductive health services, and includes the building or structure in which the facility is located.

(2) Interfere with.—The term "interfere with" means to restrict a person's freedom of movement.

(3) Intimidate.—The term "intimidate" means to place a person in reasonable apprehension of bodily harm to him-or herself or to another.

(4) Physical obstruction.—The term "physical obstruction" means rendering impassable ingress to or egress from a facility that provides reproductive health services or to or from a place of religious worship, or rendering passage to or from such a facility or place of religious worship unreasonably difficult or hazardous.

(5) Reproductive health services.—The term "reproductive health services" means reproductive health services provided in a hospital, clinic, physician's office, or other facility, and includes medical, surgical, counselling or referral services relating to the human reproductive system, including services relating to pregnancy or the termination of a pregnancy.

(6) State.—The term "State" includes a State of the United States, the District of Columbia, and any commonwealth, territory, or possession of the United States.

B. PENNSYLVANIA ABORTION CONTROL ACT: PA ST 18 PA.C.S.A. § 3202

§ 3201. Short title of chapter

This chapter shall be known and may be cited as the "Abortion Control Act."

§ 3202. Legislative intent

(a) Rights and interests.

It is the intention of the General Assembly of the Commonwealth of Pennsylvania to protect hereby the life and health of the woman subject to abortion and to protect the life and health of the child subject to abortion. It is the further intention of the General Assembly to foster the development of standards of professional conduct in a critical area of medical practice, to provide for development of statistical data and to protect the right of the minor woman voluntarily to decide to submit to abortion or to carry her child to term. The General Assembly finds as fact that the rights and interests furthered by this chapter are not secure in the context in which abortion is presently performed.

(b) Conclusions.

Reliable and convincing evidence has compelled the General Assembly to conclude and the General Assembly does hereby solemnly declare and find that:

(1) Many women now seek or are encouraged to undergo abortions without full knowledge of the development of the unborn child or of alternatives to abortion.

(2) The gestational age at which viability of an unborn child occurs has been lowering substantially and steadily as advances in neonatal medical care continue to be made.

(3) A significant number of late-term abortions result in live births, or in delivery of children who could survive if measures were taken to bring about breathing. Some physicians have been allowing these children to die or have been failing to induce breathing.

(4) Because the Commonwealth places a supreme value upon protecting human life, it is necessary that those physicians which it permits to practice medicine be held to precise standards of care in cases where their actions do or may result in the death of an unborn child.

(5) A reasonable waiting period, as contained in this chapter, is critical to the assurance that a woman elect to undergo an abortion procedure only after having the fullest opportunity to give her informed consent thereto.

(c) Construction.

In every relevant civil or criminal proceeding in which it is possible to do so without violating the Federal Constitution, the common and statutory law of Pennsylvania shall be construed so as to extend to the unborn the equal protection of the laws and to further the public policy of this commonwealth encouraging childbirth over abortion.

(d) Right of conscience.

It is the further public policy of the Commonwealth of Pennsylvania to respect and protect the right of conscience of all persons who refuse to obtain, receive, subsidize, accept or provide abortions including those persons who are engaged in the delivery of medical services and medical care whether acting individually, corporately or in association with other persons; and to prohibit all forms of discrimination, disqualification, coercion, disability or imposition of liability or financial burden upon such persons or entities by reason of their refusing to act contrary to their conscience or conscientious convictions in refusing to obtain, receive, subsidize, accept or provide abortions.

§ 3203. Definitions

The following words and phrases when used in this chapter shall have, unless the context clearly indicates otherwise, the meanings given to them in this section:

"Abortion." The use of any means to terminate the clinically diagnosable pregnancy of a woman with knowledge that the termination by those means will, with reasonable likelihood, cause the death of the unborn child except that, for the purposes of this chapter, abortion shall not mean the use of an intrauterine device or birth control pill to inhibit or prevent ovulation, fertilization or the implantation of a fertilized ovum within the uterus.

"Born alive." When used with regard to a human being, means that the human being was completely expelled or extracted from her or his mother and after such separation breathed or showed evidence of any of the following: beating of the heart, pulsation of the umbilical cord, definite movement of voluntary muscles or any brain-wave activity.

"Complication." Includes but is not limited to hemorrhage, infection, uterine perforation, cervical laceration and retained products. The department may further define complication.

"Conscience." A sincerely held set of moral convictions arising from belief in and relation to a deity or which, though not so derived, obtains from a place in the life of its possessor parallel to that filled by a deity among adherents to religious faiths.

"Department." The Department of Health of the Commonwealth of Pennsylvania.

"Facility" or "medical facility." Any public or private hospital, clinic, center, medical school, medical training institution, health care facility, physician's office, infirmary, dispensary, ambulatory surgical treatment center or other institution or location wherein medical care is provided to any person.

"Fertilization" and "conception." Each term shall mean the fusion of a human spermatozoon with a human ovum.

"First trimester." The first 12 weeks of gestation.

"Gestational age." The age of the unborn child as calculated from the first day of the last menstrual period of the pregnant woman.

"Hospital." An institution licensed pursuant to the provisions of the law of this Commonwealth.

"In vitro fertilization." The purposeful fertilization of a human ovum outside the body of a living human female.

"Medical emergency." That condition which, on the basis of the physician's good faith clinical judgment, so complicates the medical condition of a pregnant woman as to necessitate the immediate abortion of her pregnancy to avert her death or for which a delay will create serious risk of substantial and irreversible impairment of major bodily function.

"Medical personnel." Any nurse, nurse's aide, medical school student, professional or any other person who furnishes, or assists in the furnishing of, medical care.

"Physician." Any person licensed to practice medicine in this Commonwealth. The term includes medical doctors and doctors of osteopathy.

"Pregnancy" and "pregnant." Each term shall mean that female reproductive condition of having a developing fetus in the body and commences with fertilization.

"Probable gestational age of the unborn child." What, in the judgment of the attending physician, will with reasonable probability be the gestational age of the unborn child at the time the abortion is planned to be performed.

"Unborn child" and "fetus." Each term shall mean an individual organism of the species homo sapiens from fertilization until live birth.

"Viability." That stage of fetal development when, in the judgment of the physician based on the particular facts of the case before him and in light of the most advanced medical technology and information available to him, there is a reasonable likelihood of sustained survival of the unborn child outside the body of his or her mother, with or without artificial support.

§ 3204. Medical consultation and judgment

(a) Abortion prohibited; exceptions.

No abortion shall be performed except by a physician after either:

    (1) He determines that, in his best clinical judgment, the abortion is necessary; or

(2) He receives what he reasonably believes to be a written statement signed by another physician, hereinafter called the "referring
physician," certifying that in this referring physician's best clinical judgment the abortion is necessary.

(b) Requirements.

Except in a medical emergency where there is insufficient time before the
abortion is performed, the woman upon whom the abortion is to be performed
shall have a private medical consultation either with the physician who is to
perform the abortion or with the referring physician. The consultation will be
in a place, at a time and of a duration reasonably sufficient to enable the
physician to determine whether, based on his best clinical judgment, the
abortion is necessary.

(c) Factors.

In determining in accordance with subsection (a) or (b) whether an
abortion is necessary, a physician's best clinical judgment may be exercised in
the light of all factors (physical, emotional, psychological, familial and the
woman's age) relevant to the well-being of the woman. No abortion which is
sought solely because of the sex of the unborn child shall be deemed a
necessary abortion.

(d) Penalty.

Any person who intentionally, knowingly or recklessly violates the provisions of this section commits a felony of the third degree, and any physician
who violates the provisions of this section is guilty of "unprofessional conduct" and his license for the practice of medicine and surgery shall be subject
to suspension or revocation in accordance with procedures provided under the
act of October 5, 1978 (P.L. 1109, No. 261), known as the Osteopathic Medical
Practice Act, the act of December 20, 1985 (P.L. 457, No. 112), known as the
Medical Practice Act of 1985, or their successor acts.

§ 3205. Informed consent

(a) General rule.

No abortion shall be performed or induced except with the voluntary and
informed consent of the woman upon whom the abortion is to be performed or
induced. Except in the case of a medical emergency, consent to an abortion is
voluntary and informed if and only if:

(1) At least 24 hours prior to the abortion, the physician who is to
perform the abortion or the referring physician has orally informed the
woman of:

(i) The nature of the proposed procedure or treatment and of
those risks and alternatives to the procedure or treatment that a
reasonable patient would consider material to the decision of whether
or not to undergo the abortion.

(ii) The probable gestational age of the unborn child at the time the abortion is to be performed.

(iii) The medical risks associated with carrying her child to term.

(2) At least 24 hours prior to the abortion, the physician who is to perform the abortion or the referring physician, or a qualified physician assistant, health care practitioner, technician or social worker to whom the responsibility has been delegated by either physician, has informed the pregnant woman that:

(i) The department publishes printed materials which describe the unborn child and list agencies which offer alternatives to abortion and that she has a right to review the printed materials and that a copy will be provided to her free of charge if she chooses to review it.

(ii) Medical assistance benefits may be available for prenatal care, childbirth and neonatal care, and that more detailed information on the availability of such assistance is contained in the printed materials published by the department.

(iii) The father of the unborn child is liable to assist in the support of her child, even in instances where he has offered to pay for the abortion. In the case of rape, this information may be omitted.

(3) A copy of the printed materials has been provided to the pregnant woman if she chooses to view these materials.

(4) The pregnant woman certifies in writing, prior to the abortion, that the information required to be provided under paragraphs (1), (2) and (3) has been provided.

(b) Emergency.

Where a medical emergency compels the performance of an abortion, the physician shall inform the woman, prior to the abortion if possible, of the medical indications supporting his judgment that an abortion is necessary to avert her death or to avert substantial and irreversible impairment of major bodily function.

(c) Penalty.

Any physician who violates the provisions of this section is guilty of "unprofessional conduct" and his license for the practice of medicine and surgery shall be subject to suspension or revocation in accordance with procedures provided under the act of October 5, 1978 (P.L. 1109, No. 261), known as the Osteopathic Medical Practice Act, the act of December 20, 1985 (P.L. 457, No. 112), known as the Medical Practice Act of 1985, or their successor acts. Any physician who performs or induces an abortion without first obtaining the certification required by subsection (a)(4) or with knowledge or reason to know that the informed consent of the woman has not been obtained shall for the first offense be guilty of a summary offense and for each subsequent offense be guilty of a misdemeanor of the third degree. No physician shall be guilty of violating this section for failure to furnish the information required by subsection (a) if he or she can demonstrate, by a preponderance of the evidence, that he or she reasonably believed that furnishing the information would have resulted in a severely adverse effect on the physical or mental health of the patient.

(d) Limitation on civil liability.—

Any physician who complies with the provisions of this section may not be held civilly liable to his patient for failure to obtain informed consent to the abortion within the meaning of that term as defined by the act of October 15, 1975 (P.L. 390, No. 111), known as the Health Care Services Malpractice Act.

§ 3206. Parental consent

(a) General rule.

Except in the case of a medical emergency, or except as provided in this section, if a pregnant woman is less than 18 years of age and not emancipated, or if she has been adjudged an incapacitated person under *20 Pa.C.S. § 5511* (relating to petition and hearing; independent evaluation), a physician shall not perform an abortion upon her unless, in the case of a woman who is less than 18 years of age, he first obtains the informed consent both of the pregnant woman and of one of her parents; or, in the case of a woman who is an incapacitated person, he first obtains the informed consent of her guardian. In deciding whether to grant such consent, a pregnant woman's parent or guardian shall consider only their child's or ward's best interests. In the case of a pregnancy that is the result of incest where the father is a party to the incestuous act, the pregnant woman need only obtain the consent of her mother.

(b) Unavailability of parent or guardian.

If both parents have died or are otherwise unavailable to the physician within a reasonable time and in a reasonable manner, consent of the pregnant woman's guardian or guardians shall be sufficient. If the pregnant woman's parents are divorced, consent of the parent having custody shall be sufficient. If neither any parent nor a legal guardian is available to the physician within a reasonable time and in a reasonable manner, consent of any adult person standing in loco parentis shall be sufficient.

(c) Petition to court for consent.

If both of the parents or guardians of the pregnant woman refuse to consent to the performance of an abortion or if she elects not to seek the consent of either of her parents or of her guardian, the court of common pleas of the judicial district in which the applicant resides of in which the abortion is sought shall, upon petition or motion, after an appropriate hearing, authorize a physician to perform the abortion if the court determines that the pregnant woman is mature and capable of giving informed consent to the proposed abortion, and has, in fact, given such consent.

(d) Court order.

If the court determines that the pregnant woman is not mature and capable of giving informed consent or if the pregnant woman does not claim to be mature and capable of giving informed consent, the court shall determine whether the performance of an abortion upon her would be in her best interests. If the court determines that the performance of an abortion would be in the best interests of the woman, it shall authorize a physician to perform the abortion.

(e) Representation in proceedings.

The pregnant woman may participate in proceedings in the court on her own behalf and the court may appoint a guardian ad litem to assist her. The court shall, however, advise her that she has a right to court appointed counsel, and shall provide her with such counsel unless she wishes to appear with private counsel or has knowingly and intelligently waived representation by counsel.

(f) Proceedings.

(1) Court proceedings under this section shall be confidential and shall be given such precedence over other pending matters as will ensure that the court may reach a decision promptly and without delay in order to serve the best interests of the pregnant woman. In no case shall the court of common pleas fail to rule within three business days of the date of application. A court of common pleas which conducts proceedings under this section shall make in writing specific factual findings and legal conclusions supporting its decision and shall, upon the initial filing of the minor's petition for judicial authorization of an abortion, order a sealed record of the petition, pleadings, submissions, transcripts, exhibits, orders, evidence and any other written material to be maintained which shall include its own findings and conclusions.

(2) The application to the court of common pleas shall be accompanied by a non-notarized verification stating that the information therein is true and correct to the best of the applicant's knowledge, and the application shall set forth the following facts:

(i) The initials of the pregnant woman.

(ii) The age of the pregnant woman.

(iii) The names and addresses of each parent, guardian or, if the minor's parents are deceased and no guardian has been appointed, any other person standing in loco parentis to the minor.

(iv) That the pregnant woman has been fully informed of the risks and consequences of the abortion.

(v) Whether the pregnant woman is of sound mind and has sufficient intellectual capacity to consent to the abortion.

(vi) A prayer for relief asking the court to either grant the pregnant woman full capacity for the purpose of personal consent to the abortion, or to give judicial consent to the abortion under subsection (d) based upon a finding that the abortion is in the best interest of the pregnant woman.

(vii) That the pregnant woman is aware that any false statements made in the application are punishable by law.

(viii) The signature of the pregnant woman. Where necessary to serve the interest of justice, the orphans' court division, or, in Philadelphia, the family court division, shall refer the pregnant woman to the appropriate personnel for assistance in preparing the application.

(3) The name of the pregnant woman shall not be entered on any docket which is subject to public inspection. All persons shall be excluded from hearings under this section except the applicant and such other persons whose presence is specifically requested by the applicant or her guardian.

(4) At the hearing, the court shall hear evidence relating to the emotional development, maturity, intellect and understanding of the pregnant woman, the fact and duration of her pregnancy, the nature, possible consequences and alternatives to the abortion and any other evidence that the court may find useful in determining whether the pregnant woman should be granted full capacity for the purpose of consenting to the abortion or whether the abortion is in the best interest of the pregnant woman. The court shall also notify the pregnant woman at the hearing that it must rule on her application within three business days of the date of its filing and that, should the court fail to rule in favor of her application within the allotted time, she has the right to appeal to the Superior Court.

(g) Coercion prohibited.

Except in a medical emergency, no parent, guardian or other person standing in loco parentis shall coerce a minor or incapacitated woman to undergo an abortion. Any minor or incapacitated woman who is threatened with such coercion may apply to a court of common pleas for relief. The court shall provide the minor or incapacitated woman with counsel, give the matter expedited consideration and grant such relief as may be necessary to prevent such coercion. Should a minor be denied the financial support of her parents by reason of her refusal to undergo abortion, she shall be considered emancipated for purposes of eligibility for assistance benefits.

(h) Regulation of proceedings.

No filing fees shall be required of any woman availing herself of the procedures provided by this section. An expedited confidential appeal shall be available to any pregnant woman whom the court fails to grant an order authorizing an abortion within the time specified in this section. Any court to which an appeal is taken under this section shall give prompt and confidential attention thereto and shall rule thereon within five business days of the filing of the appeal. The Supreme Court of Pennsylvania may issue such rules as may further assure that the process provided in this section is conducted in such a manner as will ensure confidentiality and sufficient precedence over other pending matters to ensure promptness of disposition.

 (i) Penalty.

Any person who performs an abortion upon a woman who is an unemancipated minor or incapacitated person to whom this section applies either with knowledge that she is a minor or incapacitated person to whom this section applies, or with reckless disregard or negligence as to whether she is a minor or incapacitated person to whom this section applies, and who intentionally, knowingly or recklessly fails to conform to any requirement of this section is guilty of "unprofessional conduct" and his license for the practice of medicine and surgery shall be suspended in accordance with procedures provided under the act of October 5, 1978 (P.L. 1109, No. 261), known as the Osteopathic Medical Practice Act, the act of December 20, 1985 (P.L. 457, No. 112), known as the Medical Practice Act of 1985, or their successor acts, for a period of at least three months. Failure to comply with the requirements of this section is prima facie evidence of failure to obtain informed consent and of interference with family relations in appropriate civil actions. The law of this Commonwealth shall not be construed to preclude the award of exemplary damages or damages for emotional distress even if unaccompanied by physical complications in any appropriate civil action relevant to violations of this section. Nothing in this section shall be construed to limit the common law rights of parents.

§ 3207. Abortion facilities

 (a) Regulations.

The department shall have power to make rules and regulations pursuant to this chapter, with respect to performance of abortions and with respect to facilities in which abortions are performed, so as to protect the health and safety of woman having abortions and of premature infants aborted alive. These rules and regulations shall include, but not be limited to, procedures, staff, equipment and laboratory testing requirements for all facilities offering abortion services.

 (b) Reports.

Within 30 days after the effective date of this chapter, every facility at which abortions are performed shall file, and update immediately upon any change, a report with the department, containing the following information:

  (1) Name and address of the facility.

  (2) Name and address of any parent, subsidiary or affiliated organizations, corporations or associations.

(3) Name and address of any parent, subsidiary or affiliated organizations, corporations or associations having contemporaneous commonality of ownership, beneficial interest, directorship or officership with any other facility.

The information contained in those reports which are filed pursuant to this subsection by facilities which receive State appropriated funds during the 12–calendar-month period immediately preceding a request to inspect or copy such reports shall be deemed public information. Reports filed by facilities which do not receive State appropriated funds shall only be available to law enforcement officials, the State Board of Medicine and the State Board of Osteopathic Medicine for use in the performance of their official duties. Any facility failing to comply with the provisions of this subsection shall be assessed by the department a fine of $500 for each day it is in violation hereof.

§ 3208. Printed information

(a) General rule.

The department shall cause to be published in English, Spanish and Vietnamese, within 60 days after this chapter becomes law, and shall update on an annual basis, the following easily comprehensible printed materials:

(1) Geographically indexed materials designed to inform the woman of public and private agencies and services available to assist a woman through pregnancy, upon childbirth and while the child is dependent, including adoption agencies, which shall include a comprehensive list of the agencies available, a description of the services they offer and a description of the manner, including telephone numbers, in which they might be contacted, or, at the option of the department, printed materials including a toll-free, 24–hour a day telephone number which may be called to obtain, orally, such a list and description of agencies in the locality of the caller and of the services they offer.

The materials shall provide information on the availability of medical assistance benefits for prenatal care, childbirth and neonatal care, and state that it is unlawful for any individual to coerce a woman to undergo abortion, that any physician who performs an abortion upon a woman without obtaining her informed consent or without according her a private medical consultation may be liable to her for damages in a civil action at law, that the father of a child is liable to assist in the support of that child, even in instances where the father has offered to pay for an abortion and that the law permits adoptive parents to pay costs of prenatal care, childbirth and neonatal care.

(2) Materials designed to inform the woman of the probable anatomical and physiological characteristics of the unborn child at two-week gestational increments from fertilization to full term, including pictures representing the development of unborn children at two-week gestational increments, and any relevant information on the possibility of the unborn child's survival; provided that any such pictures or drawings must contain the dimensions of the fetus and must be realistic and appropriate for

the woman's stage of pregnancy. The materials shall be objective, non-judgmental and designed to convey only accurate scientific information about the unborn child at the various gestational ages. The material shall also contain objective information describing the methods of abortion procedures commonly employed, the medical risks commonly associated with each such procedure, the possible detrimental psychological effects of abortion and the medical risks commonly associated with each such procedure and the medical risks commonly associated with carrying a child to term.

(b) Format.

The materials shall be printed in a typeface large enough to be clearly legible.

(c) Free distribution.

The materials required under this section shall be available at no cost from the department upon request and in appropriate number to any person, facility or hospital.

§ 3208.1. Commonwealth interference prohibited

The Commonwealth shall not interfere with the use of medically appropriate methods of contraception or the manner in which medically appropriate methods of contraception are provided.

§ 3209. Spousal notice

(a) Spousal notice required.

In order to further the Commonwealth's interest in promoting the integrity of the marital relationship and to protect a spouse's interests in having children within marriage and in protecting the prenatal life of that spouse's child, no physician shall perform an abortion on a married woman, except as provided in subsections (b) and (c), unless he or she has received a signed statement, which need not be notarized, from the woman upon whom the abortion is to be performed, that she has notified her spouse that she is about to undergo an abortion. The statement shall bear a notice that any false statement made therein is punishable by law.

(b) Exceptions.

The statement certifying that the notice required by subsection (a) has been given need not be furnished where the woman provides the physician a signed statement certifying at least one of the following:

(1) Her spouse is not the father of the child.

(2) Her spouse, after diligent effort, could not be located.

(3) The pregnancy is a result of spousal sexual assault as described in section 3128 (relating to spousal sexual assault), which has been reported to a law enforcement agency having the requisite jurisdiction.

(4) The woman has reason to believe that the furnishing of notice to her spouse is likely to result in the infliction of bodily injury upon her by her spouse or by another individual.

Such statement need not be notarized, but shall bear a notice that any false statements made therein are punishable by law.

(c) Medical emergency.

The requirements of subsection (a) shall not apply in case of a medical emergency.

(d) Forms.

The department shall cause to be published forms which may be utilized for purposes of providing the signed statements required by subsections (a) and (b). The department shall distribute an adequate supply of such forms to all abortion facilities in this Commonwealth.

(e) Penalty; civil action.

Any physician who violates the provisions of this section is guilty of "unprofessional conduct," and his or her license for the practice of medicine and surgery shall be subject to suspension or revocation in accordance with procedures provided under the act of October 5, 1978 (P.L. 1109, No. 261), known as the Osteopathic Medical Practice Act, the act of December 20, 1985 (P.L. 457, No. 112), known as the Medical Practice Act of 1985, or their successor acts. In addition, any physician who knowingly violates the provisions of this section shall be civilly liable to the spouse who is the father of the aborted child for any damages caused thereby and for punitive damages in the amount of $5,000, and the court shall award a prevailing plaintiff a reasonable attorney fee as part of costs.

§ 3210.   Determination of gestational age

(a) Requirement.

Except in the case of a medical emergency which prevents compliance with this section, no abortion shall be performed or induced unless the referring physician or the physician performing or inducing it has first made a determination of the probable gestational age of the unborn child. In making such determination, the physician shall make such inquiries of the patient and perform or cause to be performed such medical examinations and tests as a prudent physician would consider necessary to make or perform in making an accurate diagnosis with respect to gestational age. The physician who performs or induces the abortion shall report the type of inquiries made and the type of examinations and tests utilized to determine the gestational age of the unborn child and the basis for the diagnosis with respect to gestational age on forms provided by the department.

(b) Penalty.

Failure of any physician to conform to any requirement of this section constitutes "unprofessional conduct" within the meaning of the act of October 5, 1978 (P.L. 1109, No. 261), known as the Osteopathic Medical Practice Act, the act of December 20, 1985 (P.L. 457, No. 112), known as the Medical Practice Act of 1985, or their successor acts. Upon a finding by the State Board of Medicine or the State Board of Osteopathic Medicine that any physician has failed to conform to any requirement of this section, the board shall not fail to suspend that physician's license for a period of at least three months. Intentional, knowing or reckless falsification of any report required under this section is a misdemeanor of the third degree.

§ 3211. Abortion on unborn child of 24 or more weeks gestational age

(a) Prohibition.

Except as provided in subsection (b), no person shall perform or induce an abortion upon another person when the gestational age of the unborn child is 24 or more weeks.

(b) Exceptions.

(1) It shall not be a violation of subsection (a) if an abortion is performed by a physician and that physician reasonably believes that it is necessary to prevent either the death of the pregnant woman or the substantial and irreversible impairment of a major bodily function of the woman. No abortion shall be deemed authorized under this paragraph if performed on the basis of a claim or a diagnosis that the woman will engage in conduct which would result in her death or in substantial and irreversible impairment of a major bodily function.

(2) It shall not be a violation of subsection (a) if the abortion is performed by a physician and that physician reasonably believes, after making a determination of the gestational age of the unborn child in compliance with section 3210 (relating to determination of gestational age), that the unborn child is less than 24 weeks gestational age.

(c) Abortion regulated.

Except in the case of a medical emergency which, in the reasonable medical judgment of the physician performing the abortion, prevents compliance with a particular requirement of this subsection, no abortion which is authorized under subsection (b)(1) shall be performed unless each of the following conditions is met:

(1) The physician performing the abortion certifies in writing that, based upon his medical examination of the pregnant woman and his medical judgment, the abortion is necessary to prevent either the death of the pregnant woman or the substantial and irreversible impairment of a major bodily function of the woman.

(2) Such physician's judgment with respect to the necessity for the abortion has been concurred in by one other licensed physician who certifies in writing that, based upon his or her separate personal medical examination of the pregnant woman and his or her medical judgment, the abortion is necessary to prevent either the death of the pregnant woman or the substantial and irreversible impairment of a major bodily function of the woman.

(3) The abortion is performed in a hospital.

(4) The physician terminates the pregnancy in a manner which provides the best opportunity for the unborn child to survive, unless the physician determines, in his or her good faith medical judgment, that termination of the pregnancy in that manner poses a significantly greater risk either of the death of the pregnant woman or the substantial and irreversible impairment of a major bodily function of the woman than would other available methods.

(5) The physician performing the abortion arranges for the attendance, in the same room in which the abortion is to be completed, of a second physician who shall take control of the child immediately after complete extraction from the mother and shall provide immediate medical care for the child, taking all reasonable steps necessary to preserve the child's life and health.

(d) Penalty.

Any person who violates subsection (a) commits a felony of the third degree. Any person who violates subsection (c) commits a misdemeanor of the second degree for the first offense and a misdemeanor of the first degree for subsequent offenses.

§ 3212. Infanticide

(a) Status of fetus.

The law of this Commonwealth shall not be construed to imply that any human being born alive in the course of or as a result of an abortion or pregnancy termination, no matter what may be that human being's chance of survival, is not a person under the Constitution and laws of this Commonwealth.

(b) Care required.

All physicians and licensed medical personnel attending a child who is born alive during the course of an abortion or premature delivery, or after being carried to term, shall provide such child that type and degree of care and treatment which, in the good faith judgment of the physician, is commonly and customarily provided to any other person under similar conditions and circumstances. Any individual who intentionally, knowingly or recklessly violates the provisions of this subsection commits a felony of the third degree.

(c) Obligation of physician.

Whenever the physician or any other person is prevented by lack of parental or guardian consent from fulfilling his obligations under subsection (b), he shall nonetheless fulfill said obligations and immediately notify the juvenile court of the facts of the case. The juvenile court shall immediately institute an inquiry and, if it finds that the lack of parental or guardian consent is preventing treatment required under subsection (b), it shall immediately grant injunctive relief to require such treatment.

§ 3213. Prohibited acts

(a) Payment for abortion.

Except in the case of a pregnancy which is not yet clinically diagnosable, any person who intends to perform or induce abortion shall, before accepting payment therefor, make or obtain a determination that the woman is pregnant. Any person who intentionally or knowingly accepts such a payment without first making or obtaining such a determination commits a misdemeanor of the second degree. Any person who makes such a determination erroneously either knowing that it is erroneous or with reckless disregard or negligence as to whether it is erroneous, and who either:

(1) Thereupon or thereafter intentionally relies upon that determination in soliciting or obtaining any such payment; or

(2) intentionally conveys that determination to any person or persons with knowledge that, or with reckless disregard as to whether, that determination will be relied upon in any solicitation or obtaining of any such payment; commits a misdemeanor of the second degree.

(b) Referral fee.

The payment or receipt of a referral fee in connection with the performance of an abortion is a misdemeanor of the first degree. For purposes of this section, "referral fee" means the transfer of anything of value between a physician who performs an abortion or an operator or employee of a clinic at which an abortion is performed and the person who advised the woman receiving the abortion to use the services of that physician or clinic.

(c) Regulations.

The department shall issue regulations to assure that prior to the performance of any abortion, including abortions performed in the first trimester of pregnancy, the maternal Rh status shall be determined and that anti-Rh sensitization prophylaxis shall be provided to each patient at risk of sensitization unless the patient refuses to accept the treatment. Except when there exists a medical emergency or, in the judgment of the physician, there exists no possibility of Rh sensitization, the intentional, knowing, or reckless failure to conform to the regulations issued pursuant to this subsection constitutes "unprofessional conduct" and his license for the practice of medicine and surgery shall be subject to suspension or revocation in accordance with procedures provided under the act of October 5, 1978 (P.L. 1109, No. 261), known as the Osteopathic Medical Practice Act, the act of December 20, 1985 (P.L. 457, No. 112), known as the Medical Practice Act of 1985, or their successor acts.

(d) Participation in abortion.

Except for a facility devoted exclusively to the performance of abortions, no medical personnel or medical facility, nor any employee, agent or student thereof, shall be required against his or its conscience to aid, abet or facilitate performance or an abortion or dispensing of an abortifacient and failure or refusal to do so shall not be a basis for any civil, criminal, administrative or disciplinary action, penalty or proceeding, nor may it be the basis for refusing to hire or admit anyone. Nothing herein shall be construed to limit the provisions of the act of October 27, 1955 (P.L. 744, No. 222), known as the "Pennsylvania Human Relations Act." Any person who knowingly violates the provisions of this subsection shall be civilly liable to the person thereby injured and, in addition, shall be liable to that person for punitive damages in the amount of $5,000.

(e) In vitro fertilization.

All persons conducting, or experimenting in, in vitro fertilization shall file quarterly reports with the department, which shall be available for public inspection and copying, containing the following information:

(1) Names of all persons conducting or assisting in the fertilization or experimentation process.

(2) Locations where the fertilization or experimentation is conducted.

(3) Name and address of any person, facility, agency or organization sponsoring the fertilization or experimentation except that names of any persons who are donors or recipients of sperm or eggs shall not be disclosed.

(4) Number of eggs fertilized.

(5) Number of fertilized eggs destroyed or discarded.

(6) Number of women implanted with a fertilized egg.

Any person required under this subsection to file a report, keep records or supply information, who willfully fails to file such report, keep records or supply such information or who submits a false report shall be assessed a fine by the department in the amount of $50 for each day in which that person is in violation hereof.

(f) Notice.

(1) Except for a facility devoted exclusively to the performance of abortions, every facility performing abortions shall prominently post a notice, not less than eight and one-half inches by eleven inches in size, entitled "Right of Conscience," for the exclusive purpose of informing medical personnel, employees, agents and students of such facilities of their rights under subsection (d) and under section 5.2 of the Pennsylvania Human Relations Act. The facility shall post the notice required by this subsection in a location or locations where notices to employees, medical personnel and students are normally posted or, if notices are not normally posted, in a location or locations where the notice required by this subsection is likely to be seen by medical personnel, employees or students of the facility. The department shall prescribe a model notice which may be used by any facility, and any facility which utilizes the model notice or substantially similar language shall be deemed in compliance with this subsection.

(2) The department shall have the authority to assess a civil penalty of up to $5,000 against any facility for each violation of this subsection, giving due consideration to the appropriateness of the penalty with respect to the size of the facility, the gravity of the violation, the good faith of the facility and the history of previous violations. Civil penalties due under this subsection shall be paid to the department for deposit in the State Treasury and may be collected by the department in the appropriate court of common pleas. The department shall send a copy of its model notice to every facility which files a report under section 3207(b) (relating to abortion facilities). Failure to receive a notice shall not be a defense to any civil action brought pursuant to this subsection.

§ 3214. Reporting

(a) General rule.

For the purpose of promotion of maternal health and life by adding to the sum of medical and public health knowledge through the compilation of relevant data, and to promote the Commonwealth's interest in protection of the unborn child, a report of each abortion performed shall be made to the department on forms prescribed by it. The report forms shall not identify the individual patient by name and shall include the following information:

(1) Identification of the physician who performed the abortion, the concurring physician as required by section 3211(c)(2) (relating to abortion on unborn child of 24 or more weeks gestational age), the second physician as required by section 3211(c)(5) and the facility where the abortion was performed and of the referring physician, agency or service, if any.

(2) The county and state in which the woman resides.

(3) The woman's age.

(4) The number of prior pregnancies and prior abortions of the woman.

(5) The gestational age of the unborn child at the time of the abortion.

(6) The type of procedure performed or prescribed and the date of the abortion.

(7) Pre-existing medical conditions of the woman which would complicate pregnancy, if any, and, if known, any medical complication which resulted from the abortion itself.

(8) The basis for the medical judgment of the physician who performed the abortion that the abortion was necessary to prevent either the death of the pregnant woman or the substantial and irreversible impairment of a major bodily function of the woman, where an abortion has been performed pursuant to section 3211(b)(1).

(9) The weight of the aborted child for any abortion performed pursuant to section 3211(b)(1).

(10) Basis for any medical judgment that a medical emergency existed which excused the physician from compliance with any provision of this chapter.

(11) The information required to be reported under section 3210(a) (relating to determination of gestational age).

(12) Whether the abortion was performed upon a married woman and, if so, whether notice to her spouse was given. If no notice to her spouse was given, the report shall also indicate the reason for failure to provide notice.

(b) Completion of report.

The reports shall be completed by the hospital or other licensed facility, signed by the physician who performed the abortion and transmitted to the department within 15 days after each reporting month.

(c) Pathological examination.

When there is an abortion performed during the first trimester of pregnancy, the tissue that is removed shall be subjected to a gross or microscopic examination, as needed, by the physician or a qualified person designated by the physician to determine if a pregnancy existed and was terminated. If the examination indicates no fetal remains, that information shall immediately be made known to the physician and sent to the department within 15 days of the analysis. When there is an abortion performed after the first trimester of pregnancy where the physician has certified the unborn child is not viable, the dead unborn child and all tissue removed at the time of the abortion shall be submitted for tissue analysis to a board eligible or certified pathologist. If the report reveals evidence of viability or live birth, the pathologist shall report such findings to the department within 15 days and a copy of the report shall also be sent to the physician performing the abortion. Intentional, knowing, reckless or negligent failure of the physician to submit such an unborn child or such tissue remains to such a pathologist for such a purpose, or intentional, knowing or reckless failure of the pathologist to report any evidence of live birth or viability to the department in the manner and within the time prescribed is a misdemeanor of the third degree.

(d) Form.

The department shall prescribe a form on which pathologists may report any evidence of absence of pregnancy, live birth or viability.

1481

(e) Statistical reports; public availability of reports.

(1) The department shall prepare a comprehensive annual statistical report for the General Assembly based upon the data gathered under subsections (a) and (h). Such report shall not lead to the disclosure of the identity of any person filing a report or about whom a report is filed, and shall be available for public inspection and copying.

(2) Reports filed pursuant to subsection (a) or (h) shall not be deemed public records within the meaning of that term as defined by the act of June 21, 1957 (P.L. 390, No. 212), referred to as the Right-to-Know Law, and shall remain confidential, except that disclosure may be made to law enforcement officials upon an order of a court of common pleas after application showing good cause therefor. The court may condition disclosure of the information upon any appropriate safeguards it may impose.

(3) Original copies of all reports filed under subsections (a), (f) and (h) shall be available to the State Board of Medicine and the State Board of Osteopathic Medicine for use in the performance of their official duties.

(4) Any person who willfully discloses any information obtained from reports filed pursuant to subsection (a) or (h), other than that disclosure authorized under paragraph (1), (2) or (3) hereof or as otherwise authorized by law, shall commit a misdemeanor of the third degree.

(f) Report by facility.

Every facility in which an abortion is performed within this Commonwealth during any quarter year shall file with the department a report showing the total number of abortions performed within the hospital or other facility during that quarter year. This report shall also show the total abortions performed in each trimester of pregnancy. Any report shall be available for public inspection and copying only if the facility receives State-appropriated funds within the 12–calendar-month period immediately preceding the filing of the report. These reports shall be submitted on a form prescribed by the department which will enable a facility to indicate whether or not it is receiving State-appropriated funds. If the facility indicates on the form that it is not receiving State-appropriated funds, the department shall regard its report as confidential unless it receives other evidence which causes it to conclude that the facility receives State-appropriated funds.

(g) Report of maternal death.

After 30 days' public notice, the department shall henceforth require that all reports of maternal deaths occurring within the Commonwealth arising from pregnancy, childbirth or intentional abortion in every case state the cause of death, the duration of the woman's pregnancy when her death occurred and whether or not the woman was under the care of a physician during her pregnancy prior to her death and shall issue such regulations as are necessary to assure that such information is reported, conducting its own investigation if necessary in order to ascertain such data. A woman shall be deemed to have been under the care of a physician prior to her death for the purpose of this chapter when she had either been examined or treated by a physician, not including any examination or treatment in connection with emergency care for complications of her pregnancy or complications of her abortion, preceding the woman's death at any time which is both 21 or more days after the time she became pregnant and within 60 days prior to her death. Known incidents of maternal mortality of nonresident women arising from induced abortion performed in this Commonwealth shall be included as incidents of maternal mortality arising from induced abortions. Incidents of maternal morality arising from continued pregnancy or childbirth and occurring after induced abortion has been attempted but not completed, including deaths occurring after induced abortion has been attempted but not completed as a result of ectopic pregnancy, shall be included as incidents of maternal morality arising from induced abortion. The department shall annually compile a statistical report for the General Assembly based upon the data gathered under this subsection, and all such statistical reports shall be available for public inspection and copying.

(h) Report of complications.

Every physician who is called upon to provide medical care or treatment to a woman who is in need of medical care because of a complication or complications resulting, in the good faith judgment of the physician, from having undergone an abortion or attempted abortion shall prepare a report thereof and file the report with the department within 30 days of the date of his first examination of the woman, which report shall be on forms prescribed by the department, which forms shall contain the following information, as received, and such other information except the name of the patient as the department may from time to time require:

(1) Age of patient.

(2) Number of pregnancies patient may have had prior to the abortion.

(3) Number and type of abortions patient may have had prior to this abortion.

(4) Name and address of the facility where the abortion was performed.

(5) Gestational age of the unborn child at the time of the abortion, if known.

(6) Type of abortion performed, if known.

(7) Nature of complication or complications.

(8) Medical treatment given.

(9) The nature and extent, if known, of any permanent condition caused by the complication.

(i) Penalties.

(1) Any person required under this section to file a report, keep any records or supply any information, who willfully fails to file such report, keep such records or supply such information at the time or times required by law or regulation is guilty of "unprofessional conduct" and his license for the practice of medicine and surgery shall be subject to suspension or revocation in accordance with procedures provided under the act of October 5, 1978 (P.L. 1109, No. 261), known as the Osteopathic Medical Practice Act, the act of December 20, 1985 (P.L. 457, No. 112), known as the Medical Practice Act of 1985, or their successor acts.

(2) Any person who willfully delivers or discloses to the department any report, record or information known by him to be false commits a misdemeanor of the first degree.

(3) In addition to the above penalties, any person, organization or facility who willfully violates any of the provisions of this section requiring reporting shall upon conviction thereof:

(i) For the first time, have its license suspended for a period of six months.

(ii) For the second time, have its license suspended for a period of one year.

(iii) For the third time, have its license revoked.

§ 3215. Publicly owned facilities; public officials and public funds

(a) Limitations.

No hospital, clinic or other health facility owned or operated by the Commonwealth, a county, a city or other governmental entity (except the government of the United States, another state or a foreign nation) shall:

(1) Provide, induce, perform or permit its facilities to be used for the provision, inducement or performance of any abortion except where necessary to avert the death of the woman or where necessary to terminate pregnancies initiated by acts of rape or incest if reported in accordance with requirements set forth in subsection (c).

(2) Lease or sell or permit the subleasing of its facilities or property to any physician or health facility for use in the provision, inducement or performance of abortion, except abortion necessary to avert the death of the woman or to terminate pregnancies initiated by acts of rape or incest if reported in accordance with requirements set forth in subsection (c).

(3) Enter into any contract with any physician or health facility under the terms of which such physician or health facility agrees to provide, induce or perform abortions, except abortion necessary to avert the death of the woman or to terminate pregnancies initiated by acts of rape or incest if reported in accordance with requirements set forth in subsection (c).

(b) Permitted treatment.

Nothing in subsection (a) shall be construed to preclude any hospital, clinic or other health facility from providing treatment for post-abortion complications.

(c) Public funds.

No Commonwealth funds and no Federal funds which are appropriated by the Commonwealth shall be expended by any State or local government agency for the performance of abortion, except:

(1) When abortion is necessary to avert the death of the mother on certification by a physician. When such physician will perform the abortion or has a pecuniary or proprietary interest in the abortion there shall be a separate certification from a physician who has no such interest.

(2) When abortion is performed in the case of pregnancy caused by rape which, prior to the performance of the abortion, has been reported, together with the identity of the offender, if known, to a law enforcement agency having the requisite jurisdiction and has been personally reported by the victim.

(3) When abortion is performed in the case of pregnancy caused by incest which, prior to the performance of the abortion, has been personally reported by the victim to a law enforcement agency having the requisite jurisdiction, or, in the case of a minor, to the county child protective service agency and the other party to the incestuous act has been named in such report.

(d) Health plans.

No health plan for employees, funded with any Commonwealth funds, shall include coverage for abortion, except under the same conditions and requirements as provided in subsection (c). The prohibition contained herein shall not apply to health plans for which abortion coverage has been expressly bargained for in any collective bargaining agreement presently in effect, but shall be construed to preclude such coverage with respect to any future agreement.

(e) Insurance policies.

All insurers who make available health care and disability insurance policies in this Commonwealth shall make available such policies which contain an express exclusion of coverage for abortion services not necessary to avert the death of the woman or to terminate pregnancies caused by rape or incest.

(f) Public officers; ordering abortions.

Except in the case of a medical emergency, no court, judge, executive officer, administrative agency or public employee of the Commonwealth or of any local governmental body shall have power to issue any order requiring an abortion without the express voluntary consent of the woman upon whom the abortion is to be performed or shall coerce any person to have an abortion.

(g) Public officers; limiting benefits prohibited.

No court, judge, executive officer, administrative agency or public employee of the Commonwealth or of any local governmental body shall withhold, reduce or suspend or threaten to withhold, reduce or suspend any benefits to

1485

which a person would otherwise be entitled on the ground that such person chooses not to have an abortion.

(h) Penalty.

Whoever orders an abortion in violation of subsection (f) or withholds, reduces or suspends any benefits or threatens to withhold, reduce or suspend any benefits in violation of subsection (g) commits a misdemeanor of the first degree.

(i) Public funds for legal services.

No Federal or State funds which are appropriated by the Commonwealth for the provision of legal services by private agencies, and no public funds generated by collection of interest on lawyer's trust accounts, as authorized by statute previously or subsequently enacted, may be used, directly or indirectly, to:

(**1**) Advocate the freedom to choose abortion or the prohibition of abortion.

(**2**) Provide legal assistance with respect to any proceeding or litigation which seeks to procure or prevent any abortion or to procure or prevent public funding for any abortion.

(**3**) Provide legal assistance with respect to any proceeding or litigation which seeks to compel or prevent the performance or assistance in the performance of any abortion, or the provision of facilities for the performance of any abortion.

Nothing in this subsection shall be construed to require or prevent the expenditure of funds pursuant to a court order awarding fees for attorney's services under the Civil Rights Attorney's Fees Awards Act of 1976 (*Public law 94–559*, 90 Stat. 2641), nor shall this subsection be construed to prevent the use of public funds to provide court appointed counsel in any proceeding authorized under section 3206 (relating to parental consent).

(j) Required statements.

No Commonwealth agency shall make any payment from Federal or State funds appropriated by the Commonwealth for the performance of any abortion pursuant to subsection (c)(2) or (3) unless the Commonwealth agency first:

(**1**) receives from the physician or facility seeking payment a statement signed by the physician performing the abortion stating that, prior to performing the abortion, he obtained a non-notarized, signed statement from the pregnant woman stating that she was a victim of rape or incest, as the case may be, and that she reported the crime, including the identity of the offender, if known, to a law enforcement agency having the requisite jurisdiction or, in the case of incest where a pregnant minor is the victim, to the county child protective service agency and stating the name of the law enforcement agency or child protective service agency to which the report was made and the date such report was made;

(2) receives from the physician or facility seeking payment, the signed statement of the pregnant woman which is described in paragraph (1). The statement shall bear the notice that any false statements made therein are punishable by law and shall state that the pregnant woman is aware that false reports to law enforcement authorities are punishable by law; and

(3) verifies with the law enforcement agency or child protective service agency named in the statement of the pregnant woman whether a report of rape or incest was filed with the agency in accordance with the statement.

The Commonwealth agency shall report any evidence of false statements, of false reports to law enforcement authorities or of fraud in the procurement or attempted procurement of any payment from Federal or State funds appropriated by the Commonwealth pursuant to this section to the district attorney of appropriate jurisdiction and, where appropriate, to the Attorney General.

§ 3216. Fetal experimentation

(a) Unborn or live child.

Any person who knowingly performs any type of nontherapeutic experimentation or nontherapeutic medical procedure (except an abortion as defined in this chapter) upon any unborn child, or upon any child born alive during the course of an abortion, commits a felony of the third degree. "Nontherapeutic" means that which is not intended to preserve the life or health of the child upon whom it is performed.

(b) Dead child.

The following standards govern the procurement and use of any fetal tissue or organ which is used in animal or human transplantation, research or experimentation:

(1) No fetal tissue or organs may be procured or used without the written consent of the mother. No consideration of any kind for such consent may be offered or given. Further, if the tissue or organs are being derived from abortion, such consent shall be valid only if obtained after the decision to abort has been made.

(2) No person who provides the information required by section 3205 (relating to informed consent) shall employ the possibility of the use of aborted fetal tissue or organs as an inducement to a pregnant woman to undergo abortion except that payment for reasonable expenses occasioned by the actual retrieval, storage, preparation and transportation of the tissues is permitted.

(3) No remuneration, compensation or other consideration may be paid to any person or organization in connection with the procurement of fetal tissue or organs.

1487

(4) All persons who participate in the procurement, use or transplantation of fetal tissue or organs, including the recipients of such tissue or organs, shall be informed as to whether the particular tissue or organ involved was procured as a result of either:

(i) stillbirth;

(ii) miscarriage;

(iii) ectopic pregnancy;

(iv) abortion; or

(v) any other means.

(5) No person who consents to the procurement or use of any fetal tissue or organ may designate the recipient of that tissue or organ, nor shall any other person or organization act to fulfill that designation.

(6) The department may assess a civil penalty upon any person who procures, sells or uses any fetal tissue or organs in violation of this section or the regulations issued thereunder. Such civil penalties may not exceed $5,000 for each separate violation. In assessing such penalties, the department shall give due consideration to the gravity of the violation, the good faith of the violator and the history of previous violations. Civil penalties due under this paragraph shall be paid to the department for deposit in the State Treasury and may be enforced by the department in the Commonwealth Court.

(c) Construction of section.

Nothing in this section shall be construed to condone or prohibit the performance of diagnostic tests while the unborn child is in utero or the performance of pathological examinations on an aborted child. Nor shall anything in this section be construed to condone or prohibit the performance of in vitro fertilization and accompanying embryo transfer.

§ 3217. Civil penalties

Any physician who knowingly violates any of the provisions of section 3204 (relating to medical consultation and judgment) or 3205 (relating to informed consent) shall, in addition to any other penalty prescribed in this chapter, be civilly liable to his patient for any damages caused thereby and, in addition, shall be liable to his patient for punitive damages in the amount of $5,000, and the court shall award a prevailing plaintiff a reasonable attorney fee as part of costs.

§ 3218. Criminal penalties

(a) Application of chapter.

Notwithstanding any other provision of this chapter, no criminal penalty shall apply to a woman who violates any provision of this chapter solely in order to perform or induce or attempt to perform or induce an abortion upon herself. Nor shall any woman who undergoes an abortion be found guilty of having committed an offense, liability for which is defined under section 306 (relating to liability for conduct of another; complicity) or Chapter 9 (relating to inchoate crimes), by reason of having undergone such abortion.

(b) False statement, etc.

A person commits a misdemeanor of the second degree if, with intent to mislead a public servant in performing his official function under this chapter, such person:

> **(1)** makes any written false statement which he does not believe to be true; or

> **(2)** submits or invites reliance on any writing which he knows to be forged, altered or otherwise lacking in authenticity.

(c) Statements "under penalty."

A person commits a misdemeanor of the third degree if such person makes a written false statement which such person does not believe to be true on a statement submitted as required under this chapter, bearing notice to the effect that false statements made therein are punishable.

(d) Perjury provisions applicable.

Section 4902(c) through (f) (relating to perjury) apply to subsections (b) and (c).

§ 3219. State Board of Medicine: State Board of Osteopathic Medicine

(a) Enforcement.

It shall be the duty of the State Board of Medicine and the State Board of Osteopathic Medicine to vigorously enforce those provisions of this chapter, violation of which constitutes "unprofessional conduct" within the meaning of the act of October 5, 1978 (P.L. 1109, No. 261), known as the Osteopathic Medical Practice Act, the act of December 20, 1985 (P.L. 457, No. 112), known as the Medical Practice Act of 1985, or their successor acts. Each board shall have the power to conduct, and its responsibilities shall include, systematic review of all reports filed under this chapter.

(b) Penalties.

Except as otherwise herein provided, upon a finding of "unprofessional conduct" under the provisions of this chapter, the board shall, for the first such offense, prescribe such penalties as it deems appropriate; for the second such offense, suspend the license of the physician for at least 90 days; and, for the third such offense, revoke the license of the physician.

(c) Reports.

The board shall prepare and submit an annual report of its enforcement efforts under this chapter to the General Assembly, which shall contain the following items:

> **(1)** number of violations investigated, by section of this chapter;

(2) number of physicians complained against;

(3) number of physicians investigated;

(4) penalties imposed; and

(5) such other information as any committee of the General Assembly shall require.

Such reports shall be available for public inspection and copying.

§ 3220. Construction

(a) Referral to coroner.

The provisions of section 503(3) of the act of June 29, 1953 (P.L. 304, No. 66), known as the "Vital Statistics Law of 1953," shall not be construed to require referral to the coroner of cases of abortions performed in compliance with this chapter.

(b) Other laws unaffected.

Apart from the provisions of subsection (a) and section 3214 (relating to reporting) nothing in this chapter shall have the effect of modifying or repealing any part of the "Vital Statistics Law of 1953" or section 5.2 of the act of October 27, 1955 (P.L. 744, No. 222), known as the "Pennsylvania Human Relations Act."

(c) Required statement.

When any provision of this chapter requires the furnishing or obtaining of a nonnotarized statement or verification, the furnishing or acceptance of a notarized statement or verification shall not be deemed a violation of that provision.

C. UNIFORM PARENTAGE ACT (2000)

§ 102. Definitions

In this [Act]:

(1) "Acknowledged father" means a man who has established a father-child relationship under [Article] 3.

(2) "Adjudicated father" means a man who has been adjudicated by a court of competent jurisdiction to be the father of a child.

(3) "Alleged father" means a man who alleges himself to be, or is alleged to be, the genetic father or a possible genetic father of a child, but whose paternity has not been determined. The term does not include:

(A) a presumed father;

(B) a man whose parental rights have been terminated or declared not to exist; or

(C) a male donor.

(4) "Assisted reproduction" means a method of causing pregnancy other than sexual intercourse. The term includes:

    (A) intrauterine insemination;

    (B) donation of eggs;

    (C) donation of embryos;

    (D) in-vitro fertilization and transfer of embryos; and

    (E) intracytoplasmic sperm injection.

(5) "Child" means an individual of any age whose parentage may be determined under this [Act].

(6) "Commence" means to file the initial pleading seeking an adjudication of parentage in [the appropriate court] of this State.

(7) "Determination of parentage" means the establishment of the parent-child relationship by the signing of a valid acknowledgment of paternity under [Article] 3 or adjudication by the court.

(8) "Donor" means an individual who produces eggs or sperm used for assisted reproduction, whether or not for consideration. The term does not include:

    (A) a husband who provides sperm, or a wife who provides eggs, to be used for assisted reproduction by the wife; or

    (B) a woman who gives birth to a child by means of assisted reproduction [, except as otherwise provided in [Article] 8].

(9) "Ethnic or racial group" means, for purposes of genetic testing, a recognized group that an individual identifies as all or part of the individual's ancestry or that is so identified by other information.

(10) "Genetic testing" means an analysis of genetic markers to exclude or identify a man as the father or a woman as the mother of a child. The term includes an analysis of one or a combination of the following:

    (A) deoxyribonucleic acid; and

    (B) blood-group antigens, red-cell antigens, human-leukocyte antigens, serum enzymes, serum proteins, or red-cell enzymes.

(11) "Gestational mother" means a woman who gives birth to a child under a gestational agreement.

(12) "Intended parents" means individuals who enter into an agreement providing that they will be the parents of a child born to a gestational mother by means of assisted reproduction, whether or not either of them has a genetic relationship with the child.

(13) "Man" means a male individual of any age.

(14) "Parent" means an individual who has established a parent-child relationship under Section 201.

(15) "Parent-child relationship" means the legal relationship between a child and a parent of the child. The term includes the mother-child relationship and the father-child relationship.

(16) "Paternity index" means the likelihood of paternity calculated by computing the ratio between:

(A) the likelihood that the tested man is the father, based on the genetic markers of the tested man, mother, and child, conditioned on the hypothesis that the tested man is the father of the child; and

(B) the likelihood that the tested man is not the father, based on the genetic markers of the tested man, mother, and child, conditioned on the hypothesis that the tested man is not the father of the child and that the father is of the same ethnic or racial group as the tested man.

(17) "Presumed father" means a man who, by operation of law under Section 204, is recognized as the father of a child until that status is rebutted or confirmed in a judicial proceeding.

(18) "Probability of paternity" means the measure, for the ethnic or racial group to which the alleged father belongs, of the probability that the man in question is the father of the child, compared with a random, unrelated man of the same ethnic or racial group, expressed as a percentage incorporating the paternity index and a prior probability.

(19) "Record" means information that is inscribed on a tangible medium or that is stored in an electronic or other medium and is retrievable in perceivable form.

(20) "Signatory" means an individual who authenticates a record and is bound by its terms.

(21) "State" means a State of the United States, the District of Columbia, Puerto Rico, the United States Virgin Islands, or any territory or insular possession subject to the jurisdiction of the United States.

(22) "Support-enforcement agency" means a public official or agency authorized to seek:

(A) enforcement of support orders or laws relating to the duty of support;

(B) establishment or modification of child support;

(C) determination of parentage; or

(D) location of child-support obligors and their income and assets.

§ 103. Scope of [Act]; Choice of Law

(a) This [Act] governs every determination of parentage in this State.

(b) The court shall apply the law of this State to adjudicate the parent-child relationship. The applicable law does not depend on:

    (1) the place of birth of the child; or

    (2) the past or present residence of the child.

    (c) This [Act] does not create, enlarge, or diminish parental rights or duties under other law of this State.

    (d) This [Act] does not authorize or prohibit an agreement between a woman and intended parents in which the woman relinquishes all rights as a parent of a child conceived by means of assisted reproduction, and which provides that the intended parents become the parents of the child. If a birth results under such an agreement and the agreement is unenforceable under [the law of this State], the parent-child relationship is determined as provided in [Article 2.]

* * *

§ 105. Protection of Participants

    Proceedings under this [Act] are subject to other law of this state governing the health, safety, privacy, and liberty of a child or other individual who could be jeopardized by disclosure of identifying information, including address, telephone number, place of employment, social security number, and the child's day-care facility and school.

§ 106. Determination of Maternity

    Provisions of this [Act] relating to determination of paternity apply to determinations of maternity.

§ 201. Establishment of Parent–Child Relationship

    (a) The mother-child relationship is established between a woman and a child by:

        (1) the woman's having given birth to the child [, except as otherwise provided in [Article] 8];

        (2) an adjudication of the woman's maternity; [or]

        (3) adoption of the child by the woman [; or

        (4) an adjudication confirming the woman as a parent of a child born to a gestational mother if the agreement was validated under [Article] 8 or is enforceable under other law].

    (b) The father-child relationship is established between a man and a child by:

        (1) an unrebutted presumption of the man's paternity of the child under Section 204;

        (2) an effective acknowledgment of paternity by the man under [Article] 3, unless the acknowledgment has been rescinded or successfully challenged;

(3) an adjudication of the man's paternity;

(4) adoption of the child by the man; [or]

(5) the man's having consented to assisted reproduction by his wife under [Article] 7 which resulted in the birth of the child [; or

(6) an adjudication confirming the man as a parent of a child born to a gestational mother if the agreement was validated under [Article] 8 or is enforceable under other law].

§ 202. No Discrimination Based on Marital Status

A child born to parents who are not married to each other has the same rights under the law as a child born to parents who are married to each other.

§ 203. Consequences of Establishment of Parentage

Unless parental rights are terminated, a parent-child relationship established under this [Act] applies for all purposes, except as otherwise specifically provided by other law of this state.

§ 204. Presumption of Paternity in Context of Marriage

(a) A man is presumed to be the father of a child if:

(1) he and the mother of the child are married to each other and the child is born during the marriage;

(2) he and the mother of the child were married to each other and the child is born within 300 days after the marriage is terminated by death, annulment, declaration of invalidity, or divorce [, or after a decree of separation];

(3) before the birth of the child, he and the mother of the child married each other in apparent compliance with law, even if the attempted marriage is or could be declared invalid, and the child is born during the invalid marriage or within 300 days after its termination by death, annulment, declaration of invalidity, or divorce [, or after a decree of separation]; or

(4) after the birth of the child, he and the mother of the child married each other in apparent compliance with law, whether or not the marriage is or could be declared invalid, and he voluntarily asserted his paternity of the child, and:

(A) the assertion is in a record filed with [state agency maintaining birth records];

(B) he agreed to be and is named as the child's father on the child's birth certificate; or

(C) he promised in a record to support the child as his own.

(b) A presumption of paternity established under this section may be rebutted only by an adjudication under [Article] 6.

§ 301. Acknowledgment of Paternity

The mother of a child and a man claiming to be the father of the child conceived as the result of his sexual intercourse with the mother may sign an acknowledgment of paternity with intent to establish the man's paternity.

§ 302. Execution of Acknowledgment of Paternity

(a) An acknowledgment of paternity must:

(1) be in a record;

(2) be signed, or otherwise authenticated, under penalty of perjury by the mother and by the man seeking to establish his paternity;

(3) state that the child whose paternity is being acknowledged:

(A) does not have a presumed father, or has a presumed father whose full name is stated; and

(B) does not have another acknowledged or adjudicated father;

(4) state whether there has been genetic testing and, if so, that the acknowledging man's claim of paternity is consistent with the results of the testing; and

(5) state that the signatories understand that the acknowledgment is the equivalent of a judicial adjudication of paternity of the child and that a challenge to the acknowledgment is permitted only under limited circumstances and is barred after two years.

(b) An acknowledgment of paternity is void if it:

(1) states that another man is a presumed father, unless a denial of paternity signed or otherwise authenticated by the presumed father is filed with the [agency maintaining birth records];

(2) states that another man is an acknowledged or adjudicated father; or

(3) falsely denies the existence of a presumed, acknowledged, or adjudicated father of the child.

(c) A presumed father may sign or otherwise authenticate an acknowledgment of paternity.

§ 303. Denial of Paternity

A presumed father may sign a denial of his paternity. The denial is valid only if:

(1) an acknowledgment of paternity signed, or otherwise authenticated, by another man is filed pursuant to Section 305;

(2) the denial is in a record, and is signed, or otherwise authenticated, under penalty of perjury; and

(3) the presumed father has not previously:

(A) acknowledged his paternity, unless the previous acknowledgment has been rescinded pursuant to Section 307 or successfully challenged pursuant to Section 308; or

(B) been adjudicated to be the father of the child.

§ 304. Rules for Acknowledgment and Denial of Paternity

(a) An acknowledgment of paternity and a denial of paternity may be contained in a single document or may be signed in counterparts, and may be filed separately or simultaneously. If the acknowledgement and denial are both necessary, neither is valid until both are filed.

(b) An acknowledgment of paternity or a denial of paternity may be signed before the birth of the child.

(c) Subject to subsection (a), an acknowledgment of paternity or denial of paternity takes effect on the birth of the child or the filing of the document with the [agency maintaining birth records], whichever occurs later.

(d) An acknowledgment of paternity or denial of paternity signed by a minor is valid if it is otherwise in compliance with this [Act].

§ 305. Effect of Acknowledgment or Denial of Paternity

(a) Except as otherwise provided in Sections 307 and 308, a valid acknowledgment of paternity filed with the [agency maintaining birth records] is equivalent to an adjudication of paternity of a child and confers upon the acknowledged father all of the rights and duties of a parent.

(b) Except as otherwise provided in Sections 307 and 308, a valid denial of paternity by a presumed father filed with the [agency maintaining birth records] in conjunction with a valid acknowledgment of paternity is equivalent to an adjudication of the nonpaternity of the presumed father and discharges the presumed father from all rights and duties of a parent.

§ 306. No Filing Fee

The [agency maintaining birth records] may not charge for filing an acknowledgment of paternity or denial of paternity.

§ 307. Proceeding for Rescission

A signatory may rescind an acknowledgment of paternity or denial of paternity by commencing a proceeding to rescind before the earlier of:

(1) 60 days after the effective date of the acknowledgment or denial, as provided in Section 304; or

(2) the date of the first hearing, in a proceeding to which the signatory is a party, before a court to adjudicate an issue relating to the child, including a proceeding that establishes support.

§ 308. Challenge After Expiration of Period for Rescission

(a) After the period for rescission under Section 307 has expired, a signatory of an acknowledgment of paternity or denial of paternity may commence a proceeding to challenge the acknowledgment or denial only:

    (1) on the basis of fraud, duress, or material mistake of fact; and

    (2) within two years after the acknowledgment or denial is filed with the [agency maintaining birth records].

(b) A party challenging an acknowledgment of paternity or denial of paternity has the burden of proof.

§ 309. Procedure for Rescission Challenge

(a) Every signatory to an acknowledgment of paternity and any related denial of paternity must be made a party to a proceeding to rescind or challenge the acknowledgment or denial.

(b) For the purpose of rescission of, or challenge to, an acknowledgment of paternity or denial of paternity, a signatory submits to personal jurisdiction of this State by signing the acknowledgment or denial, effective upon the filing of the document with the [agency maintaining birth records].

(c) Except for good cause shown, during the pendency of a proceeding to rescind or challenge an acknowledgment of paternity or denial of paternity, the court may not suspend the legal responsibilities of a signatory arising from the acknowledgment, including the duty to pay child support.

(d) A proceeding to rescind or to challenge an acknowledgment of paternity or denial of paternity must be conducted in the same manner as a proceeding to adjudicate parentage under [Article] 6.

(e) At the conclusion of a proceeding to rescind or challenge an acknowledgment of paternity or denial of paternity, the court shall order the [agency maintaining birth records] to amend the birth record of the child, if appropriate.

§ 310. Ratification Barred

A court or administrative agency conducting a judicial or administrative proceeding is not required or permitted to ratify an unchallenged acknowledgment of paternity.

§ 311. Full Faith and Credit

A court of this State shall give full faith and credit to an acknowledgment of paternity or denial of paternity effective in another State if the acknowledgment or denial has been signed and is otherwise in compliance with the law of the other State.

§ 312. Forms for Acknowledgment and Denial of Paternity

(a) To facilitate compliance with this [article], the [agency maintaining birth records] shall prescribe forms for the acknowledgment of paternity and the denial of paternity.

(b) A valid acknowledgment of paternity or denial of paternity is not affected by a later modification of the prescribed form.

§ 313. Release of Information

The [agency maintaining birth records] may release information relating to the acknowledgment of paternity or denial of paternity to a signatory of the acknowledgment or denial and to courts and [appropriate state or federal agencies] of this or another State.

§ 314. Adoption of Rules

The [agency maintaining birth records] may adopt rules to implement this [article].

§ 401. Establishment of Registry

A registry of paternity is established in the [agency maintaining the registry].

§ 402. Registration for Notification

(a) Except as otherwise provided in subsection (b) or Section 405, a man who desires to be notified of a proceeding for adoption of, or termination of parental rights regarding, a child that he may have fathered must register in the registry of paternity before the birth of the child or within 30 days after the birth.

(b) A man is not required to register if

(1) a father-child relationship between the man and the child has been established under this [Act] or other law or

(2) the man commences a proceeding to adjudicate his paternity before the court has terminated his parental rights.

(c) A registrant shall promptly notify the registry in a record of any change in the information registered. The [agency maintaining the registry] shall incorporate all new information received into its records but need not affirmatively seek to obtain current information for incorporation in the registry.

§ 403. Notice of Proceeding

Notice of a proceeding for the adoption of, or termination of parental rights regarding, a child must be given to a registrant who has timely registered. Notice must be given in a manner prescribed for service of process in a civil action.

§ 404. Termination of Parental Rights: Child Under One Year of Age

The parental rights of a man who may be the father of a child may be terminated without notice if:

(1) the child has not attained one year of age at the time of the termination of parental rights;

(2) the man did not register timely with the [agency maintaining the registry]; and

(3) the man is not exempt from registration under Section 402.

§ 405. Termination of Parental Rights: Child at Least One Year of Age

(a) If a child has attained one year of age, notice of a proceeding for adoption of, or termination of parental rights regarding, the child must be given to every alleged father of the child, whether or not he has registered with the [agency maintaining the registry].

(b) Notice must be given in a manner prescribed for service of process in a civil action.

§ 411. Required Form

The [agency maintaining the registry] shall prepare a form for registering with the agency. The form must require the signature of the registrant. The form must state that the form is signed under penalty of perjury. The form must also state that:

(1) a timely registration entitles the registrant to notice of a proceeding for adoption of the child or termination of the registrant's parental rights;

(2) a timely registration does not commence a proceeding to establish paternity;

(3) the information disclosed on the form may be used against the registrant to establish paternity;

(4) services to assist in establishing paternity are available to the registrant through the support-enforcement agency;

(5) the registrant should also register in another State if conception or birth of the child occurred in the other State;

(6) information on registries of other States is available from [appropriate state agency or agencies]; and

(7) procedures exist to rescind the registration of a claim of paternity.

§ 412. Furnishing of Information; Confidentiality

(a) The [agency maintaining the registry] need not seek to locate the mother of a child who is the subject of a registration, but the [agency maintaining the registry] shall send a copy of the notice of registration to a mother if she has provided an address.

(b) Information contained in the registry is confidential and may be released on request only to:

    (1) a court or a person designated by the court;

    (2) the mother of the child who is the subject of the registration;

    (3) an agency authorized by other law to receive the information;

    (4) a licensed child-placing agency;

    (5) a support-enforcement agency;

    (6) a party or the party's attorney of record in a proceeding under this [Act] or in a proceeding for adoption of, or for termination of parental rights regarding, a child who is the subject of the registration; and

    (7) the registry of paternity in another State.

§ 413. Penalty for Releasing Information

An individual commits a [appropriate level misdemeanor] if the individual intentionally releases information from the registry to another individual or agency not authorized to receive the information under Section 412.

§ 414. Rescission of Registration

A registrant may rescind his registration at any time by sending to the registry a rescission in a record signed or otherwise authenticated by him, and witnessed or notarized.

§ 415. Untimely Registration

If a man registers more than 30 days after the birth of the child, the [agency] shall notify the registrant that on its face his registration was not filed timely.

§ 416. Fees for Registry

(a) A fee may not be charged for filing a registration or a rescission of registration.

(b) [Except as otherwise provided in subsection (c), the] [The] [agency maintaining the registry] may charge a reasonable fee for making a search of the registry and for furnishing a certificate.

(c) A support-enforcement agency [is] [and other appropriate agencies, if any, are] not required to pay a fee authorized by subsection (b).

§ 421. Search of Appropriate Registry

(a) If a father-child relationship has not been established under this [Act] for a child under one year of age, a [petitioner] for adoption of, or termination of parental rights regarding, the child, must obtain a certificate of search of the registry of paternity.

(b) If a [petitioner] for adoption of, or termination of parental rights regarding, a child has reason to believe that the conception or birth of the child may have occurred in another State, the [petitioner] must also obtain a certificate of search from the registry of paternity, if any, in that State.

§ 422. Certificate of Search of Registry

(a) The [agency maintaining the registry] shall furnish to the requester a certificate of search of the registry on request of an individual, court, or agency identified in Section 412.

(b) A certificate provided by the [agency maintaining the registry] must be signed on behalf of the [agency] and state that:

(1) a search has been made of the registry; and

(2) a registration containing the information required to identify the registrant:

(A) has been found and is attached to the certificate of search; or

(B) has not been found.

(c) A [petitioner] must file the certificate of search with the court before a proceeding for adoption of, or termination of parental rights regarding, a child may be concluded.

§ 423. Admissibility of Registered Information

A certificate of search of the registry of paternity in this or another State is admissible in a proceeding for adoption of, or termination of parental rights regarding, a child and, if relevant, in other legal proceedings.

§ 501. Scope of Article

This [article] governs genetic testing of an individual to determine parentage, whether the individual:

(1) voluntarily submits to testing; or

(2) is tested pursuant to an order of the court or a support-enforcement agency.

§ 502. Order for Testing

(a) Except as otherwise provided in this [article] and [Article] 6, the court shall order the child and other designated individuals to submit to genetic testing if the request for testing is supported by the sworn statement of a party to the proceeding:

(1) alleging paternity and stating facts establishing a reasonable probability of the requisite sexual contact between the individuals; or

(2) denying paternity and stating facts establishing a possibility that sexual contact between the individuals, if any, did not result in the conception of the child.

(b) A support-enforcement agency may order genetic testing only if there is no presumed, acknowledged, or adjudicated father.

(c) If a request for genetic testing of a child is made before birth, the court or support-enforcement agency may not order in-utero testing.

(d) If two or more men are subject to court-ordered genetic testing, the testing may be ordered concurrently or sequentially.

§ 503. Requirements for Genetic Testing

(a) Genetic testing must be of a type reasonably relied upon by experts in the field of genetic testing and performed in a testing laboratory accredited by:

(1) the American Association of Blood Banks, or a successor to its functions;

(2) the American Society for Histocompatibility and Immunogenetics, or a successor to its functions; or

(3) an accrediting body designated by the federal Secretary of Health and Human Services.

(b) A specimen used in genetic testing may consist of one or more samples, or a combination of samples, of blood, buccal cells, bone, hair, or other body tissue or fluid. The specimen used in the testing need not be of the same kind for each individual undergoing genetic testing.

(c) Based on the ethnic or racial group of an individual, the testing laboratory shall determine the databases from which to select frequencies for use in calculation of the probability of paternity. If there is disagreement as to the testing laboratory's choice, the following rules apply:

(1) The individual objecting may require the testing laboratory, within 30 days after receipt of the report of the test, to recalculate the probability of paternity using an ethnic or racial group different from that used by the laboratory.

(2) The individual objecting to the testing laboratory's initial choice shall:

(A) if the frequencies are not available to the testing laboratory for the ethnic or racial group requested, provide the requested frequencies compiled in a manner recognized by accrediting bodies; or

(B) engage another testing laboratory to perform the calculations.

(3) The testing laboratory may use its own statistical estimate if there is a question regarding which ethnic or racial group is appropriate. If available, the testing laboratory shall calculate the frequencies using statistics for any other ethnic or racial group requested.

(d) If, after recalculation using a different ethnic or racial group, genetic testing does not rebuttably identify a man as the father of a child under Section 505, an individual who has been tested may be required to submit to additional genetic testing.

§ 504. Report of Genetic Testing

(a) A report of genetic testing must be in a record and signed under penalty of perjury by a designee of the testing laboratory. A report made under the requirements of this [article] is self-authenticating.

(b) Documentation from the testing laboratory of the following information is sufficient to establish a reliable chain of custody that allows the results of genetic testing to be admissible without testimony:

(1) the names and photographs of the individuals whose specimens have been taken;

(2) the names of the individuals who collected the specimens;

(3) the places and dates the specimens were collected;

(4) the names of the individuals who received the specimens in the testing laboratory; and

(5) the dates the specimens were received.

§ 505. Genetic Testing Results; Rebuttal

(a) Under this [Act], a man is rebuttably identified as the father of a child if the genetic testing complies with this [article] and the results disclose that:

(1) the man has at least a 99 percent probability of paternity, using a prior probability of 0.50, as calculated by using the combined paternity index obtained in the testing; and

(2) a combined paternity index of at least 100 to 1.

(b) A man identified under subsection (a) as the father of the child may rebut the genetic testing results only by other genetic testing satisfying the requirements of this [article] which:

(1) excludes the man as a genetic father of the child; or

(2) identifies another man as the possible father of the child.

1503

(c) Except as otherwise provided in Section 510, if more than one man is identified by genetic testing as the possible father of the child, the court shall order them to submit to further genetic testing to identify the genetic father.

§ 506. Cost of Genetic Testing

(a) Subject to assessment of costs under [Article] 6, the cost of initial genetic testing must be advanced:

    (1) by a support-enforcement agency in a proceeding in which the support-enforcement agency is providing services;

    (2) by the individual who made the request;

    (3) as agreed by the parties; or

    (4) as ordered by the court.

(b) In cases in which the cost is advanced by the support-enforcement agency, the agency may seek reimbursement from a man who is rebuttably identified as the father.

§ 507. Additional Genetic Testing

The court or the support-enforcement agency shall order additional genetic testing upon the request of a party who contests the result of the original testing. If the previous genetic testing identified a man as the father of the child under Section 505, the court or agency may not order additional testing unless the party provides advance payment for the testing.

§ 508. Genetic Testing When Specimens Not Available

(a) Subject to subsection (b), if a genetic-testing specimen is not available from a man who may be the father of a child, for good cause and under circumstances the court considers to be just, the court may order the following individuals to submit specimens for genetic testing:

    (1) the parents of the man;

    (2) brothers and sisters of the man;

    (3) other children of the man and their mothers; and

    (4) other relatives of the man necessary to complete genetic testing.

(b) Issuance of an order under this section requires a finding that a need for genetic testing outweighs the legitimate interests of the individual sought to be tested.

§ 509. Deceased Individual

For good cause shown, the court may order genetic testing of a deceased individual.

§ 510. Identical Brothers

(a) The court may order genetic testing of a brother of a man identified as the father of a child if the man is commonly believed to have an identical brother and evidence suggests that the brother may be the genetic father of the child.

(b) If each brother satisfies the requirements as the identified father of the child under Section 505 without consideration of another identical brother being identified as the father of the child, the court may rely on nongenetic evidence to adjudicate which brother is the father of the child.

§ 511. Confidentiality of Genetic Testing

(a) Release of the report of genetic testing for parentage is controlled by applicable state law.

(b) An individual who intentionally releases an identifiable specimen of another individual for any purpose other than that relevant to the proceeding regarding parentage without a court order or the written permission of the individual who furnished the specimen commits a [appropriate level misdemeanor].

§ 601. Proceeding Authorized

A civil proceeding may be maintained to adjudicate the parentage of a child. The proceeding is governed by the [rules of civil procedure].

§ 602. Standing to Maintain Proceeding

Subject to [Article] 3 and Sections 607 and 609, a proceeding to adjudicate parentage may be maintained by:

(1) the child;

(2) the mother of the child;

(3) a man whose paternity of the child is to be adjudicated;

(4) the support-enforcement agency [or other governmental agency authorized by other law];

(5) an authorized adoption agency or licensed child-placing agency; [or]

(6) a representative authorized by law to act for an individual who would otherwise be entitled to maintain a proceeding but who is deceased, incapacitated, or a minor [; or

(7) an intended parent under [Article] 8].

§ 603. Parties to Proceeding

The following individuals must be joined as parties in a proceeding to adjudicate parentage:

(1) the mother of the child; and

(2) a man whose paternity of the child is to be adjudicated.

§ 604. Personal Jurisdiction

(a) An individual may not be adjudicated to be a parent unless the court has personal jurisdiction over the individual.

(b) A court of this State having jurisdiction to adjudicate parentage may exercise personal jurisdiction over a nonresident individual, or the guardian or conservator of the individual, if the conditions prescribed in [Section 201 of the Uniform Interstate Family Support Act] are fulfilled.

(c) Lack of jurisdiction over one individual does not preclude the court from making an adjudication of parentage binding on another individual over whom the court has personal jurisdiction.

§ 605. Venue

Venue for a proceeding to adjudicate parentage is in the [county] of this State in which:

(1) the child resides or is found;

(2) the [respondent] resides or is found if the child does not reside in this State; or

(3) a proceeding for probate or administration of the presumed or alleged father's estate has been commenced.

§ 606. No Limitation: Child Having No Presumed, Acknowledged, or Adjudicated Father

A proceeding to adjudicate the parentage of a child having no presumed, acknowledged, or adjudicated father may be commenced at any time, even after:

(1) the child becomes an adult; or

(2) an earlier proceeding to adjudicate paternity has been dismissed based on the application of a statute of limitation then in effect.

§ 607. Limitation: Child Having Presumed Father

(a) Except as otherwise provided in subsection (b), a proceeding brought by a presumed father, the mother, or another individual to adjudicate the parentage of a child having a presumed father must be commenced not later than two years after the birth of the child.

(b) A proceeding seeking to disprove the father-child relationship between a child and the child's presumed father may be maintained at any time if the court determines that:

(1) the presumed father and the mother of the child neither cohabited nor engaged in sexual intercourse with each other during the probable time of conception; and

(2) the presumed father never openly treated the child as his own.

§ 608. Authority to Deny Motion for Genetic Testing

(a) In a proceeding to adjudicate parentage under circumstances described in Section 607, the court may deny a motion seeking an order for genetic testing of the mother, the child, and the presumed father if the court determines that:

(1) the conduct of the mother or the presumed father estops that party from denying parentage; and

(2) it would be inequitable to disprove the father-child relationship between the child and the presumed father.

(b) In determining whether to deny a motion seeking an order for genetic testing under this section, the court shall consider the best interest of the child, including the following factors:

(1) the length of time between the proceeding to adjudicate parentage and the time that the presumed father was placed on notice that he might not be the genetic father;

(2) the length of time during which the presumed father has assumed the role of father of the child;

(3) the facts surrounding the presumed father's discovery of his possible nonpaternity;

(4) the nature of the relationship between the child and the presumed father;

(5) the age of the child;

(6) the harm that may result to the child if presumed paternity is successfully disproved;

(7) the nature of the relationship between the child and any alleged father;

(8) the extent to which the passage of time reduces the chances of establishing the paternity of another man and a child-support obligation in favor of the child; and

(9) other factors that may affect the equities arising from the disruption of the father-child relationship between the child and the presumed father or the chance of other harm to the child.

(c) In a proceeding involving the application of this section, a minor or incapacitated child must be represented by a guardian ad litem.

(d) Denial of a motion seeking an order for genetic testing must be based on clear and convincing evidence.

(e) If the court denies a motion seeking an order for genetic testing, it shall issue an order adjudicating the presumed father to be the father of the child.

§ 609. Limitation: Child Having Acknowledged or Adjudicated Father

(a) If a child has an acknowledged father, a signatory to the acknowledgment of paternity or denial of paternity may commence a proceeding seeking to rescind the acknowledgement or denial or challenge the paternity of the child only within the time allowed under Section 307 or 308.

(b) If a child has an acknowledged father or an adjudicated father, an individual, other than the child, who is neither a signatory to the acknowledgment of paternity nor a party to the adjudication and who seeks an adjudication of paternity of the child must commence a proceeding not later than two years after the effective date of the acknowledgment or adjudication.

§ 610. Joinder of Proceedings

(a) Except as otherwise provided in subsection (b), a proceeding to adjudicate parentage may be joined with a proceeding for adoption, termination of parental rights, child custody or visitation, child support, divorce, annulment, [legal separation or separate maintenance,] probate or administration of an estate, or other appropriate proceeding.

(b) A [respondent] may not join a proceeding described in subsection (a) with a proceeding to adjudicate parentage brought under [the Uniform Interstate Family Support Act].

§ 611. Proceeding Before Birth

A proceeding to determine parentage may be commenced before the birth of the child, but may not be concluded until after the birth of the child. The following actions may be taken before the birth of the child:

(1) service of process;

(2) discovery; and

(3) except as prohibited by Section 502, collection of specimens for genetic testing.

§ 612. Child as Party; Representation

(a) A minor child is a permissible party, but is not a necessary party to a proceeding under this [article].

(b) The court shall appoint an [attorney ad litem] to represent a minor or incapacitated child if the child is a party or the court finds that the interests of the child are not adequately represented.

§ 621. Admissibility of Results of Genetic Testing; Expenses

(a) Except as otherwise provided in subsection (c), a record of a genetic-testing expert is admissible as evidence of the truth of the facts asserted in the report unless a party objects to its admission within [14] days after its receipt by the objecting party and cites specific grounds for exclusion. The admissibility of the report is not affected by whether the testing was performed:

> **(1)** voluntarily or pursuant to an order of the court or a support-enforcement agency; or

> **(2)** before or after the commencement of the proceeding.

(b) A party objecting to the results of genetic testing may call one or more genetic-testing experts to testify in person or by telephone, videoconference, deposition, or another method approved by the court. Unless otherwise ordered by the court, the party offering the testimony bears the expense for the expert testifying.

(c) If a child has a presumed, acknowledged, or adjudicated father, the results of genetic testing are inadmissible to adjudicate parentage unless performed:

> **(1)** with the consent of both the mother and the presumed, acknowledged, or adjudicated father; or

> **(2)** pursuant to an order of the court under Section 502.

(d) Copies of bills for genetic testing and for prenatal and postnatal health care for the mother and child which are furnished to the adverse party not less than 10 days before the date of a hearing are admissible to establish:

> **(1)** the amount of the charges billed; and

> **(2)** that the charges were reasonable, necessary, and customary.

§ 622. Consequences of Declining Genetic Testing

(a) An order for genetic testing is enforceable by contempt.

(b) If an individual whose paternity is being determined declines to submit to genetic testing ordered by the court, the court for that reason may adjudicate parentage contrary to the position of that individual.

(c) Genetic testing of the mother of a child is not a condition precedent to testing the child and a man whose paternity is being determined. If the mother is unavailable or declines to submit to genetic testing, the court may order the testing of the child and every man whose paternity is being adjudicated.

§ 623. Admission of Paternity Authorized

(a) A [respondent] in a proceeding to adjudicate parentage may admit to the paternity of a child by filing a pleading to that effect or by admitting paternity under penalty of perjury when making an appearance or during a hearing.

(b) If the court finds that the admission of paternity satisfies the requirements of this section and finds that there is no reason to question the admission, the court shall issue an order adjudicating the child to be the child of the man admitting paternity.

§ 624. Temporary Order

(a) In a proceeding under this [article], the court shall issue a temporary order for support of a child if the order is appropriate and the individual ordered to pay support is:

(1) a presumed father of the child;

(2) petitioning to have his paternity adjudicated;

(3) identified as the father through genetic testing under Section 505;

(4) an alleged father who has declined to submit to genetic testing;

(5) shown by clear and convincing evidence to be the father of the child; or

(6) the mother of the child.

(b) A temporary order may include provisions for custody and visitation as provided by other law of this State.

§ 631. Rules of Adjudication of Paternity

The court shall apply the following rules to adjudicate the paternity of a child:

(1) The paternity of a child having a presumed, acknowledged, or adjudicated father may be disproved only by admissible results of genetic testing excluding that man as the father of the child or identifying another man as the father of the child.

(2) Unless the results of genetic testing are admitted to rebut other results of genetic testing, a man identified as the father of a child under Section 505 must be adjudicated the father of the child.

(3) If the court finds that genetic testing under Section 505 neither identifies nor excludes a man as the father of a child, the court may not dismiss the proceeding. In that event, the results of genetic testing, and other evidence, are admissible to adjudicate the issue of paternity.

(4) Unless the results of genetic testing are admitted to rebut other results of genetic testing, a man excluded as the father of a child by genetic testing must be adjudicated not to be the father of the child.

§ 632. Jury Prohibited

The court, without a jury, shall adjudicate paternity of a child.

§ 633. Hearings; Inspection of Records

(a) On request of a party and for good cause shown, the court may close a proceeding under this [article].

(b) A final order in a proceeding under this [article] is available for public inspection. Other papers and records are available only with the consent of the parties or on order of the court for good cause.

§ 634. Order on Default

The court shall issue an order adjudicating the paternity of a man who:

(1) after service of process, is in default; and

(2) is found by the court to be the father of a child.

§ 635. Dismissal for Want of Prosecution

The court may issue an order dismissing a proceeding commenced under this [Act] for want of prosecution only without prejudice. An order of dismissal for want of prosecution purportedly with prejudice is void and has only the effect of a dismissal without prejudice.

§ 636. Order Adjudicating Parentage

(a) The court shall issue an order adjudicating whether a man alleged or claiming to be the father is the parent of the child.

(b) An order adjudicating parentage must identify the child by name and date of birth.

(c) Except as otherwise provided in subsection (d), the court may assess filing fees, reasonable attorney's fees, fees for genetic testing, other costs, and necessary travel and other reasonable expenses incurred in a proceeding under this [article]. The court may award attorney's fees, which may be paid directly to the attorney, who may enforce the order in the attorney's own name.

(d) The court may not assess fees, costs, or expenses against the support-enforcement agency of this State or another State, except as provided by other law.

(e) On request of a party and for good cause shown, the court may order that the name of the child be changed.

(f) If the order of the court is at variance with the child's birth certificate, the court shall order [agency maintaining birth records] to issue an amended birth registration.

§ 637. Binding Effect of Determination of Parentage

(a) Except as otherwise provided in subsection (b), a determination of parentage is binding on:

(1) all signatories to an acknowledgement or denial of paternity as provided in [Article] 3; and

(2) all parties to an adjudication by a court acting under circumstances that satisfy the jurisdictional requirements of [Section 201 of the Uniform Interstate Family Support Act].

(b) A child is not bound by a determination of parentage under this [Act] unless:

(1) the determination was based on an unrescinded acknowledgment of paternity and the acknowledgement is consistent with the results of genetic testing;

(2) the adjudication of parentage was based on a finding consistent with the results of genetic testing and the consistency is declared in the determination or is otherwise shown; or

(3) the child was a party or was represented in the proceeding determining parentage by an [attorney ad litem].

(c) In a proceeding to dissolve a marriage, the court is deemed to have made an adjudication of the parentage of a child if the court acts under circumstances that satisfy the jurisdictional requirements of [Section 201 of the Uniform Interstate Family Support Act], and the final order:

(1) expressly identifies a child as a "child of the marriage," "issue of the marriage," or similar words indicating that the husband is the father of the child; or

(2) provides for support of the child by the husband unless paternity is specifically disclaimed in the order.

(d) Except as otherwise provided in subsection (b), a determination of parentage may be a defense in a subsequent proceeding seeking to adjudicate parentage by an individual who was not a party to the earlier proceeding.

(e) A party to an adjudication of paternity may challenge the adjudication only under law of this State relating to appeal, vacation of judgments, or other judicial review.

§ 701. Scope of Article

This [article] does not apply to the birth of a child conceived by means of sexual intercourse[, or as the result of a gestational agreement as provided in [Article] 8].

§ 702. Parental Status of Donor

A donor is not a parent of a child conceived by means of assisted reproduction

§ 703. Husband's Paternity of Child of Assisted Reproduction

If a husband provides sperm for, or consents to, assisted reproduction by his wife as provided in Section 704, he is the father of a resulting child.

§ 704.   Consent to Assisted Reproduction

(a) Consent by a married woman to assisted reproduction must be in a record signed by the woman and her husband. This requirement does not apply to the donation of eggs by a married woman for assisted reproduction by another woman.

(b) Failure of the husband to sign a consent required by subsection (a), before or after birth of the child, does not preclude a finding that the husband is the father of a child born to his wife if the wife and husband openly treated the child as their own.

§ 705.   Limitation on Husband's Dispute of Paternity

(a) Except as otherwise provided in subsection (b), the husband of a wife who gives birth to a child by means of assisted reproduction may not challenge his paternity of the child unless:

(1) within two years after learning of the birth of the child he commences a proceeding to adjudicate his paternity; and

(2) the court finds that he did not consent to the assisted reproduction, before or after birth of the child.

(b) A proceeding to adjudicate paternity may be maintained at any time if the court determines that:

(1) the husband did not provide sperm for, or before or after the birth of the child consent to, assisted reproduction by his wife;

(2) the husband and the mother of the child have not cohabited since the probable time of assisted reproduction; and

(3) the husband never openly treated the child as his own.

(c) The limitation provided in this section applies to a marriage declared invalid after assisted reproduction.

§ 706.   Effect of Dissolution of Marriage

(a) If a marriage is dissolved before placement of eggs, sperm, or embryos, the former spouse is not a parent of the resulting child unless the former spouse consented in a record that if assisted reproduction were to occur after a divorce, the former spouse would be a parent of the child.

(b) The consent of a former spouse to assisted reproduction may be withdrawn by that individual in a record at any time before placement of eggs, sperm, or embryos.

§ 707.   Parental Status of Deceased Spouse

If a spouse dies before placement of eggs, sperm, or embryos, the deceased spouse is not a parent of the resulting child unless the deceased spouse consented in a record that if assisted reproduction were to occur after death, the deceased spouse would be a parent of the child.

§ 801.   Gestational Agreement Authorized

(a) A prospective gestational mother, her husband if she is married, a donor or the donors, and the intended parents may enter into a written agreement providing that:

> **(1)** the prospective gestational mother agrees to pregnancy by means of assisted reproduction;

> **(2)** the prospective gestational mother, her husband if she is married, and the donors relinquish all rights and duties as the parents of a child conceived through assisted reproduction; and

> **(3)** the intended parents become the parents of the child.

(b) The intended parents must be married, and both spouses must be parties to the gestational agreement.

(c) A gestational agreement is enforceable only if validated as provided in Section 803.

(d) A gestational agreement does not apply to the birth of a child conceived by means of sexual intercourse.

(e) A gestational agreement may provide for payment of consideration.

(f) A gestational agreement may not limit the right of the gestational mother to make decisions to safeguard her health or that of the embryos or fetus.

§ 802.   Requirements of Petition

(a) The intended parents and the prospective gestational mother may commence a proceeding in the [appropriate court] to validate a gestational agreement.

(b) A proceeding to validate a gestational agreement may not be maintained unless:

> **(1)** the mother or the intended parents have been residents of this State for at least 90 days;

> **(2)** the prospective gestational mother's husband, if she is married, is joined in the proceeding; and

> **(3)** a copy of the gestational agreement is attached to the [petition].

§ 803.   Hearing to Validate Gestational Agreement

(a) If the requirements of subsection (b) are satisfied, a court may issue an order validating the gestational agreement and declaring that the intended parents will be the parents of a child born during the term of the of the agreement.

(b) The court may issue an order under subsection (a) only on finding that:

(1) the residence requirements of Section 802 have been satisfied and the parties have submitted to the jurisdiction of the court under the jurisdictional standards of this [Act];

(2) medical evidence shows that the intended mother is unable to bear a child or is unable to do so without unreasonable risk to her physical or mental health or to the unborn child;

(3) unless waived by the court, the [relevant child-welfare agency] has made a home study of the intended parents and the intended parents meet the standards of fitness applicable to adoptive parents;

(4) all parties have voluntarily entered into the agreement and understand its terms;

(5) the prospective gestational mother has had at least one pregnancy and delivery and her bearing another child will not pose an unreasonable health risk to the unborn child or to the physical or mental health of the prospective gestational mother;

(6) adequate provision has been made for all reasonable health-care expense associated with the gestational agreement until the birth of the child, including responsibility for those expenses if the agreement is terminated; and

(7) the consideration, if any, paid to the prospective gestational mother is reasonable.

(c) Whether to validate a gestational agreement is within the discretion of the court, subject to review only for abuse of discretion.

§ 804.   Inspection of Records

The proceedings, records, and identities of the individual parties to a gestational agreement under this [article] are subject to inspection under the standards of confidentiality applicable to adoptions as provided under other law of this State.

§ 805.   Exclusive, Continuing Jurisdiction

Subject to the jurisdictional standards of [Section 201 of the Uniform Child Custody Jurisdiction and Enforcement Act], the court conducting a proceeding under this [article] has exclusive, continuing jurisdiction of all matters arising out of the gestational agreement until a child born to the gestational mother during the period governed by the agreement attains the age of 180 Days.

§ 806.   Termination of Gestational Agreement

(a) After issuance of an order under this [article], but before the prospective gestational mother becomes pregnant by means of assisted reproduction, the prospective gestational mother, her husband, or either of the intended parents may terminate the gestational agreement by giving written notice of termination to all other parties.

(b) The court for good cause shown may terminate the gestational agreement.

(c) An individual who terminates a gestational agreement shall file notice of the termination with the court. On receipt of the notice, the court shall vacate the order issued under this [article]. An individual who does not notify the court of the termination of the agreement is subject to appropriate sanctions.

(d) Neither a prospective gestational mother nor her husband, if any, is liable to the intended parents for terminating a gestational agreement pursuant to this section.

§ 807. Parentage Under Validated Gestational Agreement

(a) Upon birth of a child to a gestational mother, the intended parents shall file notice with the court that a child has been born to the gestational mother within 300 days after assisted reproduction. Thereupon, the court shall issue an order:

(1) confirming that the intended parents are the parents of the child;

(2) if necessary, ordering that the child be surrendered to the intended parents; and

(3) directing the [agency maintaining birth records] to issue a birth certificate naming the intended parents as parents of the child.

(b) If the parentage of a child born to a gestational mother is alleged not to be the result of assisted reproduction, the court shall order genetic testing to determine the parentage of the child.

§ 808. Gestational Agreement: Effect of Subsequent Marriage

After the issuance of an order under this [article], subsequent marriage of the gestational mother does not affect the validity of a gestational agreement, her husband's consent to the agreement is not required, and her husband is not a presumed father of the resulting child.

§ 809. Effect of Nonvalidated Gestational Agreement

(a) A gestational agreement, whether in a record or not, that is not judicially validated is not enforceable.

(b) If a birth results under a gestational agreement that is not judicially validated as provided in this [article], the parent-child relationship is determined as provided in [Article] 2.

(c) Individuals who are parties to a nonvalidated gestational agreement as intended parents may be held liable for support of the resulting child, even if the agreement is otherwise unenforceable. The liability under this subsection includes assessing all expenses and fees as provided in Section 636.

§ 901. Uniformity of Application and Construction

In applying and construing this Uniform Act, consideration must be given to the need to promote uniformity of the law with respect to its subject matter among States that enact it.

§ 902. Severability Clause

If any provision of this [Act] or its application to an individual or circumstance is held invalid, the invalidity does not affect other provisions or applications of this [Act] which can be given effect without the invalid provision or application, and to this end the provisions of this [Act] are severable.

§ 904. Repeal

The following acts and parts of acts are repealed:

(1) [Uniform Act on Paternity, 1960]

(2) [Uniform Parentage Act, 1973]

(3) [Uniform Putative and Unknown Fathers Act, 1988]

(4) [Uniform Status of Children of Assisted Conception Act, 1988]

(5) [other inconsistent statutes]

§ 905. Transitional Provision

A proceeding to adjudicate parentage which was commenced before the effective date of this [Act] is governed by the law in effect at the time the proceeding was commenced.

XII. STATE STATUTES RELATING TO PUBLIC HEALTH

A. MASSACHUSETTS PUBLIC HEALTH ACT: MASS. STAT. 111 § 7, INVESTIGATION OF CONTAGIOUS OR INFECTIOUS DISEASES

If smallpox or any other contagious or infectious disease declared by the department to be dangerous to the public health exists or is likely to exist in any place within the commonwealth, the department shall make an investigation thereof and of the means of preventing the spread of the disease, and shall consult thereon with the local authorities. It shall have co-ordinate powers as a board of health, in every town, with the board of health thereof. It may require the officers in charge of any city or state institution, charitable institution, public or private hospital, dispensary or maternity hospital, or any board of health, or the physicians in any town to give notice of cases of any disease declared by the said department to be dangerous to the public health. Such notice shall be given in such manner as the department may deem advisable. If any such officer, board or physician refuses or neglects to give such notice, he or they shall forfeit not less than fifty nor more than two hundred dollars.

B. TEXAS HEALTH AND SAFETY CODE § 81.085: AREA QUARANTINE

(a) If an outbreak of communicable disease occurs in this state, the commissioner or one or more health authorities may impose an area quarantine coextensive with the area affected. A health authority may impose the quarantine only within the boundaries of the health authority's jurisdiction.

(b) A health authority may not impose an area quarantine until the authority consults with and obtains the approval of the commissioner and of the governing body of each county and municipality in the health authority's jurisdiction that has territory in the affected area.

(c) Absent preemptive action by the board under this chapter or by the governor under Chapter 418, Government Code (Texas Disaster Act of 1975), a health authority may impose in a quarantine area under the authority's jurisdiction additional disease control measures that the health authority considers necessary and most appropriate to arrest, control, and eradicate the threat to the public health.

(d) If an affected area includes territory in an adjacent state, the department may enter into cooperative agreements with the appropriate officials or agencies of that state to:

(1) exchange morbidity, mortality, and other technical information;

(2) receive extrajurisdictional inspection reports;

(3) coordinate disease control measures;

(4) disseminate instructions to the population of the area, operators of interstate private or common carriers, and private vehicles in transit across state borders; and

(5) participate in other public health activities appropriate to arrest, control, and eradicate the threat to the public health.

(e) The department or health authority may use all reasonable means of communication to inform persons in the quarantine area of the board's or health authority's orders and instructions during the period of area quarantine. The department or health authority shall publish at least once each week during the area quarantine period, in a newspaper of general circulation in the area, a notice of the orders or instructions in force with a brief explanation of their meaning and effect. Notice by publication is sufficient to inform persons in the area of their rights, duties, and obligations under the orders or instructions.

(f) The commissioner or, with the commissioner's consent, a health authority may terminate an area quarantine.

(g) To provide isolation and quarantine facilities during an area quarantine, the commissioner's court of a county, the governing body of a municipality, or the governing body of a hospital district may suspend the admission of patients desiring admission for elective care and treatment, except for needy or indigent residents for whom the county, municipality, or district is constitutionally or statutorily required to care.

(h) A person commits an offense if the person knowingly fails or refuses to obey a rule, order, or instruction of the board or an order or instruction of a health authority issued under a board rule and published during an area quarantine under this section. An offense under this subsection is a felony of the third degree.

C. MICHIGAN PUBLIC HEALTH ACT: MICH. STAT. SEC. 333.5111, COMMUNICABLE DISEASES

333.5111. Rules

(1) In carrying out its authority under this article, the department may promulgate rules to:

(a) Designate and classify communicable, serious communicable, chronic, other noncommunicable diseases, infections, and disabilities.

(b) Establish requirements for reporting and other surveillance methods for measuring the occurrence of diseases, infections, and disabilities and the potential for epidemics. Rules promulgated under this subdivision may require a licensed health professional or health facility to submit to the department or a local health department, on a form provided by the department, a report of the occurrence of a communicable disease, serious communicable disease or infection, or disability. The rules promulgated under this subdivision may require a report to be submitted to the department not more than 24 hours after a licensed health professional or health facility determines that an individual has a serious communicable disease or infection.

(c) Investigate cases, epidemics, and unusual occurrences of diseases, infections, and situations with a potential for causing diseases.

(d) Establish procedures for control of diseases and infections, including, but not limited to, immunization and environmental controls.

(e) Establish procedures for the prevention, detection, and treatment of disabilities and rehabilitation of individuals suffering from disabilities or disease, including nutritional problems.

(f) Establish procedures for control of rabies and the disposition of nonhuman agents carrying disease, including rabid animals.

(g) Establish procedures for the reporting of known or suspected cases of lead poisoning or undue lead body burden.

(h) Designate communicable diseases or serious communicable diseases or infections for which local health departments are required to furnish care including, but not limited to, tuberculosis and venereal disease.

(i) Implement this part and parts 52 and 53 including, but not limited to, rules for the discovery, care, and reporting of an individual having or suspected of having a communicable disease or a serious communicable disease or infection, and to establish approved tests under section 5125 and approved prophylaxes under section 5127.

(2) The department shall promulgate rules to provide for the confidentiality of reports, records, and data pertaining to testing, care, treatment, reporting, and research associated with communicable diseases and serious communicable diseases or infections. The rules shall specify the communicable diseases and serious communicable diseases or infections covered under the rules and shall include, but are not limited to, hepatitis B, venereal disease, and tuberculosis. The rules shall not apply to the serious communicable diseases or infections of HIV infection, or acquired immunodeficiency syndrome. * * *

†